Preface

There has been a growing demand, particularly among foreigners, of a new comprehensive English-Korean dictionary. It is our intention to meet this need for those who wish, as foreigners, to understand and speak Korean. The dictionary contains over 12, 000 entry words more than any other English-Korean dictionary for foreigners in Korea. Special efforts were made to select more useful words and to take most commonly used meaning in English for the equivalent Korean word.

The McCune-Reischauer system, favored by many publishers, was adopted. Thus, Korean equivalents for selected English words were romanized in the context of McCune-Reischauer system, with a few exceptions to avoid the complexity of the system.

One of the most important features of this dictionary is the detailed and yet simplified explanation of words. English idioms and proverbs were used in illustrative sentences for those commonly used entries. The user will find that each entry word contains English synonyms with English pronunciation of Korean word.

The editor wishes to express a special appreciation to the people for their tireless assistance and suggestions which made this publication available to the public.

B. J. Jones

Korean Alphabet I

	ㄱ k(g)	ㄴ n	ㄷ t(d)	ㄹ r(l)	ㅁ m	ㅂ p(b)	ㅅ s(sh)
ㅏ a	가 k(g)a	나 na	다 t(d)a	라 r(l)a	마 ma	바 p(b)a	사 sa
ㅑ ya	갸 k(g)ya	냐 nya	댜 t(d)ya	랴 r(l)ya	먀 mya	뱌 p(b)ya	샤 sya
ㅓ ŏ	거 k(g)ŏ	너 nŏ	더 t(d)ŏ	러 r(l)ŏ	머 mŏ	버 p(b)ŏ	서 sŏ
ㅕ yŏ	겨 k(g)yŏ	녀 nyŏ	뎌 t(d)yŏ	려 r(l)yŏ	며 myŏ	벼 p(b)yŏ	셔 syŏ
ㅗ o	고 k(g)o	노 no	도 t(d)o	로 r(l)o	모 mo	보 p(b)o	소 so
ㅛ yo	교 k(g)yo	뇨 nyo	됴 t(d)yo	료 r(l)yo	묘 myo	뵤 p(b)yo	쇼 syo
ㅜ u	구 k(g)u	누 nu	두 t(d)u	루 r(l)u	무 mu	부 p(b)u	수 su
ㅠ yu	규 k(g)yu	뉴 nyu	듀 t(d)yu	류 r(l)yu	뮤 myu	뷰 p(b)yu	슈 syu
ㅡ ŭ	그 k(g)ŭ	느 nŭ	드 t(d)ŭ	르 r(l)ŭ	므 mŭ	브 p(b)ŭ	스 sŭ
ㅣ i	기 k(g)i	니 ni	디 t(d)i	리 r(l)i	미 mi	비 p(b)i	시 shi

Mini Dictionary
of
English-Korean
Korean-English

Romanized

Edited by
B.J. Jones & Gene S. Rhie

HOLLYM

Korean Alphabet II

ㅇ ng	ㅈ ch (j)	ㅊ ch'	ㅋ k'	ㅌ t'	ㅍ p'	ㅎ h
아 a	자 ch (j) a	차 ch'a	카 k'a	타 t'a	파 p'a	하 ha
야 ya	쟈 ch (j) ya	챠 ch'ya	캬 k'ya	탸 t'ya	퍄 p'ya	햐 hya
어 ŏ	저 ch (j) ŏ	쳐 ch'ŏ	커 k'ŏ	터 t'ŏ	퍼 p'ŏ	허 hŏ
여 yŏ	져 ch (j) yŏ	쳐 ch'yŏ	켜 k'yŏ	텨 t'yŏ	펴 p'yŏ	혀 hyŏ
오 o	조 ch (j) o	초 ch'o	코 k'o	토 t'o	포 p'o	호 ho
요 yo	죠 ch (j) yo	쵸 ch'yo	쿄 k'yo	툐 t'yo	표 p'yo	효 hyo
우 u	주 ch (j) u	추 ch'u	쿠 k'u	투 t'u	푸 p'u	후 hu
유 yu	쥬 ch (j) yu	츄 ch'yu	큐 k'yu	튜 t'yu	퓨 p'yu	휴 hyu
으 ŭ	즈 ch (j) ŭ	츠 ch'ŭ	크 k'ŭ	트 t'ŭ	프 p'ŭ	흐 hŭ
이 i	지 ch (j) i	치 ch'i	키 k'i	티 t'i	피 p'i	히 hi

The Korean Alphabet and Their Sounds

(1) Vowels

1) Simple:

Korean Letter		Romanization	English sound
ㅏ	아	a	as *ah*
ㅓ	어	ŏ	as h*u*t
ㅗ	오	o	as *oh*
ㅜ	우	u	as d*o*
ㅡ	으	ŭ	as tak*e*n
ㅣ	이	i	as *i*nk
ㅐ	애	ae	as h*a*nd
ㅔ	에	e	as m*e*t
ㅚ	외	oe	as K*ö*ln

2) Compound:

Korean Letter		Romanization	English sound
ㅑ	야	ya	as *ya*rd
ㅕ	여	yŏ	as *yea*rn
ㅛ	요	yo	as *yo*ke
ㅠ	유	yu	as *you*
ㅒ	애	yae	as *ya*m
ㅖ	예	ye	as *ye*s
ㅟ	위	wi	as *wie*ld
ㅢ	의	ŭi	as tak*e*n+*we*
ㅘ	와	wa	as *wa*n
ㅙ	왜	wae	as *wa*g
ㅝ	워	wo	as *wo*n
ㅞ	웨	we	as *we*t

(2) Consonants

1) Simple:

Korean Letter	Romanization	English sound
ㄱ	k (g)	as *k*ing or *g*rocer
ㄴ	n	as *n*ame
ㄷ	t (d)	as *t*oy or *d*epend
ㄹ	r (l)	as *r*ain or *l*ily
ㅁ	m	as *m*other
ㅂ	p (b)	as *p*in or *b*ook
ㅅ	s (sh)	as *s*peech
ㅇ	ng	as *ah* or ki*ng*
ㅈ	ch (j)	as *J*ohn
ㅊ	ch'	as *church*
ㅋ	k'	as *k*ite
ㅌ	t'	as *t*ank
ㅍ	p'	as *p*um*p*
ㅎ	h	as *h*igh

2) Double:

Korean Letter	Romanization	English sound
ㄲ	kk	as *sk*y or Ja*ck*
ㄸ	tt	as *st*ay
ㅃ	pp	as *sp*y
ㅆ	ss	as e*ss*ential
ㅉ	tch	as *j*oy

Guidelines for the Romanization of Korean

(1) Basic Principles for Transcription

1) Romanization is based on standard Korean pronunciation.
2) No symbols except Roman letters are used, so far as possible.
3) Romanization follows the principle of 'one letter (or set of letters) per phoneme.'

(2) Summary of the Transcription System

1) Vowels are transcribed as follows:

simple vowels ㅏ ㅓ ㅗ ㅜ ㅡ ㅣ ㅐ ㅔ ㅚ
a ŏ o u ŭ i ae e oe

diphthongs ㅑ ㅕ ㅛ ㅠ ㅒ ㅖ ㅢ ㅘ ㅝ ㅙ ㅞ ㅟ
ya yŏ yo yu yae ye ŭi wa wo wae we wi

[Note] Long vowels are not marked in transcription.

2) Consonants are transcribed as follows:

plosives (stops)	ㄱ	ㄲ	ㅋ
	k, g	kk	k'
	ㄷ	ㄸ	ㅌ
	t, d	tt	t'
	ㅂ	ㅃ	ㅍ
	p, b	pp	p'
affricates	ㅈ	ㅉ	ㅊ
	ch, j	tch	ch'
fricatives	ㅅ	ㅆ	ㅎ
	s, sh	ss	h

nasals   ㅁ   ㄴ   ㅇ
                 m   n   ng

liquids   ㄹ
                 r, l

[Note 1] ㄱ, ㄷ, ㅂ and ㅈ are transcribed respectively as *g*, *d*, *b* and *j*, between vowels, or between ㄴ, ㄹ, ㅁ, or ㅇ and a vowel; otherwise they are transcribed as *k, t, p,* and *ch.*

e. g. 가구 kagu 바둑 paduk 갈비 kalbi
제주 Cheju 담배 tambae 받침 patch'im

[Note 2] ㅅ is transcribed as *s* except in the case of 시, when it is transcribed as *sh.*

e. g. 시루 shiru 신안 Shinan 신촌 Shinch'on
부산 Pusan 상표 sangp'yo 황소 hwangso

[Note 3] ㄹ is transcribed as *r* before a vowel, and as *l* before a consonant or at the end of a word: ㄹㄹ is transcribed as *ll.*

e. g. 사랑 sarang 물건 mulgŏn 발 pal
진달래 chindallae

(3) **Special Provisions for·Transcription**

1) When Korean sound values change as in the following cases, the results of those changes are transcribed as follows:

1. The case of assimilation of adjacent consonants

e. g. 냇 물 naenmul   부엌문 puŏngmun
낚는다 nangnŭnda   닫는다 tannŭnda
갚는다 kamnŭnda   진 리 chilli
심 리 shimni   압 력 amnyŏk

독 립 tongnip

2. The case of the epenthetic ㄴ and ㄹ

    e.g. 가랑잎 karangnip   낮 일 nannil

         담 요 tamnyo   홑이불 honnibul

         풀 잎 p'ullip   물 약 mullyak

3. The case of palatalization

    e.g. 굳 이 kuji   해돋이 haedoji

         같 이 kach'i

4. The case when ㄱ, ㄷ, ㅂ and ㅈ are adjacent to ㅎ

    e.g. 국 화 kuk'wa   낳 다 nat'a

         밟히다 palp'ida   맞히다 mach'ida

[Note] The tense (or glottalized) sounds, which occur in cases when morphemes are compounded as in the examples below, are transcribed by voiceless consonants.

    e.g. 장기 (長技) changki   사 건 sakŏn

         냇 가 naetka   작 두 chaktu

         신 다 shinta   산 불 sanpul

2) When there is a possibility of confusion in pronunciation, or a need for segmentation, a hyphen '-' may be used.

    e.g. 연 구 yŏn-gu   잔기 (殘期) chan-gi

         물가에 mulka-e   종로에 Chongno-e

[Note] In the transcription of personal names and names of administrative units, assimilated sound changes before or after a hyphen are not transcribed.

    e.g. 김복남 Kim Pok-nam

         사북면 Sabuk-myŏn

3) The first letter is capitalized in proper names.

    e.g. 인 천 Inch'ŏn   대 구 Taegu

세 종 Sejong

4) Personal names are written by family name first, followed by a space and then the given name. A hyphen will separate given names, except that non-Sino-Korean given names may be joined without a hyphen.

e. g. 김정호 Kim Chŏng-ho
남궁 동자 Namgung Tong-cha
손 미희자 Son Mi-hŭi-cha
정 마리아 Chŏng Maria

5) In spite of the Note to 2) above, administrative units such as 도, 시, 군, 구, 읍, 면, 리, 동 and 가 are transcribed respectively as *do, shi, gun, gu, ŭp, myŏn, ri, dong*, and *ga* and are preceded by a hyphen.

e. g. 충청북도 Ch'ungch'ŏngbuk-do
제 주 도 Cheju-do
의정부시 Ŭijŏngbu-shi
파 주 군 P'aju-gun
도 봉 구 Tobong-gu
신 창 읍 Shinch'ang-ŭp
주 내 면 Chunae-myŏn
인 왕 리 Inwang-ri
당 산 동 Tangsan-dong
봉천 2 동 Pongch'ŏn 2-dong
종로 2 가 Chongno 2-ga
퇴계로 5 가 T'oegyero 5-ga

〔Note〕 Terms for administrative units such as 특별시, 직할시, 시, 군, 읍 and so on may be omitted.

e. g. 부산직할시 Pusan　신창읍 Shinch'ang

6) Names of geographic features, cultural prop-

erties, and man-made structures may be written
without hyphens.

e. g. 남　산 Namsan
속 리 산 Songnisan
금　강 Kŭmgang
독　도 Tokto
해 운 대 Haeundae
경 복 궁 Kyŏngbokkung
도산서원 Tosansŏwon
불 국 사 Pulguksa
현 충 사 Hyŏnch'ungsa
독 립 문 Tongnimmun

[Note] Hyphens may be inserted in words of
five syllables or more.

e. g. 금동 미륵보살 반가상 Kŭmdong-mirŭk-
posal-pan-gasang

7) Some proper names, which cannot be abruptly
changed in view of international practices and
common longstanding transcriptions, may be
written as follows:

e. g. 서　울 Seoul　　　이순신 Yi Sun-shin
연　세 Yonsei　　　이　화 Ewha
이승만 Syngman Rhee

8) When they are difficult to print or to type-
write, the breve '˘' in $\check{o}, \check{u}, y\check{o}$, and $\check{u}i$, and
the apostrophe ' ' in k', t', p', and ch', may
be omitted as long as there is no confusion in
meaning.

Mini Dictionary
of
English-Korean

Romanized

Edited by B. J. Jones

HOLLYM

A

a *art.* not normally used in Korean.—*a book* ch'aek 책 /*a dog* kae 개 ; When *a* means each, it may be translated by *han* 한 or *il* 일 : ～*week* il chu-il 일 주 일 ; (*a certain*) ŏ-ddŏn 어떤.

abacus *n.* chu-p'an 주판.

abalone *n.* chŏn-bok 전복.

abandon *v.* pŏ-ri-da 버리다, p'o-gi-ha-da 포기하다.

abate *v.* ① (*decrease*) ppae-da 빼다, kam-ha-da 감하 다. ② (*weaken*) yak-hae-ji-da 약해지다.

abbess *n.* yŏ-ja tae-su-do-wŏn-jang 여자 대수도원장.

abbey *n.* tae-su-do-wŏn 대수도원.

abbot *n.* tae-su-do-wŏn-jang 대수도원장.

abbreviate *v.* (*words*) saeng-ryak-ha-da 생략하다; (*shorten*) chu-ri-da 줄이다.

abbreviation *n.* saeng-ryak 생략, (*word*) yak-ŏ 약어.

abdicate *v.* mul-rŏ-na-da 물러나다 ; pŏ-ri-da 버리다.

abdomen *n.* pae 배, pok-bu 복부.

abduct *v.* yu-goe-ha-da 유괴하다.

abet *v.* sŏn-dong-ha-da 선동하다, ch'u-gi-da 추기다.

abhor *v.* mop-si si-rŏ-ha-da 몹시 싫어하다.

abide *v.* mŏ-mu-ru-da 머무르다 ; sal-da 살다. 「수완가.

ability *n.* nŭng-ryŏk 능력 : *a man of* ～ su-wan-ga

abject *adj.* ch'ŏn-bak-han 천박한, pi-ch'am-han 비참한.

able *adj.* hal su it-nŭn 할 수 있는, yu-nŭng-han 유능한.

abnormal *adj.* i-sang-han 이상한, pyŏn-ch'ik-ŭi 변칙의.

aboard *adv. & prep.* (*on board*) …ŭl t'a-go …을 타고.

abode *n.* chu-so 주소, kŏ-ch'ŏ 거처.

abolish *v.* p'ye-ji[ch'ŏl-p'ye]-ha-da 폐지[철폐]하다.

abolition *n.* p'ye-ji 폐지, ch'ŏl-p'ye 철폐.
A-bomb *n.* (*atomic bomb*) wŏn-ja-p'ok-t'an 원자폭탄.
abominable *adj.* chi-gŭt-ji-gŭt-han 지긋지긋한, chi-dok-han 지독한, chi-gyŏ-un 지겨운.
aboriginal *adj.* t'o-ch'ak-ŭi 토착의. —*n.* t'o-ch'ak-min 토착민.
abortion *n.* yu-san 유산(流産).
abound *v.* p'ung-bu-ha-da 풍부하다.
about *prep.* (*concerning*) …e tae-ha-yŏ …에 대하여. —*adv.* ① (*approximately*) yak 약. ② (*around*) chu-wi-e 주위에. 「wi-ŭi 위의.
above *prep.* …wi-e …위에. —*adv.* wi-ro 위로. —*adj.*
abridge *v.* (*shorten*) yo-yak-ha-da 요약하다.
abroad *adv.* hae-oe-e 해외에 ; nŏl-ri 널리.
abrogate *v.* p'ye-ji-ha-da 폐지하다. 「뜻밖의.
abrupt *adj.* kap-jak-sŭ-rŏ-un 갑작스러운, ttŭt-ba-ggŭi
abscess *n.* pu-sŭ-rŏm 부스럼.
absence *n.* kyŏl-sŏk 결석, pu-jae 부재(不在).
absent *adj.* kyŏl-sŏk-han 결석한. —*v.* kyŏl-sŏk-ha-da 결석하다, kyŏl-gŭn-ha-da 결근하다.
absent-minded *adj.* mŏng-ha-go it-nŭn 멍하고 있는.
absolute *adj.* chŏl-dae-ŭi 절대의, chŏn-je-jŏk 전제적.
absolutely *adv.* chŏl-dae-ro 절대로.
absolution *n.* sa-myŏn 사면. 「면하다.
absolve *v.* yong-sŏ-ha-da 용서하다, sa-myŏn-ha-da 사
absorb *v.* hŭp-su-ha-da 흡수하다.
abstain *v.* chŏl-je-ha-da 절제하다, sam-ga-da 삼가다.
abstinence *n.* chŏl-je 절제 ; kŭm-ju 금주(禁酒).
abstract *adj.* ch'u-sang-jŏk-in 추상적인. —*n.* ch'u-sang 추상 ; (*summary*) chŏk-yo 적요(摘要).
absurd *adj.* (*unreasonable*) pul-hap-ri-han 불합리한 ; (*foolish*) ŏ-i-ŏp-nŭn 어이없는.

abundance *n.* p'ung-bu 풍부, yun-t'aek 윤택.
abundant *adj.* p'ung-bu-han 풍부한, man-ŭn 많은.
abuse *n.* (*of authority*) nam-yong 남용 ; (*verbal*) mo-yok 모욕. —*v.* (*revile*) mo-yok-ha-da 모욕하다 ; (*misuse*) nam-yong-ha-da 남용하다.
abusive *adj.* ip-jŏng sa-na-un 입정 사나운, yok-ha-nŭn 욕하는 : *use ~ language* yok-ŭl ha-da 욕을 하다.
acacia *n.* a-k'a-si-a 아카시아.
academy *n.* hak-sul-wŏn 학술원, a-k'a-de-mi 아카데미 ; (*school*) hak-wŏn 학원 ; (*society*) hak-hoe 학회.
accede *v.* tong-ŭi-ha-da 동의하다. 「가속(加速)하다.
accelerate *v.* ppa-rŭ-ge ha-da 빠르게 하다, ka-sok-ha-da
accent *n.* aek-sŏn-t'ŭ 액센트, kang-se 강세.
accept *v.* pat-a-dŭ-ri-da 받아들이다, pat-da 받다.
acceptable *adj.* su-rak-hal man-han 수락할 만한, ma-ŭm-e tŭ-nŭn 마음에 드는, man-jok-han 만족한.
access *n.* ① (*approach*) chŏp-gŭn 접근. ② (*admittance*) ch'u-rip 출입. ③ (*entrance*) ip-gu 입구.
accessary·accessory *n.* pu-sok-p'um 부속품, aek-se-sŏ-ri 액세서리. —*adj.* po-jo-jŏk-in 보조적인.
accessible *adj.* ka-gga-i-hal su it-nŭn 가까이할 수 있는.
accession *n.* (*reaching*) to-dal 도달 ; (*enthronement*) chŭk-wi 즉위 ; (*acquisition*) ch'wi-dŭk 취득.
accident *n.* ① (*unexpected event*) sa-go 사고. ② (*chance*) u-yŏn 우연 : *by ~* u-yŏn-hi 우연히.
accidental *adj.* u-yŏn-han 우연한, ttŭt-ba-ggŭi 뜻밖의.
accidentally *adv.* u-yŏn-hi 우연히.
acclaim *v.* hwan-ho-ha-da 환호하다 ; oe-ch'i-da 외치다.
accommodate *v.* (*admit*) su-yong-ha-da 수용하다 ; (*adapt*) chŏk-ŭng-si-k'i-da 적응시키다. 「숙소.
accommodation *n.* chŏk-ŭng 적응 ; (*lodgings*) suk-so
accompaniment *n.* pu-su-mul 부수물 ; (*music*) pan-ju

반주. 「da 동반하다.
accompany *v.* ham-gge ka-da 함께 가다, tong-ban-ha-
accomplice *n.* kong-bŏm-ja 공범자.
accomplish *v.* i-ru-da 이루다, wan-sŏng-ha-da 완성하다.
accomplishment *n.* sŏng-ch'wi 성취, wan-sŏng 완성.
accord *n.* il-ch'i 일치. —*v.* il-ch'i-ha-da 일치하다.
according *adv.* ~ *to* …e tta-ra …에 따라.
accordingly *adv.* kŭ-rŏ-mŭ-ro 그러므로. 「코오디언.
accordion *n.* son-p'ung-gŭm 손풍금, a-k'o-o-di-ŏn 아
account *v.* kye-san-ha-da 계산하다 ; …i-ra-go saeng-
gak-ha-da …이라고 생각하다. —*n.* kye-san 계산.
accountant *n.* hoe-gye-sa 회계사, kye-ri-sa 계리사.
·accumulate *v.* ch'uk-jŏk-ha-da 축적하다.
accuracy *n.* (*correctness*) chŏng-hwak 정확, (*precision*) chŏng-mil-do 정밀도. 「정밀한.
accurate *adj.* chŏng-hwak-han 정확한, chŏng-mil-han
accusation *n.* ① (*indictment*) ko-bal 고발. ② (*blame*)
pi-nan 비난, hil-ch'aek 힐책.
accuse *v.* ko-bal-ha-da 고발하다, pi-nan-ha-da 비난하다.
accustom *v.* ik-hi-da 익히다, sŭp-gwan-dŭ-ri-da 습관들
ace *n.* e-i-sŭ 에이스, u-su-sŏn-su 우수선수. 「이다.
ache *v.* a-p'ŭ-da 아프다. —*n.* a-p'ŭm 아픔.
achieve *v.* i-ru-da 이루다, tal-sŏng-ha-da 달성하다.
achievement *n.* ① sŏng-ch'wi 성취, tal-sŏng 달성. ②
(*merit*) kong-jŏk 공적, ŏp-jŏk 업적.
acid *adj.* sin 신. —*n.* san 산(酸). 「ha-da 감사하다.
acknowledge *v.* ① in-jŏng-ha-da 인정하다. ② kam-sa-
acorn *n.* to-t'o-ri 도토리. 「알리다.
acquaint *v.* …ŭl ch'in-hi al-da …을 친히 알다, al-ri-da
acquaintance *n.* a-nŭn sa-i 아는 사이, ch'in-ji 친지.
acquiesce *v.* muk-in-ha-da 묵인하다.
acquire *v.* ŏt-da 얻다, sŭp-dŭk-ha-da 습득하다.

acquit *v.* ① mu-joe-ro ha-da 무죄로 하다, pang-myŏn-ha-da 방면(放免)하다. ② (*pay*) kap-da 갚다.
acre *n.* e-i-k'ŏ 에이커 ; (*pl.*) non-bat 논밭.
acrid *adj.* mae-un 매운, (*bitter*) ssŭn 쓴.
acrobat *n.* kok-ye-sa 곡예사, kwang-dae 광대.
across *prep. & adv.* kŏn-nŏ-sŏ 건너서.
act *v.* haeng-ha-da 행하다. —*n.* (*deed*) haeng-wi 행위 ; (*law*) pŏp-ryŏng 법령, cho-rye 조례 ; (*scene*) mak 막.
acting *adj.* ① chak-yong-ha-nŭn 작용하는. ② (*substitute*) tae-ri-ŭi 대리의 : *the ~ chairman* ŭi-jang sŏ-ri 의장 서리(署理).
action *n.* ① haeng-dong 행동, haeng-wi 행위. ② (*play*) yŏn-gi 연기(演技).
active *adj.* ① hwal-dong-jŏk-in 활동적인, hwal-bal-han 활발한. ② chŏk-gŭk-jŏk-in 적극적인.
activity *n.* hwal-dong 활동, hwal-yak 활약.
actor *n.* nam(-bae)-u 남(배)우.
actress *n.* yŏ(-bae)-u 여(배)우.　　　　　「현행의.
actual *adj.* sil-je-ŭi 실제의 ; (*present*) hyŏn-haeng-ŭi
acute *adj.* nal-k'a-ro-un 날카로운, mo-jin 모진.
adapt *v.* (*fit*) chŏk-ŭng-si-k'i-da 적응시키다.
add *v.* tŏ-ha-da 더하다.
addict *v.* ppa-ji-ge ha-da 빠지게 하다.
addition *n.* pu-ga 부가(附加) ; tŏt-sem 덧셈.　　「가세.
additional *adj.* ch'u-ga-ŭi 추가의 : ~ *tax* pu-ga-se 부
address *v.* (*speak to*) yŏn-sŏl-ha-da 연설하다 ; (*letter*) chu-so sŏng-myŏng-ŭl ssŭ-da 주소 성명을 쓰다. —*n.* ① chu-so 주소. ② (*speech*) yŏn-sŏl 연설.
addressee *n.* su-sin-in 수신인, pat-nŭn-i 받는이.
adequate *adj.* ŏ-ul-ri-nŭn 어울리는, chŏk-dang-han 적당한 ; (*sufficient*) ch'ung-bun-han 충분한.
adhere *v.* tŭl-rŏ-but-da 들러붙다 ; ko-su-ha-da 고수하다.

adhesion *n*. pu-ch'ak 부착, ko-ch'ak 고착.

adhesive plaster pan-ch'ang-go 반창고.

adjacent *adj*. pu-gŭn-ŭi 부근의, in-jŏp-han 인접한.

adjective *n*. hyŏng-yong-sa 형용사.

adjoin *v*. chŏp-ha-da 접하다, in-jŏp-ha-da 인접하다.

adjourn *v*. (*put off*) yŏn-gi-ha-da 연기하다 ; (*recess*) hyu-hoe-ha-da 휴회하다. 「조정하다.

adjust *v*. chŏng-don-ha-da 정돈하다 ; cho-jŏng-ha-da

adjutant *n*. pu-gwan 부관.

adjutant general ko-gŭp pu-gwan 고급 부관.

administer *v*. (*superintend*) kam-dok-ha-da 감독하다, (*manage*) kwal-li-ha-da 관리하다.

administration *n*. ① haeng-jŏng 행정, t'ong-ch'i 통치. ② (*management*) kwal-li 관리, kyŏng-yŏng 경영.

administrator *n*. haeng-jŏng-gwan 행정관.

admirable *adj*. kam-t'an-hal man-han 감탄할 만한, hul-ryung-han 훌륭한, chang-han 장한.

admiral *n*. hae-gun-dae-jang 해군대장 ; che-dok 제독.

admiration *n*. kam-t'an 감탄, ch'ing-ch'an 칭찬.

admire *v*. kam-t'an-ha-da 감탄하다 ; (*praise*) ch'ing-ch'an-ha-da 칭찬하다.

admission *n*. ① (*school*) ip-hak 입학, (*theater etc.*) ip-jang 입장. ② (*fee*) ip-hak-gŭm 입학금.

admit *v*. ① (*let in*) tŭ-ri-da 들이다. ② (*recognize*) in-jŏng-ha-da 인정하다. ③ (*concede*) yang-bo-ha-da

admittance *n*. ip-jang(-hŏ-ga) 입장(허가). 「양보하다.

admonish *v*. t'a-i-rŭ-da 타이르다, kwŏn-go-ha-da 권고

admonition *n*. ch'ung-go 충고, kyŏng-go 경고. 「하다.

ado *n*. (*fuss*) so-dong 소동 ; (*trouble*) su-go 수고.

adolescence *n*. ch'ŏng-nyŏn-gi 청년기.

adopt *v*. (*accept*) ch'ae-yong[ch'ae-t'aek]-ha-da 채용 [채택]하다 ; (*a son*) yang-ja-ro sam-da 양자로 삼다.

adopted son yang-ja 양자.

adoration *n.* chon-gyŏng 존경, sung-bae 숭배. 「하다.

adore *v.* sung-bae-ha-da 숭배하다, hŭm-mo-ha-da 흠모

adorn *v.* kku-mi-da 꾸미다, chang-sik-ha-da 장식하다.

adrift *adv.* p'yo-ryu-ha-yŏ 표류하여.

adroit *adj.* som-ssi-it-nŭn 솜씨있는, ki-min-han 기민한.

adulation *n.* a-ch'ŏm 아첨, a-yang 아양.

adult *n.* ŏ-rŭn 어른, sŏng-in 성인 : ~ *education* sŏng-in-gyo-yuk 성인교육.　　　　　「질을 저하시키다.

adulterate *v.* (*debase*) p'um-jil-ŭl chŏ-ha-si-k'i-da 품

adultery *n.* kan-t'ong 간통, kan-ŭm 간음.

advance *v.* (*move forward*) chŏn-jin-ha-da 전진하다 ; (*propose*) chu-jang-ha-da 주장하다 ; (*promote*) sŭng-jin-si-k'i-da 승진시키다.　　　　　「wi 전위(前衛).

advanced *adj.* chin-bo-han 진보한 : *an* ~ *guard* chŏn-

advantage *n.* i-ik 이익, yu-ri 유리(有利).

advantageous *adj.* yu-ri-han 유리한.

Adventism *n.* ye-su chae-rim-sŏl 예수 재림설.

adventure *n.* mo-hŏm 모험, mo-hŏm-dam 모험담.

adventurer *n.* mo-hŏm-ga 모험가, t'u-gi-sa 투기사.

adverb *n.* pu-sa 부사(副詞).

adversary *n.* (*enemy*) wŏn-su 원수, chŏk 적 ; (*opponent*) sang-dae 상대.

adverse *adj.* ① (*opposed*) pan-dae-ŭi 반대의. ② (*unfortunate*) pu-run-han 불운한 ; (*unfavorable*) pul-ri-han 불리한. ③ (*confronting*) tae-ŭng-ha-nŭn 대응

adversity *n.* yŏk-gyŏng 역경 ; ko-nan 고난.　　　「하는.

advertise *v.* kwang-go-ha-da 광고하다.

advertisement *n.* kwang-go 광고, kong-si 공시.

advice *n.* ch'ung-go 충고 ; (*information*) al-rim 알림.

advisable *adj.* ① kwŏn-hal man-han 권할 만한. ② (*wise*) hyŏn-myŏng-han 현명한.

advise *v.* ch'ung-go-ha-da 충고하다.
adviser *n.* cho-ŏn-ja 조언자, ko-mun 고문(顧問) : *a legal* ～ pŏp-ryul ko-mun 법률 고문.
advocate *v.* ch'ang-do-ha-da 창도하다. —*n.* (*upholder*) ch'ang-do-ja 창도자 ; (*pleader*) pyŏl-lon-ja 변론자.
adz(e) *n.* son-do-ggi 손도끼, kka-ggwi 까뀌.
aerial *adj.* ① kong-gi-ŭi 공기의, ki-ch'e-ŭi 기체의. ② kong-jung-ŭi 공중의 : ～ *attack* kong-sŭp 공습.
aeroplane *n.* (*Brit.*) pi-haeng-gi 비행기.
afar *adv.* mŏl-ri 멀리, a-dŭk-hi 아득히.
affable *adj.* sang-nyang-han 상냥한.
affair *n.* (*business*) il 일 ; (*event*) sa-gŏn 사건.
affect *v.* yŏng-hyang-ŭl chu-da 영향을 주다.
affectation *n.* kku-mi-nŭn t'ae-do 꾸미는 태도, (*false show*) hŏ-sik 허식.
affection *n.* ① (*love*) ae-jŏng 애정. ② kam-jŏng 감정. ③ (*disease*) chil-byŏng 질병.
affectionate *adj.* ta-jŏng-han 다정한.
affectionately *adv.* chŏng-dap-ge 정답게. 「하다.
affirm *v.* hwak-ŏn-ha-da 확언하다, tan-jŏng-ha-da 단정
affix *v.* ch'ŏm-bu-ha-da 첨부하다, pu-ch'i-da 붙이다.
afflict *v.* koe-rop-hi-da 괴롭히다, kol-ri-da 곯리다.
affliction *n.* (*suffering*) ko-t'ong 고통 ; (*calamity*) chae-nan 재난. 「chu-da 주다.
afford *v.* …hal yŏ-yu-ga it-da …할 여유가 있다 ; (*give*)
affront *n.* (*open insult*) mo-yok 모욕. —*v.* mo-yok-ha-da 모욕하다, yok-bo-i-da 욕보이다.
afire *adv.* pul-t'a-go 불타고, hŭng-bun-ha-yŏ 흥분하여 : *set* ～ t'a-o-rŭ-ge ha-da 타오르게 하다.
aflame *adj. & adv.* pul-t'a-ol-ra 불타올라.
afloat *adj.* ttŏ-it-nŭn 떠있는. —*adv.* sŏn〔ham〕-sang-e 선〔함〕상에 ; hae-sang-e 해상에.

afraid *adj.* mu-sŏ-wŏ-ha-nŭn 무서워하는, u-ryŏ-ha-nŭn 우려하는.
A-frame *n.* chi-ge 지게.
after *adv.* (*behind*) twi-e 뒤에 ; (*time*) hu-e 후에. — *prep.* …ŭi twi-e …의
afternoon *n.* o-hu 오후. ⌐뒤에.
afterward(s) *adv.* hu-e 후에.
again *adv.* ta-si 다시, tto 또.

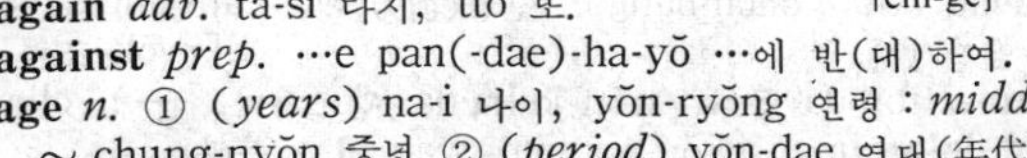
[chi-ge]

against *prep.* …e pan(-dae)-ha-yŏ …에 반(대)하여.
age *n.* ① (*years*) na-i 나이, yŏn-ryŏng 연령 : *middle* ~ chung-nyŏn 중년. ② (*period*) yŏn-dae 연대(年代) : *the Atomic A*~ wŏn-ja-ryŏk-si-dae 원자력시대.
aged *adj.* na-i-mŏk-ŭn 나이먹은, nŭl-gŭn 늙은.
agency *n.* ① tae-ri(-jŏm) 대리(점) : *a general* ~ ch'ong-dae-ri-jŏm 총대리점. ② (*of government*) ki-gwan 기관. ⌐협의 사항.
agenda *n.* ŭi-sa il-jŏng 의사 일정, hyŏp-ŭi sa-hang
agent *n.* tae-ri-in 대리인 : *secret* ~ mil-jŏng 밀정.
aggravate *v.* ak-hwa-si-k'i-da 악화시키다.
aggregate *adj.* (*collective*) chip-hap-jŏk-in 집합적인 ; (*total*) ch'ong-gye-ŭi 총계의.
aggression *n.* kong-gyŏk 공격 ; ch'im-ryak 침략.
aggressive *adj.* ch'im-ryak-jŏk 침략적. ⌐하다.
aggrieve *v.* koe-rop-hi-da 괴롭히다, hak-dae-ha-da 학대
agile *adj.* (*deft*) min-ch'ŏp-han 민첩한 ; (*nimble*) yŏng-ri-han 영리한. ⌐뒤흔들다.
agitate *v.* sŏn-dong-ha-da 선동하다 ; twi-hŭn-dŭl-da
ago *adv.* (chi-gŭm-bu-t'ŏ) … chŏn-e (지금부터) … 전에 : *ten years* ~ sip-nyŏn chŏn 10년 전.
agony *n.* ko-min 고민, ko-t'ong 고통.
agrarian *adj.* t'o-ji-ŭi 토지의, nong-ŏp-ŭi 농업의.
agree *v.* tong-ŭi-ha-da 동의하다, ŭng-ha-da 응하다.

agreeable *adj.* ma-ŭm-e tŭ-nŭn 마음에 드는, (*willing*) k'wae-hi ŭng-ha-nŭn 쾌히 응하는.

agreement *n.* (*treaty*) hyŏp-yak 협약 ; (*assent*) tong-ŭi 동의 ; (*concord*) il-ch'i 일치. 「의.

agricultural *adj.* nong-ŏp-ŭi 농업의, nong-hak-ŭi 농학

agriculture *n.* nong-ŏp 농업 ; nong-hak 농학.

ague *n.* ① hak-jil 학질. ② o-han 오한(惡寒).

ahead *adv.* chŏn-bang-e 전방(前方)에, ap-jang-sŏ-sŏ 앞장서서. 「ryŏk 조력.

aid *v.* top-da 돕다, wŏn-jo-ha-da 원조하다. —*n.* cho-

aid-de-camp *n.* chŏn-sok pu-gwan 전속 부관.

ail *v.* koe-rop-hi-da 괴롭히다 ; pyŏng-dŭl-da 병들다.

ailment *n.* (*illness*) pyŏng 병.

aim *v.* kyŏ-nu-da 겨누다. —*n.* mok-jŏk 목적.

aimless *adj.* mok-jŏk-ŏp-nŭn 목적없는.

air *n.* ① (*atmosphere*) kong-gi 공기. ② (*open space*) kong-jung 공중. ③ (*manner*) t'ae-do 태도.

air base kong-gun ki-ji 공군 기지.

air conditioning naeng-nan-bang 냉난방.

airplane *n.* pi-haeng-gi 비행기.

airport *n.* kong-hang 공항(空港).

air pressure ki-ap 기압.

aisle *n.* (chwa-sŏk sa-i-ŭi) t'ong-ro (좌석 사이의) 통로.

akin *adj.* (*of kin*) tong-jok-ŭi 동족의 ; (*resembling*) yu-sa-han 유사한. 「민활하게.

alacrity *n.* min-hwal 민활 : *with* ~ min-hwal-ha-ge

alarm *v.* (*frighten*) kkam-jjak nol-ra-ge ha-da 깜짝 놀라게 하다 ; (*warn*) wi-gŭp-ham-ŭl al-ri-da 위급함을 알리다. —*n.* nol-ram 놀람, kyŏng-bo 경보.

alarm clock cha-myŏng-jong 자명종.

alarming *adj.* nol-ra-un 놀라운, wi-gŭp-han 위급한.

alas *int.* a-i-go 아이고, a-a 아아, sŭl-p'ŭ-da 슬프다.

album *n.* ael-bŏm 앨범, sa-jin-ch'ŏp 사진첩, u-p'yo-
alcohol *n.* al-k'o-ol 알코올. ⌞ch'ŏp 우표첩.
alcoholism *n.* al-k'o-ol chung-dok 알코올 중독.
alder *n.* o-ri-na-mu 오리나무. ⌜주.
ale *n.* maek-ju 맥주 : *bottled* ～ pyŏng-maek-ju 병맥
alehouse *n.* maek-ju-jip 맥주집, pi-ŏ hQ-ol 비어 호올.
alert *adj.* chu-ŭi-gi-p'ŭn 주의깊은 ;chae-bba-rŭn 재빠른.
algebra *n.* tae-su-hak 대수학(代數學).
alibi *n.* al-ri-ba-i 알리바이.
alien *n.* oe-guk-in 외국인. —*adj.* oe-guk-in-ŭi 외국인의.
alienate *v.* mŏl-ri-ha-da 멀리하다, tta-dol-ri-da 따돌리다.
alight *v.* ① nae-ri-da 내리다, ha-ch'a-ha-da 하차하다.
  ② (*settle*) nae-ryŏ-an-da 내려앉다.
alike *adj.* (*like each other*) kkok tal-mŭn 꼭 닮은.
  —*adv.* (*similarly*) pi-sŭt-ha-ge 비슷하게.
alive *adj.* ① (*living*) sa-ra-it-nŭn 살아있는. ② (*active*)
  hwal-bal-han 활발한.
all *adj.* mo-dŭn 모든. —*n.* chŏn-bu 전부. —*adv.*
  (*completely*) chŏn-hyŏ 전혀, t'ong-t'ŭ-rŏ 통틀어.
allege *v.* (*assert*) chu-jang-ha-da 주장하다 ; (*declare*)
  sil-lip-ha-da 신립(申立)하다.
alleged *adj.* chu-jang-doen 주장된 ; i-rŭn-ba 이른바.
allegiance *n.* ch'ung-sŏng 충성, ch'ung-sil 충실.
alley *n.* (*path*) o-sol-gil 오솔길, (*back street*) twit-
  gol-mok 뒷골목.
alliance *n.* ① yŏn-hap 연합. ② tong-maeng-guk 동맹국.
alligator *n.* ak-ŏ 악어.
all-important *adj.* a-ju chung-yo-han 아주 중요한.
allot *v.* ① (*assign*) hal-dang-ha-da 할당하다, pun-bae-
  ha-da 분배하다. ② chi-jŏng-ha-da 지정하다.
allow *v.* (*permit*) hŏ-rak-ha-da 허락하다, (*grant*) chi-
  gŭp-ha-da 지급하다.

allowance *n.* ① (*share allotted*) il-jŏng-ryang 일정량. ② (*compensation*) su-dang 수당.

allude *v.* ŏn-gŭp-ha-da 언급하다, am-si-ha-da 암시하다.

allure *v.* kkoe-da 꾀다, yu-hok-ha-da 유혹하다. —*n.* mae-hok 매혹, (*charm*) ae-gyo 애교.

allusion *n.* am-si 암시, ŏn-gŭp 언급.

ally *n.* tong-maeng-guk 동맹국. —*v.* tong-maeng-ha-da 동맹하다, che-hyu-ha-da 제휴하다.

almanac *n.* tal-ryŏk 달력 ; yŏn-gam 연감.

almighty *adj.* chŏn-nŭng-ŭi 전능의 ; tae-dan-han 대단한. —*n.* (*God*) chŏn-nŭng-ŭi sin 전능의 신.

almost *adv.* kŏ-ŭi 거의, tae-ch'e-ro 대체로. 「함.

alms *n.* ŭi-yŏn-gŭm 의연금 : ～ *box* cha-sŏn-ham 자선

aloft *adv.* wi-ro 위로 ; (*high up*) no-p'i 높이.

aloha *int.* an-nyŏng! 안녕 !

alone *adj.* hol-ro-ŭi 홀로의. —*adv.* hol-ro 홀로.

along *prep.* & *adv.* tta-ra-sŏ 따라서.

aloud *adv.* k'un so-ri-ro 큰 소리로, so-ri-no-p'i 소리높

alphabet *n.* al-p'a-bet 알파벳. 「이.

alphabetically *adv.* al-p'a-bet sun-ŭ-ro 알파벳 순으로.

alpine *adj.* no-p'ŭn san-ŭi 높은 산의 ; (*A～*) al-p'ŭ-sŭ san-ŭi 알프스 산의 : *an ～ club* san-ak-hoe 산악회.

alpinist *n.* tŭng-san-ga 등산가.

already *adv.* pŏl-ssŏ 벌써, i-mi 이미.

also *adv.* yŏk-si 역시, ma-ch'an-ga-ji-ro 마찬가지로.

altar *n.* che-dan 제단(祭壇).

alter *v.* pyŏn-gyŏng-ha-da 변경하다, pa-ggu-da 바꾸다.

alteration *n.* pyŏn-gyŏng 변경, kae-jo 개조.

alternate *v.* kyo-dae〔kyo-ch'e〕-ha-da 교대〔교체〕하다.

alternation *n.* kyo-dae 교대, kyo-ch'e 교체.

alternative *n.* yang-ja-t'aek-il 양자택일.

although *conj.* pi-rok …il-ji-ra-do 비록 …일지라도.

altitude *n.* no-p'i 높이, ko-do 고도 ; hae-bal 해발.

altogether *adv.* (*entirely*) chŏn-hyŏ 전혀, (*in all*) t'ong-t'ŭ-rŏ 통틀어 ; (*on the whole*) tae-ch'e-ro 대체로.

aluminium *n.* al-ru-mi-nyum 알루미늄.

alumnus *n.* cho-rŏp-saeng 졸업생, tong-ch'ang-saeng 동창생 : ~ *association* tong-ch'ang-hoe 동창회.

always *adv.* hang-sang 항상, ŏn-je-na 언제나. 「하다.

amalgamate *v.* hap-dong〔hap-byŏng〕-ha-da 합동〔합병〕

amass *v.* ① (*pile up*) ssa-t'a 쌓다, (*accumulate*) ch'uk-jŏk-ha-da 축적하다. ② (*collect*) su-jip-ha-da 수

amateur *n.* a-ma-t'yu-ŏ 아마튜어.　　　　　　└집하다.

amaze *v.* nol-ra-ge ha-da 놀라게 하다.

amazement *n.* nol-ra-um 놀라움, kyŏng-ak 경악.

amazing *adj.* nol-ra-un 놀라운, koeng-jang-han 굉장한.

ambassador *n.* tae-sa 대사(大使).

amber *n.* ho-bak 호박.　　　　　　「an-ŭn 분명치 않은.

ambiguous *adj.* ae-mae-han 애매한, pun-myŏng-ch'i

ambition *n.* (*strong desire*) ya-mang 야망, ung-ji 웅지, p'o-bu 포부.

ambitious *adj.* ya-sim-jŏk-in 야심적인 : *Boys, be* ~ ! So-nyŏn-dŭl-i-yŏ tae-mang-ŭl ka-jyŏ-ra! 소년들이여, 대망을 가져라 !　　　　　　「앰뷸런스.

ambulance *n.* ku-gŭp-ch'a 구급차, aem-byul-rŏn-sŭ

ambush *n.* cham-bok 잠복, pok-byong 복병. —*v.* mae-bok-ha-da 매복(埋伏)하다.

amen *int.* a-men 아멘.

amend *v.* ko-ch'i-da 고치다, su-jŏng-ha-da 수정하다.

amendment *n.* su-jŏng 수정, kyo-jŏng 교정.

amends *n.* pae-sang 배상, pŏl-ch'ung 벌충.

America *n.* mi-guk 미국, a-me-ri-k'a 아메리카.

American *adj.* mi-guk-ŭi 미국의. —*n.* ① (*person*) mi-guk-in 미국인. ② (*language*) mi-guk-ŏ 미국어.

amiable *adj.* (*lovable*) kwi-yŏm-sŏng-it-nŭn 귀염성있는, sa-rang-sŭ-rŏ-un 사랑스러운.
amicable *adj.* u-ho-jŏk-in 우호적인, on-hwa-han 온화한.
amid(st) *prep.* …ŭi ka-un-de …의 가운데.
ammonia *n.* am-mo-ni-a 암모니아.
ammunition *n.* t'an-yak 탄약, kun-su-p'um 군수품.
amnesty *n.* t'ŭk-sa 특사(特赦), tae-sa 대사(大赦) : *general* ～ il-ban sa-myŏn 일반 사면.
among(st) *prep.* ka-un-de 가운데. 「반한.
amorous *adj.* ho-saek-ŭi 호색의 ; (*enamoured*) pan-han
amour *n.* chŏng-sa 정사(情事), mil-t'ong 밀통.
amount *n.* (*altogether*) ch'ong-gye 총계 ; (*quantity*) aek-su 액수, yang 양(量). —*v.* i-rŭ-da 이르다, toe-da
ample *adj.* ch'ung-bun-han 충분한. 「되다.
amplifier *n.* aem-p'ŭ 앰프, hwak-sŏng-gi 확성기.
amplify *v.* hwak-dae-ha-da 확대하다 ; (*more details*) sang-se-hi sŏl-myŏng-ha-da 상세히 설명하다.
amputate *v.* chŏl-dan-ha-da 절단하다, chal-ra-nae-da
amputation *n.* chŏl-dan 절단. 「잘라내다.
amulet *n.* pu-jŏk 부적(符籍), aek-mak-i 액막이.
amuse *v.* chae-mi-na-ge ha-da 재미나게 하다.
amusement *n.* (*enjoyment*) hŭng 흥 ; (*entertainment*) o-rak 오락. 「거운.
amusing *adj.* chae-mi-it-nŭn 재미있는, chŭl-gŏ-un 즐
an *art.* not normally used in Korean. —(*one*) han 한, (*a certain*) ŏ-ddŏn 어떤.
anachronism *n.* si-dae ch'ak-o 시대 착오.
an(a)emia *n.* pin-hyŏl-jŭng 빈혈증.
analogy *n.* (*similarity*) yu-sa 유사, yu-ch'u 유추.
analyse·analyze *v.* pun-hae〔pun-sŏk〕-ha-da 분해〔분석〕-ha-da
analysis *n.* pun-hae 분해, pun-sŏk 분석. 「하다.
anarchism *n.* mu-jŏng-bu-ju-ŭi 무정부주의.

anarchist *n.* mu-jŏng-bu-ju-ŭi-ja 무정부주의자.
anarchy *n.* mu-jŏng-bu 무정부.
anatomy *n.* hae-bu 해부, hae-bu-hak 해부학.
ancestor *n.* sŏn-jo 선조(先祖), cho-sang 조상.
ancestral *adj.* sŏn-jo-ŭi 선조의, cho-sang-ŭi 조상의.
ancestry *n.* cho-sang 조상 ; (*family descent*) ka-gye 가계(家系), mun-bŏl 문벌.
anchor *n.* tat 닻. —*v.* ta-ch'ŭl nae-ri-da 닻을 내리다; chŏng-bak-ha-da 정박하다.
anchorage *n.* chŏng-bak 정박, chŏng-bak-ji 정박지.
ancient *adj.* o-rae-doen 오래된, yet-nal-ŭi 옛날의.
and *conj.* (*between noun and noun*) …wa …와, (*everywhere else*) tto 또, kŭ-ri-go 그리고.
anecdote *n.* il-hwa 일화(逸話), ki-dam 기담(奇談).
anesthesia *n.* ma-ch'wi 마취, mu-gam-gak 무감각.
anesthetic *n.* ma-ch'wi-je 마취제.
anew *adv.* sae-ro 새로, ta-si han-bŏn 다시 한번.
angel *n.* ch'ŏn-sa 천사. 「하다.
anger *n.* no-yŏ-um 노여움. —*v.* no-ha-ge ha-da 노하게
angle *n.* ① (*corner*) mo-t'ung-i 모퉁이. ② kak-do 각도. ③ (*fishhook*) nak-si 낚시. —*v.* ① (*fish*) nak-si-jil-ha-da 낚시질하다. ② kkoe-ŏ-nae-da 꾀어내다.
angler *n.* nak-sit-gun 낚싯군.
Anglican Church sŏng-gong-hoe 성공회(聖公會).
Anglo-American *adj.* yŏng-mi-ŭi 영미의.
angry *adj.* sŏng-nan 성난, no-han 노한.
anguish *n.* sim-han ko-t'ong 심한 고통, pi-t'ong 비통.
animal *n.* tong-mul 동물, chim-sŭng 짐승.
animate *v.* ① saeng-myŏng-ŭl pu-rŏ-nŏ-t'a 생명을 불어넣다. ② (*inspire*) ko-mu-ha-da 고무하다.
animism *n.* mul-hwal-ron 물활론(物活論).
animosity *n.* wŏn-han 원한, chŭng-o-sim 증오심.

ankle *n.* pal-mok 발목 : ～ *bone* pok-sa-bbyŏ 복사뼈.

annals *n.* yŏn-dae-p'yo 연대표, yŏn-bo 연보.

annex *v.* (*add*) pu-ga〔ch'ŏm-ga〕-ha-da 부가〔첨가〕하다. —*n.* ① (*affix*) pu-rok 부록. ② (*subsidiary building*) pyŏl-gwan 별관.

annexation *n.* hap-byŏng 합병, pu-ga 부가.

annihilate *v.* chŏn-myŏl-si-k'i-da 전멸시키다 ; (*annul*) p'ye-gi-ha-da 폐기하다.

anniversary *n.* ki-nyŏm-il 기념일, ki-il 기일(忌日).

announce *v.* ① (*give notice of*) al-ri-da 알리다. ② (*publish*) pal-p'yo-ha-da 발표하다.

announcer *n.* ŏ-na-un-sŏ 어나운서.

annoy *v.* koe-rop-hi-da 괴롭히다, sok-t'ae-u-da 속태우다.

annoyance *n.* koe-rop-him 괴롭힘.

annual *adj.* hae-ma-da 해마다 : ～ *income* yŏn-su 연수 (年收)/～ *rings* yŏl-lyun 연륜.

another *adj.* ① tto ha-na-ŭi 또 하나의. ② (*different*) ta-rŭn 다른. —*n.* (*one more thing or person*) tto ha-na 또 하나, tto han sa-ram 또 한 사람.

answer *v.* tae-dap-ha-da 대답하다. —*n.* tae-dap 대답.

ant *n.* kae-mi 개미.

antagonism *n.* chŏk-dae 적대, tae-rip 대립.

antagonist *n.* (*opponent*) pan-dae-ja 반대자, kyŏng-jaeng-ja 경쟁자, chŏk-su 적수.

antarctic *adj.* nam-gŭk-ui 남극의. —*n.* nam-gŭk 남극.

antecedent *adj.* ap-sŏn 앞선 ; sŏn-haeng-ha-nŭn 선행 하는. —*n.* (*ancestry*) cho-sang 조상.

anthem *n.* sŏng-ga 성가 : *national* ～ kuk-ga 국가.

anthology *n.* (*collection of poems*) myong-si-sŏn 명 시선(名詩選) ; sŏn-jip 선집, mun-jip 문집.

anthropology *n.* il-lyu-hak 인류학.

anti-aircraft *adj.* tae-gong-ŭi 대공(對空)의, pang-

gong-ŭi 방공(防空)의. 　　　　　　　「하다.
anticipate *v.* ye-gi-ha-da 예기하다, ye-sang-ha-da 예상
anticipation *n.* ye-gi 예기, ki-dae 기대.
anti-Communism *n.* pan-gong 반공(反共).
antidote *n.* hae-dok-je 해독제, che-hae-mul 제해물.
antipathy *n.* pan-gam 반감 ; hyŏm-o 혐오.
antique *adj.* ko-dae-ŭi 고대의 ; (*old-fashioned*) ku-sik-
ŭi 구식의. —*n.* kol-dong-p'um 골동품.
antiquity *n.* (*old times*) ko-dae 고대(古代) ; (*relics*)
ko-dae yu-mul 고대 유물.
antiseptic *n.* pang-bu-je 방부제.
antler *n.* nok-yong 녹용, ka-ji-jin ppul 가지진 뿔.
anus *n.* hang-mun 항문(肛門).
anxiety *n.* ① (*uneasiness*) kŭn-sim 근심, kŏk-jŏng 걱
정. ② (*eager desire*) yŏl-mang 열망. 「nŭn 갈망하는.
anxious *adj.* kŏk-jŏng-doe-nŭn 걱정되는 ; kal-mang-ha-
anxiously *adv.* yŏm-ryŏ-sŭ-rŏ-un tŭ-si 염려스러운 듯이.
any *adj.* ŏ-ddŏn 어떤, mu-sŭn 무슨.
anybody *pron.* nu-gun-ga 누군가, a-mu-do 아무도.
anyhow *adv.* a-mu-t'ŭn 아뭏든, chwa-u-gan 좌우간.
anyone *pron.* nu-gu-dŭn-ji 누구든지, a-mu-do 아무도,
nu-gun-ga 누군가. 　　　　　　　「do 아무것도.
anything *pron.* mu-ŏ-si-dŭn-ji 무엇이든지, a-mu-gŏt-
anyway *adv.* ŏ-jjaet-dŭn 어쨌든, ha-yŏ-t'ŭn 하여튼.
anywhere *adv.* ŏ-di-dŭn-ji 어디든지.
anywise *adv.* a-mu-rae-do 아무래도, kyŏl-k'o 결코.
apart *adv.* ttŏ-rŏ-jyŏ-sŏ 떨어져서, tta-ro-dda-ro 따로따
로 : *live* ～ tta-ro sal-da 따로 살다. 　　　　　「방.
apartment *n.* ① a-p'a-a-t'ŭ 아파아트. ② (*room*) pang
ape *n.* wŏn-sung-i 원숭이.
apiece *adv.* kak-gak 각각, tta-ro-dda-ro 따로따로.
apologize *v.* (*excuse*) sa-gwa-ha-da 사과하다, (*ex-*

plain) pyŏn-myŏng-ha-da 변명하다.
apology *n.* sa-gwa 사과, pyŏn-myŏng 변명.
apoplexy *n.* chol-do 졸도(卒倒) : *cerebral* ~ noe-il-hyŏl
apostle *n.* sa-do 사도(使徒).　　　　　└뇌일혈.
apostrophe *n.* ŏ-p'o-sŭ-t'ŭ-rŏ-p'i 어포스트러피.
apothecary *n.* yak-jong-sang 약종상.
appal(l) *v.* (*terrify*) sŏm-ddŭk-ha-ge ha-da 섬뜩하게
하다 ; (*dismay*) tang-hwang-k'e ha-da 당황케 하다.
appalling *adj.* so-rŭm-ggi-ch'i-nŭn 소름끼치는.
apparatus *n.* ki-gu 기구, chang-ch'i 장치.
apparent *adj.* myŏng-baek-han 명백한.　　　「외견상.
apparently *adv.* myŏng-baek-hi 명백히 ; oe-gyŏn-sang
apparition *n.* (*ghost*) yu-ryŏng 유령.
appeal *v.* ho-so-ha-da 호소하다, ae-wŏn-ha-da 애원하
다 ; (*law*) sang-go-ha-da 상고하다. —*n.* ① ho-so 호
소. ② (*attraction*) mae-ryŏk 매력.　　　　　「다.
appear *v.* na-t'a-na-da 나타나다, …ro po-i-da …로 보이
appearance *n.* ① ch'ul-hyŏn 출현. ② oe-gwan 외관.
appease *v.* tal-rae-da 달래다, wi-ro-ha-da 위로하다.
appendicitis *n.* maeng-jang-yŏm 맹장염.
appendix *n.* pu-rok 부록, ch'u-ga 추가.　　　　「망.
appetite *n.* ① sik-yok 식욕. ② (*craving*) kal-mang 갈
applause *n.* pak-su kal-ch'ae 박수 갈채, ch'an-yang
찬양, ch'ing-ch'an 칭찬.
apple *n.* sa-gwa 사과, nŭng-gŭm 능금.
appliance *n.* (*apparatus*) ki-gu 기구, sŏl-bi 설비.
applicant *n.* chi-wŏn-ja 지원자, ŭng-mo-ja 응모자.
application *n.* sin-ch'ŏng 신청, chi-wŏn 지원.
applied *adj.* chŏk-yong-doe-nŭn 적용되는, ŭng-yong-ŭi
응용의 : ~ *chemistry* ŭng-yong-hwa-hak 응용화학.
apply *v.* ① chŏk-yong-ha-da 적용하다. ② (*make appli-*
cation) sin-ch'ŏng-ha-da 신청하다.

appoint *v.* ① (*nominate*)chi-myŏng[im-myŏng]-ha-da 지명[임명]하다. ② (*fix*) chi-jŏng-ha-da 지정하다.

appointed *adj.* ① chi-jŏng-doen 지정된, yak-sok-han 약속한. ② (*equipped*) sŏl-bi-doen 설비된.

appointment *n.* ① (*nomination*) im-myŏng 임명 ; (*designation*) chi-jŏng 지정. ② (*promise*) yak-sok 약속.

appraise *v.* kap-sŭl mae-gi-da 값을 매기다.

appreciable *adj.* p'yŏng-ga-hal su it-nŭn 평가할 수 있는 ; (*noticeable*) a-ra-bol su it-nŭn 알아볼 수 있는.

appreciate *v.* ① (*enjoy*) kam-sang-ha-da 감상하다; (*assess*) p'yŏng-ga-ha-da 평가하다. ② (*feel grateful for*) kam-sa-ha-da 감사하다.

appreciation *n.* ① kam-sang 감상. ② kam-sa 감사.

apprehend *v.* ① (*arrest*) ch'e-p'o-ha-da 체포하다. ② (*understand*) i-hae-ha-da 이해하다. ③ (*fear*) u-ryŏ-ha-da 우려하다. 「p'o 체포.

apprehension *n.* ① i-hae 이해. ② pu-ran 불안. ③ ch'e-

apprehensive *adj.* ① (*anxious*) u-ryŏ-ha-nŭn 우려하는. ② (*intelligent*) yŏng-ri-han 영리한.

apprentice *n.* to-je 도제(徒弟), kyŏn-sŭp-saeng 견습생, (*novice*) ch'o-sim-ja 초심자.

approach *v.* ka-gga-i ka-da 가까이 가다, chŏp-gŭn-ha-da 접근하다. —*n.* chŏp-gŭn 접근.

appropriate *adj.* chŏk-dang-han 적당한. —*v.* ch'ung-dang-ha-da 충당하다.

approval *n.* sŭng-in 승인, (*sanction*) in-ga 인가.

approve *v.* sŭng-in-ha-da 승인하다.

approximately *adv.* (*almost*) tae-gang 대강, kŏ-ŭi 거의.

apricot *n.* sal-gu 살구. 「의.

April *n.* sa-wŏl 사월.

apron *n.* ap-ch'i-ma 앞치마, e-i-p'ŭ-rŏn 에이프런.

apt *adj.* (*inclined*)…ha-gi swi-un …하기 쉬운 ; (*suitable*) chŏk-dang-han 적당한.

aquarium *n.* su-jok-gwan 수족관, yang-ŏ-jang 양어장.

arabesque *adj.* (*decoration*) tang-ch'o-mu-nŭi-ŭi 당초 (唐草)무늬의 ; (*fanciful*) koe-sang-han 피상한.

arable land kyŏng-jak-ji 경작지.

arbitrary *adj.* im-ŭi-ŭi 임의의, tok-dan-jŏk-in 독단적인.

arbitrate *v.* chung-jae-ha-da 중재하다.

arbor *n.* su-mok 수목 : *A~ Day* sik-mok-il 식목일.

arc *n.* ho 호(弧), kung-hyŏng 궁형(弓形).

arch *n.* a-a-ch'i 아아치.

archaeology *n.* ko-go-hak 고고학(考古學).

archbishop *n.* tae-ju-gyo 대주교, tae-sa-gyo 대사교.

archery *n.* kung-sul 궁술, kung-do 궁도(弓道).

architect *n.* kŏn-ch'uk-ga 건축가.

architecture *n.* kŏn-ch'uk(-sul) 건축(술).   「북극.

arctic *adj.* puk-gŭk-ŭi 북극의. —*n.* (*the A~*) puk-gŭk

ardent *adj.* yŏl-ryŏl-han 열렬한.   「지구.

area *n.* ① (*space*) myŏn-jŏk 면적. ② (*district*) chi-gu

argue *v.* (*discuss*) non-ha-da 논하다, non-jaeng-ha-da 논쟁하다 ; (*contend*) chu-jang-ha-da 주장하다.

argument *n.* non-jaeng 논쟁 ; (*reason*) non-jŭng 논증.

arise *v.* i-rŏ-na-da 일어나다, pal-saeng-ha-da 발생하다.

aristocrat *n.* kwi-jok 귀족, kwi-jok-jŏk-in sa-ram 귀 족적인 사람 ; kwi-jok-jŏng-ch'i-ju-ŭi-ja 귀족정치주의자.

arithmetic *n.* san-su 산수.

arm *n.* ① p'al 팔. ② pyŏng-gi 병기, mu-gi 무기. —*v.* mu-jang-ha-da 무장하다.

armament *n.* chang-bi 장비, mu-gi 무기, kun-bi 군비.

armchair *n.* al-lak-ŭi-ja 안락의자.

armed *adj.* mu-jang-han 무장한.

armistice *n.* hyu-jŏn 휴전 ; chŏng-jŏn 정전.

armo(u)r *n.* kap-ot 갑옷, kap-ju 갑주.

armo(u)red vehicle chang-gap-ch'a 장갑차.

army *n.* yuk-gun 육군.　　　　　　　　　「jjŭm 쯤.

around *adv. & prep.* tul-re-e 둘레에 ; (*about*) yak 약,

arouse *v.* kak-sŏng-ha-da 각성하다, kkae-u-da 깨우다;
(*excite*) pun-gi-si-k'i-da 분기시키다.

arrange *v.* ① (*put in order*) chŏng-don-ha-da 정돈하
다. ② (*make ready for*) chun-bi-ha-da 준비하다.

arrangement *n.* ① chŏng-don 정돈. ② (*preparation*)
chun-bi 준비. ③ (*agreement*) t'a-hyŏp 타협.

array *n.* ① (*dress up*) kku-mi-da 꾸미다. ② (*place
in order*) chŏng-ryŏl-si-k'i-da 정렬시키다.

arrest *v.* ch'e-p'o-ha-da 체포하다. —*n.* ch'e-p'o 체포.

arrival *n.* to-ch'ak 도착, to-dal 도달.

arrive *v.* to-ch'ak-ha-da 도착하다, to-dal-ha-da 도달하

arrogance *n.* o-man 오만, kŏ-man 거만.　　　　「다.

arrow *n.* hwa-sal 화살.

arsenal *n.* pyŏng-gi-go 병기고.

art *n.* ye-sul 예술, mi-sul 미술 ; (*craft*) ki-sul 기
술. —*v.* (~ *up*) ki-gyo-rŭl pu-ri-da 기교를 부리다.

artery *n.* tong-maek 동맥.

artful *adj.* (*ingenious*) kyo-myo-han 교묘한 ; (*sly*)
kyo-hwal-han 교활한.

article *n.* ① (*newspaper*) ki-sa 기사. ② (*things*) mul-
p'um 물품. ③ (*provision*) cho-hang 조항.

artificial *adj.* in-gong-jŏk 인공적, mo-jo-ŭi 모조의.

artillery *n.* ① tae-p'o 대포. ② (*branch of service*) p'o-
byŏng 포병 : ~ *fire* p'o-hwa 포화(砲火).

artisan *n.* (*mechanic*) chik-gong 직공 ; (*handicrafts-
man*) ki-gong 기공(技工).

artist *n.* ye-sul-ga 예술가, hwa-ga 화가(畵家).

as *adv.* …wa kat-ge …와 같게, …ka-t'ŭl man-k'ŭm
…같을 만큼. —*conj.* …man-k'ŭm …만큼, …chŏng-do

…정도. —*prep.* …ch'ŏ-rŏm …처럼, …wa ka-ch'i …와 같이, …ro-sŏ …로서. —*rel. pron.* …wa ka-t'ŭn …와 같은, …ha-nŭn pa-ŭi …하는 바의.

as far as (*and including*) kka-ji-nŭn 까지는, (ha-nŭn) han-e-sŏ-nŭn (하는) 한에서는.

as much as …man-k'ŭm …만큼.

ascend *v.* (*rise*) ol-ra-ga-da 올라가다, (*climb*) tŭng-ban-ha-da 등반하다 ; (*promote*) sŭng-jin-ha-da 승진하다 : ~ *a mountain* tŭng-san-ha-da 등산하다.

ascent *n.* sang-sŭng 상승 ; (*advancement*) sŭng-jin 승진 ; (*upward slope*) o-rŭ-mak-gil 오르막길.

ascertain *v.* hwak-in-ha-da 확인하다, a-ra-nae-da 알아

ascetic *n.* kŭm-yok-ju-ŭi-ja 금욕주의자.   ㄴ내다.

ascribe *v.* …t'a-sŭ-ro ha-da …탓으로 하다.

ash *n.* chae 재 ; (*pl.*) (*remains*) yu-gol 유골.

ashamed *adj.* pu-ggŭ-rŏ-un 부끄러운, su-jŭp-ŏ-ha-nun

ashore *adv.* hae-byŏn-e 해변에.   ㄴ수줍어하는.

ash tray chae-ddŏ-ri 재떨이.

Asia *n.* a-si-a 아시아 : *Southeast* ~ tong-nam-a 동남아.

aside *adv.* ① kyŏ-t'ŭ-ro 곁으로. ② (*apart*) pyŏl-do-ro 별도로. ③ (*except for*) …ŭl che-ha-go …을 제하고.

ask *v.* ch'ŏng-ha-da 청하다 ; (*inquire*) mut-da 묻다.

asleep *adv.* cham-dŭ-rŏ 잠들어.

asparagus *n.* a-sŭ-p'a-ra-gŏ-sŭ 아스파라거스.

aspect *n.* ① (*look*) yŏng-mo 용모. ② (*appearance*) mo-yang 모양. ③ (*phase*) kuk-myŏn 국면.

asphalt n. a-sŭ-p'al-t'ŭ 아스팔트.   「동경하다.

aspire *v.* yŏl-mang-ha-da 열망하다, tong-gyŏng-ha-da

ass *n.* ① (*donkey*) na-gwi 나귀. ② (*stupid*) pa-bo 바보. ③ (*arse*) ŏng-dŏng-i 엉덩이.

assail *v.* ① kong-gyŏk-ha-da 공격하다, sŭp-gyŏk-ha-da 습격하다. ② ta-gga-se-u-da 닦아세우다.

assassin *n.* am-sal-ja 암살자, cha-gaek 자객.
assassinate *v.* am-sal-ha-da 암살하다.
assassination *n.* am-sal 암살.
assault *n.* tol-gyŏk 돌격 ; sŭp-gyŏk 습격.
assemble *v.* mo-i-da 모이다, mo-ŭ-da 모으다.
assembly *n.* chip-hoe 집회, ŭi-hoe 의회(議會).
assent *n.* tong-ŭi 동의. —*v.* tong-ŭi-ha-da 동의하다.
assert *v.* tan-ŏn-ha-da 단언하다 ; (*maintain*) chu-jang-
　ha-da 주장하다. 「ha-da 부과하다.
assess *v.* p'yŏng-ga-ha-da 평가하다 ; (*impose*) pu-gwa-
assets *n.* cha-san 자산, chae-san 재산.
assign *v.* (*allot*) hal-dang-ha-da 할당하다 ; (*appoint*)
　chi-myŏng-ha-da 지명하다.
assimilate *v.* (*absorb*) tong-hwa-ha-da 동화하다; (*make
　like*) kat-ge ha-da 같게 하다.
assist *v.* top-da 돕다, kŏ-dŭl-da 거들다.
assistance *n.* cho-ryŏk 조력, wŏn-jo 원조.
assistant *n.* cho-su 조수, po-jo-ja 보조자.
associate *v.* ① (*keep company*) kyo-je-ha-da 교제하
　다. ② (*combine*) yŏn-hap-ha-da 연합하다. —*n.* tong-
　ryo 동료 ; tong-ŏp-ja 동업자.
association *n.* ① (*connection*) yŏn-hap 연합. ② (*soci-
　ety*) hyŏp-hoe 협회. ③ (*companionship*) kyo-je 교제.
assort *v.* (*classify*) pul-lyu-ha-da 분류하다 ; (*group*)
　jjak-ŭl mat-ch'u-da 짝을 맞추다. 「래다.
assuage *v.* wan-hwa-si-k'i-da 완화시키다, tal-rae-da 달
assume *v.* ttŏ-mat-da 떠맡다 ; (*pretend*) ka-jang-ha-
　da 가장하다, (*presume*) ka-jŏng-ha-da 가정(假定)하다.
assumption *n.* ① ŏk-ch'uk 억측. ② hoeng-ryŏng 횡령.
assurance *n.* po-jŭng 보증 ; hwak-sin 확신.
assure *v.* po-jŭng-ha-da 보증하다, hwak-sil-ha-ge ha-da
asthma *n.* ch'ŏn-sik 천식(喘息). 　　　　「확실하게 하다.

astonish *v.* nol-ra-ge ha-da 놀라게 하다.
astonishment *n.* nol-ra-um 놀라움, kyŏng-ak 경악.
astound *v.* kkam-jjak nol-ra-ge ha-da 깜짝 놀라게 하다.
astray *adj. & adv.* (*off the right way*) kil-ŭl il-k'o 길을 잃고 : *go* ~ he-mae-da 헤매다.
astrology *n.* chŏm-sŏng-hak 점성학(占星學).
astronomer *n.* ch'ŏn-mun-hak-ja 천문학자.
astronomy *n.* ch'ŏn-mun-hak 천문학.　　「ŭn 약은.
astute *adj.* (*keen*) ki-min-han 기민한 ; (*crafty*) yak-
asunder *adv.* san-san-i hŭ-t'ŏ-jyŏ 산산이 흩어져.
asylum *n.* su-yong-so 수용소 ; yang-yuk-wŏn 양육원 : *lunatic* ~ chŏng-sin-byong-wŏn 정신병원.
at *prep.* …e …에, …e-sŏ …에서, …ŭ-ro …으로, …chung-e …중에, …ŭl …을.
atheism *n.* mu-sil-lon 무신론, mu-sin-ang 무신앙.
athlete *n.* un-dong-ga 운동가, kyŏng-gi-ja 경기자.
athletics *n.* un-dong kyŏng-gi 운동 경기.
Atlantic *n.* tae-sŏ-yang 대서양.
atlas *n.* ① chi-do-ch'aek 지도책. ② to-hae 도해(圖解).
atmosphere *n.* ① (*air*) tae-gi 대기(大氣). ② (*environment*) pun-wi-gi 분위기, hwan-gyŏng 환경.
atom *n.* wŏn-ja 원자, a-t'om 아톰.
atomic *adj.* wŏn-ja-ŭi 원자의 : ~ *energy* won-ja-ryŏk 원자력 / ~ *bomb* wŏn-ja-p'ok-t'an 원자폭탄 / ~ *pile* wŏn-ja-ro 원자로(爐).
atrocity *n.* p'o-hak 포학, hyung-ak 흉악.
attach *v.* pu-ch'i-da 붙이다, ch'ŏm-bu-ha-da 첨부하다.
attaché *n.* tae-sa[kong-sa]-gwan-wŏn 대사〔공사〕관원.
attachment *n.* ① pu-ch'ak 부착. ② pu-sok-p'um 부속품. ③ (*affection*) ae-ch'ak 애착.　　「공격.
attack *v.* kong-gyŏk-ha-da 공격하다. —*n.* kong-gyŏk
attain *v.* (*gain*) …ŭl tal-sŏng-ha-da …을 달성하다.

attainment *n*. tal-sŏng 달성, to-dal 도달.
attempt *v*. si-do-ha-da 시도하다. —*n*. ki-do 기도(企圖).
attend *v*. ① (*be present at*) ch'ul-sŏk-ha-da 출석하다.
  ② (*wait upon*) mo-si-da 모시다.
attendance *n*. ① ch'ul-sŏk 출석. ② si-jung 시중.
attendant *n*. su-haeng-wŏn 수행원.
attention *n*. chu-ŭi 주의 : *A*~! Ch'a-ryŏ 차려 !
attentive *adj*. cho-sim-sŏng-it-nŭn 조심성있는.
attest *v*. chŭng-myŏng-ha-da 증명하다 ; (*put on oath*)
  maeng-se-si-k'i-da 맹세시키다.
attic *n*. ta-rak-bang 다락방, ko-mi-da-rak 고미다락.
attitude *n*. t'ae-do 태도, cha-se 자세.
attorney *n*. ① (*deputy*) tae-ri-in 대리인. ② (*lawyer*)
  pyŏn-ho-sa 변호사.
attorney general kŏm-ch'al-ch'ong-jang 검찰총장.
attract *v*. kkŭl-da 끌다, yu-in-ha-da 유인하다; (*entice*)
  mae-hok-ha-da 매혹하다.
attraction *n*. il-lyŏk 인력(引力), mae-ryŏk 매력.
attribute *v*. …ŭi t'a-sŭ-ro ha-da …의 탓으로 하다.
  —*n*. (*property*) sok-sŏng 속성.
auction *n*. & *v*. kyŏng-mae(-ha-da) 경매(하다).
audacity *n*. (*boldness*) tae-dam-mu-ssang 대담무쌍 ;
  (*impudence*) an-ha-mu-in 안하무인.
audible *adj*. tŭl-ri-nŭn 들리는.
audience *n*. ch'ŏng-jung 청중.
audit *v*. hoe-gye-gam-sa-ha-da 회계감사하다. —*n*. ①
  hoe-gye-gam-sa 회계감사. ② kyŏl-san 결산.
auditor *n*. kam-sa(-yŏk) 감사(역). 「dang 강당.
auditorium *n*. ch'ŏng-jung-sŏk 청중석 ; (*hall*) kang-
auditory *adj*. kwi-ŭi 귀의, ch'ŏng-gak-ŭi 청각의.
augment *v*. chŭng-ga-ha-da 증가하다, nŭl-da 늘다.
August *n*. p'al-wŏl 팔월.

aunt *n.* suk-mo 숙모, a-ju-mŏ-ni 아주머니.
aural *adj.* kwi-ŭi 귀의, ch'ŏng-gak-ŭi 청각의.
auspice *n.* ① (*omen*) chŏn-jo 전조, kil-jo 길조. ②
 (*patronage*) hu-wŏn 후원.
austere *adj.* ① (*stern*) ŏm-gyŏk-han 엄격한. ② (*simple*)
 tam-baek-han 담백한. ③ (*sour*) sin 신.
authentic *adj.* (*trustworthy*) mit-ŭl man-han 믿을 만
 한 ; (*genuine*) chin-jja-ŭi 진짜의.
author *n.* chŏ-ja 저자, chak-ga 작가.
authorities *n.* tang-guk 당국, kwan-hŏn 관헌.
authority *n.* kwŏn-wi 권위, kwŏn-han 권한.
authorized *adj.* in-ga-rŭl pat-ŭn 인가를 받은, kong-in-
autobiography *n.* cha-sŏ-jŏn 자서전.　ㄴdoen 공인된.
automatically *adv.* cha-dong-jŏk-ŭ-ro 자동적으로.
automobile *n.* cha-dong-ch'a 자동차.
autumn *n.* ka-ŭl 가을.
avail *v.* ssŭl-mo-it-da 쓸모있다, yu-yong-ha-da 유용하다.
available *adj.* i-yong-hal su it-nŭn 이용할 수 있는.
avalanche *n.* sa-t'ae 사태, swae-do 쇄도.
avarice *n.* hŏ-yok 허욕, t'am-yok 탐욕.　「원수를 갚다.
avenge *v.* pok-su-ha-da 복수하다, wŏn-su-rŭl kap-da
avenue *n.* ka-ro-su-gil 가로수길 ; tae-ro 대로.
average *n.* p'yŏng-gyun 평균. —*adj.* p'yŏng-gyun-ŭi
avert *v.* pi-k'i-da 비키다, p'i-ha-da 피하다.　 ㄴ평균의.
aviation *n.* pi-haeng 비행, hang-gong 항공.
aviator *n.* pi-haeng-sa 비행사, pi-haeng-ga 비행가.
avoid *v.* p'i-ha-da 피하다, hoe-p'i-ha-da 회피하다.
avow *v.* (*declare openly*) kong-ŏn-ha-da 공언하다 ;
 (*confess*)cha-baek-ha-da 자백하다.
await *v.* …ŭl ki-da-ri-da …을 기다리다.
awake *v.* cham-ŭl kkae-da 잠을 깨다. —*adj.* kkae-ŏ-
 it-nŭn 깨어있는.

award *n.* sang-p'um 상품(賞品). —*v.* (*adjudge*) su-yŏ-ha-da 수여하다, sang-ŭl chu-da 상을 주다.

aware *adj.* al-go-sŏ 알고서 ; kkae-dat-go 깨닫고 : *be* ~ *of* …ŭl al-go it-da …을 알고 있다. 「멀리.

away *adv.* (*off*) ttŏ-rŏ-jyŏ-sŏ 떨어져서 ; (*far*) mŏl-ri

awe *n.* tu-ryŏ-um 두려움. 「시한.

awful *adj.* tu-ryŏ-un 두려운, mu-si-mu-si-han 무시무

awhile *adv.* cham-ggan 잠깐, cham-si 잠시.

awkward *adj.* (*embarrassing*) kŏ-buk-han 거북한; (*clumsy*) sŏ-t'u-rŭn 서투른, kkol-sa-na-un 꼴사나운.

awl *n.* song-got 송곳. 「자르다.

ax(e) *n.* to-ggi 도끼. —*v.* to-kki-ro cha-rŭ-da 도끼로

axis *n.* kul-dae 굴대, ch'uk 축(軸).

axle *n.* kul-dae 굴대, ch'a-ch'uk 차축(車軸).

azalea *n.* chin-dal-rae 진달래, ch'ŏl-jjuk 철쭉.

B

babe *n.* kat-nan-a-gi 갓난아기 ; p'ut-na-gi 풋나기.

baby *n.* a-gi 아기 ; yu-a 유아 ; (*girl friend*)ae-in 애인.

bachelor *n.* ① ch'ong-gak 총각, tok-sin nam-ja 독신 남자. ② (*university graduate*) hak-sa 학사.

back *n.* (*of body*) tŭng 등 ; twi 뒤. —*adj. & adv.* twi-ŭi 뒤의, twi-ro 뒤로. —*v.* hu-t'oe-ha-da 후퇴하다.

backbone *n.* ch'ŏk-ch'u 척추, tŭng-bbyŏ 등뼈.

background *n.* pae-gyŏng 배경, i-myŏn 이면.

backward(s) *adv.* twi-ro 뒤로, kŏ-ggu-ro 거꾸로. —*adj.* twi-jjok-ŭi 뒤쪽의, (*late*) twi-jin 뒤진.

bacon *n.* pe-i-k'ŏn 베이컨.

bacteria *n.* se-gyun 세균, pak-t'e-ri-a 박테리아.

bad *adj.* na-bbŭn 나쁜, (*severe*) sim-han 심한.

badge *n.* hwi-jang 휘장, pae-ji 배지.

badger *n.* o-so-ri 오소리.
badly *adv.* (*wrongly*) na-bbŭ-ge 나쁘게 ; (*very much*) tae-dan-hi 대단히, mae-u 매우.
baffle *v.* (*frustrate*) chwa-jŏl-si-k'i-da 좌절시키다.
bag *n.* cha-ru 자루, ka-bang 가방, paek 백.
baggage *n.* su-ha-mul 수하물.
baggage check su-ha-mul-p'yo 수하물표.
baggage room su-ha-mul ch'wi-gŭp-so 수하물 취급소.
bail *n.* po-sŏk 보석 ; po-sŏk-gŭm 보석금. —*v.* po-sŏk-ŭl hŏ-ga-ha-da 보석을 허가하다. 「피다.
bait *n.* mi-ggi 미끼. —*v.* mi-ggi-ro kkoe-da 미끼로
bake *v.* kup-da 굽다, t'ae-u-da 태우다.
baker *n.* ppang kup-nŭn sa-ram 빵 굽는 사람.
bakery *n.* ppang-jip 빵집, che-bbang-so 제빵소.
balance *n.* ① (*equality*) kyun-hyŏng 균형. ② (*scales*) chŏ-ul 저울. —*v.* (*settle*) kyŏl-san-ha-da 결산하다.
balcony *n.* pal-k'o-ni 발코니, no-dae 노대(露台).
bald *adj.* tae-mŏ-ri-ŭi 대머리의, pŏ-sŏ-jin 벗어진.
bale *n.* kku-rŏ-mi 꾸러미, (*pl.*) hwa-mul 화물.
baleful *adj.* hae-ro-un 해로운, ka-yŏp-sŭn 가엾은.
ball *n.* ① kong 공, po-ol 보올. ② (*social dancing*) mu-do-hoe 무도회.
ballad *n.* min-yo 민요, pal-ra-a-dŭ 발라아드.
ballet *n.* pal-re 발레, pal-re-dan 발레단.
balloon *n.* ki-gu 기구(氣球), p'ung-sŏn 풍선.
ballot *n.* & *v.* t'u-p'yo(-ha-da) 투표(하다).
ballroom *n.* *mu-do*-jang 무도장, taen-sŭ-ho-ol 댄스호올.
balm *n.* hyang-yu 향유, (*pleasant smell*) pang-hyang 방향(芳香). 「sun 죽순.
bamboo *n.* tae 대(竹), ch'am-dae 참대 : ~ *shoots* chŭk-
ban *v.* kŭm-ji-ha-da 금지하다. —*n.* kŭm-ji 금지 ; (*of religion*) p'a-mun 파문(破門).

banana *n*. pa-na-na 바나나.

band *n*. ① (*sash*) tti 띠. ② (*group*) tte 떼, mu-ri 무리. ③ (*music*) ak-dae 악대. —*v*. kkŭn-ŭ-ro muk-da 끈으로 묶다, (*unite*) tan-gyŏl-ha-da 단결하다.

bandage *n*. pung-dae 붕대. —*v*. pung-dae-ro kam-da 붕대로 감다. 「san-jŏk 산적.

bandit *n*. ① (*ruffian*) ak-dang 악당. ② (*brigand*)

bang *n*. t'ang ha-nŭn so-ri 탕 하는 소리 ; p'o-sŏng 포성. —*v*. t'ang so-ri na-da 탕 소리 나다.

banish *v*. ch'u-bang-ha-da 추방하다, nae-jjot-da 내쫓다.

banishment *n*. ch'u-bang 추방, yu-hyŏng 유형.

bank *n*. ① ŭn-haeng 은행. ② (*of river*) tuk 둑, che-bang 제방.

bankbook *n*. ŭn-haeng-t'ong-jang 은행통장.

banker *n*. ŭn-haeng-ga 은행가, ŭn-haeng-ŏp-ja 은행업자.

bank note chi-p'ye 지폐, ŭn-haeng-gwŏn 은행권.

bankruptcy *n*. p'a-san 파산, to-san 도산.

banner *n*. (*flag*) ki 기(旗), (*colors*) kun-gi 군기.

banquet *n*. yŏn-hoe 연회, hyang-yŏn 향연.

baptism *n*. se-rye 세례, yŏng-se 영세.

Baptist *n*. ch'im-rye-gyo-do 침례교도.

baptize *v*. se-rye-rŭl pe-p'ul-da 세례를 베풀다.

bar *n*. ① (*stick*) mong-dung-i 몽둥이. ② (*for drinks*) pa-a 바아, sul-jip 술집. —*v*. ka-ro-mak-da 가로막다.

barbarian *n*. ya-man-in 야만인. —*adj*. ya-man-sŭ-rŏn 야만스런, mi-gae-in-ŭi 미개인의. 「개한.

barbarous *adj*. ya-man-jŏk-in 야만적인, mi-gae-han 미

barber *n*. i-bal-sa 이발사: ~'s *shop* i-bal-gwan 이발관.

barbed wire ka-si-ch'ŏl-sa-jul 가시철사줄, chŏl-jo-

bare *adj*. pŏl-gŏ-bŏ-sŭn 벌거벗은. 「mang 철조망.

barefoot *adj*. & *adv*. maen-bal-ŭi〔ro〕 맨발의〔로〕.

barely *adv*. kyŏ-u 겨우, kan-sin-hi 간신히.

bargain *n.* (*transaction*) hŭng-jŏng 홍정, (*cheap purchase*) ssan mul-gŏn 싼 물건 : ~ *sale* yŏm-ga-p'an-mae 염가판매. —*v.* hŭng-jŏng-ha-da 홍정하다.

barge *n.* kŏ-rut-bae 거룻배, chim-bae 짐배.

bark *v.* (*bay*) chit-da 짖다. —*n.* (*wood*) na-mu kkŏp-jil 나무 껍질, su-p'i 수피.

barley *n.* po-ri 보리 : ~ *tea* po-ri-ch'a 보리차.

barn *n.* hŏt-gan 헛간, kwang 광.

barometer *n.* ki-ap-gye 기압계, ch'ŏng-u-gye 청우계, pa-ro-mi-t'ŏ 바로미터 ; chi-p'yo 지표.

baron *n.* nam-jak 남작(男爵). 「바라크.

barracks *n.* mak-sa 막사, pyŏng-yŏng 병영, pa-ra-k'ŭ

barrage *n.* t'an-mak 탄막, yŏn-sok an-t'a 연속 안타.

barrel *n.* ① wŏn-t'ong 원통, t'ong 통. ② han pae-rŏl 한 배럴. ③ (*of gun*) ch'ong-sin 총신, p'o-sin 포신.

barren *adj.* (*unproductive*) pul-mo-ŭi 불모의 ; (*sterile*) im-sin mot-ha-nŭn 임신 못하는.

barricade *n.* t'ong-haeng ch'a-dan-mul 통행 차단물.

barrier *n.* ul-t'a-ri 울타리, pang-ch'aek 방책 ; (*obstacle*) chang-hae 장해. 「다).

barter *n & v.* mul-mul-gyo-hwan(-ha-da) 물물교환(하

base *n.* ① ki-ch'o 기초. ② (*of operations*) ki-ji 기지 (基地). —*adj.* (*mean*) ch'ŏn-han 천한.

baseball *n.* ya-gu 야구, ya-gu-gong 야구공.

baseless *adj.* kŭn-gŏ-ŏp-nŭn 근거없는.

basement *n.* chi-ha-sil 지하실 ; ch'oe-ha-bu 최하부.

bashful *adj.* (*shy*) pu-ggŭ-rŏ-wŏ-ha-nŭn 부끄러워하는, su-jup-ŏ-ha-nŭn 수줍어하는.

basic *adj.* ki-bon-jŏk 기본적, ki-ch'o-jŏk 기초적.

basin *n.* ① (*for washing*) se-su tae-ya 세수 대야. ② (*bowl*) tae-jŏp 대접. ③ pun-ji 분지(盆地).

basis *n.* ki-ch'o 기초 ; (*army*) ki-ji 기지.

bask *v.* (*in the sun*) jjoe-da 쬐다.

basket *n.* pa-gu-ni 바구니, kwang-ju-ri 광주리.

basketball *n.* nong-gu 농구.

bass *n.* ① (*fish*) nong-ŏ 농어. ② (*sound*) chŏ-ŭm(-bu) 저음(부).

bastard *n.* (*illegitimate child*) sa-saeng-a 사생아 ; sŏ-ja 서자(庶子) ; (*chap*)kae-ja-sik 개자식.

baste *v.* ① (*clothes*) si-ch'i-da 시치다. ② (*meat*) ki-rŭm-ŭl pa-rŭ-da 기름을 바르다.

bat *n.* ① pae-t'ŭ 배트, t'a-bong 타봉. ② (*animal*) pak-jwi 박쥐.

bath *n.* mok-yok 목욕.

bathe *v.* mok-yok-ha-da 목욕하다 ; tam-gŭ-da 담그다.

bathing *n.* mok-yok 목욕, su-yŏng 수영.

bathrobe *n.* hwa-jang-bok 화장복.

bathroom *n.* mok-yok-sil 목욕실, hwa-jang-sil 화장실.

baton *n.* chi-hwi-bong 지휘봉 ; pa-t'ong 바통.

battalion *n.* tae-dae 대대(大隊).

batter *v.* tu-dŭl-gi-da 두들기다.

battery *n.* ① (*electric*) chŏn-ji 전지. ② (*artillery*) p'o-byŏng-jung-dae 포병중대. ③ (*law*) ku-t'a 구타.

battle *n.* (*fight*) ssa-um 싸움, chŏn-t'u 전투. —*v.* ssa-u-da 싸우다, pun-t'u-ha-da 분투하다.

battlefield *n.* ssa-um-t'ŏ 싸움터, chŏn-jaeng-t'ŏ 전쟁터.

battle line chŏn-sŏn 전선.

battlement *n.* hyung-byŏk 흉벽(胸壁).

battleship *n.* chŏn-t'u-ham 전투함, chŏn-ham 전함.

bawdy *adj.* ŭm-t'ang-han 음탕한, oe-sŏl-sŭ-rŏn 외설스런.

bawl *v.* ko-ham-ch'i-da 고함치다, oe-ch'i-da 외치다.

bay *n.* ① (*gulf*) man 만(灣). ② (*fix*) kung-ji 궁지. ③ (*bark*) chit-nŭn so-ri 짖는 소리.

bayonet *n.* ch'ong-gŏm 총검. —*v.* ch'ong-gŏm-ŭ-ro jji-rŭ-da 총검으로 찌르다.

baza(a)r *n.* ① sang-jŏm-ga 상점가. ② (*fancy fair*)

pa-ja 바자, cha-sŏn-si 자선시(慈善市).

be *v.* ① (*existence*) it-da 있다. ② (*predicative*) i-da 이다. ③ (*honorific*) kye-si-da 계시다.

beach *n.* hae-byŏn 해변, mul-ga 물가, pa-dat-ga 바닷가.

beacon *n.* (*signal fire*) hwaet-bul 횃불, pong-hwa 봉화.

bead *n.* yŏm-ju-al 염주알, ku-sŭl 구슬 ; (*pl.*) yŏm-ju 염주.

beak *n.* (*bill*) chu-dung-i 주둥이, pu-ri 부리.

beam *n.* ① (*wood*) tae-dŭl-bo 대들보, to-ri 도리. ② (*of light*) kwang-sŏn 광선.

[yŏm-ju]

beaming *adj.* ① (*radiant*) pit-na-nŭn 빛나는. ② (*benign*) on-hwa-han 온화한.

bean *n.* k'ong 콩 : *soy* ~s tae-du 대두(大豆)/~ *sprouts* k'ong-na-mul 콩나물.

bear *n.* kom 곰. —*v.* ① (*endure*) kyŏn-di-da 견디다. ② (*yield*) maet-da 맺다. ③ (*a child*) na-t'a 낳다. ④ (*carry*) na-rŭ-da 나르다. 「러기.

beard *n.* ① su-yŏm 수염. ② (*awn*) kkŏ-ggŭ-rŏ-gi 꺼끄

bearer *n.* un-ban-in 운반인 ; chi-ch'am-in 지참인, so-ji-ja 소지자.

bearing *n.* ① t'ae-do 태도. ② (*direction*) pang-wi 방위. ③ (*relationship*) kwan-gye 관계.

beast *n.* chim-sŭng 짐승, ya-su 야수.

beat *v.* ① (*hit*) ttae-ri-da 때리다. ② (*defeat*) chi-u-da 지우다. —*n.* (*of music*) pak-ja 박자.

beater *n.* ① ch'i-nŭn sa-ram 치는 사람. ② (*chaser*) mo-rit-gun 몰잇군. ③ t'a-bong 타봉.

beau *n.* ① (*dandy*) mŏt-jang-i 멋장이. ② (*male lover*) chŏng-bu 정부(情夫).

beautiful *adj.* a-rŭm-da-un 아름다운.
beautify *v.* a-rŭm-dap-ge ha-da 아름답게 하다.
beauty *n.* ① a-rŭm-da-um 아름다움, mi 미(美). ② mi-in 미인 : ~ *contest* mi-in tae-hoe 미인 대회.
beauty parlor mi-jang-wŏn 미장원.
because *conj.* ⋯i-gi ttae-mun-e ⋯이기 때문에, wae-nya-ha-myŏn 왜냐하면.
beckon *v.* ① son-ji-sŭ-ro pu-rŭ-da 손짓으로 부르다. ② (*lure*) yu-hok-ha-da 유혹하다. 「어울리다.
become *v.* ① ⋯i toe-da ⋯이 되다. ② (*suit*) ŏ-ul-ri-da
becoming *adj.* (*suitable*) ŏ-ul-ri-nŭn 어울리는.
bed *n.* ch'im-dae 침대 ; hwa-dan 화단.
bedbug *n.* pin-dae 빈대.
bedclothes *n.* ch'im-gu 침구, kŭm-ch'im 금침.
bedding *n.* ① (*bedclothes and mattress*) ch'im-gu-ryu 침구류. ② (*foundation*) t'o-dae 토대.
bedridden *adj.* nu-wŏ-man it-nŭn 누워만 있는.
bedroom *n.* ch'im-sil 침실, ch'im-bang 침방.
bedstead *n.* ch'im-dae-t'ŭl 침대틀.
bee *n.* kkul-bŏl 꿀벌 : *a queen* ~ yŏ-wang-bŏl 여왕벌.
beech *n.* nŏ-do-bam-na-mu 너도밤나무.
beef *n.* soe-go-gi 쇠고기, ko-gi 고기.
beefsteak *n.* pi-i-p'ŭ-sŭ-t'e-i-k'ŭ 비이프스테이크.
beehive *n.* (kkul-)pŏl-jip (꿀)벌집, pŏl-t'ong 벌통.
beer *n.* maek-ju 맥주 : ~ *hall* pi-ŏ ho-ol 비어 호올.
beet *n.* sa-t'ang-mu-u 사탕무우, kŭn-dae 근대.
beetle *n.* ttak-jŏng-bŏl-re 딱정벌레.
befall *v.* ⋯ŭi sin-sang-e tak-ch'i-da ⋯의 신상에 닥치다.
before *adv.* a-p'e 앞에, mŏn-jŏ 먼저. —*prep.* (*time*) chŏn-e 전에, pŏl-ssŏ 벌써 ; (*place*) a-p'e 앞에. —*conj.* ⋯ha-gi chŏn-e ⋯하기 전에.
beforehand *adv.* mi-ri 미리, sa-jŏn-e 사전에.

befriend *v*. tol-bwa-ju-da 돌봐주다 ; …ŭi p'yŏn-ŭl tŭl-da …의 편을 들다.

beg *v*. ① ku-gŏl-ha-da 구걸하다. ② (*beseech*) ch'ŏng-ha-da 청하다, kan-ch'ŏng-ha-da 간청하다.

beget *v*. (*procreate*) na-t'a 낳다 ; (*cause*) saeng-gi-ge ha-da 생기게 하다, ch'o-rae-ha-da 초래하다.

beggar *n*. kŏ-ji 거지, pi-rŏng-baeng-i 비렁뱅이.

begin *v*. si-jak-ha-da 시작하다, kae-si-ha-da 개시하다.

beginner *n*. ① (*novice*) ch'o-bo-ja 초보자. ② (*originator*) ch'ang-si-ja 창시자.

beginning *n*. si-jak 시작, si-ch'o 시초, pal-dan 발단.

beguile *v*. ① (*cheat*) sok-i-da 속이다. ② (*pass time*) ·sim-sim-p'u-ri-ha-da 심심풀이하다.

behalf *n*. (*interest*) i-ik 이익 : *in*[*on*] ~ *of* …ŭl tae-sin-ha-yŏ …을 대신하여 ; …ŭl wi-ha-yŏ …을 위하여.

behave *v*. ① ch'ŏ-sin-ha-da 처신하다, haeng-dong-ha-da 행동하다. ② (*work*) ki-dong-ha-da 기동하다.

behavior *n*. ch'ŏ-sin 처신, haeng-wi 행위.

behead *v*. mok-ŭl pe-da 목을 베다.

behind *adv*. twi-e 뒤에. —*prep*. …ŭi twi-e …의 뒤에.

behold *v*. po-da 보다. —*int*. po-ra 보라.

being *n*. ① (*existence*) sil-jae 실재(實在). ② (*human life*) in-saeng 인생. ③ (*essence*) pon-jil 본질.

belch *v*. t'ŭ-rim-ha-da 트림하다. —*n*. t'ŭ-rim 트림.

belief *n*. ① (*conviction*) hwak-sin 확신. ② (*trust*) sin-yong 신용. ③ (*faith*) mit-ŭm 믿음, sin-ang 신앙.

believe *v*. mit-da 믿다 ; saeng-gak-ha-da 생각하다.

bell *n*. chong 종, pel 벨.

bellow *v*. (*roar*) ul-bu-jit-da 울부짖다.

bellows *n*. p'ul-mu 풀무.

belly *n*. pae 배, pok-bu 복부.

belong *v*. sok-ha-da 속하다.

beloved *adj.* ka-jang sa-rang-ha-nŭn 가장 사랑하는, kwi-yŏ-un 귀여운. —*n.* (*darling*) ae-in 애인.

below *adv.* a-rae-e 아래에, mi-t'e 밑에.

belt *n.* ① hyŏk-dae 혁대, pel-t'ŭ 벨트. ② (*area*) chi-dae 지대 : *green* ~ nok-ji-dae 녹지대.

bench *n.* kin kŏl-sang 긴 걸상, pen-ch'i 벤치.

bend *v.* ku-bu-ri-da 구부리다, (*twist*) hwi-da 휘다.

beneath *adv. & prep.* a-rae-jjok-e 아래쪽에, …ŭi pa-ro a-rae-e …의 바로 아래에.

benediction *n.* ch'uk-bok 축복, ŭn-ch'ong 은총.

benefactor *n.* ŭn-in 은인 ; hu-wŏn-ja 후원자.

beneficial *adj.* yu-ik-han 유익한, i-ro-un 이로운.

benefit *n.* ① (*profit*) i-ik 이익. ② (*favor*) hye-t'aek 혜택. —*v.* …e-ge i-rop-da …에게 이롭다.

benevolence *n.* cha-sŏn 자선, pak-ae 박애.

benevolent *adj.* in-ja-han 인자한, cha-ae-ro-un 자애로운.

benign *adj.* in-ja-han 인자한, on-hwa-han 온화한.

benumb *v.* (*make numb*) ma-bi-si-k'i-da 마비시키다.

bequeath *v.* (*leave behind*) yu-jŭng-ha-da 유증(遺贈)하다, nam-gi-da 남기다.

bequest *n.* yu-san 유산 ; yu-mul 유물.

bereave *v.* il-k'e ha-da 잃게 하다, ppae-at-da 빼앗다.

berry *n.* chang-gwa 장과(漿果), ttal-gi 딸기.

berth *n.* ① (*ship or train*) ch'im-dae 침대. ② (*lodging*) suk-so 숙소.

beseech *v.* t'an-wŏn-ha-da 탄원하다, kan-ch'ŏng-ha-da 간청하다.

beset *v.* ① (*surround*) p'o-wi-ha-da 포위하다. ② (*attack*) sŭp-gyŏk-ha-da 습격하다.

beside *prep.* …yŏ-p'e …옆에, kyŏ-t'e 곁에.

besides *prep.* (*otherwise*) kŭ-ba-gge 그밖에 ; (*moreover*) tŏ-u-gi 더우기, ke-da-ga 게다가.

besiege *v.* ① p'o-wi-ha-da 포위하다. ② (*crowd around*) mil-ryŏ-o-da 밀려오다, swae-do-ha-da 쇄도하다.

best *adj.* ka-jang cho-ŭn 가장 좋은. —*adv.* ka-jang chal 가장 잘. —*n.* ch'oe-sŏn 최선, ch'oe-sang 최상.

bestow *v.* ① (*confer*) chu-da 주다, su-yŏ-ha-da 수여하다. ② (*place*) no-t'a 놓다.

bet *n.* nae-gi 내기. —*v.* (ton-ul) kŏl-da (돈을) 걸다.

betray *v.* ① pae-ban-ha-da 배반하다. ② chŏ-bŏ-ri-da 저버리다. ③ (*reveal*) nu-sŏl-ha-da 누설하다.

betroth *v.* yak-hon-ha-da 약혼하다.

better *adj.* tŏ-uk cho-ŭn 더욱 좋은. —*adv.* tŏ-uk cho-k'e 더욱 좋게. —*n.* po-da na-ŭn kŏt 보다 나은 것.

bettor *n.* nae-gi-ha-nŭn sa-ram 내기하는 사람.

between *prep.* …sa-i-e …사이에. —*adv.* sa-i-e 사이에.

beverage *n.* (*drink*) ŭm-ryo 음료, ma-sil kŏt 마실 것.

bewail *v.* (*lament*) sul-p'ŭm-e cham-gi-da 슬픔에 잠기다, pi-t'an-ha-da 비탄하다.

beware *v.* cho-sim〔chu-ŭi〕-ha-da 조심〔주의〕하다 : *B~ ~ of the dog!* Kae cho-sim! 개 조심!

bewilder *v.* ŏ-ri-dung-jŏl-ha-ge ha-da 어리둥절하게 하다, tang-hwang-k'e ha-da 당황케 하다.

beyond *prep.* …ŭi chŏ-jjok-e …의 저쪽에, (*past*) …ŭl nŏm-ŏ-sŏ …을 넘어서. —*adv.* chŏ-jjok-e 저쪽에.

bias *n.* sa-sŏn 사선 ; ch'i-u-ch'im 치우침, p'yŏn-gyŏn

bib *n.* t'ŏk-ba-ji 턱받이. 〔편견.

Bible *n.* sŏng-gyŏng 성경, sŏng-sŏ 성서.

bicycle *n.* cha-jŏn-gŏ 자전거.

bid *v.* ① (*price*) kap-sŭl mae-gi-da 값을 매기다, ip-ch'al-ha-da 입찰하다. ② (*command*) myŏng-ryŏng-ha-da 명령하다. —*n.* (*tender*) ip-ch'al 입찰.

biennial *adj.* i-nyŏn-ma-da-ŭi 2년마다의.

bier *n.* ① sang-yŏ 상여. ② (*corpse*) si-ch'e 시체.

big *adj.* ① k'ŭn 큰 ; chung-yo-han 중요한. ② kwa-

bigot *n.* ko-jip-jang-i 고집장이. ⌐jang-han 과장한.

bill *n.* ① kye-san-sŏ 계산서. ② (*of bank*) ŏ-ŭm 어음. ③ (*deed*) chŭng-sŏ 증서: ~ *of lading* sŏn-ha chŭng-gwŏn 선하 증권. ④ (*animal's*) pu-ri 부리.

billiards *n.* tang-gu 당구 : ~ *table* tang-gu-dae 당구대.

billion *n.* ① (*a thousand millions*) sip-ŏk 10억. ② (*a million millions*) il-jo 1조(兆).

billow *n.* & *v.* k'ŭn p'a-do(-ga il-da) 큰 파도(가 일다).

bimonthly *adj.* tu tal-ma-da-ŭi 두 달마다의, kyŏk-wŏl-ŭi 격월의.

bind *v.* muk-da 묶다, ku-sok-ha-da 구속하다.

binoculars *n.* ssang-an-gyŏng 쌍안경.

biography *n.* chŏn-gi 전기(傳記), il-dae-gi 일대기.

biology *n.* saeng-mul-hak 생물학.

bipartisan *adj.* ch'o-dang-p'a-jŏk 초당파적 : ~ *diplomacy* ch'o-dang-p'a-jŏk oe-gyo 초당파적 외교.

birch *n.* cha-jak-na-mu 자작나무.

bird *n.* sae 새, nal-jim-sŭng 날짐승. ⌐t'ae-saeng 태생.

birth *n.* ch'ul-san 출산, t'an-saeng 탄생 ; (*descent*)

birthday *n.* saeng-il 생일 : *a* ~ *present* saeng-il-sŏn-

birthplace *n.* ch'ul-saeng-ji 출생지. ⌐mul 생일선물.

birthright *n.* t'a-go-nan kwŏl-li 타고난 권리.

biscuit *n.* pi-sŭ-k'it 비스킷.

bishop *n.* sŭng-jŏng 승정 ; chu-gyo 주교 ; sa-gyo 사교.

bit *n.* (*small piece*) chak-ŭn cho-gak 작은 조각 ; (*small quantity*) cho-gŭm 조금, yak-gan 약간.

bite *v.* ① (*sting*) mul-da 물다. ② (*corrode*) pu-sik-ha-da 부식하다. —*n.* mul-gi 물기.

bitter *adj.* ① ssŭn 쓴. ② (*harsh*) chi-dok-han 지독한.

bitterly *adv.* mop-si 몹시, sim-ha-ge 심하게.

black *adj.* kŏm-ŭn 검은. —*v.* kka-ma-k'e ha-da 까맣

게 하다. —*n.* hŭk-saek 흑색.

blackboard *n.* ch'il-p'an 칠판, hŭk-p'an 흑판.

blacken *v.* kka-ma-k'e ha-da 까맣게 하다.

black market am-si-jang 암시장.

blacksmith *n.* tae-jang-jang-i 대장장이, ch'ŏl-gong 철공 : *a ~'s shop* tae-jang-gan 대장간.

bladder *n.* pang-gwang 방광(膀胱).

blade *n.* ① (*of knife*) k'al-nal 칼날, (*sword*) k'al 칼. ② (*of grass*) p'ul-ip 풀잎.

blame *v.* pi-nan-ha-da 비난하다. —*n.* pi-nan 비난.

blameless *adj.* hŭm-ŏp-nŭn 흠없는.

blanch *v.* pa-rae-da 바래다, p'yo-baek-ha-da 표백하다 ; ch'ang-baek-hae-ji-da 창백해지다.

blank *n.* paek-ji 백지. —*adj.* paek-ji-ŭi 백지의, kong-baek-ŭi 공백의.

blanket *n.* tam-yo 담요.

blaspheme *v.* (*curse and swear*) (sin-ŭl) mo-dok-ha-da (신을) 모독하다.

blast *v.* (*blow up*) p'ok-p'a-ha-da 폭파하다. —*n.* tol-p'ung 돌풍, p'ok-p'a 폭파.

blaze *n.* pul-ggot 불꽃. —*v.* t'a-o-rŭ-da 타오르다.

bleach *v.* (*make white*) p'yo-baek-ha-da 표백하다.

bleak *adj.* (*cold*) ssa-nŭl-han 싸늘한 ; (*desolate*) hwang-p'ye-han 황폐한, ssŭl-ssŭl-han 쓸쓸한.

bleat *v.* (*sheep, goat etc.*) mae-ae-mae-ae ul-da 매애매애 울다. —*n.* u-rŭm-so-ri 울음소리.

bleed *v.* p'i-rŭl hŭl-ri-da 피를 흘리다.

blend *v.* twi-sŏk-da 뒤섞다, hon-hap-ha-da 혼합하다.

bless *v.* ch'uk-bok-ha-da 축복하다, ŭn-ch'ong-ŭl pil-da 은총을 빌다 ; ch'an-mi-ha-da 찬미하다.

blessing *n.* (*benediction*) ch'uk-bok 축복, (*devine favor*) ch'ŏn-hye 천혜(天惠).

blind *adj.* nun-mŏn 눈먼, chang-nim-ŭi 장님의.

blindman *n.* chang-nim 장님, so-gyŏng 소경.
blindness *n.* sil-myŏng 실명 ; maeng-mok 맹목.
blink *v.* nun-ŭl kkam-bak-gŏ-ri-da 눈을 깜박거리다.
bliss *n.* (*great enjoyment*) ta-si-ŏp-nŭn chŭl-gŏ-um 다
시없는 즐거움 ; chi-bok 지복(至福).   「집이 생기다.
blister *n.* mul-jip 물집. —*v.* mul-jip-i saeng-gi-da 물
bloc *n.* tan 단, kwŏn 권(圈), pŭl-rok 블록.
block *n.* ① (*of wood*) na-mu-t'o-mak 나무토막;(*lump*)
  tŏng-ŏ-ri 덩어리. ② (*area*) ku-hoek 구획. —*v.* (*obstruct*) mak-da 막다, (*check*) pang-hae-ha-da 방해하
blockade *n.* pong-swae 봉쇄, tu-jŏl 두절.   「다.
blockhead *n.* mŏng-ch'ŏng-i 멍청이, pa-bo 바보.
blood *n.* p'i 피 ; (*lineage*) hyŏl-t'ong 혈통.
blood vessel hyŏl-gwan 혈관.
bloody *adj.* (*bleeding*) p'i-na-nŭn 피나는 ; (*with much
  bloodshed*) p'i-t'u-sŏng-i-ŭi 피투성이의.   「영하다.
bloom *v.* kko-ch'i p'i-da 꽃이 피다, pŏn-yŏng-ha-da 번
blossom *n.* kkot 꽃, kae-hwa 개화(開花).
blot *n.* ŏl-ruk 얼룩, o-jŏm 오점(汚點), kyŏl-jŏm 결점.
  —*v.* (*stain*) ŏl-ruk-ji-ge ha-da 얼룩지게 하다.
blotter *n.* ap-ji 압지(押紙).
blouse *n.* pŭl-ra-u-sŭ 블라우스, chak-ŏp-bok 작업복.
blow *v.* pul-da 불다; (*explode*) p'ok-bal-ha-da 폭발하다.
  —*n.* (*knock*) t'a-gyŏk 타격.
blue *adj.* p'u-rŭn 푸른 ; (*dismal*) ch'im-ul-han 침울한.
bluebell *n.* to-ra-ji 도라지.
blueprint *n.* ch'ŏng-sa-jin 청사진, kye-hoek 계획.
bluff *n.* ① (*cliff*) chŏl-byŏk 절벽, pyŏ-rang 벼랑. ②
  (*bravado*) hŏ-se 허세.   「실수를 하다.
blunder *n.* k'ŭn sil-su 큰 실수. —*v.* sil-su-rŭl ha-da
blunt *adj.* (*dull*) mu-din 무딘 ; mu-dduk-dduk-han 무
  뚝뚝한 ; (*outspoken*) sol-jik-han 솔직한.

bluntly *adv.* t'ung-myŏng-sŭ-rŏp-ge 퉁명스럽게.
blur *v.* hŭ-ri-ge ha-da 흐리게 하다 ; ŏl-ruk-ji-ge ha-da 얼룩지게 하다. —*n.* (*blot*) ŏl-ruk 얼룩.
blush *v.* (*be shamed*) na-ch'ŭl pul-k'i-da 낯을 붉히다, ppal-gae-ji-da 빨개지다. —*n.* (*rosy glow*) hong-jo 홍조, pul-gŭ-re-ham 불그레함.
bluster *v.* kŏ-se-ge mo-ra-ch'i-da 거세게 몰아치다.
boar *n.* su-t'wae-ji 수돼지 : *wild* ~ met-dwae-ji 멧돼지.
board *n.* ① (*thin plank*) p'an-ja 판자. ② (*committee*) wi-wŏn-hoe 위원회 : ~ *of directors* i-sa-hoe 이사회. —*v.* ① (*embark on*) ol-ra-t'a-da 올라타다. ② (*lodge*) ha-suk-ha-da 하숙하다.
boarder *n.* ha-suk-in 하숙인, ki-suk-saeng 기숙생.
boardinghouse *n.* ha-suk-jip 하숙집.
boast *v.* cha-rang-ha-da 자랑하다, ttŏ-bŏl-ri-da 떠벌리다. —*n.* cha-rang 자랑 ; hŏ-p'ung 허풍.
boastful *adj.* cha-rang-ha-nŭn 자랑하는.
boat *n.* chak-ŭn ki-sŏn 작은 기선, po-u-t'ŭ 보우트.
boatman *n.* paet-sa-gong 뱃사공. 「sil-p'ae 실패.
bobbin *n.* ① (*sewing machine*) puk 북. ② (*spool*)
bodily *adj.* sin-ch'e[yuk-ch'e]-ŭi 신체[육체]의. —*adv.* (*as a whole*) song-du-ri-jjae 송두리째.
body *n.* ① yuk-ch'e 육체 ; (*corpse*) si-ch'e 시체. ② (*group*) tan-ch'e 단체. ③ (*letter*) pon-mun 본문.
bodyguard *n.* ho-wi-byŏng 호위병, kyŏng-ho-in 경호인.
bog *n.* su-rŏng 수렁, nŭp 늪.
bogus *adj.* ka-jja-ŭi 가짜의, wi-jo-ŭi 위조의.
boil *v.* ① (*liquid*) kkŭl-t'a 끓다. ② (*solids*) sam-da 삶다. —*n.* (*tumor*) chong-gi 종기, pu-sŭ-rŏm 부스럼.
boiler *n.* po-il-rŏ 보일러.
boisterous *adj.* kŏ-ch'in 거친, nan-p'ok-han 난폭한.
bold *adj.* tae-dam-han 대담한.

bolt *n.* ① (*dart*) hwa-sal 화살. ② (*of a gate*) pit-jang 빗장. ③ (*lightning*) pŏn-gaet-bul 번갯불.

bomb *n.* p'ok-t'an 폭탄 : *hydrogen* ~ su-so p'ok-t'an 수소 폭탄/*incendiary* ~ so-i-t'an 소이탄. —*v.* p'ok-gyŏk-ha-da 폭격하다.

bonanza *n.* no-da-ji 노다지 ; (*run of luck*) ttŭt-ba-ggŭi haeng-un 뜻밖의 행운.

bond *n.* ① (*tie*) kyŏl-sok 결속. ② (*fetters*) sok-bak 속박. ③ (*finance*) chŭng-gwŏn 증권.

bondage *n.* no-ye-ŭi sin-se 노예의 신세 ; kul-jong 굴종.

bone *n.* ppyŏ 뼈, kol-gyŏk 골격.

bonfire *n.* mo-dak-bul 모닥불, hwa-t'ot-bul 화톳불.

bonnet *n.* po-nit 보닛.

bonus *n.* po-u-nŏ-sŭ 보우너스, sang-yŏ-gŭm 상여금 ; pae-dang-gŭm 배당금.

book *n.* ch'aek 책. —*v.* (*record*) ki-ip-ha-da 기입하다.

bookcase *n.* ch'aek-jang 책장, ch'aek-ggo-ji 책꽂이.

bookkeeping *n.* pu-gi 부기(簿記).

booklet *n.* so-ch'aek-ja 소책자, p'am-p'ŭl-ret 팜플렛.

bookstore *n.* sŏ-jŏm 서점, ch'aek-bang 책방.

boom *n.* (*in market value*) pyŏ-rak kyŏng-gi 벼락 경기 ; kŭp-dŭng 급등. 　　　　　　「을 올리다.

boost *v.* mi-rŏ-ol-ri-da 밀어올리다, kap-sŭl ol-ri-da 값

boot *n.* chang-hwa 장화, pan-jang-hwa 반(半)장화.

bootblack *n.* ku-du-da-ggi 구두닦기.

booth *n.* ① p'an-ja-jip 판자집. ② (*stand*) no-jŏm 노점 : *telephone* ~ kong-jung chŏn-hwa 공중 전화.

booty *n.* chŏl-li-p'um 전리품, no-hoek-mul 노획물.

boracic acid pung-san 붕산.

border *n.* ① ka-jang-ja-ri 가장자리, t'e-du-ri 테두리. ② kyŏng-gye 경계. —*v.* (*adjoin*) chŏp-ha-da 접하다.

bore *v.* ① (*annoy*) sil-jŭng-na-ge ha-da 싫증나게 하다.

② (*drill*) ku-mŏng ttul-t'a 구멍 뚫다.
born *adj.* t'a-go-nan 타고난, ch'ŏn-sŏng-ŭi 천성의.
borrow *v.* pil-ri-da 빌리다, ch'a-yong-ha-da 차용하다.
bosom *n.* ka-sŭm 가슴. —*adj.* (*cherished*) ka-sŭm-e
kan-jik-han 가슴에 간직한 : *a ~ friend* ch'in-u 친우.
boss *n.* tu-mok 두목, chu-in 주인, po-sŭ 보스. —*v.*
(*control*) t'ong-sol-ha-da 통솔하다.
botanical garden sik-mul-wŏn 식물원.
botany *n.* sik-mul-hak 식물학.
both *adj.* yang-jjok-ŭi 양쪽의. —*pron.* tul ta 둘 다.
—*adv.* ···do ···do ···도 ···도.
bother *v.* (*annoy*) kwi-ch'an-k'e ha-da 귀찮게 하다:
~ about kŏk-jŏng-ha-da 걱정하다.　　　「병마개 뽑이.
bottle *n.* pyŏng 병 : *a ~ opener* pyŏng-ma-gae ppop-i
bottom *n.* mit-ba-dak 밑바닥 ; ki-ch'o 기초.
bottomless *adj.* mit-ba-dak-i ŏp-nŭn 밑바닥이 없는.
bough *n.* k'ŭn ka-ji 큰 가지.
boulder *n.* tung-gŭn tol 둥근 돌, p'yo-sŏk 표석.
bounce *v.* t'wi-da 튀다, ttwi-ŏ-o-rŭ-da 뛰어오르다.
bound *v.* (*leap*) t'wi-da 튀다. —*n.* kyŏng-gye 경계,
pŏm-wi 범위. —*adj.* mu-ggin 묶인.
boundary *n.* kyŏng-gye 경계, pŏm-wi 범위.
boundless *adj.* han-i ŏp-nŭn 한이 없는.
bountiful *adj.* (*generous*) kwan-dae-han 관대한.
bouquet *n.* kkot-da-bal 꽃다발 ; hyang-gi 향기.
bow *n.* ① (*archery*) hwal 활. ② (*of
the head*) chŏl 절. —*v.* (*for salutation*) chŏl-ha-da 절하다.
bowels *n.* nae-jang 내장.
bower *n.* (*arbor*) chŏng-ja 정자(亭子) ;
ch'o-so 처소.
bowl *n.* sa-bal 사발, kong-gi 공기.

[chŏng-ja]

box *n.* sang-ja 상자 ; (*theater*) t'ŭk-byŏl-sŏk 특별석 ;
　(*witness box*) chŭng-in-sŏk 증인석.
boxer *n.* kwŏn-t'u-sŏn-su 권투선수, pok-sŏ 복서.
boxing *n.* kwŏn-t'u 권투, pok-sing 복싱.
box office mae-p'yo-so 매표소.
boy *n.* ① so-nyŏn 소년, nam-ja a-i 남자 아이. ② a-dŭl
　아들, nam-ja 남자. ③ (*young servant*) kŭp-sa 급사.
boycott *n.* pul-mae tong-maeng 불매 동맹, po-i-k'ot
boyhood *n.* so-nyŏn-gi 소년기.　　　　　　　　⌐보이콧.
boy scouts so-nyŏn-dan 소년단.
brace *v.* (*support*) pŏ-t'i-da 버티다. —*n.* pŏ-t'im-dae
　버팀대, chi-ju 지주 ; mel-bbang 멜빵.
bracelet *n.* p'al-jji 팔찌.　　　　　　　　　　⌐괄호.
bracket *n.* ① kka-ch'i-bal 까치발. ② (*marks*) kwal-ho
brackish *adj.* (*salty*) jjap-jjal-han 짭짤한.
brag *v.* cha-rang-ha-da 자랑하다 ; (*boast of*) ppom-
　nae-da 뽐내다. —*n.* cha-rang 자랑, hŏ-p'ung 허풍.
braggart *n.* (*boaster*) hŏ-p'ŭng-sŏn-i 허풍선이.
braid *v.* tta-t'a 땋다. —*n.* kkon kkŭn 꼰 끈.
brain *n.* noe 뇌, tu-noe 두뇌 ; chi-ryŏk 지력.
brainwash *n. & v.* se-noe(-ha-da) 세뇌(하다).
brake *n.* che-dong-gi 제동기, pŭ-re-i-k'ŭ 브레이크.
bramble *n.* ka-si-dŏm-bul 가시덤불, tŭl-jang-mi 들장미.
bran *n.* kyŏ 겨, mil-gi-ul 밀기울.
branch *n.* ① (*of tree*) ka-ji 가지. ② (*office*) chi-jŏm
　지점. —*v.* kal-ra-ji-da 갈라지다.
brand *n.* ① (*trademark*) sang-p'yo 상표. ② (*stigma*)
　nak-in 낙인, o-myŏng 오명(汚名).
brandy *n.* pŭ-raen-di 브랜디.　　　　　　⌐ŭi 신품의.
brand-new *adj.* a-ju sae-ro-un 아주 새로운, sin-p'um-
brass *n.* not-soe 놋쇠.　　　　　　　　⌐dŭ 브라스밴드.
brass band ch'wi-ju-ak-dan 취주악단, pŭ-ra-sŭ-baen-

brave *adj.* yong-gam-han 용감한. —*v.* yong-gam-ha-ge mat-sŏ-da 용감하게 맞서다.

bravery *n.* yong-gam 용감, yong-maeng 용맹.

brawl *n. & v.* mal-da-t'um(-ha-da) 말다툼(하다).

bray *n.* (*donkey*) u-rŭm-so-ri 울음소리.

brazier *n.* ① hwa-ro 화로. ② not-gat-jang-i 놋갓장이.

breach *n.* kkae-ddŭ-rim 깨뜨림, wi-ban 위반 ; pul-hwa 불화(不和) : *a* ~ *of contract* kye-yak-wi-ban 계약위 [반.

bread *n.* ppang 빵, sik-bbang 식빵.

breadth *n.* p'ok 폭, na-bi 나비.

break *v.* ① pu-su-da 부수다 ; jjo-gae-da 쪼개다. ② wi-ban-ha-da 위반하다. ③ chung-ji-ha-da 중지하다. —*n.* ① (*rupture*) p'a-goe 파괴. ② (*gap*) kal-ra-jin t'ŭm 갈라진 틈. ③ (*pause*) chung-dan 중단.

breakdown *n.* ① ko-jang 고장. ② p'a-son 파손. ③ pung-goe 붕괴.

breakfast *n.* cho-ban 조반.

breakwater *n.* pang-p'a-je 방파제. 「젖.

breast *n.* ka-sŭm 가슴 ; (*woman*) yu-bang 유방, chŏt

breastwork *n.* hyung-byŏk 흉벽.

breath *n.* sum 숨, ho-hŭp 호흡.

breathe *v.* sum-swi-da 숨쉬다, ho-hŭp-ha-da 호흡하다.

breathless *adj.* sum-ga-bbŭn 숨가쁜.

breeches *n.* jjal-bŭn yang-bok-ba-ji 짧은 양복바지.

breed *v.* ① (*keep cattle*) ki-rŭ-da 기르다. ② (*propagate*) pŏn-sik-ha-da 번식하다. —*n.* chong-jok 종족.

breeze *n.* san-dŭl-ba-ram 산들바람, mi-p'ung 미풍.

brethren *n.* ① tong-p'o 동포. ② tong-ŏp-ja 동업자.

brevity *n.* kan-gyŏl 간결, kal-lyak 간략.

brew *v.* yang-jo-ha-da 양조하다, pit-da 빚다.

brewery *n.* yang-jo-jang 양조장. 「주다.

bribe *n.* noe-mul 뇌물. —*v.* noe-mul-ŭl chu-da 뇌물을

bribery *n.* chŭng-hoe 증회, su-hoe 수회.

brick *n.* pyŏk-dol 벽돌.
brickyard *n.* pyŏk-dol kong-jang 벽돌 공장.
bride *n.* sin-bu 신부(新婦), sae-saek-si 새색시.
bridegroom *n.* sil-lang 신랑.
bridesmaid *n.* sin-bu tŭl-rŏ-ri 신부 들러리.
bridesman *n.* sil-lang tŭl-rŏ-ri 신랑 들러리.
bridge *n.* ta-ri 다리, kyo-ryang 교량.
bridgehead *n.* kyo-du-bo 교두보.   「ku-sok 구속.
bridle *n.* mal-gul-re 말굴레, ko-bbi 고삐 ; (*restraint*)
brief *adj.* kan-dan-han 간단한, kan-gyŏl-han 간결한.
brier *n.* jjil-re 찔레, (*wild rose*) tŭl-jang-mi 들장미.
brigade *n.* yŏ-dan 여단(旅團) ; tae 대(隊).
brigadier general yuk-gun-jun-jang 육군준장.
bright *adj.* pit-na-nŭn 빛나는, mal-gŭn 맑은 ; k'wae-
    hwal-han 쾌활한 ; ch'ong-myŏng-han 총명한.
brighten *v.* pit-na-ge ha-da 빛나게 하다 ; chŭl-gŏp-ge
    ha-da 즐겁게 하다.   「릉한.
brilliant *adj.* ch'al-lan-han 찬란한, hul-ryung-han 훌
brim *n.* ka-jang-ja-ri 가장자리, (*projecting rim*) t'e 테.
brimful *adj.* nŏm-ch'il tŭt-han 넘칠 듯한.
brine *n.* jjan-mul 짠물, kan-mul 간물.
bring *v.* (*of things*) ka-jyŏ-o-da 가져오다, (*of person*)
    te-ryŏ-o-da 데려오다 ; ch'o-rae-ha-da 초래하다.
brink *n.* ① ka-jang-ja-ri 가장자리. ② mul-ga 물가.
brisk *adj.* hwal-bal-han 활발한; sang-k'wae-han 상쾌한.
briskly *adv.* hwal-bal-ha-ge 활발하게.   「(剛毛).
bristle *n.* ppŏt-bbŏt-han t'ŏl 뻣뻣한 털, kang-mo 강모
Britain *n.* tae-yŏng-je-guk 대영제국, yŏng-guk 영국.
brittle *adj.* ① kkae-ji-gi swi-un 깨지기 쉬운. ② (*tran-*
    sitory) hŏ-mang-han 허망한.
broad *adj.* nŏl-bŭn 넓은, kwan-dae-han 관대한 ;
    (*plain*) myŏng-baek-han 명백한.

broadcast *v.* ① pang-song-ha-da 방송하다. ② (*spread*) yu-p'o-ha-da 유포하다. —*n.* pang-song 방송.
broadcasting station pang-song-guk 방송국.
brocade *n.* su-no-ŭn pi-dan 수놓은 비단.
brochure *n.* so-ch'aek-ja 소책자, p'am-p'ŭl-ret 팜플렛.
broil *v.* (*grill*) kup-da 굽다. —*n.* ① (*roast meat*) pul-go-gi 불고기. ② ssa-um 싸움.
broken *adj.* ① pu-sŏ-jin 부서진. ② (*weakened*) nak-sim-han 낙심한 : *a ~ heart* si-ryŏn 실연.
broker *n.* chung-gae-in 중개인, pŭ-ro-u-k'ŏ 브로우커.
bronchia *n.* ki-gwan-ji 기관지(氣管支).
bronchitis *n.* ki-gwan-ji-yŏm 기관지염. 「ŭi 청동의.
bronze *n.* ch'ŏng-dong 청동(青銅). —*adj.* ch'ŏng-dong-
brooch *n.* pŭ-ro-u-ch'i 브로우치.
brood *n.* han-bae sae-ggi 한배 새끼. —*v.* (*meditate deeply*) kom-gom-i saeng-gak-ha-da 곰곰이 생각하다.
brook *n.* si-nae 시내, sil-gae-ch'ŏn 실개천.
broom *n.* pi 비. —*v.* (*sweep*) ssŭl-da 쓸다, ch'ŏng-so-ha-da 청소하다.
broth *n.* (*thin soup*) ko-git-guk 고깃국.
brothel *n.* mae-ŭm-gul 매음굴, kal-bo-jip 갈보집.
brother *n.* hyŏng-je 형제 : *elder ~* (*for men*) hyŏng-nim 형님 ; (*for women*) o-bba 오빠/ *younger ~* tong-saeng 동생, a-u 아우.
brother-in-law *n.* (*husband's elder brother*) a-ju-bŏ-ni 아주버니 ; (*husband's younger brother*) si-dong-saeng 시동생 ; (*wife's brother*) ch'ŏ-nam 처남 ; (*sister's husband*) mae-bu 매부.
brow *n.* (*forehead*) i-ma 이마 ; (*eye*) nun-ssŏp 눈썹.
brown *n. & adj.* kal-saek(-ŭi) 갈색(의), ko-dong-saek (-ŭi) 고동색(의). 「da 상처를 내다.
bruise *n.* t'a-bak-sang 타박상. —*v.* sang-ch'ŏ-rŭl nae-

brush *n.* ① sol 솔, pŭ-rŏ-si 브러시. ② (*for painting, writing*) put 붓. —*v.* sol-jil-ha-da 솔질하다.

brutal *adj.* ya-su-jŏk-in 야수적인 ; (*cruel*) chan-in-han 잔인한, ya-bi-han 야비한.

brutality *n.* chan-in 잔인, mu-ja-bi 무자비.

brute *n.* ① (*beast*) chim-sŭng 짐승 ; ch'uk-saeng 축생. ② (*cruel person*) pi-in-gan 비인간.

bubble *n.* kŏ-p'um 거품 : ki-p'o 기포.

bubonic plague hŭk-sa-byŏng 흑사병, p'e-sŭ-t'ŭ 페스트.

buck *n.* ① su-sa-sŭm 수사슴. ② (*dollar*) tal-rŏ 달러(弗).

bucket *n.* yang-dong-i 양동이, pŏ-k'it 버킷.

buckle *n.* mul-rim-soe 물림쇠, hyŏk-dae-soe 혁대쇠, pŏ-k'ŭl 버클.

buckwheat *n.* me-mil 메밀.

bud *n.* pong-o-ri 봉오리, ssak 싹.

Buddha *n.* pu-ch'ŏ 부처.

Buddhism *n.* pul-gyo 불교.

Buddhist *n.* pul-gyo-do 불교도, pul-gyo sin-ja 불교신자.

Buddhist scripture pul-gyŏng 불경

Buddhist temple chŏl 절.   [pu-ch'ŏ]

buddy *n.* (*mate*) tong-ryo 동료, jjak-p'ae 짝패.

budget *n.* ye-san 예산, ye-san-an 예산안.

buffer *n.* wan-ch'ung-gi 완충기.

bug *n.* pŏl-re 벌레 ; (*bedbug*) pin-dae 빈대.

bugle *n.* na-p'al 나팔, kak-jŏk 각적(角笛).

build *v.* se-u-da 세우다, kŏn-sŏl-ha-da 건설하다.

building *n.* kŏn-mul 건물, pil-ding 빌딩.   「전구.

bulb *n.* ① ku-gŭn 구근(球根). ② (*electric*) chŏn-gu

bulge *n.* pu-p'um 부품. —*v.* pu-p'ul-da 부풀다.

bulk *n.* (*volume*) yong-jŏk 용적, (*size*) k'ŭ-gi 크기,

(*cargo*) paet-jim 뱃짐.

bulky *adj.* pu-p'i-ga k'ŭn 부피가 큰.

bull *n.* hwang-so 황소;(*animal*)su-k'ŏt 수컷.「위협하다.

bulldoze *v.* kang-haeng-ha-da 강행하다, wi-hyŏp-ha-da

bullet *n.* ch'ong-al 총알, t'an-hwan 탄환.

bulletin *n.* kong-bo 공보(公報), hoe-bo 회보: *a* ~ *board* ke-si-p'an 게시판.

bullfrog *n.* sik-yong kae-gu-ri 식용 개구리.

bully *n.* kol-mok-dae-jang 골목대장; kkang-p'ae 깡패.

bump *v.* pu-dit-ch'i-da 부딪치다. —*n.* ① ch'ung-dol 충돌. ② (*swelling*) hok 혹.　　　　　「da-bal 꽃다발.

bunch *n.* song-i 송이, ta-bal 다발: *a* ~ *of flower* kkot-

bundle *n.* ta-bal 다발, kku-rŏ-mi 꾸러미.　　　「대.

buoy *n.* pu-p'yo 부표(浮標), ku-myŏng-bu-dae 구명부

buoyant *adj.* ① chal ttŭ-nŭn 잘 뜨는. ② (*merry*) k'wae-hwal-han 쾌활한, hwal-gi-it-nŭn 활기있는.

burden *n.* mu-gŏ-un chim 무거운 짐, pu-dam 부담.

burdensome *adj.* pu-dam-i toe-nŭn 부담이 되는, kwi-ch'an-ŭn 귀찮은, sŏng-ga-sin 성가신.

bureau *n.* ① (*dresser*) ot-jang 옷장. ② (*office*) kuk 국(局), an-nae-so 안내소: *an employment* ~ chik-ŏp so-gae-so 직업 소개소.

burglar *n.* kang-do 강도, pam-do-duk 밤도둑.

burial *n.* mae-jang 매장(埋葬).

burn *v.* pul-t'a-da 불타다, hwa-sang-ŭl ip-da 화상을 입다, kŭ-ŭl-da 그을다. —*n.* hwa-sang 화상(火傷).

burnish *v.* ① (*polish*) tak-da 닦다. ② (*become bright*) pit-na-da 빛나다. —*n.* yun 윤, kwang-t'aek 광택.

burrow *n.* kul 굴. —*v.* kul-ŭl p'a-da 굴을 파다.

burst *v.* t'ŏ-ji-da 터지다; pyŏ-ran-gan na-t'a-na-da 별안간 나타나다. —*n.* p'ok-bal 폭발.

bury *v.* p'a-mut-da 파묻다, mae-jang-ha-da 매장하다.

ɔus *n.* pŏ-sŭ 버스.

ɔush *n.* su-p'ul 수풀, tŏm-bul 덤불.　　　「sa-ŏp 사업.

ɔusiness *n.* chik-ŏp 직업 ; ŏp-mu 업무 ; chang-sa 장사 ;

ɔust *n.* ① pan-sin-sang 반신상(半身像), hyung-sang 흉상. ② (*failure*) sil-p'ae 실패.　　　「큰 소동.

ɔustle *v.* pŏp-sŏk-dae-da 법석대다. —*n.* k'ŭn so-dong

ɔusy *adj.* pa-bbŭn 바쁜, pŏn-ch'ang-han 번창한.

ɔut *conj.* kŭ-rŏ-na 그러나. —*prep.* …oe-e-nŭn …외에 는. —*adv.* ta-man 다만, tan-ji 단지.　　　「점.

ɔutcher *n.* p'u-ju(-han) 푸주(한) ; chŏng-yuk-jŏm 정육

butler *n.* chip-sa 집사, ch'ŏng-ji-gi 청지기.

butter *n.* bŏ-t'ŏ 버터.　　　　　　　　　「泳).

butterfly *n.* na-bi 나비 : ～ *stroke* chŏp-yŏng 접영(蝶

button *n.* tan-ch'u 단추. —*v.* tan-ch'u-rŭl ch'ae-u-da 〔tal-da〕 단추를 채우다〔달다〕.

buttonhole *n.* tan-ch'u ku-mŏng 단추 구멍.

buy *v.* sa-da 사다, ku-ip-ha-da 구입하다. —*n.* mae-ip

buyer *n.* sa-nŭn sa-ram 사는 사람, pa-i-ŏ 바이어. 「매입.

buzz *v.* (*bees*) wing-wing so-ri-nae-da 윙윙 소리내다. —*n.* wing-wing-gŏ-ri-nŭn so-ri 윙윙거리는 소리 ; (*humming*) so-ŭm 소음.

by *adv.* kyŏ-t'e 곁에. —*prep.* ① …yŏ-p'e …옆에. ② (*by means of*) …e-ŭi-ha-yŏ …에 의하여. ③ (*before*) kka-ji-e-nŭn 까지에는.

by-product *n.* pu-san-mul 부산물.　　　　　　「관자.

bystander *n.* ku-gyŏng-gun 구경군 ; pang-gwan-ja 방

bystreet *n.* twit-gol-mok 뒷골목, twit-gil 뒷길.

C

cab *n.* ① t'aek-si 택시. ② ma-ch'a 마차.

cabbage *n.* yang-bae-ch'u 양배추, k'ae-bi-ji 캐비지.

cabin *n.* ① (*hut*) o-du-mak-jip 오두막집. ② (*ship*) sŏn-sil 선실. ③ (*signal* ~) sin-ho-so 신호소.

cabinet *n. & adj.* ① chang 장(欌). ② (*governmental*) nae-gak(ŭi) 내각(의) : *a C*~ *minister* kak-ryo 각료.

cable *n.* (*rope*) kul-gŭn pat-jul 굵은 밧줄, k'e-i-bŭl 케이블 ; (*underwater*) hae-jŏ chŏn-sŏn 해저 전선.

cable car k'e-i-bŭl k'a-a 케이블 카아.

cablegram *n.* hae-oe-jŏn-bo 해외전보, oe-jŏn 외전.

cadence *n.* un-yul 운율(韻律), ŏk-yang 억양.

cadet *n.* sa-gwan saeng-do 사관 생도, sa-gwan[kan-bu] hu-bo-saeng 사관[간부] 후보생.

cage *n.* ① (*bird*) sae-jang 새장. ② kam-ok 감옥.

cake *n.* ① kwa-ja 과자, k'e-i-k'ŭ 케이크. ② (*solid mass*) tŏng-ŏ-ri 덩어리.

calamity *n.* chae-nan 재난, pul-haeng 불행.

calculate *v.* ① kye-san-ha-da 계산하다, ye-sang-ha-da 예상하다. ② (*rely*) ki-dae-ha-da 기대하다.

calculation *n.* kye-san 계산 ; (*forecast*) ye-sang 예상.

calendar *n.* tal-ryŏk 달력, k'ael-rin-dŏ 캘린더.

calf *n.* ① song-a-ji 송아지. ② (*leg*) chong-a-ri 종아리.

calico *n.* ok-yang-mok 옥양목.

call *v.* ① pu-rŭ-da 부르다. ② (*visit*) pang-mun-ha-da 방문하다. ③ (*telephone*) chŏn-hwa-rŭl kŏl-da 전화를 걸다. —*n.* (*visit*) pang-mun 방문.

calling *n.* ① so-jip 소집. ② (*occupation*) chik-ŏp 직업.

calm *adj.* ko-yo-han 고요한, on-hwa-han 온화한.

camel *n.* nak-t'a 낙타.

camera *n.* sa-jin-gi 사진기, k'a-me-ra 카메라.

camp *n.* ya-yŏng 야영. —*v.* ya-yŏng-ha-da 야영하다.

campaign *n.* ① chŏn-jaeng 전쟁. ② chŏng-ch'i-un-dong 정치운동 : *an election* ~ sŏn-gŏ-un-dong 선거운동.

camping *n.* ya-yŏng 야영, k'aem-p'u saeng-hwal 캠

프 생활, ch'ŏn-mak saeng-hwal 천막 생활.　「퍼스.

campus *n.* hak-gyo ku-nae 학교 구내, k'aem-p'ŏ-sŭ 캠

can *n.* kkang-t'ong 깡통. —*aux. v.* …hal su it-da …할 수 있다, (*may*) ha-yŏ-do cho-t'a 하여도 좋다.

Canadian *n.* k'ae-na-da-sa-ram 캐나다사람.　—*adj.* k'ae-na-da-ŭi 캐나다의.

canal *n.* ① un-ha 운하. ② to-gwan 도관(導管).

canary *n.* k'a-na-ri-a 카나리아.

cancel *v.* ch'wi-so-ha-da 취소하다, mal-sal-ha-da 말살 하다. —*n.* mal-sal 말살, p'ye-gi 폐기.

cancellation *n.* ch'wi-so 취소, mal-sal 말살.

cancer *n.* ① am 암 : ～ *of the lung* p'ye-am 폐암/～ *of the stomach* wi-am 위암/*uterine* ～ cha-gung-am 자궁암. ② (*C*～) ha-ji-sŏn 하지선(夏至線).

candid *adj.* sol-jik-han 솔직한, chŏng-jik-han 정직한.

candidate *n.* hu-bo-ja 후보자 ; chi-wŏn-ja 지원자.

candle *n.* ① yang-ch'o 양초. ② ch'ok-gwang 촉광.

candlelight *n.* ch'ot-bul 촛불.

candlestick *n.* ch'ot-dae 촛대.

cando(u)r *n.* sol-jik 솔직, chŏng-jik 정직.

candy *n.* sa-t'ang 사탕, k'aen-di 캔디.

cane *n.* ① chi-p'ang-i 지팡이, tan-jang 단장. ② (*stem*) chul-gi 줄기 : *sugar* ～ sa-t'ang-su-su 사탕수수.

canned goods t'ong-jo-rim che-p'um 통조림 제품.

cannibal *n.* sik-in-jong 식인종.

cannon *n.* tae-p'o 대포, ki-gwan-p'o 기관포.

cannon ball (*shell*) p'o-t'an 포탄.

cannot *v.* …hal su ŏp-da …할 수 없다.　「중한.

canny *adj.* pin-t'ŭm-ŏp-nŭn 빈틈없는, sin-jung-han 신

canoe *n.* t'ong-na-mu-bae 통나무배, k'a-nu-u 카누우.

canopy *n.* tŏp-gae 덮개, ch'ŏn-gae 천개(天蓋) ; k'ae-nŏ-p'i 캐너피.

canvas *n.* hwa-p'o 화포(畫布), k'aen-bŏ-sŭ 캔버스.

canvass *v.* ① (*examine thoroughly*) se-mil-hi cho-sa-ha-da 세밀히 조사하다. ② (*election*) yu-se-ha-da 유세하다. —*n.* sŏn-gŏ-un-dong 선거운동, yu-se 유세.

cap *n.* (*no brim*) mo-ja 모자 ; ttu-ggŏng 뚜껑.

capable *adj.* …hal su it-nŭn …할 수 있는.

capacity *n.* ① (*cubic content*) yong-jŏk 용적. ② (*ability*) chae-nŭng 재능. ③ (*function*) cha-gyŏk 자격.

cape *n.* ① ŏ-ggae mang-t'o 어깨 망토, k'e-i-p'ŭ 케이프. ② (*headland*) kot 곶(岬).

capital *adj.* chu-yo-han 주요한. —*n.* ① (*city*) su-do 수도. ② (*money*) cha-bon 자본. ③ (*letter*) tae-mun-ᒷja 대문자.

capitalism *n.* cha-bon-ju-ŭi 자본주의.

capitalist *n.* cha-bon-ga 자본가 ; cha-bon-ju-ŭi-ja 자본주ᒷ의자.

capitol *n.* kuk-hoe ŭi-sa-dang 국회 의사당.

capsule *n.* k'aep-syul 캡슐 ; kko-t'u-ri 꼬투리.

captain *n.* (*army*) tae-wi 대위 ; (*navy*) tae-ryŏng 대령 ; (*of warship*) ham-jang 함장 ; (*of merchant ship*) sŏn-jang 선장 ; (*of sport*) chu-jang 주장.

caption *n.* (*heading*) p'yo-je 표제 ; (*cinema*) cha-mak 자막(字幕).

captive *n.* p'o-ro 포로. —*adj.* sa-ro-jap-hin 사로잡힌, ᒷmu-ggin 묶인.

capture *n.* (*seizure*) p'o-hoek 포획, saeng-p'o 생포. —*v.* (*catch*) chap-da 잡다.

car *n.* ch'a 차, cha-dong-ch'a 자동차 ; chŏn-ch'a 전차.

caravan *n.* tae-sang 대상(隊商).

carbolic acid sŏk-t'an-san 석탄산.

carbon *n.* t'an-so 탄소 : ~ *paper* k'a-a-bon-ji 카아본지.

carburetor *n.* ki-hwa-gi 기화기(氣化器), k'a-a-byu-re-t'ŏ 카아뷰레터.

carcase·carcass *n.* (*animal*) si-ch'e 시체.

card *n.* ① k'a-a-dŭ 카아드. ② (*playing*) t'ŭ-rŏm-p'ŭ

트럼프. ③ (*calling*) myŏng-ham 명함.

cardboard *n.* ma-bun-ji 마분지.

cardinal *adj.* ① (*fundamental*) ki-bon-jŏk-in 기본적인. ② (*bright red*) sae-bbal-gan 새빨간.

care *v.* kŏk-jŏng-ha-da 걱정하다. —*n.* ① (*anxiety*) kŏk-jŏng 걱정. ② cho-sim 조심 : *take* ~ chu-ŭi-ha-da 주의하다. ⌐ŏp 직업.

career *n.* ① kyŏng-ryŏk 경력. ② (*occupation*) chik-

carefree *adj.* kŏk-jŏng-ŏp-nŭn 걱정없는, (*easy*) t'ae-p'yŏng-sŭ-rŏn 태평스런. ⌐소중히 하는.

careful *adj.* chu-ŭi-gi-p'ŭn 주의깊은, so-jung-hi ha-nŭn

carefully *adv.* cho-sim-sŭ-rŏp-ge 조심스럽게.

careless *adj.* cho-sim-sŏng-ŏp-nŭn 조심성없는, kyŏng-sol-han 경솔한. ⌐ge 경솔하게.

carelessly *adv.* so-hol-ha-ge 소홀하게, kyŏng-sol-ha-

carelessness *n.* pu-ju-ŭi 부주의, mu-gwan-sim 무관심.

caress *n. & v.* ae-mu(-ha-da) 애무(하다).

caretaker *n.* kwal-li-in 관리인 ; mun-ji-gi 문지기.

carfare *n.* kyo-t'ong-bi 교통비, pŏ-sŭ-yo-gŭm 버스요금.

cargo *n.* hwa-mul 화물, paet-jim 뱃짐.

carnival *n.* ch'uk-je 축제(祝祭), k'a-a-ni-bal 카아니발.

carol *n.* ch'uk-ha-ŭi no-rae 축하의 노래 : *Christmas* ~ k'ŭ-ri-sŭ-ma-sŭ ch'uk-ga 크리스마스 축가(祝歌).

carp *n.* ing-ŏ 잉어 : *the silver* ~ pung-ŏ 붕어.

carpenter *n.* mok-su 목수, mok-gong 목공(木工).

carpet *n.* yang-t'an-ja 양탄자, yung-dan 융단.

carriage *n.* ① (*transport*) un-ban 운반 ; (*coach*) ma-ch'a 마차. ② (*bearing*) t'ae-do 태도.

carrier *n.* ① un-ban-in 운반인 ; (*mail*) u-ch'e-bu 우체부 ; (*A-frame*) chi-get-gun 지겟군. ② (*germ* ~) po-gyun-ja 보균자. ③ (*aircraft* ~) hang-gong-mo-ham

carrot *n.* tang-gŭn 당근. ∟항공모함.

carry *v.* ① (*take*) na-rŭ-da 나르다, un-ban-ha-da 운반 하다 ; (*on the head*) i-da 이다 ; (*on the back*) chi-da 지다 ; (*in the arms*) an-da 안다 ; (*on the shoulder*) me-da 메다 ; (*in the hand*) tŭl-da 들다 ; (*in the belt*) ch'a-da 차다. ② hyu-dae-ha-da 휴대하다.

cart *n.* ch'a 차 ; chim-ma-ch'a 짐마차.

cartoon *n.* p'ung-ja-man-hwa 풍자만화.

cartridge *n.* t'an-yak-t'ong 탄약통, yak-p'o 약포.

carve *v.* cho-gak-ha-da 조각하다, sae-gi-da 새기다.

carver *n.* cho-gak-ga 조각가.

carving *n.* cho-gak 조각, cho-gak-sul 조각술.

case *n.* ① (*box*) sang-ja 상자. ② (*condition*) kyŏng-u 경우. ③ (*affair*) sa-gŏn 사건. ④ (*patient*) hwan-ja ⌐환자.

casement *n.* yŏ-da-ji ch'ang-mun 여닫이 창문.

cash *n.* hyŏn-gŭm 현금, hyŏn-ch'al 현찰. —*v.* (*exchange*) hyŏn-gŭm-ŭ-ro pa-ggu-da 현금으로 바꾸다.

cashier *n.* ch'ul-nap-gye 출납계, hoe-gye-wŏn 회계원.

cask *n.* t'ong 통 : *a wine* ~ sul-t'ong 술통.

casket *n.* chak-ŭn sang-ja 작은 상자 ; (*coffin*) kwan 관.

cast *v.* ① (*throw*) tŏn-ji-da 던지다. ② (*found*) chu-jo-ha-da 주조하다. —*n.* ① (*mold*) chu-hyŏng 주형 (鑄型). ② (*of play*) pae-yŏk 배역. ⌐jŏn 궁전.

castle *n.* ① sŏng 성(城), sŏng-gwak 성곽. ② kung-

castor oil a-ju-gga-ri ki-rŭm 아주까리 기름, p'i-ma-ja-yu 피마자유.

casual *adj.* u-yŏn-han 우연한, ttŭt-ba-ggŭi 뜻밖의.

cat *n.* ① ko-yang-i 고양이. ② (*guy*) nom 놈.

catalog(ue) *n.* mok-rok 목록, *k'a-t'al-ro-gŭ* 카탈로그.

catastrophe *n.* ① (*a great misfortune*) k'ŭn chae-nan 큰 재난. ② (*drama*) tae-dan-wŏn 대단원.

catch ① (*seize*) chap-da 잡다. ② (*overtake*) ch'u-wŏl-ha-da 추월하다. ③ (*be attacked*) kam-yŏm-ha-da 감염하다. ④ (*arrest*) chu-ŭi-rŭl kkŭl-da 주의를 끌다. ⑤ (*understand*) i-hae-ha-da 이해하다.

category *n.* pŏm-ju 범주, k'ae-t'i-go-ri 캐티고리.

caterpillar *n.* p'ul-sswae-gi 풀쌔기, mo-ch'ung 모충.

cathedral *n.* tae-sŏng-dang 대성당.

Catholic *adj.* (*Roman*) ch'ŏn-ju-gyo-ŭi 천주교의. —*n.* ch'ŏn-ju-gyo-do 천주교도, ku-gyo-do 구교도.

cattle *n.* so 소 ; (*livestock*) ka-ch'uk 가축.

cause *v.* i-rŭ-k'i-da 일으키다. —*n.* ① (*reason*) wŏn-in 원인 ; (*motive*) tong-gi 동기. ② tae-ŭi 대의(大義).

caution *n.* ① cho-sim 조심. ② (*warning*) kyŏng-go 경고. ③ (*surety*) tam-bo 담보.

cautious *adj.* cho-sim-sŏng-it-nŭn 조심성있는.

cavalier *n.* ki-sa 기사(騎士), ki-ma-byŏng 기마병.

cavalry *n.* ki-byŏng 기병, ki-byŏng-dae 기병대.

cave *n.* kul 굴, tong-gul 동굴, tong-hyŏl 동혈.

cavity *n.* ku-mŏng 구멍 ; kong-dong 공동(空洞).

cease *v.* kŭ-ch'i-da 그치다, kŭ-man-du-da 그만두다.

ceasefire *n.* hyu-jŏn 휴전 : *the ~ line* hyu-jŏn-sŏn 휴

ceaseless *adj.* kkŭn-im-ŏp-nŭn 끊임없는. ⌊전선.

cedar *n.* hi-mal-ra-ya sam-mok 히말라야 삼목(杉木).

ceiling *n.* ① ch'ŏn-jang 천장. ② kkok-dae-gi 꼭대기.

celadon *n.* (*porcelain*) ch'ŏng-ja 청자(靑瓷).

celebrate *v.* ch'uk-ha-ha-da 축하하다.

celebrated *adj.* i-rŭm-no-p'ŭn 이름높은, yu-myŏng-han 유명한, chŏ-myŏng-han 저명한.

celebration *n.* ch'uk-ha 축하, che-jŏn 제전.

celebrity *n.* ① (*famous person*) myŏng-sa 명사, yu-myŏng-in 유명인. ② (*fame*) myŏng-sŏng 명성.

celery *n.* sel-rŏ-ri 셀러리.

cell *n.* ① (*small room*) chak-ŭn tok-bang 작은 독방. ② (*hermit*) am-ja 암자. ③ (*prison*) kam-bang

감방. ④ (*biol.*) se-p'o 세포.
cellar *n.* chi-ha-sil 지하실 ; um 움.
cement *n.* si-men-t'ŭ 시멘트, yang-hoe 양회.
cemetery *n.* kong-dong-myo-ji 공동묘지.
censure *n.* pi-nan 비난, kyŏn-ch'aek 견책. —*v.* pi-nan-ha-da 비난하다, na-mu-ra-da 나무라다.
census *n.* kuk-se-jo-sa 국세조사, sen-sŏ-sŭ 센서스.
cent *n.* sen-t'ŭ 센트.
centenary *adj.* paek-nyŏn-ŭi 100년의. —*n.* paek-nyŏn-gan 100년간, paek-nyŏn-je 100년제(祭).
center *n.* chung-sim 중심, sen-t'ŏ 센터.
centigrade *adj.* paek-bun-do-ŭi 백분도의 : ~ *thermometer* sŏp-ssi on-do-gye 섭씨 온도계.
centiped(e) *n.* chi-ne 지네.
central *adj.* chung-ang-ŭi 중앙의, chung-sim-ŭi 중심의.
century *n.* se-gi 세기, paek-nyŏn 100년.
cereals *n.* kok-sik 곡식, kok-mul 곡물.
ceremony *n.* ye-sik 예식, ŭi-sik 의식(儀式) : *a marriage* ~ kyŏl-hon-sik 결혼식.
certain *adj.* (*sure*) hwak-sil-han 확실한 ; (*one, some*) ŏ-ddŏn 어떤 ; (*fixed*) il-jŏng-han 일정한.
certainly *adv.* ① hwak-sil-hi 확실히. ② (*exclamation*) kŭ-rŏ-k'o-mal-go 그렇고말고.
certificate *n.* chŭng-myŏng-sŏ 증명서. 「ha-da 보증하다.
certify *v.* ① chŭng-myŏng-ha-da 증명하다. ② po-jŭng-
chain *n.* soe-sa-sŭl 쇠사슬 ; (*a long line*) yŏn-sok 연속.
chair *n.* ŭi-ja 의자, kŏl-sang 걸상 ; ŭi-jang 의장.
chairman *n.* ŭi-jang 의장, hoe-jang 회장.
chalk *n.* pun-p'il 분필, ch'o-o-k'ŭ 초오크.
challenge *n.* to-jŏn 도전. —*v.* to-jŏn-ha-da 도전하다.
chamber ① (*room*) pang 방. ② (*assembly hall*) hoe-ŭi-so 회의소 : ~ *music* sil-nae-ak 실내악.

champion *n*. chŏn-sa 전사(戰士) ; (*winner*) u-sŭng-ja 우승자, (*player*) ch'aem-p'i-ŏn 챔피언.
chance *n*. (*opportunity*) ki-hoe 기회, ch'a-an-sŭ 차안스.
change *n*. ① pyŏn-gyŏng 변경. ② (*money*) chan-don 잔돈, kŏ-sŭ-rŭm-don 거스름돈. —*v*. pyŏn-ha-da 변하다, pa-ggu-da 바꾸다.
changeable *adj*. pyŏn-ha-gi swi-un 변하기 쉬운.
channel *n*. ① hae-hyŏp 해협, su-ro 수로. ② kyŏng-ro 경로. ③ (*radio, TV*) ch'ae-nŏl 채널. 「ha-da 노래하다.
chant *n*. no-rae 노래 ; sŏng-ga 성가. —*v*. (*sing*) no-rae-
chaos *n*. hon-don 혼돈, mu-jil-sŏ 무질서.
chap *n*. (*fellow*) nyŏ-sŏk 녀석, nom 놈 : *a good* ∼ cho-ŭn nyŏ-sŏk 좋은 녀석.
chapel *n*. ye-bae-dang 예배당, (*service*) ye-bae 예배.
chaperon(e) *n*. sya-p'ŭ-rong 샤프롱.
chapter *n*. ① (*book*) chang 장(章). ② (*local divisions*) chi-bu 지부, pun-hoe 분회.
character *n*. ① sŏng-jil 성질 ; in-gyŏk 인격. ② myŏng-sŏng 명성. ③ (*letter*) kŭl-ja 글자.
charcoal *n*. sut 숯, mok-t'an 목탄.
charge *n*. ① ch'aek-im 책임. ② (*price demanded*) pu-dam 부담, yo-gŭm 요금. ③ (*accusation*) pi-nan 비난, ko-bal 고발. —*v*. (*attack*) chin-gyŏk-ha-da 진격하다.
chariot *n*. chŏn-ch'a 전차(戰車) ; ma-ch'a 마차.
charitable *adj*. in-ja-han 인자한, cha-bi-ro-un 자비로운.
charity *n*. cha-bi-sim 자비심, cha-ae 자애, sa-rang 사랑.
charm *v*. mae-hok-ha-da 매혹하다. —*n*. mae-ryŏk 매력.
charming *adj*. mae-ryŏk-jŏk-in 매력적인.
chart *n*. to-p'yo 도표, ch'a-a-t'ŭ 차아트 ; hae-do 해도 (海圖). 「hŏ-ga-jang 허가장.
charter *n*. ① hŏn-jang 헌장. ② t'ŭk-hŏ-jang 특허장,
chase *v*. twi-rŭl jjot-da 뒤를 쫓다. —*n*. ch'u-gyŏk 추격.

chaste *adj*. sun-gyŏl-han 순결한 ; ko-sang-han 고상한.
chat *n. & v*. chap-dam(-ha-da) 잡담(하다).
chatter *v*. chae-jal-jae-jal chi-ggŏ-ri-da 재잘재잘 지껄이다. —*n*. chi-ggŏ-ri-nŭn so-ri 지껄이는 소리.
chauffeur *n*. un-jŏn ki-sa 운전 기사, un-jŏn-su 운전수.
cheap *adj*. ssan 싼, kap-ssan 값싼.
cheat *v*. sok-i-da 속이다 ; sok-yŏ ppae-at-da 속여 빼앗다.
check *v*. (*prevent*) chŏ-ji-ha-da 저지하다, (*control*) ŏk-je-ha-da 억제하다 ; (*collate*) tae-jo-ha-da 대조하다, ch'e-k'ŭ-ha-da 체크하다. —*n*. ① pang-hae 방해. ② chŏm-gŏm 점검, ch'e-k'ŭ 체크. ③ (*bank*) su-p'yo 수표.
checkbook *n*. su-p'yo-jang 수표장.
checkerboard *n*. chang-gi-p'an 장기판.
checkers *n*. sŏ-yang-jang-gi 서양장기.
cheek *n*. ppyam 뺨, pol 볼.
cheer *n*. ki-bun 기분, k'wae-hwal 쾌활 ; (*applause*) kal-ch'ae 갈채. —*v*. ① (*comfort*) ki-bbŭ-ge ha-da 기쁘게 하다. ② (*animate*) ki-un-ŭl tot-gu-da 기운을 돋구다 : *C~ up!* Ki-un-ŭl nae-ra! 기운을 내라 !
cheerful *adj*. ki-bun-jo-ŭn 기분좋은 ; k'wae-hwal-han 쾌활한.
cheese *n*. ch'i-i-jŭ 치이즈.
chemical *adj*. hwa-hak-ŭi 화학의. —*n*. hwa-hak-je-p'um 화학제품, yak-p'um 약품.
chemise *n*. sok-ch'i-ma 속치마, si-mi-i-jŭ 시미이즈.
chemist *n*. hwa-hak-ja 화학자 ; (*Brit*.) yak-je-sa 약제사.
chemistry *n*. hwa-hak 화학.
cheque *n*. su-p'yo 수표.
cherish *v*. so-jung-hi ha-da 소중히 하다 ; (*foster*) ma-ŭm-e p'um-da 마음에 품다.
cherry *n*. pŏ-jji 버찌 ; (*blossom*) pŏt-ggot 벚꽃 ; (*tree*) pŏt-na-mu 벚나무. —*adj*. chin-bun-hong-ŭi 진분홍의.
chess *n*. sŏ-yang-jang-gi 서양장기, ch'e-sŭ 체스.

chest *n.* ① (*breast*) ka-sŭm 가슴. ② (*box*) kwe 궤, sang-ja 상자. ③ (*funds*) cha-gŭm 자금.

chestnut *n.* pam 밤(栗), pam-na-mu 밤나무.

chew *v.* ssip-da 씹다.

chewing gum kkŏm 껌.

chick *n.* ① pyŏng-a-ri 병아리. ② (*child*) ŏ-rin-a-i 어

chicken *n.* tak 닭, tak-go-gi 닭고기.　　　　「린아이.

chicken sexer pyŏng-a-ri kam-byŏl-sa 병아리 감별사.

chief *adj.* chu-yo-han 주요한, ŭ-ddŭm-ga-nŭn 으뜸가는. —*n.* u-du-mŏ-ri 우두머리, chang 장(長).

chiffonier *n.* yang-bok-jang 양복장.

child *n.* a-i 아이, ŏ-rin-i 어린이, a-dong 아동.

childhood *n.* ŏ-rin si-jŏl 어린 시절, yu-nyŏn-gi 유년기.

chill *n.* naeng-gi 냉기(冷氣); (*cold fit*) o-han 오한.

chime *v.* chong-ŭl ul-ri-da 종을 울리다. —*n.* (*bell*) chong 종, ch'a-im 차임.

chimney *n.* kul-dduk 굴뚝, yŏn-t'ong 연통.

chin *n.* t'ŏk 턱, t'ŏk-ggŭt 턱끝.

China *n.* chung-guk 중국 : *Red* ~ chung-gong 중공.

china *n.* (*porcelain*) to-ja-gi 도자기, cha-gi 자기.

Chinese *adj.* chung-guk-ŭi 중국의, chung-guk-sik-ŭi 중국식의 ; (*Communist*) chung-gong-ŭi 중공의. —*n.* (*people*) chung-guk-sa-ram 중국사람, chung-guk-in 중국인 : (*language*) chung-guk-ŏ 중국어.

chip *n.* t'o-mak 토막, na-mut-jo-gak 나뭇조각. —*v.* chal-ge ssŏl-da 잘게 썰다, kkak-da 깎다.

chirp *v.* jjaek-jjaek ul-da 짹짹 울다. —*n.* jjaek-jjaek-ha-nŭn u-rŭm-so-ri 짹짹하는 울음소리.

chisel *n.* kkŭl 끌, chŏng 정.　　　　　　　　「의협심.

chivalry *n.* ki-sa-do 기사도 ; (*gallantry*) ŭi-hyŏp-sim

chlorine *n.* yŏm-so 염소(鹽素).

chocolate *n.* ch'o-k'ŏl-rit 초컬릿.

choice *n*. sŏn-t'aek 선택, ko-rŭn kŏt 고른 것.

choir *n*. hap-ch'ang-dae 합창대, sŏng-ga-dae 성가대.

choke *v*. sum-mak-hi-ge ha-da 숨막히게 하다 ; ŏk-nu-rŭ-da 억누르다. —*n*. chil-sik 질식.

cholera *n*. ho-yŏl-ja 호열자, k'ol-re-ra 콜레라.

choose *v*. ① sŏn-t'aek-ha-da 선택하다 ; (*elect*) sŏn-ch'ul-ha-da 선출하다. ② (*want*) wŏn-ha-da 원하다.

chop *v*. (*cut*) cha-rŭ-da 자르다. —*n*. chŏl-dan 절단.

chopsticks *n*. chŏt-ga-rak 젓가락.

chorus *n*. hap-ch'ang 합창.

Christ *n*. kŭ-ri-sŭ-do 그리스도.

Christian *n*. ki-dok-gyo-in[sin-ja] 기독교인[신자].

[chŏt-ga-rak]

Christianity *n*. ki-dok-gyo 기독교.

Christmas *n*. sŏng-t'an-jŏl 성탄절, k'ŭ-ri-sŭ-ma-sŭ 크리스마스.

chronic *adj*. man-sŏng-ŭi 만성의, ko-jil-ŭi 고질의, (*habitual*) sang-sŭp-jŏk-in 상습적인.

chronicle *n*. ① yŏn-dae-gi 연대기. ② (*record*) ki-rok 기록.

chrysanthemum *n*. kuk-hwa 국화.

chuckle *n*. kkil-ggil u-sŭm 낄낄 웃음. —*v*. kkil-ggil ut-da 낄낄 웃다, hon-ja ut-da 혼자 웃다.

chum *n*. tan-jjak 단짝, ch'in-gu 친구.

church *n*. kyo-hoe 교회, ye-bae-dang 예배당.

cicada *n*. mae-mi 매미.

cider *n*. sa-i-da 사이다 ; sa-gwa-sul 사과술.

cigar *n*. yo-song-yŏn 여송연, si-ga-a 시가아.

cigaret(te) *n*. kwŏl-ryŏn 궐련, tam-bae 담배.

cinder *n*. sŏk-t'an chae 석탄재, ttŭn sut 뜬 숯.

cinema *n*. yŏng-hwa-gwan 영화관, yŏng-hwa 영화.

circle *n*. ① (*round*) wŏn-hyŏng 원형. ② (*group*) chip-dan 집단 ; …kye …계(界). ③ (*range*) pŏm-wi

범위. —*v.* hoe-jŏn-ha-da 회전하다.
circuit *n.* (*round*) sun-hoe 순회 ; (*circumference*) chu-wi 주위 ; (*electric*) hoe-ro 회로.
circular *adj.* wŏn-hyŏng-ŭi 원형의, tung-gŭn 둥근; sun-hwan-ha-nŭn 순환하는. —*n.* hoe-ram-jang 회람장.
circulate *v.* sun-hwan-ha-da 순환하다, tol-ri-da 돌리다.
circulation *n.* sun-hwan 순환, yu-t'ong 유통.
circumference *n.* wŏn-dul-re 원둘레 ; chu-wi 주위.
circumstance *n.* sa-jŏng 사정 ; hwan-gyŏng 환경.
circus *n.* kok-ma-dan 곡마단, sŏ-ŏ-k'ŏ-sŭ 서어커스.
cistern *n.* mul-t'ong 물통, mul-t'aeng-k'ŭ 물탱크.
citadel *n.* sŏng 성(城) ; pon-gŏ-ji 본거지.
citation *n.* ① (*quotation*) in-yong 인용. ② (*testimonial*) p'yo-ch'ang-jang 표창장.　　　　「하다.
cite *v.* in-yong-ha-da 인용하다 ; p'yo-ch'ang-ha-da 표창
citizen *n.* si-min 시민, kong-min 공민.　　　　「민권.
citizenship *n.* si-min-gwŏn 시민권, kong-min-gwŏn 공
city *n.* to-si 도시, si 시(市).
civic *adj.* si-min-ŭi 시민의, kong-min-ŭi 공민의.
civil *adj.* ① min-gan-ŭi 민간의. ② (*polite*) chŏng-jung-han 정중한. ③ (*law*) min-sa-ŭi 민사의.
civilian *n.* min-gan-in 민간인, mun-gwan 문관.
civilization *n.* mun-myŏng 문명, kae-hwa 개화.
civilize *v.* mun-myŏng-hwa-ha-da 문명화하다, (*enlighten*) kae-hwa-si-k'i-da 개화시키다.
claim *n.* yo-gu 요구. —*v.* ① (*insist*) chu-jang-ha-da 주장하다. ② (*demand*) yo-gu-ha-da 요구하다.
clam *n.* mu-myŏng-jo-gae 무명조개, tae-hap 대합.
clamber *v.* ki-ŏ-o-rŭ-da 기어오르다. —*n.* ki-ŏ-o-rŭ-gi 기어오르기, tŭng-ban 등반.
clamo(u)r *n.* oe-ch'i-nŭn so-ri 외치는 소리. —*v.* ttŏ-dŭl-
clan *n.* ① ssi-jok 씨족. ② tang-p'a 당파.　 ∟da 떠들다.

clap *n.* pak-su 박수. —*v.* (*hands*) pak-su-ha-da 박수하다 ; ka-byŏp-ge ch'i-da 가볍게 치다.
clarinet *n.* k'ŭl-ra-ri-net 클라리넷.　　　「sŏng 투명성.
clarity *n.* (*clearness*) myŏng-k'wae 명쾌 ; t'u-myŏng-
clash *v.* ch'ung-dol-ha-da 충돌하다, pu-dit-ch'i-da 부딪치다. —*n.* pu-dit-ch'i-nŭn so-ri 부딪치는 소리, ch'ung-dol 충돌, (*discord*) al-ryŏk 알력.　　　「포옹하다.
clasp *v.* kkwak put-jap-da 꽉 붙잡다 ; p'o-ong-ha-da
class *n.* ① kye-gŭp 계급. ② (*school*) pan 반.
classic *adj.* ① ko-jŏn-ŭi 고전의. ② il-ryu-ŭi 일류의. —*n.* ko-jŏn chak-p'um 고전 작품.
classification *n.* pul-lyu 분류, chong-byŏl 종별.
classify *v.* pul-lyu-ha-da 분류하다.
classmate *n.* tong-gŭp-saeng 동급생, tong-ch'ang-saeng
classroom *n.* kyo-sil 교실.　　　　　　　「동창생.
clatter *n.* tŏl-gŏ-dŏk-gŏ-ri-nŭn so-ri 덜거덕거리는 소리. —*v.* wak-ja-gŭ-rŭ ttŏ-dŭl-da 와자그르 떠들다.
clause *n.* ① (*provision*) cho-hang 조항. ② (*sentence*) chŏl 절. ③ (*music*) ak-gu 악구(樂句).
claw *n.* pal-t'op 발톱 ; chip-ge-bal 집게발.
clay *n.* chin-hŭk 진흙, ch'al-hŭk 찰흙.
clean *adj.* kkae-ggŭt-han 깨끗한. —*v.* kkae-ggŭ-si ha-da 깨끗이 하다, tak-da 닦다.
cleaner *n.* ① ch'ŏng-so-bu 청소부. ② so-je-gi 소제기.
cleaning *n.* ch'ŏng-sŏ 청소 ; k'ŭl-ri-i-ning 클리이닝.
cleanse *v.* ① (*clean*) kkae-ggŭ-si ha-da 깨끗이 하다. ② (*purge*) so-dok-ha-da 소독하다.
clear *adj.* mal-gŭn 맑은. —*v.* mal-ge ha-da 맑게 하다.
clearance sale chae-go chŏng-ri 재고 정리.
clearly *adv.* pal-ge 밝게, pun-myŏng-hi 분명히.
cleave *v.* ① (*split*) jjo-gae-da 쪼개다, tte-ŏ-no-t'a 떼어놓다. ② (*stick*) tal-ra-but-da 달라붙다.

clench *v.* kkwak choe-da 꽉 죄다.

clergyman *n.* mok-sa 목사, sŏng-jik-ja 성직자.

clerk *n.* sa-mu-wŏn 사무원, chŏm-wŏn 점원.

clever *adj.* yŏng-ri-han 영리한, hyŏn-myŏng-han 현명한.

cleverness *n.* yŏng-ri-ham 영리함.

client *n.* ① so-song ŭi-roe-in 소송 의뢰인. ② tan-gol son-nim 단골 손님, ko-gaek 고객.

cliff *n.* nang-ddŏ-rŏ-ji 낭떠러지, chŏl-byŏk 절벽.

climate *n.* ki-hu 기후, p'ung-t'o 풍토.

climax *n.* chŏl-jŏng 절정, k'ŭl-ra-i-maek-sŭ 클라이맥스.

climb *n.* ki-ŏ-o-rŭ-da 기어오르다. —*n.* tŭng-ban 등반.

cling *v.* tal-ra-but-da 달라붙다, mil-ch'ak-ha-da 밀착하다.

clinic *n.* chil-lyo-so 진료소, pyŏng-wŏn 병원.

clip *n.* k'ŭl-rip 클립. —*v.* (*cut*) ka-wi-ro cha-rŭ-da 가위로 자르다 ; (*grip*) kkwak chwi-da 꽉 쥐다.

cloak *n.* oe-t'u 외투, mang-t'o 망토.

clock *n.* kwae-jong-si-gye 괘종시계.

clog *n.* ① chang-ae-mul 장애물. ② na-mak-sin 나막신.

cloister *n.* ① hoe-rang 회랑. ② (*monastery*) su-do-wŏn 수도원, sŭng-wŏn 승원(僧院).

close *v.* (*shut*) tat-da 닫다 ; (*finish*) ma-ch'i-da 마치다. —*adv.* ka-gga-i 가까이. —*adj.* (*near*) ka-gga-un 가까운 ; (*intimate*) ch'in-han 친한.

closely *adv.* (*nearly*) ka-ggap-ge 가깝게 ; (*strictly*) ŏm-mil-hi 엄밀히 ; (*tightly*) tan-dan-hi 단단히.

closet *n.* ① sa-sil 사실(私室). ② pyŏk-jang 벽장. ③ pyŏn-so 변소.

clot *n.* ŏng-gin tŏng-ŏ-ri 엉긴 덩어리.

cloth *n.* ch'ŏn 천, ot-gam 옷감.

clothe *v.* (*dress*) o-sŭl ip-da 옷을 입다.

clothes *n.* ot 옷 ; (*bedclothes*) ch'im-gu 침구.

clothing *n.* (*collective*) ŭi-ryu 의류, ŭi-bok 의복.

cloud *n.* ① ku-rŭm 구름. ② (*flock*) tte 떼.

cloudless *adj*. ku-rŭm-ŏp-nŭn 구름없는.
cloudy *adj*. ku-rŭm-ggin 구름낀, hŭ-rin 흐린.
clover *n*. k'ŭl-ro-u-bŏ 클로우버.
clown *n*. ① (*jester*) ik-sal-gun 익살군, kwang-dae 광대. ② (*rustic*) si-gol-ddŭ-gi 시골뜨기.
club *n*. ① (*heavy stick*) kon-bong 곤봉. ② (*association*) k'ŭl-rŏp 클럽, tong-ho-hoe 동호회.
clue *n*. sil-ma-ri 실마리, tan-sŏ 단서.
clump *n*. ① (*thicket*) su-p'ul 수풀, tŏm-bul 덤불. ② (*lump*) tŏng-ŏ-ri 덩어리.
clumsy *adj*. (*unskilful*) sŏ-t'u-rŭn 서투른, ŏ-saek-han 어색한, (*tactless*) ŏl-bba-jin 얼빠진.
cluster *n*. song-i 송이 ; (*crowd*) mu-ri 무리, tt'e 떼. —*v*. (*round*) tte-rŭl ji-ŏ mo-i-da 떼를 지어 모이다.
coach *v*. chi-do-ha-da 지도하다, k'o-u-ch'i-ha-da 코우치하다. —*n*. ① tae-hyŏng-ma-ch'a 대형마차 ; (*railway*) kaek-ch'a 객차. ② (*athletic*) k'o-u-ch'i 코우치.
coal *n*. sŏk-t'an 석탄 : ～ *field* t'an-jŏn 탄전(炭田).
coalition *n*. yŏn-hap 연합, hap-dong 합동.
coal mine t'an-gwang 탄광, t'an-gaeng 탄갱(炭坑).
coarse *adj*. kŏ-ch'in 거친, hŏ-rŭm-han 허름한.
coast *n*. hae-an 해안, yŏn-an 연안(沿岸).
coat *n*. ut-ot 웃옷, sang-ŭi 상의, oe-t'u 외투.
cobbler *n*. ku-du 구두 ; (*shoemaker*) ku-du su-ri-gong 구두 수리공, sin-gi-ryo chang-su 신기료 장수.
cobweb *n*. kŏ-mi-jul 거미줄, kŏ-mi-jip 거미집. 「꼭지.
cock *n*. ① su-t'ak 수탉 ; su-k'ŏt 수컷. ② (*tap*) kkok-ji
coconut *n*. ya-ja yŏl-mae 야자 열매, k'o-k'o-nŏt 코코넛.
cocoon *n*. (*silkworm*) ko-ch'i 고치.
cod *n*. (*codfish*) tae-gu 대구.
code *n*. ① pŏp-jŏn 법전(法典). ② (*rules*) kwal-lye 관례, kyu-yak 규약. ③ (*cipher*) am-ho 암호.

cod-liver oil kan-yu 간유.

co-ed *n*. (nam-nyo kong-hak-ŭi) yŏ-hak-saeng (남녀 공 「학의) 여학생.

coeducation *n*. nam-nyŏ kong-hak 남녀 공학.

coerce *v*. kang-yo-ha-da 강요하다, wi-ap-ha-da 위압하다.

coffee *n*. k'o-o-p'i 코오피.

coffin *n*. kwan 관(棺), nŏl 널.　　　　　　「il 코일.

coil *v*. tul-dul kam-da 둘둘 감다. —*n*. sa-ri 사리 ; k'o-

coin *n*. ton 돈, hwa-p'ye 화폐 ; *copper* ～ tong-jŏn 동전.

coincide *v*. il-ch'i-ha-da 일치하다, pu-hap-ha-da 부합하

coincidence *n*. il-ch'i 일치, pu-hap 부합.　　　　「다.

coke *n*. k'o-u-k'ŭ-sŭ 코우크스, hae-t'an 해탄(骸炭).

cold *adj*. ch'an 찬, ch'a-ga-un 차가운 : *be* ～ ch'up-da
　춥다 ; (*of hands and feet*) si-ri-da 시리다. —*n*. kam-
　gi 감기 : *catch* ～ kam-gi tŭl-da 감기 들다.　「하다.

collapse *v*. mu-nŏ-ji-da 무너지다 ; soe-t'oe-ha-da 쇠퇴

collar *n*. k'al-ra 칼라, kit 깃.

colleague *n*. tong-ryo 동료, tong-ŏp-ja 동업자.

collect *v*. mo-ŭ-da 모으다, su-jip-ha-da 수집하다.

collection *n*. su-jip 수집, su-jip-p'um 수집품.

collective security (*of U.N.*) chip-dan an-jŏn-bo-jang
　집단 안전보장.

college *n*. tan-gwa-dae-hak 단과대학.　　　　　　「딪치다.

collide *v*. ch'ung-dol-ha-da 충돌하다, pu-dit-ch'i-da 부

collision *n*. ch'ung-dol 충돌, sang-ch'ung 상충.

colloquial *adj*. ku-ŏ(-ch'e)-ŭi 구어(체)의.

colonel *n*. yuk-gun-dae-ryŏng 육군대령.

colonist *n*. sik-min-ji kae-ch'ŏk-ja 식민지 개척자 ; hae-
　oe i-ju-min 해외 이주민.　　　　　　　　　　「집단.

colony *n*. ① sik-min-ji 식민지. ② (*group*) chip-dan

colossal *adj*. kŏ-dae-han 거대한, pang-dae-han 방대한.

colo(u)r *n*. ① pit-ggal 빛깔, k'ŏl-rŏ 컬러. ② (*pl*.)
　kun-gi 군기(軍旗). —*v*. saek-ch'il-ha-da 색칠하다.

colt *n.* mang-a-ji 망아지 ; p'ut-na-gi 풋나기.
column *n.* ① (*pillar*) ki-dung 기둥. ② (*of newspaper*) nan 난(欄). ③ (*mil.*) chong-dae 종대(縱隊).
comb *n.* pit 빗. —*v.* pit-da 빗다.
combat *n.* (*fight*) chŏn-t'u 전투 ; (*struggle*) t'u-jaeng 투쟁. —*v.* kyŏk-t'u-ha-da 격투하다.
combination *n.* ① kyŏl-hap 결합, jja-mat-ch'u-gi 짜맞추기. ② k'om-bi-ne-i-syŏn 콤비네이션. 「합하다.
combine *v.* kyŏl-hap-ha-da 결합하다, yŏn-hap-ha-da 연
come *v.* ① o-da 오다. ② (*happen*) i-rŏ-na-da 일어나다. ③ (*be caused by*) yu-rae-ha-da 유래하다. ④ (*become*) …i toe-da …이 되다. ⑤ (*amount to*) …e tal-ha-da …에 달하다. 「디언.
comedian *n.* hŭi-gŭk pae-u 희극 배우, k'o-mi-di-ŏn 코미
comedy *n.* hŭi-gŭk 희극, k'o-mi-di 코미디.
comet *n.* hye-sŏng 혜성, sal-byŏl 살별.
comfort *n.* (*consolation*) wi-an 위안 ; (*ease*) al-lak 안락, —*v.* (*console*) wi-ro-ha-da 위로하다.
comfortable *adj.* p'yŏn-an-han 편안한, al-lak-han 안락한, ki-bun-jo-ŭn 기분좋은. 「배우.
comic *adj.* hŭi-gŭk-ŭi 희극의. —*n.* hŭi-gŭk pae-u 희극
command *n.* myŏng-ryŏng 명령. —*v.* myŏng-ryŏng-ha-da 명령하다 ; chi-hwi-ha-da 지휘하다.
commander *n.* ① chi-hwi-gwan 지휘관, sa-ryŏng-gwan 사령관. ② (*navy*) chung-ryŏng 중령 : ~ *in chief* ch'ong-sa-ryŏng-gwan 총사령관.
commandment *n.* kye-myŏng 계명, kye-yul 계율.
commemorate *v.* ki-nyŏm-ha-da 기념하다 ; (*celebrate*) kyŏng-ch'uk-ha-da 경축하다. 「da 개시하다.
commence *v.* (*start*) si-jak-ha-da 시작하다, kae-si-ha-
commencement *n.* cho-rŏp-sik 졸업식.
commend *v.* ① ch'u-ch'ŏn-ha-da 추천하다. ② (*praise*)

ch'ing-ch'an-ha-da 칭찬하다. 「논평.
comment *v.* non-p'yŏng-ha-da 논평하다. —*n.* non-p'yŏng
commerce *n.* sang-ŏp 상업, (*trade*) mu-yŏk 무역.
commercial *adj.* sang-ŏp-ŭi 상업의. —*n.* (*broadcasting*)
  kwang-go pang-song 광고 방송.
commission *n.* ① wi-im 위임.② (*fee*) su-su-ryo 수수료.
commissioner *n.* wi-wŏn 위원, i-sa 이사.
commit *v.* ① (*entrust*) wi-t'ak-ha-da 위탁하다. ② (*do
  wrong*) pŏm-ha-da 범하다, chŏ-ji-rŭ-da 저지르다.
committee *n.* wi-wŏn-hoe 위원회. 「dae 세면대.
commode *n.* ① ot-jang 옷장. ② (*washstand*) se-myŏn-
commodity *n.* sang-p'um 상품 ; i-ryong-p'um 일용품.
common *adj.* kong-t'ong-ŭi 공통의 ; po-t'ong-ŭi 보통의.
commonplace *adj.* p'yŏng-bŏm-han 평범한.
commons *n.* p'yŏng-min 평민, sŏ-min 서민.
common sense sang-sik 상식, yang-sik 양식(良識).
commonwealth *n.* (*nation*) kuk-ga 국가, kong-hwa-
  guk 공화국 ; (*union of states*) yŏn-bang 연방.
commotion *n.* tong-yo 동요(動搖), so-dong 소동.
communicate *v.* al-ri-da 알리다, chŏn-ha-da 전하다 ;
  t'ong-sin-ha-da 통신하다.
communication *n.* t'ong-sin 통신 ; kyo-t'ong 교통.
communion *n.* ① (*close relation*) ch'in-gyo 친교. ②
  (*church*) sŏng-ch'an-sik 성찬식.
communism *n.* kong-san-ju-ŭi 공산주의.
communist *n.* kong-san-ju-ŭi-ja 공산주의자, (*C~*) kong-
  san-dang-wŏn 공산당원 : *C~ Party* kong-san-dang 공
  산당/ ~ *camp* kong-san chin-yŏng 공산 진영.
community *n.* sa-hoe 사회, kong-dong-sa-hoe 공동사회,
  chi-yŏk-sa-hoe 지역사회.
compact *adj.* ① (*close*) cho-mil-han 조밀한 ; (*dense*)
  mil-jip-han 밀집한. ② (*concise*) kan-gyŏl-han 간결한.

companion *n.* tong-ryo 동료, ch'in-gu 친구.
company *n.* ① (*association*) kyo-je 교제 ; (*companions*) tong-ryo 동료. ② (*firm*) hoe-sa 회사. ③ (*army*) chung-dae 중대. 「간.
comparatively *adv.* pi-gyo-jŏk 비교적, ta-so-gan 다소
compare *v.* pi-gyo-ha-da 비교하다, pi-yu-ha-da 비유하다.
comparison *n.* ① pi-gyo 비교. ② yu-sa 유사(類似).
compartment *n.* ku-hoek 구획, kan-mak-i 간막이.
compass *n.* ① (*extent*) pŏm-wi 범위. ② na-ch'im-ban 나
compassion *n.* tong-jŏng 동정, yŏn-min 연민. ⌊침반.
compatriot *n.* tong-guk-in 동국인, tong-p'o 동포.
compel *v.* kang-yo-ha-da 강요하다.
compensate *v.* kap-da 갚다, po-sang-ha-da 보상하다.
compete *v.* kyŏng-jaeng-ha-da 경쟁하다.
competent *adj.* (*capable*) cha-gyŏk-it-nŭn 자격있는.
competition *n.* kyŏng-jaeng 경쟁, si-hap 시합.
compile *v.* p'yŏn-ch'an-ha-da 편찬하다. 「호소하다.
complain *v.* pul-p'yŏng-ha-da 불평하다 ; ho-so-ha-da
complement *n.* po-ch'ung 보충, po-wan 보완. —*v.* po-ch'ung-ha-da 보충하다.
complete *v.* wan-sŏng-ha-da 완성하다. —*adj.* wan-jŏn-han 완전한, (*whole*) chŏn-bu-ŭi 전부의.
complex *adj.* pok-jap-han 복잡한 ; pok-hap-ŭi 복합의.
complexion *n.* ① an-saek 안색. ② (*aspect*) mo-yang 모양, oe-gwan 외관.
complicate *v.* pok-jap-ha-ge ha-da 복잡하게 하다.
complication *n.* pok-jap 복잡 ; (*tangle*) pun-gyu 분규.
compliment *n.* (*praise*) ch'an-sa 찬사 ; (*greetings*) in-sa 인사. —*v.* ch'ing-ch'an-ha-da 칭찬하다.
complimentary *adj.* ch'ing-ch'an-ha-nŭn 칭찬하는 ; ch'uk-ha-ŭi 축하의, in-sa-ŭi 인사의.
comply *v.* ŭng-ha-da 응하다, tong-ŭi-ha-da 동의하다.

compose *v.* ku-sŏng-ha-da 구성하다, mat-ch'u-ŏ jja-da 맞추어 짜다 ; (*music*) chak-gok-ha-da 작곡하다.
composer *n.* chak-gok-ga 작곡가.
composition *n.* ① ku-sŏng 구성. ② (*written*) chak-mun 작문. ③ (*music*) chak-gok 작곡.
composure *n.* (*calmness*) ch'im-ch'ak 침착, naeng-jŏng 냉정 ; (*self-control*) cha-je 자제.
compound *v.* hon-hap-ha-da 혼합하다. —*adj.* hap-sŏng-ŭi 합성의. —*n.* hon-hap-mul 혼합물.
comprehend *v.* ① al-da 알다, i-hae-ha-da 이해하다. ② p'o-ham-ha-da 포함하다, nae-p'o-ha-da 내포하다.
compress *v.* ap-ch'uk-ha-da 압축하다.
compromise *n.* & *v.* t'a-hyŏp(-ha-da) 타협(하다).
compulsion *n.* kang-je 강제, kang-yo 강요.
compulsory *adj.* kang-je-jŏk-in 강제적인 ; ŭi-mu-jŏk-in 의무적인, p'il-su-ŭi 필수의.
compute *n.* ① (*reckon*) sem-ha-da 셈하다. ② (*estimate*) ch'u-jŏng-ha-da 추정하다.
computer *n.* kye-san-gi 계산기, k'ŏm-p'yu-t'ŏ 컴퓨터: *an electronic* ∼ chŏn-ja kye-san-gi 전자 계산기.
comrade *n.* pŏt 벗, tong-ji 동지.
conceal *v.* kam-ch'u-da 감추다, sum-gi-da 숨기다.
concede *v.* yang-bo-ha-da 양보하다.　　　　　「(奇想).
conceit *n.* cha-bu-sim 자부심 ; (*fancy*) ki-sang 기상
conceive *v.* ① (*imagine*) sang-sang-ha-da 상상하다. ② (*child*) a-gi-rŭl pae-da 아기를 배다.
concentrate *v.* chip-jung-ha-da 집중하다.
concern *n.* ① (*relation*) kwan-gye 관계. ② (*anxiety*) kŭn-sim 근심. —*v.* (*relate to*) kwan-gye-ha-da 관계하다, kwan-sim-ŭl kat-da 관심을 갖다.
concerning *prep.* …e kwan-ha-yŏ …에 관하여.
concert *n.* ŭm-ak-hoe 음악회, k'on-sŏ-ŏ-t'ŭ 콘서어트.

concession *n.* (*yielding*) yang-bo 양보.
conciliate *v.* tal-rae-da 달래다, mu-ma-ha-da 무마하다.
concise *adj.* kan-gyŏl-han 간결한.
conclude *v.* ① …ŭi kyŏl-mal-ŭl chit-da …의 결말을 짓다. ② (*settle*) ch'e-gyŏl-ha-da 체결하다. 「체결.
conclusion *n.* ① chong-gyŏl 종결.② (*treaty*) ch'e-gyŏl
conclusive *adj.* kyŏl-jŏng-jŏk-in 결정적인, kyŏl-ron-jŏk-in 결론적인, chong-guk-ŭi 종국의.
concord *n.* ① (*agreement*) il-ch'i 일치, hwa-hap 화합. ② (*treaty*) hyŏp-jŏng 협정.
concrete *adj.* ku-ch'e-jŏk-in 구체적인. —*n.* k'on-k'ŭ-ri-i-t'ŭ 콘크리이트. —*v.* kut-hi-da 굳히다.
concubine *n.* ch'ŏp 첩, so-ga 소가(小家).
concussion *n.* ① chin-dong 진동. ② noe-jin-t'ang 뇌진탕.
condemn *v.* ① (*blame*) pi-nan-ha-da 비난하다.② (*sentence*) sŏn-go-ha-da 선고하다.
condense *v.* ap-ch'uk-si-k'i-da 압축시키다.
condescend *v.* kong-son-hi tae-ha-da 공손히 대하다.
condition *n.* ① (*state*) sang-t'ae 상태. ② (*in contracts*) cho-gŏn 조건. ③ (*rank*) sin-bun 신분. 「da 문상하다.
condole *v.* cho-wi-ha-da 조위(吊慰)하다, mun-sang-ha-
conduct *n.* haeng-wi 행위. —*v.* (*direct*) chi-hwi-ha-da 지휘하다 ; (*lead*) in-do-ha-da 인도하다.
conductor *n.* ① chi-hwi-ja 지휘자. ② ch'a-jang 차장.
cone *n.* wŏn-bbul 원뿔, wŏn-ch'u 원추. 「상의하다.
confer *v.* ① chu-da 주다. ② (*consult*) sang-ŭi-ha-da
confess *v.* cha-baek-ha-da 자백하다, ko-baek-ha-da 고백하다 ; (*recognize*) cha-in-ha-da 자인하다.
confession *n.* ko-baek 고백, cha-baek 자백.
confide *v.* ① (*put trust*) sin-yong-ha-da 신용하다. ② (*share secret*) pi-mil-ŭl t'ŏ-rŏ-no-t'a 비밀을 털어놓다.
confidence *n.* (*trust*) sin-yong 신용 ; (*assurance*) cha-

sin 자신, hwak-sin 확신.
confine *v.* han-jŏng-ha-da 한정하다 ; ka-du-da 가두다.
confirm *v.* ① (*verify*) hwak-jŭng-ha-da 확증하다. ② (*fortify*) kong-go-hi ha-da 공고히 하다. 「하다.
confiscate *v.* mol-su-ha-da 몰수하다, ap-su-ha-da 압수
conflagration *n.* k'ŭn-bul 큰불, tae-hwa 대화(大火).
conflict *n.* t'u-jaeng 투쟁, ch'ung-dol 충돌. —*v.* ta-t'u-da 다투다, ch'ung-dol-ha-da 충돌하다.
conform *v.* il-ch'i-si-k'i-da 일치시키다 ; tta-rŭ-da 따르다.
confound *v.* (*confuse*) hon-dong-ha-da 혼동하다 ; (*perplex*) tang-hwang-k'e hà-da 당황케 하다.
confront *v.* …ŭi ma-jŭn-p'yŏn-e it-da …의 맞은편에 있다, chik-myŏn-ha-da 직면하다.
confuse *v.* hol-lan-si-k'i-da 혼란시키다 ; hon-dong-ha-da 혼동하다, ŏ-ji-rŏp-hi-da 어지럽히다.
confusion *n.* hol-lan 혼란, tang-hwang 당황.
congratulate *v.* ch'uk-ha-ha-da 축하하다.
congratulation *n.* ch'uk-ha 축하 ; ch'uk-sa 축사.
congress *n.* (*meeting*) hoe-ŭi 회의, tae-hoe 대회 ; (*national assembly*) kuk-hoe 국회. 「민의원.
congressman *n.* kuk-hoe-ŭi-wŏn 국회의원, min-ŭi-wŏn
conjunction *n.* ① kyŏl-hap 결합. ② chŏp-sok-sa 접속사.
connect *v.* yŏn-gyŏl-ha-da 연결하다, it-da 잇다.
connection *n.* ① yŏn-gyŏl 연결. ② kwan-gye 관계. ③ (*relative*) yŏn-jul 연줄, yŏn-go 연고.
connotation *n.* ham-ch'uk-sŏng 함축성.
conquer *v.* chŏng-bok-ha-da 정복하다, sŭng-ri-ha-da 승
conqueror *n.* chŏng-bok-ja 정복자. 「리하다.
conquest *n.* chŏng-bok 정복, hoek-dŭk 획득.
conscience *n.* yang-sim 양심, to-ŭi-sim 도의심.
conscientious *adj.* yang-sim-jŏk-in 양심적인.
conscious *adj.* chi-gak-i it-nŭn 지각이 있는, ŭi-sik-jŏk-

in 의식적인.
consciousness *n*. ŭi-sik 의식, cha-gak 자각.
conscript *n*. ching-jip-byong 징집병. —*v*. (*draft*)
ching-bal-ha-da 징발하다, ching-jip-ha-da 징집하다.
consecrate *v*. pa-ch'i-da 바치다, pong-hŏn-ha-da 봉헌하다.
consent *v*. sŭng-nak-ha-da 승낙하다, tong-ŭi-ha-da 동
의하다. —*n*. sŭng-nak 승낙 ; tong-ŭi 동의.
consequence *n*. kyŏl-gwa 결과 ; chung-yo-sŏng 중요성.
conserve *v*. po-jon-ha-da 보존하다. 「하다.
consider *v*. suk-go-ha-da 숙고하다, pae-ryŏ-ha-da 배려
considerable *adj*. sang-dang-han 상당한.
consign *v*. wi-t'ak-ha-da 위탁하다, mat-gi-da 맡기다.
consist *v*. ① …ŭ-ro i-ru-ŏ-ji-da …으로 이루어지다. ②
…e it-da …에 있다. ③ yang-rip-ha-da 양립하다.
console *v*. wi-ro-ha-da 위로하다. 「하는.
consonant *n*. cha-ŭm 자음. —*adj*. il-ch'i-ha-nŭn 일치
conspicuous *adj*. nun-e chal ttŭi-nŭn 눈에 잘 띄는 ;
chŏ-myŏng-han 저명한, hyŏn-jŏ-han 현저한.
consort *n*. pae-u-ja 배우자 ; tong-ryo 동료.
conspirator *n*. kong-mo-ja 공모자, ŭm-mo-ja 음모자.
conspire *v*. (*plot*) kong-mo-ha-da 공모하다.
constable *n*. kyŏng-gwan 경관, sun-gyŏng 순경.
constant *adj*. ① (*same*) han-gyŏl-ga-t'ŭn 한결같은. ②
(*continuous*) pu-dan-han 부단한.
constellation *n*. sŏng-jwa 성좌, pyŏl-ja-ri 별자리.
constituent *n*. ① sŏng-bun 성분. ② sŏn-gŏ-in 선거인.
constitute *v*. ① (*compose*) ku-sŏng-ha-da 구성하다.
② (*enact*) che-jŏng-ha-da 제정하다. ③ (*set up*) sŏl-
rip-ha-da 설립하다.
constitution *n*. ① sŏl-rip 설립. ② (*law*) hŏn-bŏp 헌법.
③ (*composition*) ku-sŏng 구성. 「하다.
construct *v*. kŏn-sŏl-ha-da 건설하다, kŏn-jo-ha-da 건조

construction *n.* ① ku-jo 구조. ② kŏn-sŏl 건설. ③ (*syntax*) ku-mun 구문. 「sŏng-ŭi 구성의.
constructive *adj.* ① kŏn-sŏl-jŏk-in 건설적인. ② ku-
consul *n.* yŏng-sa 영사(領事).
consulate *n.* yŏng-sa-gwan 영사관.
consult *v.* ① sang-ŭi-ha-da 상의하다. ② chin-ch'al-ŭl pat-da 진찰을 받다. ③ (*refer to*) ch'am-go-ha-da 참
consume *v.* so-bi-ha-da 소비하다. 「고하다.
consumption *n.* ① so-bi 소비. ② (*tuberculosis*) p'ye-gyŏl-haek 폐결핵, p'ye-byŏng 폐병.
contact *n.* chŏp-ch'ok 접촉, kyo-je 교제.
contagion *n.* chŏn-yŏm(-byŏng) 전염(병).
contagious *adj.* chŏn-yŏm-sŏng-ŭi 전염성의. 「있다.
contain *v.* p'o-ham-ha-da 포함하다, tam-go it-da 담고
contaminate *v.* tŏ-rŏp-hi-da 더럽히다, o-yŏm-si-k'i-da 오염시키다 ; t'a-rak-si-k'i-da 타락시키다.
contemplate *v.* ① sim-sa-suk-go-ha-da 심사숙고하다. ② (*look at*) ŭng-si-ha-da 응시하다.
contemporary *adj.* ka-t'ŭn si-dae-ŭi 같은 시대의, tang-
contempt *n.* kyŏng-myŏl 경멸. 「dae-ŭi 당대의.
contend *v.* ① (*struggle*) ta-t'u-da 다투다, kyŏ-ru-da 겨루다. ② (*insist*) chu-jang-ha-da 주장하다.
content *adj.* (*satisfied*) man-jok-han 만족한. —*n.* ① man-jok 만족. ② nae-yong 내용.
contentment *n.* man-jok 만족.
contest *n.* non-jaeng 논쟁, ta-t'um 다툼. —*v.* ta-t'u-da 다투다, kyŏ-ru-da 겨루다. 「ryuk 아시아 대륙.
continent *n.* tae-ryuk 대륙 : *the ~ of Asia* a-si-a tae-
continue *v.* kye-sok〔yŏn-sok〕-ha-da 계속〔연속〕하다.
continuous *adj.* kye-sok-jŏk-in 계속적인.
contraband *n.* mil-su 밀수, (*smuggled goods*) mil-su-p'um 밀수품. —*adj.* kŭm-ji-doen 금지된.

contract *n.& v.* kye-yak(-ha-da) 계약(하다).
contradict *v.* pan-bak-ha-da 반박하다, mo-sun-doe-da
contrary *adj.* pan-dae-ŭi 반대의. 「모순되다.
contrast *n.* tae-jo 대조, tae-bi 대비(對比).
contribute *v.* ① (*money etc.*) ki-bu-ha-da 기부하다 ;
　(*conduce*) kong-hŏn-ha-da 공헌하다. ② (*write for*)
　ki-go-ha-da 기고하다. 「기고.
contribution *n.* ① ki-bu 기부 ; kong-hŏn 공헌. ② ki-go
contrive *v.* ① (*invent*) ko-an-ha-da 고안하다. ② (*manage*) yong-k'e hae-ch'i-u-da 용케 해치우다.
control *v.* chi-bae-ha-da 지배하다 ; (*hold in check*)
　ŏk-je-ha-da 억제하다. —*n.* t'ong-je 통제.
controversy *n.* non-jaeng 논쟁, t'o-ron 토론.
convenience *n.* p'yŏn-ŭi 편의, pyŏl-li 편리.
convenient *adj.* p'yŏl-li-han 편리한.
convent *n.* su-nyŏ-wŏn 수녀원, su-do-wŏn 수도원.
convention *n.* ① (*custom*) in-sŭp 인습, kwal-lye 관
　례. ② (*session*) hoe-ŭi 회의, chip-hoe 집회.
conversation *n.* hoe-hwa 회화, tam-hwa 담화.
convert *v.* ① chŏn-hwan-ha-da 전환하다. ② (*religion*)
　kae-jong-si-k'i-da 개종(改宗)시키다.
convey *v.* na-rŭ-da 나르다, chŏn-dal-ha-da 전달하다.
convict *v.* yu-joe-ro p'an-gyŏl-ha-da 유죄로 판결하다.
　—*n.* choe-in 죄인, choe-su 죄수.
convince *v.* hwak-sin-ŭl ka-ji-ge ha-da 확신을 가지게
　하다 ; nap-dŭk-si-k'i-da 납득시키다. 「송하다.
convoy *n.* ho-song-dae 호송대. —*v.* ho-song-ha-da 호
cook *v.* yo-ri-ha-da 요리하다. —*n.* yo-ri-sa 요리사.
cool *adj.* sŏ-nŭl-han 서늘한 ; naeng-jŏng-han 냉정한.
　—*v.* sik-hi-da 식히다.
coop *n.* tung-u-ri 둥우리, tak-jang 닭장.
co(-)operate *v.* hyŏp-dong-ha-da 협동하다, hyŏp-ryŏk-

ha-da 협력하다.

cope *v.* ① tae-hang-ha-da 대항하다, mat-sŏ-da 맞서다.
② tae-ch'ŏ-ha-da 대처하다. 「동판.

copper *n.* ku-ri 구리, tong 동(銅) : ~ *plate* tong-p'an

copy *v.* pe-ggi-da 베끼다. —*n.* sa-bon 사본 ; (*book*)

coral *n.* san-ho 산호. ⌊kwŏn 권 ; ch'o-go 초고.

cord *n.* ① (*thick string*) kul-gŭn kkŭn 굵은 끈. ②
(*small rope*) ka-nŭn pat-jul 가는 밧줄.

cordial *adj.* chin-sim-e-sŏ u-rŏ-na-nŭn 진심에서 우러
나는. —*n.* kang-sim-je 강심제.

core *n.* sok 속, haek-sim 핵심(核心), kol-ja 골자.

cork *n.* k'o-rŭ-k'ŭ 코르크. 「옥수수.

corn *n.* (*Am.*) kok-sik 곡식, kok-mul 곡물 ; ok-su-su

corner *n.* ① mo-t'ung-i 모퉁이, k'o-o-nŏ 코오너. ②
(*angle*) kak 각. ③ (*commerce*) mae-jŏm 매점.

coronation *n.* tae-gwan-sik 대관식, chŭk-wi-sik 즉위식.

corporal *n.* ha-sa 하사(下士), sang-byŏng 상병.

corporation *n.* pŏp-in 법인, yu-han-hoe-sa 유한회사.

corps *n.* kun-dan 군단, pyŏng-dan 병단.

corpse *n.* si-ch'e 시체, song-jang 송장.

correct *adj.* pa-rŭn 바른. —*v.* ko-ch'i-da 고치다.

correspond *v.* il-ch'i-ha-da 일치하다, pu-hap-ha-da 부
합하다 : ~ *with* t'ong-sin-ha-da 통신하다.

correspondence *n.* ① (*agreement*) il-ch'i 일치, sang-
ŭng 상응. ② (*communication*) t'ong-sin 통신.

corridor *n.* pok-do 복도, hoe-rang 회랑.

corrupt *adj.* (*rotten*) ssŏk-ŭn 썩은. —*v.* ssŏk-da 썩
다 ; (*become debased*) t'a-rak-ha-da 타락하다.

cosmetic *adj.* (*beautifying*) mi-yong-ŭi 미용의, hwa-
jang-yong-ŭi 화장용의. —*n.* hwa-jang-p'um 화장품.

cosmopolitan *adj.* se-gye-jŏk-in 세계적인. —*n.* se-gye-
in 세계인, se-gye-ju-ŭi-ja 세계주의자.

cost *v.* ① kap-na-ga-da 값나가다. ② (*require*) tŭl-da 들다, yo-ha-da 요하다. ③ hŭi-saeng-si-k'i-da 희생시키다. —*n.* (*expense*) pi-yong 비용, (*price*) kap 값.

costly *adj.* kap-bi-ssan 값비싼, ho-hwa-ro-un 호화로운.

costume *n.* pok-jang 복장, ŭi-sang 의상.

cosy *adj.* a-nŭk-han 아늑한, a-dam-han 아담한.

cot *n.* kan-i ch'im-dae 간이 침대 ; u-ri 우리.

cottage *n.* o-du-mak-jip 오두막집, nong-ga 농가.

cotton *n.* ① som 솜. ② (*cloth*) mu-myŏng 무명.

couch *n.* ch'im-sang 침상, kin ŭi-ja 긴 의자.

cough *n.* ki-ch'im 기침. —*v.* ki-ch'im-ha-da 기침하다.

council *n.* p'yŏng-ŭi-hoe 평의회, hyŏp-ŭi-hoe 협의회.

counsel *n.* (*consultation*) ŭi-non 의논 ; (*advice*) kwŏn-go 권고. —*v.* cho-ŏn-ha-da 조언하다, kwŏn-ha-da 권하다 ; hyŏp-ŭi-ha-da 협의하다.

count *v.* se-da 세다, kye-san-ha-da 계산하다 : ~ *for much* chung-yo-ha-da 중요하다. —*n.* kye-san 계산.

counter *n.* kye-san-gi 계산기, kye-san-dae 계산대. —*adj.* (*opposite*) pan-dae-ŭi 반대의, yŏk-ŭi 역(逆)의.

counteract *v.* pang-hae-ha-da 방해하다.

counterfeit *adj.* ka-jja-ŭi 가짜의. —*n.* ka-jja 가짜, mo-jo-p'um 모조품, wi-jo-p'um 위조품.

countess *n.* paek-jak pu-in 백작 부인.

country *n.* ① si-gol 시골, kyo-oe 교외. ② chi-bang 지방, chi-yŏk 지역. ③ (*nation*) na-ra 나라, kuk-ga 국가.

county *n.* kun 군(郡), (*Brit.*) chu 주(州).

couple *n.* han ssang 한 쌍, pu-bu 부부.

coupon *n.* k'u-u-p'on 쿠우폰, kyŏng-p'um-gwŏn 경품권.

courage *n.* yong-gi 용기, pae-jjang 배짱.

course *n.* ① (*route*) chil-lo 진로, k'ŏ-o-sŭ 코오스. ② (*of study*) kang-jwa 강좌, kwa-jŏng 과정.

court *n.* ① (*law*) chae-p'an-so 재판소. ② k'o-o-t'ŭ 코

오트 : *a tennis* ～ t'e-ni-sŭ k'o-o-t'ŭ 테니스 코오트.
courtesy *n.* ye-jŏl 예절 ; chŏng-jung 정중 ; ho-ŭi 호의.
courthouse *n.* ① pŏp-wŏn 법원. ② kun-ch'ŏng 군청.
court-martial *n.* kun-bŏp-hoe-ŭi 군법회의.
courtship *n.* (*wooing*) ku-hon 구혼, ku-ae 구애(求愛).
courtyard *n.* an-ddŭl 안뜰, ap-ma-dang 앞마당.
cousin *n.* sa-ch'on 사촌, chong-hyŏng-je 종형제.
cover *v.* ① tŏp-da 덮다. ② (*hide*) kam-ch'u-da 감추다.
  ③ (*extend over*) chŏn-myŏn-e kŏl-ch'i-da 전면에 걸
  치다 ; p'o-ham-ha-da 포함하다. —*n.* tŏp-gae 덮개.
coverlet *n.* tŏp-gae 덮개, i-bul 이불.
covet *v.* mop-si t'am-nae-da 몹시 탐내다.
cow *n.* am-so 암소 : ～ *boy* mok-dong 목동.
coward *n.* kŏp-jang-i 겁장이. —*adj.* kŏp-man-ŭn 겁많은.
cower *v.* um-ch'ŭ-ri-da 움츠리다 ; chil-ri-da 질리다.
crab *n.* ① ke 게. ② (*winch*) win-ch'i 윈치.
crack *n.* ① t'ŭm 틈, kŭm 금. ② (*shot*) pal-sa 발사.
  —*v.* (*break*) jjo-gae-da 쪼개다, kkae-ji-da 깨지다.
cracker *n.* ① (*firecracker*)p'ok-juk 폭죽.② p'a-swae-
  gi 파쇄기. ③ (*biscuit*) k'ŭ-rae-k'ŏ 크래커.
cradle *n.* ① yo-ram 요람(搖籃). ② pal-sang-ji 발상지.
craft *n.* ① (*skill*) ki-gyo 기교, son-jae-ju 손재주 ;
  (*cunning*) sul-ch'aek 술책. ② kong-ye 공예.
craftsman *n.* ki-nŭng-gong 기능공, chang-in 장인.
crafty *adj.* kan-sa-han 간사한.　　　　　　「기중기.
crane *n.* ① (*bird*) hak 학. ② (*machine*) ki-jung-gi
crash *n.* ① to-san 도산. ② ch'ung-dol 충돌. —*v.* wa-
  rŭ-rŭ mu-nŏ-ji-da 와르르 무너지다.
crate *n.* kwe-jjak 궤짝, tae-ba-gu-ni 대바구니.
crave *v.* kan-ch'ŏng-ha-da 간청하다, kal-mang-ha-da
  갈망하다.　　　　　　　　「ri-da 느릿느릿 달리다.
crawl *v.* ki-da 기다, (*move slowly*) nŭ-rit-nŭ-rit tal-

crayon *n.* k'ŭ-re-yong 크레용.

crazy *adj.* (*insane*) mi-ch'in 미친 ; (*madly eager*) yŏl-gwang-ha-nŭn 열광하는.

creak *v.* ppi-gŏk-gŏ-ri-da 삐걱거리다.

cream *n.* k'ŭ-ri-im 크리임, yu-ji 유지.

crease *n.* chu-rŭm 주름, chŏp-ŭn kŭm 접은 금. 「하다.

create *v.* ch'ang-jo-ha-da 창조하다 ; sŏl-rip-ha-da 설립

creative *adj.* ch'ang-jo-jŏk-in 창조적인.   「조물주.

creator *n.* ch'ang-jo-ja 창조자, (*the C∼*) cho-mul-ju

creature *n.* ① (*anything created*) ch'ang-jo-mul 창조물. ② (*living being*) saeng-mul 생물. ③ (*domestic animal*) ka-ch'uk 가축. ④ (*human being*) in-gan 인

credentials *n.* sin-im-jang 신임장.   「간.

credible *adj.* sin-yong-hal su it-nŭn 신용할 수 있는.

credit *n.* ① ch'ae-gwŏn 채권. ② (*belief*) sin-yong 신용. ③ (*honor*) myŏng-ye 명예.

creditable *adj.* ch'ing-ch'an-hal man-han 칭찬할 만한.

credulous *adj.* swip-sa-ri mit-nŭn 쉽사리 믿는, chal sok-nŭn 잘 속는.

creed *n.* sin-jo 신조 ; (*principle*) chu-ŭi 주의(主義).

creek *n.* sil-gae-ch'ŏn 실개천, k'ŭ-ri-i-k'ŭ 크리이크.

creel *n.* tong-bal 통발, mul-go-gi pa-gu-ni 물고기 바구

creep *v.* ki-da 기다, p'o-bok-ha-da 포복하다.   「니.

cremate *v.* hwa-jang-ha-da 화장(火葬)하다.

crepe *n.* k'ŭ-re-i-p'ŭ 크레이프.

crescent *n.* ch'o-sŭng-dal 초승달, sin-wŏl 신월(新月).

crest *n.* ① (*comb*) pyŏt 벗, to-ga-mŏ-ri 도가머리. ② (*head*) kkok-dae-gi 꼭대기, chŏng-sang 정상.

crevice *n.* kal-ra-jin t'ŭm 갈라진 틈, kŭm 금.

crew *n.* ① sŭng-mu-wŏn 승무원. ② p'ae-gŏ-ri 패거리.

cricket *n.* ① (*insect*) kwi-ddu-ra-mi 귀뚜라미. ② (*game*) k'ŭ-ri-k'et 크리켓.

crime *n.* choe 죄, pŏm-joe 범죄.

criminal *adj.* pŏm-joe-ŭi 범죄의, hyŏng-sa-sang-ŭi 형사상의. —*n.* choe-in 죄인. 「새빨간.

crimson *n.* chin-hong-saek 진홍색. —*adj.* sae-bbal-gan

cripple *n.* chŏl-rŭm-ba-ri 절름발이, pul-gu-ja 불구자.

crisis *n.* wi-gi 위기 ; (*decisive moment*) chung-dae-si-guk 중대시국, (*turning point*) kal-rim-gil 갈림길.

crisp *adj.* ① pa-sak-ba-sak-ha-nŭn 바삭바삭하는, kop-sŭl-gop-sŭl-han 곱슬곱슬한. ② sang-k'wae-han 상쾌한.

criterion *n.* p'yo-jun 표준, ki-jun 기준.

critic *n.* pi-p'yŏng-ga 비평가, kam-jŏng-ga 감정가 : *an art* ~ mi-sul p'yŏng-ron-ga 미술 평론가.

critical *adj.* ① pi-p'yŏng-jŏk-in 비평적인. ② chung-dae-han 중대한. ③ wi-gŭp-han 위급한. 「난하다.

criticize *v.* pi-p'yŏng-ha-da 비평하다 ; pi-nan-ha-da 비

croak *v.* kae-gol-gae-gol ul-da 개골개골 울다, t'u-dŏl-

crocodile *n.* ak-ŏ 악어. 「dae-da 투덜대다.

crony *n.* (*chum*) yet-bŏt 옛벗, ch'in-gu 친구.

crooked *adj.* ku-bu-rŏ-jin 구부러진, pi-ddu-rŏ-jin 비뚤어진 ; (*deformed*) ki-hyŏng-ŭi 기형의.

crop *n. & v.* su-hwak(-ha-da) 수확(하다).

cross *n.* sip-ja-ga 십자가. —*v.* kŏn-nŏ-da 건너다 ; (*intersect*) kyo-ch'a-ha-da 교차하다. 「mok 건널목.

crossing *n.* hoeng-dan 횡단 ; kyo-ch'a 교차 ; kŏn-nŏl-

crossroad *n.* ne-gŏ-ri 네거리, sip-ja-ro 십자로.

crouch *v.* (*bend down*) ung-k'ŭ-ri-da 웅크리다.

crow *n.* kka-ma-gwi 까마귀. —*v.* (*cock*) ul-da 울다.

crowd *n.* ① kun-jung 군중. ② (*throng*) hon-jap 혼잡. —*v.* (*swarm*) pum-bi-da 붐비다.

crown *n.* ① wang-gwan 왕관. ② (*top*) kkok-dae-gi 꼭대기. —*v.* kwan-ŭl ssŭi-u-da 관을 씌우다.

crude *adj.* ka-gong-ha-ji an-ŭn 가공하지 않은 ; it-nŭn

kŭ-dae-ro-ŭi 있는 그대로의 ; mi-suk-han 미숙한.
cruel *adj.* chan-in-han 잔인한 ; mu-jŏng-han 무정한.
cruelty *n.* chan-in-sŏng 잔인성, mu-ja-bi 무자비.
cruise *v.* (*sail*) sun-hang-ha-da 순항하다.
cruiser *n.* sun-yang-ham 순양함(巡洋艦).
crumb *n.* ① ppang pu-sŭ-rŏ-gi 빵 부스러기, ppang ka-ru 빵 가루. ② (*bit*) so-ryang 소량.
crumble *v.* ① pu-sŭ-rŏ-ddŭ-ri-da 부스러뜨리다, pu-su-da 부수다. ② (*perish*) mang-ha-da 망하다.
crumple *v.* ku-gyŏ-ji-da 구겨지다, ku-gi-da 구기다.
crunch *v.* u-du-duk kkae-mul-da 우두둑 깨물다.
crusade *n.* sip-ja-gun 십자군, sŏng-jŏn 성전(聖戰).
crush *v.* nul-rŏ pu-sŭ-rŏ-ddŭ-ri-da 눌러 부스러뜨리다, jji-gŭ-rŏ-ddŭ-ri-da 찌그러뜨리다.
crust *n.* ① ppang kkŏp-jil 빵 껍질. ② (*hardened surface*) kut-ŏ-jin p'yo-myŏn 굳어진 표면.
crutch *n.* ① mok-bal 목발. ② (*prop*) pŏ-t'im 버팀.
cry *v.* ul-da 울다 ; (*shout*) so-ri chi-rŭ-da 소리 지르다. —*n.* u-rŭm-so-ri 울음소리 ; pu-rŭ-ji-jŭm 부르짖음.
crying *adj.* ① u-nŭn 우는, ul-bu-jit-nŭn 울부짖는. ② (*urgent*) kin-gŭp-han 긴급한.
crystal *n.* ① su-jŏng 수정(水晶), k'ŭ-ri-sŭ-t'al 크리스탈. ② kyŏl-jŏng-ch'e 결정체. —*adj.* t'u-myŏng-han 투명한.
cube *n.* ip-bang 입방, ip-bang-ch'e 입방체.
cubism *n.* ip-ch'e-p'a 입체파, k'yu-bi-jŭm 큐비즘.
cuckoo *n.* ppŏ-gguk-sae 뻐꾹새, ppŏ-ggu-gi 뻐꾸기.
cucumber *n.* o-i 오이 : *as cool as a* ~ naeng-jŏng-han 냉정한, t'ae-yŏn-ja-yak-han 태연자약한.
cuff *n.* so-maet-bu-ri 소맷부리, k'ŏ-p'ŭ-sŭ 커프스.
culprit *n.* hyŏng-sa p'i-go-in 형사 피고인, choe-in 죄인.
cultivate *v.* ① kyŏng-jak-ha-da 경작하다 ; ki-rŭ-da 기르다. ② kyo-hwa-ha-da 교화(敎化)하다.

ːultivation *n.* ① (*tilling*) kyŏng-jak 경작, chae-bae 재배. ② yang-sŏng 양성. 「yang 교양.
culture *n.* ① mun-hwa 문화. ② (*refinement*) kyo-
cunning *adj.* kyo-hwal-han 교활한, kan-sa-han 간사한.
cup *n.* chan 잔, k'ŏp 컵 ; sang-bae 상배(賞杯).
cupboard *n.* ch'an-jang 찬장.
cure *n.* (*remedy*) ch'i-ryo 치료, ch'i-yu 치유. —*v.* (*heal*) ko-ch'i-da 고치다, nat-da 낫다. 「간 통행금지.
curfew *n.* so-dŭng 소등, ya-gan t'ong-haeng-gŭm-ji 야
curio *n.* kol-dong-p'um 골동품, mi-sul-p'um 미술품 : ~ *dealer* kol-dong-p'um-sang 골동품상.
curiosity *n.* ① ho-gi-sim 호기심. ② (*rare thing*) chin-gi-han mul-gŏn 진기한 물건.
curious *adj.* ho-gi-sim-e ch'an 호기심에 찬 ; (*eccentric*) koe-sang-han 괴상한, chin-gi-han 진기한.
curl *n.* kop-sŭl-mŏ-ri 곱슬머리. —*v.* kop-sŭl-gop-sŭl-ha-ge ha-da 곱슬곱슬하게 하다, k'ŏ-ŏl-ha-da 커얼하다.
curly *adj.* kop-sŭl-gop-sŭl-han 곱슬곱슬한.
currant *n.* kŏn-p'o-do 건포도.
current *n.* ① hŭ-rŭm 흐름, p'ung-jo 풍조. ② (*electricity*) chŏl-lyu 전류. —*adj.* ① yu-t'ong-doe-nŭn 유통되는. ② (*present*) hyŏn-jae-ŭi 현재의.
curriculum *n.* kyo-gwa-gwa-jŏng 교과과정, k'ŏ-ri-k'yul-rŏm 커리큘럼 : ~ *vitae* i-ryŏk-sŏ 이력서.
curse *n.* & *v.* chŏ-ju(-ha-da) 저주(하다).
curtain *n.* k'ŏ-ŏ-t'ŭn 커어튼, chang-mak 장막.
curve *n.* kok-sŏn 곡선. —*v.*(*bend*) ku-bu-ri-da 구부리다.
cushion *n.* pang-sŏk 방석, k'u-syŏn 쿠션.
custody *n.* ① (*safe keeping*) po-gwan 보관, kwal-li 관리. ② (*detention*) ku-sok 구속, kam-gŭm 감금.
custom *n.* ① sŭp-gwan 습관, kwal-lye 관례. ② (*import duties*) kwan-se 관세(關稅).

customer *n.* ko-gaek 고객, tan-gol-son-nim 단골손님.
customhouse *n.* se-gwan 세관.
cut *v.* ① pe-da 베다, kkŭn-t'a 끊다, sak-gam-ha-da 삭
감하다 ; (*carve*) sae-gi-da 새기다. ② (*absent from*)
kyŏl-sŏk-ha-da 결석하다. —*n.* (*gash*) sang-ch'ŏ 상처.
cute *adj.* ① kwi-yŏ-un 귀여운. ② (*shrewd*) ki-min-
han 기민한, pin-t'ŭm-ŏp-nŭn 빈틈없는.
cutlery *n.* k'al-bu-ch'i 칼붙이, k'al che-jo-ŏp 칼 제조업.
cycle *n.* ① chu-gi 주기. ② (*bicycle*) cha-jŏn-gŏ 자전거.
③ (*electricity*) chu-p'a 주파(周波), sa-i-k'ŭl 사이클.
cynical *adj.* pi-ggo-nŭn 비꼬는, naeng-so-jŏk-in 냉소
적인.

---- **D** ----

daffodil *n.* su-sŏn-hwa 수선화(水仙花).
dagger *n.* tan-do 단도, tan-gŏm 단검, pi-su 비수.
dahlia *n.* ta-al-ri-a 다알리아.
daily *adj.* mae-il-ŭi 매일의, il-sang-ui 일상의. —*adv.*
nal-ma-da 날마다. —*n.* il-gan-sin-mun 일간신문.
dainty *adj.* (*delicious*) ma-sit-nŭn 맛있는 ; (*elegant*)
u-a-han 우아한. —*n.* (*delicacy*) chin-mi 진미.
dairy *n.* nak-nong-jang 낙농장, nak-nong-ŏp 낙농업 :
～ *products* yu-je-p'um 유제품.
daisy *n.* sil-guk-hwa 실국화, te-i-ji 데이지.
dale *n.* chak-ŭn kol-jja-gi 작은 골짜기, kye-gok 계곡.
dam *n.* taem 댐, tuk 둑. —*v.* (*block up*) mak-da 막다.
damage *n.* son-hae 손해, son-hae-bae-sang 손해배상.
—*v.* son-hae-rŭl ip-hi-da 손해를 입히다.
dame *n.* kwi-bu-in 귀부인, suk-nyŏ 숙녀.
damn *v.* chŏ-ju-ha-da 저주하다, hok-p'yŏng-ha-da 혹
평하다 : *D～ it!* Chen-jang 젠장 !

damp *adj*. ch'uk-ch'uk-han 축축한, p'ul-i chuk-ŭn 풀
이 죽은. —*n*. sŭp-gi 습기, (*fog*) an-gae 안개.
dance *n*. ch'um 춤, mu-yong 무용, mu-do-hoe 무도회.
—*v*. ch'um-ŭl ch'u-da 춤을 추다.
dancer *n*. mu-yong-ga 무용가, taen-sŏ 댄서.
dandelion *n*. min-dŭl-re 민들레.
dandy *n*. mŏt-jang-i 멋장이. —*adj*. mŏ-sit-nŭn 멋있는.
danger *n*. (*risk*) wi-hŏm 위험 ; (*menace*) wi-hyŏp
위협, wi-hŏm-mul 위험물. 「로운.
dangerous *adj*. wi-hŏm-han 위험한, wi-t'ae-ro-un 위태
dangle *v*. mae-dal-da 매달다, pu-t'ŏ-da-ni-da 붙어다니다.
dare *v*. kam-hi …ha-da 감히 …하다.
daring *adj*. tae-dam-han 대담한, yong-gam-han 용감한.
dark *adj*. ŏ-du-un 어두운, (*dismal*) ŭm-ch'im-han
음침한. —*n*. ŏ-dum 어둠, am-hŭk 암흑.
darken *v*. ŏ-du-wŏ-ji-da 어두워지다.
darkness *n*. ŏ-dum 어둠 ; (*ignorance*) mu-ji 무지.
darling *adj*. sa-rang-ha-nŭn 사랑하는. —*n*. kwi-yŏ-un
sa-ram 귀여운 사람 : *my* ~ yae-ya 애야 ; yŏ-bo 여보,
tang-sin 당신.
darn *v*. kkwe-mae-da 꿰매다. —*n*. kip-gi 깁기.
dart *n*. tol-jin 돌진. —*v*. tol-jin-ha-da 돌진하다 ; (*go
rapidly*) na-ra-ga-da 날아가다.
dash *v*. (*fling away*) nae-dŏn-ji-da 내던지다 ; (*rush
against*) tol-jin-ha-da 돌진하다. —*n*. tol-jin 돌진.
data *n*. ① cha-ryo 자료, te-i-t'ŏ 데이터. ② chŏng-bo
정보 ; chi-sik 지식. ③ (*notes*) pi-mang-rok 비망록.
date *n*. ① nal-jja 날짜. ② te-i-t'ŭ 데이트 ; man-nal
yak-sok 만날 약속. —*v*. …e-sŏ pi-rot-doe-da …에서
daughter *n*. ttal 딸. 「비롯되다.
daughter-in-law *n*. myŏ-nŭ-ri 며느리,' ŭi-but-ddal 의
daunt *v*. wi-hyŏp-ha-da 위협하다. 「붓딸.

dawn *n.* sae-byŏk 새벽. —*v.* nal-i sae-da 날이 새다.
day *n.* ① nal 날, ha-ru 하루. ② (*daytime*) nat 낮. ③ (*epoch*) si-dae 시대.
daybreak *n.* sae-byŏk 새벽, tong-t'ŭl-nyŏk 동틀녘.
daylight *n.* haet-bit 햇빛 ; (*daytime*) chu-gan 주간.
daze *v.* nun-bu-si-ge ha-da 눈부시게 하다 ; mŏng-ha-ge ha-da 멍하게 하다. —*n.* hyŏn-hok 현혹.
dazzle *v.* nun-i pu-si-da 눈이 부시다, hyŏn-hok-si-k'i-da 현혹시키다. —*n.* nun-bu-sin pit 눈부신 빛.
dead *adj.* chuk-ŭn 죽은 ; hwal-bal-ch'i mot-han 활발치 못한 : *a ~ season* han-san-han ch'ŏl 한산한 철.
deadly *adj.* ch'i-myŏng-jŏk-in 치명적인.　　　「리의.
deaf *adj.* kwi-mŏk-ŭn 귀먹은, kwi-mŏ-gŏ-ri-ŭi 귀머거
deal *v.* ① ta-ru-da 다루다. ② (*trade*) kŏ-rae-ha-da 거래하다. ③ (*deliver*) chu-da 주다. —*n.* (*treatment*) ch'wi-gŭp 취급 ; (*amount*) pul-lyang 분량.
dealer *n.* sang-in 상인, chang-su 장수.　　　「학장.
dean *n.* ① pu-gam-dok 부감독. ② (*college*) hak-jang
dear *adj.* ① ch'in-ae-ha-nŭn 친애하는. ② (*expensive*) pi-ssan 비싼. —*n.* ae-in 애인. —*int.* ŏ-mŏ-na 어머나.
death *n.* chuk-ŭm 죽음, sa-mang 사망.
debase *v.* (*depreciate*) ttŏ-rŏ-ddŭ-ri-da 떨어뜨리다 ; (*degrade*) ch'ŏn-ha-ge man-dŭl-da 천하게 만들다.
debate *v.* t'o-ron-ha-da 토론하다. —*n.* t'o-ron 토론, non-jaeng 논쟁.　　　「hye 은혜.
debt *n.* ① pit 빚, pu-ch'ae 부채. ② (*obligation*) ŭn-
debut *n.* ch'ŏt-mu-dae 첫무대, te-bwi 데뷔.
decade *n.* sip-nyŏn-gan 10년간 : *the first ~* ch'oe-ch'o-ŭi sip-nyŏn-gan 최초의 10년간.
decay *n.* ① pu-p'ae 부패. ② (*decline*) soe-t'oe 쇠퇴. —*v.* ssŏk-da 썩다 ; soe-t'oe-ha-da 쇠퇴하다.
decease *v.* chuk-da 죽다. —*n.* sa-mang 사망.

deceit *n*. ki-man 기만, sa-gi 사기.　　　　　「다.
deceive *v*. sok-i-da 속이다 ; hyŏn-hok-si-k'i-da 현혹시키
December *n*. sip-i-wŏl 12월, sŏt-dal 섣달.
decent *adj*.　chŏm-jan-ŭn 점잖은, ye-ŭi-ba-rŭn 예의바
　른 ; (*fair*) sang-dang-han 상당한.
deception *n*. ki-man 기만, sa-gi 사기, sok-im-su 속임수.
decide *v*. kyŏl-jŏng-ha-da 결정하다.　　　　　「결.
decision *n*. kyŏl-jŏng 결정, (*judgment*) p'an-gyŏl 판
decisive *adj*. kyŏl-jŏng-jŏk-in 결정적인.
deck *n*. kap-p'an 갑판. —*v*. (*adorn*) kku-mi-da 꾸미다.
declaration *n*. sŏn-ŏn 선언, kong-p'yo 공표.
declare *v*. sŏn-ŏn-ha-da 선언하다, tan-ŏn-ha-da 단언하다.
decline *v*. (*bend down*) ki-ul(-i)-da 기울(이)다, soe-t'oe-
　ha-da 쇠퇴하다 ; (*refuse*) kŏ-jŏl-ha-da 거절하다. —*n*.
　kyŏng-sa 경사, soe-t'oe 쇠퇴.
decorate *v*. kku-mi-da 꾸미다.　　　　　　　「훈장.
decoration *n*. ① chang-sik 장식. ② (*medal*) hun-jang
decorum *n*. (*etiquette*) ye-jŏl 예절, (*pl*.) ye-bŏp 예법 ;
　(*decency*) tan-jŏng 단정.
decoy *n*. (*bait*) mi-ggi 미끼, (*lure*) yu-in-mul 유인물.
decrease *v*. chul-da 줄다, kam-so-ha-da 감소하다. —*n*.
　kam-so 감소, ch'uk-so 축소.
decree *n*. pŏp-ryŏng 법령, p'o-go-ryŏng 포고령.
dedicate *v*. pa-ch'i-da 바치다, hŏn-nap-ha-da 헌납하다 ;
　(*give up*) nae-dŏn-ji-da 내던지다.
deduct *v*. ppae-da 빼다, kong-je-ha-da 공제하다.
deed *n*. ① haeng-wi 행위. ② kong-jŏk 공적.　「하다.
deem *v*. saeng-gak-ha-da 생각하다, kan-ju-ha-da 간주
deep *adj*. ki-p'ŭn 깊은, sim-wŏn-han 심원한.
deer *n*. sa-sŭm 사슴.　　　　　　　　「chi-u-da 지우다.
defeat *n*. p'ae-bae 패배. —*v*. ch'yŏ-bu-su-da 쳐부수다 ;
defect *n*. kyŏl-jŏm 결점, kyŏl-ham 결함.

defence·defense *n.* pang-wi 방위, su-bi 수비.

defenceless *adj.* pang-bi-ŏp-nŭn 방비없는, mu-bang-bi-ŭi 무방비의.　　「하다.

defend *v.* pang-ŏ-ha-da 방어하다, pyŏn-ho-ha-da 변호

defendant *n.* p'i-go 피고.　　「보하다.

defer *v.* ① yŏn-gi-ha-da 연기하다. ② yang-bo-ha-da 양

defiance *n.* to-jŏn 도전, kong-gong-yŏn-han pan-hang 공공연한 반항 ; (*disregard*) mu-si 무시.

deficient *adj.* pu-jok-han 부족한, mo-ja-ra-nŭn 모자라는.

defile *v.* tŏ-rŏp-hi-da 더럽히다 ; mo-dok-ha-da 모독하다.

define *v.* chŏng-ŭi-rŭl nae-ri-da 정의를 내리다.

definite *adj.* myŏng-hwak-han 명확한, il-jŏng-han 일정한 ; han-jŏng-doen 한정된.　　「syŏn 디플레이션.

deflation *n.* t'ong-hwa su-ch'uk 통화 수축, ti-p'ŭl-re-i-

deformity *n.* pul-gu 불구, ki-hyŏng 기형.

deft *adj.* som-ssi-jo-ŭn 솜씨좋은, (*skillful*) nŭng-suk-han 능숙한, nŭng-ran-han 능란한.

defy *v.* to-jŏn-ha-da 도전하다 ; kŏ-bu-ha-da 거부하다.

degeneration *n.* t'a-rak 타락, t'oe-bo 퇴보.

degrade *v.* kyŏk-ha-ha-da 격하하다, kang-dŭng-ha-da 강등하다 ; (*debase*) t'a-rak-si-k'i-da 타락시키다.

degree *n.* ① (*extent*) to 도(度), chŏng-do 정도. ② (*school*) hak-wi 학위. ③ (*rank*) tŭng-gŭp 등급.

deity *n.* sin 신(神), sang-je 상제(上帝).

delay *v.* yŏn-gi-si-k'i-da 연기시키다 ; kku-mul-gŏ-ri-da 꾸물거리다. —*n.* chi-ch'e 지체, yŏn-gi 연기.

delegate *n.* tae-p'yo 대표. —*v.* tae-p'yo-ro nae-se-u-da 대표로 내세우다, (*commit*) wi-im-ha-da 위임하다.

deliberate *v.* sin-jung-hi saeng-gak-ha-da 신중히 생각하다. —*adj.* sin-jung-han 신중한.　　「의로.

deliberately *adv.* sin-jung-ha-ge 신중하게, ko-ŭi-ro 고

delicate *adj.* chŏng-gyo-han 정교한 ; (*slender*) ka-

nyal-p'ŭn 가냘픈 ; (*sensitive*) min-gam-han 민감한.
delicious *adj*. ma-sit-nŭn 맛있는.
delight *v*. chŭl-gŏp-ge ha-da 즐겁게 하다. —*n*. ki-bbŭm 기쁨, hwan-hŭi 환희. 「bbŭn 기쁜.
delightful *adj*. (mae-u) chŭl-gŏ-un (매우) 즐거운, ki-
deliver *v*. ① (*relieve*) ku-hae-nae-da 구해내다. ② (*distribute*) pae-dal-ha-da 배달하다. ③ (*utter*) chin-sul-ha-da 진술하다. ④ (*toss*) tŏn-ji-da 던지다.
deliverance *n*. ① ku-jo 구조. ② sŏk-bang 석방.
delivery *n*. ① (*letter*) pae-dal 배달. ② (*childbirth*) ch'ul-san 출산.
delta *n*. sam-gak-ju 삼각주(三角洲), tel-t'ŏ 델터.
delude *v*. sok-i-da 속이다, hyŏn-hok-ha-da 현혹하다.
delusion *n*. ki-man 기만, ch'ak-gak 착각.
demand *n*. & *v*. yo-gu(-ha-da) 요구(하다). 「민주정체.
democracy *n*. min-ju-ju-ŭi 민주주의, min-ju-jŏng-ch'e
democratic *adj*. min-ju-jŏng-ch'e-ŭi 민주정체의, min-ju-jŏk-in 민주적인, tae-jung-jŏk-in 대중적인.
demon *n*. ak-ma 악마, to-ggae-bi 도깨비.
demonstrate *v*. ip-jŭng-ha-da 입증하다, si-ryŏn-ha-da 실연(實演)하다, si-wi-ha-da 시위하다.
demonstration *n*. (*proof*) chŭng-myŏng 증명 ; (*mass meeting*) si-wi-un-dong 시위운동, te-mo 데모.
den *n*. kul 굴, u-ri 우리, so-gul 소굴.
denomination *n*. ① (*title*) myŏng-ch'ing 명칭. ② (*kind*) chong-ryu 종류. ③ (*units*) tan-wi 단위. ④ (*religious sect*) chong-p'a 종파.
denote *v*. p'yo-si-ha-da 표시하다, na-t'a-nae-da 나타내다.
denounce *v*. (*blame*) pi-nan-ha-da 비난하다, ko-bal-ha-da 고발하다 ; (*repudiate*) p'ye-gi-ha-da 폐기하다.
dense *adj*. mil-jip-han 밀집한, cho-mil-han 조밀한 ; chi-t'ŭn 짙은 : *a ~ forest* mil-rim 밀림.

dentist *n.* ch'i-gwa-ŭi-sa 치과의사.

deny *v.* pu-in-ha-da 부인하다, kŏ-jŏl-ha-da 거절하다.

depart *v.* ttŏ-na-da 떠나다, ch'ul-bal-ha-da 출발하다; (*pass away*) se-sang-ŭl tt'ŏ-na-da 세상을 떠나다.

department *n.* pu-mun 부문; (*suffix*) …pu …부, …kuk …국(局), …kwa …과.

department store paek-hwa-jŏm 백화점.

departure *n.* ch'ul-bal 출발, ttŏ-nam 떠남.

depend *v.* ŭi-ji-ha-da 의지하다, ŭi-jon-ha-da 의존하다.

dependent *n.* pu-yang ka-jok 부양 가족, sik-gaek 식객.

depict *v.* (*portray*) kŭ-ryŏ-nae-da 그려내다, myo-sa-ha-da 묘사하다, (*describe*) sŏ-sul-ha-da 서술하다.

deplore *v.* sŭl-p'ŏ-ha-da 슬퍼하다, ae-do-ha-da 애도하다.

deposit *n.* (*in a bank*) ye-gŭm 예금; (*sediment*) ang-gŭm 앙금, jji-ggi 찌끼. —*v.* ye-gŭm〔kong-t'ak〕-ha-da 예금〔공탁〕하다.

deprave *v.* t'a-rak-si-k'i-da 타락시키다, ak-hwa-si-k'i-da 악화시키다.

depress *v.* ① ŏk-ap-ha-da 억압하다. ② pul-gyŏng-gi-ro man-dŭl-da 불경기로 만들다.

depression *n.* ① (*commercial*) pul-gyŏng-gi 불경기. ② (*mental*) nak-sim 낙심, u-ul 우울.

deprive *v.* ppae-at-da 빼앗다, pak-t'al-ha-da 박탈하다.

depth *n.* ki-p'i 깊이, ki-p'ŭn kot 깊은 곳.

deputy *n.* tae-ri(-in) 대리(인), sŏ-ri 서리(署理). —*adj.* tae-ri-ŭi 대리의, pu-ŭi 부(副)의.

deride *v.* pi-ut-da 비웃다, cho-rong-ha-da 조롱하다.

derive *v.* i-ggŭ-rŏ-nae-da 이끌어내다.

descend *v.* ① nae-ryŏ-o-da 내려오다, pi-t'al-ji-da 비탈지다. ② chŏn-ha-yŏ-ji-da 전하여지다.

descendant *n.* cha-son 자손, hu-ye 후예.

descent *n.* ① (*coming down*) kang-ha 강하. ② (*lineage*) ka-gye 가계(家系), hyŏl-t'ong 혈통.

describe *v.* ① sŏ-sul-ha-da 서술하다, myo-sa-ha-da 묘사하다. ② (*trace*) kŭ-ri-da 그리다.

description *n.* sŏ-sul 서술, sŏl-myŏng-sŏ 설명서.

desert *n.* sa-mak 사막. —*adj.* pul-mo-ŭi 불모의. —*v.* (*forsake*) pŏ-ri-da 버리다 ; t'al-ch'ul-ha-da 탈출하다.

deserter *n.* to-mang-ja 도망자, to-mang-byŏng 도망병.

deserve *v.* …hal ka-ch'i-ga it-da …할 가치가 있다, …ŭl pat-ŭl ka-ch'i-ga it-da …을 받을 가치가 있다.

design *n.* sŏl-gye 설계, ku-sang 구상 ; ŭi-do 의도. —*v.* sŏl-gye-ha-da 설계하다, ti-ja-in-ha-da 디자인하다.

designate *v.* chi-jŏng[chi-myŏng]-ha-da 지정[지명]하다, im-myŏng-ha-da 임명하다.　　　　　「rŏn 소망스런.

desirable *adj.* pa-ram-jik-han 바람직한, so-mang-sŭ-

desire *n.* yok-mang 욕망, so-mang 소망, yo-gu 요구. —*v.* pa-ra-da 바라다, yo-mang-ha-da 요망하다.

desk *n.* ch'aek-sang 책상.

despair *n.* chŏl-mang 절망. —*v.* chŏl-mang-ha-da 절망하다, tan-nyŏm-ha-da 단념하다.

desperate *adj.* chŏl-mang-jŏk-in 절망적인, p'il-sa-jŏk-in 필사적인, cha-p'o-ja-gi-ŭi 자포자기의.

despise *v.* myŏl-si-ha-da 멸시하다, kkal-bo-da 깔보다.

despite *prep.* …e-do pul-gu-ha-go …에도 불구하고.

despond *v.* sil-mang-ha-da 실망하다, nak-sim-ha-da 낙심하다, ki-ga chuk-da 기가 죽다.

despot *n.* chŏn-je-gun-ju 전제군주, (*tyrant*) p'ok-gun 폭군.

dessert *n.* ti-jŏ-ŏ-t'ŭ 디저어트.

destination *n.* mok-jŏk-ji 목적지 ; ye-jŏng 예정.

destitute *adj.* ka-nan-han 가난한, kung-p'ip-han 궁핍한 : *a ~ family* kŭk-bin ka-jŏk 극빈 가족.

destroy *v.* p'a-goe-ha-da 파괴하다, mu-nŏ-ddŭ-ri-da 무너뜨리다 ; (*kill*) chuk-i-da 죽이다.　　　　　「축함.

destroyer *n.* ① p'a-goe-ja 파괴자. ② ku-ch'uk-ham 구

destruction *n.* p'a-goe 파괴, p'a-myŏl 파멸.

detach *v.* (*seperate*) tte-ŏ-nae-da 떼어내다,　pul-li-ha-da 분리하다 ; (*dispatch*) p'a-gyŏn-ha-da 파견하다.

detail *v.* ① sang-se-hi mal-ha-da 상세히 말하다. ② t'ŭk-p'a-ha-da 특파하다. —*n.* se-bu 세부(細部).

detain *v.* (*hold in custody*) ku-ryu-ha-da 구류하다 ; (*keep waiting*) ki-da-ri-ge ha-da 기다리게 하다.

detect *v.* a-ra-nae-da 알아내다, t'am-ji-ha-da 탐지하다.

detective *n.* t'am-jŏng 탐정 ; hyŏng-sa 형사.

determination *n.* kyŏl-sim 결심.　　　　「da 결심하다.

determine *v.* kyŏl-jŏng-ha-da 결정하다,　kyŏl-sim-ha-

detest *v.* mop-si mi-wŏ-ha-da 몹시 미워하다.

devastate *v.* yu-rin-ha-da 유린하다,　hwang-p'ye-k'e ha-da 황폐케 하다.

develop *v.* ① pal-dal-ha-da 발달하다. ② (*photo*) hyŏn-sang-ha-da 현상하다.　　　　「*to*) hyŏn-sang 현상.

development *n.* ① pal-dal 발달, kae-bal 개발. ② (*pho-*

deviate *v.* pit-na-ga-da 빗나가다, pŏ-sŏ-na-da 벗어나다.

device *n.* (*scheme*) ko-an 고안, (*apparatus*) chang-ch'i 장치 ; kung-ri 궁리 ; ŭi-jang 의장(意匠),　kye-ch'aek

devil *n.* ak-ma 악마, kwi-sin 귀신.　　　　「계책.

devise *v.* ko-an-ha-da 고안하다, kung-ri-ha-da 궁리하다.

devote *v.* pa-ch'i-da 바치다 ; mat-gi-da 맡기다.

devotion *n.* hŏn-sin 헌신 ; (*piety*) sin-sim 신심.

devour *v.* ① (*eat hungrily*) ke-gŏl-sŭ-re mŏk-da 게걸스레 먹다. ② t'am-dok-ha-da 탐독하다.

dew *n.* i-sŭl 이슬, pang-ul 방울.

dexterous *adj.* son-jae-ju-it-nŭn 손재주있는.

diagram *n.* (*figure*) to-p'yo 도표, to-hyŏng 도형, to-sik 도식 ; (*drawing*) chak-do 작도.　　　　「다이얼.

dial *n.* hae-si-gye 해시계,　p'yo-si-p'an 표시판, ta-i-ŏl

dialect *n.* sa-t'u-ri 사투리 ; kwan-yong-ŏ 관용어.

dialog(ue) *n.* tae-hwa 대화, mun-dap 문답.
diameter *n.* chi-rŭm 지름, chik-gyŏng 직경. 「아몬드.
diamond *n.* kŭm-gang-sŏk 금강석, ta-i-a-mon-dŭ 다이
diaper *n.* ① ma-rŭm-mo-ggol mu-nŭi 마름모꼴 무늬.
  ② (*breechcloth*) ki-jŏ-gwi 기저귀. 「다.
diarrhoea *n.* sŏl-sa 설사 : *have* ～ sŏl-sa-ha-da 설사하
diary *n.* il-gi 일기, il-ji 일지.
dice *n.* chu-sa-wi 주사위, chu-sa-wi no-ri 주사위 놀이.
dictate *v.* ① pat-a-ssŭ-da 받아쓰다. ② (*order*) myŏng-
  ryŏng-ha-da 명령하다. 「ryŏng 명령.
dictation *n.* pat-a-ssŭ-gi 받아쓰기; (*command*) myŏng-
dictator *n.* tok-jae-ja 독재자, chi-ryŏng-ja 지령자.
dictatorship *n.* tok-jae 독재, tok-jae-gwŏn 독재권.
dictionary *n.* sa-jŏn 사전(辭典), cha-jŏn 자전.
die *v.* chuk-da 죽다. —*n.* chu-sa-wi 주사위.
diet *n.* ① kuk-hoe 국회. ② (*food*) ŭm-sik-mul 음식물.
differ *v.* ta-rŭ-da 다르다, t'ŭl-ri-da 틀리다.
difference *n.* ch'a-i 차이; (*discord*) pul-hwa 불화.
different *adj.* ta-rŭn 다른, sang-i-han 상이한.
difficult *adj.* ŏ-ryŏ-un 어려운, kka-da-ro-un 까다로운.
difficulty *n.* ŏ-ryŏ-um 어려움, kol-lan 곤란.
diffident *adj.* cha-sin-ŏp-nŭn 자신없는, su-jup-ŭn 수줍은.
diffuse *v.* (*scatter*) ppu-ri-da 뿌리다, po-gŭp-ha-da 보
  급하다. —*adj.* san-man-han 산만한. 「하다.
dig *v.* p'a-da 파다, k'ae-da 캐다; t'am-gu-ha-da 탐구
digest *v.* ① so-hwa-ha-da 소화하다. ② (*simplify*) yo-
  yak-ha-da 요약하다. —*n.* ① so-hwa 소화. ② kae-yo
digestion *n.* so-hwa 소화; tong-hwa 동화(同化). 「개요.
digger *n.* ① kwang-bu 광부. ② kong-bu pŏl-re 공부 벌레.
dignity *n.* wi-ŏm 위엄, wi-p'ung 위풍; (*high position*)
  ko-wi 고위, ko-gwan 고관.
dike·dyke *n.* to-rang 도랑, tuk 둑; che-bang 제방.

diligence *n.* pu-ji-rŏn-ham 부지런함, kŭn-myŏn 근면.

diligent *adj.* pu-ji-rŏn-han 부지런한, kŭn-myŏn-ha 근면한, kong-bu-ha-nŭn 공부하는.　　　　「다.

dilute *v.* mul-gge ha-da 묽게 하다, hŭi-sŏk-ha-da 희석ㅎ

dim *adj.* ŏ-dum-ch'im-ch'im-han 어둠침침한 ; hŭi-mi han 희미한.　　　　「jŏk 면적, yong-jŏk 용적.

dimension *n.* ① ch'i-su 치수 ; ch'a-wŏn 차원. ② myŏn

diminish *v.* chu-ri-da 줄이다, tŏl-da 덜다.　　　「결.

dimple *n.* ① po-jo-gae 보조개. ② chan-mul-gyŏl 잔물

din *n.* si-ggŭ-rŏ-un so-ri 시끄러운 소리, so-ŭm 소음.

dine *v.* chŏng-ch'an-ŭl tŭl-da 정찬을 들다, chŏ-nyŏk sik-sa-rŭl ha-da 저녁 식사를 하다.

dining *n.* sik-sa 식사 : ~ *car* sik-dang-ch'a 식당차/ ~ *room* sik-dang 식당/~ *table* sik-t'ak 식탁.

dinner *n.* chŏng-ch'an 정찬, man-ch'an 만찬 : *a* ~ *party* man-ch'an-hoe 만찬회, o-ch'an-hoe 오찬회.

dip *v.* chŏk-si-da 적시다, tam-gŭ-da 담그다.

diphtheria *n.* ti-p'ŭ-t'e-ri-a 디프테리아.

diploma *n.* myŏn-hŏ-jang 면허장 ; cho-rŏp-jang 졸업장.

diplomacy *n.* oe-gyo 외교, oe-gyo-sul 외교술.

diplomat *n.* oe-gyo-gwan 외교관, oe-gyo-ga 외교가.

dipper *n.* kuk-ja 국자, chu-gŏk 주걱.　　　　「처참한.

dire *adj.* mu-si-mu-si-han 무시무시한, ch'o-ch'am-han

direct *adv.* (*immediate*) chik-jŏp-jŏk-in 직접적인 ; (*frank*) sol-jik-han 솔직한 ; (*straight*) ttok-ba-rŭn 똑 바른. —*v.* (*order*) chi-si-ha-da 지시하다, myŏng- ryŏng-ha-da 명령하다 ; chi-do-ha-da 지도하다.

direction *n.* ① pang-hyang 방향. ② (*instruction*) chi- si-sŏ 지시서 ; sa-yong-bŏp 사용법.

directly *adv.* chik-jŏp 직접, chŭk-si 즉시.

director *n.* ① chi-do-ja 지도자. ② (*manager*) chung-yŏk 중역 ; chi-bae-in 지배인. ③ (*cinema*) kam-dok 감독.

directory *n.* in-myŏng-rok 인명록, (*telephone*) chŏn-hwa pŏn-ho-bu 전화 번호부.

dirt *n.* ssŭ-re-gi 쓰레기 ; chin-hŭk 진흙 ; o-mul 오물.

dirty *adj.* (*unclean*) tŏ-rŏ-un 더러운, (*base*) ch'ŏn-han 천한, sang-sŭ-rŏ-un 상스러운.

disable *v.* pul-gu-ro man-dŭl-da 불구로 만들다.

disadvantage *n.* pul-ri 불리, son-hae 손해.

disagree *v.* (*differ*) ŭi-gyŏn-i ta-rŭ-da 의견이 다르다 ; (*unsuitable*) chŏk-hap-ha-ji an-t'a 적합하지 않다.

disagreeable *adj.* pul-k'wae-han 불쾌한, si-rŭn 싫은.

disappear *v.* sa-ra-ji-da 사라지다, so-myŏl-ha-da 소멸

disappearance *n.* so-sil 소실, sil-jong 실종. ⌊하다.

disappoint *v.* sil-mang-k'e ha-da 실망케 하다, chŏ-bŏ-ri-da 저버리다, chwa-jŏl-si-k'i-da 좌절시키다.

disappointment *n.* sil-mang 실망, nak-sim 낙심.

disapproval *n.* pul-ch'an-sŏng 불찬성, pu-dong-ŭi 부동의(不同意), pul-man 불만.

disapprove *v.* ① ch'an-sŏng-ha-ji an-t'a 찬성하지 않다. ② (*condemn*) pi-nan-ha-da 비난하다.

disarm *v.* ① kun-bi-ch'uk-so-ha-da 군비축소하다. ② mu-jang-ŭl hae-je-ha-da 무장을 해제하다.

disaster *n.* chae-nan 재난, pul-haeng 불행. ⌈한.

disastrous *adj.* chae-nan-ŭi 재난의 ; pi-ch'am-han 비참

disbelieve *v.* mit-ji an-t'a 믿지 않다.

discern *v.* ① sik-byŏl〔pun-byŏl〕-ha-da 식별〔분별〕하다, pun-gan-ha-da 분간하다. ② in-sik-ha-da 인식하다.

discharge *v.* (*electricity*) pang-jŏn-ha-da 방전하다 ; (*from army*) che-dae-ha-da 제대하다 ; (*dismiss*) hae-go-ha-da 해고하다. —*n.* (*shoot*) pal-sa 발사, (*release*) hae-je 해제 ; (*performance*) su-haeng 수행.

disciple *n.* che-ja 제자, mun-ha-saeng 문하생.

discipline *n.* hul-lyŏn 훈련 ; (*public morals*) p'ung-gi 풍기. —*v*. (*train*) hul-lyŏn-ha-da 훈련하다 ; (*rep-rimand*) ching-gye-ha-da 징계하다.

disclose *v*. p'ok-ro-ha-da 폭로하다, tŭl-ch'u-ŏ-nae-da 들추어내다 ; ch'ŏn-myŏng-ha-da 천명하다.

discomfort *n*. pul-k'wae 불쾌, pu-ran 불안. 「케 하다.

disconcert *v*. (*embarrass*) tang-hwang-k'e ha-da 당황

discontent *n*. pul-man 불만, pul-p'yŏng 불평.

discontented *adj*. pul-man-sŭ-rŏ-un 불만스러운. 「치다.

discontinue *v*. chung-ji-ha-da 중지하다, kŭ-ch'i-da 그

discord *n*. ① pu-ril-ch'i 불일치. ② pul-hyŏp-hwa-ŭm 불협화음. —*v*. il-ch'i-ha-ji an-t'a 일치하지 않다 ; sa-i-ga na-bbŭ-da 사이가 나쁘다.

discount *n*. & *v*. ha-rin(-ha-da) 할인(하다).

discourage *v*. sil-mang-k'e ha-da 실망케 하다 ; (*thwart*) pang-hae-ha-da 방해하다. 「하다.

discourse *n*. tam-hwa 담화. —*v*. i-ya-gi-ha-da 이야기

discourtesy *n*. sil-rye 실례, (*rude act*) mu-rye 무례.

discourteous *adj*. pŏ-rŭt-ŏp-nŭn 버릇없는.

discover *v*. ① pal-gyŏn-ha-da 발견하다. ② kkae-dat-

discovery *n*. pal-gyŏn 발견. 「da 깨닫다.

discreet *adj*. sa-ryŏ-gi-p'ŭn 사려깊은, yong-ŭi-ju-do-han 용의주도한, sin-jung-han 신중한.

discretion *n*. sa-ryŏ pun-byŏl 사려 분별, sik-byŏl 식별.

discriminate *v*. sik-byŏl-ha-da 식별하다 ; ch'a-byŏl-ha-da 차별하다. —*adj*. ch'a-byŏl-jŏk-in 차별적인.

discrimination *n*. ch'a-byŏl 차별 ; ku-byŏl 구별.

discuss *v*. ŭi-non-ha-da 의논하다, t'o-ron-ha-da 토론하

discussion *n*. ŭi-non 의논, t'o-ŭi 토의. 「다.

disdain *v*. myŏl-si-ha-da 멸시하다. —*n*. myŏl-si 멸시.

disease *n*. pyŏng 병, chil-hwan 질환.

disgrace *v*. mang-sin-si-k'i-da 망신시키다. —*n*. pul-myŏng-ye 불명예, ch'i-yok 치욕.

disgraceful *adj.* su-ch'i-sŭ-rŏ-un 수치스러운.
disguise *v.* pyŏn-jang-ha-da 변장하다, ka-jang-ha-da 가장하다. —*n.* pyŏn-jang 변장, ka-myŏn 가면.
disgust *n.* sil-jŭng 싫증, hyŏm-o 혐오.
dish *n.* ① chŏp-si 접시. ② yo-ri 요리.
dishonest *adj.* chŏng-jik-ha-ji mot-han 정직하지 못한.
dishonesty *n.* pu-jŏng-jik 부정직, pul-sŏng-sil 불성실.
dishonor *n.* pul-myŏng-ye 불명예, ch'i-yok 치욕. —*v.* ch'ang-p'i-rŭl chu-da 창피를 주다.
disillusion *n.* hwan-myŏl 환멸, kak-sŏng 각성. —*v.* hwan-sang-e-sŏ kkae-ŏ-na-da 환상에서 깨어나다.
disinterested *adj.* (*unselfish*) sa-sim-i ŏp-nŭn 사심이 없는 ; (*impartial*) kong-p'yŏng-han 공평한.
disk *n.* wŏn-ban 원반, re-k'o-o-dŭ 레코오드.
dislike *n.* si-rŭm 싫음, hyŏm-o 혐오. —*v.* si-rŏ-ha-da 싫어하다, mi-wŏ-ha-da 미워하다.
disloyal *adj.* ch'ung-sŏng-sŭ-rŏp-ji mot-han 충성스럽지 못한, pul-sŏng-sil-han 불성실한.
dismal *adj.* (*gloomy*) ŭm-ch'im-han 음침한, u-ul-han 우울한 ; mu-si-mu-si-han 무시무시한.
dismay *n.* tang-hwang 당황 ; (*fear*) nol-ram 놀람. —*v.* tang-hwang-k'e ha-da 당황케 하다.
dismiss *v.* ① (*send away*) mul-rŏ-na-ge ha-da 물러나게 하다, hae-go-ha-da 해고하다. ② (*disband*) hae-san-si-k'i-da 해산시키다. ③ (*reject*) ki-gak-ha-da 기각하다.
dismount *v.* nae-ri-da 내리다, ha-ch'a-ha-da 하차하다.
disobedience *n.* pul-bok-jong 불복종, wi-ban 위반.
disobedient *adj.* sun-jong-ha-ji an-nŭn 순종하지 않는, mal-ŭl tŭt-ji an-nŭn 말을 듣지 않는.
disobey *v.* mal-ŭl tŭt-ji an-t'a 말을 듣지 않다, sun-jong-ch'i an-t'a 순종치 않다, ŏ-gi-da 어기다.
disorder *n.* nan-jap 난잡, mu-jil-sŏ 무질서. —*v.* ŏ-ji-

rŏp-hi-da 어지럽히다.

dispatch *n.* kŭp-song 급송, kŭp-p'a 급파; (*express delivery*) sok-dal-u-p'yŏn 속달우편. —*v.* p'a-gyŏn-ha-da 파견하다; (*goods*) pal-song-ha-da 발송하다.

dispel *v.* jjo-ch'a-bŏ-ri-da 쫓아버리다, ŏp-sae-da 없애다.

dispense *v.* ① (*distribute*) na-nwŏ-ju-da 나눠주다. ② (*do without*) ŏp-si kyŏn-di-da 없이 견디다. ③ (*put up*) cho-je-ha-da 조제하다.　「하다.

disperse *v.* hŭ-t'ŏ-ji-da 흩어지다, hae-san-ha-da 해산

displace *n.* ① pa-ggu-ŏ no-t'a 바꾸어 놓다. ② (*remove from office*) hae-im-ha-da 해임하다.

display *n.* chin-yŏl 진열. —*v.* na-t'a-nae-da 나타내다.

disposal *n.* ch'ŏ-bun 처분, ch'ŏ-ch'i 처치.

dispose *v.* ① (*arrange*) pae-ch'i-ha-da 배치하다. ② (*deal with*) ch'ŏ-ri-ha-da 처리하다.

disposition *n.* ① ki-jil 기질. ② ch'ŏ-ri 처리.

dispute *n.* mal-da-t'um 말다툼, non-jaeng 논쟁. —*v.* mal-da-t'um-ha-da 말다툼하다.

disregard *v.* mu-si-ha-da 무시하다. —*n.* mu-si 무시.

disrespect *n.* mu-rye 무례, sil-rye 실례.　「다.

dissatisfy *v.* pul-man-ŭl p'um-ge ha-da 불만을 품게 하

dissect *v.* ka-rŭ-da 가르다, hae-bu-ha-da 해부하다.

dissipate *v.* hŭt-ddŭ-ri-da 흩뜨리다, il-so-ha-da 일소하

dissipated *adj.* pang-t'ang-han 방탕한.　　　└다.

dissolution *n.* hae-san 해산; so-myŏl 소멸.

dissolve *v.* ① nok-da 녹다. ② hae-san-ha-da 해산하다.

dissuade *v.* t'a-il-rŏ kŭ-man-du-ge ha-da 타일러 그만 두게 하다, tan-nyŏm-si-k'i-da 단념시키다.

distance *n.* kŏ-ri 거리, kan-gyŏk 간격.

distant *adj.* ① (*space*) mŏl-ri-it-nŭn 멀리있는. ② (*time*) o-raen 오랜. ③ (*relationship*) ch'on-su-ga mŏn 촌수가 먼. ④ (*not familiar*) sŏ-rŭm-han 서름한.

distaste *n*. si-rŭm 싫음, hyŏm-o 혐오.

distil(l) *v*. chŭng-ryu-ha-da 증류하다, ppum-da 뿜다.

distinct *adj*. ① myŏng-baek-han 명백한, sŏn-myŏng-han 선명한. ② (*seperate*) pyŏl-gae-ŭi 별개의.   「한.

distinctive *adj*. ku-byŏl-i pun-myŏng-han 구별이 분명

distinctly *adv*. pun-myŏng-hi 분명히, (*definitely*) ttok-ddok-ha-ge 똑똑하게, myŏng-baek-ha-ge 명백하게.

distinguish *v*. ku-byŏl-ha-da 구별하다.   「저한.

distinguished *adj*. i-rŭm-nan 이름난 ; hyŏn-jŏ-han 현

distort *v*. ① twi-t'ŭl-da 뒤틀다, jji-gŭ-rŏ-ddŭ-ri-da 찌그러뜨리다. ② kok-hae-ha-da 곡해하다.

distract *v*. hŭt-ddŭ-ri-da 흩뜨리다.

distress *n*. kŭn-sim 근심, ko-t'ong 고통 ; kon-gung 곤궁. —*v*. koe-rop-hi-da 괴롭히다, sŭl-p'ŭ-ge ha-da 슬프게 하다.

distribute *v*. na-nu-ŏ-ju-da 나누어주다.

distribution *n*. pun-bae 분배, pae-gŭp 배급.

district *n*. ① ku-yŏk 구역. ② (*region*) chi-bang 지방.

distrust *n*. pul-sin 불신. —*v*. mit-ji an-t'a 믿지 않다.

disturb *v*. ŏ-ji-rŏp-ge ha-da 어지럽게 하다, kyo-ran-ha-da 교란하다 ; pang-hae-ha-da 방해하다.

ditch *n*. to-rang 도랑, kae-ch'ŏn 개천.

dive *n*. cham-su 잠수. —*v*. mul-e ttwi-ŏ-dŭl-da 물에 뛰어들다, cham-su-ha-da 잠수하다.

diverse *adj*. (*different*) ta-rŭn 다른 ; (*varied*) ta-yang-han 다양한, ka-ji-gak-saek-ŭi 가지각색의.

divert *v*. ① (*turn aside*) chŏn-hwan-ha-da 전환하다. ② (*entertain*) ki-bun-ŭl p'ul-da 기분을 풀다.

divide *v*. na-nu-da 나누다, pul-li-ha-da 분리하다.

divine *adj*. sin-ŭi 신의 ; (*holy*) sin-sŏng-han 신성한. —*v*. (*foretell*) ye-ŏn-ha-da 예언하다.

division *n*. ① pun-hal 분할. ② (*boundary*) kyŏng-gye 경계. ③ (*portion*) ku-hoek 구획. ④ (*mil.*) sa-dan 사단.

divorce *n.* i-hon 이혼. —*v.* i-hon-ha-da 이혼하다.

dizzy *adj.* ŏ-ji-rŏ-un 어지러운, hyŏn-gi-jŭng na-nŭn 현기증 나는. —*v.* ŏ-ji-rŏp-ge ha-da 어지럽게 하다.

do *v.* ① (*act*) ha-da 하다. ② (*confer*) chu-da 주다. ③ (*make*) man-dŭl-da 만들다. ④ (*finish*) kkŭt-nae-da 끝내다. ⑤ (*enough*) ch'ung-bun-ha-da 충분하다.

docile *adj.* ka-rŭ-ch'i-gi swi-ŭn 가르치기 쉬운, ta-ru-gi swi-un 다루기 쉬운, yu-sun-han 유순한.

dock *n.* ① (*artificial basin*) tok 독, sŏn-gŏ 선거(船渠), pu-du 부두. ② (*law*) p'i-go-sŏk 피고석.

dockyard *n.* cho-sŏn-so 조선소(造船所).

doctor *n.* ① ŭi-sa 의사. ② (*degree*) pak-sa 박사. —*v.* ch'i-ryo-ha-da 치료하다.　　　　　　　　　　　「교훈.

doctrine *n.* kyo-ri 교리 ; chu-ŭi 주의(主義) ; kyo-hun

document *n.* mun-sŏ 문서, chŭng-sŏ 증서.

dodge *v.* sal-jjak p'i-ha-da 살짝 피하다.

doe *n.* ① am-no-ru 암노루. ② am-k'ŏt 암컷.

dog *n.* kae 개 : *a dirty* ~ tŏ-rŏ-un nyŏ-sŏk 더러운 녀석.

doleful *adj.* (*sad*) sŭl-p'ŭn 슬픈, u-ul-han 우울한.

doll *n.* ① in-hyŏng 인형. ② (*silly girl*) kkok-duk-gak-si 꼭둑각시.

dollar *n.* tal-rŏ 달러, pul 불(弗).

dolmen *n.* ko-in-dol 고인돌, tol-men 돌멘.

domain *n.* yŏng-t'o 영토, so-yu-ji 소유지 ; pun-ya 분야.

dome *n.* tŭng-gŭn chi-bung 둥근 지붕, (*vault*) tŭng-gŭn ch'ŏn-jang 둥근 천장.

domestic *adj.* ① (*household*) ka-jŏng-ŭi 가정의. ② (*national*) kuk-nae-ŭi 국내의. —*n.* ha-in 하인(下人).

domicile *n.* chu-so 주소, pon-jŏk-ji 본적지.

dominate *v.* (*rule*) chi-bae-ha-da 지배하다, (*rise above*) u-dduk sot-da 우뚝 솟다.

dominion *n.* chu-gwŏn 주권, t'ong-ch'i-gwŏn 통치권.

donate *v.* chŭng-yŏ-ha-da 증여하다, ki-jŭng-ha-da 기증하다, ki-bu-ha-da 기부하다.

donkey *n.* ① tang-na-gwi 당나귀. ② pa-bo 바보.

doom *n.* ①(*fate*)un-myŏng 운명, p'a-myŏl 파멸. ②(*sentence*) sŏn-go 선고. —*v.* un-myŏng-jit-da 운명짓다.

door *n.* mun 문, ch'u-rip-gu 출입구, to-ŏ 도어: ~ *keeper* mun-ji-gi 문지기, su-wi 수위/~ *knob* son-jap-i 손잡이/ *out of* ~*s* chip pa-gge-sŏ 집 밖에서.

doorbell *n.* ch'o-in-jong 초인종.

doorway *n.* tae-mun-gan 대문간, ch'u-rip-gu 출입구.

dormitory *n.* ki-suk-sa 기숙사, hap-suk-so 합숙소.

dose *n.* (*medicine*) il-hoe-bun 1회분 ; pok-yong-ryang 복용량. —*v.* t'u-yak-ha-da 투약(投藥)하다.

dot *n.* chŏm 점. —*v.* chŏm-ŭl jjik-da 점을 찍다.

dote *v.* ① mang-ryŏng-dŭl-da 망령들다, no-mang-ha-da 노망하다. ② sa-rang-e ppa-ji-da 사랑에 빠지다.

double *adj.* tu kop-ŭi 두 곱의. —*v.* pae-ro-ha-da 배로 하다. —*n.* kop 곱, pae 배(倍). 「의심하다.

doubt *n.* ŭi-sim 의심, ŭi-hok 의혹. —*v.* ŭi-sim-ha-da

doubtful *adj.* ŭi-sim-sŭ-rŏ-un 의심스러운. 「hi 확실히.

doubtless *adj.* ŭi-sim-ŏp-nŭn 의심없는. —*adv.* hwak-sil-

dough *n.* mil-ga-ru pan-juk 밀가루 반죽.

dove *n.* ① (*pigeon*) pi-dul-gi 비둘기. ② (*Holy Spirit*) sŏng-ryŏng 성령. 「mi-t'e 밑에.

down *adv. & adj.* a-rae-ro(-ŭi) 아래로(의). —*prep.*

downcast *v.* p'ul-i chuk-ŭn 풀이 죽은.

downstairs *n.* a-rae-ch'ŭng 아래층, ha-ch'ung 하층.

downtown *n.* to-sim-ji 도심지, pŏn-hwa-ga 번화가, (*business part of a city*) sang-ga 상가.

downward *adv.* a-rae-jjok-ŭ-ro 아래쪽으로.

downy *adj.* som-t'ŏl-ga-t'ŭn 솜털같은, p'ok-sin-p'ok-sin-han 폭신폭신한.

dowry *n.* (*bride*) chi-ch'am-gŭm 지참금.
doze *v.* chol-da 졸다, sŏn-jam-ja-da 선잠자다.
dozen *n.* yŏl-du-gae 12개, ta-sŭ 다스, t'a 타(打).
draft·draught *n.* ① (*rough copy*) ch'o-an 초안. ②
  (*conscription*) ching-byŏng 징병. ③ (*bank*) hwan-ŏ-
  ŭm 환어음. ④ t'ong-p'ung 통풍. —*v.* ① ki-ch'o-ha-
  da 기초(起草)하다. ② ching-jip-ha-da 징집하다.
drag *v.* kkŭl-da 끌다, kkŭ-rŏ-dang-gi-da 끌어당기다.
dragnet *n.* ① ye-in-mang 예인망. ② su-sa-mang 수사망.
dragon *n.* yong 용.
dragonfly *n.* cham-ja-ri 잠자리.
drain *n.* pae-su 배수(排水). —*v.* ① mul-ŭl ppae-da
  물을 빼다 ; jjuk tŭ-ri-k'i-da 쭉 들이키다.
drake *n.* (*male duck*) su-o-ri 수오리. 「sa-gŭk 사극.
drama *n.* kŭk 극, tŭ-ra-ma 드라마 : *the historical* ~
dramatic *adj.* yŏn-gŭk-ŭi 연극의, kŭk-jŏk-in 극적인.
drape *n.* p'o-jang 포장, hwi-jang 휘장. —*v.* tŏp-da 덮다.
drapery *n.* (*textile fabrics*) p'i-ryuk 피륙, ot-gam 옷감.
drastic *adj.* maeng-ryŏl-han 맹렬한, ch'ŏl-jŏ-han 철저한.
draw *v.* ① (*pull*) kkŭl-da 끌다. ② (*pictures*) kŭ-ri-
  da 그리다. ③ (*inhale*) sum-ŭl swi-da 숨을 쉬다. 「애.
drawback *n.* kyŏl-jŏm 결점 ; (*hindrance*) chang-ae 장
drawer *n.* ① sŏ-rap 서랍. ② (*pl.*) p'aen-ch'ŭ 팬츠.
drawing *n.* che-do 제도(製圖), kŭ-rim 그림.
drawing room ŭng-jŏp-sil 응접실.
dread *n.* tu-ryŏ-um 두려움, kong-p'o 공포. —*v.* mu-
  sŏ-wŏ-ha-da 무서워하다, tu-ryŏ-wŏ-ha-da 두려워하다.
dreadful *adj.* mu-sŏ-un 무서운, tu-ryŏ-un 두려운.
dream *n.* kkum 꿈 ; kong-sang 공상. —*v.* kkum-ŭl
  kku-da 꿈을 꾸다, mong-sang-ha-da 몽상하다.
dreary *adj.* ssŭl-ssŭl-han 쓸쓸한, hwang-ryang-han
  황량한 ; (*dull*) chi-ru-han 지루한.

dredger *n.* (*persons*) chun-sŏl in-bu 준설 인부 ; (*ships*) chun-sŏl-sŏn 준설선, ye-mang-ŏ-sŏn 예망어선.

dreg *n.* jji-ggŏ-gi 찌꺼기, ang-gŭm 앙금.

drench *v.* mul-e tam-gŭ-da 물에 담그다, hŭm-bbŏk chŏk-si-da 흠뻑 적시다. —*n.* mul-yak 물약.

dress *n.* ot 옷, ŭi-bok 의복. —*v.* ① (*put on*) ip-da 입다. ② (*adorn*) kku-mi-da 꾸미다, son-jil-ha-da 손질하다.

dresser *n.* ① ot ip-hi-nŭn sa-ram 옷 입히는 사람. ② (*dandy*) mŏt-jang-i 멋장이. ③ (*dressing table*) kyŏng-dae 경대, hwa-jang-dae 화장대.

drift *v.* p'yo-ryu-ha-da 표류하다, ttŏ-dol-da 떠돌다.

drill *n.* ① song-got 송곳. ② (*practice*) yŏn-sŭp 연습. —*v.* ① (*hole*) ku-mŏng-ŭl ttŭl-t'a 구멍을 뚫다. ② (*training*) hul-lyŏn-si-k'i-da 훈련시키다.

drink *v.* ma-si-da 마시다. —*n.* ŭm-ryo 음료.

drip *n.* (*of liquid*) pang-ul 방울. —*v.* (*from a height*) ttŏ-rŏ-ji-da 떨어지다.

drive *v.* mol-da 몰다, (*car*) un-jŏn-ha-da 운전하다. —*n.* ① tŭ-ra-i-bŭ 드라이브. ② (*path*) ch'a-do 차도. ③ (*campaign*) un-dong 운동.

driver *n.* un-jŏn-su 운전수 ; mal-mo-rit-gun 말몰잇군.

drizzle *n.* i-sŭl-bi 이슬비, ka-rang-bi 가랑비, po-sŭl-bi 보슬비. —*v.* i-sŭl-bi-ga nae-ri-da 이슬비가 내리다.

droop *v.* a-rae-ro ch'ŏ-ji-da 아래로 처지다, su-gŭ-rŏ-ji-da 수그러지다 ; (*flower*) si-dŭl-da 시들다.

drop *n.* pang-ul 방울, mul-bang-ul 물방울. —*v.* ttok-ddok ttŏ-rŏ-ji-da 똑똑 떨어지다.

drought *n.* (*dry weather*) ka-mum 가뭄, han-bal 한발.

drown *v.* mul-e ppa-ji-da 물에 빠지다.

drowsy *adj.* chol-ri-nŭn 졸리는, cho-rŭm-i o-nŭn 졸음이 오는, na-rŭn-han 나른한.

drug *n.* yak 약, yak-p'um 약품. —*v.* yak-ŭl mŏk-i-da

약을 먹이다.   「mak 고막.
drum *n*. ① puk 북, tŭ-rŏm 드럼. ② (*eardrum*) ko-
drummer *n*. ko-su 고수(鼓手), tŭ-rŏ-mŏ 드러머.
drunkard *n*. chu-jŏng-gun 주정군, sul-go-rae 술고래.
dry *v*. mal-ri-da 말리다. —*adj*. ma-rŭn 마른, kŏn-jo-
    han 건조한.
dual *adj*. i-jung-ŭi 이중의, i-wŏn-jŏk-in 이원적인 : ~
    personality i-jung-in-gyŏk 이중인격.   「수상한.
dubious *adj*. ŭi-sim-sŭ-rŏ-un 의심스러운, su-sang-han
duck *n*. o-ri 오리 : *the domestic* ~ chip-o-ri 집오리.
due *adj*. man-gi-ga toen 만기가 됨 ; chi-dang-han 지당
    한 ; to-ch'ak ye-jŏng-in 도착 예정인. —*adv*. pa-ro 바로.
duel *n*. kyŏl-t'u 결투, si-hap 시합. —*v*. kyŏl-t'u-ha-da
duet *n*. i-jung-ch'ang 이중창, i-jung-ju 이중주. 「결투하다.
duke *n*. kong-jak 공작(公爵).
dull *adj*. tun-han 둔한, mu-din 무딘.
duly *adv*. ① chŏng-dang-ha-ge 정당하게. ② che-si-
    gan-e 제시간에. ③ sun-sŏ-dae-ro 순서대로.   「하는.
dumb *adj*. pŏng-ŏ-ri-ŭi 벙어리의, mal mot-ha-nŭn 말 못
dumbbell *n*. a-ryŏng 아령(啞鈴).
dunce *n*. chŏ-nŭng-a 저능아, mŏng-ch'ŏng-i 멍청이.
dung *n*. ttong 똥 ; (*manure*) kŏ-rŭm 거름.
dungeon *n*. ① (*underground prison*) chi-ha kam-
    ok 지하 감옥. ② (*donjon*) a-sŏng 아성(牙城).
duplicate *n*. sa-bon 사본 ; pok-sa 복사. —*v*. i-jung-ŭ-ro
    ha-da 이중으로 하다 ; pok-sa-ha-da 복사하다.
duration *n*. chi-sok 지속 ; ki-gan 기간.
during *prep*. …ha-nŭn tong-an …하는 동안.
dusk *n*. ttang-gŏ-mi 땅거미, hwang-hon 황혼.
dust *n*. mŏn-ji 먼지. —*v*. mŏn-ji-rŭl ttŏl-da 먼지를 떨다.
dustbin *n*. ssŭ-re-gi-t'ong 쓰레기통.
duster *n*. ch'ong-ch'ae 총채, mŏn-ji-ddŏ-ri 먼지떨이.

dusty *adj.* mŏn-ji t'u-sŏng-i-ŭi 먼지 투성이의.

dutiful *adj.* ŭi-mu-gam-i kang-han 의무감이 강한, pon-bun-ŭl chi-k'i-nŭn 본분(本分)을 지키는.

duty *n.* ① ŭi-mu 의무. ② (*tax*) se-gŭm 세금.

dwarf *n.* nan-jang-i 난장이. —*adj.* wae-so-han 왜소한, chak-ŭn 작은. —*v.* chak-ge ha-da 작게 하다.

dwell *v.* ① sal-da 살다. ② mŏ-mu-rŭ-da 머무르다.

dwindle *v.* ① (chŏm-jŏm) chak-a-ji-da (점점) 작아지다, chul-da 줄다. ② (*waste away*) ya-wi-da 야위다.

dye *v.* mul-dŭ-ri-da 물들이다. —*n.* mul-gam 물감.

dynasty *n.* wang-jo 왕조.

dysentery *n.* i-jil 이질, sŏl-sa-byŏng 설사병.

E

each *adj.* kak-gak-ŭi 각각의, kak-ja-ŭi 각자의. —*pron.* kak-ja 각자, che-gak-gi 제각기.

eager *adj.* yŏl-jung-ha-nŭn 열중하는, yŏl-sim-in 열심인.

eagerly *adv.* yŏl-sim-hi 열심히, kan-jŏl-hi 간절히.

eagerness *n.* yŏl-sim 열심, kal-mang 갈망.

eagle *n.* tok-su-ri 독수리 ; (*emblem*) tok-su-ri-p'yo 독

ear *n.* ① kwi 귀. ② (*corn, etc.*) i-sak 이삭. ⌊수리표.

early *adj.* i-rŭn 이른. —*adv.* il-jji-gi 일찌기.

earn *v.* (*by labor*) pŏl-da 벌다 ; (*obtain*) ŏt-da 얻다 ; (*deserve*) pat-ŭl man-ha-da 받을 만하다.

earnest *adj.* chin-ji-han 진지한, yŏl-sim-in 열심인. —*n.* chin-ji-ham 진지함, chin-sim 진심.

earnestly *adv.* yŏl-sim-hi 열심히, chin-ji-ha-ge 진지하게, chin-sim-ŭ-ro 진심으로.

earnings *n.* so-dŭk 소득, (*wage*) im-gŭm 임금.

earphone *n.* su-sin-gi 수신기, su-hwa-gi 수화기.

earring *n.* kwi-go-ri 귀고리, i-ŏ-ring 이어링.

earth *n*. ① (*globe*) chi-gu 지구. ② (*ground*) tae-ji 대
지 ; (*soil*) hŭk 흙. ③ (*this world*) i se-sang 이 세상.
earthen *adj*. hŭl-gŭ-ro man-dŭn 흙으로 만든.
earthenware *n*. chil-gŭ-rŭt 질그릇, t'o-gi 토기(土器).
earthly *adj*. i se-sang-ŭi 이 세상의, sok-se-ŭi 속세의.
earthquake *n*. chi-jin 지진.　　　　「pi-yŏl-han 비열한.
earthworm *n*. ① chi-rŏng-i 지렁이. ② (*mean person*)
ease *n*. ① al-lak 안락 , p'yŏn-an 편안. ② an-sim 안심.
—*v*. ① (*make comfortable*) p'yŏn-ha-ge ha-da 편하
게 하다. ② (*make easy*) an-sim-si-k'i-da 안심시키다.
easily *adv*. swip-ge 쉽게, yong-i-ha-ge 용이하게.
east *n*. tong-jjok 동쪽. —*adv*. tong-jjok-ŭ-ro 동쪽으로:
　Far E~ kŭk-dong 극동/*E*~ *Asia* tong-a-si-a 동아
Easter *n*. pu-hwal-jŏl 부활절.　　　　　　　　└시아.
eastern *adj*. tong-jjok-ŭi 동쪽의, tong-bang-ŭi 동방의.
eastward *adj*. tong-jjok-ŭ-ro-ŭi 동쪽으로의.
easy *adj*. swi-un 쉬운 ; p'yŏn-han 편한 ; nŏ-gŭ-rŏ-un
너그러운. —*adv*. su-wŏl-ha-ge 수월하게.
easy chair al-lak-ŭi-ja 안락의자.
eat *v*. ① mŏk-da 먹다, (*honorific*) chap-su-si-da 잡수
시다. ② (*gnaw*) ch'im-sik-ha-da 침식하다, pu-sik-ha-
da 부식하다.
eaves *n*. ch'ŏ-ma 처마, ch'aeng 쳉.
ebb *n*. (*reflux of tide*) ssŏl-mul
썰물, kan-jo 간조(干潮). —*v*. ppi-
da 삐다 ; soe-t'oe-ha-da 쇠퇴하다.

ebony *n*. hŭk-dan 흑단(黑檀).
eccentric *adj*. pyŏl-nan 별난, koe-sang-han 괴상한.
—*n*. koe-jja 괴짜, ki-in 기인(奇人).
echo *n*. me-a-ri 메아리, pan-hyang 반향. —*v*. me-a-
ri-ch'i-da 메아리치다.
eclipse *n*. (*solar*) il-sik 일식 ; (*lunar*) wŏl-sik 월식 ;

(*total*) kae-gi-sik 개기식(皆旣蝕). 「학의.
economic *adj*. kyŏng-je-ŭi 경제의, kyŏng-je-hak-ŭi 경제
economical *adj*. kyŏng-je-jŏk-in 경제적인 ; (*thrifty*)
　검소한, chŏl-yak-ha-nŭn 절약하는.
economics *n*. kyŏng-je-hak 경제학. 「ga 검약가.
economist *n*. ① kyŏng-je-hak-ja 경제학자. ② kŏm-yak-
economize *v*. kyŏng-je-jŏk-ŭ-ro ssŭ-da 경제적으로 쓰다,
　chŏl-yak-ha-da 절약하다.
economy *n*. kyŏng-je 경제, (*frugality*) chŏl-yak 절약.
ecstasy *n*. hwang-hol-gyŏng 황홀경, kwang-hŭi 광희
　(狂喜), mu-han-han ki-bbŭm 무한한 기쁨.
eddy *n*. so-yong-do-ri 소용돌이, hoe-o-ri 회오리.
edge *n*. ① ka-jang-ja-ri 가장자리. ② (*blade*) nal 날.
　—*v*. nal-ŭl se-u-da 날을 세우다, kal-da 갈다.
edible *adj*. mŏk-ŭl su it-nŭn 먹을 수 있는, sik-yong-
　ui 식용의. —*n*. sik-ryo-p'um 식료품.
edict *n*. ch'ik-ryŏng 칙령, (*decree*) p'o-go 포고.
edifice *n*. kŏn-mul 건물, tae-jŏ-t'aek 대저택. 「다.
edify *v*. kyo-hwa-ha-da 교화하다, kye-bal-ha-da 계발하
edit *v*. p'yŏn-jip[p'yŏn-ch'an]-ha-da 편집[편찬]하다.
editor *n*. p'yŏn-jip-ja 편집자.
editorial *n*. sa-sŏl 사설, non-sŏl 논설. —*adj*. p'yŏn-jip
　(-ja)-ŭi 편집(자)의. 「훈련하다.
educate *v*. kyo-yuk-ha-da 교육하다, hul-lyŏn-ha-da
education *n*. kyo-yuk 교육, hun-yuk 훈육, to-ya 도야.
eel *n*. paem-jang-ŏ 뱀장어.
efface *v*. chi-u-da 지우다, mal-sal-ha-da 말살하다.
effect *n*. kyŏl-gwa 결과 ; yŏng-hyang 영향. —*v*. i-rŭ-
　k'i-da 일으키다, tal-sŏng-ha-da 달성하다. 「적인.
effective *adj*. yu-hyo-han 유효한, hyo-gwa-jŏk-in 효과
efficacy *n*. hyo-ryŏk 효력, hyo-nŭng 효능.
efficiency *n*. nŭng-ryul 능률, hyo-yul 효율.

effort *n.* no-ryŏk 노력, no-go 노고, su-go 수고.
egg *n.* al 알, (*of hen*) tal-gyal 달걀, kye-ran 계란.
eggplant *n.* (*vegetable*) ka-ji 가지.
egoism *n.* i-gi-ju-ŭi 이기주의, cha-gi pon-wi 자기 본위.
egotism *n.* ① cha-gi chung-sim 자기 중심. ② cha-man
Egypt *n.* i-jip-t'ŭ 이집트.　　　　　　　　└자만.
eight *n.* yŏ-dŏl 여덟, p'al 8.
eighteen *n.* yŏl-yŏ-dŏl 열여덟, sip-p'al 18.
eighty *n.* yŏ-dŭn 여든, p'al-sip 80.
either *pron. & adj.* ŏ-nŭ han-jjok 어느 한쪽. —*adv.*
　& conj. ···gŏ-na ···gŏ-na ···거나 ···거나.
ejaculate *v.* kap-ja-gi so-ri chi-rŭ-da 갑자기 소리 지르다.
eject *v.* ① ch'u-bang-ha-da 추방하다, myŏn-jik-si-k'i-
　da 면직시키다. ② (*emit*) ppum-ŏ-nae-da 뿜어내다.
elaborate *adj.* chŏng-sŏng-dŭ-rin 정성들인; chŏng-
　gyo-han 정교한. —*v.* chŏng-gyo-ha-ge man-dŭl-da
　정교하게 만들다, ta-dŭm-da 다듬다.
elapse *v.* (*pass away*) kyŏng-gwa-ha-da 경과하다.
elastic *n.* ko-mu-ggŭn 고무끈. —*adj.* t'al-lyŏk-sŏng-
　it-nŭn 탄력성있는, sin-ch'uk-sŏng-it-nŭn 신축성있는.
elate *v.* ki-un-ŭl puk-do-du-da 기운을 북돋우다, ŭi-gi-
　yang-yang-ha-ge ha-da 의기양양하게 하다.
elbow *n.* p'al-ggum-ch'i 팔꿈치. —*v.* p'al-ggum-ch'i-ro
　ttŏ-mil-da 팔꿈치로 떠밀다.
elder *adj.* (*older*) son-wi-ŭi 손위의, yŏn-jang-ŭi 연장
　의. —*n.* yŏn-jang-ja 연장자, sŏn-bae 선배.
elder brother (*male's*) hyŏng-nim 형님; (*female's*)
　o-bba 오빠.
elderly *adj.* ① na-i-ga chi-gŭt-han 나이가 지긋한, ch'o-
　ro-ŭi 초로(初老)의. ② ku-sik-ŭi 구식의.　　「언니.
elder sister (*male's*) nu-nim 누님; (*female's*) ŏn-ni
eldest daughter k'ŭn-ddal 큰딸, chang-nyŏ 장녀.

eldest son k'ŭn-a-dŭl 큰아들, chang-nam 장남.

elect *v.* (*choose*) ppop-da 뽑다, sŏn-gŏ-ha-da 선거하다.
　—*adj.* tang-sŏn-doen 당선된. 　　　　　　「총선거.

election *n.* sŏn-gŏ 선거 : *a general* ～ ch'ong-sŏn-gŏ

electric *adj.* chŏn-gi-ŭi 전기의 : ～ *bulb* chŏn-gu 전구/
　 ～ *current* chŏl-lyu 전류/ ～ *fan* sŏn-p'ung-gi 선풍
　기/ ～ *heater* chŏn-yŏl-gi 전열기/ ～ *light* chŏn-dŭng
　전등/～ *power house* pal-jŏn-so 발전소.

electrician *n.* chŏn-gi ki-sa 전기 기사.

electricity *n.* chŏn-gi 전기, chŏn-gi-hak 전기학.

electron *n.* chŏn-ja 전자(電子), el-rek-t'ŭ-ron 엘렉트론.

elegant *adj.* u-a-han 우아한, ko-sang-han 고상한.

elegy *n.* pi-ga 비가, ae-ga 애가(哀歌).

element *n.* yo-so 요소, wŏn-so 원소, sŏng-bun 성분.

elementary *adj.* ki-bon-jŏk-in 기본적인, ch'o-bo-ŭi 초보

elementary school kuk-min-hak-gyo 국민학교. 　　「의.

elephant *n.* k'o-ggi-ri 코끼리.

elevate *v.* ① ol-ri-da 올리다 ; sŭng-jin-si-k'i-da 승진시
　키다. ② (*excite*) ko-mu-ha-da 고무하다. 　　「이터.

elevator *n.* sŭng-gang-gi 승강기, el-ri-be-i-t'ŏ 엘리베

eleven *n.* yŏl-ha-na 열하나, sip-il 11. 　　「이 있는.

eligible *adj.* p'i-sŏn-gŏ cha-gyŏk-i it-nŭn 피선거 자격

eliminate *v.* ① che-gŏ-ha-da 제거하다, sak-je-ha-da 삭
　제하다. ② (*ignore*) mu-si-ha-da 무시하다.

elite *n.* el-ri-t'ŭ 엘리트, chŏng-su 정수(精粹).

elm *n.* nŭ-rŭp-na-mu 느릅나무.

eloquent *adj.* mal chal-ha-nŭn 말 잘하는, ung-byŏn-
　jŏk-in 웅변적인, sŏl-dŭk-ryŏk-it-nŭn 설득력있는.

else *adv.* kŭ-ba-gge 그밖에 : *or* ～ kŭ-rŏ-ch'i an-ŭ-myŏn
　그렇지 않으면. 　　　　　「u-e 다른 경우에.

elsewhere *adv.* ta-rŭn kŏ-se 다른 곳에 ; ta-rŭn kyŏng-

embankment *n.* che-bang 제방, tuk 둑.

embark *v*. ① (*board*) pae-rŭl t'a-da 배를 타다. ② (*start*) ch'ul-bal-ha-da 출발하다.

embarrass *v*. nan-ch'ŏ-ha-ge ha-da 난처하게 하다, hol-lan-k'e ha-da 혼란케 하다 ; pang-hae-ha-da 방해하다.

embassy *n*. tae-sa-gwan 대사관.

embellish *v*. (*decorate*) a-rŭm-dap-ge ha-da 아름답게 하다 ; chang-sik-ha-da 장식하다.

emblem *n*. (*symbol*) sang-jing 상징 ; (*type*) chŏn-hyŏng 전형 ; (*mark*) p'yo-ji 표지. 「da 구현하다.

embody *v*. ku-ch'e-hwa-ha-da 구체화하다, ku-hyŏn-ha-

embrace *n*. p'o-ong 포옹. —*v*. kkyŏ-an-da 껴안다.

embroider *v*. su-no-t'a 수놓다, yun-saek-ha-da 윤색하다.

embroidery *n*. su 수(繡), cha-su 자수.

embryo *n*. ① t'ae-a 태아. ② pae-a 배아(胚芽).

emerald *n*. e-mŏ-ral-dŭ 에머랄드, ch'wi-ok 취옥.

emerge *v*. na-t'a-na-da 나타나다 ; pŏ-sŏ-na-da 벗어나다.

emergency *n*. pi-sang-sa-t'ae 비상사태, kin-gŭp-sa-t'ae 긴급사태, wi-gi 위기.

emigrant *n*. i-ju-min 이주민. —*adj*. i-min-ŭi 이민의.

emigrate *v*. i-min-ha-da 이민하다, i-ju-ha-da 이주하다.

eminence *n*. ① (*high position*) ko-wi 고위. ② (*superiority*) t'ak-wŏl 탁월. ③ (*lofty place*) ko-ji 고지.

eminent *adj*. ① chŏ-myŏng-han 저명한 ; t'ak-wŏl-han 탁월한. ② (*prominent*) t'wi-ŏ-na-on 튀어나온.

emotion *n*. chŏng-sŏ 정서 ; kam-dong 감동 ; kam-jŏng 감정.

emperor *n*. hwang-je 황제, che-wang 제왕. 「감정.

emphasize *v*. kang-jo-ha-da 강조하다, yŏk-sŏl-ha-da 역설하다.

empire *n*. che-guk 제국, che-jŏng 제정(帝政).

employ *v*. ch'ae-yong-ha-da 채용하다 ; (*use*) sa-yong-ha-da 사용하다. —*n*. ko-yong 고용 ; kŭn-mu 근무.

employe(e) *n*. ko-yong-in 고용인, chong-ŏp-wŏn 종업원.

employer *n.* ko-yong-ju 고용주, chu-in 주인.
employment *n.* ko-yong 고용, chik-ŏp 직업.
empress *n.* hwang-hu 황후, wang-bi 왕비.
empty *adj.* pin 빈 ; hŏt-doen 헛된. —*v.* pi-u-da 비우다.
emulate *v.* ① kyŏ-ru-da 겨루다, kyŏng-jaeng-ha-da
경쟁하다. ② …wa tong-gyŏk-i-da …와 동격이다.
enable *v.* …hal su it-ge ha-da …할 수 있게 하다.
enact *v.* ① (*decree*) che-jŏng-ha-da 제정하다, kyu-jŏng-
ha-da 규정하다. ② (*act*) sang-yŏn-ha-da 상연하다.
enamel *n.* e-na-mel 에나멜. —*v.* e-na-mel-ŭl ip-hi-da
에나멜을 입히다. 「hok-ha-da 매혹하다.
enchant *v.* hwang-hol-ha-ge ha-da 황홀하게 하다, mae-
encircle *v.* tul-rŏ-ssa-da 둘러싸다. 「워싸다.
enclose *v.* pong-hae nŏ-t'a 봉해 넣다, e-wŏ-ssa-da 에
encompass *v.* tul-rŏ-ssa-da 둘러싸다.
encore *int.* ang-k'o-o-rŭ 앙코오르. 「닥치다.
encounter *v.* ma-ju-ch'i-da 마주치다, pu-dak-ch'i-da 부
encourage *v.* yong-gi-rŭl chu-da 용기를 주다 ; chang-
ryŏ-ha-da 장려하다 ; cho-jang-ha-da 조장하다.
encouragement *n.* chang-ryŏ 장려, kyŏk-ryŏ 격려.
encroach *v.* ch'im-ip-ha-da 침입하다, ch'im-hae-ha-da
encyclopaedia *n.* paek-gwa-sa-jŏn 백과사전. 「침해하다.
end *n.* kkŭt 끝 ; (*purpose*) mok-jŏk 목적; (*close*) kyŏl-
mal 결말. —*v.* kkŭt-nae-da 끝내다.
endanger *v.* wi-t'ae-rop-ge ha-da 위태롭게 하다.
endear *v.* ae-jŏng-ŭl nŭ-ggi-ge ha-da 애정을 느끼게 하다.
endeavo(u)r *n.* (*effort*) no-ryŏk 노력 ; si-do 시도.
—*v.* no-ryŏk-ha-da 노력하다 ; si-do-ha-da 시도하다.
ending *n.* (*termination*) kyŏl-mal 결말, ma-ji-mak 마
지막 ; (*death*) chuk-ŭm 죽음.
endless *adj.* kkŭt-ŏp-nŭn 끝없는, mu-han-han 무한한.
endorse *v.* ① i-sŏ-ha-da 이서(裏書)하다. ② po-jŭng-ha-

da 보증하다. ③ chi-ji-ha-da 지지하다.
endow *v.* (*give*) chu-da 주다, pu-yŏ-ha-da 부여하다,
ki-bu-ha-da 기부하다. 「내(력).
endurance *n.* ch'am-ŭl-sŏng 참을성, in-nae(-ryŏk) 인
endure *v.* kyŏn-di-da 견디다, chi-t'aeng-ha-da 지탱하다.
enemy *n.* chŏk 적, chŏk-gun 적군, chŏk-guk 적국.
energy *n.* him 힘, e-nŏ-ji 에너지.
enforce *v.* ① sil-si-ha-da 실시하다, si-haeng-ha-da 시
행하다. ② (*impose*) kang-yo-ha-da 강요하다.
engage *v.* ① chong-sa-ha-da 종사하다. ② yak-sok-ha-
da 약속하다. ③ (*betroth*) yak-hon-ha-da 약혼하다.
engagement *n.* ① yak-hon 약혼. ② yak-sok 약속.
engine *n.* ki-gwan 기관, pal-dong-gi 발동기.
engineer *n.* ki-sa 기사, kong-hak-ja 공학자(工學者).
England *n.* yŏng-guk 영국, ing-gŭl-raen-dŭ 잉글랜드.
English *n.* & *adj.* (*language*) yŏng-ŏ(-ui) 영어(의).
Englishman *n.* yŏng-guk-sa-ram 영국사람.
engrave *v.* cho-gak-ha-da 조각하다, sae-gi-da 새기다.
engross *v.* ① (*fill one's mind*) yŏl-jung-k'e ha-da 열중
케 하다. ② (*monopolize*) tok-jŏm-ha-da 독점하다.
enhance *v.* no-p'i-da 높이다, ang-yang-ha-da 앙양하다.
enjoin *v.* pu-gwa-ha-da 부과하다 ; myŏng-ha-da 명하다.
enjoy *v.* chŭl-gi-da 즐기다, (*possess*) nu-ri-da 누리다.
enjoyment *n.* hyang-rak 향락, hyang-yu 향유(享有).
enlarge *v.* k'ŭ-ge ha-da 크게 하다, hwak-dae〔chŭng-
dae〕-ha-da 확대〔증대〕하다. 「교화하다.
enlighten *v.* kye-mong-ha-da 계몽하다, kyo-hwa-ha-da
enlist *v.* ① (*in army*) ŭng-mo-ha-da 응모하다, ip-dae-
ha-da 입대하다. ② to-um-ŭl pat-da 도움을 받다.
enmity *n.* chŭng-o 증오, chŏk-ŭi 적의(敵意).
enormous *adj.* kŏ-dae-han 거대한, mak-dae-han 막대
한 : ~ *profits* mak-dae-han i-ik 막대한 이익.

enough *adj*. ch'ung-bun-han 충분한. —*adv*. nŏk-nŏk-ha-ge 넉넉하게. —*n*. ch'ung-bun-ham 충분함.

enrage *v*. kyŏk-bun-si-k'i-da 격분시키다, no-ha·ge ha-da 노하게 하다.

enrich *v*. pu-yu-ha·ge ha-da 부유하게 하다.

enrol(l) *v*. ① tŭng-rok-ha-da 등록하다, pyŏng-jŏk-e ol-ri-da 병적에 올리다. ② (*in school*) ip-hak-si-k'i-da 입학시키다.

ensign *n*. ① (*badge*) ki-jang 기장. ② (*flag*) ki 기.

ensure *v*. ① (*protect*) po-ho-ha-da 보호하다. ② (*make certain of*) hwak-sil-ha·ge ha-da 확실하게 하다. ③ (*guarantee*) po-jŭng-ha-da 보증하다.

entangle *v*. ŏl-k'i-ge ha-da 얽히게 하다, nan-ch'ŏ-ha-ge ha-da 난처하게 하다.

enter *v*. ① (*go into*) tŭ-rŏ-ga-da 들어가다 ; (*start*) si-jak-ha-da 시작하다. ② (*join*) ka-ip-ha-da 가입하다. ③ (*record*) ki-ip-ha-da 기입하다.

enterprise *n*. sa-ŏp 사업, ki-ŏp 기업, ki-hoek 기획.

entertain *v*. ① (*amuse*) hŭng-gyŏp-ge ha-da 흥겹게 하다. ② (*hospitality*) hwan-dae-ha-da 환대하다. ③ (*harbor*) ma-ŭm-e p'um-da 마음에 품다.

entertainment *n*. chŏp-dae 접대, hwan-dae 환대.

enthusiasm *n*. yŏl-gwang 열광, yŏl-sim 열심.

enthusiastic *adj*. yŏl-gwang-jŏk-in 열광적인.

entice *v*. yu-hok-ha-da 유혹하다, kkoe-da 꾀다.

entire *adj*. chŏn-ch'e-ŭi 전체의, wan-jŏn-han 완전한.

entirely *adv*. wan-jŏn-hi 완전히, chŏn-hyŏ 전혀.

entitle *v*. cha-gyŏk-ŭl chu-da 자격을 주다, myŏng-ch'ing-ŭl pu-ch'i-da 명칭을 붙이다.

entrails *n*. nae-jang 내장, ch'ang-ja 창자.

entrance *n*. ① ip-jang 입장(入場), ip-hoe 입회. ② (*door*) ip-gu 입구 : ~ *fee* ip-jang-ryo 입장료.

entreat *v.* kan-ch'ŏng-ha-da 간청하다.
entrust *v.* wi-im-ha-da 위임하다, mat-gi-da 맡기다.
enumerate *v.* se-da 세다 ; yŏl-gŏ-ha-da 열거하다.
envelop *v.* ssa-da 싸다, pong-ha-da 봉하다.
envelope *n.* pong-t'u 봉투, (*wrapper*) ssa-gae 싸개.
envious *adj.* pu-rŏ-wŏ-ha-nŭn 부러워하는, sae-am-ha-nŭn 새암하는 ; chil-t'u-sim-i kang-han 질투심이 강한.
environment *n.* hwan-gyŏng 환경.
envy *n.* chil-t'u 질투, si-gi 시기, sŏn-mang 선망. —*v.* pu-rŏ-wŏ-ha-da 부러워하다.
epidemic *n.* yu-haeng-byŏng 유행병, chŏn-yŏm-byŏng 전염병. —*adj.* yu-haeng-sŏng-ŭi 유행성의.
Episcopalian Church kam-dok-gyo-hoe 감독교회.
episode *n.* sap-hwa 삽화, e-p'i-so-u-dŭ 에피소우드.
epitaph *n.* pi-mun 비문, pi-myŏng 비명(碑銘).
epoch *n.* (*new era*) sin-gi-wŏn 신기원, sin-si-dae 신시대 ; (*age*) si-dae 시대.
epoch-making *adj.* hoek-gi-jŏk-in 획기적인.
equal *adj.* ka-t'ŭn 같은, tong-dŭng-han 동등한.
equality *n.* p'yŏng-dŭng 평등, kyun-dŭng 균등. 「하게.
equally *adv.* ttok-ga-ch'i 똑같이, kyun-dŭng-ha-ge 균등
equation *n.* pang-jŏng-sik 방정식, tŭng-sik 등식.
equator *n.* chŏk-do 적도.   「춘〔추〕분.
equinox *n.* *the vernal*〔*autumnal*〕 ～ ch'un〔ch'u〕-bun
equip *v.* chun-bi-ha-da 준비하다, kat-ch'u-da 갖추다.
equipment *n.* sŏl-bi 설비, chang-gu 장구(裝具).
equivalent *adj.* tong-dŭng-han 동등한.
era *n.* ki-wŏn 기원(紀元), yŏn-dae 연대, si-dae 시대.
erase *v.* chi-u-da 지우다, sak-je-ha-da 삭제하다.
eraser *n.* chi-u-gae 지우개, ko-mu-ji-u-gae 고무지우개.
erect *adj.* kot-ŭn 곧은. —*v.* se-u-da 세우다.
err *v.* kŭ-rŭ-ch'i-da 그르치다, t'ŭl-ri-da 틀리다.

rrand *n.* sim-bu-rŭm 심부름 ; (*mission*) sa-myŏng 사명 ; (*business*) pol-il 볼일, yong-gŏn 용건.

error *n.* chal-mot 잘못, (*fault*) e-rŏ 에러.

erupt *v.* t'ŏ-jyŏ na-o-da 터져 나오다, p'ok-bal-ha-da 폭발하다, pun-ch'ul-ha-da 분출하다.

eruption *n.* ① p'ok-bal 폭발. ② (*volcano*) pun-hwa 분화(噴火). ③ (*rash*) pal-jin 발진(發疹).

escape *n.* & *v.* to-mang(-ga-da) 도망(가다).

escort *v.* ho-song-ha-da 호송하다, ho-wi-ha-da 호위하다.

especial *adj.* t'ŭk-byŏl-han 특별한, t'ŭk-su-han 특수한.

espionage *n.* kan-ch'ŏp (haeng-wi) 간첩 (행위).

espouse *v.* (*take a wife*) chang-ga-dŭl-da 장가들다.

essay *n.* non-mun 논문, su-p'il 수필.

essence *n.* ① pon-jil 본질, chin-su 진수 : *the ~ of happiness* haeng-bok-ŭi pon-jil 행복의 본질. ② (*extract*) ek-sŭ 엑스.　　　　　「주요점.

essential *adj.* pon-jil-jŏk-in 본질적인. —*n.* chu-yo-jŏm

establish *v.* ① (*found*) sŏl-rip-ha-da 설립하다. ② (*constitute*) che-jŏng-ha-da 제정하다. ③ (*prove*) hwak-jŭng-ha-da 확증하다.

establishment *n.* ① sŏl-rip 설립, hwak-rip 확립. ② (*system*) che-do 제도. ③ si-sŏl 시설.

estate *n.* ① (*land*) t'o-ji 토지 ; (*property*) chae-san 재산. ② (*rank*) sin-bun 신분, chi-wi 지위.

esteem *n.* chon-jung 존중, chon-gyŏng 존경. —*v.* ① chon-gyŏng-ha-da 존경하다. ② (*consider*) kan-ju-ha-da 간주하다, yŏ-gi-da 여기다.

estimate *v.* p'yŏng-ga-ha-da 평가하다. —*n.* (*of cost*) kyŏn-jŏk 견적(見積) : *a written ~* kyŏn-jŏk-sŏ 견적서.

estrange *v.* (*turn away*) sa-i-rŭl na-bbŭ-ge ha-da 사이를 나쁘게 하다, i-gan-ha-da 이간하다.

et cetera ki-t'a tŭng-dŭng 기타 등등, tta-wi 따위.

eternal *adj.* yŏng-wŏn-han 영원한, pul-hu-ŭi 불후의.
eternity *n.* yŏng-wŏn 영원, mu-gung 무궁.
ethics *n.* yul-li-(hak) 윤리(학).
Ethiopia *n.* i-di-o-p'i-a 이디오피아.
etiquette *n.* ye-ŭi pŏm-jŏl 예의 범절, e-t'i-k'et 에티켓.
etymology *n.* ŏ-wŏn 어원(語源), ŏ-wŏn-hak 어원학.
Europe *n.* yu-rŏp 유럽, ku-ju 구주.　　　　「유럽사람.
European *adj.* yu-rŏp-ŭi 유럽의. —*n.* yu-rŏp-sa-ram
evacuation *n.* ch'ŏl-gŏ 철거, myŏng-do 명도.
evade *v.* p'i-ha-da 피하다, t'al-ch'ul-ha-da 탈출하다.
evangelist *n.* pok-ŭm chŏn-do-ja 복음 전도자.
evaporate *v.* ① chŭng-bal-ha-da 증발하다, so-san-ha-
　da 소산(消散)하다. ② t'al-su-ha-da 탈수하다.　　.
eve *n.* chŏn-ya 전야, chŏn-nal-bam 전날밤 : *Christmas*
　~ k'ŭ-ri-sŭ-ma-sŭ chŏn-ya 크리스마스 전야.
even *adj.* (*level*) p'yŏng-p'yŏng-han 평평한. —*adv.*
　pi-rok 비록, …cho-ch'a-do …조차도.
evening *n.* chŏ-nyŏk 저녁, hae-jil-nyŏk 해질녘.
event *n.* ① sa-gŏn 사건. ② (*outcome*) sŏng-gwa 성과.
　③ (*in sport*) kyŏng-gi chong-mok 경기 종목.
eventually *adv.* kyŏl-guk 결국, ma-ch'im-nae 마침내.
ever *adv.* ① yŏ-t'ae-ggŏt 여태껏, il-jji-gi 일찌기. ②
　(*always*) ŏn-je-na 언제나.
everlasting *adj.* kkŭt-ŏp-nŭn 끝없는, yŏng-wŏn-han
　영원한. —*n.* yŏng-gu 영구, yŏng-wŏn 영원.
evermore *adv.* hang-sang 항상, yŏng-wŏn-hi 영원히.
every *adj.* mo-dŭn 모든, (*all possible*) on-gat 온갖 ;
　mae… 매…, …ma-da …마다 : ~ *day* mae-il 매일/
　~ *four day* na-hŭl-jjae-ma-da 나흘째마다.
everybody *pron.* nu-gu-na 누구나, che-gak-gi 제각기.
everyday *adj.* nal-ma-da-ŭi 날마다의, mae-il-ŭi 매일의.
everyone *pron.* nu-gu-na 누구나, kak-ja 각자.

everything *pron.* ① mu-ŏ-si-dŭn-ji 무엇이든지, man-sa 만사. ② ka-jang chung-yo-han kŏt 가장 중요한 것.
everywhere *adv.* ŏ-di-dŭn-ji 어디든지, to-ch'ŏ-e 도처에.
evidence *n.* chŭng-gŏ 증거, (*pl.*) ching-hu 징후.
evident *adj.* myŏng-baek-han 명백한, pun-myŏng-han 분명한, tt'u-ryŏt-han 뚜렷한.
evil *adj.* na-bbŭn 나쁜, sa-ak-han 사악한, pul-gil-han 불길한. —*n.* ak 악, chae-hae 재해. 「기시키다.
evoke *v.* pul-rŏ-nae-da 불러내다, hwan-gi-si-k'i-da 환
evolution *n.* chin-hwa 진화(進化), chŏn-gae 전개.
evolve *v.* ① chŏn-gae-ha-da 전개하다. ② chin-hwa-ha-da 진화하다. ③ (*give off*) pang-ch'ul-ha-da 방출하다.
exact *adj.* chŏng-hwak-han 정확한, chŏng-mil-han 정밀한 ; ŏm-gyŏk-han 엄격한. 「si 틀림없이.
exactly *adv.* chŏng-hwak-ha-ge 정확하게, t'ŭl-rim-ŏp-
exaggerate *v.* kwa-jang-ha-da 과장하다.
exalt *v.* ① (*raise high*) no-p'i-da 높이다. ② sŭng-jin-si-k'i-da 승진시키다. ③ ch'ing-ch'an-ha-da 칭찬하다.
examination *n.* ① si-hŏm 시험, kŏm-sa 검사. ② kŏm-t'o 검토. ③ sin-mun 신문.
examine *v.* ① si-hŏm-ha-da 시험하다, sim-sa-ha-da 심사하다. ② kŏm-t'o-ha-da 검토하다, cho-sa-ha-da 조사
example *n.* po-gi 보기, sil-rye 실례, mo-bŏm 모범. 「하다.
exasperate *v.* yak-o-rŭ-ge ha-da 약오르게 하다, hwa-na-ge ha-da 화나게 하다.
excavate *v.* (*dig*) p'a-da 파다, pal-gul-ha-da 발굴하다.
exceed *v.* nŏm-da 넘다, nŭng-ga-ha-da 능가하다.
exceedingly *adv.* chi-gŭk-hi 지극히, mop-si 몹시.
excel *v.* (po-da) nat-da (보다) 낫다, nŭng-ga-ha-da 능가하다, t'ak-wŏl-ha-da 탁월하다.
excellent *adj.* u-su-han 우수한, hul-ryung-han 훌륭한.
except *prep.* …ŭl che-oe-ha-go …을 제외하고. —*v.*

che-oe-ha-da 제외하다.
exception *n.* ye-oe 예외, che-oe 제외.
exceptional *adj.* ye-oe-jŏk-in 예외적인, tŭ-mun 드문.
excess *n.* ch'o-gwa 초과, kwa-da 과다 ; yŏ-bun 여분.
exchange *n.* & *v.* kyo-hwan(-ha-da) 교환(하다).
excite *v.* cha-gŭk-ha-da 자극하다, i-rŭ-k'i-da 일으키다.
excitement *n.* hŭng-bun 흥분, cha-gŭk 자극.
exclaim *v.* (*cry out*) oe-ch'i-da 외치다.
exclamation *n.* ① oe-ch'im 외침. ② kam-t'an 감탄.
exclude *v.* nae-jjot-da 내쫓다, pae-ch'ŏk-ha-da 배척하다.
excursion *n.* so-p'ung 소풍, yu-ram 유람.
excuse *n.* ku-sil 구실, p'ing-gye 핑계. —*v.* ① yong-sŏ-ha-da 용서하다. ② pyŏn-myŏng-ha-da 변명하다.
execute *v.* ① (*carry out*) sil-haeng-ha-da 실행하다. ② (*punish*) ch'ŏ-hyŏng-ha-da 처형하다.
execution *n.* ① (*performance*) su-haeng 수행. ② (*punishment*) sa-hyŏng chip-haeng 사형 집행.
executioner *n.* ① su-haeng-ja 수행자. ② (*hangman*) sa-hyŏng chip-haeng-ja 사형 집행자.
executive *adj.* haeng-jŏng-jŏk-in 행정적인. —*n.* haeng-jŏng-gwan 행정관 ; kan-bu yŏk-wŏn 간부 역원.
exercise *n.* un-dong 운동 ; yŏn-sŭp 연습. —*v.* un-dong-ha-da 운동하다 ; yŏn-sŭp-ha-da 연습하다.
exert *v.* him-ŭl nae-da 힘을 내다 ; (*put forth*) pal-hwi-ha-da 발휘하다 ; hwi-du-rŭ-da 휘두르다.
exertion *n.* no-ryŏk 노력, pun-bal 분발.
exhaust *v.* ① ssŏ-bŏ-ri-da 써버리다, t'ang-jin-ha-da 탕진하다. ② (*tire out*) chi-ch'i-ge ha-da 지치게 하다.
exhaustion *n.* so-mo 소모 ; p'i-ro 피로.
exhibit *v.* chŏn-si-ha-da 전시하다, chŏl-lam-ha-da 전람하다. —*n.* ch'ul-p'um 출품. 「회.
exhibition *n.* chŏl-lam-hoe 전람회, pak-ram-hoe 박람

exile *n*. ① ch'u-bang 추방. ② (*person*) mang-myŏng-ja 망명자. —*v*. ch'u-bang-ha-da 추방하다.
exist *v*. chon-jae-ha-da 존재하다, sa-ra-it-da 살아있다.
existence *n*. chon-jae 존재, sil-jae 실재. 「da 퇴장하다.
exit *n*. ch'ul-gu 출구 ; t'oe-jang 퇴장. —*v*. t'oe-jang-ha-
expand *v*. p'ŏ-ji-da 퍼지다, hwak-jang-ha-da 확장하다, p'aeng-ch'ang-ha-da 팽창하다.
expect *v*. ki-dae-ha-da 기대하다, ye-gi-ha-da 예기하다.
expectation *n*. ki-dae 기대, ye-sang 예상.
expedient *adj*. p'yŏl-li-han 편리한 ; chŏk-dang-han 적당한. —*n*. pang-p'yŏn 방편.
expedition *n*. wŏn-jŏng 원정 ; t'am-hŏm 탐험.
expel *v*. ① ch'u-bang-ha-da 추방하다. ② (*from school*) t'oe-hak-si-k'i-da 퇴학시키다.
expense *n*. pi-yong 비용 ; (*expenditure*) chi-ch'ul 지출.
expensive *adj*. kap-bi-ssan 값비싼.
experience *n*. kyŏng-hŏm 경험, ch'e-hŏm 체험. —*v*. kyŏng-hŏm〔ch'e-hŏm〕-ha-da 경험〔체험〕하다.
experiment *n*. & *v*. sil-hŏm(-ha-da) 실험(하다).
expert *adj*. ik-suk-han 익숙한, no-ryŏn-han 노련한. —*n*. chŏn-mun-ga 전문가, myŏng-su 명수.
expire *v*. ① sum-ŭl nae-swi-da 숨을 내쉬다. ② (*terminate*) man-gi-ga toe-da 만기가 되다. ③ (*die out*) so-myŏl-ha-da 소멸하다, chuk-da 죽다.
explain *v*. sŏl-myŏng-ha-da 설명하다, pal-k'i-da 밝히다.
explanation *n*. sŏl-myŏng 설명, hae-sŏl 해설.
explicit *adj*. (*clear*) myŏng-baek-han 명백한, (*out-spoken*) sum-gim-ŏp-nŭn 숨김없는. 「하다.
explode *v*. p'ok-bal-ha-da 폭발하다, p'a-yŏl-ha-da 파열
exploit *n*. kong-jŏk 공적, kong-hun 공훈. —*v*. ① i-yong-ha-da 이용하다. ② (*cultivate*) kae-bal-ha-da 개발하다. ③ (*extract*) ch'ak-ch'wi-ha-da 착취하다.

exploration *n*. t'am-hŏm 탐험, tap-sa 답사.

explore *v*. t'am-hŏm-ha-da 탐험하다 ; (*search into*) t'am-gu-ha-da 탐구하다, cho-sa-ha-da 조사하다.

explorer *n*. t'am-hŏm-ga 탐험가, t'am-gu-ja 탐구자.

explosion *n*. p'ok-bal 폭발, p'a-yŏl 파열.   「수출품.

export *v*. su-ch'ul-ha-da 수출하다. —*n*. su-ch'ul-p'um

expose *v*. no-ch'ul-ha-da 노출하다, tŭ-rŏ-nae-da 드러

exposure *n*. no-ch'ul 노출, p'ok-ro 폭로.   └내다.

express *v*. p'yo-hyŏn-ha-da 표현하다, na-t'a-nae-da 나 타내다. —*adj*. t'ŭk-byŏl-han 특별한. —*n*. ① kŭp- haeng-yŏl-ch'a 급행열차. ② sok-dal 속달.

expression *n*. ① p'yo-hyŏn 표현. ② p'yo-jŏng 표정.

exquisite *adj*. chŏng-gyo-han 정교한, sŏm-se-han 섬세 한 ; (*sharp*) nal-k'a-ro-un 날카로운.

extend *v*. nŭ-ri-da 늘이다, hwak-jang-ha-da 확장하다 ; (*reach*) …e i-rŭ-da …에 이르다.

extensive *adj*. nŏl-bŭn 넓은, tae-gyu-mo-ŭi 대규모의.

extent *n*. nŏl-bi 넓이, p'ŏm-wi 범위 ; chŏng-do 정도.

exterior *adj*. pa-gga-t'ŭi 바깥의, oe-gwan-sang-ŭi 외관 상의. —*n*. oe-bu 외부, oe-mo 외모.

exterminate *v*. chŏn-myŏl-si-k'i-da 전멸시키다.

external *adj*. ① oe-bu-ŭi 외부의. ② hyŏng-sik-jŏk-in 형식적인. —*n*. oe-bu 외부, oe-mo 외모.

extinguish *v*. kkŭ-da 끄다 ; so-myŏl-si-k'i-da 소멸시키다.

extol(l) *v*. kyŏk-ch'an-ha-da 격찬하다.

extra *adj*. yŏ-bun-ŭi 여분의. —*n*. ① (*newspaper*) ho-oe 호외. ② ek-sŭ-t'ŭ-rŏ 엑스트러.

extract *v*. ppop-da 뽑다, pal-ch'we-ha-da 발췌하다. —*n*. ch'u-ch'ul-mul 추출물, (*excerpt*) pal-ch'we 발췌.

extraordinary *adj*. ① pi-sang-han 비상한, (*uncom- mon*) pi-bŏm-han 비범한, ŏm-ch'ŏng-nan 엄청난. ② (*additional*) im-si-ŭi 임시의.

extravagant *adj.* sa-ch'i-sŭ-rŏn 사치스런 ; t'ŏ-mu-ni-ŏp-nŭn 터무니없는, ŏm-ch'ŏng-nan 엄청난.

extreme *adj.* kŭk-dan-jŏk-in 극단적인 ; kwa-gyŏk-han 과격한 ; ch'oe-jong-ŭi 최종의. —*n.* kŭk-dan 극단.

eye *n.* nun 눈 : *artificial* ∼ ŭi-an 의안(義眼).

eyebrow *n.* nun-ssŏp 눈썹 : ∼ *pencil* nun-ssŏp ku-ri-gae 눈썹 그리개.

eyelash *n.* sok-nun-ssŏp 속눈썹.

eyelid *n.* nun-ggŏ-p'ul 눈꺼풀.

eyesight *n.* si-ryŏk 시력 ; si-gye 시계(視界).

F

fable *n.* u-hwa 우화(寓話).

fabric *n.* ① (*texture*) chik-mul 직물. ② (*building*) kŏn-mul 건물. ③ (*structure*) ku-jo 구조.

face *n.* ① ŏl-gul 얼굴. ② (*surface*) p'yo-myŏn 표면. —*v.* …e chik-myŏn-ha-da …에 직면하다.

facility *n.* ① yong-i-ham 용이함. ② (*skill*) chae-gan 재간. ③ (*convenience*) p'yŏn-ŭi 편의. ④ sŏl-bi 설비.

fact *n.* sa-sil 사실, sil-je 실제, chin-sang 진상.

faction *n.* tang-p'a(-sim) 당파(심), pun-jaeng 분쟁.

factor *n.* yo-so 요소, yo-in 요인, wŏn-dong-ryŏk 원동력.

factory *n.* kong-jang 공장, che-jak-so 제작소.

faculty *n.* ① chae-nŭng 재능. ② (*college*) hak-bu 학부.

fade *v.* si-dŭl-da 시들다, pa-rae-da 바래다.

fail *v.* sil-p'ae-ha-da 실패하다 ; pu-jok-ha-da 부족하다.

failure *n.* sil-p'ae 실패 ; nak-je 낙제.

faint *adj.* ① hŭi-mi-han 희미한; ka-nyal-p'ŭn 가냘픈. ② hyŏn-gi-jŭng-i na-nŭn 현기증이 나는. —*v.* ① hŭi-mi-hae-ji-da 희미해지다. ② ki-jŏl-ha-da 기절하다.

fair *adj.* ① a-rŭm-da-un 아름다운. ② (*just*) kong-p'yŏng-han 공평한. —*n.* si-jang 시장(市場) ; (*exhibi-

tion) kong-jin-hoe 공진회.

fairly *adv.* ① kong-jŏng-ha-ge 공정하게. ② (*pretty*) sang-dang-hi 상당히, kkwae 꽤.

fairy *n.* yo-jŏng 요정. —*adj.* yo-jŏng-ŭi 요정의.

faith *n.* sin-ang 신앙, sin-nyŏm 신념, ch'ung-sil 충실.

faithful *adj.* ch'ung-sil-han 충실한, sil-loe-hal su it-nŭn 신뢰할 수 있는, mit-ŭm-i kut-ŭn 믿음이 굳은.

faithless *adj.* sin-ŭi-ga ŏp-nŭn 신의가 없는, pul-sil-han [불실한.

falcon *n.* song-gol-mae 송골매.

fall *v.* ttŏ-rŏ-ji-da 떨어지다. —*n.* ① ch'u-rak 추락. ② (*autumn*) ka-ŭl 가을. ③ (*pl.*) p'ok-p'o 폭포.

false *adj.* (*untrue*) kŏ-ji-sŭi 거짓의, (*wrong*) ku-rŭt-doen 그릇된, (*unfaithful*) pul-sŏng-sil-han 불성실한.

falsehood *n.* kŏ-jit-mal 거짓말, hŏ-wi 허위.

falter *v.* ① (*stumble*) pi-t'ŭl-gŏ-ri-da 비틀거리다. ② (*stammer*) mal-ŭl tŏ-dŭm-da 말을 더듬다.

fame *n.* myŏng-sŏng 명성, se-p'yŏng 세평.

famed *adj.* i-rŭm-nan 이름난, yu-myŏng-han 유명한.

familiar *adj.* ch'in-han 친한 ; chal al-go it-nŭn 잘 알고 있는 ; hŭn-han 흔한.

family *n.* ka-jok 가족, ka-jŏng 가정.

famine *n.* ki-gŭn 기근, ki-a 기아.

famous *adj.* yu-myŏng-han 유명한.

fan *n.* pu-ch'ae 부채, p'aen 팬. —*v.* pu-ch'ae-jil-ha-da 부채질하다 ; sŏn-dong-ha-da 선동하다.

fancy *n.* kong-sang 공상 ; pyŏn-dŏk 변덕. —*v.* kong-sang-ha-da 공상하다.

[pu-ch'ae]

fantastic *adj.* kong-sang-jŏk-in 공상적인, (*capricious*) pyŏn-dŏk-sŭ-rŏ-un 변덕스러운, pyŏl-nan 별난.

far *adj.* mŏn 먼 ; yo-wŏn-han 요원한. —*adv.* mŏl-ri 멀리 : ~ *away* mŏl-ri-e 멀리에.

farce *n.* so-gŭk 소극(笑劇), ik-sal 익살.

fare *n.* ① (*carriage*) un-im 운임, yo-gŭm 요금. ② (*passenger*) sŭng-gaek 승객. ③ (*food*) um-sik-mul 음식물 : *good* ~ sŏng-ch'an 성찬.

farewell *int.* an-nyŏng 안녕. —*n.* chak-byŏl 작별.

farm *n.* ① nong-jang 농장. ② yang-sik-jang 양식장. —*v.* kyŏng-jak-ha-da 경작하다.

farmer *n.* nong-bu 농부, nong-min 농민. 「머슴.

farm hand nong-jang no-dong-ja 농장 노동자, mŏ-sŭm

farmhouse *n.* nong-ga 농가. 「농경.

farming *n.* nong-ŏp 농업, nong-sa 농사, nong-gyŏng

farmyard *n.* nong-ga-ŭi ma-dang 농가의 마당.

far-reaching *adj.* kwang-bŏm-wi-han 광범위한, mŏl-ri-gga-ji mi-ch'i-nŭn 멀리까지 미치는.

far-sighted *adj.* ① wŏn-si-ŭi 원시(遠視)의. ② (*far-seeing*) sŏn-gyŏn-ji-myŏng-i it-nŭn 선견지명이 있는.

farther *adj.* tŏ mŏn 더 먼. —*adv.* tŏ mŏl-ri 더 멀리.

fascinate *v.* mae-hok-ha-da 매혹하다, hwang-hol-k'e ha-da 황홀케 하다, noe-swae-ha-da 뇌쇄하다.

fashion *n.* ① yu-haeng 유행. ② (*mode*) pang-sik 방식 ; hyŏng 형. —*v.* hyŏng-sŏng-ha-da 형성하다.

fashionable *adj.* yu-haeng-e mat-nŭn 유행에 맞는.

fast *adj.* ppa-rŭn 빠른 ; tan-dan-han 단단한; pul-byŏn-ŭi 불변의. —*adv.* (*tight*) tan-dan-hi 단단히. —*n.* tan-sik 단식. —*v.* tan-sik-ha-da 단식하다.

fasten *v.* tong-yŏ-mae-da 동여매다, cham-gŭ-da 잠그다.

fastidious *adj.* kka-da-ro-un 까다로운.

fasting *n.* tan-sik 단식. —*adj.* tan-sik-ŭi 단식의 : *a* ~ *cure* tan-sik yo-bŏp 단식 요법.

fat *adj.* sal-jjin 살찐 ; (*fertile*) pi-ok-han 비옥한. —*n.* kut-gi-rŭm 굳기름, chi-bang 지방. 「명적인.

fatal *adj.* un-myŏng-ŭi 운명의, ch'i-myŏng-jŏk-in 치

fate *n.* ① un-myŏng 운명 ; ak-un 악운. ② chuk-ŭm 죽음.

father *n.* ① a-bŏ-ji 아버지, pu-ch'in 부친. ② (*founder*) si-jo 시조. ③ (*priest*) sin-bu 신부.

father-in-law ① (*man's*) chang-in 장인. ② (*woman's*) si-a-bŏ-ji 시아버지. ③ (*stepfather*) kye-bu 계부.

fathom *n.* kil 길 (6 *feet*). —*v.* ki-p'i-rŭl chae-da 깊이 를 재다, he-a-ri-da 헤아리다.

fatigue *n.* p'i-gon 피곤, p'i-ro 피로, no-go 노고(勞苦).

fault *n.* ① (*defect*) hŭm 흠, kyŏl-jŏm 결점. ② (*mistake*) kwa-o 과오, sil-su 실수. ③ (*sin*) choe 죄.

faultless *adj.* hŭm-ŏp-nŭn 흠없는, wan-jŏn-han 완전한.

favo(u)r *n.* ho-ŭi 호의, ch'ong-ae 총애 ; pu-t'ak 부탁. —*v.* ch'an-sŏng-ha-da 찬성하다 ; ch'in-jŏl-hi tae-ha-da 친절히 대하다, top-da 돕다.

favo(u)rite *adj.* ma-ŭm-e tŭ-nŭn 마음에 드는, a-ju cho-a-ha-nŭn 아주 좋아하는. —*n.* (*thing*) ma-ŭm-e tŭ-nŭn kŏt 마음에 드는 것 ; (*person*) ch'ong-a 총아.

fawn *n.* sae-ggi sa-sŭm 새끼 사슴.

fear *n.* kong-p'o 공포, kŏk-jŏng 걱정. —*v.* tu-ryŏ-wŏ-ha-da 두려워하다, kŏk-jŏng-ha-da 걱정하다.

feast *n.* ① ch'uk-je 축제, ch'uk-je-il 축제일. ② hyang-yŏn 향연, chan-ch'i 잔치. —*v.* (*regale*) sŏng-ch'an-ŭl tae-jŏp-ha-da 성찬을 대접하다. 「gi 묘기.

feat *n.* kong-jŏk 공적(功績) ; (*surprising trick*) myo-

feather *n.* (*plume*) kit 깃, kit-t'ŏl 깃털.

feature *n.* ① (*characteristic*) t'ŭk-jing 특징. ② (*appearance*) yong-mo 용모. ③ (*scoop*) t'ŭk-jong-gi-sa 특종기사 ; in-gi p'ŭ-ro 인기 프로.

February *n.* i-wŏl 2월. 「yŏn-bang-ŭi 연방의.

federal *adj.* ① yŏn-hap-ui 연합의. ② (*F~*) (*Am.*)

fee *n.* yo-gŭm 요금 : *an admission* ~ ip-jang-ryo 입장료 / *school* ~s su-ŏp-ryo 수업료.

feeble *adj.* yak-han 약한, ka-nyal-p'ŭn 가냘픈.
feed *v.* ① mŏk-i-da 먹이다; ki-rŭ-da 기르다. ②(*supply*) kong-gŭp-ha-da 공급하다. —*n.* ① (*for fowl*) mo-i 모이. ② (*for cattle, horses*) kkol 꼴, yŏ-mul 여물. ③ (*for dogs, cats*) pap 밥.
feel *v.* ① man-jyŏ po-da 만져 보다. ② (*with senses*) nŭ-ggi-da 느끼다. —*n.* nŭ-ggim 느낌.　「감정.
feeling *n.* nŭ-ggim 느낌, kam-gak 감각, (*pl.*) kam-jŏng
feign *v.* ① ka-jang-ha-da 가장(假裝)하다, …in ch'e-ha-da …인 체하다. ② (*forge*) wi-jo-ha-da 위조하다.
fellow *n.* ① ch'in-gu 친구, tong-ryo 동료; nom 놈, nyŏ-sŏk 녀석. ② (*man*) nam-ja 남자, sa-na-i 사나이.
female *n.* yŏ-sŏng 여성, yŏ-ja 여자. —*adj.* ① (*used as animals*) am-k'ŏ-sŭi 암컷의. ② (*people*) yŏ-sŏng-ŭi 여성의 : ~ *dress* pu-in-bok 부인복.
fence *n.* ① (*hedge*) ul-t'a-ri 울타리, (*wall*) tam 담. ② (*fencing*) kŏm-sul 검술.　「효소.
ferment *v.* pal-hyo-ha-da 발효(發酵)하다. —*n.* hyo-so
fern *n.* yang-ch'i-ryu 양치류, ko-sa-ri 고사리.
ferocious *adj.* ① hyung-ak-han 흉악한, chan-in-han 잔인한. ② sim-han 심한, mo-jin 모진.
ferry *n.* na-rut-bae 나룻배, na-ru-t'ŏ 나루터. —*v.* pae-ro kŏn-nŏ-da 배로 건너다.
ferryboat *n.* na-rut-bae 나룻배, yŏl-lak-sŏn 연락선.
ferryman *n.* na-rut-bae sa-gong 나룻배 사공.
fertile *adj.* ① (*productive*) ki-rŭm-jin 기름진, pi-ok-han 비옥한. ② (*prolific*) ta-san-ŭi 다산의.
fertilizer *n.* (*manure*) kŏ-rŭm 거름, pi-ryo 비료.
fervo(u)r *n.* yŏl-ryŏl 열렬, yŏl-jŏng 열정.
festival *n.* ch'uk-je(-il) 축제(일), chan-ch'i 잔치.
fetch *v.* ① ka-sŏ ka-jyŏ[te-ri-go]-o-da 가서 가져[데리고]오다. ② (*take out*) kkŏ-nae-da 꺼내다.

fetter *n.* ch'a-ggo 차꼬, chok-swae 족쇄. —*v.* ch'a-ggo-rŭl ch'ae-u-da 차꼬를 채우다, sok-bak-ha-da 속박하다.
feudal *adj.* yŏng-ji-ŭi 영지의, pong-gŏn-jŏk-in 봉건적인 : *the* ~ *system* pong-gŏn-je-do 봉건제도.
fever *n.* ko-yŏl 고열, yŏl-byŏng 열병 ; yŏl-gwang 열광.
few *adj.* so-su-ŭi 소수의, kŏ-ŭi ŏp-nŭn 거의 없는. —*n.* so-su 소수, tu-sŏ-nŏt 두서넛.
fiance *n.* (*male*) yak-hon-ja 약혼자.
fiber·fibre *n.* sŏm-yu 섬유, sŏm-yu-jil 섬유질.
fickle *adj.* (*changeable*) pyŏn-dŏk-sŭ-rŏ-un 변덕스러운, pyŏn-ha-gi swi-un 변하기 쉬운. 「sŏl 소설.
fiction *n.* ① (*invention*) hŏ-gu 허구. ② (*novel*) so-
fiddle *n.* che-gŭm 제금, (*violin*) pa-i-ol-rin 바이올린.
fidelity *n.* ch'ung-sil 충실, ch'ung-sŏng 충성.
field *n.* ① tŭl 들. ② (*scope*) pun-ya 분야.
field hospital ya-jŏn pyŏng-wŏn 야전 병원.
field marshal yuk-gun wŏn-su 육군 원수. 「(狂).
fiend *n.* (*devil*) ak-ma 악마, ma-gwi 마귀, kwang 광
fierce *adj.* sa-na-un 사나운, chi-dok-han 지독한.
fiery *adj.* pul-ga-t'ŭn 불같은, yŏl-ryŏl-han 열렬한 : ~ *heat* jji-nŭn-dŭt-han tŏ-wi 찌는듯한 더위.
fifteen *n.* yŏl-da-sŏt 열다섯, sip-o 15.
fifty *n.* swin 쉰, o-sip 50. —*adj.* man-ŭn 많은.
fig *n.* mu-hwa-gwa 무화과.
fight *v.* ssa-u-da 싸우다. —*n.* ① ssa-um 싸움, kyŏk-t'u 격투. ② (*contest*) sŭng-bu 승부.
figure *n.* ① (*form*) hyŏng-sang 형상, mo-yang 모양. ② (*appearance*) oe-no 외모, oe-gwan 외관. ③ (*design*) to-hae 도해, kŭ-rim 그림. ④ (*numeral*) sut-ja 숫자. —*v.* kŭ-ri-da 그리다. 「men-t'ŭ 필라멘트.
filament *n.* ① sŏm-yu-ŭi han ol 섬유의 한 올. ② p'il-la-
file *v.* ① (*papers*) ch'ŏl-ha-da 철하다. ② (*send in*)

che-ch'ul-ha-da 제출하다. —*n.* ① (*tool*) chul 줄. ②
(*for papers*) sŏ-ryu-ch'ŏl 서류철. ③ (*mil.*) tae-yŏl
대열.
filial *adj.* cha-sik-ŭ-ro-sŏ-ŭi 자식으로서의, hyo-sŏng-
sŭ-rŏ-un 효성스러운 : ~ *piety* hyo-do 효도.
filibuster *n.* ŭi-sa pang-hae-ja 의사(議事) 방해자.
fill *v.* ch'ae-u-da 채우다, me-u-da 메우다. —*n.* ch'ungbun 충분 ; (*satiety*) p'o-sik 포식.
film *n.* yŏl-bŭn mak 엷은 막 ; p'il-rŭm 필름.
filter *v.* kŏ-rŭ-da 거르다. —*n.* yŏ-gwa-gi 여과기.
filth *n.* ① ssŭ-re-gi 쓰레기, o-mul 오물 ; pun-nyŏ 분뇨.
  ② (*nasty language*) ŭm-dam-p'ae-sŏl 음담패설.
filthy *adj.* pul-gyŏl-han 불결한, ch'u-jap-han 추잡한.
fin *n.* chi-nŭ-rŏ-mi 지느러미. 「정적인.
final *adj.* ma-ji-mak-ŭi 마지막의, kyŏl-jŏng-jŏk-in 결
finally *adv.* ch'oe-hu-ro 최후로, ma-ch'im-nae 마침내.
finance *n.* ① chae-jŏng 재정, (*science*) chae-jŏng-hak
  재정학. ② (*pl.*) (*funds*) chae-wŏn 재원.
find *v.* ① pal-gyŏn-hae-nae-da 발견해내다. ② (*something lost*) ch'at-da 찾다. ③ (*learn*) al-da 알다.
fine *adj.* ① hul-ryung-han 훌륭한, u-su-han 우수한. ②
  (*very thin*) ka-nŭ-da-ran 가느다란. ③ (*handsome*)
  a-rŭm-da-un 아름다운. —*n.* pŏl-gŭm 벌금.
finger *n.* son-ga-rak 손가락 : *the ring* ~ mu-myŏng-ji
fingernail *n.* son-t'op 손톱. 「무명지.
fingerprint *n.* chi-mun 지문(指紋).
finish *v.* kkŭt-nae-da 끝내다, wan-sŏng-ha-da 완성하
  다. —*n.* kkŭt 끝, chong-gyŏl 종결, ma-mu-ri 마무리.
fir *n.* chŏn-na-mu 전나무.
fire *n.* pul 불, (*conflagration*) hwa-jae 화재. —*v.*
  ① (*set on fire*) pul no-t'a 불 놓다. ② (*a gun*)
  sso-da 쏘다. ③ (*from job*) hae-go-ha-da 해고하다.

fire alarm hwa-jae kyŏng-bo-gi 화재 경보기.
fire bomb so-i-t'an 소이탄.
fire brigade so-bang-dae 소방대.
firecracker *n.* p'ok-juk 폭죽, ttak-ch'ong 딱총.
fire engine so-hwa p'ŏm-p u 소화 펌프.
fire escape pi-sang-gu 비상구, so-bang sa-da-ri 소방 사
fire exit pi-sang-gu 비상구.　　　　　　　　└다리.
fire extinguisher so-hwa-gi 소화기(消火器).
firefly *n.* kae-ddong-bŏl-re 개똥벌레.
fireman *n.* ① so-bang-su 소방수. ② hwa-bu 화부.
fireplace *n.* nal-lo 난로, pyŏk-nal-lo 벽난로.
firewood *n.* chang-jak 장작, ttael-na-mu 땔나무.
firm *n.* sang-sa 상사, hoe-sa 회사. —*adj.* kyŏn-go-
　han 견고한, an-jŏng-doen 안정된.
first *adj.* ch'ŏt-jjae-ŭi 첫째의, che-il-ŭi 제일의. —*adv.*
　ch'ŏt-jjae-ro 첫째로. —*n.* ch'ŏt-jjae 첫째, che-il 제일.
fiscal *adj.* kuk-go-ŭi 국고의 ; chae-jŏng-sang-ŭi 재정
　상의 : *a* ~ *stamp* su-ip-in-ji 수입인지.
fish *n.* mul-go-gi 물고기, saeng-sŏn 생선. —*v.* nak-da
　낚다, ko-gi-rŭl chap-da 고기를 잡다.
fisherman *n.* ŏ-bu 어부 ; (*angler*) nak-sit-gun 낚싯군.
fishery *n.* ŏ-ŏp 어업, su-san-ŏp 수산업.
fishing *n.* ko-gi-jap-i 고기잡이, ŏ-ŏp 어업 : ~ *boat* ŏ-
　sŏn 어선/~ *line* nak-sit-jul 낚싯줄/~ *rod* nak-sit-
　dae 낚싯대/~ *village* ŏ-ch'on 어촌.　　　 └으로 치다.
fist *n.* chu-mŏk 주먹. —*v.* chu-mŏk-ŭ-ro ch'i-da 주먹
fit *adj.* chŏk-dang-han 적당한, al-ma-jŭn 알맞은 ; ŏ-
　ul-ri-nŭn 어울리는. —*v.* al-mat-da 알맞다, mat-ch'u-
　da 맞추다. —*n.* (*convulsion*) pal-jak 발작.
five *n.* ta-sŏt 다섯, o 5.　　　　　　　 └da 수리하다.
fix *v.* ko-jŏng-si-k'i-da 고정시키다 ; (*repair*) su-ri-ha-
flag *n.* ki 기 : *national* ~ kuk-gi 국기(國旗).

flail *n.* to-ri-ggae 도리깨.
flake *n.* yŏl-bŭn cho-gak 엷은 조각 : ∼*s of snow* nun-song-i 눈송이.
flame *n.* ① pul-ggot 불꽃. ② chŏng-yŏl 정열.
flank *n.* ① yŏp-gu-ri 옆구리. ② (*side*) ch'ŭk-myŏn 측면.
flannel *n.* p'ŭl-ran-nel 플란넬.
flap *v.* ① (*slap*) ch'al-ssak ttae-ri-da 찰싹 때리다. ② (*flutter*) na-p'ul-gŏ-ri-da 나풀거리다. ③ (*birds*) nal-gae-ch'i-da 날개치다.　[to-ri-ggae]
flare *n.* ① nŏ-ul-gŏ-ri-nŭn pul-ggot 너울거리는 불꽃. ② (*skirt*) p'ŭl-re-ŏ 플레어. —*v.* hwŏl-hwŏl t'a-o-rŭ-da 훨훨 타오르다, pŏn-jjŏk-i-da 번쩍이다.
flash *v.* pŏn-jjŏk-i-da 번쩍이다, hoek chi-na-ga-da 획 지나가다. —*n.* sŏm-gwang 섬광(閃光).
flask *n.* p'ŭl-ra-sŭ-k'ŭ 플라스크, t'an-yak-t'ong 탄약통.
flat *adj.* ① p'yŏng-p'yŏng-han 평평한. ② (*plain*) sol-jik-han 솔직한. —*n.* p'yŏng-myŏn 평면.
flatten *v.* p'yŏng-p'yŏng-ha-ge p'yŏ-da 평평하게 펴다, mu-mi-ha-ge ha-da 무미하게 하다.　「아첨하다.
flatter *v.* al-rang-gŏ-ri-da 알랑거리다, a-ch'ŏm-ha-da
flatterer *n.* a-ch'ŏm-gun 아첨군, ch'u-jong-ja 추종자.
flattery *n.* a-ch'ŏm 아첨, al-rang-dae-gi 알랑대기.
flaunt *n.* & *v.* kwa-si(-ha-da) 과시(하다), tŭ-rŏ-nae po-i-da 드러내 보이다, cha-rang-ha-da 자랑하다.
flavo(u)r *v.* yang-nyŏm-ha-da 양념하다. —*n.* mat 맛, p'ung-mi 풍미 ; (*fragrance*) hyang-gi 향기.
flaw *n.* hŭm 흠, kyŏl-jŏm 결점, kyŏl-ham 결함.
flax *n.* a-ma 아마 : ∼ *line* a-ma-sa 아마사(糸), sam-
flea *n.* pyŏ-ruk 벼룩.　　　　　　　　　　　　Lsil 삼실.
flee *v.* to-mang-ha-da 도망하다, ta-ra-na-da 달아나다.
fleece *n.* yang-t'ŏl 양털. —*v.* t'ŏl-ŭl kkak-da 털을 깎다.

fleet *n.* ham-dae 함대 : *a combined* ～ yŏn-hap-ham-dae 연합함대.　　　　　　　　　「ch'e 육체.

flesh *n.* ① ko-gi 고기, sal 살. ② (*human body*) yuk-

flexible *adj.* hwi-gi swi-un 휘기 쉬운, (*pliant*) ta-ru-gi swi-un 다루기 쉬운, yu-yŏn-han 유연한.

flicker *v.* kkam-bak-i-da 깜박이다, myŏng-myŏl-ha-da 명멸하다. —*n.* kkam-bak-im 깜박임.

flight *n.* ① (*airplane*) pi-haeng 비행. ② (*flee*) to-mang 도망. ③ (*stairs*) ch'ŭng-gye 층계.

flimsy *adj.* yal-bŭn 얇은, ka-nyal-p'ŭn 가냘픈.

fling *v.* ① tŏn-ji-da 던지다. ② (*dash*) tol-jin-ha-da 돌진하다. —*n.* t'u-ch'ŏk 투척.　　　　　　　「고한 사람.

flint *n.* ① pu-sit-dol 부싯돌. ② wan-go-han sa-ram 완

flirt *v.* (*play at love*) hŭi-rong-ha-da 희롱하다. —*n.* (*coquette*) pa-ram-dung-i 바람둥이.　　　　　「훨 날다.

flit *v.* na-ra-da-ni-da 날아다니다, hwŏl-hwŏl nal-da 훨

float *n.* (*buoy*) pu-p'yo 부표. —*v.* ttŭ-da 뜨다.

flock *n.* tte 떼, kun-jung 군중. —*v.* mo-i-da 모이다.

flog *v.* mae-jil〔ch'ae-jjik-jil〕-ha-da 매질〔채찍질〕하다.

flood *n.* hong-su 홍수. —*v.* pŏm-ram-ha-da 범람하다.

floodlight *n.* kang-ryŏk cho-myŏng 강력 조명, il-gwang 일광(溢光).

floor *n.* ma-ru 마루 ; ch'ŭng 층 ; mit-ba-dak 밑바닥.

flop *v.* k'wang nŏm-ŏ-ddŭ-ri-da 쾅 넘어뜨리다.

flounder *n.* ① mom-bu-rim 몸부림. ② (*fish*) nŏp-ch'i 넙치. —*v.* mom-bu-rim-ch'i-da 몸부림치다.

flour *n.* mil-ga-ru 밀가루, ka-ru 가루, pun-mal 분말.

flourish *v.* mu-sŏng-ha-da 무성하다.

flow *v.* hŭ-rŭ-da 흐르다, nŏm-ch'yŏ-hŭ-rŭ-da 넘쳐흐르다. —*n.* hŭ-rŭm 흐름, yu-ch'ul 유출(流出).

flower *n.* kkot 꽃 : *artificial* ～ cho-hwa 조화/～ *arrangement* kkot-ggo-ji 꽃꽂이.

flowerpot *n.* hwa-bun 화분.
flu *n.* (*influenza*) yu-haeng-sŏng kam-gi 유행성 감기.
fluctuate *v.* pyŏn-dong-ha-da 변동하다, p'a-dong-ha-
fluent *adj.* yu-ch'ang-han 유창한. ⌐da 파동하다.
fluid *n.* aek-ch'e 액체, yu-dong-ch'e 유동체. —*adj.*
  (*liquid*) yu-dong-sŏng-ŭi 유동성의. ⌐하는.
fluorescent *adj.* hyŏng-gwang-ŭl pal-ha-nŭn 형광을 발
flush *v.* ① ssi-sŏ-nae-ri-da 씻어내리다. ② (*be red*) pul-
  gŏ-ji-da 붉어지다. —*n.* ① (*rush of water*) pae-su
  배수(排水). ② (*blush*) hong-jo 홍조(紅潮).
flute *n.* p'i-ri 피리, p'ŭl-ru-u-t'ŭ 플루우트.
flutter *v.* nal-gae-ch'i-da 날개치다. —*n.* ① p'ŏ-dŏk-
  gŏ-rim 퍼덕거림. ② (*stir*) tae-so-dong 대소동.
fly *n.* ① (*insect*) p'a-ri 파리. ② (*flight*) pi-haeng 비
  행. —*v.* ① (*bird*) nal-da 날다. ② (*kite*) nal-ri-da 날
  리다. ③ (*run away*) ta-ra-na-da 달아나다.
flypaper *n.* p'a-ri-yak chong-i 파리약 종이. ⌐일다.
foam *n.* kŏ-p'um 거품. —*v.* kŏ-p'um-i il-da 거품이
focus *n.* ch'o-jŏm 초점, p'o-u-k'ŏ-sŭ 포우커스.
fodder *n.* kkol 꼴, ma-ch'o 마초, sa-ryo 사료(飼料).
foe *n.* wŏn-su 원수, (*enemy*) chŏk 적.
fog *n.* an-gae 안개, yŏn-mu 연무(煙霧).
foil *n.* (*thin sheet of metal*) pak 박(箔) : *gold* ∼
  kŭm-bak 금박/*silver* ∼ ŭn-bak 은박.
fold *n.* chu-rŭm 주름. —*v.* chŏp-da 접다.
foliage *n.* (mu-sŏng-han) na-mut-ip (무성한) 나뭇잎.
folk *n.* (*people*) sa-ram-dŭl 사람들, (*pl.*) ka-jok 가족.
follow *v.* tta-ra-ga-da 따라가다, tta-rŭ-da 따르다 ; (*pursue*) ch'u-gu-ha-da 추구하다. ⌐수행원.
follower *n.* pu-ha 부하, (*attendant*) su-haeng-wŏn
folly *n.* ŏ-ri-sŏk-ŭm 어리석음, (*stupidity*) u-mae 우매.
fond *adj.* cho-a-ha-nŭn 좋아하는, chŏng-da-un 정다운.

food *n.* ŭm-sik 음식 : ~ *stuff* sik-ryang 식량, sik-ryo-p'um 식료품. 「da 속이다.

fool *n.* pa-bo 바보, mŏng-ch'ŏng-i 멍청이. —*v.* sok-i-

foolish *adj.* ŏ-ri-sŏk-ŭn 어리석은.

foot *n.* ① (*of the body*) pal 발. ② (*bottom*) mit 밑. ③ (*measure*) p'i-i-t'ŭ 피이트. ④ (*infantry*) po-byŏng 보병.

football *n.* ch'uk-gu 축구, p'ut-bo-ol 풋보올 ; ch'uk-gu-gong 축구공. 「ba-ri 삼발이.

footman *n.* ① chong-bok 종복 ; ma-bu 마부. ② sam-

footpath *n.* o-sol-gil 오솔길, po-do 보도, in-do 인도.

footprint *n.* pal-ja-ch'wi 발자취, pal-ja-guk 발자국.

footstep *n.* kŏ-rŭm-gŏ-ri 걸음걸이, pal-so-ri 발소리.

fop *n.* maep-si-gun 맵시군, mŏt-jang-i 멋장이.

for *prep.* …ŭl wi-ha-yŏ …을 위하여 ; (*on account of*) ttae-mun-e 때문에 ; …tong-an …동안.

forbear *v.* (*bear with*) ch'am-go kyŏn-di-da 참고 견디다 ; (*refrain*) sam-ga-da 삼가다.

forbid *v.* kŭm-ha-da 금하다 ; pang-hae-ha-da 방해하다.

force *n.* ① him 힘. ② (*pl.*) (*troops*) kun-dae 군대. (*effect*) hyŏ-ryŏk 효력. —*v.* ŏk-ji-ro …ha-ge ha-da 억지로 …하게 하다, kang-yo-ha-da 강요하다.

forceps *n.* chok-jip-ge 족집게, p'in-set 핀셋.

forcibly *adv.* kang-je-ro 강제로. 「걸어 건너다.

ford *n.* (*shallows*) yŏ-ul 여울. —*v.* kŏ-rŏ kŏn-nŏ-da

fore *n.* ap-bu-bun 앞부분, chŏn-myŏn 전면.

forecast *v.* ye-ch'ŭk-ha-da 예측하다, ye-bo-ha-da 예보하다. —*n.* (*anticipation*) ye-sang 예상 ; ye-bo 예보.

forefather *n.* cho-sang 조상, sŏn-jo 선조.

forefinger *n.* chip-ge-son-ga-rak 집게손가락.

forehead *n.* ① i-ma 이마. ② (*front part*) ap-jjok 앞쪽.

foreign *adj.* oe-guk-ŭi 외국의, oe-rae-ŭi 외래의.

foreigner *n.* oe-guk-in 외국인, oe-in 외인.

foreleg *n.* (*of animals*) ap-da-ri 앞다리.

foreman *n.* sip-jang 십장, kam-dok 감독.

foremost *adj.* maen mŏn-jŏ-ŭi 맨 먼저의 ; il-ryu-ŭi 일류의 ; chu-yo-han 주요한. —*adv.* maen mŏn-jŏ 맨 먼저.

forenoon *n.* o-jŏn 오전, a-ch'im-na-jŏl 아침나절.

forerunner *n.* sŏn-gu-ja 선구자, chŏn-ju-ja 전주자.

foresee *v.* mi-ri al-da 미리 알다, ye-gyŏn-ha-da 예견 [하다.

forest *n.* sup 숲, sam-rim 삼림.

foretell *v.* ye-ŏn-ha-da 예언하다, ye-go-ha-da 예고하다.

forever *adv.* yŏng-gu-hi 영구히, yŏng-wŏn-hi 영원히. —*n.* yŏng-wŏn 영원, (*eternity*) yŏng-gŏp 영겁.

foreword *n.* mŏ-ri-mal 머리말, sŏ-mun 서문.

forfeit *n.* (*fine*) pŏl-gŭm 벌금, kwa-ryo 과료. —*v.* sang-sil-ha-da 상실하다 ; mol-su-dang-ha-da 몰수당하다.

forge *n.* tae-jang-gan 대장간. —*v.* ① (*steel*) pyŏ-ri-da 버리다. ② (*counterfeit*) wi-jo-ha-da 위조하다.

forgery *n.* wi-jo 위조 ; pyŏn-jo 변조. 「각하다.

forget *v.* i-jŏ-bŏ-ri-da 잊어버리다, mang-gak-ha-da 망

forgetful *adj.* chal i-jŏ-bŏ-ri-nŭn 잘 잊어버리는.

forgive *v.* ① yong-sŏ-ha-da 용서하다. ② (*remit*) myŏn-je-ha-da 면제하다, t'ang-gam-ha-da 탕감하다.

fork *n.* ① p'o-o-k'ŭ 포오크. ② kal-k'wi 갈퀴, soe-sŭ-rang 쇠스랑. —*v.* pun-gi-ha-da 분기하다.

forlorn *adj.* pŏ-rim-bat-ŭn 버림받은, (*desolate*) ko-dok-han 고독한, ssŭl-ssŭl-han 쓸쓸한.

form *n.* ① (*shape*) mo-yang 모양, hyŏng-t'ae 형태, (*appearance*) oe-gwan 외관. ② (*blank*) sŏ-sik 서식. —*v.* hyŏng-t'ae-rŭl i-ru-da 형태를 이루다.

formal *adj.* chŏng-sik-ŭi 정식의 ; (*in form*) hyŏng-sik-jŏk-in 형식적인. 「p'yŏn-dae 편대.

formation *n.* ① ku-sŏng 구성, cho-jik 조직. ② (*army*)

former *adj.* (*previous*) a-p'ŭi 앞의 ; yet-nal-ŭi 옛날의,

i-jŏn-ŭi 이전의. —*n.* (*the* ~) chŏn-ja 전자.
formidable *adj.* mu-sŏ-un 무서운 ; kam-dang-ha-gi ŏ-ryŏ-un 감당하기 어려운.　　　　　　　　　　　「처방.
formula *n.* ① kong-sik 공식. ② (*recipe*) ch'ŏ-bang
fornicate *v.* kan-ŭm-ha-da 간음하다, sa-t'ong-ha-da 사통하다.　　　　　　　　　　　「da 포기하다.
forsake *v.* chŏ-bŏ-ri-da 저버리다, (*give up*) p'o-gi-ha-
fort *n.* yo-sae 요새(要塞), sŏng-ch'ae 성채.
forth *adv.* ① a-p'ŭ-ro 앞으로, (*onward*) chŏn-bang-ŭ-ro 전방으로. ② (*abroad*) pa-ggŭ-ro 밖으로.
forthcoming *adj.* ta-ga-o-nŭn 다가오는, i-bŏn-ŭi 이번의.
fortification *n.* ① pang-bi 방비. ② (*pl.*) (*defensive works*) pang-ŏ-gong-sa 방어공사. ③ kang-hwa 강화.
fortified area yo-sae chi-dae 요새 지대.
fortify *v.* ① yo-sae-hwa-ha-da 요새화하다, kang-hwa-ha-da 강화하다. ② twit-bat-ch'im-ha-da 뒷받침하다.
fortnight *n.* i-ju-il-gan 2주일간, po-rŭm 보름.
fortress *n.* yo-sae 요새, (*stronghold*) sŏng-ch'ae 성채.
fortunate *adj.* haeng-un-ŭi 행운의, un-jo-ŭn 운좋은, chae-su-ga cho-ŭn 재수가 좋은.
fortune *n.* ① (*chance*) un 운, un-su 운수, haeng-un 행운. ② (*wealth*) chae-san 재산, pu 부(富).
forty *n.* ma-hŭn 마흔, sa-sip 40.
forward *adj.* a-p'ŭi 앞의. —*adv.* a-p'ŭ-ro 앞으로. —*v.* ch'ok-jin-ha-da 촉진하다 ; chŏn-song-ha-da 전송하다.
fossil *n.* hwa-sŏk 화석. —*adj.* ① hwa-sŏk-ŭi 화석의. ② (*antiquated*) ku-sik-ŭi 구식의.
foster *v.* ① (*rear*) ki-rŭ-da 기르다, tol-bo-da 돌보다. ② (*cherish*) so-jung-hi ha-da 소중히 하다.
foul *adj.* ① tŏ-rŏ-un 더러운, pul-gyŏl-han 불결한. ② ŭm-t'ang-han 음탕한. —*n.* kyu-ch'ik wi-ban 규칙 위반.
found *v.* ① (*establish*) ch'ang-sŏl-ha-da 창설하다. ②

(lay the base of) se-u-da 기초를 세우다.

foundation *n.* ① (*base*) ki-ch'o 기초. ② (*establishing*) kŏn-sŏl 건설. ③ (*endowment*) chae-dan 재단(財團).

founder *n.* ch'ang-rip-ja 창립자. 「주물 공장.

foundry *n.* ① chu-jo 주조(鑄造). ② chu-mul kong-jang

fountain *n.* pun-su 분수, (*spring*) saem 샘.

fountain pen man-nyŏn-p'il 만년필.

four *n.* net 넷, sa 4 : *Form* ~*s!* Sa-yŏl-ro 4열로!

fourteen *n.* yŏl-net 열넷, sip-sa 14.

fowl *n.* ① tak 닭. ② (*poultry*) ka-gŭm 가금.

fox *n.* yŏ-u 여우 ; (*sly person*) kyo-hwal-han in-gan 교활한 인간 : *a silver* ~ ŭn yŏ-u 은 여우.

fraction *n.* ① (*scrap*) p'a-p'yŏn 파편(破片), chak-ŭn cho-gak 작은 조각. ② (*math.*) pun-su 분수(分數).

fragile *adj.* pu-sŏ-ji-gi swi-un 부서지기 쉬운 ; hŏ-yak-han 허약한.

fragment *n.* ① kkae-jin cho-gak 깨진 조각, p'a-p'yŏn 파편. ② tan-jang 단장(斷章).

fragrance *n.* hyang-gi 향기 ; pang-hyang 방향.

frail *adj.* yak-han 약한, mu-rŭn 무른.

frame *n.* ① ku-jo 구조 ; ppyŏ-dae 뼈대, p'ŭ-re-im 프레임. ② (*mood*) ki-bun 기분. —*v.* (*shape*) hyŏng-sŏng-ha-da 형성하다 ; ko-an-ha-da 고안하다.

framework *n.* ① (*skeleton*) ppyŏ-dae 뼈대, kol-gyŏk 골격. ② (*system*) ch'e-gye 체계, ch'e-je 체제.

frank *adj.* sol-jik-han 솔직한 ; sum-gim-ŏp-nŭn 숨김

frantic *adj.* mi-ch'in-dŭt-han 미친듯한.   「없는.

fraternal *adj.* hyŏng-je-ŭi 형제의, ch'in-han 친한.

fraud *n.* sa-gi 사기, hyŏp-jap 협잡, sa-git-gun 사깃군.

freak *n.* ki-hyŏng 기형, pyŏn-jong 변종.

freckle *n.* chu-gŭn-ggae 주근깨, (*stain*) ŏl-ruk 얼룩.

free *adj.* cha-yu-ŭi 자유의 ; (*without payment*) muryo-ŭi 무료의. —*v.* hae-bang-ha-da 해방하다.

freedom *n.* cha-yu 자유, cha-ju 자주(自主). 「다.

freeze *v.* ① ŏl-da 얼다. ② tong-gyŏl-si-k'i-da 동결시키

freight *n.* ① hwa-mul 화물. ② (*charges*) un-im 운임.

freight car hwa-mul-ch'a 화물차.

frequent *adj.* pin-bŏn-han 빈번한, (*habitual*) sang-sŭp-jŏk-in 상습적인. —*v.* cha-ju ka-da 자주 가다.

fresh *adj.* sin-sŏn-han 신선한, sing-sing-han 싱싱한.

freshman *n.* sin-ip-saeng 신입생, il-nyŏn-saeng 1년생.

fret *v.* ae-t'ae-u-da 애태우다, (*become irritated*) cho-ba-sim-ha-da 조바심하다. —*n.* ch'o-jo 초조.

friction *n.* (*rubbing*) ma-ch'al 마찰 ; al-ryŏk 알력.

Friday *n.* kŭm-yo-il 금요일.

friend *n.* ch'in-gu 친구, tong-mu 동무, pŏt 벗.

friendly *adj.* ch'in-han 친한, u-ho-jŏk-in 우호적인.

friendship *n.* u-jŏng 우정, u-ae 우애, ch'in-gyo 친교.

fright *n.* nol-ram 놀람, kong-p'o 공포.

frighten *n.* kkam-jjak nol-ra-ge ha-da 깜짝 놀라게 하다.

frigid *adj.* mop-si ch'u-un 몹시 추운, (*chilling*) ssal-ssal-han 쌀쌀한 ; (*formal*) ttak-ddak-han 딱딱한.

fringe *n.* ① (*tuft*) sul 술, ka-du-ri chang-sik 가두리 장식. ② (*border*) ka-jang-ja-ri 가장자리.

frivolous *adj.* kyŏng-sol-han 경솔한, (*silly*) pa-bo-ga-t'ŭn 바보같은, (*trivial*) si-si-han 시시한.

frog *n.* kae-gu-ri 개구리.

from *prep.* ···ro-bu-t'ŏ ···로부터, ···e-sŏ ···에서.

front *n.* ① ap 앞, (*forward part*) chŏng-myŏn 정면, ap-myŏn 앞면. ② (*fighting*) il-sŏn 일선.

frontier *n.* kuk-gyŏng 국경, pyŏn-gyŏng 변경.

frost *n.* sŏ-ri 서리. —*v.* sŏ-ri-ga nae-ri-da 서리가 내리다 ; (*freeze*) ŏl-ge ha-da 얼게 하다. 「sang 우거지상.

frown *v.* jji-p'u-ri-da 찌푸리다. —*n.* (*scowl*) u-gŏ-ji-

frozen *adj.* ŏn 언, (*congealed*) naeng-dong-han 냉동한.
frugal *adj.* kŏm-so-han 검소한, al-ddŭl-han 알뜰한 : *a*
~ *meal* kŏm-so-han sik-sa 검소한 식사.
fruit *n.* kwa-il 과일, kwa-sil 과실 ; (*plant products*)
san-mul 산물 : ~ *shop* kwa-il ka-ge 과일 가게.
frustration *n.* ① chwa-jŏl 좌절, sil-p'ae 실패 ; mu-hyo
무효. ② (*psych.*) yok-gu-bul-man 욕구불만.
fry *v.* ki-rŭm-e t'wi-gi-da 기름에 튀기다, p'ŭ-ra-i-ha-
da 프라이하다. —*n.* t'wi-gim-yo-ri 튀김요리.
frying pan p'ŭ-ra-i nam-bi 프라이 남비, p'ŭ-ra-i-p'aen
프라이팬. 「炭).
fuel *n.* yŏl-lyo 연료, chang-jak 장작, sin-t'an 신탄(薪
fugitive *adj.* ta-ra-na-nŭn 달아나는, mang-myŏng-ŭi 망
명의. —*n.* to-mang-ja 도망자, mang-myŏng-ja 망명자.
fulfil *v.* ① su-haeng-ha-da 이행하다 ; kkŭt-nae-da 끝내
다. ② (*satisfy*) ch'ung-jok-si-k'i-da 충족시키다.
full *adj.* ka-dŭk-ch'an 가득찬, ch'ung-bun-han 충분한.
—*adv.* ka-dŭk-hi 가득히. —*n.* chŏn-bu 전부.
full moon po-rŭm-dal 보름달, man-wŏl 만월.
fume *n.* ① (*vapor*) yŏn-gi 연기, an-gae 안개, (*incense*)
hyang-gi 향기. ② (*anger*) no-gi 노기.
fun *n.* chang-nan 장난, nong-dam 농담, chae-mi 재미.
function *n.* ki-nŭng 기능, chik-nŭng 직능, yŏk-hal 역
할. —*v.* (*work*) chak-yong-ha-da 작용하다.
fund *n.* cha-gŭm 자금, (*pl.*) chae-wŏn 재원.
fundamental *adj.* ki-bon-jŏk-in 기본적인, kŭn-wŏn-
jŏk-in 근원적인. —*n.* ki-bon 기본, ki-ch'o 기초.
funeral *n.* chang-rye-sik 장례식. —*adj.* chang-rye-ŭi 장
fungus *n.* kyul-lyu 균류(菌類), pŏ-sŏt 버섯. ㄴ례의.
funnel *n.* ① (*boat*) yŏn-t'ong 연통. ② (*pouring*)
kkal-ddae-gi 깔때기. ③ t'ong-p'ung-t'ong 통풍통.
funny *adj.* ① (*comical*) ik-sal-ma-jŭn 익살맞은, chae-

mi-it-nŭn 재미있는. ② (*queer*) koe-sang-han 괴상한, ki-myo-han 기묘한. 「소설가.
funnyman *n*. kwang-dae 광대 ; hae-hak so-sŏl-ga 해학
fur *n*. mo-p'i 모피. 「da 닦다.
furbish *v*. (*polish*) kwang-ŭl nae-da 광을 내다, tak-
furious *adj*. kyŏk-bun-han 격분한, maeng-ryŏl-han 맹
furl *v*. (*roll*) mal-da 말다, (*fold*) chŏp-da 접다. 렬한.
furlough *n*. (*mil*.) hyu-ga 휴가. 「광로.
furnace *n*. hwa-ro 화로 ; (*smelter*) yong-gwang-ro 용
furnish *v*. ① (*supply*) kong-gŭp-ha-da 공급하다, tae-ju-da 대주다. ② (*equip*) pi-ch'i-ha-da 비치하다.
furnishings *n*. ka-gu-ryu 가구류, se-gan 세간. ‚
furniture *n*. ka-gu 가구, se-gan 세간, pi-p'um 비품.
furrow *n*. ko-rang 고랑 ; (*wrinkle*) chu-rŭm 주름.
furry *adj*. mo-p'i-ro tŏ-p'in 모피로 덮인, mo-p'i-ro man-dŭn 모피로 만든.
further *adj*. kŭ wi-ŭi 그 위의, kŭ i-sang-ŭi 그 이상의. —*adv*. kŭ wi-e 그 위에, ke-da-ga 게다가.
furthermore *adv*. tŏ-gun-da-na 더군다나. 「한.
furtive *adj*. mol-rae-ha-nŭn 몰래하는, ŭn-mil-han 은밀
fury *n*. ① kyŏk-jŏng 격정, kyŏk-bun 격분. ② maeng-ryŏl 맹렬, (*violence*) kwang-p'o 광포.
fuse *n*. ① (*electric*) p'yu-jŭ 퓨즈. ② (*ordnance*) sin-gwan 신관(信管), to-hwa-sŏn 도화선. —*v*. (*melt*) nok-i-da 녹이다, (*blend*) yung-hwa-ha-da 융화하다.
fusion *n*. ① yong-hae 용해. ② hap-dong 합동.
fuss *n*. ya-dan-bŏp-sŏk 야단법석, so-dong 소동. —*v*. ttŏ-dŭl-da 떠들다, an-dal-bok-dal-ha-da 안달복달하다.
futile *adj*. so-yong-ŏp-nŭn 소용없는, mu-ik-han 무익한 : *a* ～ *attempt* hŏt-doen si-do 헛된 시도.
future *n*. chang-rae 장래, mi-rae 미래. —*adj*. mi-rae-ŭi 미래의 ; nae-se-ŭi 내세의.

G

gabble *v*. chi-ggŏ-ri-da 지껄이다, chong-al-gŏ-ri-da 종알거리다. —*n*. chae-jal-gŏ-rim 재잘거림. 「부속품.
gadget *n*. chang-ch'i 장치 ; (*accessory*) pu-sok-p'um
gaiety *n*. myŏng-rang 명랑, yu-k'wae 유쾌.
gaily *adv*. k'wae-hwal-ha-ge 쾌활하게. 「이득.
gain *v*. ŏt-da 언다, (*win*) i-gi-da 이기다. —*n*. i-dŭk
gait *n*. kŏ-rŭm-gŏ-ri 걸음걸이, po-jo 보조(步調).
gale *n*. kang-p'ung 강풍, chil-p'ung 질풍.
gallant *adj*. ① yong-gam-han 용감한, ssik-ssik-han 씩씩한. ② ch'in-jŏl-han 친절한. —*n*. mŏt-jang-i 멋장이.
gallery *n*. ① hwa-rang 화랑(畫廊). ② (*corridor*) pok-do 복도. ③ (*theater*) kwal-lam-sŏk 관람석.
gallon *n*. kal-ron 갈론(=3.785 *l*).
gallop *n*. chil-ju 질주. —*v*. chil-ju-ha-da 질주하다.
gallows *n*. kyo-su-dae 교수대, kyo-su-hyŏng 교수형.
galvanized iron ham-sŏk 함석.
gamble *n*. & *v*. to-bak(-ha-da) 도박(하다). 「사냥감.
game *n*. ① yu-hŭi 유희, o-rak 오락. ② sa-nyang-gam
gang *n*. (*a group*) han p'ae 한 패 ; kaeng 갱.
gangster *n*. kaeng 갱, ak-dang 악당.
gap *n*. (*opening*) t'ŭm 틈, (*interval*) kan-gyŏk 간격.
gape *v*. ip-ŭl k'ŭ-ge pŏl-ri-da 입을 크게 벌리다, (*yawn*) ha-p'um-ha-da 하품하다.
garage *n*. ch'a-go 차고 ; kyŏk-nap-go 격납고.
garbage *n*. ssŭ-re-gi 쓰레기, jji-ggŏ-gi 찌꺼기.
garden *n*. ① ttŭl 뜰, chŏng-wŏn 정원. ② (*pl.*) yu-wŏn-ji 유원지.
gardener *n*. chŏng-wŏn-sa 정원사.
gargle *v*. yang-ch'i-jil-ha-da 양치질하다.

garland *n.* hwa-hwan 화환, hwa-gwan 화관.
garlic *n.* ma-nŭl 마늘.
garment *n.* kin ot 긴 옷, (*pl.*) ŭi-bok 의복, ŭi-sang 의상.
garnet *n.* sŏk-ryu-sŏk 석류석(石榴石).　「mul 장식물.
garnish *v.* chang-sik-ha-da 장식하다. —*n.* chang-sik-
garrison *n.* su-bi-dae 수비대, chu-dun-gun 주둔군.
garret *n.* ta-rak-bang 다락방, ko-mi-da-rak-bang 고미
garter *n.* yang-mal tae-nim 양말 대님.　　「다락방.
gas *n.* ga-sŭ 가스 : *natural* ～ ch'ŏn-yŏn-ga-sŭ 천연가스.
gasoline *n.* hwi-bal-yu 휘발유, ka-sol-rin 가솔린.
gasp *v.* ① hŏl-ddŏk-gŏ-ri-da 헐떡거리다. ② (*desire*)
　kal-mang-ha-da 갈망하다.　　　　　　　「궤양.
gastric *adj.* wi-ŭi 위(胃)의 : ～*ulcer* wi-gwe-yang 위
gate *n.* mun 문, (*portal*) ch'u-rip-mun 출입문.
gather *v.* ① mo-ŭ-da 모으다, mo-i-da 모이다. ② (*creas-
　ing*) chu-rŭm-ŭl chap-da 주름을 잡다.
gathering *n.* mo-im 모임, hoe-hap 회합 ; su-jip 수집.
gaudy *adj.* ya-han 야한, hwa-ryŏ-han 화려한.
ga(u)ge *n.* kye-gi 계기(計器), ke-i-ji 게이지, p'yo-jun-
　ch'i-su 표준치수.　　　　　　　　　「시무시한.
gaunt *adj.* yŏ-win 여윈 ; (*grim*) mu-si-mu-si-han 무
gauze *n.* yal-bŭn ch'ŏn 얇은 천, ka-a-je 가아제.
gay *adj.* k'wae-hwal-han 쾌활한 ; (*showy*) ya-han 야한.
gaze *v.* ŭng-si-ha-da 응시하다, chi-k'yŏ-bo-da 지켜보
　다. —*n.* (*steady look*) ŭng-si 응시, chu-si 주시.
gear *n.* t'op-ni-ba-k'wi 톱니바퀴, chang-ch'i 장치, ki-
gelatin(e) *n.* a-gyo 아교, chel-ra-t'in 젤라틴.　「gu 기구.
gem *n.* po-sŏk 보석, ok 옥 ; il-p'um 일품(逸品).
gender *n.* sŏng 성(性), (*sex*) sŏng-byŏl 성별.　「bo 족보.
genealogy *n.* ① ka-gye 가계, hyŏl-t'ong 혈통. ② chok-
general *n.* chang-gun 장군. —*adj.* il-ban-jŏk-in 일반
　적인, chŏn-ban-jŏk-in 전반적인.

general election ch'ong-sŏn-gŏ 총선거.
generate *v.* ① na-t'a 낳다 ; pal-saeng-ha-da 발생하다.
　② (*electricity*) pal-jŏn-ha-da 발전하다.
generation *n.* ① il-dae 일대(一代), se-dae 세대 ; tong-si-
　dae-ŭi sa-ram-dŭl 동시대의 사람들. ② pal-saeng 발생.
generator *n.* pal-jŏn-gi 발전기, pal-saeng-gi 발생기.
generosity *n.* kwan-yong 관용, a-ryang 아량.
generous *adj.* ① kwan-dae-han 관대한, nŏ-gŭ-rŏ-un
　너그러운. ② (*unsparing*) a-ggim-ŏp-nŭn 아낌없는.
genial *adj.* on-hwa-han 온화한, ch'in-jŏl-han 친절한.
genius *n.* ch'ŏn-jae 천재 ; ch'ŏn-sŏng 천성 ; t'ŭk-jing 특징.
genteel *adj.* p'um-wi-it-nŭn 품위있는, u-a-han 우아한.
gentle *adj.* on-hwa-han 온화한, chŏm-jan-ŭn 점잖은.
gentleman *n.* sin-sa 신사.
gentlewoman *n.* suk-nyŏ 숙녀, kwi-bu-in 귀부인.
gently *adj.* sang-nyang-ha-ge 상냥하게, chŏm-jan-k'e
　점잖게 ; (*quietly*) cho-yong-ha-ge 조용하게.　「류 사회.
gentry *n.* sin-sa kye-gŭp 신사 계급, sang-ryu sa-hoe 상
genuine *adj.* chin-jŏng-han 진정한, chin-jja-ŭi 진짜의.
geography *n.* chi-ri-hak 지리학, chi-ji 지지(地誌) ; chi-
geology *n.* chi-jil-hak 지질학.　　　　　　└se 지세(地勢).
geometry *n.* ki-ha-hak 기하학.
geophysics *n.* chi-gu-mul-ri-hak 지구물리학.
germ *n.* ① (*microbe*) pyŏng-gyun 병균, se-gyun 세균.
　② (*origin*) kŭn-wŏn 근원, ki-wŏn 기원.
German *adj.* tok-il-ŭi 독일의. —*n.* (*people*) tok-il-sa-
　ram 독일사람 ; (*language*) tok-i-rŏ 독일어.
Germany *n.* to-i-ch'i 도이치, tok-il 독일.　「(發芽)하다.
germinate *v.* ssak-i t'ŭ-da 싹이 트다, pa-ra-ha-da 발아
gesture *n.* mom-jit 몸짓, che-sŭ-ch'ŏ 제스처.
get *v.* (*acquire*) ŏt-da 얻다 ; (*arrive*) i-rŭ-da 이르다 ;
　(*induce*) ha-ge ha-da 하게 하다 ; (*become*) …i toe-

da …이 되다 : ~ *up* i-rŏ-na-da 일어나다.　「시한.
ghastly *adj.* mu-sŏ-un 무서운, mu-si-mu-si-han 무시무
ghost *n.* yu-ryŏng 유령, mang-ryŏng 망령, kwi-sin 귀
giant *n.* kŏ-in 거인. —*adj.* kŏ-dae-han 거대한.　「신.
giddy *adj.* ŏ-ji-rŏ-un 어지러운, ŏ-jil-ŏ-jil-han 어질어질한.
gift *n.* sŏn-mul 선물 ; (*natural ability*) ch'ŏn-bu-ŭi
　chae-nŭng 천부의 재능.
gifted *adj.* chae-nŭng-i it-nŭn 재능이 있는.　「한.
gigantic *adj.* kŏ-in-ga-t'ŭn 거인같은, kŏ-dae-han 거대
giggle *v.* k'il-k'il ut-da 킬킬 웃다.
gild *v.* kŭm-bak-ŭl ip-hi-da 금박을 입히다, to-gŭm-ha-
gills *n.* (*fish*) a-ga-mi 아가미.　　　　　｟da 도금하다.
ginger *n.* sae-ang 새앙, saeng-gang 생강 : ~ *group*
　kŭp-jin-p'a 급진파.　　　　　　　「ha-ge 신중하게.
gingerly *adj.* sin-jung-han 신중한. —*adv.* sin-jung-
gingko·ginkgo *n.* ŭn-haeng-na-mu 은행나무.
ginseng *n.* in-sam 인삼 : *a Korean* ~ ko-ryŏ in-sam
gipsy·gypsy *n.* chip-si 집시.　　　　　｟고려 인삼.
giraffe *n.* ki-rin 기린, chi-ra-p'ŭ 지라프.
gird *v.* (*encircle*) tu-rŭ-da 두르다, chol-ra-mae-da 졸라
　매다 ; (*equip*) kŏl-ch'i-da 걸치다, ch'a-da 차다
girdle *n.* tti 띠, hŏ-ri-tti 허리띠. —*v.* tu-rŭ-da 두르다.
girl *n.* so-nyŏ 소녀, kye-jip-a-i 계집아이, ae-in 애인.
girlhood *n.* so-nyŏ si-jŏl 소녀 시절 ; so-nyŏ-dŭl 소녀들.
give *v.* chu-da 주다, pe-p'ul-da 베풀다 ; (*hold*) yŏl-da
　열다 ; (*entrust*) mat-gi-da 맡기다 : ~ *up* p'o-gi-ha-da
　포기하다, tan-nyŏm-ha-da 단념하다.　　　　　「자.
giver *adj.* chu-nŭn sa-ram 주는 사람, ki-jŭng-ja 기증
glacier *n.* ping-ha 빙하.
glad *adj.* ki-bbŭn 기쁜, chŭl-gŏ-un 즐거운.
gladden *v.* ki-bbŭ-ge ha-da 기쁘게 하다.
gladness *n.* ki-bbŭm 기쁨, chŭl-gŏ-um 즐거움.

glamo(u)r *n*. ma-ryŏk 마력, mae-ryŏk 매력 : *a ~ girl* mae-hok-jŏk-in yŏ-ja 매혹적인 여자.

glance *v*. hil-ggŭt-bo-da 힐끗보다. —*n*. hil-ggŭt-bo-gi 힐끗보기, (*meaning look*) nun-jit 눈짓.

gland *n*. sŏn 선(腺): *lymphatic ~s* im-p'a-sŏn 임파선.

glare *v*. (*light*) nun-i pu-si-da 눈이 부시다 ; (*stare fiercely*) no-ryŏ-bo-da 노려보다. —*n*. nun-bu-sin pit 눈부신 빛, (*fierce stare*) sso-a-bo-gi 쏘아보기.

glass *n*. ① yu-ri 유리 ; k'ŏp 컵. ② (*drinking*) sul 술, ŭm-ju 음주. ③ (*spectacles*) an-gyŏng 안경.

glassware *n*. yu-ri kŭ-rŭt 유리 그릇.

glazed *adj*. yun-t'aek-na-nŭn 윤택나는, kwang-t'aek-it-nun 광택있는, mae-ggŭn-mae-ggŭn-han 매끈매끈한.

gleam *n*. pit-nam 빛남 ; ŏ-ryŏm-p'ut-han pit 어렴풋한 빛, mi-gwang 미광. —*v*. pŏn-jjŏk-i-da 번쩍이다.

glean *v*. ① i-sak-ŭl chup-da 이삭을 줍다. ② su-jip-ha-da 수집하다.

glee *n*. ki-bbŭm 기쁨, hwan-hŭi 환희.

glen *n*. kol-jja-gi 골짜기, chop-ŭn kye-gok 좁은 계곡.

glide *v*. mi-ggŭ-rŏ-ji-da 미끄러지다, hwal-ju-ha-da 활주하다. —*n*. hwal-ju 활주.

glim *n*. tŭng-bul 등불, ch'ot-bul 촛불, pul-bit 불빛.

glimmer *v*. ka-mul-ga-mul pi-ch'i-da 가물가물 비치다, kkam-bak-i-da 깜박이다. —*n*. hŭ-rit-han pit 흐릿한 빛.

glimpse *n*. hil-ggŭt-bo-gi 힐끗보기, il-byŏl 일별.

glisten *v*. pan-jjak-i-da 반짝이다, pit-na-da 빛나다.

glitter *v*. pan-jjak-ban-jjak pit-na-da 반짝반짝 빛나다.

globe *n*. kong 공 ; (*the earth*) chi-gu 지구.

gloom *n*. ŏ-dum 어둠 ; u-ul 우울. —*v*. o-du-wŏ-ji-da 어두워지다.

gloomy *adj*. ŏ-du-un 어두운, ch'im-ul-han 침울한.

glorify *v*. ch'an-mi-ha-da 찬미하다. yŏng-gwang-ŭl pe-p'ul-da 영광을 베풀다.

glorious *adj*. yŏng-gwang-sŭ-rŏ-un 영광스러운.

glory *n.* yŏng-gwang 영광, yŏng-ye 영예 ; yŏng-hwa 영화(榮華), yung-sŏng 융성, nun-bu-sim 눈부심.

gloss *n.* kwang-t'aek 광택 ; (*specious show*) hŏ-sik 허식 ; (*comment*) chu-hae 주해(註解).

glossary *n.* so-sa-jŏn 소사전, yong-ŏ p'u-ri 용어 풀이.

glove *n.* chang-gap 장갑, kŭl-rŏ-bŭ 글러브.

glow *v.* ppal-ga-k'e ta-ra-o-rŭ-da 빨갛게 달아오르다. —*n.* paek-yŏl 백열, hong-jo 홍조.

glue *n.* a-kyo 아교, p'ul 풀. —*v.* a-gyo-ro pu-ch'i-da 「아교로 붙이다.

gnat *n.* mo-gi 모기, kak-da-gwi 각다귀.

gnaw *v.* mu-rŏ kkŭn-t'a 물어 끊다 ; ssol-da 쏠다.

go *v.* ① (*proceed*) ka-da 가다. ② (*work*) um-jik-i-da 움직이다. ③ (*elapse*) chi-na-ga-da 지나가다.

goal *n.* kyŏl-sŭng-jŏm 결승점, mok-p'yo 목표, mok-jŏk-ji 목적지.

goat *n.* yŏm-so 염소.

gobble *v.* ke-gŏl-sŭ-rŏp-ge mŏk-da 게걸스럽게 먹다.

go-between *n.* chung-gae-in 중개인, chung-mae-ja 중매자 ; (*pander*) ttu-jang-i 뚜장이.

goblin *n.* yo-gwi 요귀, ma-gwi 마귀, ak-gwi 악귀.

god *n.* sin 신(神), (*G~*) ha-nŭ-nim 하느님.

goddess *n.* yŏ-sin 여신.

godlike *adj.* sin-gwa ka-t'ŭn 신과 같은, chon-ŏm-han 존엄한.

godliness *n.* kyŏng-gŏn 경건, kyŏng-sin 경신(敬神).

gold *n.* kŭm 금, (*coin*) kŭm-hwa 금화 ; (*color*) kŭm-bit 금빛.

golden *adj.* ① kŭm-bi-ch'ŭi 금빛의. ② (*precious*) kwi-jung-han 귀중한. ③ yung-sŏng-han 융성한.

goldfish *n.* kŭm-bung-ŏ 금붕어.

golf *n.* kol-p'ŭ 골프.

gong *n.* ching 징, pa-ra 바라.

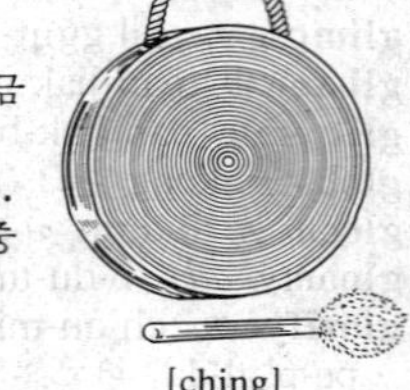

[ching]

good *n.* ch'ak-ham 착함. —*adj.* cho-ŭn 좋은, (*kind*) ch'in-jŏl-han 친절한 ; (*skilled*) nŭng-suk-han 능숙한.

good-by(e) *n.* chak-byŏl in-sa 작별 인사. —*int.* an-nyŏng-hi ka-sip-si-o 안녕히 가십시오, an-nyŏng-hi kye-sip-si-o 안녕히 계십시오.

goodness *n.* ch'ak-ham 착함, mi-dŏk 미덕 ; (*kindness*) ch'in-jŏl 친절 ; (*excellence*) u-ryang 우량.

goods *n.* mul-p'um 물품, sang-p'um 상품.

goose *n.* kŏ-wi 거위 : *wild* ~ ki-rŏ-gi 기러기.

gorgeous *adj.* ch'al-lan-han 찬란한, hwa-ryŏ-han 화려한 ; hul-ryung-han 훌륭한.

gosh *int.* ŏ-ma 어마, a-i-go 아이고, chŏ-rŏn 저런.

gospel *n.* pok-ŭm 복음.

gossip *n.* chap-dam 잡담, twit-gong-ron 뒷공론, ko-sip 고십 : *the* ~ *column* ko-sip-ran 고십란(欄).

gourd *n.* ho-ri-byŏng-bak 호리병박, cho-rong-bak 조롱박 : *the sponge* ~ su-se-mi-oe 수세미외.

gourmet *n.* sik-do-rak 식도락, mi-sik-ga 미식가.

govern *v.* ① chi-bae-ha-da 지배하다, ta-sŭ-ri-da 다스리다. ② (*determine*) kyŏl-jŏng-ha-da 결정하다.

government *n.* chŏng-bu 정부. chŏng-ch'i 정치.

governor *n.* t'ong-ch'i-ja 통치자, chi-sa 지사. 「스.

gown *n.* kin kŏt-ot 긴 겉옷, ka-un 가운, tu-re-sŭ 드레

grab *v.* um-k'yŏ-jap-da 움켜잡다, put-jap-da 붙잡다.

grace *n.* ① ŭn-ch'ong 은총, ho-ŭi 호의. ② (*elegance*) ki-p'um 기품, u-a 우아. ③ (*prayer*) ki-do 기도.

graceful *adj.* u-a-han 우아한, chŏm-jan-ŭn 점잖은.

gracious *adj.* (*merciful*) in-ja-han 인자한, cha-bi-ro-un 자비로운, (*courteous*) chŏng-jung-han 정중한.

grade *n.* (*degree*) tŭng-gŭp 등급, p'yŏng-jŏm 평점 ; (*form*) hak-gŭp 학급. —*v.* (*mark*) tŭng-gŭp-ŭl mae-gi-da 등급을 매기다.

gradual *adj*. chŏm-ch'a-jŏk-in 점차적인.

graduate *n*. cho-rŏp-saeng 졸업생. —*v*. cho-rŏp-ha-da 졸업하다, hak-wi-rŭl su-yŏ-ha-da 학위를 수여하다.

graduation *n*. cho-rŏp(-sik) 졸업(식).

graft *v*. chŏp-bu-ch'i-da 접붙이다. —*n*. chŏp-mok 접목.

grain *n*. ① kok-mul 곡물, nat-al 낟알. ② al-gaeng-i 알갱이. ③ kŭk-so-ryang 극소량. ④ (*temper*) ki-jil 기질.

grammar *n*. mun-bŏp 문법, ŏ-bŏp 어법.

grammatical *adj*. mun-bŏp(-sang)-ŭi 문법(상)의.

gramophone *n*. ch'uk-ŭm-gi 축음기. 「곡창.

granary *n*. kok-mul ch'ang-go 곡물 창고, kok-ch'ang

grand *adj*. ung-dae-han 웅대한, (*majestic*) tang-dang-han 당당한 ; ho-hwa-ro-un 호화로운.

grandchild *n*. son-ja 손자, son-nyŏ 손녀.

granddaughter *n*. son-nyŏ 손녀, son-ja-ddal 손자딸.

grandfather *n*. ha-ra-bŏ-ji 할아버지, cho-bu 조부.

grandmother *n*. hal-mŏ-ni 할머니, cho-mo 조모.

grandson *n*. son-ja 손자.

grandstand *n*. t'ŭk-byŏl kwal-lam-sŏk 특별 관람석.

granite *n*. hwa-gang-sŏk 화강석, ssuk-dol 쑥돌.

grant *v*. ① (*give*) chu-da 주다, su-yŏ-ha-da 수여하다. ② (*admit*) si-in-ha-da 시인하다, hŏ-ga-ha-da 허가하다.

grape *n*. p'o-do 포도 : ~ *sugar* p'o-do-dang 포도당.

grapevine *n*. p'o-do-dŏng-gul 포도덩굴.

grapple *v*. kkwak put-jap-da 꽉 붙잡다 ; (*fight*) kyŏk-t'u-ha-da 격투하다. —*n*. kyŏk-t'u 격투.

grasp *v*. ① kkwak chwi-da 꽉 쥐다. ② (*understand*) i-hae-ha-da 이해하다. —*n*. ① p'o-ch'ak 포착. ② (*power*) kwŏl-lyŏk 권력. ③ (*understanding*) i-hae

grasping *adj*. yok-sim-i man-ŭn 욕심이 많은. 「이해.

grass *n*. ① p'ul 풀, mok-ch'o 목초. ② (*meadow*) mok-jang 목장. ③ (*sod*) chan-di 잔디.

grasshopper *n.* me-ddu-gi 메뚜기, yŏ-ch'i 여치.
grassy *adj.* p'ul-i u-gŏ-jin 풀이 우거진, pul-ŭi 풀의.
grate *v.* mun-ji-rŭ-da 문지르다, kal-da 갈다.
grateful *adj.* ko-map-ge yŏ-gi-nŭn 고맙게 여기는 : *a ~ letter* kam-sa-ŭi p'yŏn-ji 감사의 편지. 「기쁘게 하다.
gratify *v.* man-jok-si-k'i-da 만족시키다, ki-bbŭ-ge ha-da
gratitude *n.* kam-sa 감사, sa-ŭi 사의(謝意).
grave *n.* mu-dŏm 무덤, myo 묘. —*adj.* (*critical*) chung-dae-han 중대한, chang-jung-han 장중한.
gravel *n.* cha-gal 자갈. 「yŏ 정색하여.
gravely *adv.* ŏm-suk-ha-ge 엄숙하게, chŏng-saek-ha-
gravestone *n.* myo-bi 묘비, pi-sŏk 비석.
graveyard *n.* myo-ji 묘지. 「yong 인력 작용.
gravitation *n.* chung-ryŏk 중력(重力), il-lyŏk chak-
gravity *n.* ① chung-ryŏk 중력. ② il-lyŏk 인력 ; (*weight*) chung-ryang 중량.
gravy *n.* ko-gi kuk-mul 고기 국물.
graze *n.* (*cattle*) p'ul-ŭl ttŭt-ŏ-mŏk-da 풀을 뜯어먹다.
grease *v.* ki-rŭm 기름, chi-bang 지방, kŭ-ri-i-sŭ 그리이스. —*v.* ki-rŭm-ŭl ch'i-da 기름을 치다.
great *adj.* k'ŭn 큰, wi-dae-han 위대한 ; (*numerous*) man-ŭn 많은 ; (*important*) chung-dae-han 중대한.
great-grandchild *n.* chŭng-son-ja 증손자.
great-grandfather *n.* chŭng-jo-bu 증조부.
great-grandmother *n.* chŭng-jo-mo 증조모. 「게.
greatly *adv.* tae-dan-hi 대단히, mae-u 매우, k'ŭ-ge 크
greatness *n.* wi-dae-ham 위대함, kŏ-dae-ham 거대함.
greed *n.* yok-sim 욕심, t'am-yok 탐욕. 「nŭn 갈망하는.
greedy *adj.* yok-sim-man-ŭn 욕심많은, kal-mang-ha-
green *adj.* ① ch'o-rok-saek-ŭi 초록색의, nok-saek-ŭi 녹색의. ② (*unripe*) sŏl-ik-ŭn 설익은. —*n.* ① ch'o-rok 초록, nok-saek 녹색. ② (*vegetables*) ch'ae-so 채소.

greenhorn *n.* p'ut-na-gi 풋나기, ch'o-sim-ja 초심자.
greenhouse *n.* on-sil 온실. 「da 영접하다.
greet *v.* in-sa-ha-da 인사하다, (*receive*) yŏng-jŏp-ha-
greeting *n.* in-sa 인사, (*pl.*) in-sa-jang 인사장.
grey·gray *n.* hoe-saek 회색. —*adj.* hoe-saek-ŭi 회
색의 ; (*dull*) u-jung-ch'ung-han 우중충한.
grief *n.* sŭl-p'ŭm 슬픔, pi-t'ong 비통, ko-noe 고뇌.
grieve *v.* sŏ-rŏ-wŏ-ha-da 서러워하다.
grill *n.* ① sŏk-soe 석쇠. ② ku-un ko-gi 구운 고기.
grim *adj.* ŏm-han 엄한, mu-sŏ-un 무서운.
grimace *n.* jji-p'u-rin ŏl-gul 찌푸린 얼굴. —*v.* ŏl-gul-
ŭl jji-p'u-ri-da 얼굴을 찌푸리다. 「히다.
grime *n.* ttae 때, mŏn-ji 먼지. —*v.* tŏ-rŏp-hi-da 더럽
grimly *adv.* ŏm-gyŏk-ha-ge 엄격하게.
grin *v.* sing-gŭt ut-da 싱긋 웃다.
grind *v.* ppa-t'a 빻다, kal-da 갈다.
grindstone *n.* maet-dol 맷돌.
grip *v.* kkwak put-jap-da 꽉 붙잡다.
—*n.* p'a-ak 파악, i-hae 이해.
groan *n.* sin-ŭm-so-ri 신음소리. —*v.*
sin-ŭm-ha-da 신음하다.

[maet-dol]

grocer *n.* sik-ryo-p'um chang-su 식료품 장수.
groceries *n.* sik-ryo-p'um 식료품, sik-p'um-jŏm 식품점.
groom *n.* ① sil-lang 신랑. ② (*footman*) ma-bu 마부.
grope *v.* son-ŭ-ro tŏ-dŭm-da 손으로 더듬다.
gross *adj.* (*big*) k'ŭn 큰 ; (*total*) ch'ong-gye-ŭi 총계의.
grotesque *adj.* koe-sang-han 괴상한, u-sŭ-un 우스운.
ground *n.* ttang 땅 ; (*play*) un-dong-jang 운동장.
ground floor il-ch'ŭng 일층.
group *n.* mu-ri 무리, chip-dan 집단. —*v.* ① tte-rŭl
chit-da 떼를 짓다. ② (*classify*) pul-lyu-ha-da 분류하
grove *n.* chak-ŭn sup 작은 숲, su-p'ul 수풀. 「다.

grow *v.* cha-ra-da 자라다 ; (*cultivate*) chae-bae-ha-da 재배하다 ; (*become*) ha-ge toe-da 하게 되다.

growl *v.* ŭ-rŭ-rŏng-gŏ-ri-da 으르렁거리다, t'u-dŏl-gŏ-ri-da 투덜거리다. —*n.* ŭ-rŭ-rŏng-gŏ-ri-nŭn so-ri 으르렁거리는 소리. 「sŏng-in 성인.

grown-up *adj.* sŏng-jang-han 성장한. —*n.* ŏ-rŭn 어른,

growth *n.* ① sŏng-jang 성장, pal-jŏn 발전. ② (*cultivation*) chae-bae 재배. ③ chong-yang 종양(腫瘍).

grub *n.* yu-ch'ung 유충, kum-beng-i 굼벵이.

grudge *n.* wŏn-han 원한, ak-ŭi 악의. —*v.* ha-go sip-ji an-t'a 하고 싶지 않다, a-gga-wa-ha-da 아까와하다.

gruel *n.* (mul-gŭn) chuk (묽은) 죽. 「불평하다.

grumble *v.* t'u-dŏl-dae-da 투덜대다, pul-p'yŏng-ha-da

grunt *v.* kkul-ggul-gŏ-ri-da 꿀꿀거리다 ; p'u-nyŏm-ha-da 푸념하다. —*n.* pul-p'yŏng 불평.

guarantee *v.* po-jŭng-ha-da 보증하다. —*n.* po-jŭng 보증.

guarantor *n.* po-jŭng-in 보증인, tam-bo-in 담보인.

guard *n.* p'a-su-gun 파수군. su-wi 수위 ; (*conductor*) ch'a-jang 차장. —*v.* p'a-su-bo-da 파수보다, pang-wi-ha-da 방위하다. 「인.

guardian *n.* po-ho-ja 보호자 ; (*legal*) hu-gyŏn-in 후견

guess *v.* ch'u-ch'ŭk-ha-da 추측하다, (*Am.*) (*think*) saeng-gak-ha-da 생각하다. —*n.* ch'u-ch'ŭk 추측.

guest *n.* son-nim 손님, nae-bin 내빈, kaek 객(客).

guide *n.* an-nae-ja 안내자, ka-i-dŭ 가이드, p'yŏl-lam 편람. —*v.* an-nae-ha-da 안내하다, in-do-ha-da 인도하

guidebook *n.* yŏ-haeng an-nae-sŏ 여행 안내서. 「다.

g(u)ild *n.* kil-dŭ 길드, tong-ŏp cho-hap 동업 조합.

guilt *n.* choe 죄, yu-joe 유죄, pŏm-joe-haeng-wi 범죄

guilty *adj.* yu-joe-ŭi 유죄의, choe-it-nŭn 죄있는. 「행위.

guise *n.* (*appearance*) kŏt-bo-gi 겉보기, oe-gwan 외관 ; (*disguise*) ka-jang 가장, pyŏn-jang 변장.

gulf *n.* man 만(灣). —*v.* sam-k'i-da 삼키다.

gull *n.* kal-mae-gi 갈매기 ; (*dupe*) ŏl-gan-i 얼간이, sa-git-gun 사깃군. —*v.* sok-i-da 속이다.

gum *n.* ① ko-mu-p'ul 고무풀, ko'mu 고무 : ~*boots* ko-mu-sin 고무신. ② (*of the mouth*) it-mom 잇몸 ; (*o the eye*) nun-ggop 눈꼽. ③(*chewing* ~) kkŏm 껌.

gun *n.* ch'ong 총 : *air* ~ kong-gi-ch'ong 공기총/*squirt* ~ mul-ch'ong 물총.

gunner *n.* p'o-su 포수, ch'ong-sa-nyang-gun 총사냥군.

gunpowder *n.* hwa-yak 화약.

gush *v.* ssot-a-jyŏ na-o-da 쏟아져 나오다, nae-bbum-da 내뿜다. —*n.* so-sa-na-om 솟아나옴, pun-ch'ul 분출.

gust *n.* tol-p'ung 돌풍, chil-p'ung 질풍 ; (*outburst*) kyŏk-bal 격발, tol-bal 돌발. 「ha-su-do 하수도.

gutter *n.* ① (*groove*) hom-t'ong 홈통. ② (*ditch*)

guttural *adj.* mok-gu-mŏng-ŭi 목구멍의, mok-gu-mŏng so-ri-ŭi 목구멍 소리의.

gymnasium *n.* ch'e-yuk-gwan 체육관.

gymnastics *n.* ch'e-jo 체조, ch'e-yuk 체육.

gyroscope *n.* hoe-jŏn-ŭi 회전의(回轉儀), cha-i-ro-sŭ-k'o-u-p'ŭ 자이로스코우프.

H

habit *n.* pŏ-rŭt 버릇, sŭp-gwan 습관, sŭp-sŏng 습성.

habitable *adj.* sŭp-gwan-jŏk-in 습관적인 ; sang-sŭp-jŏk-in 상습적인 ; (*usual*) p'yŏng-so-ŭi 평소의.

hack *v.* cha-rŭ-da 자르다, nan-do-jil-ha-da 난도질하다.

haggard *adj.* yŏ-win 여윈, su-ch'ŏk-han 수척한.

hail *n.* ssa-rak-nun 싸락눈. —*v.* ① ssa-rak-nun-i nae-ri-da 싸락눈이 내리다. ② (*call*) pu-rŭ-da 부르다.

hair *n.* t'ŏl 털, mŏ-ri-t'ŏl 머리털, tu-bal 두발.

hairbrush *n.* mŏ-ri-sol 머리솔.

hairdresser *n.* i-bal-sa 이발사, mi-yong-sa 미용사.

hale *adj.* kŏn-jang-han 건장한, t'ŭn-t'ŭn-han 튼튼한.

half *n. & adj.* pan 반, chŏl-ban(-ŭi) 절반(의).

half brother pae-da-rŭn hyŏng-je 배다른 형제, ŭi-but hyŏng-je 의붓 형제.　　　　　　　　　　　「han 미지근한.

half-hearted *adj.* yŏ-rŭi-ŏp-nŭn 열의없는, mi-ji-gŭn-

half holiday pan-gong-il 반공일, pan-hyu-il 반휴일.

half-mast *n.* pan-gi-ŭi wi-ch'i 반기(半旗)의 위치 : *a flag at* ~ pan-gi 반기, cho-gi 조기(吊旗).

half-moon *n.* pan-dal 반달.　　　　　　　「cha-mae 의붓 자매.

half sister pae-da-rŭn cha-mae 배다른 자매, ŭi-but

halfway *adj. & adv.* chung-do-ŭi〔-e-sŏ〕 중도의〔에서〕.

half-wit *n.* (*fool*) pan-p'yŏn 반편, ŏl-gan-i 얼간이.

hall *n.* (*auditorium*) kang-dang 강당 ; (*corridor*) pok-do 복도, t'ong-ro 통로 : *city* ~ si-ch'ŏng 시청 / *music* ~ ŭm-ak-dang 음악당.

hallo(a) *int.* yŏ-bo 여보, i-rŏn 이런.

hallow *v.* (*make holy*) sin-sŏng-ha-ge ha-da 신성하게 하다, sin-e-ge pa-ch'i-da 신에게 바치다.

halo *n.* tal〔hae〕-mu-ri 달〔해〕무리, hu-gwang 후광.

halt *v.* (*army*) chu-dun-ha-da 주둔하다 ; (*stop*) mŏm-ch'u-da 멈추다. —*n.* chŏng-ji 정지 : *Company,* ~*!* Chung-dae sŏ 중대 서 !

halve *v.* i-dŭng-bun-ha-da 이등분하다, pan-ssik na-nu-

ham *n.* haem 햄.　　　　　　　　　　　└da 반씩 나누다.

hamlet *n.* chak-ŭn ma-ŭl 작은 마을, ch'ol-lak 촌락.

hammer *n.* mang-ch'i 망치, hae-mŏ 해머. —*v.* mang-ch'i-jil-ha-da 망치질하다.　　　　　　　　　　「하다.

hamper *n.* chok-swae 족쇄. —*v.* pang-hae-ha-da 방해

hand *n.* ① (*of the body*) son 손. ② (*laborer*) il-son 일손, (*skill*) som-ssi 솜씨. ③ (*timepiece*) si-gye-ba-nŭl 시계바늘. —*v.* kŏn-ne-ju-da 건네주다.

handbag *n.* son-ga-bang 손가방, haen-dŭ-baek 핸드백.

handbook *n.* p'yŏl-lam 편람, an-nae-sŏ 안내서.

handcart *n.* chim-su-re 짐수레, son-su-re 손수레.

handcuff *n.* su-gap 수갑, soe-go-rang 쇠고랑.

handful *n.* han chum 한 줌 ; so-su 소수, so-ryang 소량: *a ~ of children* so-su-ŭi a-i-dŭl 소수의 아이들.

handicap *n.* pul-ri-han cho-gŏn 불리한 조건, chang-ae 장애, haen-di-k'aep 핸디캡.

handicraft *n.* su-ye 수예, su-se-gong 수세공(手細工).

handily *adv.* p'yŏl-li-ha-ge 편리하게, kyo-myo-ha-ge ⌞교묘하게.

handkerchief *n.* son-su-gŏn 손수건.

handle *n.* son-jap-i 손잡이, haen-dŭl 핸들. —*v.* cho-jong-ha-da 조종하다, ta-ru-da 다루다 ; mae-mae-ha-da

handshake *n.* ak-su 악수. ⌞매매하다.

handsome *adj.* chal saeng-gin 잘 생긴, tang-dang-han 당당한 ; (*generous*) a-ryang-it-nŭn 아량있는.

handy *adj.* p'yŏl-li-han 편리한, kan-p'yŏn-han 간편한.

hang *v.* kŏl-da 걸다, mae-dal-da 매달다 ; (*remain in suspense*) mang-sŏ-ri-da 망설이다.

hangar *n.* kyŏk-nap-go 격납고, ch'a-go 차고.

Hangul *n.* (*Korean*) han-gŭl 한글.

hanker *v.* kal-mang〔yŏl-mang〕-ha-da 갈망〔열망〕하다.

happen *v.* i-rŏ-na-da 일어나다, saeng-gi-da 생기다, u-yŏn-hi …ha-da 우연히 …하다.

happiness *n.* haeng-bok 행복, haeng-un 행운.

happy *adj.* haeng-bok-han 행복한, ki-bbŭn 기쁜 ; (*lucky*) ta-haeng-han 다행한. ⌜ha-da 침공하다.

harass *v.* koe-rop-hi-da 괴롭히다 ; (*raid*) ch'im-gong-

harbo(u)r *n.* hang-gu 항구, (*refuge*) p'i-nan-ch'ŏ 피난처. —*v.* sum-gi-da 숨기다.

hard *adj.* (*solid*) tan-dan-han 단단한 ; (*difficult*) ŏ-ryŏ-

un 어려운. —*adv.* (*earnestly*) yŏl-sim-hi 열심히.
hardly *adv.* kŏ-ŭi …a-ni-da 거의 …아니다.
hardship *n.* ko-ch'o 고초, ko-nan 고난, hak-dae 학대.
hardware *n.* ch'ŏl-mul 철물, ha-a-dŭ-we-ŏ 하아드웨어.
hardworking *adj.* kŭn-myŏn-han 근면한.
hardy *adj.* t'ŭn-t'ŭn-han 튼튼한, nae-gu-ryŏk-i it-nŭn 내구력이 있는 ; (*daring*) tae-dam-han 대담한.
hare *n.* t'o-ggi 토끼, san-t'o-ggi 산토끼.
hark *v.* tŭt-da 듣다, kwi-rŭl ki-u-ri-da 귀를 기울이다.
harlot *n.* mae-ch'un-bu 매춘부, ch'ang-bu 창부.
harm *n.* hae 해, son-hae 손해, son-sang 손상. —*v.* hae-ch'i-da 해치다, son-sang-ha-da 손상하다.
harmony *n.* cho-hwa 조화 ; (*music*) hwa-sŏng 화성.
harness *n.* (*horse equipment*) ma-gu 마구.
harp *n.* ha-a-p'ŭ 하아프 ; (*Korean*) kŏ-mun-go 거문고.
harrow *n.* ① ssŏ-re 써레, —*v.* ssŏ-re-jil-ha-da 써레질하다. ② (*torment*) mot-sal-ge kul-da 못살게 굴다.
harsh *adj.* kŏ-ch'in 거친 ; ka-hok-han 가혹한 ; (*discordant*) kwi-e kŏ-sŭl-ri-nŭn 귀에 거슬리는.
harshly *adv.* kŏ-ch'il-ge 거칠게, ŏm-ha-ge 엄하게.
hart *n.* (*stag*) su-sa-sŭm 수사슴.
harvest *n.* su-hwak 수확 ; (*result*) kyŏl-gwa 결과 : *good* ~ p'ung-nyŏn 풍년/*poor* ~ hyung-nyŏn 흉년.
haste *n.* sŏ-du-rŭm 서두름, kyŏng-sol 경솔.
hasten *v.* sŏ-du-rŭ-da 서두르다, (*speed up*) mo-ra-se-u-da 몰아세우다, chae-ch'ok-ha-da 재촉하다.
hastily *adv.* pa-bbi 바삐, cho-gŭp-hi 조급히.
hasty *adj.* kŭp-han 급한, sŏng-gŭp-han 성급한.
hat *n.* mo-ja 모자 : *My* ~*!* Ŏ-mŏ-na! 어머나 !
hatch *n.* ① (*ships*) sŭng-gang-gu 승강구. ② (*incubation*) pu-hwa 부화. —*v.* pu-hwa-ha-da 부화하다; (*contrive*) ko-an-ha-da 고안하다.

hatchet *n.* son-do-ggi 손도끼.

hate *v.* mi-wŏ-ha-da 미워하다, si-rŏ-ha-da 싫어하다.

hateful *adj.* mi-un 미운, chi-gyŏ-un 지겨운.

hatred *n.* mi-um 미움, chŭng-o 증오, hyŏm-o 혐오.

haughty *adj.* kyo-man-han 교만한, o-man-han 오만한: *a* ~ *air* o-man-han t'ae-do 오만한 태도.

haul *v.* chap-a-ggŭl-da 잡아끌다, kkŭ-rŏ-dang-gi-da 끌어당기다.

haunch *n.* ŏng-dŏng-i 엉덩이.

haunt *v.* cha-ju tŭ-na-dŭl-da 자주 드나들다, tal-ra-but-da 달라붙다. —*n.* cha-ju ta-ni-nŭn kot 자주 다니는 곳.

have *v.* (*possess*) ka-ji-da 가지다 ; (*eat*) mŏk-da 먹다 ; (*drink*) ma-si-da 마시다 ; (*obtain*) ŏt-da 얻다 ; (*wear*) ip-da 입다.

haven *n.* hang-gu 항구 ; (*shelter*) p'i-nan-ch'ŏ 피난처.

havoc *n.* p'a-goe 파괴, hwang-p'ye 황폐.

hawk *n.* mae 매(鷹).

hay *n.* kŏn-ch'o 건초, kkol 꼴.

haystack *n.* kŏn-ch'o ka-ri 건초 가리, kŏn-ch'o-dŏ-mi 건초더미.

hazard *n.* wi-hŏm 위험, mo-hŏm 모험, (*chance*) un 운. —*v.* mo-hŏm-ŭl ha-da 모험을 하다.

haze *n.* a-ji-raeng-i 아지랭이, an-gae 안개.

hazel *n.* kae-am(-na-mu) 개암(나무) ; (*light brown*) tam-gal-saek 담갈색.

hazy *adj.* an-gae kkin 안개 낀 : ~ *weather* hŭ-rin nal-ssi 흐린 날씨.

H-bomb *n.* su-so-p'ok-t'an 수소폭탄, su-so-t'an 수소탄.

he *pron.* kŭ-nŭn[-ga] 그는[가], chŏ-sa-ram-ŭn[-i] 저 사람은[이]. —*n.* nam-ja 남자, su-k'ŏt 수컷.

head *n.* mŏ-ri 머리, (*intellect*) tu-noe 두뇌, chi-ryŏk 지력 ; (*chief*) su-ryŏng 수령, chang 장(長).

headache *n.* tu-t'ong 두통, tu-t'ong-gŏ-ri 두통거리.

headlight *n.* he-dŭ-ra-i-t'ŭ 헤드라이트, chang-dŭng 장등(牆燈).

headline *n.* p'yo-je 표제, che-mok 제목.

headlong *adv*. kŏ-ggu-ro 거꾸로, kon-du-bak-i-ro 곤두박이로 ; (*rashly*) mu-t'ŏk-dae-go 무턱대고.
head office pon-jŏm 본점, pon-sa 본사.　　　「화기.
headphone *n*. mŏ-ri-e kŏ-nŭn su-hwa-gi 머리에 거는 수
headquarters *n*. pon-bu 본부, sa-ryŏng-bu 사령부: *general* ∼ ch'ong-sa-ryŏng-bu 총사령부.
headstrong *adj*. wan-go-han 완고한, ko-jip sen 고집 센.
heal *v*. ① (*cure*) ko-ch'i-da 고치다. ② (*appease*) hwa-hae-si-k'i-da 화해시키다, mu-ma-ha-da 무마하다.
health *n*. ① kŏn-gang 건강. ② wi-saeng 위생.　　「한.
healthy *adj*. kŏn-gang-han 건강한, t'ŭn-t'ŭn-han 튼튼
heap *n*. ① tŏ-mi 더미, mu-dŏ-gi 무더기. ② (*a lot*) ta-ryang 다량, ta-su 다수. —*v*. ssa-a-ol-ri-da 쌓아올리다.
hear *v*. tŭt-da 듣다 ; (*law*) sim-mun-ha-da 심문하다.
hearer *n*. ch'ŏng-ch'wi-ja 청취자, pang-ch'ŏng-in 방청
hearing *n*. tŭt-gi 듣기, ch'ŏng-ch'wi 청취.　　└인.
hearse *n*. yŏng-gu-ch'a 영구차 ; kwan 관.
heart *n*. sim-jang 심장, (*mind*) ma-ŭm 마음.
heartbroken *adj*. ae-ggŭn-nŭn 애끊는, pi-t'an-e cham-gin 비탄에 잠긴.　　　　　　　　　　　　「불평.
heartburn *n*. ① ka-sŭm-a-ri 가슴앓이. ② pul-p'yŏng
heart disease sim-jang-byŏng 심장병.
heart failure sim-jang-ma-bi 심장마비.
hearth *n*. nal-lo 난로 ; (*fireside*) no-byŏn 노변.
heartily *adv*. chin-sim-ŭ-ro 진심으로, mae-u 매우.
heartless *adj*. ① mu-jŏng-han 무정한, mo-rin-jŏng-han 몰인정한. ② yong-gi-ga ŏp-nŭn 용기가 없는.
hearty *adj*. ① ma-ŭm-e-sŏ u-rŏ-nan 마음에서 우러난 ; ch'in-jŏl-han 친절한. ② (*robust*) ki-un-ch'an 기운찬.
heat *n*. ① yŏl 열(熱) ; on-do 온도. ② (*anger*) kyŏk-no 격노. ③ (*zeal*) yŏl-sim 열심. —*v*. te-u-da 데우다, ttŭ-gŏp-ge ha-da 뜨겁게 하다.

heater *n*. nan-bang-jang-ch'i 난방장치, hi-i-t'ŏ 히이터.
heath *n*. hi-i-dŭ 히이드 ; (*wilderness*) hwang-ya 황야.
heathen *adj*. (*pagan*) i-gyo(-do)-ŭi 이교(도)의. —*n*.
i-gyo-do 이교도, i-bang-in 이방인.
heave *v*. ① (*lift*) tŭ-rŏ-ol-ri-da 들어올리다. ② (*throw*)
tŏn-ji-da 던지다. ③ (*pull*) chap-a-ggŭl-da 잡아끌다.
heaven *n*. ha-nŭl 하늘, ch'ŏn-guk 천국.
heavenly *adj*. ha-nŭl-ŭi 하늘의, ch'ŏl-lae-ŭi 천래의 ;
(*holy*) sin-sŏng-han 신성한, kŏ-ruk-han 거룩한.
heavily *adv*. mu-gŏp-ge 무겁게 ; sim-ha-ge 심하게.
heavy *adj*. mu-gŏ-un 무거운 ; (*violent*) maeng-ryŏl-
han 맹렬한 : *a ~ rain* p'ok-u 폭우. 「장벽.
hedge *n*. san-ul-t'a-ri 산울타리 ; (*barrier*) chang-byŏk
heed *v*. chu-ŭi-ha-da 주의하다, cho-sim-ha-da 조심하다.
heedful *adj*. cho-sim-sŏng-it-nŭn 조심성있는, chu-ŭi-
gi-p'ŭn 주의깊은, cho-sim-ha-nŭn 조심하는.
heel *n*. twi-ggum-ch'i 뒤꿈치, kup 굽, twi-ch'uk 뒤축.
heifer *n*. am-song-a-ji 암송아지.
height *n*. ① no-p'i 높이 ; (*stature*) k'i 키. ② ko-ji 고지.
heighten *v*. no-p'i-da 높이다.
heir *n*. sang-sok-in 상속인, hu-gye-ja 후계자. 「동산.
heirloom *n*. ka-bo 가보, sang-jŏn tong-san 상전(相傳)
heiress *n*. yŏ-ja sang-sok-in 여자 상속인, yŏ-ja hu-gye-
helicopter *n*. hel-ri-k'op-t'ŏ 헬리콥터. └ja 여자 후계자.
hell *n*. chi-ok 지옥, chŏ-sŭng 저승, hwang-ch'ŏn 황천.
hello *int*. (*telephone*) yŏ-bo-se-yo 여보세요 ; (*greeting*)
an-nyŏng-ha-sip-ni-gga 안녕하십니까.
helm *n*. (*of ship*) k'i (배의) 키, cho-t'a-gi 조타기.
—*v*. k'i-rŭl cho-jong-ha-da 키를 조종하다.
helmet *n*. ch'ŏl-mo 철모, t'u-gu 투구, hel-met 헬멧.
help *n*. to-um 도움, (*remedy*) ku-je-ch'aek 구제책.
—*v*. top-da 돕다, to-wa-ju-da 도와주다.

helper *n.* top-nŭn sa-ram 돕는 사람, cho-ryŏk-ja 조력자.
helpful *adj.* to-um-i toe-nŭn 도움이 되는, (*useful*)
　yu-yong-han 유용한, p'yŏl-li-han 편리한.
helpless *adj.* ŏ-jji-hal su ŏp-nŭn 어찌할 수 없는.
hem *n.* (*cloth*) ka-jang-ja-ri 가장자리, ot-dan 옷단.
hemisphere *n.* pan-gu 반구(半球).
hemp *n.* sam 삼, tae-ma 대마.
hen *n.* am-t'ak 암탉, (*fowl*) am-k'ŏt 암컷.
hence *adv.* (*from now*) i-je-bu-t'ŏ 이제부터, yŏ-gi-sŏ-
　bu-t'ŏ 여기서부터; (*therefore*) kŭ-rŏ-mŭ-ro 그러므로.
henchman *n.* ① ch'u-jong-ja 추종자. ② hu-wŏn-ja 후원
hencoop *n.* tak-jang 닭장, tung-u-ri 둥우리.　　　└자.
henhouse *n.* tak-jang 닭장.
her *pron.* kŭ yŏ-ja-ŭi〔rŭl, e-ge〕 그 여자의〔를, 에게〕.
herald *n.* chŏn-dal-ja 전달자; (*harbinger*) sŏn-gu-ja
　선구자. —*v.* (*announce*) al-ri-da 알리다.
herb *n.* ch'o-bon 초본(草本): *a medicinal* ～ yak-ch'o
　약초/*a poisonous* ～ tok-ch'o 독초.
herd *n.* ① chim-sŭng-ŭi tte 짐승의 떼. ② (*mob*) kun-
　·jung 군중. ③ (*rabble*) ha-ch'ŭng-min 하층민.
herdsman *n.* mok-dong 목동, mok-ja 목자(牧者).
here *adv.* yŏ-gi-e 여기에, i-go-se 이곳에.
hereafter *adv.* chi-gŭm-bu-t'ŏ 지금부터, kŭm-hu 금후.
heredity *n.* yu-jŏn 유전.
heresy *n.* i-gyo 이교, i-dan 이단; i-ron 이론(異論).
heritage *n.* sang-sok chae-san 상속 재산, yu-san 유산.
hermit *n.* ŭn-dun-ja 은둔자(隱遁者), ŭn-ja 은자.　「공.
hero *n.* ① yŏng-ung 영웅. ② (*story*) chu-in-gong 주인
heroic *adj.* yŏng-ung-jŏk-in 영웅적인, yong-gam-han
heroine *n.* yŏ-jang-bu 여장부, yŏ-gŏl 여걸.　　└용감한.
heron *n.* wae-ga-ri 왜가리.
herring *n.* ch'ŏng-ŏ 청어.

hers *pron.* kŭ yŏ-ja-ŭi kŏt 그 여자의 것.

herself *pron.* kŭ yŏ-ja cha-sin 그 여자 자신.

hesitate *v.* chu-jŏ-ha-da 주저하다, mang-sŏ-ri-da 망설이다, kyŏl-dan-ŭl mot nae-ri-da 결단을 못 내리다.

hew *v.* (*cut*) pe-da 베다, (*chop*) jjik-da 찍다, ssŏl-da 썰다.

hey *int.* i-bwa 이봐, ŏ-i 어이 ; ya-a 야아.

hiccough·hiccup *n.* ttal-gguk-jil 딸꾹질.

hide *v.* kam-ch'u-da 감추다, sum-da 숨다. —*n.* ka-juk 가죽, p'i-hyŏk 피혁.

hideous *adj.* mu-si-mu-si-han 무시무시한, mip-sal-sŭ-rŏ-un 밉살스러운.

high *adj.* no-p'ŭn 높은 ; ko-gŭp-ŭi 고급의 ; (*intense*) kang-ryŏl-han 강렬한 : *a ~ words* kwa-gyŏk-han mal 과격한 말. —*adv.* (*intensely*) sim-ha-ge 심하게 ; (*luxuriously*) sa-ch'i-sŭ-rŏp-ge 사치스럽게.

highland *n.* ko-ji 고지, san-gan chi-yŏk 산간 지역.

highly *adv.* no-p'i 높이, mae-u 매우.

highway *n.* kan-sŏn to-ro 간선 도로, kong-ro 공로.

hijack *v.* kong-jung nap-ch'i-ha-da 공중 납치하다.

hike *n.* ① to-bo yŏ-haeng 도보 여행. ② (*increase*) in-sang 인상. —*v.* kkŭ-rŏ-ol-ri-da 끌어올리다.

hill *n.* ŏn-dŏk 언덕, chak-ŭn san 작은 산.

him *pron.* kŭ-rŭl 그를, kŭ-e-ge 그에게.

himself *pron.* kŭ cha-sin 그 자신.

hind *adj.* twi-jjok-ŭi 뒤쪽의. —*n.* (*doe*) am-sa-sŭm 암사슴.

hinder *adj.* twi-ŭi 뒤의, hu-bang-ŭi 후방의. —*v.* pang-hae-ha-da 방해하다.

hindrance *n.* pang-hae 방해.

hinge *n.* tol-jjŏ-gwi 돌쩌귀, kyŏng-ch'ŏp 경첩. —*v.* (*on*) …yŏ-ha-e tal-ryŏ-it-da …여하에 달려있다.

hint *n.* am-si 암시. —*v.* am-si-rŭl chu-da 암시를 주다.

hip *n.* ŏng-dŏng-i 엉덩이, kung-dung-i 궁둥이.

hire *n.* ko-yong 고용 ; im-dae 임대(賃貸) ; sak 삯. —*v.*

(*engage*) ko-yong-ha-da 고용하다.

his *pron.* kŭ-ŭi 그의.　　　　　　「nae-da 쉿 소리 내다.

hiss *n.* swit ha-nŭn so-ri 쉿 하는 소리. —*v.* swit so-ri

historian *n.* yŏk-sa-ga 역사가, sa-hak-ja 사학자.

historic *adj.* yŏk-sa-sang yu-myŏng-han 역사상 유명한.

historical *adj.* yŏk-sa-ŭi 역사의, sa-hak-ŭi 사학(史學)의.

history *n.* ① yŏk-sa 역사. ② kyŏng-ryŏk 경력, nae-ryŏk 내력 : *one's personal* ~ i-ryŏk-sŏ 이력서.「하다.

hit *v.* (*strike*) ch'i-da 치다, myŏng-jung-ha-da 명중

hitch *v.* ① hwaek um-jik-i-da 홱 움직이다. ② (*tie*) mae-da 매다. ③ (*key*) kŏl-da 걸다.

hither *adv.* i-jjok-ŭ-ro 이쪽으로. —*adj.* i-jjok-ŭi 이쪽의.

hitherto *adv.* yŏ-t'ae-gga-ji 여태까지.

hive *n.* pŏl-jip 벌집, pŏl-t'ong 벌통.

hives *n.* tu-dŭ-rŏ-gi 두드러기.

hoard *n.* chŏ-jang 저장. —*v.* chŏ-jang-ha-da 저장하다.

hoarse *adj.* mok-swin 목쉰, mok-swin so-ri-ŭi 목쉰 소리의, (*rough*) kwi-e kŏ-sŭl-ri-nŭn 귀에 거슬리는.

hoary *adj.* (*white*) ha-yan 하얀 ; paek-bal-ŭi 백발의.

hobble *v.* chŏl-rŭm-gŏ-ri-da 절름거리다.

hobby *n.* ① (*taste*) ch'wi-mi 취미, to-rak 도락. ② (*hobbyhorse*) mok-ma 목마.

hockey *n.* ha-k'i 하키 : *ice* ~ a-i-sŭ ha-k'i 아이스 하키.

hoe *n.* kwaeng-i 괭이. —*v.* kwaeng-i-jil-ha-da 괭이질 하다 : ~ *up weeds* chap-ch'o-rŭl p'a-he-ch'i-da 잡초

hog *n.* (*pig*) twae-ji 돼지.　　　　　　└를 파헤치다.

hoist *v.* no-p'i ol-ri-da 높이 올리다, (*lift up*) tŭ-rŏ-ol-ri-da 들어올리다. —*n.* (*crane*) ki-jung-gi 기중기.

hold *v.* ① (*keep*) chi-ni-da 지니다. ② (*open*) kae-ch'oe-ha-da 개최하다. ③ (*grasp*) put-jap-da 붙잡다. ④ (*support*) chi-t'aeng-ha-da 지탱하다. —*n.* ① (*grasp*) p'o-ch'ak 포착. ② (*ship*) sŏn-ch'ang 선창.

holder *n.* ① (*person*) po-yu-ja 보유자. ② (*thing*) pat-ch'i-nŭn mul-gŏn 받치는 물건, yong-gi 용기(容器).

hole *n.* ku-mŏng 구멍.

holiday *n.* hyu-il 휴일, ch'uk-je-il 축제일.

holiness *n.* sin-sŏng-ham 신성함.

Holiness Church sŏng-gyo-hoe-p'a 성교회파(聖敎會派).

hollow *n.* u-muk-han kot 우묵한 곳. —*adj.* (*empty*) pin 빈, (*sunken*) o-mok-hi tŭ-rŏ-gan 오목히 들어간. —*v.* (*excavate*) to-ryŏ-nae-da 도려내다.

hollyhock *n.* chŏp-si-ggot 접시꽃.

holy *adj.* sin-sŏng-han 신성한, kŏ-ruk-han 거룩한.

homage *n.* chŏn-gyŏng 존경, kyŏng-ŭi 경의(敬意) : *pay ～ to* kyŏng-ŭi-rŭl p'yo-ha-da 경의를 표하다.

home *n.* ka-jŏng 가정 ; (*native land*) pon-guk 본국.

homeland *n.* cha-gi na-ra 자기 나라, ko-guk 고국(故國).

homely *adj.* su-su-han 수수한 ; ka-jŏng-jŏk-in 가정적인 ; hŭn-hi it-nŭn 혼히 있는. 「hyang-ŭi 망향의.

homesick *adj.* hyang-su-byŏng-ŭi 향수병의, mang-

homesickness *n.* hyang-su 향수(鄕愁). 「p'ŏn 호움스펀.

homespun *adj.* son-ŭ-ro jjan 손으로 짠. —*n.* ho-um-sŭ-

homework *n.* ① suk-je 숙제. ② ka-nae kong-ŏp 가내

homicide *n.* sa-rin(-bŏm) 살인(범). 「공업.

hone *n.* sut-dol 숫돌. —*v.* sut-dol-ro kal-da 숫돌로 갈다.

honest *adj.* chŏng-jik-han 정직한, sŏng-sil-han 성실한 ; (*legitimate*) chŏng-dang-han 정당한.

honesty *n.* chŏng-jik 정직, song-sil 성실.

honey *n.* ① kkul 꿀. ② (*darling*) ae-in 애인.

honeycomb *n.* pŏl-jip 벌집. 「신혼 여행.

honeymoon *n.* mil-wŏl 밀월 : ～ *trip* sin-hon yŏ-haeng

hono(u)r *n.* ① myŏng-ye 명예, (*esteem*) kyŏng-ŭi 경의. ② (*pl.*) hun-jang 훈장. ③ (*top grade*) u-dŭng 우등. —*v.* chon-gyŏng-ha-da 존경하다.

honorable *adj*. chon-gyŏng-hal man-han 존경할 만한.

hood *n*. tu-gŏn 두건, tŏp-gae 덮개.

hoof *n*. pal-gup 발굽, mal pal-gup 말 발굽 : *a cloven* ～ kal-ra-jin pal-gup 갈라진 발굽.

hook *n*. kal-go-ri 갈고리, huk 훅, (*for fishing*) nak-si-ba-nŭl 낚시바늘. —*v*. ku-bu-rŏ-ji-da 구부러지다, kal-go-ri-ro kŏl-da 갈고리로 걸다.

hoop *n*. t'e 테, soe-t'e 쇠테 ; (*plaything*) kul-rŏng-soe 굴렁쇠, hu-u-p'ŭ 후우프.

hop *v*. ① kkang-ch'ong-ggang-ch'ong ttwi-da 깡총깡총 뛰다. ② (*jump on one leg*) han-bal-ro ttwi-da 한 발로 뛰다. —*n*. ang-gam-jil 앙감질.

hope *n*. hŭi-mang 희망, so-mang 소망. —*v*. pa-ra-da 바라다, hŭi-mang-ha-da 희망하다. 「희망에 찬.

hopeful *adj*. yu-mang-han 유망한, hŭi-mang-e ch'an

hopeless *adj*. hŭi-mang-i ŏp-nŭn 희망이 없는. 「선.

horizon *n*. chi-p'yŏng-sŏn 지평선, su-p'yŏng-sŏn 수평

horizontal *adj*. su-p'yŏng-ŭi 수평의, (*level*) p'yŏng-p'yŏng-han 평평한 : ～ *bar* ch'ŏl-bong 철봉.

hormone *n*. ho-rŭ-mon 호르몬. 「호른.

horn *n*. ① ppul 뿔. ② (*bugle*) na-p'al 나팔, ho-rŭn

horrible *adj*. kkŭm-jjik-han 끔찍한, mu-sŏ-un 무서운.

horrid *adj*. mu-si-mu-si-han 무시무시한, chin-jŏ-ri-na-nŭn 진저리나는.

horrify *v*. so-rŭm-ggi-ch'i-ge ha-da 소름끼치게 하다.

horror *n*. kong-p'o 공포, chŏn-yul 전율.

horse *n*. mal 말 : ～ *opera* sŏ-bu-gŭk 서부극.

horse chestnut ma-ro-ni-e 마로니에.

horsefly *n*. mal-p'a-ri 말파리, tŭng-e 등에.

horseman *n*. ki-su 기수, sŭng-ma-ja 승마자.

horsepower *n*. ma-ryŏk 마력(馬力).

horse race kyŏng-ma 경마.

horseshoe *n.* p'yŏn-ja 편자, che-ch'ŏl 제철.
horticulture *n.* wŏn-ye 원예.   「mal 긴양말.
hose *n.* ① ho-o-sŭ 호오스. ② (*stockings*) kin-yang-
hospitable *adj.* ① tae-u-ga cho-ŭn 대우가 좋은, (*gen-erous*) hu-dae-ha-nŭn 후대하는. ② ho-ŭi-jŏk-in 호의
hospital *n.* (chong-hap) pyŏng-wŏn (종합) 병원. ⌊적인.
hospitality *n.* hwan-dae 환대, hu-dae 후대.
host *n.* ① chu-in 주인. ② (*majority*) ta-su 다수.
hostage *n.* in-jil 인질, (*pledge*) chŏ-dang 저당.
hostel *n.* hap-suk-so 합숙소, (*inn*) yŏ-in-suk 여인숙.
hostess *n.* an-ju-in 안주인, yŏ-ju-in 여주인.
hostile *adj.* chŏk-ŭi-e ch'an 적의에 찬, (*opposed*) pan-dae-ha-nŭn 반대하는, chŏk-ŭi 적의.
hot *adj.* ① (*temperature*) to-un 더운, ttŭ-gŏ-un 뜨거운; (*taste*) mae-un 매운. ② (*fresh*) kat-na-on 갓나온.
hotel *n.* ho-t'el 호텔, yŏ-gwan 여관.   「천장.
hot spring on-ch'ŏn 온천 : *a ~ resort* on-ch'ŏn-jang 온
hound *n.* sa-nyang-gae 사냥개 ; yŏl-jung-ha-nŭn sa-ram 열중하는 사람 : *a jazz ~* chae-jŭ-gwang 재즈광(狂).
hour *n.* si-gan 시간 : (*o'clock*) si 시(時).
house *n.* ① chip 집, ka-ok 가옥. ② (*A~*)ŭi-hoe 의회.
household *n. & adj.* ka-jok(-ŭi) 가족(의).
housekeeper *n.* chu-bu 주부, ka-jŏng-bu 가정부.
housemaid *n.* ha-nyŏ 하녀, sik-mo 식모.
house-rent *n.* chip-se 집세.   「jit-go-ri 반짇고리.
housewife *n.* ① chu-bu 주부. ② (*a sewing box*) pan-
hover *v.* ha-nŭl-ŭl nal-da 하늘을 날다 ; (*linger*) sŏ-sŏng-gŏ-ri-da 서성거리다. —*n.* pae-hoe 배회.
how *adv.* (*in what state*) ŏ-ddŏ-k'e 어떻게 ; (*to what extent*) ŏ-nŭ chŏng-do 어느 정도 ; (*why*) wae 왜. —*int.* ya 야, a-i ch'am 아이 참. —*n.* (*means*) pang-bŏp 방법, pang-sik 방식.

however *adv.* a-mu-ri ···hae-do 아무리 ···해도. —*conj.* (*though*) kŭ-rŏ-na 그러나, kŭ-rŏ-ch'i-man 그렇지만.

howl *v.* (*of animals*) chit-da 짖다, ul-bu-jit-da 울부짖다; (*of the wind*) mop-si pul-da 몹시 불다.

huddle *v.* ma-gu kŭl-gŏ-mo-ŭ-da 마구 긁어모으다; (*curl up*) tung-gŭl-ge ku-bu-ri-da 둥글게 구부리다. —*n.* (*confusion*) hon-jap 혼잡, pum-bim 붐빔.

hue *n.* (*color*) pit-ggal 빛깔, saek-jo 색조.

hug *v.* kkok kkyŏ-an-da 꼭 껴안다, p'um-da 품다.

huge *adj.* kŏ-dae-han 거대한, mak-dae-han 막대한.

hull *v.* kkŏp-jil-ŭl pŏt-gi-da 껍질을 벗기다. —*n.* ① (*husk*) kkŏp-jil 껍질. ② (*ship*) sŏn-ch'e 선체(船體).

hum *v.* wing-wing-gŏ-ri-da 윙윙거리다, k'ot-no-rae-rŭl pu-rŭ-da 콧노래를 부르다.

human *n.* in-gan 인간. —*adj.* in-gan-ŭi 인간의, in-gan-da-un 인간다운. 「비로운.

humane *adj.* in-jŏng-it-nŭn 인정있는, cha-bi-ro-un 자

humble *adj.* (*lowly*) pi-ch'ŏn-han 비천한; (*modest*) kyŏm-son-han 겸손한. 「눅한.

humid *adj.* ch'uk-ch'uk-han 축축한, nuk-nuk-han 눅

humility *n.* kyŏm-son 겸손; pi-ha 비하(卑下).

humo(u)r *n.* ① (*mood*) ki-jil 기질; ki-bun 기분. ② ik-sal 익살, yu-u-mŏ 유우머. 「리다.

hump *n.* hok 혹, yuk-bong 육봉. —*v.* ku-bu-ri-da 구부

humpback *n.* kkop-ch'u 꼽추, kop-sa-dŭng-i 곱사등이.

hundred *n.* paek 백. 「mang 간절한 소망.

hunger *n.* ① kum-ju-rim 굶주림. ② kan-jŏl-han so-

hungry *adj.* pae-go-p'ŭn 배고픈, kum-ju-rin 굶주린: *go* [*be*] ~ pae-go-p'ŭ-da 배고프다.

hunt *n.* sa-nyang 사냥, (*search*) ch'u-jŏk 추적. —*v.* sa-nyang-ha-da 사냥하다: ~ *for* ch'at-da 찾다.

hunter *n.* sa-nyang-gun 사냥군, t'am-gu-ga 탐구가.

hunting *n*. sa-nyang 사냥, su-ryŏp 수렵 ; (*pursuit*) t'am-gu 탐구, ch'u-gu 추구.

hurdle *n*. pa-ja(-ul) 바자(울), chang-ae-mul 장애물.

hurl *v*. nae-dŏn-ji-da 내던지다, p'aeng-gae-ch'i-da 팽개

hurrah·hurray *int*. man-se 만세, hu-ra 후라.　└치다.

hurricane *n*. p'ok-p'ung 폭풍, t'ae-p'ung 태풍.

hurry *v*. sŏ-du-rŭ-da 서두르다. —*n*. (*haste*) sŏ-du-rŭm 서두름, kŭp-sok 급속 : *in a* ～ kŭp-hi 급히.

hurt *v*. (*injure*) hae-ch'i-da 해치다, (*pain*) a-p'ŭ-da 아프다. —*n*. (*wound*) sang-ch'ŏ 상처 ; (*damage*) son-hae 손해 ; (*pain*) ko-t'ong 고통.　　└하다.

husband *n*. nam-p'yŏn 남편. —*v*. chŏl-yak-ha-da 절약

husbandry *n*. ① (*farming*) nong-ŏp 농업, kyŏng-jak 경작. ② (*thrift*) kŏm-yak 검약.

hush *v*. cho-yong-ha-ge ha-da 조용하게 하다, ip-ŭl ta-mul-ge ha-da 입을 다물게 하다. —*int*. swit 쉿.

husk *n*. kkŏp-jil 껍질, oe-p'i 외피(外皮).

hustle *v*. ttŏ-mil-da 떠밀다 ; nan-p'ok-ha-ge mil-da 난폭하게 밀다. —*n*. mil-ch'i-gi 밀치기.

hut *n*. o-du-mak-jip 오두막집, im-si mak-sa 임시 막사.

hybrid *n*. chap-jong 잡종, hon-hyŏ-ra 혼혈아. —*adj*. chap-jong-ŭi 잡종의, hon-hap-ŭi 혼합의.

hydrant *n*. kŭp-su-jŏn 급수전 ; so-hwa-jŏn 소화전.

hydrogen *n*. su-so 수소 : *H*～ *bomb* su-so-p'ok-t'an 수소폭탄／*heavy* ～ chung-su-so 중수소.

hydroplane *n*. su-sang pi-haeng-gi 수상 비행기.

hygiene *n*. kŏn-gang-bŏp 건강법 ; (*sanitary science*) wi-saeng-hak 위생학, sŏp-saeng-bŏp 섭생법.

hymn *n*. ch'an-song-ga 찬송가. —*v*. ch'an-song-ha-da

hyphen *n*. ha-i-p'ŭn 하이픈.　　　　　　└찬송하다.

hypocrite *n*. wi-sŏn-ja 위선자.　　　　┌병적 흥분.

hysteria *n*. hi-sŭ-t'e-ri 히스테리, pyŏng-jŏk hŭng-bun

⟨ I ⟩

I *pron.* na-nŭn 나는, nae-ga 내가.   「da 얼리다.
ice *n.* ŏ-rŭm 얼음, ping-su 빙수. —*v.* (*freeze*) ŏl-ri-
iceberg *n.* ping-san 빙산, yu-bing 유빙(流氷).
icebox *n.* naeng-jang-go 냉장고, naeng-jang-gwe 냉장
ice cream a-i-sŭ-k'ŭ-rim 아이스크림.   └궤.
icehouse *n.* ŏ-rŭm ch'ang-go 얼음 창고, ping-go 빙고
ice water ŏ-rŭm-mul 얼음물, ping-su 빙수.   └(氷庫).
icicle *n.* ko-dŭ-rŭm 고드름.   「쌀쌀한.
icy *adj.* ŏ-rŭm-ga-t'ŭn 얼음같은, (*cold*) ssal-ssal-han
idea *n.* ① (*conception*) kwan-nyŏm 관념, (*thought*)
    sa-sang 사상, (*notion*) saeng-gak 생각. ② (*opinion*)
    ŭi-gyŏn 의견. ③ (*plan*) kye-hoek 계획.
ideal *n.* i-sang 이상(理想). —*adj.* i-sang-jŏk-in 이상적
    인 ; to-hal na-wi-ŏp-nŭn 더할 나위없는.
identical *adj.* (*exactly alike*) tong-il-han 동일한, ttok-
    ga-t'ŭn 똑같은, pa-ro kŭ 바로 그.
identification card sin-bun-jŭng 신분증.
identify *v.* tong-il-si-ha-da 동일시하다, tong-il-ham-ŭl
    chŭng-myŏng-ha-da 동일함을 증명하다.
idiom *n.* suk-ŏ 숙어, kwan-yong-ŏ 관용어.
idiot *n.* ch'ŏn-ch'i 천치, paek-ch'i 백치, pa-bo 바보.
idiotic *adj.* paek-ch'i-ga-t'ŭn 백치같은.
idle *adj.* ke-ŭ-rŭn 게으른 ; (*worthless*) mu-ik-han 무
    익한 ; (*baseless*) kŭn-gŏ-ŏp-nŭn 근거없는. —*v.* ke-
    ŭ-rŭm-p'i-u-da 게으름피우다.
idleness *n.* ke-ŭ-rŭm 게으름, t'ae-man 태만.
idler *n.* ke-ŭ-rŭm-baeng-i 게으름뱅이, kŏn-dal 건달.
idol *n.* u-sang 우상, sung-bae-mul 숭배물.
idolatry *n.* u-sang sung-bae 우상 숭배.

if *conj.* ① (*in case that*) man-il…i-ra-myŏn 만일…이라면. ② (*even if*) …il-ji-ra-do …일지라도. ③ (*whether*) in-ji ŏ-ddŏn-ji 인지 어떤지. 「da 점화하다.

ignite *v.* pul-ŭl pu-ch'i-da 불을 붙이다, chŏm-hwa-ha-

ignoble *adj.* ch'ŏn-han 천한, pi-yŏl-han 비열한.

ignominy *n.* (*dishonor*) pul-myŏng-ye 불명예, ch'i-yok 치욕 ; (*misconduct*) ch'u-haeng 추행.

ignorance *n.* mu-sik 무식, mu-ji 무지.

ignorant *adj.* mu-sik-han 무식한. 「른 체하다.

ignore *v.* mu-si-ha-da 무시하다, mo-rŭn ch'e-ha-da 모

ill *adj.* ① (*sick*) pyŏng-dŭn 병든. ② (*bad*) na-bbŭn 나쁜. ③ (*malevolent*) sim-sul-gu-jŭn 심술궂은. ─*n.* (*evil*) ak 악, (*misfortune*) pul-haeng 불행.

ill-bred *adj.* pŏ-rŭt-ŏp-si cha-ran 버릇없이 자란.

illegal *adj.* pul-bŏp-ŭi 불법의, pi-hap-bŏp-jŏk-in 비합법적인 : *an* ~ *act* pul-bŏp haeng-wi 불법 행위.

ill-fated *adj.* pul-haeng-han 불행한.

illiteracy *n.* mu-sik 무식, mun-maeng 문맹.

illiterate *adj.* mu-sik-han 무식한, mun-maeng-ŭi 문맹의. ─*n.* mun-maeng-ja 문맹자, mu-sik-ja 무식자.

ill-natured *adj.* sim-sul-gu-jŭn 심술궂은.

illness *n.* (*disease*) pyŏng 병, p'yŏn-ch'an-ŭm 편찮음.

ill-treatment *n.* p'u-dae-jŏp 푸대접, hak-dae 학대.

illuminate *v.* pi-ch'u-da 비추다, cho-myŏng-ha-da 조명(照明)하다. 「루미네이션.

illumination *n.* cho-myŏng 조명, il-ru-mi-ne-i-syŏn 일

illusion *n.* hwan-sang 환상, ch'ak-gak 착각.

illustrate *v.* ① (*example*) ye-rŭl tŭ-rŏ sŏl-myŏng-ha-da 예를 들어 설명하다, ye-jŭng-ha-da 예증(例證)하다. ② (*picture*) kŭ-rim-ŭl nŏ-t'a 그림을 넣다.

illustration *n.* ① (*example*) ye-jŭng 예증(例證). ② (*picture*) sap-hwa 삽화, sŏl-myŏng-do 설명도.

illustrious *adj.* ① (*famous*) yu-myŏng-han 유명한. ② (*glorious*) pit-na-nŭn 빛나는.

image *n.* ① yŏng-sang 영상, (*statue*) cho-sang 조상 (彫像). ② (*symbol*) sang-jing 상징. ③ (*form*) mo-yang 모양. —*v.* sang-sang-ha-da 상상하다.

imaginary *adj.* sang-sang-jŏk-in 상상적인.

imagination *n.* sang-sang 상상, sang-sang-ryŏk 상상력.

imagine *v.* sang-sang-ha-da 상상하다, (*think*) saeng-gak-ha-da 생각하다. 「모방하다.

imitate *v.* hyung-nae-nae-da 흉내내다, mo-bang-ha-da

imitation *n.* mo-bang 모방, hyung-nae 흉내.

immeasurable *adj.* he-a-ril su ŏp-nŭn 헤아릴 수 없는.

immediate *adj.* (*direct*) chik-jŏp-jŏk-in 직접적인 ; (*instant*) chŭk-sok-ŭi 즉석의.

immediately *adv.* kot 곧, pa-ro 바로, chŭk-si 즉시.

immense *adj.* mak-dae-han 막대한, mu-han-han 무한한.

immigrant *n.* i-min 이민, i-ju-ja 이주자.

immigrate *v.* i-ju-ha-yŏ o-da 이주하여 오다.

imminent *adj.* (*impending*) im-bak-han 임박한, chŏl-bak-han 절박한. 「룻없는.

immodest *adj.* mu-rye-han 무례한, pŏ-rŭt-ŏp-nŭn 버

immoral *adj.* pu-do-dŏk-han 부도덕한.

immortal *adj.* pul-sa-ŭi 불사의, pul-myŏl-ŭi 불멸의.

immovable *adj.* um-jik-il su ŏp-nŭn 움직일 수 없는.

imp *n.* (*little devil*) kko-ma to-ggae-bi 꼬마 도깨비.

impair *v.* ① (*injure*) hae-ch'i-da 해치다, son-sang-ha-da 손상하다. ② (*reduce*) chu-ri-da 줄이다.

impart *v.* na-nu-ŏ-ju-da 나누어주다 ; al-ri-da 알리다.

impartial *adj.* kong-p'yŏng-han 공평한, ch'i-u-ch'i-ji an-ŭn 치우치지 않은. 「han 침착한.

impassive *adj.* mu-gam-gak-han 무감각한; ch'im-ch'ak-

impatient *adj.* ch'am-ŭl-sŏng-ŏp-nŭn 참을성없는, sŏng-

gŭp-han 성급한, sŏng-ma-rŭn 성마른.   「규탄하다.
impeach *v.* t'an-haek-ha-da 탄핵하다, kyu-t'an-ha-da
impediment *n.* (*obstacle*) pang-hae 방해.
impel *v.* ch'u-jin-si-k'i-da 추진시키다 ; (*urge*) chae-
ch'ok-ha-da 재촉하다.   「im-bak-han 임박한.
impending *adj.* kot i-rŏ-nal tŭt-han 곧 일어날 듯한,
imperative *adj.* myŏng-ryŏng-jŏk-in 명령적인.
imperceptible *adj.* kam-ji-hal su ŏp-nŭn 감지할 수 없
는, nun-e po-i-ji an-nŭn 눈에 보이지 않는.
imperfect *adj.* pul-wan-jŏn-han 불완전한.
imperial *adj.* (*of an empire*) che-guk-ŭi 제국의,
hwang-je-ŭi 황제의 ;(*majestic*) tang-dang-han 당당한 ;
imperialism *n.* che-guk-ju-ŭi 제국주의.
imperishable *adj.* pul-myŏl-ŭi 불멸의, pul-hu-ŭi 불후의.
impersonal *adj.* pi-gae-in-jŏk-in 비개인적인, pi-in-gyŏk-
jŏk-in 비인격적인.
impertinent *adj.* (*insolent*) kŏn-bang-jin 건방진, chŏk-
jŏl-ha-ji an-ŭn 적절하지 않은; mu-rye-han 무례한.
impetuous *adj.* (*violent*) maeng-ryŏl-han 맹렬한, (*rash*)
sŏng-gŭp-han 성급한, ch'ung-dong-jŏk-in 충동적인.
impious *adj.* sin-ang-sim-ŏp-nŭn 신앙심없는; pul-gyŏng-
ŭi 불경의 ; (*wicked*) sa-ak-han 사악한.   「han 엄한.
implacable *adj.* tal-rae-gi him-dŭn 달래기 힘든 ; ŏm-
implement *n.* to-gu 도구, (*instrument*) ki-gu 기구.
—*v.* ① wan-sŏng-ha-da 완성하다, su-haeng-ha-da 수
행하다. ② (*satisfy*) man-jok-si-k'i-da 만족시키다.
implicate *v.* (*entangle*) ŏl-k'i-ge ha-da 얽히게 하다,
kwal-lyŏn-si-k'i-da 관련시키다.
implore *v.* (*entreat*) kan-ch'ŏng-ha-da 간청하다.
imply *v.* ŭi-mi-ha-da 의미하다 ; (*hint*) am-si-ha-da 암
impolite *adj.* pŏ-rŭt-ŏp-nŭn 버릇없는.   L시하다.
import *v.* (*bring in*) su-ip-ha-da 수입하다. —*n.* ① su-

ip 수입. ② (*meaning*) ŭi-mi 의미. ③ (*importance*)
chung-yo-sŏng 중요성.
importance *n*. chung-yo(-sŏng) 중요(성).   「중대한.
important *adj*. chung-yo-han 중요한, chung-dae-han
impose *v*. pu-gwa-ha-da 부과하다, kang-yo-ha-da 강요
impossible *adj*. pul-ga-nŭng-han 불가능한.   └하다.
impotent *adj*. mu-ryŏk-han 무력한. —*n*. hŏ-yak-ja 허약
impractical *adj*. sil-je-jŏk-i a-nin 실제적이 아닌.   └자.
impress *v*. in-sang-ŭl chu-da 인상을 주다.
impression *n*. in-sang 인상, kam-myŏng 감명.
impressive *adj*. in-sang-jŏk-in 인상적인.   「옥하다.
imprison *v*. kam-gŭm-ha-da 감금하다, t'u-ok-ha-da 투
improper *adj*. pu-jŏk-dang-han 부적당한 ; kŭ-rŭt-doen
그릇된, (*indecent*) pŏ-rŭt-ŏp-nŭn 버릇없는.
improve *v*. ① kae-sŏn-ha-da 개선하다, cho-a-ji-da 좋
아지다. ② (*use well*) i-yong-ha-da 이용하다.
improvement *n*. kae-sŏn 개선, kae-ryang 개량.
imprudence *n*. kyŏng-sol 경솔, so-hol 소홀.
imprudent *adj*. (*rash*) kyŏng-sol-han 경솔한, (*indiscreet*) pun-byŏl-ŏp-nŭn 분별없는.   「러운.
impudent *adj*. (*insolent*) ppŏn-bbŏn-sŭ-rŏ-un 뻔뻔스
impulse *n*. ch'ung-dong 충동, (*stimulus*) cha-gŭk 자
극, (*a driving force*) ch'u-jin-ryŏk 추진력.
impunity *n*. myŏn-bŏl 면벌(免罰).   「불결한.
impure *adj*. pul-sun-han 불순한, (*dirty*) pul-gyŏl-han
impute *v*. (*attribute*) …ŭi t'a-sŭ-ro tol-ri-da …의 탓으
로 돌리다, ttŏ-mat-gi-da 떠맡기다.   「[으로].
in *prep*. …ŭi an-e …의 안에. —*adv*. an-e[ŭ-ro] 안에
inability *n*. mu-nŭng 무능, mu-ryŏk 무력.   「린.
inaccurate *adj*. pu-jŏng-hwak-han 부정확한, t'ŭl-rin 틀
inactive *adj*. hwal-bal-ha-ji an-ŭn 활발하지 않은, (*motionless*) hwal-dong-ha-ji an-ŭn 활동하지 않은.

inadequate *adj*. pu-jŏk-dang-han 부적당한; (*insufficient*) pul-ch'ung-bun-han 불충분한.

inattention *n*. pu-ju-ŭi 부주의, pang-sim 방심.

inaudible *adj*. a-ra-dŭ-rŭl su ŏp-nŭn 알아들을 수 없는.

inaugurate *v*. ch'wi-im-sik-ŭl ha-da 취임식을 하다; (*open*) kae-si-ha-da 개시하다. 「성식.

inauguration *n*. ch'wi-im-sik 취임식, nak-sŏng-sik 낙

incapable *adj*. …hal nŭng-ryŏk-i ŏp-nŭn …할 능력이 없는; mu-nŭng-han 무능한.

incendiary *n*. (*arsonist*) pang-hwa-bŏm 방화범; (*bomb*) so-i-t'an 소이탄. —*adj*. pang-hwa-ŭi 방화의.

incense *n*. hyang 향: ~ *burner* hyang-ro 향로.

incentive *adj*. cha-gŭk-jŏk 자극적. —*n*. (*stimulus*) cha-gŭk 자극; (*motive*) tong-gi 동기.

incessant *adj*. kkŭn-im-ŏp-nŭn 끊임없는, yŏn-sok-jŏk-
inch *n*. in-ch'i 인치(＝2.54cm). 「in 연속적인.

incident *n*. sa-gŏn 사건, sa-byŏn 사변.

inclination *n*. ① (*slope*) kyŏng-sa 경사. ② (*tendency*) kyŏng-hyang 경향. ③ (*liking*) ki-ho 기호.

incline *v*. ki-ul-da 기울다; (*be disposed*) ma-ŭm-i ssol-ri-da 마음이 쏠리다. —*n*. kyŏng-sa-myŏn 경사면.

include *v*. p'o-ham-ha-da 포함하다: *postage* ~*d* u-song-ryo p'o-ham-ha-yŏ 우송료 포함하여.

incoherent *adj*. cho-ri-ga sŏ-ji an-nŭn 조리가 서지 않는, ap-dwi-ga mat-ji an-nŭn 앞뒤가 맞지 않는.

income *n*. su-ip 수입, so-dŭk 소득.

incomparable *adj*. pi-gyo-ga an-doe-nŭn 비교가 안되는; yu-rye-ŏp-nŭn 유례없는. 「는, mo-sun-doen 모순된.

incompatible *adj*. yang-rip-hal su ŏp-nŭn 양립할 수 없

incomplete *adj*. pul-wan-jŏn-han 불완전한, mi-wan-sŏng-ŭi 미완성의. 「sol-han 경솔한.

inconsiderate *adj*. chi-gak-ŏp-nŭn 지각없는, kyŏng-

inconsistent *adj.* (*contradictory*) il-ch'i-ha-ji an-nŭn 일치하지 않는, mo-sun-doen 모순된.

inconvenience *n.* pul-p'yŏn 불편, pu-ja-yu 부자유.

inconvenient *adj.* pul-p'yŏn-han 불편한 ; (*causing trouble*) p'ye-ga toe-nŭn 폐가 되는.

incorporate *adj.* pŏp-in-jo-jik-ŭi 법인조직의. —*v.* (*combine*) hap-dong-ha-da 합동하다 ; chu-sik-hoe-sa-ro ha-da 주식회사로 하다.

incorporation *n.* hoe-sa 회사, pŏp-in tan-ch'e 법인 단체.

incorrect *adj.* pu-jŏng-hwak-han 부정확한, t'ŭl-rin 틀린, ol-ch'i an-ŭn 옳지 않은.　　　　「증가.

increase *v.* chŭng-ga-ha-da 증가하다. —*n.* chŭng-ga

incredible *adj.* mit-ŭl su ŏp-nŭn 믿을 수 없는.

incubate *v.* (*hatch*) al-ŭl kka-da 알을 까다.

incubator *n.* pu-hwa-gi 부화기, po-yuk-gi 보육기.

incur *v.* ch'o-rae-ha-da 초래하다, ip-da 입다.

incurable *adj.* ko-ch'il su ŏp-nŭn 고칠 수 없는, pul-ch'i-ŭi 불치의. —*n.* pul-ch'i pyŏng-ja 불치 병자.

indebted *adj.* pu-ch'ae-ga it-nŭn 부채가 있는 ; (*owing gratitude*) ŭn-hye-rŭl ip-ŭn 은혜를 입은.

indecent *adj.* (*ill-bred*) pŏ-rŭt-ŏp-nŭn 버릇없는 ; (*immodest*) ch'u-jap-han 추잡한.

indecisive *adj.* u-mul-jju-mul-ha-nŭn 우물쭈물하는.

indeed *adv.* ch'am-ŭ-ro 참으로, kwa-yŏn 과연.

indefinite *adj.* ① (*not precise*) myŏng-hwak-ha-ji an-nŭn 명확하지 않는. ② (*unlimited*) pu-jŏng-ŭi 부정의.

independent *adj.* tok-rip-han 독립한.

indescribable *adj.* hyŏng-ŏn-hal su ŏp-nŭn 형언할 수

indestructible *adj.* pul-myŏl-ŭi 불멸의.　　　　「없는.

index *n.* saek-in 색인, in-dek-sŭ 인덱스.

India *n.* in-do 인도 : ～ *ink* mŏk 먹.

indicate *v.* chi-jŏk-ha-da 지적하다, ka-ri-k'i-da 가리키다 ;

(*show*) p'yo-si-ha-da 표시하다.

indict *v*. ko-bal-ha-da 고발하다, ki-so-ha-da 기소하다.

indifferent *adj*. mu-gwan-sim-han 무관심한 ; (*careless*) kae-ŭi-ch'i an-nŭn 개의치 않는.

indigenous *adj*. t'o-ch'ak-ŭi 토착의, chi-bang ko-yu-ui 지방 고유의.

indigestion *n*. so-hwa pul-ryang 소화 불량.

indignant *adj*. hwa-ga nan 화가 난, kyŏk-bun-han 격분한.

indigo *n*. nam-saek 남색, jjok-bit 쪽빛, in-di-go 인디고.

indirect *adj*. kan-jŏp-jŏk-in 간접적인 ; (*roundabout*) u-hoe-jŏk-in 우회적인.

indiscreet *adj*. pun-byŏl-ŏp-nŭn 분별없는, mu-mo-han 무모한, (*not prudent*) kyŏng-sol-han 경솔한.

indiscriminate *adj*. ch'a-byŏl-ŏp-nŭn 차별없는, ka-ri-ji an-nŭn 가리지 않는 ; (*random*) nan-jap-han 난잡한.

indispensable *adj*. chŏl-dae p'i-ryo-han 절대 필요한, (*unavoidable*) p'i-hal su ŏp-nŭn 피할 수 없는.

indisputable *adj*. (*unquestionable*) non-ŭi-hal yŏ-ji-ŏp-nŭn 논의할 여지없는, myŏng-baek-han 명백한.

indistinct *adj*. ttu-ryŏt-ha-ji an-ŭn 뚜렷하지 않은, pun-myŏng-ch'i an-ŭn 분명치 않은, hŭi-mi-han 희미한.

individual *adj*. tan-dok-jŏk-in 단독적인, kae-in-jŏk-in 개인적인. —*n*. kae-in 개인, kae-ch'e 개체.

individualism *n*. kae-in-ju-ŭi 개인주의.

indolent *adj*. ke-ŭ-rŭn 게으른, t'ae-man-han 태만한.

indomitable *adj*. kul-ha-ji an-nŭn 굴하지 않는.

indoor *adj*. chip-an-ŭi 집안의, ok-nae-ŭi 옥내의, sil-nae-ŭi 실내의 : ~ *sports* sil-nae-un-dong 실내운동.

indoors *adv*. ok-nae-e-sŏ 옥내에서, sil-nae-e-sŏ 실내에서.

indorse *v*. i-sŏ-ha-da 이서(裏書)하다.

induce *v*. (*exhort*) kwŏn-yu-ha-da 권유하다 ; (*persuade*) sŏl-dŭk-ha-da 설득하다.

induct *v*. (*place*) chik-wi-e an-ch'i-da 직위에 앉히다 ;

(*introduce*) to-ip-ha-da 도입하다.

induction *n.* ① (*introduction*) kkŭ-rŏ-dŭ-rim 끌어들임, to-ip 도입. ② (*logic*) kwi-nap-pŏp 귀납법.

indulge *v.* …e ppa-ji-da …에 빠지다.

industrial *adj.* san-ŏp-ŭi 산업의, kong-ŏp-ŭi 공업의.

industrious *adj.* pu-ji-rŏn-han 부지런한.　　「근면.

industry *n.* ① san-ŏp 산업. ② (*diligence*) kŭn-myŏn

inefficient *adj.* mu-nŭng-han 무능한, (*wasteful*) pi-nŭng-ryul-jŏk-in 비능률적인.　　「석은.

inept *adj.* pu-jŏk-dang-han 부적당한, ŏ-ri-sŏk-ŭn 어리

inequality *n.* ① (*unfairness*) pul-p'yŏng-dŭng 불평등. ② (*disparity*) pu-dong 부동(不同).

inert *adj.* saeng-gi-ga ŏp-nŭn 생기가 없는 ; (*inactive*) t'a-sŏng-jŏk-in 타성적인 ; tun-han 둔한.

inescapable *adj.* p'i-hal su ŏp-nŭn 피할 수 없는.

inestimable *adj.* p'yŏng-ga-hal su ŏp-nŭn 평가할 수

inevitable *adj.* p'i-hal su ŏp-nŭn 피할 수 없는. 「없는.

inexcusable *adj.* yong-sŏ-hal su ŏp-nŭn 용서할 수 없는, pyŏn-myŏng-hal to-ri-ga ŏp-nŭn 변명할 도리가 없는.

inexhaustible *adj.* ① ta ssŭl su ŏp-nŭn 다 쓸 수 없는, mu-jin-jang-ŭi 무진장의. ② (*indefatigable*) pul-gul-ŭi

inexorable *adj.* ka-hok-han 가혹한.　　「불굴의.

inexperienced *adj.* kyŏng-hŏm-ŏp-nŭn 경험없는.

inexplicable *adj.* sŏl-myŏng-hal su ŏp-nŭn 설명할 수 없는 ; (*unaccountable*) pul-ga-hae-han 불가해한.

infamous *adj.* ak-myong-i no-p'ŭn 악명이 높은. 「추문.

infamy *n.* pul-myŏng-ye 불명예, (*disgrace*) ch'u-mun

infant *n.* yu-a 유아, so-a 소아, a-dong 아동.

infantile *adj.* yu-a-ŭi 유아의 : ~ *paralysis* so-a-ma-bi

infantry *n.* po-byŏng 보병(步兵).　　「소아마비.

infect *v.* chŏn-yŏm-si-k'i-da 전염시키다.

infection *n.* chŏn-yŏm 전염, chŏn-yŏm-byŏng 전염병.

infer *v*. ch'u-ron-ha-da 추론하다 ; am-si-ha-da 암시하다.
inferior *adj*. ha-wi-ŭi 하위의 ; yŏl-dŭng-han 열등한.
—*n*. a-raet-sa-ram 아랫사람, yŏl-dŭng-ja 열등자.
infernal *adj*. ① (*of hell*) chi-ok-ŭi 지옥의. ② (*hellish*)
chi-dok-han 지독한, kŭk-ak-ŭi 극악의.
infest *v*. tŭl-ggŭl-t'a 들끓다 ; mol-ryŏ-dŭl-da 몰려들다.
infinitive *n*. pu-jŏng-sa 부정사(不定詞).
inflation *n*. p'aeng-ch'ang 팽창, in-p'ŭl-re 인플레.
inflict *v*. (*impose*) kwa-ha-da 과하다 : (*lay on*) chu-da
주다 ; (*cause*) ip-hi-da 입히다.
influence *n*. ① yŏng-hyang 영향. ② yu-ryŏk-ja 유력
자. —*v*. yŏng-hyang-ŭl kki-ch'i-da 영향을 끼치다.
influenza *n*. yu-haeng-sŏng kam-gi 유행성 감기.
inform *v*. al-ri-da 알리다, t'ong-ji-ha-da 통지하다.
informal *adj*. pi-gong-sik-ŭi 비공식의, yak-sik-ŭi 약식의.
information *n*. ① (*news*) so-sik 소식. ② (*report*) po-
go 보고. ③ (*intelligence*) chŏng-bo 정보 : ~ *bureau*
chŏng-bo-bu 정보부. ④ (*knowledge*) chi-sik 지식.
ingratitude *n*. pae-ŭn-mang-dŏk 배은망덕.
ingredient *n*. sŏng-bun 성분, yo-in 요인, yo-so 요소.
inhabit *v*. (*live in*) kŏ-ju-ha-da 거주하다, sal-da 살다.
inhabitant *n*. chu-min 주민, kŏ-ju-ja 거주자.
inhale *v*. (*breathe in*) ppa-ra-dŭ-ri-da 빨아들이다.
inherent *adj*. (*natural*) t'a-go-nan 타고난, ch'ŏn-bu-
ŭi 천부의 ; (*inborn*) ko-yu-ŭi 고유의.
inherit *v*. sang-sok-ha-da 상속하다, i-ŏ-bat-da 이어받다.
inhibit *v*. kŭm-ha-da 금하다, che-ji-ha-da 제지하다.
inhospitable *adj*. pul-ch'in-jŏl-han 불친절한.
iniquity *n*. pu-jŏng 부정 ; (*wickedness*) sa-ak 사악.
initial *adj*. ch'ŏ-ŭm-ŭi 처음의, pal-dan-ŭi 발단의. —*n*.
mŏ-rit-gŭl-ja 머릿글자. 「키다.
initiate *v*. si-jak-ha-da 시작하다 ; ka-ip-si-k'i-da 가입시

initiative *adj.* ch'ŏ-ŭm-ŭi 처음의. —*n.* ① (*lead*) sol-sŏn 솔선. ② (*first step*) che-il-bo 제일보. ③ (*leadership*) chu-do-gwŏn 주도권.

inject *v.* ① chu-sa-ha-da 주사하다. ② (*interject*) mal-ch'am-gyŏn-ha-da 말참견하다. 「(灌腸).

injection *n.* chu-sa 주사, chu-ip 주입, kwan-jang 관장

injure *v.* hae-ch'i-da 해치다 ; (*hurt*) ta-ch'i-da 다치다.

injury *n.* (*harm*) sang-hae 상해, (*damage*) son-hae 손해 ; kwŏl-li-ch'im-hae 권리침해.

injustice *n.* (*unfairness*) pu-jŏng 부정.

ink *n.* ing-k'ŭ 잉크 : *India* ~ mŏk 먹.

inkstone *n.* pyŏ-ru 벼루.

inlaid *adj.* a-ro-sae-gin 아로새긴, sang-gam-ŭi 상감(象嵌)의.

inland *n. & adj.* nae-ryuk(-ŭi) 내륙(의), kuk-nae(-ŭi) 국내(의).

inlet *n.* ① hu-mi 후미. ② (*entrance*) ip-gu 입구.

inmate *n.* tong-gŏ-in 동거인, tong-suk-in 동숙인.

inn *n.* yŏ-in-suk 여인숙, yŏ-gwan 여관. 「부의.

inner *adj.* an-jjok-ŭi 안쪽의, (*interior*) nae-bu-ŭi 내

innocent *adj.* ch'ŏn-jin nan-man-han 천진 난만한, (*pure*) sun-gyŏl-han 순결한, kyŏl-baek-han 결백한.

innovate *v.* hyŏk-sin-ha-da 혁신하다. 「han 무수한.

innumerable *adj.* sel su ŏp-nŭn 셀 수 없는, mu-su-

innutrition *n.* yŏng-yang pu-jok 영양 부족.

inoculate *v.* (*vaccinate*) ye-bang-jŏp-jong-ŭl ha-da 예방접종을 하다 ; (*imbue*) chu-ip-ha-da 주입하다.

inoculation *n.* chŏp-jong 접종(接種), chong-du 종두.

inquest *n.* sim-ri 심리 ; (*jury*) pae-sim 배심.

inquire *v.* mut-da 묻다 ; cho-sa-ha-da 조사하다. 「탐구.

inquiry *n.* chil-mun 질문 ; (*investigation*) t'am-gu

inquisitive *adj.* ho-gi-sim-i kang-han 호기심이 강한.

insane *adj.* (*mad*) mi-ch'in 미친.

inscribe *v.* sae-gi-da 새기다 ; ki-ip-ha-da 기입하다.

inscription *n.* pi-mun 비문(碑文).

insect *n.* kon-ch'ung 곤충, pŏl-re 벌레.

insecticide *n.* sal-ch'ung-je 살충제.　　　　「전〕한.

insecure *adj.* pu-ran-jŏng〔pu-ran-jŏn〕-han 불안정〔불안

insensible *adj.* (*having no feelings*) mu-gam-gak-han 무감각한, in-sa-bul-sŏng-ŭi 인사불성의.

inseparable *adj.* na-nul su ŏp-nŭn 나눌 수 없는.

insert *v.* kki-wŏ-nŏ-t'a 끼워넣다, (*put into*) sap-ip-ha-da 삽입하다 ; (*publish*) ke-jae-ha-da 게재하다.

inside *n.* an-jjok 안쪽, nae-bu 내부. —*adj. & prep.* an-ŭi 안의. —*adv.* an-jjok-ŭ-ro 안쪽으로, an-e 안에.

insight *n.* t'ong-ch'al-ryŏk 통찰력, an-sik 안식(眼識).

insignia *n.* hun-jang 훈장, (*signs*) p'yo-ji 표지.

insignificant *adj.* (*meaningless*) mu-ŭi-mi-han 무의미한, (*trivial*) tae-su-rop-ji an-ŭn 대수롭지 않은.

insincere *adj.* sŏng-ŭi-ŏp-nŭn 성의없는, pul-sŏng-sil-han 불성실한 ; (*hypocritical*) wi-sŏn-jŏk-in 위선적인.

insist *v.* chu-jang-ha-da 주장하다 ; cho-rŭ-da 조르다.

insolent *adj.* kŏ-man-han 거만한, kyo-man-han 교만한.

insoluble *adj.* hae-gyŏl-hal su ŏp-nŭn 해결할 수 없는.

inspect *v.* cho-sa-ha-da 조사하다, kŏm-yŏl-ha-da 검열하다 ; si-ch'al-ha-da 시찰하다.

inspection *n.* kŏm-sa 검사 ; si-ch'al 시찰.

inspector *n.* (*of factory*) kam-dok-gwan 감독관, (*of school*) chang-hak-gwan 장학관, kŏm-sa-gwan 검사관.

inspire *v.* ko-ch'wi-ha-da 고취하다 ;(*encourage*) ko-mu-ha-da 고무하다 ; yŏng-gam-ŭl chu-da 영감을 주다.

install *v.* ① ch'wi-im-si-k'i-da 취임시키다, im-myŏng-ha-da 임명하다. ② (*set up*) sŏl-ch'i-ha-da 설치하다.

instal(l)ment *n.* pun-nap(-gŭm) 분납(금) : *monthly ~*

wŏl-bu 월부.

instance *n.* (*case*) kyŏng-u 경우 ; (*example*) po-gi 보 [기.

instant *n.* chŭk-si 즉시, sun-gan 순간.

instantaneous *adj.* sun-gan-ŭi 순간의, chŭk-sŏk-ŭi 즉

instantly *adv.* kot 곧, chŭk-gak 즉각. [적의.

instead *adv.* tae-sin-ŭ-ro 대신으로. [기에 찬.

instinct *n.* pon-nŭng 본능. —*adj.* hwal-gi-e ch'an 활.

instinctively *adv.* pon-nŭng-jŏk-ŭ-ro 본능적으로.

institute *v.* (*establish*) sŏl-rip-ha-da 설립하다. —*n.*
  (*society*) hak-hoe 학회, hyŏp-hoe 협회.

institution *n.* ① (*establishment*) sŏl-rip 설립. ② (*system*) che-do 제도. ③ (*custom*) sŭp-gwan 습관. ④
  (*society*) hak-hoe 학회, hyŏp-hoe 협회.

instruct *v.* (*teach*) ka-rŭ-ch'i-da 가르치다 ; (*direct*)
  chi-si-ha-da 지시하다 ; (*inform*) al-ri-da 알리다.

instruction *n.* ① ka-rŭ-ch'im 가르침. ② (*knowledge*)
  chi-sik 지식. ③ (*order*) hul-lyŏng 훈령.

instructor *n.* kyo-sa 교사, kang-sa 강사.

instrument *n.* ki-gu 기구 ; (*means*) su-dan 수단.

insufficient *adj.* pul-ch'ung-bun-han 불충분한, (*inadequate*) pu-jŏk-dang-han 부적당한. [립시키다.

insulate *v.* kyŏk-ri-ha-da 격리하다, ko-rip-si-k'i-da 고

insult *v.* mo-yok-ha-da 모욕하다. —*n.* (*insolence*) mo-yok 모욕 ; (*impoliteness*) mu-rye 무례.

insurance *n.* po-hŏm 보험, po-hŏm-ryo 보험료.

insure *v.* po-hŏm-e nŏ-t'a 보험에 넣다 ; po-jŭng-ha-da
  보증하다 ; (*protect*) an-jŏn-ha-ge ha-da 안전하게 하다.

insurrection *n.* p'ok-dong 폭동, pal-lan 반란.

integrity *n.* ① (*sincerity*) sŏng-sil 성실 ; (*uprightness*) ko-gyŏl 고결. ② (*completeness*) wan-jŏn 완전.

intellect *n.* ① chi-sŏng 지성, chi-ryŏk 지력, i-ji 이지
  (理智). ② chi-sik-in 지식인, chi-sŏng-in 지성인.

intelligence *n.* ① (*sagacity*) chi-hye 지혜, i-hae-ryŏk 이해력. ② (*information*) chŏng-bo 정보.

intelligent *adj.* chi-jŏk-in 지적인, i-ji-jŏk-in 이지적인; (*acute*) ch'ong-myŏng-han 총명한.

intemperance *n.* pu-jŏl-je 부절제, p'ok-ŭm 폭음.

intend *v.* …hal chak-jŏng-i-da …할 작정이다.

intendant *n.* kam-dok-gwan 감독관, kwal-li-ja 관리자.

intense *adj.* kyŏk-ryŏl-han 격렬한, (*fervent*) yŏl-ryŏl-han 열렬한; kin-jang-doen 긴장된.

intent *n.* ŭi-ji 의지, ŭi-hyang 의향. —*adj.* (*absorbed*) yŏl-jung-ha-nŭn 열중하는, mol-du-ha-nŭn 몰두하는.

intention *n.* ŭi-do 의도, ŭi-ji 의지, ŭi-hyang 의향.

intentionally *adv.* il-bu-rŏ 일부러, ko-ŭi-ro 고의로.

interact *n.* mak-gan-gŭk 막간극, mak-gan 막간.

intercept *v.* ka-ro-mak-da 가로막다, ka-ro-ch'ae-da 가

interchange *v.* kyo-hwan-ha-da 교환하다. └로채다.

intercourse *n.* kyo-je 교제, kyo-ryu 교류; sŏng-gyo 성교(性交): *social* ～ sa-gyo 사교.

interest *n.* ① hŭng-mi 흥미. ② (*money*) i-ja 이자.

interesting *adj.* chae-mi-it-nŭn 재미있는. 「정하다.

interfere *v.* kan-sŏp-ha-da 간섭하다; cho-jŏng-ha-da 조

interior *n.* nae-bu 내부. —*adj.* nae-bu-ŭi 내부의.

intermarriage *n.* kuk-je kyŏl-hon 국제 결혼.

intermission *n.* (*pause*) chung-dan 중단, chung-ji 중지; (*between acts*) mak-gan 막간.

internal *adj.* nae-bu-ŭi 내부의, kuk-nae-ŭi 국내의.

international *adj.* kuk-je-jŏk-in 국제적인.

interplanetary *adj.* hok-sŏng-gan-ŭi 혹성간의, ch'ŏn-ch'e-gan-ŭi 천체간의. 「gyŏn-ha-da 말참견하다.

interpose *v.* sap-ip-ha-da 삽입하다; (*put in*) mal-ch'am-

interpret *v.* hae-sŏk-ha-da 해석하다, t'ong-yŏk-ha-da 통역하다.

interpretation *n*. ① (*exposition*) hae-sŏk 해석, hae-sŏl 해설. ② (*translation*) t'ong-yŏk 통역.

interpreter *n*. hae-sŏl-ja 해설자 ; t'ong-yŏk-ja 통역자.

interrogation *n*. chil-mun 질문 ; sim-mun 심문.

interrupt *v*. ka-ro-mak-da 가로막다, pang-hae-ha-da 방해하다 ; (*stop*) chung-dan-ha-da 중단하다.

interruption *n*. pang-hae 방해 ; chung-dan 중단.

interval *n*. kan-gyŏk 간격 ; (*break*) hyu-sik ki-gan 휴식 기간 ; (*between acts*) mak-gan 막간.

interview *n*. ① (*meeting*) myŏn-jŏp 면접. ② (*with pressmen*) hoe-gyŏn 회견, in-t'ŏ-byu-u 인터뷰우. ③ (*with rulers of countries*) al-hyŏn 알현.

intimate *adj*. ch'in-mil-han 친밀한, ka-gga-un 가까운. —*n*. ch'in-u 친우. —*v*. (*hint*) am-si-ha-da 암시하다.

intimidate *v*. ŭ-rŭ-da 으르다, wi-hyŏp-ha-da 위협하다.

into *prep*. an-ŭ-ro 안으로, an-e 안에.

intolerable *adj*. ch'am-ŭl su ŏp-nŭn 참을 수 없는.

intonation *n*. ŏ-jo 어조, ŏk-yang 억양.

intoxicate —*v*. ch'wi-ha-ge ha-da 취하게 하다 ; to-ch'wi〔hung-bun〕-ha-da 도취〔흥분〕하다.

intricate *adj*. twi-ŏl-k'in 뒤얽힌, pok-jap-han 복잡한.

intrigue *n*. ŭm-mo 음모 ; mil-t'ong 밀통. —*v*. ŭm-mo-ha-da 음모하다 ; mil-t'ong-ha-da 밀통하다.

intrinsic *adj*. (*essential*) pon-jil-jŏk-in 본질적인, pol-lae-ŭi 본래의, (*inherent*) ko-yu-ŭi 고유의.

introduce *v*. ① so-gae-ha-da 소개하다. ② (*bring in*) i-ggŭ-rŏ-dŭ-ri-da 이끌어들이다.

introduction *n*. ① so-gae 소개. ② (*in a book*) sŏ-mun 서문, mŏ-ri-mal 머리말. ③ (*primer*) ip-mun 입문.

intrude *v*. ch'im-ip-ha-da 침입하다, mil-go tŭ-rŏ-ga-da 밀고 들어가다 ; pang-hae-ha-da 방해하다.

intuition *n*. chik-gak 직각, chik-gwan 직관.

invade *v*. ch'yŏ-dŭ-rŏ-o-da 쳐들어오다, ch'im-ip-ha-da 침입하다, (*violate*) ch'im-hae-ha-da 침해하다.

invalid *n*. hwan-ja 환자. —*adj*. ① (*feeble*) hŏ-yak-han 허약한. ② (*of no force*) mu-hyo-ŭi 무효의.

invalidate *v*. mu-hyo-ro ha-da 무효로 하다.

invaluable *adj*. a-ju kwi-jung-han 아주 귀중한.

invariable *adj*. (*unchangeable*) pul-byŏn-ŭi 불변의 ; (*constant*) il-jŏng-han 일정한.

invasion *n*. ch'im-ip 침입, ch'im-hae 침해.

invent *v*. pal-myŏng-ha-da 발명하다 ; kku-myŏ-nae-da 꾸며내다 ; (*make up*) nal-jo-ha-da 날조하다.

invention *n*. pal-myŏng(-p'um) 발명(품).

inventor *n*. pal-myŏng-ga 발명가, ko-an-ja 고안자.

inventory *n*. chae-san mok-rok 재산 목록 ; (*a stock list*) chae-go-p'um mok-rok 재고품 목록.

inverse *adj*. pan-dae-ŭi 반대의, yŏk-ŭi 역(逆)의.

invest *v*. ① (*funds*) t'u-ja-ha-da 투자하다. ② (*clothes*) ip-hi-da 입히다. ③ (*endow*) chu-da 주다. 「구하다.

investigate *v*. cho-sa-ha-da 조사하다, yŏn-gu-ha-da 연

investigation *n*. cho-sa 조사, yŏn-gu 연구.

investment *n*. t'u-ja 투자 ; (*encirclement*) p'o-wi 포위.

invigorate *v*. wŏn-gi-rŭl tot-gu-da 원기를 돋구다.

invincible *adj*. chŏng-bok-hal su ŏp-nŭn 정복할 수 없는, mu-jŏk-ŭi 무적의, pul-p'ae-ŭi 불패(不敗)의.

invisible *adj*. po-i-ji an-nŭn 보이지 않는. 「대장.

invitation *n*. ch'o-dae 초대 : ~ *card* ch'o-dae-jang 초

invite *v*. ch'o-dae-ha-da 초대하다 ; kkoe-da 꾀다.

invocation *n*. ki-wŏn 기원 ;(*spell*) chu-mun 주문(呪文).

invoice *n*. song-jang 송장(送狀).

involuntary *adj*. mu-ŭi-sik-jung-ŭi 무의식중의 ; (*un-wished for*) pon-ŭi a-nin 본의 아닌.

involve *v*. p'o-ham-si-k'i-da 포함시키다, kkŭ-rŏ-nŏ-t'a

끌어넣다 ; (*imply*) ttŭt-ha-da 뜻하다.   「적인.
inward *adj.* nae-bu-ŭi 내부의 ; (*mental*) sim-jŏk-in 심
iris *n.* ① (*plant*) put-ggot 붓꽃, ch'ang-p'o 창포. ②
    (*eye*) hong-ch'ae 홍채.
irksome *adj.* sŏng-ga-sin 성가신, kwi-ch'an-ŭn 귀찮은.
iron *n.* ① soe 쇠, ch'ŏl 철. ② (*flatiron*) ta-ri-mi 다
    리미. —*adj.* ① ch'ŏl-ŭi 철의. ② kyŏn-go-han 견고한.
ironic(al) *adj.* pin-jŏng-dae-nŭn 빈정대는, pi-ggo-nŭn
ironing *n.* ta-ri-mi-jil 다리미질.   「비꼬는.
ironmonger *n.* ch'ŏl-mul-sang 철물상.
irregular *adj.* pul-gyu-ch'ik-jŏk-in 불규칙적인, (*uneven*)
    ko-rŭ-ji an-ŭn 고르지 않은, pyŏn-ch'ik-ŭi 변칙의.
irrelevant *adj.* pu-jŏk-dang-han 부적당한.
irresistible *adj.* chŏ-hang-hal su ŏp-nŭn 저항할 수 없
    는 ; (*overmastering*) i-gyŏ-nael su ŏp-nŭn 이겨낼 수
    없는 ; kyŏn-dil su ŏp-nŭn 견딜 수 없는.
irresolute *adj.* kyŏl-dan-ryŏk-ŏp-nŭn 결단력없는, (*hesi-
    tating*) u-yu-bu-dan-han 우유부단한.
irresponsible *adj.* mu-ch'aek-im-han 무책임한.
irrigate *v.* mul-ŭl tae-da 물을 대다, ch'uk-i-da 축이다,
    (*water*) kwan-gae-ha-da 관개(灌漑)하다.
irrigation *n.* mul-daem 물댐, kwan-gae 관개.
irritable *adj.* hwa chal nae-nŭn 화 잘 내는, sŏng-ma-
    rŭn 성마른, ae-rŭl t'ae-u-nŭn 애를 태우는.
irritate *v.* (*provoke*) yak-ol-ri-da 약올리다, an-dal-na-
    ge ha-da 안달나게 하다, cha-gŭk-ha-da 자극하다.
island *n.* sŏm 섬 : *Namhae I*~ nam-hae-sŏm 남해섬.
isolate *v.* ko-rip-si-k'i-da 고립시키다, kyŏk-ri-ha-da 격
    리하다 ; (*insulate*) chŏ-ryŏn-ha-da 절연하다.
issue *n.* ① (*flowing out*) yu-ch'ul 유출(流出). ② (*exit*)
    ch'ul-gu 출구. ③ (*outcome*) kyŏl-gwa 결과. ④ (*subject
    debated*) non-jŏm 논점. ⑤ (*publication*) pal-haeng

발행. —*v.* ① (*make public*) kong-p'o-ha-da 공포하다. ② (*publish*) kan-haeng-ha-da 간행하다. ③ (*result*) i-rŏ-na-da 일어나다.

it *pron.* kŭ-gŏ-sŭn 그것은, kŭ-gŏ-si 그것이, kŭ-gŏ-sŭl 그것을.

itch *n.* ka-ryŏ-um 가려움 ; (*disease*) om 옴. —*v.* ka-ryŏ-wŏ-ha-da 가려워하다.

item *n.* cho-hang 조항, hang-mok 항목.　「반복하다.

iterate *v.* toe-p'u-ri-ha-da 되풀이하다, pan-bok-ha-da

itinerary *n.* (*plan of travel*) yŏ-haeng il-jŏng 여행 일정, yŏ-haeng an-nae 여행 안내, (*route*) yŏ-ro 여로, (*record of travel*) yŏ-haeng il-gi 여행 일기.

itinerate *v.* sun-hoe-ha-da 순회하다.

itself *pron.* kŭ cha-sin 그 자신, kŭ cha-ch'e 그 자체.

ivory *n.* sang-a 상아 ; *artificial* ～ in-jo sang-a 인조 상아/～ *tower* sang-a-t'ap 상아탑.　「담쟁이로 덮다.

ivy *n.* tam-jaeng-i 담쟁이. —*v.* tam-jaeng-i-ro tŏp-da

✦ J ✦

jab *v.* jji-rŭ-da 찌르다 ; chwi-ŏ-bak-da 쥐어박다.

jack *n.* (*tool*) chaek 잭, (*man*) nam-ja 남자, (*crew*)

jacket *n.* cha-k'et 자켓.　Lsŏn-wŏn 선원.

jade *n.* pi-ch'wi 비취, ok 옥.

jail *n.* (*prison*) kyo-do-so 교도소, kam-ok 감옥.

jailer · jailor *n.* kan-su 간수(看守).

jam *n.* ① chaem 쨈. ② (*crowdedness*) hon-jap 혼잡. ③ (*machinery*) ko-jang 고장. —*v.* ① (*press*) ssu-syŏ-nŏ-t'a 쑤셔넣다. ② (*machinery*) kŏl-ri-da 걸리다.

jangle *v.* ttaeng-gŭ-rang so-ri-na-da 땡그랑 소리나다.

janitor *n.* (*doorkeeper*) mun-ji-gi 문지기, (*guard*) su-wi 수위, kwal-li-in 관리인.

January *n.* chŏng-wŏl 정월, il-wŏl 일월.
Japan *n.* il-bon 일본(日本).
Japanese *n.* ① (*people*) il-bon-sa-ram 일본사람. ② (*lang.*) il-bon-mal 일본말. —*adj.* il-bon-ŭi 일본의.
jar *n.* tok 독, tan-ji 단지, hang-a-ri 항아리. 「설수설.
jargon *n.* hŏ-t'ŭn-so-ri 허튼소리, hoeng-sŏl-su-sŏl 횡
jarring *n.* chin-dong 진동. —*adj.* ppi-gŏk-gŏ-ri-nŭn
jaundice *n.* hwang-dal 황달. 「삐걱거리는.
jaunty *adj.* kyŏng-k'wae-han 경쾌한 ; hwal-gi-it-nŭn 활기있는 ; (*smart*) mal-ssuk-han 말쑥한.
javelin *n.* (*dart*) t'u-ch'ang 투창(投槍).
jaw *n.* t'ŏk 턱 : *Hold your* ~! tak-ch'yŏ 닥쳐 !
jazz *n.* chae-jŭ 재즈 : ~ *band* chae-jŭ-baen-dŭ 재즈밴드.
jealous *adj.* chil-t'u-sim-man-ŭn 질투심많은, si-gi-ha-nŭn 시기하는, t'u-gi-ha-nŭn 투기하는.
jealousy *n.* chil-t'u 질투, kang-jja 강짜.
jeer *v.* cho-rong-ha-da 조롱하다 ; pi-ut-da 비웃다.
jelly *n.* han-ch'ŏn 한천, u-mu 우무 ; chel-ri 젤리.
jellyfish *n.* hae-p'a-ri 해파리.
jeopardize *v.* wi-t'ae-rop-ge ha-da 위태롭게 하다.
jerk *n.* pi-t'ŭl-gi 비틀기 ; kŭn-yuk-ŭi kyŏng-ryŏn 근육의 경련. —*v.* hwaek chap-a-dang-gi-da 홱 잡아당기다.
jest *n.* & *v.* nong-dam(-ha-da) 농담(하다).
Jesus *n.* ye-su 예수, ye-su kŭ-ri-sŭ-do 예수 그리스도.
jet *v.* (*shoot*) ppŭm-ŏ-nae-da 뿜어내다, pun-ch'ul-ha-da 분출하다. —*n.* ① pun-ch'ul 분출. ② hŭk-ok 흑옥
jet plane che-t'ŭ-gi 제트기. 「(黑玉).
jetty *n.* (*breakwater*) pang-p'a-je 방파제 ; (*pier*) pu-du 부두, sŏn-ch'ang 선창. 「자.
Jew *n.* yu-t'ae-in 유태인 ; yu-t'ae-gyo sin-ja 유태교 신
jewel *n.* po-sŏk 보석, po-ok 보옥. 「보석 세공인.
jewel(l)er *n.* po-sŏk-sang 보석상, po-sŏk se-gong-in

jingle *v.* ttal-rang-ddal-rang ul-ri-da 딸랑딸랑 울리다.
jinx *n.* pul-gil-han kŏt 불길한 것, ching-k'ŭ-sŭ 징크스.
job *n.* ① (*work*) il 일, sak-il 삯일. ② (*employment*) chik-ŏp 직업. ③ (*post*) chi-wi 지위.
jocund *adj.* myŏng-rang-han 명랑한, chŭl-gŏ-un 즐거운.
join *v.* ka-ip-ha-da 가입하다, (*unite*) kyŏl-hap-ha-da 결합하다, (*connect*) yŏn-gyŏl-ha-da 연결하다.
joint *n.* ① (*of the body*) kwan-jŏl 관절. ② (*seam*) i-ŭn cha-ri 이은 자리. ③ (*connection*) chŏp-hap 접합. —*adj.* (*common*) kong-dong-ŭi 공동의.
joke *n.* nong-dam 농담. —*v.* nong-dam-ha-da 농담하다.
jolly *adj.* chŭl-gŏ-un 즐거운. —*adv.* mae-u 매우.
jolt *v.* tŏl-k'ŏng-gŏ-ri-da 덜컹거리다.
jostle *v.* ① (*push roughly*) pu-dit-ch'i-da 부딪치다. ② (*elbow*) mi-rŏ-jŏ-ch'i-da 밀어젖히다.
jot *v.* (*down*) kan-dan-ha-ge chŏk-ŏ-du-da 간단하게 적어두다. —*n.* cho-gŭm 조금, yak-gan 약간.
journal *n.* ① (*diary*) il-gi 일기, il-ji 일지. ② (*daily newspaper*) il-gan-sin-mun 일간신문. ③ (*periodical*) (chŏng-gi kan-haeng) chap-ji (정기 간행) 잡지.
journalist *n.* ki-ja 기자, chŏ-ŏ-nŏl-ri-sŭ-t'ŭ 저어널리스트.
journey *n.* yŏ-haeng 여행, yŏ-jŏng 여정(旅程). —*v.* yŏ-haeng-ha-da 여행하다. 「희
joy *n.* ki-bbŭm 기쁨, chŭl-gŏ-um 즐거움, hwan-hŭi 환
joyful *adj.* ki-bbŭn 기쁜, chŭl-gŏ-un 즐거운.
judge *n.* chae-p'an-gwan 재판관, p'an-sa 판사. —*v.* p'an-gyŏl-ha-da 판결하다.
judg(e)ment *n.* ① chae-p'an 재판. ② (*discrimination*) p'an-dan 판단. ③ (*opinion*) ŭi-gyŏn 의견.
jug *n.* ① chu-jŏn-ja 주전자, hang-a-ri 항아리, tan-ji 단지. ② cho-ggi 조끼.
juggle *n.* (*sleight of hand*) yo-sul 요술 ; (*imposture*)

sa-gi 사기. 「sa-git-gun 사깃군.
juggler *n.* ① yo-sul-jang-i 요술장이. ② (*impostor*)
juice *n.* chŭp 즙, chu-u-sŭ 주우스 : *fruit* ～ kwa-jŭp
July *n.* ch'il-wŏl 7월. 　　　　　　　　　　　 ⌐과즙.
jumble *n.* chap-dong-sa-ni 잡동사니 ; hol-lan 혼란.
jump *v.* ttwi-ŏ-o-rŭ-da 뛰어오르다, twi-ŏ-nŏm-da 뛰어
　 넘다. —*n.* (*leap*) to-yak 도약, chŏm-p'ŭ 점프.
junction *n.* chŏp-hap 접합, chŏp-hap-jŏm 접합점.
June *n.* yu-wŏl 6월.
jungle *n.* mil-rim 밀림, chŏng-gŭl 정글.
junior *n.* (*younger*) yŏn-so-ja 연소자 ; pu-ha 부하 ;
　 hu-bae 후배. —*adj.* yŏn-so-han 연소한.
junk *n.* ① chŏng-k'ŭ 정크. ② p'ye-mul 폐물.
Jupiter *n.* ① chu-p'i-t'ŏ 주피터. ② mok-song 목성(木星).
jurisdiction *n.* ① sa-bŏp-gwŏn 사법권. ② kwan-hal
jury *n.* pae-sim-wŏn 배심원. 　　　　 ⌐ku-yŏk 관할 구역.
just *adj.* (*right*) chŏng-dang-han 정당한, kong-jŏng-
　 han 공정한. —*adv.* ① (*exactly*) pa-ro 바로. ② (*hard-
　 ly*) ka-gga-sŭ-ro 가까스로.
justice *n.* chŏng-ŭi 정의, kong-jŏng 공정.
justify *v.* chŏng-dang-hwa-ha-da 정당화하다, ol-t'a-go
　 ha-da 옳다고 하다. 　　　　　　 「ch'ul-ha-da돌출하다.
jut *v.* (*project*) pul-ruk nae-mil-da 불룩 내밀다, tol-
juvenile *adj.* so-nyŏn-so-nyŏ-ŭi 소년소녀의.

—◄ K ►—

kangaroo *n.* k'aeng-gŏ-ru-u 캥거루우.
keen *adj.* ① nal-k'a-ro-un 날카로운. ② (*strong*) kang-
　 han 강한. ③ (*eager*) yŏl-mang-ha-nŭn 열망하는.
keep *v.* ① (*guard*) chi-k'i-da 지키다. ② (*raise*) ki-
　 rŭ-da 기르다. ③ (*preserve*) po-jon-ha-da 보존하다.

keeper *n.* ① (*guardian*) kwal-li-in 관리인, kam-si-ja 감시자. ② (*proprietor*) so-yu-ja 소유자.

keeping *n.* yu-ji 유지 ; po-jon 보존, pu-yang 부양.

keepsake *n.* yu-p'um 유품, ki-nyŏm-p'um 기념품.

kennel *n.* kae-jip 개집 ; (*lair*) kul 굴.

kernel *n.* kwa-sil-ŭi in 과실의 인(仁), (*grain*) al-

kerosene *n.* tŭng-yu 등유(燈油).　　　⌐maeng-i 알맹이.

kettle *n.* chu-jŏn-ja 주전자, (*pot*) sot 솥.

key *n.* ① yŏl-soe 열쇠. ② (*clue*) sil-ma-ri 실마리. ③ (*secret*) pi-gyŏl 비결. ④ (*piano*) kŏn 건.

keyhole *n.* yŏl-soe ku-mŏng 열쇠 구멍, ma-gae ku-mŏng

key industry ki-gan san-ŏp 기간 산업.　　　⌐마개 구멍.

key money kwŏl-li-gŭm 권리금, po-jŭng-gŭm 보증금.

khaki *adj.* k'a-a-k'i-saek-ŭi 카아키색의.

kick *v.* ch'a-da 차다. —*n.* pal-ro ch'a-gi 발로 차기.

kid *n.* ① (*young goat*) sae-ggi yŏm-so 새끼 염소. ② (*child*) a-i 아이. —*v.* nong-dam-ha-da 농담하다.

kidnap *v.* (*abduct*) kkoe-ŏ-nae-da 꾀어내다, yu-goe-ha-da 유괴하다, (*hijack*) nap-ch'i-ha-da 납치하다.

kidney *n.* sin-jang 신장(腎臟), k'ong-p'at 콩팥.

kill *v.* ① (*slay*) chuk-i-da 죽이다. ② (*suppress*) ŏk-nu-rŭ-da 억누르다. ③ (*consume*) so-bi-ha-da 소비하다:

killer *n.* chuk-i-nŭn sa-ram 죽이는 사람.

kiln *n.* ka-ma(-sot) 가마(솥).

kilogram *n.* k'il-ro-gŭ-raem 킬로그램.

Kimchi *n.* (*Korean*) kim-ch'i 김치.

kilometer *n.* k'il-ro-mi-t'ŏ 킬로미터.

kin *n.* (*relatives*) ch'in-ch'ŏk 친척, ch'in-jok 친족, hyŏl-jok-gwan-gye 혈족관계, (*family*) ka-mun 가문.

[ka-ma-(sot)]

kind *n.* (*sort*) chong-ryu 종류, (*character*) sŏng-jil 성질. —*adj.* ch'in-jŏl-han 친절한.

kindergarten *n.* yu-ch'i-wŏn 유치원.

kindle *v.* pul-sa-rŭ-da 불사르다; pal-gge ha-da 밝게 하다.

kindly *adj.* ch'in-jŏl-han 친절한, sang-nyang-han 상냥한. —*adv.* ch'in-jŏl-ha-ge 친절하게, ki-ggŏ-i 기꺼이.

kindness *n.* ch'in-jŏl 친절; (*love*) ae-jŏng 애정.

kindred *n.* ① (*blood relationship*) hyŏ-ryŏn 혈연; (*clan*) tong-jok 동족. ② (*likeness*) yu-sa 유사. —*àdj.* ① hyŏ-ryŏn-ŭi 혈연의. ② yu-sa-han 유사한.

king *n.* wang 왕, kuk-wang 국왕, kun-ju 군주.

kingdom *n.* wang-guk 왕국; (*realm*) ···kye ···계.

kingfisher *n.* mul-ch'ong-sae 물총새. 「당한.

kingly *adj.* wang-ŭi 왕의; (*royal*) tang-dang-han 당

kinsfolk *n.* ch'in-ch'ŏk 친척, il-ga 일가.

kiss *n.* ip-mat-ch'u-gi 입맞추기, k'i-sŭ 키스. —*v.* ip-mat-ch'u-da 입맞추다. 「취사장.

kitchen *n.* pu-ŏk 부엌, chu-bang 주방, ch'wi-sa-jang

kite *n.* ① (*toy*) yŏn 연(鳶). ② (*bird*) sol-gae 솔개. ③ (*impostor*) sa-git-gun 사깃군. 「끼.

kitten *n.* ko-yang-i sae-ggi 고양이 새

klaxon *n.* cha-dong-ch'a-ŭi kyŏng-jŏk 자동차의 경적. 「령.

[yŏn]

knack *n.* som-ssi 솜씨, yo-ryŏng 요

knapsack *n.* pae-nang 배낭, ran-do-sel 란도셀. 「견달.

knave *n.* (*rascal*) ak-han 악한(惡漢), (*rogue*) kŏn-dal

knead *v.* pan-juk-ha-da 반죽하다, kae-da 개다.

knee *n.* mu-rŭp 무릎: *on one's* ~s mu-rŭp-ŭl kkul-k'o 무릎을 꿇고.

kneel *v.* mu-rŭp-ŭl kkul-t'a 무릎을 꿇다. 「jo 흉조.

knell *n.* ① cho-jong 조종(弔鍾). ② (*evil omen*) hyung-

knife *n.* chu-mŏ-ni-k'al 주머니칼, na-i-p'ŭ 나이프.

knight *n.* ki-sa 기사(騎士).

knit *v.* ① (*yarn*) ttŭ-da 뜨다 ; jja-da 짜다. ② (*joint*)
chŏp-hap-ha-da 접합하다.
knitting *n.* ttŭ-gae-jil 뜨개질, p'yŏn-mul 편물.
knob *n.* ① son-jap-i 손잡이. ② (*lump*) hok 혹.
knock *v.* (*strike*) tu-dŭ-ri-da 두드리다. —*n.* (*stroke*)
t'a-gyŏk 타격, (*blow*) ku-t'a 구타 ; no-k'ŭ 노크.
knockout *n.* nok-a-u-t'ŭ 녹아우트, k'e-i-o-u 케이오우.
knoll *n.* (*mound*) chak-ŭn san 작은 산.
knot *n.* ① (*tie*) mae-dŭp 매듭. ② (*nautical mile*)
hae-ri 해리(海里). ③ no-t'ŭ 노트. —*v.* mae-dŭp-jit-da
매듭짓다, (*entangle*) ŏl-k'i-da 얽히다.
know *v.* ① (*understand*) al-da 알다. ② (*recognize*)
in-jŏng-ha-da 인정하다. ③ (*be acquainted with*) …wa
ch'in-han sa-i-da …와 친한 사이다.   「결.
know-how *n.* chi-sik 지식, pang-bŏp 방법, pi-gyŏl 비
knowledge *n.* (*information*) chi-sik 지식, in-sik 인식 ;
i-hae 이해 ; (*learning*) hak-mun 학문.
known *adj.* al-ryŏ-jyŏ it-nŭn 알려져 있는 : *make* ～ al-
ri-da 알리다, pal-p'yo-ha-da 발표하다.
knuckle *n.* son-ga-rak-ŭi kwan-jŏl 손가락의 관절.
Korea *n.* han-guk 한국 : tae-han-min-guk 대한민국.
Korean *n. & adj.* (*people*) han-guk-sa-ram(-ŭi) 한
국사람(의) ; (*language*) han-guk-mal(-ŭi) 한국말(의).
Kremlin *n.* k'ŭ-re-mŭl-rin kung-jŏn 크레믈린 궁전 ; so-
ryŏn chŏng-bu 소련 정부.

—◄ **L** ►—

label *n.* ttak-ji 딱지, pu-jŏn 부전, re-t'e-rŭ 레테르.
—*v.* ttak-ji-rŭl pu-ch'i-da 딱지를 붙이다.
labo(u)r *n.* no-dong 노동, (*toil*) ko-doen il 고된 일.
—*v.* il-ha-da 일하다, no-dong-ha-da 노동하다.

laboratory *n.* sil-hŏm-sil 실험실, yŏn-gu-so 연구소 :
chemical ~ hwa-hak-yŏn-gu-so 화학연구소.
laborious *adj.* him-dŭ-nŭn 힘드는, ko-doen 고된.
labo(u)r union no-dong-jo-hap 노동조합.
labyrinth *n.* (*maze*) mi-gung 미궁(迷宮), mi-ro 미로.
lace *n.* (*fabric*) re-i-sŭ 레이스, kkŭn 끈.
lack *n.* (*want*) pu-jok 부족, (*deficiency*) kyŏl-p'ip 결
핍. —*v.* pu-jok-ha-da 부족하다, mo-ja-ra-da 모자라다.
lacquer *n.* rae-k'ŏ 래커, ch'il 칠(漆), ot 옻.
lacquer ware ch'il-gi 칠기.　　　　　「sŏk 녀석.
lad *n.* chŏl-mŭn-i 젊은이, so-nyŏn 소년, (*chap*) nyŏ-
ladder *n.* ① sa-dak-da-ri 사닥다리. ② (*means*) su-dan
수단, pang-bŏp 방법.
lade *v.* (*load*) hwa-mul-ŭl sit-da 화물을 싣다 ; (*burden*) chim-ŭl chi-u-da 짐을 지우다.
laden *adj.* chim-ŭl si-rŭn 짐을 실은.
ladies and gentlemen sin-sa suk-nyŏ 신사 숙녀.
lading *n.* chim-sit-gi 짐싣기, chŏk-jae 적재 : *bill of* ~
sŏn-ha-jŭng-gwŏn 선하증권.　　　　　「내다.
ladle *n.* kuk-ja 국자. —*v.* p'u-da 푸다, p'ŏ-nae-da 퍼
lady *n.* kwi-bu-in 귀부인, suk-nyŏ 숙녀 : *a* ~ *clerk*
yŏ-sa-mu-wŏn 여사무원/*a* ~ *killer* saek-gol 색골.
lag *v.* kku-mul-gŏ-ri-da 꾸물거리다, ch'ŏ-ji-da 처지다.
lair *n.* (*den*) tŭl-jim-sŭng-ŭi kul 들짐승의 굴.
laity *n.* (*laymen*) sok-in 속인(俗人) ; p'ut-na-gi 풋나기,
a-ma-t'yu-ŏ 아마튜어.
lake *n.* ho-su 호수 ; (*pond*) mot 못, yŏn-mot 연못.
lamb *n.* ① (*young sheep*) ŏ-rin yang 어린 양. ②
(*innocent person*) yu-sun-han sa-ram 유순한 사람.
lame *adj.* chŏl-rŭm-ba-ri-ŭi 절름발이의 ; (*imperfect*)
pul-wan-jŏn-han 불완전한.　　　　　「sŭl-p'ŭm 슬픔.
lament *v.* sŭl-p'ŏ-ha-da 슬퍼하다. —*n.* pi-t'an 비탄,

lamentation *n*. pi-t'an 비탄, t'ong-gok 통곡.

lamp *n*. tŭng 등, nam-p'o 남포 : *a street* ~ ka-ro-dŭng 가로등/*a safety* ~ an-jŏn-dŭng 안전등.

lamplight *n*. tŭng-bul 등불, raem-p'ŭ-bit 램프빛.

lance *n*. ch'ang 창(槍), chak-sal 작살.

land *n*. ① ttang 땅, t'o-ji 토지. ② (*state*) na-ra 나라. —*v*. sang-ryuk-ha-da 상륙하다 ; (*alight*) ha-ch'a-ha-da 하차하다 ; (*arrive*) to-ch'ak-ha-da 도착하다.

landlady *n*. yŏ-ja-ju-in 여자주인, an-ju-in 안주인.

landlord *n*. ① (*house*) chip-ju-in 집주인 ; ka-jang 가장. ② (*property*) chi-ju 지주.

landmark *n*. ① kyŏng-gye-p'yo 경계표. ② (*outstanding event*) hoek-gi-jŏk sa-gŏn 획기적 사건.

landowner *n*. t'o-ji so-yu-ja 토지 소유자, chi-ju 지주.

landscape *n*. p'ung-gyŏng 풍경, chŏn-mang 전망.

landslide *n*. sa-t'ae 사태, san-sa-t'ae 산사태.

lane *n*. chop-ŭn kil 좁은 길, (*byway*) saet-gil 샛길.

language *n*. mal 말, ŏn-ŏ 언어, kuk-ŏ 국어.

languid *adj*. na-rŭn-han 나른한, no-gon-han 노곤한.

languish *v*. soe-yak-hae-ji-da 쇠약해지다, si-dŭl-da 시들다.

lantern *n*. ch'o-rong 초롱, k'an-del-ra 칸델라.

lap *v*. (*lick*) hal-t'a 핥다. —*n*. mu-rŭp 무릎.

lapse *v*. ① (*backslide*) t'a-rak-ha-da 타락하다. ② (*pass*) si-gan-i chi-na-da 시간이 지나다.

lard *n*. twae-ji ki-rŭm 돼지 기름, ra-a-dŭ 라아드.

large *adj*. k'ŏ-da-ran 커다란, (*spacious*) nŏl-bŭn 넓은, (*copious*) man-ŭn 많은, (*liberal*) kwan-dae-han 관대한.

lark *n*. (*skylark*) chong-da-ri 종다리, chong-dal-sae 종달새.

lascivious *adj*. ŭm-t'ang-han 음탕한.

lash *n*. ch'ae-jjik 채찍. —*v*. ① mae-jil-ha-da 매질하다. ② (*bind*) tong-yŏ-mae-da 동여매다.

lass *n*. so-nyŏ 소녀, chŏl-mŭn yŏ-ja 젊은 여자.

last *v.* (*continue*) kye-sok-ha-da 계속하다. —*adj.* ch'oe-hu-ŭi 최후의 ; (*most recent*) ch'oe-gŭn-ŭi 최근의. —*adv.* ch'oe-hu-ro 최후로. 「영속하는.

lasting *adj.* o-rae ka-nŭn 오래 가는, yŏng-sok-ha-nŭn

latch *n.* pit-jang 빗장, kŏl-soe 걸쇠.

late *adj.* ① nŭ-jŭn 늦은, chi-gak-han 지각한. ② (*recent*) ch'oe-gŭn-ŭi 최근의. ③ (*dead*) ko 고(故) : *the ~ Mr. A* ko e-i-ssi 고(故) A씨. —*adv.* nŭt-ge 늦게.

lately *adv.* yo-jŭ-ŭm 요즈음, kŭl-lae 근래.

latent *adj.* cham-bok-han 잠복한, cham-jae-jŏk 잠재적 : ~ *period* cham-bok-gi 잠복기.

latest *adj.* ch'oe-gŭn-ŭi 최근의, ch'oe-hu-ui 최후위.

lathe *n.* sŏn-ban 선반(旋盤), nok-ro 녹로.

Latin *adj.* ra-t'in-ŭi 라틴의, ra-t'in-gye-ŭi 라틴계의. —*n.* ra-t'in-ŏ 라틴어, ra-t'in-sa-ram 라틴사람.

latitude *n.* ① wi-do 위도, ssi-jul 씨줄. ② (*pl.*) chi-

latrine *n.* (*privy*) pyŏn-so 변소. ⌊dae 지대.

latter *adj.* hu-ja-ŭi 후자의. —*n.* hu-ja 후자.

lattice *n.* kyŏk-ja 격자(格子), kyŏk-ja-ch'ang 격자창.

laudable *adj.* kya-rŭk-han 갸륵한, ki-t'ŭk-han 기특한.

laugh *v.* ut-da 웃다. —*n.* u-sŭm 웃음.

laughter *n.* u-sŭm 웃음, u-sŭm-so-ri 웃음소리.

launch *v.* ① (*ship*) chin-su-ha-da 진수하다. ② (*start*) si-jak-ha-da 시작하다. —*n.* chin-su(-dae) 진수(대).

laundress *n.* se-t'ak-ha-nŭn yŏ-ja 세탁하는 여자, se-t'ak-bu 세탁부.

laundry *n.* ① se-t'ak-so 세탁소. ② se-t'ak-mul 세탁물.

laurel *n.* ① wŏl-gye-su 월계수. ② wŏl-gye-gwan 월계관. ③ (*honor*) yŏng-ye 영예. ④ (*victory*) sŭng-ri 승리.

lava *n.* yong-am 용암(溶岩). ⌊승리.

lavatory *n.* se-myŏn-so 세면소, hwa-jang-sil 화장실.

laver *n.* kim 김.

lavish *v.* a-ggim-ŏp-si chu-da 아낌없이 주다, (*squander*) nang-bi-ha-da 낭비하다. —*adj.* a-ggim-ŏp-nŭn 아낌없는 ; (*abundant*) p'ung-bu-han 풍부한.

law *n.* pop 법, pŏp-ryul 법률 : *constitutional* ~ hŏn-bŏp 헌법/*martial* ~ kun-bŏp 군법.

lawbreaker *n.* pŏm-bŏp-ja 범법자, choe-in 죄인.

lawful *adj.* hap-bŏp-jŏk-in 합법적인, (*legitimate*) chŏk-ch'ul-ŭi 적출(嫡出)의 : *a* ~ *child* chŏk-ja 적자.

lawless *adj.* mu-bŏp-ŭi 무법의, pul-bŏp-jŏk-in 불법적인.

lawn *n.* chan-di 잔디, chan-di-bat 잔디밭 : ~ *mower* chan-di kkak-nŭn ki-gye 잔디 깎는 기계.

lawyer *n.* pŏp-ryul-ga 법률가 ; pyŏn-ho-sa 변호사.

lax *adj.* nŭ-sŭn-han 느슨한 ; ae-mae-han 애매한.

lay *v.* ① (*produce*) na-t'a 낳다. ② (*put down*) no-t'a 놓다, tu-da 두다. ③ (*prepare*) chun-bi-ha-da 준비하다.

layer *n.* ① not-nŭn sa-ram 놓는 사람: *a brick* ~ pyŏk-dol ssat-nŭn sa-ram 벽돌 쌓는 사람. ② ch'ŭng 층 ; kyŏp 겹.

layman *n.* ① sok-in 속인(俗人). ② mun-oe-han 문외한.

layoff *n.* hyu-sik 휴식, il-si-jŏk hae-go 일시적 해고.

lazy *adj.* ke-ŭ-rŭn 게으른, kum-ddŭn 굼뜬, nŭ-rin 느린.

leach *v.* kŏ-rŭ-da 거르다. —*n.* yŏ-gwa-gi 여과기.

lead *v.* i-ggŭl-da 이끌다, in-do-ha-da 인도하다, ap-jang-sŏ ka-da 앞장서 가다. —*n.* ① (*direction*) sŏn-do 선도, (*command*) chi-hwi 지휘. ② (*metal*) nap 납.

leader *n.* sŏn-do-ja 선도자, t'ong-sol-ja 통솔자, chi-do-ja 지도자.

leadership *n.* chi-do 지도, t'ong-sol-ryŏk 통솔력.

leading *n.* sŏn-do 선도. t'ong-sol 통솔. —*adj.* chi-do-jŏk-in 지도적인 ; il-ryu-ŭi 일류의 ; (*chief*) chu-yo-han 주요한 ; yu-ryŏk-han 유력한.

leaf *n.* ① (*of tree*) na-mut-ip 나뭇잎. ② (*of book*)

han chang 한 장, p'e-i-ji 페이지.

leaflet *n.* ppi-ra kwang-go 삐라 광고.

league *n.* (*alliance*) yŏn-maeng 연맹, tong-maeng 동맹 : *L~ of Nations* kuk-je yŏn-maeng 국제 연맹.

leak *n.* sae-nŭn kot 새는 곳. —*v.* sae-da 새다.

lean *adj.* yŏ-win 여윈, me-ma-rŭn 메마른. —*v.* (*incline*) ki-ul-da 기울다, (*rely*) ki-dae-da 기대다.

leap *v.* ttwi-da 뛰다. —*n.* ttwi-gi 뛰기, to-yak 도약.

leap year yun-nyŏn 윤년(閏年). 「듣다.

learn *v.* pae-u-da 배우다 ; al-da 알다 ; (*hear*) tŭt-da

learned *adj.* pak-sik-han 박식한, yu-sik-han 유식한.

learning *n.* hak-mun 학문 ; hak-sŭp 학습.

lease *n.* im-dae(-ch'a) kye-yak 임대(차) 계약. —*v.* im-dae(-ch'a)-ha-da 임대(차)하다.

leash *n.* ka-juk-ggŭn 가죽끈, pat-jul 밧줄.

least *adj.* ch'oe-so-ŭi 최소의. —*adv.* ka-jang chŏk-ge 가장 적게. —*n.* ch'oe-so 최소 : *at ~* chŏk-ŏ-do 적어도.

leather *n.* ka-juk 가죽, p'i-hyŏk 피혁 : *~ belt* ka-juk hyŏk-dae 가죽 혁대.

leave *v.* (*go away*) ttŏ-na-da 떠나다 ; (*quit*) kŭ-man-tu-da 그만두다 ; nae-bŏ-ryŏ tu-da 내버려 두다. —*n.* ① (*permission*) hŏ-ga 허가. ② hyu-ga 휴가.

leaven *n.* hyo-mo 효모(酵母), nu-ruk 누룩. —*v.* pal-hyo-si-k'i-da 발효시키다.

lectern *n.* song-sŏ-dae 성서대, tok-gyŏng-dae 독경대.

lecture *n.* kang-ŭi 강의, (*speech*) kang-yŏn 강연 ; hun-gye 훈계. —*v.* kang-ŭi-ha-da 강의하다.

lecturer *n.* kang-sa 강사, yŏn-sa 연사.

ledge *n.* ① sŏn-ban 선반, si-rŏng 시렁. ② (*reef*) am-ch'o 암초. ③ (*mineral vein*) kwang-maek 광맥.

ledger *n.* chang-bu 장부, tae-jang 대장(台帳).

leek *n.* pu-ch'u 부추.

left *adv*. oen-p'yŏn-ŭ-ro 왼편으로. —*adj*. oen-jjok-ŭi 왼쪽의. —*n*. oen-p'yŏn 왼편. 「서투른.
left-handed *adj*. oen-son-jap-i-ŭi 왼손잡이의 ; sŏ-t'u-rŭn
leftover *n*. & *adj*. na-mŏ-ji(-ŭi) 나머지(의).
left wing chwa-ik 좌익, chwa-p'a 좌파.
leg *n*. ① ta-ri 다리. ② (*prop*) pŏ-t'im-dae 버팀대.
legacy *n*. yu-san 유산(遺產), yu-jŭng 유증.
legal *adj*. ① pŏp-ryul-sang-ŭi 법률상의. ② (*lawful*) hap-bŏp-jŏk-in 합법적인, chŏng-dang-han 정당한.
legation *n*. kong-sa-gwan 공사관(公使館).
legend *n*. ① chŏn-sŏl 전설. ② pŏm-rye 범례(凡例).
legible *adj*. (*of handwriting*) il-ggi swi-un 읽기 쉬운: ~ *writing* il-ggi swi-un p'il-jŏk 읽기 쉬운 필적.
legion *n*. ① kun-dan 군단. ②(*great number*) ta-su 다
legislation *n*. (*enacting of laws*) ip-bŏp 입법. 「수.
legislator *n*. ip-bŏp-ja 입법자, pŏp-ryul-je-jŏng-ja 법률
legislature *n*. ip-bŏp-bu 입법부. 「제정자.
legitimate *adj*. (*lawful*) hap-bŏp-jŏk-in 합법적인 ; (*reasonable*) hap-ri-jŏk-in 합리적인 ; (*regular*) chŏng-t'ong-ŭi 정통의 : *a* ~ *child* chŏk-ja 적자(嫡子).
leisure *n*. yŏ-ga 여가, t'ŭm 틈, (*ease*) an-il 안일.
leisurely *adj*. nŭ-rit-han 느릿한 ; ch'im-ch'ak-han 침착한. —*adv*. yu-yu-hi 유유히. 「담황색.
lemon *n*. re-mon 레몬 ; (*pale yellow*) tam-hwang-saek
lemonade *n*. re-mon-su 레몬수, ra-mu-ne 라무네.
lend *v*. pil-ryŏ-ju-da 빌려주다 ; (*add*) ch'ŏm-ga-ha-da 첨가하다 ; (*furnish*) che-gong-ha-da 제공하다. 「거리.
length *n*. ki-ri 길이 ; (*time*) tong-an 동안 ; (*space*) kŏ-ri
lenient *adj*. a-ryang-it-nŭn 아량있는, nŏ-gŭ-rŏ-un 너그러운, (*merciful*) in-jŏng-gi-p'ŭn 인정깊은.
lens *n*. ren-jŭ 렌즈, su-jŏng-ch'e 수정체.
Lent *n*. sa-sun-jŏl 사순절(四旬節).

leopard *n*. p'yo-bŏm 표범.　　　「hwan-ja 문둥병 환자.
leper *n*. na-byŏng hwan-ja 나병 환자, mun-dung-byŏng
leprosy *n*. na-byŏng 나병.　　　　「ge 보다 적게.
less *adj*. po-da chŏk-ŭn 보다 적은. —*adv*. po-da chŏk-
lessen *v*. (*make less*) kam-ha-da 감하다.
lesson *n*. (*school subject*) kyo-gwa 교과, hak-gwa 학
　과 ; su-ŏp 수업 ; (*precept*) kyo-hun 교훈.
lest *conj*. ···ha-ji an-k'e ···하지 않게.
let *v*. (*allow*) hŏ-rak-ha-da 허락하다. —*v*. ① (*allow
　to*) ···ha-ge ha-da ···하게 하다. ② (*lend*) pil-ryŏ-ju-
　da 빌려주다 : *house to* ~ set-jip 셋집.
lethargic *adj*. hon-su-sang-t'ae-ŭi 혼수상태의.
letter *n*. ① (*written message*) p'yŏn-ji 편지. ② (*al-
　phabet*) mun-ja 문자. ③ (*learning*) hak-mun 학문.
　④ (*pl*.) (*literature*) mun-hak 문학.
letter box (*mailbox*) u-ch'e-t'ong 우체통.
lettuce *n*. sang-ch'i 상치, re-t'ŏ-sŭ 레터스.
level *adj*. p'yŏng-p'yŏng-han 평평한, ko-rŭn 고른. —*n*.
　① su-p'yŏng 수평. ② (*standard*) su-jun 수준.
lever *n*. chi-ret-dae 지렛대, re-bŏ 레버.
levy *n*. ching-se 징세. —*v*. (*a tax*) pu-gwa-ha-da 부
　과하다, (*collect*) ching-su-ha-da 징수하다.
lewd *adj*. ŭm-t'ang-han 음탕한, ch'u-jap-han 추잡한.
liable *adj*. ch'aek-im-i it-nŭn 책임이 있는.
liaison *n*. yŏl-lak 연락, sŏp-oe 섭외 : ~ *officer* yŏl-
　lak-jang-gyo 연락장교.　　　　　　「풍장이].
liar *n*. kŏ-jit-mal-jang-i 거짓말장이, hŏ-p'ung-jang-i 허
liberal *adj*. tae-bŏm-han 대범한, cha-yu-ju-ŭi-ŭi 자유
　주의의. —*n*. cha-yu-ju-ŭi-ja 자유주의자.
liberate *v*. cha-yu-rop-ge ha-da 자유롭게 하다, hae-
　bang-ha-da 해방하다, sŏk-bang-ha-da 석방하다.
liberty *n*. cha-yu 자유, hae-bang 해방.

librarian *n*. to-sŏ-gwan-wŏn 도서관원 ; sa-sŏ 사서.
library *n*. ① to-sŏ-gwan 도서관, (*study*) sŏ-jae 서재.
② chang-sŏ 장서. ③ ch'ong-sŏ 총서, mun-go 문고.
libretto *n*. ka-sa-jip 가사집, ka-sa 가사(歌詞).
licence · license *n*. ① hŏ-ga 허가, in-ga 인가. ② myŏn-
hŏ-jang 면허장, hŏ-ga-jŭng 허가증.
lick *v*. ① hal-t'a 핥다. ② (*beat*) ttae-ri-da 때리다.
lid *n*. ttu-ggŏng 뚜껑 ; (*eyelid*) nun-gga-p'ul 눈까풀.
lie *n*. kŏ-jit-mal 거짓말. —*v*. ① kŏ-jit-mal-ha-da 거짓
말하다. ② (*recline*) nup-da 눕다. ③ (*exist*) chon-jae-
ha-da 존재하다, (*be situated*) wi-ch'i-ha-da 위치하다.
lieutenant *n*. ① (*1st*) chung-wi 중위, (*2nd*) so-wi
소위, (*s.g., navy*) tae-wi 대위, (*j.g., navy*) chung-
wi 중위. ② (*deputy*) pu-gwan 부관.
lieutenant colonel chung-ryŏng 중령.
lieutenant commander hae-gun so-ryŏng 해군 소령.
lieutenant general chung-jang 중장.
life *n*. ① saeng-myŏng 생명. ② (*span of*) il-saeng 일
생. ③ (*biography*) chŏn-gi 전기(傳記). ④ (*way of
living*) saeng-gye 생계. ⑤ (*energy*) hwal-gi 활기.
lifeboat *n*. ku-jo-sŏn 구조선, ku-myŏng-jŏng 구명정.
life insurance saeng-myŏng po-hŏm 생명 보험.
lifelong *adj*. p'il-saeng-ŭi 필생의.
life preserver ku-myŏng-gu 구명구(具).
life sentence mu-gi ching-yŏk 무기 징역.
lifetime *n*. saeng-ae 생애 ; p'yŏng-saeng 평생, il-saeng
일생.
lifework *n*. p'il-saeng-ŭi sa-ŏp 필생의 사업.
lift *v*. tŭ-rŏ-ol-ri-da 들어올리다, no-p'i-da 높이다 ; kŏt-
hi-da 걷히다. —*n*. ① tŭ-ro-ol-ri-gi 들어올리기. ②
sŭng-jin 승진. ③ (*elevator*) sŭng-gang-gi 승강기.
light *n*. ① pit 빛. ② (*lamp*) pul 불. —*v*. ① pul-ŭl
k'yŏ-da 불을 켜다. ② (*fire*) pul-p'i-u-da 불피우다.

—*adj*. ka-byŏ-un 가벼운.

lighten *v*. ① pi-ch'u-da 비추다. ② ka-byŏp-ge ha-da 가볍게 하다.

lighter *n*. ① (*cigarette*) ra-i-t'ŏ 라이터. ② (*barge*) kŏ-rut-bae 거룻배.

lighthouse *n*. tŭng-dae 등대.

lightly *adv*. ka-byŏp-ge 가볍게, (*easily*) swip-ge 쉽게.

lightning *n*. pŏn-gaet-bul 번갯불. —*adj*. kŭp-sok-han 급속한, chŏn-gwang-sŏk-hwa-ŭi 전광석화의.

like *v*. cho-a-ha-da 좋아하다. —*prep*. …wa ka-ch'i …와 같이, ch'ŏ-rŏm 처럼. —*adj*. tal-mŭn 닮은.

likely *adj*. kŭ-rŏl-dŭt-han 그럴듯한, i-ssŭm-jik-han 있음직한. —*adv*. a-ma 아마, ta-bun-hi 다분히.

liken *v*. (*compare*) pi-yu-ha-da 비유하다, pi-gi-da 비기다.

likeness *n*. pi-sŭt-ham 비슷함, yu-sa 유사.

likewise *adv*. ma-ch'an-ga-ji-ro 마찬가지로.

liking *n*. (*fancy*) ki-ho 기호, cho-a-ham 좋아함 : *Is it your* ~? Ma-ŭm-e tŭ-sip-ni-gga? 마음에 드십니까?

lilac *n*. cha-jŏng-hyang 자정향, ra-il-rak 라일락.

lily *n*. na-ri 나리, paek-hap 백합 : ~ *of the valley* ŭn-bang-ul-ggot 은방울꽃/*water* ~ su-ryŏn 수련.

limb *n*. ① (*branch*) k'ŭn ka-ji 큰 가지. ② (*body*) son-bal 손발, su-jok 수족, (*wing*) nal-gae 날개.

lime *n*. sŏk-hoe 석회 : *caustic* ~ saeng-sŏk-hoe 생석회.

limelight *n*. (*footlight*) kak-gwang 각광(脚光).

limestone *n*. sŏk-hoe-sŏk 석회석.

limit *v*. che-han-ha-da 제한하다. —*n*. che-han 제한 ; pŏm-wi 범위.

limitation *n*. che-han 제한, (*bounds*) han-gye 한계.

limp *v*. chŏl-rŭm-gŏ-ri-da 절름거리다, chŏl-dduk-gŏ-ri-da 절뚝거리다. —*adj*. (*flexible*) na-gŭt-na-gŭt-han 나긋나긋한. —*n*. chŏl-rŭm-ba-ri 절름발이.

line *n*. ① sŏn 선. ② (*row*) chul 줄, yŏl 열(列), haeng 행.

linen *n*. a-ma-p'o 아마포, rin-ne-rŭ 린네르.

liner *n*. chŏng-gi hang-gong-gi 정기 항공기.

linger *v.* u-mul-jju-mul-ha-da 우물쭈물하다, pin-dung-gŏ-ri-da 빈둥거리다, chil-jil kkŭl-da 질질 끌다.
lingering *adj.* kku-mul-gŏ-ri-nŭn 꾸물거리는.
linguist *n.* ŏn-ŏ-hak-ja 언어학자, ŏ-hak-ja 어학자.
liniment *n.* pa-rŭ-nŭn yak 바르는 약.
lining *n.* ① (*of dresses*) an 안, an-gam 안감. ② (*contents*) nae-yong 내용, al-maeng-i 알맹이.
link *v.* yŏn-gyŏl-ha-da 연결하다. —*n.* (*loop*) ko-ri 고리.
lion *n.* sa-ja 사자, ra-i-on 라이온.
lip *n.* ip-sul 입술, ip 입. —*adj.* (*insincere*) mal-bbun-in 말뿐인.
lipstick *n.* ip-sul-yŏn-ji 입술연지, rip-sŭ-t'ik 립스틱.
liquid *n.* aek-ch'e 액체. —*adj.* aek-ch'e-ŭi 액체의.
liquor *n.* al-k'o-ol ŭm-ryo 알코올 음료, sul 술.
lisp *v.* hyŏ-jja-rae-gi so-ri-rŭl ha-da 혀짜래기 소리를 하다. —*n.* hyŏ-jja-rae-gi so-ri 혀짜래기 소리.
list *n.* (*table*) p'yo 표, (*roll*) myŏng-bu 명부. —*v.* myŏng-bu-e chŏk-da 명부에 적다.
listen *v.* tŭt-da 듣다, kwi-rŭl ki-u-ri-da 귀를 기울이다.
literal *adj.* mun-ja kŭ-dae-ro-ŭi 문자 그대로의 ; (*accurate*) ; chŏng-hwak-han 정확한.
literary *adj.* mun-hak-ŭi 문학의, mun-ŏ-jŏk-in 문어적인 : ~ *works* mun-hak-jak-p'um 문학작품.
literate *adj.* il-ggo ssŭl su it-nŭn 읽고 쓸 수 있는, (*learned*) kyo-yang-i it-nŭn 교양이 있는.
literature *n.* ① mun-hak 문학, mun-ye 문예. ② chŏ-sul 저술. ③ (*documents*) mun-hŏn 문헌. 「석판화.
lithograph *n.* sŏk-p'an-in-swae 석판인쇄, sŏk-p'an-hwa
litre · liter *n.* ri-t'ŏ 리터. 「dong-sa-ni 잡동사니.
litter *n.* ① (*stretcher*) tŭl-gŏt 들것. ② (*mess*) chap-
little *adj.* (*size*) chak-ŭn 작은, (*amount*) chŏk-ŭn 적은 ; ŏ-rin 어린. —*n.* cho-gŭm 조금, so-ryang 소량.

live *v.* sal-da 살다, saeng-hwal-ha-da 생활하다. —*adj.*
sa-ra-it-nŭn 살아있는, hwal-gi-it-nŭn 활기있는.

livelihood *n.* saeng-gye 생계, sal-rim 살림.

lively *adj.* hwal-bal-han 활발한 ; (*vivid*) saeng-saeng-
han 생생한. —*adv.* ki-un-ch'a-ge 기운차게.

liver *n.* kan-jang 간장, kan 간 : ~ *oil* kan-bu 간유.

livestock *n.* ka-ch'uk 가축.

living *adj.* sa-ra-it-nŭn 살아있는. —*n.* saeng-gye 생계.

lizard *n.* to-ma-baem 도마뱀.

load *n.* ① (*on a cart*) chim 짐. ② (*burden*) pu-dam
부담. —*v.* chim-ŭl sit-da 짐을 싣다.

loaf *n.* (*bread*) ppang cho-gak 빵 조각. —*v.* (*spend
time idly*) nol-go chi-nae-da 놀고 지내다.

loan *n.* tae-bu 대부(貸付), kong-ch'ae 공채, ch'a-gwan
차관. —*v.* tae-bu-ha-da 대부하다.

loath *adj.* si-rŭn 싫은, yŏk-gyŏ-un 역겨운. 「싫.

lobby *n.* ro-bi 로비 ; hyu-ge-sil 휴게실 ; tae-gi-sil 대기

lobe *n.* (*of the ear*) kwit-bul 귓불.

lobster *n.* pa-da-ga-jae 바다가재, k'ŭn sae-u 큰 새우.

local *adj.* chi-bang-ŭi 지방의 : ~ *color* chi-bang-saek
지방색/*a* ~ *paper* chi-bang-sin-mun 지방신문.

locate *v.* (*be situated*) cha-ri-jap-da 자리잡다, (*find
out*) wi-ch'i-rŭl a-ra-nae-da 위치를 알아내다.

location *n.* (*position*) wi-ch'i 위치 ; ya-oe ch'wal-
yŏng-jang 야외 촬영장, ro-k'e-i-syŏn 로케이션.

lock *n.* ① cha-mul-soe 자물쇠. ② (*water*) su-mun 수
문. —*v.* cha-mul-soe-rŭl ch'ae-u-da 자물쇠를 채우다,
cham-gŭ-da 잠그다.

locker *n.* ① ro-k'ŏ 로커. ② (*cabinet to be locked*)
ch'an-jang 찬장.

locomotive *n.* ki-gwan-ch'a 기관차.

locust *n.* me-ddu-gi 메뚜기 ; (*cicada*) mae-mi 매미.

lodge *v.* muk-da 묵다, suk-bak-ha-da 숙박하다. —*n.* (*hut*) o-du-mak-jip 오두막집, su-wi-sil 수위실.
lodger *n.* suk-bak-in 숙박인, ha-suk-in 하숙인.
lodging house ha-suk-jip 하숙집.
loft *n.* ko-mi-ta-rak-bang 고미다락방, wi-ch'ŭng 위층.
lofty *adj.* ① mae-u no-p'ŭn 매우 높은. ② (*noble*) ko-sang-han 고상한. ③ (*arrogant*) kŏ-man-han 거만한.
log *n.* ① t'ong-na-mu 통나무. ② (*diary*) hang-hae-il-ji 항해일지 : ~ *cabin* t'ong-na-mu-jip 통나무집.
logic *n.* nol-li-hak 논리학.
loin *n.* hŏ-ri 허리, yo-bu 요부(腰部).
loiter *v.* pin-dung-gŏ-ri-da 빈둥거리다, ŏ-jŏng-gŏ-ri-da 「어정거리다.
loll *v.* (*hang*) ch'uk nu-rŏ-ji-da 축 늘어지다.
lone *adj.* ① ko-dok-han 고독한, ssŭl-ssŭl-han 쓸쓸한. ② oe-jin 외진. ③ (*unmarried*) tok-sin-ŭi 독신의.
loneliness *n.* ko-dok 고독, ssŭl-ssŭl-ham 쓸쓸함.
lonely *adj.* ① oe-ro-un 외로운. ② oe-ddan 외딴.
lonesome *adj.* ssŭl-ssŭl-han 쓸쓸한, oe-ro-un 외로운.
long *adj.* kin 긴, o-raen 오랜. —*adv.* kil-ge 길게, o-rae 오래. —*v.* (*yearn*) tong-gyŏng-ha-da 동경하다; yŏl-mang-ha-da 열망하다.
longevity *n.* chang-su 장수(長壽), su-myŏng 수명.
longing *n.* kal-mang 갈망, yŏl-mang 열망.
longitude *n.* kyŏng-do 경도(經度), kyŏng-sŏn 경선.
long-run *adj.* chang-gi hŭng-haeng-ŭi 장기 흥행의.
look *v.* pa-ra-bo-da 바라보다, (*stare*) yu-sim-hi po-da 유심히 보다 ; (*face*) hyang-ha-da 향하다. —*n.* ① (*glance*) il-gyŏn 일견. ② (*aspect*) yong-mo 용모.
looking glass kŏ-ul 거울, ch'e-gyŏng 체경.
lookout *n.* (*watch*) mang-bo-gi 망보기, kam-si 감시.
loom *n.* pe-t'ŭl 베틀, chik-jo-gi 직조기. —*v.* ŏ-ryŏm-p'u-si na-t'a-na-da 어렴풋이 나타나다.

loop *n.* ko-ri 고리 ; t'e 테 ; ol-ga-mi 올가미.
loophole *n.* (*outlet*) to-mang-gil 도망길.
loose *adj.* (*slack*) hŏl-gŏ-wŏ-jin 헐거워진, (*not tight*) tan-jŏng-ch'i mot-han 단정치 못한. —*v.* (*slacken*) nŭt-ch'u-da 늦추다, p'u-rŏ-ju-da 풀어주다.
loosen *v.* (*untie*) p'ul-da 풀다, nŭ-sŭn-ha-ge ha-da 느슨하게 하다, no-a-ju-da 놓아주다. 「리품.
loot *n.* (*booty*) yak-t'al-p'um 약탈품 ; chŏl-li-p'um 전
lop *v.* chal-ra-nae-da 잘라내다, (*hew*) ch'i-da 치다.
lord *n.* (*ruler*) kun-ju 군주 ; (*master*) chu-in 주인 ; kwi-jok 귀족 ; (*savior*) chu 주(主).
lordly *adj.* tang-dang-han 당당한, sung-go-han 숭고한.
lordship *n.* ① t'ong-ch'i-gwŏn 통치권, chi-bae-ryŏk 지배력. ② (*domain*) yŏng-ji 영지(領地).
lose *v.* il-t'a 잃다 ; (*be defeated*) chi-da 지다 ; (*miss*) no-ch'i-da 놓치다 ; (*waste*) hŏ-bi-ha-da 허비하다.
loser *n.* pun-sil-ja 분실자, p'ae-ja 패자.
loss *n.* pun-sil 분실, son-sil 손실 ; mol-rak 몰락. 「명의.
lost *adj.* i-rŭn 잃은, haeng-bang-bul-myŏng-ŭi 행방불
lot *n.* ① ch'u-ch'ŏm 추첨. ② (*destiny*) un-myŏng 운명. ③ (*house*) pu-ji 부지. ④ (*plenty*) man-ŭm 많음.
lotion *n.* se-je 세제(洗劑) ; hwa-jang-su 화장수.
lottery *n.* che-bi 제비, pok-gwŏn 복권.
lotus *n.* yŏn 연(蓮). 「ggŭ-rŏ-un 시끄러운.
loud *adj.* ① so-ri-ga k'ŭn 소리가 큰. ② (*noisy*) si-
loudspeaker *n.* hwak-sŏng-gi 확성기.
lounge *n.* ① (*stroll*) man-bo 만보(漫步). ② (*social hall*) sa-gyo-sil 사교실, ra-un-ji 라운지.
louse *n.* ① i 이(虱). ② ki-saeng-ch'ung 기생충.
lousy *adj.* tŏ-rŏ-un 더러운 ; ya-bi-han 야비한.
lov(e)able *adj.* sa-rang-sŭ-rŏ-un 사랑스러운.
love *n.* ① sa-rang 사랑, ae-jŏng 애정 ; cho-a-ham 좋아

함. ② (*sweetheart*) yŏn-in 연인, ae-in 애인. —*v.* sa-rang-ha-da 사랑하다. 「멋진.

lovely *adj.* ye-bbŭn 예쁜, kwi-yŏ-un 귀여운 ; mŏt-jin

lover *n.* ① ae-in 애인, yŏn-in 연인. ② (*devotee*) ae-ho-ga 애호가, ch'an-mi-ja 찬미자.

low *adj.* na-jŭn 낮은 ; kap-ssan 값싼 ; (*mean*) pi-ch'ŏn-han 비천한. —*adv.* nat-ge 낮게, ssa-ge 싸게.

lower *v.* nat-ch'u-da 낮추다, nae-ri-da 내리다, ttŏ-rŏ-ddŭ-ri-da 떨어뜨리다. —*adj.* chŏ-gŭp-han 저급한.

lowly *adj.* pi-ch'ŏn-han 비천한, (*shabby*) ch'o-ra-han 초라한 ; (*humble*) kup-sil-gŏ-ri-nŭn 굽실거리는.

loyal *adj.* ch'ung-sŏng-sŭ-rŏn 충성스런, sŏng-sil-han 성실한. —*n.* ch'ung-sin 충신 ; ae-guk-ja 애국자.

lubricant *n.* yun-hwal-yu 윤활유, yun-hwal-je 윤활제.

lubricate *v.* ki-rŭm-ŭl ch'i-da 기름을 치다. 「한.

lucid *adj.* (*clear*) mal-gŭn 맑은, t'u-myŏng-han 투명

luck *n.* un 운, haeng-un 행운, yo-haeng 요행.

luckily *adv.* ta-haeng-hi 다행히, un-jo-k'e 운좋게.

lucky *adj.* un-jo-ŭn 운좋은, haeng-un-ŭi 행운의.

lucrative *adj.* ton-i pŏl-ri-nŭn 돈이 벌리는.

ludicrous *adj.* ik-sal-sŭ-rŏn 익살스런, (*absurd*) pa-bo-ga-t'ŭn 바보같은, ssuk-sŭ-rŏ-un 쑥스러운. 「물.

luggage *n.* su-ha-mul 수하물, yŏ-haeng-ha-mul 여행하

lukewarm *adj.* mi-ji-gŭn-han 미지근한, mi-on-jŏk-in 미온적인, ma-ji-mot-hae-ha-nŭn 마지못해하는.

lull *v.* (*soothe*) tal-rae-da 달래다 ; chae-u-da 재우다. —*n.* cham-jam-ham 잠잠함, ttŭm-ham 뜸함.

lullaby *n.* (*cradle song*) cha-jang-ga 자장가.

lumber *n.* ① chae-mok 재목. ② (*rubbish*) ssŭ-re-gi 쓰레기. —*v.* k'ung-k'ung kŏt-da 쿵쿵 걷다.

luminous *adj.* pit-na-nŭn 빛나는 ; (*clear*) myŏng-

lump *n.* tŏng-ŏ-ri 덩어리, hok 혹. 「baek-han 명백한.

lunar *adj.* tal-ŭi 달의 : ~ *calendar* ŭm-ryŏk 음력.
lunatic *n.* mi-ch'in sa-ram 미친 사람. —*adj.* (*insane*)
　mi-ch'in 미친 : *a* ~ *asylum* chŏng-sin pyŏng-wŏn
lunch *n.* chŏm-sim 점심, to-si-rak 도시락.　⌐정신 병원.
lung *n.* p'ye 폐(肺), hŏ-p'a 허파.　　　　　⌐물.
lure *v.* yu-hok-ha-da 유혹하다. —*n.* yu-hok-mul 유혹
lurk *v.* sum-da 숨다, cham-jŏk-ha-da 잠적하다.
lust *n.* (*carnal desire*) saek-yok 색욕, sŏng-jŏng 성정.
lusty *adj.* ① (*strong*) t'ŭn-t'ŭn-han 튼튼한. ② (*vig-
　orous*) hwal-bal-han 활발한.　　　　　⌐産)의.
luxuriant *adj.* mu-sŏng-han 무성한 ; ta-san-ŭi 다산(多
luxurious *adj.* sa-ch'i-sŭ-rŏ-un 사치스러운, ho-sa-sŭ-
luxury *n.* sa-ch'i 사치, ho-sa 호사.　　　⌐rŏn 호사스런.
lye *n.* chaet-mul 잿물, al-k'al-ri aek 알칼리 액(液).
lynch *n. & v.* rin-ch'i(-rŭl ka-ha-da) 린치(를 가하다).
lyre *n.* su-gŭm 수금(竪琴), ra-i-ŏ 라이어.
lyric *n.* sŏ-jŏng-si 서정시. —*adj.* sŏ-jŏng-si-jŏk-in 서
　정시적인.

—◄ M ►—

machine *n.* ki-gye 기계, ki-gu 기구.
machine gun ki-gwan-ch'ong 기관총.
machinery *n.* ki-gye 기계, ki-gye chang-ch'i 기계 장치.
mackerel *n.* ko-dŭng-ŏ 고등어.
macrocosm *n.* tae-u-ju 대우주, tae-se-gye 대세계.
mad *adj.* mi-ch'in 미친 ; (*furious*) maeng-ryŏl-han 맹
　렬한 ; (*angry*) hwa-ga nan 화가 난.
madam *n.* ma-dam 마담, (*lady*) pu-in 부인.
made *adj.* (*artificially produced*) man-dŭn 만든,
　…che …제(製) : ~ *in Korea* han-guk-je 한국제/~
　in U.S.A. mi-guk-je 미국제.

madman *n.* mi-ch'in sa-ram 미친 사람, kwang-in 광인.

maestro *n.* tae-ŭm-ak-ga 대음악가, kŏ-jang 거장(巨匠).

magazine *n.* ① (*periodical*) chap-ji 잡지, chŏng-gi kan-haeng-mul 정기 간행물. ② (*army*) t'an-yak-go 탄

maggot *n.* ① ku-dŏ-gi 구더기. ② pyŏn-dŏk 변덕. 「약고.

magic *n.* ma-bŏp 마법, yo-sul 요술 ; ma-ryŏk 마력. —*adj.* ma-bŏp-ŭi 마법의, yo-sul-ŭi 요술의.

magician *n.* ma-sul-sa 마술사, ma-bŏp-sa 마법사.

magistrate *n.* haeng-jŏng-jang-gwan 행정장관, (*justice of the peace*) ch'i-an p'an-sa 치안 판사.

magnanimous *adj.* to-ryang-i k'ŭn 도량이 큰, a-ryang-it-nŭn 아량있는 ; (*noble*) ko-gyŏl-han 고결한.

magnet *n.* cha-sŏk 자석(磁石), chi-nam-ch'ŏl 지남철.

magnetic *adj.* ① cha-sŏk-ŭi 자석의, cha-gi-ŭi 자기의. ② (*attractive*) mae-ryŏk-it-nŭn 매력있는.

magnificent *adj.* chang-ŏm-han 장엄한 ; (*stately*) tang-dang-han 당당한, (*splendid*) hul-ryung-han 훌륭한.

magnify *v.* hwak-dae-ha-da 확대하다 ; (*exaggerate*) kwa-jang-ha-da 과장하다, ch'an-mi-ha-da 찬미하다.

magnitude *n.* k'ŭ-gi 크기, pang-dae 방대 ; chung-yo-ham 중요함, wi-dae-ham 위대함.　　　「ryŏn 백목련.

magnolia *n.* mok-ryŏn 목련 : *a white* ~ paek-mok-

magpie *n.* kka-ch'i 까치.　　　　　　　「하녀.

maid *n.* so-nyŏ 소녀, a-ga-ssi 아가씨 ; (*servant*) ha-nyŏ

maiden *n.* so-nyŏ 소녀, ch'ŏ-nyŏ 처녀.

maidservant *n.* ha-nyŏ 하녀.　　　　　　「하다.

mail *n.* u-p'yŏn-mul 우편물. —*v.* u-song-ha-da 우송.

mailbox *n.* u-ch'e-t'ong 우체통, u-p'yŏn-ham 우편함.

maim *v.* pyŏng-sin-ŭl man-dŭl-da 병신을 만들다.

main *adj.* chung-yo-han 중요한 ; (*leading*) yu-ryŏk-han 유력한. —*n.* ① (*might*) him 힘. ② (*principal pipe*) pon-gwan 본관(本管).

mainland *n.* pon-t'o 본토, tae-ryuk 대륙.
mainly *adv.* chu-ro 주로, tae-gae 대개, o-ro-ji 오로지.
maintain *v.* yu-ji-ha-da 유지하다 ; (*assert*) chu-jang-ha-da 주장하다 ; (*support*) pu-yang-ha-da 부양하다.
maize *n.* ok-su-su 옥수수.　　　　　　　「it-nŭn 위엄있는.
majestic *adj.* chang-ŏm-han 장엄한, (*stately*) wi-ŏm-
majesty *n.* ① chon-ŏm 존엄. ② (*sovereignty*) chu-gwŏn 주권. ③ (*title of emperor*) (*M*~) p'ye-ha 폐하.
major *n.* (*army*) yuk-gun so-ryŏng 육군 소령. —*adj.* k'ŭn p'yŏn-ŭi 큰 편의, chu-yo-han 주요한. —*v.* (*specialize*) chŏn-gong-ha-da 전공하다.
major general yuk-gun so-jang 육군 소장.
majority *n.* tae-da-su 대다수, kwa-ban-su 과반수.
make *v.* ① man-dŭl-da 만들다. ② (*compel*) …ha-ge ha-da …하게 하다, …i toe-da …이 되다. ③ (*gain*) hoek-dŭk-ha-da 획득하다. —*n.* ku-jo 구조.
make-believe *n.* ① ku-sil 구실, p'ing-gye 핑계. ② …ch'e-ha-nŭn sa-ram …체하는 사람.　「i-k'ŏ 메이커.
maker *n.* che-jak-ja 제작자, che-jo-ŏp-ja 제조업자, me-
makeshift *n.* im-si pyŏn-t'ong 임시 변통 ; mi-bong-ch'aek 미봉책.　　　　「*struction*) cho-rip 조립.
make-up *n.* ① hwa-jang 화장, pun-jang 분장. ② (*con-*
malady *n.* chil-byŏng 질병, pyŏng 병.
malaria *n.* hak-jil 학질, mal-ra-ri-a 말라리아.
male *n. & adj.* ① nam-sŏng(-ŭi) 남성(의). ② (*of animals*) su-k'ŏt(-ŭi) 수컷(의) : *a* ~ *dog* su-k'ae 수캐.
malice *n.* ak-ŭi 악의(惡意) ; wŏn-han 원한.　「악의있는.
malicious *adj.* sim-sul-gu-jŭn 심술궂은, ak-ŭi-it-nŭn
maltreat *v.* hak-dae-ha-da 학대하다, naeng-dae-ha-da
mamma *n.* ŏm-ma 엄마.　　　　　　　　　└냉대하다.
mammal *n.* p'o-yu tong-mul 포유 동물.
man *n.* ① sa-ram 사람. ② (*male*) nam-ja 남자.

manage *v.* kwal-li-ha-da 관리하다 ; (*handle*) ta-ru-da 다루다 ; kyŏng-yŏng-ha-da 경영하다.
management *n.* kwal-li 관리 ;ch'wi-gŭp 취급.
manager *n.* chi-bae-in 지배인, kyŏng-yŏng-ja 경영자,
Manchuria *n.* man-ju 만주.　　　　[kam-dok 감독.
mandate *n.* ① myŏng-ryŏng 명령.　② wi-t'ak 위탁 ; (*trusteeship*) sin-t'ak-t'ong-ch'i 신탁통치.
mandolin(e) *n.* man-dol-rin 만돌린.
mane *n.* (*horse, lion etc.*) kal-gi 갈기.
maneuver · manoeuvre *n.* ki-dong-yŏn-sŭp 기동연습. —*v.* yŏn-sŭp-ha-da 연습하다.
manful *adj.* ssik-ssik-han 씩씩한, tan-ho-han 단호한.
manger *n.* yŏ-mul-t'ong 여물통, ku-yu 구유.
mangle *v.* nan-do-jil-ha-da 난도질하다.
manhole *n.* maen-ho-ul 맨호울, cham-ip-gu 잠입구.
manhood *n.* in-gyŏk 인격 ; sŏng-nyŏn 성년 ; (*manliness*) nam-ja-da-um 남자다움.　　　「광(狂).
mania *n.* yŏl-gwang 열광, yŏl-jung 열중, …kwang …
maniac *adj.* mi-ch'in 미친. —*n.* mi-ch'i-gwang-i 미치광이, yŏl-gwang-ja 열광자.　　　「gi 손톱다듬기.
manicure *n.* mae-ni-k'yu-ŏ 매니큐어 ; son-t'op-da-dŭm-
manifest *adj.* myŏng-baek-han 명백한. —*v.* myŏng-si-ha-da 명시하다 ; na-t'a-na-da 나타나다. —*n.* chŏk-ha-mok-rok 적하목록.　　　「myŏn-ŭi 다방면의.
manifold *adj.* yŏ-rŏ ka-ji-ŭi 여러 가지의, ta-bang-
manipulate *v.* kyo-myo-ha-ge ta-ru-da 교묘하게 다루다.
mankind *n.* il-lyu 인류 ; (*male*) nam-sŏng 남성.
manlike *adj.* (*manly*) nam-ja-da-un 남자다운.　「한.
manly *adj.* nam-ja-da-un 남자다운, ssik-ssik-han 씩씩
manner *n.* pang-bŏp 방법 ; ye-jŏl 예절 ; t'ae-do 태도.
mansion *n.* tae-jŏ-t'aek 대저택.　　　　「마재비.
mantis *n.* (*insect*) sa-ma-gwi 사마귀, pŏ-ma-jae-bi 버

mantle *n.* (*cloak*) mang-t'o 망토 ; (*covering*) mak
  mak. —*v.* tŏp-da 덮다, kam-ch'u-da 감추다.
manual *adj.* son-ŭi 손의. —*n.* (*small book*) so-ch'aek-
  ja 소책자, (*handbook*) p'yŏl-lam 편람.
manufacture *n.* & *v.* che-jo(-ha-da) 제조(하다).
manufacturer *n.* che-jo-ŏp-ja 제조업자 ; kong-jang-ju
manure *n.* pi-ryo 비료, kŏ-rŭm 거름. ⌊공장주.
manuscript *n.* wŏn-go 원고(原稿), sa-bon 사본.
many *adj.* man-ŭn 많은, ta-su-ŭi 다수의.
map *n.* ① chi-do 지도(地圖). ② ch'ŏn-ch'e-do 천체도.
maple *n.* tan-p'ung(-na-mu) 단풍(나무). ⌈손하다.
mar *v.* mang-ch'yŏ-no-t'a 망쳐놓다, hwe-son-ha-da 훼
marathon *n.* (*race*) ma-ra-t'on 마라톤.
marble *n.* ① tae-ri-sŏk 대리석.② kong-gi-dol 공기돌.
March *n.* sam-wŏl 3월.
march *n.* haeng-jin 행진, chin-jŏn 진전 ;(*music*) haeng-
  jin-gok 행진곡. —*v.* haeng-jin-ha-da 행진하다.
mare *n.* (*female horse*) am-mal 암말.
margin *n.* ① (*edge*) ka-jang-ja-ri 가장자리. ② (*limit*)
  han-gye 한계. ③ (*commerce*) i-mun 이문.
marine *adj.* pa-da-ŭi 바다의 ; (*of the navy*) hae-gun-
  ŭi 해군의 : ~ *insurance* hae-sang-bo-hŏm 해상보험/
  ~ *force* hae-byŏng-dae 해병대. —*n.* sŏn-bak 선박.
Marine Corps hae-byŏng-dae 해병대.
marine products hae-san-mul 해산물.
mariner *n.* (*seaman*) sŏn-wŏn 선원, su-bu 수부.
marital *adj.* nam-p'yŏn-ŭi 남편의, pu-bu-gan-ŭi 부부간
maritime *adj.* pa-da-ŭi 바다의, hae-un-ŭi 해운의. ⌊의.
mark *n.* ① (*trace*) p'yo-jŏk 표적, cha-guk 자국. ②
  (*pl.*) ki-ho 기호 ; (*point*) chŏm-su 점수. —*v.* p'yo-
  ha-da 표하다, ma-a-k'ŭ-rŭl ha-da 마아크를 하다.
market *n.* si-jang 시장(市場), chang 장 : *black* ~ am-si-

jang 암시장/*fish* ～ ŏ-mul-si-jang 어물시장/*fruit* ～ ch'ŏng-gwa-si-jang 청과시장.

market place si-jang 시장(市場), chang-t'ŏ 장터.

market price *n.* si-se 시세, sit-ga 싯가.

marking *n.* ① (*mark*) p'yŏ 표. ② (*pattern*) mu-nŭi 무늬. —*adj.* (*prominent*) t'ŭk-ch'ul-han 특출한.

marksman *n.* ① sa-su 사수, sa-gyŏk-su 사격수. ② (*sharpshooter*) chŏ-gyŏk-byŏng 저격병.

marmot *n.* ma-a-mŏt 마아못, mo-rŭ-mo-t'ŭ <u>모르모트</u>.

marriage *n.* kyŏl-hon 결혼, (*wedding*) kyŏl-hon-sik 결혼식 ; (*close union*) hap-ch'e 합체.

marrow *n.* ① kol-su 골수, ppyŏ-gol 뼈골. ② (*essence*) chŏng-su 정수 ; (*vitality*) hwal-ryŏk 활력.

marry *v.* kyŏl-hon-ha-da 결혼하다, kyŏl-hon-si-k'i-da 결혼시키다 ; (*for man*) chang-ga-dŭl-da 장가들다 ; (*for woman*) si-jip-ga-da 시집가다.

marsh *n.* (*swamp*) nŭp 늪, (*bog*) sŭp-ji 습지.

marshal *n.* yuk-gun wŏn-su 육군 원수(元帥): *provost* ～ hŏn-byŏng-sa-ryŏng-gwan 헌병사령관.

martial *adj.* ① kun-sa-ŭi 군사의, chŏn-jaeng-ŭi 전쟁의 : ～ *law* kye-ŏm-ryŏng 계엄령/～ *rule* kun-jŏng 군정(軍政). ② (*brave*) yong-gam-han 용감한.

martyr *n.* sun-gyo-ja 순교자, (*victim*) hŭi-saeng-ja 희생자. —*v.* (*persecute*) pak-hae-ha-da 박해하다.

marvel *n.* kyŏng-t'an 경탄, nol-raem 놀램.

marvel(l)ous *adj.* nol-ra-un 놀라운, ki-i-han 기이한, mŏt-jin 멋진.

mascot *n.* ma-sŭ-k'o-t'ŭ 마스코트.

masculine *adj.* nam-sŏng-ŭi 남성의, (*manly*) nam-sŏng-da-un 남성다운, nam-ja-ga-t'ŭn 남자같은.

mask *n.* pok-myŏn 복면, ka-myŏn 가

면. —*v.* ka-myŏn-ŭl ssŭ-da 가면을 쓰다, (*disguise*) ka-jang-ha-da 가장하다, kam-ch'u-da 감추다.

mason *n.* sŏk-gong 석공(石工), sŏk-su 석수(石手).

masquerade *n.* ① (*masked assembly*) ka-jang mu-do-hoe 가장 무도회. ② (*pretence*) kŏt-ch'i-re 겉치레.

mass *n.* ① tŏng-ŏ-ri 덩어리. ② (*large number*) ta-su 다수, (*great quantity*) ta-ryang 다량. ③ (*crowd*) chip-dan 집단. ④ mi-sa 미사. —*v.* mo-ŭ-da 모으다.

massacre *n.* &. *v.* tae-hak-sal(-ha-da) 대학살(하다).

massage *n.* ma-sa-a-ji 마사아지 ; an-ma 안마.

massive *adj.* ① pu-p'i-ga k'ŭn 부피가 큰. ② (*solid*) kŏn-jang-han 건장한. ③ (*imposing*) tang-dang-han ⌐당당한.

mast *n.* tot-dae 돛대, ma-sŭ-t'ŭ 마스트.

master *n.* chu-in 주인, (*employer*) ko-yong-ju 고용주; (*teacher*) sŏn-saeng 선생.

masterpiece *n.* kŏl-jak 걸작, myŏng-jak 명작.

mat *n.* (*straw*) tot-ja-ri 돗자리 ; (*bamboo*) tae-ja-ri 대자리, kŏ-jŏk 거적, kkal-gae 깔개.

match *n.* ① sŏng-nyang 성냥. ② (*athletic*) kyŏng-gi 경기. ③ (*rival*) chŏk-su 적수. ④ (*marriage*) kyŏl-hon 결혼. —*v.* (*be equal to*) ⋯e p'il-jŏk-ha-da ⋯에 필적하다 ; (*be a rival to*) sang-dae-ga ṭoe-da 상대가 되다, (*fit*) cho-hwa-ha-da 조화하다.

matchbox *n.* sŏng-nyang-gap 성냥갑.

mate *n.* pae-p'il 배필 ; (*companion*) tong-ryo 동료.

material *adj.* ① mul-jil-ŭi 물질의. ② (*essential*) chung-yo-han 중요한. —*n.* chae-ryo 재료.

maternal *adj.* ŏ-mŏ-ni-ŭi 어머니의, mo-gye-ŭi 모계의.

maternity *n.* (*motherhood*) mo-sŏng 모성 : ~ *hospital* san-gwa pyŏng-wŏn 산과 병원.

mathematics *n.* su-hak 수학(數學). ⌐티네.

matinee *n.* chu-gan-gong-yŏn 주간공연, ma-t'i-ne 마

matron *n.* ① (*married woman*) ki-hon pu-in 기혼 부인. ② kan-ho-bu-jang 간호부장, po-mo 보모.

matter *n.* ① (*substance*) mul-jil 물질. ② (*affair*) sa-gŏn 사건. ③ (*material*) chae-ryo 재료. ④ (*constituents*) yo-so 요소. —*v.* kwan-gye-ga it-da 관계가 있다, chung-dae-ha-da 중대하다.

mattress *n.* (ch'im-dae-yong) yo (침대용) 요, mae-t'ŭ-ri-sŭ 매트리스.

mature *adj.* (*things*) ik-ŭn 익은 ; (*people*) sŏng-suk-han 성숙한.

mausoleum *n.* nŭng 능(陵), yŏng-myo 영묘(靈廟).

maxim *n.* kyŏk-ŏn 격언, (*proverb*) kŭm-ŏn 금언.

maximum *adj.* ch'oe-dae-han-ŭi 최대한의. —*n.* ch'oe-go-jŏm 최고점, ch'oe-dae-han 최대한, ch'oe-dae-ryang 최대량.

May *n.* o-wŏl 5월.

may *aux. v.* … il-ji-do mo-rŭn-da …일지도 모른다 ; …hae-do cho-t'a …해도 좋다 ; …hal su it-da …할 수 있다 ; wŏn-k'ŏn-dae …ha-gi-rŭl 원컨대 …하기를.

maybe *adv.* a-ma 아마, ŏ-jjŏ-myŏn 어쩌면.

mayor *n.* si-jang 시장(市長).

maze *n.* (*labyrinth*) mi-gung 미궁.

me *pron.* na-e-ge 나에게, na-rŭl 나를.

meadow *n.* p'ul-bat 풀밭, ch'o-wŏn 초원. mok-ch'o-ji 목초지.

meager·meagre *adj.* (*thin*) ma-rŭn 마른, yŏ-win 여윈, (*poor*) pin-yak-han 빈약한. ru 굵은 가루.

meal *n.* ① (*food*) sik-sa 식사. ② (*corn*) kul-gŭn ka-ru 굵은 가루.

mealtime *n.* sik-sa si-gan 식사 시간.

mean *adj.* ① ch'ŏn-han 천한. ② (*average*) p'yŏng-gyun-ŭi 평균의. ③ (*stingy*) in-saek-han 인색한. —*v.* ŭi-mi-ha-da 의미하다 ; (*intend*) ye-jŏng-ha-da 예정하다. —*n.* ① chung-gan 중간. ② (*pl.*) su-dan 수단.

meaning *n.* ttŭt 뜻, ŭi-mi 의미. —*adj.* (*significant*) ŭi-mi-sim-jang-han 의미심장한.

meantime *n. & adv.* kŭ tong-an(-e) 그 동안(에).

measles *n.* hong-yŏk 홍역, p'ung-jin 풍진.

measure *n.* ch'i-su 치수, ch'ŭk-jŏng 측정 ; (*pl.*) su-dan 수단. —*v.* ch'ŭk-jŏng-ha-da 측정하다.

meat *n.* ko-gi 고기 : *tender* ∼ yŏn-han ko-gi 연한 고기.

mechanic *n.* chik-gong 직공, ki-gye-gong 기계공. 「인.

mechanical *adj.* ki-gye-ŭi 기계의, ki-gye-jŏk-in 기계적

mechanism *n.* ki-gu 기구 ; ku-jo 구조 ; ki-gye-jang-ch'i 기계장치, me-k'ŏ-ni-jŭm 메커니즘.

medal *n.* hun-jang 훈장, me-dal 메달. 「르다.

meddle *v.* kan-sŏp-ha-da 간섭하다 ; chu-mu-rŭ-da 주무

medi(a)eval *adj.* chung-se-ŭi 중세의.

mediate *v.* cho-jŏng-ha-da 조정하다 ; (*intermediate*) chung-jae-ha-da 중재하다.

medical *adj.* ŭi-hak-ŭi 의학의, ŭi-sul-ŭi 의술의 : *a* ∼ *college* ŭi-gwa tae-hak 의과 대학/*a* ∼ *examination* kŏn-gang chin-dan 건강 진단.

medicine *n.* ① yak 약. ② (*science*) ŭi-hak 의학. 「통의.

mediocre *adj.* p'yŏng-bŏm-han 평범한, po-t'ong-ŭi 보

meditate *v.* ① suk-go-ha-da 숙고하다, muk-sang-ha-da 묵상하다. ② (*plan*) kkoe-ha-da 꾀하다.

Mediterranean *n.* chi-jung-hae 지중해. —*adj.* chi-jung-hae-ŭi 지중해의.

medium *n.* ① chung-gan 중간. ② mae-gae 매개, (*means*) su-dan 수단. —*adj.* chung-ch'i-ŭi 중치의.

medley *n.* chap-dong-sa-ni 잡동사니, hon-hap 혼합.

meek *adj.* (*mild*) pu-dŭ-rŏ-un 부드러운.

meet *v.* man-na-da 만나다 ; ma-ji-ha-da 맞이하다 ; (*join*) hap-ch'i-da 합치다.

meeting *n.* (*assembly*) hoe 회, hoe-hap 회합, mo-im 모임.

megaphone *n.* hwak-sŏng-gi 확성기, me-ga-p'on 메가폰.

melancholy *n. & adj.* u-ul(-han) 우울(한).

mellow *adj.* ik-ŭn 익은, pu-dŭ-rŏ-un 부드러운.
melodious *adj.* kok-jo-ga a-rŭm-da-un 곡조가 아름다운.
melodrama *n.* mel-ro-dŭ-ra-ma 멜로드라마.
melody *n.* (*harmony*) sŏn-yul 선율 ; mel-ro-di 멜로디,
  ka-rak 가락 ; (*tune*) kok-jo 곡조.
melon *n.* mel-ron 멜론, ch'am-oe 참외.　　　　「용해.
melt *v.* nok-da 녹다, nok-i-da 녹이다.　—*n.* yong-hae
member *n.* il-wŏn 일원 ; (*of a company*) sa-wŏn 사
  원 ; (*of an association*) hoe-wŏn 회원.
memorable *adj.* ki-ŏk-hal man-han 기억할 만한.
memorandum *n.* me-mo 메모 ; kak-sŏ 각서.
memorial *adj.* ki-nyŏm-ŭi 기념의.　—*n.* ki-nyŏm-mul
  기념물 ; (*monument*) ki-nyŏm-bi 기념비.
memory *n.* ki-ŏk 기억, (*recollection*) ch'u-ŏk 추억.
menace *n.* wi-hyŏp 위협.　—*v.* wi-hyŏp-ha-da 위협하다.
mend *v.* ko-ch'i-da 고치다, su-sŏn-ha-da 수선하다.
menstruation *n.* wŏl-gyŏng 월경, men-sŭ 멘스.
mental *adj.* chŏng-sin-ŭi 정신의, tu-noe-ŭi 두뇌의.
mention *v.* (*speak of*) …ŭl mal-ha-da …을 말하다.
mercantile *adj.* sang-ŏp-ŭi 상업의, sang-in-ŭi 상인의 :
  a ~ city sang-ŏp to-si 상업 도시.
merchandise *n.* (*goods*) sang-p'um 상품.
merchant *n.* sang-in 상인.　—*adj.* sang-ŏp-ŭi 상업의.
merciful *adj.* cha-bi-ro-un 자비로운 ; ta-haeng-in 다행인.
mercury *n.* ① su-ŭn 수은. ② on-do-gye 온도계.　「행운.
mercy *n.* ① cha-bi 자비, yŏn-min 연민. ② haeng-un
mere *adj.* tan-sun-han 단순한, sun-jŏn-han 순전한.
merely *adv.* tan-sun-hi 단순히, o-jik 오직.　　　　「기.
meridian *n.* ① cha-o-sŏn 자오선. ② chŏn-sŏng-gi 전성
merit *n.* ① (*forte*) chang-jŏm 장점, (*worth*) ka-ch'i
  가치. ② (*exploits*) kong-jŏk 공적.
merry *adj.* k'wae-hwal-han 쾌활한, chŭl-gŏ-un 즐거운.

mesh *n.* ① kŭ-mul-k'o 그물코. ② ol-ga-mi 올가미.

mess *n.* ① ŭm-sik-mul 음식물. ② hon-hap 혼합, twi-juk-bak-juk 뒤죽박죽 : ~ *hall* sik-dang 식당.

message *n.* so-sik 소식, t'ong-sin 통신, chŏn-gal 전갈, me-si-ji 메시지 ; (*mission*) sa-myŏng 사명.

messenger *n.* sim-bu-rŭm-gun 심부름군 ; (*envoy*) sa-ja 사자(使者) ; (*herald*) sŏn-gu-ja 선구자.

Messiah *n.* ku-se-ju 구세주, me-si-a 메시아.

messy *adj.* ŏ-ji-rŏ-un 어지러운, chi-jŏ-bun-han 지저분한.

metabolism *n.* sin-jin tae-sa 신진 대사.

metal *n.* kŭm-sok 금속, soe-bu-ch'i 쇠붙이. 「속성의.

metallic *adj.* kŭm-sok-ŭi 금속의, kŭm-sok-sŏng-ŭi 금

meteor *n.* (*shooting star*) yu-sŏng 유성(流星).

meteorology *n.* ki-sang 기상, ki-sang-hak 기상학.

meter · metre *n.* ① (*measure*) mi-t'ŏ 미터 ; (*instrument*) kye-ryang-gi 계량기. ② un-yul 운율.

method *n.* pang-bŏp 방법 ; (*order*) sun-sŏ 순서.

Methodist Church kam-ri-gyo-hoe 감리교회.

metropolis *n.* su-do 수도(首都). 「min 수도의 주민.

metropolitan *adj.* su-do-ŭi 수도의. —*n.* su-do-ŭi chu-

mew *v.* (*cat*) ya-ong-ha-go ul-da 야옹하고 울다.

microbe *n.* mi-saeng-mul 미생물 ; se-gyun 세균.

microfilm *n.* ch'uk-sa p'il-rŭm 축사(縮寫) 필름.

microphone *n.* hwak-sŏng-gi 확성기, ma-i-k'ŭ 마이크.

microscope *n.* hyŏn-mi-gyŏng 현미경.

mid *adj.* chung-ang-ŭi 중앙의, chung-gan-ŭi 중간의.

midday *n.* (*noon*) chŏng-o 정오, han-nat 한낮.

middle *n.* ka-un-de 가운데, chung-ang 중앙. —*adj.* chung-ang-ŭi 중앙의, han-ga-un-de-ŭi 한가운데의.

middle-aged *adj.* chung-nyŏn-ŭi 중년의.

middle-class *adj.* chung-ryu-ŭi 중류의, chung-san-gye-gŭp-ŭi 중산계급의.

midnight *n.* han-bam-jung 한밤중, ya-ban 야반.
midst *n.* han-ga-un-de 한가운데, pok-p'an 복판.
midsummer *n.* han-yŏ-rŭm 한여름.　　　　「중도의.
midway *adv.* chung-gan-e 중간에. —*adj.* chung-do-ŭi
midwife *n.* cho-san-wŏn 조산원, san-p'a 산파.
midwinter *n.* & *adj.* han-gyŏ-ŭl(-ŭi) 한겨울(의).
might *n.* (*power*) him 힘, nŭng-ryŏk 능력 : *M* ~ *is
right.* Him-ŭn chŏng-ŭi-da 힘은 정의다.
mighty *adj.* (*powerful*) kut-sen 굳센 ; kŏ-dae-han 거
대한 ; (*wonderful*) koeng-jang-han 굉장한.　　「하다.
migrate *v.* om-gyŏ sal-da 옮겨 살다, i-ju-ha-da 이주
mild *adj.* (*gentle*) chŏm-jan-ŭn 점잖은, (*warm*) on-
mildew *n.* kom-p'ang-i 곰팡이.　　　　⌊hwa-han 온화한.
mile *n.* ma-il 마일 (1,609.3m).　　　　「획기적 사건.
milestone *n.* i-jŏng-p'yo 이정표 ; hoek-gi-jŏk sa-gŏn
militant *adj.* ho-jŏn-jŏk-in 호전적인, t'u-jaeng-jŏk-in
militarism *n.* kun-guk-ju-ŭi 군국주의.　　　⌊투쟁적인.
military *adj.* kun-ŭi 군의 : ~ *attache* tae-sa-gwan-so-
sok mu-gwan 대사관소속 무관/~ *academy* yuk-gun
sa-gwan-hak-gyo 육군 사관학교.　　　　「gun 의용군.
militia *n.* (*citizen army*) min-byŏng 민병, ŭi-yong-
milk *n.* u-yu 우유, chŏt 젖, mil-k'ŭ 밀크.
Milky Way ŭn-ha-su 은하수.　　　　　　　　「아.
mill *n.* pang-at-gan 방앗간 : *water* ~ mul-bang-a 물방
miller *n.* ① pang-at-gan chu-in 방앗간 주인. ② che-
bun-ŏp-ja 제분업자.
millet *n.* ki-jang 기장 : *African* ~ su-su 수수.
million *n.* & *adj.* paek-man(-ŭi) 백만(의).
million(n)aire *n.* paek-man-jang-ja 백만장자.
millstone *n.* maet-dol 맷돌, yŏn-ja-mae 연자매.
mimeograph *n.* tŭng-sa-p'an 등사판, pok-sa-p'an 복사
판. —*v.* tŭng-sa〔pok-sa〕-ha-da 등사〔복사〕하다.

mimic *v.* hyung-nae-nae-da 흉내내다. —*adj.* hyung-nae-nae-nŭn 흉내내는.

mince *v.* chal-ge ssŏl-da 잘게 썰다 : ~*d meat* ta-jin ko-gi 다진 고기.

mind *n.* ma-ŭm 마음, saeng-gak 생각 ; (*intent*) ŭi-hyang 의향. —*v.* (*heed*) cho-sim-ha-da 조심하다.

mindful *adj.* chu-ŭi-gi-p’ŭn 주의깊은.

mindless *adj.* mu-sim-han 무심한, (*stupid*) ŏ-ri-sŏk-ŭn 어리석은.

mine *pron.* na-ŭi kŏt 나의 것. —*n.* kwang-san 광산 ; chi-roe 지뢰 : *a coal* ~ t’an-gwang 탄광.

miner *n.* kwang-bu 광부, kaeng-bu 갱부.

mineral *n.* kwang-mul 광물. —*adj.* kwang-mul-ŭi 광물의 : ~ *right* ch’ae-gul-gwŏn 채굴권.

mingle *v.* ① (*mix*) sŏk-da 섞다, (*unite*) hap-ch’i-da 합치다. ② (*participate*) ch’am-ga-ha-da 참가하다.

miniature *n.* se-mil-hwa 세밀화, ch’uk-do 축도, mi-ni-ŏ-ch’ŏ 미니어처. —*adj.* so-gyu-mo-ŭi 소규모의.

minimize *v.* ch’oe-so-ro ŏ-rim-jap-da 최소로 어림잡다.

minimum *n.* ch’oe-so-han-do 최소한도. —*adj.* (*smallest possible*) ch’oe-so-han-do-ŭi 최소한도의.

minimum wage ch’oe-jŏ im-gŭm 최저 임금.

mining industry kwang-ŏp 광업.

minister *n.* ① (*government*) chang-gwan 장관. ② (*church*) mok-sa 목사. ③ (*envoy*) kong-sa 공사(公使) : *the Prime M*~ kuk-mu-ch’ong-ri 국무총리.

ministry *n.* ① (*cabinet*) nae-gak 내각. ② (*of the church*) sŏng-jik 성직. ③ (*suffix*) …pu …부(部) : *the M*~ *of Education* mun-gyo-bu 문교부.

minor *adj.* (*lesser*) so-su-ŭi 소수의, (*inferior*) ha-ch’an-ŭn 하찮은. —*n.* mi-sŏng-nyŏn-ja 미성년자.

minority *n.* ① so-su 소수. ② (*legal infancy*) mi-sŏng-nyŏn 미성년. ③ (*faction*) so-su-p’a 소수파.

mint *n.* ① (*plant*) pak-ha 박하. ② (*coining money*)

cho-p'ye-guk 조폐국. —*v*. (*coin*) chu-jo-ha-da 주조하다, man-dŭ-rŏ-nae-da 만들어내다.

minus *adj*. ma-i-nŏ-sŭ-ŭi 마이너스의, pu-ŭi 부(負)의. —*prep*. ···ŭl ppaen ···을 뺀. —*n*. (*minus sign*) ma-i-nŏ-sŭ ki-ho 마이너스 기호, pu-ho 부호(負號).

minute *adj*. mi-se-han 미세한, (*detailed*) sang-se-han 상세한. —*n*. ① pun 분(分). ② sun-gan 순간.

minute hand pun-ch'im 분침, chang-ch'im 장침.

minutes *n*. (*record of proceedings*) ŭi-sa-rok 의사록.

minx *n*. mal-gwal-ryang-i 말괄량이, wal-p'ae 왈패.

miracle *n*. (*supernatural event*) ki-jŏk 기적.

miraculous *adj*. ki-jŏk-jŏk-in 기적적인.

mire *n*. (*mud*) chin-hŭk 진흙, chin-ch'ang 진창.

mirror *n*. ① kŏ-ul 거울. ② (*pattern*) mo-bŏm 모범. —*v*. (*reflect*) pan-yŏng-ha-da 반영하다.

mirth *n*. (*gaiety*) yu-k'wae 유쾌 ; hwal-lak 환락.

misapply *v*. o-yong-ha-da 오용하다.

miscarriage *n*. (*failure*) sil-su 실수, sil-ch'aek 실책.

miscellaneous *adj*. chap-jong-ŭi 잡종의.　　　　「손해.

mischief *n*. ① chang-nan 장난. ② (*damage*) son-hae

mischievous *adj*. (*annoying*) mal-ssŏng-bu-ri-nŭn 말썽부리는, (*harmful*) hae-ro-un 해로운.

misconception *n*. o-hae 오해, o-in 오인, (*false opinion*) chal-mot-doen saeng-gak 잘못된 생각.

misconduct *n*. pi-haeng 비행. —*v*. sil-su-ha-da 실수하다.

misdeed *n*. na-bbŭn chit 나쁜 짓, ak-haeng 악행.

miser *n*. ku-du-soe 구두쇠, no-rang-i 노랑이, su-jŏn-no 수전노.　　　　「행한, ka-yŏp-sŭn 가엾은.

miserable *adj*. pi-ch'am-han 비참한, pul-haeng-han 불

misery *n*. pul-haeng 불행, (*poverty*) pin-gon 빈곤.

misfortune *n*. pu-run 불운, (*adversity*) yŏk-gyŏng 역경, (*calamity*) chae-nan 재난.

mishap *n.* (*unhappiness*) pu-run 불운, (*disaster*) chae-nan 재난 ; (*accident*) ch'am-sa 참사.

misjudge *v.* o-p'an-ha-da 오판(誤判)하다.

mislay *v.* (*lose*) tu-go i-jŏ-bŏ-ri-da 두고 잊어버리다, ŏng-ddung-han ko-se tu-da 엉뚱한 곳에 두다.

mislead *v.* chal-mot in-do-ha-da 잘못 인도하다, kŭ-rŭ-ch'i-da 그르치다; (*dazzle*) hyŏn-hok-si-k'i-da 현혹시키

misplace *v.* chal-mot tu-da 잘못 두다.   └다.

misprint *n.* o-sik 오식, mi-sŭ-p'ŭ-rin-t'ŭ 미스프린트.

miss *v.* no-ch'i-da 놓치다, ‥‥i ŏp-sŏ-sŏ sŏ-un-ha-da ‥‥이 없어서 서운하다. —*n.* ① (*failure*) sil-ch'aek 실책. ② (*omission*) t'al-rak 탈락.

Miss *n.* yang 양 : ~ *Kim* kim-yang 김양.

missile *n.* & *adj.* na-ra-ga-nŭn mu-gi(-ŭi) 날아가는 무기(의), mi-sa-il(-ŭi) 미사일(의).

missing *adj.* op-so-jin 없어진, haeng-bang-bul-myŏng-ŭi 행방불명의.

mission *n.* ① (*commission*) sa-myŏng 사명. ② (*dele-gation*) sa-jŏl 사절(使節). ③ (*evangelism*) chŏn-do 전도 : ~ *school* chŏn-do-hak-gyo 전도학교.

missionary *n.* ① sŏn-gyo-sa 선교사. ② sŏn-jŏn-ja 선전자. ③ sa-jŏl 사절.

mist *n.* an-gae 안개, (*haze*) nol 눌.

mistake *n.* chal-mot 잘못, sil-su 실수. —*v.* t'ŭl-ri-da 틀리다, chal-mot saeng-gak-ha-da 잘못 생각하다.

mistaken *adj.* t'ŭl-rin 틀린, kŭ-rŭt-doen 그릇된.

mistress *n.* an-ju-in 안주인, chu-bu 주부.

mistrust *v.* (*suspect*) ŭi-sim-ha-da 의심하다. —*n.* (*distrust*) pul-sin 불신 ; (*suspicion*) ŭi-hok 의혹.

misty *adj.* an-gae kkin 안개 낀, hŭi-mi-han 희미한.

misunderstand *v.* o-hae-ha-da 오해하다.   「추다.

mitigate *v.* wan-hwa-ha-da 완화하다, nŭt-ch'u-da 늦

mix *v.* sŏk-da 섞다, hon-hap-ha-da 혼합하다.

mixer *n.* hon-hap-ha-nŭn sa-ram 혼합하는 사람 ; hon-hap-gi 혼합기, mik-sŏ 믹서.

mixture *n.* hon-hap 혼합, hon-hap-mul 혼합물.

moan *n.* & *v.* sin-ŭm(-ha-da) 신음(하다).

mob *n.* (*rioter*) p'ok-do 폭도, (*crowd*) kun-jung 군중.

mobile *adj.* (*movable*) um-jik-i-gi swi-un 움직이기 쉬운, (*fickle*) pyŏn-dŏk-sŭ-rŏ-un 변덕스러운.

mock *v.* (*ridicule*) cho-rong-ha-da 조롱하다, (*imitate*) hyung-nae-nae-da 흉내내다. —*n.* cho-rong 조롱, hyung-nae 흉내. —*adj.* ka-jja-ŭi 가짜의. 「흉내.

mockery *n.* cho-rong 조롱 ; si-nyung 시늉, hyung-nae

mockingbird *n.* ip-nae-sae 입내새, aeng-mu-sae 앵무새.

mode *n.* pang-bŏp 방법, yang-sik 양식 ; yu-haeng 유행.

model *n.* (*pattern*) mo-bŏm 모범 ; (*ideal*) p'yo-bon 표본. —*v.* pon-ddŭ-da 본뜨다.

moderate *adj.* on-gŏn-han 온건한, (*medium*) chŏk-dang-han 적당한. —*n.* on-gŏn-p'a 온건파.

moderation *n.* (*temperance*) chŏl-je 절제 ; (*mildness*) on-gŏn 온건 ; (*medium*) al-ma-jŭm 알맞음.

moderator *n.*(*chairman*) sa-hoe-ja 사회자, ŭi-jang 의장.

modern *adj.* hyŏn-dae-ŭi 현대의, sin-sik-ŭi 신식의. —*n.* hyŏn-dae-in 현대인. 「근대화.

modernization *n.* hyŏn-dae-hwa 현대화, kŭn-dae-hwa

modest *adj.* (*humble*) kyŏm-son-han 겸손한, yam-jŏn-han 얌전한 ; (*shy*) su-jup-ŭn 수줍은.

modesty *n.* kyŏm-son 겸손 ; (*decency*) chŏng-suk 정숙.

modifier *n.* su-jŏng-ja 수정자 ; su-sik-ŏ 수식어.

modify *v.* (*change*) pyŏn-gyŏng-ha-da 변경하다, su-jŏng-ha-da 수정하다 ; su-sik-ha-da 수식하다.

modulate *v.* cho-jŏl-ha-da 조절하다. 「물젖은.

moist *adj.* ch'uk-ch'uk-han 축축한 ; nun-mul-jŏ-jŭn 눈

moisture *n.* sŭp-gi 습기, mul-gi 물기.

molasses *n.* tang-mil 당밀(糖蜜).

mole *n.* ① (*on face*) sa-ma-gwi 사마귀, chu-gŭn-ggae 주근깨. ② (*animal*) tu-dŏ-ji 두더지. 「하다.

molest *v.* koe-rop-hi-da 괴롭히다, pang-hae-ha-da 방해

moment *n.* sun-gan 순간 ; (*occasion*) ki-hoe 기회, kyŏng-u 경우 ; (*element*) yo-so 요소. 「덧없는.

momentary *adj.* sun-sik-gan-ŭi 순식간의 ; tŏt-ŏp-nŭn

monarch *n.* kun-ju 군주, che-wang 제왕.

monarchy *n.* kun-ju-guk 군주국 ; kun-ju chŏng-ch'i 군

monastery *n.* su-do-wŏn 수도원. 「주 정치.

Monday *n.* wŏ-ryo-il 월요일.

money *n.* ton 돈, kŭm-jŏn 금전, (*wealth*) pu 부(富).

money changer hwan-jŏn-sang 환전상(換錢商).

money order hwan 환(換), (*postal order*) u-p'yŏn-hwan 우편환.

monitor *n.* (*in a school*) pan-jang 반장 ; (*adviser*) ch'ung-go-ja 충고자, mo-ni-t'ŏ 모니터.

monk *n.* su-do-sŭng 수도승 ; sŭng-ryŏ 승려.

monkey *n.* wŏn-sung-i 원숭이.

monolog(ue) *n.* tok-baek 독백 ; i-rin-gŭk 일인극(一人劇).

monoplane *n.* tan-yŏp pi-haeng-gi 단엽 비행기.

monopolize *v.* tok-jŏm-ha-da 독점하다.

monopoly *n.* tok-jŏm 독점, chŏn-mae 전매. 「노레일.

monorail *n.* tan-gwe-ch'ŏl-do 단궤철도, mo-no-re-il 모

monotonous *adj.* tan-jo-ro-un 단조로운, pyŏn-hwa-ga ŏp-nŭn 변화가 없는 ; chi-ru-han 지루한. 「철.

monsoon *n.* kye-jŏl-p'ung 계절풍 ; chang-ma-ch'ŏl 장마

monster *n.* koe-mul 괴물, kŏ-in 거인.

monstrous *adj.* ki-goe-han 기괴한, mu-si-mu-si-han 무시무시한, (*huge*) ŏm-ch'ŏng-nan 엄청난. 「아지.

montage *n.* hon-sŏng-hwa 혼성화, mong-t'a-a-ji 몽타

month *n.* tal 달, wŏl 월 : *this* ~ i-dal 이달/ *last* ~ chi-nan-dal 지난달/*next* ~ nae-dal 내달.

monthly *adj.* mae-dal-ŭi 매달의 : *a* ~ *salary* wŏl-gŭp 월급. —*n.* wŏl-gan chap-ji 월간 잡지.

monument *n.* ki-nyŏm-bi 기념비, myo-bi 묘비 ; ki-nyŏm-mul 기념물 : *natural* ~ ch'ŏn-yŏn ki-nyŏm-mul 천연 기념물.

monumental *adj.* ki-nyŏm-bi-ŭi 기념비의, pul-myŏl-ŭi 「불멸의.

mood *n.* ki-bun 기분, sim-jŏng 심정 ; p'ung-jo 풍조.

moon *n.* tal 달 : *a full* ~ po-rŭm-dal 보름달, man-wŏl 만월/*a new* ~ ch'o-sŭng-dal 초승달/*an old* ~ kŭ-mŭm-dal 그믐달 / *a half* ~ pan-dal 반달.

moonlight *n.* tal-bit 달빛 : *a* ~ *ramble* tal-bam-ŭi san-ch'aek 달밤의 산책. 「bak-ha-da 정박하다.

moor *n.* hwang-mu-ji 황무지. —*v.* (*anchor*) chŏng-

moot *n.* t'o-ron-hoe 토론회, t'o-ŭi 토의.

mop *n.* cha-ru kŏl-re 자루 걸레, mop 몹.

moral *adj.* yul-li-jŏk-in 윤리적인, to-dŏk-jŏk-in 도덕적인. —*n.* ① kyo-hun 교훈. ② yul-li 윤리. 「풍기.

morale *n.* (*military*) sa-gi 사기 ; (*civilian*) p'ung-gi

moralist *n.* to-dŏk-ga 도덕가, to-hak-ja 도학자, mo-ral-ri-sŭ-t'ŭ 모랄리스트. 「상도덕.

morality *n.* to-dŏk 도덕 : *commercial* ~ sang-do-dŏk

morbid *adj.* pyŏng-jŏk-in 병적인, pyŏng-ŭi 병의.

more *adj.* tŏ man-ŭn 더 많은. —*adv.* tŏ man-i 더 많이. —*n.* tŏ man-ŭn kŏt 더 많은 것.

moreover *adv.* kŭ wi-e 그 위에, ke-da-ga 게다가.

morning *n.* a-ch'im 아침, (*before noon*) o-jŏn 오전.

morphine *n.* mo-rŭ-p'in 모르핀.

morsel *n.* han ip 한 입, (*a bite*) han cho-gak 한 조각.

mortal *adj.* ① chuk-ŭl un-myŏng-ŭi 죽을 운명의. ② (*human*) in-gan-ŭi 인간의. —*n.* in-gan 인간.

mortar *n.* ① (*utensil*) chŏl-gu 절구. ② (*gun*) pak-gyŏk-p'o 박격포. ③ (*for building*) mo-rŭ-t'a-rŭ 모르타르.

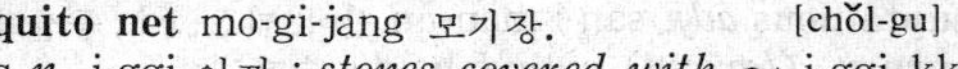
[chŏl-gu]

mortgage *n.* chŏ-dang 저당(抵當).
mortify *v.* ŏk-je-ha-da 억제하다.
mortuary *n.* si-ch'e im-si an-ch'i-so 시체 임시 안치소.
mosquito *n.* mo-gi 모기.
mosquito net mo-gi-jang 모기장.
moss *n.* i-ggi 이끼 : *stones covered with* ~ i-ggi kkin tol 이끼 낀 돌.
most *adj.* ka-jang man-ŭn 가장 많은. —*n.* ch'oe-dae-「ryang 최대량.
mostly *adv.* tae-gae 대개, tae-bu-bun 대부분.
mote *n.* (*particle*) t'i-ggŭl 티끌, mŏn-ji 먼지.
motel *n.* (*motorists' hotel*) cha-dong-ch'a yŏ-haeng-ja suk-bak-so 자동차 여행자 숙박소. 「re 좀벌레.
moth *n.* ① na-bang 나방. ② (*clothes moth*) chom-bŏl-
mother *n.* ŏ-mŏ-ni 어머니, mo-ch'in 모친. —*v.* (*bring up*) po-yuk-ha-da 보육하다.
mother country mo-guk 모국(母國), pon-guk 본국.
mother-in-law *n.* ① (*for woman*) si-ŏ-mŏ-ni 시어머니. ② (*for man*) chang-mo 장모.
mother-of-pearl *n.* chin-ju-mo 진주모, cha-gae 자개.
motif *n.* chu-je 주제, (*theme*) t'e-e-ma 테에마.
motion *n.* ① un-dong 운동. ② (*gesture*) mom-jit 몸짓. ③ (*proposal*) tong-ŭi 동의. ④ un-jŏn 운전.
motive *n.* tong-gi 동기, r ㅣo-t'i-bŭ 모티브. 「모우터.
motor *n.* (*prime mover*) pal-dong-gi 발동기, mo-u-t'ŏ
motorboat *n.* mo-u-t'ŏ-bo-u-t'ŭ 모우터보우트.
motorcade *n.* cha-dong-ch'a haeng-ryŏl 자동차 행렬.
motorcar *n.* cha-dong-ch'a 자동차. 「gŏ 자동 자전거.
motorcycle *n.* o-o-t'o-ba-i 오오토바이, cha-dong cha-jŏn-

motor pool (*motor park*) chu-ch'a-jang 주차장.

motto *n.* p'yo-ŏ 표어, ch'ŏ-se-hun 처세훈, mo-t'o 모토.

mo(u)ld *n.* ① t'ŭl 틀, kŏ-p'u-jip 거푸집. ② (*mildew*) kom-p'ang-i 곰팡이. ③ (*fertile soil*) ok-t'o 옥토.

mound *n.* ŏn-dŏk 언덕, (*raised bank*) tuk 둑.

mount *v.* o-rŭ-da 오르다. —*n.* san 산.

mountain *n.* san 산 : ~ *range* san-maek 산맥.

mountaineer *n.* tŭng-san-ga 등산가. —*v.* tŭng-san-ha-
mountainous *adj.* san-i man-ŭn 산이 많은. ⌊da 등산하다.

mourn *v.* (*lament*) sŭl-p'ŏ-ha-da 슬퍼하다.

mourner *n.* cho-gaek 조객, ae-do-ja 애도자(哀悼者) :
 the chief ~ sang-ju 상주.

mourning *n.* ae-do 애도, sang 상(喪), sang-bok 상복:
 ~ *badge* sang-jang 상장/~ *card* pu-go 부고.

mouse *n.* saeng-jwi 생쥐 : ~ *trap* chwi-dŏt 쥐덫.

m(o)ustache *n.* k'ot-su-yŏm 콧수염. ⌈동성으로.

mouth *n.* ip 입 : *with one* ~ i-gu-dong-sŏng-ŭ-ro 이구

move *v.* ① um-jik-i-da 움직이다. ② (*touch*) kam-dong-
 si-k'i-da 감동시키다. ③ (*propose*) che-ŭi-ha-da 제의
 하다. ④ (*remove*) i-sa-ha-da 이사하다.

movement *n.* ① un-dong 운동, tong-jak 동작 ; i-dong
 이동 ; (*operation*) un-jŏn 운전. ② (*pl.*) t'ae-do 태도.

movie *n.* (*motion picture*) yŏng-hwa 영화.

moving *adj.* um-jik-i-nŭn 움직이는 ; (*touching*) kam-
 dong-si-k'i-nŭn 감동시키는 : ~ *picture* hwal-dong-sa-
 jin 활동사진, yŏng-hwa 영화.

mow *v.* pe-da 베다, kŏ-du-ŏ-dŭ-ri-da 거두어들이다.
 —*n.* kok-sik-dŏ-mi 곡식더미.

mower *n.* ① (*machine*) p'ul-be-nŭn ki-gye 풀베는 기
 계. ② (*person*) p'ul-be-nŭn sa-ram 풀베는 사람.

Mr. *n.* ssi 씨, kun 군, nim 님.

Mrs. *n.* ⋯ssi pu-in ⋯씨 부인, ⋯yŏ-sa ⋯여사(女史).

much *adj*. man-ŭn 많은. —*adv*. man-i 많이.

muck *n*. (*manure*) kŏ-rŭm 거름, t'oe-bi 퇴비.

mud *n*. chin-hŭk 진흙, (*mire*) chin-ch'ang 진창.

muddle *v*. hol-lan-si-k'i-da 혼란시키다. —*n*. hol-lan 혼란, ŏng-mang-jin-ch'ang 엉망진창.

muddy *adj*. chin-hŭk t'u-sŏng-i-ŭi 진흙 투성이의.

muffle *v*. (*wrap up*) ssa-da 싸다, tŏp-da 덮다.

muffler *n*. ① (*neck scarf*) mok-do-ri 목도리, mŏ-p'ŭl-rŏ 머플러. ② so-ŭm chang-ch'i 소음 장치.

mug *n*. k'ŭn ch'at-jan 큰 찻잔, cho-ggi 조끼.

mulatto *n*. hŭk-baek hon-hyŏl-a 흑백 혼혈아.

mulberry *n*. ppong-na-mu 뽕나무 ; (*berry*) o-di 오디.

mule *n*. no-sae 노새 ; ko-jip-jang-i 고집쟁이. 「ho 대부호.

multimillionaire *n*. ch'ŏn-man-jang-ja 천만장자, tae-bu-

multiplication *n*. kop-sem 곱셈 ; chŭng-sik 증식.

multiply *v*. chŭng-ga-ha-da 증가하다, pŏn-sik-si-k'i-da 번식시키다 ; kop-sem-ha-da 곱셈하다.

multipurpose dam ta-mok-jŏk-daem 다목적댐.

multitude *n*. ① (*large number*) ta-su 다수. ② (*great crowd*) kun-jung 군중. 「da 우물거리다.

mumble *v*. chung-ŏl-gŏ-ri-da 중얼거리다, u-mul-gŏ-ri-

mummy *n*. ① mi-i-ra 미이라. ② (*mamma*) ŏm-ma 엄

munch *v*. wa-sak-wa-sak mŏk-da 와삭와삭 먹다. 「마.

municipal *adj*. si-ŭi 시(市)의 : ~ *office* si-ch'ŏng 시청.

munition *n*. ① kun-su-p'um 군수품. ② t'an-yak 탄약.

murder *n*. sa-rin 살인, sal-hae 살해. —*v*. sal-hae-ha-da 살해하다, chuk-i-da 죽이다.

murderer *n*. sa-rin-ja 살인자, ha-su-in 하수인.

murmur *n*. sok-sak-im 속삭임, chol-jol so-ri 졸졸 소리 ; (*grumble*) pul-p'yŏng 불평. —*v*. sok-sak-i-da 속삭이다, (*complain*) t'u-dŏl-gŏ-ri-da 투덜거리다. 「완력.

muscle *n*. kŭn-yuk 근육 ; (*bodily strength*) wal-lyŏk

muse *v.* saeng-gak-e cham-gi-da 생각에 잠기다.

museum *n.* pak-mul-gwan 박물관.

mushroom *n.* ① (*toadstool*) pŏ-sŏt 버섯. ② (*upstart*) pyŏ-rak-bu-ja 벼락부자.　　　　　　　　　「악곡.

music *n.* ŭm-ak 음악 ; (*musical composition*) ak-gok

musical *adj.* ŭm-ak-ŭi 음악의, (*melodious*) ŭm-ak-jŏk-in 음악적인. —*n.* (*musicale*) ŭm-ak-hoe 음악회.

musician *n.* ŭm-ak-ga 음악가, ak-sa 악사.

musk *n.* ① sa-hyang 사향. ② sa-hyang no-ru 사향 노루.

muslin *n.* mo-sŭl-rin 모슬린, ok-yang-mok 옥양목.

muss *n.* twi-juk-bak-juk 뒤죽박죽, so-dong 소동.

must *aux. v.* ···hae-ya han-da ···해야 한다 ; ···ham-e t'ŭl-rim-op-da ···함에 틀림없다. —*n.* kom-p'ang-i 곰팡이.

mustard *n.* kyŏ-ja 겨자(芥子), kat 갓.

muster *v.* pul-rŏ-mo-ŭ-da 불러모으다, so-jip-ha-da 소집하다. —*n.* so-jip 소집, chŏm-ho 점호.

mute *adj.* so-ri-ŏp-nŭn 소리없는, pŏng-ŏ-ri-ŭi 벙어리의.

mutilate *v.* chŏl-dan-ha-da 절단하다, hwe-son-ha-da 훼손하다, pul-gu-ro man-dŭl-da 불구로 만들다.

mutiny *n.* (*rebellion*) p'ok-dong 폭동. —*v.* p'ok-dong-ŭl i-rŭ-k'i-da 폭동을 일으키다 ; chŏ-hang-ha-da 저항하다.

mutter *v.* chung-ŏl-gŏ-ri-da 중얼거리다, t'u-dŏl-gŏ-ri-da 투덜거리다. —*n.* sok-sak-im 속삭임, pul-p'yŏng 불평.

mutton *n.* yang-go-gi 양고기.

mutual *adj.* sŏ-ro-ŭi 서로의, sang-ho-ŭi 상호의.

muzzle *n.* ① ip-ma-gae 입마개, chae-gal 재갈. ② (*snout*) chu-dung-i 주둥이. ③ (*gun*) ch'ong-gu 총구.

my *pron.* na-ŭi 나의. —*int.* M~!=Oh, m~! chŏ-rŏn! 저런! ŏ-mŏ-na 어머나! i-gŏt ch'am! 이것 참!

myself *pron.* na cha-sin 나 자신.

mystery *n.* sin-bi 신비, i-sang-han kŏt 이상한 것.

myth *n.* sin-hwa 신화, (*legend*) chŏn-sŏl 전설 ; yet-nal i-ya-gi 옛날 이야기.

N

nail *v.* mo-sŭl pak-da 못을 박다. —*n.* ① (*instrument*) mot 못. ② (*finger*) son-t'op 손톱 ; (*toe*) pal-t'op 발톱 : ~ *clippers* son-t'op-gga-ggi 손톱깎이.

naive *adj.* sun-jin-han 순진한, u-jik-han 우직한.

naked *adj.* pŏl-gŏ-bŏ-sŭn 벌거벗은, na-ch'e-ŭi 나체의 ; (*exposed*) no-ch'ul-doen 노출된.

name *n.* i-rŭm 이름, sŏng-myŏng 성명. —*v.* i-rŭm-jit-da 이름짓다, (*appoint*) chi-myŏng-ha-da 지명하다.

namely *adv.* chŭk 즉, ta-si mal-ha-myŏn 다시 말하면.

name plate mun-p'ae 문패, myŏng-ch'al 명찰.

nap *v.* chol-da 졸다. —*n.* ① (*of wool*) po-p'ul 보풀. ② (*short sleep*) nat-jam 낮잠, sŏn-jam 선잠.

nape *n.* mok-dŏl-mi 목덜미.

napkin *n.* naep-k'in 냅킨.

narcissus *n.* ① su-sŏn-hwa 수선화. ② (*N*~) na-rŭ-si-so-sŭ 나르시소스.　　　　　　　　　「취제.

narcotic *adj.* ma-ch'wi-ŭi 마취의. —*n.* ma-ch'wi-je 마

narrate *v.* mal-ha-da 말하다, chin-sul-ha-da 진술하다.

narration *n.* i-ya-gi 이야기, tam-hwa 담화, sŏ-sul 서술, (*gram.*) hwa-bŏp 화법(話法).　　　　「기체의.

narrative *n.* i-ya-gi 이야기. —*adj.* i-ya-gi-ch'e-ŭi 이야

narrator *n.* i-ya-gi-ha-nŭn sa-ram 이야기하는 사람, na-re-i-t'ŏ 나레이터.

narrow *adj.* chop-ŭn 좁은, p'yŏn-hyŏp-han 편협한.

narrow-minded *adj.* ma-ŭm-i chop-ŭn 마음이 좁은.

nasty *adj.* (*dirty*) tŏ-rŏ-un 더러운, pul-gyŏl-han 불결한 ; (*malicious*) sim-sul-gu-jŭn 심술궂은.

nation *n.* ① kuk-min 국민. ② (*state*) kuk-ga 국가. ③ (*race*) min-jok 민족.

national *adj.* kuk-min-ŭi 국민의, kuk-ga-ŭi 국가의 : ~ *flag* kuk-gi 국기 / ~ *anthem* kuk-ga 국가(國歌) / ~ *defence* kuk-bang 국방.

nationalism *n.* kuk-ga-ju-ŭi 국가주의, min-jok-ju-ŭi 민족주의, (*patriotism*) ae-guk-sim 애국심.

nationality *n.* kuk-jŏk 국적, kuk-min-sŏng 국민성.

nationalization *n.* kuk-min-hwa 국민화, kuk-yu-hwa 국유화, kuk-yŏng 국영(國營).

nation-wide *adj.* chŏn-guk-jŏk-in 전국적인.

native *adj.* ① (*inborn*) t'a-go-nan 타고난. ② (*aboriginal*) t'o-ch'ak-ŭi 토착의. ③ pol-lae-ŭi 본래의 : ~ *country* ko-guk 고국 / ~ *place* ko-hyang 고향.

natural *adj.* cha-yŏn-ŭi 자연의, cha-yŏn kŭ-dae-ro-ŭi 자연 그대로의, (*innate*) t'a-go-nan 타고난.

naturalization *n.* kwi-hwa 귀화(歸化).

naturally *adv.* cha-yŏn-hi 자연히, ch'ŏn-sŏng-jŏk-ŭ-ro 천성적으로, tang-yŏn-hi 당연히.

nature *n.* ① cha-yŏn 자연. ② (*character*) ch'ŏn-sŏng 천성, sŏng-jil 성질. ③ (*sort*) chong-ryu 종류.

naught·nought *n.* (*zero*) yŏng 영, mu 무(無).

naughty *adj.* (*mischievous*) chang-nan-ggu-rŏ-gi-ŭi 장난꾸러기의 ; pŏ-rŭt-ŏp-nŭn 버릇없는.

nauseous *adj.* me-sŭ-ggŏ-un 메스꺼운, si-rŭn 싫은.

naval *adj.* hae-gun-ŭi 해군의 : ~ *forces* hae-gun 해군 / N~ *Academy* hae-gun-sa-gwan-hak-gyo 해군사관학교.

navigate *v.* hang-hae-ha-da 항해하다 ; (*steer*) cho-jong-ha-da 조종하다, chin-haeng-si-k'i-da 진행시키다.

navigation *n.* hang-hae 항해 : *aerial* ~ hang-gong-sul 항공술 / ~ *company* ki-sŏn-hoe-sa 기선회사.

navy *n.* hae-gun 해군, hae-gun kun-in 해군 군인.

near *adj*. ka-gga-un 가까운. —*adv*. ka-gga-i 가까이. —*prep*. …ŭi ka-gga-i-e …의 가까이에, …ŭi kŭn-ch'ŏ-e …의 근처에.

near-by *adj*. ka-gga-un 가까운, ka-gga-i-ŭi 가까이의: *a ~ village* pa-ro i-ut ma-ŭl 바로 이웃 마을.

Near East kŭn-dong 근동(近東).

nearly *adv*. kŏ-ŭi 거의, ha-ma-t'ŏ-myŏn 하마터면.

nearsighted *adj*. kŭn-si-ŭi 근시(近視)의.

neat *adj*. cho-ch'ol-han 조촐한, san-ddŭt-han 산뜻한.

necessary *adj*. p'i-ryo-han 필요한, (*inevitable*) p'i-hal su ŏp-nŭn 피할 수 없는, p'i-ryŏn-jŏk-in 필연적인.

necessity *n*. p'i-ryo 필요 ; p'il-su-p'um 필수품.

neck *n*. mok 목, mok-dŏl-mi 목덜미. 「치프.

neckerchief *n*. mok-do-ri 목도리, ne-k'ŏ-ch'i-p'ŭ 네커

necklace *n*. mok-gŏ-ri 목걸이.

necktie *n*. nek-t'a-i 넥타이.

need *n*. ① p'i-ryo 필요 ; yo-gu 요구. ② (*poverty*) pin-gon 빈곤. —*v*. ① (*want*) p'i-ryo-ha-da 필요하다. ② (*be needy*) kon-gung-e ppa-jyŏ-it-da 곤궁에 빠져있다.

needle *n*. pa-nŭl 바늘, cha-ch'im 자침(磁針).

needlewoman *n*. ch'im-mo 침모, pa-nŭ-jil-ha-nŭn yŏ-ja

needlework *n*. pa-nŭ-jil 바느질. 「바느질하는 여자.

needy *adj*. saeng-hwal-i ttak-han 생활이 딱한.

negative *n*. ① pu-jŏng 부정(否定) ; (*refusal*) kŏ-bu 거부. ② (*film*) wŏn-p'an 원판. —*adj*. pu-jŏng-jŏk-in 부정적인 ; so-gŭk-jŏk-in 소극적인.

neglect *v*. so-hol-hi-ha-da 소홀히하다 ; mu-si-ha-da 무시하다. —*n*. t'ae-man 태만 ; (*disregard*) mu-si 무시.

negligee *n*. sil-nae-bok 실내복, ne-gŭl-ri-je 네글리제.

negligence *n*. t'ae-man 태만, pang-sim 방심.

negotiate *v*. ① (*bargain*) tam-p'an-ha-da 담판하다. ② (*arrange*) hyŏp-jŏng-ha-da 협정하다. ③ (*convert* *into cash*) ton-ŭ-ro pa-ggu-da 돈으로 바꾸다.

negotiation *n.* tam-p'an 담판 ; (*parley*) kyo-sŏp 교섭.

Negro *n.* hŭk-in 흑인, ni-gŭ-ro 니그로.

neigh *v.* (*whinny*) mal-i ul-da 말이 울다. —*n.* mal u-rŭm-so-ri 말 울음소리. 「tong-p'o 동포.

neighbo(u)r *n.* i-ut(-sa-ram) 이웃사람, (*fellowman*)

neighbo(u)rhood *n.* kŭn-ch'ŏ 근처, i-ut 이웃 ; i-ut-sa-ram-dŭl 이웃사람들. 「…도 아니다.

neither ～ **nor** …do a-ni-go …do a-ni-da …도 아니고

neon *n.* ne-on 네온 : ～ *signs* ne-on-sa-in 네온사인.

nephew *n.* cho-k'a 조카, saeng-jil 생질.

nerve *n.* sin-gyŏng 신경 ;(*vigor*)ki-ryŏk 기력 ;(*courage*) yong-gi 용기 ; (*pl.*) sin-gyŏng kwa-min 신경 과민.

nerveless *adj.* mu-gi-ryŏk-han 무기력한.

nerve war sin-gyong-jŏn 신경전, sŏn-jŏn-jŏn 선전전.

nervous *adj.* sin-gyŏng-ŭi 신경의, sin-gyŏng-jil-ŭi 신경질의.

nervousness *n.* sin-gyŏng-jil 신경질, sin-gyŏng-gwa-min 신경과민.

nest *n.* ① sae-dung-u-ri 새둥우리, sae-jip 새집. ② po-gŭm-ja-ri 보금자리. ③ (*retreat*) p'i-nan-ch'ŏ 피난처. —*v.* po-gŭm-ja-ri-rŭl chit-da 보금자리를 짓다.

nestle *v.* kit-dŭ-ri-da 깃들이다, ki-bun cho-k'e nup-da [an-da] 기분 좋게 눕다[앉다].

net *n.* ① kŭ-mul 그물. ② (*snare*) ham-jŏng 함정. —*adj.* (*business*) sun-i-ik-ŭi 순이익의.

nettle *n.* sswae-gi-p'ul 쐐기풀.

network *n.* ① kŭ-mul se-gong 그물 세공, kŭ-mul-k'o 그물코. ② (*broadcasting*) pang-song-mang 방송망.

neurosis *n.* sin-gyŏng-jŭng 신경증, no-i-ro-je 노이로제.

neuter *adj.* chung-sŏng-ŭi 중성의, chung-rip-ŭi 중립의 : *a* ～ *gender* chung-sŏng 중성(中性).

neutral *adj.* chung-rip-ŭi 중립의, pul-p'yon-bu-dang-ŭi 불편부당의 : *a ~ zone* chung-rip-ji-dae 중립지대.

neutron *n.* chung-sŏng-ja 중성자.

never *adv.* kyŏl-k'o …a-ni-da 결코 …아니다.

nevertheless *conj.* kŭ-rŏm-e-do pul-gu-ha-go 그럼에도 불구하고, ku-rŏ-ch'i-man 그렇지만.

new *adj.* sae-ro-un 새로운, sin-sik-ŭi 신식의 ; (*recently appointed*) sin-im-ŭi 신임(新任)의.

newly *adv.* sae-ro-i 새로이, (*recently*) yo-sa-i 요사이.

news *n.* nyu-u-sŭ 뉴우스, ki-sa 기사, so-mun 소문.

newspaper *n.* sin-mun 신문 : *daily ~* il-gan-sin-mun 일간신문/*~ report* sin-mun-bo-do 신문보도.

newsreel *n.* (*news film*) si-sa yŏng-hwa 시사 영화.

New Year sae-hae 새해 : *New Year's Day* sŏl-nal 설날, chŏng-wŏl ch'o-ha-ru 정월 초하루.

next *adj.* ta-ŭm-ŭi 다음의. —*adv.* ta-ŭm-e 다음에. —*prep.* …e ka-jang ka-gga-un …에 가장 가까운.

nibble *v.* ① cho-gŭm-ssik kal-ga-mŏk-da 조금씩 갉아 먹다. ② (*carp*) hŭm-jap-da 흠잡다. 「고운.

nice *adj.* cho-ŭn 좋은, kkae-ggŭt-han 깨끗한 ; ko-un

nice-looking *adj.* kwi-yŏ-un 귀여운, ko-un 고운.

nickel *n.* ni-k'el 니켈, paek-t'ong 백통(白銅).

nickname *n.* pyŏl-myŏng 별명 ; ae-ch'ing 애칭.

nicotine *n.* ni-k'o-t'in 니코틴 : *~ poisoning* ni-k'o-t'in chung-dok 니코틴 중독.

niece *n.* cho-k'a-ddal 조카딸, chil-nyŏ 질녀.

night *n.* pam 밤, ya-gan 야간, chŏ-nyŏk 저녁.

night duty ya-gŭn 야근, suk-jik 숙직.

nightgown *n.* cham-ot 잠옷. 「kong-p'o-gam 공포감.

nightmare *n.* ak-mong 악몽, ka-wi-nul-rim 가위눌림,

nimble *adj.* min-ch'ŏp-han 민첩한, (*clever*) chae-ch'i-it-nŭn 재치있는, nun-ch'i-ga ppa-rŭn 눈치가 빠른.

nine *n.* & *adj.* a-hop(-ŭi) 아홉(의), ku(-ŭi) 9(의).
ninefold *adj.* & *adv.* a-hop-bae-ŭi〔ro〕 아홉배의〔로〕.
nineteen *n.* yŏl a-hop 열 아홉, sip-gu 19.
ninety *n.* a-hŭn 아흔, ku-sip 90.　　　「tta-da 따다.
nip *v.* kko-jip-da 꼬집다 ; (*bite*) mul-da 물다 ; (*cut*)
nipple *n.* chŏt-ggok-ji 젖꼭지, yu-do 유두(乳頭).
nitrogen *n.* chil-so 질소.
no *adj.* mu-ŭi 무(無)의, ha-na-do ŏp-nŭn 하나도 없는.
　—*adv.* ① cho-gŭm-do …a-ni-da 조금도 …아니다. ②
　a-ni-o 아니오. —*n.* pu-jŏng 부정, kŏ-jŏl 거절.
noble *adj.* ko-sang-han 고상한, ko-gyŏl-han 고결한 ;
　kwi-jok-ŭi 귀족의 ; (*grand*) tang-dang-han 당당한.
nobleman *n.* (*peer*) kwi-jok 귀족.
nobody *pron.* a-mu-do … a-ni-da 아무도 … 아니다. —*n.*
　ha-ch'an-ŭn sa-ram 하찮은 사람.
nocturn(e) *n.* ① ya-gok 야곡, ya-sang-gok 야상곡 ; nok-
　t'ŏ-ŏn 녹터언. ② ya-gyŏng-hwa 야경화(夜景畫).
nod *v.* kkŭ-dŏk-i-da 끄덕이다, chol-da 졸다. —*n.* kkŭ-
　dŏk-im 끄덕임, su-gŭng 수긍 ; cho-rŭm 졸음.
noise *n.* (*clamor*) so-ŭm 소음, pŏp-sŏk 법석.
noisy *adj.* ① si-ggŭ-rŏ-un 시끄러운, ttŏ-dŭl-ssŏk-han
　떠들썩한. ② (*showy*) ya-han 야한.
nomad(e) *n.* yu-mok-min 유목민, pang-rang-ja 방랑자.
nominal *adj.* myŏng-ŭi-sang-ŭi 명의상의 ; (*gram.*)
　myŏng-sa-ŭi 명사(名詞)의.　　　　　　「지정하다.
nominate *v.* chi-myŏng-ha-da 지명하다, chi-jŏng-ha-da
nonalignment *n.* pi-dong-maeng 비동맹.
none *pron.* (*no person*) a-mu-do …an-t'a 아무도 …않다.
nonsense *n.* mu-ŭi-mi 무의미 ; hŏ-t'ŭn so-ri 허튼 소리,
　nŏn-sen-sŭ 넌센스. —*int.* pa-bo-ga-ch'i 바보같이.
nonstop *adj.* chik-haeng-ŭi 직행의 ; mu-ch'ak-ryuk-ŭi
　무착륙의 : *a ～ flight* mu-ch'ak-ryuk pi-haeng 무착

류 비행. —*adv.* chik-haeng-ŭ-ro 직행으로.
noodles *n.* kuk-su 국수.　　　　　　　「ch'ŏ 은신처.
nook *n.* ① ku-sŏk 구석 ; oe-ddan-got 외딴곳. ② ŭn-sin-
noon *n.* (*midday*) chŏng-o 정오, tae-nat 대낮.
noose *n.* ① (*slipknot*) mae-dŭp 매듭. ② (*snare*) ol-
ga-mi 올가미. ③ (*bond*) yu-dae 유대.
nor *conj.* …do tto-han …a-ni-da …도 또한 …아니다.
normal *adj.* ① chŏng-sang-ŭi 정상의, chŏng-gyu-ŭi
정규의. ② (*average*) p'yŏng-gyun-ŭi 평균의.
normal school sa-bŏm hak-gyo 사범 학교.　　　「(의).
north *n. & adj.* puk(-ŭi) 북(의), puk-jjok(-ŭi) 북쪽
northeast *n.* tong-buk 동북, tong-buk-bu 동북부. ʼ
northern *adj.* puk-ŭi 북의, puk-jjok-ŭi 북쪽의.
North Pole puk-gŭk 북극(北極).
northwest *n.* sŏ-buk 서북, sŏ-buk-bu 서북부.
nose *n.* k'o 코 ; (*sense of smell*) hu-gak 후각.
nostril *n.* k'ot-gu-mŏng 콧구멍.
not *adv.* …a-ni-da …아니다, …an-t'a …않다.
notable *adj.* chu-mok-hal man-han 주목할 만한, tu-dŭ-
rŏ-jin 두드러진. —*n.* myŏng-sa 명사(名士).
notary *n.* kong-jŭng-in 공증인(公證人).
note *n.* ① (*mark*) pu-ho 부호. ② (*memo*) 메모. ③
(*annotation*) chu-hae 주해. ④ (*short letter*) tan-sin
단신. ⑤ (*score*) ak-bo 악보. —*v.* ① (*see*) chu-mok-
ha-da 주목하다. ② (*write*) ki-rok-ha-da 기록하다.
notebook *n.* ① kong-ch'aek 공책, p'il-gi-jang 필기장,
no-u-t'ŭ 노우트. ② su-ch'ŏp 수첩, pi-mang-rok 비망
notepaper *n.* p'yŏn-ji-ji 편지지.　　　　　　　└록.
nothing *pron.* ① (*not anything*) a-mu-gŏt-do …a-
ni-da 아무것도 …아니다. ② mu 무(無). ③ (*trifle*) po-
jal-gŏt-ŏp-nŭn kŏt 보잘것없는 것. —*adv.* cho-gŭm-
do …an-t'a 조금도 …않다.

notice *n*. (*information*) t'ong-ji 통지, (*warning*) ye-go 예고; (*observation*) chu-mok 주목. —*v.* (*perceive*) a-ra-ch'ae-da 알아채다 ; chu-mok-ha-da 주목하다.

notify *v.* (*inform*) t'ong-ji-ha-da 통지하다, t'ong-go-ha-da 통고하다, kong-go-ha-da 공고하다.

notion *n.* ① (*idea*) kae-nyŏm 개념. ② (*intention*) ŭi-hyang 의향. ③ (*opinion*) kyŏn-hae 견해.

notorious *adj.* so-mun-nan 소문난, ak-myŏng-no-p'ŭn 악명높은, chu-ji-ŭi 주지의.

noun *n.* (*gram.*) myŏng-sa 명사(名詞).

nourish *v.* ① ki-rŭ-da 가르다. ② ma-ŭm-e p'um-da 마음에 품다.

novel *n.* so-sŏl 소설. —*adj.* (*new*) sae-ro-un 새로운, (*strange*) sin-gi-han 신기한, ki-bal-han 기발한.

novelette *n.* tan[chŭng]-p'yŏn so-sŏl 단[중]편 소설.

novelist *n.* so-sŏl-ga 소설가.   「je-p'um 신제품.

novelty *n.* sin-gi-ham 신기함, chin-gi-ham 진기함, sin-

November *n.* sip-il-wŏl 11월.

novice *n.* p'ut-na-gi 풋나기, ch'o-sim-ja 초심자(初心者) ; (*new convert*) sae sin-ja 새 신자.

now *adv.* i-je 이제, chi-gŭm 지금. —*n.* chi-gŭm 지금, hyŏn-jae 현재. —*conj.* …han i-sang …한 이상.

nowadays *adv.* o-nŭl-nal-e-nŭn 오늘날에는, yo-jŭm-e-nŭn 요즘에는. —*n.* hyŏn-jae 현재, o-nŭl-nal 오늘날.

nowhere *adv.* a-mu-de-do …ŏp-da 아무데도 …없다.

nuance *n.* mi-myo-han ch'a-i 미묘한 차이 ; saek-jo 색조(色調), nwi-ang-sŭ 뉘앙스.

nuclear *adj.* haek-ŭi 핵의 ; wŏn-ja-haek-ŭi 원자핵의.

nucleus *n.* haek 핵, haek-sim 핵심; wŏn-ja-haek 원자핵.

nude *adj.* na-ch'e-ŭi 나체의, pŏl-gŏ-bŏ-sŭn 벌거벗은.

nudge *v.* p'al-ggum-ch'i-ro jji-rŭ-da 팔꿈치로 찌르다.

nuisance *n.* sŏng-ga-sin il 성가신 일, tu-t'ong-gŏ-ri 두

통거리, p'ye 폐(弊).

nullify *v.* mu-hyo-ro ha-da 무효로 하다, pye-gi-ha-da 폐기하다, (*cancel*) ch'wi-so-ha-da 취소하다.

numb *adj.* kam-gak-ŭl i-rŭn 감각을 잃은.

number *n.* ① (*figure*) sut-ja 숫자. ② (*series*) pŏn-ho 번호, pŏn-ji 번지, (*suffix*) pŏn 번. 「의.

numerous *adj.* man-ŭn su-ŭi 많은 수의, ta-su-ŭi 다수

nun *n.* su-nyŏ 수녀, yŏ-sŭng 여승.

nuptial *adj.* kyŏl-hon-ŭi 결혼의, hol-lye-ŭi 혼례의 : *a* ~ *ceremony* kyŏl-hon-sik 결혼식, hol-lye 혼례.

nurse *n.* ① yu-mo 유모. ② kan-ho-wŏn 간호원. —*v.* ① (*hospital*) kan-ho-ha-da 간호하다. ② (*give suck*) chŏ-jŭl mŏk-i-da 젖을 먹이다.

nursery *n.* ŏ-rin-i pang 어린이 방, yuk-a-sil 육아실.

nursery rhyme cha-jang-ga 자장가 ; tong-yo 동요.

nut *n.* (*chestnut, walnut, filbert, etc.*) kyŏn-gwa 견과 (堅果) ; na-mu yŏl-mae 나무 열매. 「물.

nutrition *n.* yŏng-yang 영양, (*food*) ŭm-sik-mul 음식

nylon *n.* na-il-ron 나일론. 「미소녀.

nymph *n.* nim-p'ŭ 님프, yo-jŏng 요정(妖精) ; mi-so-nyŏ

—◄◉►—

oaf *n.* ki-hyŏng-a 기형아, (*idiot*) paek-ch'i 백치.

oak *n.* ch'am-na-mu 참나무, ttŏk-gal-na-mu 떡갈나무.

oar *n.* no 노.

oat *n.* kwi-ri 귀리. 「yak-ha-da 서약하다.

oath *n.* maeng-se 맹세, sŏ-yak 서약 : *make an* ~ sŏ-

oatmeal *n.* o-u-t'ŭ-mil 오우트밀. 「고한.

obdurate *adj.* ko-jip-i sen 고집이 센, wan-go-han 완

obedience *n.* pok-jong 복종, sun-jong 순종.

obedient *adj.* pok-jong-ha-nŭn 복종하는, sun-song-ha-nŭn 순종하는, (*filial*) hyo-sŏng-sŭ-rŏ-un 효성스러운.

obey *v.* pok-jong-ha-da 복종하다, tta-rŭ-da 따르다.

obituary *n.* pu-go 부고, sa-mang ki-sa 사망 기사. —*adj.* sa-mang-ŭi 사망의.

object *n.* ① (*aim*) mok-jŏk 목적. ② (*thing*) mul-ch'e 물체. ③ (*gram.*) mok-jŏk-ŏ 목적어. —*v.* pan-dae-ha-da 반대하다, hang-ŭi-ha-da 항의하다.

objection *n.* pan-dae 반대, hang-ŭi 항의.

objective *adj.* kaek-gwan-jŏk-in 객관적인. —*n.* (*aim*) mok-jŏk 목적 ; (*gram.*) mok-jŏk-ŏ 목적어.

objector *n.* pan-dae-ja 반대자.

obligation *n.* ① (*duty*) ŭi-mu 의무. ② (*debt*) ch'ae-mu 채무. ③ (*debt of gratitude*) ŭn-hye 은혜.

oblige *v.* ① ŭi-mu-rŭl chi-u-da 의무를 지우다. ② (*favor*) ŭn-hye-rŭl pe-p'ul-da 은혜를 베풀다.

oblivion *n.* mang-gak 망각 ; kŏn-mang 건망(健忘).

oblong *n.* chang-bang-hyŏng 장방형.

obscene *adj.* ŭm-t'ang-han 음탕한, ch'u-jap-han 추잡한.

obscure *adj.* ae-mae-han 애매한 ; (*dim*) hŭ-rin 흐린, (*unknown*) mu-myŏng-ŭi 무명의.

observance *n.* ① chun-su 준수. ② ŭi-sik 의식(儀式).

observation *n.* (*notice*) kwan-ch'al 관찰, kwan-ch'ŭk 관측 ; (*experiment*) sil-hŏm kwan-ch'al 실험 관찰.

observatory *n.* ① (*astron.*) ch'ŏn-mun-dae 천문대. ② (*meteor.*) ch'ŭk-hu-so 측후소.

observe *v.* ① kwan-ch'al-ha-da 관찰하다. ② (*obey*) chun-su-ha-da 준수하다. ③ (*remark*) mal-ha-da 말하다, chin-sul-ha-da 진술하다.

observer *n.* kwan-ch'ŭk-ja 관측자, chun-su-ja 준수자 ; (*witness*) ip-hoe-in 입회인, ŏp-jŏ-ŏ-bŏ 업저어버.

obstacle *n.* chang-ae 장애, pang-hae 방해.

obstetrics *n.* san-gwa-hak 산과학(産科學).

obstinate *adj.* ko-jip-sen 고집센, wan-go-han 완고한.
obstruct *v.* pang-hae-ha-da 방해하다.
obstruction pang-hae 방해, chi-jang 지장.
obtain *v.* ŏt-da 얻다, son-e nŏ-t'a 손에 넣다.
obvious *adj.* myŏng-baek-han 명백한, ppan-han 빤한.
occasion *n.* ki-hoe 기회 ; (*case*) kyŏng-u 경우.
occasionally *adv.* ttae-ddae-ro 때때로, ka-ggŭm 가끔.
Occident *n.* sŏ-yang 서양, sŏ-gu 서구.
occidental *adj.* sŏ-yang-ŭi 서양의, ku-mi-ŭi 구미의.
occupant *n.* ① (*inhabitant*) kŏ-ju-ja 거주자. ② (*occupier*) chŏm-yu-ja 점유자, chŏm-gŏ-ja 점거자.
occupation *n.* ① (*work*) chik-ŏp 직업. ② (*military*) chŏm-ryŏng 점령, chŏm-gŏ 점거.
occupational disease chik-ŏp-byŏng 직업병.
occupy *v.* ① chŏm-ryŏng-ha-da 점령하다. ② chong-sa-ha-da 종사하다.
occur *v.* i-rŏ-na-da 일어나다 ; saeng-gi-da 생기다.
occurrence *n.* pal-saeng 발생, (*accident*) sa-gŏn 사건.
ocean *n.* tae-yang 대양 : *Atlantic O~* tae-sŏ-yang 대서양/*Pacific O~* t'ae-p'yŏng-yang 태평양.
o'clock *n.* …si …시(時).
octave *n.* ok-t'a-bŭ 옥타브, che-p'al-ŭm 제8음.
October *n.* si-wŏl 10월.
octopus *n.* mun-ŏ 문어, nak-ji 낙지.
oculist *n.* an-gwa ŭi-sa 안과(眼科) 의사.
odd *adj.* ① (*strange*) i-sang-han 이상한. ② (*extra*) yŏ-bun-ŭi 여분의. ③ (*not even*) ki-su-ŭi 기수(奇數)의.
odds *n.* (*inequalities*) pul-p'yŏng-dŭng 불평등.
odious *adj.* si-rŭn 싫은, (*hateful*) mi-un 미운.
odo(u)r *n.* hyang-gi 향기, naem-sae 냄새. 「…로 된.
of *prep.* ① (*poss.*) …ŭi …의. ② (*made of*) …ro toen
off *adv.* ttŏ-rŏ-jyŏ 떨어져, mŏl-ri 멀리.

offence · offense *n.* ① pŏm-joe 범죄. ② (*attack*) kong-gyŏk 공격. ③ (*foul*) pan-ch'ik 반칙.

offend *v.* ① no-ha-ge ha-da 노하게 하다. ② (*transgress*) pŏm-ha-da 범하다, ŏ-gi-da 어기다.

offensive *adj.* ① si-rŭn 싫은, (*unpleasant*) pul-k'wae-han 불쾌한. ② (*attack*) kong-gyŏk-jŏk 공격적.

offer *v.* che-ch'ul-ha-da 제출하다 ; che-ŭi-ha-da 제의하다 ; (*show*) p'yo-si-ha-da 표시하다. —*n.* che-an 제안, sin-ch'ŏng 신청.   「mul 제물.

offering *n.* (*church*) hŏn-gŭm 헌금 ; (*to a diety*) che-

office *n.* ① (*room*) sa-mu-sil 사무실. ② (*section*) …kwa …과, …pu …부, …ch'ŏng …청, …kuk …국.

office boy sa-hwan 사환, kŭp-sa 급사.

officer *n.* ① (*civil*) kwal-li 관리, kong-mu-wŏn 공무원. ② (*army*) chang-gyo 장교.

official *adj.* (*formal*) kong-sik-ŭi 공식의 ; (*public*) kong-mu-sang-ŭi 공무상의. —*n.* kwal-li 관리, kong-mu-wŏn 공무원, chik-wŏn 직원.

off limits ch'u-rip kum-ji(-gu-yŏk) 출입 금지(구역).

often *adv.* ka-ggŭm 가끔, chong-jong 종종, cha-ju 자주.

oil *n.* & *v.* ki-rŭm(-ŭl ch'i-da) 기름(을 치다). 「주.

oily *adj.* ① ki-rŭm-ŭl pa-rŭn 기름을 바른, ki-rŭm t'u-sŏng-i-ŭi 기름 투성이의. ② ku-byŏn-i cho-ŭn 구변이 좋은.

ointment *n.* yŏn-go 연고.

old *adj.* (*person*) nŭl-gŭn 늙은 ; (*thing*) nal-gŭn 낡은.

older brother (*boy*) hyŏng-nim 형님 ; (*girl*) o-bba 오빠.

older sister (*girl*) ŏn-ni 언니 ; (*boy*) nu-nim 누님.

old-fashioned *adj.* ku-sik-ŭi 구식의, ko-p'ung-ŭi 고풍의.

Old Testament ku-yak sŏng-sŏ 구약 성서.

olive *n.* ol-ri-bŭ 올리브, kam-ram 감람(橄欖).

Olympics *n.* (=*Olympic games*) ol-rim-p'ik kyŏnggi 올림픽 경기.

omen *n.* (*foreboding*) chŏn-jo 전조, ching-jo 징조 : *good* ~ kil-jo 길조/*bad* ~ hyung-jo 흉조.

omission *n.* saeng-ryak 생략, nu-rak 누락.

omit *v.* ① saeng-ryak-ha-da 생략하다, ppa-ddŭ-ri-da 빠뜨리다. ② (*neglect*) ke-ŭl-ri-ha-da 게을리하다.

omnibus *n.* hap-sŭng cha-dong-ch'a 합승 자동차.

on *prep.* …wi-e …위에, …e kwan-ha-yŏ …에 관하여.

once *adv.* han pŏn 한 번 ; (*formerly*) il-jji-gi 일찌기.

one *adj.* ha-na-ŭi 하나의. —*n.* ha-na 하나, il 일.

oneself *pron.* cha-gi cha-sin-i 자기 자신이, sŭ-sŭ-ro 스스로, cha-gi cha-sin-ŭl[e] 자기 자신을[에].

one-sided *adj.* han-jjok-ŭ-ro ki-un 한쪽으로 기운.

one-way *adj.* il-bang-t'ong-haeng-ŭi 일방통행의 : *a* ~ *ticket* p'yŏn-do ch'a-p'yo 편도 차표.

onion *n.* yang-p'a 양파, p'a 파.

onlooker *n.* ku-gyŏng-gun 구경군, mok-gyŏk-ja 목격자.

only *adj.* yu-il-han 유일한. —*adv.* ta-man 다만.

onset *n.* sŭp-gyŏk 습격, kong-gyŏk 공격. 「향상하는.

onward *adv.* a-p'ŭ-ro 앞으로. —*adj.* hyang-sang-ha-nŭn

opal *n.* tan-baek-sŏk 단백석, o-p'al 오팔.

open *v.* yŏl-da 열다. —*adj.* yŏl-rin 열린.

opening *n.* ① (*beginning*) si-jak 시작. ② (*meeting*) kae-hoe 개회. ③ (*open space*) ku-mŏng 구멍.

openwork *n.* (*sculpture*) to-rim-jil se-gong 도림질 세공.

opera *n.* ka-gŭk 가극, o-p'e-ra 오페라.

opera house o-p'e-ra kŭk-jang 오페라 극장.

operate *v.* ① (*mech.*) un-jŏn-ha-da 운전하다. ② (*surg.*) su-sul-ha-da 수술하다.

operation *n.* ① (*surg.*) su-sul 수술. ② (*milit.*) chak-jŏn 작전. ③ (*function*) chak-yong 작용. ④ (*mech.*) un-jŏn 운전. ⑤ (*management*) kyŏng-yŏng 경영.

operator *n.* un-jŏn-ja 운전자, ki-sa 기사 : *telegraph* ~ chŏn-sin ki-sa 전신 기사/*telephone* ~ chŏn-hwa kyo-hwan-su 전화 교환수. 「소신.

opinion *n.* ŭi-gyŏn 의견, kyŏn-hae 견해, (*pl.*) so-sin

opium *n.* a-p'yŏn 아편.

opponent *n.* pan-dae-ja 반대자, chŏk-su 적수 ; kyŏng-jaeng-ja 경쟁자. —*adj.* chŏk-dae-ha-nŭn 적대하는.

opportunist *n.* ki-hoe-ju-ŭi-ja 기회주의자.

opportunity *n.* ki-hoe 기회, ho-gi 호기(好機).

oppose *v.* pan-dae-ha-da 반대하다, chŏ-hang-ha-da 저항하다, (*hinder*) pang-hae-ha-da 방해하다.

opposite *adj.* chŏng-ban-dae-ŭi 정반대의 ; chŏ-jjok-ŭi 저쪽의 ; (*front*) ma-jŭn-p'yŏn-ŭi 맞은편의.

opposition *n.* ① pan-dae 반대. ② ya-dang 야당.

oppress *v.* ap-bak-ha-da 압박하다, hak-dae-ha-da 학대

optical *adj.* nŭn-ŭi 눈의, si-gak-ŭi 시각의. 「하다.

optimism *n.* nak-ch'ŏn-ju-ŭi 낙천주의.

or *conj.* tto-nŭn 또는, hok-ŭn 혹은.

oracle *n.* sin-t'ak 신탁, t'ak-sŏn 탁선(託宣).

oral *adj.* (*spoken*) ku-du-ŭi 구두의. —*n.* (*oral exam.*) ku-du si-hŏm 구두 시험. 「bi-ch'ŭi 오렌지빛의.

orange *n.* kyul 귤, o-ren-ji 오렌지. —*adj.* o-ren-ji-

orator *n.* yŏn-sŏl-ja 연설자, pyŏn-sa 변사. 「눈구멍.

orbit *n.* ① kwe-do 궤도. ② (*eye socket*) nun-gu-mŏng

orchard *n.* kwa-su-wŏn 과수원, kwa-su 과수(果樹).

orchestra *n.* kwan-hyŏn-ak-dan 관현악단, o-k'e-sŭ-t'ŭ-ra 오케스트라.

orchid *n.* nan 난(蘭), nan-ch'o 난초.

ordain *v.* ① (*appoint*) im-myŏng-ha-da 임명하다. ② (*estab.*) che-jŏng-ha-da 제정하다. ③ (*order*) myŏng-ha-da 명하다 ; (*destine*) un-myŏng-ji-u-da 운명지우다.

order *n.* ① (*command*) myŏng-ryŏng 명령. ② (*se-

quence) sun-sŏ 순서. ③ (*commission to supply*) chu-mun 주문. ④ (*decoration*) hun-jang 훈장. —*v.* ①
(*command*) myŏng-ryŏng-ha-da 명령하다. ② (*goods*)
chu-mun-ha-da 주문하다.

orderly *adj.* tan-jŏng-han 단정한. —*n.* (*messenger*)
chŏl-lyŏng 전령, yŏl-lak-byŏng 연락병.
ordinance *n.* ① pŏp-ryŏng 법령. ② (*rite*) ŭi-sik 의식.
ordinary *adj.* po-t'ong-ŭi 보통의, p'yŏng-bŏm-han 평
범한. —*n.* ① po-t'ong-il 보통일. ② chŏng-sik 정식(定
ordnance *n.* p'o 포, (*weapons*) pyŏng-gi 병기. 「(食.
ore *n.* kwang-sŏk 광석, wŏn-gwang 원광.
organ *n.* ① (*music*) o-rŭ-gan 오르간. ② (*of body*) ki-
gwan 기관(器官). ③ (*agent*) ki-gwan 기관(機關).
organization *n.* (*system*) cho-jik 조직, tan-ch'e 단체;
(*outfit*) ki-gu 기구. 「립하다.
organize *v.* cho-jik-ha-da 조직하다 ; ch'ang-rip-ha-da 창
orgie·orgy *n.* pŏp-sŏk 법석, puk-sae 북새.
orient *n.* tong-yang 동양. —*adj.* tong-yang-ŭi 동양의.
oriental *adj.* tong-yang-ŭi 동양의. —*n.* tong-yang-in
동양인, a-si-a-in 아시아인.
origin *n.* kŭn-wŏn 근원, pal-dan 발단.
original *adj.* ch'oe-ch'o-ŭi 최초의 ; tok-ch'ang-jŏk-in 독
창적인. —*n.* wŏn-mun 원문, wŏn-hyŏng 원형.
originality *n.* tok-ch'ang-sŏng 독창성, ch'ang-ŭi-ryŏk
창의력 ; ch'am-sin 참신, sin-gi 신기(新奇).
ornament *n.* chang-sik 장식. —*v.* kku-mi-da 꾸미다.
orphan *n.* ko-a 고아. —*adj.* pu-mo-ŏp-nŭn 부모없는.
orphanage *n.* ko-a-wŏn 고아원.
orthodox *adj.* chŏng-t'ong-ŭi 정통의, pon-sik-ŭi 본식의.
ostensible *adj.* p'yo-myŏn-sang-ŭi 표면상의, oe-yang-
ostrich *n.* t'a-jo 타조. 「man-ŭi 외양만의.
other *adj.* ta-rŭn 다른, ttan 딴, kŭ-ba-ggŭi 그밖의.

otherwise *adj*. kŭ-rŏ-ch'i an-ŭ-myŏn 그렇지 않으면.

ought *aux. v.* …ha-yŏ-ya han-da …하여야 한다, …ha-nŭn kŏ-si tang-yŏn-ha-da …하는 것이 당연하다.

ounce *n*. on-sŭ 온스.

our *pron*. u-ri-ŭi 우리의, u-ri-dŭl-ŭi 우리들의.

ours *pron*. u-ri kot 우리 것, u-ri-dŭl-ŭi kŏt 우리들의 것.

out *adv*. pa-gge 밖에, pa-ggŭ-ro 밖으로. —*adj*. pa-ggŭi 밖의. —*prep*. …e-sŏ …에서. —*n*. pak 밖.

outbreak *n*. tol-bal 돌발, pal-bal 발발.

outcast *n*. pu-rang-ja 부랑자 ; pang-rang-ja 방랑자.

outcome *n*. kyŏl-gwa 결과 ; sŏng-gwa 성과.

outcry *n*. ko-ham 고함, a-u-sŏng 아우성.

outdoors *adv*. chip pa-gge-sŏ 집 밖에서, ok-oe-e-sŏ 옥외에서. —*n*. ok-oe 옥외, mun-bak 문밖 ; se-sang 세상.

outfit *n*. chang-bi 장비, ch'ae-bi 채비, yong-p'um 용품.

outing *n*. so-p'ung 소풍, na-dŭ-ri 나들이.

outline *n*. yun-gwak 윤곽. —*v*. yun-gwak-ŭl kŭ-ri-da 윤곽을 그리다. 「ya 시야.

outlook *n*. kyŏng-ch'i 경치, chŏn-mang 전망 ; (*view*) si-

out-of-date *adj*. si-dae-e twi-jin 시대에 뒤진.

outpost *n*. chŏn-ch'o 전초(前哨).

output *n*. saeng-san-go 생산고 ; ch'ul-ryŏk 출력(出力).

outrage *n*. p'ok-haeng 폭행, mo-yok 모욕.

outright *adj*. sol-jik-han 솔직한 ; ttok-ba-rŭn 똑바른. —*adv*. t'ŏ-no-k'o 터놓고 ; chŭk-sŏk-e-sŏ 즉석에서.

outside *n*. oe-bu 외부, pa-ggat 바깥. —*prep*. …ŭi pa-ggŭi …의 밖의. —*adv*. chip pa-ggŭ-ro 집 밖으로. —*adj*. pa-ggŭi 밖의, oe-bu-ŭi 외부의. 「한.

outstanding *adj*. ttu-ryŏt-han 뚜렷한, hyŏn-jŏ-han 현저

outward *adj*. oe-bu-ŭi 외부의, oe-myŏn-jŏk-in 외면적인.

oval *adj*. t'a-wŏn-hyŏng-ŭi 타원형의.

oven *n*. sot 솥, ka-ma 가마(釜), hwa-dŏk 화덕.

over *prep.* ···ŭi wi-e ···의 위에. —*adv.* to-ch'ŏ-e 도처
에, kkŭt-na-go 끝나고.
overall *adj.* chŏn-ch'e-ŭi 전체의.
overalls *n.* chak-ŏp-bok 작업복, kŏt-ot 겉옷.
overcast *v.* ku-rŭm-ŭ-ro ka-ri-da 구름으로 가리다.
overcoat *n.* oe-t'u 외투.
overcome *v.* i-gi-da 이기다, kŭk-bok-ha-da 극복하다.
overcrowded *adj.* ch'o-man-wŏn-ŭi 초만원의, hon-jap-
han 혼잡한.
overflow *v.* nŏm-ch'i-da 넘치다, pŏm-ram-ha-da 범람
하다. —*n.* ① hong-su 홍수. ② (*excess*) kwa-ing 과잉.
overgrow *v.* ① cha-ra-sŏ twi-dŏp-da 자라서 뒤덮다, mu-
sŏng-ha-da 무성하다. ② nŏ-mu k'ŏ-ji-da 너무 커지다.
overhang *v.* ···ŭi wi-e kŏl-ch'i-da ···의 위에 걸치다.
overhead *adv.* mŏ-ri wi-e 머리 위에 ; ha-nŭl-e 하늘에.
—*adj.* mŏ-ri wi-ŭi 머리 위의. 「듣다.
overhear *v.* yŏt-dŭt-da 엿듣다, mol-rae tŭt-da 몰래
overlook *v.* pa-ra-bo-da 바라보다, nae-ryŏ-da-bo-da 내
려다보다 ; nun-gam-a-ju-da 눈감아주다.
oversea(s) *adv.* hae-oe-ro 해외로, hae-oe-e-sŏ 해외에서.
—*adj.* hae-oe-ŭi 해외의, hae-oe-ro ka-nŭn 해외로 가는.
oversee *v.* kam-dok-ha-da 감독하다.
overshoe *n.* tŏt-sin 덧신, o-u-bŏ-syu-u-jŭ 오우버슈우즈.
overtake *v.* tta-ra-jap-da 따라잡다 ; ch'u-wŏl-ha-da 추
overturn *v.* twi-jip-ŏ-no-t'a 뒤집어놓다. 「월하다.
overwhelm *v.* ap-do-ha-da 압도하다, twi-ŏp-da 뒤엎다,
wi-ch'uk-si-k'i-da 위축시키다. 「과로.
overwork *v.* kwa-ro-si-k'i-da 과로시키다. —*n.* kwa-ro
owe *v.* pi-jŭl chi-da 빚을 지다, him-ip-da 힘입다.
owing to ··· ttae-mun-e ··· 때문에.
owl *n.* ol-bbae-mi 올빼미, pu-ŏng-i 부엉이.
own *adj.* cha-gi cha-sin-ŭi 자기 자신의. —*v.* ① so-yu-

ha-da 소유하다. ② cha-baek-ha-da 자백하다.
owner *n.* im-ja 임자, so-yu-ja 소유자.
ox *n.* hwang-so 황소 ; su-so 수소.
oxcart *n.* u-ch'a 우차(牛車), tal-gu-ji 달구지.
oxygen *n.* san-so 산소 : ~ *breathing apparatus* san-so ho-hŭp-gi 산소 호흡기.
oyster *n.* kul 굴 ; *raw* ~ saeng-gul 생굴.

P

pace *n.* kŏ-rŭm 걸음, po-jo 보조(步調), kŏt-nŭn sok-do 걷는 속도. —*v.* kŏ-rŭm-ŭ-ro chae-da 걸음으로 재다.
pacific *adj.* p'yŏng-on-han 평온한, t'ae-p'yong-han 태
Pacific Ocean t'ae-p'yŏng-yang 태평양.   「평한.
pack *n.* chim 짐, (*bundle*) ta-bal 다발, (*gang*) han p'ae 한 패. —*v.* p'o-jang-ha-da 포장하다.   「포장.
package *n.* (*parcel*) so-p'o 소포, chim 짐 ; p'o-jang
packet *n.* so-ha-mul 소하물, (*bundle*) ta-bal 다발.
packing *n.* p'o-jang 포장 : ~ *charge* p'o-jang-ryo 포장료.
pad *v.* sok-ŭl ch'ae-u-da 속을 채우다. —*n.* mit-bat-ch'im 밑받침, tŏt-dae-nŭn mul-gŏn 덧대는 물건.
padded clothes som-ot 솜옷.
padding *n.* sim-nŏ-k'i 심넣기 ; sim 심.
paddle *n.* no 노. —*v.* no-ro chŏt-da 노로 젓다.
paddyfield *n.* (*rice field*) non 논.
padlock *n.* maeng-ggong-i cha-mul-soe 맹꽁이 자물쇠.
pagan *n.* (*heathen*) i-gyo-do 이교도.   「사환.
page *n.* ① p'e-i-ji 페이지, myŏn 면. ② (*boy*) sa-hwan
pageant *n.* ya-oe-gŭk 야외극, mi-gwan 미관(美觀) ; (*parade*) ho-hwa haeng-jin 호화 행진.   「층탑.
pagoda *n.* t'ap 탑 : *a five-storeyed* ~ o-ch'ŭng-t'ap 오
pail *n.* mul-t'ong 물통.

pain *n.* ① ko-t'ong 고통, a-p'ŭm 아픔. ② kŭn-sim 근심.

painful *adj.* ① a-p'ŭn 아픈, koe-ro-un 괴로운. ② (*toilsome*) him-i tŭ-nŭn 힘이 드는.

painkiller *n.* chin-t'ong-je 진통제.

paint *n.* kŭ-rim-mul-gam 그림물감, p'e-in-t'ŭ 페인트. —*v.* ch'il-ha-da 칠하다, kŭ-ri-da 그리다.

paintbrush *n.* kŭ-rim put 그림 붓, hwa-p'il 화필.

painter *n.* ① hwa-ga 화가. ② ch'il-jang-i 칠장이.

painting *n.* ① kŭ-rim 그림. ② p'e-in-t'ŭ-ch'il 페인트 칠 : *oil* ~ yu-hwa 유화/*water color* ~ su-ch'ae-hwa

paintress *n.* yŏ-ryu hwa-ga 여류 화가. ㄴ수채화.

pair *n.* han ssang 한 쌍, (*couple*) pu-bu 부부.

pal *n.* ch'in-gu 친구, tong-a-ri 동아리, jjak-p'ae 짝패.

palace *n.* kung-jŏn 궁전, kung-gwŏl 궁궐.

palanquin *n.* ka-ma 가마.

palate *n.* ① ip-ch'ŏn-jang 입천장, ku-gae 구개(口蓋). ② mi-gak 미각.

pale *adj.* (*wan*) ch'ang-baek-han 창백한. —*n.* ul-t'a-ri 울타리.

pallbearer *n.* sang-yŏ-gun 상여군.

palm *n.* ① (*of hand*) son-ba-dak 손바닥. ② (*tree*) ya-ja-su 야자수.

[ka-ma]

palmist *n.* son-gŭm-jang-i 손금장이, su-sang-ga 수상가.

pamphlet *n.* p'am-p'ŭl-ret 팜플렛.

pan *n.* nam-bi 남비 : *frying* ~ p'ŭ-ra-i-p'aen 프라이팬.

pane *n.* p'an-yu-ri 판유리, ch'ang-yu-ri 창유리.

panel *n.* p'ae-nŏl 패널, hwa-p'an 화판.

pang *n.* ko-t'ong 고통 ; pi-t'ong 비통 ; sang-sim 상심.

panic *n.* ① (*sudden alarm*) tang-hwang 당황 ; kong-p'o 공포. ② (*commerce*) kong-hwang 공황.

panorama *n.* chŏn-gyŏng 전경, p'a-no-ra-ma 파노라마.

pansy *n.* ho-jŏp che-bi-ggot 호접 제비꽃, p'aen-ji 팬지.

pant *v.* hŏl-ddŏk-gŏ-ri-da 헐떡거리다. —*n.* hŏl-ddŏk-gŏ-rim 헐떡거림 ; ko-dong 고동, tong-gye 동계(動悸).

panther *n.* p'yo-bŏm 표범, p'yu-u-ma 퓨우마.

pantry *n.* sik-ryo-p'um-sil 식료품실, sik-gi-sil 식기실.

pants *n.* pa-ji 바지, p'aen-ch'ŭ 팬츠.

papa *n.* (*dad, daddy*) a-bba 아빠. 「non-mun 논문.

paper *n.* ① chong-i 종이 ; sin-mun-ji 신문지. ② (*essay*)

paper file chong-i kko-ji 종이 꽂이.

paper mill che-ji kong-jang 제지 공장.

papeterie *n.* (*stationary case*) mun-gap 문갑(文匣), sŏ-ryu-ham 서류함.

parachute *n.* nak-ha-san 낙하산, p'a-ra-swi-t'ŭ 파라쉬트.

parade *n.* haeng-ryŏl 행렬, yŏl-byŏng-sik 열병식, p'ŏ-re-i-dŭ 퍼레이드. —*v.* haeng-ryŏl-ha-da 행렬하다.

paradise *n.* nak-wŏn 낙원 ; (*Budd.*) kŭk-rak 극락.

paragraph *n.* tal-lak 단락, chŏl 절(節), hang 항.

parallel *adj.* p'yŏng-haeng-ŭi 평행의. —*n.* (*latitude*) wi-do-sŏn 위도선 : *38th P*～ sam-p'al·sŏn 삼팔선.

paralysis *n.* ma-bi 마비, chung-p'ung 중풍.

paramount *adj.* ch'oe-go-ŭi 최고의, chi-sang-ŭi 지상(至上)의. —*n.* ch'oe-go kwŏn-wi-ja 최고 권위자.

parapet *n.* ① nan-gan 난간. ② hyung-jang 흉장(胸檣).

paraphrase *n.* swip-ge pa-ggu-ŏ ssŭ-gi 쉽게 바꾸어 쓰기, ŭi-yŏk 의역(意譯). —*v.* pa-ggu-ŏ ssŭ-da〔mal-ha-da〕 바꾸어 쓰다〔말하다〕.

parasite *n.* ① (*insect*) ki-saeng-ch'ung 기생충. ② (*tree*) kyŏ-u-sa-ri 겨우살이. ③ (*person*) sik-gaek 식객.

parasol *n.* yang-san 양산, p'a-ra-sol 파라솔.

parcel *n.* (*post*) so-p'o 소포, so-ha-mul 소하물.

parch *v.* ① (*roast*) pok-da 볶다, kup-da 굽다. ② (*dry up*) pa-ssak mal-ri-da 바싹 말리다.

pardon *n.* & *v.* yong-sŏ(-ha-da) 용서(하다) : *I beg your*

~. Choe-song-hap-ni-da. 죄송합니다.
pare *v.* (*cut*) kkak-da 깎다, chal-ra-nae-da 잘라내다, (*strip*) kkŏp-jil-ŭl pŏt-gi-da 껍질을 벗기다.
parent *n.* ŏ-bŏ-i 어버이, yang-ch'in 양친.
parenthesis *n.* ① kwal-ho 괄호. ② sap-ip-gu 삽입구.
parish *n.* kyo-gu 교구(敎區). 「ch'a-jang 주차장.
park *n.* ① kong-wŏn 공원. ② (*for motorcars*) chu-
parliament *n.* kuk-hoe 국회, ŭi-hoe 의회.
parlo(u)r *n.* kaek-sil 객실, kŏ-sil 거실, ŭng-jŏp-sil 응
parole *n.* sŏ-yak 서약, maeng-se 맹세. 「접실.
parrot *n.* aeng-mu-sae 앵무새.
parson *n.* kyo-gu mok-sa 교구 목사, mok-sa 목사.
part *n.* ① pu-bun 부분, pu 부, p'yŏn 편. ② chi-yŏk 지역. ③ (*role*) yŏk-hal 역할. —*v.* (*seperate*) na-nu-da 나누다, kal-ra-ji-da 갈라지다. 「han 불공평한.
partial *adj.* ① pu-bun-jŏk 부분적. ② pul-gong-p'yŏng-
participate *v.* ch'am-ga-ha-da 참가하다.
participle *n.* (*gram.*) pun-sa 분사(分詞).
particle *n.* ip-ja 입자(粒子), mi-bun-ja 미분자.
particular *adj.* ① (*individual*) kak-gak-ŭi 각각의. ② (*special*) kak-byŏl-han 각별한. ③ (*detailed*) sang-se-han 상세한. —*n.* (*details*) sa-hang 사항.
parting *n.* chak-byŏl 작별, (*division*) pun-hal 분할.
partisan *n.* han p'ae 한 패, to-dang 도당 ; (*guerilla*) yu-gyŏk-dae 유격대, ppal-ch'i-san 빨치산.
partition *n.* ku-bun 구분, ku-hoek 구획 ; pun-hal 분할.
partly *adv.* pu-bun-jŏk-ŭ-ro 부분적으로.
partner *n.* ① tong-mu 동무, jjak-p'ae 짝패, p'a-a-t'ŭ-nŏ 파아트너. ② cho-hap-wŏn 조합원.
partnership *n.* ① yŏn-hap 연합, hyŏp-ryŏk 협력. ② hap-myŏng-hoe-sa 합명회사, cho-hap 조합.
part-time *adj.* ŏ-nŭ si-gan-man il-ha-nŭn 어느 시간만

일하는, p'a-a-t'ŭ-t'a-im-ŭi 파아트타임의.

party *n.* ① (*entertainment*) yŏn-hoe 연회, p'a-a-t'i 파아티. ② (*polit.*) chŏng-dang 정당.

pass *n.* hap-gyŏk 합격, p'ae-sŭ 패스 ; (*of admission*) ip-jang-gwŏn 입장권. —*v.* ① t'ong-gwa-ha-da 통과하다, chi-na-da 지나다.. ② (*die*) chuk-da 죽다.

passage *n.* ① (*passing*) t'ong-gwa 통과. ② (*voyage*) hang-hae 항해. ③ (*way*) t'ong-ro 통로.

passenger *n.* sŭng-gaek 승객, yŏ-gaek 여객.

passer-by *n.* chi-na-ga-nŭn sa-ram 지나가는 사람, t'ong-haeng-in 통행인. 「jae-ŭi 현재의.

passing *adj.* chi-na-ga-nŭn 지나가는, (*current*) hyŏn-

passion *n.* chŏng-yŏl 정열(情熱), (*zeal*) yŏl-sim 열심.

passionate *adj.* yŏl-ryŏl-han 열렬한.

passive *adj.* su-dong-jŏk 수동적, p'i-dong-jŏk 피동적 : (*gram.*) ~ *voice* su-dong-t'ae 수동태.

Passover *n.* yu-wŏl-jŏl 유월절(逾越節).

passport *n.* yŏ-gwŏn 여권, p'ae-sŭ-p'o-o-t'ŭ 패스포오트.

password *n.* am-ho 암호. 「—*n.* kwa-gŏ 과거.

past *adj.* chi-na-gan 지나간. —*prep.* chi-na-sŏ 지나서.

paste *n.* p'ul 풀(糊). —*v.* p'ul-ch'il-ha-da 풀칠하다.

pasteboard *n.* ma-bun-ji 마분지, p'an-ji 판지(板紙).

pastime *n.* so-il-gŏ-ri 소일거리, ki-bun-jŏn-hwan 기분

pastor *n.* (*minister*) mok-sa 목사. 「전환.

pastry *n.* pan-juk kwa-ja 반죽 과자, saeng-gwa-ja 생과자, p'e-sŭ-t'ŭ-ri 페스트리.

pasture *n.* mok-jang 목장, mok-ch'o(-ji) 목초(지).

pat *n.* t'uk-t'uk-ch'i-gi 툭툭치기. —*v.* ka-byŏp-ge ch'i-da 가볍게 치다 ; ssŭ-da-dŭm-da 쓰다듬다.

patch *n.* hŏng-gŏp cho-gak 헝겊 조각. —*v.* kip-da 깁다.

patent *n.* chŏn-mae t'ŭk-hŏ 전매 특허. 「부성애.

paternal *adj.* a-bŏ-ji-ŭi 아버지의 : ~ *love* pu-sŏng-ae

path *n.* kil 길, (*footpath*) po-do 보도 ; (*course in life*)
 in-saeng haeng-ro 인생 행로. 「감상적인.
pathetic *adj.* ae-ch'ŏ-ro-un 애처로운 ; kam-sang-jŏk-in
pathos *n.* pi-ae 비애, p'a-t'o-sŭ 파토스.
pathway *n.* o-sol-gil 오솔길, chop-ŭn kil 좁은 길.
patience *n.* in-nae 인내, ch'am-ŭl-sŏng 참을성.
patient *adj.* ch'am-ŭl-sŏng-it-nŭn 참을성있는. —*n.* hwan-
 ja 환자, pyŏng-ja 병자.
patina *n.* p'u-rŭn nok 푸른 녹, nok-ch'ŏng 녹청(綠靑).
patrimony *n.* se-sŭp chae-san 세습 재산.
patriot *n.* ae-guk-ja 애국자, chi-sa 지사(志士).
patriotic *adj.* ae-guk-sim-i kang-han 애국심이 강한.
patriotism *n.* ae-guk-sim 애국심, u-guk-sim 우국심.
patrol *n.* & *v.* sun-ch'al(-ha-da) 순찰(하다).
patrolman *n.* sun-ch'al-dae-wŏn 순찰대원.
patron *n.* ① po-ho-ja 보호자, hu-wŏn-ja 후원자. ② tan-
 gol son-nim 단골 손님, p'ae-t'ŭ-rŏn 패트런. 「하다.
patronize *v.* hu-wŏn-ha-da 후원하다, po-ho-ha-da 보호
patten *n.* tŏt-na-mak-sin 덧나막신, na-mak-sin 나막신.
pattern *n.* mo-bŏm 모범, (*model*) kyŏn-bon 견본.
pauper *n.* kŭk-bin-ja 극빈자, pin-min 빈민.
pause *n.* mŏm-ch'um 멈춤, chung-dan 중단 ; hyu-sik
 휴식. —*v.* mŏm-ch'u-da 멈추다, (*rest*) swi-da 쉬다.
pave *v.* p'o-jang-ha-da 포장(鋪裝)하다.
pavement *n.* p'o-jang 포장, p'o-jang-do-ro 포장도로.
pavilion *n.* ① (*arbor*) chŏng-ja 정자. ② pyŏl-gwan
 별관. ③ (*large tent*) k'ŭn ch'ŏn-mak 큰 천막.
paw *n.* ap-bal 앞발. —*v.* ap-bal-ro kŭk-da 앞발로 긁다.
pawn *n.* & *v.* (*pledge*) chŏn-dang (chap-da) 전당 (잡다).
pawnshop *n.* chŏn-dang-p'o 전당포.
pay *n.* chi-bul 지불 ; (*salary*) pong-gŭp 봉급, po-su 보
 수. —*v.* chi-bul-ha-da 지불하다.

paymaster *n.* hoe-gye-wŏn 회계원, kyŏng-ri-gwa-jang 경리과장, (*mil.*) chae-jŏng-gwan 재정관.

payment *n.* chi-bul 지불, chi-bul-gŭm 지불금.

pea *n.* wan-du-k'ong 완두콩.

peace *n.* p'yŏng-hwa 평화, p'yŏng-on 평온 ; (*reconciliation*) kang-hwa 강화(講和).　　　　　　　「온화한.

peaceful *adj.* p'yŏng-hwa-rŏ-un 평화로운, on-hwa-han

peach *n.* pok-sung-a 복숭아, pok-sung-a-na-mu 복숭아

peacock *n.* kong-jak 공작.　　　　　　　　　　「나무.

peak *n.* kkok-dae-gi 꼭대기, pong-u-ri 봉우리 ; ch'oe-go-jŏm 최고점.

peal *n.* u-rŏng-ch'an so-ri 우렁찬 소리. —*v.* ul-ryŏ-p'ŏ-ji-da 울려퍼지다, p'ŏ-ddŭ-ri-da 퍼뜨리다.

peanut *n.* ttang-k'ong 땅콩, nak-hwa-saeng 낙화생.

peapod *n.* wan-du-ggo-t'u-ri 완두꼬투리.

pear *n.* pae 배(梨), (*plant*) pae-na-mu 배나무.

pearl *n.* chin-ju 진주 : *artificial* ～ in-jo chin-ju 인조 진주/*black* ～ hŭk-jin-ju 흑진주.

peasant *n.* ① nong-bu 농부. ② si-gol-ddŭ-gi 시골뜨기.

peat *n.* t'o-t'an 토탄, i-t'an 이탄(泥炭).

pebble *n.* cha-gal 자갈, cho-yak-dol 조약돌.

peck *v.* jjo-da 쪼다, jjo-a-mŏk-da 쪼아먹다.

peculiar *adj.* tok-t'ŭk-han 독특한, t'ŭk-yu-han 특유한.

pecuniary *adj.* ton-ŭi 돈의, kŭm-jŏn-sang-ŭi 금전상의.

pedagog(ue) *n.* sŏn-saeng 선생 ; hyŏn-hak-ja 현학자.

pedal *n.* pal-p'an 발판 ; p'e-dal 페달.

pedant *n.* a-nŭn ch'e-ha-nŭn sa-ram 아는 체하는 사람.

peddler *n.* (*bell ringer*) haeng-sang-in 행상인, (*hawker*) to-bu-jang-su 도부장수.

pedestal *n.* chu-ch'ut-dae 주춧대 ; tae-jwa 대좌(台座).

pedestrian *n.* po-haeng-ja 보행자.　　　　　　「t'ong 혈통.

pedigree *n.* (*genealogy*) chok-bo 족보; (*lineage*) hyŏl-

peel *n.* kkŏp-jil 껍질. —*v.* kkŏp-jil-ŭl pŏt-gi-da 껍질을
peep *n.* yŏt-bom 엿봄. —*v.* yŏt-bo-da 엿보다. ⌊벗기다.
peer *v.* cha-se-hi po-da 자세히 보다. —*n.* ① (*equal*)
  tong-ryo 동료. ② (*nobleman*) kwi-jok 귀족. ⌈쌍의.
peerless *adj.* yu-rye-op-nŭn 유례없는, mu-ssang-ŭi 무
peevish *adj.* sŏng-ma-rŭn 성마른 ; pul-p'yŏng-ha-nŭn
peg *n.* na-mu-mot 나무못, mal-dduk 말뚝. ⌊불평하는.
peke *n.* (*Pekinese dog*) pal-ba-ri 발바리.
pen *n.* ① p'en 펜, ch'ŏl-p'il 철필. ② (*writing*) mun-
  p'il 문필. ③ (*fold*) u-ri 우리, ul-t'a-ri 울타리.
penalty *n.* ① hyŏng-bŏl 형벌. ② (*fine*) pŏl-gŭm 벌금.
  ③ (*sport*) p'e-nŏl-t'i 페널티.
penance *n.* (*repentance*) ch'am-hoe 참회, hoe-gae 회개.
pencil *n.* yŏn-p'il 연필 : ~ *sharpener* yŏn-p'il-gga-ggi
  연필깎이.
pencil case (yŏn-)p'il-t'ong (연)필통.
pendant *n.* mok-gŏ-ri 목걸이, p'en-dŏn-t'ŭ 펜던트.
pending *adj.* (*undecided*) mi-gyŏl-ŭi 미결의 : *a* ~
  question hyŏn-an mun-je 현안 문제.
pendulum *n.* si-gye-ch'u 시계추.　　　　　⌈투시하다.
penetrate *v.* kwan-t'ong-ha-da 관통하다, t'u-si-ha-da
penholder *n.* p'en-dae 펜대, p'en-gŏ-ri 펜걸이.
peninsula *n.* pan-do 반도(半島).
penis *n.* cha-ji 자지, ŭm-gyŏng 음경, p'e-ni-sŭ 페니스.
penitence *n.* nwi-u-ch'im 뉘우침. ⌈ko-hae-ja 고해자.
penitent *adj.* nwi-u-ch'i-nŭn 뉘우치는. —*n.* (*Cath.*)
penman *n.* sŏ-ga 서가(書家), sŭp-ja kyo-sa 습자 교사.
penmanship *n.* sŭp-ja 습자, sŏ-do 서도 ; (*style of*
  handwriting) p'il-jŏk 필적.　　　　　⌈im 펜네임.
pen name p'il-myŏng 필명, a-ho 아호(雅號), p'en-ne-
penniless *adj.* han-p'un-ŏp-nŭn 한푼없는, mu-il-p'un-
  ŭi 무일푼의.

penny *n.* p'e-ni 페니. 「給).

pension *n.* (*annuity*) yŏn-gŭm 연금, ŭn-gŭp 은급(恩

pensive *adj.* ① (*thoughtful*) saeng-gak-e cham-gin 생각에 잠긴. ② (*sad*) ku-sŭl-p'ŭn 구슬픈.

pentagon *n.* ① o-gak-hyŏng 5각형. ② (*Am.*) kuk-bang-sŏng 국방성.

peony *n.* chak-yak 작약.

people *n.* sa-ram-dŭl 사람들 ; kuk-min 국민.

pepper *n.* ① (*black*) hu-ch'u 후추. ② (*red*) ko-ch'u

peppermint *n.* pak-ha 박하. 「고추.

peppery *adj.* (*pungent*) mae-un 매운, a-ral-han 알알한.

perceive *v.* chi-gak-ha-da 지각(知覺)하다 ; i-hae-ha-da 이해하다; (*discern*) sik-byŏl-ha-da 식별하다.

percent *n.* p'ŏ-sen-t'ŭ 퍼센트(%) ; paek-bun-yul 백분율.

percentage *n.* ① (*proportion*) paek-bun-yul 백분율 ; pi-yul 비율. ② (*commission*) su-su-ryo 수수료.

perch *v.* ol-ra-an-da 올라앉다. —*n.* ① (*roost*) hwaet-dae 홰대. ② no-p'ŭn chi-wi 높은 지위.

percolate *v.* kŏ-rŭ-da 거르다, yŏ-gwa-ha-da 여과하다.

perennial *adj.* sa-ch'ŏl ma-ru-ji an-nŭn 사철 마르지 않는 ; ta-nyŏn-saeng-ŭi 다년생의. 「완성하다.

perfect *adj.* wan-jŏn-han 완전한. —*v.* wan-sŏng-ha-da

perform *v.* ① (*accomplish*) su-haeng-ha-da 수행하다, (*do*) ha-da 하다, i-haeng-ha-da 이행하다. ② (*play*) yŏn-ju[kong-yŏn]-ha-da 연주〔공연〕하다.

performance *n.* ① i-haeng 이행, sil-haeng 실행. ② (*drama*) yŏn-gi 연기 ;(*entertainment*) yŏ-hŭng 여흥.

perfume *n.* hyang-su 향수, pang-hyang 방향(芳香).

perhaps *adv.* a-ma 아마, ŏ-jjŏ-myŏn 어쩌면.

peril *n.* (*danger*) wi-hŏm 위험 ; mo-hŏm 모험. 「지부.

period *n.* ① ki-gan 기간 ; si-dae 시대. ② chong-ji-bu 종

periodical *n.* chŏng-gi kan-haeng-mul 정기 간행물.

periscope *n.* cham-mang-gyŏng 잠망경.

perish *v.* (*die*) chuk-da 죽다 ; (*pass away*) sa-ra-ji-da 사라지다 ; myŏl-mang-ha-da 멸망하다.

permanent *adj.* yŏng-sok-ha-nŭn 영속하는, yŏng-gu-jŏk-in 영구적인, pyŏn-ham-ŏp-nŭn 변함없는.

permanent tooth yŏng-gu-ch'i 영구치(永久齒).

permission *n.* hŏ-ga 허가 ; (*licence*) myŏn-hŏ 면허 : *without* ～ mu-dan-hi 무단히. 「ha-da 허락하다.

permit *n.* (*licence*) hŏ-ga-jŭng 허가증. —*v.* hŏ-rak-

perpendicular *adj.* (*vertical*) su-jik-ŭi 수직의, kka-gga se-un tŭt-han 깎아 세운 듯한. —*n.* su-jik 수직.

perpetual *adj.* yŏng-wŏn-han 영원한 ; (*incessant*) kkŭn-im-ŏp-nŭn 끊임없는 ; chong-sin-ŭi 종신(終身)의.

perplex *v.* ŏ-ri-dung-jŏl-ha-ge ha-da 어리둥절하게 하다.

perplexity *n.* ① tang-hwang 당황, nang-p'ae 낭패. ② (*dilemma*) nan-guk 난국. 「da 괴롭히다.

persecute *v.* ① pak-hae-ha-da 박해하다. ② koe-rop-hi-

perseverance *n.* ch'am-ŭl-sŏng 참을성, in-nae 인내.

persevere *v.* ch'am-da 참다, kyŏn-di-da 견디다.

persimmon *n.* kam 감 : *dried* ～ kot-gam 곶감.

persist *v.* ko-jip-ha-da 고집하다 ; chi-sok-ha-da 지속하다.

person *n.* sa-ram 사람, in-mul 인물 ; in-p'um 인품.

personal *adj.* kae-in-ŭi 개인의, il-sin-sang-ŭi 일신상의.

personality *n.* kae-sŏng 개성, in-gyŏk 인격.

personnel *n.* chik-wŏn 직원 : ～ *office* in-sa-ch'ŏ 인사처.

perspective *n.* chŏn-mang 전망 ; wŏn-gŭn-bŏp 원근법.

perspiration *n.* (*sweat*) ttam 땀, pal-han 발한.

perspire *v.* ttam-nae-da 땀내다, ttam-i na-da 땀이 나다.

persuade *v.* sŏl-bok-si-k'i-da 설복시키다.

persuasion *n.* sŏl-dŭk 설득 ; (*conviction*) hwak-sin 확신.

pertain *v.* ① sok-ha-da 속하다. ② ŏ-ul-ri-da 어울리다.

pertinent *adj.* chŏk-jŏl-han 적절한 ; kwal-lyŏn-doen

관련된. —*n.* (*pl.*) pu-sok-mul 부속물.

perusal *n.* chŏng-dok 정독(精讀), suk-dok 숙독.

pervade *v.* po-gŭp-ha-da 보급하다, ko-ru mi-ch'i-da 고루 미치다, ch'im-t'u-ha-da 침투하다. 「고집의.

perverse *adj.* sim-sul-gu-jŭn 십술궂은, oe-go-jip-ŭi 외

pessimism *n.* yŏm-se-ju-ŭi 염세주의.

pessimist *n.* pi-gwal-lon-ja 비관론자, yŏm-se-ju-ŭi-ja 염세주의자.

pest *n.* ① hae-ch'ung 해충 ; (*nuisance*) kol-ch'it-gŏ-ri 골칫거리. ② (*plague*) hŭk-sa-byŏng 흑사병, p'e-sŭ- 「t'ŭ 페스트.

pesticide *n.* sal-ch'ung-je 살충제.

pestilence *n.* hŭk-sa-byŏng 흑사병, p'e-sŭ-t'ŭ 페스트.

pestle *n.* chŏl-gut-gong-i 절굿공이, mak-ja 막자.

pet *adj.* kwi-yŏ-un 귀여운. —*n.* ae-wan-dong-mul 애완동물 ; kwi-yŏm-dong-i 귀염둥이, p'e-t'ŭ 페트. —*v.* kwi-yŏ-wŏ-ha-da 귀여워하다, ch'ong-ae-ha-da 총애하다.

petal *n.* kkot-ip 꽃잎.

petition *n.* (*appeal*) t'an-wŏn 탄원, ch'ŏng-wŏn 청원. —*v.* t'an-wŏn-ha-da 탄원하다. 「솔린.

petrol *n.* (*gasoline*) hwi-bal-yu 휘발유, ka-sol-rin 가

petroleum *n.* sŏk-yu 석유 : *crude* ～ wŏn-yu 원유.

petticoat *n.* sok-ch'i-ma 속치마, sŭ-k'ŏ-ŏ-t'ŭ 스커어트.

petty *adj.* chak-ŭn 작은, sa-so-han 사소한.

pew *n.* chwa-sŏk 좌석, kŏl-sang 걸상, cha-ri 자리.

phantasy *n.* kong-sang 공상, hwan-sang 환상.

phantom *n.* ① (*vision*) hwan-yŏng 환영, (*image*) yŏng-sang 영상. ② (*spectre*) yu-ryŏng 유령.

pharmacist *n.* yak-je-sa 약제사.

pharmacy *n.* ① cho-je-bŏp 조제법. ② yak-guk 약국.

phase *n.* ① tan-gye 단계, kuk-myŏn 국면. ② (*aspect*) myŏn 면, sang 상(相).

pheasant *n.* kkwŏng 꿩.

phenomenon *n.* (*of nature*) hyŏn-sang 현상.
philanthropy *n.* pak-ae 박애(博愛), in-ja 인자.
philosopher *n.* ch'ŏl-hak-ja 철학자, hyŏn-in 현인.
philosophy *n.* ch'ŏl-hak 철학, ch'ŏl-ri 철리.
phoenix *n.* pul-sa-jo 불사조 ; pong-hwang-sae 봉황새.
phone *n.* chŏn-hwa(-gi) 전화(기). —*v.* chŏn-hwa-rŭl
   kŏl-da 전화를 걸다. 「가(音價).
phonetic *adj.* ŭm-sŏng-ŭi 음성의 : ~ *value* ŭm-ga 음
phonograph *n.* ch'uk-ŭm-gi 축음기.
photograph *n.* sa-jin 사진. —*v.* sa-jin-ŭl jjik-da 사진
   을 찍다, ch'wal-yŏng-ha-da 촬영하다.
phrase *n.* ku 구, suk-ŏ 숙어, kwan-yong-gu 관용구.
physical *adj.* ① cha-yŏn-ŭi 자연의. ② (*body*) sin-ch'e-
   ŭi 신체의 : ~ *beauty* yuk-ch'e-mi 육체미 /~ *exami-*
   nation sin-ch'e kŏm-sa 신체 검사 /~ *exercise* ch'e-
   jo 체조. ③ mul-ri-hak-ŭi 물리학의. 「사.
physician *n.* (*internist*) nae-gwa-ŭi 내과의, ŭi-sa 의
physics *n.* (*science*) mul-ri-hak 물리학.
physiology *n.* saeng-ri-hak 생리학. 「피아노 연주자.
pianist *n.* p'i-a-ni-sŭ-t'ŭ 피아니스트, p'i-a-no yŏn-ju-ja
pick *n.* (*pickaxe*) kok-gwaeng-i 곡괭이. —*v.* ① (*poke*)
   ssu-si-da 쑤시다. ② (*dig into*) p'a-da 파다. ③ (*gather*)
   mo-ŭ-da 모으다. ④ (*choose*) ko-rŭ-da 고르다.
pickle *n.* chŏ-rin kŏt 절인 것, chang-a-jji 장아찌.
pickpocket *n.* so-mae-ch'i-gi 소매치기.
picnic *n.* so-p'ung 소풍, tŭl-no-ri 들놀이, p'i-k'ŭ-nik 피
   크닉 : *go on a* ~ so-p'ung-ga-da 소풍가다.
picture *n.* kŭ-rim 그림 ; sa-jin 사진 ; yŏng-hwa 영화.
pie *n.* p'a-i 파이 : *apple* ~ sa-gwa p'a-i 사과 파이.
piece *n.* han cho-gak 한 조각 ; p'a-p'yŏn 파편.
pier *n.* pu-du 부두, sŏn-ch'ang 선창. 「하다.
pierce *v.* kkwe-ddŭl-t'a 꿰뚫다, kwan-t'ong-ha-da 관통

piety *n.* ① (*godliness*) kyŏng-gŏn 경건. ② ch'ung-jŏl 충절. ③ (*devotion*) sin-sim 신심.

pig *n.* (*swine, hog*) twae-ji 돼지, (*pork*) twae-ji-go-gi 돼지고기.

pigeon *n.* pi-dul-gi 비둘기 : ∼ *hole* pi-dul-gi-jang 비둘기장/*carrier* ∼ chŏn-sŏ-gu 전서구(傳書鳩).

pigment *n.* ① kŭ-rim mul-gam 그림 물감 ; (*paint*) al-lyo 안료. ② (*biol.*) saek-so 색소.

pigtail *n.* (*queue*) pyŏn-bal 변발(辮髮).

pike *n.* (*spear*) ch'ang 창. —*v.* ch'ang-ŭ-ro jji-rŭ-da 창으로 찌르다.

pile *n.* ① mu-dŏ-gi 무더기, tae-ryang 대량. ② (*stake*) mal-ddŭk 말뚝. —*v.* ssa-a-ol-ri-da 쌓아올리다.

pilgrim *n.* sul-lye-ja 순례자, na-gŭ-ne 나그네.

pilgrimage *n.* sul-lye 순례(巡禮).

piling *n.* (*piles*) mal-dduk 말뚝.　　　　　　「da 약탈하다.

pill *n.* hwan-yak 환약, al-yak 알약. —*v.* yak-t'al-ha-

pillage *n.* (*plunder*) yak-t'al 약탈, (*booty*) yak-t'al-p'um 약탈품. —*v.* yak-t'al-ha-da 약탈하다.

pillar *n.* ki-dung 기둥, chu-sŏk 주석(柱石).

pillow *n.* pe-gae 베개 ; mok-ch'im 목침.　　　「커버.

pillowcase *n.* pe-gaet-it 베갯잇, pe-gae k'ŏ-bŏ 베개

pilot *n.* (*plane*) cho-jong-sa 조종사, p'a-il-rŏt 파일럿 ; (*ship*) su-ro an-nae-in 수로 안내인.

pimp *n.* ttu-jang-i 뚜장이 ; (*pander*) p'o-ju 포주.

pimple *n.* yŏ-dŭ-rŭm 여드름, ppyo-ru-ji 뽀루지. 「전핀.

pin *n.* p'in 핀, ap-p'in 압핀 : *safety* ∼ an-jŏn-p'in 안

pincers *n.* mot-bbop-i 못뽑이, (*nippers*) ppen-jji 뻰찌.

pinch *n.* (*with nails*) kko-jip-da 꼬집다, choe-da 죄다.

pine *n.* so-na-mu 소나무. —*v.* yŏn-mo-ha-da 연모하다 ; (*yearn*) kal-mang-ha-da 갈망하다.

pineapple *n.* p'a-in-ae-p'ŭl 파인애플.

ping-pong *n.* (*table tennis*) t'ak-gu 탁구, p'ing-p'ong 핑퐁 : *a* ～ *table* t'ak-gu-dae 탁구대.

pink *adj.* pun-hong-bi-ch'ŭi 분홍빛의. —*n.* ① (*color*) pun-hong-saek 분홍색. ② (*flower*) p'ae-raeng-i-ggot 패랭이꽃, sŏk-juk 석죽. 「대기.

pinnacle *n.* ① ppyo-jok-t'ap 뾰족탑. ② kkok-dae-gi 꼭

pin-up *n.* in-gi-it-nŭn mi-in sa-jin 인기있는 미인 사진.

pioneer *n.* kae-ch'ŏk-ja 개척자.

pious *adj.* sin-ang-i tu-t'ŏ-un 신앙이 두터운 ; kyŏng-gŏn-han 경건한 ; (*worthy*) kya-rŭk-han 갸룩한.

pipe *n.* ① (*for smoking*) tam-baet-dae 담뱃대. ② (*for liquid, gas*) p'a-i-p'ŭ 파이프, kwan 관(管) : *water* ～ su-do-gwan 수도관. 「*ment*) pun-no 분노.

pique *n.* (*enmity*) chŏk-ŭi 적의, ak-gam 악감, (*resent-*

pirate *n.* ① hae-jŏk 해적. ② p'yo-jŏl-ja 표절자.

piss *v.* o-jum-nu-da 오줌누다, so-byŏn-bo-da 소변보다.

pistil *n.* am-sul 암술.

pistol *n.* kwŏn-ch'ong 권총, p'i-sŭ-t'ol 피스톨.

piston *n.* p'i-sŭ-t'on 피스톤.

pit *n.* ① ku-mŏng 구멍 ; (*pitfall*) ham-jŏng 함정. ② kaeng 갱(坑). ③ u-muk-han kot 우묵한 곳.

pitch *n.* ① (*tar*) song-jin 송진. ② (*throw*) tŏn-ji-gi 던지기. —*v.* tŏn-ji-da 던지다 ; ch'i-da 치다.

pitcher *n.* ① mul-ju-jŏn-ja 물주전자. ② (*baseball*) t'u-su 투수, p'i-ch'ŏ 피처.

pitchfork *n.* soe-sŭ-rang 쇠스랑, (*rake*) kal-k'wi 갈퀴.

piteous *adj.* pul-ssang-han 불쌍한, ka-yŏp-sŭn 가엾은.

pity *n.* pul-ssang-hi yŏ-gim 불쌍히 여김, yŏn-min 연민. —*v.* pul-ssang-hi yŏ-gi-da 불쌍히 여기다.

pivot *n.* ch'uk 축(軸), chung-sim-jŏm 중심점.

placard *n.* ① p'ŭl-rae-k'a-a-dŭ 플래카아드. ② pyŏk-bo 벽보. ③ p'o-sŭ-t'ŏ 포스터, ppi-ra 삐라.

place *n.* chang-so 장소. —*v.* tu-da 두다.

placid *adj.* p'yŏng-on-han 평온한; cho-yong-han 조용한.

plague *n.* (*epidemic*) hŭk-sa-byŏng 흑사병.

plain *adj.* ① (*clear*) myŏng-baek-han 명백한. ② (*flat*) p'yŏng-p'yŏng-han 평평한. ③ (*simple*) su-su-han 수수한. —*n.* (*moor*) p'yŏng-ya 평야.

plait *n.* ① chu-rŭm 주름. ② kkon kkŭn 꼰 끈. —*v.* chu-rŭm-jap-da 주름잡다 ; tta-t'a 땋다.

plan *n.* ① (*drawing*) to-myŏn 도면. ② (*project*) kye-hoek 계획. —*v.* kye-hoek-ha-da 계획하다.

plane *n.* ① (*flat*) p'yŏng-myŏn 평면. ② (*aviation*) pi-haeng-gi 비행기. ③ (*carpenter*) tae-p'ae 대패. —*v.* tae-p'ae-jil-ha-da 대패질하다.

planet *n.* yu-sŏng 유성(遊星), hok-sŏng 혹성.

plank *n.* (*board*) nŏl 널, nŏl-bban-ji 널빤지.

plant *n.* ① (*vegetable*) sik-mul 식물. ② (*mill*) kong-jang 공장. —*v.* sim-da 심다, (*sow*) ppu-ri-da 뿌리다.

plantation *n.* nong-wŏn 농원, chae-bae-ji 재배지.

plaster *n.* ① sŏk-go 석고. ② (*med.*) ko-yak 고약. —*v.* hoe-ch'il-ŭl ha-da 회칠을 하다.

plastic *adj.* p'ŭl-ra-sŭ-t'ik-ŭi 플라스틱의 ; (*formative*) hyŏng-sŏng-jŏk-in 형성적인 ; (*pliable*) yu-yŏn-han 유연한. —*n.* hap-sŏng-su-ji che-p'um 합성수지 제품.

plate *n.* ① (*dish*) chŏp-si 접시. ② (*of metal*) p'an 판 : *silver* ~ ŭn-ban 은반(銀盤).

platform *n.* ① (*stage*) yŏn-dan 연단. ② (*station*) p'ŭl-raet-p'o-om 플랫포옴. ③ (*plank*) chŏng-gang 정강.

plausible *adj.* kŭ-rŏl-dŭt-han 그럴듯한.

play *n.* ① un-dong 운동, kyŏng-gi 경기. ② yŏn-gŭk 연극. —*v.* ① nol-da 놀다. ② yon-ju-ha-da 연주하다 ; (*act*) yŏn-gi-rŭl ha-da 연기를 하다.

playboy *n.* nan-bong-gun 난봉군, pa-ram-dung-i 바람

둥이, p'ŭl-re-i-bo-i 플레이보이.

player *n.* (*of sport*) sŏn-su 선수 ; (*actor*) pae-u 배우; (*of instrument*) yŏn-ju-ja 연주자.

playground *n.* un-dong-jang 운동장, no-ri-t'ŏ 놀이터.

playmate *n.* no-ri ch'in-gu 놀이 친구, so-ggop-dong-mu 소꼽동무. 「노리개.

plaything *n.* (*toy*) chang-nan-gam 장난감, no-ri-gae

playwright *n.* kŭk-jak-ga 극작가.

plaza *n.* ① kwang-jang 광장. ② (*market*) si-jang 시장.

plea *n.* ch'ŏng-wŏn 청원 ; (*in law*) so-song 소송.

plead *v.* ① t'an-wŏn-ha-da 탄원하다. ② chu-jang-ha-da 주장하다 ; pyŏn-ho-ha-da 변호하다. 「쾌한.

pleasant *adj.* ki-bun-jo-ŭn 기분좋은, yu-k'wae-han 유

please *v.* ① chŭl-gŏp-ge ha-da 즐겁게 하다. ② (*in Korean, a suffix*) …chu-sip-si-o …주십시오. 「족한.

pleased *adj.* ki-bbŏ-ha-nŭn 기뻐하는, man-jok-han 만

pleasing *adj.* yu-k'wae-han 유쾌한, chŭl-gŏ-un 즐거운.

pleasure *n.* chŭl-gŏ-um 즐거움, k'wae-rak 쾌락.

pleasure boat yu-ram-sŏn 유람선.

pledge *n.* ① sŏ-yak 서약. ② chŏ-dang-mul 저당물.

plentiful *adj.* p'ung-bu-han 풍부한, nŏk-nŏk-han 넉넉한 : *a ~ harvest* p'ung-jak 풍작.

plenty *n.* man-ŭm 많음, p'ung-bu 풍부, ta-ryang 다량.

pleurisy *n.* nŭk-mak-yŏm 늑막염. 「이어.

pliers *n.* chip-ge 집게, ppen-jji 뻰찌, p'ŭl-ra-i-ŏ 플라

plight *n.* kon-gyŏng 곤경, kung-ji 궁지.

plod *v.* ①ttu-bŏk-ddu-bŏk kŏt-da 뚜벅뚜벅 걷다. ②kkŭn-gi-it-ge il〔kong-bu〕-ha-da 끈기있게 일〔공부〕하다.

plot *n.* ① (*conspiracy*) mo-ryak 모략. ② (*ground*) t'ŏ 터, chi-myŏn 지면. —*v.* ŭm-mo-ha-da 음모하다.

plough · plow *n.* chaeng-gi 쟁기. —*v.* kal-da 갈다.

pluck *v.* (*pull off*) ttŭt-da 뜯다, tta-da 따다.

plug *n.* ma-gae 마개. —*v.* ma-gae-rŭl kki-u-da 마개를
끼우다, t'ŭ-rŏ-mak-da 틀어막다.
plum *n.* o-yat 오얏 : ∼ *blossom* mae-hwa 매화.
plumage *n.* kit-t'ŏl 깃털, u-mo 우모(羽毛).
plumb *n.* ch'u 추, (∼ *bob*) pun-dong 분동(分銅).
plumber *n.* yŏn-gong 연공(鉛工).
plumb line ch'u-sŏn 추선(錘線), ta-rim-jul 다림줄 ;
(*plumb rule*) mŏk-jul-ch'u 먹줄추.
plump *adj.* sal-jjin 살찐, t'o-sil-t'o-sil-han 토실토실한.
plunder *v.* yak-t'al-ha-da 약탈하다.
plunge *v.* ① jji-rŭ-da 찌르다. ② ttwi-ŏ-dŭ-rŏ-ga-da 뛰
.어들어가다, tol-jin-ha-da 돌진하다. —*n.* ① jji-rŭ-gi
찌르기. ② ttwi-ŏ-dŭ-rŏ-ga-gi 뛰어들어가기.
plural *adj.* pok-su-ŭi 복수의. —*n.* (*gram.*) pok-su 복수.
plus *prep.* tŏ-ha-yŏ 더하여. —*adj.* tŏ-ha-gi-ŭi 더하기의.
—*n.* p'ŭl-rŏ-sŭ ki-ho 플러스 기호. 「재벌
plutocrat *n.* pu-ho-jŏng-ch'i-ga 부호정치가, chae-bŏl
ply *v.* yŏl-sŏng-ŭl nae-da 열성을 내다, (*wield diligently*)
pu-ji-rŏn-hi nol-ri-da 부지런히 놀리다.
pneumonia *n.* p'ye-ryŏm 폐렴.
pocket *n.* ho-ju-mŏ-ni 호주머니, p'o-k'et 포켓.
pocketbook *n.* chi-gap 지갑 ; su-ch'ŏp 수첩.
pocketmoney *n.* yong-don 용돈.
pockmark *n.* kom-bo 곰보, ma-ma-ja-guk 마마자국.
pod *n.* (*seed vessel*) kkak-ji 깍지, kko-t'u-ri 꼬투리.
poem *n.* si 시(詩) : *a prose* ∼ san-mun-si 산문시.
poet *n.* si-in 시인. 「sa-si 서사시.
poetry *n.* si 시 : *lyric* ∼ sŏ-jŏng-si 서정시/*epic* ∼ sŏ-
poignant *adj.* ① (*bitter*) kyŏk-ryŏl-han 격렬한. ②
(*keen*) ye-ri-han 예리한 ; (*pungent*) sso-nŭn 쏘는.
point *n.* ① (*dot*) chŏm 점. ② (*end*) kkŭt 끝. ③ (*view*)
kyŏn-hae 견해. —*v.* (*with hand*) ka-ri-k'i-da 가리키다.

poison *n.* tok-yak 독약. —*v.* tok-ŭl nŏ-t’a 독을 넣다.

poisonous *adj.* yu-dok-han 유독한, hae-ro-un 해로운.

poke *v.* jji-rŭ-da 찌르다, ssu-si-da 쑤시다, ssu-syŏ i-rŭ-k’i-da 쑤셔 일으키다.

poker *n.* (*for stove*) pu-ji-ggaeng-i 부지깽이 ; (*for brazier*) hwa-jŏt-ga-rak 화젓가락.　　　　「극의.

polar *adj.* kŭk-ji-ŭi 극지의, nam[puk]-gŭk-ŭi 남[북]

pole *n.* ① chang-dae 장대, mak-dae-gi 막대기. ② kŭk 극, (*plus*) yang-gŭk 양극, (*minus*) ŭm-gŭk 음극 : *South P*~ nam-gŭk 남극.

police *n.* kyŏng-ch’al 경찰 : *the chief of* ~ kyŏng-ch’al-sŏ-jang 경찰서장/~ *box* p’a-ch’ul-so 파출소.

policeman *n.* kyŏng-ch’al-gwan 경찰관, sun-gyŏng 순

police station kyŏng-ch’al-sŏ 경찰서.　　　　　　「경.

policy *n.* chŏng-ch’aek 정책, pang-ch’im 방침.

polish *n.* ① yun 윤, kwang-t’aek 광택. ② yŏn-ma-je 연마제. —*v.* tak-da 닦다, ta-dŭm-da 다듬다.

polite *adj.* kong-son-han 공손한 ; se-ryŏn-doen 세련된.

politeness *n.* kong-son 공손, chŏng-jung 정중.

political *adj.* chŏng-ch’i-ŭi 정치의 : ~ *economy* kyŏng-je-hak 경제학/~ *party* chŏng-dang 정당.

politician *n.* chŏng-ch’i-ga 정치가, chŏng-gaek 정객.

politics *n.* chŏng-ch’i 정치, chŏng-ch’i-hak 정치학.

poll *n.* t’u-p’yo 투표. —*v.* t’u-p’yo-ha-da 투표하다.

pollen *n.* kkot-ga-ru 꽃가루, hwa-bun 화분.

pollution *n.* o-yŏm 오염 : *air* ~ tae-gi o-yŏm 대기 오

pond *n.* mot 못(池), yŏn-mot 연못, nŭp 늪.　　「염.

ponder *v.* ki-p’i saeng-gak-ha-da 깊이 생각하다, muk-sang-ha-da 묵상하다, suk-go-ha-da 숙고하다.

pontoon *n.* kŏ-rut-bae 거룻배 : ~ *bridge* pu-gyo 부교 (浮橋).

pony *n.* cho-rang-mal 조랑말, p’o-u-ni 포우니.

pool *n.* ① mul-ung-dŏng-i 물웅덩이. ② p'u-ul 푸울.
poor *adj.* ka-nan-han 가난한; (*pitiable*) ka-yŏp-sŭn 가
  엾은 ; (*inferior*) yŏl-dŭng-han 열등한.
pop *n.* ① (*music*) yu-haeng-ga 유행가, tae-jung-ga-yo
  대중가요. ② (*dad*) a-bba 아빠. —*v.* p'ŏng-ha-go t'ŏ-
  ji-da 펑하고 터지다.   「팝코온.
popcorn *n.* t'wi-gim ok-su-su 튀김 옥수수, p'ap-k'o-on
Pope *n.* ro-ma kyo-hwang 로마 교황.
poplar *n.* p'o-p'ŭl-ra 포플라.   「hong-saek 진홍색.
poppy *n.* ① yang-gwi-bi 양귀비. ② (*scarlet*) chin-
popular *adj.* t'ong-sok-jŏk 통속적 ; in-gi-it-nŭn 인기있는.
popularity *n.* in-gi 인기, p'yŏng-p'an 평판 ; yu-haeng
  유행 : *win* ~ in-gi-rŭl ŏt-da 인기를 얻다.
population *n.* in-gu 인구.
porcelain *n.* sa-gi kŭ-rŭt 사기 그릇, cha-gi 자기(瓷器).
porch *n.* hyŏn-gwan 현관, (*Am.*) pe-ran-da 베란다.
pore *n.* t'ŏl-gu-mŏng 털구멍. —*v.* yŏl-jung-ha-da 열중
  하다 ; kom-gom-i saeng-gak-ha-da 곰곰이 생각하다.
pork *n.* twae-ji-go-gi 돼지고기.   「리지.
porridge *n.* o-o-t'ŭ-mil chuk 오오트밀 죽, p'o-ri-ji 포
port *n.* ① hang-gu 항구. ② (~ *wine*) p'o-o-t'ŭ-wa-in
  포오트와인. ③ (*bearing*) t'ae-do 태도. 「bŭl 포오터블.
portable *adj.* hyu-dae-yong-ŭi 휴대용의. —*n.* p'o-o-t'ŏ-
portal *n.* chŏng-mun 정문(正門), ip-gu 입구.
porter *n.* ① (*gatekeeper*) mun-ji-gi 문지기. ② (*carrier*)
  chim-gun 짐군, un-ban-in 운반인.   「gŭm 지참금.
portion *n.* ① pu-bun 부분. ② mok 몫. ③ chi-ch'am-
portrait *n.* ch'o-sang-hwa 초상화 ; sa-jin 사진.
portray *v.* kŭ-ri-da 그리다, myo-sa-ha-da 묘사하다.
pose *n.* cha-se 자세, p'o-u-jŭ 포우즈.   「ch'aek 직책.
position *n.* ① wi-ch'i 위치. ② sin-bun 신분. ③ chik-
positive *adj.* ① (*definite*) myŏng-hwak-han 명확한 ;

(*active*) chŏk-gŭk-jŏk-in 적극적인. ② (*photo*) yang-hwa-ŭi 양화(陽畵)의. —*n.* yang-hwa 양화.

positively *adv.* chŏk-gŭk-jŏk-ŭ-ro 적극적으로, hwak-⌊sil-hi 확실히.

possess *v.* so-yu-ha-da 소유하다.

possession *n.* so-yu 소유, chŏm-yu 점유 ; chae-san 재산.

possibility *n.* ka-nŭng-sŏng 가능성, ka-mang 가망.

possible *adj.* ka-nŭng-han 가능한.

possibly *adv.* a-ma 아마, ŏ-jjŏ-myŏn 어쩌면.

post *n.* ① (*mail*) u-p'yŏn 우편 : *parcel* ~ so-p'o 소포. ② (*pole*) ki-dung 기둥. ③ (*station*) pu-sŏ 부서(部署). —*v.* u-song-ha-da 우송하다.

postage *n.* u-p'yŏn-yo-gŭm 우편요금 : ~ *due* song-ryo ⌊mi-dal 송료 미달.

postage stamp u-p'yo 우표.

postcard *n.* u-p'yŏn yŏp-sŏ 우편 엽서.

poster *n.* p'o-sŭ-t'ŏ 포스터, pyŏk-bo 벽보.

posterity *n.* cha-son 자손, hu-se 후세. ⌈유복자.

posthumous *adj.* sa-hu-ŭi 사후의 : *a* ~ *child* yu-bok-ja

postman *n.* u-p'yŏn pae-dal-bu 우편 배달부, u-ch'e-bu 우체부, chip-bae-wŏn 집배원.

postmark *n. & v.* so-in(-ŭl jjik-da) 소인(을 찍다).

post office u-ch'e-guk 우체국.

postpone *v.* yŏn-gi-ha-da 연기하다, mi-ru-da 미루다.

postscript *n.* ch'u-sin 추신(追申), hu-gi 후기. ⌈상태.

posture *n.* ① cha-se 자세, t'ae-do 태도. ② sang-t'ae

postwar *adj.* chŏn-hu-ŭi 전후의 : ~ *days* chŏn-hu 전후.

pot *n.* (*jar*) tan-ji 단지, (*pan*) nam-bi 남비, (*bowl*) sa-bal 사발 : *a flower* ~ hwa-bun 화분(花盆).

potato *n.* kam-ja 감자 : *sweet* ~ ko-gu-ma 고구마.

potential *adj.* ① (*possible*) ka-nŭng-han 가능한. ② (*latent*) cham-jae-jŏk-in 잠재적인.

pottery *n.* to-gi 도기(陶器), chil-gŭ-rŭt 질그릇.

pouch *n.* chak-ŭn chu-mŏ-ni 작은 주머니, ssam-ji 쌈지:

tobacco ~ tam-bae ssam-ji 담배 쌈지.   「닭.
poultry *n.* (*domestic fowls*) ka-gŭm 가금(家禽), tak
pounce *v.* wa-rak tŏm-byŏ-dŭl-da 와락 덤벼들다.
pound *n.* ① (*weight*) p'a-un-dŭ 파운드. ② ul-t'a-ri 울
타리. —*v.* tu-dŭl-gi-da 두들기다.
pour *v.* ① (*flow*) p'ŏ-but-da 퍼붓다, ssot-da 쏟다, tta-
rŭ-da 따르다. ② (*shed*) pal-san-ha-da 발산하다.
poverty *n.* ① ka-nan 가난, pin-gon 빈곤, (*scarcity*)
kyŏl-p'ip 결핍. ② (*inferiority*) yŏl-dŭng 열등.
powder *n.* ① (*dust*) ka-ru 가루. ② (*explosive*) hwa-
yak 화약 : *toilet* ~ pun 분(粉).
power *n.* him 힘, nŭng-ryŏk 능력 : *electric* ~ chŏllyŏk 전력 / *horse* ~ ma-ryŏk 마력.
powerful *adj.* kang-ryŏk-han 강력한 : *a* ~ *nation*
kang-ryŏk-han min-jok 강력한 민족.
power house pal-jŏn-so 발전소.   「용적인.
practical *adj.* sil-je-jŏk-in 실제적인, si-ryong-jŏk-in 실
practice *n.* ① (*exercise*) yŏn-sŭp 연습. ② (*habit*)
sŭp-gwan 습관. ③ (*business*) ŏp-mu 업무.
practise·practice *v.* sil-haeng-ha-da 실행하다 ; yŏn-sŭp-
ha-da 연습하다.
practitioner *n.* kae-ŏp-ŭi 개업의, pyŏn-ho-sa 변호사.
pragmatism *n.* si-ryong-ju-ŭi 실용주의.
prairie *n.* tae-ch'o-wŏn 대초원, mok-jang 목장.
praise *n.* ch'an-yang 찬양 ; sung-bae 숭배. —*v.* ch'ing-
ch'an-ha-da 칭찬하다, ch'an-yang-ha-da 찬양하다.
prank *n.* chang-nan 장난, nong-dam 농담.
prate *v.* chi-ggŏ-ri-da 지껄이다. —*n.* su-da 수다.
pray *v.* pil-da 빌다, ki-do-ha-da 기도하다.   「도문.
prayer *n.* ① ki-do 기도, ki-wŏn 기원. ② ki-do-mun 기
prayer book ki-do-sŏ 기도서.   「하다.
preach *v.* sŏl-gyo-ha-da 설교하다 ; chŏn-do-ha-da 전도

preacher *n.* chŏn-do-sa 전도사, sŏl-gyo-ja 설교자.
precaution *n.* cho-sim 조심, kyŏng-gye 경계. 「하다.
precede *v.* ap-sŏ-da 앞서다, ···e u-sŏn-ha-da ···에 우선
precedent *n.* chŏl-lye 전례, kwal-lye 관례 : *without*
 ~ chŏl-lye-ga ŏp-nŭn 전례가 없는.
preceding *adj.* chŏn-ŭi 전의, ap-sŏn 앞선 ; chŏn-sul-
 han 전술한 : ~ *year* chŏn-nyŏn 전년. 「hun 교훈.
precept *n.* (*maxim*) kyŏk-ŏn 격언, (*instruction*) kyo-
precinct *n.* ① kyong-nae 경내, ku-nae 구내. ② kwan-
 hal-gu 관할구, (*Am.*) sŏn-gŏ-gu 선거구.
precious *adj.* ① kwi-jung-han 귀중한, ka-ch'i-it-nŭn
 가치있는. ② (*gross*) tae-dan-han 대단한.
precipice *n.* chŏl-byŏk 절벽, nang-ddŏ-rŏ-ji 낭떠러지.
precipitate *v.* ① (*throw down*) ttŏ-rŏ-ddŭ-ri-da 떨어
 뜨리다. ② (*urge*) chae-ch'ok-ha-da 재촉하다. 「정밀한.
precise *adj.* chŏng-hwak-han 정확한, chŏng-mil-han
precocious *adj.* ol-doen 올된, cho-suk-han 조숙한.
predecessor *n.* ① (*senior*) chŏn-im-ja 전임자, sŏn-
 bae 선배. ② (*forefather*) sŏn-jo 선조.
predestination *n.* suk-myŏng 숙명 ; ye-jŏng 예정.
predicate *n.* (*gram.*) sul-bu 술부.
predict *v.* ye-ŏn-ha-da 예언하다, ye-bo-ha-da 예보하다.
pre-election *n.* ye-sŏn 예선, ye-bi sŏn-gŏ 예비 선거.
preface *n.* mŏ-ri-mal 머리말, sŏ-mun 서문.
prefecture *n.* hyŏn 현, to 도(道).
prefer *v.* ① ···jjok-ŭl cho-a-ha-da ···쪽을 좋아하다. ②
 (*present*) che-ch'ul-ha-da 제출하다.
prefix *n.* chŏp-du-sa 접두사(接頭辭).
pregnant *adj.* ① im-sin-han 임신한. ② (*filled*) ka-
 dŭk-ch'an 가득찬, ch'ung-man-han 충만한.
prejudice *n.* p'yŏn-gyŏn 편견, sŏn-ip-gwan 선입관. 「의.
preliminary *adj.* ① ye-bi-jŏk 예비적. ② sŏ-mun-ŭi 서문

prelude *n.* sŏ-mak 서막, (*overture*) sŏ-gok 서곡. 「이른.
premature *adj.* cho-suk-han 조숙한, nŏ-mu i-rŭn 너무
premier *n.* kuk-mu-ch'ong-ri 국무총리, su-sang 수상.
premium *n.* ① p'ŭ-ri-mi-ŏm 프리미엄. ② sang-yŏ-gŭm
  상여금(賞與金). ③ po-hŏm-ryo 보험료.
preoccupy *v.* ma-ŭm-ŭl ppae-at-da 마음을 빼앗다.
preparation *n.* chun-bi 준비, ma-ryŏn 마련.
prepare *v.* chun-bi-ha-da 준비하다, ma-ryŏn-ha-da 마
preposition *n.* (*gram.*) chŏn-ch'i-sa 전치사. 「련하다.
prerogative *n.* (*privilege*) t'ŭk-gwŏn 특권.
Presbyterian *n.* chang-ro-gyo hoe-wŏn 장로교 회원.
  —*adj.* chang-ro-gyo-hoe-ŭi 장로교회의 : ～ *Church*
  chang-ro-gyo-hoe 장로교회.
prescribe *v.* (*med.*) ch'ŏ-bang-ha-da 처방하다; (*ordain*)
  kyu-jŏng-ha-da 규정하다.
prescription *n.* ① kyu-jŏng 규정. ② (*med.*) ch'ŏ-bang
  처방 : ～ *slip* ch'ŏ-bang-jŏn 처방전.
presence *n.* ① (*being*) chon-jae 존재. ② (*attendance*)
  ch'ul-sŏk 출석. ③ (*bearing*) t'ae-do 태도.
present *v.* chŭng-jŏng-ha-da 증정하다, sŏn-sa-ha-da 선
  사하다. —*adj.* ch'ul-sŏk-han 출석한 ; (*current*) hyŏn-
  jae-ŭi 현재의. —*n.* sŏn-mul 선물.
presently *adv.* i-nae 이내, kot 곧 ; hyŏn-jae 현재.
preserve *v.* po-jon-ha-da 보존하다. 「(主宰)하다.
preside *v.* sa-hoe-ha-da 사회하다, chu-jae-ha-da 주재
president *n.* tae-t'ong-ryŏng 대통령 ; (*of company*) sajang 사장 ; (*of bank*) ch'ong-jae 총재.
press *v.* ① nu-rŭ-da 누르다. ② (*urge*) ch'ok-gu-ha-da
  촉구하다. —*n.* (*newspapers*) sin-mun 신문.
pressing *adj.* (*urgent*) kin-gŭp-han 긴급한.
pressure *n.* ap-ryŏk 압력, ap-bak 압박 : *atmospheric*
  ～ ki-ap 기압.

prestige *n.* ① (*power*) wi-ryŏk 위력, wi-sin 위신. ②
(*fame*) myŏng-sŏng 명성. ③ (*credit*) sin-mang 신망.
presume *v.* ① ch'u-ch'ŭk-ha-da 추측하다, chim-jak-ha-
da 짐작하다. ② i-yong-ha-da 이용하다.
pretend *v.* ⋯ch'e-ha-da ⋯체하다. 「변명.
pretext *n.* p'ing-gye 핑계, ku-sil 구실, pyŏn-myŏng
pretty *adj.* ko-un 고운, ŏ-yŏ-bbŭn 어여쁜, (*fine*) hul-
ryung-han 훌륭한. —*adv.* (*fairly*) kkwae 꽤.
prevail *v.* ① u-se-ha-da 우세하다. ② yu-haeng-ha-da
prevent *v.* pang-ji-ha-da 방지하다. 「유행하다.
prevention *n.* ① ye-bang 예방, pang-ji 방지. ② (*hin-
dering*) pang-hae 방해.
previous *adj.* i-jŏn-ŭi 이전의, mŏn-jŏ-ŭi 먼저의.
prey *v.* chap-a-mŏk-da 잡아먹다. —*n.* mŏk-i 먹이.
price *n.* ① kap 값, ka-gyŏk 가격. ② (*reward*) po-sang
price index mul-ga chi-su 물가 지수. 「보상.
priceless *adj.* mop-si kwi-jung-han 몹시 귀중한.
price tag chŏng-ga-p'yo 정가표, chŏng-ch'al 정찰.
prick *v.* jji-rŭ-da 찌르다 ; ko-t'ong-ŭl chu-da 고통을
주다. —*n.* jji-rŭ-gi 찌르기, ka-si 가시. 「다.
prickle *n.* ka-si 가시, pa-nŭl 바늘. —*v.* jji-rŭ-da 찌르
pride *n.* cha-bu-sim 자부심, cha-rang 자랑, kŭng-ji 긍
지. —*v.* cha-rang-ha-da 자랑하다.
priest *n.* (*monk*) sŭng-ryŏ 승려, su-do-ja 수도자 ;
(*minister*) mok-sa 목사, sa-je 사제.
primary *adj.* pol-lae-ŭi 본래의, ch'o-bo-ŭi 초보의 : ~
school kuk-min-hak-gyo 국민학교.
prime *adj.* ch'ŏt-jjae-ŭi 첫째의 ; chu-yo-han 주요한 ;
pol-lae-ŭi 본래의 : ~ *minister* su-sang 수상.
primer *n.* ip-mun-(sŏ) 입문(서). 「시인.
primitive *adj.* wŏn-si-ŭi 원시의 : ~ *man* wŏn-si-in 원
primrose *n.* aeng-ch'o 앵초, tal-ma-ji-ggot 달맞이꽃.

prince *n.* ① wang-ja 왕자. ② (*duke*) kong-jak 공작.
princess *n.* ① kong-ju 공주. ② wang-bi 왕비.
principal *adj.* chung-yo-han 중요한 ; che-il-ŭi 제일의.
　—*n.* ① u-du-mŏ-ri 우두머리. ② kyo-jang 교장.
principle *n.* wŏn-ch'ik 원칙 ; (*doctrine*) chu-ŭi 주의.
print *n.* ① (*mark*) cha-guk 자국. ② (*printing*) in-
　swae 인쇄. —*v.* in-swae-ha-da 인쇄하다.
printer *n.* in-swae-ŏp-ja 인쇄업자 ; in-swae-gi 인쇄기.
printing *n.* in-swae 인쇄.
prior *adj.* ① (*former*) a-p'ŭi 앞의, i-jŏn-ŭi 이전의. ②
　(*more important*) po-da chung-yo-han 보다 중요한.
priority *n.* u-sŏn-gwŏn 우선권, sang-wi 상위(上位).
prism *n.* p'ŭ-ri-jŭm 프리즘.
prison *n.* kam-ok 감옥, kyo-do-so 교도소.
prisoner *n.* choe-su 죄수 : ~ *of war* p'o-ro 포로.「생활.
privacy *n.* sa-jŏk cha-yu 사적 자유, sa-saeng-hwal 사
private *adj.* sa-jŏk-in 사적인, pi-mil-ŭi 비밀의. —*n.*
　pyŏng-sa 병사(兵士), pyŏng-jol 병졸.
privilege *n.* t'ŭk-gwŏn 특권, t'ŭk-jŏn 특전 ; ŭn-jŏn 은
　전. —*v.* t'ŭk-gwŏn-ŭl chu-da 특권을 주다.
privy *adj.* sum-ŭn 숨은, pi-mil-ŭi 비밀의. —*n.*(*latrine*)
　pyŏn-so 변소.
prize *n.* ① (*reward*) sang 상. ② (*booty*) chŏl-li-p'um
　전리품. —*v.* so-jung-hi ha-da 소중히 하다.
pro *n.* chik-ŏp sŏn-su 직업 선수, p'ŭ-ro 프로.
probable *adj.* ① (*likely*) i-ssŭm-jik-han 있음직한, kŭ-
　rŏl-ssa-han 그럴싸한. ② yu-mang-han 유망한.
probably *adv.* a-ma 아마, sip-jung-p'al-gu 십중팔구.
problem *n.* mun-je 문제 ; nan-mun 난문.
procedure *n.* sun-sŏ 순서, chŏl-ch'a 절차.　　「하다.
proceed *v.* na-a-ga-da 나아가다, chin-haeng-ha-da 진행
proceedings *n.* ŭi-sa-rok 의사록, hoe-ŭi-rok 회의록.

process *n*. chin-haeng 진행, kwa-jŏng 과정 ; (*method*) pang-bŏp 방법. —*v*. ka-gong-ha-da 가공하다.

procession *n*. haeng-ryŏl 행렬, haeng-jin 행진.

proclaim *v*. kong-p'yo-ha-da 공표하다, sŏn-ŏn-ha-da 선언하다. 「myŏng 성명.

proclamation *n*. ① sŏn-ŏn 선언, p'o-go 포고. ② sŏng-

procurator *n*. so-song tae-ri-in 소송 대리인.

procure *v*. son-e nŏ-t'a 손에 넣다, ŏt-da 얻다.

prodigal *adj*. ① (*wasteful*) nang-bi-ha-nŭn 낭비하는. ② (*dissipated*) pang-t'ang-han 방탕한.

prodigious *adj*. kŏ-dae-han 거대한; i-sang-han 이상한.

prodigy *n*. ① kyŏng-i 경이(驚異). ② ch'ŏn-jae 천재.

produce *v*. saeng-san〔san-ch'ul〕-ha-da 생산〔산출〕하다.

producer *n*. saeng-san-ja 생산자, che-jak-ja 제작자, p'ŭ-ro-dyu-u-sŏ 프로듀우서. 「성과.

product *n*. san-mul 산물, che-p'um 제품 ; song-gwa

production *n*. ① saeng-san 생산. ② yŏn-ch'ul 연출.

productive *adj*. saeng-san-jŏk-in 생산적인.

profane *adj*. (*irreverent*) mo-dok-jŏk-in 모독적인.

profanity *n*. mo-dok 모독. 「백하다.

profess *v*. kong-ŏn-ha-da 공언하다 ; ko-baek-ha-da 고

profession *n*. ① chik-ŏp 직업. ② kong-ŏn 공언(公言).

professor *n*. kyo-su 교수 : *assistant* ~ cho-gyo-su 조교수/*associate* ~ pu-gyo-su 부교수. 「하다.

proffer *v*. che-gong-ha-da 제공하다 ; che-ŭi-ha-da 제의

proficient *adj*. ik-suk-han 익숙한, nŭng-ran-han 능란한.

profile *n*. ① (*of person's face*) yŏp mo-sŭp 옆 모습, p'ŭ-ro-u-p'il 프로우필. ② (*outline*) yun-gwak 윤곽.

profit *n*. i-ik 이익, i-dŭk 이득. 「있는.

profitable *adj*. yu-ri-han 유리한, i-mun-i it-nŭn 이문이

profiteer *n*. pu-dang i-dŭk-ja 부당 이득자.

profound *adj*. ki-p'ŭn 깊은, sim-wŏn-han 심원한;(*very*

learned) hae-bak-han 해박한.

profuse *adj.* (*generous*) t'ong-i k'ŭn 통이 큰 ; nang-bi-ha-nŭn 낭비하는 ;(*abundant*) p'ung-bu-han 풍부한.

progeny *n.* cha-son 자손 ; (*outcome*) so-san 소산.

program(me) *n.* p'ŭ-ro-gŭ-raem 프로그램 ; (*schedule*) ye-jŏng-p'yo 예정표.　　　　　　　　　　「da 나아가다.

progress *n.* pal-dal 발달, chin-bo 진보.　—*v.* na-a-ga-

progressive *adj.* chin-bo-jŏk-in 진보적인.

prohibit *v.* kŭm-ha-da 금하다 ;pang-hae-ha-da 방해하다.

prohibition *n.* kŭm-ji 금지, kŭm-ji-ryŏng 금지령.

project *n.* kye-hoek 계획 ; sŏl-gye 설계.　—*v.* ① (*on screen*) yŏng-sa-ha-da 영사하다. ② (*jut out*) tol-ch'ul-ha-da 돌출하다.　　　　　　　　　　　「han 장황한.

prolix *adj.* (*tedious*) chi-ru-han 지루한, chang-hwang-

prolog(ue) *n.* mŏ-ri-mal 머리말, sŏ-ŏn 서언 ; sŏ-gok 서

prolong *v.* yŏn-jang-ha-da 연장하다.　　　　　　「곡.

promenade *n.* san-ch'aek-gil 산책길, san-ch'aek 산책.

prominent *adj.* t'wi-ŏ-na-on 튀어나온 ; (*distinguished*) chŏ-myŏng-han 저명한, t'ak-wŏl-han 탁월한.

promise *n. & v.* yak-sok(-ha-da) 약속(하다).

promising *adj.* (*hopeful*) yu-mang-han 유망한.

promote *v.* ① (*raise*) sŭng-jin-si-k'i-da 승진시키다. ② (*further*) ch'ok-jin-si-k'i-da 촉진시키다.

promotion *n.* sŭng-jin 승진, chin-gŭp 진급.

prompt *adj.* ppa-rŭn 빠른 ; chŭk-sŏk-ŭi 즉석의.　—*v.* ch'ok-jin-ha-da 촉진하다, cha-gŭk-ha-da 자극하다.

prone *adj.* …ha-gi swi-un …하기 쉬운, ŏp-dŭ-rin 엎드

pronoun *n.* (*gram.*) tae-myŏng-sa 대명사.　　　「린.

pronounce *v.* pa-rŭm-ha-da 발음하다.

pronunciation *n.* pa-rŭm 발음.

proof *n.* ① (*evidence*) chŭng-gŏ 증거. ② (*of book*) kyo-jŏng(-swae) 교정(쇄).

prop *n.* (*support*) pŏ-t'im-mok 버팀목.
propaganda *n.* sŏn-jŏn 선전(宣傳). 「da 보급시키다.
propagate *v.* pŏn-sik-si-k'i-da 번식시키다, po-gŭp-si-k'i-
propel *v.* ch'u-jin-ha-da 추진하다, a-p'ŭ-ro mil-da 앞으
propeller *n.* p'ŭ-ro-p'el-rŏ 프로펠러. 「로 밀다.
proper *adj.* chŏk-dang-han 적당한; tok-t'ŭk-han 독특한.
properly *adv.* chŏk-dang-hi 적당히.
property *n.* chae-san 재산, so-yu-mul 소유물.
prophecy *n.* ye-ŏn 예언, ye-ŏn-sŏ 예언서. 「다.
prophesy *v.* ye-ŏn-ha-da 예언하다, ye-bo-ha-da 예보하
prophet *n.* ye-ŏn-ja 예언자, sŏn-ji-ja 선지자.
proportion *n.* ① (*ratio*) pi-yul 비율 ; (*share*) mok 몫.
　② (*balance*) kyun-hyŏng 균형.
proposal *n.* sin-ch'ŏng 신청, che-ŭi 제의; (*plan*)an 안.
propose *v.* ① che-ŭi-ha-da 제의하다. ② (*woo*) ku-hon-
　ha-da 구혼하다. 「kye-hoek 계획.
proposition *n.* ① (*assertion*) chu-jang 주장. ② (*plan*)
proprietor *n.* so-yu-ja 소유자 ; chi-ju 지주(地主).
propriety *n.* ① chŏk-dang 적당. ② (*decency*) ye-jŏl 예
prose *n.* san-mun(-ch'e) 산문(체). 「절.
prosecute *v.* ① (*carry out*) su-haeng-ha-da 수행하다,
　chong-sa-ha-da 종사하다. ② (*sue*) ki-so-ha-da 기소
prosecutor *n.* kŏm-sa 검사(檢事). 「하다.
prospect *n.* ① (*scene*) cho-mang 조망. ② (*expectation*)
　ye-sang 예상. —*v.* ① (*promise*) yu-mang-ha-da 유
　망하다. ② (*explore*) tap-sa-ha-da 답사하다.
prosper *v.* ① pŏn-ch'ang〔pŏn-yŏng〕-ha-da 번창〔번영〕
　하다. ② (*succeed*) sŏng-gong-ha-da 성공하다.
prosperity *n.* pŏn-ch'ang 번창 ; sŏng-gong 성공.
prosperous *adj.* pŏn-ch'ang-han 번창한.
prostitute *n.* ch'ang-nyŏ 창녀, mae-ch'un-bu 매춘부.
prostrate *adj.* ŏp-dŭ-rin 엎드린, kul-bok-han 굴복한.

protagonist *n.* (*leading actor*) chu-yŏk 주역.
protect *v.* po-ho-ha-da 보호하다, (*defend*) mak-da 막
protection *n.* po-ho 보호, pang-ŏ 방어.   ㄴ다.
protector *n.* po-ho-ja 보호자, ong-ho-ja 옹호자.
protectory *n.* so-nyŏn-wŏn 소년원, po-yuk-wŏn 보육원.
protein *n.* tan-baek-jil 단백질.
protest *v.* hang-ŭi-ha-da 항의하다. —*n.* hang-ŭi 항의.
Protestant *n.* sin-gyo-do 신교도.
prototype *n.* wŏn-hyŏng 원형, (*pattern*) p'yo-jun 표준.
protract *v.* (*lengthen*) o-rae kkŭl-da 오래 끌다, (*extend*) yŏn-jang-ha-da 연장하다.
proud *adj.* ① cha-rang-ha-nŭn 자랑하는. ② (*haughty*) kŏ-man-han 거만한. ③ (*grand*) tang-dang-han 당당한.
prove *v.* chŭng-myŏng-ha-da 증명하다.
proverb *n.* sok-dam 속담, (*wise saying*) kŭm-ŏn 금언.
provide *v.* (*supply*) kong-gŭp-ha-da 공급하다 ; (*prepare*) chun-bi-ha-da 준비하다.
provided *conj.* man-yak …i-ra-myŏn 만약 …이라면, …i-ra-nŭn cho-gŏn-ŭ-ro …이라는 조건으로.
providence *n.* sŏp-ri 섭리, sin-ŭi 신의(神意).
province *n.* to 도(道) ; (*state*) chu 주 ; chi-bang 지방.
provision *n.* ① chun-bi 준비, kong-gŭp 공급. ② (*supplies of food*) sik-ryang 식량.
provisional *adj.* im-si-ŭi 임시의.   「노하게 하다.
provoke *v.* cha-gŭk-ha-da 자극하다 ; no-ha-ge ha-da
prowess *n.* yong-gam 용감 ; (*excellence*) t'ak-wŏl 탁월.
prowl *v.* (*wander*) pae-hoe-ha-da 배회하다, to-ra-da-ni-da 돌아다니다, sŏ-sŏng-gŏ-ri-da 서성거리다.
prudence *n.* sin-jung 신중, cho-sim 조심.   「별있는.
prudent *adj.* sin-jung-han 신중한, pun-byŏl-it-nŭn 분
pry *v.* yŏt-bo-da 엿보다, sal-p'i-da 살피다.
psalm *n.* ch'an-song-ga 찬송가, sŏng-ga 성가.

psychology *n.* sim-ri-hak 심리학.

psychosis *n.* chŏng-sin-byŏng 정신병.

puberty *n.* (*sexual maturity*) sa-ch'un-gi 사춘기.

public *adj.* kong-jung-ŭi 공중(公衆)의.

publication *n.* ① pal-p'yo 발표. ② ch'ul-p'an 출판.

publish *v.* ① (*books*) ch'ul-p'an-ha-da 출판하다. ②
 pal-p'yo-ha-da 발표하다.   「행자.

publisher *n.* ch'ul-p'an-ŏp-ja 출판업자, pal-haeng-ja 발

publishing *n.* ch'ul-p'an 출판.

pucker *n.* chu-rŭm 주름. —*v.* chu-rŭm-sal-ji-ge ha-da
 주름살지게 하다.

pudding *n.* p'u-ding 푸딩.

puddle *n.* mul ung-dŏng-i 물 웅덩이.   「혹 내불다.

puff *n.* huk nae-bul-gi 혹 내불기. —*v.* huk nae-bul-da

pull *v.* kkŭl-da 끌다, tang-gi-da 당기다.

pulley *n.* hwal-ch'a 활차(滑車), to-rŭ-rae 도르래.

pulp *n.* ① p'ŏl-p'ŭ 펄프. ② (*fruit*)kwa-yuk 과육(果肉).

pulpit *n.* sŏl-gyo-dan 설교단.

pulsate *v.* ttwi-da 뛰다 ; chin-dong-ha-da 진동하다.

pulse *n.* maek-bak 맥박, ko-dong 고동.

pump *n.* p'ŏm-p'ŭ 펌프 : *fire* ～ so-bang-p'ŏm-p'ŭ 소방
 펌프. —*v.* p'ŏm-p'ŭ-jil-ha-da 펌프질하다.

pumpkin *n.* ho-bak 호박.

punch *v.* ① (*a hole*) ttul-t'a 뚫다. ② (*hit*) t'a-gyŏk-
 ŭl chu-da 타격을 주다. —*n.* p'ŏn-ch'i 펀치.

punctual *adj.* si-gan-ŭl ŏm-su-ha-nŭn 시간을 엄수하는.

punctuality *n.* si-gan ŏm-su 시간 엄수.

punctuation *n.* ku-du-jŏm 구두점, ku-du-bŏp 구두법.

puncture *n.* ppang-ggu 빵꾸.

punish *v.* pŏl-ju-da 벌주다, ch'ŏ-bŏl-ha-da 처벌하다.

punishment *n.* hyŏng-bŏl 형벌, ch'ŏ-bŏl 처벌.

pupa *n.* pŏn-de-gi 번데기.

pupil *n.* saeng-do 생도 ; che-ja 제자(弟子).

puppet *n.* ① (*doll*) in-hyŏng 인형. ② (*marionette*) kkok-duk-gak-si 꼭둑각시 ; kŏe-roe 괴뢰.

puppy *n.* (*young dog*) kang-a-ji 강아지. 「ip 구입.

purchase *v.* sa-da 사다, ku-ip-ha-da 구입하다. —*n.* ku-

pure *adj.* sun-su-han 순수한, sun-gyŏl-han 순결한.

purely *adv.* sun-su-ha-ge 순수하게.

purge *v.* ① (*cleanse*) kkae-ggŭ-si ha-da 깨끗이 하다. ② (*expel*) suk-ch'ŏng-ha-da 숙청하다.

purify *v.* kkae-ggŭ-si〔mal-gge〕 ha-da 깨끗이〔맑게〕 하 다, chŏng-hwa-ha-da 정화하다.

Puritan *n.* ch'ŏng-gyo-do 청교도.

purity *n.* sun-su 순수, sun-gyŏl 순결, kyŏl-baek 결백.

purple *n.* & *adj.* cha-jut-bit(-ŭi) 자주빛(의).

purpose *n.* (*aim*) mok-jŏk 목적, (*intention*) ŭi-do 의 도 ; (*effect*) hyo-gwa 효과.

purposely *adv.* il-bu-rŏ 일부러, ko-ŭi-ro 고의로.

purr *v.* kŭ-rŭ-rŏng-gŏ-ri-da 그르렁거리다.

purse *n.* chi-gap 지갑. 「행하다.

pursue *v.* ch'u-jŏk-ha-da 추적하다 ; su-haeng-ha-da 수

pursuit *n.* ① ch'u-jŏk 추적 ; su-haeng 수행. ② (*occu-*

pus *n.* ko-rŭm 고름. 「*pation*) chik-ŏp 직업.

push *n.* mil-gi 밀기, ap-ryŏk 압력. —*v.* mil-da 밀다.

push-over *n.* a-ju swi-un il 아주 쉬운 일.

puss *n.* ① (*cat*) ko-yang-i 고양이. ② so-nyŏ 소녀.

pussyfoot *v.* sal-gŭm-sal-gŭm kŏt-da 살금살금 걷다.

put *v.* ① (*place*) nŏ-t'a 놓다. ② (*cause*) …si-k'i-da …시키다. ③ (*express*) p'yo-hyŏn-ha-da 표현하다. ④ (*entrust*) mat-gi-da 맡기다.

puzzle *n.* su-su-gge-ggi 수수께끼, k'wi-jŭ 퀴즈. —*v.* tang-hwang-ha-da 당황하다.

pyramid *n.* kŭm-ja-t'ap 금자탑 ; p'i-ra-mit 피라밋.

—◄ **Q** ►—

quack *n.* tol-p'a-ri ŭi-sa 돌팔이 의사 ; (*imposter*) sa-git-gun 사깃군.

quadrangle *n.* sa-gak-hyŏng 사각형, sa-byŏn-hyŏng 사변형.

quadruped *n.* ne-bal chim-sŭng 네발 짐승.

quail *n.* me-ch'u-ra-gi 메추라기.

quaint *adj.* ki-myo-han 기묘한, chin-gi-han 진기한.

quake *v.* hŭn-dŭl-ri-da 흔들리다 ; ttŏl-da 떨다.

Quaker *n.* k'we-i-k'ŏ kyo-do 퀘이커 교도.

qualification *n.* ① cha-gyŏk 자격 : *a medical* ∼ ŭi-sa myŏn-hŏ-jang 의사 면허장. ② (*adaptation*) chŏk-ŭng 적응. ③ (*faculty*) nŭng-ryŏk 능력.

qualify *v.* ① cha-gyŏk-ŭl chu-da 자격을 주다. ② (*gram.*) (*modify*) su-sik-ha-da 수식하다.

quality *n.* p'um-jil 품질, t'ŭk-sŏng 특성.

quantity *n.* (*amount*) yang 양(量), (*numbers*) su-ryang 수량, (*pl.*) ta-su 다수, ta-ryang 다량.

quarantine *n.* (*medical inspection*) kŏm-yŏk 검역.

quarrel *n.* & *v.* mal-da-t'um(-ha-da) 말다툼(하다).

quarrelsome *adj.* si-bi〔ta-t'u-gi〕-rŭl cho-a-ha-nŭn 시비〔다투기〕를 좋아하는, si-bi-jo-ŭi 시비조의.

quarry *v.* tol-ŭl ttŏ-nae-da 돌을 떠내다. —*n.* ① ch'ae-sŏk-jang 채석장. ② (*source*) ch'ul-ch'ŏ 출처.

quarter *n.* ① (1/4) sa-bun-ŭi il 4분의 1. ② (*district*) chi-bang 지방. ③ (*lodge*) suk-so 숙소.

quarterly *n.* kye-gan chap-ji 계간 잡지.

quartz *n.* sŏk-yŏng 석영(石英).

quay *n.* pu-du 부두, pang-p'a-je 방파제.

queen *n.* yŏ-wang 여왕, wang-bi 왕비 : *a* ∼ *of beauty* mi-ŭi yŏ-wang 미의 여왕.

queer *adj*. i-sang-han 이상한, myo-han 묘한.
quest *n*. t'am-saek 탐색, t'am-gu 탐구.
question *n*. ① chil-mun 질문, ŭi-mun 의문. ② (*prob-lem*) non-jŏm 논점. —*v*. chil-mun-ha-da 질문하다.
question mark mu-rŭm-p'yo 물음표(?).
question(n)aire *n*. chil-mun-sŏ 질문서.
queue *n*. (*pigtail*) pyŏn-bal 변발 ; (*waiting line*) haeng-ryŏl 행렬. —*v*. yŏl-ŭl chit-da 열을 짓다.
quick *adj*. ppa-rŭn 빠른, min-gam-han 민감한.
quicken *v*. ppal-ra-ji-da 빨라지다 ; sal-ri-da 살리다.
quick-eyed *adj*. nun-ch'i-bba-rŭn 눈치빠른.
quickly *adv*. ppal-ri 빨리, sin-sok-hi 신속히.
quicksilver *n*. (*mercury*) su-ŭn 수은.
quiet *adj*. (*still*) ko-yo-han 고요한, (*gentle*) on-hwa-han 온화한, (*peaceful*) p'yŏng-hwa-sŭ-rŏn 평화스런. —*n*. ko-yo 고요, p'yŏng-on 평온.
quilt *n*. i-bul 이불, nu-bi i-bul 누비 이불.
quinine *n*. kŭm-gye-rap 금계랍, k'i-ni-ne 키니네.
quit *v*. kŭ-man-du-da 그만두다, ttŏ-na-da 떠나다.
quite *adv*. a-ju 아주, chŏn-hyŏ 전혀.   「da 떨다.
quiver *n*. hwa-sal-t'ong 화살통. —*v*. (*tremble*) ttŏl-
quota *n*. mok 몫, mo-ga-ch'i 모가치, hal-dang-ryang 할당량.
quotation *n*. ① in-yong 인용(引用). ② (*current price*) si-se 시세, si-ga 시가(時價).
quote *v*. in-yong-ha-da 인용하다.

—✠ **R** ✠—

rabbit *n*. chip-t'o-ggi 집토끼, t'o-ggi 토끼.
race *n*. ① (*contest*) kyŏng-ju 경주. ② (*the human*) in-jong 인종. —*v*. kyŏng-ju-ha-da 경주하다.

racial *adj.* in-jong-ŭi 인종의, chong-jok-ŭi 종족의.
rack *n.* kŭ-mul si-rŏng 그물 시렁, sŏn-ban 선반 : *a hat* ∼ mo-ja-gŏ-ri 모자걸이.
racket *n.* ① ra-k'et 라켓. ② (*din*) so-dong 소동.
radar *n.* chŏn-p'a t'am-ji-gi 전파 탐지기, re-i-da-a 레이다아 : ∼ *fence* re-i-da-a-mang 레이다아망(網).
radiant *adj.* pit-na-nŭn 빛나는 ; (*phys.*) pang-sa-ha-nŭn 방사(放射)하는 : ∼ *heat* pang-sa-yŏl 방사열.
radiate *v.* (*send forth*)pang-sa-ha-da 방사(放射)하다 ; (*emit*) pal-san-ha-da 발산하다.
radiator *n.* ra-di-e-i-t'ŏ 라디에이터, pang-yŏl-gi 방열기.
radical *adj.* (*fundamental*) kŭn-bon-jŏk-in 근본적인 ; (*extreme*) kŭp-jin-jŏk-in 급진적인.
radio *n.* ra-di-o 라디오 ; mu-sŏn-jŏn-sin 무선전신.
radioactivity *n.* pang-sa-nŭng 방사능.
radish *n.* mu-u 무우 : *red* ∼ hong-dang-mu 홍당무.
radium *n.* ra-di-um 라디움. 「범위.
radius *n.* pan-ji-rŭm 반지름, pan-gyŏng 반경, pŏm-wi
raft *n.* ① ttet-mok 뗏목. ② (*abundance*) ta-ryang 다
rafter *n.* sŏ-gga-rae 서까래. 「량.
rag *n.* nŏng-ma 넝마, nu-dŏ-gi 누더기.
rage *n.* kyŏk-bun 격분 ; (*enthusiasm*) yŏ-rŭi 열의. —*v.* sa-nap-ge nal-ddwi-da 사납게 날뛰다 ; (*scold*) ya-dan-ch'i-da 야단치다.
ragged *adj.* nu-dŏ-gi-rŭl ip-ŭn 누더기를 입은 ; hŏp-su-ruk-han 헙수룩한, t'ŏp-su-ruk-han 텁수룩한.
raid *n.* & *v.* sŭp-gyŏk(-ha-da) 습격(하다) ; (*search*) su-saek(-ha-da) 수색(하다). 「gan 난간.
rail *n.* ① sŏl-lo 선로, re-il 레일. ② (*handrail*) nan-
railing *n.* ① nan-gan 난간. ② (*jeers*) cho-rong 조롱.
railroad *n.* ch'ŏl-do 철도, ch'ŏl-ro 철로.
rain *n.* pi 비 : *a drizzling* ∼ ka-rang-bi 가랑비/*a fine*

~ i-sŭl-bi 이슬비. —*v.* pi-ga o-da 비가 오다.

rainbow *n.* mu-ji-gae 무지개.

raincoat *n.* pi-ot 비옷, re-in-k'o-u-t'ŭ 레인코우트.

raindrop *n.* pit-bang-ul 빗방울, nak-su-mul 낙수물.

rainfall *n.* kang-u 강우, kang-u-ryang 강우량. 「방수용.

rainproof *adj.* pi-rŭl mak-nŭn 비를 막는, pang-su-yong

rainstorm *n.* pi-ba-ram 비바람, p'ok-p'ung-u 폭풍우.

rainy *adj.* pi-ga o-nŭn 비가 오는 : *a* ~ *day* pi-o-nŭn nal 비오는 날, u-ch'ŏn 우천. 「*up*) ki-rŭ-da 기르다.

raise *v.* ① i-rŭ-k'i-da 일으키다, ol-ri-da 올리다. ② (*bring*

raisin *n.* kŏn-p'o-do 건포도.

rake *n.* (*implement*) kal-k'wi 갈퀴, soe-sŭ-rang 쇠스랑.

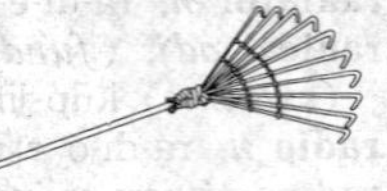

[kal-k'wi]

rally *v.* ta-si mo-ŭ-da 다시 모으다. —*n.* (*mass meeting*) kun-jung tae-hoe 군중 대회.

ram *n.* su-yang 수양. —*v.* pu-dit-ch'i-da 부딪치다.

ramble *v.* ① kŏ-nil-da 거닐다. ② (*digress*) yŏ-dam-ha-da 여담하다. —*n.* san-ch'aek 산책, so-yo 소요.

ramp *n.* pi-t'al-gil 비탈길. 「pang-ŏ-ha-da 방어하다.

rampart *n.* (*bulwark*) sŏng-byŏk 성벽. —*v.* (*defend*)

ranch *n.* nong-jang 농장, mok-jang 목장.

random *adj.* tak-ch'i-nŭn-dae-ro-ŭi 닥치는대로의. —*n.* *at* ~ toe-nŭn-dae-ro 되는대로.

range *n.* ① (*scope*) pŏm-wi 범위. ② (*mount.*) san-maek 산맥. ③ (*distance*) kŏ-ri 거리.

rank *n.* ① (*row*) yŏl 열. ② (*station*) chi-wi 지위.

ransack *v.* sat-sa-ch'i twi-ji-da 샅샅이 뒤지다 ; (*plunder*) yak-t'al-ha-da 약탈하다.

ransom *n.* mom-gap 몸값. —*v.* mom-gap-sŭl ch'i-rŭ-go toe-ch'at-da 몸값을 치르고 되찾다.

rap *v.* (*tap*) ttok-ddok tu-dŭ-ri-da 똑똑 두드리다.

rape *v.* (*violate*) kang-gan-ha-da 강간하다. ;(*plunder*)
yak-t'al-ha-da 약탈하다.

rapid *adj.* (*quick*) ppa-rŭn 빠른 ; (*steep*) ka-p'a-rŭn
가파른 : *a* ~ *slope* ka-p'a-rŭn pi-t'al 가파른 비탈. —*n.*
(*swift current*) yŏ-ul 여울.　　　　　　　　　　　「하게.

rapidly *adv.* chae-bbal-ri 재빨리, sin-sok-ha-ge 신속

rapt *adj.* nŏk-sŭl ppae-at-gin 넋을 빼앗긴.

rapture *n.* (*ecstasy*) hwan-hŭi 환희, hwang-hol 황홀.

rare *adj.* (*scarce*) tŭ-mun 드문, chin-gi-han 진기한 ;
(*thin*) hŭi-bak-han 희박한.

rare book chin-bon 진본.

rarely *adv.* chom-ch'e-ro … an-k'e 좀체로 …않게, tŭ-

rarity *n.* chin-p'um 진품(珍品).　　　　　⌊mul-ge 드물게.

rascal *n.* pul-ryang-bae 불량배, ak-han 악한.

rash *adj.* sŏng-gŭp-han 성급한, kyŏng-sol-han 경솔한.
—*n.* (*eruption*) pal-jin 발진, ppyo-ru-ji 뽀루지.

rashly *adv.* kyŏng-sol-ha-ge 경솔하게, mu-mo-ha-ge 무

raspberry *n.* na-mu-ddal-gi 나무딸기.　　　　　⌊모하게.

rasping *adj.* pak-bak kŭk-nŭn 박박 긁는.

rat *n.* chwi 쥐 : *like a drowned* ~ mul-e ppa-jin saeng-
jwi-ch'ŏ-rŏm 물에 빠진 생쥐처럼.

rate *n.* ① (*ratio*) pi-yul 비율. ② (*grade*) tŭng-gŭp
등급. ③ (*charge*) yo-gŭm 요금. —*v.* p'yŏng-ga-ha-
da 평가하다, ŏ-rim-jap-da 어림잡다.　　　　　　「매.

rather *adv.* o-hi-ryŏ 오히려, ch'a-ra-ri 차라리, kkwae

ratification *n.* pi-jun 비준(批准), chae-ga 재가.

ratify *v.* (*sanction*) pi-jun-ha-da 비준하다.

ratio *n.* (*proportion*) pi 비(比), pi-yul 비율.

ration *n.* pae-gŭp(-ryang) 배급(량), ha-ru-bun-ŭi sik-
ryang 하루분의 식량, (*provision*) yang-sik 양식.

rational *adj.* hap-ri-jŏk-in 합리적인, i-sŏng-jŏk-in 이성

rationalism *n.* hap-ri-ju-ŭi 합리주의.　　　　　⌊적인.

rat poison chwi-yak 쥐약.

rattle *v*. tŏl-gŏk-tŏl-gŏk so-ri-nae-da 덜걱덜걱 소리내다.

ravage *n*. p'a-goe 파괴, (*ruin*) hwang-p'ye 황폐. —*v*. hwang-p'ye-ha-ge ha-da 황폐하게 하다.

raven *n*. (*bird*) kal-ga-ma-gwi 갈가마귀.

ravenous *adj*. (*greedy*) ke-gŏl-sŭ-rŏ-un 게걸스러운.

ravine *n*. (*deep gully*) ki-p'ŭn kye-gok 깊은 계곡 ; (*gorge*) hyŏp-gok 협곡.

raw *adj*. nal-gŏ-sŭi 날것의, mi-suk-han 미숙한 : ~ *materials* wŏl-lyo 원료/*a* ~ *recruit* sin-byŏng 신병.

rawhide *n*. saeng-ga-juk 생가죽. 「sa-ha-da 방사하다.

ray *n*. kwang-sŏn 광선. —*v*. pal-sa-ha-da 발사하다, pang-

rayon *n*. (*artificial silk*) in-jo-gyŏn-sa 인조견사, re-i-

razor *n*. myŏn-do-k'al 면도칼. 「on 레이온.

reach *v*. to-ch'ak-ha-da 도착하다, tang-do-ha-da 당도하다 ; (*extend*) nae-bbŏt-da 내뻗다.

react *v*. pan-dong-ha-da 반동하다. 「bal 반발.

reaction *n*. pan-dong 반동, pan-jak-yong 반작용, pan-

reactionary *adj*. pan-dong-ŭi 반동의, pan-ŭng-ŭi 반응

read *v*. ik-da 읽다, tok-sŏ-ha-da 독서하다. 「의.

reader *n*. tok-ja 독자 ; (*book*) tok-bon 독본.

readily *adv*. swip-sa-ri 쉽사리 ; k'wae-hi 쾌히.

reading *n*. il-ggi 읽기, nang-dok 낭독, tok-sŏ 독서.

ready *adj*. chun-bi-ga toen 준비가 된.

ready-made *adj*. ki-sŏng-p'um-ŭi 기성품의, man-dŭ-rŏ no-ŭn 만들어 놓은.

ready money mat-don 맞돈, hyŏn-gŭm 현금.

real *adj*. ① chin-sil-ŭi 진실의 ; sil-je-ŭi 실제의. ② pu-dong-san-ŭi 부동산의 : ~ *estate* pu-dong-san 부동산.

realism *n*. sa-sil-ju-ŭi 사실주의, hyŏn-sil-ju-ŭi 현실주의.

reality *n*. hyŏn-sil-sŏng 현실성 ; chin-sil 진실.

realization *n*. sil-hyŏn 실현, hyŏn-sil-hwa 현실화.

realize *v.* sil-hyŏn-ha-da 실현하다; kkae-dat-da 깨닫다.
really *adv.* ch'am-ŭ-ro 참으로, chŏng-mal-ro 정말로.
realm *n.* yŏng-yŏk 영역 ; wang-guk 왕국.
reap *v.* (*cut*) pe-da 베다, su-hwak-ha-da 수확하다, kŏ-du-ŏ-dŭ-ri-da 거두어들이다: ~ *a harves t*nong-jak-mul-ŭl kŏ-du-ŏ-dŭ-ri-da 농작물을 거두어들이다.
reappear *v.* chae-hyŏn〔chae-bal〕-ha-da 재현〔재발〕하다.
rear *n.* twi 뒤. —*adj.* pae-hu-ŭi 배후의. —*v.* ① (*bring up*) ki-rŭ-da 기르다. ② (*raise*) ol-ri-da 올리다.
rearrange *v.* ta-si pa-ro-jap-da 다시 바로잡다.
reason *n.* (*cause*) i-yu 이유 ; (*rationality*) i-sŏng 이성.
reasonable *adj.* (*rational*) hap-ri-jŏk-in 합리적인, (*moderate*) al-ma-jŭn 알맞은 ; hap-dang-han 합당한.
reassure *v.* (*give courage*) an-sim-si-k'i-da 안심시키다.
rebel *n.* pan-yŏk-ja 반역자. —*v.* (*revolt*) pan-yŏk-ha-da 반역하다, pae-ban-ha-da 배반하다.
rebellion *n.* pal-lan 반란, p'ok-dong 폭동.
rebuff *n.* kŏ-jŏl 거절, t'oe-jja 퇴짜. —*v.* t'oe-jja-no-t'a 퇴짜놓다, (*check*) chŏ-ji-ha-da 저지하다.「축하다.
rebuild *v.* chae-gŏn-ha-da 재건하다, kae-ch'uk-ha-da 개
rebuke *v.* kku-jit-da 꾸짖다, ching-gye-ha-da 징계하다. —*n.* pi-nan 비난, kyŏn-ch'aek 견책.
recall *n.* & *v.* ① (*call back*) so-hwan(-ha-da) 소환(하다). ② (*recollect*) sang-gi(-ha-da) 상기(하다).
recapture *v.* t'al-hwan-ha-da 탈환하다.
recede *v.* ① mul-rŏ-na-da 물러나다, son-ŭl tte-da 손을 떼다. ② (*return*) pan-hwan-ha-da 반환하다.
receipt *n.* yŏng-su-jŭng 영수증.
receive *v.* pat-da 받다, yŏng-su-ha-da 영수하다.
receiver *n.* ① (*recipient*) su-ryŏng-in 수령인. ② (*of telephone*) su-hwa-gi 수화기.
recent *adj.* ch'oe-gŭn-ŭi 최근의, yo-jŭm-ŭi 요즘의 ;

(*new*) sae-ro-un 새로운.

reception *n.* (*welcoming*) chŏp-dae 접대 ; (*party*) hwan-yŏng-hoe 환영회, ri-sep-syŏn 리셉션.

receptivity *n.* kam-su-sŏng 감수성, i-hae-ryŏk 이해력.

recess *n.* swi-nŭn si-gan 쉬는 시간, hyu-hoe 휴회.

recipe *n.* ch'ŏ-bang 처방, cho-ri-bŏp 조리법.　　「器).

recipient *n.* ① su-ryŏng-ja 수령자. ② yong-gi 용기(容

reciprocal *adj.* (*mutual*) sang-ho-ŭi 상호의 ; (*compensatory*) po-sang-jŏk-in 보상적(補償的)인.　　　　「창회.

recital *n.* (*mus.*) tok-ju-hoe 독주회, tok-ch'ang-hoe 독

recitation *n.* nang-dok 낭독, am-song 암송.

recite *v.* oe-da 외다, nang-dok-ha-da 낭독하다, (*narrate*) i-ya-gi-ha-da 이야기하다.

reckless *adj.* mu-mo-han 무모한, pun-byŏl-ŏp-nŭn 분별 없는 : *a* ～ *fellow* tang-dol-han nom 당돌한 놈.

reckon *v.* (*count*) kye-san-ha-da 계산하다, sem-ha-da 셈하다. ch'u-jŏng-ha-da 추정하다.

reclaim *v.* ① (*bring back*) to-ro ch'at-da 도로 찾다 ; ② (*reform*) kae-sŏn-ha-da 개선하다.

recline *v.* ki-dae-da 기대다, ŭi-ji-ha-da 의지하다. 「다.

recognize *v.* a-ra-bo-da 알아보다, in-jŏng-ha-da 인정하

recoil *v.* twi-ro mul-rŏ-na-da 뒤로 물러나다 ; um-jjil-ha-da 움찔하다.　　　　　　　　「da 다시 모으다.

recollect *v.* ① hoe-sang-ha-da 회상하다. ② ta-si mo-ŭ-

recollection *n.* hoe-sang 회상, ch'u-ŏk 추억.

recommend *v.* ch'u-ch'ŏn-ha-da 추천하다, (*advise*) kwŏn-go-ha-da 권고하다.　　　　　　「ch'ŏn-sŏ 추천서.

recommendation *n.* ch'u-ch'ŏn 추천 : *letter of* ～ ch'u-

recompense *v.* po-dap-ha-da 보답하다, po-sang-ha-da 보상하다. —*n.* po-su 보수, po-sang 보상.

reconcile *v.* hwa-hae-si-k'i-da 화해시키다, chung-jae-ha-da 중재하다, (*adjust*) cho-jŏng-ha-da 조정하다.

reconnaissance *n.* chŏng-ch'al 정찰.

reconsider *v.* chae-go-ha-da 재고하다.

reconstruct *v.* chae-gŏn-ha-da 재건하다, pu-hŭng-ha-da 「부흥하다.

record *n.* ① (*written note*) ki-rok 기록. ② (*phonograph*) re-k'o-o-dŭ 레코오드, ŭm-ban 음반. ③ (*personal history*) kyŏng-ryŏk 경력. —*v.* ki-rok-ha-da 기록하다.

recount *n.* cha-se-hi mal-ha-da 자세히 말하다.

recover *v.* hoe-bok-ha-da 회복하다, toe-ch'at-da 되찾다.

recovery *n.* hoe-bok 회복 ; pok-gu 복구.

recreation *n.* ki-bun chŏn-hwan 기분 전환 ; o-rak 오락, re-k'ŭ-ri-e-i-syŏn 레크리에이션.

recruit *n.* sin-byŏng 신병(新兵). —*v.* sin-byŏng-ŭl mo-jip-ha-da 신병을 모집하다.

rectangle *n.* chik-sa-gak-hyŏng 직사각형.

rectify *v.* ko-ch'i-da 고치다, kae-jŏng-ha-da 개정하다.

rector *n.* ① (*clergyman*) kyo-gu mok-sa 교구 목사, su-do-wŏn-jang 수도원장. ② (*college*) hak-jang 학장.

recuperate *v.* hoe-bok-doe-da 회복되다, nat-da 낫다.

recur *v.* toe-do-ra-ga-da 되돌아가다 ; hoe-sang-ha-da 회상하다 ; chae-bal-ha-da 재발하다.

red *adj.* ppal-gan 빨간 : *R~ China* chung-gong 중공/ *R~ Cross* chŏk-sip-ja 적십자. —*n.* chŏk-saek 적색.

redeem *v.* toe-sa-da 되사다 ; sok-joe-ha-da 속죄하다.

redemption *n.* (*from sin*) sok-joe 속죄.

reduce *v.* chul-da 줄다, kam-so-ha-da 감소하다.

reduction *n.* ch'uk-so 축소 ; (*discount*) ha-rin 할인.

redundant *adj.* yŏ-bun-ŭi 여분의, kwa-da-han 과다한.

reed *n.* kal-dae 갈대.

reef *n.* am-ch'o 암초.

reel *n.* (*spool*) ŏl-re 얼레, sil-gam-gae 실감개. —*v.* kam-da 감다.

[ŏl-re]

re-elect *v.* chae-sŏn-ha-da 재선하다. 「da 재건하다.
re-establish *v.* pu-hŭng-ha-da 부흥하다, chae-gŏn-ha-
re-examine *v.* chae-gŏm-t'o-ha-da 재검토하다.
refectory *n.* sik-dang 식당 ; ta-sil 다실.
refer *v.* ① cho-hoe-ha-da 조회하다. ② (*attribute*) …e
  tol-ri-da …에 돌리다. ③ ch'am-jo-ha-da 참조하다.
referee *n.* sim-p'an 심판, re-p'ŏ-ri 레퍼리.
reference *n.* ch'am-go 참고 ; (*inquiry*) cho-hoe 조회 ;
  (*testimonial*) chŭng-myŏng-sŏ 증명서.
referendum *n.* kuk-min t'u-p'yo 국민 투표.
refine *v.* ① se-ryŏn-ha-da 세련하다. ② (*purify*) chŏng-
  je-ha-da 정제하다, mal-gge-ha-da 맑게하다.
refined *adj.* se-ryŏn-doen 세련된, chŏng-je-doen 정제된.
refinement *n.* se-ryŏn 세련 ; ki-p'um ; 기품 ; u-a 우아.
reflect *v.* pan-sa-ha-da 반사하다 ; pi-ch'u-da 비추다.
reflection *n.* pan-sa 반사, pan-yŏng 반영 ; pan-sŏng
  반성. 「—*n.* kae-ryang 개량.
reform *v.* kae-hyŏk〔kae-ryang〕-ha-da 개혁〔개량〕하다.
reformation *n.* kae-hyŏk 개혁, kae-sŏn 개선. 「화원.
reformatory *n.* so-nyŏn-wŏn 소년원, kam-hwa-wŏn 감
refrain *v.* sam-ga-da 삼가다, cha-je-ha-da 자제하다.
refresh *v.* hwal-gi-ddi-ge ha-da 활기띠게 하다 ; (*renew*)
  sae-rop-ge ha-da 새롭게 하다.
refreshment *n.* ① wŏn-gi-hoe-bok 원기회복 ; hyu-yang
  휴양. ② (*pl.*) (*light meal*) ŭm-sik-mul 음식물.
refrigerate *v.* naeng-gak-si-k'i-da 냉각시키다, naeng-
  dong〔naeng-jang〕-ha-da 냉동〔냉장〕하다.
refrigerator *n.* naeng-jang-go 냉장고.
refuge *n.* p'i-nan-ch'ŏ 피난처, tae-p'i-so 대피소.
refugee *n.* ① p'i-nan-min 피난민. ② mang-myŏng-ja
refusal *n.* kŏ-jŏl 거절, sa-t'oe 사퇴. 「망명자.
refuse *v.* kŏ-jŏl-ha-da 거절하다, kŏ-bu-ha-da 거부하다.

—*n.* (*rubbish*) ssŭ-re-gi 쓰레기, p'ye-mul 폐물.
refute *v.* (*disprove*) pan-bak-ha-da 반박하다.
regain *v.* toe-ch'at-da 되찾다; (*recover*) hoe-bok-ha-da 회복하다 ; pok-gwi-ha-da 복귀하다.
regard *v.* yŏ-gi-da 여기다 ; (*respect*) chon-jung-ha-da 존중하다 ; (*heed*) chu-ŭi-ha-da 주의하다. —*n.* (*consideration*) ko-ryŏ 고려 ; chon-gyŏng 존경.
regarding *prep.* ⋯e kwan-ha-yŏ ⋯에 관하여.
regatta *n.* (*boat, etc.*) kyŏng-jo 경조.
regenerate *v.* chae-saeng-si-k'i-da 재생시키다.
regime *n.* (*system*) che-do 제도 ; (*political system*) chŏng-ch'e 정체.　　　　「gu-dan 야구단.
regiment *n.* ① (*army*) yŏn-dae 연대. ② (*Am.*) ya-
region *n.* chi-bang 지방, yŏng-yŏk 영역.
register *v.* tŭng-gi-ha-da 등기하다, tŭng-rok-ha-da 등록하다. —*n.* tŭng-gi 등기, tŭng-rok 등록.
registrar *n.* ho-jŏk-gye-won 호적계원 ; (*of school*) kyo-mu-ch'ŏ-jang 교무처장.
registration *n.* ki-jae 기재, tŭng-rok 등록.
registry office ho-jŏk tŭng-gi-so 호적 등기소.
regret *v.* yu-gam-ŭ-ro saeng-gak-ha-da 유감으로 생각하다. —*n.* (*remorse*) yu-gam 유감 ; hu-hoe 후회.
regular *adj.* kyu-ch'ik-jŏk-in 규칙적인, chŏng-gi-jŏk-in 정기적인. —*n.* (*pl.*) chŏng-gyu-byŏng 정규병.
regulate *v.* kyu-jŏng-ha-da 규정하다 ; (*moderate*) cho-jŏl-ha-da 조절하다, (*control*) tan-sok-ha-da 단속하다.
regulation *n.* kyu-ch'ik 규칙, kyu-yul 규율.
rehabilitate *v.* pok-gu-si-k'i-da 복구시키다.
rehabilitation *n.* pok-gu 복구, pu-hŭng 부흥.
rehearsal *n.* yŏn-sŭp 연습, ri-hŏ-sŏl 리허설.
rehearse *v.* yŏn-sŭp-ha-da 연습하다, si-yŏn-ha-da 시연(試演)하다 ; (*recite*) am-song-ha-da 암송하다.

reign *n*. t'ong-ch'i 통치. —*v*. t'ong-ch'i-ha-da 통치하다.
rein *n*. ko-bbi 고삐 ; (*pl*.) kyŏn-je 견제.
reindeer *n*. sul-lok 순록(馴鹿), mal-sa-sŭm 말사슴.
reinforce *v*. po-gang-ha-da 보강하다.
reiterate *n*. pan-bok-ha-da 반복하다.
reject *v*. kŏ-jŏl-ha-da 거절하다, kŏ-bu-ha-da 거부하다 ; (*refuse to grant*) kak-ha-ha-da 각하하다.
rejection *n*. kŏ-jŏl 거절, pu-gyŏl 부결, ki-gak 기각.
rejoice *v*. ki-bbŏ-ha-da 기뻐하다.
relapse *v*. ① toe-do-ra-ga-da 되돌아가다. ② t'a-rak-ha-da 타락하다. —*n*. chae-bal 재발 ; t'a-rak 타락.
relate *v*. ① chin-sul-ha-da 진술하다, i-ya-gi-ha-da 이야기하다. ② (*connect*) kwal-lyŏn-si-k'i-da 관련시키다.
relation *n*. ① (*connection*) kwan-gye 관계. ② (*kinsman*) ch'in-ch'ŏk 친척. ③ chin-sul 진술.
relationship *n*. (ch'in-ch'ŏk) kwan-gye (친척) 관계.
relative *n*. ch'in-ch'ŏk 친척 ; (*gram*.) kwan-gye-sa 관계사. —*adj*. (*comparative*) sang-dae-jŏk-in 상대적인.
relax *v*. (*loosen*) nŭt-ch'u-da 늦추다. 「중계.
relay *v*. chung-gye-ha-da 중계하다. —*n*. chung-gye
release *v*. p'u-rŏ-no-t'a 풀어놓다, sŏk-bang-ha-da 석방하다 ; (*remit*) myŏn-je-ha-da 면제하다. 「지다.
relent *v*. sun-hae-ji-da 순해지다. nu-gŭ-rŏ-ji-da 누그러
relevant *adj*. chŏk-jŏl-han 적절한. 「han 확실한.
reliable *adj*. mit-ŭl su it-nŭn 믿을 수 있는 ; hwak-sil-
relic *n*. yu-mul 유물, yu-jŏk 유적 ; (*pl*.) yu-gol 유골.
relief *n*. ① ku-je 구제. ② (*removal*) che-gŏ 제거. ③ (*comfort*) wi-an 위안. ④ yang-gak 양각(陽刻).
relieve *v*. ku-je-ha-da 구제하다 ; (*make less*) tŏ-rŏ-ju-da 덜어주다 ; p'yŏn-an-ha-ge ha-da 편안하게 하다.
religion *n*. chong-gyo 종교. 「ki-p'ŭn 신앙심이 깊은.
religious *adj*. chong-gyo-jŏk-in 종교적인 ; sin-ang-sim-i

relinquish *v*. (*give up*) p'o-gi-ha-da 포기하다, pŏ-ri-da 버리다 : (*loosen*) no-t'a 놓다.
relish *n*. (*taste*) mat 맛, (*flavor*) p'ung-mi 풍미 ; (*liking*) ki-ho 기호, —*v*. mat-bo-da 맛보다, (*enjoy*) chŭl-gi-da 즐기다.
reluctant *adj*. (*unwilling*) si-rŏ-ha-nŭn 싫어하는.
rely *v*. ŭi-ji-ha-da 의지하다. mit-da 믿다.
remain *v*. mŏ-mu-rŭ-da 머무르다 ; nam-da 남다.
remainder *n*. ① na-mŏ-ji 나머지. ② chal-lyu-ja 잔류자. ③ (*relics*) yu-jŏk 유적.
remand home im-si su-yong-so 임시 수용소.
remark *v*. ① chu-mok-ha-da 주목하다. ② (*speak*) mal-ha-da 말하다. —*n*. pa-rŏn 발언 ; pi-p'yŏng 비평.
remarkable *adj*. hyŏn-jŏ-han 현저한. 「재혼.
remarry *v*. chae-hon-ha-da 재혼하다. —*n*. chae-hon
remedy *n*. (*med*.) ŭi-yak 의약 ; (*cure*) yo-bŏp 요법. —*v*. ko-ch'i-da 고치다. 「da 상기하다.
remember *v*. (*recall*) ki-ŏk-ha-da 기억하다, sang-gi-ha-
remembrance *n*. (*memory*) ki-ŏk 기억 ; (*souvenir*) ki-nyŏm-p'um 기념품. 「u-ch'i-da 깨우치다.
remind *v*. saeng-gak-na-ge ha-da 생각나게 하다, kkae-
reminiscence *n*. hoe-sang 회상, (*pl*.) hoe-go-dam 회고담.
remission *n*. yong-sŏ 용서, sa-myŏn 사면.
remit *v*. ① (*send*) song-gŭm-ha-da 송금하다. ② (*abate*) wan-hwa-ha-da 완화하다. ③ (*pardon*) yong-sŏ-ha-da 용서하다. 「*ic* ~ chŏn-sin-hwan 전신환.
remittance *n*. (*of money*) song-gŭm 송금 : *telegraph-*
remnant *n*. na-mŏ-ji 나머지 ; (*relic*) yu-mul 유물.
remonstrate *v*. ch'ung-go-ha-da 충고하다, kan-ha-da 간(諫)하다 ; (*protest*) hang-ŭi-ha-da 항의하다.
remorse *n*. hu-hoe 후회, nwi-u-ch'im 뉘우침.
remote *adj*. (*distant*) mŏn 먼, mŏn-go-sŭi 먼곳의.

removal *n.* (*transfer*) i-dong 이동, i-sa 이사 ; (*dismissal*) hae-im 해임, che-gŏ 제거.
remove *v.* om-gi-da 옮기다 ; ch'i-u-da 치우다.
Renaissance *n.* mun-ye-bu-hŭng 문예부흥.
render *v.* ① (*give back*) tol-ryŏ-ju-da 돌려주다. ② (*make*) ···toe-ge ha-da ···되게 하다. ③ (*submit*) che-ch'ul-ha-da 제출하다. ④ pŏn-yŏk-ha-da 번역하다.
rendezvous *n.* rang-de-bu 랑데부 ; hoe-hap chang-so 회합 장소 ; mil-hoe chang-so 밀회 장소.
renew *v.* sae-rop-ge ha-da 새롭게 하다 ; hoe-bok-ha-da 회복하다, pok-gu-si-k'i-da 복구시키다.
renounce *v.* p'o-gi-ha-da 포기하다 ; pu-in-ha-da 부인하다.
renown *n.* myŏng-sŏng 명성, yu-myŏng 유명.
rent *n.* ① (*house*) chip-se 집세 ; (*land*) chi-dae 지대 (地代) ; im-dae-ryo 임대료. ② (*gap*) kal-ra-jin t'ŭm 갈라진 틈. —*v.* (*to somebody*) pil-ryŏ-ju-da 빌려주다, (*from somebody*) pil-ri-da 빌리다.
reorganize *v.* chae-p'yŏn-sŏng-ha-da 재편성하다.
repair *v.* (*mend*) su-sŏn-ha-da 수선하다, kyo-jŏng-ha-da 교정하다 ; (*restore*) hoe-bok-ha-da 회복하다.
reparation *n.* pae-sang 배상, (*pl.*) pae-sang-gŭm 배상금.
repast *n.* (*meal*) sik-sa 식사.
repatriate *v.* pon-guk-ŭ-ro song-hwan-ha-da 본국으로 송환하다. —*n.* kwi-hwan tong-p'o 귀환 동포.
repay *v.* kap-da 갚다, po-dap-ha-da 보답하다.
repeal *n.* (*annul*) p'ye-ji-ha-da 폐지하다, ch'wi-so-ha-da 취소하다. —*n.* p'ye-ji 폐지, ch'wi-so 취소.
repeat *n. & v.* toe-p'u-ri(-ha-da) 되풀이(하다).
repel *v.* kyŏk-t'oe-ha-da 격퇴하다.
repent *v.* (*regret*) nwi-u-ch'i-da 뉘우치다, hu-hoe-ha-da 후회하다.
repetition *n.* toe-p'u-ri 되풀이, pan-bok 반복.
replace *v.* che-ja-ri-e kat-da tu-da 제자리에 갖다 두다 ;

(*repay*) tol-ryŏ-ju-da 돌려주다.
replacement *n.* kyo-dae 교대 ; (*substitute*) tae-ch'i 대치, kyo-ch'e-ja〔mul〕 교체자〔물〕.
replay *n.* & *v.* chae-si-hap(-ha-da) 재시합(하다).
replenish *n.* po-ch'ung-ha-da 보충하다.
reply *n.* & *v.* tae-dap(-ha-da) 대답(하다).
report *n.* & *v.* po-go(-ha-da) 보고(하다).
report card sŏng-jŏk-p'yo 성적표, t'ong-sin-bu 통신부.
reporter *n.* po-go-ja 보고자 ; (*jour.*) ki-ja 기자.
repose *v.* ① hyu-sik-ha-da 휴식하다 ; cha-da 자다. ② (*re-ly*) ŭi-ji-ha-da 의지하다. —*n.* hyu-sik 휴식 ; cham 잠.
reprehend *v.* kku-jit-da 꾸짖다, pi-nan-ha-da 비난하다.
represent *v.* ① sŏl-myŏng-ha-da 설명하다, myo-sa-ha-da 묘사하다. ② (*stand for*) tae-p'yo-ha-da 대표하다.
representative *n.* tae-p'yo-ja 대표자, tae-ri-in 대리인.
repress *v.* ŏk-nu-rŭ-da 억누르다, chin-ap-ha-da 진압하다.
reprieve *n.* chip-haeng-yu-ye 집행유예.
reprimand *v.* (*censure*) ching-gye-ha-da 징계하다.
reprint *n.* & *v.* chae-p'an(-ha-da) 재판(再版)(하다).
reproach *v.* kku-jit-da 꾸짖다, pi-nan-ha-da 비난하다.
reproduce *v.* pok-sa-ha-da 복사하다, chae-saeng-ha-da 재생하다. 「pok-je 복제.
reproduction *n.* chae-saeng 재생, chae-hyŏn 재현 ;
reproof *n.* (*censure*) kyŏn-ch'aek 견책.
reprove *v.* pi-nan-ha-da 비난하다 ; kku-jit-da 꾸짖다.
reptile *n.* (*crawling animal*) p'a-ch'ung-ryu 파충류.
republic *n.* kong-hwa-guk 공화국. 「da 거부하다.
repudiate *v.* in-yŏn-ŭl kkŭn-t'a 인연을 끊다 ; kŏ-bu-ha-
repulse *v.* ① kyŏk-t'oe-ha-da 격퇴하다, mul-ri-ch'i-da 물리치다. ② (*refute*) non-bak-ha-da 논박하다.
reputation *n.* p'yŏng-p'an 평판, myŏng-sŏng 명성.
request *n.* yo-mang 요망, yo-gu 요구. —*v.* kan-ch'ŏng-

ha-da 간청하다, yo-gu-ha-da 요구하다.
require *v.* p'i-ryo-ro ha-da 필요로 하다 ; yo-gu-ha-da 요
구하다. 「p'il-su-p'um 필수품.
requisite *adj.* p'i-ryo-han 필요한, p'il-su-ŭi 필수의. —*n.*
requite *v.* ① (*reward*) po-dap-ha-da 보답하다. ②
(*avenge*) po-bok-ha-da 보복하다. 「다.
rescue *v.* ku-ch'ul-ha-da 구출하다, ku-jo-ha-da 구조하
research *n.* (*investigation*) cho-sa-yŏn-gu 조사연구.
—*v.* cho-sa-yŏn-gu-ha-da 조사연구하다.
resemblance *n.* yu-sa(-jŏm) 유사(점), tal-mŭm 닮음.
resemble *v.* pi-sŭt-ha-da 비슷하다, tam-da 닮다.
resent *v.* pun-gae-ha-da 분개하다, wŏn-mang-ha-da 원
망하다. 「ryu 보류.
reservation *n.* (*of hotel room, etc.*) ye-yak 예약 ; po-
reserve *v.* (*keep*) po-jon-ha-da 보존하다 ; (*retain*) po-
ryu-ha-da 보류하다 ; ye-yak-ha-da 예약하다.
residence *n.* chu-t'aek 주택 ; chu-so 주소.
resident *n.* ① kŏ-ju-ja 거주자. ② kŏ-ryu-min 거류민.
resign *v.* ① tan-nyŏm-ha-da 단념하다. ② sa-jik-ha-da 사
resignation *n.* sa-jik 사직, sa-p'yo 사표. 「직하다.
resist *v.* chŏ-hang-ha-da 저항하다, (*repel*) mul-ri-ch'i-
da 물리치다 ; (*withstand*) kyŏn-di-da 견디다.
resistance *n.* chŏ-hang 저항, hang-jaeng 항쟁.
resolute *adj.* tan-ho-han 단호한, hwak-go-han 확고한.
resolution *n.* kyŏ-rŭi 결의, kyŏl-sim 결심.
resolve *v.* ① (*decide*) kyŏl-sim-ha-da 결심하다. ②
(*solve*) hae-gyŏl-ha-da 해결하다.
resort *n.* yu-hŭng-ji 유흥지 ; hyu-yang-ji 휴양지. —*v.*
cha-ju ta-ni-da 자주 다니다.
resound *v.* (*echo*) ul-ri-da 울리다.
resource *n.* ① cha-wŏn 자원(資源) ; cha-gŭm 자금. ②
(*means*) su-dan 수단, pang-p'yŏn 방편.

respect *v.* ① chon-gyŏng-ha-da 존경하다. ② (*regard*) ko-ryŏ-ha-da 고려하다. —*n.* chon-jung 존중.

respectable *adj.* chon-gyŏng-hal man-han 존경할 만한.

respectful *adj.* (*polite*) kong-son-han 공손한, chŏng-jung-han 정중한.　　　　　　　「ro 따로따로.

respectively *adj.* kak-gak 각각, kak-ja 각자 ; tta-ro-dda-

respiration *n.* ho-hŭp 호흡, sum 숨 : *artificial* ～ in-gong-ho-hŭp 인공호흡.

respire *v.* sum-swi-da 숨쉬다, ho-hŭp-ha-da 호흡하다.

respite *n.* & *v.* yu-ye(-ha-da) 유예(하다).

respond *v.* tae-dap-ha-da 대답하다, ŭng-ha-da 응하다.

respondent *n.* (*defendant*) p'i-go 피고. —*adj.* tae-dap-ha-nŭn 대답하는, ŭng-dap-ha-nŭn 응답하는.

response *n.* ŭng-dap 응답 ; (*reaction*) pan-ŭng 반응.

responsibility *n.* ch'aek-im 책임 ; chik-ch'aek 직책.

responsible *adj.* ch'aek-im-it-nŭn 책임있는.

rest *v.* swi-da 쉬다 ; ki-dae-da 기대다. —*n.* ① (*repose*) hyu-sik 휴식. ② (*remainder*) na-mŏ-ji 나머지.

restaurant *n.* yo-jŏng 요정 ; ŭm-sik-jŏm 음식점, re-sŭ-t'o-rang 레스토랑.　　　　　　　「한.

restless *adj.* tŭl-ddŏ-it-nŭn 들떠있는, pu-ran-han 불안

restoration *n.* hoe-bok 회복 ; su-bok 수복.　　「복하다.

restore *v.* hoe-bok-si-k'i-da 회복시키다 ; su-bok-ha-da 수

restrain *v.* ① (*hold back*) ŏk-je-ha-da 억제하다. ② (*check*) kŭm-ji-ha-da 금지하다.　　　　　「하다.

restrict *v.* che-han-ha-da 제한하다 ; sok-bak-ha-da 속박

result *n.* kyŏl-gwa 결과, sŏng-jŏk 성적. —*v.* (*follow*) kyŏl-gwa-ro i-rŏ-na-da 결과로 일어나다.

resume *v.* ① (*begin again*) chae-gae-ha-da 재개하다. ② (*reoccupy*) ta-si ch'a-ji-ha-da 다시 차지하다.

resumption *n.* chae-gae 재개, hoe-bok 회복.

resurrection *n.* pu-hwal 부활, chae-saeng 재생.

retail *n.* & *v.* so-mae(-ha-da) 소매(하다).
retain *v.* ① po-ryu-ha-da 보류하다, po-yu-ha-da 보유하다. ② (*keep in mind*) ki-ŏk-ha-da 기억하다.
retaliate *v.* po-bok-ha-da 보복하다.   「방해하다.
retard *v.* (*delay*) nŭt-ch'u-da 늦추다 ; pang-hae-ha-da
reticent *adj.* mal-i ŏp-nŭn 말이 없는.
retire *v.* mul-rŏ-ga-da 물러가다, t'oe-gŏ-ha-da 퇴거하다 ; (*from office*) t'oe-jik-ha-da 퇴직하다.
retirement *n.* t'oe-gŏ 퇴거 ; (*seclusion*) ŭn-t'oe 은퇴.
retort *v.* mal-dae-ggu-ha-da 말대꾸하다. —*n.* pan-bak
retouch *n.* & *v.* su-jŏng(-ha-da) 수정(하다).   「반박.
retrace *v.* toe-do-ra-ga-da 되돌아가다, hoe-go-ha-da 회고하다.   「*draw*) um-ch'ŭ-ri-da 움츠리다.
retract *v.* ① (*recant*) ch'wi-so-ha-da 취소하다. ② (*with-*
retreat *n.* & *v.* hu-t'oe(-ha-da) 후퇴(하다).
retrieve *v.* (*recover*) hoe-bok-ha-da 회복하다.
retroactive *adj.* so-gŭp-ha-nŭn 소급하는 ; pan-jak-yong-ha-nŭn 반작용하는.   「상.
retrospect *v.* hoe-go-ha-da 회고하다. —*n.* hoe-sang 회
return *v.* to-ra-o-da 돌아오다 ; pan-hwan-ha-da 반환하다. —*n.* ① pok-gwi 복귀. ② (*profit*) su-ik 수익.
reunion *n.* chae-hoe 재회(再會), yung-hwa 융화.
reunite *v.* ta-si kyŏl-hap-si-k'i-da 다시 결합시키다 ; hwa-hae-si-k'i-da 화해시키다.   「ro-ha-da 폭로하다.
reveal *v.* na-t'a-nae-da 나타내다, po-i-da 보이다 ; p'ok-
revel *v.* ma-si-go hŭng-ch'ŏng-gŏ-ri-da 마시고 흥청거리다, chŭl-gŏ-wŏ-ha-da 즐거워하다. —*n.* (*carousal*) sul-jan-ch'i 술잔치.   「p'ok-ro 폭로.
revelation *n.* ① (*of God*) kye-si 계시. ② (*disclosure*)
revenge *n.* & *v.* pok-su(-ha-da) 복수(하다).
revenue *n.* (*annual income*) se-ip 세입 ; (*income*) su-ip 수입 : ~ *stamp* su-ip-in-ji 수입인지.

revere *v.* sung-bae-ha-da 숭배하다.

reverence *n.* chon-gyŏng 존경, sung-bae 숭배.

reverend *adj.* chong-gyŏng-hal man-han 존경할 만한.

reverie·revery *n.* (*deep musing*) myŏng-sang 명상 ; (*daydream*) paek-il-mong 백일몽, hwan-sang 환상.

reverse *v.* kŏ-ggu-ro ha-da 거꾸로 하다, yŏk-dong-si-k'i-da 역동시키다. —*n.* yŏk 역(逆), pan-dae 반대.

revert *v.* (*return*) toe-do-ra-ga-da 되돌아가다.

review *v.* ① (*book*) p'yŏng-ron-ha-da 평론하다. ② (*lessons*) pok-sŭp-ha-da 복습하다. ③ (*troops*) yŏl-byŏng-ha-da 열병하다. —*n.* pok-sŭp 복습.

revile *v.* yok-ha-da 욕하다, yok-sŏl-ha-da 욕설하다.

revise *v.* kyo-jŏng-ha-da 교정하다.

revision *n.* kyo-jŏng 교정 ; (*book*) kae-jŏng-p'an 개정판.

revival *n.* pu-hwal 부활, chae-saeng 재생.

revive *v.* so-saeng-ha-da 소생하다, pu-hwal-ha-da 부활하다 ; pu-hŭng-ha-da 부흥하다.   「pal-lan 반란.

revolt *v.* pan-yŏk-ha-da 반역하다. —*n.* (*rebellion*)

revolution *n.* hyŏk-myŏng 혁명, hoe-jŏn 회전 : *the Industrial R~* san-ŏp hyŏk-myŏng 산업 혁명.

revolve *v.* tol-da 돌다, hoe-jŏn-ha-da 회전하다.

revolver *n.* yŏn-bal kwŏn-ch'ong 연발 권총.

reward *n.* ① po-su 보수, sang 상(賞). ② hyŏn-sang-gŭm 현상금. —*v.* po-su-rŭl chu-da 보수를 주다.

rewrite *v.* ta-si ssŭ-da 다시 쓰다, ko-ch'yŏ ssŭ-da 고

rheumatism *n.* ryu-mŏ-t'i-jŭm 류머티즘.   「쳐 쓰다.

rhythm *n.* yul-dong 율동, ŭm-yul 음율, ri-dŭm 리듬.

rib *n.* kal-bit-dae 갈빗대, nŭk-gol 늑골.

ribbon *n.* ri-bŏn 리번, tti 띠.

rice *n.* ssal 쌀, (*cooked*) pap 밥, (*cooked, polite form*) chin-ji 진지 ; (*unshelled*) pyŏ 벼.

rich *adj.* ton-man-ŭn 돈많은 ; p'ung-bu-han 풍부한 ;

(*color*) chi-t'ŭn 짙은.
riches *n.* chae-san 재산, chae-mul 재물, pu 부(富).
rick *n.* (*stack*) chip-ga-ri 짚가리.　　　　「곱사등.
rickets *n.* ku-ru-byŏng 구루병(佝僂病), kop-sa-dŭng
rid *v.* (*free*) myŏn-ha-ge ha-da 면하게 하다, che-gŏ-
　ha-da 제거하다 : *get* ~ *of* pŏ-sŏ-na-da 벗어나다.
riddle *n.* su-su-gge-ggi 수수께끼, nan-mun 난문.
ride *v.* t'a-da 타다. —*n.* sŭng-ch'a 승차 ; sŭng-ma 승마.
ridge *n.* (*of mountain*) san-ma-ru 산마루, san-dŭng-
　sŏng-i 산등성이 ; (*of roof*) yong-ma-ru 용마루.
ridicule *n.* cho-rong 조롱. —*v.* cho-rong-ha-da 조롱하다.
ridiculous *adj.* u-sŭ-ggwang-sŭ-rŏ-un 우스꽝스러운.
rifle *n.* so-ch'ong 소총, ra-i-p'ŭl ch'ong 라이플 총.
rift *n.* kal-ra-jin t'ŭm 갈라진 틈. —*v.* jjo-gae-da 쪼개다.
rig *v.* chang-bi[ch'ae-bi]-ha-da 장비[채비]하다.
right *adj.* ① o-rŭn 옳은, chŏng-dang-han 정당한. ② o-
　rŭn-jjok-ŭi 오른쪽의. —*n.* kwŏl-li 권리.　　　　「게.
rightly *adv.* pa-rŭ-ge 바르게, kong-jŏng-ha-ge 공정하
right-wing *n.* u-ik 우익(右翼), po-su-p'a 보수파.
rigid *adj.* kut-ŭn 굳은, (*strict*) ŏm-gyŏk-han 엄격한.
rigo(u)r *n.* ŏm-gyŏk 엄격 ; hok-dok-ham 혹독함.
rim *n.* ka-jang-ja-ri 가장자리, t'e 테.
rind *n.* (*skin, bark, peel*) kkŏp-jil 껍질.
ring *n.* (*circle*) ko-ri 고리 ; (*finger*) pan-ji 반지 ; (*ear*)
　kwi-go-ri 귀고리. —*v.* ul-ri-da 울리다.
rink *n.* sŭ-k'e-i-t'ŭ-jang 스케이트장.
rinse *v.* heng-gu-da 헹구다, ssit-da 씻다.
riot *n.* p'ok-dong 폭동, so-dong 소동. —*v.* p'ok-dong-
　ŭl i-rŭ-k'i-da 폭동을 일으키다.
rip *v.* jjit-da 찢다. —*n.* (*rent*) jjae-jin t'ŭm 째진 틈.
ripe *adj.* ik-ŭn 익은, wŏn-suk-han 원숙한.
ripen *v.* ik-da 익다, ik'hi-da 익히다.

ripple *n.* chan-mul-gyŏl 잔물결.

rise *v.* ol-ra-ga-da 올라가다 ; i-rŏ-na-da 일어나다 ; (*sun*) ttŭ-da 뜨다. —*n.* sang-sŭng 상승, o-rŭm 오름.

risk *n.* wi-hŏm 위험. —*v.* (*venture*) nae-gŏl-da 내걸 다 : ~ *one's life* mok-sum-ŭl kŏl-da 목숨을 걸다.

rite *n.* ŭi-sik 의식 ; kwan-sŭp 관습.

rival *n.* kyŏng-jaeng-ja 경쟁자 ; chŏk-su 적수. —*v.* kyŏng-jaeng-ha-da 경쟁하다, kyŏ-ru-da 겨루다.

river *n.* kang 강, nae 내.

rivulet *n.* si-nae 시내, sil-gae-ch'ŏn 실개천, kae-ul 개울.

road *n.* ① kil 길, chil-lo 진로. ② (*way*) pang-bŏp 방법.

roadside *n.* kil-ga 길가, no-byŏn 노변. 「하다.

roam *v.* to-ra-da-ni-da 돌아다니다, pae-hoe-ha-da 배회

roar *v.* pu-rŭ-jit-da 부르짖다. —*n.* ① (*of animals*) ŭ-rŭ-rŏng-gŏ-rim 으르렁거림. ② (*of inanimate nature*) no-ho 노호. ③ (*of cannon*) p'o-sŏng 포성.

roast *n.* ku-un-go-gi 구운고기. —*v.* kup-da 굽다. —*adj.* ku-un 구운 : ~ *beef* pul-go-gi 불고기.

rob *v.* kang-t'al-ha-da 강탈하다, hum-ch'i-da 훔치다.

robber *n.* (*bandit*) kang-do 강도, to-duk 도둑.

robbery *n.* kang-t'al 강탈, yak-t'al 약탈.

robe *n.* ka-un 가운 ; (*pl.*) ye-bok 예복, pŏp-bok 법복.

robot *n.* ro-bot 로봇, in-jo in-gan 인조 인간.

robust *adj.* kang-gŏn-han 강건한, t'ŭn-t'ŭn-han 튼튼한.

rock *n.* pa-wi 바위. —*v.* hŭn-dŭl-da 흔들다.

rocket *n.* ① ro-k'et 로켓. ② (*beacon*) pong-hwa 봉화.

rod *n.* chang-dae 장대, (*stick*) mak-dae-gi 막대기.

rogue *n.* ak-han 악한(惡漢), kkang-p'ae 깡패.

roll *n.* ① (*of paper*) tu-ru-ma-ri 두루마리. ② (*list of names*) myŏng-bu 명부. ③ (*of ship*) yo-dong 요동. —*v.* ① kul-ri-da 굴리다. ② u-rŭ-rŭ ul-ri-da 우르르

roller *n.* ro-ul-rŏ 로울러.   「울리다.

romantic *adj.* nang-man-jŏk-in 낭만적인.　「괄량이.
romp *v.* ttwi-nol-da 뛰놀다.　—*n.* mal-gwal-ryang-i 말
roof *n.* ① chi-bung 지붕. ② (*summit*) kkok-dae-gi 꼭
　대기 : *live under the same* ~ tong-gŏ-ha-da 동거하다.
rook *n.* (*crow*) ttang-gga-ma-gwi 땅까마귀.
room *n.* ① (*chamber*) pang 방. ② (*space*) yŏ-ji 여지.
roommate *n.* han-bang ch'in-gu 한방 친구, tong-suk-
roost *n.* hwae 홰, po-gŭm-ja-ri 보금자리.　└ja 동숙자.
rooster *n.* su-t'ak 수탉.　「wŏn 근원.
root *n.* ① ppu-ri 뿌리, ki-ch'o 기초. ② (*cause*) kŭn-
rope *n.* pat-jul 밧줄, sae-ggi 새끼.
rosary *n.* (*Cath.*)(*beads*) ro-ja-ri-o 로자리오 ; (*Budd.*)
　(*beads*) yŏm-ju 염주.　「무궁화.
rose *n.* chang-mi 장미 : ~ *of Sharon* mu-gung-hwa
rostrum *n.* yŏn-dan 연단, sŏl-gyo-dan 설교단.
rosy *adj.* ① chang-mi-bi-ch'ŭi 장미빛의, pal-gŭ-re-han
　발그레한. ② (*promising*) yu-mang-han 유망한.
rot *v.* ssŏk-da 썩다, pu-p'ae-ha-da 부패하다.
rotary *adj.* hoe-jŏn-ha-nŭn 회전하는.
rotate *v.* ① tol-da 돌다. ② kyo-dae-ha-da 교대하다.
rotation *n.* hoe-jŏn 회전, cha-jŏn 자전 ; sun-hwan 순
　환 ; (*change in turn*) kyo-dae 교대.
rotten *adj.* ssŏk-ŭn 썩은, pu-p'ae-han 부패한.
rouge *n.* yŏn-ji 연지, ru-u-jŭ 루우즈.
rough *adj.* ① kŏ-ch'in 거친 ;(*uneven*) ul-t'ung-bul-t'ung-
　-han 울퉁불퉁한. ② (*rude*) pŏ-rŭt-ŏp-nŭn 버릇없는.
round *adj.* tung-gŭn 둥근. —*prep.* chu-wi-e 주위에.
　—*adv.* to-ra-sŏ 돌아서. —*n.* il-hoe-jŏn 일회전.
roundabout *adj.* to-ra-sŏ ka-nŭn 돌아서 가는.
roundup *n.* kŏm-gŏ 검거, ch'e-p'o 체포.
rouse *v.* kkae-u-da 깨우다 ; cha-gŭk-ha-da 자극하다.
route *n.* kil 길, (*line*) hang-ro 항로, no-sŏn 노선.

routine *n.* il-gwa 일과 ; ki-gye-jŏk chŏl-ch'a 기계적 절차.
rove *v.* (*wander about*) pae-hoe-ha-da 배회하다.
row *n.* ① (*line*) chul 줄, yŏl 열(列). ② (*disturbance*) pŏp-sŏk 법석. —*v.* no-jŏt-da 노젓다.
royal *adj.* kuk-wang-ŭi 국왕의 ; wi-ŏm-it-nŭn 위엄있는.
royalty *n.* ① wang-gwŏn 왕권. ② (*to owner*) sa-yong-ryo 사용료. ③ (*on a book*) in-se 인세(印稅).
rub *v.* pi-bi-da 비비다. —*n.* ma-ch'al 마찰.
rubber *n.* ko-mu 고무, chi-u-gae 지우개.
rubbish *n.* ssŭ-re-gi 쓰레기 ; chap-dong-sa-ni 잡동사니.
ruby *n.* hong-ok 홍옥, ru-u-bi 루우비.
rucksack *n.* pae-nang 배낭, ruk-jak 룩작.
rudder *n.* (*boat*) k'i 키, (*airplane*) pang-hyang-t'a 방향타.
ruddy *adj.* pul-gŭ-re-han 불그레한 ; hong-an-ŭi 홍안의 : ~ *cheeks* hong-an 홍안(紅顏).
rude *adj.* mu-rye-han 무례한, (*uneducated*) kyo-yang-ŏp-nŭn 교양없는 ; (*rough*) nan-p'ok-han 난폭한.
rue *v.* nwi-u-ch'i-da 뉘우치다, hu-hoe-ha-da 후회하다.
ruffian *n.* ak-dang 악당, kkang-p'ae 깡패.
ruffle *v.* hŭ-t'ŭ-rŏ-ddŭ-ri-da 흐트러뜨리다.
rug *n.* yang-t'an-ja 양탄자, ma-ru kkal-gae 마루 깔개.
rugged *adj.* ul-t'ung-bul-t'ung-han 울퉁불퉁한.
ruin *n.* ① (*destruction*) p'a-myŏl 파멸. ② (*impairment*) hwe-son 훼손. ③ (*remains*) p'ye-hŏ 폐허. —*v.* p'a-goe-ha-da 파괴하다, mang-ch'i-da 망치다.
rule *n.* ① kyu-ch'ik 규칙. ② (*control*) chi-bae 지배. —*v.* chi-bae-ha-da 지배하다 ; p'an-gyŏl-ha-da 판결하다.
ruler *n.* ① chi-bae-ja 지배자, t'ong-ch'i-ja 통치자. ② (*measure*) cha 자.
rumble *v.* u-rŭ-rŭ ul-ri-da 우르르 울리다. —*n.* tŏl-gŏ-dŏk so-ri 덜거덕 소리.
rumo(u)r *n.* so-mun 소문, p'ung-mun 풍문.
run *v.* ① tal-ri-da 달리다. ② (*flee*) to-mang-ga-da 도

망가다. ③ (*manage*) kyŏng-yŏng-ha-da 경영하다.

rural *adj*. si-gol-ŭi 시골의, chŏn-wŏn-ŭi 전원의 : ~ *life* chŏn-wŏn-saeng-hwal 전원생활.

ruse *n*. (*trick*) mo-ryak 모략, ch'aek-ryak 책략.

rush *n*. tol-jin 돌진, pun-mang 분망 : ~ *hour* hon-jap-han si-gan 혼잡한 시간, rŏ-si-a-wŏ 러시아워. —*v*. tol-jin-ha-da 돌진하다 ; tal-ryŏ-dŭl-da 달려들다.

rust *n*. nok 녹. —*v*. nok-sŭl-da 녹슬다.

rustic *adj*. si-gol-ddŭ-gi-ŭi 시골뜨기의.　　「리가 나다.

rustle *v*. sal-rang-sal-rang so-ri-ga na-da 살랑살랑 소

rusty *adj*. nok-sŭ-rŭn 녹슬은 ; (*old*) nal-gŭn 낡은.

rut *n*. (*wheel track*) pa-k'wi cha-guk 바퀴 자국.

ruthless *adj*. mu-ja-bi-han 무자비한, in-jŏng-ŏp-nŭn 인정없는, (*cruel*) chan-in-han 잔인한.

rye *n*. ho-mil 호밀, ssal-bo-ri 쌀보리.

⊷✦ S ✦⊶

Sabbath *n*. an-sik-il 안식일.

saber · sabre *n*. kun-do 군도, sa-a-bŭ-rŭ 사아브르.

sabotage *n*. t'ae-ŏp 태업(怠業), sa-bo-t'a-a-ji 사보타아지.

saccharin *n*. sa-k'a-rin 사카린.

sack *n*. cha-ru 자루, pu-dae 부대, pong-ji 봉지.

sack dress cha-ru-ot 자루옷, saek-dŭ-re-sŭ 색드레스.

sacrament *n*. sŏng-rye 성례, sŏng-sa 성사(聖事).

sacred *adj*. sin-sŏng-han 신성한, kŏ-ruk-han 거룩한 ; (sin-e-ge) pa-ch'in (신에게) 바친.　　「하다.

sacrifice *n*. hŭi-saeng 희생. —*v*. hŭi-saeng-ha-da 희생

sad *adj*. sŭl-p'ŭn 슬픈, pi-ch'am-han 비참한.

saddle *n*. an-jang 안장, kil-ma 길마. —*v*. an-jang-ŭl no-t'a 안장을 놓다.　　「pi-t'an 비탄.

sadness *n*. sŭl-p'ŭm 슬픔, pi-ae 비애 ; (*mournfulness*)

safe *adj*. an-jŏn-han 안전한. —*n*. kŭm-go 금고.

safe-conduct *n*. an-jŏn t'ong-haeng-gwŏn〔jŭng〕안전 통행권〔증〕.

safeguard *n*. po-ho 보호, ho-wi 호위.

safely *adv*. an-jŏn-ha-ge 안전하게, mu-sa-hi 무사히.

safety *n*. an-jŏn 안전 : ～ *belt* ku-myŏng-dae 구명대.

safety pin an-jŏn-p'in 안전핀. 「영리한.

sagacious *adj*. ch'ong-myŏng-han 총명한, yŏng-ri-han

sage *adj*. sŭl-gi-ro-un 슬기로운. —*n*. (*wise man*) hyŏn-in 현인(賢人), sŏng-in 성인.

sail *n*. tot 돛. —*v*. (*navigate*) hang-hae-ha-da 항해하다 ; (*airplane*) cho-jong-ha-da 조종하다.

sailing *n*. ch'ul-bŏm 출범, hang-hae 항해.

sailing boat tot-bae 돛배, pŏm-sŏn 범선.

sailor *n*. (*seaman*) sŏn-wŏn 선원 ; su-byŏng 수병.

saint *n*. sŏng-in 성인(聖人), sŏng-ja 성자.

sake *n*. mok-jŏk 목적 ; i-yu 이유 ; (*interest*) i-ik 이익 : *for the* ～ *of* …ŭl wi-ha-yŏ …을 위하여.

salad *n*. sael-rŏ-dŭ 샐러드, saeng-ch'ae-yo-ri 생채요리.

salary *n*. pong-gŭp 봉급, kŭp-ryo 급료 : *get a high* ～ wŏl-gŭp-ŭl man-i pat-da 월급을 많이 받다.

sale *n*. p'an-mae 판매 : *bargain* ～ ssa-gu-ryŏ p'an-mae 싸구려 판매, yŏm-ga p'an-mae 염가 판매.

salesman·saleswoman *n*. p'an-mae-wŏn 판매원, chŏm-wŏn 점원 ; (*Am*.) oe-p'an-wŏn 외판원.

salient *adj*. hyŏn-jŏ-han 현저한, (*projecting*) tol-ch'ul-han 돌출한.

saliva *n*. ch'im 침, t'a-aek 타액.

salmon *n*. yŏn-ŏ 연어.

saloon *n*. ① (*hall*) tae-ch'ŏng 대청. ② tam-hwa-sil 담화실. ③ (*barroom*) sul-jip 술집.

salt *n*. so-gŭm 소금 ; *the* ～ *of the earth* se-sang-ŭi so-gŭm 세상의 소금. —*v*. so-gŭm-ŭl ch'i-da 소금을 치다.

saltation *n*. (*leaping*) ttwi-gi 뛰기, to-yak 도약.

salty *adj.* jjan 짠, jjap-jjal-han 짭짤한.

salutation *n.* in-sa 인사, kyong-rye 경례 : *return one's* ~ tap-rye-ha-da 답례하다. 「rye 경례.

salute *v.* in-sa-ha-da 인사하다. —*n.* chŏl 절, kyŏng-

salvage *v.* (*salve*) ku-jo-ha-da 구조하다. —*n.* hae-nan-gu-jo 해난구조. 「gun 구세군.

salvation *n.* (*rescue*) ku-je 구제 : *S*~ *Army* ku-se-

salve *n.* ko-yak 고약. —*v.* ① ko-yak-ŭl pa-rŭ-da 고약을 바르다. ② (*soothe*) tal-rae-da 달래다.

salvo *n.* ① il-je sa-gyŏk 일제 사격. ② ye-p'o 예포.

same *adj.* ka-t'ŭn 같은, tong-il-han 동일한.

sample *n.* kyŏn-bon 견본, p'yo-bon 표본.

sanatorium *n.* ① yo-yang-so 요양소. ② p'i-sŏ-ji 피서지.

sanctify *v.* sin-sŏng-hwa-ha-da 신성화하다.

sanction *n.* ① (*approval*) in-ga 인가 ; (*consent*) ch'an-sŏng 찬성. ② (*penalty*) che-jae 제재.

sanctuary *n.* sŏng-yŏk 성역, kŏ-ruk-han kot 거룩한 곳.

sand *n.* mo-rae 모래, (*pl.*) mo-rae-t'ŏp 모래톱.

sandbag *n.* mo-rae pu-dae 모래 부대, sa-nang 사낭.

sand bar mo-rae-t'op 모래톱, sa-ju 사주(砂洲).

sandstorm *n.* mo-rae p'ok-p'ung 모래 폭풍.

sandwich *n.* saen-dŭ-wi-ch'i 샌드위치.

sandy *adj.* mo-rae-ŭi 모래의, mo-rae-bi-ch'ŭi 모래빛의.

sane *adj.* (*sound*) che-jŏng-sin-ŭi 제정신의.

sanguine *adj.* ta-hyŏl-jil-ŭi 다혈질의, p'i-ŭi 피의.

sanitary *adj.* wi-saeng-ŭi 위생의 ; *a* ~ *inspector* wi-saeng kŏm-sa-gwan 위생 검사관.

sanitation *n.* kong-jung wi-saeng 공중 위생. 「미치다.

sanity *n.* che-jŏng-sin 제정신 : *lose one's* ~ mi-ch'i-da

Santa Claus san-t'a-k'ŭl-ro-o-sŭ ha-ra-bŏ-ji 산타클로오스 할아버지. 「ryŏk 활력.

sap *n.* (*of trees*) su-aek 수액(樹液) ; (*vigor*) hwal-

sapling *n.* ① (*tree*) ŏ-rin-na-mu 어린나무. ② (*youth*) p'ut-na-gi 풋나기, ae-song-i 애송이.

sapphire *n.* sa-p'a-i-ŏ 사파이어, ch'ŏng-ok 청옥(靑玉).

sarcastic *adj.* pi-ggo-nŭn 비꼬는, pin-jŏng-dae-nŭn 빈정대는, (*mocking*) nol-ri-nŭn 놀리는.

sardine *n.* chŏng-ŏ-ri 정어리.

sarira *n.* (*Sans.*) (*Buddha's bone*) sa-ri 사리(舍利).

sash *n.* ① chang-sik-ddi 장식띠, (*shoulder strap*) kyŏn-jang 견장(肩章). ② (*of window*) sae-si 새시.

Satan *n.* ak-ma 악마, sa-t'an 사탄.

satchel *n.* hak-saeng ka-bang 학생 가방, chak-ŭn ka-bang 작은 가방.

satellite *n.* wi-sŏng 위성.

satellite communication wi-sŏng t'ong-sin 위성 통신.

satin *n.* kong-dan 공단, su-ja 수자.

satire *n.* p'ung-ja 풍자, pin-jŏng-daem 빈정댐.

satisfaction *n.* man-jok 만족, hŭp-jok 흡족.

satisfactory *adj.* ① man-jok-han 만족한, ch'ung-bun-han 충분한. ② (*adequate*) chŏk-jŏl-han 적절한.

satisfy *v.* man-jok-si-k'i-da 만족시키다.

saturate *v.* p'uk chŏk-si-da 푹 적시다, tam-gŭ-da 담그다.

Saturday *n.* t'o-yo-il 토요일.

sauce *n.* sŏ-yang kan-jang 서양 간장, so-o-sŭ 소오스.

saucepan *n.* sŭ-t'yu-u nam-bi 스튜우 남비.

saucer *n.* pat-ch'im chŏp-si 받침 접시.

saucy *adj.* ① (*pert*) kŏn-bang-jin 건방진; yŏm-ch'i-ŏp-nŭn 염치없는. ② (*smart*) nal-ssin-han 날씬한.

sausage *n.* so-si-ji 소시지, sun-dae 순대.

savage *adj.* ya-man-ŭi 야만의. —*n.* ya-man-in 야만인.

save *v.* ① ku-ha-da 구하다. ② (*hoard*) chŏ-ch'uk-ha-da 저축하다. —*prep.* …ŭl che-oe-ha-go …을 제외하고.

savings *n.* chŏ-gŭm 저금, chŏ-ch'uk 저축.

savings bank chŏ-ch'uk ŭn-haeng 저축 은행.

savio(u)r *n.* (*Jesus Christ*) ku-se-ju 구세주, kŭ-ri-sŭ-do 그리스도 ; (*rescuer*) ku-jo-ja 구조자.

savo(u)r *n.* mat 맛, p'ung-mi 풍미, hyang-gi 향기.

saw *n.* t'op 톱. —*v.* t'op-jil-ha-da 톱질하다. 「제재용 톱.

sawmill *n.* ① che-jae-so 제재소. ② che-jae-yong t'op

say *v.* mal-ha-da 말하다 ; i-rŭl-t'e-myŏn 이를테면 ; i-bwa 이봐, cham-ggan-man 잠깐만.

saying *n.* mal 말 ; (*proverb*) sok-dam 속담.

scab *n.* sang-ch'ŏ-ŭi ttak-ji 상처의 딱지 ; om 옴.

scabbard *n.* (*sheath*) k'al-jip 칼집.

scabby *adj.* ttak-ji-t'u-sŏng-i-ŭi 딱지투성이의, tŏ-rŏ-un

scabies *n.* om 옴. 「더러운 ; in-saek-han 인색한.

scaffold *n.* ① pal-p'an 발판. ② kyo-su-dae 교수대.

scald *v.* te-ge ha-da 데게 하다, te-ch'i-da 데치다.

scale *n.* ① (*of fish*) pi-nŭl 비늘. ② (*map*) ch'ŏk-do 척도 ; kyu-mo 규모. ③ (*weighing machine*) chŏl-ul

scamper *v.* kŭp-hi tal-ri-da 급히 달리다. 「저울.

scan *v.* cha-se-hi cho-sa-ha-da 자세히 조사하다.

scandal *n.* (*disgrace*) ch'u-mun 추문, ch'ang-p'i 창피, sŭ-k'aen-dŭl 스캔들. 「han 인색한.

scanty *adj.* mo-ja-ra-nŭn 모자라는 ; (*sparing*) in-saek-

scar *n.* hyung-t'ŏ 흉터, hŭm 흠 ; hŭn-jŏk 흔적.

scarce *adj.* pu-jok-han 부족한, (*rare*) tŭ-mun 드문.

scarcely *adv.* kan-sin-hi 간신히 ; ka-gga-sŭ-ro 가까스로 ; kŏ-ŭi ···ŏp-da 거의 ···없다.

scarcity *n.* pu-jok 부족 ; sik-ryang-nan 식량난.

scare *v.* nol-ra-ge ha-da 놀라게 하다. —*n.* kong-p'o 공

scarecrow *n.* hŏ-su-a-bi 허수아비. 「포.

scarf *n.* mok-do-ri 목도리, sŭ-k'a-a-p'ŭ 스카아프.

scarlet *n.* chin-hong-saek 진홍색. 「하다.

scatter *v.* hŭt-bbu-ri-da 흩뿌리다, pun-san-ha-da 분산

scene *n.* ① kwang-gyŏng 광경. ② (*theatre*) mu-dae 무

대. ③ (*movie*) chang-myŏn 장면.
scenery *n.* kyŏng-ch'i 경치, p'ung-gyŏng 풍경.
scent *n.* naem-sae 냄새, (*perfume*) hyang-su 향수.
sceptical *adj.* ŭi-sim-man-ŭn 의심많은.
schedule *n.* si-gan-p'yŏ 시간표, ye-jŏng-p'yo 예정표.
scheme *n.* ① (*plan*) kye-hoek 계획. ② (*intrigue*) ŭm-mo 음모. ③ (*system*) ch'e-gye 체계. 「do 학도.
scholar *n.* (*learned man*) hak-ja 학자 ; (*student*) hak-
scholarship *n.* ① (*learning*) hak-mun 학문, hak-sik 학식. ② (*grant*) chang-hak-gŭm 장학금.
school *n.* ① hak-gyo 학교, su-ŏp 수업 : *primary* ~ kuk-min-hak-gyo 국민학교/*middle* ~ chung-hak-gyo 중학교/*high* ~ ko-dŭng-hak-gyo 고등학교/*a graduate* ~ tae-hak-wŏn 대학원. ② (*doctrinal faction*)
schoolboy *n.* nam-hak-saeng 남학생. 「hak-p'a 학파.
schoolfellow *n.* tong-ch'ang 동창, hak-u 학우.
schoolgirl *n.* yŏ-hak-saeng 여학생. 「sa 교장 관사.
schoolhouse *n.* ① kyo-sa 교사(校舍). ② kyo-jang kwan-
school inspector *n.* chang-hak-sa〔gwan〕 장학사〔관〕.
schoolmaster *n.* kyo-wŏn 교원 ; kyo-jang 교장.
schoolmate *n.* tong-ch'ang 동창, hak-u 학우.
schoolroom *n.* (*classroom*) kyo-sil 교실.
science *n.* kwa-hak 과학, hak-sul 학술, …hak …학 (學) : *political* ~ chŏng-ch'i-hak 정치학. 「과학 소설.
science fiction *n.* (kong-sang) kwa-hak so-sŏl (공상)
scientific *adj.* kwa-hak-jŏk-in 과학적인, kwa-hak-ŭi
scientist *n.* kwa-hak-ja 과학자. 「과학의.
scissors *n.* ka-wi 가위.
scoff *n.* & *v.* (*jeer*) cho-rong(-ha-da) 조롱(하다).
scold *v.* kku-jit-da 꾸짖다, ya-dan-ch'i-da 야단치다.
scoop *n.* kuk-ja 국자, pu-sap 부삽.
scope *n.* (*range*) pŏm-wi 범위 ; (*room*) yŏ-ji 여지.

scorch *v*. kŭ-sŭl-ri-da 그슬리다, te-da 데다.

score *n*. tŭk-jŏm 득점 ; (*pl*.) ta-su 다수. —*v*. tŭk-jŏm-ha-da 득점하다, ki-rok-ha-da 기록하다.

scorn *n*. & *v*. myŏl-si(-ha-da) 멸시(하다).

scorpion *n*. chŏn-gal 전갈.

scoundrel *n*. ak-dang 악당, ak-han 악한.「샅샅이 뒤지다.

scour *v*. kal-go tak-da 갈고 닦다, sat-sa-ch'i twi-ji-da

scout *n*. chŏng-ch'al-byŏng 정찰병 ; so-nyŏn〔so-nyŏ〕tan-wŏn 소년〔소녀〕단원. —*v*. sŭ-k'a-u-t'ŭ-ha-da 스카

scowl *v*. jji-p'u-ri-da 찌푸리다.   〔우트하다.

scramble *v*. ① (*climb*) ki-ŏ-o-rŭ-da 기어오르다. ② (*struggle*) ta-t'u-ŏ ppae-at-da 다투어 빼앗다.

scrap *n*. cho-gak 조각, sŭ-k'ŭ-raep 스크랩.

scrape *v*. mun-ji-rŭ-da 문지르다, kŭk-da 긁다.

scratch *n*. kŭl-ggi 긁기. —*v*. kŭk-da 긁다.

scream *n*. a-u-sŏng 아우성, pi-myŏng 비명. —*v*. a-u-sŏng-ch'i-da 아우성치다.

screen *n*. ① pyŏng-p'ung 병풍, kan-mak-i 간막이. ② (*movie*) yŏng-sa-mak 영사막, sŭ-k'ŭ-ri-in 스크리인.

screw *n*. na-sa 나사, sŭ-k'ŭ-ru-u 스크루우.

screwdriver *n*. na-sa tol-ri-gae 나사 돌리개 ; tŭ-ra-i-bŏ 드라이버. 〔pyŏng-p'ung〕

scribble *n*. nan-p'il 난필. —*v*. kal-gyŏ ssŭ-da 갈겨 쓰다.

scribe *n*. tae-so 대서(代書), p'il-gi-ja 필기자, sŏ-gi 서기 ; (*Judaism*) yul-bŏp-hak-ja 율법학자.

script *n*. ① ssŭn kŭl-ja 쓴 글자, p'il-gi-ch'e hwal-ja 필기체 활자. ② (*play*) kak-bon 각본, tae-bon 대본, sŭ-k'ŭ-rip-t'ŭ 스크립트.

scripture *n*. sŏng-gyŏng 성경, (*sacred books*) kyŏng-jŏn 경전.

scroll *n.* ① tu-ru-ma-ri 두루마리. ② mok-rok 목록.
scrub *n.* tŏm-bul 덤불. —*v.* puk-buk mun-ji-rŭ-da 북
　북 문지르다, puk-buk tak-da 북북 닦다. 「한.
scrupulous *adj.* sin-jung-han 신중한, se-sim-han 세심
scrutiny *n.* ① myŏn-mil-han cho-sa 면밀한 조사 ; ŭm-
　mi 음미. ② t'u-p'yo chae-gŏm-sa 투표 재검사.
sculptor *n.* cho-gak-ga 조각가.
sculpture *n.* cho-gak 조각, cho-gak-sul 조각술.
scurry *v.* chong-jong-gŏ-rŭm-ŭ-ro tal-ri-da　종종걸음으
scythe *n.* (*sickle*) k'ŭn nat 큰 낫. 「로 달리다.
sea *n.* pa-da 바다 : *the East S~* tong-hae 동해.
sea bathing hae-su-yok 해수욕.
seacoast *n.* pa-dat-ga 바닷가, hae-an 해안, hae-byŏn 해
sea gull kal-mae-gi 갈매기. 「변.
seal *n.* ① (*animal*) pa-da-p'yo-bŏm 바다표범. ② (*mark*)
　to-jang 도장, pong-in 봉인. —*v.* na-rin-ha-da 날인하
　다 ; pong-in-ha-da 봉인하다.
seam *n.* sol-gi 솔기. —*v.* kkwe-mae-da 꿰매다.
seaman *n.* sŏn-wŏn 선원, su-byŏng 수병. 「재봉사.
seamstress *n.* ch'im-mo 침모 ; yŏ-ja chae-bong-sa 여자
search *v.* ch'at-da 찾다, su-saek-ha-da 수색하다. —*n.*
　su-saek 수색, t'am-saek 탐색. 「어치라이트.
searchlight *n.* t'am-jo-dŭng 탐조등, sŏ-ŏ-ch'i-ra-i-t'ŭ 서
seashore *n.* hae-byŏn 해변, hae-an 해안, pa-dat-ga 바
seasickness *n.* paet-mŏl-mi 뱃멀미. 「닷가.
season *n.* ① kye-jŏl 계절. ② (*right time*) ho-gi 호기.
　—*v.* (*flavor*) kan-ŭl mat-ch'u-da 간을 맞추다.
seat *n.* cha-ri 자리. —*v.* an-ch'i-da 앉히다 : *Please ~*
　yourself. Pu-di an-jŭ-se-yo. 부디 앉으세요.
seaweed *n.* hae-ch'o 해초 : *brown ~* mi-yŏk 미역.
seclude *v.* (*separate*) tte-ŏ-no-t'a 떼어놓다 ; (*withdraw*)
　ŭn-t'oe-si-k'i-da 은퇴시키다.

second *adj.* tul-jjae-ŭi 둘째의. —*n.* (*time*) ch'o 초(秒).
secondary *adj.* che i-wi-ŭi 제 2위의, pu-ch'a-jŏk 부차적.
second-hand *adj.* muk-ŭn 묵은, chung-go-ŭi 중고의.
　　—*n.* ① chung-go-p'um 중고품. ② (*clock*) ch'o-ch'im
secrecy *n.* pi-mil 비밀, ŭn-mil 은밀. 　　　　　⌊초침.
secret *n.* pi-mil 비밀. —*adj.* pi-mil-ŭi 비밀의.
secretary *n.* pi-sŏ 비서, sŏ-gi 서기, pi-sŏ-gwan 비서관;
　　(*Am. gov.*) chang-gwan 장관 : *the S～ of State*
　　kuk-mu-jang-gwan 국무장관.
secretion *n.* ① pun-bi(-mul) 분비(물). ② ŭn-nik 은닉.
sect *n.* kyo-p'a 교파 ; tang-p'a 당파 ; hak-p'a 학파.
section *n.* ku-bun 구분 ; (*area*) chi-gu 지구 ; (*office*)
　　kwa〔pu〕 과〔부〕. —*v.* ku-bun〔ku-hoek〕-ha-da 구분
　　〔구획〕하다 : *a personnel ～* in-sa-gwa 인사과.
secular *adj.* se-sok-jŏk 세속적, hyŏn-se-ŭi 현세의.
secure *v.* (*make safe*) an-jŏn-ha-ge ha-da 안전하게 하
　　다 ; (*obtain*) hoek-dŭk-ha-da 획득하다. —*adj.* an-jŏn-
　　han 안전한, (*sure*) hwak-sil-han 확실한.
security *n.* an-jŏn 안전, po-jŭng 보증 : *S～ Council*(*U.*
　　N.) an-jŏn-bo-jang i-sa-hoe 안전보장 이사회.
seduce *v.* yu-hok-ha-da 유혹하다, kkoe-da 꾀다.
see *v.* ① po-da 보다. ② (*meet*) man-na-da 만나다. ③
　　(*understand*) i-hae-ha-da 이해하다. ④ (*escort*) pae-
　　ung-ha-da 배웅하다. ⑤ (*attend*) tol-bo-da 돌보다.
seed *n.* ssi 씨, yŏl-mae 열매, chong-ja 종자.
seeing *n.* po-gi 보기, si-gak 시각(視覺) : *S～ is be-*
　　lieving. Paek-mun-i pu-ryŏ-il-gyŏn. 백문이 불여일견.
seek *v.* ch'at-da 찾다, (*ask for*) ku-ha-da 구하다.
seem *v.* (*appear*) …ch'ŏ-rŏm po-i-da …처럼 보이다.
seeming *adv. & adj.* oe-gwan-sang(-ŭi) 외관상(의).
　　—*n.* oe-gwan 외관, oe-yang 외양.
seesaw *n.* si-i-so-o 시이소오, nŏl-ddwi-gi 널뛰기.

segment *n.* kkŭn·ŭn cho-gak 끊은 조각 ; pun-jŏl 분절.
segregate *v.* kyŏk-ri-ha-da 격리하다.
seize *v.* ① (*grasp*) chap-da 잡다. ② (*understand*)
　p'a-ak-ha-da 파악하다. ③ (*arrest*) ch'e-p'o-ha-da 체
seizure *n.* ap-ryu 압류, kang-t'al 강탈.　　　└포하다.
seldom *adj.* tŭ-mul-ge 드물게, kan-hok 간혹, chom-ch'ŏ-
　rŏm ···an-nŭn 좀처럼 ···않는.
select *v.* ko-rŭ-da 고르다, sŏn-t'aek-ha-da 선택하다.
　—*adj.* ch'u-ryŏ-naen 추려낸.
self *n.* cha-gi 자기, cha-a 자아(自我).
self-centred *adj.* cha-gi chung-sim-ŭi 자기 중심의.
self-confident *adj.* cha-sin-it-nŭn 자신있는.
self-education *n.* tok-hak 독학, ko-hak 고학.
self-indulgence *n.* oe-go-jip 외고집, pang-jong 방종.
self-interest *n.* sa-ri 사리, sa-yok 사욕.
selfish *adj.* i-gi-jŏk 이기적, i-gi-ju-ŭi-jŏk-in 이기주의적인.
self-satisfaction *n.* cha-gi man-jok 자기 만족.
sell *v.* p'al-da 팔다, (*be sold*) p'al-ri-da 팔리다.
seller *n.* p'a-nŭn sa-ram 파는 사람, p'an-mae-in 판매
semblance *n.* yu-sa 유사 ; oe-gwan 외관.　　　└인.
semester *n.* hak-gi 학기(學期).
seminar *n.* yŏn-gu-ban 연구반, se-mi-na-a 세미아나.
seminary *n.* (*a divinity school*) sin-hak-gyo 신학교 ;
　hak-wŏn 학원 ; yang-sŏng-so 양성소.
senate *n.* ① wŏl-lo-wŏn 원로원. ② sang-wŏn 상원.
senator *n.* sang-wŏn ŭi-wŏn 상원 의원.
send *v.* po-nae-da 보내다, pu-ch'i-da 부치다.
sender *n.* ① po-nae-nŭn sa-ram 보내는 사람, pal-song-
　in 발송인. ② song-sin-gi 송신기.
senior *adj.* son-wi-ŭi 손위의, yŏn-sang-ŭi 연상의. —*n.*
　(*elder*) yŏn-jang-ja 연장자, sŏn-bae 선배.
sensation *n.* ① kam-gak 감각. ② k'ŭn hwa-je 큰 화제,

sen-se-i-syŏn 센세이션.
sense *n.* ① kam-gak 감각 ; (*five senses*) o-gwan 오관 ; pun-byŏl 분별. ② (*meaning*) ttŭt 뜻.
senseless *adj.* mu-gam-gak-ŭi 무감각의. 「식한.
sensible *adj.* pun-byŏl-it-nŭn 분별있는 ; ŭi-sik-han 의
sensitive *adj.* min-gam-han 민감한, sin-gyŏng-gwa-min-ŭi 신경과민의. 「음란한.
sensual *adj.* kwan-nŭng-jŏk-in 관능적인, ŭm-ran-han
sentence *n.* ① mun-jang 문장. ② (*for crime*) sŏn-go 선고, ŏn-do 언도. —*v.* sŏn-go-ha-da 선고하다.
sentiment *n.* kam-jŏng 감정, chŏng-sŏ 정서.
sentimental *adj.* kam-sang-jŏk-in 감상적인.
sentry *n.* po-ch'o 보초, p'a-su-byŏng 파수병. 「수도.
Seoul *n.* sŏ-ul 서울 ; tae-han-min-guk su-do 대한민국
separate *v.* tte-ŏ-no-t'a 떼어놓다, pul-li-ha-da 분리하다. —*adj.* pul-li-doen 분리된.
separation *n.* pul-li 분리, pul-lyu 분류(分類).
September *n.* ku-wŏl 구월.
sequel *n.* kye-sok 계속 ; sok-p'yŏn 속편, hu-p'yŏn 후편.
sequence *n.* yŏn-sok 연속 ; sun-sŏ 순서.
serenade *n.* so-ya-gok 소야곡, se-re-na-dŭ 세레나드.
serene *adj.* ch'ŏng-myŏng-han 청명한, hwa-ch'ang-han 화창한 ; (*tranquil*) ch'im-ch'ak-han 침착한.
serf *n.* nong-no 농노(農奴) ; no-ye 노예.
serge *n.* sa-a-ji 사아지, se-ru 세루. 「sa 중사.
sergeant *n.* ha-sa-gwan 하사관, sang-sa 상사, chung-
serial *adj.* yŏn-sok-jŏk-in 연속적인 : ~ *number* il-ryŏn pŏn-ho 일련 번호 : kun-bŏn 군번(軍番).
sericulture *n.* yang-jam-ŏp 양잠업(養蠶業).
series *n.* yŏn-sok 연속 ; ch'ong-sŏ 총서.
serious *adj.* (*grave*) chin-ji-han 진지한 ; (*critical*) chung-dae-han 중대한 : *a* ~ *illness* chung-byŏng 중병.

seriously *adv*. sim-gak-ha-ge 심각하게, chin-ji-ha-ge 진지하게.

sermon *n*. sŏl-gyo 설교, hun-gye 훈계.

serpent *n*. (*snake*) paem 뱀.

servant *n*. ha-in 하인, chong 종 : *a man* ~ ha-in 하인, mŏ-sŭm 머슴/*a maid* ~ ha-nyŏ 하녀.

serve *v*. sŏm-gi-da 섬기다, si-jung-ŭl tŭl-da 시중을 들다.

service *n*. ① (*employ*) ko-yong 고용, pong-sa 봉사. ② (*devotion to God*) ye-bae 예배. ③ (*official duty*) kŭn-mu 근무. ④ (*conscription*) pyŏng-yŏk 병역. ⑤ (*treatment in hotels*) chŏp-dae 접대.

serviceable *adj*. (*useful*) ssŭl-mo-it-nŭn 쓸모있는, p'yŏl-li-han 편리한 ; (*obliging*) ch'in-jŏl-han 친절한.

service station chu-yu-so 주유소.

session *n*. (*cong*.) kae-hoe 개회 ; hoe-gi 회기.

set *v*. ① (*put*) tu-da 두다. ② (*start*) ch'ak-su-ha-da 착수하다. ③ (*impose*) pu-gwa-ha-da 부과하다. —*adj*. (*fixed*) ko-jŏng-doen 고정된. —*n*. han cho 한 조(組).

setback *n*. pang-hae 방해 ; yŏk-ryu 역류(逆流).

setting *n*. (*plays*) mu-dae chang-ch'i 무대 장치.

settle *v*. cha-ri-jap-da 자리잡다 ; (*decide*) kyŏl-jŏng-ha-da 결정하다 ; (*solve*) hae-gyŏl-ha-da 해결하다.

settlement *n*. chŏng-ch'ak 정착(定着) ; (*conclusion*) hae-gyŏl 해결 ; (*colony*) kŏ-ryu-ji 거류지.

settler *n*. kae-ch'ŏk-min 개척민, i-ju-min 이주민.

seven *n*. & *adj*. il-gop(-ŭi) 일곱(의), ch'il 7.

seventeen *n*. yŏl-il-gop 열일곱, sip-ch'il 17.

Seventh-Day Adventists an-sik-gyo 안식교.

seventy *n*. & *adj*. il-hŭn(-ŭi) 일흔(의), ch'il-sip(-ui) 70(의).

sever *v*. kkŭn-t'a 끊다, chŏl-dan-ha-da 절단하다.

several *adj*. myŏt-myŏ-ch'ŭi 몇몇의. —*n*. myŏt kae 몇 개.

severe *adj*. ŏm-gyŏk-han 엄격한, sim-han 심한.

severity *n*. ŏm-gyŏk 엄격 ; hok-dok 혹독.

sew *v.* pa-nŭ-jil-ha-da 바느질하다, chae-bong-ha-da 재

sewage *n.* si-gung-ch'ang 시궁창. ㄴ봉하다.

sewer *n.* ① (*ditch*) ha-su-do 하수도. ② (*butler*) u-du-mŏ-ri kŭp-sa 우두머리 급사. ③ (*seamstress*) chae-bong-sa 재봉사, ch'im-mo 침모.

sewing *n.* pa-nŭ-jil 바느질, chae-bong 재봉 : ~ *machine* chae-bong-t'ŭl 재봉틀. 「sŏng 남성.

sex *n.* sŏng 성(性), sŏng-byŏl 성별 : *the male* ~ nam-

sexual *adj.* nam-nyŏ-ŭi 남녀의, sŏng-jŏk-in 성적인 : ~ *appetite* sŏng-yok 성욕/~ *disease* sŏng-byŏng 성병.

shabby *adj.* ch'o-ra-han 초라한, kkoe-joe-han 꾀죄한.

shack *n.* p'an-ja-jip 판자집, t'ong-na-mu-jip 통나무집.

shackle *n.* su-gap 수갑, soe-go-rang 쇠고랑.

shade *n.* kŭ-nŭl 그늘 ; (*blind*) ch'a-yang 차양.

shadow *n.* kŭ-rim-ja 그림자. 「su-sang-han 수상한.

shady *adj.* kŭ-nŭl-jin 그늘진 ; (*of dubious character*)

shaft *n.* hwa-sal-dae 화살대, kul-dae 굴대.

shaggy *adj.* t'ŏl-i man-ŭn 털이 많은. 「수하다.

shake *v.* hŭn-dŭl-da 흔들다 ; (*hands*) ak-su-ha-da 악

shall *aux.v.* …il〔hal〕 kŏ-si-da …일〔할〕 것이다.

shallow *adj.* ya-t'ŭn 얕은 ; ch'ŏn-bak-han 천박한 : *a* ~ *mind* ch'ŏn-bak-han ma-ŭm 천박한 마음.

sham *n. & adj.* sok-im-su(-ŭi) 속임수(의), ka-jja(-ŭi) 가짜(의) : *a* ~ *exam* mo-ŭi si-hŏm 모의 시험.

Shamanism *n.* mu-gyo 무교, sya-mŏn-gyo 샤먼교.

shamble *n.* to-sal-jang 도살장, su-ra-jang 수라장.

shame *n.* pu-ggŭ-rŏ-um 부끄러움, su-ch'i 수치.

shamefaced *adj.* su-jup-ŏ-ha-nŭn 수줍어하는, am-ddin

shameful *adj.* su-ch'i-sŭ-rŏ-un 수치스러운. ㄴ암떤.

shameless *adj.* yŏm-ch'i-ŏp-nŭn 염치없는.

shampoo *v.* mŏ-ri-rŭl kam-da 머리를 감다. —*n.* syaem-p'u-u 샘푸우.

shank *n.* ① (*shin*) chŏng-gang-i 정강이. ② (*handle*) cha-ru 자루, son-jap-i 손잡이.

shape *n.* mo-yang 모양. —*v.* hyŏng-sŏng-ha-da 형성하다.

share *n.* ① mok 몫. ② (*stock*) chu-sik 주식. —*v.* ① pae-dang-ha-da 배당하다. ② ka-ch'i-ha-da 같이하다.

sharecropper *n.* so-jak-in 소작인.

shark *n.* ① sang-ŏ 상어. ② yok-sim-jang-i 욕심장이.

sharp *adj.* nal-k'a-ro-un 날카로운. —*adv.* nal-k'a-rop-ge 날카롭게 : *Look* ~! Cho-sim-ha-yŏ-ra! 조심하여라!

sharpen *v.* nal-k'a-rop-ge ha-da 날카롭게 하다 ; kal-da 갈다 ; kkak-da 깎다.

shatter *v.* pu-su-da 부수다 ; kkŏk-da 꺾다 : ~ *one's hopes* hŭi-mang-ŭl kkŏk-da 희망을 꺾다.

shave *v.* myŏn-do-ha-da 면도하다. —*n.* myŏn-do 면도.

shawl *n.* syo-ol 쇼올, ŏ-ggae-gŏ-ri 어깨걸이.

she *pron.* kŭ-nyŏ-nŭn[ga] 그녀는[가].

sheaf *n.* ta-bal 다발, mu-ggŭm 묶음.

shear *v.* pe-da 베다, cha-rŭ-da 자르다. —*n.* k'ŭn ka-「wi 큰 가위.

sheath *n.* k'al-jip 칼집, (*cover*) chip 집.

shed *v.* (*drop off*) t'ŏl-da 털다 ; (*tears*) hŭl-ri-da 흘리다. —*n.* (*hut*) o-du-mak 오두막, hŏt-gan 헛간.

sheen *n.* kwang-ch'ae 광채, (*lustre*) yun 윤.

sheep *n.* yang 양, myŏn-yang 면양.

sheer *adj.* sun-jŏn-han 순전한 ; (*steep*) ka-p'a-rŭn 가파른: *a* ~ *cliff* ka-p'a-rŭn pyŏ-rang 가파른 벼랑.

sheet *n.* hot-i-bul 홑이불, si-i-t'ŭ 시이트 ; (*piece of paper*) chong-i han chang 종이 한 장.

shelf *n.* sŏn-ban 선반, si-rŏng 시렁.

shell *n.* ① kkŏp-jil 껍질. ② (*gun*) p'o-t'an 포탄. ③ cho-「gae 조개.

shellfire *n.* p'o-hwa 포화(砲火).

shelter *n.* tae-p'i-so 대피소, p'i-nan-ch'ŏ 피난처. —*v.* p'i-nan-ha-da 피난하다 ; sum-gi-da 숨기다.

shelve *v.* sŏn-ban-e ŏn-da 선반에 얹다 ; po-ryu-ha-da 보류하다 ; (*ignore*) muk-sal-ha-da 묵살하다.

shepherd *n.* yang-ch'i-nŭn sa-ram 양치는 사람.

sheriff *n.* (*Am.*) kun po-an-gwan 군(郡) 보안관 ; chu chang-gwan 주(州) 장관.

shield *v.* po-ho-ha-da 보호하다. —*n.* pang-p'ae 방패.

shiftless *adj.* sok-su-mu-ch'aek-ŭi 속수무책의.

shimmer *n.* ka-mul-gŏ-ri-nŭn pit 가물거리는 빛. —*v.* ka-mul-gŏ-ri-da 가물거리다.

shin *n.* chŏng-gang-i 정강이. —*v.* (*climb*) ki-ŏ-o-rŭ-da 「기어오르다.

shine *v.* ① pit-na-da 빛나다, pan-jjak-i-da 반짝이다. ② (*polish*) tak-da 닦다. —*n.* haet-bit 햇빛, il-gwang 일광.

ship *n.* pae 배. —*v.* su-song-ha-da 수송하다 : *sailing* ~ pŏm-sŏn 범선. 「주.

shipowner *n.* sŏn-bak so-yu-ja 선박 소유자, sŏn-ju 선

shipping company hae-un-hoe-sa 해운회사.

shipwreck *n.* nan-p'a 난파(難破) ; nan-p'a-sŏn 난파선.

shipyard *n.* cho-sŏn-so 조선소.

shirk *v.* (*evade*) p'i-ha-da 피하다, hoe-p'i-ha-da 회피

shirt *n.* wa-i-syŏ-ŏ-ch'ŭ 와이셔어츠. 「하다.

shiver *v.* ttŏl-da 떨다. —*n.* chŏn-yul 전율.

shoal *n.* yŏ-ul 여울 ; (*crowd*) tte 떼, mu-ri 무리.

shock *n.* ch'ung-gyŏk 충격, syo-k'ŭ 쇼크.

shoe *n.* ku-du 구두, tan-hwa 단화, (*Korean*) sin 신 : *rubber* ~s ko-mu-sin 고무신.

shoebrush *n.* ku-dut-sol 구둣솔.

shoehorn *n.* ku-dut-ju-gŏk 구둣주걱.

shoelace *n.* (*shoestring*) ku-du-ggŭn 구두끈.

shoemaker *n.* ku-du ko-ch'i-nŭn sa-ram 구두 고치는 사람, che-hwa-gong 제화공.

shoe polish ku-du-yak 구두약.

shoeshine *n.* ku-du-dak-ggi 구두닦기.

shoot *n.* sa-gyŏk 사격. —*v.* sso-da 쏘다.
shooting *n.* sa-gyŏk 사격, (*hunting*) sa-nyang 사냥.
shop *n.* ka-ge 가게, sang-jŏm 상점 ; (*workshop*) kong-jang 공장 ; chak-ŏp-jang 작업장.
shopkeeper *n.* ka-ge chu-in 가게 주인, (*retailer*) so-mae sang-in 소매 상인.　　　　　　　「주인.
shopman *n.* ① chŏm-wŏn 점원. ② ka-ge chu-in 가게
shopping *n.* chang-bo-gi 장보기, mul-gŏn sa-gi 물건 사기, syo-p'ing 쇼핑.
shore *n.* mul〔kang〕-ga 물〔강〕가, hae-an 해안.
short *adj.* jjal-bŭn 짧은 ; pu-jok-han 부족한 ; (*blunt*) mu-dduk-dduk-han 무뚝뚝한. —*n.* (*pl.*) pan-ba-ji 반
shortage *n.* pu-jok 부족, kyŏl-p'ip 결핍.　　　└바지.
shorten *v.* jjal-gge ha-da 짧게 하다, chul-da 줄다.
shorthand *n.* sok-gi-sul 속기술.
shorts *n.* jjal-bŭn pa-ji 짧은 바지, pan-ba-ji 반바지.
short-sighted *adj.* kŭn-si-ŭi 근시(近視)의.
shot *n.* ① t'an-hwan 탄환, p'o-t'an 포탄. ② (*shooting*) sa-gyŏk 사격. ③ (*marksman*) sa-su 사수.
shoulder *n.* ŏ-ggae 어깨. —*v.* me-da 메다.
shout *n.* ko-ham 고함. —*v.* oe-ch'i-da 외치다.
shove *v.* ttŏ-mil-da 떠밀다, mi-rŏ-nŏ-t'a 밀어넣다.
shovel *n.* sap 삽, pu-sap 부삽, ka-rae 가래.
show *v.* po-i-da 보이다, ka-ri-k'i-da 가리키다. —*n.* kwa-si 과시 ; ku-gyŏng-gŏ-ri 구경거리.
shower *n.* so-na-gi 소나기 ; (*bath*) sya-u-ŏ 샤우어.
showy *adj.* tu-dŭ-rŏ-jin 두드러진 ; ya-han 야한.
shred *n.* han cho-gak 한 조각, p'a-p'yŏn 파편 ; (*bit*) yak-gan 약간. —*v.* chal-ge jji-t'a 잘게 찢다.
shrewd *adj.* pin-t'ŭm-ŏp-nŭn 빈틈없는.
shriek *n.* nal-k'a-ro-un so-ri 날카로운 소리, pi-myŏng 비명. —*v.* pi-myŏng-ŭl ol-ri-da 비명을 올리다.

shrill *adj*. jjae-nŭn tŭt-han 째는 듯한.　—*v*. nal-k'a-ro-un so-ri-rŭl nae-da 날카로운 소리를 내다.　「이.

shrimp *n*. ① sae-u 새우.　② (*dwarf*) nan-jang-i 난장

shrine *n*. sa-dang 사당, myo 묘(廟) ; sŏng-dang 성당.

shrink *v*. o-gŭ-ra-dŭl-da 오그라들다.

shroud *n* su-ŭi 수의(壽衣).　—*v*. (*cover*) tŏ-p'ŏ ssŭi-u-da 덮어 씌우다, ssa-da 싸다.

shrub *n*. kwan-mok 관목, tŏm-bul 덤불.

shrug *v*. ŏ-ggae-rŭl ŭ-ssŭk-ha-da 어깨를 으쓱하다.

shudder *v*. mom-sŏ-ri-ch'i-da 몸서리치다.

shuffle *v*. ① pal-ŭl kkŭl-go ka-da 발을 끌고 가다.　② (*cards*) sŏk-da 섞다.　③ ŏl-bŏ-mu-ri-da 얼버무리다.

shun *v*. p'i-ha-da 피하다, pi-ggi-da 비끼다 : ～ *danger* wi-hŏm-ŭl p'i-ha-da 위험을 피하다.

shut *v*. tat-da 닫다, cham-gŭ-da 잠그다.

shutter *n*. tŏt-mun 덧문, syŏ-t'ŏ 셔터.　　　「왕복 열차.

shuttle *n*. ① (*loon*) puk 북.　② wang-bok yŏl-ch'a

shy *adj*. su-jup-ŭn 수줍은, am-ddin 암띤.

sick *adj*. ① pyŏng-dŭn 병든 ; (*nauseating*) me-sŭ-ggŏ-un 메스꺼운.　② (*longing*) kŭ-ri-wŏ-ha-nŭn 그리워하는.

sickle *n*. chak-ŭn nat 작은 낫.

sickness *n*. pyŏng 병(病) ; yok-ji-gi 욕지기.

side *n*. jjok 쪽, myŏn 면 ; (*flank*) yŏp-gu-ri 옆구리.

sideboard *n*. ch'an-jang 찬장, sal-gang 살강.

sidewalk *n*. po-do 보도, in-do 인도.

sideways *adv*. yŏ-p'ŭ-ro 옆으로, pi-sŭ-dŭm-hi 비스듬히.

siege *n*. p'o-wi kong-gyŏk 포위 공격.

sieve *n*. ① ch'e 체.　② (*person*) ip-i ka-byŏ-un sa-ram 입이 가벼운 사람.　—*v*. ch'e-jil-ha-da 체질하다.

sift *v*. ch'e-ro ch'i-da 체로 치다, ko-rŭ-da 고르다.

sigh *n*. han-sum 한숨.　—*v*. han-sum-ŭl swi-da 한숨을 쉬다, t'an-sik-ha-da 탄식하다.

sight *n.* ① si-ryŏk 시력. ② kwang-gyŏng 광경, kyŏng-ch'i 경치. —*v.* a-ra-bo-da 알아보다.

sightseeing *n.* ku-gyŏng 구경, kwan-gwang 관광.

sign *n.* (*token*) ching-jo 징조; (*signal*) sin-ho 신호; (*symbol*) pu-ho 부호. —*v.* sŏ-myŏng-ha-da 서명하다.

signal *n. & v.* sin-ho(-ha-da) 신호(하다).

signal fire pong-hwa 봉화. 「주제 음악.

signature *n.* sŏ-myŏng 서명: ~ *tune* chu-je ŭm-ak

signboard *n.* kan-p'an 간판, ke-si-p'an 게시판.

signet *n.* mak-do-jang 막도장, (*seal*) in-jang 인장.

significant *adj.* chung-yo-han 중요한.

signify *v.* ŭi-mi-ha-da 의미하다; na-t'a-nae-da 나타내다.

silence *n.* ch'im-muk 침묵, chŏng-jŏk 정적.

silent *adj.* ko-yo-han 고요한, mal-ŏp-nŭn 말없는.

silently *adv.* cho-yong-hi 조용히, cham-ja-k'o 잠자코.

silk *n.* pi-dan 비단; (*Korean*) myŏng-ju 명주.

silkworm *n.* nu-e 누에.

sill *n.* mun-ji-bang 문지방, ch'ang-t'ŏk 창턱.

silly *adj.* ŏ-ri-sŏk-ŭn 어리석은: *Don't be* ~! Ŏ-ri-sŏk-ŭn chit ma-ra! 어리석은 짓 마라!

silver *n.* ŭn 은: ~ *screen* ŭn-mak 은막.

silvery *adj.* ŭn-bi-ch'ŭi 은빛의: ~ *hair* ŭn-bal 은발.

similar *adj.* tal-mŭn 닮은, yu-sa-han 유사한.

simple *adj.* kan-dan-han 간단한, tan-sun-han 단순한; (*plain*) so-bak-han 소박한: ~ *manner* kku-mim-ŏp-nŭn t'ae-do 꾸밈없는 태도.

simplicity *n.* kan-dan 간단; tan-sun 단순; sun-jin 순진.

simplify *v.* kan-dan-ha-ge ha-da 간단하게 하다.

simply *adv.* kan-dan-hi 간단히; (*plainly*) so-bak-ha-ge 소박하게; (*only*) ta-man 다만.

simultaneous *adj.* tong-si-jŏk-in 동시적인.

sin *n.* choe 죄; kwa-sil 과실, (*offense*) wi-ban 위반.

since *conj.* ① (*because*) ···ttae-mun-e ···때문에. ② (*time*) ···i-hu ···이후. —*prep.* ···i-rae ···이래.

sincere *adj.* chin-sil-han 진실한, sŏng-sil-han 성실한.

sincerely *adv.* sŏng-sil-ha-ge 성실하게, chin-jŏng-ŭ-ro [진정으로.

sinew *n.* kŏn 건(腱) ; (*pl.*) kŭn-yuk 근육.

sinful *adj.* choe-man-ŭn 죄많은.

sing *v.* ① no-rae-ha-da 노래하다, (*chirp*) chi-jŏ-gwi-da 지저귀다, ul-da 울다. ② (*ring*) wing-wing-gŏ-ri-da 윙윙거리다. ③ (*praise*) ye-ch'an-ha-da 예찬하다.

singe *v.* kŭ-ŭl-da 그을다, chi-ji-da 지지다.

singer *n.* ka-su 가수, sŏng-ak-ga 성악가.

singing *n.* no-rae-bu-rŭ-gi 노래부르기, ch'ang-ga 창가.

single *adj.* tan-il-ŭi 단일의, tan ha-na-ŭi 단 하나의 ; (*unmarried*) tok-sin-ŭi 독신의. —*n.* han kae 한 개.

singular *adj.* koe-sang-han 괴상한. —*n.* tan-su 단수.

sinister *adj.* pul-gil-han 불길한, chae-su-ŏp-nŭn 재수 없는 ; ak-ŭi-rŭl p'um-ŭn 악의(惡意)를 품은.

sink *n.* sŏl-gŏ-ji-t'ŏng 설겆이통 ; (*drain*) su-ch'ae 수채, ha-su-gu 하수구. —*v.* ka-ra-an-da 가라앉다.

sip *v.* hol-jjak-hol-jjak ma-si-da 홀짝홀짝 마시다, ppal-da 빨다. —*n.* han mo-gŭm 한 모금.

siphon *n.* sa-i-p'ŏn 사이펀.

sir *n.* (*Korean polite title*) nim 님 ; sŏn-saeng 선생.

siren *n.* sa-i-ren 사이렌, ho-jŏk 호적(號笛).

sister *n.* yŏ-ja hyŏng-je 여자 형제, cha-mae 자매(姉妹) ; (*boy's older sister*) nu-nim 누님, (*boy's younger sister*) nu-i tong-saeng 누이 동생 ; (*girl's younger sister*) tong-saeng 동생, (*girl's older sister*) ŏn-ni 언니.

sister-in-law *n.* ① of a man (*elder brother's wife*) hyŏng-su 형수, (*younger brother's wife*) kye-su 계수, (*wife's older sister*) ch'ŏ-hyŏng 처형, (*wife's* *younger sister*) ch'ŏ-je 처제. ② of a woman (*elder brother's wife*) ol-k'e 올케, (*younger brother's wife*) a-u-nim 아우님, (*husband's sister*) si-nu-i 시누이.

sit *v.* an-da 앉다 : ~ *down* an-da 앉다/~ *for* ch'i-rŭ-da 치르다/~ *on*[*upon*] …ŭl cho-sa-ha-da …을 조사하다/~ *up* i-rŏ-na an-da 일어나 앉다.

situation *n.* ch'ŏ-ji 처지 ; (*place*) chang-so 장소.

six *n.* yŏ-sŏt 여섯, yuk 6. —*adj.* yŏ-sŏ-sŭi 여섯의.

sixteen *n. & adj.* yŏl-yŏ-sŏt(-ŭi) 열여섯(의), sip-yuk

sixty *n.* ye-sun 예순, yuk-sip 60.   ⌊(-ŭi)16(의).

size *n.* k'ŭ-gi 크기, ch'i-su 치수.

skate *n.* sŭ-k'e-i-t'ŭ 스케이트. —*v.* sŭ-k'e-i-t'ŭ-rŭl t'a-da 스케이트를 타다, ŏ-rŭm-ŭl chi-ch'i-da 얼음을 지치다.

skating *n.* ŏ-rŭm chi-ch'i-gi 얼음 지치기, sŭ-k'e-i-t'ing 스케이팅, sŭ-k'e-i-t'ŭ 스케이트.

skeleton *n.* ① hae-gol 해골. ② kol-gyŏk 골격.

sketch *n.* (*rough drawing*) sŭ-k'e-ch'i 스케치 ; (*outline*) kae-yo 개요 ; ch'o-an 초안.

ski *n. & v.* sŭ-k'i-i(-rŭl t'a-da) 스키이(를 타다).

skil(l)ful *adj.* nŭng-suk-han 능숙한, som-ssi-it-nŭn 솜

skill *n.* suk-ryŏn 숙련, som-ssi 솜씨.   ⌊씨있는.

skim *v.* sŭ-ch'yŏ chi-na-ga-da 스쳐 지나가다, (*read hastily*) tae-ch'ung il-dda 대충 읽다.   ⌈p'i-bu 피부.

skin *n.* kkŏp-jil 껍질, (*animal*) ka-juk 가죽 ; (*human*)

skip *v.* kkang-ch'ung-ggang-ch'ung ttwi-da 깡충깡충 뛰다 ; (*leave out*) ppa-ddŭ-ri-da 빠뜨리다.

skirmish *n.* so-ch'ung-dol 소충돌. —*v.* chak-ŭn ch'ung-dol-ŭl ha-da 작은 충돌을 하다.

skirt *n.* ① cha-rak 자락. ② sŭ-k'ŏ-ŏ-t'ŭ 스커어트, ch'i-ma 치마. ③ (*border*) pyŏn-du-ri 변두리, ka-jang-ja-

skull *n.* tu-gae-gol 두개골.   ⌊ri 가장자리.

sky *n.* ha-nŭl 하늘 ; (*weather*) nal-ssi 날씨.
skylark *n.* chong-dal-sae 종달새, chong-da-ri 종다리.
skylight *n.* ch'ŏn-ch'ang 천창(天窓).
skyscraper *n.* ma-ch'ŏl-lu 마천루, ko-ch'ŭng 고층.
slab *n.* p'yŏng-p'an 평판, sŏk-p'an 석판 ; sŭl-raep 슬
랩 : *a ～ of marble* tae-ri-sŏk-p'an 대리석판.
slack *adj.* nŭ-sŭn-han 느슨한, nŭ-rin 느린.
slacken *v.* nŭ-sŭn-hae-ji-da 느슨해지다, nŭt-ch'u-da 늦
추다 ; (*neglect*) ke-ŭl-ri-ha-da 게을리하다.
slacks *n.* pa-ji 바지, sŭl-raek-sŭ 슬랙스.　　　　「때리다.
slam *v.* ① (*bang*)k'wang tat-da 쾅 닫다. ② ttae-ri-da
slander *n.* & *v.* chung-sang(-ha-da) 중상(中傷)(하다).
slang *n.* sok-ŏ 속어, sŭl-raeng 슬랭.
slant *n.* pi-t'al 비탈, kyŏng-sa 경사. —*v.* ki-u-ri-da 기
울이다. —*adj.* ki-u-rŏ-jin 기울어진.
slap *n.* ch'al-ssak tu-dŭl-gim 찰싹 두들김. —*v.* ch'al-
ssak ch'i-da 찰싹 치다. —*adv.* ch'al-ssak 찰싹.
slash *v.* ① (*hack violently*) ki-p'i pe-da 깊이 베다, nan-
dol-jil-ha-da 난도질하다. ② (*lash*) 매질하다. —*n.* ①
il-gyŏk 일격. ② k'ŭn sang-ch'ŏ 큰 상처.
slate *n.* sŏk-p'an 석판, sŭl-re-i-t'ŭ 슬레이트.
slaughter *n.* to-sal 도살, (*carnage*) sal-ryuk 살륙.
slave *n.* no-ye 노예.　　　　　　　　「ri-nŭn 침을 흘리는.
slavery *n.* no-ye che-do 노예 제도. —*adj.* ch'im-ŭl hŭl-
slay *v.* chuk-i-da 죽이다, sal-hae-ha-da 살해하다.
sled *n.* ssŏl-mae 썰매. —*v.* ssŏl-mae-rŭl t'a-da 썰매를
타다.　　　　　　　　　　　　　　「nŭn 광택이 나는.
sleek *adj.* mae-ggŭ-rŏ-un 매끄러운, kwang-t'aek-i na-
sleep *n.* cham 잠, su-myŏn 수면. —*v.* cha-da 자다.
sleeping car ch'im-dae-ch'a 침대차.　　　　　　「듯한.
sleepy *adj.* chol-ri-nŭn 졸리는, cha-nŭn tŭt-han 자는
sleet *n.* chin-nun-ggae-bi 진눈깨비.

sleeve *n.* so-mae 소매, so-maet-ja-rak 소맷자락.

sleigh *n.* ssŏl-mae 썰매. —*v.* ssŏl-mae-rŭl t'a-da 썰매를 타다, ssŏl-mae-ro na-rŭ-da 썰매로 나르다.

slender *adj.* hol-jjuk-han 홀쭉한, pin-yak-han 빈약한: *a ~ income* pin-yak-han su-ip 빈약한 수입.

slice *n.* yal-bŭn cho-gak 얇은 조각. —*v.* yal-gge ssŏl-da 얇게 썰다.

slicker *n.* pi-ot 비옷, re-in-k'o-u-t'ŭ 레인코우트.

slide *v.* mi-ggŭ-rŏ-ji-da 미끄러지다. —*n.* hwal-ju 활주, sŭl-ra-i-dŭ 슬라이드.

slight *adj.* yak-gan-ŭi 약간의, kŭn-so-han 근소한. —*v.* kyŏng-si-ha-da 경시하다. —*n.* kyŏng-myŏl 경멸.

slightly *adv.* cho-gŭm 조금, ka-nyal-p'ŭ-ge 가냘프게.

slim *adj.* ka-nŭ-da-ran 가느다란, ho-ri-ho-ri-han 호리

slime *n.* chin-hŭk 진흙.   ⌐호리한.

sling *n.* t'u-sŏk-gi 투석기. —*v.* tŏn-ji-da 던지다.

slink *v.* sal-myŏ-si to-mang-ch'i-da 살며시 도망치다.

slip *v.* mi-ggŭ-rŏ-ji-da 미끄러지다. —*n.* sil-su 실수.

slipper *n.* sŭl-ri-p'ŏ 슬리퍼.

slippery *adj.* mi-ggŭ-rŏ-un 미끄러운.

slit *n.* kal-ra-jin t'ŭm 갈라진 틈, t'ŭm-sae 틈새.

slogan *n.* p'yo-ŏ 표어, sŭl-ro-u-gŏn 슬로우건.

slope *n.* pi-t'al 비탈, kyŏng-sa 경사. —*v.* kyŏng-sa-ji-da 경사지다, pi-t'al-ji-da 비탈지다.

sloth *n.* ke-ŭ-rŭm 게으름, t'ae-man 태만, na-t'ae 나태.

slow *adj.* nŭ-rin 느린, tŏ-din 더딘. —*v.* sok-ryŏk-ŭl nŭt-ch'u-da 속력을 늦추다.

slowly *adv.* ch'ŏn-ch'ŏn-hi 천천히, nŭ-rit-nŭ-rit 느릿느릿.

slug *n.* ① (*animal*) min-dal-p'aeng-i 민달팽이. ② (*idler*) nŭ-ri-gwang-i 느리광이.

sluggard *n.* (*idler*) ke-ŭ-rŭm-baeng-i 게으름뱅이 ; nom-p'ang-i 놈팡이, (*lounger*) kŏn-dal 건달.

sluggish *adj*. nŭ-rin 느린, ke-ŭ-rŭn 게으른.

slum *n*. pin-min-gul 빈민굴, pin-min-ga 빈민가.

slumber *n*. sŏn-jam 선잠, su-myŏn 수면. —*v*. kku-bŏk-ggu-bŏk chol-da 꾸벅꾸벅 졸다.

slump *n*. p'ok-rak 폭락; pu-jin-sang-t'ae 부진상태.

sly *adj*. kyo-hwal-han 교활한, ŏng-k'ŭm-han 엉큼한; mol-rae 몰래 : *on the* ~ ŭn-mil-hi 은밀히.

smack *n*. ① (*taste*) mat 맛, p'ung-mi 풍미. ② (*loud kiss*) jjok-ha-nŭn k'i-sŭ 쪽하는 키스. —*v*. ip-ma-sŭl ta-si-da 입맛을 다시다.

small *adj*. (*not large*) chak-ŭn 작은, (*little*) chŏk-ŭn 적은 ; (*trivial*) po-jal-gŏt-ŏp-nŭn 보잘것없는.

smallpox *n*. ma-ma 마마, ch'ŏn-yŏn-du 천연두.

smart *adj*. chae-ch'i-it-nŭn 재치있는 ; mŏt-jin 멋진.

smash *v*. pun-swae-ha-da 분쇄하다, tu-dŭl-gyŏ p'ae-da 두들겨 패다. 「히다. —*n*. ŏl-ruk 얼룩.

smear *v*. ch'il-ha-da 칠하다 ; (*stain*) tŏ-rŏp-hi-da 더럽

smell *n*. naem-sae 냄새. —*v*. naem-sae mat-da 냄새 맡다, naem-sae-ga na-da 냄새가 나다.

smelt *v*. che-ryŏn-ha-da 제련하다, (*fuse*) yong-hae-ha-da 용해하다. 「gŭt ut-da 생긋 웃다.

smile *n*. mi-so 미소. —*v*. mi-so-ha-da 미소하다, saeng-

smiling *adj*. mi-so-ha-nŭn 미소하는.

smith *n*. (*blacksmith*) tae-jang-jang-i 대장장이.

smoke *n*. yŏn-gi 연기. —*v*. yŏn-gi-nae-da 연기내다; (*cigarette*) tam-bae p'i-u-da 담배 피우다.

smoker *n*. tam-bae p'i-nŭn sa-ram 담배 피는 사람, hŭp-yŏn-ga 흡연가.

smoking *n*. hŭp-yŏn 흡연 : *No* ~. Kŭm-yŏn 금연.

smooth *adj*. mae-ggŭ-rŏ-un 매끄러운, sun-t'an-han 순탄한 : *a* ~ *road* p'yŏng-p'yŏng-han kil 평평한 길. —*v*. mae-ggŭ-rŏp-ge ha-da 매끄럽게 하다.

smother *v.* sum-ŭl mak-da 숨을 막다, chil-sik-si-k'i-da 질식시키다.　　　　　　　　　　　　　「nŭn 뻬기는.

smug *adj.* chal-nan ch'e-ha-nŭn 잘난 체하는, ppŏ-gi-

smuggle *v.* mil-su-ip〔ch'ul〕-ha-da 밀수입〔출〕하다.

smuggler *n.* mil-su-ja 밀수자, mil-su-sŏn 밀수선 : *a ring of* ∼*s* mil-su-dan 밀수단.

snack *n.* kan-dan-han sik-sa 간단한 식사.

snail *n.* tal-p'aeng-i 달팽이.

snake *n.* paem 뱀.

snap *v.* (*break*) t'ak kkŏk-da 탁 꺾다 ; (*dog*) tŏp-sŏk mul-da 덥석 물다. —*n.* ① choem-soe 죔쇠, kŏl-soe 걸쇠. ② (*picture*) sŭ-naep sa-jin 스냅 사진.

snappy *adj.* ki-un-ch'an 기운찬, p'al-p'al-han 팔팔한 : *Make it* ∼*!* Ŏ-sŏ hae-ra! 어서 해라!

snare *n.* tŏt 덫, ol-ga-mi 올가미.

snarl *v.* ŭ-rŭ-rŏng-gŏ-ri-da 으르렁거리다 ; hol-lan 혼란.

snatch *v.* chap-a-ch'ae-da 잡아채다, tal-ryŏ-dŭl-da 달려들다. —*n.* kang-t'al 강탈 ; (*a short period*) cham-ggan 잠깐 ; (*fragments*) tan-p'yŏn 단편.

sneak *v.* (*slink*) sal-gŭm-sal-gŭm ta-ni-da 살금살금 다니다 ; (*cringe*) kup-sil-gŏ-ri-da 굽실거리다.

sneer *v.* pi-ut-da 비웃다, kyŏng-myŏl-ha-da 경멸하다. —*n.* naeng-so 냉소.

sneeze *n.* chae-ch'ae-gi 재채기. —*v.* ① chae-ch'ae-gi-ha-da 재채기하다. ② (*despise*) kkal-bo-da 깔보다.

sniff *v.* k'o-rŭl k'ŭng-k'ŭng-gŏ-ri-da 코를 킁킁거리다, naem-sae-rŭl mat-da 냄새를 맡다.

snip *n.* cho-gak 조각. —*v.* cha-rŭ-da 자르다.　　　「속물.

snob *n.* sa-i-bi sin-sa 사이비 신사 ; (*worldling*) sok-mul

snore *n.* k'o-go-nŭn so-ri 코고는 소리. —*v.* k'o-rŭl kol-da 코를 골다.

snout *n.* ① k'o 코. ② (*muzzle*) chu-dung-i 주둥이.

snow *n.* nun 눈. —*v.* nun-i o-da 눈이 오다.

snowball *n.* nun-mung-ch'i 눈뭉치, nun-dŏng-i 눈덩이.

snowdrift *n.* nun-dŏ-mi 눈더미.

snowfall *n.* kang-sŏl 강설, kang-sŏl-ryang 강설량.

snowflake *n.* nun-song-i 눈송이.

snowman *n.* nun-sa-ram 눈사람.

snowplough·snowplow *n.* che-sŏl-gi 제설기(除雪機).

snowslide *n.* (*avalanche*) nun-sa-t'ae 눈사태.

snowstorm *n.* nun-bo-ra 눈보라.

snowy *adj.* nun-i man-ŭn 눈이 많은, sae-ha-yan 새하얀.

snuff *v.* k'o-ro tŭ-ri-ma-si-da 코로 들이마시다. —*n.* k'o-dam-bae 코담배. 「다.

snuffle *n.* k'ot-so-ri 콧소리. —*v.* k'o-ga me-da 코가 메

snug *adj.* a-nŭk-han 아늑한, al-lak-han 안락한.

so *adv.* kŭ-rŏ-k'e 그렇게. —*conj.* kŭ-rŏ-mŭ-ro 그러므로. —*pron.* kŭ-wa ka-t'ŭn kŏt 그와 같은 것.

soak *n.* tam-gŭ-da 담그다, chŏk-si-da 적시다 ; (*permeate*) sŭ-myŏ-dŭl-da 스며들다. 「누.

soap *n.* pi-nu 비누 : *toilet* ~ hwa-jang pi-nu 화장 비

soapsuds *n.* pi-nu kŏ-p'um 비누거품, pi-nut-mul 비눗물.

soar *v.* no-p'i nal-da 높이 날다 ; ch'i-sot-da 치솟다.

sob *n.* hŭ-nŭ-ggim 흐느낌. —*v.* hŭ-nŭ-ggyŏ ul-da 흐느껴 울다, mok-me-ŏ ul-da 목메어 울다.

sober *adj.* chin-ji-han 진지한, kŭn-sil-han 근실한, ch'wi-ha-ji an-ŭn 취하지 않은.

so-called *adj.* i-rŭn-ba 이른바, so-wi 소위.

sociable *adj.* sa-gyo-jŏk-in 사교적인, sa-gŭn-sa-gŭn-han 사근사근한, pu-ch'im-sŏng-it-nŭn 붙임성있는.

social *adj.* sa-hoe-ŭi 사회의, sa-gyo-jŏk-in 사교적인.

society *n.* sa-hoe 사회 ; (*institution*) hak-hoe 학회.

sociology *n.* sa-hoe-hak 사회학.

sock *n.* jjal-bŭn yang-mal 짧은 양말.

socket *n.* (kki-u-nŭn) ku-mŏng (끼우는) 구멍, so-k'et [소켓.

sod *n.* chan-di 잔디, tte 떼.

soda *n.* t'an-san-su 탄산수, so-o-da 소오다.

soever *adv.* pi-rok …il-ji-ra-do 비록 …일지라도.

sofa *n.* kin al-lak-ŭi-ja 긴 안락의자, so-p'a 소파.

soft *adj.* pu-dŭ-rŏ-un 부드러운, on-hwa-han 온화한.

soften *v.* pu-dŭ-rŏp-ge ha-da 부드럽게 하다.

softly *adv.* pu-dŭ-rŏp-ge 부드럽게.

soil *n.* *n.* ① hŭk 흙, t'o-ji 토지. ② (*dirt*) o-mul 오물.
 —*v.* tŏ-rŏp-hi-da 더럽히다. 「ch'e-jae 체재.

sojourn *v.* ch'e-ryu-ha-da 체류하다. —*n.* ch'e-ryu 체류,

solace *n.* wi-ro 위로, wi-an 위안. —*v.* wi-ro-ha-da 위
 로하다, wi-an-i toe-da 위안이 되다.

solar *adj.* t'ae-yang-ŭi 태양의 : ~ *calendar* yang-ryŏk
 양력(陽曆)/~ *eclipse* il-sik 일식.

soldier *n.* kun-in 군인, sa-byŏng 사병.

sole *n.* ① (*one and only*) tan ha-na 단 하나. ② (*of
 shoes*) ch'ang 창. ③ (*of foot*) pal-ba-dak 발바닥.

solely *adv.* o-jik 오직, ta-man 다만, hon-ja-sŏ 혼자서.

solemn *adj.* ŏm-suk-han 엄숙한, chang-ŏm-han 장엄한.

solicit *v.* ① (*entreat*) kan-ch'ŏng-ha-da 간청하다. ②
 (*ask earnestly*) cho-rŭ-da 조르다.

solid *adj.* ko-ch'e-ŭi 고체의 ; tan-dan-han 단단한 ; kyŏn-
 go-han 견고한. —*n.* ko-ch'e 고체.

solidarity *n.* tan-gyŏl 단결, yŏn-dae-ch'aek-im 연대책임.

solidify *v.* (*make solid*) kut-hi-da 굳히다, ko-ch'e-
 hwa-ha-da 고체화하다.

solitary *adj.* ko-dok-han 고독한, oe-ro-un 외로운.

solitude *n.* ① ko-dok 고독. ② oe-ddan kot 외딴 곳.

solo *n.* (*vocal*) tok-ch'ang 독창, (*inst.*) tok-ju 독주.

solstice *n.* (*winter*) tong-ji 동지, (*summer*) ha-ji 하지.

solution *n.* ① hae-gyŏl 해결. ② yong-hae 용해.

solve *v.* hae-gyŏl-ha-da 해결하다.

somber·sombre *adj.* ch'im-ch'im-han 침침한.

some *adj.* ŏ-ddŏn 어떤, yak-gan-ŭi 약간의. —*pron.* 약간, ta-so 다소, ŏ-ddŏn kŏt 어떤 것.

somebody *n. & pron.* ŏ-ddŏn sa-ram 어떤 사람 ; (*person of some note*) sang-dang-han in-mul 상당한 인물.

somehow *adj.* ŏ-ddŏ-k'e-dŭn 어떻게든.

somersault *n.* chae-ju-nŏm-gi 재주넘기, (*handspring*) kong-jung-je-bi 공중제비.

something *pron.* ŏ-ddŏn kŏt 어떤 것, (*thing of some value*) sang-dang-han kŏt 상당한 것.

sometime *adj.* ŏn-jen-ga 언젠가, ŏn-je-go 언제고.

sometimes *adv.* ttae-ddae-ro 때때로, i-dda-gŭm 이따금.

somewhat *adv.* ŏl-ma-gan 얼마간, ta-so 다소.

somewhere *adv.* ŏ-di-ron-ga 어디론가, ŏ-din-ji 어딘지.

son *n.* a-dŭl 아들, cha-son 자손.

song *n.* ① no-rae 노래. ② (*birds*) u-nŭn so-ri 우는 소 「리.

son-in-law *n.* sa-wi 사위 ; (*adopted son*) yang-ja 양자.

sonnet *n.* sip-sa-haeng-si 14행시(行詩), so-ne-t'ŭ 소네트.

soon *adv.* kot 곧, i-nae 이내, ppal-ri 빨리.

soot *n.* kŏm-daeng 검댕, mae-yŏn 매연. 「키다.

soothe *v.* tal-rae-da 달래다, chin-jŏng-si-k'i-da 진정시

sophisticated *adj.* yak-sak-bba-rŭn 약삭빠른, ki-gyo-e ch'i-u-ch'in 기교에 치우친, sok-im-su-ŭi 속임수의.

soprano *n.* so-p'ŭ-ra-no 소프라노.

sorcerer *n.* ma-sul-sa 마술사, ma-bŏp-sa 마법사.

sorceress *n.* mu-dang 무당.

sordid *adj.* (*dirty*) tŏ-rŏ-un 더러운, nu-ch'u-han 누추한 ; t'am-yok-sŭ-rŏ-un 탐욕스러운.

sore *adj.* ① (*painful to the touch*) a-p'ŭn 아픈, ssŭ-ra-rin 쓰라린. ② (*sorrowful*) sŭl-p'ŭn 슬픈.

sorrow *n.* sŭl-p'ŭm 슬픔. —*v.* sŭl-p'ŏ-ha-da 슬퍼하다.

sorry *adj.* sŏp-sŏp-han 섭섭한, (*feeling regret*) yu-gam-sŭ-rŏn 유감스런 : *I am* ~. ① (*my fault*) Mi-an-hap-ni-da. 미안합니다. ② (*not my fault*) An-dwae-ssŭm-ni-da. 안됐읍니다.

sort *n.* chong-ryu 종류. — *v.* pul-lyu-ha-da 분류하다.

soul *n.* ① yŏng-hon 영혼, chŏng-sin 정신. ② (*person*) sa-ram 사람. 「so-ri-ga na-da 소리가 나다.

sound *adj.* kŏn-jŏn-han 건전한. —*n.* so-ri 소리. —*v.*

soundproof *adj.* pang-ŭm-jang-ch'i-ga toen 방음장치가 된, pang-ŭm-ŭi 방음의.

soup *n.* kuk 국, su-u-p'ŭ 수우프.

sour *adj.* (*acid*) sin 신, si-k'ŭm-han 시큼한.

source *n.* kŭn-wŏn 근원, ch'ul-ch'ŏ 출처.

south *n.* nam-jjok 남쪽. —*adj.* nam-jjok-ŭi 남쪽의.

southeast *n.* tong-nam 동남, tong-nam-bu 동남부.

southern *adj.* nam-jjok-ŭi 남쪽의. 「jjok-ŭi 남쪽의.

southward *adv.* nam-jjok-ŭ-ro 남쪽으로. —*adj.* nam-

souvenir *n.* ki-nyŏm-p'um 기념품 ; sŏn-mul 선물.

sovereign *n.* chu-gwŏn-ja 주권자, kun-ju 군주.

sow *v.* ssi-rŭl ppu-ri-da 씨를 뿌리다, p'ŏ-ddŭ-ri-da 퍼뜨리다. —*n.* (*a female hog*) am-t'wae-ji 암돼지.

soy *n.* (*sauce*) kan-jang 간장.

soy(a)bean *n.* k'ong 콩 : ~ *paste* toen-jang 된장.

space *n.* (*interval*) kan-gyŏk 간격 ; (*celestial*) kong-gan 공간 ; (*universe*) u-ju 우주.

spacious *adj.* nŏl-bŭn 넓은, kwang-dae-han 광대한.

spade *n.* sap 삽, ka-rae 가래.

span *n.* han ppyŏm 한 뼘 ; (*short distance*) jjal-bŭn kŏ-ri 짧은 거리. —*v.* son-ga-rak-ŭ-ro chae-da 손가락으로 재다, (*extend*) ···e mi-ch'i-da ···에 미치다.

spangle *n.* pŏn-jjŏk-gŏ-ri-nŭn chang-sik 번쩍거리는 장식. —*v.* pŏn-jjŏk-i-da 번쩍이다.

Spanish *n*. sŭ-p'e-in-ŏ 스페인어 ; (*people*) sŭ-p'e-in-sa-ram 스페인사람. —*adj*. sŭ-p'e-in-ŭi 스페인의.

spank *v*. ch'al-ssak ttae-ri-da 찰싹 때리다.

spare *adj*. (*scanty*) pu-jok-han 부족한 ; (*reserved*) ye-bi-ŭi 예비의. —*v*. a-ggyŏ ssŭ-da 아껴 쓰다.

spark *n*. pul-ggot 불꽃, pul-ddong 불똥.

sparkle *n*. pul-t'i 불티, sŏm-gwang 섬광. —*v*. (*glitter*) pŏn-jjŏk-gŏ-ri-da 번쩍거리다.

sparrow *n*. ch'am-sae 참새. 「드문드문한.

sparse *adj*. (*thin*) sŏng-gin 성긴, tŭ-mun-dŭ-mun-han

spasm *n*. kyŏng-ryŏn 경련, pal-jak 발작.

speak *v*. mal-ha-da 말하다, (*converse*) i-ya-gi-ha-da 이야기하다 ; (*speech*) yŏn-sŏl-ha-da 연설하다.

speaker *n*. ① yŏn-sa 연사, pyŏn-sa 변사. ② hwak-

spear *n*. ch'ang 창. 「sŏng-gi 확성기.

special *adj*. t'ŭk-byŏl-han 특별한. 「의(醫).

specialist *n*. chŏn-mun-ga 전문가 ; chŏn-mun-ŭi 전문

specialize *v*. chŏn-mun-ŭ-ro yŏn-gu-ha-da 전문으로 연구하다, chŏn-gong-ha-da 전공하다.

specially *adv*. t'ŭk-byŏl-hi 특별히, t'ŭk-hi 특히.

species *n*. chong 종(種), chong-ryu 종류.

specific *adj*. t'ŭk-jong-ŭi 특종의 ; (*explicit*) myŏng-hwak-han 명확한. —*n*. t'ŭk-hyo-yak 특효약.

specify *v*. cha-se-hi ki-ip-ha-da 자세히 기입하다.

specimen *n*. kyŏn-bon 견본, p'yo-bon 표본.

speck *n*. ŏl-ruk 얼룩, pan-jŏm 반점 ; o-jŏm 오점.

speckle *n*. chak-ŭn pan-jŏm 작은 반점.

spectacle *n*. ① kwang-gyŏng 광경. ② an-gyŏng 안경.

spectacled *adj*. an-gyŏng-ŭl kkin 안경을 낀.

spectator *n*. ku-gyŏng-gun 구경군, kwan-gaek 관객.

spectroscope *n*. pun-gwang-gi 분광기.

speculate *v*. sa-saek-ha-da 사색하다 ; (*gamble in*

stocks) t'u-gi-ha-da 투기하다.
speculation *n.* ① (*meditation*) sa-saek 사색, suk-go 숙고. ② (*stockjobbing*) t'u-gi 투기.
speech *n.* (*address*) yŏn-sŏl 연설 ; (*language*) ŏn-ŏ 언어, mal 말 ; (*gram.*) hwa-bŏp 화법.　「sok 신속.
speed *n.* sok-do 속도, sok-ryŏk 속력. (*swiftness*) sin-
spell *n.* ① chu-mun 주문(呪文). ② (*short period*) cham-si 잠시. —*v.* ch'ŏl-ja-ha-da 철자하다.
spelling *n.* ch'ŏl-ja(-bŏp) 철자(법).　　「다.
spend *v.* so-bi-ha-da 소비하다 ; (*time*) po-nae-da 보내
spendthrift *n.* nang-bi-ga 낭비가 ; pang-t'ang-a 방탕아.
sphere *n.* ① (*globe*) ku-ch'e 구체(球體), ku-hyŏng 구형. ② (*scope*) pŏm-wi 범위, pun-ya 분야.
spice *n.* yang-nyŏm 양념, hyang-ryo 향료.
spider *n.* ① kŏ-mi 거미. ② sam-ba-ri 삼발이. 「파이크.
spike *n.* (*nail*) mot 못 ; (*for shoes*) su-p'a-i-k'ŭ 스
spill *v.* ŏp-ji-rŭ-da 엎지르다, hŭl-ri-da 흘리다.
spin *v.* (*yarn*) chat-da 잣다, pang-jŏk-ha-da 방적하다 ; (*a top*) tol-ri-da 돌리다. —*n.* hoe-jŏn 회전.
spinach *n.* si-gŭm-ch'i 시금치.
spinal *adj.* ch'ŏk-ch'u-ŭi 척추의.
spindle *n.* puk 북.
spine *n.* ch'ŏk-ch'u 척추.
spinning wheel mul-re 물레.
spinster *n.* (*old maid*) no-ch'ŏ-nyŏ 노처녀, o-ul-dŭ-mi-sŭ 오울드미스.　[mul-re]
spire *n.* ppyo-jok-t'ap 뾰족탑, ch'ŏm-t'ap 첨탑.
spirit *n.* ① (*soul*) chŏng-sin 정신 ; (*ghost*) mang-ryŏng 망령 ; (*vigor*) ki-un 기운. ② al-k'o-ol 알코올. —*v.* (*animate*) hwal-gi-rŭl tti-ge ha-da 활기를 띠게 하다.
spiritual *adj.* chŏng-sin-jŏk-in 정신적인, yŏng-jŏk-in 영적인. —*n.* yŏng-ga 영가(靈歌).

spit *v.* ch'im-ŭl paet-da 침을 뱉다. —*n.* ch'im 침.
spite *n.* ak-ŭi 악의, wŏn-han 원한. —*v.* (*vex*) koe-rop-hi-da 괴롭히다, hak-dae-ha-da 학대하다.
spiteful *adj.* sim-sul-gu-jŭn 심술궂은, ang-sim-gi-p'ŭn
spittoon *n.* t'a-gu 타구(唾具).　　　　　　　└앙심깊은.
splash *v.* (*spatter*) t'wi-gi-da 튀기다.
spleen *n.* pi-jang 비장(脾臟) ; (*ill humor*) ul-hwa 울화.
splendid *adj.* (*fine*) hul-ryung-han 훌륭한, (*grand*) tang-dang-han 당당한, koeng-jang-han 굉장한.
splendo(u)r *n.* kwang-ch'ae 광채, pit-nam 빛남.
splice *v.* it-da 잇다, kyŏp-ch'yŏ it-da 겹쳐 잇다.
splinter *n.* na-mu cho-gak 나무 조각, t'o-mak 토막 ; (*thorn*) ka-si 가시. —*v.* jjo-gae-da 쪼개다.
split *v.* jjo-gae-da 쪼개다, jjit-da 찢다. —*n.* ① kal-ra-jin t'ŭm 갈라진 틈. ② (*rupture*) pul-hwa 불화.
spoil *n.* yak-t'al-p'um 약탈품. —*v.* (*ruin*) mang-ch'i-da 망치다 ; (*damage*) son-sang-ha-da 손상하다.
spokesman *n.* tae-byŏn-in〔ja〕 대변인〔자〕.
sponge *n.* hae-myŏn 해면, sŭ-p'ŏn-ji 스펀지.
spongy *adj.* hae-myŏn mo-yang-ŭi 해면 모양의 ; p'ok-sin-p'ok-sin-han 폭신폭신한.
sponsor *n.* (*supporter*) hu-wŏn-ja 후원자 ; (*promoter*) pal-gi-in 발기인 ; kwang-go-ju 광고주. —*v.* ① hu-wŏn-ha-da 후원하다. ② kwang-go-rŭl ha-da 광고를 하다.
spontaneous *adj.* (*voluntary*) cha-bal-jŏk-in 자발적인, (*natural*) cha-yŏn-jŏk-in 자연적인.
spool *n.* sil-p'ae 실패, sil-gam-gae 실감개.
spoon *n.* sut-ga-rak 숟가락. sŭ-p'u-un 스푸운.
sporadic *adj.* ka-ggŭm i-rŏ-na-nŭn 가끔 일어나는.
sport *n.* un-dong 운동 ; (*pastime*) no-ri 놀이 ; (*jest*)
sportsman *n.* un-dong-ga 운동가.　　　└nong-dam 농담.
sportsmanship *n.* un-dong-ga chŏng-sin 운동가 정신,

sŭ-p'o-ch'ŭ-maen-sip 스포츠맨십.

spot *n.* (*place*) chi-jŏm 지점 ; (*dot*) ŏl-ruk 얼룩. —*v.* tŏ-rŏ-wŏ-ji-da 더러워지다.　「nŭn 흠이 없는.

spotless *adj.* ŏl-ruk-i ŏp-nŭn 얼룩이 없는, hŭm-i ŏp-

spouse *n.* pae-u-ja 배우자, (*pl.*) pu-bu 부부.

spout *v.* nae-bbum-da 내뿜다. —*n.* chu-dung-i 주둥이.

sprain *n.* chŏp-jil-rim 접질림. —*v.* ppi-da 삐다.

sprawl *v.* son-bal-ŭl jjuk ppŏt-da 손발을 쭉 뻗다 ; (*scramble*) ki-ŏ-da-ni-da 기어다니다.

spray *n.* ① (*from water*) mul-bo-ra 물보라. ② (*small branch*) chak-ŭn ka-ji 작은 가지. —*v.* mul-bo-ra-rŭl nal-ri-da 물보라를 날리다, ppum-da 뿜다.

spread *v.* ppu-ri-da 뿌리다, p'ŏ-ddŭ-ri-da 퍼뜨리다.

sprig *n.* chan-ga-ji 잔가지, ŏ-rin ka-ji 어린 가지.

sprightly *adj.* (*gay*) k'wae-hwal-han 쾌활한.

spring *n.* ① (*fountain*) saem 샘. ② (*season*) pom 봄. ③ (*wire*) sŭ-p'ŭ-ring 스프링. —*v.* ttwi-da 뛰다.

sprinkle *v.* ppu-ri-da 뿌리다, kki-ŏn-da 끼얹다.

sprout *v.* ssak-i na-da 싹이 나다. —*n.* ssak 싹 ; (*bean sprouts*) k'ong-na-mul 콩나물.

spur *n.* pak-ch'a 박차. —*v.* (*urge*) pak-ch'a-rŭl ka-ha-da 박차를 가하다. ko-mu-ha-da 고무하다.

spurn *v.* jjo-ch'a-bŏ-ri-da 쫓아버리다. —*n.* kŏ-jŏl 거절.

sputter *v.* ch'im-ŭl t'wi-gi-da 침을 튀기다.

spy *n.* kan-ch'ŏp 간첩, sŭ-p'a-i 스파이. —*v.* chŏng-t'am-ha-da 정탐하다, ch'a-ja-nae-da 찾아내다.

spyglass *n.* chak-ŭn mang-wŏn-gyŏng 작은 망원경.

squad *n.* pan 반(班), pun-dae 분대.　「대.

squadron *n.* pi-haeng chung-dae 비행 중대 ; ham-dae 함

square *n.* ne-mo-ggol 네모꼴, chŏng-bang-hyŏng 정방형 ; (*open space*) kwang-jang 광장.

squash *n.* sŏ-yang ho-bak 서양 호박. —*v.* jji-gŭ-rŏ-ddŭ-ri-da 찌그러뜨리다.

squat *v.* ung-k'ŭ-ri-go an-da 웅크리고 앉다.

squawk *v.* kkak-ggak ul-da 깍깍 울다.

squeak *v.* ppi-gŏk-bbi-gŏk so-ri nae-da 삐걱삐걱 소리 내다 ; (*peach*) ko-ja-jil-ha-da 고자질하다.

squeal *n.* a-u-sŏng 아우성. —*v.* kkik-ggik-gŏ-ri-da 끽 끽거리다 ; pul-p'yŏng-ha-da 불평하다.

squeeze *v.* jja-da 짜다, kkwak choe-da 꽉 죄다.

squint *n.* sa-p'al-nun 사팔눈, kyŏt-nun-jil 곁눈질. —*v.* kyŏt-nun-jil-ha-da 곁눈질하다. 「주.

squire *n.* chi-bang myŏng-sa 지방 명사, tae-ji-ju 대지

squirm *v.* kkum-t'ŭl-gŏ-ri-da 꿈틀거리다.

squirrel *n.* ta-ram-jwi 다람쥐. 「출하다.

squirt *v.* ppum-ŏ-nae-da 뿜어내다, pun-ch'ul-ha-da 분

stab *v.* jji-rŭ-da 찌르다, (*pierce*) kkwe-da 꿰다.

stability *n.* an-jŏng 안정, kyŏn-go 견고.

stable *adj.* kyŏn-go-han 견고한 ; an-jŏng-doen 안정된. —*n.* ma-gut-gan 마굿간, oe-yang-gan 외양간.

stack *n.* nat-ga-ri 낟가리, tŏ-mi 더미.

stadium *n.* kyŏng-gi-jang 경기장, sŭ-t'a-di-um 스타디움.

staff *n.* ① (*pole*) mak-dae-gi 막대기, chang-dae 장대. ② pu-wŏn 부원, chik-wŏn 직원. ③ (*army*) ch'am-mo 참모 : *chief of* ~ ch'am-mo-ch'ong-jang 참모총장.

stag *n.* su-sa-sŭm 수사슴.

stage *n.* ① mu-dae 무대, sŭ-t'e-i-ji 스테이지, pal-p'an 발판. ② (*period*) si-gi 시기 ; tan-gye 단계. 「설이다.

stagger *v.* pi-t'ŭl-gŏ-ri-da 비틀거리다 ; mang-sŏ-ri-da 망

stagnant *adj.* koe-ŏ-it-nŭn 괴어있는 ; (*slump*) pul-gyŏng-gi-ŭi 불경기의. 「doen 고정된.

staid *adj.* ch'im-ch'ak-han 침착한 ; (*fixed*) ko-jŏng-

stain *v.* tŏ-rŏp-hi-da 더럽히다. —*n.* ① (*spot*) ŏl-ruk 얼룩, tŏ-rŏm 더럼. ② (*blot*) o-jŏm 오점.

stainless *adj.* nok-sŭl-ji an-nŭn 녹슬지 않는, ŏl-ruk-ji-ji an-ŭn 얼룩지지 않은.

stair *n.* sa-da-ri 사다리, kye-dan 계단.

staircase *n.* kye-dan 계단, ch'ŭng-gye 층계. 「판돈.

stake *n.* ① (*post*) mal-dduk 말뚝. ② (*wager*) p'an-don

stale *adj.* sang-han 상한, (*flat*) kim-bba-jin 김빠진 ; (*trite*) k'ye-k'ye-muk-ŭn 케케묵은.

stalk *n.* chul-gi 줄기. —*v.* sal-gŭm-sal-gŭm ka-da 살금살금 가다 ; (*stride*) hwal-bo-ha-da 활보하다.

stall *n.* ① (*stable*) ma-gut-gan 마굿간. ② (*stand*) mae-jŏm 매점. —*v.* (*bogged down*) o-do-ga-do mot-ha-da 오도가도 못하다, chŏ-ji-ha-da 저지하다.

stalwart *adj.* t'ŭn-t'ŭn-han 튼튼한, kŏn-jang-han 건장

stamen *n.* (*of flower*) su-sul 수술. 「한.

stammer *v.* mal-ŭl tŏ-dŭm-da 말을 더듬다.

stamp *n.* (*postage*) u-p'yo 우표, in-ji 인지 ; (*seal*) to-jang 도장. —*v.* (*impress*) jjik-da 찍다 ; (*feet*) pal-ŭl ku-rŭ-da 발을 구르다, kŏt-da 걷다.

stand *n.* (*position*) ip-jang 입장 ; (*support*) tae 대(臺). —*v.* ① sŏ-da 서다. ② (*endure*) ch'am-da 참다.

standard *n.* ① p'yo-jun 표준. ② (*flag*) kun-gi 군기.

standing *n.* (*standing place*) sŏn chang-so 선 장소 ; (*rank*) chi-wi 지위, myŏng-mang 명망.

staple *n.* chu-san-mul 주산물, (*raw material*) wŏl-lyo 원료. —*adj.* (*principal*) chu-yo-han 주요한.

star *n.* ① pyŏl 별 ; (*destiny*) un-myŏng 운명. ② (*popular actor, actress*) sŭ-t'a-a 스타아.

starch *n.* nok-mal 녹말, (*paste*) p'ul 풀. —*v.* p'ul-ŭl mŏk-i-da 풀을 먹이다. 「다. —*n.* ŭng-si 응시.

stare *v.* no-ryŏ-bo-da 노려보다, ppan-hi po-da 빤히 보

starry *adj.* pyŏl-ŭi 별의 ; pyŏl-i pan-jjak-i-nŭn 별이 반짝이는 ; pyŏl-bit pal-gŭn 별빛 밝은.

start *n.* ① si-jak 시작, (*in races*) ch'ul-bal 출발. ②
(*shock*) kkam-jjak nol-ram 깜짝 놀람. —*v.* si-jak-ha-
da 시작하다, ch'ul-bal-ha-da 출발하다.
starting point ch'ul-bal-jŏm 출발점.
startle *v.* kkam-jjak nol-ra-ge ha-da 깜짝 놀라게 하다.
starvation *n.* kum-ju-rim 굶주림, ki-a 기아.
starve *v.* kum-ju-ri-da 굶주리다 ; kal-mang-ha-da 갈망
하다 : ~ *to death* kul-mŏ chuk-da 굶어 죽다.
state *n.* (*body politic*) kuk-ga 국가 ; (*a province*)
chu 주(州) : (*condition*) sang-t'ae 상태. —*v.* (*express
formally*) chin-sul-ha-da 진술하다.　　　　　　「있는.
stately *adj.* tang-dang-han 당당한, wi-ŏm-it-nŭn 위엄
statement *n.* chin-sul 진술 ; sŏng-myŏng 성명.
stateroom *n.* t'ŭk-dŭng-sil 특등실, chŏn-yong-sil 전용
statesman *n.* chŏng-ch'i-ga 정치가.　　　　　　　　「실.
station *n.* (*of a railway*) chŏng-gŏ-jang 정거장 ; (*position*) wi-ch'i 위치 ; (*rank*) sin-bun 신분. —*v.* chu-
dun-ha-da 주둔하다, pae-ch'i-ha-da 배치하다.
stationary *adj.* um-jik-i-ji an-nŭn 움직이지 않는, chŏng-
ji-doen 정지된 ; sang-bi-ŭi 상비(常備)의.
stationery *n.* p'yŏn-ji-ji 편지지, mun-bang-gu 문방구.
statistical *adj.* t'ong-gye-ŭi 통계의.
statistics *n.* ① t'ong-gye(-p'yo) 통계(표). ② (*science*)
t'ong-gye-hak 통계학.　　　　　　　　　　　　　「상.
statue *n.* cho-sang 조상(彫像) : *bronze* ~ tong-sang 동
stature *n.* sin-jang 신장(身長), k'i 키.
status *n.* (*rank*) sin-bun 신분 ; (*condition*) sang-t'ae
statute *n.* pŏp-ryŏng 법령, pŏp-gyu 법규.　　　　「상태.
stay *v.* mŏ-mu-rŭ-da 머무르다, (*stop*) mŏm-ch'u-da 멈추
다. —*n.* ch'e-ryu 체류 ; chŏng-ji 정지.　　「대신하여.
stead *n.* tae-sin 대신 : *in* ~ *of* …ŭl tae-sin-ha-yŏ …을
steadfast *adj.* hwak-go-han 확고한, pul-byŏn-ŭi 불변의.

steady *adj.* (*firm*) tan-dan-han 단단한, (*faithful*) ch'ak-sil-han 착실한, han-gyŏl-ga-t'ŭn 한결같은.
steak *n.* sŭ-t'e-i-k'ŭ 스테이크, pul-go-gi 불고기.
steal *adj.* hum-ch'i-da 훔치다. —*n.* chŏl-do 절도.
steam *n.* chŭng-gi 증기, kim 김. —*v.* jji-da 찌다.
steam engine chŭng-gi ki-gwan 증기 기관.
steamer *n.* ① ki-sŏn 기선. ② si-ru 시루.
steamship *n.* ki-sŏn 기선, sang-sŏn 상선.
steed *n.* (*for horse riding*) mal 말, kun-ma 군마.
steel *n.* kang-ch'ŏl 강철, kang 강(鋼).
steelyard *n.* tae-jŏ-ul 대저울.
steep *adj.* hŏm-han 험한, ka-p'a-rŭn 가파른 : *a ~ mountain* ka-p'a-rŭn san 가파른 산.
steeple *n.* ppyo-jok-t'ap 뾰족탑, ch'ŏm-t'ap 첨탑.
steer *v.* ① cho-jong-ha-da 조종하다 ; (*direct*) tol-ri-da 돌리다. ② (*conduct oneself*) ch'ŏ-sin-ha-da 처신하다.
stem *n.* (*of plants*) chul-gi 줄기. —*v.* (*stop*) mak-a-nae-da 막아내다, (*resist*) chŏ-hang-ha-da 저항하다.
stenographer *n.* sok-gi-sa 속기사.
stenography *n.* sok-gi 속기, sok-gi-sul 속기술.
step *v.* (*walk*) kŏt-da 걷다 ; na-a-ga-da 나아가다 ; (*tread*) pap-da 밟다. —*n.* kŏ-rŭm-sae 걸음새.
stepbrother *n.* i-bok-hyŏng-je 이복형제.
stepchild *n.* ŭi-but-ja-sik 의붓자식.
stepdaughter *n.* ŭi-but-ddal 의붓딸.
stepfather *n.* ŭi-but-a-bŏ-ji 의붓아버지, kye-bu 계부.
stepmother *n.* ŭi-but-ŏ-mŏ-ni 의붓어머니, kye-mo 계모.
sterile *adj.* (*barren*) me-ma-rŭn 메마른 ; pu-rim-ŭi 불임의 ; (*unable to produce*) pul-mo-ŭi 불모의.
stern *adj.* ŏm-gyŏk-han 엄격한. —*v.* (*of a ship*) ko-mul 고물, sŏn-mi 선미(船尾).
steward *n.* (*of ship*) sŏn-sil-gye 선실계 ; (*in hotels*)

po-i 보이, chŏp-dae-wŏn 접대원.

stewardess *n.* sŭ-t'yu-ŏ-di-sŭ 스튜어디스.

stick *n.* chi-p'ang-i 지팡이. —*v.* (*to*) put-da 붙다 ; (*into*) jji-rŭ-da 찌르다 ; (*catch*) kŏl-ri-da 걸리다.

sticking plaster pan-ch'ang-go 반창고.

sticky *adj.* kkŭn-jŏk-ggŭn-jŏk-han 끈적끈적한.

stiff *adj.* (*hard*) kut-ŭn 굳은, ttak-ddak-han 딱딱한, ppŏt-bbŏt-han 뻣뻣한 ; (*dense*) kŏl-jjuk-han 걸쭉한.

stifle *v.* ① chil-sik-si-k'i-da 질식시키다. ② (*put out*) kkŭ-da 끄다. ③ (*repress*) ŏk-nu-rŭ-da 억누르다.

stigma *n.* (*stain*) o-myŏng 오명 ; ch'i-yok 치욕.

stile *n.* ti-dim-p'an 디딤판.

still *adj.* ko-yo-han 고요한, chŏng-ji-han 정지한. —*adv.* tŏ-uk 더욱, sang-gŭm 상금 ; a-jik-do 아직도.

stillness *n.* ko-yo 고요, ch'im-muk 침묵.

stimulant *n.* hŭng-bun-je 흥분제 ; (*pl.*) sul 술.

stimulate *v.* (*excite*) cha-gŭk-ha-da 자극하다, (*animate*) hwal-gi-ddi-ge ha-da 활기띠게 하다.

sting *n.* jjil-rin sang-ch'ŏ 찔린 상처, (*pain*) sim-han ko-t'ong 심한 고통. —*v.* (*prick*) jji-rŭ-da 찌르다 ; sso-da 쏘다.

stingy *adj.* ① in-saek-han 인색한 : ～ *man* ku-du-soe 구두쇠. ② sso-nŭn 쏘는.

stink *v.* ak-ch'wi-rŭl ppum-da 악취를 뿜다. —*n.* ak-ch'wi 악취 ; ku-rin-nae 구린내.

stint *v.* (*grudge*) chu-gi si-rŏ-ha-da 주기 싫어하다.

stipend *n.* pong-gŭp 봉급, (*salary*) kŭp-ryo 급료.

stipulate *v.* (*require*) kyu-jŏng-ha-da 규정하다, yak-jŏng-ha-da 약정하다, (*specify*) myŏng-gi-ha-da 명기하 [다.

stir *v.* hwi-jŏt-da 휘젓다 ; um-jik-i-da 움직이다.

stitch *v.* (*sew*) kkwe-mae-da 꿰매다.

stock *n.* (*goods for business*) chae-go-p'um 재고품 ;

(*lineage*) hyŏl-t'ong 혈통, ka-mun 가문.
stocking *n.* yang-mal 양말, (*Korean*) pŏ-sŏn 버선.
stomach *n.* wi 위, (*belly*) pae 배.
stone *n.* tol 돌, tol-meng-i 돌멩이, sŏk-jae 석재.
stone coal (*anthracite*) mu-yŏn-t'an 무연탄.
stonemason *n.* sŏk-su 석수, sŏk-gong 석공.
stonework *n.* sŏk-jo-mul 석조물 ; tol-se-gong 돌세공.
stony *adj.* tol-ŭi 돌의, tol-i man-ŭn 돌이 많은 ; (*merciless*) naeng-hok-han 냉혹한 ; (*motionless*) um-jik-i-ji an-nŭn 움직이지 않는.
stool *n.* kŏl-sang 걸상 ; (*commode*) pyŏn-gi 변기.
stoop *v.* kku-bu-ri-da 구부리다. —*n.* sae-u-dŭng 새우등.
stop *n.* (*pause*)chung-ji 중지 ; (*stopping place*) chŏng-gŏ-jang 정거장. —*v.* mŏm-ch'u-da 멈추다.
store *n.* sang-jŏm 상점. —*v.* chŏ-jang-ha-da 저장하다.
storehouse *n.* ch'ang-go 창고, kwang 광.
stor(e)y *n.* ch'ŭng 층, kye-ch'ŭng 계층 : *a house of one* ~ tan-ch'ŭng-jip 단층집/*the first* ~ il-ch'ŭng 1층.
stork *n.* hwang-sae 황새.
storm *n.* p'ok-p'ung-u 폭풍우 ; so-dong 소동 : *a* ~ *warning* p'ok-p'ung chu-ŭi-bo 폭풍 주의보. —*v.* (*weather*) sa-na-wa-ji-da 사나와지다.
stormy *adj.* p'ok-p'ung-u-ŭi 폭풍우의.
story *n.* ① (*tale*) i-ya-gi 이야기, sŏl-hwa 설화. ② (*plot*) chul-gŏ-ri 줄거리. ③ (*report*) so-mun 소문.
stout *adj.* kŏn-gang-han 건강한, kang-in-han 강인한.
stove *n.* nal-lo 난로 : *cooking* ~ hwa-dŏk 화덕/*electric* ~ chŏn-gi nal-lo 전기 난로.
stovepipe *n.* sŭ-t'o-o-bŭ-ŭi yŏn-t'ong 스토오브의 연통.
stowaway *n.* mil-hang-ja 밀항자.
straight *adj.* (*erect*) ttok-ba-rŭn 똑바른, (*upright*) su-jik-ŭi 수직의. —*n.* chik-sŏn 직선. —*adv.* ttok-

ba-ro 똑바로, (*honestly*) sol-jik-ha-ge 솔직하게.

strain *n*. (*tension*) kin-jang 긴장 ; (*overwork*) kwa-ro 과로. —*v*. kin-jang-si-k'i-da 긴장시키다 ; kwa-ro-si-k'i-da 과로시키다.

strainer *n*. (*sieve*) ch'e 체, yŏ-gwa-gi 여과기.

strait *n*. ① hae-hyŏp 해협. ② (*pl*.) kon-gyŏng 곤경.

strand *v*. chwa-ch'o-ha-da 좌초하다. —*n*. mul-ga 물가.

strange *adj*. i-sang-han 이상한, nat-sŏn 낯선.

stranger *n*. mo-rŭ-nŭn sa-ram 모르는 사람 ; mun-oe-han 문외한 ; (*foreigner*) oe-guk-in 외국인.

strangle *v*. mok-jol-ra chuk-i-da 목졸라 죽이다, chil-sik-si-k'i-da 질식시키다.

strap *n*. ka-juk-ggŭn 가죽끈. —*v*. ka-juk-ggŭn-ŭ-ro mae-da 가죽끈으로 매다.

stratagem *n*. chŏl-lyak 전략, ch'aek-ryak 책략.

strategy *n*. chŏl-lyak 전략, pyŏng-bŏp 병법.

straw *n*. chip 짚, mil-jip 밀짚 : ~ *bag* 가마니.

strawberry *n*. ttal-gi 딸기, yang-ddal-gi 양딸기.

straw vote pi-gong-sik t'u-p'yo 비공식 투표.

stray *v*. kil-ŭl il-t'a 길을 잃다, (*go wrong*) kil-ŭl chal-mot tŭl-da 길을 잘못 들다. —*n*. mi-a 미아(迷兒).

streak *n*. ① chul-mu-nŭi 줄무늬. ② ki-jil 기질.

stream *n*. (*current*) hŭ-rŭm 흐름 ; (*small river*) kae-ul 개울, nae 내. —*v*. hŭ-rŭ-da 흐르다.

streamline *n*. yu-sŏn-hyŏng 유선형(流線型).

street *n*. kŏ-ri 거리 ; ka-ro 가로.

streetcar *n*. (*tramcar*) si-ga chŏn-ch'a 시가 전차.

street lamp ka-ro-dŭng 가로등.

strength *n*. him 힘, se-ryŏk 세력.

strengthen *v*. kang-ha-ge ha-da 강하게 하다.

strenuous *adj*. pun-t'u-jŏk-in 분투적인 : *make ~ effort* mu-ch'ŏk no-ryŏk-ha-da 무척 노력하다.

stress *n.* ap-bak 압박. —*v.* kang-jo-ha-da 강조하다.
stretch *v.* (*spread*) nŭl-ri-da 늘리다 ; (*reach out*) nae-mil-da 내밀다. —*n.* nŏl-bi 넓이, pŏm-wi 범위.
strew *v.* ppu-ri-da 뿌리다, kki-ŏn-da 끼얹다.
strict *adj.* ŏm-gyŏk-han 엄격한 ; chŏng-mil-han 정밀한.
stride *v.* sŏng-k'ŭm-sŏng-k'ŭm kŏt-da 성큼성큼 걷다.
strife *n.* ssa-um 싸움, pun-t'u 분투 ; ch'ung-dol 충돌.
strike *v.* ttae-ri-da 때리다, tu-dŭ-ri-da 두드리다. —*n.* (*industry*) tong-maeng-p'a-ŏp 동맹파업.
string *n.* kkŭn 끈 : *shoe* ～ ku-du-ggŭn 구두끈.
strip *v.* pŏt-gi-da 벗기다. —*n.* (*of cloth*) cho-gak 조각.
stripe *n.* chul 줄, chul-mu-nŭi 줄무늬 : *the Stars and S*～ sŏng-jo-gi 성조기.
strive *v.* no-ryŏk-ha-da 노력하다, ae-ssŭ-da 애쓰다.
stroke *n.* ① (*of Korean characters*) hoek 획. ② (*illness*) chol-do 졸도. —*v.* ssŭ-da-dŭm-da 쓰다듬다.
stroll *n. & v.* san-ch'aek(-ha-da) 산책(하다).
strong *adj.* (*powerful*) kang-han 강한, (*tough*) t'ŭn-t'ŭn-han 튼튼한, (*robust*) kŏn-gang-han 건강한 ; (*thick*) chin-han 진한.
structure *n.* ku-jo 구조 ; (*building*) kŏn-mul 건물.
struggle *n.* ssa-um 싸움 ; no-ryŏk 노력. —*v.* no-ryŏk-ha-da 노력하다 ; (*fight*) ta-t'u-da 다투다.
strut *v.* ppom-nae-myŏ kŏt-da 뽐내며 걷다. —*n.* ppom-naen kŏ-rŭm-gŏ-ri 뽐낸 걸음걸이.
stub *n.* kŭ-ru-t'ŏ-gi 그루터기, tong-gang 동강.
stubborn *adj.* wan-go-han 완고한, ko-jip-sen 고집센.
stud *n.* ① (*of shirt*) tan-ch'u 단추. ② (*nail head*) mot 못. ③ (*horse*) mal-dde 말떼. 「연구가.
student *n.* hak-saeng 학생 ; (*investigator*) yŏn-gu-ga
studio *n.* sŭ-t'yu-di-o 스튜디오, pang-song-sil 방송실 ; hwa-sil 화실 ; sa-jin-gwan 사진관.

study *n.* ① kong-bu 공부. ② (*room*) sŏ-jae 서재. —*v.* kong-bu-ha-da 공부하다, yŏn-gu-ha-da 연구하다.

stuff *n.* (*material*) chae-ryo 재료 ; mul-ja 물자 ; (*rubbish*) p'ye-mul 폐물. —*v.* ch'ae-u-da 채우다.

stumble *v.* (kŏl-ryŏ) nŏm-ŏ-ji-da (걸려) 넘어지다 ; pi-t'ŭl-gŏ-ri-da 비틀거리다. —*n.* sil-p'ae 실패.

stump *n.* kŭ-ru-t'ŏ-gi 그루터기, mong-dang yŏn-p'il 몽

stun *v.* ki-jŏl-si-k'i-da 기절시키다. 「당 연필.

stupefy *v.* ma-bi-si-k'i-da 마비시키다.

stupendous *adj.* (*amazing*) nol-ral-man-han 놀랄만한, ŏm-ch'ŏng-nan 엄청난, kŏ-dae-han 거대한.

stupid *adj.* ŏ-ri-sŏk-ŭn 어리석은, u-dun-han 우둔한.

sturdy *adj.* sil-han 실한, t'ŭn-t'ŭn-han 튼튼한.

stutter *v.* (*stammer*) mal-ŭl tŏ-dŭm-da 말을 더듬다.

sty *n.* ① (*for pigs*) twae-ji-u-ri 돼지우리. ② (*eye*) da-rae-ggi 다래끼. 「(*of writing*) mun-ch'e 문체.

style *n.* (*manner*) mo-yang 모양, (*mode*) hyŏng 형 ;

stylus *n.* ch'ŏl-p'il 철필 ; (*phonograph*) pa-nŭl 바늘.

subdue *v.* (*suppress*) chin-ap-ha-da 진압하다.

subject *n.* ① (*of a country*) sin-ha 신하, paek-sŏng 백성. ② (*theme*) chu-je 주제 ; (*of study*) hak-gwa 학과, kwa-mok 과목 ; (*gram.*) chu-ŏ 주어.

subjugate *v.* pok-jong-si-k'i-da 복종시키다.

subjunctive *n.* (*gram.*) ka-jŏng-bŏp 가정법. 「한.

sublime *adj.* chang-ŏm-han 장엄한, sung-go-han 숭고

submarine *adj.* pa-da-mi-t'ŭi 바다밑의, hae-jŏ-ŭi 해저의. —*n.* cham-su-ham 잠수함.

submerge *v.* mul-sok-e cham-gŭ-da 물속에 잠그다.

submission *n.* pok-jong 복종, hang-bok 항복.

submit *v.* ① (*present*) che-ch'ul-ha-da 제출하다. ② (*surrender*) kul-bok-ha-da 굴복하다.

subordinate *adj.* chong-sok-ha-nŭn 종속하는 ; ha-wi-ŭi

하위의. —*n.* pu-ha 부하(部下).

subscribe *v.* ① (*pre-engage*) ye-yak-ha-da 예약하다. ② (*contribute*) ki-bu-ha-da 기부하다.③ (*sign*) sŏ-myŏng-ha-da 서명하다. ④ (*take in*) ku-dok-ha-da 구독하다.

subscription *n.* ye-yak 예약 ; ki-bu 기부 ; sŏ-myŏng 서명 : ～ *edition* ye-yak-p'an 예약판.

subsequent *adj.* kŭ hu-ŭi 그 후의. 「잠잠해지다.

subside *v.* -ka-ra-an-da 가라앉다, cham-jam-hae-ji-da

subsidize *v.* po-jo-gŭm-ŭl chu-da 보조금을 주다.

subsidy *n.* po-jo-gŭm 보조금, chang-ryŏ-gŭm 장려금.

subsist *v.* (*continue to live*) saeng-jon-ha-da 생존하다 ; (*maintain*) mŏk-yŏ sal-ri-da 먹여 살리다.

subsistence *n.* saeng-jon 생존, saeng-gye 생계.

substance *n.* ① sil-ch'e 실체. ② mul-jil 물질.

substantial *adj.* (*actual*) sil-jae-ha-nŭn 실재하는, (*solid*) sil-sok-it-nŭn 실속있는, kyŏn-sil-han 견실한.

substitute *n.* (*a person*) tae-ri 대리 ; (*a thing*) tae-yong-p'um 대용품. —*v.* tae-ch'i-ha-da 대치하다.

substitution *n.* tae-ch'i 대치 ; tae-ri 대리.

subtle *adj.* (*delicate*) mi-myo-han 미묘한 ; min-gam-han 민감한 ; (*elaborate*) chŏng-gyo-han 정교한.

subtract *v.* ppae-da 빼다, kam-ha-da 감하다.

subtraction *n.* sak-gam 삭감, (*math.*) kam-bŏp 감법, 「ppae-gi 빼기.

suburb *n.* kyo-oe 교외(郊外).

subversive *adj.* twi-jip-ŏ ŏp-nŭn 뒤집어 엎는.

subway *n.* (*underground passage*) chi-ha-do 지하도 ; (*underground railway*) chi-ha-ch'ŏl 지하철.

succeed *v.* ① sŏng-gong-ha-da 성공하다. ② (*follow*) it-da-ra i-rŏ-na-da 잇달아 일어나다 ; (*be successor to*) sang-sok[kye-sŭng]-ha-da 상속[계승]하다.

success *n.* sŏng-gong 성공, sŏng-ch'wi 성취.

successful *adj.* sŏng-gong-jŏk-in 성공적인.

succession *n*. (*inheritance*) sang-sok 상속, kye-sŭng 계승 ; (*continuation*) yŏn-sok 연속.

successive *adj*. yŏn-sok-jŏk-in 연속적인.

successor *n*. hu-gye-ja 후계자, sang-sok-in 상속인.

succumb *v*. (*yield*) kul-bok-ha-da 굴복하다.

such *adj*. kŭ-rŏ-han 그러한, i-rŏ-han 이러한.

suck *v*. ppal-da 빨다 : chŏ-jŭl mŏk-da 젖을 먹다.

sudatorium *n*. han-jŭng-mak 한증막, chŭng-gi-t'ang 증기탕.　　　　　　　　　　「뜻밖의, to-ryŏn-han 돌연한.

sudden *adj*. kap-jak-sŭ-rŏ-un 갑작스러운, ttŭt-ba-ggŭi

suddenly *adv*. kap-ja-gi 갑자기, to-ryŏn 돌연.

sue *v*. ① ko-so-ha-da 고소하다.② (*beseech*) kan-ch'ŏng-ha-da 간청하다. ③ (*court*) ku-hon-ha-da 구혼하다.

suet *n*. soe-gi-rŭm 쇠기름, yang-gi-rŭm 양기름.

suffer *v*. (*undergo*) kyŏk-da 겪다, (*bear pain*) koe-ro-wa-ha-da 괴로와하다 ; (*tolerate*) ch'am-da 참다.

suffering *n*. (*pain*) ko-t'ong 고통 ; (*loss*) son-hae 손해.

suffice *v*. man-jok-si-k'i-da 만족시키다, ch'ung-bun-ha-da 충분하다, (*be enough*) chok-ha-da 족하다.

sufficient *adj*. ch'ung-bun-han 충분한, man-ŭn 많은.

suffix *n*. (*gram.*) chŏp-mi-ŏ 접미어(接尾語).

suffocate *v*. (*choke*) chil-sik-si-k'i-da 질식시키다, sum-ŭl mak-da 숨을 막다 ; (*extinguish*) kkŭ-da 끄다.

suffrage *n*. t'u-p'yo 투표, sŏn-gŏ-gwŏn 선거권.

sugar *n*. sŏl-t'ang 설탕 : *cube* ～ kak-sŏl-t'ang 각설탕.

sugar cane sa-t'ang-su-su 사탕수수.

suggest *v*. am-si-ha-da 암시하다;che-an-ha-da 제안하다.

suggestion *n*. am-si 암시 ; che-ŭi 제의.　　　　「하다.

suicide *n*. cha-sal 자살 : *commit* ～ cha-sal-ha-da 자살

suit *n*. ① (*law*) so-song 소송, ko-so 고소. ② (*clothes*) han pŏl 한 벌. —*v*. chŏk-hap-ha-da 적합하다.　　「는.

suitable *adj*. chŏk-dang-han 적당한 ; ŏ-ul-ri-nŭn 어울리

suitor *n.* ① (*for marriage*) ku-hon-ja 구혼자. ② (*law*)
so-song-in 소송인.　　　　　　　　　　　「da 뽀로통해지다.
sulk *v.* sael-jjuk-ha-da 샐쭉하다, ppyo-ro-t'ong-hae-ji-
sulky *adj.* sael-jjuk-han 샐쭉한, ttung-han 뚱한.
sullen *adj.* si-mu-ruk-han 시무룩한, mu-dduk-dduk-han
sulphur · sulfur *n.* yu-hwang 유황.　　　　　　　 「무뚝뚝한.
sultry *adj.* mu-dŏ-un 무더운, hu-dŏp-ji-gŭn-han 후덥지
근한 : ~ *weather* mu-dŏ-un nal-ssi 무더운 날씨.
sum *n.* ① (*total amount*) hap-gye 합계. ② (*outline*)
kae-yo 개요. ③ (*pl.*) (*calculation*) kye-san 계산.
summarize *v.* yo-yak-ha-da 요약하다.
summary *n.* yo-yak 요약, chŏk-yo 적요(摘要). —*adj.*
yo-yak-han 요약한, tae-gang-ŭi 대강의.
summer *n.* yŏ-rŭm 여름, yŏ-rŭm-ch'ŏl 여름철.
summit *n.* chŏng-sang 정상, kkok-dae-gi 꼭대기 : *a* ~
talk chŏng-sang-hoe-dam 정상회담.
summon *v.* so-hwan-ha-da 소환하다, so-jip-ha-da 소집
하다. —*n.* (*a writ*) so-hwan-jang 소환장.
sumptuous *adj.* kap-bi-ssan 값비싼 ; sa-ch'i-han 사치한.
sun *n.* hae 해, t'ae-yang 태양, haet-bit 햇빛.
sunbeam *n.* haet-sal 햇살, t'ae-yang kwang-sŏn 태양
sunburn *v.* haet-byŏ-t'e t'a-da 햇볕에 타다.　　　 「광선.
Sunday *n.* i-ryo-il 일요일, kong-il 공일, chu-il 주일.
Sunday best na-dŭ-ri-ot 나들이옷, cho-ŭn ot 좋은 옷.
sundial *n.* hae-si-gye 해시계.
sunflower *n.* hae-ba-ra-gi 해바라기.
sunlight *n.* haet-bit 햇빛, il-gwang 일광.
sunny *adj.* haet-byŏt jjoe-nŭn 햇볕 쬐는, yang-ji-ba-
rŭn 양지바른.
sunrise *n.* hae-do-ji 해돋이, sae-byŏk-nyŏk 새벽녘.
sunset *n.* hae-jil-nyŏk 해질녘, hae-gŏ-rŭm 해거름.
sunshade *n.* (*parasol*) yang-san 양산, ch'a-yang 차양.

sunshine *n.* haet-byŏt 햇볕, il-gwang 일광.
sunspot *n.* t'ae-yang-ŭi hŭk-jŏm 태양의 흑점.
sunstroke *n.* il-sa-byŏng 일사병. 「훌륭한.
superb *adj.* ch'oe-go-gŭp-ŭi 최고급의, hul-ryung-han
superficial *adj.* p'yo-myŏn-ŭi 표면의 ; p'i-sang-jŏk-in
  피상적인 ; (*shallow*) ch'ŏn-bak-han 천박한.
superfluous *adj.* yŏ-bun-ŭi 여분의, nam-a-do-nŭn 남아도
superintendent *n.* kam-dok(-ja) 감독(자). 「는.
superior *adj.* hul-ryung-han 훌륭한, u-su-han 우수한.
  —*n.* wit-sa-ram 윗사람, sang-gwan 상관, sŏn-bae 선
superiority *n.* u-wŏl 우월, u-wi 우위. 「배.
superlative *adj.* ch'oe-go-ŭi 최고의. —*n.* ch'oe-go 최고.
supermarket *n.* syu-u-p'ŏ-ma-a-k'it 슈우퍼마아킷.
superstition *n.* mi-sin 미신.
supervise *v.* kam-dok〔kwal-li〕-ha-da 감독〔관리〕하다.
supervisor *n.* kam-dok-ja 감독자, kwal-li-in 관리인.
supper *n.* chŏ-nyŏk-sik-sa 저녁식사.
supple *adj.* ① na-gŭt-na-gŭt-han 나긋나긋한, yu-sun-
  han 유순한. ② (*flexible*) chal hwi-nŭn 잘 휘는.
supplement *n.* pu-rok 부록 ; (*addition*) ch'u-ga 추가.
supplication *n.* t'an-wŏn 탄원, ae-wŏn 애원.
supply *n.* (*supplying*) kong-gŭp 공급 ; (*stock*) chae-
  go-p'um 재고품 ; (*provisions*) yang-sik 양식. —*v.*
  kong-gŭp-ha-da 공급하다. 「jo-ha-da 원조하다.
support *n.* chi-ji 지지. —*v.* chi-ji-ha-da 지지하다, wŏn-
supporter *n.* ① (*prop*) chi-ju 지주(支柱). ② (*sus-*
  tainer) pu-yang-ja 부양자. ③ pak-dae 박대.
suppose *v.* (*assume*) ka-jŏng-ha-da 가정하다 ; (*think*)
  saeng-gak-ha-da 생각하다, ch'u-ch'ŭk-ha-da 추측하다.
supposition *n.* ch'u-ch'ŭk 추측, ka-jŏng 가정.
suppress *v.* (*subdue*) chin-ap-ha-da 진압하다 ; (*stop*)
  kŭm-ha-da 금하다 ; (*conceal*) sum-gi-da 숨기다.

supreme *adj*. ch'oe-go-ŭi 최고의, kŭk-do-ŭi 극도의 : *the S~ Court* tae-bŏp-wŏn 대법원.

sure *adj*. hwak-sil-han 확실한, (*reliable*) mit-ŭl su it-nŭn 믿을 수 있는 ; (*safe*) an-jŏn-han 안전한.

surely *adv*. hwak-sil-hi 확실히 ; (*answer*) a-mu-ryŏm 아무렴 ; mul-ron 물론.

surety *n*. (*sponsor*) po-jŭng-in 보증인, tam-bo 담보.

surf *n*. mil-ryŏ-o-nŭn p'a-do 밀려오는 파도.

surface *n*. p'yo-myŏn 표면, oe-gwan 외관.

surge *n*. kŏ-sen p'a-do 거센 파도.　　　　　　　「군의관.

surgeon *n*. ① oe-gwa ŭi-sa 외과 의사. ② kun-ŭi-gwan

surly *adj*. mu-dduk-dduk-han 무뚝뚝한, ku-jŭn 굳은.

surmise *n. & v*. ch'u-ch'ŭk(-ha-da) 추측(하다).

surmount *v*. nŏm-da 넘다 ; kŭk-bok-ha-da 극복하다.

surname *n*. sŏng 성(姓) ; pyŏl-myŏng 별명.

surpass *v*. …po-da nat-da …보다 낫다, …ŭl nŭng-ga-ha-da …을 능가하다. —*adj*. ttwi-ŏ-nan 뛰어난.

surplus *n*. yŏ-bun 여분, na-mŏ-ji 나머지.　　　　「하다.

surprise *n*. nol-ram 놀람. —*v*. nol-ra-ge ha-da 놀라게

surprising *adj*. nol-ral-man-han 놀랄만한, nun-bu-sin

surrender *n. & v*. hang-bok(-ha-da) 항복(하다). 「눈부신.

surround *v*. tul-rŏ-ssa-da 둘러싸다, e-wŏ-ssa-da 에워 싸다 ; p'o-wi-ha-da 포위하다.

surroundings *n*. chu-wi 주위, hwan-gyŏng 환경.

surtax *n*. pu-ga-se 부가세, nu-jin-se 누진세.

survey *v*. ① (*look over*) tul-ro-bo-da 둘러보다. ② (*examine*) cho-sa-ha-da 조사하다. ③ (*measure*) ch'ŭk-ryang-ha-da 측량하다. —*n*. ① kae-gwan 개관. ② ch'ŭk-ryang 측량.　　　　　　　　「da 살아 남다.

survive *v*. po-da o-rae sal-da 보다 오래 살다, sa-ra nam-

susceptible *adj*. min-gam-han 민감한, (*liable*) …e kŏl-ri-gi swi-un …에 걸리기 쉬운.

suspect *v.* ŭi-sim-ha-da 의심하다, su-sang-hi yŏ-gi-da 수상히 여기다. —*n.* hyŏm-ŭi-ja 혐의자.

suspend *v.* ① (*hang*) ta-ra-mae-da 달아매다. ② (*from work*) chŏng-jik-si-k'i-da 정직(停職)시키다 ; (*stop temporarily*) chung-ji-ha-da 중지하다. ③ (*delay*) yŏn-gi-ha-da 연기하다.

suspenders *n.* mel-bbang 멜빵. 「pu-ran 불안.

suspense *n.* ① (*pending*) mi-gyŏl 미결. ② (*anxiety*)

suspension *n.* (*hanging up*) mae-dal-gi 매달기 ; (*pending question*) mi-gyŏl 미결 ; (*from office*) chŏng-jik 정직, (*from school*) chŏng-hak 정학.

suspicion *n.* ŭi-sim 의심, hyŏm-ŭi 혐의.

suspicious *adj.* ŭi-sim-man-ŭn 의심많은, ŭi-sim-sŭ-rŏ-un 의심스러운, su-sang-jjŏk-ŭn 수상쩍은.

sustain *v.* kyŏn-di-da 견디다, yu-ji-ha-da 유지하다.

sustenance *n.* ① saeng-gye 생계. ② (*nourishment*) yŏng-yang-mul 영양물. ③ (*support*) yu-ji 유지.

swagger *v.* hwal-bo-ha-da 활보하다. —*n.* hwal-bo 활보.

swallow *n.* che-bi 제비. —*v.* sam-k'i-da 삼키다.

swallowtail *n.* che-bi kkong-ji 제비 꽁지.

swamp *n.* (*bog*) nŭp 늪, (*marsh*) sŭp-ji 습지.

swan *n.* paek-jo 백조.

swarm *n.* tte 떼. —*v.* mo-yŏ-dŭl-da 모여들다.

sway *v.* hŭn-dŭl-ri-da 흔들리다, hŭn-dŭl-da 흔들다.

swear *v.* ① maeng-se-ha-da 맹세하다. ② (*curse*) yok-ŭl ha-da 욕을 하다. —*n.* ① sŏn-sŏ 선서. ② chŏ-ju 저

sweat *n.* ttam 땀. —*v.* ttam hŭl-ri-da 땀 흘리다. 「주.

sweater *n.* (*jersey*) sŭ-we-t'ŏ 스웨터.

sweep *v.* ssŭl-da 쓸다, ch'ŏng-so-ha-da 청소하다 ; (*remove*) il-so-ha-da 일소하다. —*n.* ch'ŏng-so 청소.

sweet *adj.* tal-k'om-han 달콤한 ; hyang-gi-ro-un 향기로운 ; (*pleasing*) yu-k'wae-han 유쾌한.

sweetheart *n.* (*lover*) ae-in 애인, yŏn-in 연인.

sweetly *adv.* (*fragrantly*) hyang-gi-rop-ge 향기롭게 ; sang-nyang-ha-ge 상냥하게, kwi-yŏp-ge 귀엽게.

sweet potato ko-gu-ma 고구마.

swell *v.* pu-p'ul-da 부풀다, k'ŏ-ji-da 커지다.

swelter *v.* mu-dŏp-da 무덥다, tŏ-wi-mŏk-da 더위먹다.

swerve *v.* pit-na-ga-da 빗나가다, pŏ-sŏ-na-da 벗어나다.

swift *adj.* ppa-rŭn 빠른, sin-sok-han 신속한.

swiftly *adv.* ppa-rŭ-ge 빠르게, sin-sok-hi 신속히.

swim *v.* he-ŏm-ch'i-da 헤엄치다 ; (*float*) ttŭ-da 뜨다.

swimming *n.* su-yŏng 수영.

swimming bath sil-nae su-yŏng-jang 실내 수영창.

swindle *v.* sok-i-da 속이다, sa-ch'wi-ha-da 사취하다.

swine *n.* (*pigs*) twae-ji 돼지.

swing *n.* ① chin-dong 진동. ② kŭ-ne 그네. —*v.* hŭn-dŭl-da 흔들다 ; (*on swing*) kŭ-ne-rŭl ttwi-da 그네를 뛰다.

swirl *v.* so-yong-do-ri-ch'i-da 소용돌이치다.

switch *n.* sŭ-wi-ch'i 스위치, kae-p'ye-gi 개폐기. —*v.* ① chŏn-hwan-ha-da 전환하다, pa-ggu-da 바꾸다. ② (*whip*) mae-jil-ha-da 매질하다.　　　　「환대.

switchboard *n.* pae-jŏn-p'an 배전판 ; kyo-hwan-dae 교

swoon *n. & v.* (*faint*) ki-jŏl(-ha-da) 기절(하다).

swoop *v.* nae-ri-dŏp-ch'i-da 내리덮치다.　　　　「검무.

sword *n.* k'al 칼 : ~ *dance* k'al-ch'um 칼춤, kŏm-mu

syllable *n.* ŭm-jŏl 음절, ch'ŏl-ja 철자.

syllabus *n.* kae-yo 개요 ; tae-gang 대강.　　　　「기호.

symbol *n.* (*emblem*) sang-jing 상징 ; (*mark*) ki-ho

symbolize *v.* sang-jing-ha-da 상징하다.

symmetry *n.* kyun-hyŏng 균형, tae-ch'ing 대칭.

sympathetic *adj.* tong-jŏng-ha-nŭn 동정하는 ; (*congenial*) ma-ŭm-e tŭ-nŭn 마음에 드는.

sympathize *v.* ① tong-jŏng-ha-da 동정하다. ② (*agree*

with) tong-ŭi-ha-da 동의하다, ch'an-sŏng-ha-da 찬성하다. ③ (*condole*) wi-ro-ha-da 위로하다.
sympathy *n.* tong-jŏng 동정, kong-myŏng 공명(共鳴).
symphony *n.* kyo-hyang-ak 교향악, sim-p'o-ni 심포니.
synonym *n.* tong-ŭi-ŏ 동의어, yu-ŏ 유어(類語).
syntax *n.* ku-mun-ron 구문론, mun-jang-ron 문장론.
syphilis *n.* mae-dok 매독, ch'ang-byŏng 창병.
system *n.* cho-jik 조직, ch'e-gye 체계 ; (*method*) pang-bŏp 방법, pang-sik 방식.　　　　　「체계적인.
systematic *adj.* cho-jik-jŏk-in 조직적인, ch'e-gye-jŏk-in

—⟪ T ⟫—

table *n.* t'ak-ja 탁자, (*food*) sik-t'ak 식탁.
tablecloth *n.* sik-t'ak-bo 식탁보.
tablespoon *n.* k'ŭn sut-ga-rak 큰 숟가락, t'e-i-bŭl sŭ-p'u-un 테이블 스푸운.　　　　　「chŏng-je 정제.
tablet *n.* ① p'yŏng-p'an 평판(平板), p'ae 패. ② (*med.*)
taboo *n.* (*ban*) kŭm-gi 금기, kŭm-je 금제.
tacit *adj.* mu-ŏn-ŭi 무언의 ; cham-jam-han 잠잠한.
taciturn *adj.* ip-i mu-gŏ-un 입이 무거운.
tack *n.* ① nap-jak-mot 납작못, ap-jŏng 압정. ② chu-rŭm 주름.
tackle *n.* to-gu 도구, yŏn-jang 연장 : *fishing* ∼ nak-si to-gu 낚시 도구. —*v.* tal-ryŏ-dŭl-da 달려들다.
tact *n.* chae-ch'i 재치 ; som-ssi 솜씨.
tactics *n.* ① (*strategy*) chŏn-sul 전술, pyŏng-bŏp 병법. ② (*tricks*) sul-ch'aek 술책, ch'aek-ryak 책략.
tadpole *n.* ol-ch'aeng-i 올챙이.
tag *n.* ① kko-ri-p'yo 꼬리표. ② sul-rae-jap-gi 술래잡기.
tail *n.* kko-ri 꼬리 ; kkŭ-t'ŭ-mŏ-ri 끄트머리.
tailor *n.* chae-bong-sa 재봉사, yang-bok-jŏm 양복점.

taint *n.* (*stain*) o-jŏm 오점, tŏ-rŏ-um 더러움. —*v.* tŏ-rŏp-hi-da 더럽히다.

take *v.* (*seize*) chwi-da 쥐다, (*grasp*) chap-da 잡다 ; (*carry*) ka-ji-go ka-da 가지고 가다; (*go on board*) t'a-da 타다 ; (*eat*) mŏk-da 먹다.　　　「흉내.

take-off *n.* ① to-yak 도약, i-ryuk 이륙. ② hyung-nae

tale *n.* i-ya-gi 이야기, (*rumor*) so-mun 소문.

talent *n.* ① chae-nŭng 재능, su-wan 수완. ② (*person of* ～) in-jae 인재, t'ael-rŏn-t'ŭ 탤런트.

talisman *n.* pu-jŏk 부적, ho-bu 호부(護符).

talk *n.* i-ya-gi 이야기, sang-dam 상담. —*v.* mal-ha-da 말하다, i-ya-gi-ha-da 이야기하다.

talkative *adj.* su-da-sŭ-rŏ-un 수다스러운.

tall *adj.* k'i-ga k'ŭn 키가 큰 ; ŏm-ch'ŏng-nan 엄청난.

tallow *n.* su-ji 수지(獸脂); chim-sŭng ki-rŭm 짐승 기름.

talon *n.* (*animal*) pal-t'op 발톱.

tame *adj.* kil-dŭ-rin 길들인. —*v.* kil-dŭ-ri-da 길들이다.

tan *n.* hwang-gal-saek 황갈색, (*pl.*) kal-saek ku-du 갈색 구두. —*v.* (*leather*) mu-du-jil-ha-da 무두질하다; (*body*) haet-byŏ-t'e t'ae-u-da 햇볕에 태우다.

tangle *v.* ŏng-k'ŭ-rŏ-ji-da 엉클어지다. 「chŏn-ch'a 전차.

tank *n.* ① t'aeng-k'ŭ 탱크, mul-t'ong 물통. ② (*army*)

tap *v.* ka-byŏp-ge tu-dŭ-ri-da 가볍게 두드리다. —*n.* (*faucet*) chu-dung-i 주둥이, kkok-ji 꼭지.

tape *n.* ① t'e-i-p'ŭ 테이프. ② chul-ja 줄자.

tape measure chul-ja 줄자.　　　　　　「먹인 심지.

taper *n.* ka-nŭn ch'o 가는 초, ch'o mŏk-in sim-ji 초

tapestry *n.* pyŏk-gŏ-ri yung-dan 벽걸이 융단.

tar *n.* t'a-a-rŭ 타아르.　　　　　　　　　「jŭn 늦은.

tardy *adj.* (*slow*) nŭ-rin 느린, tŏ-din 더딘 ; (*late*) nŭ-

target *n.* p'yo-jŏk 표적, kwa-nyŏk 과녁.

tariff *n.* ① kwan-se 관세, se 세. ② (*a price list*)

yo-gŭm-p'yo 요금표, un-im-p'yo 운임표.

task *n.* (*job*) il 일, (*duty*) chik-mu 직무, (*lesson*) kwa-ŏp 과업 : *a home* ~ suk-je 숙제.

task force (*mil.*) ki-dong pu-dae 기동 부대.

tassel *n.* sul 술 ; (*plant*) song-i-ggot 송이꽃.

taste *n.* mat 맛, mi-gak 미각 ; (*liking*) ch'wi-mi 취미, ki-ho 기호. —*v.* mat-bo-da 맛보다.

tatter *n.* nŏng-ma 넝마, nu-dŏ-gi-ot 누더기옷.

taunt *v.* cho-rong-ha-da 조롱하다 ; tta-ji-da 따지다.

tavern *n.* (*public house*) sŏn-sul-jip 선술집, chu-mak 주막 ; (*inn*) yŏ-in-suk 여인숙.

tax ·*n.* se-gŭm 세금. —*v.* kwa-se-ha-da 과세하다.

taxi *n.* t'aek-si 택시.　　　　　　　　　　　　　「차.

tea *n.* ch'a 차, hong-ch'a 홍차 : *coarse* ~ yŏp-ch'a 엽

teach *v.* ka-rŭ-ch'i-da 가르치다, sŏl-myŏng-ha-da 설명

teacher *n.* sŏn-saeng 선생, kyo-sa 교사.　　　　「하다.

teacup *n.* ch'a-jan 차잔, ch'a-jong 차종.

teakettle *n.* chu-jŏn-ja 주전자.

team *n.* t'i-im 티임, (*group*) p'ae 패.

teapot *n.* ch'a-ju-jŏn-ja 차주전자, ch'a-byong 차병.

tear *n.* ① (*drop*) nun-mul 눈물. ② (*rip*) jjae-jin t'ŭm 째진 틈. —*v.* jjit-da 찢다.

tearoom *n.* ta-bang 다방.　　　　　　　「da 성가시게 굴다.

tease *v.* chi-bun-gŏ-ri-da 지분거리다, sŏng-ga-si-ge kul-

technic *n.* su-bŏp 수법, (*pl.*) ki-gyo 기교.

technical *adj.* ki-sul-jŏk-in 기술적인, chŏn-mun-jŏk-in 전문적인 : ~ *terms* chŏn-mun-ŏ 전문어, su-rŏ 술어.

technology *n.* kong-ŏp ki-sul 공업 기술.

tedious *adj.* chi-ru-han 지루한, chi-gyŏ-un 지겨운.

teem *v.* (*abound*) ch'ung-man-ha-da 충만하다.

teen-age *adj.* sip-dae-ŭi 10대의.

teens *n.* sip-dae 10대.

telegram *n.* chŏn-bo 전보. 「전보를 치다.
telegraph *n.* chŏn-sin 전신. —*v.* chŏn-bo-rŭl ch'i-da
telepathy *n.* chŏng-sin kam-ŭng 정신 감응.
telephone *n.* chŏn-hwa 전화 : ~ *booth* kong-jung chŏn-hwa-sil 공중 전화실/~ *directory* chŏn-hwa-bu 전화부/~ *operator* kyo-hwan-su 교환수/*public* ~ kong-jung chŏn-hwa 공중 전화. —*v.* chŏn-hwa-rŭl kŏl-da
telescope *n.* mang-wŏn-gyŏng 망원경. 「전화를 걸다.
television *n.* t'el-ri-bi-jyŏn 텔리비젼.
tell *v.* mal-ha-da 말하다, i-ya-gi-ha-da 이야기하다 ; al-ri-da 알리다 : myŏng-ha-da 명하다.
temper *n.* ki-jil 기질, sŏng-mi 성미, (*anger*) no-gi 노
temperament *n.* ch'e-jil 체질, ki-jil 기질. 「기.
temperance *n.* (*moderation*) chŏl-je 절제 ; (*liquor*) chŏl-ju 절주, kŭm-ju 금주. 「화한.
temperate *adj.* chŏl-je-it-nŭn 절제있는, on-hwa-han 온
temperature *n.* on-do 온도 ; ch'e-on 체온.
tempest *n.* tae-p'ok-p'ung-u 대폭풍우.
temple *n.* ① kwan-ja-no-ri 관자놀이. ② (*rel.*) sin-jŏn 신전(神殿), sa-wŏn 사원, chŏl 절. 「世)의.
temporal *adj.* il-si-jŏk-in 일시적인, hyŏn-se-ŭi 현세(現
temporary *adj.* il-si-jŏk-in 일시적인, im-si-ŭi 임시의.
tempt *v.* yu-hok-ha-da 유혹하다, pu-ch'u-gi-da 부추기
temptation *n.* yu-hok 유혹. 「다.
ten *n.* & *adj.* yŏl(-ŭi) 열(의), sip(-ŭi) 10(의).
tenacious *adj.* wan-gang-han 완강한, wan-go-han 완고한. 「ja 차용자.
tenant *n.* (*farmer*) so-jak-in 소작인 ;(*hirer*) ch'a-yong-
tend *v.* ① …ŭi kyŏng-hyang-i it-da …의 경향이 있다. ② tol-bo-da 돌보다, chi-k'i-da 지키다.
tendency *n.* kyŏng-hyang 경향, sŏng-hyang 성향.
tender *adj.* (*soft*) pu-dŭ-rŏ-un 부드러운, mu-rŭn 무른.

tenderness *n.* pu-dŭ-rŏ-um 부드러움.

tenement *n.* ch'a-yong-ji 차용지, set-jip 셋집.

tennis *n.* chŏng-gu 정구, t'e-ni-sŭ 테니스.

tense *adj.* kin-jang-han 긴장한, p'aeng-p'aeng-han 팽팽한. —*n.* (*gram.*) si-je 시제(時制).

tent *n.* ch'ŏn-mak 천막, t'en-t'ŭ 텐트.

tenth *adj.* yŏl-bŏn-jjae-ŭi 열번쩨의.

term *n.* ① (*school*) hak-gi 학기. ② (*period*) ki-han 기한. ③ (*tech.*) yong-ŏ 용어. ④ (*pl.*) cho-gŏn 조건. —*v.* (*name*) ch'ing-ha-da 칭하다.

terminal *n.* chong-jŏm 종점, chong-ch'ak-yŏk 종착역, t'ŏ-ŏ-mi-nŏl 터어미널. 「종결시키다.

terminate *v.* kkŭt-nae-da 끝내다, chong-gyŏl-si-k'i-da

terrace *n.* (*height*) tae-ji 대지, ko-ji 고지 ; no-dae 노대(露臺) ; t'e-ra-sŭ 테라스.

terrapin *n.* (*turtle*) sik-yong kŏ-buk 식용 거북.

terrible *adj.* mu-sŏ-un 무서운, ka-gong-hal 가공할.

terrify *v.* (*frighten*) nol-ra-da 놀라다, kŏp-na-ge ha-da 겁나게 하다.

territory *n.* yŏng-t'o 영토 ; chi-yŏk 지역.

terror *n.* kong-p'o 공포, kong-p'o-ŭi ssi 공포의 씨.

test *n. & v.* si-hŏm(-ha-da) 시험(하다).

testament *n.* (*will*) yu-ŏn(-jang) 유언(장) : *the Old* [*New*] *T*~ ku[sin]-yak sŏng-sŏ 구[신]약 성서.

testify *v.* (*give evidence*) chŭng-ŏn-ha-da 증언하다, ip-jŭng-ha-da 입증하다.

testimony *n.* chŭng-ŏn 증언, chŭng-gŏ 증거.

text *n.* ① wŏn-mun 원문, pon-mun 본문. ② kyo-gwa-
textbook *n.* kyo-gwa-sŏ 교과서.   ⌞sŏ 교과서.

than *conj.* …po-da-do …보다도.

thank *v.* kam-sa-ha-da 감사하다 : *T*~ *you.* Ko-map-sŭp-ni-da 고맙습니다, Kam-sa-hap-ni-da 감사합니다.

thankful *adj.* kam-sa-ha-nŭn 감사하는, ko-ma-wa-ha-nŭn 고마와하는.
thanks *n.* kam-sa 감사, sa-rye 사례.
Thanksgiving Day ch'u-su kam-sa-jŏl 추수 감사절.
that *adj.* kŭ 그, chŏ 저. —*pron.* kŭ-gŏt 그것, chŏ-gŏt 저것. —*adv.* kŭ-rŏ-k'e 그렇게. —*conj.* …ha-da-nŭn[i-ra-nŭn] kŏt …하다는 〔이라는〕 것.
thatch *n.* i-ŏng 이엉.
thaw *v.* nok-da 녹다, nok-i-da 녹이다, (*soften*) p'ul-ri-da 풀리다.
the *art.* kŭ 그, chŏ 저.
theatre · theater *n.* kŭk-jang 극장.
theft *n.* to-duk-jil 도둑질, chŏl-do 절도.
their *pron.* kŭ-dŭl-ŭi 그들의.
theirs *pron.* kŭ-dŭl-ŭi kŏt 그들의 것.
them *pron.* kŭ-dŭl-ŭl 그들을, kŭ-dŭl-e-ge 그들에게.
theme *n.* chu-je 주제, non-je 논제, t'e-e-ma 테에마, chu-sŏn-yul 주선율(主旋律) : ～ *song* chu-je-ga 주제가.
themselves *pron.* kŭ-dŭl cha-sin 그들 자신.
then *adv.* kŭ-ddae 그때, kŭ-ri-go-nŭn 그리고는, kŭ ta-ŭm-e 그 다음에, kŭ-rae-sŏ 그래서.
theology *n.* sin-hak 신학.
theoretical *adj.* i-ron-jŏk-in 이론적인.　　　　「의견.
theory *n.* i-ron 이론 ; hak-sŏl 학설 ; (*opinion*) ŭi-gyŏn
there *adv.* kŏ-gi-e 거기에, kŏ-gi-sŏ 거기서.
therefore *adv.* kŭ-rŏ-mŭ-ro 그러므로, tta-ra-sŏ 따라서.
thermal *adj.* yŏl-ŭi 열(熱)의, on-do-ŭi 온도의.
thermometer *n.* han-nan-gye 한난계 ; on-do-gye 온도계.
these *pron.* i-gŏt-dŭl 이것들. —*adj.* i-gŏt-dŭl-ŭi 이것들의 : ～ *days* yo-jŭ-ŭm 요즈음.
they *pron.* kŭ-dŭl 그들, ku-dŭl-ŭn 그들은.
thick *adj.* tu-ggŏ-un 두꺼운 ; (*dense*) chin-han 진한.

—*adv*. tu-ggŏp-ge 두껍게, chin-ha-ge 친하게.
thicket *n*. su-p'ul 수풀, chap-mok sup 잡목 숲.
thickness *n*. tu-gge 두께, kul-ggi 굵기 ; (*liquid, color*) nong-do 농도.
thief *v*. to-duk 도둑, chom-do-duk 좀도둑.
thieve *v*. hum-ch'i-da 훔치다. 「가랑이.
thigh *n*. nŏp-jŏk-da-ri 넓적다리, ka-rang-i
thimble *n*. kol-mu 골무.
thin *adj*. yal-bŭn 얇은 ; (*slender*) yŏ-win 여윈 ; (*sparse*) tŭ-mun-dŭ-mun-han 드문드문한.

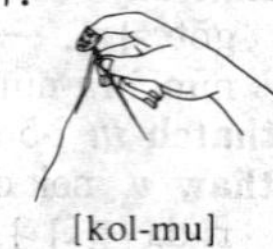

thing *n*. mul-gŏn 물건, mul-ch'e 물체, sa-mul 사물.
think *v*. saeng-gak-ha-da 생각하다.
thinker *n*. sa-sang-ga 사상가. 「제(의).
third *n*. & *adj*. che sam(-ŭi) 제 3 (의), se-jjae(-ŭi) 세
third-class *adj*. sam-dŭng-ŭi 삼등의 ; sam-ryu-ŭi 삼류의.
thirst *n*. kal-jŭng 갈증, mok-ma-rŭm 목마름. —*v*. mok-ma-rŭ-da 목먀르다 ; kal-mang-ha-da 갈망하다.
thirsty *adj*. mok-ma-rŭn 목마른, kal-jŭng-nan 갈증난.
thirteen *n*. & *adj*. yŏl-set(-ŭi) 열셋 (의), sip-sam(-ŭi)
thirty *n*. sŏ-rŭn 서른, sam-sip 30. ⌊13(의).
this *adj*. i 이, kŭm 금(今). —*pron*. i-gŏt 이것.
thistle *n*. ŏng-gŏng-k'wi 엉겅퀴.
thorn *n*. ① ka-si 가시. ② (*pain*) ko-t'ong 고통.
thorough *adj*. wan-jŏn-han 완전한 ; ch'ŏl-jŏ-han 철저한.
thoroughfare *n*. han-gil 한길, tae-ro 대로 : (*notice*) *No* ~. T'ong-haeng kŭm-ji 통행 금지.
thoroughly *adv*. wan-jŏn-hi 완전히 ; ch'ŏl-jŏ-hi 철저히.
those *pron*. kŭ-gŏt-dŭl 그것들. —*adj*. kŭ-gŏt-dŭl-ŭi 그것들의. 「pul-gu-ha-go …에도 불구하고.
though *adv*. kŭ-rŏ-na 그러나. —*conj*. (*even if*) …e-do
thought *n*. sa-sang 사상, saeng-gak 생각.

thoughtful *adj*. saeng-gak-i ki-p'ŭn 생각이 깊은, saeng-gak-e cham-gin 생각에 잠긴. 「ŏp-nŭn 지각없는.

thoughtless *adj*. pun-byŏl-ŏp-nŭn 분별없는, chi-gak-

thousand *n*. & *adj*. ch'ŏn(-ŭi) 천(의) : *ten* ~ man 만.

thrash *v*. (*beat*) ttae-ri-da 때리다, tu-dŭ-ri-da 두드리다.

thrasher *n*. (*machine*) t'al-gok-gi 탈곡기.

thread *n*. sil 실 : *a spool of* ~ sil-pae 실패. —*v*. sil-ŭl kkwe-da 실을 꿰다.

threadbare *adj*. (*worn-out*) nal-ga-bba-jin 낡아빠진.

threat *n*. wi-hyŏp 위협, hyŏp-bak 협박.

threaten *v*. wi-hyŏp-ha-da 위협하다, ŭ-rŭ-da 으르다.

threatening *adj*. (*weather*) hŏm-ak-han 험악한.

three *n*. & *adj*. set(-ŭi) 셋(의), sam(-ŭi) 3 (의).

threescore *n*. yuk-sip 60, yuk-sip-se 60세.

thresh *v*. (*thrash*) kok-sik-ŭl tu-dŭ-ri-da 곡식을 두드리다, t'a-jak-ha-da 타작하다.

threshold *n*. mun-ji-bang 문지방, mun-gan 문간.

thrice *adv*. (*three times*) se-bŏn 세번, sam-hoe 3 회, se-bae-ro 세배로.

thrift *n*. chŏl-yak 절약, kŏm-yak 검약. 「낭비하는.

thriftless *adj*. chŏl-je-ŏp-nŭn 절제없는. nang-bi-ha-nŭn

thrifty *adj*. ① chŏl-yak-ha-nŭn 절약하는, kŏm-so-han 검소한. ② (*prosper*) pŏn-ch'ang-ha-nŭn 번창하는.

thrill *n*. tŭ-ril 드릴, chŏn-yul 전율, kam-dong 감동.

thrive *v*. (*prosper*) pŏn-ch'ang-ha-da 번창하다.

throat *n*. mok-gu-mŏng 목구멍. 「가슴이 두근거리다.

throb *n*. ko-dong 고동. —*v*. ka-sŭm-i tu-gŭn-gŏ-ri-da

throne *n*. wang-jwa 왕좌, wang-wi 왕위.

throng *n*. kun-jung 군중. —*v*. mo-yŏ-dŭl-da 모여들다.

through *prep*. & *adv*. …ŭl t'ong-ha-yŏ …을 통하여.

throughout *prep*. & *adv*. to-ch'ŏ-e 도처에, nae-nae

throw *v*. nae-dŏn-ji-da 내던지다. 「내내.

thrust *v.* (*push*) mil-da 밀다, mil-ch'i-da 밀치다.
thumb *n.* ŏm-ji son-ga-rak 엄지 손가락.
thump *v.* t'ak ttae-ri-da 탁 때리다.
thunder *n.* ch'ŏn-dung 천둥, pyŏ-rak 벼락, u-roe 우뢰.
　—*v.* ch'ŏn-dung-ch'i-da 천둥치다.
thunderbolt *n.* pyŏ-rak 벼락, nak-roe 낙뢰(落雷).
thundering *n.* & *adj.* ch'ŏn-dung(-ch'i-nŭn) 천둥(치는).
thunderous *adj.* ch'ŏn-dung-ŭi 천둥의, u-roe-ga-t'ŭn 우
　뢰같은.
thunderstorm *n.* noe-u 뇌우(雷雨).
Thursday *n.* mok-yo-il 목요일.
thus *adv.* i-wa ka-ch'i 이와 같이, tta-ra-sŏ 따라서.
thwart *v.* (*hinder*) ka-ro-mak-da 가로막다, pang-hae-
　ha-da 방해하다.
tick *n.* (*mite*) chin-dŭ-gi 진드기. —*v.* ttok-ddak so-ri-
　nae-da 똑딱 소리내다.
ticket *n.* p'yo 표 ; ip-jang-gwŏn 입장권 : *single* ～
　p'yŏn-do sŭng-ch'a-gwŏn 편도 승차권.
tickle *v.* kan-ji-ri-da 간질이다 ; (*amuse*) ki-bbŭ-ge-ha-
　da 기쁘게 하다.
tide *n.* ① cho-su 조수. ② (*tendency*) p'ung-jo 풍조 :
　ebb ～ ssŏl-mul 썰물/*flood* ～ mil-mul 밀물.
tidings *n.* (*news*) so-sik 소식, ki-byŏl 기별.
tidy *adj.* chŏng-don-doen 정돈된, mal-ssuk-han 말쑥한.
tie *v.* mae-da 매다, muk-da 묶다. —*n.* nek-t'a-i 넥타이.
tiger *n.* ho-rang-i 호랑이, pŏm 범.
tiger cat sal-gwaeng-i 삵괭이, sŭ-ra-so-ni 스라소니.
tiger lily ch'am-na-ri 참나리.
tight *adj.* (*firm*)tan-dan-han 단단한 ; (*tense*) p'aeng-
　p'aeng-han 팽팽한 ; (*close-fitting*) kkok mat-nŭn 꼭
tighten *v.* choe-da 죄다.　　　　　　　　　　└맞는.
tightly *adv.* tan-dan-hi 단단히 ; kkok mat-ge 꼭 맞게.

tile *n.* (*of roof*) ki-wa 기와, t'a-il 타일.
till *prep.* …kka-ji …까지. —*v.* (*culti-vate*) kyŏng-jak-ha-da 경작하다.
timber *n.* chae-mok 재목.
time *n.* si-gan 시간, ttae 때.
timely *adj.* ttae-e al-ma-jŭn 때에 알맞은, chŏk-si-ŭi 적시(適時)의.

[ki-wa]

times *n.* ① si-dae 시대. ② (*arith.*) pae 배(倍).
timid *adj.* kŏp-man-ŭn 겁많은, su-jup-ŭn 수줍은.
tin *n.* chu-sŏk 주석 ; yang-ch'ŏl 양철.
tinge *n.* pit-ggal 빛깔 ; (*trace*) ki-mi 기미.
tingle *v.* ŏ-rŏl-ha-da 얼얼하다, a-ri-da 아리다.
tint *n.* pit-ggal 빛깔. —*v.* mul-dŭ-ri-da 물들이다.
tiny *adj.* chak-ŭn 작은, cho-gŭ-ma-han 조그마한.
tip *n.* ① kkŭ-t'ŭ-mŏ-ri 끄트머리. ② (*money*) t'ip 팁.
    —*v.* t'ip-ŭl chu-da 팁을 주다.
tipsy *adj.* ŏl-gŭn-han 얼근한 ; (*unsteady*) pi-t'ŭl-gŏ-ri-nŭn 비틀거리는.   「끝으로 걷다.
tiptoe *n.* pal-ggŭt 발끝. —*v.* pal-ggŭ-t'ŭ-ro kŏt-da 발
tire *n.* t'a-i-ŏ 타이어. —*v.* (*fatigue*) p'i-gon-ha-da 피곤하다, (*fore*) sil-jŭng-na-da 싫증나다.
tiresome *adj.* chi-ru-han 지루한 ; sŏng-ga-sin 성가신.
tissue *n.* yal-bùn chik-mul 얇은 직물 ; (*cell*) cho-jik 조직 ; pak-yŏp-ji 박엽지.
title *n.* che-mok 제목, ch'ing-ho 칭호.
to *prep.* ① (*up to and including*) …kka-ji …까지. ② (*place*) …ŭ-ro …으로. ③ …ŭl wi-ha-yŏ …을 위하여.
toad *n.* tu-ggŏ-bi 두꺼비.
toadstool *n.* pŏ-sŏt 버섯, tok-bŏ-sŏt 독버섯.
toast *n.* ① t'o-u-sŭ-t'ŭ 토우스트. ② ch'uk-bae 축배. —*v.* ① kup-da 굽다. ② ch'uk-bae-rŭl dŭl-da 축배를 들다.
tobacco *n.* tam-bae 담배 ; hŭp-yŏn 흡연.

tobacco pouch tam-bae ssam-ji 담배 쌈지.　「늘날.
today *n.* ① o-nŭl 오늘. ② hyŏn-jae 현재, o-nŭl-nal 오
toddle *n.* a-jang-a-jang kŏt-da 아장아장 걷다.
toe *n.* pal-ga-rak 발가락.
together *adv.* ham-gge 함께, ta ka-ch'i 다 같이.
toil *n.* no-go 노고, (*effort*) ae 애, no-yŏk 노역(勞役).
　—*v.* (*labor*) ae-ssŏ il-ha-da 애써 일하다.
toilet *n.* (*lavatory*) pyŏn-so 변소, hwa-jang-sil 화장실.
toilet paper hyu-ji 휴지.
toilet room hwa-jang-sil 화장실.　「nyŏm-p'um 기념품.
token *n.* p'yo 표, t'o-u-k'ŭn 토우큰 ; (*keepsake*) ki-
tolerable *adj.* ch'am-ŭl su it-nŭn 참을 수 있는 ; wen-
　man-han 웬만한, kwaen-ch'an-ŭn 괜찮은.
tolerance *n.* kwan-yong 관용, a-ryang 아량.
tolerate *v.* ① (*allow*) nŏ-gŭ-rŏp-ge po-a chu-da 너그럽
　게 보아 주다. ② (*endure*) ch'am-da 참다, kyŏn-di-da
　견디다.
toll *n.* (*passage money*) t'ong-haeng-se 통행세.
tomato *n.* t'o-ma-t'o 토마토.
tomb *n.* (*grave*) mu-dŏm 무덤, myo 묘.
tombstone *n.* tol-bi-sŏk 돌비석, myo-bi 묘비.
tomorrow *n.* nae-il 내일 : *the day after* ∼ mo-re 모레 /
　two days after ∼ kŭl-p'i 글피.
ton *n.* t'on 톤.
tone *n.* ① (*sound*) ŭm-jo 음조(音調). ② (*hue*) saek-jo
　색조. —*v.* (*attune*) cho-yul-ha-da 조율(調律)하다.
tongs *n.* pu-jŏt-ga-rak 부젓가락, chip-ge 집게.
tongue *n.* ① hyŏ 혀. ② (*language*) mal 말 : *mother*
tonic *n.* kang-jang-je 강장제.　└∼ mo-guk-ŏ 모국어.
tonight *n. & adv.* o-nŭl-bam(-e) 오늘밤(에).
too *adv.* (*also*) tto-han 또한 ; nŏ-mu 너무.
tool *n.* yŏn-jang 연장, to-gu 도구.

tooth *n.* i 이, i-bbal 이빨.
toothache *n.* ch'i-t'ong 치통.
tooth-brush *n.* ch'it-sol 칫솔.
toothpick *n.* i-ssu-si-gae 이쑤시개.
top *n.* ① (*summit*) kkok-dae-gi 꼭
대기, (*head*) su-sŏk 수석. ②
(*toy*) p'aeng-i 팽이.

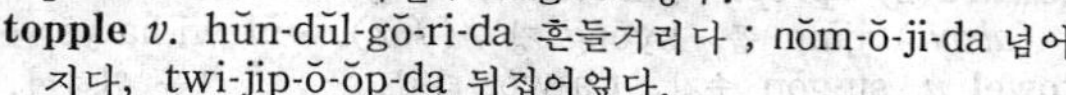

topic *n.* hwa-je 화제, non-je 논제.
topknot *n.* ta-bal 다발 ; sang-t'u 상투.
topple *v.* hŭn-dŭl-gŏ-ri-da 흔들거리다 ; nŏm-ŏ-ji-da 넘어
지다, twi-jip-ŏ-ŏp-da 뒤집어엎다.
torch *n.* ① hwaet-bul 횃불. ② tŭng-bul 등불.
torment *n.* ko-t'ong 고통 ; (*torture*) ka-ch'aek 가책.
—*v.* koe-rop-hi-da 괴롭히다.
torpedo *n.* ŏ-roe 어뢰, su-roe 수뢰.
torpedo boat ŏ-roe-jŏng 어뢰정.
torrent *n.* ① kŭp-ryu 급류. ② (*pl.*) ŏk-su 억수.
torrid *adj.* (*very hot*) mop-si tŏ-un 몹시 더운 ; *the
T~ Zone* yŏl-dae chi-bang 열대 지방.
tortoise *n.* kŏ-buk 거북.
torture *n. & v.* ko-mun(-ha-da) 고문(拷問)하다.
toss *v.* ① (*throw*) tŏn-jyŏ-ol-ri-da 던져올리다. ②
(*tossup*) tong-jŏn-dŏn-ji-gi 동전던지기.
total *n. & adj.* ch'ong-gye(-ŭi) 총계(의) : *the ~ number*
ch'ong-su 총수. —*v.* hap-gye-ha-da 합계하다.
totalitarianism *n.* chŏn-ch'e-ju-ŭi 전체주의.
totally *adv.* a-ju 아주 ; chŏn-jŏk-ŭ-ro 전적으로.
totem *n.* t'o-t'em 토템. 「da 아장아장 걷다.
totter *v.* pi-t'ŭl-gŏ-ri-da 비틀거리다, a-jang-a-jang kŏt-
touch *v.* (*with hand*) tae-da 대다. man-ji-da 만지다.
—*n.* ① chŏp-ch'ok 접촉. ② (*dash*) p'il-ch'i 필치.
touching *adj.* kam-dong-si-k'i-nŭn 감동시키는 ; (*pitiful*)

ae-ch'ŏ-ro-un 애처로운.

tough *adj.* (*hard*) tan-dan-han 단단한, (*strong*) t'ŭn-t'ŭn-han 튼튼한 ; (*sturdy*) wan-gang-han 완강한.

tour *n.* yu-ram 유람, yŏ-haeng 여행. —*v.* yu-ram-ha-da 유람하다, yŏ-haeng-ha-da 여행하다.

tourist *n.* kwan-gwang-gaek 관광객.

tournament *n.* kyŏng-gi 경기, si-hap 시합.

tow *v.* (*pull*) kkŭl-go ka-da 끌고 가다.

toward(s) *prep.* (*direction*) …jjok-ŭ-ro …쪽으로 ; (*about*) jjŭm 쯤, kyŏng 경 ; (*for*) …ŭl wi-ha-yŏ … ㄴ을 위하여.

towel *n.* su-gŏn 수건, t'a-wŏl 타월.

tower *n.* t'ap 탑. —*v.* u-dduk sot-da 우뚝 솟다.

town *n.* ŭp 읍 ; (*big* ∼) to-hoe-ji 도회지.

toy *n.* chang-nan-gam 장난감.

toyshop *n.* chang-nan-gam ka-ge 장난감 가게.

trace *n.* hŭn-jŏk 흔적. —*v.* ch'u-jŏk-ha-da 추적하다.

track *n.* ① pal-ja-guk 발자국. ② (*railway*) ch'ŏl-do 철도. —*v.* twi-rŭl jjot-da 뒤를 쫓다.

tractor *n.* t'ŭ-raek-t'ŏ 트랙터, kyŏn-in-ch'a 견인차.

trade *n.* sang-ŏp 상업, mu-yŏk 무역. —*v.* chang-sa-ha-da 장사하다 ; (*barter*) kyo-hwan-ha-da 교환하다.

trademark *n.* sang-p'yo 상표.

trader *n.* sang-in 상인, mu-yŏk-ŏp-ja 무역업자 ; (*trading vessel*) mu-yŏk-sŏn 무역선.

tradition *n.* chŏn-t'ong 전통, kwan-sŭp 관습.

traffic *n.* ① kyo-t'ong 교통. ② (*trade*) mae-mae 매매, kŏ-rae 거래. —*v.* kŏ-rae-ha-da 거래하다.

tragedy *n.* pi-gŭk 비극 ; ch'am-sa 참사.

tragic *adj.* pi-gŭk-ŭi 비극의, pi-gŭk-jŏk-in 비극적인.

trail *v.* (*drag*) (chil-jil) kkŭl-da (질질) 끌다.

train *n.* ki-ch'a 기차, yŏl-ch'a 열차. —*v.* (*teach*) hul-lyŏn-ha-da 훈련하다.

trainer *n.* hul-lyŏn-ja 훈련자, t'ŭ-re-i-nŏ 트레이너.

training *n.* hul-lyŏn 훈련, yŏn-sŭp 연습 ; tal-lyŏn 단련 : ～ *school* yang-sŏng-so 양성소.

trait *n.* t'ŭk-saek 특색, t'ŭk-jing 특징.

traitor *n.* pan-yŏk-ja 반역자, pae-ban-ja 배반자.

tram *n.* (*streetcar*) si-ga chŏn-ch'a 시가 전차.

tramp *n.* ① (*vagabond*) pang-rang-ja 방랑자. ② (*trudge*) to-bo yŏ-haeng 도보 여행. —*v.* pap-da 밟다.

trample *v.* chit-bap-da 짓밟다.

trance *n.* mong-hwan 몽환(夢幻) ; hwang-hol 황홀.

tranquil *adj.* cho-yong-han 조용한, p'yŏng-on-han 평온한, (*calm*) ch'im-ch'ak-han 침착한. 「하다.

transact *v.* ch'ŏ-ri-ha-da 처리하다 ; kŏ-rae-ha-da 거래

transaction *n.* ① (*conducting*) ch'ŏ-ri 처리. ② (*business*) kŏ-rae 거래. ③ (*pl.*) (*proceedings*) ui-sa-rok 의사록. 「nŭng-ga-ha-da 능가하다.

transcend *v.* (*go beyond*) ch'o-wŏl-ha-da 초월하다,

transcribe *v.* pok-sa-ha-da 복사하다, pe-ggi-da 베끼다.

transcript *n.* sa-bon 사본, tŭng-bon 등본.

transfer *n.* i-jŏn 이전(移轉). —*v.* (*convey*) om-gi-da 옮기다 ; (*make over*) yang-do-ha-da 양도하다.

transform *v.* pyŏn-hyŏng-ha-da 변형하다.

transformer *n.* pyŏn-ap-gi 변압기. 「없는.

transient *adj.* sun-gan-jŏk-in 순간적인, tŏt-ŏp-nŭn 덧

transit *n.* t'ong-gwa 통과, t'ong-haeng 통행.

translate *v.* pŏn-yŏk-ha-da 번역하다, hae-sŏk-ha-da 해

translation *n.* pŏn-yŏk 번역. 「석하다.

transmission *n.* chŏn-dal 전달 ; yang-do 양도.

transmit *v.* chŏn-dal-ha-da 전달하다, chŏn-ha-da 전하다.

transmitter *n.* song-sin〔song-hwa〕-gi 송신〔송화〕기.

transparent *adj.* t'u-myŏng-han 투명한. 「식하다.

transplant *v.* om-gyŏ sim-da 옮겨 심다, i-sik-ha-da 이

transport *v.* (*convey*) su-song-ha-da 수송하다.
transportation *n.* su-song 수송, un-song 운송.
trap *n.* tŏt 덫. —*v.* tŏ-ch'ŭ-ro chap-da 덫으로 잡다.
trash *n.* ssŭ-re-gi 쓰레기. jji-ggi 찌끼.
travel *n.* & *v.* yŏ-haeng(-ha-da) 여행(하다).
travel(l)er *n.* yŏ-haeng-ja 여행자, na-gŭ-ne 나그네.
traverse *v.* hoeng-dan-ha-da 횡단하다.
tray *n.* chaeng-ban 쟁반 : *ash* ~ chae-ddŏ-ri 재떨이.
treacherous *adj.* pae-ban-ha-nŭn 배반하는, pae-sin-ha-nŭn 배신하는 ; mit-ŭl su ŏp-nŭn 믿을 수 없는.
treachery *n.* pae-sin 배신, pae-ban 배반.
tread *v.* (*walk*) kŏt-da 걷다, (*trample*) pap-da 밟다.
treason *n.* pan-yŏk 반역, pul-sin 불신. 「hwa 재화.
treasure *n.* po-mul 보물, po-sŏk 보석, (*wealth*) chae-
treasurer *n.* hoe-gye-wŏn 회계원, kŭm-go-gye 금고계.
treasury *n.* kuk-go 국고(國庫) ; po-go 보고.
treat *v.* ① ch'wi-gŭp-ha-da 취급하다 ; tae-jŏp-ha-da 대접하다. ② (*cure*) ch'i-ryo-ha-da 치료하다.
treatise *n.* non-mun 논문. 「료.
treatment *n.* ① tae-u 대우. ② (*medical*) ch'i-ryo 치
treaty *n.* (*agreement*) cho-yak 조약, yak-jŏng 약정.
treble *adj.* se-gop-ŭi 세곱의, se-bae-ŭi 세배의.
tree *n.* na-mu 나무, su-mok 수목.
tremble *v.* ttŏl-da 떨다, ttŏl-ri-da 떨리다.
tremendous *adj.* (*awful*) mu-sŏ-un 무서운 ; (*huge*) koeng-jang-han 굉장한.
tremulous *adj.* ttŏl-ri-nŭn 떨리는, kŏp-man-ŭn 겁많은.
trench *n.* (*mil.*) ch'am-ho 참호 ; (*ditch*) to-rang 도랑.
trend *n.* kyŏng-hyang 경향, ch'u-se 추세.
trespass *v.* (*invade*) ch'im-ip-ha-da 침입하다.
trial *n.* ① (*test*) si-do 시도. ② (*hardship*) si-ryŏn 시련. ③ (*law*) kong-p'an 공판.

triangle *n.* sam-gak-hyŏng 3각형.

tribe *n.* chong-jok 종족, pu-jok 부족.

tribunal *n.* pŏp-jŏng 법정, p'an-sa-sŏk 판사석.

tribute *n.* ① kong-mul 공물. ② ch'an-sa 찬사.

trick *n.* kye-ryak 계략. —*v.* sok-i-da 속이다.

trickle *v.* ttuk-dduk ttŏ-rŏ-ji-da 뚝뚝 떨어지다.「발 자전거.

tricycle *n.* sam-ryun-ch'a 3륜차, se-bal cha-jŏn-gŏ 세

trifle *n.* sa-so-han il 사소한 일, so-ryang 소량. —*v.*
nang-bi-ha-da 낭비하다, chang-nan-ha-da 장난하다.

trifling *adj.* si-si-han 시시한, ha-ch'an-ŭn 하찮은.

trigger *n.* pang-a-soe 방아쇠, che-dong-gi 제동기.

trilogy *n.* sam-bu-jak 3부작, sam-bu-gŭk 3부극.

trim *adj.* mal-ssuk-han 말쑥한, chŏng-don-doen 정돈된.
—*v.* chal-ra pŏ-ri-da 잘라 버리다, ka-ji-rŏn-hi ha-da
가지런히 하다, ta-dŭm-da 다듬다.

trinity *n.* sam-wi-il-ch'e 3위일체.

trio *n.* (*persons*) sam-in-jo 3인조 ; (*singers or mu-
sicians*) sam-jung-ju 3중주. 「디다.

trip *n.* yŏ-haeng 여행. —*v.* chal-mot ti-di-da 잘못 디

triple *adj.* se-gyŏp-ŭi 세겹의 ; (*three times*) se-bae-ŭi
세배의. 「bu-han 진부한.

trite *adj.* (*stale*) k'ye-k'ye-muk-ŭn 케케묵은, chin-

triumph *n.* sŭng-ri 승리. —*v.* sŭng-ri-ha-da 승리하다,
kae-sŏn-ha-da 개선하다. 「양양한.

triumphant *adj.* i-gin 이긴, ŭi-gi-yang-yang-han 의기

trivial *adj.* si-si-han 시시한, ha-ch'an-ŭn 하찮은 : *a* ~
matters si-si-han il 시시한 일.

trolley *n.* t'ŭ-rol-ri 트롤리, si-ga chŏn-ch'a 시가 전차.

troop *n.* ① (*band*) tte 떼. ② (*pl.*) kun-dae 군대.

trooper *n.* ki-ma kyŏng-gwan 기마 경관 ; (*parachutist*)
nak-ha-san-byŏng 낙하산병. 「t'ŭ-ro-p'i 트로피.

trophy *n.* chŏl-li-p'um 전리품 ; u-sŭng-p'ae 우승패,

tropic *n.* ① hoe-gwi-sŏn 회귀선(回歸線). ② yŏl-dae
tropical *adj.* yŏl-dae-ŭi 열대의. 「열대.
tropics *n.* yŏl-dae chi-bang 열대 지방. 「리다.
trot *n.* sok-bo 속보. —*v.* sok-bo-ro tal-ri-da 속보로 달
trouble *n.* ① kŏk-jŏng 걱정, kŭn-sim 근심, ko-noe 고뇌.
② (*disease*) pyŏng 병. —*v.* koe-rop-hi-da 괴롭히다.
troublesome *adj.* kka-da-ro-un 까다로운, kwi-ch'an-
ŭn 귀찮은, sŏng-ga-sin 성가신.
trough *n.* yŏ-mul-t'ong 여물통, ku-yu 구유.
trousers *n.* yang-bok pa-ji 양복 바지, chŭ-bong 즈봉.
trousseau *n.* hon-su-gam 혼수감, hon-su ot-ga-ji 혼수
trout *n.* song-ŏ 송어. 「옷가지.
trowel *n.* hŭk-son 흙손, mo-jong-sap 모종삽.
truant *n.* ① ke-ŭ-rŭm-baeng-i 게으름뱅이. ② (*absentee*)
mu-dan kyŏl-sŏk-ja 무단 결석자.
truce *n.* hyu-jŏn 휴전 : *a* ~ *line* hyu-jŏn-sŏn 휴전선.
truck *n.* hwa-mul cha-dong-ch'a 화물 자동차, t'ŭ-rŏk
트럭 ; son-su-re 손수레. 「ŭi 실제의.
true *adj.* ch'am-doen 참된, chin-jŏng-ŭi 진정의 ; sil-je-
truly *adv.* chin-sil-ro 진실로 ; (*loyally*) ch'ung-sil-hi
충실히 ; (*correctly*) chŏng-hwak-hi 정확히.
trump *n.* t'ŭ-rŏm-p'ŭ 트럼프, ŭ-ddŭm-p'ae 으뜸패.
trumpet *n.* na-p'al 나팔, t'ŭ-rŏm-p'et 트럼펫. —*v.* na-
p'al-ŭl pul-da 나팔을 불다. 「기.
trunk *n.* ① t'ŭ-rŏng-k'ŭ 트렁크. ② (*tree*) chul-gi 줄
trust *n.* (*belief*) sin-yong 신용 ; (*responsibility*) sin-
t'ak 신탁. —*v.* mit-da 믿다, sin-yong-ha-da 신용하다.
trustee *n.* ① po-gwan-in 보관인, su-t'ak-ja 수탁자. ②
(*univ.*) p'yŏng-ŭi-wŏn 평의원, i-sa 이사.
trustful *adj.* mit-nŭn 믿는, sil-loe-ha-nŭn 신뢰하는.
truth *n.* chil-li 진리, chin-sil-sŏng 진실성, sa-sil 사실.
truthful *adj.* sŏng-sil-han 성실한, ch'am-doen 참된.

try *v.* ① si-do-ha-da 시도하다, (*endeavor*) no-ryŏk-ha-da 노력하다. ② (*law*) chae-p'an-ha-da 재판하다.
tub *n.* t'ong 통 : *bath* ~ mok-yok-t'ong 목욕통.
tube *n.* kwan 관, t'yu-u-bŭ 튜우브.
tuberculosis *n.* p'ye-byŏng 폐병, kyŏl-haek 결핵.
tuck *v.* kŏt-ŏ ol-ri-da 걷어 올리다, ch'aeng-gyŏ nŏ-t'a
Tuesday *n.* hwa-yo-il 화요일.　　　　　　 ⌞챙겨 넣다.
tuft *n.* song-i 송이, tŏm-bul 덤불.
tug *n.* (*boat*) ye-in-sŏn 예인선. —*v.* (*drag*) tang-gi-da 당기다, kkŭ-rŏ-dang-gi-da 끌어당기다.
tuition *n.* su-ŏp 수업, su-ŏp-ryo 수업료.
tulip *n.* t'yu-ul-rip 튜울립.　　　　　　 ⌜떨어지다.
tumble *v.* nŏm-ŏ-ji-da 넘어지다, kul-rŏ ttŏ-rŏ-ji-da 굴러
tumbler *n.* ① k'ŏp 컵. ② (*acrobat*) kok-ye-sa 곡예사.
tumo(u)r *n.* chong-gi 종기, chong-yang 종양.
tumult *n.* so-dong 소동, so-ran 소란, tong-ran 동란.
tuna *n.* ta-rang-ŏ 다랑어.
tune *n.* (*melody*) kok-jo 곡조, (*tone*) ka-rak 가락. —*v.* kok-jo-rŭl mat-ch'u-da 곡조를 맞추다.
tunic *n.* kun-bok chŏ-go-ri 군복 저고리.　　⌜을 파다.
tunnel *n.* t'ŏ-nŏl 터널, kul 굴. —*v.* kul-ŭl p'a-da 굴
turbulent *adj.* si-ggŭ-rŏ-un 시끄러운 ; (*violent*) sa-na-
turf *n.* chan-di 잔디, chan-di-bat 잔디밭. ⌞un 사나운.
turkey *n.* ch'il-myŏn-jo 칠면조.
turmoil *n.* so-ran 소란, so-dong 소동, hol-lan 혼란.
turn *v.* ① hoe-jŏn-ha-da 회전하다, to-ra-sŏ-da 돌아서다. ② (*curve*) ku-bu-rŏ-ji-da 구부러지다. ③ (*change*) pyŏn-ha-da 변하다. —*n.* ① hoe-jŏn 회전. ② kul-gok 굴곡. ③ pyŏn-hwa 변화. ④ (*order*) ch'a-rye 차례.
turning point chŏn-hwan-jŏm 전환점, pun-gi-jŏm 분
turnip *n.* sun-mu 순무.　　　　　　　　 ⌞기점.
turpentine *n.* t'e-re-bin-yu 테레빈유(油).

turret *n.* chak-ŭn t'ap 작은 탑 ; (*gun*) p'o-t'ap 포탑.
turtle *n.* pa-da-gŏ-buk 바다거북.
tusk *n.* ŏm-ni 엄니 ; ppŏ-dŭ-rŏng-ni 뻐드렁니.
tussle *n.* tŭ-jap-i 드잡이, nan-t'u 난투.
tutor *n.* ka-jŏng-gyo-sa 가정교사, kang-sa 강사.
tweezers *n.* chok-jip-ge 족집게, p'in-set 핀셋.
twelve *n.* yŏl-dul 열둘, sip-i 12.
twenty *n.* sŭ-mul 스물, i-sip 20.
twice *adv.* tu-bae-ro 두배로, tu-bŏn 두번, i-hoe 2회.
twig *n.* chan-ga-ji 잔가지, ka-nŭn ka-ji 가는 가지.
twilight *n.* hwang-hon 황혼, ttang-gŏ-mi 땅거미.
twin *n.* ssang-dong-i 쌍동이, ssang-saeng-a 쌍생아.
twine *n.* no-ggŭn 노끈, kkon sil 꼰 실.　「깜박이다.
twinkle *v.* pan-jjak-gŏ-ri-da 반짝거리다, kkam-bak-i-da
twirl *v.* ping-bing tol-ri-da 빙빙 돌리다.
twist *v.* kko-da 꼬다, (*distort*) pi-t'ŭl-da 비틀다.
twitch *v.* (*pull at*)chap-a-ggŭl-da 잡아끌다.
twitter *v.* ① chi-jŏ-gwi-da 지저귀다. ② (*excited*) hŭng-
bun-ha-yŏ mom-ŭl ttŏl-da 흥분하여 몸을 떨다.
two *n.* tul 둘, i 2. —*adj.* tu-gae-ŭi 두개의.
type *n.* ① (*sort*) hyŏng 형, yu-hyŏng 유형. ② (*printing*) hwal-ja 활자. —*v.* t'a-i-p'ŭ-ra-i-t'ŏ-ro ch'i-da
타이프라이터로 치다.　　　　　　　　　　　「라이터.
typewriter *n.* t'a-ja-gi 타자기, t'a-i-p'ŭ-ra-i-t'ŏ 타이프
typhoid *n.* chang-t'i-p'u-sŭ 장티푸스.
typhoon *n.* t'ae-p'ung 태풍.
typhus *n.* pal-jin-t'i-p'u-sŭ 발진티푸스.　「in 대표적인.
typical *adj.* chŏn-hyŏng-jŏk-in 전형적인, tae-p'yo-jŏk-
typist *n.* t'a-ja-su 타자수, t'a-i-p'i-sŭ-t'ŭ 타이피스트.
tyranny *n.* ① p'o-hak 포학. ② p'ok-jŏng 폭정 ; chŏn-
je chŏng-ch'i 전제 정치.
tyrant *n.* p'ok-gun 폭군, chŏn-je kun-ju 전제 군주.

⟶◂ U ▸⟵

udder *n.* (*cow*) chŏt-t'ong 젖통, yu-bang 유방.
ugly *adj.* ch'u-ak-han 추악한, mot saeng-gin 못 생긴.
ulcer *n.* kwe-yang 궤양, chong-gi 종기.
ultimate *adj.* ch'oe-hu-ŭi 최후의, kung-gŭk-ŭi 궁극의;
 (*fundamental*) kŭn-bon-jŏk-in 근본적인.
ultimatum *n.* ch'oe-hu t'ong-ch'ŏp 최후 통첩.
umbrella *n.* (*for rain*) u-san 우산, pak-jwi-u-san 박
 쥐우산, (*for sunlight*) yang-san 양산.
umpire *n.* sim-p'an(-gwan) 심판(관).
unable *adj.* hal su ŏp-nŭn 할 수 없는. ⌜없는.
unaccountable *adj.* sŏl-myŏng-hal su ŏp-nŭn 설명할 수
unacquainted *adj.* nat-sŏn 낯선, saeng-so-han 생소한.
unaffected *adj.* kku-mim-ŏp-nŭn 꾸밈없는.
unanimous *adj.* man-jang-il-ch'i-ŭi 만장일치의.
unarm *v.* mu-jang-hae-je-ha-da 무장해제하다.
unavoidable *adj.* p'i-hal su ŏp-nŭn 피할 수 없는, p'i-
 ch'i-mot-hal 피치못할, pul-ga-p'i-han 불가피한.
unaware *adj.* al-ji mot-ha-nŭn 알지 못하는.
unbearable *adj.* kyŏn-dil su ŏp-nŭn 견딜 수 없는.
unbelievable *adj.* mit-ŭl su ŏp-nŭn 믿을 수 없는.
unceasing *adj.* kkŭn-im-ŏp-nun 끊임없는, pu-dan-ŭi
uncertain *adj.* pul-hwak-sil-han 불확실한. ⌞부단의.
uncle *n.* a-jŏ-ssi 아저씨, (*sup.*) paek-bu 백부, (*inf.*)
 suk-bu 숙부.
unclean *adj.* tŏ-rŏ-un 더러운, pul-gyŏl-han 불결한.
uncomfortable *adj.* pul-yu-k'wae-han 불유쾌한, pul-
 k'wae-han 불쾌한; pul-p'yŏn-han 불편한.
uncommon *adj.* pi-bŏm-han 비범한, chin-gi-han 진기한.
unconscious *adj.* mu-ŭi-sik-ŭi 무의식의.

uncouth *adj.* t'u-bak-han 투박한, kŏ-ch'in 거친.
uncover *v.* pŏt-gi-da 벗기다 ; (*disclose*) p'ok-ro-ha-da 폭로하다, tŭ-rŏ-nae-da 드러내다.
under *prep. & adv.* a-rae-e 아래에, mi-t'e 밑에.
underclothes *n.* sok-ot 속옷, nae-ŭi 내의.
underdeveloped *adj.* chŏ-gae-bal-ŭi 저개발의.
undergo *v.* (*experience*) kyŏk-da 겪다. (*suffer*) tang-ha-da 당하다 ; (*endure*) kyŏn-di-da 견디다.
undergraduate *n.* tae-hak chae-hak-saeng 대학 재학생.
underground *adj.* chi-ha-ŭi 지하의. —*n.* (*Am.*) (*subway*) chi-ha-ch'ŏl 지하철. 「래에.
underneath *adv.* a-rae-ro 아래로. —*prep.* a-rae-e 아
understand *v.* i-hae-ha-da 이해하다, al-da 알다.
undertake *v.* mat-da 맡다 ; ch'ak-su-ha-da 착수하다.
undertaker *n.* ① (*of funerals*) chang-ŭi-sa 장의사. ② (*contractor*) to-gŭp-ja 도급자, ch'ŏng-bu-in 청부인.
underwear *n.* sok-ot 속옷, nae-ŭi 내의.
undo *v.* wŏn-sang-dae-ro ha-da 원상대로 하다.
undoubted *adj.* ŭi-sim-ŏp-nŭn 의심없는, hwak-sil-han
undress *v.* o-sŭl pŏt-da 옷을 벗다. 「확실한.
undue *adj.* pu-dang-han 부당한, kwa-do-ŭi 과도의.
uneasy *adj.* pu-ran-han 불안한. p'yŏn-ch'an-ŭn 편찮은.
unemployment *n.* si-rŏp 실업, sil-jik 실직.
unequal *adj.* pul-gong-p'yong-han 불공평한.
uneven *adj.* ko-rŭ-ji an-ŭn 고르지 않은.
unexpected *adj.* ye-gi-ch'i an-ŭn 예기치 않은, ttŭt-ba-ggŭi 뜻밖의, ŭi-oe-ŭi 의외의. 「히.
unexpectedly *adv.* ttŭt-ba-gge 뜻밖에. to-ryŏn-hi 돌연
unfair *adj.* pul-gong-p'yŏng-han 불공평한.
unfaithful *adj.* sŏng-sil-ch'i mot-han 성실치 못한, pul-sil-han 불실한, pu-jŏng-han 부정(不貞)한.
unfavorable *adj.* pul-ri-han 불리한: ~ *balance of trade*

mu-yŏk yŏk-jo 무역 역조.　　　　　　「적임어 아닌.
unfit *adj*. pu-jŏk-dang-han 부적당한, chŏk-im-i a-nin
unfold *v*. p'yŏ-da 펴다, yŏl-da 열다.
unforeseen *adj*. ye-ch'ŭk-mot-han 예측못한.
unfortunate *adj*. pu-run-han 불운한, pul-haeng-han
　불행한. —*n*. pul-haeng-han sa-ram 불행한 사람.
unfrequented *adj*. in-jŏk-i tŭ-mun 인적이 드문.
unfriendly *adj*. u-ae-ŏp-nŭn 우애없는, pak-jŏng-han
　박정한, pul-ch'in-jŏl-han 불친절한.
unfurl *v*. (*spread*) p'yŏ-da 펴다, p'ŏl-rŏk-i-da 펄럭이다.
ungrateful *adj*. ŭn-hye-rŭl mo-rŭ-nŭn 은혜를 모르는 ;
　(*unrewarding*) po-ram-ŏp-nŭn 보람없는.
unhappy *adj*. pul-haeng-han 불행한.
unheard *adj*. tŭl-ri-ji an-nŭn 들리지 않는 ; al-ryŏ-ji-ji
　an-nŭn 알려지지 않는.
unidentified *adj*. sin-wŏn-mi-sang-ŭi 신원미상의, mi-
　hwak-in-ŭi 미확인의.
uniform *adj*. han-mo-yang-ŭi 한모양의, han-gyŏl-ga-
　t'ŭn 한결같은. —*n*. che-bok 제복.　　　　　　「하다.
unify *v*. t'ong-il-ha-da 통일하다, t'ong-hap-ha-da 통합
unilateral *adj*. il-bang-jŏk-in 일방적인.
unimportant *adj*. chung-yo-ha-ji an-ŭn 중요하지 않은.
union *n*. ① kyŏl-hap 결합. ② (*trade* ～) cho-hap 조
　합. ③ (*marriage*) kyŏl-hon 결혼. ④ (*league*) yŏn-
　hap 연합. ⑤ (*concord*) il-ch'i 일치.
unique *adj*. yu-il-han 유일한, tok-t'ŭk-han 독특한.
unison *n*. ① cho-hwa 조화. ② (*mus*.) che-ch'ang 제창.
unit *n*. ① tan-wi 단위. ② (*mil*.) pu-dae 부대.
unite *v*. kyŏl-hap-ha-da 결합하다, hap-ch'i-da 합치다.
United Nations kuk-je yŏn-hap 국제 연합.
universal *adj*. u-ju-ŭi 우주의 ; po-p'yŏn-jŏk-in 보편적인.
universe *n*. u-ju 우주, chŏn-se-gye 전세계.

university *n*. chong-hap tae-hak-gyo 종합 대학교.
unjust *adj*. ol-ch'i an-ŭn 옳지 않은, pu-jŏng-han 부정
　한 ; (*unfair*) pul-gong-p'yŏng-han 불공평한.
unkind *adj*. pul-ch'in-jŏl-han 불친절한.
unknown *adj*. al-ryŏ-ji-ji an-ŭn 알려지지 않은.
unlatch *v*. kŏl-soe-rŭl pŏt-gi-da 걸쇠를 벗기다.
unlawful *adj*. pul-bŏp-ŭi 불법의, wi-bŏp-ŭi 위법의.
unlearned *adj*. mu-sik-han 무식한.
unless *conj*. ···i a-ni-myŏn ···이 아니면.
unlike *adj*. kat-ji an-ŭn 같지 않은, ta-rŭn 다른. —
　prep. ···tap-ji an-k'e ···답지 않게.
unload *v*. (chim-ŭl) pu-ri-da (짐을) 부리다.　　　「나쁜.
unlucky *adj*. pu-run-han 불운한, un-i na-bbŭn 운이
unmanly *adj*. nam-ja-dap-ji an-ŭn 남자답지 않은.
unnatural *adj*. pu-ja-yŏn-han 부자연한, ki-goe-han 기
unnecessary *adj*. pul-p'i-ryo-han 불필요한.　　　└괴한.
unnoticed *adj*. nam-ŭi nun-e ttŭi-ji an-nŭn 남의 눈에
　띄지 않는.　　　　　　　　　　　　「it-nŭn 비어있는.
unoccupied *adj*. im-ja-ŏp-nŭn 임자없는 ; (*vacant*) pi-ŏ-
unofficial *adj*. pi-gong-sik-ŭi 비공식의.
unpack *v*. chim-ŭl p'ul-da 짐을 풀다.　　　　「ŭi 미불의.
unpaid *adj*. chi-bul-ha-ji an-ŭn 지불하지 않은, mi-bul-
unpardonable *adj*. yong-sŏ-hal su ŏp-nŭn 용서할 수 없는.
unpleasant *adj*. pul-yu-k'wae-han 불유쾌한.
unprecedented *adj*. chŏl-lye-ŏp-nŭn 전례없는.
unquestionable *adj*. ŭi-sim-hal yŏ-ji ŏp-nŭn 의심할 여
　지 없는, hwak-sil-han 확실한.
unravel *v*. p'ul-da 풀다, kkŭ-rŭ-da 끄르다.
unreasonable *adj*. pul-hap-ri-han 불합리한 ; pu-dang-
　han 부당한 ; t'ŏ-mu-ni-ŏp-nŭn 터무니없는.
unroll *v*. p'ul-da 풀다, p'yŏl-ch'i-da 펼치다.
unseen *adj*. po-i-ji an-nŭn 보이지 않는.

unselfish *adj.* sa-sim-i ŏp-nŭn 사심이 없는.
unskilled *adj.* mi-suk-han 미숙한. 「p'ae-han 실패한.
unsuccessful *adj.* sŏng-gong mot-han 성공 못한, sil-
untie *v.* kkŭ-rŭ-da 끄르다, p'ul-da 풀다.
until *prep.* …kka-ji …까지.
untimely *adj.* ttae a-nin 때 아닌, ch'ŏl a-nin 철 아닌.
untrue *adj.* hŏ-wi-ŭi 허위의.
unusual *adj.* i-sang-han 이상한 ; tŭ-mun 드문.
unwelcome *adj.* hwan-yŏng-bat-ji mot-ha-nŭn 환영받
지 못하는, tal-gap-ji an-ŭn 달갑지 않은.
unwilling *adj.* ma-ŭm nae-k'i-ji an-nŭn 마음 내키지
않는, si-rŏ-ha-nŭn 싫어하는. 「한.
unwise *adj.* ŏ-ri-sŏk-ŭn 어리석은, ch'ŏn-bak-han 천박
unworthy *adj.* ka-ch'i-ŏp-nŭn 가치없는.
up *adv. & prep.* …wi-e …위에 ; …ŭi wi-ro…의 위로.
uphill *adj.* ol-ra-ga-nŭn 올라가는, o-rŭ-mak-ŭi 오르막의.
uphold *v.* (*support*) chi-ji-ha-da 지지하다.
upon *prep.* …wi-e …위에.
upper *adj.* wi-jjok-ŭi 위쪽의, sang-wi-ŭi 상위의.
upright *adj.* ttok-ba-rŭn 똑바른 ; chŏng-jik-han 정직한.
uprising *n.* p'ok-dong 폭동 ; pal-lan 반란.
uproar *n.* k'ŭn so-dong 큰 소동 ; so-ŭm 소음.
uproot *v.* ppu-ri ppop-da 뿌리 뽑다 ; kŭn-jŏl-ha-da 근절
하다, mo-ra-nae-da 몰아내다. 「복.
upset *v.* twi-jip-ŏ ŏp-da 뒤집어 엎다. —*n.* chŏn-bok 전
upside-down *adj.* twi-jip-ŏ-jin 뒤집어진 ; chŏn-do-doen
전도된 ; ŏng-mang-in 엉망인.
upstairs *adj.* wi-ch'ŭng-ŭi 위층의, i-ch'ŭng-ŭi 2층의.
—*n.* wi-ch'ŭng 위층, i-ch'ŭng 2층. 「대적인.
up-to-date *adj.* ch'oe-sin-ŭi 최신의, hyŏn-dae-jŏk-in 현
upward *adj.* wi-ro hyang-han 위로 향한.
upwards *adv.* wi-rŭl hyang-ha-yŏ 위를 향하여, wi-jjok-

ŭ-ro 위쪽으로.

urban *adj.* to-si-ŭi 도시의, to-hoe-p'ung-ŭi 도회풍의.

urge *v.* kwŏn-go-ha-da 권고하다, (*push*) chae-ch'ok-ha-da 재촉하다, kyŏk-ryŏ-ha-da 격려하다.

urgent *adj.* kin-gŭp-han 긴급한, chŏl-bak-han 절박한.

urn *n.* (*vase*) hang-a-ri 항아리, tan-ji 단지, tok 독.

us *pron.* (*accus.*) u-ri-rŭl 우리를, (*dat.*) u-ri-e-ge 우리에게. 「다, sa-yong-ha-da 사용하다.

use *n.* sa-yong 사용, yong-bŏp 용법. —*v.* ssŭ-da 쓰

useful *adj.* yu-yong-han 유용한, ssŭl-mo-it-nŭn 쓸모

useless *adj.* ssŭl-mo-ŏp-nŭn 쓸모없는. 「있는.

usher *n.* an-nae-in 안내인, mun-ji-gi 문지기.

usual *adj.* po-t'ong-ŭi 보통의, p'yong-so-ŭi 평소의.

usually *adv.* po-t'ong 보통, tae-gae 대개.

utensil *n.* kŭ-rŭt 그릇, ki-gu 기구 ; pu-ŏk ki-gu 부엌 기구 : *farming* ∼*s* nong-gi-gu 농기구.

utilize *v.* i-yong-ha-da 이용하다.

utmost *adj.* kŭk-do-ŭi 극도의, ch'oe-go-do-ŭi 최고도의.

Utopia *n.* i-sang-hyang 이상향, yu-t'o-p'i-a 유토피아.

utter *adj.* wan-jŏn-han 완전한 ; (*total*) chŏn-jŏk-in 전 적인. —*v.* (*speak*) pa-rŏn-ha-da 발언하다.

utterance *n.* pa-rŏn 발언, mal-ssi 말씨.

utterly *adv.* a-ju 아주, wan-jŏn-hi 완전히.

V

vacancy *n.* kong-hŏ 공허 ; (*vacant post*) kong-sŏk 공석, (*blank*) pin-t'ŭm 빈틈.

vacant *adj.* pin 빈 : *a* ∼ *house* pin-jip 빈집.

vacate *v.* pi-u-da 비우다 ; mul-rŏ-na-da 물러나다.

vacation *n.* hyu-ga 휴가, pang-hak 방학.

vaccinate *v.* chong-du-rŭl no-t'a 종두를 놓다.

vaccination *n.* chong-du 종두, u-du 우두.

vacuum *n.* chin-gong 진공(眞空).

vagabond *n.* pang-rang-ja 방랑자.　　　　「모호한.

vague *adj.* mak-yŏn-han 막연한 ; (*obscure*) mo-ho-han

vain *adj.* hŏt-doen 헛된, kong-hŏ-han 공허한.

vainly *adv.* kong-yŏn-hi 공연히, hŏt-doe-i 헛되이.

valiant *adj.* ssik-ssik-han 씩씩한, yong-gam-han 용감한.

valid *adj.* yu-hyo-han 유효한 ; hwak-sil-han 확실한.

valley *n.* kol-jja-gi 골짜기, kye-gok 계곡.

valor *n.* yong-gi 용기, yong-maeng 용맹.　　　「귀중품.

valuable *adj.* kwi-jung-han 귀중한. —*n.* kwi-jung-p'um

value *n.* ka-ch'i 가치. —*v.* ① chon-jung-ha-da 존중하
다. ② (*appraise*) p'yŏng-ga-ha-da 평가하다.

valve *n.* p'an 판(瓣) : *safety* ～ an-jŏn-p'an 안전판.

vamp *n.* yo-bu 요부, t'ang-nyŏ 탕녀.

vampire *n.* ① (*bloodsucker*) hŭp-hyŏl-gwi 흡혈귀. ②
(*enchantress*) yo-bu 요부(妖婦).

vane *n.* pa-ram-gae-bi 바람개비, p'ung-hyang-gye 풍향
계, p'ung-sin-gi 풍신기.

vanguard *n.* chŏn-wi 전위(前衛), sŏn-bong 선봉.

vanish *v.* sa-ra-ji-da 사라지다, ŏp-sŏ-ji-da 없어지다.

vanity *n.* hŏ-yŏng 허영, kong-hŏ 공허.

vanquish *v.* chŏng-bok-ha-da 정복하다, i-gyŏ-nae-da 이

vantage *n.* yu-ri 유리(有利), i-dŭk 이득.　　　Ｌ겨내다.

vapid *adj.* kim ppa-jin 김 빠진, hŭng-mi-op-nŭn 흥미

vaporize *v.* chŭng-bal-si-k'i-da 증발시키다.　　　Ｌ없는.

vapo(u)r *n.* chŭng-gi 증기, kim 김.　　　　「채로운.

varied *adj.* yŏ-rŏ ka-ji-ŭi 여러 가지의, ta-ch'ae-ro-un 다

variety *n.* pyŏn-hwa 변화 ; ta-yang(-sŏng) 다양(성).

various *adj.* yŏ-rŏ ka-ji-ŭi 여러 가지의.

vary *v.* (*change*) pyŏn-gyŏng-ha-da 변경하다 ; (*diver-
sify*) ta-ch'ae-rop-ge ha-da 다채롭게 하다.

vase *n.* pyŏng 병, hang-a-ri 항아리, tan-ji 단지 ; (*for flower*) kkot-byŏng 꽃병.

vassal *n.* (*subject*) sin-ha 신하, (*servant*) ha-in 하인.

vast *adj.* nŏl-bŭn 넓은, kwang-dae-han 광대한.

vault *n.* ① tung-gŭn ch'ŏn-jang 둥근 천장. ② (*cellar*) chi-ha-sil 지하실. —*v.* (*jump*) ttwi-da 뛰다.

vegetable *n.* ya-ch'ae 야채, ch'ae-so 채소.

vegetation *n.* sik-mul 식물, ch'o-mok 초목.

vehicle *n.* ch'a-ryang 차량, t'al kŏt 탈 것.

veil *v.* kam-ch'u-da 감추다, tŏp-da 덮다. —*n.* pe-il 베일, nŏ-ul 너울, chang-mak 장막.

vein *n.* hyŏl-gwan 혈관, chŏng-maek 정맥.

velocity *n.* (*speed*) sok-ryŏk 속력, sok-do 속도.

velvet *n.* u-dan 우단, pil-ro-o-do 빌로오도, pel-bet 벨벳.

venerable *adj.* ① chon-gyŏng-hal man-han 존경할 만한. ② (*ancient*) yu-sŏ-gi-p'ŭn 유서깊은.

venerate *v.* (*respect*) chon-gyŏng-ha-da 존경하다.

vengeance *n.* pok-su 복수, ang-ga-p'ŭm 앙갚음.

venom *n.* ① tok 독, tok-aek 독액. ② (*spite*) wŏn-han 원한.

vent *n.* ku-mŏng 구멍, pae-ch'ul-gu 배출구.

ventilate *v.* hwan-gi-ha-da 환기하다.

ventilation *n.* hwan-gi 환기, t'ong-p'ung 통풍.

venture *n.* mo-hŏm 모험. —*v.* wi-hŏm-ŭl mu-rŭp-ssŭ-da 위험을 무릅쓰다, kam-haeng-ha-da 감행하다.

veranda(h) *n.* pe-ran-da 베란다 ; t'oet-ma-ru 툇마루.

verb *n.* (*gram.*) tong-sa 동사.

verbal *adj.* mal-ŭi 말의, ŏn-ŏ-ŭi 언어의 ; *a ~ explanation* ku-du-sŏl-myŏng 구두설명.

verdict *n.* (*law*) p'yŏng-gyŏl 평결 ; p'an-dan 판단.

verge *n.* pyŏn-du-ri 변두리, ka-jang-ja-ri 가장자리.

verify *v.* hwak-in-ha-da 확인하다, (*prove*) chŭng-myŏng[ip-jŭng]-ha-da 증명[입증]하다.

vernacular *n.* ① kuk-ŏ 국어. ② sa-t'u-ri 사투리. —*adj.* (*native*) pon-guk-ŭi 본국의.
vernal equinox ch'un-bun 춘분(春分).
verse *n.* sit-gwi 싯귀(詩句), un-mun 운문.
versed *adj.* (*skilled*) chŏng-t'ong-han 정통한.
very *adj.* ch'am-da-un 참다운, pa-ro kŭ 바로 그. — *adv.* tae-dan-hi 대단히, mae-u 매우.
vessel *n.* ① kŭ-rŭt 그릇. ② (*ship*) pae 배.
vest *n.* (*waistcoat*) cho-ggi 조끼.
veteran *n.* no-ryŏn-ga 노련가. —*adj.* no-ryŏn-han 노련한. 「다.
veto *n.* kŏ-bu-gwŏn 거부권. —*v.* kŏ-bu-ha-da 거부하
vex *v.* (*provoke*) sŏng-na-ge ha-da 성나게 하다, (*annoy*) sŏng-ga-si-ge kul-da 성가시게 굴다.
vexation *n.* sok-sang-ham 속상함 ; ae-t'am 애탐.
via *prep.* (*by way of*) …ŭl kŏ-ch'yŏ-sŏ …을 거쳐서, …kyŏng-yu-ha-yŏ …경유하여.
vibrate *v.* chin-dong-ha-da 진동하다, ttŏl-ri-da 떨리다.
vibration *n.* chin-dong 진동, tong-yo 동요.
vicar *n.* (kyo-gu) mok-sa (교구) 목사.
vice *n.* ① ak-dŏk 악덕. ② (*tool*) kkŏk-soe 꺾쇠.
vice-president *n.* pu-t'ong-ryŏng 부통령.
vicinity *n.* pu-gŭn 부근, kŭn-ch'ŏ 근처.
vicious *adj.* ak-dŏk-ŭi 악덕의, sa-ak-han 사악한.
vicissitude *n.* pyŏn-hwa 변화, hŭng-mang 흥망.
victim *n.* hŭi-saeng-ja 희생자, su-nan-ja 수난자.
victor *n.* sŭng-ri-ja 승리자, chŏng-bok-ja 정복자.
victorious *adj.* sŭng-ri-ŭi 승리의, i-gin 이긴.
victory *n.* sŭng-ri 승리, u-sŭng 우승.
vie *v.* kyŏ-ru-da 겨루다, kyŏng-jaeng-ha-da 경쟁하다.
view *n.* ① (*scene*) kyŏng-ch'i 경치. ② (*opinion*) ŭi-gyŏn 의견. —*v.* kwan-ch'al-ha-da 관찰하다.

vigil *n.* pam-sae-um 밤새움, ch'ŏ-rya 철야.

vigorous *adj.* chŏng-ryŏk wang-sŏng-han 정력 왕성한, (*lively*) ki-un-ch'an 기운찬.

vigo(u)r *n.* hwal-ryŏk 활력, wŏn-gi 원기.

vile *adj.* (*base*) pi-yŏl-han 비열한 ; ch'ŏn-han 천한.

villa *n.* pyŏl-jang 별장, pyŏl-jŏ 별저(別邸).

village *n.* ma-ŭl 마을, ch'ol-lak 촌락.

villager *n.* ma-ŭl sa-ram 마을 사람, ch'on-min 촌민.

villain *n.* ak-han 악한, ak-dang 악당.　　「호하다.

vindicate *v.* pyŏn-ho-ha-da 변호하다, ong-ho-ha-da 옹

vine *n.* tŏng-gul 덩굴 ; p'o-do-na-mu 포도나무.

vinegar *n.* ch'o 초, sik-ch'o 식초.

vineyard *n.* p'o-do-wŏn[bat] 포도원[밭].

viola *n.* pi-ol-ra 비올라.

violate *v.* ① wi-ban-ha-da 위반하다, ŏ-gi-da 어기다 ; ② (*profane*) tŏ-rŏp-hi-da 더럽히다.

violence *n.* p'ok-haeng 폭행, p'ok-ryŏk 폭력.

violent *adj.* ① maeng-ryŏl-han 맹렬한, nan-p'ok-han 난폭한. ② (*unnatural*) pu-ja-yŏn-han 부자연한.

violet *n.* o-rang-k'ae-ggot 오랑캐꽃, che-bi-ggot 제비꽃.

violin *n.* pa-i-ŏl-rin 바이얼린 ; che-gŭm 제금(提琴).

viper *n.* tok-sa 독사, sal-mu-sa 살무사.

virgin *n.* ch'ŏ-nyŏ 처녀. —*adj.* sun-gyŏl-han 순결한; (*untrodden*) chŏn-in mi-dap-ŭi 전인 미답의 : ~ *gold* sun-gŭm 순금/ ~ *paper* paek-ji 백지.

virtual *adj.* sa-sil[sil-je]-sang-ŭi 사실[실제]상의.

virtue *n.* (*goodness*) tŏk 덕(德) ; (*chastity*) chŏng-jo 정조 ; (*merit*) mi-dŏk 미덕.

virtuous *adj.* tŏk-i no-p'ŭn 덕이 높은, ko-gyŏl-han 고결한, (*chaste*) chŏng-suk-han 정숙한.

visible *adj.* nun-e po-i-nŭn 눈에 보이는.

vision *n* si-gak 시각 ; (~ *for future*) mi-rae-sang 미

래상 ; (*imagination*) hwan-yŏng 환영.
visit *n. & v.* pang-mun(-ha-da) 방문(하다).
visitor *n.* pang-mun-gaek 방문객, son-nim 손님.
visor *n.* (*peak of cap*) mo-ja-ŭi ch'aeng 모자의 챙.
visual *adj.* si-gak-ŭi 시각의, nun-e po-i-nŭn 눈에 보이는.
vital *adj.* ① (*of life*) saeng-myŏng-ŭi 생명의. ② (*fatal*) ch'i-myŏng-jŏk-in 치명적인.
vitality *n.* saeng-myŏng-ryŏk 생명력, hwal-gi 활기.
vivid *adj.* (*lively*) saeng-saeng-han 생생한 ; (*clear*) sŏn-myŏng-han 선명한.
vocabulary *n.* ŏ-hwi 어휘, yong-ŏ 용어.
vocal *adj.* mok-so-ri-ŭi 목소리의 :~ *cords* sŏng-dae 성대.
vocalist *n.* sŏng-ak-ga 성악가, ka-su 가수.
vocation *n.* ch'ŏn-jik 천직, chik-ŏp 직업.
vogue *n.* (*fashion*) yu-haeng 유행 ; in-gi 인기.
voice *n.* mok-so-ri 목소리, ŭm-sŏng 음성.
void *adj.* (*empty*) kong-hŏ-han 공허한 ; (*not binding*) mu-hyo-ŭi 무효의. —*n.* kong-gan 공간.
volcano *n.* hwa-san 화산.
volley *n.* ① il-je sa-gyŏk 일제 사격. ② (*tennis*) pal-ri
volleyball *n.* pae-gu 배구.   └발리.
voltage *n.* chŏn-ap 전압, chŏn-ap-ryang 전압량.
volume *n.* ① (*quantity*) yang 양, (*bulk, size*) pu-p'i 부피, k'ŭ-gi 크기. ② (*book*) kwŏn 권.
voluntary *adj.* cha-bal-jŏk-in 자발적인.   「원하다.
volunteer *n.* chi-wŏn-ja 지원자. —*v.* chi-wŏn-ha-da 지
vomit *v.* (*spew*) t'o-ha-da 토하다, ke-u-da 게우다, nae-bbum-da 내뿜다. —*n.* ku-t'o 구토.
vote *n. & v.* t'u-p'yo(-ha-da) 투표(하다).
voter *n.* t'u-p'yo-ja 투표자, yu-gwŏn-ja 유권자.
vouch *v.* (*guarantee*) po-jŭng-ha-da 보증하다 ; (*assert*) tan-ŏn-ha-da 단언하다.

vow *n.* & *v.* maeng-se(-ha-da) 맹세(하다).
vowel *n.* mo-ŭm 모음 ; mo-ŭm-ja 모음자.
voyage *n.* & *v.* hang-hae(-ha-da) 항해(하다).
vulgar *adj.* (*base*) pi-ch'ŏn-han 비천한, chŏ-sok-han 저속한. —*n.* (*common people*) sŏ-min 서민.
vulgarity *n.* ya-bi 야비 ; ch'ŏn-bak 천박.
vulture *n.* tok-su-ri 독수리 ; (*a greedy person*) yok-sim-jang-i 욕심장이.

W

waddle *v.* a-jang-a-jang kŏt-da 아장아장 걷다.
wade *v.* mul-sok-ŭl kŏ-rŏ-ga-da 물속을 걸어가다.
waft *v.* ttŏ-dol-da 떠돌다; pu-dong-ha-da 부동(浮動)하다.
wag *v.* hŭn-dŭl-da 흔들다.
wage *n.* im-gŭm 임금(賃金) : *a ~ raise* im-gŭm in-sang 임금 인상. —*v.* (*carry on*) haeng-ha-da 행하다.
wageworking *n.* im-gŭm no-dong 임금 노동.
wag(g)on *n.* su-re 수레, chim-ma-ch'a 짐마차.
wag(g)oner *n.* ma-ch'a-gun 마차군. 「부짖음.
wail *v.* t'ong-gok-ha-da 통곡하다. —*n.* ul-bu-ji-jŭm 울
waist *n.* hŏ-ri 허리, yo-bu 요부(腰部).
waistcoat *n.* cho-ggi 조끼. 「da 시중들다.
wait *v.* ① ki-da-ri-da 기다리다. ② (*serve*) si-jung-dŭl-
waiter *n.* kŭp-sa 급사, we-i-t'ŏ 웨이터.
waiting room tae-hap-sil 대합실.
waitress *n.* yŏ-gŭp 여급, we-i-t'ŭ-re-sŭ 웨이트레스.
wake *v.* kkae-da 깨다, kkae-u-da 깨우다.
waken *v.* kkae-u-da 깨우다, i-rŭ-k'i-da 일으키다.
walk *n.* kŏ-rŭm 걸음, po-haeng 보행 ; (*stroll*) san-ch'aek 산책 ; (*path*) po-do 보도. —*v.* kŏ-rŏ-ga-da 걸어가다.
wall *n.* pyŏk 벽, tam 담 ; (*pl.*) sŏng-byŏk 성벽.

wallet *n.* chi-gap 지갑, ton-ju-mŏ-ni 돈주머니.
walnut *n.* ho-du 호두, ho-du-na-mu 호두나무.
wan *adj.* ch'ang-baek-han 창백한 ; na-yak-han 나약한.
wand *n.* mak-dae-gi 막대기, chi-p'ang-i 지팡이.
wander *v.* he-mae-da 헤매다, kil-ŭl il-t'a 길을 잃다.
wane *v.* i-ul-da 이울다, soe-t'oe-ha-da 쇠퇴하다. —*n.*
　i-ji-rŏ-jim 이지러짐, soe-t'oe 쇠퇴.
want *n.* p'i-ryo 필요 ; (*lack*) kyŏl-p'ip 결핍. —*v.* ①
　wŏn-ha-da 원하다. ② (*need*) p'i-ryo-ha-da 필요하다.
wanton *adj.* pyŏn-dŏk-sŭ-rŏ-un 변덕스러운 ; (*lewd*)
　ŭm-t'ang-han 음탕한. —*n.* pa-ram-dung-i 바람둥이.
war *n.* chŏn-jaeng 전쟁, t'u-jaeng 투쟁.　　「저럼.
warble *v.* chi-jŏ-gwi-da 지저귀다. —*n.* chi-jŏ-gwim 지
ward *n.* ① (*in hosp.*) pyŏng-sil 병실, pyŏng-dong 병
　동. ② (*guard*) kam-si 감시, kam-dok 감독.
wardrobe *n.* ot-jang 옷장, yang-bok-jang 양복장.
ware *n.* ① (*pl.*) sang-p'um 상품. ② ki-mul 기물:
　silver ～ ŭn-je-p'um 은제품.　　　　　「도매 상점.
warehouse *n.* ① ch'ang-go 창고. ② to-mae sang-jŏm
warfare *n.* chŏn-jaeng 전쟁, chŏn-t'u 전투.
warm *adj.* tta-ddŭt-han 따뜻한, tŏ-un 더운. —*v.* tta-
　ddŭt-ha-ge ha-da 따뜻하게 하다, te-u-da 데우다.
warm-hearted *adj.* tong-jŏng-sim-man-ŭn 동정심많은,
　ch'in-jŏl-han 친절한.
warmth *n.* tta-ddŭt-ham 따뜻함, on-gi 온기(溫氣).
warn *v.* kyŏng-go-ha-da 경고하다, t'a-i-rŭ-da 타이르다.
warning *n.* kyŏng-go 경고, hun-gye 훈계.
warp *v.* hwi-da 휘다, twi-t'ŭl-da 뒤틀다.
warrant *n.* & *v.* po-jŭng(-ha-da) 보증(하다).
warrant officer (*mil.*) chun-wi 준위(准尉).
warrior *n.* kun-in 군인, chŏn-sa 전사, yong-sa 용사.
warship *n.* kun-ham 군함.

wary *adj*. cho-sim-sŏng‑it-nŭn 조심성있는, (*cautious*) sin-jung-han 신중한.

wash *n*. se-t’ak 세탁. —*v*. ① (*self*) ssit-da 씻다. ② (*clothes*) se-t’ak-ha-da 세탁하다.

washerman *n*. se-t’ak-ŏp-ja 세탁업자.

washerwoman *n*. se-t’ak-bu 세탁부.

washing *n*. ppal-rae 빨래: ∼ *machine* se-t’ak-gi 세탁기.

washroom *n*. yok-sil 욕실(浴室), pyŏn-so 변소.

washstand *n*. se-myŏn-dae 세면대.

wasp *n*. mal-bŏl 말벌, na-na-ni-bŏl 나나니벌.

waste *adj*. hwang-p’ye-han 황폐한. —*v*. nang-bi-ha-da 낭비하다.—*n*. ① nang-bi 낭비. ② hwang-mu-ji 황무지.

watch *n*. ① hoe-jung-si-gye 회중시계. ② (*look out*) kam-si 감시. —*v*. chi-k’yŏ-bo-da 지켜보다.

watchful *adj*. cho-sim-ha-nŭn 조심하는.

watchman *n*. kam-si-in 감시인, p’a-su-gun 파수군.

watchtower *n*. mang-ru 망루, kam-si-t’ap 감시탑.

water *n*. mul 물. —*v*. kŭp-su-ha-da 급수하다.

water colo(u)r su-ch’ae-hwa 수채화.

water dropper (*for inkstone*) yŏn-jŏk 연적(硯滴).

[yŏn-jŏk]

waterfall *n*. p’ok-p’o 폭포.

water gate su-mun 수문.

water lily su-ryŏn 수련.

watermelon *n*. su-bak 수박.

water mill mul-bang-a 물방아, mul-re-bang-a 물레방아.

waterproof *adj*. pang-su-ŭi 방수의. —*n*. (*clothes*) pang-su-bok 방수복.

wave *n*. mul-gyŏl 물결, p’a-do 파도. —*v*. mul-gyŏl-ch’i-da 물결치다 p’ŏl-rŏk-i-da 펄럭이다.

wax *n*. mil 밀, mil-ch’o 밀초. (*tom*) sŭp-gwan 습관.

way *n*. ① kil 길. ② (*method*) pang-bŏp 방법. ③ (*cus-*

waylay *v.* sum-ŏ ki-da-ri-da 숨어 기다리다, cham-bok-ha-da 잠복하다 ; yo-gyŏk-ha-da 요격하다.

wayside *n.* kil-ga 길가, no-byŏn 노변. —*adj.* kil-ga-ŭi 길가의, no-byŏn-ŭi 노변의.

wayward *adj.* pyŏn-dŏk-sŭ-rŏ-un 변덕스러운 ; sun-jong-ch'i an-nŭn 순종치 않는.

we *pron.* u-ri-ga〔nŭn〕 우리가〔는〕.

weak *adj.* ka-nyal-p'ŭn 가냘픈, yak-han 약한.

weaken *v.* yak-ha-ge ha-da 약하게 하다.

weakness *n.* hŏ-yak 허약, pak-yak 박약.

wealth *n.* chae-san 재산 ; pu 부(富) ; p'ung-jok 풍족.

weathy *adj.* chae-san-i man-ŭn 재산이 많은, pu-yu-han 부유한 : *a ~ person* pu-ja 부자. 「키다.

wean *v.* chŏ-jŭl tte-da 젖을 떼다, i-yu-si-k'i-da 이유시

weapon *n.* mu-gi 무기, pyŏng-gi 병기.

wear *v.* ① (*clothes*) ip-da 입다. ② hae-ŏ-ji-da 해어지다.

weary *adj.* chi-ch'in 지친, sil-jŭng-i nan 싫증이 난. —*v.* chi-ch'i-da 지치다, sil-jŭng-na-da 싫증나다.

weasel *n.* chok-je-bi 족제비.

weather *n.* nal-ssi 날씨, il-gi 일기.

weather-beaten *adj.* p'ung-u-e si-dal-rin 풍우에 시달린.

weathercock *n.* ① pa-ram-gae-bi 바람개비, p'ung-hyang-gye 풍향계. ② pyŏn-dŏk-jang-i 변덕장이.

weather forecast il-gi ye-bo 일기 예보.

weave *v.* ① jja-da 짜다, ttŭ-da 뜨다. ② yŏk-da 엮다.

web *n.* ① kŏ-mi-jul 거미줄. ② p'i-ryuk 피륙.

wed *v.* kyŏl-hon-ha-da 결혼하다.

wedding *n.* kyŏl-hon 결혼, hol-lye 혼례.

wedding card kyŏl-hon ch'ŏng-ch'ŏp-jang 결혼 청첩장.

wedding ring kyŏl-hon-ban-ji 결혼반지.

wedge *n.* ① sswae-gi 쐐기. ② hwe-bang 훼방.

Wednesday *n.* su-yo-il 수요일.

weed *n.* chap-ch'o 잡초. —*v.* p'ul-ŭl ppop-da 풀을 뽑다.
week *n.* chu 주(週), chu-gan 주간.
weekend *n.* chu-mal 주말. 「gan-ji 주간지.
weekly *adv.* & *adj.* mae-ju-(ŭi) 매주(의). —*n.* chu-
weep *v.* ul-da 울다, sŭl-p'ŏ-ha-da 슬퍼하다.
weeping willow su-yang-bŏ-dŭl 수양버들.
weigh *v.* ① mu-ge-rŭl tal-da 무게를 달다. ② (*consider*) chung-yo-si-ha-da 중요시하다.
weight *n.* ① ɪnu-ge 무게. ② chung-yo-sŏng 중요성.
weir *n.* ① tuk 둑 ; taem 댐. ② ŏ-sal 어살.
weird *n.* (*fate*) un-myŏng 운명 ; (*omen*) chŏn-jo 전조.
—*adj.* mu-si-mu-si-han 무시무시한.
welcome *n.* & *v.* hwan-yŏng(-ha-da) 환영(하다).
weld *v.* yong-jŏp-ha-da 용접하다.
welfare *n.* hu-saeng 후생, pok-ji 복지.
well *n.* u-mul 우물. —*adv.* hul-ryung-hi 훌륭히. —*v.*
so-sa-na-o-da 솟아나오다.
well-being *n.* an-nyŏng 안녕, pok-ji 복지, pok-ri 복리.
well-born *adj.* chip-an-i cho-ŭn 집안이 좋은, myŏng-
mun t'ae-saeng-ŭi 명문 태생의.
well-bred *adj* pon-de it-ge cha-ran 본데 있게 자란 ;
ye-jŏl-ba-rŭn 예절바른.
well-disposed *adj.* ma-ŭm-ssi ko-un 마음씨 고운.
wellknown *adj.* yu-myŏng-han 유명한.
west *n.* sŏ-jjok 서쪽, sŏ-bu 서부. —*adj.* sŏ-jjok-ŭi 서
쪽의. —*adv.* sŏ-jjok-ŭ-ro 서쪽으로.
western *adj.* sŏ-jjok-ŭi 서쪽의, sŏ-yang-ŭi 서양의.
westward *adj.* & *adv.* sŏ-bang-ŭi[ŭ-ro] 서방의[으로].
wet *adj.* chŏ-jŭn 젖은. —*v.* chŏk-si-da 적시다.
whale *n.* ko-rae 고래.
wharf *n.* pu-du 부두, (*quay*) sŏn-ch'ang 선창.
what *adj.* ŏ-ddŏn 어떤. —*pron.* mu-ŏt 무엇.

whatever *adj.* ŏ-nŭ ⋯i-ra-do 어느 ⋯이라도.　—*pron.*
　ŏ-nŭ kŏ-si-ra-do 어느 것이라도.
wheat *n.* mil 밀, so-maek 소맥.
wheel *n.* pa-k'wi 바퀴. ch'a-ryun 차륜.
wheeze *v.* ssi-gŭn-gŏ-ri-da 씨근거리다.
when *adv.* ŏn-je 언제, ⋯hal ttae ⋯할 때. —*conj.* ttae-
　e 때에. —*n.* (*time*) ttae 때 ; kyong-u 경우.
whence *adv.* ŏ-di-e-sŏ 어디에서, ŏ-jjae-sŏ 어째서.
whenever *adv.* ŏn-je-na 언제나.
where *adv.* ŏ-di-sŏ 어디서, ŏ-di-e 어디에, ŏ-di-ro 어디로.
whereabouts *adv.* ŏ-di-jjŭm-e 어디쯤에. —*n.* haeng-
wherever *adv.* ŏ-di-dŭn-ji 어디든지.　　⌊bang 행방.
whether *conj.* ⋯in-ji ŏ-ddŏn-ji ⋯인지 어떤지.
whetstone *n.* (*grindstone*) sut-dol 숫돌.
which *adj. & pron.* ŏ-nŭ (kŏt) 어느 (것).
whichever *adj.* ŏ-nŭ kŏ-si-dŭn-ji 어느 것이든지.
whiffle *v.* na-p'ul-gŏ-ri-da 나풀거리다.
while *n.* tong-an 동안, cham-si tong-an 잠시 동안.
　—*conj.* ⋯ha-nŭn tong-an-e ⋯하는 동안에.
whim *n.* (*caprice*) pyŏn-dŏk 변덕.
whimper *v.* hŭ-nŭ-ggyŏ ul-da 흐느껴 울다.　　⌈별난.
whimsical *adj.* pyŏn-dŏk-sŭ-rŏ-un 변덕스러운, pyŏl-nan
whine *v.* ① sŭl-p'i ul-da 슬피 울다. ② (*dog*) kking-
　gging-gŏ-ri-da 낑낑거리다.
whinny *v.* (*neigh*) (mal-i) ul-da (말이) 울다.
whip *n.* ch'ae-jjik 채찍. —*v.* mae-jil-ha-da 매질하다.
whirl *v.* ping-bing tol-da 빙빙 돌다. —*n.* hoe-jŏn 회전.
whirlpool *n.* so-yong-do-ri 소용돌이.
whirlwind *n.* hoe-o-ri-ba-ram 회오리바람.
whiskers *n.* ① ku-re-na-rut 구레나룻. ② su-yŏm 수염.
whisper *n.* sok-sak-im 속삭임, kwi-et-mal 귀엣말.
　—*v.* sok-sak-i-da 속삭이다.

whistle *n.* ho-gak 호각 ; hwi-p'a-ram 휘파람, hwi-sŭl 휘슬. —*v.* (*mouth*) hwi-p'a-ram-ŭl pul-da 휘파람을 불다 ; ki-jŏk-ŭl ul-ri-da 기적을 울리다.

white *adj.* hŭin 흰, (*pale*) ch'ang-baek-han 창백한. —*n.* hŭin-saek 흰색 ; hŭin-ot 흰옷.

who *pron.* nu-gu 누구, ŏ-ddŏn sa-ram 어떤 사람.

whoever *pron.* nu-gu-dŭn-ji 누구든지.

whole *n. & adj.* chŏn-ch'e(-ŭi) 전체(의). 「도매.

wholesale *adj.* to-mae-ha-nŭn 도매하는. —*n.* to-mae

wholesome *adj.* (*healthy*) kŏn-gang-e cho-ŭn 건강에 좋은, kŏn-jŏn-han 건전한.

wholly *adv.* chŏn-hyŏ 전혀, wan-jŏn-hi 완전히.

whom *pron.* nu-gu-rŭl 누구를 : *for* ～? nu-gu-rŭl wi-ha-yŏ 누구를 위하여? / *from* ～? nu-gu-e-ge-sŏ 누구에게서 ? /*to* ～? nu-gu-e-ge 누구에게 ?

whooping cough paek-il-hae 백일해.

whose *pron.* nu-gu-ŭi 누구의, ŏ-nŭ pun-ŭi 어느 분의.

why *adv.* wae 왜. —*int.* ŏ-ma 어마.

wick *n.* (*candle or oil lamp*) sim-ji 심지.

wicked *adj.* na-bbŭn 나쁜, (*evil*) sa-ak-han 사악한.

wickedness *n.* sa-ak 사악, sim-sul 심술.

wicket *n.* chak-ŭn mun 작은 문, jjok-mun 쪽문.

wide *adj.* nŏl-bŭn 넓은. —*adv.* nŏl-gge 넓게.

widen *v.* nŏl-p'i-da 넓히다. 「리 퍼진.

widespread *adj.* po-gŭp-doen 보급된, nŏl-ri p'ŏ-jin 널

widow *n.* kwa-bu 과부, mi-mang-in 미망인.

widower *n.* ho-ra-bi 홀아비.

width *n.* nŏl-bi 넓이, p'ok 폭(幅).

wield *v.* hwi-du-rŭ-da 휘두르다, chi-bae-ha-da 지배하다.

wife *n.* ① (*own*) a-nae 아내, ma-nu-ra 마누라, chip-sa-ram 집사람. ② (*another's*) pu-in 부인.

wig *n.* ka-bal 가발(假髮).

wild *adj.* ① ya-saeng-ŭi 야생의. ② (*savage*) mi-gae-han 미개한. ③ (*furious*) nan-p'ok-han 난폭한. —*n.* (*desert*) hwang-mu-ji 황무지.

wild boar san-dwae-ji 산돼지, met-dwae-ji 멧돼지.

wildcat *n.* sal-k'waeng-i 삵괭이.

wilderness *n.* hwang-mu-ji 황무지, kwang-ya 광야.

wile *n.* kan-gye 간계(奸計).

wilful *adj.* ko-ŭi-ŭi 고의의, kye-hoek-jŏk-in 계획적인.

will *aux. v.* ···hal kŏ-si-da ···할 것이다, ···hal chak-jŏng-i-da ···할 작정이다. —*n.* ① ŭi-sa 의사, ŭi-ji 의지. ② (*testament*) yu-ŏn(-jang) 유언(장). —*v.* (*bequeath*) yu-ŏn-ha-da 유언하다.

willing *adj.* ki-ggŏ-i ···ha-nŭn 기꺼이 ···하는.

willingly *adv.* ki-ggŏ-i 기꺼이, chŭl-gŏ-i 즐거이.

willow *n.* pŏ-dŭl 버들.

wilt *v.* si-dŭl-da 시들다, i-ul-da 이울다.

wily *adj.* kyo-hwal-han 교활한.

win *v.* (*races*) i-gi-da 이기다, (*gain*) ŏt-da 얻다.

wince *v.* chu-ch'um-ha-da 주춤하다, chil-ri-da 질리다.

wind *n.* pa-ram 바람. —*v.* kam-da 감다.

winding *adj.* kku-bul-ggu-bul-han 꾸불꾸불한, kup-i-ch'i-nŭn 굽이치는. —*n.* kul-gok 굴곡.

windmill *n.* p'ung-ch'a 풍차(風車).

window *n.* ch'ang 창, ch'ang-mun 창문.

windowpane *n.* ch'ang-yu-ri 창유리.

windpipe *n.* ki-gwan-ji 기관지, sum-t'ong 숨통.

windshield *n.* (*motorcar*) pang-p'ung yu-ri 방풍 유리.

windy *adj.* pa-ram-bu-nŭn 바람부는 : ～ *weather* pa-ram-bu-nŭn nal-ssi 바람부는 날씨.

wine *n.* sul 술, (*from grapes*) p'o-do-ju 포도주.

wing *n.* (*of bird*) nal-gae 날개 ; (*of political party*) ik 익(翼) : *the left* ～ chwa-ik 좌익.

wink *n.* nun-ŭl kkam-bak-gŏ-rim 눈을 깜박거림. —*v.*
kkam-bak-gŏ-ri-da 깜박거리다, nun-jit-ha-da 눈짓하다.
winner *n.* sŭng-ri-ja 승리자.
winnow *v.* k'i-jil-ha-da 키질하다.
winter *n.* kyŏ-ul 겨울, tong-gye 동계(冬季).
wipe *v.* ssi-sŏ-nae-da 씻어내다, tak-da 닦다.
wire *n.* ① ch'ŏl-'sa 철사. ② (*teleg.*) chŏn-bo 전보.
—*v.* chŏn-bo-rŭl ch'i-da 전보를 치다.
wireless *n. & adj.* mu-sŏn chŏn-sin(-ui) 무선 전신의.
wisdom *n.* chi-hye 지혜 ; (*learning*) chi-sik 지식.
wise *adj.* hyŏn-myŏng-han 현명한, ŏ-jin 어진.
wisecrack *n.* ik-sal 익살, u-sŭ-gaet-so-ri 우스갯소리.
wise guy kŏn-bang-jin sa-na-i 건방진 사나이.
wish *n.* so-wŏn 소원, so-mang 소망. —*v.* (*desire*) hŭi-
mang-ha-da 희망하다, pa-ra-da 바라다.
wisteria *n.* tŭng-na-mu 등나무.
wistful *adj.* t'am-nae-nŭn tŭt-han 탐내는 듯한 ; saeng-
gak-e cham-gi-nŭn 생각에 잠기는.
wit *n.* ki-ji 기지, chae-ch'i 재치 ; chae-sa 재사(才士).
witch *n.* mu-dang 무당, ma-sul-jang-i 마술장이.
witchcraft *n.* ma-bŏp 마법, ma-sul 마술.
with *prep.* …wa ham-gge …와 함께, …ro …로.
withdraw *v.* mul-rŏ-na-da 물러나다, ch'ŏl-su-ha-da 철
수하다, (*mil.*) ch'ŏl-byŏng-ha-da 철병하다.
wither *v.* si-dŭl-da 시들다, i-ul-da 이울다.
withhold *v.* po-ryu-ha-da 보류하다. 「—*n.* nae-bu 내부.
within *adv.* an-e 안에, sok-e 속에 ; chip an-e 집 안에.
without *prep.* ŏp-si 없이, …ŭi pa-gge-sŏ …의 밖에서.
—*adv.* pa-ggŭn 밖은. —*n.* oe-bu 외부.
withstand *v.* chŏ-hang-ha-da 저항하다, (*endure*) kyŏn-
di-ŏ-nae-da 견디어내다.
witness *n.* chŭng-gŏ 증거 ; (*person*) chŭng-in 증인.

—*v.* mok-gyŏk-ha-da 목격하다, ip-jŭng-ha-da 입증하다.
witty *adj.* chae-ch'i-it-nŭn 재치있는.
wizard *n.* yo-sul-jang-i 요술장이, ma-bŏp-sa 마법사.
woe *n.* ① (*grief*) pi-t'ong 비통. ② (*calamity*) ; chae-
wolf *n.* i-ri 이리, nŭk-dae 늑대.   ⌞ang 재앙.
woman *n.* yŏ-ja 여자, pu-in 부인.   「〔답게〕.
womanly *adj. & adv.* yŏ-sŏng-da-un〔dap-ge〕 여성다운
womb *n.* cha-gung 자궁, t'ae-nae 태내(胎內).
wonder *n.* nol-ra-um 놀라움, kyŏng-i 경이. —*v.* kyŏng-
  t'an-ha-da 경탄하다.
wonderful *adj.* nol-ral-man-han 놀랄만한 ; (*remarka-*
  ble) kŭn-sa-han 근사한, hul-ryung-han 훌륭한.
wondrous *adj.* nol-ral-man-han 놀랄만한 ; pul-ga-sa-ŭi-
  han 불가사의한.
woo *v.* ku-ae-ha-da 구애하다, ku-hon-ha-da 구혼하다.
wood *n.* sup 숲 ; na-mu 나무, (*timber*) mok-jae 목재.
woodcutter *n.* na-mut-gun 나뭇군.
wooden *adj.* na-mu-ŭi 나무의, mok-jae-ŭi 목재의.
woodland *n.* sam-rim-ji-dae 삼림지대.
woodpecker *n.* (*bird*) ttak-da-gu-ri 딱다구리.
wool *n.* yang-t'ŏl 양털, yang-mo 양모.
woollen *adj.* yang-mo-ŭi 양모의, mo-jik-ŭi 모직의.
woozy *adj.* mŏng-ch'ŏng-han 멍청한.   「sok 약속.
word *n.* ① mal 말, nat-mal 낱말. ② (*promise*) yak-
work *n.* ① (*labor*) il 일, no-dong 노동. ② che-jak-mul
  제작물. ③ (*factory*) kong-jang 공장. —*v.* il-ha-da 일
  하다, no-dong-ha-da 노동하다.
workaday *adj.* p'yŏng-il-ŭi 평일(平日)의.
worker *n.* il-gun 일군, no-mu-ja 노무자.
workman *n.* no-dong-ja 노동자, chik-gong 직공.
workmanship *n.* som-ssi 솜씨, ki-ryang 기량.
workshop *n.* kong-jang 공장 ; yŏn-gu-hoe 연구회.

world *n.* ① (*phys.*) se-gye 세계. ② (*abs.*) se-sang 세
상 ; se-in 세인(世人). ③ (*sphere*) pun-ya 분야.

worldly *adj.* se-sok-jŏk-in 세속적인.

world-wide *adj.* se-gye-jŏk-in 세계적인.

worm *n.* pŏl-re 벌레 : *earth* ~ chi-rŏng-i 지렁이.

worn-out *adj.* nal-ga-bba-jin 낡아빠진.

worry *v.* ① koe-rop-hi-da 괴롭히다. ② kŏk-jŏng-ha-da
격정하다. —*n.* kŏk-jŏng 격정. 　　　　　「신.

worrying *adj.* kwi-ch'an-ŭn 귀찮은, sŏng-ga-sin 성가

worse *adj.* po-da na-bbŭn 보다 나쁜, ak-hwa-doen 악
화된. —*adv.* po-da na-bbŭ-ge 보다 나쁘게.

worship *n.* sung-bae 숭배 ; chon-gyŏng 존경, ye-bae
예배. —*v.* ye-bae-ha-da 예배하다 ; pil-da 빌다 ; (*others*) sung-bae-ha-da 숭배하다.

worship(p)er *n.* ye-bae-ja 예배자, sung-bae-ja 숭배자.

worst *adj.* ka-jang na-bbŭn 가장 나쁜.

worsted *n.* tŏl-sil 털실. so-mo-sa 소모사.

worth *n.* & *adj.* ka-ch'i(-it-nŭn) 가치(있는).

worthless *adj.* ka-ch'i-ŏp-nŭn 가치없는, mu-ik-han 무

worthy *adj.* ka-ch'i-it-nŭn 가치있는. 　　　　「익한.

wound *n.* & *v.* pu-sang(-ha-da) 부상(하다).

wrangle *n.* ŏn-jaeng 언쟁. —*v.* mal-da-t'um-ha-da 말
다툼하다, ta-t'u-da 다투다.

wrap *v.* ssa-da 싸다, tu-rŭ-da 두르다, mal-da 말다.

wrath *n.* (*rage*) kyŏk-bun 격분, pun-no 분노.

wreath *n.* hwa-hwan 화환, hwa-gwan 화관.

wreck *n.* ① (*shipwreck*) nan-p'a-sŏn 난파선. ② (*ruin*)
p'a-goe 파괴. —*v.* ① nan-p'a-ha-da 난파하다. ②
(*destroy*) p'a-goe-ha-da 파괴하다.

wren *n.* kul-dduk-sae 굴뚝새.

wrench *n.* sŭ-p'ae-nŏ 스패너, ren-ch'i 렌치. —*v.* pi-
t'ŭl-da 비틀다, pi-ggo-da 비꼬다.

wrest *v.* ① pi-t'ŭl-da 비틀다. ② ppae-at-da 빼앗다.

wrestle *v.* ssi-rŭm-ha-da 씨름하다. —*n.* ssi-rŭm 씨름.

wrestling *n.* re-sŭl-ring 레슬링, ssi-rŭm 씨름.

wretch *n.* pul-ssang-han sa-ram 불쌍한 사람 ; (*scoundrel*) pi-yŏl-han in-gan 비열한 인간.

wretched *adj.* pul-ssang-han 불쌍한.

wriggle *v.* kkum-t'ŭl-gŏ-ri-da 꿈틀거리다. —*n.* kkum-t'ŭl-gŏ-rim 꿈틀거림, mom-bu-rim 몸부림.

wring *v.* jja-nae-da 짜내다 ; pi-t'ŭl-da 비틀다.

wrinkl e*n.* chu-rŭm 주름, ku-gim-sal 구김살. —*v.* chu-rŭm-jap-da 주름잡다.

wrist *n.* son-mok 손목, p'al-mok 팔목.

wristwatch *n.* p'al-mok si-gye 팔목 시계.

writ *n.* yŏng-jang 영장(令狀) ; (*document*) sŏ-ryu 서류 : *a ~ of summon* so-hwan-jang 소환장.

write *v.* ssŭ-da 쓰다, ki-rok-ha-da 기록하다.

writer *n.* chŏ-ja 저자, chak-ga 작가, mun-p'il-ga 문필가.

writhe *v.* mom-bu-rim-ch'i-da 몸부림치다.

writings *n.* chŏ-jak 저작 ; (*lit. prod.*) chak-p'um 작품.

wrong *adj.* na-bbŭn 나쁜, t'ŭl-rin 틀린. —*adv.* na-bbŭ-ge 나쁘게. —*n.* pu-dang 부당, chal-mot 잘못. —*v.* pu-jŏng-ŭl chŏ-ji-rŭ-da 부정을 저지르다.

wrongdoer *n.* pi-haeng-ja 비행자(非行者).

wry *adj.* twi-t'ŭl-rin 뒤틀린 ; jji-p'u-rin 찌푸린.

—◄◄ **X** ►►—

Xmas *n.* (*Christmas*) k'ŭ-ri-sŭ-ma-sŭ 크리스마스, sŏng-t'an-jŏl 성탄절.

x-ray *n.* roen-t'ŭ-gen sŏn 뢴트겐 선, ek-sŭ-re-i 엑스레이.

xylophone *n.* mok-gŭm 목금(木琴), sil-ro-p'on 실로폰.

❧ Y ❧

yacht *n.* yo-t'ŭ 요트, k'wae-sok-jŏng 쾌속정.
yachtsman *n.* yo-t'ŭ sŏn-su 요트 선수.
Yalu *the* ∼ ap-rok-gang 압록강(鴨綠江).
yam *n.* (*sweet potato*) ko-gu-ma 고구마.
yank *v.* hwak chap-a-dang-gi-da 확 잡아당기다.
yard *n.* ① ma-dang 마당. ② (*measure*) ya-a-dŭ 야아드.
yardstick *n.* ya-a-dŭ cha 야아드 자(尺).
yarn *n.* ① pang-sa 방사(紡糸) : *cotton* ∼ myŏn-sa 면
사/*woolen* ∼ t'ŏl-sil 털실. ② (*tale*) i-ya-gi 이야기.
yawn *n. & v.* ha-p'um(-ha-da) 하품(하다).
yea *int.* ye 예, (*yes*) kŭ-rŏ-so 그렇소.
year *n.* ① hae 해. ② (*in comp.*) nyŏn 년 : *last* ∼
chak-nyŏn 작년/*next* ∼ nae-nyŏn 내년/*this* ∼ kŭmnyŏn 금년. ③ (*pl.*) yŏn-ryŏng 연령.
yearbook *n.* yŏn-gam 연감, yŏn-bo 연보.
yearlong *adj.* il-nyŏn tong-an-ŭi 1년 동안의.
yearly *adj.* hae-ma-da-ŭi 해마다의. —*adv.* hae-ma-da
해마다. —*n.* yŏn-gan-ji 연간지(年刊誌). 「동경하다.
yearn *v.* kŭ-ri-wŏ-ha-da 그리워하다, tong-gyŏng-ha-da
yearning *n.* tong-gyŏng 동경, yŏl-mang 열망. —*adj.*
tong-gyŏng[yŏl-mang]-ha-nŭn 동경[열망]하는.
yeast *n.* nu-ruk 누룩, hyo-mo 효모(酵母).
yell *n.* ko-ham 고함. —*v.* oe-ch'i-da 외치다.
yellow *adj.* no-ran 노란. —*n.* hwang-saek 황색.
yelp *v.* nal-k'a-rop-ge oe-ch'i-da 날카롭게 외치다 ; chi-
jŏ-dae-da 짖어대다. —*n.* chit-nŭn so-ri 짖는 소리.
yes *adv.* ye 예, kŭ-rŏ-sŭp-ni-da 그렇습니다.
yes man kup-sil-dae-nŭn sa-ram 굽실대는 사람. 「저께.
yesterday *n.* ŏ-je 어제 : *the day before* ∼ kŭ-jŏ-gge 그

yet *adv.* a-jik 아직, yŏ-jŏn-hi 여전히. —*conj.* kŭ-rŏm-e-do pul-gu-ha-go 그럼에도 불구하고.

yield *v.* ① (*produce*) san-ch'ul-ha-da 산출하다. ② (*surrender*) kul-bok-ha-da 굴복하다. —*n.* (*crop*) su-hwak 수확.

YMCA *n.* ki-dok-gyo ch'ŏng-nyŏn-hoe 기독교 청년회.

yoke *n.* ① mŏng-e 멍에. ② (*clothes*) yo-u-k'ŭ 요우크. —*v.* mŏng-e-rŭl me-u-da 멍에를 메우다.

yolk *n.* no-rŭn-ja-wi 노른자위.

yonder *adj.* chŏ-jjok-ŭi 저쪽의. —*adv.* chŏ-jjok-e 저쪽에.

you *pron.* tang-sin(-dŭl) 당신(들), (*to inf.*) cha-ne (-dŭl) 자네(들), nŏ-hŭi(-dŭl) 너희(들).

young *adj.* chŏl-mŭn 젊은, ŏ-rin 어린.

youngster *n.* a-i 아이, chŏl-mŭn-i 젊은이.

your *pron.* tang-sin(-dŭl)-ŭi 당신(들)의, (*to inf.*) cha-ne(-dŭl)-ŭi 자네(들)의, nŏ(-hŭi-dŭl)-ŭi 너(희들)의.

yours *pron.* tang-sin(-dŭl)-ŭi kŏt 당신(들)의 것, (*to inf.*) cha-ne(-dŭl)-ŭi kŏt 자네(들)의 것, nŏ-hŭi(-dŭl)-ŭi kŏt 너희(들)의 것.

yourself *pron.* tang-sin cha-sin 당신 자신.

youth *n.* ch'ŏng-ch'un 청춘, chŏl-mŭm 젊음.

youthful *adj.* chŏl-mŭn 젊은 ; pal-ral-han 발랄한.

yow *int.* a-yu 아유, e-gŭ-mŏ-ni 에그머니 .

yule *n.* k'ŭ-ri-sŭ-ma-sŭ kye-jŏl 크리스마스 계절.

YWCA *n.* ki-dok-gyo yŏ-ja ch'ŏng-nyŏn-hoe 기득교 여자 청년회.

Z

zeal *n.* yŏl-sim 열심, yŏl-jung 열중.

zealous *adj.* yŏl-jung-ha-nŭn 열중하는, yŏl-sŏng-jŏk-in

zealously *adv.* yŏl-sim-hi 열심히.   ㄴ열성적인.

zebra *n.* ŏl-ruk-mal 얼룩말.

zenith *n.* chŏng-jŏm 정점 ; chŏl-jŏng 절정.

zero *n.* yŏng 영(零), che-ro 제로.

zest *n.* (*relish*) p'ung-mi 풍미, mat 맛.

zigzag *adj.* chi-gŭ-jae-gŭ-ŭi 지그재그의, kal-ji-ja hyŏng-ŭi 갈지자 형의.

zinc *n.* a-yŏn 아연(亞鉛), ham-sŏk 함석.

Zionism *n.* si-on-ju-ŭi 시온주의.

zipper *n.* chi-p'ŏ 지퍼, (*slide fastener*) cha-k'ŭ 자크.

zodiac *n.* sip-i-gung 십이궁(十二宮), hwang-do-dae 황도대(黃道帶).

zone *n.* chi-dae 지대, (*in comp.*) tae 대(帶) : *safety ∼* an-jŏn chi-dae 안전 지대.

zoo *n.* tong-mul-wŏn 동물원.

zoological *adj.* tong-mul-hak-ŭi 동물학의 : ∼ *garden*(s) tong-mul-wŏn 동물원.

zoology *n.* tong-mul-hak 동물학.

zoom *n.* ① pung so-ri-nae-da 붕 소리내다. ② kŭp-sang-sŭng-ha-da 급상승하다.

zyme *n.* (*ferment*) hyo-so 효소.

Mini Dictionary
of
Korean-English

ROMANIZED

Edited by
Gene S. Rhie (이 시진) & B. J. Jones

HOLLYM

A

a 아 Ah!; Oh!; O dear; O!; Dear me!

aböji 아버지 father; papa; daddy; dad.

abu 아부 flattery. *abuhada* 아부하다 flatter; fawn.

ach'im 아침 morning. *ach'ime* 아침에 in the morning.

ach'im chŏnyŏk 아침 저녁 morning and evening.

ach'ŏm 아첨 →**abu** 아부.

adamhada 아담하다 (be) refined; elegant; tidy; neat; cozy.

adong 아동 child; juvenile. *adongŭi* 아동의 juvenile.

adŭk'ada 아득하다 (be) far; distant; remote; dim. *adŭk'an yennal* 아득한 옛날 dim past.

adŭl 아들 son; boy. *adŭlttal* 아들딸 son(s) and daughter(s).

aech'ak 애착 attachment; affection; love.

aech'o 애초. *aech'o-e* 애초에 at first; at the start.

aech'ŏ 애처 one's (beloved) wife. *aech'ŏga* 애처가 devoted husband.

aech'ŏropta 애처롭다 (be) pitiful; pitiable; touching.

aedangch'o 애당초 →**aech'o** 애초.

aedo 애도 condolence; grief; mourning. *aedohada* 애도하다 mourn; lament; grieve.

aedok 애독. *aedok'ada* 애독하다 read with pleasure. *aedokcha* 애독자 (regular) reader; subscriber.

aeguk 애국 love of one's country; patriotism. *aeguk-chŏk* 애국적 patriotic. *aegukcha* 애국자 patriot.

aegukka 애국가 national anthem.

aegyo 애교 charms. *aegyo innŭn* 애교 있는 attractive; charming.

aeho 애호 love; liking. *aehohada* 애호하다 love;

be fond (of).

aein 애인 (her) lover; (his) lover; sweetheart.

aejijungjihada 애지중지하다 prize; cherish; treasure; think[make] much of; set high value(upon).

aejŏng 애정 love; affection. *aejŏngi innŭn* 애정이 있는 affectionate.

aeju 애주. *aejuhada* 애주하다 be fond of liquor.

aek 액 amount; sum. *saengsan[sobi]aek* 생산[소비]액 amount of production[consumption].

aekch'e 액체 liquid; fluid. *aekch'e yŏllyo* 액체 연료 liquid fuel.

aekku 애꾸 one-eyed person; blind of an[one] eye.

aeksu 액수 sum; amount.

aemae 애매. *aemaehan* 애매한 vague; ambiguous.

aemŏgida 애먹이다 harass; annoy; bewilder; embarrass.

aemŏkta 애먹다 have a hard time (with); have bitter experience.

aengmusae 앵무새 parrot.

aengmyŏn 액면 face-value; par value; denomination.

aero 애로 narrow path; bottleneck.

aesŏk 애석. *aesŏk'ada* 애석하다 sad; sorrowful; mournful; regrettable.

aessŭda 애쓰다 exert[strain] oneself; make effort.

aet'ada 애타다 be anxious (about); be nervous[much worried] (about).

aewŏn 애원 supplication; entreaty. *aewŏnhada* 애원하다 entreat; implore; supplicate.

agassi 아가씨 ① young lady; girl; maid(en) ② Miss; young lady!

agi 아기 ① baby; infant ② (daughter; daughter-in-law) dear; darling.

agin 악인 bad[wicked] man; villain.
agŭi 악의 evil intention; ill will; malice.
agun 악운 ill luck; bad fortune; evil fate.
agungi 아궁이 fuel hole; furnace.
agyo 아교 glue.
ahop 아홉 nine. *ahoptchae* 아홉째 the ninth.
ahŭn 아흔 ninety. *ahŭntchae* 아흔째 the ninetieth.
ahŭre 아흐레 nine days; the ninth day (of a month).
ai 아이 child; kid; boy-child; boy; girl-child; girl.
ajanggŏrida 아장거리다 toddle; totter; shamble.
ajik 아직 yet; as yet; still.
ajikkaji 아직까지 so[thus] far; up to now; till now; up to the present.
aju 아주 very; quite; utterly; exceedingly.
ajumŏni 아주머니 aunt; auntie.
ak 악 badness; evil; wrong; vice; wickedness.
akchil 악질. *akchirŭi* 악질의 vicious; ill-natured; evil. *akchil punja* 악질 분자 bad elements.
akch'wi 악취 bad[nasty] smell; offensive odo(u)r; stink; stench.
akkapta 아깝다 ① (be) pitiful; regrettable ② (be) dear; precious. *akkapkedo* 아깝게도 regrettably; lamentably.
akki 악기 musical instrument.
akkida 아끼다 ① grudge; spare; be stingy ② value; prize; hold (a thing) dear.
akkimŏpshi 아낌없이 unsparingly; ungrudgingly; without stint.
akpo 악보 musical note; sheet music; score. *akpojip* 악보집 music book.
akp'yŏng 악평 bad reputation; ill repute. *akp'yŏng hada* 악평하다 speak ill of.

aksa 악사 band(s) man; musician.
aksu 악수 handshake. *aksuhada* 악수하다 shake hand (with).
aktae 악대 (musical) band; brass band.
aktan 악단 orchestra. *kyohyangaktan* 교향악단 symphony orchestra.
aktŏk 악덕 vice; immorality. *aktŏk sangin* 악덕 상인 wicked dealers.
al 알 egg; spawn; roe. *arŭl nat'a* 알을 낳다 lay an egg; spawn.
alda 알다 know; be informed of; be aware of.
allak 안락 ease; comfort. *allak'ada* 안락하다 (be) easy; comfortable.
allida 알리다 let (a person) know; inform; notify.
allŭnsori 앓는소리 moaning; groaning, *allŭnsori- hada* 앓는소리하다 moan; groan.
allyak 알약 tablet; tabloid.
allyŏjida 알려지다 be[become] known (to); come to light. *chal allyŏjin* 잘 알려진 well-known; famous.
allyŏk 알력 friction; discord; strife.
almatta 알맞다 (be) fit; becoming; suitable.
alt'a 앓다 be ill (with); be sick; suffer from.
altcha 알짜 cream; essence; choice.
alttŭrhada 알뜰하다 (be) thrifty; frugal; econom- ical. *alttŭrhi* 알뜰히 frugally; thriftily.
am 암 cancer. *wi*[*p'ye, chagung*]*am* 위〔폐, 자궁〕 암 stomach[lung, uterine] cancer.
ama 아마 probably; perhaps; maybe; possibly; presumably.
amch'o 암초 reef; (sunken) rock.
amgi 암기. *amgihada* 암기하다 learn[get] by heart;

memorize (*Am.*).
amho 암호 code; cipher; password.
amk'ae 암캐 she-dog; bitch.
ammŏri 앞머리 forehead; forefront.
amu ttae 아무 때 any time; any day; whenever; always; all the time.
amnal 앞날 future; days ahead[to come].
amnyŏk 압력 pressure; stress. *amnyŏgŭl kahada* 압력을 가하다 give[apply] pressure (to). *amnyŏk-sot* 압력솥 pressure cooker.
amp'yosang 암표상 ticket broker; speculator(*Am.*).
amsal 암살 assassination. *amsarhada* 암살하다 assassinate; murder. *amsalcha* 암살자 assassin.
amsan 암산 mental arithmetic. *amsanhada* 암산하다 do (a sum) in mental arithmetic.
amshi 암시 hint; suggestion. *amshihada* 암시하다 hint (at); suggest.
amshijang 암시장 black market.
amt'ak 암탉 hen; pullet.
amtallŏ 암달러 black-market dollar.
amugae 아무개 Mr. [Mrs., Miss] So and so; certain person. *Kim amugae* 김 아무개 certain Mr. Kim; one Kim.
amulda 아물다 heal (up); be healed (of a wound).
amuraedo 아무래도 anyhow; anyway; for anything; come what may.
amuri 아무리 however much; no matter how.
amutchorok 아무쪼록 by all means; as much as one can; in any case; at any cost.
an 안 ① inside; interior ② in; within; less than. *ane* 안에 within; inside; in. *anŭrobut'ŏ* 안으로부터 from the inside; from within.

anae 아내 wife; better-half; spouse.

anangne 아낙네 woman; wife.

anchuin 안주인 lady of the house; hostess.

andoeda 안되다 ① must not; shall not ② be sorry;

an-gae 안개 fog; mist. ⌞be a pity.

anggap'ŭm 앙갚음 revenge; retaliation. *anggap'ŭm-hada* 앙갚음하다 revenge oneself; get revenge.

an-gida 안기다 (be) embraced; be in (a person's) arms[bosom].

angma 악마 evil spirit; devil; demon.

angmong 악몽 bad[evil] dream; nightmare.

angshim 앙심 grudge; enmity. *angshimŭl p'umta* 앙심을 품다 bear[nurse] a grudge against.

an-gyŏng 안경 spectacles; glasses.

anikkopta 아니꼽다 ① (be) sickening; disgusting ② be nauseated; be sick.

anjŏlbujŏl mot'ada 안절부절 못하다 be restless [nervous]; flutter; be irritated.

anjŏn 안전 safety; security. *anjŏnhan* 안전한 safe; secure. *anjŏnhi* 안전히 safely; securely.

anjŏng 안정 stability; steadiness.

annyŏng 안녕 public peace. *Annyŏnghashimnikka?* 안녕하십니까? ① How are you? ② Good morning [afternoon, evening]. *Annyonghi ka[kye]shipshio.* 안녕히 가[계]십시오. Good-bye.

anju 안주 appetizer dishes; side dish.

anma 안마 massage. *anmahada* 안마하다 massage.

annae 안내 guidance; leading. *annaehada* 안내하다 guide; conduct. *annaeyang* 안내양 conductress.

anp'ak 안팎 ① interior and exterior; inside and outside. ② about; some; around(*Am.*).

ansaek 안색 complexion; countenance.

anshikku 안식구 female members of a family.
anshim 안심 relief; peace[ease] of mind. *anshim-hada* 안심하다 feel at rest; feel easy (about).
ansonnim 안손님 lady visitor; woman caller.
anta 안다 ① hold[carry] in one's arm(s); embrace; hug. ② answer for; take charge of.
anta 앉다 sit down; take a seat; be seated.
ant'akkapta 안타깝다 ① (be) impatient; irritated ② (be) pitiful; pitiable.
anŭk'ada 아늑하다 (be) cozy; snug; comfortable.
anyak 안약 eye-water[lotion]; eye drops.
ap 앞 front; fore. *ap'ŭi* 앞의 front; preceding. *ap'e* 앞에 in front of; ahead.
apchabi 앞잡이 agent; tool; cat's-paw.
apchi 압지 blotting paper; (paper) blotter.
apch'ima 앞치마 apron. *apch'imarŭl turŭda* 앞치마를 두르다 put on[wear] an apron.
apchip 앞집 house in front.
apch'uk 압축 compression; condensation. *apch'uk'ada* 압축하다 compress; condense.
apkasŭm 앞가슴 breast; chest (part).
appa 아빠 papa; daddy; dad; pop(*Am.*).
appak 압박 pressure; oppression. *appak'ada* 압박하다 oppress; suppress.
appak'wi 앞바퀴 fore wheel; front wheel.
appal 앞발 paw; forefoot; foreleg.
apsŏ 앞서 before; previously; already.
apsu 압수 confiscation; seizure. *apsuhada* 압수하다 seize; confiscate.
aptanggida 앞당기다 move[carry] up; advance.
apto 압도. *aptohada* 압도하다 overwhelm; overcome; overpower. *aptojŏk[ŭro]* 압도적[으로]

overwhelming[ly]; sweeping[ly].

aptwi 앞뒤 before and behind; front and rear.

ap'ŭda 아프다 (be) painful; sore; have[feel] a pain.

ap'yŏn 아편 opium; opiate.

arae 아래 low part; foot; bottom; base. *araeŭi* 아래의 lower; under. *araee* 아래에 down; under; beneath; below.

araech'ŭng 아래층 downstairs. *araech'ŭngesŏ[ŭro]* 아래층에서[으로] downstairs.

araessaram 아랫사람 one's junior; one's inferior; subordinate.

araewi 아래위 up and down; above and below; high and low.

arajuda 알아주다 acknowledge; recognize; appreciate.

aramach'ida 알아맞히다 guess right; make a good guess.

aranaeda 알아내다 find out; make out; detect.

arida 아리다 ① (be) smarting; tingling ② (be) pungent; acrid.

arisonghada 아리송하다 (be) ambiguous; vague; obscure; indistinct.　　　　　　　　　　　「side job.

arŭbait'ŭ 아르바이트 Arbeit (*Ger.*); part-time Job;

arŭmdapta 아름답다 ① (be) beautiful; pretty; lovely; fair ② (be) handsome; good-looking. *arŭmdapke* 아름답게 beautifully; prettily.

arŭn-gŏrida 아른거리다 flicker; flit; glimmer.

asa 아사 death from hunger[by starvation] *asahada* 아사하다 die of[from] hunger.

ashwipta 아쉽다 miss; feel the lack of; (be) inconvenient; (feel) regret.

at 앗 Oh!; O dear!; O my!; Heaven!

au 아우 man's younger brother; woman's younger sister.

ausŏng 아우성 shouting a clamor; scream. *ausŏng-ch'ida* 아우성치다 clamor; scream.

ayang 아양 coquetry. *ayang ttŏlda* 아양 떨다 play the coquette.

⚫ C ⚫ 【ch】

cha 자 foot rule; rule; measure.

chabadanggida 잡아당기다 pull; draw; tug; jerk.

chabaek 자백 confession; profession. *chabaek'ada* 자백하다 confess; make a clean breast.

chabamaeda 잡아매다 tie up; bind; fasten.

chabamŏkta 잡아먹다 slaughter; butcher; prey on.

chabi 자비 mercy; charity; benevolence. *chabiroun* 자비로운 merciful; compassionate; tenderhearted.

chabi 자비. *chabiro* 자비로 at one's own expense.

chabon 자본 capital; funds. *chabon-ga* 자본가 capitalist *chabonjuŭi* 자본주의 capitalism.

chabŭm 잡음 noise; dissenting voices.

chach'i 자치 self-government; autonomy. *chach'i-hada* 자치하다 govern oneself.

chach'o 자초. *chach'ohada* 자초하다 bring on oneself.

chach'wi 자취. *chach'wihada* 자취하다 do one's own cooking; cook for oneself.

chach'wi 자취 traces; vestiges; marks.

chada 자다 sleep; go to bed; go to sleep; be in bed.

chadong 자동. *chadongjŏgin* 자동적인 automatic. *chadongjŏgŭro* 자동적으로 automatically. *chadong-*

mun 자동문 automatic door.

chadongch'a 자동차 motorcar; automobile(*Am.*).

chae 재 ashes. *tambaetchae* 담뱃재 cigarette ash.

chaebae 재배 cultivation; culture. *chaebaehada* 재배하다 cultivate; grow.

chaebal 재발 recurrence. *chaebarhada* 재발하다 recur; return; have a relapse.

chaebŏl 재벌 financial clique[combine]; plutocracy.

chaebong 재봉 sewing; needlework. *chaebonghada* 재봉하다 sew; do needlework.

chaebongt'ŭl 재봉틀 sewing machine.

chaech'a 재차 twice; again; a second time.

chaech'i 재치 wit; cleverness; resources. *chaech'i innŭn* 재치 있는 quick-witted; smart.

chaech'ok 재촉 pressing; urging. *chaech'ok'ada* 재촉하다 press; urge.

chaeda 재다 measure; weigh; gauge.

chaedan 재단 foundation. *chaedan pŏbin* 재단 법인 juridical foundation.

chaegae 재개 reopening; resumption. *chaegaehada* 재개하다 open again; reopen.

chaegŏn 재건 reconstruction. *chaegŏnhada* 재건하다 rebuild; reconstruct.

chaehae 재해 calamity; disaster.

chaehyang kunin 재향 군인 exsoldier; veteran(*Am.*).

chaeil 재일. *chaeirŭi* 재일의 in Japan. *chaeil kyop'o* 재일 교포 Korean residents in Japan.

chaejangnyŏn 재작년 the year before last.

chaejik 재직. *chaejik'ada* 재직하다 hold office; be in office[service].

chaejŏng 재정 finance; financial affairs.

chaeju 재주 ability; talent; gifts. *chaeju innŭn* 재

주 있는 talented; able; gifted.
chaemi 재미 interest; amusement; enjoyment; fun.
chaemiitta 재미있다 be interesting.
chaemi 재미. *chaemi kyop'o* 재미 교포 Korean residents in America. *chaemi yuhaksaeng* 재미 유학생 Korean students studying in America.
chaemok 재목 wood; lumber (*Am.*); timber (*Eng.*) →**mokchae** 목재.
chaemul 재물 property; fortune; means; treasures.
chaenan 재난 misfortune; calamity; disaster.
chaengban 쟁반 tray; salver.
chaenggi 쟁기 plow; plough (*Eng.*).
chaenŭng 재능 → **chaeju** 재주.
chaeoe 재외. *chaeoeŭi* 재외의 abroad; overseas. *chaeoe konggwan* 재외 공관 embassies and legations abroad; diplomatic establishment abroad.
chaep'an 재판 trial; judgement. *chaep'anhada* 재판하다 try; judge; decide on; pass judgment on. *chaep'anil* 재판일 court day.
chaepssada 잽싸다 (be) nimble; quick; agile.
chaerae 재래. *chaeraeŭi* 재래의 conventional. *chaeraeshik* 재래식 conventional type.
chaeryo 재료 material; raw material; stuff; data. *chaeryobi* 재료비 material costs.
chaeryŏk 재력 financial power; means; wealth.
chaesa 재사 man of talent[ability].
chaesan 재산 property; fortune; assets; wealth.
chaesu 재수 luck; fortune.
chaetpit 잿빛 ash color; grey; gray (*Am.*).
chaewon 재원 gifted[talented] young lady.
chagae 자개 mother of pearl; nacre.
chagaek 자객 assassin; assassinator.

chagal 자갈 gravel; pebbles.

chagayong 자가용 private car; one's own car.

chagi 자기 oneself; self; ego. *chagiŭi* 자기의 one's own (self); personal.

chagi 자기 porcelain; china(ware); ceramics.

chagŏp 작업 work; operations. *chagŏp'ada* 작업하다 work; conduct operations.

chaguk 자국 mark; traces; scar; track; stain.

chagŭk 자극 stimulus; impulse. *chagŭk'ada* 자극하다 stimulate; irritate; incite; give an impetus.

chagŭm 자금 funds; capital; fund.

chagŭmahada 자그마하다 (be) smallish; small; short.

chagŭnabŏji 작은아버지 uncle; one's father's younger brother.

chagung 자궁 womb; uterus. *chagungam* 자궁암 uterine cancer.

chagŭnŏmŏni 작은어머니 aunt; wife of one's father's younger brother.

chagwi 작위 peerage; title and rank of nobility.

chagyŏk 자격 qualification; eligibility. *chagyŏgi itta* 자격이 있다. be qualified; be eligible (for).

chagyong 작용 action; operation. *chagyonghada* 작용하다 act; operate on.

chahwasang 자화상 self-portrait.

chajae 자재 materials. *kŏnch'uk chajae* 건축 자재 construction material.

chajak 자작 viscount. *chajak puin* 자작 부인 viscountess.

chajangga 자장가 lullaby; cradlesong.

chaje 자제 self-control[-restraint]. *chajehada* 자제하다 control[restrain] oneself.

chaje 자제 sons; children; young people.

chaji 자지 penis; cock (*Am.*).

chajilgurehada 자질구레하다 (be) small; trifling.

chajŏn 자전 →**sajŏn** 사전.

chajŏng 자정 midnight.

chajŏn-gŏ 자전거 bicycle; bike.

chajonshim 자존심 self-respect; pride.

chaju 자주 often; frequently.

chakchŏn 작전 (military) operations; strategy. *chakchŏnsang* 작전상 strategically; tactically.

chakka 작가 writer; author; artist. *inki chakka* 인기 작가 popular[favorite] writer.

chakkok 작곡 (musical) composition. *chakkok'ada* 작곡하다 compose. *chakkokka* 작곡가 composer.

chakku 자꾸 ① constantly; incessantly; always ② eagerly; strongly.

chakpu 작부 barmaid; waitress.

chakp'um 작품 work. *munhak chakp'um* 문학 작품 literary work.

chakpyŏl 작별 farewell; parting; leave-taking. *chakpyŏrhada* 작별하다 take leave.

chakta 작다 (be) small; little; tiny; young.

chaktonghada 작동하다 operate; move; come into action; start.

chal 잘 well; nicely; skilfully.

challada 잘나다 ① (be) handsome; good-looking ② (be) distinguished; great.

challok'ada 잘록하다 (be) slender; constricted (in the middle).

chalmot 잘못 fault; error; blunder; mistake. *chalmot'ada* 잘못하다 do wrong; make a mistake.

chalsaenggida 잘생기다 → **challada** 잘나다 ①.

cham 잠 sleep; nap; slumber; doze. *chamjada* 잠자다 sleep; go to sleep.

chamae 자매 sisters. *chamae hakkyo* 자매 학교 sister school.

chaman 자만 self-conceit; vanity; boast. *chamanhada* 자만하다 be conceited; be vain.

chambangi 잠방이 (farmer's) knee-breeches.

chambok 잠복. *chambok'ada* 잠복하다 conceal oneself; lie hidden.

chamdŭlda 잠들다 ① fall[drop] asleep; drop off to sleep ② lie (in the churchyard).

chamgŭda 잠그다 lock (up); fasten; bolt.

chamgyŏl 잠결 while asleep.

chamjada 잠자다 → **cham** 잠.

chamjak'o 잠자코 without a word; silently; without objection.

chamjamhada 잠잠하다 ① silent; mute; tacit ② be hushed; subside; become quiet[still, calm].

chamjari 잠자리 dragonfly. *koch'u jamjari* 고추 잠자리 red dragonfly.

chamkkan 잠깐 (for) a while; (for) a moment; (for) some time; for a (short) time.

chamkkodae 잠꼬대 sleep talking. *chamkkodaehada* 잠꼬대하다 talk in one's sleep; talk nonsense.

chammok 잡목 miscellaneous wood; scrubs.

chammu 잡무 miscellaneous[add] business[duties].

chamnyŏm 잡념 worldly[earthly] thoughts; idle thoughts.

chamŏn 잠언 aphorism; maxim.

chamot 잠옷 nightclothes; pajamas; nightgown.

chamshi 잠시 short time[while]; (little) while. *chamshi hue* 잠시 후에 after a while.

chamsu 잠수 diving. *chamsuhada* 잠수하다 dive; submerge. *chamsubu* 잠수부 diver.

chamulsoe 자물쇠 lock; padlock.

chamun 자문 consultation. *chamunhada* 자문하다 inquire; consult.

chamyŏl 자멸 self-destruction. *chamyŏrhada* 자멸하다 destroy[ruin] oneself; perish.

chan 잔 (wine) cup; glass. *ch'atchan* 찻잔 teacup.

chanaek 잔액 balance; remainder.

chanakkaena 자나깨나 (whether) awake or asleep; night and day; always.

chanch'i 잔치 feast; banquet; party. *saengil chanch'i* 생일 잔치 birthday party.

chandi 잔디 lawn; sod; turf. *chandibat* 잔디밭 lawn; grassplot.

chane 자네 you.

chang 장 head; chief; chieftain; boss (*Am.*).

chang 장 soy (sauce). *toenjang* 된장 bean paste.

chang 장 intestines; bowels; entrails.

chang 장 wardrobe; chest of drawers; cabinet; bureau (*Am.*).

changae 장애 obstacle; hindrance; impediment. *changaemul* 장애물 obstacle; obstruction.

changbal 장발 long hair. *changbarŭi* 장발의 long-haired. *changbaljok* 장발족 long-hair group.

changbonin 장본인 ringleader; prime mover.

changbu 장부 (account) book; ledger.

changbyŏng 장병 officers and men; soldiers.

changch'i 장치 apparatus; equipment; installation. *changch'ihada* 장치하다 equip; install; fit.

changch'im 장침 →**punch'im** 분침.

changchŏm 장점 merit; strong[good] point; one's

forte. *changdanchŏm* 장단점 strong and weak points.
changch'ong 장총 (long-barreled) rifle.
changdam 장담 assurance; assertion. *changdam-hada* 장담하다 assure; vouch (for).
changdori 장도리 hammer; claw hammer.
changga 장가 marriage. *changga kada*[*tŭlda*] 장가 가다[들다] marry; get married; take a wife.
changgap 장갑 (a pair of) gloves[mittens].
changgi 장기 (game of) Korean chess. *changgi-p'an* 장기판 chessboard.
changgi 장기 long time[period, term]. *changgiŭi* 장기의 long(-dated).
changgŏri 장거리 long distance[range]. *changgŏri chŏnhwa* 장거리 전화 long-distance call [telephone] (*Am.*); trunk-call (*Eng.*).
changgu 장구 (Korean) hourglass drum.
changgun 장군 general.
changgwan 장관 grand sight; magnificent view [spectacle].
changgwan 장관 minister (of state); Cabinet member; secretary.
changgyo 장교 officer; commissioned officer.
changhak 장학. *changhakkŭm* 장학금 scholarship. *changhaksaeng* 장학생 scholarship student[holder].
changhwa 장화 top[high] boots; boots (*Am.*).
changja 장자 eldest son.
changji 장지 burial place[ground].
changki 장기 one's forte; special skill [ability]; one's speciality; one's great forte.
changma 장마 long rain; spell of wet weather. *changmach'ŏl* 장마철 the rainy[wet] season.

changman 장만. *changmanhada* 장만하다 prepare; provide oneself.
changmi 장미 rose. *tŭlchangmi* 들장미 wild rose.
changmo 장모 wife's mother; man's mother-in-law.
changmun 작문 composition.
changnae 장래 future. *changnaeŭi* 장래의 future; prospective. *changnaee* 장래에 in the future.
changnam 장남 eldest son.
changnan 장난 game; play; mischief; joke. *chang-nanhada* 장난하다 do mischief; play a trick.
changnankam 장난감 plaything; toy; sport.
changnim 장님 blind man; the blind.
changnong 장롱 wardrobe; bureau (*Am.*); dresser.
changnye 장례 funeral [burial] service.
changnyŏ 장녀 eldest daughter.
changnyŏ 장려 encouragement. *changnyŏhada* 장려하다 encourage; promote.
changnyŏn 작년 last year; past year.
chan-go 잔고 balance; remainder → **chanaek** 잔액.
changŏ 장어 eel. *changŏ kui* 장어 구이 broiled eels.
changsa 장사 funeral. *changsa chinaeda* 장사 지내다 hold a funeral.
changsa 장사 man of great strength; powerful man.
changsa 장사 trade; business; commerce. *chang-sahada* 장사하다 do[engage in] business.
changshigan 장시간 for many hours.
changshik 장식 decoration; adornment; ornament. *changshik'ada* 장식하다 ornament; decorate; adorn.
changshin-gu 장신구 accessories; trinkets; furnishings; fancy goods.
changso 장소 place; spot; location; site.
changsŏ 장서 collection of books; one's library.

changtae 장대 (bamboo) pole; rod.

changt'ŏ 장터 market place[site].

changŭi 장의 →**changnye** 장례. *changŭisa* 장의사 undertaker's shop; funeral parlor (*Am.*).

chan-gŭm 잔금 balance; remainder.

chanin 잔인. *chaninhan* 잔인한 cruel; atrocious; brutal; merciless; harsh.

chanjae 잔재 leftovers; dregs; remnants; waste matter.

chanjaeju 잔재주 petty artifice; trick. *chanjaeju purida* 잔재주 부리다 play petty tricks.

chanjurŭm 잔주름 fine wrinkles.

chanshimburŭm 잔심부름 sundry errands[jobs].

chanson 잔손 elaborate care. *chansonjil* 잔손질 small touch; piecework.

chansori 잔소리 scolding; rebuke; complaint. *chansorihada* 잔소리하다 scold; nag; rebuke.

chanyŏ 자녀 children; sons and daughters.

chaoesŏn 자외선 ultraviolet rays.

chapchi 잡지 magazine; journal; periodical.

chapch'ida 잡치다 ① harm; hurt; injure ② fail (to); (make a) mistake[error] ③ spoil; ruin; mar.

chapch'o 잡초 weeds.

chapchong 잡종 hybrid; cross; half[mixed] breed.

chap'ida 잡히다 be caught[arrested; apprehended; seized]; get captured; fall into.

chap'il 자필 one's own handwriting; autograph.

chapkok 잡곡 (miscellaneous) cereals; minor grains.

chappajida 자빠지다 ① fall on one's back; fall backward. ② lie down.

chappi 잡비 sundries.

chappugŭm 잡부금 miscellaneous fees.

chapta 잡다 butcher; kill; slaughter.

chapta 잡다 ① catch; seize; grip; hold; grasp ② capture; arrest.

chapt'ang 잡탕 mixed soup.

chaptongsani 잡동사니 sundries; odds and ends.

chap'wa 잡화 miscellaneous[sundry] goods. *chap'wasang* 잡화상 grocer's.

chara 자라 snapping turtle; terrapin.

charada 자라다 grow (up); be bred; be brought up.

charak 자락 skirt; foot; bottom; train.

charang 자랑 pride; boast. *charanghada* 자랑하다 boast; be proud (of).

charhada 잘하다 ① do well[nicely, skilfully] ② do often; do a lot.

chari 자리 ① seat; one's place ② status.

charijapta 자리잡다 take one's seat; be situated.

charip 자립 independence; self-reliance[-support]. *charip'ada* 자립하다 establish oneself.

charu 자루 sack; bag. *ssalcharu* 쌀자루 rice bag.

charu 자루 handle; haft; hilt; shaft.

charŭda 자르다 cut (off); chop; sever.

charyo 자료 material; data.

charyŏk 자력. *charyŏgŭro* 자력으로 by one's own efforts; for oneself.

chasal 자살 suicide. *chasarhada* 자살하다 kill oneself; commit suicide.

chasan 자산 property; fortune; asset.

chasang 자상. *chasanghada* 자상하다 (be) detailed; thoughtfully kind.

chase 자세. *chasehan* 자세한 detailed; minute. *chasehi* 자세히 in detail; minutely.

chase 자세 posture[pose]; attitude. *ko[chŏ]jase* 고[저]자세 haughty[humble] attitude.

chashik 자식 ① one's children; offspring ② chap; wretch; "bastard".

chashin 자신 self-confidence. *chashin innŭn* 자신 있는 self-confident.

chashin 자신 one's self; oneself. *chashinŭi* 자신의 one's own. *chashini* 자신이 (by) oneself; in person.

chasŏjŏn 자서전 autobiography; life story.

chasŏk 자석 magnet. *chasŏgŭi* 자석의 magnetic.

chason 자손 descendants; posterity; offspring.

chasŏn 자선 charity; benevolence. *chasŏn nambi* 자선 남비 charity pot.

chasu 자수 self-surrender; (voluntary) confession. *chasuhada* 자수하다 deliver oneself to justice.

chasu 자수 embroidery. *chasuhada* 자수하다 embroider. *chasuhan* 자수한 embroidered.

chasujŏng 자수정 amethyst; violet quartz.

chat'aek 자택 one's own house[home].

chatta 잦다 (be) frequent; (be) quick; rapid.

chatta 잣다 ① pump[suck; draw] up ② spin; make yarn.

chaŭm 자음 consonant.

chawon 자원 resources. *inchŏk[mulchŏk] chawon* 인적[물적] 자원 human[material] resources.

chayŏn 자연 nature. *chayŏnŭi* 자연의 natural. *chayŏnhi* 자연히 naturally; of itself.

chayu 자유 freedom; liberty. *chayuŭi[roun]* 자유의[로운] free; liberal. *chayuro(i)* 자유로(이) freely; as one pleases.

chean 제안 proposal; suggestion. *cheanhada* 제안하다 propose.

chebal 제발 kindly; please; pray. *Chebal yong-*

sŏhashio 제발 용서하시오 Excuse me, please.

chebang 제방 bank; embankment; dike.

chebi 제비 swallow.

chebi 제비 lot; lottery; lottery-ticket. *chebi ppop-ta* 제비 뽑다 draw lots.

chebikkot 제비꽃 violet; pansy.

chebok 제복 uniform. *chebogŭl ibŭn* 체복을 입은 uniformed; in uniform.

chebon 제본 bookbinding. *chebonhada* 제본하다 bind (a book). *chebonso* 제본소 bookbindery.

chebŏp 제법 nicely; quite (good); pretty. *Chebŏp tŏpta* 제법 덥다. It is quite warm.

chech'il 제 7 the seventh; number seven 〔No. 7〕.

chech'ul 제출 presentation; submission. *chech'ur-hada* 제출하다 present; submit; bring forward.

chech'yŏnot'a 제쳐놓다 put〔lay〕 aside; set apart.

chedae 제대 discharge from military service.

chedan 제단 altar.

chedo 제도 system; institution. *chedosangŭi* 제도상의 institutional.

chedo 제도 drafting; drawing; cartography. *chedo-hada* 제도하다 draw 〔draft〕 a plan.

chedok 제독 admiral; commodore (*Am.*).

chedong 제동 braking. *chedongŭl kŏlda* 제동을 걸다 put on〔apply〕 the brake.

chedŭng 제등 paper lantern. *chedŭng haengnyŏl* 제등 행렬 lantern procession〔parade〕.

chegi 제기, **chegiral** 제기랄 Shucks!; Phew; Damn 〔Hang〕 it!; Ugh!; Tut!; Pshaw.

chegŏ 제거. *chegŏhada* 제거하다 get rid of; eliminate; exclude; remove.

chegong 제공 offer; supply. *chegonghada* 제공하다

(make an) offer; proffer.
chegop 제곱 square. *chegop'ada* 제곱하다 square [multiply] (a number).
cheguk 제국 empire. *chegugŭi* 제국의 imperial.
chegwa 제과 confectionery. *chegwa hoesa*; 제과 회사 confectionery company.
chehŏn 제헌 establishment of a constitution. *chehŏnjŏl* 제헌절 Constitution Day.
chehan 제한 restriction; limitation. *chehanhada* 제한하다 restrict; limit; restrain. *sana chehan* 산아 제한 birthcontrol.
chehyu 제휴 cooperation; concert. *chehyuhada* 제휴하다 cooperate (with); act in concert with. *kisul chehyu* 기술 제휴 technical tie-up.
chei 제2 the second; number two [No. 2].
cheil 제1 the first; number one [No. 1].
cheja 제자 pupil; disciple; follower.
chejae 제재 sawing; lumbering. *chejaeso* 제재소 sawmill; lumbermill.
chejak 제작 manufacture; production. *chejak'ada* 제작하다 manufacture; produce; make.
cheji 제지 restraint; control. *chejihada* 제지하다 control; check; restrain.
chejo 제조 making; manufacture. *chejohada* 제조하다 make; manufacture; turn out.
chejŏn 제전 festival; fete.
chemak 제막. *chemak'ada* 제막하다 unveil. *chemakshik* 제막식 unveiling ceremony.
chemok 제목 subject; theme; title; caption.
chemyŏng 제명 title. *…ŭi chemyŏngŭro* …의 제명으로 under the title of ….
chemyŏng 제명 expulsion. *chemyŏnghada* 제명하다

strike a name off; expel.

chenjang 젠장 Hang it!; Damn it!; Hell!

cheo 제5 the fifth; number five[No. 5].

cheoe 제외. *cheoehada* 제외하다 except; exclude; save; exempt; rule out.

chep'um 제품 manufactured goods; product. *oeguk chep'um* 외국 제품 foreign products.

cheryŏn 제련 refining. *cheryŏnhada* 제련하다 refine. *cheryŏnso* 제련소 refinery.

chesa 제사 religious service; sacrificial rite.

cheya 제야 New Year's Eve; watch night.

cheyak 제약 medicine manufacture; pharmacy. *cheyak hoesa* 제약 회사 pharmaceutical company.

chibae 지배 control; rule. *chibaehada* 지배하다 govern; rule. *chibaein* 지배인 manager.

chiban 지반 base; foundation; foothold. *chibanŭl takta* 지반을 닦다 establish one's foothold.

chiban 집안 family; household. *chiban shikku* 집안 식구 (members of) a family.

chibang 지방 district; region; locality. *chibangjŏk* 지방적 local; provincial. *chibang sat'uri* 지방 사투리 local accent.

chibang 지방 fat; grease; lard.

chibu 지부 branch (office); chapter.

chibul 지불 payment; discharge. *chibur.hada* 지불하다 pay; discharge.

chibung 지붕 roof; roofing; housetop. *kiwa chibung* 기와 지붕 tiled roof.

chibyŏng 지병 chronic disease; old complaint.

chich'ida 지치다 be[get] tired; be exhausted; be worn out; be done up.

chich'ida 지치다 slide on[over]; skate on.

chich'ul 지출 expense; outgo. *chich'urhada* 지출하다 expend; pay.

chida 지다 be[get] defeated; lose; yield (to). *kyŏnggie chida* 경기에 지다 lose in a contest.

chida 지다 ① bear; carry on the back ② owe; be indebted.

chida 지다 ① fall; fade and fall ② set; sink; go down.

chidae 지대 zone; region; belt. *pimujang chidae* 비무장 지대 demilitarized zone[DMZ].

chidaegong 지대공. *chidaegong misail* 지대공 미사일 ground-to-air missile.

chido 지도 map. *chidoch'aek* 지도책 atlas.

chido 지도 guidance; directions. *chidohada* 지도하다 guide; lead; coach.

chidok 지독. *chidok'ada* 지독하다 (be) vicious; severe; awful. *chidok'an ch'uwi*[*tŏwi*] 지독한 추위[더위] severe cold[heat].

chigak 지각. *chigak'ada* 지각하다 be[come] late; be behind time; be tardy.

chigap 지갑 purse; pocketbook.

chigekkun 지게꾼 A-frame man; burden carrier.

chigŏp 직업 occupation; calling; profession; vocation; business.

chigu 지구 the earth; the globe.

chigu 지구 district; zone; region; area; section. *sangŏp*[*chut'aek*] *chigu* 상업[주택] 지구 business[residence] zone[area].

chiguk 지국 branch[district] office.

chigŭm 지금 now; the present; this moment. *chigŭmkkaji* 지금까지 till now; up to the present. *chigŭmbut'ŏ* 지금부터 from now on; after this.

chigŭp 지급. *chigŭbŭi* 지급의 urgent; pressing; express. *chigŭp chŏnbo* 지급 전보 urgent telegram.
chigwon 직원 personnel; staff-member; employee.
chigyŏpta 지겹다 (be) tedious; tiresome; detestable.
chiha 지하. *chihaŭi*[*-e*, *-esŏ*] 지하의〔에, 에서〕 underground.
chihwi 지휘 command; orders; direction. *chihwihada* 지휘하다 command; order; lead.
chihye 지혜 wisdom; sense; intelligence. *chihye innŭn* 지혜 있는 wise; intelligent.
chijang 지장 obstacle; difficulty. *chijangi ŏpsŭmyŏn* 지장이 없으면 if it is convenient to you.
chiji 지지 support; backing. *chijihada* 지지하다 support; back (up); uphold.
chijida 지지다 stew; panfry; frizzle.
chijin 지진 earthquake.
chijŏbunhada 지저분하다 (be) messy; disordered; untidy; dirty(-looking).
chijŏm 지점 branch shop[office, house]. *chijŏmjang* 지점장 branch manager.
chijŏng 지정 appointment; designation. *chijŏnghada* 지정하다 appoint; fix; designate.
chiju 지주 landowner; landlord.
Chijunghae 지중해 Mediterranean Sea.
chik'aeng 직행. *chik'aenghada* 직행하다 go straight 〔direct, nonstop〕; run 〔go〕 through *chik'aeng pŏsŭ* 직행 버스 nonstop bus.
chikchang 직장 one's place of work; one's post.
chikchŏp 직접 directly; firsthand; personally. *chikchŏpchŏk* 직접적 direct; personal; firsthand.
chik'ida 지키다 ① protect; defend ② watch; guard ③ keep; observe.

chikkak 직각 right angle.

chikkong 직공 worker; workman; factory hand.

chikkŏrida 지껄이다 chatter; chat; gabble.

chikkyŏng 직경 diameter.

chiksŏn 직선 straight line; beeline. *chiksŏn k'osŭ* 직선 코스 straight course.

chikt'ong 직통. *chikt'onghada* 직통하다 communicate directly. *chikt'ong chŏnhwa* 직통 전화 direct telephone line[service].

chil 질 quality. *chilchŏgin* 질적인 qualitative. *chilchŏgŭro* 질적으로 qualitatively.

chilgida 질기다 (be) tough; durable; tenacious.

chilgŭrŭt 질그릇 clayware; unglazed earthenware.

chilli 진리 truth. *kwahagŭi chilli* 과학의 진리 the truth of science.

chillida 질리다 ① become disgusted with; get sick of ② turn pale.

chillo 진로 course (to advance); one's path in life.

chillyŏ 질녀 niece.

chilmŏjida 짊어지다 bear; carry on one's back; shoulder.

chilmun 질문 question; inquiry. *chilmunhada* 질문하다 ask a question.

chilshik 질식 suffocation. *chilshik'ada* 질식하다 be suffocated; be choked.

chilsŏ 질서 order; system. *chilsŏ innŭn* 질서 있는 orderly; systematic; methodical.

chilt'u 질투 jealousy. *chilt'uhada* 질투하다 be jealous (of); envy; be envious of.

chim 짐 load; cargo; luggage; baggage (*Am.*).

chimang 지망 wish; desire; choice. *chimanghada* 지망하다 desire; apply for; choose. *chimangja*

지망자 applicant; candidate.

chimch'a 짐차 goods wagon[van]; freight car; truck.

chimjak 짐작 guess; conjecture. *chimjak'ada* 짐작하다 guess; conjecture.

chimkkun 짐꾼 porter; luggage porter.

chimmach'a 짐마차 cart; wagon.

chimsŭng 짐승 beast; brute; animal.

chimtchak 짐짝 package; parcel; piece of baggage.

chimun 지문 fingerprint; finger mark.

chimyŏn 지면 surface; ground.

chimyŏng 지명 nomination. *chimyŏnghada* 지명하다 nominate; name.

chimyŏng 지명 place name; name of a place.

chinach'ida 지나치다 ① go too far; exceed; do too much ② pass through. *chinach'in* 지나친 excessive. *chinach'ige* 지나치게 excessively.

chinada 지나다 ① pass by; go past; pass through ② expire; terminate; be out.

chinaeda 지내다 ① spend[pass] one's time; get along ② hold; observe.

chinanbŏn 지난번 last; last time; the other day. *chinanbŏnŭi* 지난번의 last; previous; recent.

chinbo 진보 progress; advance. *chinbohada* 진보하다 make progress; improve.

chinch'al 진찰 medical examination. *chinch'arhada* 진찰하다 examine. *chinch'alkwŏn* 진찰권 consultation ticket.

chinch'ang 진창 mud; mire. *chinch'angkil* 진창길 muddy road.

chindallae 진달래 azalea.

chindan 진단 diagnosis. *chindanhada* 진단하다 di-

agnose. *chindansŏ* 진단서 medical certificate.
chindong 진동 vibration; shock. *chindonghada* 진동하다 shake; quake; vibrate.
chindŭgi 진드기 tick; mite.
ching 징 hobnail; clout nail.
ching 징 gong.
chin-gae 진개 dust; dirt; garbage.
chingbyŏng 징병 conscription; military draft (*Am.*). *chingbyŏng kŏmsa* 징병 검사 physical examination for conscription.
chinggŏmdari 징검다리 steppingstone.
chinggŭrŏpta 징그럽다 (be) creepy; crawly; uncanny; disgusting.
chin-gi 진기. *chin-gihan* 진기한 new; novel; rare; uncommon; strange.
chingmu 직무 duties; work; job. *chingmusangŭi* 직무상의 official.
chingmul 직물 cloth; textile fabrics. *chingmul kongjang* 직물 공장 textile factory[mill].
chingmyŏn 직면. *chingmyŏnhada* 직면하다 face; confront; be faced[confronted] (with).
chin-gong 진공 vacuum. *chin-gongŭi* 진공의 vacuous. *chin-gonggwan* 진공관 vacuum tube[bulb].
chin-gŭp 진급 promotion. *chin-gŭp'ada* 진급하다 be [get] promoted (to); win promotion.
chingyŏk 징역 penal servitude. *chingyŏksari* 징역살이 prison life; imprisonment.
chinhaeje 진해제 cough remedy.
chinhŭk 진흙 mud; mire; dirt.
chinhwa 진화 evolution. *chinhwahada* 진화하다 evolve. *chinhwaron* 진화론 evolutionism.
chinjŏlmŏri 진절머리. *chinjŏlmŏrinada* 진절머리나

다 be sick of; be disgusted with.
chinjŏng 진정 petition; appeal. *chinjŏnghada* 진정하다 make a petition; appeal. *chinjŏngsŏ* 진정서 written petition.
chinju 진주 pearl. *chinju mokkŏri* 진주 목걸이 pearl necklace *chinju chjogae* 진주 조개 pearl oyster.
chinka 진가 true[real] value; true worth[merit].
chinmaek 진맥. *chinmaek'ada* 진맥하다 feel[examine] pulse.
chinnunkkaebi 진눈깨비 sleet.
chinsang 진상 truth; actual fact; what's what.
chinshil 진실 fact; truth; reality. *chinshirhan* 진실한 true; real. *chinshillo* 진실로 in fact; really.
chinshim 진심 true heart; sincerity. *chinshimŭro* 진심으로 heartily; sincerely.
chinsul 진술 statement. *chinsurhada* 진술하다 state; give an account of.
chint'ang 진탕 to one's heart's content; to the full. *chint'ang mŏkta[mashida]* 진탕 먹다[마시다] eat[drink] one's fill.
chintcha 진짜 genuine article; real thing; real stuff (*Am.*).
chint'ongje 진통제 pain-killing drug; pain-killer.
chinŭng 지능 intelligence; mental faculties; intellect *chinŭng chisu* 지능 지수 intelligence quotient
chinŭrŏmi 지느러미 fin. ⌊[I. Q.].
chinyŏl 진열 exhibition; show; display. *chinyŏrhada* 진열하다 exhibit; display.
chinyŏng 진영 camp; bloc; quarters. *minju chinyŏng* 민주 진영 democratic camp.
chiok 지옥 hell; inferno; Hades *kyot'ong chiok* 교통 지옥 traffic jam.

chiŏnaeda 지어내다 make up; invent; fabricate.

chip 집 house; home. *kiwa[ch'oga]jip* 기와[초가]집 tile[thatch] roofed house. *yangokchip* 양옥집 western style building.

chip 짚 straw. *milchip* 밀짚 wheat straw. *milchip moja* 밀짚 모자 straw hat.

chip'angi 지팡이 (walking) stick; cane.

chipch'ak 집착 attachment. *chipch'ak'a da* 집착하다 be attached; cling[stick] to; be stubbornly bent.

chipchŏkkŏrida 집적거리다 tease; provoke; vex.

chipchuin 집주인 owner of a house; head of a family; landlord; landlady.

chipke 집게 tongs; nippers; tweezers; pincers. *pujipke* 부집게 fire tongs.

chipkesonkarak 집게손가락 index finger; forefinger.

chip'oe 집회 meeting; assembly. *chip'oehada* 집회하다 meet together; gather. *chip'oe changso* 집회 장소 meeting place; assembly hall.

chipp'il 집필 writing. *chipp'irhada* 집필하다 write. *chipp'ilja* 집필자 writer.

chipse 집세 (house) rent; house-rent.

chipshin 짚신 straw sandles[shoes].

chipta 집다 pick up; take up. *chipkero chipta* 집게로 집다 pick up with tongs.

chiptan 집단 group; mass; collective body.

chip'ye 지폐 paper money[currency]; (bank) note (*Eng.*); bill (*Am.*).

chip'yŏngsŏn 지평선 horizon; horizontal line.

chiri 지리 geography; topography.

chiroe 지뢰 (land) mine.

chirŭda 지르다. (*sorirŭl*) *chirŭda* (소리를) 지르다 yell; cry aloud; scream; shout.

chirŭmkil 지름길 shortcut; shorter way.
chiryŏng 지령 order; instruction. *chiryŏnghada* 지령하다 order; direct; give instruction.
chisa 지사 (provincial) governor →**tojisa** 도지사.
chisa 지사 branch (office).
chisang 지상 ground. *chisangŭi* 지상의 earthly; terrestrial. *chisangkwŏn* 지상권 surface rights.
chishi 지시 directions; indication. *chishihada* 지시하다 direct; indicate; point out.
chishik 지식 knowledge; information; learning. *chishik kyegŭp* 지식 계급 the educated classes; the intelligentsia; highbrows. ⌈station.
chisŏ 지서 *kyŏngch'al chisŏ* 경찰 지서 police sub-
chisŏng 지성 intellect; intelligence. *chisŏngin* 지성인 intellectual; highbrow.
chitkutta 짓궂다 (be) annoying; bothersome; harassing; ill-natured; spiteful.
chitta 짖다 bark; bay; howl.
chitta 짙다 (be) dark; deep; thick; dense.
chitta 짓다 ① boil; cook (rice) ② compose (composition) ③ raise; grow (barley) ④ commit (crime) ⑤ wear (smile) ⑥ build; construct (house).
chiuda 지우다 erase; rub〔wipe〕out; cross out.
chiugae 지우개 eraser.
chiwi 지위 position; status; rank; post; situation.
chiwon 지원 application; volunteering. *chiwonhada* 지원하다 apply for; volunteer for. *chiwonja* 지원자 applicant; candidate.
chiyŏk 지역 area; region; zone. *chiyŏkchŏk* 지역적 local; regional.
cho 조 million million; billion(*Eng.*); trillion(*Am.*).
chŏ 저 (pair of) chopsticks →**chŏtkarak** 젓가락.

chǒ 저 that. *chǒ saram* 저 사람 that man. *chǒgǒt* 저것 that thing[one].

choahada 좋아하다 ① like; love; prefer ② be pleased[delighted, glad].

chǒbǒn 저번 last time; the other day. *chǒbǒnǔi* 저 번의 last; recent; previous.

chobu 조부 grandfather.→**harabǒji** 할아버지.

chǒch'uk 저축 saving; savings. *chǒch'uk'ada* 저축 하다 save; lay by[aside, up]; store up.

chǒdang 저당 mortgage; security. *chǒdanghada* 저 당하다 mortgage.

choe 죄 crime; sin; offense; guilt. *choerǔl pǒmhada* 죄를 범하다 commit a crime[sin].

choeda 죄다 ① tighten; make tight ② feel anxious.

choein 죄인 criminal; convict; offender; sinner.

choga 조가 dirge; elegy.

chogabi 조가비 clam shell; shell.

chogae 조개 shellfish; clam.

chogaek 조객 condoler; caller for condolence.

chogak 조각 piece; bit; fragment; splinter.

chogak 조각 sculpture; carving; engraving. *chogak'ada* 조각하다 sculpture; carve; engrave.

chogamdo 조감도 bird's-eye-view.

chogan 조간. *chogan shinmun* 조간 신문 morning paper.

chogi 조기 mourning flag; flag at half-mast.

chǒgi 저기 that place; there. *chǒgie* 저기에 there; over[up, down] there.

chǒgiap 저기압 low (atmospheric) pressure.

chǒgǒdo 적어도 at (the) least.

chǒgori 저고리 coat; Korean jacket.

chǒgǔi 적의 hostility; enmity. *chǒgǔi innǔn* 적의

있는 hostile; inimical.

choguk 조국 fatherland; one's native land.

chŏgŭm 저금 saving; savings; deposit. *chŏgŭmha-da* 저금하다 save; deposit.

chogŭm 조금 ① small quantity; a little ② small number; a few ③ somewhat; a bit.

chŏgŭp 저급 low grade. *chŏgŭp'ada* 저급하다 (be) inferior; vulgar; low (-grade); lowbrow.

chogyo 조교 assistant (teacher, instruction).

chŏgyong 적용 application. *chŏgyonghada* 적용하다 apply (to).

chogyosu 조교수 assistant professor.

chŏhang 저항 resistance; opposition. *chŏhanghada* 저항하다 resist; oppose; fight against.

chohap 조합 association; partnership; union; guild; league. *hyŏptong chohap* 협동 조합 cooperative association[union]; co-op.

chŏhŭidŭl 저희들 we. *chŏhŭidŭrŭi* 저희들의 our. *chŏhŭidŭrŭl* 저희들을 us.

chohwa 조화 harmony. *chohwahada* 조화하다 harmonize (with); be in harmony.

chohwa 조화 artificial flower.

choin 조인 signature; signing. *choinhada* 조인하다 seal; sign; affix one's seal.

chŏja 저자 writer; author; authoress.

chojak 조작 invention; fabrication. *chojak'ada* 조작하다 fabricate; invent.

chŏjang 저장 storage; storing. *chŏjanghada* 저장하다 store; preserve.

chŏji 저지. *chŏjihada* 저지하다 hinder; obstruct; prevent; arrest; check.

chojik 조직 organization; system. *chojik'ada* 조직

하다 organize; form; set up; compose.
chojim 조짐 symptoms; omen; signs.
chojŏl 조절 accommodation; adjustment.
chŏjŏllo 저절로 of itself; naturally; of its own accord; spontaneously; automatically.
chojŏn 조전 telegram of condolence.
chojong 조종 management; operation. *chojonghada* 조종하다 manage; operate.
chojŏng 조정 regulation; adjustment. *chojŏnghada* 조정하다 regulate; adjust.
chŏju 저주 curse; imprecation. *chŏjuhada* 저주하다 curse; imprecate; wish ill of.
chŏk 적 enemy; foe; opponent; rival. *chayuŭi chŏk* 자유의 적 enemy of freedom.
chok'a 조카 nephew. *chok'attal* 조카딸 niece.
chokcha 족자 hanging roll[scroll].
chŏkcha 적자 red figures; deficit; loss.
chokchipke 족집게 (hair) tweezers.
chŏkchŏl 적절. *chŏkchŏrhan* 적절한 fitting; proper; adequate. *chŏkchŏrhi* 적절히 properly; aptly.
chokki 조끼 vest (*Am.*); waistcoat.
chokki 조끼 jug; mug; pitcher. *maekchu han chokki* 맥주 한 조끼 a jug(ful) of beer.
chŏkkuk 적국 enemy country; hostile power.
chŏkkŭk 적극. *chŏkkŭkchŏgin* 적극적인 positive; active; (very) energic. *chŏkkŭkchŏgŭro* 적극적으로 positively; actively.
chokŏn 조건 condition; term; stipulation. *nodong chokŏn* 노동 조건 labor condition.
chokpo 족보 genealogy; pedigree; family tree.
chŏksaek 적색 red (color); crimson *chŏksaek punja* 적색 분자 Red; communist.

chŏksan 적산 enemy property.

chŏkshida 적시다 wet; moisten; drench; soak.

chŏkshinho 적신호 red[danger] signal.

chŏkshipcha 적십자 the Red Cross.

chŏksŏng 적성 hostility. *chŏksŏng kukka* 적성 국가 hostile country.

chŏksŏng 적성 aptitude. *chŏksŏng kŏmsa* 적성 검사 aptitude test.

chŏksu 적수 match; opponent; rival; antagonist. *hojŏksu* 호적수 good rival.

chŏkta 적다 write[put] down; record; describe.

chŏkta 적다 (be) few; little; rare; scanty. *chŏkchianŭn* 적지않은 not a few[little].

chŏktang 적당. *chŏktanghan* 적당한 suitable; fit (for); proper; competent; appropriate. *chŏktanghage* 적당하게 suitably; properly; adequately.

chŏkto 적도 equator. *chŏktoŭi* 적도의 equatorial.

chŏl 절 bow; salutation. *chŏrhada* 절하다 bow; make a bow; salute.

chŏl 절 Buddhist temple.

chŏlbyŏk 절벽 precipice; cliff; bluff.

chŏlch'a 절차 process; procedure; formalities. *segwan[yŏkwŏn] chŏlch'a* 세관[여권] 절차 customs [passport] formalities.

cholchak 졸작 poor work; trash; rubbish.

chŏlchŏng 절정 summit; peak; zenith; climax. *inkiŭi chŏlchŏng* 인기의 절정 zenith of one's popularity.

cholda 졸다 doze; take a nap.

chŏlda 절다 walk lame; limp; hobble.

chŏlgu 절구 mortar. *chŏlgut'ong* 절구통 body of a mortar.

chŏlgyo 절교 break of friendship; rupture. *chŏlgyohada* 절교하다 cut one's acquaintance with.

chŏllam 전람 exhibition; show. *chŏllamhoe* 전람회 exhibition; exposition.

chollamaeda 졸라매다 tie up; tighten; fasten.

chŏllyak 전략 strategy; tactics. *chŏllyakchŏk* 전략적 strategic *chŏllyaksang* 전략상 strategically.

chŏllye 전례 precedent. *chŏllyega ŏmnŭn* 전례가 없는 unprecedented.

chŏllyŏk 전력 electric power; electricity.

chŏllyŏk 전력 all one's strength[power]. *chŏllyŏgul tahayŏ* 전력을 다하여 with all one's might.

chŏlmang 절망 despair; hopelessness. *chŏlmanghada* 절망하다 despair; lose hope. *chŏlmangjŏgin* 절망적인 hopeless; desperate.

chŏlsu 절수 water saving

chŏltae 절대. *chŏltaeŭi* 절대의 absolute; unconditional. *chŏltaero* 절대로 absolutely; positively.

cholto 졸도 faint; swoon. *choltohada* 졸도하다 faint; (fall into a) swoon.

chŏlto 절도 thief. *chŏltobŏm* 절도범 larceny.

chŏlttukkŏrida 절뚝거리다 →**chŏlda** 절다.

chom 좀 clothes moth; bookworm.

chŏm 점 divination; fortunetelling. *chŏmch'ida* 점치다 tell fortune; divine.

chŏm 점 ① spot; point ② mark; score.

chomajoma 조마조마. *chomajomahada* 조마조마하다 (be) uneasy; feel nervous.

chŏmch'a 점차 gradually; by steps[degrees].

chŏmho 점호 roll call. *chŏmhohada* 점호하다 call [take] the roll.

chomi 조미. *chomihada* 조미하다 season; flavor.

chomiryo 조미료 seasonings; spices.
chŏmida 저미다 cut thin; slice.
chŏmjangi 점장이 fortuneteller; diviner.
chŏmjant'a 점잖다 (be) dignified; genteel; decent. *chŏmjanŭn saram* 점잖은 사람 decent man.
chŏmjŏm 점점 by degrees; gradually; more and more; less and less.
chŏmnyŏng 점령 occupation. *chŏmnyŏnghada* 점령하다 occupy; take possession of; capture.
chomo 조모 grandmother. →**halmŏni** 할머니.
chomok 조목 article; clause; item.
chŏmp'o 점포 shop; store.
chŏmshim 점심 lunch(eon). *chŏmshimŭl mŏkta* 점심을 먹다 have[take] lunch.
chŏmsŏn 점선 dotted[perforated] line.
chŏmsu 점수 marks; score; points. →**chŏm** 점.
chŏmta 젊다 (be) young; youthful. *chŏlmŭni* 젊은이 young man; youth.
chŏmulda 저물다 get[grow] dark[dusk].
chomun 조문 call of condolence. *chomunhada* 조문하다 make a call of condolence.
chŏmwon 점원 shop-assistant; (shop) clerk. *yŏjŏmwon* 여점원 shopgirl.
chomyŏng 조명 lighting; illumination. *chomyŏnghada* 조명하다 light up; illuminate.
chŏn 전 all; whole; entire; total. *chŏn-gungmin* 전국민 whole nation. *chŏnjaesan* 전재산 entire fortune.
chŏn 전. *chŏnŭi* 전의 previous; former; last. *chŏne* 전에 before; previously.
chŏnaek 전액 total[full] amount; sum total.
chonham 존함 your (honorable) name.

chonan 조난 disaster. *chonanhada* 조난하다 meet with a disaster[accident].

chŏnbang 전방 front (line). *chŏnbangŭi* 전방의 front; forward. *chŏnbange* 전방에 ahead.

chŏnbo 전보 telegram; wire. *chŏnbo ch'ida* 전보 치다 telegraph; send a telegram.

chŏnbu 전부 all; whole. *chŏnbuŭi* 전부의 all; whole; total. *chŏnbu hapch'yŏ* 전부 합쳐 in all; altogether; in full.

chŏnch'a 전차 tank. *chŏnch'a pudae* 전차 부대 tank corps. *taejŏnch'ap'o* 대전차포 antitank gun.

chŏnch'a 전차 electric car; tramcar (*Eng.*).

chŏnch'e 전체 the whole; all. *chŏnch'eŭi* 전체의 whole; entire; general. *chŏnch'ejŏgŭro* 전체적으로 generally; as a whole.

chonch'ing 존칭 title of hono(u)r; honorific title.

chŏnch'isa 전치사 preposition.

chŏnch'ŏl 전철 electric railway.

chŏnchu 전주 last week; preceding week.

chŏnch'uk 전축 record player; electric phonograph.

chondae 존대. *chondaehada* 존대하다 treat with respect. *chondaeŏ* 존대어 term of respect.

chŏndal 전달 delivery; conveyance. *chŏndarhada* 전달하다 deliver; convey; transmit.

chŏndang 전당. *chŏndang chap'ida* 전당 잡히다 pawn; put in pawn. *chŏndangp'o* 전당포 pawnshop.

chŏndo 전도 one's future; prospects. *chŏndo yumanghan* 전도 유망한 promising.

chŏndŭng 전등 electric light[lamp]. *hoejung chŏndŭng* 회중 전등 flashlight.

chong 종 bell. *chongŭl ullida* 종을 울리다 ring [strike, toll] a bell.

chong 종 servant; slave; maid(servant); help.

chŏng 정 tablet; tabloid; pill.

chongalgŏrida 종알거리다 mutter; murmur; prate.

chongari 종아리 calf of the leg; calf.

chŏngbak 정박 anchorage; mooring. *chŏngbak'ada* 정박하다 cast anchor; moor.

chŏngbanghyŏng 정방형 →**chŏngsagak'yŏng** 정사각형.

chŏngbi 정비 adjustment; equipment. *chŏngbihada* 정비하다 fully equip; fix. *chadongch'a chŏngbigong* 자동차 정비공 car mechanic.

chŏngbo 정보 information; report; news. *chungang chŏngbobu* 중앙 정보부 Central Intelligence Agency (C. I. A.).

chŏngbok 정복 conquest. *chŏngbok'ada* 정복하다 conquer; subjugate; master.

chŏngbok 정복 formal dress. *chŏngbok kyŏngch'algwan* 정복 경찰관 policeman in full uniform.

chŏngbu 정부 paramour; (secret) lover; mistress.

chŏngbu 정부 government; administration. *chŏngbuŭi* 정부의 governmental; ministerial. *Han-guk chŏngbu* 한국 정부 Korean government.

chŏngbyŏn 정변 political change; coup d'état (*Fr.*).

chŏngch'a 정차 →**chŏnggŏ** 정거. *chŏngch'a shigan* 정차 시간 stoppage time.

chŏngch'aek 정책 policy.

chŏngch'al 정찰 reconnaissance; scouting. *chŏngch'arhada* 정찰하다 reconnoiter; scout.

chŏngch'al 정찰 price label[mark, tag]. *chŏngch'alje* 정찰제 price tag[fixed price] system.

chongch'angnyŏk 종착역 terminal station; terminus.

chŏngch'i 정치 politics; government. *chŏngch'ijŏ-*

gin 정치적인 political.
chongchŏm 종점 terminal (station); terminus (*Eng.*).
chongdalsae 종달새 skylark; lark.
chŏngdang 정당 political party. *posu*[*hyŏkshin*] *chŏngdang* 보수[혁신] 정당 conservative[progressive] party.
chŏngdang 정당. *chŏngdanghan* 정당한 just; fair; proper; right. *chŏngdanghage* 정당하게 justly; rightly; lawfully.
chŏngdap 정답 correct[right] answer.
chŏngdapta 정답다 (be) affectionate; tender; loving. *chŏngdapke* 정답게 affectionately; warmly.
chŏngdo 정도 grade; degree; standard; extent.
chŏngdon 정돈 order; arrangement. *chŏngdonhada* 정돈하다 arrange; put in order.
chŏnggak 정각 ① fixed time ② exact time. *chŏnggage* ① 정각에 at the appointed time ② just; punctually, sharp.
chŏnggang 정강 political principle; party platform.
chŏnggangi 정강이 shin; shank.
chonggi 종기 swell(ing); boil; tumo(u)r.
chŏnggi 정기. *chŏnggiŭi* 정기의 regular; periodical. *chŏnggijŏgŭro* 정기적으로 regularly; periodically; at a fixed period. *chŏnggi kanhaengmul* 정기 간행물 periodical publications.
chŏnggŏ 정거 stop; stoppage. *chŏnggŏjang* 정거장 station depot (*Am.*); stand.
chŏnggu 정구 tennis. *chŏngguhada* 정구하다 play tennis. *chŏnggujang* 정구장 tennis court.
chŏngguk 정국 political situation. *chŏnggugŭi puranjŏng*[*wigi*] 정국의 불안정[위기] instability [crisis] of a political situation.

chǒnggye 정계 political circles[world].

chonggyo 종교 religion. *chonggyosangǔi* 종교상의 religious. *chonggyo chaep'an* 종교 재판 the Inquisition.

chǒnggyǒn 정견 one's political view. *chǒnggyǒn palp'yohoe* 정견 발표회 campaign meeting.

chǒnggyu 정규 regularity; formality. *chǒnggyuǔi* 정규의 regular; formal.

chǒnghada 정하다 decide; fix; determine; settle; arrange; appoint.

chǒnghak 정학 suspension from school. *chǒnghaktanghada* 정학당하다 be suspended from school.

chonghap 종합 synthesis. *chonghapchǒk* 종합적 synthetic; composite. *chonghap pyǒngwon* 종합 병원 general hospital.

chǒnghwak 정확 correctness; accuracy; precision. *chǒnghwak'an[k'i]* 정확한[히] correct[ly]; exact [ly]; accurate[ly].

chǒnghyǒng 정형. *chǒnghyǒng susul[oekwa]* 정형 수술[외과] orthopedic operation[surgery].

chongi 종이 paper. *chongi han chang* 종이 한 장 a sheet of paper. *saekchongi* 색종이 colored paper.

chǒn-gi 전기 biography; life story.

chǒn-gi 전기 electricity. *chǒn-giǔi* 전기의 electric; electrical. *chǒn-girǔl k'yǒda[kkǔda]* 전기를 켜다 [끄다] turn[switch] on[off] the electrical light.

chongil 종일 all day (long); whole day; from morning till night; throughout the day.

chongja 종자 seed. →**ssi** 씨.

chǒngja 정자 pavilion; arbor.

chǒngje 정제 tablet; tabloid; pill.

chǒngji 정지 stop; suspension. *chǒngjihada* 정지하다 stop; suspend.

chongjibu 종지부 full stop. →**mach'imp'yo** 마침표.

chǒngjik 정직 honesty. *chǒngjik'an[k'age]* 정직한 [하게] honest[ly].

chǒngjo 정조 chastity; virginity.

chǒngjǒk 정적 political opponent[rival, enemy].

chǒngjǒn 정전 stoppage of electric current; power failure.

chǒngjǒn 정전 ceasefire; truce. *chǒngjǒnhada* 정전 하다 have a truce; suspend hostilities. *chǒngjǒn hoedam* 정전 회담 ceasefire conference[order]

chǒngjǒng 정정 correction; *chǒngjǒnghada* 정정하 다 correct; revise; amend.

chǒngjǒngdangdang 정정당당. *chǒngjǒngdangdang-han* 정정당당한 fair and square. *chǒngjǒngdang-danghi* 정정당당히 fairly (and squarely).

chǒngka 정가 fixed[set, regular, list] price. *chǒng-kap'yo* 정가표 price list[tag].

chǒngkwon 정권 political power[regime]. *chǒng-kwon kyoch'e* 정권 교체 change of regime.

chǒngmaek 정맥 vein. *chǒngmaek chusa* 정맥 주사 venous injection.

chǒngmal 정말. *chǒngmallo* 정말로 really; quite; indeed; actually; truly.

chǒngmi 정미 net content[weight].

chǒngmil 정밀 minuteness; precision. *chǒngmirhan* [*hi*] 정밀한[히] minute[ly]; accurate[ly].

chongmok 종목 item; lines. *yǒngǒp chongmok* 영업 종목 lines of business.

chǒngmun 정문 front gate; main entrance.

chǒngmyǒn 정면 front; facade(*Fr.*). *chǒngmyǒnǔi* 정면의 front; frontal. *chǒngmyǒn ch'ungdol* 정면 충돌 head-on collision.

chŏngni 정리 arrangement. *chŏngnihada* 정리하다 put in order; adjust; arrange.

chongnyŏ 종려 hemp palm; palm. *chongnyŏnamu* 종려나무 palm tree.

chŏngnyŏk 정력 energy; vigo(u)r; vitality. *chŏngnyŏkchŏgin* 정력적인 energetic; vigorous.

chŏngnyŏl 정열 passion; ardor. *chŏngnyŏlchŏgin* 정열적인 passionate; ardent.

chŏngnyŏn 정년 retirement age; age limit. *chŏngnyŏn t'oejik* 정년 퇴직 retirement under the age limit.

chongnyu 종류 kind; sort. *on-gat chongnyuŭi* 온갖 종류의 all kinds[sorts] of.

chŏngnyu 정류. *chŏngnyujang* 정류장 stop; station.

chŏngo 정오 (high) noon; midday. *chŏngo-e* 정오에 at noon; at midday.

chŏn-gong 전공 special study. *chŏn-gonghada* 전공하다 specialize[major] (in).

chongŏbwon 종업원. employee; worker; operative; hands. 종업원 대표 *chongŏbwòn taep'yo* spokesman of the workingmen.

chŏngŏri 정어리 sardine. *chŏngŏri t'ongjorim* 정어리 통조림 canned sardines.

chongsa 종사. *chongsahada* 종사하다 engage in; pursue; follow; devote; be employed. 「affair.

chŏngsa 정사 ① love suicide; double suicide. ② love

chŏngsagak'yŏng 정사각형 regular[perfect] square.

chŏngsang 정상 normalcy; normality. *chŏngsangjŏk* 정상적 normal. *chŏngsanghwa* 정상화 normalization.

chŏngsang 정상 top; summit; peak. *chŏngsang hoedam* 정상 회담 summit meeting[conference].

chŏngse 정세 situation; conditions. *kungnae[kukche]*

chŏngse 국내〔국제〕 정세 domestic〔international〕 situation.

chŏngshik 정식 formality. *chŏngshigŭi* 정식의 formal; due. *chŏngshik susok* 정식 수속 formal process〔procedure〕.

chŏngshik 정식 regular meal; ordinary (*Eng.*).

chongshin 종신 (whole) life. *chongshinŭi* 종신의 life-long; life.

chŏngshin 정신 mind; spirit; soul. *chŏngshinjŏgin* 정신적인 spiritual; mental.

chŏngsuk 정숙 chastity; female virtue. *chŏngsuk'an* 정숙한 chaste; virtuous; faithful.

chŏngt'ong 정통. *chŏngt'onghada* 정통하다 be well versed〔informed〕 (in); have a thorough knowledge.

chŏn-gu 전구 electric bulb; light bulb.

chŏngŭi 정의 definition.

chŏngŭi 정의 justice; righteousness. *chŏngŭigam* 정의감 sense of justice.

chŏn-guk 전국 whole country〔nation〕. *chŏn-gugŭi* 전국의 nation-wide; national.

chŏn-gŭn 전근 transference. *chŏn-gŭnhada* 전근하다 be〔get〕 transferred to (another office).

chŏngwol 정월 January. *chŏngwol ch'oharu* 정월 초하루 New Year's Day.

chŏngwon 정원 garden. *chŏngwonsa* 정원사 (landscape) gardener.

chŏngwon 정원 the full member; regular staff.

chongyang 종양 tumor. *aksŏng chongyang* 악성 종양 malignant tumor.

chŏngyok 정욕 sexual〔sensual, carnal〕 desire; lust.

chon-gyŏng 존경 respect; reverence. *chon-gyŏnghada* 존경하다 respect; esteem. *chon-gyŏnghal man-*

han 존경할 만한 honorable; respectable.
chǒngyuk 정육. *chǒngyukchǒm* 정육점 butcher's (shop); meat market (*Am.*).
chǒnhada 전하다 ① convey[deliver] a message. ② hand down; transmit.
chǒnhak 전학. *chǒnhak'ada* 전학하다 change[transfer] to another school.
chǒnhu 전후 front and rear; before and behind.
chǒnhu 전후. *chǒnhuŭi* 전후의 postwar; after the war. *chǒnhup'a* 전후파 postwar generation.
chǒnhwa 전화 telephone; phone. *chǒnhwahada* 전화하다 (tele)phone; call; call[ring] up.
chǒnhyǒ 전혀 entirely; completely; utterly, quite.
chǒnhyǒng 전형 model; pattern; type. *chǒnhyǒngjǒk* 전형적 typical; model.
chǒnim 전임. *chǒnimŭi* 전임의 former. *chǒnimja* 전임자 predecessor in office.
chǒnim 전임 full-time service[employment]. *chǒnim kangsa* 전임 강사 full-time instructor.
chǒnja 전자 electron. *chǒnja kyesan-gi* 전자 계산기 electronic computer.
chonjae 존재 existence. *chonjaehada* 존재하다 exist.
chǒnjaeng 전쟁 war; warfare; battle; fight.
chǒnji 전지 change of air. *chǒnji yoyang* 전지 요양 change of air for one's health.
chǒnji 전지 electric cell; battery. *kǒnjǒnji* 건전지 dry battery.
chǒnjik 전직 one's former occupation[office]. *chǒnjik changgwan* 전직 장관 ex-minister.
chǒnjik 전직. *chǒnjik'ada* 전직하다 change one's occupation; switch jobs (to).
chǒnjin 전진 advance; progress. *chǒnjinhada* 전진

하다 advance; march forward.
chŏnjo 전조 sign; omen; foreboding; premonition.
chŏnju 전주 electric pole; telegraph[telephone, electric-light] pole.
chŏnju 전주 financier; capitalist.
chŏnjugok 전주곡 prelude; overture.
chonjung 존중 respect; esteem. *chonjunghada* 존중하다 respect; value.
chŏnmang 전망 view; prospect; outlook.
chŏnmun 전문 speciality; major. *chŏnmunŭro* 전문으로 specially; professionally. *chŏnmun-ga* 전문가 specialist; professional; expert.
chŏnmyŏl 전멸 complete[total] destruction; annihilation. *chŏnmyŏrhada* 전멸하다 be completely destroyed.
chŏnnal 전날 the other day; some time[days] ago; previous[preceding] day.
chŏnnap 전납 advance payment. *chŏnnap'ada* 전납하다 pay in advance; prepay.
chŏnnyŏn 전년 the previous year; the year before.
chŏnp'a 전파 electric wave. *chŏnp'a t'amjigi* 전파 탐지기 radar.
chŏnp'a 전파 transmission; propagation. *chŏnp'ahada* 전파하다 be propagated; be disseminated.
chŏnp'yo 전표 chit; ticket; slip. *maech'ul chŏnp'yo* 매출 전표 sales check.
chŏnsa 전사. *chŏnsahada* 전사하다 be killed in action[battle].
chŏnsa 전사 fighter; warrior; combatant.
chŏnse 전세. *chŏnsechip* 전세집 house for rent (*Am.*); house to let (*Eng.*). *chŏnse pŏsŭ* 전세 버스 chartered bus.

chŏnsegye 전세계 whole world. *chŏnsegyee* 전세계
에 all over[through] the world.
chŏnshi 전시 exhibition; display. *chŏnshihada* 전
시하다 exhibit.
chŏnshi 전시 wartime. *chŏnshi naegak* 전시 내각
war cabinet.
chŏnshi 전시 whole city. *chŏnshimin* 전시민 all the
citizens.
chŏnshin 전신 whole body. *chŏnshine* 전신에 all
over the body.
chŏnsŏl 전설 legend; tradition. *chŏnsŏlchŏk* 전설적
legendary; traditional.
chŏnsŏn 전선 electric wire[cord]; cable.
chŏnsong 전송 send-off. *chŏnsonghada* 전송하다 see
(a person) off; give a send-off.
chŏnsongnyŏk 전속력 full speed. *chŏnsongnyŏgŭro*
전속력으로 at full speed.
chŏnsul 전술 tactics; art of war. *chŏnsulsangŭi* 전
술상의 tactical.
chŏnt'ong 전통 tradition. *chŏnt'ongjŏgin[ŭro]* 전통
적인[으로] traditional[ly].
chŏnt'u 전투 battle; fight. *chŏnt'uhada* 전투하다
fight; battle. *chŏnt'ugi* 전투기 fighter.
chŏnŭng 저능. *chŏnŭnghan* 저능한 weak-[feeble-]
minded. *chŏnŭnga* 저능아 imbecile child.
chŏnwi 전위 advance(d) guard; vanguard.
chŏnwon 전원 all (the) members; entire staff. *chŏnwon ilch'iro* 전원 일치로 unanimously.
chŏnyŏk 저녁 evening. *chŏnyŏkttaee* 저녁때에 toward evening.
chŏnyŏm 전염 contagion; infection. *chŏnyŏmhada*
전염하다 be contagious[infectious]. *chŏnyŏm-*

pyǒng 전염병 infectious[contagious] disease; epidemic.

chǒnyǒn 전연 →**chǒnhyǒ** 전혀.

chǒnyong 전용 exclusive use. *chǒnyongǔi* 전용의 private; exclusive. *chǒnyongch'a* 전용차 private car.

choǒn 조언 advice; counsel. *choǒnhada* 조언하다 advise; give (a person) advice.

chǒon 저온 low temperature.

chǒpcha'k 접착 adhesion; glueing.

chǒpch'akche 접착제 adhesive (agent); cement.

chǒpch'ok 접촉 contact; touch. *chǒpch'ok'ada* 접촉하다 touch; come into contact[touch] (with).

chǒpchong 접종 inoculation; vaccination. *chǒpchonghada* 접종하다 inoculate; vaccinate.

chǒpkǔn 접근 approach; access. *chǒpkǔnhada* 접근하다 approach; draw[get] near.

chǒp'ada 접하다 touch; adjoin; border (on); be adjacent (to).

chǒpshi 접시 plate; dish; saucer; platter.

chǒpsu 접수 receipt; acceptance. *chǒpsuhada* 접수하다 receive; accept. *chǒpsugu* 접수구 usher's window[desk].

chopta 좁다 (be) narrow; small; limited.

chǒpta 접다 fold (up); furl; double; turn up[down].

chǒptae 접대 reception. *chǒptaehada* 접대하다 receive; entertain.

chorida 졸이다 ① boil down ② feel nervous[anxious]

chǒrida 저리다 be benumbed; become numbed.

chǒrida 절이다 pickle; salt (vegetable).

chorigae 조리개 thin cord; tightening string.

chorim 조림 hard-boiled food. *t'ongjorim* 통조림 canned food.

chorip 조립 assembly; framework. *chorip'ada* 조립하다 assemble; put[fit] together.

chorong 조롱 ridicule; sneer. *choronghada* 조롱하다 ridicule; make fun of; laugh at.

chorŏp 졸업 graduation. *chorŏp'ada* 졸업하다 finish; graduate from. *chorŏpsaeng* 졸업생 graduate.

chorŭda 조르다 ① tighten; strangle ② importune; press.

chŏryak 절약 saving; economy; thrift. *chŏryak'ada* 절약하다 economize; save; spare.

choryŏk 조력 help; aid; assistance. *choryŏk'ada* 조력하다 help; aid; assist.

chosa 조사 investigation; inquiry. *chosahada* 조사하다 inquire; investigate.

chosan 조산 premature birth. *chosanhada* 조산하다 give premature birth to.

chosang 조상 ancestor; forefather.

chosanwón 조산원 midwife; maternity nurse.

choshim 조심 caution; heed; care. *choshimhada* 조심하다 take care; be careful[cautious].

chŏsŏ 저서 one's writings; work; book.

chosu 조수 assistant; helper. *unjŏn chosu* 운전 조수 assistant driver.

chŏsuji 저수지 reservoir.

chosuk 조숙 early maturity. *chosuk'an* 조숙한 premature; precocious.

chŏt 젖 milk. *chŏtkkokchi* 젖꼭지 teat; nipple. *chŏsso* 젖소 milch cow.

chŏt 젓 pickled[salted] fish. *saeujŏt* 새우젓 pickled shrimps.

chot'a 좋다 (be) good; fine; nice. *kajang chŏun* 가장 좋은 best.

chŏt'aek 저택 mansion; residence. *chŏt'aekka* 저택가 residential quarters.

chŏtchok 저쪽 there; over there; the opposite side.

chŏtkarak 젓가락 (pair of) chopsticks.

chŏtta 젓다 ① row ② stir ③ wave.

chŏtta 젖다 get wet; be damp; be soaked[drenched]. *chŏjŭn* 젖은 wet; damp.

chot'oe 조퇴. *chot'oehada* 조퇴하다 leave (school, office) earlier (than usual).

chŏui 조의 condolence. *chŏuirŭl p'yohada* 조의를 표하다 express one's condolence.

chŏul 저울 balance; scales; weighing beam.

choyak 조약 treaty; pact. *p'yŏnghwa choyak* 평화조약 peace treaty.

choyaktol 조약돌 gravel; pebbles.

choyonghada 조용하다 (be) quiet; silent; still; tranquil; placid.

chu 주 share; stock. *ŭnhaengju* 은행주 bank stocks. →**chushik** 주식.

chubin 주빈 guest of honor; principal guest.

chubu 주부 mistress of a house; housewife.

chubyŏn 주변 circumference; environs; outskirts.

chuch'a 주차 parking. *chuch'ahada* 주차하다 park.

chuch'oe 주최 auspices. *chuch'oehada* 주최하다 sponsor. *chuch'oero* 주최로 under the auspices of.

chuda 주다 give; bestow; award. *kihoerŭl chuda* 기회를 주다 give[afford] a chance.

chudan 주단 silks and satins; silk goods.

chudong 주동 leadership. *chudonghada* 주동하다 take the lead.

chudun 주둔 stationing. *chudunhada* 주둔하다 be stationed. *chudun-gun* 주둔군 stationary troops.

chudungi 주둥이 mouth; beak; mouthpiece.

chugan 주간 week. *toksŏ chugan* 독서 주간 book week. *chugan nonp'yŏng* 주간 논평 weekly review.

chugan 주간 daytime; day; diurnal. *chugan kŭnmu* 주간 근무 day-duty.

chugida 죽이다 kill; slay; murder.

chugŭm 죽음 death. *chugŭmŭl murŭpssŭgo* 죽음을 무릅쓰고 at the risk of one's death.

chugŭp 주급 weekly wages[pay, salary].

chuil 주일 week(day). *ibŏn* [*chinan, taŭm*] *chuil* 이번[지난, 다음] 주일 this [last, next] week.

chuim 주임 person in charge; head; chief.

chuin 주인 master; employer; host.

chuin-gong 주인공 hero; heroine.

chujang 주장 assertion; claim. *chujanghada* 주장하다 assert; claim.

chuje 주제 main subject; theme; motif.

chujenŏmta 주제넘다 (be) forward; cheeky; impudent; pert; saucy.

chuji 주지 chief[head] priest.

chujŏ 주저 hesitation. *chujŏhada* 주저하다 hesitate.

chujŏanta 주저앉다 fall down; sit down plump.

chujŏm 주점 tavern; pub; grogshop; wineshop.

chujŏnja 주전자 (copper, brass) kettle; teakettle.

chuju 주주 shareholder (*Eng.*); stockholder (*Am.*).

chuk 죽 (rice) gruel; porridge.

chŭk 즉 namely; that is; so to speak.

chŭkkak 즉각 on the spot; at once; instantly.

chŭksa 즉사 instantaneous death. *chŭksahada* 즉사하다 die on the spot.

chuksun 죽순 bamboo shoot[sprout].

chukta 죽다 die; pass away; be killed; lose one's life. *chugŭn* 죽은 dead; deceased; the late.

chul 줄 rope; cord; string; line.

chulda 줄다 decrease; diminish; lessen.

chuldarigi 줄다리기 tug of war. *chuldarigihada* 줄다리기하다 play at a tug of war.

chŭlgida 즐기다 enjoy oneself; take pleasure in; amuse oneself.

chŭlgŏpta 즐겁다 (be) pleasant; delightful; glad. *chŭlgŏi* 즐거이 happily; pleasantly; cheerfully.

chulgot 줄곧 all the time[way]; all along[through].

chumak 주막 tavern; inn. *chumak chuin* 주막 주인 innkeeper.

chumal 주말 weekend. *chumare* 주말에 on weekends.

chumi 주미. *chumiŭi* 주미의 stationed[resident] in America. *chumi Han-guk taesa* 주미 한국 대사 Korean Ambassador to[in] the United States.

chumin 주민 inhabitants; residents.

chumok 주목 attention; notice. *chumok'ada* 주목하다 pay attention to.

chumŏk 주먹 (clenched) fist.

chumŏni 주머니 bag; sack; pouch; purse.

chumun 주문 order; request. *chumunhada* 주문하다 order; give an order.

chumurŭda 주무르다 finger; fumble with.

chunbi 준비 preparation; arrangements; provision. *chunbihada* 준비하다 prepare; arrange; provide for; get ready for.

chunjang 준장 brigadier general (*army*); commodore (*navy*).

chung 중 Buddhist priest; monk; bonze.

chungang 중앙 center; middle; heart. *chungangŭi* 중앙의 central; middle.

chŭngbal 증발 evaporation. *chŭngbarhada* 증발하다 evaporate; vaporize.

chungbok 중복 duplication. *chungbok'ada* 중복하다 overlap; duplicate.

chungbyŏng 중병 serious[severe] illness. *chungbyŏnge kŏllida* 중병에 걸리다 fall[get] seriously ill. *chungbyŏng hwanja* 중병 환자 serious case.

chungdae 중대 company. *chungdaejang* 중대장 company commander.

chungdae 중대 importance. *chungdaehan* 중대한 important; serious; grave.

chungdan 중단 discontinuance. *chungdanhada* 중단하다 discontinue; suspend; break off.

chungdo 중도. *chungdo-esŏ* 중도에서 halfway; midway; in the middle.

chungdok 중독 poisoning; toxication. *chungdok-toeda* 중독되다 be poisoned. *shikchungdok* 식중독 food-poisoning.

chŭngga 증가 increase; addition. *chŭnggahada* 증가하다 increase; rise; grow.

chunggan 중간 middle; midway. *chungganŭi* 중간의 middle; midway; interim; intermediate.

chŭnggi 증기 steam; vapor.

chunggo 중고. *chunggoŭi* 중고의 used; old; second-hand. *chunggop'um* 중고품 second-hand article. *chunggoch'a* 중고차 used car.

chŭnggŏ 증거 evidence; proof; testimony.

Chunggong 중공 Communist[Red] China.

chunggongŏp 중공업 heavy industry.

Chungguk 중국 China.

chunggyŏn 중견 backbone; main body. *chunggyŏn inmul* 중견 인물 leading figures.

chunggyŏngsang 중경상 serious and slight injuries [wounds].

chunghakkyo 중학교 middle school; junior high school (*Am.*).

Chunghwamin-guk 중화민국 (Rep. of) China.

chunghwanja 중환자 serious case.

chŭngin 증인 witness; attestor.

chungjae 중재 arbitration. *chungjaehada* 중재하다 mediate; arbitrate.

chungjang 중장 lieutenant general (*army*); vice admiral (*navy*).

chungji 중지 suspension; discontinuance. *chungjihada* 중지하다 stop; suspend; discontinue.

chungjin-guk 중진국 semi-developed country.

chingjip 징집 enlistment; enrollment; recruiting. *chingjip'ada* 징집하다 levy; enlist; recruit.

chungchŏm 중점 importance; emphasis; stress. *…e chungchŏmŭl tuda* …에 중점을 두다 lay emphasis [stress] on.

chungjŏlmo 중절모 soft hat; felt hat.

chŭngjŏng 증정 presentation. *chŭngjŏnghada* 증정하다 present; make a present.

chŭngkwon 증권 bill; securities. *chŭngkwon hoesa* 증권 회사 stock company; security corporation.

chungmae 중매 matchmaking. *chungmaehada* 중매하다 make a match.

Chungmi 중미 Central America.

chŭngmyŏng 증명 proof; evidence. *chŭngmyŏnghada* 증명하다 prove; show; verify.

chungnip 중립 neutrality. *chungnipchŏk* 중립적

neutral. *chungnipkuk* 중립국 neutral power (state).

chungnyŏng 중령 lieutenant colonel (*army*); commander (*navy*).

chungnyu 중류 middle class. *chungnyu kajŏng* 중류 가정 middle class family.

chŭngnyu 증류 distillation. *chŭngnyuhada* 증류하다 distill. *chŭngnyuju* 증류주 spirituous liquor.

chŭngŏn 증언 testimony; witness; (verbal) evidence. *chŭngŏnsŏ* 증언서 written testimony.

chungp'ung 중풍 palsy; paralysis.

chungsang 중상 slander. *chungsanghada* 중상하다 slander. *chungsangjŏgin* 중상적인 slanderous.

chungsanmo 중산모 derby (*Am.*); bowler (*Eng.*).

chungse 중세 the Middle Ages; medieval times. *chungseŭi* 중세의 medieval.

chŭngse 증세 symptoms; condition of a patient.

chungshi 중시 serious consideration. *chungshihada* 중시하다 attach importance to; take a serious view (of); make much (of).

chungshim 중심 center; focus; core. *kongŏbŭi chungshim* 공업의 중심 industrial center.

chŭngsŏ 증서 deed; bond; certificate; voucher.

chungsun 중순 second[middle] ten days of a month.

chungt'ae 중태 serious[critical] condition.

chungwi 중위 first lieutenant (*Am. army*); lieutenant junior grade (*Am. navy*).

chungyo 중요. *chungyohan* 중요한 important; essential; momentous. *chungyoshihada* 중요시하다 make[think] much of. →**chungshi** 중시.

chun-gyŏlsŭngjŏn 준결승전 semifinal game[match].

chunusŭng 준우승 coming out second best.

chungyǒk 중역 director. → **isa** 이사.
chungyu 중유 crude[raw] petroleum; heavy oil.
chuǒ 주어 subject.
chŭp 즙 juice; sap. *p'odo[sagwa]jŭp* 포도[사과] 즙 grape[apple] juice.
chupta 줍다 pick up; gather (up); find.
churida 줄이다 reduce; decrease; diminish.
churo 주로 mainly; chiefly; principally.
churŭm 주름 wrinkles; crumples. *churŭmjin ŏlgul* 주름진 얼굴 wrinkled[furrowed] face.
churye 주례 officiator. *churyerŭl sŏda* 주례를 서다 officiate at a marriage.
churyǒk 주력. *churyǒk'ada* 주력하다 exert oneself (for).
churyǒk 주력 main force. *churyǒk pudae* 주력 부대 main force unit.
churyu 주류 main current; mainstream. *churyup'a* 주류파 leading faction.
chusa 주사 injection; shot (*Am.*). *chusahada* 주사하다 inject. *yebang chusa* 예방 주사 preventive injection.
chusan 주산 abacus calculation.
chusawi 주사위 die.
chushi 주시 steady look; gaze. *chushihada* 주시하다 gaze at; watch carefully.
chushik 주식 shares (*Eng.*); stock (*Am.*).
chuso 주소 one's residence[abode]; address.
chusǒngbun 주성분 chief[main] ingredient.
chut'aek 주택 house; residence. *hohwa chut'aek* 호화 주택 luxurious house[mansion].
chuŭi 주의 attention; care. *chuŭihada* 주의하다 be careful of; take care of.

chuŭi 주의 principle; doctrine; ism; cause.
chuwi 주위 circumference. *chuwiŭi* 주위의 neighboring.
chuya 주야 day and night.
chuyŏk 주역 leading title[part, role].
chwach'ŏn 좌천 relegation; demotion. *chwach'ŏnhada* 좌천하다 relegate; demote (*Am.*).
chwach'ŭk 좌측 left (side). *chwach'ŭk t'onghaeng* 좌측 통행 "Keep to the left."
chwadam 좌담 table-talk. *chwadamhoe* 좌담회 roundtable talk; symposium.
chwaik 좌익 left wing. *chwaik punja* 좌익 분자 left-wing element.
chwajŏl 좌절 frustration; setback. *chwajŏrhada* 좌절하다 get ruined; be frustrated.
chwasŏk 좌석 seat. *chwasŏksu* 좌석수 seating capacity.
chwau 좌우 right and left. *chwaue* 좌우에 on right and left.
chwaugan 좌우간 anyhow; in any case; at any rate.
chwi 쥐 rat; mouse. *chwiyak* 쥐약 rat poison.
chwida 쥐다 hold; take hold of; grasp; seize.

⟆ C ⟂ 〔ch'〕

ch'a 차 (motor)car; auto(mobile). *ch'arŭl t'ada* 차를 타다 take a car. *ch'asago* 차사고 vehicular accident.
ch'abi 차비 carfare; train[railway, bus] fare.
ch'abyŏl 차별 distinction; discrimination. *ch'abyŏrhada* 차별하다 discriminate.
ch'ada 차다 ① kick; give a kick. ② click (tongue).

ch'ada 차다 carry; wear; put on.

ch'ada 차다 (be) full (of); be filled (with); be jammed[overcrowded].

ch'ada 차다 (be) cold; chilly; icy. *ch'anbaram* 찬바람 chilly[cold] wind.

ch'ado 차도 roadway; carriageway; track.

ch'aegim 책임 responsibility; liability. *ch'aegimi innŭn* 책임이 있는 responsible.

ch'aejip 채집 collection. *ch'aejip'ada* 채집하다 collect; gather.

ch'aek 책 book; volume. *yŏngŏch'aek* 영어책 English book.

ch'aekcha 책자 book; pamphlet; leaflet.

ch'aekchang 책장 bookcase; bookshelf.

ch'aekchang 책장 leaf of a book; pages.

ch'aekkoji 책꽂이 bookshelf; bookcase.

ch'aekpang 책방 bookstore; bookshop. →**sŏjŏm** 서점.

ch'aeksang 책상 desk; (writing) table[bureau].

ch'aemu 채무 debt; obligation; liabilities. *ch'aemuja* 채무자 debtor.

ch'aeso 채소 vegetables; greens. →**yach'ae** 야채.

ch'aetchik 채찍 whip; lash; rod.

ch'aeyong 채용 adoption. *ch'aeyonghada* 채용하다 adopt.

ch'ago 차고 car shed; garage; carport.

ch'agwan 차관 loan. *ch'agwanŭl ŏtta* 차관을 얻다 obtain a loan.

ch'ai 차이 difference; disparity. *ŭigyŏnŭi ch'ai* 의견의 차이 difference of opinion.

ch'ail 차일 sunshade; awning; tent.

ch'ajanaeda 찾아내다 find out; discover; detect.

ch'ajang 차장 conductor(*Am.*); guard (*Eng.*). *yŏ-*

ch'ajang 여차장 conductress.
ch'ajihada 차지하다 occupy; hold; take; possess.
ch'ak'ada 착하다 (be) good; nice; kind-hearted. *ch'ak'an saram* 착한 사람 good-natured person.
ch'akch'wi 착취 exploitation. *ch'akch'wihada* 착취하다 exploit; squeeze.
ch'akkak 착각 illusion. *ch'akkak'ada* 착각하다 have [be under] an illusion.
ch'akshil 착실. *ch'akshirhada* 착실하다 (be) steady; trustworthy; faithful; sound. *ch'akshirhi* 착실히 steadily; faithfully.
ch'alssak 찰싹 with a slap →**ch'ŏlssŏk** 철썩.
ch'alttŏk 찰떡 glutinous rice cake.
ch'amhada 참하다 (be) nice and pretty; charming; good-looking. *ch'amhan agassi* 참한 아가씨 pretty girl.
ch'amga 참가 participation. *ch'amgahada* 참가하다 participate[take part] (in); join.
ch'amgo 참고 reference. *ch'amgohada* 참고하다 refer; consult. *ch'amgosŏ* 참고서 reference book.
ch'amhok 참혹. *ch'amhok'an* 참혹한 cruel; brutal. *ch'amhok'age* 참혹하게 cruelly; brutally.
ch'ammal 참말 true remark[story]; truth. *ch'ammallo* 참말로 truly; really; indeed.
ch'amp'ae 참패 crushing defeat. *ch'amp'aehada* 참패하다 suffer a crushing defeat.
ch'amsae 참새 sparrow.
ch'amsŏk 참석 attendance. *ch'amsŏk'ada* 참석하다 attend; be present; take part in.
ch'amta 참다 bear; endure; tolerate; stand.
ch'amŭro 참으로 really; truly; indeed.
ch'anae 차내 inside[interior] of a car.

ch'ang 창 window. *yurich'ang* 유리창 glass window. *ch'angŭl yŏlda* [*tatta*] 창을 열다 [닫다] open [close] a window.

ch'ang 창 spear; lance. *ch'angdŏnjigi* 창던지기 javelin throw.

ch'angbu 창부 →**ch'angnyŏ** 창녀.

ch'anggo 창고 warehouse; storehouse.

ch'anggŭk 창극 Korean classical opera.

ch'angja 창자 intestines; bowels; entrails.

ch'angjak 창작 original work; creation. *ch'angjak'ada* 창작하다 create; write (a novel).

ch'angjo 창조 creation. *ch'angjohada* 창조하다 create. *ch'angjojŏk* 창조적 creative.

ch'angmun 창문 →**ch'ang** 창.

ch'angnip 창립 foundation; establishment *ch'angnip'ada* 창립하다 found; establish.

ch'angnyŏ 창녀 prostitute; whore; street girl.

ch'angp'i 창피 shame; dishonor. *ch'angp'ihada* 창피하다 (be) shameful; humiliating.

ch'anjo 찬조 support; patronage. *ch'anjohada* 찬조하다 support; back up.

ch'anmul 찬물 cold water. →**naengsu** 냉수.

ch'ansong 찬송. *ch'ansonghada* 찬송하다 praise; chant. *ch'ansongga* 찬송가 hymn; psalm.

ch'ansŏng 찬성 approval; agreement. *ch'ansŏnghada* 찬성하다 approve of; agree.

ch'ap'yo 차표 ticket. *wangbok ch'ap'yo* 왕복 차표 round-trip ticket (*Am.*); return ticket (*Eng.*).

ch'aryang 차량 vehicles; cars; carriage.

ch'arye 차례 order; turn. *ch'aryero* 차례로 in order; by [in] turns.

ch'assak 찻삯 (car)fare. →**ch'abi** 차비.

ch'atta 찾다 search[hunt, look] (for); seek (for, after); look out.

ch'atchan 찻잔 teacup.

ch'atchip 찻집 tea[coffee] house; tea[coffee] shop; tearoom. →**tabang** 다방.

ch'atkil 찻길 roadway; carriageway; track.

ch'ayong 차용 borrowing; loan. *ch'ayonghada* 차용하다 borrow; have the loan.

ch'e 체 sieve; bolter; riddle. *ch'ero ch'ida* 체로 치다 sieve; screen; sift.

ch'ejung 체중 (body) weight. *ch'ejungŭl talda* 체중을 달다 weigh[measure] oneself.

ch'egye 체계 system. *ch'egyejŏk(ŭro)* 체계적(으로) systematic(ally).

ch'egyŏk 체격 physique; build; constitution.

ch'ejo 체조 gymnastics; gym; physical exercises. *kigye ch'ejo* 기계 체조 heavy gymnastics.

ch'eon 체온 temperature; body heat. *ch'eon-gye* 체온계 clinical thermometer.

ch'ep'o 체포 arrest; capture. *ch'ep'ohada* 체포하다 arrest; capture.

ch'eryŏk 체력 physical strength[stamina]. *ch'eryŏk kŏmsa* 체력 검사 strength test.

ch'eyuk 체육 physical education. *ch'eyuk'oe* 체육회 athletic association.

ch'ian 치안 public peace. *ch'ian-guk* 치안국 Headquarters of National police.

ch'ibun 치분 tooth powder. →**ch'iyak** 치약.

ch'ida 치다 strike; hit; beat.

ch'ida 치다 ① attack; assault ② cut; trim ③ denounce; charge.

ch'ida 치다 send (a telegram).

ch'ida 치다 put (soy) into[in, on].

ch'ida 치다 put up; hang; draw. *k'ŏt'ŭnŭl ch'ida* 커튼을 치다 draw a curtain.

ch'ikwa 치과. *ch'ikwa pyŏngwon* 치과 병원 dental clinic. *ch'ikwa ŭisa* 치과 의사 dentist; dental surgeon.

ch'ilgi 칠기 lacquer(ed) ware.

ch'ilmyŏnjo 칠면조 turkey.

ch'ilp'an 칠판 blackboard.

ch'ilship 칠십 (70) seventy. *che ch'ilshibŭi* 제 칠십의 the seventieth.

ch'im 침 spittle; saliva. *ch'imŭl paetta* 침을 뱉다 spit.

ch'im 침 ① needle; pin ② hand ③ prickle ④ hook.

ch'im 침 acupuncture. *ch'imŭl not'a* 침을 놓다 acupuncture; apply acupuncture.

ch'ima 치마 skirt.

ch'imch'imhada 침침하다 (be) dark; gloomy; dim. *ch'imch'imhan pang* 침침한 방 dimly-lit room.

ch'imdae 침대 bed; berth. *ch'imdaech'a* 침대차 sleeping car.

ch'imgu 침구 bedding; bedclothes.

ch'imip 침입 invasion. *ch'imip'ada* 침입하다 invade.

ch'immuk 침묵 silence. *ch'immuk'ada* 침묵하다 be silent; hold one's tongue.

ch'imnyak 침략 aggression; invasion. *ch'imnyak'ada* 침략하다 invade.

ch'imnye 침례. *ch'imnye kyohoe* 침례 교회 Baptist Church.

chimshil 침실 bedroom; bedchamber.

ch'imt'u 침투 permeation; penetration. *ch'imt'uhada* 침투하다 permeate; penetrate.

ch'imul 침울. *ch'imurhan* 침울한 melancholy; gloomy.

ch'inch'ŏk 친척 relation; relative; kinsman.

ch'ingch'an 칭찬 praise; applause. *ch'ingch'anhada* 칭찬하다 praise; admire; speak highly of.

ch'ingŏlgŏrida 칭얼거리다 whimper; whine; fret.

ch'in-gu 친구 friend; companion; pal. *yŏja ch'in-gu* 여자 친구 girl friend.

ch'inhada 친하다 (be) intimate; friendly. *ch'inhan pŏt* 친한 벗 intimate friend.

ch'inil 친일. *ch'inirŭi* 친일의 pro-Japanese. *ch'inil-p'a* 친일파 pro-Japanese (group).

ch'injŏl 친절 kindness. *ch'injŏrhan* 친절한 kind. *ch'injŏrhi* 친절히 kindly.

ch'inmi 친미. *ch'inmiŭi* 친미의 pro-American. *ch'inmip'a* 친미파 pro-Americans.

ch'inmok 친목. *ch'inmok'oe* 친목회 social meeting [gathering]; sociable (*Am.*).

ch'insŏ 친서 autograph letter; personal letter.

ch'insŏn 친선 goodwill; friendship; amity. *ch'insŏn kyŏnggi* 친선 경기 friendly match.

ch'iril 칠일 seventh (of the month); seven days.

chirwol 칠월 July.

ch'iryo 치료 medical treatment. *ch'iryohada* 치료하다 treat; cure.

ch'isol 치솔 toothbrush.

ch'isu 치수 measurement; size; dimensions.

ch'it'ong 치통 toothache.

ch'iuda 치우다 put in order; tidy up; clear away.

ch'iyak 치약 tooth paste.

ch'o 초 candle. *ch'otpul* 촛불 candlelight.

ch'o 초 vinegar. *chorŭl chida* 초를 치다 add vinegar.

ch'ŏ 처 wife; one's better-half. →**anae** 아내.

ch'obo 초보 first steps; rudiment. *ch'oboŭi* 초보의 elementary; rudimentary.

ch'ŏbŏl 처벌 punishment; penalty. *ch'ŏbŏrhada* 처벌하다 punish.

ch'ŏbun 처분 disposal; management. *ch'ŏbunhada* 처분하다 dispose of; do[deal] with.

ch'och'im 초침 second-hand (of a watch).

ch'ochŏm 초점 focus.

ch'och'ŏng 초청 invitation. *ch'och'ŏnghada* 초청하다 invite. *ch'och'ŏngchang* 초청장 letter of invitation.

ch'odae 초대 invitation. *ch'odaehada* 초대하다 invite. *ch'odaekwŏn* 초대권 complimentary ticket. *ch'odaechang* 초대장 invitation card.

ch'ŏdinsang 첫인상 one's first impression.

ch'oeak 최악. *ch'oeagŭi* 최악의 the worst. *ch'oeagŭi kyŏnguenŭn* 최악의 경우에는 in the worst case.

ch'oech'o 최초 first; beginning. *ch'oech'oŭi* 최초의 first. *ch'oech'o-e* 최초에 in the first place.

ch'oego 최고. *ch'oegoŭi* 최고의 highest; maximum.

ch'oeha 최하 lowest. *ch'oeha kagyŏk* 최하 가격 lowest price.

ch'oehu 최후 the last; the end. *ch'oehuŭi* 최후의 the last; final.

ch'oejŏ 최저. *ch'oejŏŭi* 최저의 lowest; minimum. *ch'oejŏ imgŭm* 최저 임금 minimum[floor] wages.

ch'oejong 최종. *ch'oejongŭi* 최종의 last; final.

ch'oegŭn 최근. *ch'oegŭnŭi* 최근의 recent; late; up-to-date. *ch'oegŭne* 최근에 recently; lately.

ch'oemyŏnsul 최면술 hypnotism; mesmerism.

ch'oeshin 최신. *ch'oeshinŭi* 최신의 newest; latest;

up-to-date. *ch'oeshinshik* 최신식 latest fashion; newest style.

ch'ogi 초기 early days; first[early] stage.

ch'ogŭp 초급 beginner's class; junior course. *ch'ogŭp taehak* 초급 대학 junior college.

ch'ogwa 초과 excess; surplus. *ch'ogwahada* 초과하다 exceed.

ch'oharunnal 초하룻날 first day of the month.

ch'ŏji 처지 situation; circumstances; condition.

ch'ŏjida 처지다 hang down; droop; sag.

ch'ojo 초조 fret; impatience. *ch'ojohada* 초조하다 (be) fretful; irritated.

ch'ojŏnyŏk 초저녁 early evening; early hours of evening; toward evening.

ch'ŏkch'u 척추 backbone; spinal column.

ch'ŏl 철 iron; steel. *ch'ŏrŭi changmak* 철의 장막 the Iron Curtain. *ch'ŏlmun* 철문 iron gate.

ch'ŏl 철 season. *sach'ŏl* 사철 four seasons.

ch'ŏlbŏkkŏrida 철벅거리다 splash; dabble in.

ch'ŏlbong 철봉 iron rod[bar]; horizontal[exercise] bar.

ch'ŏlchŏ 철저 thoroughness. *ch'ŏlchŏhan* 철저한 thorough(going). *ch'ŏlchŏhi* 철저히 thoroughly.

ch'ŏlchomang 철조망 (barbed) wire entanglements.

ch'ŏlgŏ 철거 withdrawal. *ch'ŏlgŏhada* 철거하다 withdraw; remove.

ch'ŏlgong 철공 ironworker. *ch'ŏlgongso* 철공소 ironworks. *ch'ŏlgongŏp* 철공업 iron manufacture.

ch'ŏlgwan 철관 iron pipe[tube].

ch'ŏlgyo 철교 iron bridge; railway bridge.

ch'ŏlmang 철망 wire-netting; wire net; wire gauze.

ch'ŏlmo 철모 helmet; steel[iron] cap.

ch'ŏlssa 철사 wire. *ch'ŏlssa kat'ŭn* 철사 같은 wiry.

ch'ŏlto 철도 railway; railroad(*Am.*). *ch'ŏlto sago* 철도 사고 railroad accident.

ch'ŏma 처마 eaves. *ch'ŏma mit'e* 처마 밑에 under the eaves.

ch'ŏmbu 첨부 appending; annexing. *ch'ŏmbuhada* 첨부하다 attach; append. *ch'ŏmbu sŏryu* 첨부 서류 attached[accompanying] papers.

ch'omch'omhada 촘촘하다 (be) close; dense; thick.

ch'ŏn 천 cloth; fabric; (woven) stuff; texture.

ch'ŏn 천(1,000) a thousand. *such'ŏnŭi* 수천의 thousands of. *ch'ŏllian* 천리안 clairvoyance.

ch'ŏnch'e 천체 heavenly body.

ch'ŏnch'ŏnhi 천천히 slowly; leisurely; without hur- ⌜ry

ch'ŏndang 천당 Heaven; Paradise. →**ch'ŏn-guk** 천국.

ch'ŏndung 천둥 thunder. *ch'ŏndungch'ida* 천둥치다 thunder; roll; grumble.

ch'ong 총 gun; rifle. *ch'ongŭl ssoda* 총을 쏘다 shoot[fire] a gun.

ch'ong 총 all; whole; total; general. *ch'ongin-gu* 총인구 total population.

ch'ŏng 청 request; one's wishes. *ch'ŏnghada* 청하다 ask; beg; request.

ch'ongaek 총액 total amount; sum[grand] total.

ch'ongal 총알 bullet; shot. →**t'anhwan** 탄환.

ch'ŏngbu 청부 contract. *ch'ŏngbuŏp* 청부업 contracting business. *ch'ŏngbuŏpcha* 청부업자 contractor.

ch'ŏngch'ŏpchang 청첩장 letter of invitation; invitation card.

ch'ŏngch'un 청춘 youth; springtime of life. *ch'ŏngch'un-gi* 청춘기 adolescence.

ch'ŏngdong 청동 bronze. *ch'ŏngdong hwaro* 청동 화

로 bronze brazier.

ch'ŏnggu 청구 demand; claim. *ch'ŏngguhada* 청구하다 request; demand. *ch'ŏnggusŏ* 청구서 request; demand bill[draft, note, loan].

ch'ŏnggwa 청과 vegetables and fruits. *ch'ŏnggwa shijang* 청과 시장 vegetable and fruit market.

ch'onggye 총계 total amount; (sum) total. *ch'onggyehada* 총계하다 totalize; sum up.

ch'ŏnggyodo 청교도 Puritan. *ch'ŏnggyodojŏk* 청교도적 puritanical.

ch'ŏnggyŏl 청결 cleanliness; purity. *ch'ŏnggyŏrhada* 청결하다 (be) clean; neat; pure. *ch'ŏnggyŏrhi* 청결히 cleanly.

ch'ŏn-guk 천국 Heaven; Paradise.

ch'onghoe 총회 general meeting; plenary session.

ch'ŏnghon 청혼 propose; proposal of marriage.

ch'ŏngja 청자 celadon porcelain. *Koryŏ ch'ŏngja* 고려 청자 Koryŏ celadon.

ch'ongjae 총재 president; governor. *puch'ongjae* 부총재 vice-president.

ch'ongjang 총장 ① president (*university*) ② secretary general (*business, office work*).

ch'ŏngju 청주 refined rice wine.

ch'ŏngjung 청중 audience; attendance.

ch'ongmyŏng 총명 cleverness. *ch'ongmyŏnghan* 총명한 wise; sagacious; intelligent.

ch'ongni 총리 premier; prime minister.

ch'ŏngnyŏn 청년 young man; youth.

ch'ŏngsaek 청색 blue (color).

ch'ŏngsajin 청사진 blueprint.

ch'ŏngsan 청산 liquidation. *ch'ŏngsanhada* 청산하다 liquidate; pay off.

ch'ŏngso 청소 cleaning. *ch'ŏngsohada* 청소하다 clean; sweep. *ch'ŏngsobu* 청소부 scavenger. *ch'ŏngsoch'a* 청소차 refuse cart; sewage truck.

ch'ongsŏn-gŏ 총선거 general election.

ch'ŏngsonyŏn 청소년 youth; younger generation; teenagers.

ch'ongyŏngsa 총영사 consul general. *ch'ongyŏngsagwan* 총영사관 consulate general.

ch'ŏnhada 천하다 ① (be) humble; low(ly) ② (be) vulgar; mean.

ch'ŏnjae 천재 genius. *ch'ŏnjaejŏk* 천재적 gifted; talented.

ch'ŏnjae 천재 (natural) calamity[disaster].

ch'ŏnjang 천장 ceiling.

ch'ŏnji 천지 ① heaven and earth; universe ② world ③ top and bottom.

ch'ŏnju 천주 Lord of Heaven; God; Creator.

ch'ŏnjugyo 천주교 Roman Catholicism. *ch'ŏnjugyohoe* 천주교회 Roman Catholic Church.

ch'ŏnmak 천막 tent; marquee; awning.

ch'ŏnmin 천민 man of humble[lowly] birth.

ch'ŏnmunhak 천문학 astronomy.

ch'ŏnnal 첫날 first day; opening day.

ch'ŏnnalpam 첫날밤 bridal[wedding] night.

ch'onnom 촌놈 country fellow; rustic.

ch'ŏnnun 첫눈 the first sight[glance]. *ch'ŏnnune* 첫눈에 at first sight; at a glance; on sight.

ch'ŏnnun 첫눈 first snow (of the season). ⌜gelic.

ch'ŏnsa 천사 angel. *ch'ŏnsa kat'ŭn* 천사 같은 an-
ch'onttŭgi 촌뜨기 →**ch'onnom** 촌놈.

ch'ŏnyŏ 처녀 virgin; maiden. *ch'ŏnyŏŭi* 처녀의 virgin; maiden. *ch'ŏnyŏji* 처녀지 virgin soil.

ch'ŏnyŏn 천연. *ch'ŏnyŏnŭi* 천연의 natural. *ch'ŏnyŏn kasŭ* 천연 가스 natural gas. *ch'ŏnyŏnsaek* 천연색 natural color.

ch'ŏnyŏndu 천연두 smallpox.

ch'ŏp 첩 concubine; (secret, kept) mistress.

ch'orahada 초라하다 (be) shabby; poor-looking.

ch'ŏrhak 철학 philosophy. *ch'ŏrhak paksa* 철학 박사 doctor of philosophy.

ch'ŏrya 철야. *ch'ŏryahada* 철야하다 sit[stay] up all night; keep vigil.

ch'osanghwa 초상화 portrait.

ch'ŏssarang 첫사랑 one's first love; calf love.

ch'osok 초속 velocity[speed] per second.

ch'ŏt'ae 첫해 first year.

ch'ŏtkŏrŭm 첫걸음 first step; start; ABC (of).

ch'ŏtpŏn 첫번 first time. *ch'ŏtpŏnenŭn* 첫번에는 at first; in the beginning.

ch'otpul 촛불 candlelight.

ch'ŏtchae 첫째 first (place); No. 1; top. *ch'ŏtchaeŭi* 첫째의 first; primary. *ch'ŏtchaero* 첫째로 first of all; to begin with.

ch'ŏŭm 처음 beginning; start[outset]; origin. *ch'ŏŭmŭi* 처음의 first; initial; early. *ch'ŏŭme* 처음에 at the beginning; first. *ch'ŏŭmŭn* 처음은 at first. *ch'ŏŭmbut'ŏ* 처음부터 from the first[beginning].

ch'u 추 weight; bob; plummet.

ch'uch'ŏm 추첨 drawing; lottery. *ch'uch'ŏmhada* 추첨하다 draw lots.

ch'uch'ŏn 추천 recommendation. *ch'uch'ŏnhada* 추천하다 recommend

ch'uch'ŭk 추측 guess; conjecture. *ch'uch'ŭk'ada* 추측하다 guess; suppose.

ch'ŭk'u 측후. *ch'ŭk'uso* 측후소 meteorological station.

ch'ulch'urhada 출출하다 feel a bit hungry.

ch'udo 추도 mourning. *ch'udohada* 추도하다 mourn. *ch'udoshik* 추도식 memorial service.

ch'uhada 추하다 ① (be) dirty; filthy ② (be) mean; base; vulgar; coarse.

ch'ujap 추잡. *ch'ujap'ada* 추잡하다 (be) filthy; foul; indecent.

ch'uk'a 축하 congratulation; celebration. *ch'uk'a-hada* 축하하다 congratulate; celebrate.

ch'ukcheil 축제일 public holiday; gala day.

ch'ukchŏn 축전 congratulatory telegram.

ch'ukch'uk'ada 축축하다 (be) moist; damp; wet.

ch'ukku 축구 football; soccer. *ch'ukku sŏnsu* 축구 선수 football player.

ch'ukpae 축배 toast. *ch'ukpaerŭl tŭlda* 축배를 들다 drink a toast.

ch'uksa 축사 congratulatory address; greetings.

ch'ukso 축소 reduction; curtailment. *ch'uksohada* 축소하다 reduce; curtail.

ch'uktae 축대 terrace; embankment.

ch'ugu 추구 pursuit. *ch'uguhada* 추구하다 pursue.

ch'ulbal 출발 departure; start. *ch'ulbarhada* 출발하다 start; set out; leave.

ch'ulchang 출장 official[business] trip. *ch'ulchang-gada* 출장가다 go on a business[an official] trip.

ch'ulgu 출구 exit; way out; outlet. *pisang ch'ulgu* 비상 출구 fire escape[exit].

ch'ulguk 출국. *ch'ulguk'ada* 출국하다 depart from [leave] the country.

ch'ulgŭn 출근 attendance. *ch'ulgŭnhada* 출근하다 attend one's office.

ch'ulma 출마. *ch'ulmahada* 출마하다 run〔stand〕 for; offer oneself as a candidate.

ch'ulp'an 출판 publication. *ch'ulp'anhada* 출판하다 publish; issue.

ch'ulsan 출산 childbirth; delivery. *ch'ulsanhada* 출산하다 give birth to.

ch'ulse 출세 success in life. *ch'ulsehada* 출세하다 rise in the world.

ch'ulshin 출신 ① native ② graduate ③ birth. *ch'ulshinida* 출신이다 come from; be a graduate of. *ch'ulshin-gyo* 출신교 one's Alma Mater.

ch'ulsŏk 출석 attendance; presence. *ch'ulsŏk'ada* 출석하다 attend; be present at.

ch'um 춤 dancing; dance. *ch'umch'uda* 춤추다 dance.

ch'umun 추문 scandal; ill fame.

ch'ŭng 층 story; floor; stairs. *ilch'ŭng* 1층 first floor (*Am.*); ground floor (*Eng.*).

ch'ungbun 충분. *ch'ungbunhan* 충분한 sufficient; enough; full. *ch'ungbunhi* 충분히 enough; sufficiently; fully.

ch'ungch'i 충치 decayed tooth.

ch'ungch'unghada 충충하다 (be) dark; dim; gloomy; dusky.

ch'ungdol 충돌 collision; conflict. *ch'ungdorhada* 충돌하다 collide with.

ch'unggo 충고 advice; counsel. *ch'unggohada* 충고하다 advise; counsel.

ch'ŭnggye 층계 stairs; staircase; stairway. *ch'ŭnggyech'am* 층계참 landing.

ch'ŭngnyang 측량 surveying; measuring. *ch'ŭngnyanghada* 측량하다 survey; measure.

ch'ungshil 충실 faithfulness. *ch'ungshirhan*[*hi*] 충실한[히] faithful[ly].

ch'ungsŏng 충성 loyalty; devotion; allegiance. *ch'ungsŏngsŭrŏun* 충성스러운 loyal; devoted.

ch'unwha 춘화 obscene picture; pornography.

ch'unyŏ 추녀 ugly[unlovely] woman.

ch'unyŏm 추념 *ch'unyŏmsa* 추념사 memorial address.

ch'uŏ 추어 loach. *ch'uŏt'ang* 추어탕 loach soup.

ch'uŏk 추억 remembrance; memory.

ch'ubang 추방 exile; purge. *ch'ubanghada* 추방하다 expel; banish.

ch'upta 춥다 (be) cold; chilly; feel cold.

ch'urak 추락 fall; drop. *ch'urak'ada* 추락하다 fall; crash.

ch'urhang 출항 departure (of a ship from port). *ch'urhanghada* 출항하다 leave port; set sail.

ch'urhyŏn 출현 appearance. *ch'urhyŏnhada* 출현하다 appear; turn[show] up.

ch'uri 추리. *ch'urihada* 추리하다 reason; infer. *ch'uri sosŏl* 추리 소설 mystery[detective] story.

ch'urip 출입. *ch'urip'ada* 출입하다 go[come] in and out. *ch'uripku* 출입구 entrance.

ch'uryŏn 출연 performance. *ch'uryŏnhada* 출연하다 appear on the stage; perform.

ch'usŏk 추석 Harvest Moon Day[Festival].

ch'usu 추수 harvest. *ch'usuhada* 추수하다 harvest.

ch'uwi 추위 cold; coldness *shimhan ch'uwi* 심한 추위 intense[bitter] cold.

ch'waryŏng 촬영 photographing. *ch'waryŏnghada* 촬영하다 take a photo(graph).

ch'wihada 취하다 get drunk; become intoxicated [tipsy]; feel high.

ch'wiim 취임 inauguration. *ch'wiimhada* 취임하다 take[assume] office.

ch'wiip 취입. *ch'wiip'ada* 취입하다 put (a song) on a record; make a record (of).

ch'wijik 취직. *ch'wijik'ada* 취직하다 find[get] employment; get a job[position].

ch'wiju 취주. *ch'wijuak* 취주악 wind-instrument music. *ch'wijuaktae* 취주악대 brass band.

ch'wimi 취미 taste; hobby. *ch'wimi saenghwal* 취미 생활 dilettante life.

ch'wisa 취사 cooking. *ch'wisa tangbŏn* 취사 당번 cook's duty. *ch'wisa togu* 취사 도구 cooking utensils.

ch'wiso 취소 cancellation; withdrawal. *ch'wisohada* 취소하다 cancel; withdraw.

ch'yŏdaboda 쳐다보다 look up; stare[gaze] (at).

❈ E ❈

ege 에게 to; for; with; from.

en-ganhada 엔간하다 (be) proper; suitable; be considerable; passable.

enuri 에누리 ① overcharge; two prices ② discount; reduction.

esŏ 에서 ① at; in. ② from; out of.

ewossada 에워싸다 surround; enclose; encircle.

❈ H ❈

habok 하복 summer clothes[wear, uniform]; summer suit.

hach'a 하차. *hach'ahada* 하차하다 leave[get off] (the car); alight from.

hada 하다 do; act; try; play; practice.

hadŭng 하등. *hadŭngŭi* 하등의 low; inferior; vulgar. *hadŭngp'um* 하등품 inferior article.

hae 해 sun. *haega ttŭda[chida]* 해가 뜨다[지다] sun rises[sets].

hae 해 year. *chinanhae* 지난해 last year. *haemada* 해마다 every year.

hae 해 injury; harm; damage. *haerŭl chuda* 해를 주다 do harm (to). *haerŭl ipta* 해를 입다 suffer damage.

haean 해안 seashore; coast; seaside.

haebang 해방 liberation; release. *haebanghada* 해방하다 liberate; release.

haebu 해부 anatomy. *haebuhada* 해부하다 dissect.

haebyŏn 해변 beach; seashore; coast.

haebyŏng 해병 marine. *haebyŏngdae* 해병대 marine corps.

haech'o 해초 seaweeds; sea plants; algae.

haego 해고 discharge; dismissal. *haegohada* 해고하다 dismiss; discharge; fire.

haegyŏl 해결 solution. *haegyŏrhada* 해결하다 solve.

haegun 해군 navy. *haegunŭi* 해군의 naval; navy.

haehak 해학 joke; jest; humo(u)r. *haehakchŏgin* 해학적인 humorous; witty.

haehyŏp 해협 straits; channel.

haeje 해제. *haejehada* 해제하다 cancel; release; remove. *mujang haeje* 무장 해제 disarm.

haejŏ 해저 bottom of the sea; sea bottom.

haejŏk 해적 pirate. *haejŏkp'an* 해적판 pirate edition. *hajŏksŏn* 해적선 pirate ship.

haek 핵 nucleus. *haengmugi* 핵무기 nuclear weapons. *haek shirhŏm* 핵실험 nuclear test. *haekchŏnjaeng*

핵전쟁 nuclear war.

haemyŏn 해면 sponge.

haengbang 행방 one's whereabouts. *haengbangŭl kamch'uda* 행방을 감추다 disappear.

haengbok 행복 happiness; welfare. *haengbok'an* 행복한 happy; blessed; fortunate. *haengbok'age* 행복하게 happily.

haengdong 행동 action; conduct; deed. *haengdong-hada* 행동하다 act.

haenghada 행하다 act; do; carry out; practice.

haengjin 행진 march; parade. *haengjinhada* 행진하다 march; parade; proceed.

haengjŏng 행정 administration. *haengjŏng kwar-ch'ŏng* 행정 관청 government office.

haengnyŏl 행렬 procession; parade; queue. *kajang haengnyŏl* 가장 행렬 fancy parade.

haengsang 행상 peddling. *haengsangin* 행상인 peddler.

haengun 행운 good fortune; good luck. *haengunŭi* 행운의 fortunate; lucky.

haengwi 행위 act; action; deed. *pulpŏp haengui* 불법 행위 illegal[unlawful] act.

haenyŏ 해녀 woman diver.

haeoe 해외. *haeoeŭi* 해외의 oversea(s); foreign. *haeoee* 해외에 abroad; overseas.

haeŏjida 해어지다 wear[be worn] out; get tattered.

haepssal 햅쌀 new rice; the year's new crop of rice.

haeropta 해롭다 (be) injurious; harmful; bad.

haesanmul 해산물 marine products.

haesŏk 해석 interpretation; explanation. *haesŏk'ada* 해석하다 interpret; explain.

haesu 해수 sea[salt] water. *haesuyok* 해수욕 sea-bathing. *haesuyokchang* 해수욕장 bathing resort.

haetpit 햇빛 sunshine; sunlight.

haetpyŏt 햇볕 sunbeams; heat of the sunlight.

haeyak 해약 cancellation of a contract. *haeyak'a-da* 해약하다 cancel[break] a contract.

hagi 하기 summer (time). *hagi panghak* 하기 방학 summer vacation. →**hagye** 하계.

hagŭp 하급 lower[low] class. *hagŭpsaeng* 하급생 lower class student.

hajik 하직 leave-taking; a farewell.

hak 학 crane; stork.

hakcha 학자 scholar; learned man.

hakchang 학장 dean; rector; president.

hakchil 학질 malaria. *hakchire kŏllida* 학질에 걸리다 be infected with malaria.

hakki 학기 (school) term; semester (*Am.*).

hakkwa 학과 subject of study. *hakkwa shihŏm* 학과 시험 achievement test.

hakkye 학계 learned circles; academic world.

hakkyo 학교 school; college. *hakkyo-e tanida* 학교에 다니다 attend[go to] school.

hakpŏl 학벌 academic clique.

hakpuhyŏng 학부형 parents of students.

hakpyŏng 학병 student soldier.

haksaeng 학생 student. *haksaeng shijŏl* 학생 시절 school days.

haktae 학대 ill-treatment; maltreatment. *haktae-hada* 학대하다 ill-treat; maltreat.

halk'wida 할퀴다 scratch; claw.

hallan-gye 한란계 thermometer; mercury. → **ondo-gye** 온도계.

halmŏni 할머니 ① grandmother; grandma; granny

② old lady[woman].

halt'a 핥다 lick; lap.

haltang 할당 assignment; allotment. *haltanghada* 할당하다 assign; allot; divide.

hamburo 함부로 at random; indiscriminately; without reason.

hamjŏng 함정 pitfall; pit; trap. *hamjŏnge ppajida* 함정에 빠지다 fall in a pit.

hamkke 함께 together (with, along); in company with.

hamnyang 함량 content. *alk'ol hamnyang* 알콜 함량 alcohol content.

hamsŏk 함석 zinc; galvanized iron.

hamul 하물 luggage (*Eng.*); baggage (*Am.*).

han 한 ① one; a. *han saram* 한 사람 one man. *han madi* 한 마디 one word ② about; nearly; some.

hana 하나 one. *hanaŭi* 하나의 one; a.

hanbamchung 한밤중 midnight; the middle of the night.

hanbok 한복 Korean clothes.

hanbŏn 한번 once; one time. *tan hanbon* 단 한번 only once. *hanbŏne* 한번에 at a time. *hanbŏn tŏ* 한번 더 once more.

hancha 한자 Chinese character.

hanch'ang 한창 height; peak; bloom. *hanch'ang-ida* 한창이다 be at its height.

handu 한두 one or two; couple. *handu saram* 한두 사람 one or two persons. *handu pŏn* 한두 번 once or twice.

han-gaji 한가지 ① a kind[sort] of ② the same.

hangbok 항복 surrender. *hangbok'ada* 항복하다 surrender; submit.

hanggong 항공 aviation; flight. *hanggong up'yŏn* 항공 우편 airmail.

hanggu 항구 port; harbor.

hanghae 항해 voyage; navigation. *hanghaehada* 항해하다 navigate; sail for.

han-gil 한길 main street[road]; thoroughfare; highway.

hangmun 학문 learning; study. *hangmuni innŭn* 학문이 있는 educated.

hangno 항로 sea route; course; line.

hangnyŏk 학력 school career; academic background.

hangnyŏn 학년 school year; grade (*Am.*); form (*Eng.*).

hangsang 항상 always; at all times; usually.

hangŭi 항의 protest; objection. *hangŭihada* 항의 하다 make a protest; object to.

Han-guk 한국 Korea; Republic of Korea (R. O. K.).

han-gŭl 한글 Korean alphabet; *han-gŭl*.

han-gye 한계 limits; bounds. *han-gyerŭl nŏmta* 한 계를 넘다 pass[exceed] the limit.

hanhwa 한화 Korean money[currency].

hanil 한일. *hanirŭi* 한일의 Korean-Japanese. *hanil hoedam* 한일 회담 Korean-Japanese Conference.

hankkŏbŏne 한꺼번에 at a time; at once; at a clip.

hanmi 한미 Korea and America. *hanmiŭi* 한미의 Korean-American.

han ssang 한 쌍 pair; couple. *han ssangŭi* 한 쌍의 a pair[couple] of.

hansum 한숨 (heavy) sigh. *hansum shwida* 한숨 쉬 다 (heave[draw] a) sigh.

hant'ŏk 한턱 treat; entertainment. *hant'ŏk naeda* 한턱 내다 give a treat.

hanttae 한때 ① a short time[while]; for a time ② once; (at) one time.

hanŭl 하늘 sky; air; heaven.

hanŭnim 하느님 (Lord of) Heaven; God.

hanyak 한약 Chinese[herb] medicine. *hanyakpang* 한약방 herb shop.

hanyŏng 한영. *hanyŏngŭi* 한영의 Korean-English. *hanyŏng sajŏn* 한영 사전 Korean-English dictionary.

hao 하오 afternoon. →**ohu** 오후.

hapch'ang 합창 chorus. *hapch'anghada* 합창하다 sing together[in chorus]. *hapch'angdan[dae]* 합창단[대] chorus.

hapch'ida 합치다 ① put together; joint together; unite; combine ② sum up.

hapchu 합주 concert; ensemble. *i[sam]bu hapchu* 2[3]부 합주 duet[trio].

hapkye 합계 total; sum total. *hapkyehada* 합계하다 sum[add] up.

hapkyŏk 합격. *hapkyŏk'ada* 합격하다 pass; be successful; be accepted.

hapsuk 합숙. *hapsuk'ada* 합숙하다 lodge together. *hapsuk hullyŏn* 합숙 훈련 camp training.

hapsŭng 합승. *hapsŭnghada* 합승하다 ride together. *hapsŭng t'aekshi* 합승 택시 jitney (cab).

hap'um 하품 yawn; gape. *hap'umhada* 하품하다 yawn; gape.

harabŏji 할아버지 ① grandfather; grandpa ② old man.

harin 할인 discount; deduction. *harinhada* 할인하다 discount; reduce.

haru 하루 a[one] day. *haru chongil* 하루 종일

all day long.

haruach'im 하루아침 one morning. *haruach'ime* 하루아침에 in a day; all of a sudden.

harubappi 하루바삐 as soon as possible.

harutpam 하룻밤 one [a] night. *harutpam saie* 하룻밤 사이에 in a single night.

hasagwan 하사관 noncommissioned[petty] officer.

hasoyŏn 하소연 appeal; petition. *hasoyŏnhada* 하소연하다 appeal to; complain of.

hasuk 하숙 lodging; boarding. *hasuk'ada* 하숙하다 lodge; board; room (*Am.*). *hasukchip* 하숙집 lodging[boarding. rooming (*Am.*)] house.

hayat'a 하얗다 (be) pure white; snow white.

hearida 헤아리다 ① fathom; conjecture ② count; calculate.

hech'ida 헤치다 push aside; make one's way (through).

hemaeda 헤매다 wander[roam] about; rove.

heŏjida 헤어지다 part from; separate; part company (with).

heŏm 헤엄 swimming; swim. *heŏmch'ida* 헤엄치다 swim.

him 힘 ① strength; force; might ② power; energy.

himch'ada 힘차다 (be) powerful; forceful. *himch'age* 힘차게 powerfully; strongly.

himchul 힘줄 ① muscle; sinew ② fiber; string.

himdŭlda 힘들다 (be) tough; laborious; toilsome.

himkkŏt 힘껏 with all one's might[strength].

himseda 힘세다 (be) strong; mighty; powerful.

himssŭda 힘쓰다 ① exert oneself; make efforts ② be industrious; be diligent (in).

hobak 호박 pumpkin; squash.

hobak 호박 amber. *hobaksaegŭi* 호박색의 amber-colored.

hodu 호두 walnut.

hoe 회 sliced[slices of] raw fish.

hoebi 회비 (membership) fee; dues.

hoebok 회복 recovery; restoration. *hoebok'ada* 회복하다 restore; recover; get better.

hoech'ori 회초리 switch; whip; lash.

hoedam 회담 talk; conversation. *hoedamhada* 회담하다 have a talk; interview.

hoedap 회답 reply; answer. *hoedap'ada* 회답하다 reply; answer.

hoegap 회갑 one's 60th birthday anniversary.

hoego 회고 reflection; recollection. *hoegohada* 회고하다 look back; recollect.

hoegye 회계 account(ing); finance. *hoegyehada* 회계하다 account; count.

hoehap 회합 meeting; gathering. *hoehap'ada* 회합하다 meet; assemble.

hoehwa 회화 conversation; talk; dialogue. *hoehwahada* 회화하다 converse[talk] (with). *Yŏngŏ hoehwa* 영어 회화 English conversation.

hoehwa 회화 →**kŭrim** 그림.

hoejang 회장 president; chairman.

hoejang 회장 place of meeting.

hoejŏn 회전 revolution; rotation. *hoejŏnhada* 회전하다 revolve; rotate.

hoejung 회중 one's pocket. *hoejung shigye* 회중 시계 watch. *hoejung chŏndŭng* 회중 전등 flashlight.

hoengdan 횡단. *hoengdanhada* 횡단하다 cross; run across. *hoengdan podo* 횡단 보도 pedestrian crossing; crosswalk (*Am.*).

hoeram 회람. *hoeramhada* 회람하다 circulate.

hoesa 회사 company; corporation; firm. *hoesawŏn* 회사원 company employee; office worker.

hoesukwŏn 회수권 commutation ticket(*Am.*); book of tickets (*Eng.*).

hoeŭi 회의 meeting; conference. *hoeŭihada* 회의하다 confer (with); hold a conference.

hoewon 회원 member(of a society). *hoewoni toeda* 회원이 되다 become a member.

hŏga 허가 permission; approval. *hŏgahada* 허가하다 permit; allow; approve.

hogak 호각 whistle.

hogishim 호기심 curiosity. *hogishimi kanghan* 호기심이 강한 curious; inquisitive.

hohŭp 호흡 breath; breathing. *hohŭp'ada* 호흡하다 breathe.

hohwa 호화. *hohwasŭrŏun* 호화스러운 splendid; luxurious. *hohwap'an* 호화판 de luxe edition.

hojŏk 호적 (census) register. *hojŏk tŭng[ch'o]bon* 호적 등[초]본 copy[abstract] of one's family register.

hojumŏni 호주머니 pocket.

hok 혹 wen; lump; bump.

hoekkijŏk 획기적 epoch-making; epochal.

hŏlda 헐다 destroy; demolish; pull down.

hollan 혼란 confusion; disorder. *hollanhada* 혼란하다 be confused.

holsu 홀수 odd number.

hom 홈 groove. *homŭl p'ada* 홈을 파다 hollow out [cut] a groove.

homi 호미 weeding hoe.

hŏmurŏjida 허물어지다 collapse; fall[break] down;

crumble.

hon 혼 soul; spirit.

hŏn 헌 old; shabby; worn-out; secondhand. *hŏn ot* 헌 옷 old clothes. *hŏn ch'aek* 헌 책 secondhand book.

honhap 혼합. *honhap'ada* 혼합하다 mix; mingle; compound.

hŏnbyŏng 헌병 military police (M. P.).

hondong 혼동. *hondonghada* 혼동하다 confuse; mix up.

hongbaek 홍백 red and white. *hongbaekchŏn* 홍백전 contest between red and white teams.

hongbo 홍보 public information. *hongbo hwaltong* 홍보 활동 information activities.

hongch'a 홍차 black tea.

hongsaek 홍색 red; red color.

hongsu 홍수 flood. *hongsuga nada* 홍수가 나다 have a flood.

honhyŏl 혼혈 mixed blood[breed]. *honhyŏra* 혼혈아 a half-breed; interracial child.

hŏnhyŏl 헌혈 donation of blood. *hŏnhyŏrhada* 헌혈하다 donate blood.

honja 혼자 alone; by oneself; for oneself. *honja salda* 혼자 살다 live alone.

honjap 혼잡 confusion; disorder. *honjap'an* 혼잡한 confused; congested.

honnada 혼나다 ① get frightened; become startled ② have bitter experiences.

hŏnpŏp 헌법 constitution.

hooe 호외 extra (edition).

hoŏn 호언 big[tall] talk. *hoŏn changdamhada* 호언장담하다 talk big; boast.

horabi 홀아비 widower.

hŏrak 허락 consent; assent; permission. *hŏrak'ada* 허락하다 consent to; permit.

horangi 호랑이 tiger; tigress.

hŏri 허리 waist; loins; hip. *hŏritti* 허리띠 belt; sash; band.

horihorihada 호리호리하다 (be) (tall and) slender; slim.

horŏmi 홀어미 widow. →**kwabu** 과부.

horyŏng 호령 command; order. *horyŏnghada* 호령하다 order; command.

hŏse 허세 bluff; (false) show of power〔influence〕.

hoso 호소 appeal; petition; complaint. *hosohada* 호소하다 appeal (to).

hŏssori 헛소리. *hŏssorihada* 헛소리하다 talk in delirium; talk nonsense.

hŏssugo 헛수고 vain effort; lost labor. *hŏssugohada* 헛수고하다 make vain efforts.

hŏsuabi 허수아비 ① scarecrow ② dummy; puppet.

hŏtkan 헛간 barn; open shed.

hoŭi 호의 goodwill; good wishes. *hoŭijŏgin* 호의적인 kind; warm-hearted.

howi 호위 guard; escort. *howihada* 호위하다 guard; escort. *howibyŏng* 호위병 (body)guard.

hoyŏlcha 호열자 cholera.

hŏyŏng 허영 vanity. *hŏyŏngshim* 허영심 (sense of) vanity.

hu 후 after; afterward(s); later. *kŭ hu* 그 후 after that; since then.

hubae 후배 one's junior. *hakkyo hubae* 학교 후배 one's junior in school.

huban 후반 latter〔second〕half. *hubanjŏn* 후반전

second half of the game
hubang 후방 rear. *hubangŭi* 후방의 rear; back; backward. *hubange* 후방에 in[at] the rear. *hubangŭro* 후방으로 rearward; backward.
hubida 후비다 scoop[scrape, dig] out; pick
hubo 후보 candidate. *hubo sŏnsu* 후보 선수 substitute.
huch'u 후추 black pepper. *huch'urŭl ch'ida* 후추를 치다 sprinkle pepper.
hudŭlgŏrida 후들거리다 tremble; shake; shiver.
hŭgin 흑인 Negro; colored person; nigger. *hŭginjong* 흑인종 black race.
huhoe 후회 repentance; regret. *huhoehada* 후회하다 repent of; regret.
hŭida 희다 (be) white; fair.
hŭigok 희곡 drama; play.
hŭigŭk 희극 comedy. *hŭigŭkchŏk* 희극적 comic(al).
huil 후일 later days; some (other) day; (the) future.
hŭimang 희망 hope; wish; desire. *hŭimanghada* 희망하다 hope (for); wish; desire.
hŭimi 희미. *hŭimihan* 희미한 faint; dim; vague. *hŭimihage* 희미하게 faintly; dimly.
hŭinjawi 흰자위 ① white of the eye ② white of an egg.
hŭisaeng 희생 sacrifice; victim. *hŭisaenghada* 희생하다 sacrifice. *hŭisaengjŏgin* 희생적인 sacrificial.
huja 후자 the latter; the other one.
hujin 후진. *hujinŭi* 후진의 backward; underdeveloped. *hujin-guk* 후진국 backward[underdeveloped] nation.

hŭk 흙 earth; soil; ground.

hŭkp'an 흑판 blackboard.

hŭkt'usŏngi 흙투성이. *hŭkt'usŏngiga toeda* 흙투성이가 되다 be covered with mud.

hŭlgida 흘기다 look askance; glare fiercely at.

hŭllida 흘리다 ① spill; drop; shed ② lose ③ take no notice (of).

hullyŏn 훈련 training; exercise. *hullyŏnhada* 훈련하다 train. *hullyŏnso* 훈련소 training school[center].

hullyunghada 훌륭하다 (be) fine; splendid. *hullyunghi* 훌륭히 nicely; splendidly.

hult'a 훑다 thresh; strip; hackle.

hŭm 흠 ① scar ② flaw; crack. *hŭmi innŭn* 흠이 있는 flawed; bruised.

humch'ida 훔치다 ① steal ② wipe (off).

hŭmut'ada 흐뭇하다 (be) pleasing; satisfied.

hŭndŭlda 흔들다 shake; wave; swing; rock.

hŭngbun 흥분 excitement. *hŭngbunhada* 흥분하다 be excited; become warm.

hŭngmi 흥미 interest; zest. *hŭngmi innŭn* 흥미 있는 (be) interesting.

hŭngŏlgŏrida 흥얼거리다 hum; croon; sing to oneself.

hŭngshinso 흥신소 inquiry agency; credit bureau.

hunjang 훈장 decoration; order; medal.

hunnal 훗날 later days; some (other) day. *hunnare* 훗날에 some (other) day; in (the) future.

hŭnŭkkida 흐느끼다 sob; whimper; weep softly.

hŭpsa 흡사. *hŭpsahada* 흡사하다 resemble closely; (be) exactly alike.

hŭpsu 흡수 absorption. *hŭpsuhada* 흡수하다 absorb; suck in.

hŭrida 흐리다 ① (be) cloudy; overcast ② (be) vague; dim; faint.

hŭrŭda 흐르다 flow; stream; run (down).

huryŏnhada 후련하다 feel refreshed[unburdened].

husaeng 후생 public[social] welfare. *husaeng saŏp* 후생 사업 welfare work.

huson 후손 descendants; posterity; offspring.

hut'oe 후퇴 retreat. *hut'oehada* 후퇴하다 retrograde; recede; retreat.

hŭt'ŏjida 흩어지다 be scattered; be dispersed.

huwi 후위 back player; rear guard.

huwŏn 후원 support; backing; patronage. *huwŏnhada* 후원하다 support; back (up).

hwa 화 disaster; calamity. *hwarŭl ipta* 화를 입다 meet with a calamity.

hwabo 화보 pictorial; graphic; illustrated magazine [news].

hwabun 화분 flowerpot.

hwabyŏng 화병 (flower) vase.

hwach'o 화초 flower; flowering plant. *hwach'o chaebae* 화초 재배 floriculture.

hwadan 화단 flower bed; flower garden.

hwae 홰 perch.

hwaetpul 횃불 torchlight; torch.

hwaga 화가 painter; artist.

hwagin 확인 confirmation; affirmation. *hwaginhada* 확인하다 confirm; affirm.

hwagyo 화교 Chinese residents abroad.

hwahae 화해 reconciliation; compromise. *hwahaehada* 화해하다 compromise with; make peace with.

hwahak 화학 chemistry. *hwahagŭi* 화학의 chemical. *hwahak yakp'um* 화학 약품 chemicals.

hwahwan 화환 wreath; garland; lei.

hwajae 화재 fire; conflagration. *hwajae kyŏngbogi* 화재 경보기 fire alarm.

hwajang 화장 toilet; make up. *hwajanghada* 화장하다 make one's toilet; make up one's face.

hwajang 화장 cremation. *hwajanghada* 화장하다 cremate; burn to ashes.

hwaje 화제 subject[topic, theme] of conversation.

hwakchang 확장 extension; expansion. *hwakchanghada* 확장하다 extend; enlarge; widen.

hwakchŏng 확정 decision; settlement. *hwakchŏnghada* 확정하다 decide; confirm; fix.

hwaktae 확대 magnification; enlargement. *hwaktaehada* 확대하다 magnify; expand; spread.

hwakshil 확실. *hwakshirhan* 확실한 sure; certain. *hwakshirhi* 확실히 certainly; surely.

hwakshin 확신 conviction; firm belief. *hwakshinhada* 확신하다 be convinced of; be sure of.

hwaksŏnggi 확성기 loudspeaker; megaphone.

hwal 활 bow. *hwarŭl ssoda* 활을 쏘다 shoot an arrow.

hwalbal 활발. *hwalbarhan* 활발한 active; brisk; vigorous ; lively. *hwalbarhi* 활발히 briskly; actively.

hwalcha 활자 type; printing type.

hwalch'ok 활촉 arrowhead.

hwalchuro 활주로 runway; landing strip.

hwalgi 활기 vigor; life; activity. *hwalgi innŭn* 활기 있는 active; lively.

hwaltong 활동 activity; action. *hwaltongjŏgin* 활동적인 active; dynamic. *hwaltongga* 활동가 man of action.

hwamul 화물 goods; freight (*Am.*); cargo. *hwamul-sŏn* 화물선 cargo boat. *hwamul chadongch'a* 화물자동차 truck.

hwan 환 (note of) exchange; check; money order.

hwanaeda 화내다 get angry (at, with); loose one's temper.

hwandŭng 환등 film slide; magic lantern.

hwanggŭm 황금 gold. *hwanggŭmŭi* 황금의 gold; golden.

hwan-gi 환기 ventilation. *hwan-gihada* 환기하다 ventilate. *hwan-git'ong* 환기통 ventilator.

hwangje 황제 emperor.

hwangnip 확립 establishment. *hwangnip'ada* 확립하다 establish.

hwangsaek 황색 yellow; yellow color. *hwangsaek injong* 황색 인종 yellow race.

hwangt'aeja 황태자 Crown Prince.

hwangya 황야 wilderness; desert land.

hwan-gyŏng 환경 environment; circumstance. *hwan-gyŏng oyŏm* 환경 오염 environmental pollution.

hwanhada 환하다 (be) bright; light. *hwanhan pang* 환한 방 well-lighted room.

hwanja 환자 patient; case. *k'ollera hwanja* 콜레라 환자 cholera patient[case].

hwanmyŏl 환멸 disillusion. *hwanmyŏrŭl nŭkkida* 환멸을 느끼다 be disillusioned.

hwansang 환상 illusion; vision. *hwansanggok* 환상곡 fantasy; fantasia.

hwansong 환송 farewell; send-off. *hwansonghada* 환송하다 give (a person) a hearty send-off. *hwansonghoe* 환송회 farewell party.

hwanyak 환약 pill; globule.

hwanyŏng 환영 welcome. *hwanyŏnghada* 환영하다 welcome; receive warmly. *hwanyŏnghoe* 환영회 reception.

hwanyul 환율 exchange rate. *hwanyul insang* 환율 인상 raise in exchange rates.

hwap'ye 화폐 money; currency; coinage.

hwaro 화로 brazier; fire pot.

hwasal 화살 arrow. *hwasalt'ong* 화살통 quiver. *hwasalpy'o* 화살표 arrow.

hwasan 화산 volcano.

hwasang 화상 burn; scald. *hwasangŭl ipta* 화상을 입다 get burned[scalded].

hwashil 화실 studio; *atelier.*

hwasŏng 화성 Mars. *hwasŏngin* 화성인 Martian.

hwassi 화씨 Fahrenheit. *hwassi hallan-gye* 화씨 한란계 Fahrenheit thermometer.

hwat'u 화투 Korean playing cards; "flower cards".

hwawon 화원 flower garden.

hwayak 화약 (gun) powder. *hwayakko* 화약고 powder magazine.

hwayoil 화요일 Tuesday (Tues.).

hwibal 휘발. *hwiballyu* 휘발유 gasoline; volatile oil.

hwida 휘다 bend; curve; warp; be bent.

hwidurŭda 휘두르다 brandish; flourish; throw a-bout. *p'arŭl hwidurŭda* 팔을 휘두르다 flourish one's arms.

hwigamta 휘감다 wind around; tie[fasten] round.

hwijang 휘장 badge; insignia.

hwijŏtta 휘젓다 stir (up); churn; beat up.

hwinallida 휘날리다 flap; fly; flutter; wave.

hwip'aram 휘파람 whistle. *hwip'aram pulda* 휘파

람 불다 (give a) whistle.

hwipssŭlda 휩쓸다 ① sweep (away, up, off) ② overrun.

hwŏlssin 훨씬 by far; very much; greatly.

hyanggi 향기 fragrance; perfume; scent; sweet odor. *hyanggiropta* 향기롭다 (be) fragrant; sweet-smelling.

hyangnak 향락 enjoyment; pleasure. *hyangnak saenghwal* 향락 생활 gay life.

hyangno 향로 incense burner.

hyangnyo 향료 ① spice; spicery ② perfume; aromatic.

hyangsang 향상 elevation; improvement. *hyangsanghada* 향상하다 rise; be elevated; improve.

hyangsu 향수 perfume; scent.

hyangt'o 향토 one's native place. *hyangt'osaek* 향토색 local colo(u)r.

hyet'aek 혜택 favo(u)r; benefit; benevolence. *munmyŏngŭi hyet'aek* 문명의 혜택 benefit of civilization.

hyŏ 혀 tongue. *hyŏrŭl naemilda* 혀를 내밀다 put out one's tongue.

hyokwa 효과 effect; efficacy. *hyokwa innŭn* 효과 있는 effective.

hyŏlgwan 혈관 blood vessel.

hyŏlsŏ 혈서. *hyŏlsŏrŭl ssŭda* 혈서를 쓰다 write in blood.

hyŏlt'ong 혈통 blood; lineage; pedigree.

hyŏmnyŏk 협력 cooperation. *hyŏmnyŏk'ada* 협력하다 cooperate with; work together.

hyŏmŭi 혐의 suspicion; charge. *hyŏmŭiro* 혐의로 on the suspicion of. *hyŏmŭija* 혐의자 suspect.

hyŏnak 현악 string music. *hyŏnakki* 현악기 stringed instrument.

hyŏnch'ungil 현충일 the Memorial Day.

hyŏndae 현대 present age[day]; modern times; today. *hyŏndaeŭi* 현대의 current; modern. *hyŏndaehwa* 현대화 modernization.

hyŏngbŏl 형벌 punishment; penalty.

hyŏngbu 형부 brother-in-law; husband of one's[a girl's] elder sister.

hyŏnggwang 형광. *hyŏnggwangdŭng[p'an]* 형광등 [판] fluorescent lamp[plate].

hyŏngje 형제 brothers; sisters. *hyŏngje chamae* 형제 자매 brothers and sisters.

hyŏngmuso 형무소 prison; jail. →**kyodoso** 교도소.

hyŏngmyŏng 혁명 revolution. *hyŏngmyŏngjŏgin* 혁명적인 revolutionary.

hyŏngp'yŏn 형편 situation; condition; circumstance.

hyŏngsa 형사 (police) detective.

hyŏngshik 형식 form; formality; mode. *hyŏngshikchŏgin* 형식적인 formal. *hyŏngshikchŏgŭro* 형식적으로 formally.

hyŏngsu 형수 sister-in law; elder brother's wife.

hyŏngt'ae 형태 form; shape.

hyŏn-gŭm 현금 cash; ready money. *hyŏn-gŭmŭro* 현금으로 in cash. *hyŏn-gum chibul* 현금 지불 cash payment.

hyŏn-gwan 현관 porch; entryway; entrance hall.

hyŏngyong 형용 description. *hyŏngyonghada* 형용 하다 describe; modify.

hyŏnjae 현재 the present time; now; at present. *hyŏnjaekkaji* 현재까지 up to now. *hyŏnjaeŭi* 현재의 present.

hyŏnjang 현장 spot; scene (of action). *hyŏnjang-esŏ* 현장에서 on the spot.

hyŏnmigyŏng 현미경 microscope.

hyŏnmyŏng 현명. *hyŏnmyŏnghan* 현명한 wise; sagacious; advisable.

hyŏnsang 현상 the present state[situation].

hyŏnsang 현상. *hyŏnsang mojip* 현상 모집 prize contest. *hyŏnsanggŭm* 현상금 prize money.

hyŏnshil 현실 actuality. *hyŏnshirŭi* 현실의 actual; real. *hyŏnshilchŏgŭro* 현실적으로 actually; really. *hyŏnshiljuŭi* 현실주의 realism.

hyŏnyŏk 현역 active service. *hyŏnyŏk kunin* 현역 군인 soldier on service.

hyŏpchugok 협주곡 concerto.

hyŏp'oe 협회 society; association. *kŏnch'uk hyŏp'oe* 건축 협회 building society.

hyŏppak 협박 threat; menace. *hyŏppak'ada* 협박하다 threaten; intimidate.

hyŏraek 혈액 blood. *hyŏraek kŏmsa* 혈액 검사 blood test. *hyŏraek ŭnhaeng* 혈액 은행 blood bank. *hyŏraek'yŏng* 혈액형 blood type.

hyŏrap 혈압 blood pressure. *ko[chŏ]hyŏrap* 고[저] 혈압 high[low] blood pressure.

hyudae 휴대. *hyudaehada* 휴대하다 carry; take with. *hyudaeyongŭi* 휴대용의 portable.

hyuga 휴가 holidays; vacation. *yŏrŭm hyuga* 여름 휴가 summer vacation.

hyuge 휴게 rest; recess. *hyuge shigan* 휴게 시간 recess. *hyugeshil* 휴게실 rest room; lounge.

hyuji 휴지 toilet paper; waste paper. *hyujit'ong* 휴지통 waste(paper) basket.

hyujŏn 휴전 truce; armistice. *hyujŏnsŏn* 휴전선

truce line. *hyujŏn hoedam* 휴전 회담 truce[ar-
mistice] talks.

hyung 흉 scar. *hyungi innŭn ŏlgul* 흉이 있는 얼굴
scarred face.

hyungak 흉악. *hyungak'an* 흉악한 wicked; atrocious.

hyungboda 흉보다 speak ill of; disparage.

hyungnae 흉내 imitation; mimicry. *hyungnaenaeda*
흉내내다 imitate; mimic.

hyuŏp 휴업 closing; suspension of business[trading].
hyuŏp'ada 휴업하다 close (office, factory).

hyushik 휴식 rest; repose; recess. *hyushik'ada* 휴
식하다 (take a) rest.

❧ Ⅰ ❧

i 이 this; present; current. *idal* 이달 this month.
i ch'aek 이 책 this book.

i 이, 2 two; the second.

i 이 tooth. *iŭi* 이의 dental. *iga ap'ŭda* 이가 아프
다 have a toothache.

ibal 이발 haircut(ting); hairdressing. *ibarhada* 이
발하다 have one's hair cut. *ibalso* 이발소 barber-
shop.

ibŏn 이번 this time; now. *ibŏnŭi* 이번의 new; present. *ibŏn iryoil* 이번 일요일 this coming Sunday.

ibu 이부 two parts; second part. *ibuje* 이부제 two
shift system.

ibul 이불 overquilt; quilt; coverlet.

ibwon 입원. *ibwŏnhada* 입원하다 enter[be sent to]
hospital.

ibyang 입양 adoption. *ibyanghada* 입양하다 adopt

(a son); affiliate.

ibyŏl 이별 parting; separation. *ibyŏrhada* 이별하다 part; separate.

ich'a 이차 second; secondary. *ich'a taejŏn* 이차 대전 Second World War; World War Ⅱ.

ich'i 이치 reason; principle. *ich'ie matta* 이치에 맞다 be reasonable.

ichŏm 이점 advantage; vantage point. .

ich'ŏrŏm 이처럼 thus; like this; in this way.

ich'ŭng 이층 second floor[story] (*Am.*); first floor [storey] (*Eng.*).

idal 이달 this month; the current month. *idal shiboire* 이달 15일에 on the 15th of this month.

idong 이동 transfer; movement. *idonghada* 이동하다 move; transfer.

idŭng 2등 second; second class [grade, prize, place].

idŭn(ji) 이든(지) whether ...or; either...or.

igach'i 이같이 like this; thus; in this way[manner].

igi 이기. *igijŏk* 이기적 selfish; egoistic. *igijuŭi* 이기주의 egoism.

igida 이기다 win; gain a victory; defeat.

igong 이공 science and engineering. *igong taehak* 이공 대학 science and engineering college.

igot 이곳 this place; here. *igose* 이곳에 here; in this place.

igŏt 이것 this; this one. *igŏsŭro* 이것으로 with this; now. *igŏt chom pwa* 이것 좀 봐 I say; Look here.

iha 이하. *ihaŭi* 이하의 less than; under; below.

ihae 이해 understanding; comprehension. *ihaehada* 이해하다 understand; comprehend.

ihae 이해 interests; advantages and disadvantages.

ihon 이혼 divorce. *ihonhada* 이혼하다 divorce.

ihu 이후 after this; from now on; hereafter. *kŭ ihu* 그 이후 since then; thereafter.

iik 이익 profit; gain. *iigi innŭn* 이익이 있는 profitable; paying.

iin 이인 two persons[men]. *iinsŭng* 2인승 two-seater. *iinjo* 이인조 duo.

ija 이자 interest. *ijaga putta* 이자가 붙다 yield interest.

iji 이지 intellect; intelligence. *ijijŏk* 이지적 intellectual.

ijŏn 이전. *ijŏnŭi* 이전의 previous; former. *ijŏne* 이전에 before; formerly; once.

ijŏn 이전 removal; moving (*Am.*); transfer. *ijŏnhada* 이전하다 remove; transfer.

iju 이주 removal; migration. *ijuhada* 이주하다. move (*Am.*); remove (*Eng.*); migrate.

ijung 이중. *ijungŭi* 이중의 double; twofold; dual. *ijung kukchŏk* 이중 국적 dual nationality. *ijung-ju[ch'ang]* 이중주[창] duet.

ikki 이끼 moss. *ikki kkin* 이끼 낀 mossy; moss-grown.

ikkŭlda 이끌다 guide; conduct; lead; show[usher] in.

iksa 익사 drowning. *iksahada* 익사하다 be drowned (to death).

iksal 익살 joke; jest; humor. *iksal purida* 익살 부리다 crack jokes; jest; be funny.

iksuk'ada 익숙하다 (be) familiar; be skilled in; be at home in.

ikta 읽다 read; peruse. *chalmot ikta* 잘못 읽다

misread; read wrong. *ta ikta* 다 읽다 read through.

ikta 익다 ripen; mature; become[get] ripe. *igŭn* 익은 ripe; mellow.

il 일, 1 one, *cheil* 제일 the first.

il 일 work; task; labo(u)r. *irhada* 일하다 work.

ilban 일반. *ilbanŭi* 일반의 general; universal. *ilban-jŏgŭro* 일반적으로 generally; in general.

ilbang 일방 one side; one hand; one way. *ilbang t'onghaeng* 일방 통행 one-way traffic.

Ilbon 일본 Japan. *Ilbonŭi* 일본의 Japanese. *Ilbon-mal* 일본말 Japanese (language). *Ilbonin* 일본인 Japanese.

ilbŏn 일번 first; No. 1. *ilbŏnŭi* 1번의 first; top.

ilbu 일부 part; portion. *ilbuŭi* 일부의 partial; divisional.

ilburŏ 일부러 on purpose; intentionally; purposely.

ilcha 일자 →**naltcha** 날짜.

ilchari 일자리 job; position. *ilcharirŭl ŏtta* 일자리를 얻다 take[get] a job.

ilche 일제. *ilcheŭi* 일제의 of Japanese manufacture; made in Japan.

ilche 일제. *ilchehi* 일제히 altogether; in a chorus.

ilch'e 일체. ① all; everything. *ilch'eŭi* 일체의 all; every; whole. ② entirely; wholly; altogether. *ilch'e chungsaeng* 일체 중생 all living beings.

ilchi 일지 diary; journal →**ilgi** 일기.

ilch'i 일치 coincidence; agreement; consent. cooperation. *ilch'ihada* 일치하다 agree (with); accord (with); coincide (with); consent to; cooperate (with).

ilchik 일직 day duty; day watch. *ilchik'ada* 일직하다 be on day duty.

ilchŏn 일전 the other day; some time ago.
ilchong 일종 kind; sort; species. *ilchongŭi* 일종의 a kind[sort] of.
ilchŏng 일정 day's program(me)[schedule].
ilchŏng 일정. *ilchŏnghan* 일정한 fixed; definite; regular; settled.
ilchu 일주 round; tour. *ilchuhada* 일주하다 go [travel] round.
ilch'ŭng 일층 ① first floor (*Am.*); ground floor (*Eng.*) ② more; still more.
ilgan 일간 daily publication[issue].
ilgi 일기 weather. *ilgi yebo* 일기 예보 weather forecast[report].
ilgi 일기 diary; journal. *ilgijang* 일기장 diary.
ilgop 일곱 seven. *ilgoptchae* 일곱째 the seventh.
ilgŭp 일급 daily wages; day's wage.
ilgŭp 일급 first class. *ilgŭbŭi* 일급의 first-class.
ilgwa 일과 daily lesson[work]; (daily) routine.
ilgwang 일광 sunlight; sunshine. *ilgwangnyok* 일광욕 sun bath(ing).
ilkŏri 일거리 piece of work; task; things to do.
ilkun 일군 workman; worker; laborer; coolie.
illiri 일일이 one by one; in detail; everything.
illŏjuda 일러주다 let know; tell; notify; advise.
illu 일루 first base.
illyŏk 인력 gravitation; magnetism.
illyŏkkŏ 인력거 ricksha(w).
illyŏl 일렬 line; row; file. *illyŏllo* 일렬로 in a row [line]; in a file.
illyŏn 일년 a[one] year. *illyŏnŭi* 일년의 yearly; annual.
illyu 일류. *illyuŭi* 일류의 first-class[rate]; top-

ranking; leading.

illyu 인류 human race; mankind; human beings. *illyuŭi* 인류의 human; racial.

ilmak 일막 one act. *ilmakkŭk* 일막극 one-act play.

ilp'a 일파 school; party; sect.

ilp'um 일품. *ilp'um yori* 일품 요리 one-course dinner. *ch'ŏnha ilp'um* 천하 일품 article of peerless quality.

ilsaeng 일생 lifetime; one's(whole) life. *ilsaengŭi* 일생의 lifelong.

ilsang 일상 every day; daily; usually. *ilsangŭi* 일상의 daily; everyday.

ilsapyŏng 일사병 sunstroke; heatstroke.

ilshi 일시 at one time; for a time[while]. *ilshijŏk* 일시적 momentary; temporary.

ilshik 일식 solar eclipse; eclipse of the sun.

ilsŏn 일선 fighting line; front.

ilsu 일수 daily installment; day-to-day loan.

ilt'a 잃다 lose; miss; be deprived [bereft] of.

iltae 일대 whole area[district]; neighborhood (of).

iltae 일대 a[one] generation; one's lifetime. *iltaegi* 일대기 life story; biography.

iltan 일단 once (at least); for the moment; first.

iltang 일당 daily allowance[pay, wages]; day's wage; per diem (*Am.*). →**ilgŭp** 일급.

iltchigi 일찌기 early; once; formerly; one time.

iltŭng 일등 first class; first rank[grade]. *iltŭng-sang* 일등상 first prize.

ima 이마 forehead; brow.

imamttae 이맘때 about[around] this time; at this time[moment, point] of day[night, year].

imank'ŭm 이만큼 this[so] much[many, big, long];

to this extent.

imbu 임부 pregnant woman; woman with child.

imdae 임대. *imdaehada* 임대하다 lease[rent] out; hire out. *imdaeryo* 임대료 rent.

imgi 임기 term of service[office].

imgŏm 임검 official inspection. *imgŏmhada* 임검하다 visit and inspect.

imgŭm 임금 wages; pay. *imgŭm insang* 임금 인상 wage increase[raise].

imgŭm 임금 king; sovereign.

imi 이미 already; now; yet.

imin 이민 emigration; immigration. *iminhada* 이민하다 emigrate (to); immigrate (from).

imja 임자 owner; possessor; proprietor.

imji 임지 one's post; place of one's appointment.

imjil 임질 gonorrhea.

imjong 임종 hour of death; dying hour; one's deathbed.

immat 입맛 appetite; taste.

immatch'uda 입맞추다 kiss; give (a person) a kiss.

immu 임무 duty; task; mission. *chungdae immu* 중대 임무 important duty.

immun 입문 introduction; guide; primer.

immyŏng 임명 appointment; nomination. *immyŏng- hada* 임명하다 appoint to; nominate.

imshi 임시. *imshiŭi* 임시의 temporary; provisional. *imshiro* 임시로 specially; temporarily.

imshin 임신 pregnancy; conception. *imshinhada* 임신하다 become[be] pregnant; conceive.

imŭi 임의. *imŭiŭi* 임의의 free; optional; voluntary. *imŭiro* 임의로 at will; as one pleases.

imyŏn 이면 the back; the reverse; the inside.

inbu 인부 labo(u)rer; coolie; hand.

inch'e 인체 human body; (human) flesh.

indo 인도. *indohada* 인도하다 deliver; turn[hand] over; transfer.

in-ga 인가 approval; authorization. *in-gahada* 인가하다 approve; authorize.

in-gam 인감 seal impression. *in-gam tojang* 인감 도장 one's registered seal.

in-gan 인간 human being; man. *in-ganŭi* 인간의 human; mortal.

ingŏ 잉어 carp.

in-gong 인공. *in-gongŭi*[*jŏk*] 인공의[적] artificial; unnatural. *in-gong wisŏng* 인공 위성 artificial satellite.

ingt'ae 잉태 conception; pregnancy. *ingt'aehada* 잉태하다 conceive. →**imshin** 임신.

in-gu 인구 population. *in-gu chosa* 인구 조사 census.

in-gye 인계. *in-gyehada* 인계하다 hand over; transfer.

inha 인하. *inhahada* 인하하다 pull[draw] down; lower. *imgŭm inha* 임금 인하 wage cut.

inhada 인하다 be due (to); be caused (by); be attributable (to).

inhyŏng 인형 doll. *inhyŏng kat'ŭn* 인형 같은 doll-like.

injang 인장 seal. →**tojang** 도장.

inji 인지 (paper) stamp. *suip inji* 수입 인지 revenue stamp.

injong 인종 (human) race. *injong ch'abyŏl* 인종 차별 racial discrimination.

injŏng 인정 recognition; acknowledgement. *injŏng-hada* 인정하다 recognize; acknowledge; approve.

injŏng 인정 humanness; sympathy; humanity.

inju 인주 red stamping ink.

inki 인기 popularity. *inki innŭn* 인기 있는 popular; favorite.

inkwon 인권 human rights; rights of man.

inkyŏk 인격 personality; character. *inkyŏkcha* 인격자 man of character.

inmul 인물 man; person. *k'ŭn inmul* 큰 인물 great man[figure].

ingmyŏng 익명 anonymity. *ingmyŏngŭi* 익명의 anonymous. *ingmyŏngŭro* 익명으로 anonymously.

innae 인내 patience; endurance. *innaehada* 인내하다 endure; be patient with.

inal 이날 ① today; this day ② that day; the (very) day.

inp'um 인품 personality; character.

insa 인사 greeting; salution; bow. *insahada* 인사하다 greet; salute; (make a) bow.

insaeng 인생 life; human[man's] life. *insaenggwan* 인생관 view of life.

insam 인삼 ginseng.

insang 인상 impression. *insangjŏgin* 인상적인 impressive. *ch'ŏdinsang* 첫인상 first impression.

inse 인세 royalty; stamp duty.

inshim 인심 man's minds; people's hearts. *inshimi chot'a* 인심이 좋다 be good-hearted.

insol 인솔. *insorhada* 인솔하다 lead. *insolcha* 인솔자 leader.

insu 인수. *insuhada* 인수하다 undertake; take charge of; accept.

inswae 인쇄 printing; print. *inswaehada* 인쇄하다 print. *inswaemul* 인쇄물 printed matter.

inwon 인원 number of persons[men]; staff; personnel.

inyang 인양 pulling up; salvage. *inyanghada* 인양하다 pull up; salvage.

inyŏm 이념 idea; ideology.

inyŏn 인연 affinity; connection; relation. *inyŏnŭl maetta* 인연을 맺다 form relations.

inyong 인용 quotation; citation. *inyonghada* 인용하다 quote; cite.

ioe 이외. *ioeŭi* 이외의 with the exception (of); except for. *ioee* 이외에 except; but; save.

iŏng 이엉 straw thatch.

ip 입 mouth. *ibŭl pŏllida[tamulda]* 입을 벌리다[다물다] open[shut] one's mouth.

ip 잎 leaf; foliage.

ipchang 입장 entrance; admission. *ipchanghada* 입장하다 enter; be admitted. *ipchangnyo* 입장료 admission fee. *ipchangkwon* 입장권 admission ticket.

ipch'e 입체 solid (body).

ipchu 입주. *ipchuhada* 입주하다 move in; live in.

ipchŭng 입증. *ipchŭnghada* 입증하다 prove; give proof; testify.

ipku 입구 entrance; way in. *ipkuesŏ* 입구에서 at the entrance[door].

ipkuk 입국 entrance into a country. *ipkuk'ada* 입국하다 enter a country. *ipkuk sachŭng* 입국 사증 entry visa. *ipkuk chŏlch'a* 입국 절차 formalities for entry.

ipkŭm 입금 receipts; receipt of money. *ipkŭmhada* 입금하다 receive (some money).

ipkwan 입관. *ipkwanhada* 입관하다 place in a

coffin.

ip'ak 입학 entrance. *ip'ak'ada* 입학하다 enter a school. *ip'ak shihŏm* 입학 시험 entrance examination.

ipch'al 입찰 tender (*Eng.*); bid (*Am.*). *ipch'arhada* 입찰하다 tender [bid] for.

ip'ida 입히다 ① dress; clothe; put on ② plate; coat; gild.

ip'oe 입회 admission; joining. *ip'oehada* 입회하다 join [enter]; become a member of.

ippŏrŭt 입버릇 way [habit] of saying; one's manner of speech.

ip'yŏn 이편 this side [way].

ipsa 입사. *ipsahada* 입사하다 enter [join] a company. *ipsa shihŏm* 입사 시험 employment examination.

ipsagwi 잎사귀 leaf; leaflet.

ipsang 입상 winning a prize. *ipsanghada* 입상하다 win [get] a prize.

ipshi 입시 entrance examination. →**ip'ak shihŏm** 입학 시험.

ipsŏn 입선. *ipsŏnhada* 입선하다 be accepted; be selected.

ipsongmal 입속말 murmur; mutter. *ipsongmarhada* 입속말하다 mutter; grumble; murmur.

ipsu 입수. *ipsuhada* 입수하다 receive; get; obtain.

ipsul 입술 lip. *win [araen] ipsul* 윗 [아랫] 입술 upper [lower] lip.

ipsŏn 입선. *ipsŏnhada* 입선하다 (be) accepted [select-[ed].

ipta 입다 ① put on; wear; be dressed in ② owe; be indebted to.

iptae 입대 enlistment. *iptaehada* 입대하다 join

[enter] the army.

iptam 입담 skill at talking; eloquence.

ip'ubo 입후보. *ip'ubohada* 입후보하다 stand for; run for. *ip'uboja* 입후보자 candidate.

irang 이랑 ridge and furrow.

ire 이레 the seventh day (of the month); seven days.

irhada 일하다 work; labor; do one's work.

irhaeng 일행 party; company; one's suite; troupe.

irhal 일할 ten percent; 10%.

irho 일호 number one; No. 1.

irhŭn 일흔 seventy; three score and ten.

irhwa 일화 anecdote; episode.

irhwa 일화 Japanese money.

iri 이리 wolf. *iritte* 이리떼 pack of wolves.

irijŏri 이리저리 this way and that; here and there; up and down.

irin 일인 one person. *irindang* 일인당 for each (person); per head.

irŏn 이런 such; like this; of this kind.

irŏk'e 이렇게 thus; like; this; in this way; so.

iron 이론 theory. *ironsang*[*jŏgŭro*] 이론상[적으로] *theoretically*; in theory.

irŏnada 일어나다 ① rise; get up; stand up; arise ② happen; occur; break out.

irŏnajŏrŏna 이러나저러나 at any rate; in any case; anyway; anyhow.

irŏsŏda 일어서다 stand up; rise (to one's feet); get up.

iru 이루 second base. *irusu* 이루수 second baseman.

iruda 이루다 accomplish; achieve; attain.

irŭda 이르다 ① (be) early; premature. *irŭn ach'im*

이른 아침 early morning ② arrive.

irŭk'ida 일으키다 ① raise[set] up ② wake up; awake ③ establish; found.

irŭm 이름 name; full name.

irŭnba 이른바 so-called; what is called.

irwi 일위 first[foremost] place; first rank; No. 1.

irwol 일월 January.

iryoil 일요일 Sunday. *taŭm*[*chinan*] *iryoire* 다음 [지난] 일요일에 next[last] Sunday.

iryŏk 이력 one's personal history; one's career[record]. *iryŏksŏ* 이력서 personal history.

iryong 일용 everyday[daily] use. *iryongp'um* 일 용품 daily necessities.

iryu 이류. *iryŭi* 이류의 second-class[rate]; minor; inferior. *iryu hot'el* 이류 호텔 second-class hotel.

isa 이사 removal; moving. *isahada* 이사하다 move.

isa 이사 director; trustee. *isahoe* 이사회 board of directors.

isam 이삼 two or three; few. *isamil* 이삼일 two or three[few] days.

isan 이산. *isanhada* 이산하다 be scattered; be dispersed. *isan kajok* 이산 가족 dispersed[separated] families. *isan kajok ch'atki undong* 이산 가족 찾기 운동 Campaign for reunion of dispersed family members.

isang 이상 strangeness; abnormality. *isangsŭrŏun* 이상스러운 odd; strange; queer.

isang 이상 ideal. *isangjŏg*(*ŭro*) 이상적 (으로) ideal-(ly). *isangjuŭi* 이상주의 idealism.

isang 이상 more than; over; above; beyond. *shimnyŏn isang* 십년 이상 more than 10 years.

isŏ 이서 endorsement. *isŏhada* 이서하다 endorse.

isŏng 이성 reason. *isŏngjŏgin* 이성적인 rational.
isŏng 이성 the other[opposite] sex.
issushigae 이쑤시개 toothpick.
isŭl 이슬 dew; dewdrops.
isŭlbi 이슬비 drizzle; mizzle; misty rain.
itchok 이쪽 this side[way]; our side.
itta 있다 ① be; there is [are]; exist ② stay; remain ③ stand; be situated; be located ④ consist
  (in); lie (in).
itta 잇다 join; put together; connect; link.
itta 잊다 ① forget; slip one's mind ② leave behind.
  ijŭl su ŏmnŭn 잊을 수 없는 unforgettable.
ittae 이때 (at) this time[moment]; then. *ittae-
  kkaji* 이때까지 until now; to this time.
ittagŭm 이따금 from time to time; now and then;
  at times.
it'ŭl 이틀 ① two days ② second day (of month).
it'ŭnnal 이튿날 next[following] day.
iut 이웃 neighbo(u)rhood. *iutchip* 이웃집 neighbo(u)r-
  ing house; next door.
iwol 이월 February.
iyagi 이야기 talk; conversation; chat. *iyagihada*
  이야기하다 speak; talk; have a chat.
iyŏk 이역 foreign[alien] country[land].
iyong 이용 use; utilization. *iyonghada* 이용하다
  make use of; utilize.
iyu 이유 reason; cause; motive; grounds; pretext;
  why. *iyu ŏpshi* 이유없이 without (good) reason.
  …ŭi iyuro …의 이유로 by reason of …. *iyurŭl
  mutta* 이유를 묻다 inquire into the reason of.
iyul 이율 (the rate of) interest.
iyun 이윤 profit; gain. →**iik** 이익.

K

ka, kajangjari 가, 가장자리 edge; verge; brink; margin.

ka- 가- temporary; provisional. *kagyeyak* 가계약 provisional contract.

-k(g)a -가 street; district. *oga* 5가 the fifth street.

kabal 가발 wig; false hair.

kabang 가방 bag; satchel; trunk; suitcase. *sonka-bang* 손가방 valise; handbag.

kabong 가봉 basting; fitting. *kabonghada* 가봉하다 baste; tack.

kabo 가보 family treasure; heirloom.

kabot 갑옷 suit[piece] of armor. *kabotkwa t'ugu* 갑옷과 투구 armor and helmet.

kabul 가불 advance; advance payment.

kabyŏpke 가볍게 lightly; slightly; rashly.

kabyŏpta 가볍다 (be)light; not heavy; not serious.

kach'i 가치 value; worth; merit. *kach'i innŭn* 가치 있는 valuable; worthy. *kach'i ŏmnŭn* 가치 없는 worthless; of no value.

kach'i 같이 ① like; as; likewise; similarly; in the same way; equally ② (along, together) with; in company with.

kach'ida 갇히다 be confined; be shut in (up); be kept indoors; be imprisoned.

kach'uk 가축 domestic cattle; livestock. *kach'uk pyŏngwon* 가축 병원 veterinary hospital; pet's hospital.

kach'ul 가출 disappearance from home. *kach'urhada* 가출하다 run away from home. *kach'ul sonyŏ*

가출 소녀 runaway girl.

kach'urok 가출옥 release on parole; provisional release.

kada 가다 go; proceed; visit.

kadong 가동 operation; work. *kadonghada* 가동하다 operate; run.

kadu 가두 street. *kadu yŏnsŏl* 가두 연설 wayside speech.

kaduda 가두다 shut in (up); lock in (up); confine; imprison.

kadŭk 가득 full *kadŭk ch'ada* 가득 차다 be full to the brim.

kae 개 dog; hound; puppy. *suk'ae* 수캐 male dog *amk'ae* 암캐 bitch.

kae 개 piece; unit. *pinu tasŏt kae* 비누 다섯 개 five pieces[cakes] of soap.

kaebal 개발 exploitation; reclamation; development. *kaebarhada* 개발하다 develop; exploit; improve.

kaebang 개방. *kaebanghada* 개방하다 (leave) open; throw open (a place) to the public.

kaebi 개비 piece (of split wood); stick. *sŏngnyang-kaebi* 성냥개비 matchstick.

kaebok susul 개복 수술 abdominal operation; celiotomy.

kaebong 개봉 (cinema) release. *kaebonghada* 개봉하다 release (a film).

kaech'al 개찰 examination of tickets. *kaech'arhada* 개찰하다 examine[punch] tickets. *kaech'algu* 개찰구 wicket; ticket gate.

kaech'oe 개최. *kaech'oehada* 개최하다 hold; have; open. *kaech'oeil* 개최일 the day fixed for a meeting; fixture. *kaech'oeji*[*changso*] 개최지[장소] site (of an exposition).

kaech'ŏk 개척 cultivation; reclamation; clearing; exploitation. *kaech'ŏk'ada* 개척하다 open up; bring (land) under cultivation; exploit.

kaech'ŏnjŏl 개천절 the National Foundation Day (of Korea); the Foundation Day of Korea.

kaeda 개다 fold (up); wrap up. *ibujarirŭl kaeda* 이부자리를 개다 fold up[turn down] the beddings[bedclothes].

kaeda 개다 knead (flour); mix up; work. *milkarurŭl kaeda* 밀가루를 개다 knead dough.

kaeda 개다 clear up; become clear. *Piga kaetta* 비가 갰다 The rain is over.

kaegak 개각 cabinet reshuffle; cabinet shake-up.

kaegan 개간 reclamation; land cleaning. *kaeganhada* 개간하다 clear (the land); reclaim.

kaegang 개강. *kaeganghada* 개강하다 open a course; begin a series of one's lecture.

kaegi 개기 total eclipse. *kaegi il*[*wol*]*shik* 개기 일 [월]식 total solar[lunar] eclipse.

kaegolch'ang 개골창 ditch; drain; gutter.

kaegujangi 개구장이 naughty boy; urchin.

kaeguri 개구리 frog. *shigyong kaeguri* 식용 개구리 edible frog; table frog.

kaegwan 개관 general survey[view]; outline. *kaegwanhada* 개관하다 survey; take a bird's-eye view of.

kaegyo 개교 opening of a school. *kaegyohada* 개교하다 open a school

kaehak 개학 beginning of school. *kaehak'ada* 개학하다 begin school; school begins.

kaehoe 개회. *kaehoehada* 개회하다 open a meeting; go into session. *kaehoesa* 개회사 opening address. *kaehoeshik* 개회식 opening ceremony.

kaehŏn 개헌 constitutional amendment[revision]. *kaehŏnhada* 개헌하다 revise a constitution.

kaehwa 개화 enlightenment; civilization. *kaehwahada* 개화하다 get civilized[enlightened]. *kaehwahan* 개화한 civilized; enlightened.

kaehyŏk 개혁 reform; innovation. *kaehyŏk'ada* 개혁하다 reform; innovate.

kaein 개인 individual; private person. *kaeinjŏk* 개인적 individual; private; personal.

kaeinjŏn 개인전 one-man show; private exhibition.

kaeinjuŭi 개인주의 individualism. *kaeinjuŭija* 개인주의자 individualist. *kaeinjuŭijŏgin* 개인주의적인 individualistic.

kaeip 개입 intervention; meddling. *kaeip'ada* 개입하다 intervene in; meddle in.

kaejashik 개자식 son-of-bitch.

kaejo 개조 remodeling; reconstruction; rebuilding. *kaejohada* 개조하다 remodel; reorganize; rebuild.

kaejŏm 개점 opening[establishment] of a shop [store]. *kaejŏmhada* 개점하다 open[start] a shop [store]; set up in business.

kaejŏng 개정 revision. *kaejŏnghada* 개정하다 revise. *kaejŏngp'an* 개정판 revised edition; revision.

kaejugŭm 개죽음 throwing away one's life. *kaejugŭmhada* 개죽음하다 die in vain; die to no purpose.

kaekch'a 객차 passenger car[train]; coach (*Am.*).

kaekchi 객지 strange[alien] land; one's staying place on a journey.

kaek'ida 개키다 fold (up). *ibujarirŭl kaek'ida* 이부자리를 개키다 fold up beddings.

kaekkwan 객관. *kaekkwanjŏk* 객관적 objective. *kaekkwanshik shihŏm* 객관식 시험 objective test.

kaekshil 객실 (*hotel*) guest room; (*boat*, *etc.*) passenger cabin.

kaeksŏk 객석 seat for a guest.

kaemak 개막 raising the curtain. *kaemak'ada* 개막하다 raise the curtain; commence[begin] the performance.

kaemi 개미 ant. *kaemitte* 개미떼 swarm of ants. *kaemit'ap* 개미탑 ant hill.

kaemŏri 개머리 gunstock; butt. *kaemŏrip'an* 개머리판 the butt of a rifle.

kaenari 개나리 golden forsythia.

kaeng 갱 pit; shaft. *kaengdo* 갱도 drift; gallery.

kaengji 갱지 pulp paper; rough paper.

kaengnyŏn-gi 갱년기 the turn[change] of (one's) life; climacteric.

kaengshin 갱신 renewal; renovation.

kaenyŏm 개념 concept; general idea; notion.

kaeŏp 개업 opening[commencement] of business [trade]. *kaeŏp'ada* 개업하다 open[start] business; begin business; (*lawyer*, *docter*) start[set up a] practice.

kaep'ittŏk 개피떡 rice-cake stuffed with bean jam.

kaep'yo 개표 ballot counting; official canvass of the votes (*Am.*). *kaep'yohada* 개표하다 count the ballots [votes]; make a canvass (*Am.*).

kaeron 개론 outline; introduction; survey; general remarks. *yŏngmunhak kaeron* 영문학 개론 an introduction to English literature.

kaeryak 개략 outline; summary; resume.
kaeryang 개량 improvement; reform. *kaeryanghada* 개량하다 improve; reform; (make) better.
kaesalgu 개살구 wild apricot.
kaeshi 개시 opening; beginning; start. *kaeshihada* 개시하다 begin; commence; open (game).
kaeshik 개식 the opening ceremony. *kaeshiksa* 개식 사 opening address[speech].
kaesŏn 개선 improvement; betterment. *kaesŏnhada* 개선하다 improve; amend; reform.
kaesŏng 개성 individuality; personality; individual character.
kaesunmul 개숫물 dishwater; slops.
kaesut'ong 개수통 dishpan; slop-basin.
kaet'an 개탄 deploring; lamentation; regret. *kaet'anhada* 개탄하다 deplore; lament. *kaet'anhal manhan* 개탄할 만한 deplorable; lamentable.
kaetka 갯가 shore of an estuary.
kaet'ong 개통. *kaet'onghada* 개통하다 be opened to [for] traffic; be installed. *kaet'ongshik* 개통식 opening ceremony.
kaettongbŏlle 개똥벌레 firefly; glowworm.
kaeul 개울 brook; rivulet; creek; streamlet.
kaeunhada 개운하다 feel refreshed[relieved, well].
kaeyo 개요 outline; summary; epitome.
kage 가게 shop; store (*Am.*). *kumŏng kage* 구멍 가게 penny candy store.
kago 각오 preparedness; resolution. *kagohada* 각오하다 be ready[prepared] for.
kagok 가곡 song; lied. *kakokchip* 가곡집 collection of songs.
kagong 가공 processing. *kagonghada* 가공하다 pro-

cess; work upon. *kagong shikp'um* 가공 식품 processed foodstuffs.

kagu 가구 furniture; upholstery. *kagujŏm*〔*sang*〕가구점〔상〕furniture store.

kagŭk 가극 opera; lyric drama. *kagŭktan* 가극단 opera company.

kagye 가계 housekeeping. *kagyebu* 가계부 housekeeping book.

kagyŏk 가격 price; cost. *tomae*〔*somae*〕*kagyŏk* 도매〔소매〕가격 wholesale〔retail〕price.

kahada 가하다 add (up); sum up. *amnyŏgŭl kahada* 압력을 가하다 give〔apply〕pressure (to).

kahok 가혹. *kahok'an* 가혹한 severe; cruel; harsh; merciless.

kahun 가훈 family precept; family code of conduct.

kaip 가입 joining; affiliation; subscription. *kaip'ada* 가입하다 join; become a member of; affiliate oneself with; subscribe for.

kajae 가재 household goods; furniture and effects.

kajak 가작 fine piece of work; work of merits.

kajang 가장 disguise; masquerade. *kajanghada* 가장하다 disguise oneself. *kajang haengnyŏl* 가장 행렬 fancy procession.

kajang 가장 most; extremely; exceedingly. *kajang arŭmdaun* 가장 아름다운 the most beautiful.

kajangjari 가장자리 edge; verge; margin; border.

kaji 가지 eggplant; egg apple.

kaji 가지 kind; sort; class. *se kaji* 세 가지 three kinds. *kajigajiŭi* 가지가지의 various; diverse; sundry.

kaji 가지 branch; bough; limb.

kajida 가지다 have; hold; carry; possess.

kajigaksaek 가지각색 (of) every kind and description. *kajigaksaegŭi* 가지각색의 various; of all kinds.

kajirŏnhada 가지런하다 (be) trim; even; equal; uniform. *kajirŏnhi* 가지런히 trimly; evenly.

kajok 가족 family; members of a family. *kajok kyehoek* 가족 계획 family planning.

kajŏn chep'um 가전 제품 electric home appliance.

kajŏng 가정 home; family. *kajŏng kyosa* 가정 교사 private teacher. *kajŏng kyoyuk* 가정 교육 home education; discipline.

kajŏng 가정 housekeeping; household management. *kajŏngkwa* 가정과 department of domestic science. *kajŏngbu* 가정부 housekeeper.

kajŏng 가정 assumption; supposition. *kajŏnghada* 가정하다 assume; suppose; presume.

kajuk 가죽 skin; hide; leather.

kajŭn 갖은 all; all sorts of; every. *kajŭn kosaeng* 갖은 고생 all sorts of hardship.

kajyŏgada 가져가다 take[carry] away; take along; carry.

kajyŏoda 가져오다 bring (over); bring (a thing *with one)*; take (a thing) along; fetch.

kak 각 each; every. *kakkuk* 각국 every country; each nation.

kak 각 ① horn ② corner; turn ③ angle.

kak'a 각하 (2 *nd person*) Your Excellency; (3 *rd person*) His[Her] Excellency. *taet'ongnyŏng kak'a* 대통령 각하 Your[His] Excellency the President.

kakcha 각자 each; each[every] one; individually; respectively.

kakchi 각지 every[each] place; various places

[quarters].

kakch'ŏ 각처 every[each] place; various places. *kakch'ŏe* 각처에 everywhere; in all[various] places.

kakchong 각종 every kind; various kinds; all kinds[sorts]. *kakchongŭi* 각종의 all sorts of; various.

kakch'ŭng 각층 ① each[every] floor ② each stratum (of society).

kakkaein 각개인 each one[individual]; each; each person.

kakkai 가까이 near; close by[to]; nearly; almost. *kakkai oda* 가까이 오다 come up close. *paengmyŏng kakkai* 백명 가까이 nearly one hundred persons.

kakkak 각각 separately; respectively; apart. *kakkagŭi* 각각의 respective.

kakkapta 가깝다 (be) near; be close by; be at home.

kakki 각기 beriberi. *kakkie kŏllida* 각기에 걸리다 have an attack of beriberi.

kakkŭm 가끔 occasionally; from time to time; now and then.

kakkwang 각광 footlights; highlight. *kakkwangŭl patta* 각광을 받다 be in the limelight.

kakkye 각계 all walks of life; every field[sphere] of life.

kakp'a 각파 each party; all political parties [groups]; each faction; all sects; all schools.

kak pangmyŏn 각 방면 every direction [quarter]; all directions. *sahoe kak pangmyŏn* 사회 각 방면 all strata of society.

kakpon 각본 playbook; scenario; script.

kakpu 각부 each section; every department[min-istry].

kak pubun 각 부분 each[every] part; various parts.

kaksat'ang 각사탕 cube[lump] sugar; sugar cubes.

kakshi 각시 maiden doll; doll bride.

kaksŏ 각서 memorandum; memo; note.

kaksŏnmi 각선미 beauty of leg line.

kakto 각도 angle; degrees of an angle.

kaltŭng 갈등 complications; discord; trouble(s).

kalbi 갈비 ribs. *kalbit'ang* 갈비탕 beef-rib soup.

kalch'ae 갈채 cheer; applause. *kalch'aehada* 갈채하다 applause; cheer; give cheer.

kalchŭng 갈증 thirst. *kalchŭngi nada* 갈증이 나다 feel thirsty.

kalda 갈다 ① sharpen; grind ② polish; burnish ③ rub; chafe.

kalda 갈다 change; replace; substitute; alter.

kalda 갈다 till; cultivate; plow.

kalgamagwi 갈가마귀 jackdaw.

kalgamŏkta 갉아먹다 nibble (at); gnaw (upon); bite (at).

kalgida 갈기다 ① strike; beat ② kick ③ cut; slash ④ scrawl; scribble; dash off.

kalgorangi 갈고랑이 hook; crook; gaff.

kalgyŏssŭda 갈겨쓰다 scrawl; scribble; dash off.

kallae 갈래 fork; branch; division. *se kallae kil* 세 갈래 길 three forked[trifurcated] road; junction.

kallajida 갈라지다 ① split; cleave; crack ② part; fork ③ be divided ④ be separated.

kallida 갈리다 (be) divided into; break into; fork. *kallimkil* 갈림길 branch road; forked road.

kalmaegi 갈매기 (sea) gull.

kalmanghada 갈망하다 be anxious (for); long [yearn, thirst, crave] (for).

kalp'angjilp'ang 갈팡질팡 confusedly; in a flurry; pellmell; this way and that. *kalp'angjilp'ang- hada* 갈팡질팡하다 go this way and that; run pellmell; be at a loss.

kalsaek 갈색 brown. *kalsaek injong* 갈색 인종 brown races.

kalsurok 갈수록 as time goes by; more and more. *nari kalsurok* 날이 갈수록 as days go by.

kaltae 갈대 reed. *kaltaebal* 갈대발 reed blind.

kam 감 persimmon.

kam 감 material; stuff. *otkam* 옷감 (dress) mate- rial; cloth.

kama 가마 palanquin; sedan chair.

kama(sot) 가마(솥) iron pot; kettle; oven; kiln.

kamanhi 가만히 still; quietly; silently. *kamanhi itta* 가만히 있다 keep still; be[remain] motionless [quiet].

kamani 가마니 straw bag; bale; sack.

kama ollida 감아 올리다 roll up; wind up; hoist.

kambang 감방 cell; ward.

kamch'al 감찰 license plate; license. *yŏngŏp kam- ch'al* 영업 감찰 trade[business] license.

kamch'o 감초 licorice root. *yakpangŭi kamch'o* 약 방의 감초 Jack-of-all-trades.

kamch'ok 감촉 touch; feeling. *kamch'ogi pudŭrŏpta* 감촉이 부드럽다 It feels soft(to the touch).

kamchŏm 감점 demerit mark. *kamchŏmhada* 감점 하다 give (a person) a demerit mark.

kamch'uda 감추다 ① hide; conceal; put out of

sight; keep secret ② cover; veil; cloak; disguise.

kamch'ida 감치다 hem; sew up.

kamdok 감독 superintendence; supervision. *yŏng-hwa kamdok* 영화 감독 director of a film.

kamdong 감동 deep emotion; impression. *kamdong-hada* 감동하다 (be) impressed (with, by); (be) moved[touched, affected] (by).

kamgae 감개 deep emotion. *kamgae muryanghada* 감개 무량하다 My heart is filled with deep emotion.

kamgak 감각 sense; sensation; feeling; sensibility. *kamgagi yemin[tun]hada* 감각이 예민[둔]하다 have keen[dull] senses.

kamgi 감기 cold; influenza; flu. *kamgie kŏllida* 감기에 걸리다 catch[take] (a) cold.

kamgŭm 감금 confinement; detention. *kamgŭmhada* 감금하다 confine; detain; imprison.

kamgyŏk 감격 deep emotion; strong feeling. *kam-gyŏk'ada* 감격하다 be deeply moved[touched].

kamhada 감하다 decrease; deduct; reduce; sub-tract; diminish; decline; fall off.

kamhaeng 감행 decisive[resolute] action. *kamhaeng-hada* 감행하다 venture; dare; carry out resolutely.

kamhi 감히 boldly; daringly. *kamhi ...hada* 감히 ...하다 dare[venture] to (do).

kamhwa 감화 influence; (moral) reform. *kamhwa-rŭl patta* 감화를 받다 be influenced[affected] (by). *kamhwahada* 감화하다 influence; exert influence upon (a person).

kamihada 가미하다 season; flavor.

kamja 감자 potato; white potato.

kamjilnada 감질나다 feel insatiable; never feel satisfied; feel tantalized.

kamjŏn 감전 (receiving) an electric shock. *kamjŏn-doeda* 감전되다 receive an electric shock.

kamjŏng 감정 judgment; appraisal. *kamjŏnghada* 감정하다 judge; appraise.

kamjŏng 감정 feeling; emotion; passion; sentiment. *kamjŏngjŏk* 감정적 emotional; sentimental.

kamjŏng 감정 ill feeling; grudge. *kamjŏngŭl sada* 감정을 사다 earn[incur] (a person's) grudge.

kamjŏngga 감정가 judge; connoisseur; appraiser.

kamjŏngin 감정인 →**kamjŏngga** 감정가.

kamnigyo 감리교 Methodist church. 「이 prison life.

kamok 감옥 prison; gaol (*Eng.*). *kamoksari* 감옥살

kamsa 감사 inspection; audit. *kamsahada* 감사하다 inspect; audit (accounts).

kamsa 감사 thanks; gratitude; appreciation. *kamsahada* 감사하다 thank; feel grateful[thankful].

kamsa 감사 inspector; auditor; supervisor.

kamsaek 감색 dark[deep, navy] blue; indigo.

kamsang 감상 appreciation. *kamsanghada* 감상하다 appreciate; enjoy.

kamsang 감상 sentimentality. *kamsangjŏgin* 감상적 인 sentimental. *kamsangjuŭija* 감상주의자 sentimentalist.

kamshi 감시 watch; lookout; vigil; observation *kamshihada* 감시하다 watch; keep watch (on, over); observe.

kamso 감소 diminution; decrease; decline; drop. *kamsohada* 감소하다 diminish; decrease; lessen.

kamsŏng 감성 sensitivity; sense; sensibility.

kamssada 감싸다 protect; shield; shelter; take (a person) under one's wing.

kamsu 감수. *kamsuhada* 감수하다 submit to; put up

with; be ready to suffer.
kamta 감다 wind; roll (up); coil; twine.
kamta 감다 shut[close] (one's eyes).
kamta 감다 wash; bathe; have a bath. *mŏrirŭl kamta* 머리를 감다 wash one's hair.
kamt'an 감탄 admiration; wonder. *kamt'anhada* 감탄하다 admire; marvel (at); wonder (at). *kamt'anhal manhan* 감탄할 만한 admirable; wonderful.
kamtchokkatta 감쪽같다 ① be perfect in (mending); be just as it was ② (be) complete; perfect.
kamt'oe 감퇴 decrease; decline; recession. *kamt'oehada* 감퇴하다 decrease; fall of. *chŏngnyŏgŭi kamt'oe* 정력의 감퇴 decline in energy.
kamt'u 감투 government post; high office. *kamt'urŭl ssŭda* 감투를 쓰다 assume office; hold a prominent post.
kamulda 가물다 (be) droughty; dry; have a spell of dry weather.
kamulgŏrida 가물거리다 ① (*light*) flicker; gleam ② (*spirit*) have a dim consciousness[memory].
kamun 가문 one's family; birth; lineage.
kamurŏjida, kkamurŏjida 가무러지다, 까무러지다 faint; swoon; lose one's senses.
kamwon 감원 personnel cut; reduction of staff. *kamwonhada* 감원하다 lay off; reduce the personnel.
kamyŏm 감염 infection; contagion. *kamyŏmhada [doeda]* 감염하다[되다] get infected(with); catch.
kamyŏn 가면 mask; disguise; cloak. *kamyŏnŭl ssŭda* 가면을 쓰다 wear a mask; make one's face.
kamyŏng 가명 assumed name; alias.
kan 간 ① liver ② courage; pluck. *kanam* 간암

cancer of the liver; liver cancer.

kan 간 seasoning; salty taste; saltiness. *kanŭl ch'ida* 간을 치다 apply salt (to); season.

kanan 가난 poverty; want. *kananhada* 가난하다 (be) poor; needy.

kananbaengi 가난뱅이 poor man; pauper.

kanbam 간밤 last night〔evening〕.

kanbu 간부 members of the executive; the managing staff.

kanbu 간부 (*male*) adulterer; (*female*) adulteress.

kanch'ŏk 간척 land reclamation (by drainage).

kanch'ŏng 간청 entreaty; earnest request. *kanch'ŏnghada* 간청하다 entreat; implore; solicit.

kanch'ŏp 간첩 spy; secret〔espionage〕agent. *mujang kanch'ŏp* 무장 간첩 armed espionage agent.

kandan 간단 brevity; simplicity. *kandanhan* 간단한 brief; simple; light. *kandanhan shiksa* 간단한 식사 light meal; quick meal; snack (lunch).

kandejokchok 간데족족 everywhere; wherever one goes.

kandŭlgŏrida 간들거리다 ① (*wind*) blow gently; breeze ② (*behavior*) act coquettishly; put on coquettish air.

kandŭrŏjida 간드러지다 (be) charming; coquettish; fascinating. *kandŭrŏjige utta* 간드러지게 웃다 laugh coquettishly.

kang 강 river. *kang kŏnnŏ* 강 건너 across the river. *kangŭl ttara* 강을 따라 along a river.

kangaji 강아지 pup; puppy.

kan-gani 간간이 occasionally; now and then; from time to time; at times.

kangap 강압 oppression; repression; coercion;

pressure. *kangapchŏgin* 강압적인 oppressive; highhanded.

kangbyŏn 강변 riverside; riverbank. *kangbyŏn toro* 강변 도로 riverside road[drive].

kangch'ŏl 강철 steel. *kangch'ŏlp'an* 강철판 steel plate[plank].

kangch'uwi 강추위 spell of dry cold weather; intense[bitter] cold.

kangdaehada 강대하다 (be) big and strong; mighty; powerful. *kangdaeguk* 강대국 powerful country; big power.

kangdan 강단 (lecture) platform; rostrum.

kangdang 강당 (lecture) hall; auditorium (*Am.*); assembly hall (*Eng.*).

kangdo 강도 burglar; robber. *kwŏnch'ong kangdo* 권총 강도 holdup (man).

kangdo 강도 intensity; degree of strength. *kangdoŭi* 강도의 intense; strong; powerful.

kanggan 강간 rape; violation; outrage. *kangganhada* 강간하다 violate; rape.

kanggŏn 강건 robustness; sturdiness. *kanggŏnhada* 강건하다 (be) strong; robust; healthy.

kangguk 강국 great[strong] power.

kanghada 강하다 (be) strong; powerful; mighty. *kanghage* 강하게 hard; severely; strongly.

kanghwa 강화 peace; peace negotiations. *kanghwahada* 강화하다 make[conclude] peace (with).

kangja 강자 strong man; the powerful. *kangjawa yakcha* 강자와 약자 the strong and the weak.

kangjangje 강장제 tonic; invigorant; restorative.

kangje 강제 compulsion; coercion; constraint. *kangjehada* 강제하다 force; compel; coerce. *kangje·*

jŏgin 강제적인 compulsory; forced.

kangjo 강조 stress; emphasis. *kangjohada* 강조하다 stress; emphasize; accentuate.

kangjwa 강좌 lecture; course. *radio Yŏngŏ kangjwa* 라디오 영어 강좌 radio English course.

kangka 강가 riverside; riverbank. →**kangbyŏn** 강변.

kangmae 강매 high-pressure salesmanship (*Am.*). *kangmaehada* 강매하다 force a sale (on); force (a thing) upon (a person).

kangmul 강물 river; stream; river water.

kangnamk'ong 강남콩 kidney bean; French bean.

kangnyo 각료 Cabinet members[ministers]; ministers of state.

kangnyŏng 강령 general principles; platform. *chŏngdangŭi kangnyŏng* 정당의 강령 party platform.

kangp'an 강판 grater.

kangparam 강바람 river wind; dry wind.

kangp'ung 강풍 strong[high] wind; gale.

kangsa 강사 lecturer; instructor *shigan*[*chŏnim*] *kangsa* 시간[전임] 강사 part-time[full-time] lecturer.

kangshimje 강심제 heart stimulant; cardiac; cordial.

kangsŭp 강습 short training course. *kangsŭbŭl patta* 강습을 받다 take a course (in). *kangsŭpso* 강습소 institute; training school.

kangt'a 강타 heavy[hard] flow; fatal blow. *kangt'ahada* 강타하다 give[deal] (a person) a heavy blow.

kangt'al 강탈 seizure; extortion; robbery; plunder. *kangt'arhada* 강탈하다 plunder[loot; despoil; rob]

kangtcha 강짜. *kangtchaburida* 강짜부리다 show

unreasonable jealousy.

kangtuk 강둑 river imbankment; levee.

kangu 강우 rainfall. *kanguryang* 강우량 amount of rainfall.

kangŭi 강의 lecture; discourse. *kangŭihada* 강의하다 lecture (on); give a lecture.

kangŭm 강음 accent; stress. *kangŭm puho* 강음 부호 accent mark.

kangyo 강요 enforcement; extortion; exaction *kangyohada* 강요하다 exact; force; compel.

kan-gyŏk 간격 space; interval; gap. *imit'ŏ kan-gyŏgŭro* 2미터 간격으로 at intervals of two meters.

kan-gyŏl 간결 conciseness; brevity. *kan-gyŏrhada* 간결하다 (be) concise; terse; brief.

kangyŏn 강연 lecture; address; discourse. *kangyŏnhada* 강연하다 (give a) lecture; address (an audience). *kangyŏnhoe* 강연회 lecture meeting.

kanhaeng 간행 publication. *kanhaenghada* 간행하다 publish; issue; bring out.

kanho 간호 nursing; care (of the sick). *kanhohada* 간호하다 nurse; tend.

kanhok 간혹 sometimes; occasionally; now and then; once in a while.

kani 간이 simplicity. *kani shiktang* 간이 식당 quick-lunch room; snack bar; cafeteria.

kanjang 간장 liver. *kanjangpyŏng* 간장병 liver troubles[complaint]. *kanjangyŏm* 간장염 inflammation of the liver; hepatitis.

kanjang 간장 soy; soybean sauce.

kanjik'ada 간직하다 ① keep; store; save; treasure (up) ② hold in mind; cherish; entertain.

kanjirida 간질이다 tickle; titillate.

kanjirŏpta 간지럽다 (be) ticklish; feel ticklish.

kanjittae 간젓대 (long) bamboo pole.

kanjŏp 간접 indirectness. *kanjŏpchŏgin* 간접적인 indirect; roundabout. *kanjŏpchŏgŭro* 간접적으로 indirectly.

kanjugok 간주곡 interlude; intermezzo.

kanmagi 간막이 ① partition; division ② screen.

kanman 간만 ebb and flow.

kan match'uda 간 맞추다 salt properly; season well.

kanmul 간물 salty water; brine.

kanp'an 간판 signboard; billboard.

kanp'yŏn 간편 convenience; handiness. *kanp'yŏn-hada* 간편하다 (be) convenient; simple; easy.

kansa 간사 executive secretary; manager. *kansa-jang* 간사장 chief secretary.

kansahada 간사하다 (be) cunning; sly; foxy.

kanse 간세 indirect tax.

kanshik 간식 eating between meals; snack. *kanshi-k'ada* 간식하다 have a snack.

kanshinhi 간신히 with difficulty; barely; narrowly.

kanso 간소 simplicity. *kansohada* 간소하다 (be) simple; plain.

kansŏn 간선 trunk[main] line. *kansŏn toro* 간선 도로 trunk road.

kansŏp 간섭 interference; intervention. *kansŏp'ada* 간섭하다 interfere; intervene. *muryŏk kansŏp* 무력 간섭 armed[military] intervention.

kansu 간수 (prison) guard; warder; jailer (*Am.*); gaoler (*Eng.*).

kant'ong 간통 adultery; illicit intercourse. *kant'ong-hada* 간통하다 commit adultery (with).

kanŭlda 가늘다 (be) thin; fine; slender. *kanŭn*

moksori 가는 목소리 thin voice. *kanŭn shil* 가는 실 fine thread. *kanŭn hŏri* 가는 허리 slender waist.

kanŭm 간음 adultery; illicit intercourse. *kanŭmhada* 간음하다 commit adultery.

kanŭng 가능. *kanŭnghan* 가능한 possible. *kanŭnghadamyŏn* 가능하다면 if (it is) possible.

kanyŏm 간염 hepatitis; inflammation of the liver.

kanyu 간유 (cod-)liver oil. *kanyugu* 간유구 sugar-coated cod-liver oil pills.

kaok 가옥 house; building. *kaokse* 가옥세 house tax.

kap 값 price; cost; charge. *kapshi ssada[pissada]* 값이 싸다[비싸다] be cheap[expensive].

kap 갑 casket; box; pack. *tambaetkap* 담뱃갑 cigarette case; tobacco box.

kapchŏl 갑절→**pae** 배.

kapkap'ada 갑갑하다 (be) tedious; stuffy; irksome; boring. *kasŭmi kapkap'ada* 가슴이 갑갑하다 feel heavy in the chest.

kapkapchŭng 갑갑증 ennui; boredom; tedium.

kapp'an 갑판 deck. *kapp'an sŭngganggu* 갑판 승강구 hatchway. *kapp'anjang* 갑판장 boatswain.

kappŭda 가쁘다 be out of breath; be short of wind; pant.

kappu 갑부 the richest man; millionaire; plutes (*Am.*).

kap'arŭda 가파르다 (be) steep; precipitous.

kapchagi 갑자기 suddenly; all of a sudden; all at once; abruptly.

kapsa 갑사 fine gauze.

kapsangsŏn 갑상선 thyroid gland. *kapsangsŏn horŭ-*

mon 갑상선 호르몬 thyroxine.
kapta 갚다 ① pay back; repay ② return; give (something) in return; reward ③ retaliate; revenge.
kap'ulmak 가풀막 steep slope[ascent].
kap'ung 가풍 family tradition[custom].
karaanta 가라앉다 sink; go down; go to the bottom.
karae 가래 spade; plow; plough.
karae 가래 phlegm; sputum. *karaerŭl paetta* 가래를 뱉다 spit (out).
karaech'im 가래침 spit; spittle.
karaipta 갈아입다 change (one's) clothes.
karakchi 가락지 ring; set of twin rings.
karangbi 가랑비 drizzle.
karangi 가랑이 fork; crotch.
karangnun 가랑눈 fine[powdery] snow.
karat'ada 갈아타다 change cars[trains]; transfer (to another train).
karida 가리다 hide; conceal; screen; cover.
karigae 가리개 twofold screen.
karik'ida 가리키다 point to; indicate; point out; show.
karo 가로 street; road. *karodŭng* 가로등 street lamp. *karosu* 가로수 street[roadside] trees.
karo 가로 width; breadth. *karo ip'it'ŭ* 가로 2피트 two feet in width.
karomakta 가로막다 interrupt; hinder; block.
karu 가루 flour; meal; powder; dust. *karupinu* 가루비누 powder soap.
karŭch'ida 가르치다 teach; instruct; educate.
karŭda 가르다 divide; part; sever; split; distribute.

karyŏpta 가렵다 (be) itchy; itching; feel itchy.
kasa 가사 household affairs; domestic duties; family concerns.
kasa 가사 words[text] of a song.
kasang 가상 imagination; supposition. *kasanghada* 가상하다 imagine; suppose. *kasang chŏk* 가상 적 imaginary enemy.
kashi 가시 thorn; prickle; bur. *kashidŏmbul* 가시 덤불 thorn thicket.
kashich'ŏl 가시철 barbed wire. *kashich'ŏlmang* 가시철망 (barbed) wire entanglement.
kasok 가속 acceleration. *kasokto* 가속도 degree of
kasŏkpang 가석방 release on parole. ⌊acceleration.
kasŏl 가설 construction; installation. *kasŏrhada* 가설하다 build; construct; install; lay on.
kasŏl 가설 hypothesis. *kasoljŏgin* 가설적인 hypothetical.
kasŏl 가설 temporary installation. *kasŏrhada* 가설하다 install temporarily. *kasŏl kŭkchang* 가설 극장 temporary theater.
kasollin 가솔린 gasoline; gas.
kasu 가수 singer; (*female*) songstress; vocalist. *yuhaeng kasu* 유행 가수 popular song singer; crooner (*Am.*).
kasŭ 가스 gas; natural gas; coal gas. *kasŭ chungdok* 가스 중독 gas-poisoning.
kasŭm 가슴 breast; chest. *kasŭmi ap'ŭda* 가슴이 아프다 have a pain in the chest.
kasŭmari 가슴앓이 heartburn; pyrosis.
kasŭmdulle 가슴둘레 girth of chest; bust.
kat 갓 Korean top hat (made of horsehair).
kat'aek susaek 가택 수색 house-searching.

katcha 가짜 imitation; sham; bogus; fake.

katch'uda 갖추다 ① get ready; prepare; furnish; equip; provide ② possess; have; be endowed (with). *chunbirŭl katch'uda* 준비를 갖추다 prepare for; make full preparation.

katkaji 갖가지 various kinds; all sorts; every kind.

kat'ollikkyo 가톨릭교 Catholicism. *kat'ollik kyodo* 가톨릭 교도 (Roman) Catholic.

katta 같다 ① be the same; (be) identical ② (be) equal (to); uniform; equivalent ③ similar; like; alike. *ttokkatta* 똑같다 be the very same; be just the same.

kat'ŭn kapshimyŏn 같은 값이면 if...at all; other things being equal; if it is all the same.

kaŭl 가을 autumn; fall (*Am.*). *kaŭl param* 가을 바람 autumn wind.

kaunde 가운데 ① middle; midway; center ② interior; inside ③ between; among.

kaundessonkarak 가운뎃손가락 middle finger.

kawi 가위 scissors; shears; clippers.

kawinnal 가윗날 →**ch'usŏk** 추석.

kayagŭm 가야금 Korean harp.

kayo 가요 song; ballad; lied. *kayoje* 가요제 popular song festival. ⌈miserable.

kayŏpta 가엾다 (be) poor; pitiable; pitiful; sad;

ke 게 crab. *kettakchi* 게딱지 crust of a crab.

kedaga 게다가 besides; moreover; what is more; in addition (to that).

kejae 게재. *kejaehada* 게재하다 publish[print] (in a newspaper); insert (an advertisement in a magazine).

kera 게라 printing galley; galley proof[sheet].

kerilla 게릴라 guerrilla. *kerillajŏn* 게릴라전 guerrilla warfare.

keshi 게시 notice; bulletin. *keshihada* 게시하다 post [put up] a notice. *keship'an* 게시판 bulletin board.

keuda 게우다 vomit; throw up; fetch up. ⌊board.

keŭllihada 게을리하다 neglect (one's work); be negligent (of duty).

keŭrŭda 게으르다 (be) idle; lazy; indolent.

keŭrŭm 게으름 laziness; idleness; indolence. *keŭrŭmp'iuda* 게으름피우다 be lazy; be idle.

keŭrŭmbaengi 게으름뱅이 idler; lazybone; idle [lazy] fellow.

keyang 게양. *keyanghada* 게양하다 hoist; raise; fly; display (a flag).

ki 기 flag; banner; colo(u)rs. *kirŭl talda[naerida]* 기를 달다[내리다] hoist[lower] a flag.

kia 기아 abandoned child; foundling.

kiak 기악 instrumental music.

kiap 기압 atmospheric pressure. *ko[chŏ]giap* 고[저]기압 high[low] atmospheric pressure.

kibon 기본 foundation; basis. *kibonjŏgin* 기본적인 fundamental; basic; standard.

kibu 기부 contribution; donation. *kibugŭm* 기부금 contribution; subscription.

kibun 기분 feeling; humor; mood.

kibyŏl 기별 notice; information. *kibyŏrhada* 기별하다 inform[notify].

kibyŏng 기병 cavalryman; horseman; cavalry.

kich'a 기차 train; railway carriage; railroad car (*Am.*). *kich'aro* 기차로 by train.

kich'im 기침 cough; coughing. *kich'imhada* 기침하다 have a cough.

kich'o 기초 foundation; basis; base.

kida 기다 crawl; creep; go on all fours.

kidae 기대 expectation; anticipation. *kidaehada* 기대하다 expect; look forward to.

kidaeda 기대다 lean(against); rest against; recline on; lean over.　　　　　　　　　　「forward to.

kidarida 기다리다 wait for; await; expect; look

kido 기도 prayer; grace. *kidohada* 기도하다 pray; offer[give] prayers; say grace.

kidokkyo 기독교 Christianity; Christian religion [faith]. *kidokkyoŭi* 기독교의 Christian. *kidokkyodo* 기독교도 Christian.

kidongch'a 기동차 diesel train.

kidung 기둥 pillar; pole; post.

kigan 기간 period; term.

kigo 기고 contribution. *kigohada* 기고하다 contribute (to); write (for).

kigu 기구 utensil; implement; apparatus. *chŏn-gi kigu* 전기 기구 electrical appliance.

kigu 기구 structure; organization; machinery. *kukche kigu* 국제 기구 international organization.

kigŭm 기금 fund; foundation; endowment.

kigwan 기관 organ. *kamgak kigwan* 감각 기관 sense organs.

kigwan 기관 ① engine; machine ② organ; means; facilities. *kyoyuk kigwan* 교육 기관 educational facilities.

kigwanch'a 기관차 engine(*Eng.*); locomotive(*Am.*). *chŏn-gi kigwanch'a* 전기 기관차 electric locomotive.

kigwanch'ong 기관총 machine gun.

kigye 기계 machine; machinery. *kigyejŏgin* 기계적인 mechanical. *kigyejŏgŭro* 기계적으로 mechani-

cally; automatically.
kigye 기계 instrument; appliance; apparatus.
kigyo 기교 art; technique; trick; technical skill.
kiyŏ 기여 contribution; service. *kiyŏhada* 기여하다 contribute; render services.
kihan 기한 term; period; time limit.
kihang 기항. *kihanghada* 기항하다 put in; call. *kihangji* 기항지 port of call.
kiho 기호 mark; sign; symbol. *hwahak kiho* 화학 기호 chemical symbol.
kihoe 기회 opportunity; chance. *kihoerŭl chapta* 기회를 잡다 seize a chance. *kihoejuŭija* 기회주의 자 opportunist.
kihoek 기획 planning; plan. *kihoek'ada* 기획하다 (make a) plan; work out a program.
kihu 기후 weather; climate.
kiil 기일 fixed date; time limit; appointed day.
kiip 기입 entry. *kiip'ada* 기입하다 enter; fill up.
kija 기자 journalist; pressman (*Eng.*); newspaper-man (*Am.*).
kiji 기지 base. *haegun kiji* 해군 기지 naval base.
kijil 기질 disposition; temper; nature; spirit. *hak-saeng kijil* 학생 기질 spirit of the student.
kijŏgwi 기저귀 diaper; (baby's) napkin.
kijŏk 기적 (steam) whistle; siren (*Am.*).
kijŏk 기적 miracle; wonder. *kijŏkchŏk(-ŭro)* 기적 적 (으로) miraculous(ly).
kijŏl 기절 fainting; swoon. *kijŏrhada* 기절하다 faint (away); go faint; swoon.
kijun 기준 standard; basis. *kijunŭi* 기준의 stand-ard; basic; base.
kijŭng 기증 contribution; donation. *kijŭnghada* 기

증하다 present; contribute; donate.
kijunggi 기중기 crane; derrick; hoist.
kikkŏi 기꺼이 willingly; with pleasure; readily.
kikkŏt'aeya 기껏해야 at (the) most; at (the) best; at the outside.
kikwon 기권 abstention; renunciation. *kikwonhada* 기권하다 abstain; withdraw one's entry.
kil 길 road; way; street. *kanŭn kire* 가는 길에 on the way. *kirŭl mutta* 길을 묻다 ask the way.
kilda 길다 (be) long; lengthy. *kin tari* 긴 다리 long legs.
kildŭrida 길들이다 ① tame; domesticate; train; break in. ② accustom; acclimate[acclimatize].
kim 김 steam; vapor. *kimi nada* 김이 나다 steam; reek. *kimppajida* 김빠지다 lose its flavo(u)r.
kim 김 laver; dried laver.
kima 기마 horse riding.
kimak'ida 기막히다 ① stifle; feel stifled[suffocated; choked] ② (be) amazed; stunned.
kimch'i 김치 pickles; pickled vegetables.
kimin 기민 smartness, sharpness. *kiminhan* 기민한 quick; prompt; sharp. ⌈curious.
kimyo 기묘. *kimyohan* 기묘한 strange; queer; odd;
kin-gŭp 긴급 emergency; urgency. *kin-gŭp'an* 긴급한 urgent; pressing; emergent.
kinjang 긴장 tension; strain. *kinjanghada* 긴장하다 become tense; be strained. *kinjangdoen* 긴장된 strained; tense.
kinmil 긴밀. *kinmirhan* 긴밀한 close[intimate].
kinŭng 기능 ability; capacity; skill. *kinŭng ollim-p'ik* 기능 올림픽 Olympics in Technology.
kinyŏm 기념 commemoration; memory. *kinyŏmha-*

da 기념하다 commemorate; honor the memory of. *kinyŏmŭro* 기념으로 in memory [commemoration] of.

kiŏk 기억 memory; remembrance. *kiŏk'ada* 기억하다 remember; bear in mind.

kion 기온 temperature. *kion pyŏnhwa* 기온 변화 change of [in] temperature.

kiŏp 기업 enterprise; undertaking. *kiŏpka* 기업가 enterpriser.

kip'i 기피 evasion. *kip'ihada* 기피하다 evade; shirk; dodge.

kipŏp 기법 techniques.

kippŭda 기쁘다 (be) glad; delightful; happy; pleased.

kipta 깊다 (be) deep; profound; close. *kip'i* 깊이 deep(ly).

kipta 깁다 sew (together); stitch; patch up.

kiri 길이 length; extent.

kirin 기린 giraffe.

kiroe 기뢰 mine. *kiroerŭl pusŏrhada* 기뢰를 부설하다 lay [place] mines (in the sea).

kirok 기록 record; document; archives. *kirok'ada* 기록하다 record; write down; register.

kirŭda 기르다 ① bring up; rear; breed; raise ② keep; grow; cultivate.

kirŭm 기름 ① oil ② fat; lard ③ grease; pomade.

kiryŏk 기력 energy; spirit; vigo(u)r. *kiryŏgi wangsŏnghan* 기력이 왕성한 energetic; vigorous.

kiryu 기류 air current. *sangsŭng [hagang] kiryu* 상승「하강」 기류 ascending [descending] current.

kisa 기사 engineer; technician. *t'omok kisa* 토목 기사 civil engineer.

kisa 기사 article; account; news. *shinmun kisa* 신문 기사 newspaper account.

kiso 기소 prosecution; litigation. *kisohada* 기소하다 prosecute; indict.

kisuk 기숙. *kisuk'ada* 기숙하다 lodge[board] (at, with a person) *kisuksa* 기숙사 dormitory.

kisul 기술 art; technique; skill. *kisulcha* 기술자 technician; engineer.

kit 깃 feather; plume.

kitpal 깃발 flag; banner. →**ki** 기.

kittae 깃대 flagstaff; flagpole.

kiulda 기울다 incline (to); lean(to); slant; tilt.

kiun 기운 ① (physical) strength; energy; force ② vigor; spirit. *kiunch'an* 기운찬 vigorous; energetic.

kiuttunggŏrida 기우뚱거리다 sway from side to side; rock; totter.

kkaburŭda 까부르다 winnow; fan.

kkach'i 까치 magpie.

kkada 까다 peel; husk; pare. *kyurŭl kkada* 귤을 까다 peel an orange.

kkadak 까닭 reason; why; cause. *musŭn kkadalgŭro* 무슨 까닭으로 why; for what reason.

kkadaropta 까다롭다 (be) particular; fastidious; overnice.

kkae 깨 sesame. *ch'amkkae* 참깨 sesame. *tŭlkkae* 들깨 wild sesame.

kkaech'ida 깨치다 learn; understand; comprehend; master. *han-gŭrŭl kkaech'ida* 한글을 깨치다 learn [master] Korean language.

kkaeda 깨다 break; crush; smash. *kŭrŭsŭl kkaeda* 그릇을 깨다 break a dish.

kkaeda 깨다 ① wake up; awake ② become sober; sober (up) ③ have one's eyes opened.

kkaeda 깨다 (be) hatched; hatch.

kkaedatta 깨닫다 see; perceive; realize; understand; sense; be aware of.

kkaejida 깨지다 ① break; be broken[smashed] ② fail; come to a rupture ③ be spoiled.

kkaekkŭshi 깨끗이 clean(ly); neatly; tidily. *kkaekkŭshi takta* 깨끗이 닦다 wipe (a thing) cleanly.

kkaekkŭt'ada 깨끗하다 ① (be) clean; cleanly; tidy; neat ② (be) pure; clean; innocent; chaste ③ (be) fair; clean.

kkaemulda 깨물다 bite (on); gnaw (at). *ipsurŭl kkaemulda* 입술을 깨물다 bite[gnaw] one's lips.

kkaenada 깨나다 return to consciousness; recover one's senses; come to oneself; awake from.

kkaesogŭm 깨소금 powdered sesame mixed with salt; sesame-salt.

kkaettŭrida 깨뜨리다 ① break; crush; destroy; crash; smash ② baffle; frustrate; disturb; spoil.

kkaeuch'ida 깨우치다 wake up; awake; (a) rouse; call (a person's) attention.

kkaeuda 깨우다 ① wake up; awaken; arouse ② bring (a person) to his sense; get[make] sober.

kkaji 까지 ① till; until; up to; by (*time*) ② to; up to; as far as (*place*) ③ even; so far as (*extent*).

kkakchŏngi 깍정이 miser; skinflint; crafty fellow.

kkakkŭragi 까끄라기 awn; beard.

kkakta 깍다 shave; sharpen; cut down.

kkaktugi 깍두기 white-radish pickles.

kkalboda 깔보다 make light of; look down upon.

kkalda 깔다 ① spread; stretch ② pave; cover ③ sit on (a cushion).

kkalgae 깔개 cushion.

kkalkkal 깔깔. *kkalkkal utta* 깔깔 웃다 laugh loudly [aloud].

kkalkkarhada 깔깔하다 (be) coarse; rough.

kkalkkŭmhada 깔끔하다 ① (be) smart; neat and tidy ② sharp; harsh.

kkalttaegi 깔때기 funnel.

kkamagwi 까마귀 crow; raven.

kkambakkŏrida 깜박거리다 twinkle; blink; flicker; glitter.

kkamkkamhada 깜깜하다 ① (be) pitch-dark ② (be) ignorant.

kkamtchakkamtchak 깜짝깜짝 with repeated starts. *kkamtchakkamtchak nollada* 깜짝깜짝 놀라다 be startled again and again.

kkamtchakkŏrida 깜짝거리다 blink repeatedly; wink.

kkamtchik'ada 깜찍하다 (be) clever for one's age; (be) precocious.

kkamtchiksŭrŏpta 깜찍스럽다 →**kkamtchik'ada** 깜찍하다.

kkangsul 깡술 drink without any food. *kkangsurŭl mashida* 깡술을 마시다 drink liquor without food.

kkangt'ong 깡통 can (*Am.*); tin (can) (*Eng.*). *kkangt'ong ttagae* 깡통 따개 can[tin] opener. *pin kkangt'ong* 빈 깡통 empty can[tin].

kkattagŏpta 까딱없다 (be) safe and sound.

kkat'uri 까투리 hen pheasant.

kkida 끼다 ① hold (a thing) (under) ② put on; pull on; wear.

kkiŏnta 끼얹다 pour; shower; splash.

kkiuda 끼우다 put[hold] between; insert; fit into.

kkoch'aengi 꼬챙이 spit; skewer; prod.

kkoda 꼬다 ① twist; twine ② writhe; wriggle. *saekkirŭl kkoda* 새끼를 꼬다 make[twist] a rope.

kkodŭgida 꼬드기다 incite; urge; egg [set] (a person on to do).

kkoe 꾀 ① wit; resources ② trick; trap; artifice.

kkoebyŏng 꾀병 feigned[pretended] illness; fake sickness (*Am.*).

kkoeda 꾀다 tempt; entice; lure; seduce.

kkoekkori 꾀꼬리 (Korean) nightingale; oriole.

kkŏjida 꺼지다 ① go[die] out; be put out; be extinguished ② cave[fall] in; sink; subside.

kkojipta 꼬집다 pinch; nip.

kkok 꼭 ① tightly; firmly; fast ② exactly; just ③ surely; without fail.

kkokchi 꼭지 ① (stop)cock; tap; spigot; faucet ② knob; nipple ③ stalk; stem.

kkokkaot 꼬까옷 children's gala dress.

kkokkurajida 꼬꾸라지다 ① fall; drop ② die.

kkŏkta 꺾다 ① break(off); snap ② make a turn; turn. *orŭnp'yŏnŭro kkŏkta* 오른편으로 꺾다 turn to the right; turn right.

kkoktaegi 꼭대기 top; summit; peak; crown.

kkoktukkakshi 꼭둑각시 puppet; dummy.

kkol 꼴 ① shape; form; appearance ② state; condition; situation ③ sight; spectacle. *chamdamhan kkol* 참담한 꼴 horrible sight[spectacle]. *kkolsanaun* 꼴사나운 unsightly; shabby.

kkŏlkkŏl 껄껄 ha-ha; haw-haw. *kkŏlkkŏl utta* 껄껄 웃다 laugh aloud; roar with laughter.

kkŏlkkŭrŏpta 껄끄럽다 (be) rough; coarse.

kkŏllŏngp'ae 껄렁패 good-for-nothing crew; shiftless lot.

kkolsanapta 꼴사납다 (be) ugly; unbecoming; unsightly.

kkoltchi 꼴찌 the last; the bottom; the tail end.

kkoma 꼬마 boy; (little) kid; baby miniature. *kkoma chadongch'a* 꼬마 자동차 baby car. *kkoma chŏn-gu* 꼬마 전구 miniature bulb.

kkomkkomhada 꼼꼼하다 very careful; methodical.

kkŏmkkŏmhada 껌껌하다 (be) pitch-dark; be as dark as pitch.

kkomtchak mot'ada 꼼짝 못하다 be unable to move an inch.

kkŏnaeda 꺼내다 pull[draw] out; take[bring] out; produce; whip out; pick out.

kkŏngch'ung 껑충 with a jump[leap].

kkongmuni 꽁무니 rear(end); tail (end); last.

kkŏpchil 껍질 ① bark ② rind; peel ③ husk; shell. *sagwa kkopchil* 사과 껍질 (the) rind of (an) apple.

kkŏptegi 껍데기 husk; hull; shell. →**kkŏpchil** 껍질.

kkoraksŏni 꼬락서니 (*slang*) state; condition; appearance; spectacle.

kkori 꼬리 tail; tag; brush (of fox); scut (of rabbit). *kkorirŭl chapta* 꼬리를 잡다 find (a person's) weak point; catch (a person) tripping.

kkŏrida 꺼리다 ① dislike; abhor ② avoid; shun ③ *hesitate*.

kkŏrimch'ik'ada 꺼림칙하다 feel uncomfortable [uneasy] (about).

kkorip'yo 꼬리표 address tag; label. *kkorip'yorŭl talda* 꼬리표를 달다 put on a tag.

kkot 꽃 flower; blossom; bloom. *kkoch'ŭi* 꽃의 floral. *kkottaun* 꽃다운 flowery; flowerlike. *kkotkage* 꽃가게 flowershop. *kkottabal* 꽃다발 bouquet; bunch of flowers.

-kkŏt –껏 as far as possible; to the best (of); to the utmost (of). *sŏngŭikkŏt* 성의껏 heartily; from one's heart *himkkŏt* 힘껏 as far as possible; to the best of one's ability.

kkotta 꽃다 ① stick; put[fix] in (to); prick; pin ② insert ③ drive into.

kkuda 꾸다 borrow; have[get] the loan (of).

kkŭda 끄다 put out; extinguish; flow out.

kkujitta 꾸짖다 scold; rebuke; chide.

kkujunhada 꾸준하다 (be) steady; untiring; constant. *kkujunhi* 꾸준히 untiringly; steadily.

kkul 꿀 honey; nectar. *kkulbŏl* 꿀벌 honeybee. *kkulmul* 꿀물 honeyed water.

kkŭl 끌 chisel.

kkŭlda 끌다 ① draw; pull; tug; drag ② attract; catch ③ delay; protract.

kkult'a 꿇다 kneel (down); fall[drop] on one's knees.

kkŭlt'a 끓다 boil; simmer; seethe.

kkum 꿈 ① dream ② vision; illusion. *kkum kat'ŭn* 꿈 같은 dreamlike. *kkumŭl kkuda* 꿈을 꾸다 dream; have a dream.

kkumida 꾸미다 ① decorate; ornament; adorn ② feign; pretend ③ invent; fabricate.

kkŭmtchik'ada 끔쩍하다 ① (be) awful; terrible; cruel ② (be) very hearty; warm. *kkŭmtchigi* 끔쩍이 ① awfully; terribly ② warmly; wholeheartedly.

kkumulgŏrida 꾸물거리다 ① wriggle; squirm; wiggle ② move slowly; dawdle.

kkŭnabul 끄나불 piece of string.

kkŭnimŏpta 끊임없다 (be) continuous; ceaseless; incessant. *kkŭnimŏpshi* 끊임없이 constantly; continually.

kkŭnnada 끝나다 (come to an) end; close; be over (up); be finished; expire.

kkŭnnaeda 끝내다 end; go[get] through (with); finish; complete.

kkŭnt'a 끊다 ① cut; cut off; sever ② give up; leave off.

kkŭnjŏkkŏrida 끈적거리다 be sticky; be greasy.

kkurida 꾸리다 pack[wrap] up; bundle. *chimŭl kkurida* 짐을 꾸리다 make a bundle[package].

kkŭrida 끓이다 ① boil (water); heat ② cook.

kkŭrŏanta 끌어안다 hug; embrace; draw (a person) close to one's breast.

kkŭrŏdŭrida 끌어들이다 ① draw in; pull in ② win (a person) over to one's side.

kkurŏmi 꾸러미 bundle; package; parcel. *ot kkurŏmi* 옷 꾸러미 bundle of clothes.

kkŭrŭda 끄르다 undo; untie; loosen; unfasten.

kkŭt 끝 ① end; close; final; last ② point; tip ③ result; consequence.

kkutkkut'ada 꿋꿋하다 (be) upright; firm; solid; steady.

kkwae 꽤 fairly; pretty; considerably.

kkwak 꽉 ① tightly; fast; closely ② to the full. *munŭl kkwak chamgŭda* 문을 꽉 잠그다 shut a door fast; lock a door tight.

kkweda 꿰다 run[pass] (a thing) through. *panŭre shirŭl kkweda* 바늘에 실을 꿰다 run[pass] a thread through a needle.

kkwemaeda 꿰매다 sew; stitch; darn; patch up.

kkwettult'a 꿰뚫다 pierce; pass[run] through; penetrate; shoot through.

kkyŏanta 껴안다 embrace; hug; hold (a person) in one's arms.

kkyŏipta 껴입다 wear (a coat) over another.

-ko ~고 ① height ② amount; sum. *p'yogo*[*haebal*] 표고[해발] above the sea-level. *sanch'ulgo* 산출고 product; output. *maesanggo* 매상고 the amount sold. ⌐Dr. Kim.

ko 고 the late. *ko Kim paksa* 고 김 박사 the late

koa 고아 orphan. *koawon* 고아원 orphanage; orphan asylum.

kŏaek 거액 big[colossal] sum; large amount.

koap 고압 ① high pressure ② high tension; high voltage. *koapchŏgin* 고압적인 high-handed. *koapsŏn* 고압선 high-tension[-voltage] wire.

kobaek 고백 confession. *kobaek'ada* 고백하다 confess.

kobal 고발 prosecution; indictment; complaint. *kobarhada* 고발하다 prosecute; indict.

kobi 고비 climax; crest; height; crucial moment. *kobirŭl nŏmgida* 고비를 넘기다 pass the crisis.

kobon 고본 second-hand book. *kobon kage* 고본 가게 second-hand bookshop.

kŏbu 거부 millionaire; billionaire.

kŏbu 거부 refusal; denial; rejection. *kŏbuhada* 거부하다 deny; refuse; reject; veto (a bill). *kŏbukwon* 거부권 veto; veto power.

kŏbuk 거북 tortoise; terrapin; turtle.

kŏbuk'ada 거북하다 feel awkward; feel ill at ease; feel uncomfortable.

kŏbuksŏn 거북선 "Turtle Boat."

kobun 고분 old[ancient] tomb.

koch'ida 고치다 ① cure; heal; remedy ② mend; repair; fix (up) ③ correct; reform; rectify.

kŏch'ida 거치다 pass by[through]; go by way of.

kŏch'ida 걷히다 clear up[away, off]; lift. *Kurŭmi kŏch'yŏtta* 구름이 걷혔다. The clouds have cleared away.

kŏch'ilda 거칠다 (be) coarse; rough; harsh; violent.

kŏch'imŏpta 거침없다 without a hitch; without hesitation.

koch'u 고추 red pepper; cayenne pepper. *koch'ujang* 고추장 hot pepper paste.

kŏch'ujangsŭrŏpta 거추장스럽다 (be) burdensome; cumbersome; troublesome.

koch'ŭng 고층 higher stories; upper floors. *koch'ŭng kŏnmul* 고층 건물 high[lofty] building.

koch'wihada 고취하다 inspire(a person with); instil.

kodae 고대 ancient[old] times; antiquity. *kodaeŭi* 고대의 ancient; antique.

kŏdae 거대. *kŏdaehan* 거대한 huge; gigantic; enormous; colossal.

kodaehada 고대하다 wait impatiently (for); long for; eagerly look forward to.

kodalp'ŭda 고달프다 (be) exhausted; tired out; done up.

kodam 고담 old tale[story]; folklore.

kodanhada 고단하다 (be) tired; fatigued.

kodo 고도 ① altitude; height ② high power[degree]. *kodoŭi* 고도의 high; high power.

kodo 고도 desert[isolated] island.

kodo 고도 ancient city; former capital.

kŏdŏch'ada 걸어차다 kick hard; give (a person) a hard kick.

kŏdŏch'iuda 걸어치우다 ① put[take] away; clear off; remove ② stop; quit; shut[close] up. *hadŏn irŭl kŏdŏch'iuda* 하던 일을 걸어치우다 stop doing a job.

kodoeda 고되다 (be) hard; painful. *kodoen il* 고된 일 hard work; toil.

kodok 고독 solitude; loneliness. *kodok'ada* 고독하다 (be) solitary; lonely; lone; isolated.

kodong 고동 beat; pulsation; palpitation. *kodong-ch'ida* 고동치다 beat; palpitate; throb; pulsate.

kodong 고동 steam whistle; syren; siren (*Am.*).

kodongsaek 고동색 brown; reddish brown.

kŏdot 겉옷 outer garment.

kŏdu 거두 leader; magnate. *chŏnggyeŭi kŏdu* 정계의 거두 political leader

kŏduda 거두다 ① gather; collect; harvest ② gain; obtain ③ die; expire.

kŏdŭlda 거들다 help; give help (to); assist.

kŏdŭlmŏkkŏrida 거들먹거리다 mount the high horse; give oneself airs; swagger.

kodung 고둥 roll shell; spiral shellfish.

kodŭng 고등 high grade; high class. *kodŭngui* 고등의 high; higher; advanced. *kodŭng hakkyo* 고등학교 high school.

kodŭngŏ 고등어 mackerel.

kŏdŭp 거듭 (over) again; repeatedly. *kŏdŭp'ada* 거듭하다 repeat; do again

kodŭrŭm 고드름 icicle.

kŏdŭrŭm 거드름 haughty air. *kŏdŭrŭm p'iuda* 거드

름 피우다 act proudly; hold one's head high.

koehan 괴한 ruffian; suspicious[strange] guy.

koemul 괴물 monster; goblin.

koengjanghada 굉장하다 grand; magnificent; splendid. *koengjanghi* 굉장히 magnificently; awfully; terribly.

koeropta 괴롭다 ① (be) troublesome; hard ② (be) onerous; distressing ③ (be) awkward; embarrassing.

koesang 괴상. *koesanghan* 괴상한 strange; queer; odd.

koetcha 괴짜 odd person; crank.

kogae 고개 ① nape; scruff ② (mountain) pass ③ crest; summit; peak; climax.

kogaek 고객 customer; client; patron. *oraen kogaek* 오랜 고객 old[regular] customer.

kŏgankkun 거간꾼 broker; middleman; agent.

kogi 고기 ① meat ② fish. *takkogi* 닭고기 chicken. *twaejigogi* 돼지고기 pork. *soegogi* 쇠고기 beef.

kŏgi 거기 that place; there. *kŏgie[esŏ]* 거기에[에서] in that place; there. *kŏgiro* 거기로 to that place; there. *kŏgisŏbut'ŏ[robutŏ]* 거기서부터[로부터] from there.

kogiap 고기압 high atmospheric pressure.

kogijabi 고기잡이 ① fishing; fishery ② fisherman; fisher.

kogitpae 고깃배 fishing boat; fisherboat.

kogohak 고고학 arch(a)eology *kogohakcha* 고고학자 archeologist.

kogong 고공 high sky; high altitude. *kogong pihaeng* 고공 비행 high altitude flight[flying].

kŏgu 거구 gigantic[massive] figure; big body.

koguk 고국 one's native land[country]; one's home land.

kogung 고궁 ancient[old] palace.

koguma 고구마 sweet potato *kun koguma* 군 고구마 roast[baked] sweet potato.

kogŭp 고급 high-class[-grade]; higher; senior. *kogŭp kwalli* 고급 관리 higher[high-ranking] officials. *kogŭp ch'a* 고급 차 deluxe car.

kogwan 고관 high officer[official]; dignitary. *kogwandŭl* 고관들 high functionaries; high-ups.

kogwi 고귀. *kogwihada* 고귀하다 (be) noble; high-born. *kogwihan saram* 고귀한 사람 high personage.

kogye 곡예 (acrobatic) feats; stunts; tricks. *kogye-sa* 곡예사 acrobat; tumble.

kogyŏl 고결. *kogyŏrhada* 고결하다 (be) noble; lofty; noble-minded. *kogyŏrhan inkyŏk* 고결한 인격 lofty [noble, high] character.

kohyang 고향 one's home; one's native place; one's birthplace.

kohyŏrap 고혈압 high blood pressure; hypertension.

koin 고인 the deceased[departed]; the dead.

kŏin 거인 giant; Titan; great man.

kojang 고장 ① hitch; hindrance ② accident; breakdown. *kojangnada* 고장나다 get out of order; break down; go wrong.

kojang 고장 ① locality; district ② place of production ③ native place.

kŏji 거지 beggar; mendicant.

kŏjinmal 거짓말 lie; falsehood; fabrication; fake. *kŏjinmarhada* 거짓말하다 tell a lie; lie.

kojip 고집 stubbornness; abstinacy. *kojip'ada* 고집하다 hold fast (to); adhere. *kojip sen* 고집 센

stubborn; abstinate.

kojobu 고조부 one's great-great-grandfather.

kojŏk 고적 historic remains; place of historical interest.

kŏjŏk 거적 (straw) mat. *kŏjŏgŭl kkalda* 거적을 깔다 spread a mat.

kŏjŏl 거절 refusal; rejection. *kŏjŏrhada* 거절하다 refuse; reject.

kojŏn 고전 classics. *kojŏnjŏk* 고전적 classic(al).

kŏju 거주 residence; dwelling. *kŏjuhada* 거주하다 dwell; reside; inhabit; live.

kŏjuk 거죽 ① surface; face ② right side ③ exterior.

kok 곡 tune; air; music; strains.

kŏkchŏng 걱정 ① anxiety; apprehensions ② uneasiness; fear ③ care; worry; trouble. *kŏkchŏnghada* 걱정하다 be anxious (about); be worried (by); trouble oneself about.

kŏkkuro 거꾸로 reversely; (in) the wrong way; inside out; upside down; topsyturvy.

kŏkkurŏjida 거꾸러지다 fall; fall down[over]; fall headfirst; tumble down.

kŏkkurŏttŭrida 거꾸러뜨리다 make fall flat[headfirst]; throw down; knock[strike] down.

kokkwaengi 곡괭이 pick; picker; pickax(e).

koksŏn 곡선 curve; curved line. *koksŏnmi* 곡선미 beauty of a curve line.

kol 골 anger; temper. *kori nada* 골이 나다 be angry. *kollaeda* 골내다 get[become] angry.

kŏlchak 걸작 masterpiece; fine piece of work.

kŏlch'ida 걸치다 extend (over); spread (over); range; cover.

kolda 골다 snore. *k'orŭl kolmyŏ chada* 코를 골며 자 다 sleep with (loud) snores.

kŏlda 걸다 ① hang; suspend ② speak to ③ pick; provoke ④ call to; ring up; telephone.

kŏlda 걸다 ① (be) rich; fertile ② abundant; plentiful; sumptuous.

kŏlgŏrhada 걸걸하다 (be) openhearted; free and easy. *sŏngmiga kŏlgŏrhada* 성미가 걸걸하다 be a freehearted fellow.

kolgoru 골고루 evenly among all; equally. →**koru**

kolgyŏk 골격 frame; build; bone structure.

kollan 곤란 difficulty; trouble; embarrassment. *kollanhan* 곤란한 difficult; hard; troublesome.

kŏlle 걸레 floor cloth; dustcloth; mop. *kŏllejirhada* 걸레질하다 wipe with a damp cloth; mop (the floor).

kŏllida 걸리다 ① hang ② fall ill ③ be caught ④ take ⑤ make (a person) walk.

kŏllŏ 걸러 at intervals of; skipping. *haru kŏllŏ* 하루 걸러 every other[second] day.

kolmaru 골마루 narrow corridor[hallway].

kŏlmŏjida 걸머지다 ① shoulder; bear ② contract a debt.

kolmok 골목 side street; alley; byway. *twitkolmok* 뒷골목 back street.

kŏlp'it'amyŏn 걸핏하면 too often; readily; quickly; without any reason.

kŏlsang 걸상 bench; stool; couch.

kŏlsoe 걸쇠 latch; hasp.

koltchagi 골짜기 valley; vale; ravine; dale.

kŏltchuk'ada 걸쭉하다 (be) thick; heavy. *kŏltchuk'an kuk* 걸쭉한 국 thick soup.

kŏlt'ŏanta 걸터앉다 sit (on, in); sit astride.

koltong, koltongp'um 골동, 골동품 curio; antique. *koltongp'um kage* 골동품 가게 curio store[shop].

kom 곰 bear.

kŏm 검 sword. *ch'onggŏm* 총검 bayonet. *tan-gŏm* 단검 dagger.

kŏmabi 거마비 traffic expenses; carriage.

kŏman 거만 arrogance; haughtiness; self-importance *kŏmanhada* 거만하다 be arrogant; haughty.

komapta 고맙다 ① (be) thankful; grateful ② (be) kind; nice; appreciated.

kombo 곰보 pockmarked person.

kŏmbŏsŏt 검버섯 dark spots on an old man's skin.

kŏmbukta 검붉다 (be) dark red; blackish red.

kŏmch'al 검찰. *kŏmch'algwan* 검찰관 public prosecutor[procurator]. *kŏmch'alch'ŏng* 검찰청 the (Public) Prosecutor's Office.

kŏmdaeng 검댕 soot. *kŏmdaengi mutta* 검댕이 묻다 be smeared with soot.

kŏmdo 검도 art of fencing.

kŏmdungi 검둥이 dark skinned person; Negro; nigger.

kŏmgŏ 검거 arrest; round up. *kŏmgŏhada* 검거하다 arrest; round up.

kŏmi 거미 spider. *kŏmijul* 거미줄 cobweb.

komin 고민 agony; anguish. *kominhada* 고민하다 (be) in agony; agonize.

kŏminjŏng, kŏmjŏng 검인정, 검정 official approval; authorization. *kŏminjŏng kyogwasŏ* 검인정 교과서 authorized textbook.

kŏmjin 검진 medical examination. *kŏmjinhada* 검진하다 give a medical examination; examine.

komkuk 곰국 thick beef soup.

kŏmmun 검문 examination; inspection; checkup (*Am.*). *kŏmmunhada* 검문하다 check up (passers-by). *kŏmmunso* 검문소 check point.

komo 고모 paternal aunt; one's father's sister.

komobu 고모부 husband of one's (paternal) aunt.

kŏmŏjwida 거머쥐다 grasp; grip; grab (up); seize.

komok 고목 old[aged] tree.

kŏmŏri 거머리 leech.

kŏmŏt'a, kkŏmŏt'a 거멓다, 꺼멓다 (be) deep black; jet-black.

komp'angi 곰팡이 mold; mildew; must.

kŏmp'urŭda 검푸르다 (be) dark blue; blue-black.

kŏmp'yo 검표 examination of tickets. *kŏmp'yohada* 검표하다 clip[examine] tickets.

kŏmsa 검사 public prosecutor; the prosecution. *pujang kŏmsa* 부장 검사 chief public prosecutor.

kŏmsa 검사 inspection; examination; test. *kŏmsahada* 검사하다 inspect; examine; audit; condition (merchandise).

kŏmsaek 검색 reference; search. *kŏmsaek'ada* 검색하다 refer to (a dictionary); search (a house).

kŏmsan 검산. *kŏmsanhada* 검산하다 verify[check] accounts; check one's figures.

kŏmso 검소. *kŏmsohada* 검소하다 (be) simple; frugal; plain. *kŏmsohan saenghwal* 검소한 생활 plain living.

kŏmsul 검술 fencing; swordmanship.

kŏmta 검다 (be) black; dark; sooty.

kŏmt'o 검토 examination; scrutiny. *kŏmt'ohada* 검토하다 examine; scrutinize.

komu 고무 rubber. *komugong* 고무공 rubber ball.

komushin 고무신 rubber shoes.

komul 고물 second-hand articles; used articles. *komulsang* 고물상 second-hand shop[store].

kŏmul 거물 leading[prominent] figure; bigwig.

komun 고문 adviser; counsel(l)or; consultant. *kisul komun* 기술 고문 technical adviser.

komurae 고무래 rake.

kŏmusŭrŭmhada 거무스름하다 (be) darkish; blackish.

kŏmyak 검약 thrift; (practice) economy; frugality. *kŏmyak'ada* 검약하다 economize (in); be thrifty.

kŏmyŏk 검역 quarantine; medical inspection.

kŏmyŏl 검열 censorship; inspection; review. *kŏmyŏrhada* 검열하다 censor; inspect; examine.

komyŏngttal 고명딸 the only daughter among one's many sons.

-kŏna -거나 whether...or; whatever; however; whenever. *nŏya choahagŏna malgŏna* 너야 좋아하거나 말거나 whether you like it or not.

kŏnahada 거나하다 (be) mellow; tipsy; slightly drunk[intoxicated].

konan 고난 hardship; suffering; affliction. *konanŭl kyŏkta* 고난을 겪다 undergo hardships.

kŏnban 건반 keyboard. *kŏnban akki* 건반 악기 keyboard instruments.

kŏnbangjida 건방지다 (be) impertinent; insolent; haughty. *kŏnbangjin t'aedo* 건방진 태도 haughty bearing.

konbong 곤봉 club; cudgel; stick; truncheon.

kŏnch'o 건초 hay; dry grass.

kŏnch'uk 건축 building; construction. *kŏnch'uk'ada* 건축하다 build; contruct; erect. *kŏnch'ukka* 건축

가 architect. *kŏnch'uk hoesa* 건축 회사 building company. *kŏnch'ukpŏp* 건축법 building regulation.

konch'ung 곤충 insect; bug. *konch'ung ch'aejip* 곤충 채집 insect collecting.

kŏndal 건달 libertine; scamp. *kŏndalp'ae* 건달패 a group of scamps[sluggards].

kŏndŏgi 건더기 ingredients; a piece of meat[vegetables] in soup; a piece of solid in liquid.

kŏndŭrida 건드리다 ① touch; jog ② provoke; tease; irritate.

kong 공 ball; handball. *kongŭl ch'ada* 공을 차다 kick a ball.

kŏn-gang 건강 health. *kŏn-ganghada* 건강하다 (be) well; healthy; sound. *kŏn-gang chindan* 건강 진단 medical examination.

kongbak 공박 refutation; wordy attack; charge. *kongbak'ada* 공박하다 refute; confute; argue against.

kongbi 공비 red[communist] guerillas. *mujang kongbi* 무장 공비 armed red guerillas.

kongbok 공복 empty stomach; hunger.

kongbŏm 공범 complicity; conspiracy. *kongbŏmja* 공범자 accomplice; confederate.

kongbu 공부 study; learning. *kongbuhada* 공부하다 study; work at[on]. *shihŏm kongbu* 시험 공부 study for an examination

kongbyŏng 공병 engineer; sapper. *kongbyŏngdae* 공병대 engineer corps.

kongch'ae 공채 public loan[debt]. *kongch'ae shijang* 공채 시장 bond market.

kongch'aek 공책 notebook.

kongch'ang 공창 licence prostitution.

kongch'ŏn 공천 public nomination[recommendation]. *kongch'ŏnhada* 공천하다 nominate publicly.

kongch'ŏnghoe 공청회 public[opening] hearing.

kongdong 공동 association; cooperation; union. *kongdongŭi* 공동의 common; joint; public. *kongdong pyŏnso* 공동 변소 public lavatory. *kongdong myoji* 공동 묘지 public cemetery.

konggal 공갈 threat; intimidation; blackmail. *konggarhada* 공갈하다 threaten; blackmail.

konggan 공간 space; room. *shigan-gwa konggan* 시간과 공간 time and space.

konggi 공기 air; atmosphere. *konggi oyŏm* 공기 오염 air pollution.

konggu 공구 tool; implement. *konggujŏm* 공구점 machine parts supplier.

konggŭm 공금 public money[funds].

konggun 공군 air force. *konggun kiji* 공군 기지 air base.

konggŭp 공급 supply; provision. *konggŭp'ada* 공급하다 supply[furnish, provide] (a person) with.

konggwan 공관 official residence. *chaeoe konggwan* 재외 공관 diplomatic establishment abroad.

konghae 공해 public nuisance[hazard, harm]; pollution. *maeyŏn konghae* 매연 공해 pollution caused by exhaust smoke.

konghak 공학 coeducation (*Am.*); mixed education (*Eng.*). *konghakche* 공학제 coeducationalism.

konghak 공학 engineering; technology. *t'omok[kigye, chŏn-gi] konghak* 토목[기계, 전기] 공학 civil [mechanical, electrical] engineering.

konghang 공항 airport. *kukche konghang* 국제 공항 international airport. *Kimp'o konghang* 김포 공항

Kimpo Airport.

konghŏn 공헌 contribution; service. *konghŏnhada* 공헌하다 contribute (to); make a contribution (to); render services (to, for).

konghwang 공황 panic; crisis; consternation. *kŭmnyung konghwang* 금융 공황 financial crisis *segye konghwang* 세계 공황 world crisis.

konghyuil 공휴일 legal holiday; red-letter day.

kongil 공일 ① Sunday ② holiday.

kongim 공임 wage, wages; pay.

kongja 공자 Confucius.

kongjak 공작 peacock; peahen.

kongjak 공작 prince; duke (*Eng.*). *kongjak puin* 공작 부인 princess; duchess.

kongjang 공장 factory; plant; mill; workshop. *kunsu kongjang* 군수 공장 munitions factory. *kongjang p'yesu* 공장 폐수 industrial sewage.

kongji 공지 vacant lot; vacant land.

kongjŏngdae 공정대 air-borne troops; paratroops.

kongju 공주 (royal) princess.

kongjung 공중 public. *kongjungŭi* 공중의 public; common. *kongjung chŏnhwa* 공중 전화 public telephone.

kongkwa 공과. *kongkwa taehak* 공과 대학 engineering college.

kongma 곡마 circus; equestrian feats. *kongmadan* 곡마단 circus (troupe).

kongmok 곡목 program; selection; repertoire; number.

kongmo 공모 conspiracy; collusion. *kongmohada* 공모하다 conspire with; plot together.

kongmu 공무 official business[duties]. *kongmuwŏn*

공무원 public official[servant].

kongmun 공문 official document. *kongmunsŏ* 공문
서 official document.

kongnip 공립 public; communal. *kongnip hakkyo* 공
립 학교 public school.

kongno 공로 meritorious service; merits. *kongnoja*
공로자 person of merit. *kongnosang* 공로상 distinguished service medal.

kongno 공로 airway; air route. *kongnoro* 공로로
by plane[air].

kongŏp 공업 industry. *kongŏbŭi* 공업의 industrial;
technical. *kongŏp tanji* 공업 단지 industrial complex. *kongŏp hakkyo* 공업 학교 technical school.
chung[kyŏng]gongŏp 중[경]공업 heavy[light]
industry.

kongp'o 공포 fear; terror; dread; horror. *kongp'o-
echillin* 공포에 질린 terror-[horror-, panic-] strick-
en. *kongp'ochŭng* 공포증 phobia; morbid fear.

kongp'o 공포 blank shot[cartridge]. *kongp'orŭl
ssoda* 공포를 쏘다 fire a blank shot.

kongp'yŏng 공평. *kongp'yŏnghada* 공평하다 (be)
fair; impartial; even-handed. *kongp'yŏnghage*
공평하게 fairly; impartially; justly.

kongsa 공사 (diplomatic) minister. *kongsagwan* 공
사관 legation.

kongsa 공사 construction work. *kongsabi* 공사비
cost of construction. *kongsajang* 공사장 site of
construction.

kongsandang 공산당 Communist Party. *kongsan-
dangwŏn* 공산당원 communist. *kongsanjuŭi* 공산
주의 communism.

kongsang 공상 idle fancy; daydream. *kongsang-*

hada 공상하다 fancy; daydream.

kongsanp'um 공산품 industrial products[goods].

kongshik 공식 formula. *kongshigŭi* 공식의 formal; official.

kongsŏl 공설. *kongsŏrŭi* 공설의 public; municipal. *kongsŏl kigwan* 공설 기관 public institution.

kongson 공손. *kongsonhan* 공손한 polite; courteous; civil. *kongsonhi* 공손히 politely; humbly; courteously.

kongsŭp 공습 air raid[attack]. *kongsŭp'ada* 공습하다 make an air attack (on); air-raid.

kongsup'yo 공수표 ① wind bill; fictitious bill; bad [dishonored] check. ② empty talks.

kongtcha 공짜 thing got for nothing; free charge; gratuitousness.

kongt'ong 공통. *kongt'onghada* 공통하다 be common (to). *kongt'ongŭi* 공통의 common; mutual; general.

kongŭi 공의 community doctor[physician].

kŏn-guk 건국 foundation of a country. *kŏn-guk kinyŏmil* 건국 기념일 National Foundation Day.

kongwon 공원 park; public garden. *kungnip kongwon* 국립 공원 national park.

kongyak 공약 public pledge[promise]. *kongyak'ada* 공약하다 pledge[commit] oneself (publicly).

kongye 공예 industrial arts; technology. *kongyega* 공예가 technologist. *kongyep'um* 공예품 industrial art products.

kon-gyŏng 곤경 awkward position; predicament; fix; adversity; difficult situation.

koni 고니 swan. *hŭkkoni* 흑고니 black swan.

kŏnilda 거닐다 walk[stroll] aimless; saunter; wander about.

kŏnjang 건장. *kŏnjanghan* 건장한 strong; stout; robust; sturdy. *kŏnjanghan ch'egyŏk* 건장한 체격 tough[robust] constitution.

kŏnjida 건지다 ① take[bring] out of water; pick up ② save[rescue] a person from.

kŏnjo 건조. *kŏnjohan* 건조한 dry; dried; arid. *kŏnjogi* 건조기 drier; desiccator.

kŏnjŏn 건전. *kŏnjŏnhada* 건전하다 (be) healthy; sound; wholesome. *kŏnjŏnhan sasang* 건전한 사상 wholesome ideas.

kŏnjŏnji 건전지 dry cell; battery.

kŏnmangchŭng 건망증 amnesia.

kŏnmoyang 겉모양 outward appearance; outlook; show; outside view.

kŏnmul 건물 building; structure. *sŏkcho[mokcho] kŏnmul* 석조[목조] 건물 stone[wooden] building.

kŏnnejuda 건네주다 ① pass[set] (a person) over [across]; take[ferry] over ② hand (over); deliver.

kŏnnŏgada 건너가다 go[pass] over; go across; cross (over)

kŏnnŏp'yŏn 건너편 the opposite side; the other side. *kŏnnŏp'yŏne* 건너편에 on the opposite[other] side.

kŏnnŭkta 겉늙다 look older than one's age; look old for one's age.

konoe 고뇌 suffering; distress; affliction; agony.

kŏnp'odo 건포도 raisins; dried grapes.

kŏnpy'ŏng 건평 floor space; building area.

kŏnshil 건실. *kŏnshirhada* 건실하다 (be) steady; sound; reliable. *kŏnshirhan saram* 건실한 사람 steady[reliable] person.

kŏnsŏl 건설 construction; building. *kŏnsŏrhada* 건설하다 construct; build; establish. *kŏnsŏljŏgin* 건설적인 constructive.

kŏn 건 affair; subject; item. *tonan kŏnsu* 도난 건수 number of cases of theft.

kŏnŭi 건의 proposal; suggestion. *kŏnŭihada* 건의하다 propose; recommend.

kŏnŭrida 거느리다 have (with one); lead; head; command.

kop 곱 double; times. *kop'ada* 곱하다 multiply; double. *tu kop* 두 곱 double; twice; twofold.

kŏp 겁 ① cowardice; timidity ② fear; awe; fright. *kŏbi nada* 겁이 나다 be seized with fear.

kopch'ang 곱창 chitterlings; small intestines (of cattle).

kŏpchangi 겁장이 coward; pudding heart.

koppaegi 곱배기 double measure (of wine); double-the-ordinary dish.

koppi 고삐 reins; bridle; halter.

kopsadŭngi 곱사등이 hunchback; humpback.

kopta 곱다 ① (be) beautiful; lovely; fair; fine; nice ② (be) tender; kindly. *koun maŭmssi* 고운 마음씨 tender heart.

kŏpt'al 겁탈 plunder; rape. *kŏpt'arhada* 겁탈하다 plunder; rape.

kŏp'u 거푸 again and again; over again; repeatedly.

kop'ŭda 고프다 (be) hungry. *paega kop'ŭda* 배가 고프다 feel hungry.

kŏp'um 거품 bubble; foam; froth. *mulgŏp'um* 물거품 water bubble.

korae 고래 whale. *koraejabi* 고래잡이 whale fishing.

kŏrae 거래 transactions; dealings; business; trade.

kŏraehada 거래하다 do[transact] business (with); have an account with.

korak 고락 pleasure and pain; joys and sorrows.

korang 고랑 furrow; trough.

korang 고랑 handcuffs; shackles.

kori 고리 ring; link; loop. *kwigori* 귀고리 earring.

kori 고리 high interest; usury. *kori taegŭmŏpcha* 고리 대금업자 usurer; loanshark (*Am.*).

kŏri 거리 street; road; town; quarter *shijang kŏri* 시장 거리 market street.

kŏri 거리 distance; range; interval.

kŏrikkida 거리끼다 be afraid (of doing); hesitate (to do); refrain from (doing).

korinnae 고린내 bad[foul] smell; stinking smell.

korip 고립 isolation. *korip'ada* 고립하다 stand along; be isolated; be friendless. *koriptoen* 고립된 isolated; solitary; helpless.

koritchak 고리짝 wicker trunk.

koru 고루 equally; evenly. *koru nanuda* 고루 나누다 divide equally.

kŏrŭda 거르다 filter; leach; percolate; strain (through cloth).

kŏrŭda 거르다 skip (over); omit; go without. *haru kŏllŏsŏ* 하루 걸러서 every other day.

koruk'ada 거룩하다 (be) divine; sacred; holy.

korŭm 고름 pus; (purulent) matter.

kŏrŭm 걸음 walking; stepping; step; pace. *pparŭn kŏrŭmŭro* 빠른 걸음으로 at a rapid pace.

kŏrŭm 거름 manure; muck; fertilizer.

kŏrŭmma 걸음마. *kŏrŭmmarŭl hada* 걸음마를 하다 toddle; find its feet.

kŏrutpae 거룻배 barge; lighter; sampan.

koryo 고료 fee[payment] for a manuscript.

koryŏ 고려 consideration; deliberation *koryŏhada* 고려하다 consider; deliberate; bear in mind.

Koryŏ chagi 고려 자기 Koryo ceramics; ancient Korean pottery.

koryŏng 고령 advanced age; ripe old age. *koryŏngja* 고령자 person of advanced age.

kŏryu 거류. *kŏryumin* 거류민 (foreign) residents. *kŏryu oegugin* 거류 외국인 resident foreigners.

kosa 고사 examination; test. *yebi kosa* 예비 고사 preliminary examination.

kosaeng 고생 ① hard[tough] life; hardships; sufferings ② toil; labor; pain. *kosaenghada* 고생하 다 go through hardship.

kosan 고산 high[lofty] mountain; alp. *kosan shingmul* 고산 식물 alpine plant.

kosang 고상. *kosanghan* 고상한 noble; lofty; high; elegant; refined.

kosap'o 고사포 anti-aircraft gun; A.A. gun

kosari 고사리 fernbrake; bracken.

kŏse 거세 castration; emasculation. *kŏsehada* 거세 하다 castrate.

kŏseda 거세다 (be) rough; wild; violent. *kŏsen yŏja* 거센 여자 unruly woman

koshi 고시 examination; test. *kodŭng koshi* 고등 고 시 higher civil service examination.

kŏshil 거실 sitting room; living room (*Am.*).

koso 고소 accusation; complaint; charge. *kosohada* 고소하다 accuse; bring a charge (against).

kosŏ 고서 old[ancient] books; classics.

kosok 고속 high-speed; rapid transit. *kosok toro* 고 속 도로 express highway; superhighway. *kosok* *pŏsŭ* 고속 버스 express bus.

kosŏngnŭng 고성능 high efficiency[performance]. *kosŏngnŭng sushin-gi* 고성능 수신기 high-fidelity receiver.

kŏsŭllida 거슬리다 (be) against one's taste; be unpleasant.

kŏsŭllŏ ollagada 거슬러 올라가다 ① go up stream ② go back (to the past).

kŏsŭrŏmi 거스러미 (*of finger*) agnail; hangnail; (*of lumber*) splinter.

kŏsŭrŭda 거스르다 ① oppose; go against; run counter to ② give (back) the change.

kŏsŭrŭmton 거스름돈 change.

kot 곧 ① at once; immediately; instantly ② easily; readily.

kot 곳 place; scene; locality. *kose ttara* 곳에 따라 in some places. *kotkose* 곳곳에 here and there.

kŏt 겉 face; surface; right side; exterior; outward appearance.

kŏtchang 겉장 front page; cover of a book.

kŏtch'ijang 겉치장. *kŏtch'ijanghada* 겉치장하다 dress up outside; make outward show.

kŏtch'irę 겉치레 outward show; ostentation; ostensible decoration. *kŏtch'iryehada* 겉치레하다 dress up; show off.

kotkam 곶감 dried persimmons.

kot'ong 고통 pain; suffering; agony; anguish. *kot'ongsŭrŏun* 고통스러운 painful; afflicting.

kŏtpong 겉봉 envelope. *kŏtpongŭl ttŭtta* 겉봉을 뜯다 open[break open] an envelope.

kotta 곧다 ① (be) straight; upright; erect ② (be) honest; upright.

kŏtta 걷다 walk; go on foot; stroll; trudge. *kŏrirŭl kŏtta* 거리를 걷다 walk the street.

kŏtta 걷다 ① tuck[roll] up (one's sleeves); gather up (curtains); fold up ② take away; remove. *ppallaerŭl kŏtta* 빨래를 걷다 gather up the laundry.

koŭi 고의. *koŭiŭi* 고의의 intentional; deliberate. *koŭiro* 고의로 intentionally; on purpose.

kŏŭi 거의 ① almost; nearly; practically ② hardly; scarcely; little. *kŏŭi chŏnbu* 거의 전부 almost all.

kŏul 거울 mirror; looking glass; speculum. *sonkŏul* 손거울 hand mirror. *kŏurŭl poda* 거울을 보다 look in a glass.

kowi 고위 high rank. *kowi kwalli* 고위 관리 ranking government official.

kŏwi 거위 goose (*pl.* geese).

koyak 고약 plaster; ointment.

koyangi 고양이 cat; puss(y). *koyangi saekki* 고양이 새끼 kitten; kitty.

koyo 고요. *koyohada* 고요하다 (be) quiet; still; tranquil; calm.

kŏyŏk 거역. *kŏyŏk'ada* 거역하다 disobey; oppose; offend; go against.

koyong 고용. *koyonghada* 고용하다 hire; employ; engage. *koyongin* 고용인 employee. *koyongju* 고용주 employer.

ku 구, 9 nine. *chegu* 제구 the ninth. →**ahop** 아홉.

ku 구 former; ex-; old. *kusedae* 구세대 the old generation.

kŭ 그 that; it. *kŭ saram* 그 사람 that man[woman]; he; she. *kŭŭi* 그의 his; her.

kŭ 그 that; those; the; its. *kunal* 그날 that[the] day. *kŭttae* 그때 that time; then. *kŭgach'i* 그같

이 thus; so; like that.

kuae 구애 courtship; love-making. *kuaehada* 구애하다 court; woo; make love to.

kubi 구비. *kubihada* 구비하다 possess; have; be fully equipped. *kubi sŏryu* 구비 서류 required documents.

kubun 구분 division; demarcation; classification. *kubunhada* 구분하다 divide; classify; partition.

kuburŏjida 구부러지다 bend; curve; stoop.

kubyŏl 구별 distinction; difference; discrimination; division. *kubyŏrhada* 구별하다 distinguish; discriminate.

kŭbyu 급유 oil supply; refueling. *kŭbyuhada* 급유하다 supply oil; refuel. *kŭbyuso* 급유소 oil station; gas station.

kŭch'ida 그치다 stop; cease; halt; be over; end.

kuch'uk'am 구축함 (torpedo) destroyer.

kŭdaero 그대로 as it is[stands]; intact; just like that.

kudŏgi 구더기 maggot; grub; worm.

kudok 구독 subscription. *kudok'ada* 구독하다 subscribe.

kudŏngi 구덩이 hollow; depression; pit.

kudu 구두 shoes; boots. *kudurŭl shinta[pŏtta]* 구두를 신다[벗다] put on[take off, remove] shoes. *kududakki* 구두닦기 shoeshine boy.

kudusoe 구두쇠 miser; stingy[grasping] fellow; close-fisted man.

kugak 국악 Korean classic music.

kugimsal 구김살 creases; rumples; folds.

kugŏ 국어 language; one's mother tongue; Korean language.

kugŭp 구급 relief; first-aid. *kugŭpch'a* 구급차 ambulance. *kugŭp hwanja* 구급 환자 emergency cases.
kugwang 국왕 king; monarch; sovereign.
kŭgyak 극약 powerful drug; deadly poison.
kugyo 구교 Roman Catholicism; Catholic Church. *kugyodo* 구교도 (Roman) Catholic.
kugyŏng 국영 state operation[management]. *kugyŏngŭi* 국영의 state-operated[-run].
kugyŏnghada 구경하다 see (a play); watch (a game); do the sights (of). *shinaerŭl kukyŏnghada* 시내를 구경하다 do the sights of a city.
kugyŏngkkun 구경꾼 sightseer; onlooker; spectator.
kuhada 구하다 ① pursue; ask for ② save; rescue.
kuho 구호 slogan; motto; catch phrase.
kuhon 구혼 proposal[offer] of marriage; courtship. *kuhonhada* 구혼하다 propose (to); court.
kŭ hu 그 후 after that; thereafter; (ever) since; since then.
kui 구이 meat [fish] roasted[broiled] with seasonings. *saengsŏn kui* 생선 구이 baked fish. *kalbi kui* 갈비 구이 roasted ribs.
kŭi 그이 that person; he.
kuil 구일 the ninth day. →**ahŭre** 아흐레.
kuip 구입 purchase; buying. *kuip'ada* 구입하다 purchase; buy. *kuipcha* 구입자 purchaser.
kuje 구제 relief; succor; help; aid. *kujehada* 구제하다 relieve; succor; deliver (a person) from.
kujik 구직 seeking work; job-hunting.
kujo 구조 rescue; aid; relief; succor. *kujohada* 구조하다 save; rescue; relieve.
kŭjŏkke 그저께 the day before yesterday.
kujŏn 구전 commission; brokerage (fee).

kŭjŏn 그전 former days[times]; the past.

kujŏng 구정 lunar New Year's Day.

kŭjŭŭm 그즈음 about that time; around then.

kujwa 구좌 account. →**kyejwa** 계좌.

kuk 국 soup; broth. *kugŭl mashida* 국을 마시다 sip soup.

kŭk 극 drama; play. *kŭkchŏgin* 극적인 dramatical. *kŭkchŏgŭro* 극적으로 dramatically.

kŭk 극 ① pole(s) ② height; extreme; climax. *…ŭi kŭge tarhada* …의 극에 달하다 reach the climax.

kukch'ae 국채 national debt; national loan; government bond

kukchang 국장 director of a bureau.

kŭkchang 극장 theater; playhouse.

kukche 국제. *kukchejŏk* 국제적 international; world. *kukchejŏgŭro* 국제적으로 internationally; universally.

kukche yŏnhap 국제 연합 United Nations (U.N.).

kŭkchin 극진. *kŭkchinhada* 극진하다 (be) very cordial; devoted. *kŭkchinhi* 극진히 kindly; cordially.

kukchŏk 국적 nationality; citizenship. *kukchŏk pulmyŏngŭi* 국적 불명의 of unknown nationality.

kukchŏn 국전 the National Art Exhibition.

kŭk'i 극히 extremely; highly; most; quite.

kŭkchak 극작 play writing. *kŭkchakka* 극작가 dramatist; playwright.

kukka 국가 state; nation; country. *kukkajŏk* 국가적 national; state.

kukka 국가 national anthem.

kukki 국기 national flag[colors].

kukkun 국군 national army. *kukkunŭi nal* 국군의 날 (ROK) Armed Forces Day.

kŭ kot 그 곳 that place; there. *kŭ kose* 그 곳에 in that place; there.

kukkyŏng 국경 border; national boundary

kukkyŏngil 국경일 national holiday.

kuk'oe 국회 National Assembly. *kuk'oe ŭiwŏn* 국회 의원 member of National Assembly[Congressman].

kukpang 국방 national defense. *kukpangbu* 국방부 Ministry of National Defense.

kukpap 국밥 rice-and-meat soup.

kukpi 국비 national expenditure[expenses] *kukpi yuhaksaeng* 국비 유학생 government student a-broad.

kŭkpin 극빈 extreme poverty. *kŭkpinja* 극빈자 needy[destitute] person; pauper.

kukpo 국보 national treasure[heirloom].

kŭkpok 극복 conquest. *kŭkpok'ada* 극복하다 over-come; conquer

kuksa 국사 national history; history of Korea.

kuksan 국산 home[domestic] production. *kuksan-ŭi* 국산의 homemade. *kuksanp'um* 국산품 home products; homemade articles.

kukta 굵다 (be) big; thick. *kulgŭn p'al* 굵은 팔 big arm.

kŭkta 긁다 ① scratch; scrape (off, out) ② rake up; gather up.

kŭktan 극단 dramatical[theatrical] company; the-atrical troupe.

kŭktan 극단 extreme; extremity. *kŭktanŭi* 극단의 extreme. *kŭktanŭro* 극단으로 extremely.

kukt'o 국토 country; territory; domain. *kukt'o pangwi* 국토 방위 national defense.

kŭkto 극도 extreme. *kŭktoŭi* 극도의 extreme; ut-

most. *kŭktoro* 극도로 extremely; to the utmost.
Kŭktong 극동 the Far East.
kuk'wa 국화 chrysanthemum.
kuk'wa 국화 national flower.
kul 굴 oyster. *kult'wigim* 굴튀김 fried oysters.
kul 굴 ① cave; cavern ② den; lair ③ tunnel.
kŭl 글 writings; composition; prose; sentence; letter.
kulbok 굴복 submission; surrender. *kulbok'ada* 굴복하다 submit[surrender, yield, give in].
kŭlcha 글자 letter; character; ideography.
kŭlkwi 글귀 passage; line; words; terms.
kulle 굴레 bridle. *kullerŭl ssŭiuda* 굴레를 씌우다 bridle. *kullerŭl pŏtta* 굴레를 벗다 take off a bridle.
kŭlp'i 글피 two days after tomorrow.
kŭlssi 글씨 letter; character; writing; penmanship.
kulttuk 굴뚝 chimney.
kŭm 금 gold. *kŭmŭi* 금의 gold; golden; auric. *kŭmshigye* 금시계 gold watch.
kŭm 금 ① line ② fold; crease ③ crevice; crack.
kŭmanduda 그만두다 stop; cease; quit; discontinue.
kŭmaek 금액 amount of money; sum (of money).
kŭmbal 금발 golden hair; blonde (of female); blond (of male).
kŭmbang 금방 →**panggŭm** 방금.
kŭmgangsŏk 금강석 diamond.
kŭmgo 금고 safe; strongbox; cash box; vault.
kŭmgoe 금괴 gold bullion; gold ingot; gold bar.
kŭmhada 금하다 ① → **kŭmjihada** 금지하다 ② suppress; restrain; check.
Kumi 구미 Europe and America; the West.
kŭmil 금일 today; this day. →**onŭl** 오늘.

kŭmji 금지 prohibition; ban; embargo. *kŭmjihada* 금지하다 prohibit; forbid; ban.

kŭmjŏn 금전 money; cash; gold coin. *kŭmjŏnsang-ŭi* 금전상의 monetary; financial; pecuniary.

kŭmju 금주 abstinence (from drink); total abstinence.

kŭmju 금주 this week. *kŭmju chunge* 금주 중에 some time this week.

kumjurida 굶주리다 be[go] hungry; starve; thirst (for, after).

kŭmmyŏnggan 금명간 in a day or two.

kŭmnyo 급료 pay; salary; wages. →**ponggŭp** 봉급, **imgŭm** 임금.

kŭmnyŏn 금년 this year; the current year. →**orhae** 올해.

kŭmnyu 급류 swift stream; torrents; rapids.

kŭmnyung 금융 money market; finance; monetary circulation. *kŭmnyunggye* 금융계 financial circles.

kumŏng 구멍 hole; opening; chink. *panŭl kumŏng* 바늘 구멍 eye of a needle. *kumŏngŭl ttult'a* 구멍을 뚫다 make[bore, drill] a hole.

kumŏng kage 구멍 가게 small shop[store].

kŭmp'um 금품 money and goods. *kŭmp'umŭl chuda* 금품을 주다 bribe (a person) with money and other valuables.

kŭmni 금리 interest; money rates.

kŭmsok 금속 metal. *kyŏnggŭmsok* 경금속 light metals. *kwigŭmsok* 귀금속 precious metals.

kŭmsu 금수 embargo on the exportation[importation]. *kŭmsup'ŭm* 금수품 contraband (goods).

kumta 굶다 starve; go hungry. *kulmŏ chukta* 굶어 죽다 starve to death; die of hunger.

kumt'ŭlgŏrida 굼틀거리다 wriggle; squirm; writhe.
kŭmul 그물 net; dragnet; netting.
kŭmŭmnal 그믐날 the last day (of the month).
kŭmyoil 금요일 Friday.
kun 군 ① army; force; troops ② team. *che p'algun* 제 8 군 the Eighth Army. *paekkun* 백군 white team.
kunae 구내 premises; precincts; compound. *kunae shiktang* 구내 식당 refectory.
kunak 군악 military music. *kunaktae* 군악대 military[naval] band.
kunbi 군비 armaments. *kunbi kyŏngjaeng* 군비 경쟁 armament race. *kunbi ch'ukso[hwakchang]* 군비 축소[확장] reduction[expansion] of armaments.
kunbok 군복 service[military, naval] uniform.
kŭnbon 근본 foundation; basis; origin. *kŭnbonjŏk (ŭro)* 근본적 (으로) fundamental(ly); basical(ly).
kŭnch'ŏ 근처 neighborhood; vicinity. *kŭnch'ŏŭi* 근처의 neighboring; nearby; close by. *kŭnch'ŏe* 근처에 in the neighborhood[vicinity].
kunch'uk 군축 reduction of armaments; disarmament. *kunch'uk'ada* 군축하다 reduce armament.
kŭndae 근대 modern ages; recent times. *kŭndaejŏgin* 근대적인 modernistic. *kŭndaehwahada* 근대화하다 modernize.
kundan 군단 corps; army corps.
kundo 군도 saber; service-sword.
kŭne 그네 swing; trapeze. *kŭnerŭl t'ada* 그네를 타다 get on a swing.
kungdungi 궁둥이 buttocks; hips; rump; ass.
kun-gi 군기 colors; standard.
kungji 궁지 difficult situation; predicament; fix.

kungjie ppajida 궁지에 빠지다 be in a fix[sad plight].

kŭngji 궁지 pride; dignity.

kungjŏn 궁전 (royal) palace.

kungmin 국민 nation; people. *kungminŭi* 국민의 national. *kungmin sodŭk* 국민 소득 national income.

kungmun 국문 national[Korean] language. *kungmunpŏp* 국문법 Korean grammar.

kŭngnak 극락 paradise. *kŭngnak segye* 극락 세계 abode of perfect bliss.

kungnip 국립. *kungnibŭi* 국립의 national; state. *kungnip kŭkchang[kongwŏn]* 국립 극장[공원] national theater[park].

kungnyŏk 국력 national power. *kungnyŏgŭl kirŭda* 국력을 기르다 build up national power.

kŭn-gŏ 근거 basis; base; foundation; ground. *kŭngŏga ŏmnŭn* 근거가 없는 groundless; baseless.

kungsul 궁술 archery; bowmanship.

kŭn-gyo 근교 suburbs; outskirts.

kŭnhae 근해 neighboring[home] waters; near [adjacent] seas.

kunham 군함 warship; battleship.

kunhwa 군화 military shoes; combat boats.

kunin 군인 serviceman; soldier; sailor; airman. *chigŏp kunin* 직업 군인 professional soldier.

kŭnjirŏpta 근지럽다 →**karyŏpta** 가렵다.

kunjung 군중 crowd; masses; multitude. *kunjung taehoe* 군중 대회 (mass) rally.

kunmaejŏm 군매점 canteen; post exchange (P.X.).

kŭnmu 근무 service; duty; work. *kŭnmuhada* 근무 하다 serve; work.

kunpap 군납 supply of goods and services to the

military. *kunnap ŏpcha* 군납 업자 military goods supplier.

kunpŏp 군법 military law. *kunpŏp hoeŭi* 군법 회의 court-martial.

kunsa 군사 military affairs. *kunsa komundan* 군사 고문단 the Military Advisory Group.

kŭnsa 근사. *kŭnsahan* 근사한 ① approximate; closely resembled ② fine; nice; splendid. *kŭnsahan saenggak* 근사한 생각 splendid idea.

kunsaryŏnggwan 군사령관 army commander.

kŭnshi 근시. *kŭnshiŭi* 근시의 shortsighted; nearsighted. *kŭnshi an-gyŏng* 근시 안경 glasses for short sight.

kunsu 군수. *kunsu kongjang* 군수 공장 munition factory. *kunsu sanŏp* 군수 산업 war industry.

kunŭi 군의 army[naval] doctor[surgeon]. *kunŭigwan* 군의관 medical officer.

kŭnŭl 그늘 shade. *namu kŭnŭl* 나무 그늘 shade of a tree.

kŭnwon 근원 origin; source; root; cause.

kŭnyang 그냥 as it is; as you find it; in that condition.

kŭnyŏ 그녀 she. *kŭnyŏŭi[rŭl, ege]* 그녀의[를, 에게] her.

kunyong 군용 military use. *kunyongŭi* 군용의 military. *kunyonggi* 군용기 military plane.

kŭnyuk 근육 muscle; sinews.

kup 굽 hoof; heel. *kubi nop'ŭn[najŭn] kudu* 굽이 높은[낮은] 구두 high-[low-]heeled shoes.

kŭp 급 class; grade.

kŭp'aeng 급행. *kŭp'aeng yŏlch'a* 급행 열차 express train.

kŭp'ada 급하다 (be) urgent; pressing; hasty. *kŭp'i* 급히 quickly; rapidly; hastily.

kup'ida 굽히다 bend; bow; stoop.

kŭppi 급비 supply of expenses. *kŭppisaeng* 급비생 scholar (*Eng.*); scholarship holder (*Am.*).

kŭpsu 급수 water supply[service]. *kŭpsuhada* 급수하다 supply (a town) with water.

kupta 굽다 roast; broil; bake. *chal kuwŏjin* 잘 구워진 well-done; well baked. *tŏl kuwŏjin* 덜 구워진 medium. *sŏl kuwojin* 설 구워진 rare.

kurenarut 구레나룻 whiskers.

kuri 구리 copper. *kuritpit* 구릿빛 copper-colored. *kuri ch'ŏlsa* 구리 철사 copper wire.

kŭrida 그리다 yearn after[for]; long[pine] for [after]; thirst for[after].

kŭrida 그리다 picture; draw; paint; sketch.

kŭrim 그림 picture; painting; drawing. *kŭrim yŏpsŏ* 그림 엽서 picture[post] card. *kŭrim kat'ŭn* 그림 같은 picturesque.

kŭrimja 그림자 shadow; silhouette.

kŭrŏch'i anŭmyŏn 그렇지 않으면 otherwise; unless; if...not so; (or) else.

kŭrŏk'omalgo 그렇고말고 indeed; of course; certainly.

kŭrŏlssahada 그럴싸하다 (be) plausible; likely.

kŭrŏl tŭt'ada 그럴 듯하다 →**kŭrŏlssahada** 그럴싸하다.

kŭrŏmŭro 그러므로 so; hence; therefore.

kŭrŏmyŏn 그러면 if so; in that case; then.

kŭrŏna 그러나 but; still; however; and yet.

kurŏngi 구렁이 big snake; huge serpent.

kŭru 그루 stump; stock. *namu han kŭru* 나무 한

그루 a stump of tree.

kŭrŭch'ida 그르치다 spoil; ruin; destroy; err.

kurŭm 구름 cloud. *kurŭm kkin* 구름 낀 cloudy. *kurŭm ŏmnŭn* 구름 없는 cloudless.

kurŭmdari 구름다리 overpass; land bridge.

kŭrŭrŏnggŏrida 그르렁거리다 wheeze; purr.

kŭrŭt 그릇 vessel; container. *notkŭrŭt* 놋그릇 brazen vessel.

kuse 구세 salvation (of the world). *kusegun* 구세 군 the Salvation Army. *kuseju* 구세주 Savior; Messiah.

kushil 구실 excuse; pretext; pretense. *...ŭl kushillo sama* …을 구실로 삼아 on the pretext of.

kusok 구속 ① restriction; restraint ② detention; binding. *kusok'ada* 구속하다 restrict; restrain; detain (a person) in custody.

kusŏk 구석 corner; nook. *kusŏge* 구석에 in a corner.

kusŏng 구성 constitution; composition; organization. *kusŏnghada* 구성하다 constitute; organize.

kusŭl 구슬 bead; gem.

kŭsŭllida 그슬리다 burn; scorch; singe.

kusŭlp'ŭda 구슬프다 (be) sad; sorrowful; doleful.

kut'o 구토 vomiting; nausea. *kut'ohada* 구토하다 vomit; throw up.

kŭ tongan 그 동안 the while; during that time; these[those] days.

kutta 궂다 ① (be) cross; bad ② (be) foul; nasty; rainy. *kujŭn nalssi* 궂은 날씨 nasty weather.

kŭŭlda 그을다 be sunburned; be scorched[tanned]; be sooted (up).

kuyak sŏngsŏ 구약 성서 Old Testament.

kŭyamallo 그야말로 indeed; really; quite.

kuyŏkchil 구역질 nausea. *kuyŏkchillada* 구역질나다 feel nausea; feel sick.

kwa 과 course; department; faculty. *Yŏngŏkwa* 영어과 English course[department].

kwa 과 ① lesson; subject ② section; department; division. *che igwa* 제2과 Lesson two. *ch'ongmukwa(jang)* 총무과(장) (chief[head] of a) general affairs section.

kwabu 과부 widow.

kwadae 과대 exaggeration. *kwadaehada* 과대하다 exaggerate; overstate. →**kwajang** 과장.

kwadogi 과도기 transition(al) period[stage]; age of transition.

kwaench'ant'a 괜찮다 ① (be) passable; not so bad; will do ② do not care; be all right.

kwaengi 괭이 hoe; pick. *kwaengiro p'ada* 괭이로 파다 hoe up the soil.

kwagŏ 과거 the past (days); bygone days. *kwagŏŭi* 과거의 past; bygone.

kwahada 과하다 levy (a tax); impose; assign; set; inflict. *segŭmŭl kwahada* 세금을 과하다 levy [impose] a tax on.

kwahak 과학 science. *kwahakchŏk(ŭro)* 과학적(으로) scientific(ally). *kwahak kisul* 과학 기술 science and technology. *kwahakcha* 과학자 scientist.

kwail 과일 (edible) fruit. *kwail kage* 과일 가게 fruit shop[stand]. →**kwashil** 과실.

kwaja 과자 confectionery; cake; sweets; candy. *kwajajŏm* 과자점 sweetshop; candy store(*Am.*).

kwajang 과장 exaggeration. *kwajanghada* 과장하다 exaggerate; overstate; magnify.

kwallam 관람 inspection; viewing. *kwallamhada*

관람하다 see; view; inspect. *kwallamkwŏn* 관람권 admission ticket. *kwallamnyo* 관람료 admission fee. *kwallamgaek*[*kwan-gaek*] 관람객[관객] spectator; visitor.

kwalli 관리 government official; public servant.

kwalli 관리 management; administration. *kwalli-hada* 관리하다 administer; manage. *kwalliin*[*ja*] 관리인[자] manager; superintendent.

kwallye 관례 custom; usage; precedent.

kwamok 과목 subject; lesson; course. *p'ilsu*[*sŏnt'aek*] *kwamok* 필수[선택] 과목 required[optional, elective] subject.

kwan 관 coffin; casket. *kwane nŏt'a* 관에 넣다 lay (a corpse) in a coffin.

kwanak 관악 pipe-music. *kwanakki* 관악기 wind instrument.

kwanbo 관보 official gazette.

kwanch'ŭk 관측 observation; survey. *kwanch'ŭk'ada* 관측하다 observe; make[take] an observations. *kwanch'ŭkso* 관측소 observatory.

kwandae 관대. *kwandaehada* 관대하다 (be) generous; broad-minded. *kwandaehan* 관대한 broad-minded; generous; liberal. *kwandaehi* 관대히 generously; tolerantly.

kwang 광 storeroom; storehouse; cellar.

kwan-gaek 관객 spectator; audience.

kwangbu 광부 miner; mine worker; pitman.

kwangdae 광대 clown; feat actor; acrobatic performer.

kwanggo 광고 advertisement. *kwanggohada* 광고하다 advertise; announce.

kwanggyŏng 광경 spectacle; sight; scene; view.

kwanghak 광학 optics; optical science.
kwangjang 광장 open space; (public) square; plaza.
kwangmaek 광맥 vein of ore; deposit.
kwangmul 광물 mineral. *kwangmul chawŏn* 광물 자원 mineral resources.
kwan-gongsŏ 관공서 government and public offices.
kwangŏp 광업 mining (industry).
kwangsan 광산 mine. *kwangsan kisa* 광산 기사 mining engineer. *kwangsan nodongja* 광산 노동자 mine worker; miner.
kwangshin 광신 religious fanaticism. *kwangshinja* 광신자 fanatic.
kwangsŏn 광선 light; ray; beam. *t'aeyang kwangsŏn* 태양 광선 sunlight. *eksŭ kwangsŏn* 엑스 광선 X rays.
kwangt'aek 광택 luster; gloss; shine. *kwangt'aegŭl naeda* 광택을 내다 polish; shine.
kwan-gwang 관광 sightseeing. *kwan-gwanghada* 관광하다 go sightseeing; do the sights (of). *kwan-gwanggaek* 관광객 sightseer; tourist. *kwan-gwang pŏsŭ* 관광 버스 sightseeing bus. *kwan-gwang yŏhaeng* 관광 여행 sightseeing tour. *kwan-gwangji* [*hot'el*] 관광지〔호텔〕 tourist resort〔hotel〕.
kwan-gye 관계 relation; concern(ment); connection. *kwan-gyehada* 관계하다 relate to; concern; participate in; be concerned in.
kwanhyŏn 관현 wind and string instrument. *kwanhyŏnak* 관현악 orchestra music. *kwanhyŏnaktan* 관현악단 orchestra (band).
kwannyŏm 관념 ① idea; notion ② sense.
kwansa 관사 official residence.
kwanse 관세 customs; customs duties. *suip*〔*such'ul*〕

kwanse 수입〔수출〕 관세 import〔export〕 duties.
kwansech'ŏng 관세청 the Office of Customs Administration.

kwanshim 관심 concern; interest. *···e kwanshimŭl kajida* ···에 관심을 가지다 be concerned (about).

kwanyŏk 과녁 target; mark.

kwanyong 관용. *kwanyongŭi* 관용의 common; customary. *kwanyongŏ* 관용어 idiom; idiomatic expression.

kwao 과오 fault; mistake; error. *kwaorŭl pŏmhada* 과오를 범하다 make a mistake; blunder.

kwarho 괄호 parenthesis; bracket; brace.

kwashik 과식 overeating. *kwashik'ada* 과식하다 eat too much; overeat.

kwashil 과실 fruit. *kwashilju* 과실주 fruit wine.

kwashil 과실 fault; mistake; blunder. *kwashil ch'i-sa* 과실 치사 accidental homicide.

kwasuwon 과수원 orchard; fruit garden.

kwetchak 궤짝 box; chest. *sagwa han kwetchak* 사과 한 궤짝 a box of apples.

kweyang 궤양 ulcer. *wigweyang* 위궤양 ulcer of the stomach.

kwi 귀 ear. *kwiga mŏlda* 귀가 멀다 be hard of hearing.

kwibin 귀빈 guest of honor; important guest. *kwibinsŏk〔shil〕* 귀빈석〔실〕 room for VIPs.

kwibuin 귀부인 (titled) lady; noble woman.

kwich'ant'a 귀찮다 (be) annoying; irksome. *kwich'ank'e* 귀찮게 annoyingly.

kwiguk 귀국. *kwiguk'ada* 귀국하다 return to one's country; go home.

kwigŭmsok 귀금속 precious metals.

kwihada 귀하다 ① (be) noble; honorable ② (be) deer; lovable ③ (be) rare; uncommon.

kwihwa 귀화 naturalization. *kwihwahada* 귀화하다 be naturalized.

kwijok 귀족 noble(man); peer. *kwijogŭi* 귀족의 noble; titled; aristocratic. *kwijok sahoe* 귀족 사회 aristocracy; nobility.

kwijunghada 귀중하다 (be) precious; valuable. *kwijungp'um* 귀중품 valuables.

kwimŏgŏri 귀머거리 deaf person.

kwisun 귀순 submission; allegiance. *kwisunhada* 귀순하다 defect; submit (to).

kwitkumŏng 귓구멍 ear-hole; opening of the ear; ear.

kwitpyŏng 귓병 ear disease.

kwitturami 귀뚜라미 cricket; grig.

kwiyŏpta 귀엽다 (be) lovely; charming; attractive; cute.

kwiyŏwohada 귀여워하다 love; pet; caress; hold (a person) dear.

kwolli 권리 right; claim; title; privilege.

kwollyŏk 권력 power; authority. *kwollyŏk innŭn* 권력 있는 influential; powerful. *kwollyŏkka* 권력가 man of power.

kwollyŏn 궐련 cigarette.

kwonch'ong 권총 pistol; revolver; gun (*Am.*). *kwonch'ong kangdo* 권총 강도 armed robber; gunman.

kwonhada 권하다 ① recommend ② advise; ask ③ invite; urge.

kwonse 권세 power; influence; authority. *kwonse-rŭl purida* 권세를 부리다 wield power.

kwont'ae 권태 weariness; fatigue; languor.

kwont'u 권투 boxing. *kwont'u shihap* 권투 시합 boxing match[bout]; prize-fight.

kwonwi 권위 authority; power; dignity. *kwonwi innŭn* 권위 있는 authoritative.

kwonyu 권유 inducement; solicitation; canvassing. *kwonyuhada* 권유하다 induce; canvass; solicit.

kyaltchuk'ada 걀쭉하다 somewhat long and slender; oval.

kyarŭmhada 갸름하다 somewhat long; (be) pleasantly oval. *kyarŭmhan ŏlgul* 갸름한 얼굴 oval face.

kye 계 ① section (in an office) ② charge; duty. *ch'ullapkye* 출납계 cashier's section.

kye 계 ① system ② family line; lineage ③ faction; clique. *t'aeyanggye* 태양계 solar system.

kye 계 mutual-aid society; loan club; guild. *kyeju* 계주 principal of a loan club.

-kye -계 notice; report. *kyŏlsŏkkye* 결석계 absence report. *samanggye* 사망계 notice of death.

-kye -계 circles; community; world; kingdom. *shirŏpkye* 실업계 business circle.

kyebu 계부 stepfather.

kyech'aek 계책 stratagem; plot; trick; scheme. *kyech'aegŭl ssŭda* 계책을 쓰다 adopt[use] a stratagem.

kyech'ŭng 계층 class; social stratum; walk of life.

kyedan 계단 stairs; staircase; doorstep.

kyegan 계간 quarterly publication. *kyeganji* 계간지 quarterly.

kyegi 계기 meter; gauge; scale; instrument.

kyegok 계곡 valley; glen; dale; canyon.

kyegŭp 계급 class; caste. *sangnyu[chungnyu, ha-*

ryu] *kyegŭp* 상류〔중류, 하류〕 계급 upper〔middle, lower〕 class(es).

kyehoek 계획 plan; project; scheme; program(me). *kyehoek'ada* 계획하다 plan; project; scheme; intend. *kyehoekchŏgin* 계획적인 intentional; planned. *kyehoekchŏgŭro* 계획적으로 intentionally; deliberately.

kyejang 계장 chief clerk; chief.

kyejip 계집 (*slang*) woman; female; one's wife. *kyejibai* 계집아이 girl; lass.

kyejŏl 계절 season. *kyejŏrŭi* 계절의 seasonal.

kyeju kyŏnggi 계주 경기 relay (race). *ch'ŏnmit'ŏ kyeju kyŏnggi* 1,000 미터 계주 경기 1,000 meter relay race.

kyejwa 계좌 account. *kyejwarŭl yŏlda* 계좌를 열다 open an account (with a bank).

kyemo 계모 stepmother.

kyemong 계몽 enlightenment; education. *kyemonghada* 계몽하다 enlighten; educate.

kyeŏmnyŏng 계엄령 martial law.

kyeran 계란 egg. →**talgyal** 달걀.

kyerisa 계리사 chartered accountant; certified public accountant.

kyeryanggi 계량기 meter; gauge; scale.

kyesan 계산 calculation; reckoning; counting; computation. *kyesanhada* 계산하다 count; sum up; calculate; reckon. *kyesan-gi* 계산기 adding machine; calculating machine. *kyesansŏ* 계산서 bill; account.

kyeshi 계시 revelation; apocalypse. *kyeshihada* 계시하다 reveal.

kyeshida 계시다 (*honorific*) be; stay.

kyesok 계속 continuance; continuation. *kyesok'ada* 계속하다 continue; last; go on with. *kyesokchŏgin* 계속적인 continuous; continual.

kyesu 계수 younger brother's wife; sister-in-law.

kyesŭng 계승 succession; inheritance. *kyesŭnghada* succeed to; inherit.

kyet'ong 계통 ① system ② lineage ③ party. *kyet'ongjŏk* 계통적 systematic. *kyet'ongjŏguro* 계통적으로 systematically.

kyewon 계원 clerk in charge; section man. *chŏpsu kyewon* 접수 계원 information clerk.

kyeyak 계약 contract; compact; covenant. *kyeyak'ada* 계약하다 contract; make a contract. *kyeyak-kŭm* 계약금 contract deposit. *kyeyaksŏ* 계약서 (written) contract.

kyŏ 겨 chaff, hulls[husks] of grain; bran.

kyoch'a 교차 intersection; crossing. *kyoch'ahada* 교차하다 cross[intersect] (each other). *kyoch'aro* 교차로 crossroads; intersection.

kyodae 교대 alternation; change. *kyodaehada* 교대하다 take turns; alternate. *kyodaero* 교대로 by turns; alternately.

kyodan 교단 platform. *kyodane sŏda* 교단에 서다 teach a class; be a teacher.

kyodoso 교도소 prison; jail.

kyŏdŭrangi 겨드랑이 armpit; axilla.

kyoga 교가 school[college] song; Alma Mater song.

kyŏgil 격일. *kyŏgillo* 격일로 every other day; on alternate days.

kyŏgŏn 격언 maxim; proverb; saying.

kyogwasŏ 교과서 textbook. *kŏmjŏng kyogwasŏ* 검정 교과서 authorized textbook.

kyŏgwol 격월 every other month. *kyŏgwol kanhaengmul* 격월 간행물 bimonthly (publication).

kyohoe 교회 church; chapel; cathedral. *kyohoedang* 교회당 church; chapel.

kyohun 교훈 instruction; precept; lesson.

kyohwal 교활. *kyohwarhan* 교활한 cunning; crafty; sly. *kyohwarhan nom* 교활한 놈 old fox; sly dog.

kyohwan 교환 exchange; interchange; barter. *kyohwanhada* 교환하다 exchange; barter; interchange.

kyohyangak 교향악 symphony. *kyohyangaktan* 교향악단 symphony orchestra.

kyoin 교인 believer; adherent; follower. *Kŭrisŭdo [kidok] kyoin* 그리스도[기독] 교인 believer in christianity; christian.

kyŏja 겨자 mustard.

kyojang 교장 schoolmaster; headmaster (of primary school); principal (of junior high school); director (of high school).

kyoje 교제 association; intercourse. *kyojehada* 교제하다 associate with; hold intercourse with; keep company with.

kyojŏng 교정 school grounds; campus (*Am.*); school playground.

kyojŏng 교정 proofreading. *kyojŏnghada* 교정하다 read proofs; correct (the press).

kyŏkcha 격자 lattice. *kyŏkcha munŭi* 격자 무늬 cross stripes; check.

kyŏkch'an 격찬 high praise. *kyŏkch'anhada* 격찬하다 praise highly; extol; speak highly of.

kyŏkch'im 격침 sinking, destruction. *kyŏkch'imhada* 격침하다 (attack and) sink (a ship); send (a ship) to the bottom.

kyŏkchŏn 격전 hot fight; fierce battle; hot contest.

kyŏkchu 격주. *kyŏkchuŭi* 격주의 fortnightly; bi-weekly.

kyŏkch'u 격추. *kyŏkch'uhada* 격추하다 shoot (air-planes) down; bring down.

kyŏkpun 격분 wild rage; vehement indignation. *kyŏkpunhada* 격분하다 be enraged.

kyŏkpyŏn 격변 sudden change; revulsion. *kyŏk-pyŏnhada* 격변하다 change violently.

kyŏkta 겪다 ① undergo; suffer; experience ② receive; entertain.

kyŏkt'oe 격퇴 repulse. *kyŏkt'oehada* 격퇴하다 re-pulse; drive[beat] back.

kyŏktol 격돌 crash; violent collision. *kyŏktorhada* 격돌하다 crash into[against].

kyŏkt'u 격투 grapple; (hand-to-hand) fight; scuffle. *kyŏkt'uhada* 격투하다 grapple with.

kyŏk'wa 격화. *kyŏk'wahada* 격화하다 grow more intense[violent]; intensify.

kyŏl 결 grain; texture. *pidankyŏl* 비단결 silky texture. *salkyŏl* 살결 texture of the skin.

kyŏlbaek 결백 purity; innocence; integrity. *kyŏl-baek'ada* 결백하다 (be) pure; upright; innocent.

kyŏlbu 결부. *kyŏlbushik'ida* 결부시키다 connect (A) with (B); link together.

kyŏlchae 결재 sanction; approval *kyŏlchaehada* 결재하다 decide (upon); approve; sanction.

kyŏlchŏm 결점 fault; defect; flaw.

kyŏlchŏng 결정 decision; determination; conclu-sion; settlement. *kyŏlchŏnghada* 결정하다 decide (upon); conclude; settle.

kyŏlguk 결국 after all; in the end; finally; in the long run; eventually.

kyŏlgŭn 결근 absence (from). *kyŏlgŭnhada* 결근하다 be absent[absent oneself] (from).

kyŏlgwa 결과 result; consequence; effect; fruit. ···*ŭi kyŏlgwa* ···의 결과 as a[the] result of.

kyŏlk'o 결코 never; by no means; not in the least.

kyŏllida 결리다 feel a stitch; get stiff.

kyŏllon 결론 conclusion. *kyŏllonŭl naerida* 결론을 내리다 draw[form] a conclusion.

kyŏllyŏl 결렬 rupture; breakdown. *kyŏllyŏrhada* 결렬하다 break down; be broken off.

kyŏlmal 결말 end; conclusion; result; settlement. *kyŏlmallada* 결말나다 be settled; come to a conclusion.

kyŏlsa 결사 *kyŏlsajŏk*[*ŭi*] 결사적[의] desperate; death-defying. *kyŏlsadae* 결사대 forlorn hope.

kyŏlsan 결산 settlement of accounts. *kyŏlsanhada* 결산하다 settle[balance] an account.

kyŏlshim 결심 determination; resolution. *kyŏlshimhada* 결심하다 determine; be resolved; make up one's mind.

kyŏlsŏk 결석 absence. *kyŏlsŏk'ada* 결석하다 be absent[absent oneself] (from). → **kyŏlgŭn** 결근.

kyŏlson 결손 loss; deficit. *kyŏlsonŭl naeda* 결손을 내다 run a deficit; suffer[incur] a loss.

kyŏlsŭng 결승 decision (of a contest). *kyŏlsŭngjŏn* 결승전 final game[match].

kyŏltan 결단 decision; determination; resolution. *kyŏltanŭl naerida* 결단을 내리다 reach[come to] a definite decision. ⌜duel.

kyŏlt'u 결투 duel. *kyŏlt'uhada* 결투하다 fight a

kyŏm 겸 and; in addition; concurrently. *ach'im kyŏm chŏmshim* 아침 겸 점심 brunch. *ch'imshil kyŏm kŏshil* 침실 겸 거실 bed-sitting room. *susang kyŏm oesang* 수상 겸 외상 Prime Minister and (concurrently) Foreign Minister.

kyoman 교만 pride; elation; haughtiness. *kyomanhada* 교만하다 (be) proud; haughty; arrogant.

kyŏmbi 겸비. *kyŏmbihada* 겸비하다 combine (one thing) with (another); have both.

kyomi 교미 copulation; coition. *kyomihada* 교미하다 copulate.

kyŏmim 겸임. *kyŏmimhada* 겸임하다 hold an additional post[office].

kyŏmson 겸손 modesty; humility. *kyŏmsonhada* 겸손하다 (be) modest; humble.

kyomun 교문 school gate. 「deft.

kyomyo 교묘 *kyomyohan* 교묘한 clever; skil(l)ful;

kyŏn 견 silk. *kyŏnsa* 견사 silk-thread.

kyonae 교내 campus. *kyonaeŭi* 교내의 interclass. *kyonaeesŏ* 교내에서 on[within] the campus.

kyŏnbon 견본 sample; specimen.

kyŏndida 견디다 ① bear; endure; stand ② wear; last; be good for; be equal to.

kyŏng 경 about; toward(s); around. *seshigyŏng* 세시경 about three o'clock.

kyŏng 경 Lord; Sir; you.

kyŏng 경 ① Chinese classics of Confucianism ② sutra; Buddhist scripture.

kyŏngbi 경비 expenses; cost; expenditure. *kyŏngbi chŏryak[chŏlgam]* 경비 절약[절감] curtailment of expenditure.

kyŏngbi 경비 defense; guard. *kyŏngbihada* 경비

하다 defend; keep watch.

kyŏngbo 경보 alarm; warning. *kyŏnggye kyŏngbo* 경계 경보 air defense alarm. *kongsŭp kyŏngbo* 공습 경보 air raid alarm.

kyŏngbŏmchoe 경범죄 minor[light] offense[crime]; misdemeanor.

kyŏngch'al 경찰 the police. *kyŏngch'alsŏ* 경찰서 police station. *kyŏngch'algwan* 경찰관 policeman; police officer. *kyŏngch'algwan p'ach'ulso* 경찰관 파출소 police box[station branch].

kyŏngch'i 경치 scenery; landscape; view.

kyŏngch'ing 경칭 honorific; term of respect.

kyŏngch'uk 경축 congratulation; celebration. *kyŏngch'uk'ada* 경축하다 congratulate; celebrate. *kyŏngch'ugil* 경축일 national holiday; fête day.

kyŏngdae 경대 dressing stand[table]; vanity (*Am.*); toilet table (*Eng.*).

kyŏngdan 경단 rice cake dumpling.

kyŏnggi 경기 game; match; contest; event. *kyŏnggihada* 경기하다 have[play] a game. *kyŏnggijang* 경기장 ground; field; stadium.

kyŏnggi 경기 ① business(condition); market ② the times; things. *pulgyŏnggi* 불경기 depression; recession. *hogyŏnggi* 호경기 boom; prosperity.

kyŏnggigwanch'ong 경기관총 light machine gun.

kyŏnggo 경고 warning; caution. *kyŏnggohada* 경고하다 warn(a person) against (of); give warning (to).

kyŏnggŏn 경건 piety; devotion. *kyŏnggŏnhada* 경건하다 (be) devout; pious.

kyŏnggongŏp 경공업 light industry.

kyŏnggu 경구 epigram; aphorism; witticism.

kyŏnggŭmsok 경금속 light metals.

kyŏnggwa 경과 ① progress (of a case); development (of an event) ② lapse (of time). *kyŏnggwahada* 경과하다 elapse; pass; go by; expire.

kyŏnggwan 경관 policeman; constable (*Eng.*); cop.

kyŏnggye 경계 guard; lookout; watch; precaution. *kyŏnggyehada* 경계하다 guard against; look out [watch] (for).

kyŏnggye 경계 boundary; border; frontier. *kyŏnggyesŏn* 경계선 boundary line; border line.

kyŏnghap 경합 concurrence; conflict; competition. *kyŏnghap'ada* 경합하다 concur; compete (with).

kyŏngho 경호 guard; escort. *kyŏnghohada* 경호하다 guard; convoy; escort. *kyŏnghowon* 경호원 bodyguard.

kyŏnghŏm 경험 experience. *kyŏnghŏmhada* 경험하다 experience; go through; undergo. *kyŏnghŏmi itta* 경험이 있다 have experience (in).

kyŏnghwahak kongŏp 경화학 공업 light chemical industry.

kyŏnghyang 경향 tendency; trend. *…ŭi kyŏnghyangi itta* …의 경향이 있다 tend towards; tend to (do); have a tendency to.

kyŏngi 경이 wonder; miracle. *kyŏngijŏk (in)* 경이적 (인) wonderful; marvelous; sensational.

kyŏngjaeng 경쟁 competition; rivalry; contest. *kyŏngjaenghada* 경쟁하다 compete with; contest; vie; cope.

kyŏngjak 경작 cultivation; tillage; farming. *kyŏngjak'ada* 경작하다 cultivate; till; plow; farm.

kyŏngje 경제 economy; finance. *kyŏngjeŭi* 경제의 economic; financial. *kyŏngjejŏk (ŭro)* 경제적 (으로)

economical (ly). *kyŏngjehak* 경제학 economics; political economy.

kyŏngji 경지 cultivated field[area]; arable land.

kyŏngjil 경질 change; replacement; reshuffle. *kyŏngjirhada* 경질하다 change; reshuffle.

kyŏngjŏk 경적 alarm whistle; police whistle; horn. *kyŏngjŏgŭl ullida* 경적을 울리다 whistle a warning.

kyŏngjŏn 경전 sacred books; scriptures.

kyŏngjong 경종 alarm bell; warning. *kyŏngjongŭl ullida* 경종을 울리다 ring[sound] an alarm bell.

kyŏngju 경주 race; run. *kyŏngjuhada* 경주하다 have[run] a race (with).

kyŏngk'wae 경쾌. *kyŏngk'waehada* 경쾌하다 (be) light; nimble; lighthearted.

kyŏngma 경마 horse race[racing]. *kyŏngmajang* 경마장 horse race track; turf.

kyŏngmae 경매 auction; public sale. *kyŏngmaehada* 경매하다 sell by[at] auction.

kyŏngmang 경망 *kyŏngmanghada[surŏpta]* 경망하다 [스럽다] (be) thoughtless; rash; imprudent; fickle; frivolous; flippant.

kyŏngmun 격문 manifesto; written appeal.

kyŏngmyŏl 경멸 contempt; scorn. *kyŏngmyŏrhada* 경멸하다 despise; disdain; scorn; look down upon; hold (a person) in contempt.

kyŏngnae 경내 compound; precincts; premises.

kyŏngnapko 격납고 hangar; air plane[aviation] shed.

kyŏngni 경리 accounting; management.

kyŏngni 격리 isolation; segregation (*Am.*); quarantine. *kyŏngnihada* 격리하다 isolate; segregate;

quarantine.

kyŏngno 경로 respect for the aged. *kyŏngnohoe* 경로회 respect-for-age meeting.

kyŏngnon 격론 heated argument; high words.

kyŏngnyang 경량 light weight. *kyŏngnyangkŭp* 경량급 lightweight division.

kyŏngnye 경례 salutation; salute; bow. *kyŏngnyehada* 경례하다 salute; bow; make a salute.

kyŏngnyŏ 격려 encouragement; urging. *kyŏngnyŏhada* 격려하다 encourage; spur (a person) on; cheer up.

kyŏngnyŏk 경력 career; record; personal history.

kyŏngnyŏn 경련 convulsions; spasm; fit. *kyŏngnyŏni irŏnada* 경련이 일어나다 fall into convulsions; have a spasm.

kyŏngŏ 경어 honorific (expression, word).

kyŏngp'um 경품 premium; free gift. *kyŏngp'umkwon* 경품권 premium ticket; gift coupon.

kyŏngsa 경사 inclination; slant. *kyŏngsajida* 경사지다 incline; slant; slope.

kyŏngsa 경사 police sergeant.

kyŏngsang 경상 slight wound. *kyŏngsangŭl ipta* 경상을 입다 be slightly injured[wounded].

kyŏngshi 경시. *kyŏngshihada* 경시하다 make light [little] of; despise; neglect.

kyŏngshin 경신 renewal. *kyŏngshinhada* 경신하다 renew; renovate. *kyeyagŭl kyŏngshinhada* 계약을 경신하다 renew a contract.

kyŏngsol 경솔. *kyŏngsorhada* 경솔하다 (be) rash; hasty; careless. *kyŏngsorhage[hi]* 경솔하게[히] rashly; hastily; thoughtlessly.

kyŏngt'an 경탄 wonder; admiration. *kyŏngt'an-*

hada 경탄하다 wonder[marvel] (at); admire. *kyŏngt'anhal manhan* 경탄할 만한 wonderful; admirable; marvelous.

kyŏngu 경우 occasion; time; circumstances; case. *kŭrŏn kyŏngu* 그런 경우 in such a case. *ŏttŏn kyŏnguedo* 어떤 경우에도 under any circumstances. *kyŏngue ttarasŏnŭn* 경우에 따라서는 according to [under some] circumstances.

kyŏngŭi 경의 respect; regard; homage. *kyŏngŭirŭl p'yohada* 경의를 표하다 pay one's respects.

kyŏngŭi 경의. *kyŏngŭishil* 경의실 dressing[locker] room.

kyŏngŭmak 경음악 light music.

kyŏngun-gi 경운기 cultivator.

kyŏngwi 경위 police lieutenant.

kyŏngyŏn 경연 contest. *kyŏngyŏnhada* 경연하다 compete(on the stage). *minyo kyŏngyŏn taehoe* 민요 경연 대회 folk song concours.

kyŏngyŏng 경영 management; administration. *kyŏngyŏnghada* 경영하다 manage; run; keep.

kyŏngyu 경유. *kyŏngyuhada* 경유하다 go by way of; pass[go] through. *…ŭl kyŏngyuhayŏ* …을 경유하여 via; by way of; through.

kyŏnhae 견해 opinion; one's view.

kyŏnhak 견학 inspection; study; observation. *kyŏnhak'ada* 견학하다 inspect; visit (a place) for study.

kyŏnjang 견장 shoulder strap; epaulet(te).

kyŏnje 견제 restraint; check. *kyŏnjehada* 견제하다 check; restrain; divert; curb.

kyŏnji 견지 point-of-view; standpoint; viewpoint; angle. →**ipchang** 입장.

kyŏnjingmul 견직물 silk fabrics; silk goods.

kyŏnjŏk 견적 estimate; estimation; assessment. *kyŏnjŏk'ada* 견적하다 estimate (at).

kyŏnjuda 견주다 compare (A) with (B); measure (one thing) against (another).

kyŏnmun 견문 information; knowledge. *kyŏnmuni nŏlta[chopta]* 견문이 넓다[좁다] be well informed [poorly informed].

kyŏnnun 곁눈 side glance. *kyŏnnunjirhada* 곁눈질하다 look askance[sideways] (at).

kyŏnsŭp 견습 apprenticeship; probation; apprentice. *kyŏnsŭpsaeng* 견습생 apprentice; trainee.

kyŏnuda 겨누다 ① (take) aim at; level (a gun) at ② compare (A with B); measure.

kyooe 교외 suburbs; outskirts. *kyooe saenghwal* 교외 생활 suburban life. *kyooesŏn* 교외선 suburban railway.

kyŏp 겹 fold *tu kyŏp* 두 겹 two fold. *yŏrŏ kyŏp* 여러 겹 many folds.

kyŏpch'ida 겹치다 pile[heap] up; put one upon another; overlap.

kyŏpkyŏbi 겹겹이 in many folds; fold and fold.

kyoran 교란 disturbance; derangement. *kyoranhada* 교란하다 disturb; derange; stir up.

kyŏre 겨레 brethren; one's countrymen; compatriots.

kyŏrhaek 결핵 tuberculosis; consumption. *kyŏrhaek hwanja* 결핵 환자 tuberculosis[T. B.] patient.

kyŏrham 결함 defect; fault; shortcoming; deficiency. *yukch'ejŏk[chŏngshinjŏk] kyŏrham* 육체적[정신적] 결함 physical[mental] defect[deficiency].

kyŏrhap 결합 combination; union. *kyŏrhap'ada* 결합하다 unite[combine] (with); joint together.

kyŏrhon 결혼 marriage; matrimony; wedding. *kyŏrhonhada* 결혼하다 marry; be[get] married (to). *kyŏrhonshik* 결혼식 wedding[marriage] ceremony. *kyŏrhon p'iroyŏn* 결혼 피로연 wedding reception.

kyŏruda 겨루다 compete with; contend; pit (one's skill against).

kyŏrŭi 결의 resolution; decision; vote.

kyŏrŭl 겨를 leisure; leisure time; free time; time to spare. *kyŏrŭri ŏpta* 겨를이 없다 have no leisure[time to spare].

kyŏrwon 결원 vacancy; vacant post[position].

kyŏryŏn 결연 forming a relationship. *kyŏryŏnhada* 결연하다 form a connection(with). *chamae kyŏryŏn* 자매 결연 establishment of sisterhood ties.

kyoryu 교류 interchange. *kyoryuhada* 교류하다 interchange. *Hanmi munhwa kyoryu* 한미 문화 교류 cultural exchange between Korea and America.

kyosa 교사 teacher; instructor.

kyosa 교사 school house; school building.

kyoshil 교실 classroom. *hwahak kyoshil* 화학 교실 chemistry room.

kyosŏp 교섭 negotiation(s). *kyosŏp'ada* 교섭하다 negotiate; approach (a person on a matter).

kyŏssang 곁상 side table.

kyosu 교수 ① teaching; instruction; tuition ② professor. *pugyosu* 부교수 associate professor. *chogyosu* 조교수 assistant professor.

kyŏt 곁 side. *kyŏt'e* 곁에 by (the side of). *paro kyŏt'e* 바로 곁에 hard[near, close] by.

kyot'ae 교태 coquetry; coquettish behavior[attitude]. *kyot'aerŭl purida* 교태를 부리다 play the coquette.

kyot'ong 교통 traffic; communication.

kyŏtpang 곁방 ① side chamber ② rented room. *kyŏtpangsari* 곁방살이 living in a rented room.

kyŏu 겨우 barely; narrowly; with difficulty; only.

kyŏul 겨울 winter. *kyŏurŭi*[*kat'ŭn*] 겨울의[같은] wintry. *kyŏul panghak* 겨울 방학 winter vacation.

kyŏunae 겨우내 throughout the winter; all winter through. ⌈instructor.

kyowon 교원 teacher; schoolteacher; schoolmaster;

kyoyang 교양 culture; education; refinement. *kyoyangi innŭn* 교양이 있는 educated; cultured; refined. *kyoyangi omnŭn* 교양이 없는 uneducated; uncultured.

kyoyuk 교육 education; schooling; instruction; training. *kyoyuk'ada* 교육하다 educate; instruct; train. *kajŏng kyoyuk* 가정 교육 home training [breeding].

kyuch'ik 규칙 rule; regulations. *kyuch'ikchŏk*[*ŭro*] 규칙적[으로] regular[ly]; systematical[ly].

kyul 귤 orange. *kyulkkŏpchil* 귤껍질 orange peel.

kyumo 규모 scale; scope; structure. *taegyumoro* 대규모로 on a large scale.

kyun 균 bacillus; germ; bacterium.

kyut'an 규탄 censure; denunciation. *kyut'anhada* 규탄하다 censure; denounce.

❮❮ K' ❯❯

k'aeda 캐다 dig up[out]; unearth.

k'al 칼 knife; sword; saber.

k'alguksu 칼국수 knife-cut noodles.

k'allal 칼날 blade of a knife[sword].

k'amk'amhada 캄캄하다 (be) dark; pitch-black.

k'i 키 stature; height. *k'iga k'ŭda[chakta]* 키가 크다[작다] be tall[short].

k'i 키 winnow; winnowing fan. *k'ijirhada* 키질 하다 winnow.

k'ingk'inggŏrida 킹킹거리다 whine; whimper.

k'iuda 키우다 bring up; rear; raise; breed.

k'o 코 nose. *tŭlch'angk'o* 들창코 turned-up nose. *maeburik'o* 매부리코 Roman[aquiline] nose.

k'ogolda 코골다 snore.

k'ŏjida 커지다 grow big[large]; grow up; expand.

k'okkiri 코끼리 elephant.

k'ŏlk'ŏrhada 컬컬하다 (be) thirsty; dry.

k'ollokkŏrida 콜록거리다 keep coughing[hacking].

k'ong 콩 beans; peas; soybean. *k'ongkkaenmuk* 콩 깻묵 bean cake.

k'ongnamul 콩나물 bean sprouts.

k'onnorae 콧노래 humming; hum. *k'onnoraehada* 콧노래하다 hum.

k'op'i 코피 nosebleed. *k'op'iga hŭrŭda* 코피가 흐르 다 bleed at the nose.

k'otkumŏng 콧구멍 nostrils.

k'ossuyŏm 콧수염 moustache.

k'ousŭm 코웃음 sneer. *k'ousŭmch'ida* 코웃음치다 sneer.

k'ŭda 크다 (be) big; large; great. *nŏmu k'ŭda* 너무 크다 be too large.

k'ŭgi 크기 size; dimensions. *kat'ŭn k'ŭgiŭi* 같은 크기의 of the same size.

k'ŭn-gil 큰길 main street[road]; highway; thoroughfare; avenue (*Am.*).

k'ŭnil 큰일 important affair; serious matter. *k'ŭnil-nada* 큰일 나다 serious thing happens.

k'ŭnsori 큰소리 ① loud voice; yell ② big talk; bragging.

k'waehwal 쾌활. *k'waehwarhan* 쾌활한 cheerful; gay; lively. *k'waehwarhage* 쾌활하게 cheerfully; gaily.

k'waerak 쾌락 pleasure; enjoyment. *insaengŭi k'waerak* 인생의 쾌락 pleasures[joys] of life.

k'wik'wihada 퀴퀴하다 (be) fetid; stinking; foul-smelling.

k'yŏda 켜다 light; kindle; turn[switch] on.

k'yŏlle 켤레 pair. *kudu han k'yŏlle* 구두 한 켤레 a pair of shoes.

—◄ M ►—

mabi 마비 paralysis; palsy; numbness. *mabidoeda* 마비되다 be paralyzed. *shimjang mabi* 심장 마비 heart failure.

mabu 마부 groom; stableman; coachman.

mach'a 마차 carriage; coach; cab. *chimmach'a* 짐마차 horse and van.

mach'al 마찰 friction; rubbing; trouble. *mach'arhada* 마찰하다 rub(against); chafe (the skin).

mach'i 마치 as if[though]; just like.

mach'ida 마치다 finish; complete. *hagŏbŭl mach'ida* 학업을 마치다 finish a school course.

mach'im 마침 luckily; fortunately; just in time.

mach'imnae 마침내 finally; at last; eventually.

mach'imp'yo 마침표 period; full stop.

madang 마당 garden; yard; court. *ammadang* 앞마당 front yard. *anmadang* 안마당 courtyard.

madi 마디 joint; knot; knob.

mae 매 whip; rod; cane.

maebu 매부 husband of one's sister; one's brother-in-law.

maech'un 매춘 prostitution; harlotry. *maech'unbu* 매춘부 prostitute; street girl; courtesan.

maeda 매다 tie (up); bind; fasten.

maedŭp 매듭 knot; tie; joint; macrame.

maegi p'ullida 맥이 풀리다 fall into low spirits; be dispirited.

maegŏpshi 맥없이 weakly; tiredly; helplessly.

maehok 매혹 fascination. *maehokchŏgin* 매혹적인 charming; fascinating. *maehoktoeda* 매혹되다 be charmed[fascinated].

maeil 매일 everyday; each day; daily. *maeirŭi* 매일의 everyday; daily. *maeil maeil* 매일 매일 day after day; day by day.

maejang 매장. *maejanghada* 매장하다 bury in the ground.

maejŏm 매점 stand; stall; booth.

maeju 매주 every week; each week; weekly.

maek 맥 pulse; pulsation. *maegi ttwida* 맥이 뛰다 pulsate; pulse beats.

maek'aehada 매캐하다 ① (be) smoky ② (be) musty; mouldy.

maekchu 맥주 beer; ale. *pyŏngmaekchu* 병맥주 bottled beer. *saengmaekchu* 생맥주 draft beer.

maekko moja 맥고 모자 straw hat.

maekkŭrŏpta 매끄럽다 (be) smooth; slimly; slippery.

maekpak 맥박 pulse; pulsation.

maemae 매매 trade; dealing; bargain. *maemae-hada* 매매하다 deal[trade] (in).

maemanjida 매만지다 smooth down; trim; dress.

maenbal 맨발 bare feet; barefoot. *maenballo* 맨발로 with bare[naked] feet.

maengmok 맹목 blindness. *maengmokchŏk(ŭro)* 맹목적(으로) blind(ly); reckless(ly).

maengse 맹세 oath; pledge; vow. *maengsehada* 맹세하다 swear; vow; take an oath.

maengsu 맹수 fierce animal; beast of prey.

maenyŏn 매년 every[each] year; annually; yearly.

maepshi 맵시 figure; shapeliness; smartness. *maepshi innŭn* 맵시 있는 smart; shapely; well-formed. *onmaepshi* 옷맵시 style of dressing.

maep'yoso 매표소 ① ticket[booking] office ② box office.

maeryŏk 매력 charm; fascination. *maeryŏk innŭn* 매력 있는 charming; attractive.

maesanggo, maech'uraek 매상고, 매출액 amount sold; sales; proceeds (of sale).

maesŏpta 매섭다 (be) fierce; severe; strict; stern.

maesuhada 매수하다 bribe[buy over] (a person).

maetta 맺다 ① tie (up); (make a) knot ② bear fruit ③ contract; enter relations (with).

maeu 매우 very (much); greatly; awfully.

maeŭm 매음 prostitution. →**maech'un** 매춘.

maeunt'ang 매운탕 pepper-pot soup; hot chowder.

maewol 매월 every month; each month; monthly.

magae 마개 stopper; cork; plug; stopcock. *magaerŭl ppopta* 마개를 뽑다 uncork.

magu 마구 recklessly; at random.

magu 마구 harness; horse-equipment[furniture].

magyŏnhada 막연하다 (be) vague; obscure; ambiguous.
mahŭn 마흔 forty. →**saship** 사십.
majak 마작 mahjong(g). *majak'ada* 마작하다 play
  mahjong(g).
majimak 마지막 the last; the end.
maju 마주 face to face; visavis. *maju poda* 마주
  보다 look at each other.
majuch'ida 마주치다 collide with; clash with; run
  against.
majung 마중 meeting; reception. *majung nagada*
  마중 나가다 go to meet (a person).
majŭnp'yŏn 맞은편 opposite side.
mak 막 ① curtain; hanging screen ② shed; hut;
  shack.
mak 막 just; just now; (be) about to.
mak 막 the last. *mangnae* 막내 the lastborn. *mak-
  ch'a* 막차 the last train.
mak'ida 막히다 be stopped by; be clogged[chocked].
makkŏlli 막걸리 unrefined[raw] rice liquor[wine].
makp'an 막판 the last round; the final scene; the
  last moment.
makpŏrikkun 막벌이꾼 day laborer; odd-jobber.
maksa 막사 camp; barracks.
makta 막다 ① stop (up); plug ② intercept; block
  ③ defend; keep off[away].
makta 맑다 (be) clear; clean; pure (*water*); (be)
  resonant (*sound*); (be) fine; clear (*weather*).
maktaegi 막대기 stick; rod; bar; club.
mal 말 horse. *marŭl t'ada* 말을 타다 ride[get on]
  a horse. *chongma* 종마 stallion.
mal 말 word; speech; language; term.

malch'amgyŏn 말참견 interfering; meddling. *malch'amgyŏnhada* 말참견하다 interfere; meddle in.

maldaekku 말대꾸 retort; severe reply. *maldaekkuhada* 말대꾸하다 retort.

maldat'um 말다툼 dispute; quarrel; argument. *maldat'umhada* 말다툼하다 dispute; quarrel; have an argument with.

maldŏdŭmta 말더듬다 →**tŏdŭmgŏrida** 더듬거리다.

malgup 말굽 horse's hoof; horseshoe.

malgwallyangi 말괄량이 romp; tomboy; flapper.

malkkŭmhada 말끔하다 (be) clean; neat; tidy.

mallida 말리다 dissuade (a person from doing); stop. *ssaumŭl mallida* 싸움을 말리다 stop a quarrel.

mallida 말리다 make dry; dry. *pure mallida* 불에 말리다 dry (a thing) over the fire.

mallu 만루 full base.

mallyŏn 말년 ① one's last days; the last period. ② one's declining years.

malpŏrŭt 말버릇 manner of speaking; way of talking.

malssŏng 말썽 trouble; complaint; dispute. *malssŏngŭl purida* 말썽을 부리다 complain; cause trouble.

malssuk'ada 말쑥하다 (be) clean; neat; smart.

malttuk 말뚝 pile; stake; post.

mamuri 마무리 finish; finishing (touches). *mamurihada* 마무리하다 finish (up); complete.

man 만 ten thousand; myriad. *suman* 수만 tens of thousands. *sushimman* 수십만 hundreds of thousands.

mananim 마나님 ① madam ② your lady.

manch'an 만찬 supper; dinner. *manch'anhoe* 만찬회 dinner party.

manchŏm 만점 full marks.

mandam 만담 comic chat[dialogue]. *mandamga* 만담가 comedian.

mandŭlda 만들다 make; manufacture; create; form.

mang 망 ① net; casting net ② network. *t'ongshin-[pangsong]mang* 통신[방송]망 communication [radio] network.

mangboda 망보다 keep watch; look out for; stand guard.

mangch'i 망치 hammer.

mangch'ida 망치다 spoil; ruin; destroy; make a mess (of).

manggŭrŏjida 망그러지다 break; be broken; be destroyed; ruined.

manghada 망하다 go to ruin; be ruined; perish.

man-gi 만기 expiration (of a term); maturity (of a bill).

mangmyŏng 망명 flight. *mangmyŏnghada* 망명하다 seek[take] refuge; exile oneself.

mangnyŏnhoe 망년회 year-end party.

mangshin 망신 shame; disgrace. *mangshinhada* 망신하다 disgrace oneself; be put to shame.

mangsŏrida 망설이다 hesitate; scruple; be at a loss.

mangwon-gyŏng 망원경 telescope.

manhoe 만회 recovery; retrieval. *manhoehada* 만회하다 recover; restore; revive.

manhwa 만화 caricature; cartoon.

mani 많이 much; lots; plenty; in abundance.

manil 만일 if; in case; supposing (that).
manjok 만족 satisfaction; contentment. *manjok'ada*
  만족하다 be satisfied with.
mannada 만나다 see; meet; interview.
mannal 만날 always; all the time; everyday.
mannyŏnp'il 만년필 fountain pen.
manse 만세 ① cheers; hurrah ② long live.
mant'a 많다 (be) many; much; lots of; plenty of.
manŭl 마늘 garlic.
manwon 만원 full[packed] house; capacity audience. *manwon pŏsŭ* 만원 버스 jam-packed bus.
marhada 말하다 talk (about); speak; converse;
  state; tell; say; mention.
mari 마리 number of animals; head.
maril 말일 the last day; the end. *shiwol marire*
  10월 말일에 at the end of October.
marŭda 마르다 (be) dry (up); get dry; run dry.
maryŏnhada 마련하다 prepare; arrange; raise;
  make shift.
maryŏpta 마렵다 feel an urge to urinate.
massŏda 맞서다 ① stand opposite each other ②
  stand against.
massŏn poda 맞선 보다 meet[see] each other with a
  view to marriage.
masul 마술 magic; black art. *masulsa* 마술사
  magician; sorcerer.
mat 맛 taste; flavor; savor. *matchoŭn* 맛좋은
  tasty; savory; delicious.
match'uda 맞추다 fix[fit] into; assemble; put together.
matkida 맡기다 place in custody; deposit with;
  put in charge of.

matpuditch'ida 맞부딪치다 hit against; run into [against].

matta 맞다 ① be right[correct] ② become; match ③ fit; suit ④ agree (with).

matta 맡다 ① be entrusted with ② take[be in] charge of.

mattanghi 마땅히 naturally; properly; justly.

matton 맞돈 cash (payment); hard cash; ready money.

maŭl 마을 village; hamlet. *maŭl saram* 마을 사람 villagers.

maŭm 마음 mind; spirit; heart; will. *maŭmsogŭro* 마음속으로 inwardly; in one's heart.

maŭmdaero 마음대로 as one pleases[likes, wishes].

maŭmssi 마음써 turn of mind; temper; disposition. *maŭmssiga chot'a[nappŭda]* 마음써가 좋다[나쁘다] be good-natured[ill-natured].

mayak 마약 narcotic; dope. *mayak chungdokcha* 마약 중독자 drug addict.

meari 메아리 echo. *mearich'ida* 메아리치다 echo; be echoed; resound.

mech'uragi, mech'uri 메추라기, 메추리 quail.

meda 메다 shoulder; carry on one's shoulder [back].

melppang 멜빵 shoulder strap[belt]; braces; suspenders.

mesŭkkŏpta 메스껍다 feel nausea; feel sick.

mettugi 메뚜기 grasshopper; locust.

meuda 메우다 fill up[in]; stop(up); reclaim.

mi 미 beauty; grace. *yukch'emi* 육체미 physical beauty. *chayŏnmi* 자연미 natural beauty.

mia 미아 lost[stray, missing] child.

mianhada 미안하다 (be) sorry; regrettable; repent-ant.

mich'ida 미치다 go mad[crazy]; become insane; lose one's senses.

mich'igwangi 미치광이 madman; lunatic; crazy [insane] man.

midaji 미닫이 sliding door.

midŏpta 미덥다 (be) trustworthy; reliable; depend-able; promising; hopeful.

migae 미개 *migaehan* 미개한 uncivilized; savage; barbarous. *migaein* 미개인 barbarian.

migok 미곡 rice. *migoksang* 미곡상 rice dealer.

Miguk 미국 (the United States of) America; U.S. A. *Migugŭi* 미국의 American; U.S.

Migun 미군 U.S. Armed Forces; American Forces. *chuhan Migun* 주한 미군 American Forces station-ed in Korea.

migyŏl 미결. *migyŏrŭi* 미결의 unsettled; undecided; pending.

mihon 미혼. *mihonŭi* 미혼의 unmarried; single. *mihonmo* 미혼모 unwed[unmarried] mother.

mihwa 미화 American money[currency]; American dollar.

miin 미인 beautiful woman[girl]; beauty.

mijangwon 미장원 beauty salon[parlor, shop].

Mije 미제. *Mijeŭi* 미제의 American[U.S.] made; made in U.S.A.

mijigŭnhada 미지근하다 (be) tepid; lukewarm.

mikki 미끼 ① bait ② decoy; lure; allurement.

mikkŭrŏjida 미끄러지다 slide; glide; slip; fail (in) an examination.

mikkŭrŏpta 미끄럽다 (be) smooth; slippery.

mil 밀 wheat. *milkaru* 밀가루 wheat flour.

milchip 밀짚 (wheat) straw. *milchip moja* 밀짚 모자 straw hat. →**maekko moja** 맥고 모자.

milchŏp 밀접. *milchŏp'an* 밀접한 close; intimate.

milda 밀다 push; shove; thrust; jostle.

milgam 밀감 mandarin orange.

millim 밀림 dense forest; jungle.

milsu 밀수 smuggling. *milsuhada* 밀수하다 smuggle. *milsup'um* 밀수품 smuggled goods.

mimangin 미망인 widow. *chŏnjaeng mimangin* 전쟁 미망인 war widow.

mimo 미모 beautiful[handsome] face; good looks. *mimoŭi* 미모의 beautiful; good-looking; handsome.

mimyohada 미묘하다 (be) delicate; subtle; nice.

minamja 미남자 handsome man; good-looking fellow.

minbangwi 민방위 civil defense. *minbangwidae* 민방위대 Civil Defense Corps unit.

minch'ŏp 민첩 agility, quickness. *minch'ŏp'ada* 민첩하다 (be) quick; agile; nimble; prompt.

min-gan 민간. *min-ganŭi* 민간의 civil; civilian; nongovernment.

minjok 민족 race; nation; people. *minjok undong* 민족 운동 national movement.

minju 민주 democracy. *minjujŏgin* 민주적인 democratic. *minjujuŭi* 민주주의 democracy.

minjung 민중 people; masses.

minkwon 민권 people's rights; civil rights.

minsok 민속 folklore; folkways. *minsok pangmulgwan* 민속 박물관 folklore museum.

minwon 민원 civil appeal. *minwon sangdamso* 민

원 상담소 civil affairs office.

minyo 민요 folk song; ballad.

minyŏ 미녀 beautiful woman; beauty; belle.

mion 미온. *mionjŏgin* 미온적인 lukewarm; tepid; half-hearted.

mipta 밉다 (be) hateful; abominable; detestable.

mirae 미래 future; time to come. *miraeŭi* 미래의 future; coming; to come. *miraee* 미래에 in the future. *miraep'a* 미래파 futurism.

miri 미리 beforehand; in advance; previously; in anticipation; prior to; earlier than.

miruda 미루다 ① put off; postpone; delay; defer ② shift; shuffle off.

misaengmul 미생물 microorganism; microbe; germ. *misaengmurhak* 미생물학 microbiology.

misail 미사일 missile. *misail kiji* 미사일 기지 missile base〔station〕.

mishin 미신 superstition; superstitious belief.

miso 미소 smile. *misohada* 미소하다 smile; beam.

Miso 미소. *Misoŭi* 미소의 American-Soviet; Russo-American. *Miso kwan-gye* 미소 관계 American-Soviet relations.

misŏngnyŏn 미성년 minority; under age. *misŏngnyŏnja* 미성년자 minor.

misul 미술 art; fine arts. *misurŭi* 미술의 artistic. *misulga* 미술가 artist.

mit 밑 lower part; bottom; base; foot. *mit'ŭi* 밑의 lower; subordinate; inferior. *mit'ŭro* 밑으로 down(ward). *mit'ŭrobut'ŏ* 밑으로부터 from under〔below〕.

mit 및 and; also; as well as; in addition.

mitch'ŏn 밑천 capital; funds; principal; costprice.

mitta 믿다 believe; be convinced; trust; credit. *midŭl su innŭn* 믿을 수 있는 believable.

miwansŏng 미완성. *miwansŏngŭi* 미완성의 incomplete; unfinished.

miwohada 미워하다 hate; detest; loathe.

miyŏk 미역 (outdoor) bathing; swimming; swim. *miyŏk kamta* 미역 감다 bathe; have a swim; swim.

miyok 미역 brown-seaweed.

miyong 미용. *miyongsa* 미용사 beautician (*Am.*). *miyong ch'ejo* 미용 체조 beauty exercise.

mo 모 certain person; Mr. So-and-so; certain; some. *Kim mossi* 김 모씨 certain Kim.

mobang 모방 imitation; mimicry. *mobanghada* 모방하다 imitate; copy (from, after).

mobŏm 모범 model; example; pattern. *mobŏmjŏk* 모범적 exemplary; model; typical.

moch'in 모친 →**ŏmŏni** 어머니.

modok 모독 profanation. *modok'ada* 모독하다 profane; defile.

mŏdŏpta 멋없다 (be) not smart[stylish]; insipid.

modu 모두 ① all; everything; everybody; everyone ② in all; all told ③ altogether.

modŭn 모든 all; every; each and every.

mogi 모기 mosquito. *mogijang* 모기장 mosquito net. *mogihyang* 모기향 mosquito stick[coil].

mŏgi 먹이 feed; food; fodder.

mŏgida 먹이다 let someone eat; feed (cattle on grass).

moguk 모국 one's mother country; one's native country. *mogugŏ* 모국어 one's mother tongue.

mogŭm 모금 fund raising; collection of subscriptions. *mogŭmhada* 모금하다 raise a fund.

mogyo 모교 one's alma mater; one's old school.

mogyok 목욕 bathing; bath. *mogyok'ada* 목욕하다 bathe (oneself) in; take[have] a bath.

mohŏm 모험 adventure; risk. *mohŏmhada* 모험하다 adventure; take a risk[chance]. *mohŏmjŏgin* 모험적인 adventurous; risky.

mohyŏng 모형 model; pattern; mold. *mohyŏng chut'aek* 모형 주택 model house.

moida 모이다 gather; come[get] together; flock; crowd.

moja 모자 hat, cap. *mojarŭl ssŭda*[*pŏtta*] 모자를 쓰다[벗다] put on[take off] a[one's] hat.

mojarada 모자라다 be not enough; be insufficient; be short of.

mojip 모집 collection; raising. *mojip'ada* 모집하다 collect; raise.

mojori 모조리 all; wholly; entirely; altogether; without (an) exception.

mok 목 neck.

mok 몫 share; portion; lot; allotment. *nae mok* 내 몫 my share.

mŏk 먹 inkstick; Chinese ink; Indian ink.

mokch'a 목차 (table of) contents.

mokchae 목재 wood; timber; lumber (*Am.*).

mokchang 목장 pasture; stockfarm; meadow; ranch (*Am.*).

mokcho 목조 *mokchoŭi* 목조의 wooden; made of wood. *mokcho kaok* 목조 가옥 wooden house.

mokch'o 목초 grass; pasturage. *mokch'oji* 목초지 meadow; grass land.

mokchŏk 목적 purpose; aim; object; end. *mokchŏgŭl talssŏnghada* 목적을 달성하다 attain one's object; fulfil one's purpose.

mokch'uk 목축 stock farming; cattle raising. *mok-ch'ugŏp* 목축업 stock raising.

mokkong 목공 woodworker; carpenter. *mokkongso* 목공소 woodworking shop[plant]; sawmill.

mokkŏri 목걸이 necklace; neckwear; neckpiece. *chinju mokkŏri* 진주 목걸이 pearl necklace.

mokkumŏng 목구멍 throat; gullet; windpipe.

mŏkkurŭm 먹구름 black cloud; dark clouds.

mokkyŏk 목격 observation; witnessing. *mokkyŏk'a-da* 목격하다 witness; observe.

mokp'yo 목표 mark; target; object; aim. *mokp'yo-hada* 목표하다 aim at; set the goal at.

moksa 목사 pastor; minister; parson; clergyman; vicar; rector; chaplain.

moksori 목소리 voice; tone (of voice).

moksu 목수 carpenter. →**mokkong** 목공.

moksum 목숨 life. *moksumŭl kŏlgo* 목숨을 걸고 at the risk of one's life.

mŏkta 먹다 eat; take; have. *pabŭl mŏkta* 밥을 먹다 eat rice; take a meal.

moktŏlmi 목덜미 nape of the neck.

moktong 목동 shepherd boy; cowboy; cowherd; herdboy; cowpuncher (*Am.*).

moktori 목도리 muffler; neckerchief; comforter; shawl; scarf; boa.

molda 몰다 drive; urge; chase; run after. *ch'arŭl molda* 차를 몰다 drive a car.

mollae 몰래 secretly; stealthily; in secret.

mollak 몰락 ruin; fall. *mollak'ada* 몰락하다 fall; go to ruin; be ruined.

mollyŏdanida 몰려다니다 go[move] about in crowds

〔groups〕.

mŏlmi 멀미 nausea; sickness. *paenmŏlmi* 뱃멀미 seasickness.

molsangshik 몰상식. *molsangshik'an* 몰상식한 wanting in common sense; senseless. *molsangshik'ada* 몰상식하다 be lacking in common sense; have no common sense.

molsu 몰수 confiscation; seizure. *molsuhada* 몰수하다 confiscate; seize.

mom 몸 body; physique; build; frame. *momi k'ŭn* 몸이 큰 big-bodied.

momburim 몸부림. *momburimch'ida* 몸부림치다 struggle; writhe; wriggle; flounder.

momchip 몸집 body; size; frame; build.

momchit 몸짓 gesture; motion. *momchit'ada* 몸짓하다 make gestures.

mŏmch'uda 멈추다 stop; cease; put a stop; halt.

momdanjanghada 몸단장하다 dress oneself.

momttungi 몸뚱이 body; frame. *momttungiga chakta* 몸뚱이가 작다 be small of frame.

mŏmurŭda 머무르다 stay; stop; put up (at an inn). *hot'ere mŏmurŭda* 호텔에 머무르다 stop〔put up〕 at a hotel.

momyŏn 모면 evasion; escape. *momyŏnhada* 모면하다 evade; shirk; escape.

mŏndong 먼동 dawning sky. *mŏndongi t'ŭda* 먼동이 트다 Day breaks.

mongdungi 몽둥이 stick; club; cudgel.

mongnok 목록 catalog(ue); list.

mongttang 몽땅 all; completely; entirely; wholly; in full; perfectly.

mŏnjŏ 먼저 first; first of all; above all.

monnani 못난이 stupid person; no-good; simpleton.

mop'i 모피 fur; skin.

mopshi 몹시 very (much); hard; greatly; awfully; extremely.

morae 모래 sand; grit. *moraettang* 모래땅 sandy soil. *moraet'op* 모래톱 sand-bank.

moranaeda 몰아내다 expel; drive out; eject; oust.

moranŏt'a 몰아넣다 ① drive in[into]; push into; chase into. ② corner up; drive into a corner.

more 모레 the day after tomorrow.

mŏri 머리 ① head ② brain ③ hair.

mŏrik'arak 머리카락 hair. *hŭin mŏrik'arak* 흰 머리카락 white hair.

mŏritkirŭm 머릿기름 hair oil; pomade.

morŭda 모르다 do not know; be ignorant.

moryak 모략 plot; trick; stratagem. *moryak sŏnjŏn* 모략 선전 strategical propaganda.

mosaek'ada 모색하다 grope (for); feel one's way.

mossalge kulda 못살게 굴다 tease; treat badly.

mosŭm 머슴 farm hand; farmer's man.

mosun 모순 contradiction; conflict; inconsistency. *mosundoeda* 모순되다 be inconsistent (with).

mosŭp 모습 appearance; one's features; one's image; face; look. *yenmosŭp* 옛모습 one's former self.

mot 못 nail; peg. *mosŭl ch'ida[ppaeda]* 못을 치다[빼다] drive in[pull out] a nail.

mŏt 멋 dandyism; foppery. *mŏdinnŭn* 멋있는 smart-looking; stylish; chic.

mot'ada 못하다 (be) inferior; be worse than; fall behind.

mŏtchangi 멋장이 dandy; fop; cockscomb; dude.

motpon ch'ehada 못본 체하다 pretend not to see.

mŏttaero 멋대로 in one's own way; wilfully; self-ishly.

mot'ungi 모퉁이 corner; turn; turning. *kil mot'ungi* 길모퉁이 street corner.

mŏttŭrŏjida 멋들어지다 (be) nice; smart; stylish. *mŏttŭrŏjige* 멋들어지게 smartly; nicely.

moŭda 모으다 ① gather; get (things, people) to-gether; collect ② concentrate; focus.

moyang 모양 shape; form; appearance; figure. *k'omoyang* 코모양 shape of one's nose.

moyok 모욕 insult; contempt. *moyok'ada* 모욕하다 insult.

muanhada 무안하다 be ashamed; feel shame; lose face.

mubŏp 무법. *mubŏbŭi* 무법의 unlawful; unjust; unreasonable. *mubŏpcha* 무법자 ruffian; outlaw.

much'abyŏl 무차별 indiscrimination. *much'abyŏrŭi* 무차별의 indiscriminate.

mudae 무대 stage; sphere; field. *mudae changch'i* 무대 장치 stage setting; set(s).

mudang 무당 witch; sorceress; exorcist.

mudida 무디다 ① (be) blunt; dull ② curt ③ slow; thick-headed.

mudo 무도 dance; dancing. *mudogok* 무도곡 dance music. *mudohoe* 무도회 dancing party.

mudŏgi 무더기 heap; pile; mound.

mudŏm 무덤 grave; tomb.

mudŏnhada 무던하다 (be) generous; broad-minded.

mudŏpta 무덥다 (be) sultry; sweltering; muggy.

muge 무게 weight; heaviness; burden. *mugerŭl talda* 무게를 달다 weigh (a thing).

mugi 무기 arms; weapon; ordnance.

mugimyŏng 무기명. *mugimyŏngŭi* 무기명의 unregistered; unsigned; uninscribed. *mugimyŏng t'up'yo* 무기명 투표 secret ballot[vote].

mugŏpta 무겁다 (be) heavy; weighty. *mugŏun chim* 무거운 짐 heavy[weighty] burden.

mugunghwa 무궁화 rose of Sharon(*national flower of Korea*).

mugwan 무관 military[naval, air force] officer.

mugwan 무관. *mugwanhan* 무관한 unrelated; irrelevant (to).

mugwanshim 무관심 indifference; unconcern. *mugwanshimhada* 무관심하다 (be) indifferent (to); unconcerned (with, at, about).　　　　　　「fig tree.

muhwagwa 무화과 fig. *muhwagwanamu* 무화과나무

muhan 무한 infinity. *muhanhan* 무한한 limitless; endless; infinite.

muhŭi 무희 dancing girl; dancer.

muhyo 무효 invalidity; ineffectiveness. *muhyoŭi* 무효의 invalid; unavailable.

muindo 무인도 desert island; uninhabited island.

mujagyŏk 무자격 disqualification; incapacity. *mujagyŏgŭi* 무자격의 disqualified.

mujang 무장 arms; armament. *mujanghada* 무장하다 arm; be under arms; equip (an army). *mujanghan* 무장한 armed.

muji 무지 ignorance; illiteracy. *mujihada* 무지하다 (be) ignorant; illiterate.

mujilsŏ 무질서 disorder. *mujilsŏhada* 무질서하다 (be) disordered; chaotic; lawless.

mujoe 무죄 innocence; being not guilty. *mujoeŭi* 무죄의 innocent; guiltless.

mujokŏn 무조건. *mujokŏnŭi* 무조건의 unconditional; unqualified. *mujokŏnŭro* 무조건으로 unconditionally; without reservation.

mujŏn 무전 *mujŏn yŏhaeng* 무전 여행 penniless journey; travel without money.

mujŏnghada 무정하다 (be) hard; heartless; pitiless; coldhearted.

mukta 묶다 bind; tie; fasten (together).

muksarhada 묵살하다 take no notice (of); ignore.

mul 물 water. *ch'anmul* 찬물 cold water. *tŏunmul* 더운물 hot water.

mulcha 물자 goods; commodities; (raw) materials.

mulch'e 물체 body; object.

mulchil 물질 matter; substance. *mulchiljŏgin* 물질적인 material; physical.

mulchip 물집 (water) blister. *mulchibi saenggida* 물집이 생기다 get a blister.

mulda 물다 ① bite; snap; sting ② hold[put] in the mouth.

muldŭrida 물들이다 dye; color; tint; paint.

mulgunamusŏda 물구나무서다 stand on one's (head and) hands; stand on end.

mulka 물가 prices (of commodities). *mulkago* 물가고 high prices of commodities.

mulki 물기 moisture. *mulkiga itta* 물기가 있다 be moist; damp; wet; succulent.

mulkogi 물고기 fish. →**saengsŏn** 생선.

mulkyŏl 물결 wave; billow; surf; ripple.

mullan 문란 disorder; confusion; corruption. *mullanhada* 문란하다 be in disorder.

mullebanga 물레방아 water mill.

mulli 문리 liberal arts and science(s). *mullikwa*

taehak 문리과 대학 College of Liberal Arts and Science (s).

mullich'ida 물리치다 ① decline; refuse; reject ② drive back[away]; beat off[back] ③ keep away.

mullida 물리다 get bitten. *mogie mullida* 모기에 물리다 be bitten by a mosquito.

mullihak 물리학 physics; physical science.

mullŏgada 물러가다 move backward; step back; retreat; withdraw.

mullon 물론 of course; to say nothing of; not to speak of; no doubt; needless to say; naturally.

mullyak 물약 liquid medicine.

mullyŏbatta 물려받다 inherit; take over.

mullyŏjuda 물려주다 hand[make] over; transfer; bequeath.

mulpangul 물방울 drop of water; water drop.

mulp'um 물품 articles; things; goods; commodities.

mulsaek'ada 물색하다 look for; search for; hunt [for[up].

mulso 물소 buffalo.

mult'ong 물통 water pail[bucket].

mumo 무모. *mumohada* 무모하다 (be) rash; thoughtless; reckless. *mumohage* 무모하게 recklessly; rashly; imprudently.

mumyŏng 무명 cotton. *mumyŏngshil* 무명실 cotton thread. *mumyŏngot* 무명옷 cotton clothes.

mun 문 gate; door; gateway. *chadongmun* 자동문 automatic door. *am[twin]mun* 앞[뒷]문 front [back] door.

munbanggu 문방구 stationery; writing materials. *munbanggujŏm* 문방구점 stationery shop; stationer's.

muncha 문자 letters; character; alphabet.

mungch'i 뭉치 bundle; roll; lump.

mungch'ida 뭉치다 ① lump; mass ② unite; combine.

munggaeda 뭉개다 crumple; mash; squash.

mungnyŏm 묵념 silent[tacit] prayer. *mungnyŏmhada* 묵념하다 pray silently.

mun-gongbu, munhwa kongbobu 문공부, 문화 공보부 Ministry of Culture and Information.

mungttuk'ada 뭉뚝하다 stubby; (be) stumpy; blunt.

mun-gwan 문관 civilian; civil officer.

mun-gyobu 문교부 Ministry of Education.

munhak 문학 literature; letters. *munhagŭi* 문학의 literary. *munhakcha* 문학자 literary man.

munhwa 문화 culture; civilization. *munhwa saenghwal* 문화 생활 cultural life. *munhwa chut'aek* 문화 주택 modern[up-to-date] house.

munjang 문장 sentence; composition; writing.

munje 문제 question; problem; issue. *sahoe munje* 사회 문제 social problem.

munjigi 문지기 gatekeeper; janitor; gateman; doorman; porter; guard.

munjip 문집 collection of works; anthology.

munmyŏng 문명 civilization; culture. *munmyŏnghan* 문명한 civilized; enlightened.

munŏjida 무너지다 crumble; collapse; go[fall] to pieces; give way.

munp'ae 문패 doorplate; name plate.

munpŏp 문법 grammar.

munshin 문신 tattoo. *munshinhada* 문신하다 tattoo.

munsŏ 문서 document; paper. *munsŏro* 문서로 in writing.

munŭi 무늬 pattern; design; figure.

munŭng 무능. *munŭnghan* 무능한 incapable; incompetent; good-for-nothing.

munye 문예 literary arts; art and literature. *munyeran* 문예란 literary column.

muŏn-gŭk 무언극 pantomime; dumb show.

muot 무엇 what; something; anything. *muŏshidŭn* 무엇이든 anything; whatever. *muŏtpodado* 무엇보다도 above all (things); first of all.

muri 무리. *murihan* 무리한 unreasonable; unjust; immoderate.

muroehan 무뢰한 rogue; ruffian; scoundrel; rowdy; hooligan; rascal.

murŏjuda 물어주다 pay (for); compensate.

murori 물오리 wild duck; drake.

murye 무례. *muryehan* 무례한 rude; discourteous; impolite; insolent.

muryo 무료. *muryoŭi* 무료의 free (of charge); gratuitous; cost-free.

muryŏk 무력 military power; force (of arms). *muryŏgŭro* 무력으로 by force (of arms).

muryŏk 무력. *muryŏk'an* 무력한 powerless; helpless; incompetent; impotent.

muryŏp 무렵 time; about; around; towards. *haejil muryŏbe* 해질 무렵에 toward evening.

musa 무사 warrior; soldier; knight.

musa 무사 safety; peace. *musahada* 무사하다 (be) safe; peaceful; quiet. *musahi* 무사히 safely.

musang 무상 *musangŭi* 무상의 gratis; for nothing.

mushimushihada 무시무시하다 (be) dreadful; awful; frightful; horrible.

musŏn 무선 wireless; radio. *musŏn kisa* 무선 기사 wireless[radio] operator.

musŏnghada 무성하다 (be) thick; dense; luxuriant.
musŏpta 무섭다 (be) fearful; terrible; dreadful; horrible.
musosok 무소속. *musosogŭi* 무소속의 independent; neutral. *musosok ŭiwŏn* 무소속 의원 independent member; nonaffiliated members.
musŏwohada 무서워하다 (be) afraid (of); fear; be fearful (of); be frightened (at).
musul 무술 military arts.
musŭn 무슨 what; what sort[kind] of. *musŭn illo* 무슨 일로 on what business.
musŭngbu 무승부 draw; drawn game; tie. *musŭngburo kkŭnnada* 무승부로 끝나다 end in a tie [draw].
mut 뭍 land; the shore.
mut 뭇 many; numerous. *mussaram* 뭇사람 people of all sorts.
mutta 묻다 ask; question; inquire.
mutta 묻다 bury; inter.
mut'ŏktaego 무턱대고 blindly; recklessly.
muŭishik 무의식 unconsciousness. *muŭishikchŏk (ŭro)* 무의식적 (으로) unconscious(ly).
muyŏk 무역 trade; commerce. *muyŏk'ada* 무역하다 trade(with); engage in foreign trade.
muyong 무용 dancing; dance. *muyonghada* 무용하다 dance; perform a dance.
myo 묘 grave; tomb. *myochari* 묘자리 grave site.
myobi 묘비 tombstone; gravestone. *myobimyŏng* 묘비명 epitaph; inscription (on tomb).
myŏch'il 며칠 what day of the month; how many days; how long; a few days. *myŏch'il chŏn* 며칠 전 a few days ago.

myogi 묘기 exquisite skill; wonderful performance.

myoji 묘지 graveyard; cemetery. *kongdong myoji* 공동 묘지 public cemetery.

myŏksal 멱살 throat; collar. *myŏksarŭl chapta* 멱살을 잡다 seize (a person) by the collar.

myŏlmang 멸망 fall; ruin; destruction. *myŏlmang-hada* 멸망하다 fall; be ruined; be destroyed.

myŏlshi 멸시 contempt; disdain. *myŏlshihada* 멸시하다 despise; disdain.

myomok 묘목 young plant; sapling; seedling.

myŏn 면 cotton.

myŏndam 면담 interview; talk. *myŏndamhada* 면담하다 have an interview (with).

myŏndo 면도 shaving. *myŏndohada* 면도하다 shave oneself; get a shave. *myŏndok'al* 면도칼 razor.

myŏngbok 명복 heavenly bliss.

myŏngch'al 명찰 identification tag; name plate.

myŏngch'ang 명창 great[noted] singer.

myŏngdan 명단 list of names; roll; roster.

myŏnggok 명곡 famous music; musical classics.

myŏngham 명함 (name) card; visiting card; calling card(*Am.*); business card.

myŏngjak 명작 masterpiece; excellent work.

myŏngjŏl 명절 festival[festive] days; gala days.

myŏngju 명주 silk. *myŏngjushil* 명주실 silk thread.

myŏngjung 명중 hit. *myŏngjunghada* 명중하다 hit (the mark); strike.

myŏngmok 명목 name; title; pretext. *myŏngmok-sangŭi* 명목상의 nominal; in name only.

myŏngmul 명물 special product; speciality.

myŏngnang 명랑. *myŏngnanghan* 명랑한 gay; merry; bright; light-hearted.

myŏngnyŏng 명령 order; command. *myŏngnyŏng-hada* 명령하다 order; command.

myŏngsa 명사 man of note; distinguished[noted, celebrated] person; celebrity.

myŏngsesŏ 명세서 detailed statement[account];specifications.

myŏngso 명소 noted place; beauty[scenic] spot; sights.

myŏngsŏng 명성 fame; reputation; renown. *myŏngsŏngŭl ŏtta* 명성을 얻다 gain[win] fame[a reputation].

myŏngsŭng 명승 *myŏngsŭng kojŏk* 명승 고적 places of scenic beauty and historic interest. *myŏngsŭngji* 명승지 beautiful place.

myŏngye 명예 honor; credit; glory. *myŏngyeroun* 명예로운 honorable.

myŏnhada 면하다 escape; avoid; get rid of.

myŏnhŏ 면허 license; permission. *myŏnhŏchŭng* 면허증 license card.

myŏnhoe 면회 interview. *myŏnhoehada* 면회하다 meet; see; have an interview.

myŏnjŏk 면적 area. *kyŏngjak myŏnjŏk* 경작 면적 area under cultivation.

myŏnmok 면목 ① countenance; looks; features ② face; honor; prestige; credit. *myŏnmok ŏpta* 면목 없다 be ashamed of oneself.

myŏnmyŏt 몇몇 some; several.

myŏnse 면세 tax exemption. *myŏnsehada* 면세하다 exempt(a person) from taxes. *myŏnsep'um* 면세품 tax-exempt[free] articles.

myŏnŭri 며느리 daughter-in-law; one's son's wife.

myŏnyŏk 면역 immunity. *myŏnyŏgi toeda* 면역이 되다 become[be] immune (from).

myosa 묘사 description; depiction. *myosahada* 묘사하다 draw; sketch; paint; describe.

myŏt 몇 ① some; a few; several ② how many; how much.

N

na 나 I; myself. *naŭi* 나의 my. *na-ege[rŭl]* 나에게[를] me.

naagada 나아가다 advance; proceed; march; go forward; move on.

naajida 나아지다 become[get] better; improve; make a good progress.

nabal 나발 trumpet. →**nap'al** 나팔.

nabi 나비 butterfly.

nabukkida 나부끼다 flutter; flap; wave.

nach'e 나체 naked body; nudity.

nach'imban 나침반 compass.

nada 나다 ① be born ② be out; come into (*bud*, *leaf*) ③ produce; yield ④ smell; taste.

nadal 낟알 grain.

nadŭri 나들이 going out; outing. *nadŭrihada* 나들이하다 go on a visit.

nae 내 stream; brook; creek (*Am.*).

naebin 내빈 guest. *naebinsŏk* 내빈석 guests' seat. *naebinshil* 내빈실 reception room.

naebonaeda 내보내다 ① let out; let go out ② dismiss; fire (*Am.*).

naebu 내부 inside; interior. *naebuŭi* 내부의 inside; internal; inner. *naebue* 내부에 inside; within.

naehunyŏn 내후년 the year after next.

naeil 내일 tomorrow. *naeil chŏnyŏk* 내일 저녁 to-morrow evening.

naejang 내장 internal organs; intestines.

naeju 내주 next week. *naeju woryoil* 내주 월요일 Monday next week; next Monday.

naejuda 내주다 ① take[bring] (a thing) out and give it; give away ② resign[surrender] (one's seat to a person).

naemak 내막 inside facts; private circumstances; the inside.

naemsae 냄새 smell; odo(u)r; scent; fragrance; perfume; stink; reek. *naemsaenada* 냄새나다 smell (of tobacco). *choŭn[nappŭn] naemsae* 좋은 [나쁜] 냄새 sweet[bad] smell.

naemu 내무 home[domestic] affairs. *naemubu* 내무부 Ministry of Home Affairs; Home Office (*Eng.*); Department of Interior (*Am.*).

naengbang 냉방 unheated room. *naengbang changch'i* 냉방 장치 air-conditioning; air conditioner; air cooler.

naengch'a 냉차 iced tea; ice[cold] tea.

naengdae 냉대 →**p'udaejŏp** 푸대접.

naengdong 냉동 refrigeration, freezing. *naengdonghada* 냉동하다 cool down; refrigerate. *naengdong shikp'um* 냉동 식품 frozen foodstuffs.

naenggak 냉각 cooling; refrigeration. *naenggakki* 냉각기 freezer.

naengjang 냉장 cold storage; refrigeration. *naengjanggo* 냉장고 refrigerator; freezer; icebox.

naengjŏn 냉전 cold war.

naengjŏng 냉정 calmness; composure; coolness.

naengjŏnghan 냉정한 calm; cool. *naengjŏnghi* 냉정히 calmly; cooly.

naengsu 냉수 cold water. *naengsu mach'al* 냉수 마찰 cold-water rubbing.

naeppaeda 내빼다 free; run away.

naeppumta 내뿜다 gush out; spout; shoot up (smoke).

naerida 내리다 ① descend; come down; get off; dismount ② drop; fall.

naeshil 내실 inner room; women's quarters.

naesŭp 내습 attack; raid. *naesŭp'ada* 내습하다 attack; raid.

naetchotta 내쫓다 ① expel; turn[send, drive] out ② dismiss; fire.

naetka 냇가 riverside; bank[edge] of a river.

naeŭi 내의 undergarment; undershirt; underwear.

naewang 내왕 comings and goings; traffic; intercourse. *naewanghada* 내왕하다 come and go; pass.

naeyong 내용 contents; substance.

nagada 나가다 go[come, get] out; be present; leave.

nagŭne 나그네 travel(l)er; vagabond; tourist.

nagwi 나귀 donkey; ass.

nagwon 낙원 paradise; Eden.

nagyŏp 낙엽 fallen[dead] leaves.

nahŭl 나흘 four days; the fourth day of the month.

nai 나이 age; years.

najŏn 나전 mother of pearl (*Am.*); nacre. *najŏn ch'ilgi* 나전 칠기 lacquerwork inlaid with mother of pearl.

najung 나중. *najunge* 나중에 later (on); afterwards;

after some time. *najung kŏt* 나중 것 the latter.

nak'asan 낙하산 parachute; chute. *nak'asan pudae* 낙하산 부대 paratroops; parachute troop.

nakch'al 낙찰 successful bid. *nakch'arhada* 낙찰하다 make a successful bid.

nakche 낙제 failure in an examination. *nakchehada* 낙제하다 fail in an exam.

nakchin 낙진 fallout. *pangsasŏng nakchin* 방사성 낙진 (radioactive) fallout.

nakkwan 낙관 optimism. *nakkwanhada* 낙관하다 be optimistic.

nakshijil 낚시질 angling; fishing. *nakshijirhada* 낚시질하다 fish; angle.

naksŏ 낙서 scribble; scrawl.

naksŏn 낙선. *naksŏnhada* 낙선하다 be defeated in an election. *naksŏnja* 낙선자 unsuccessful candidate.

nakta 낡다 ① (be) old; used; worn ② (be) old-fashioned; be out of date.

nakt'a 낙타 camel.

nakt'ae 낙태 abortion; miscarriage. *nakt'ae* 낙태하다 have an abortion.

nakto 낙도 remote island.

nak'wasaeng 낙화생 peanut; ground nut; monkey-nut(*Eng.*). →**ttangk'ong** 땅콩.

nal 날 ① day; date; time ② time when; in time of. *nallo* 날로 day by day.

nal 날 edge; blade. *k'allal* 칼날 blade of a knife.

nalch'igi 날치기 snatching; snatcher (person). *nalch'igirŭl tanghada* 날치기를 당하다 have (a purse) snatched.

nalchimsŭng 날짐승 fowls; birds; the feathered

tribe.

nalda 날다 fly; soar; flutter[flit] about.

nalgae 날개 wing. *nalgae tallin* 날개 달린 winged.

nalk'aropta 날카롭다 (be) sharp; keen; acute; pointed. *nalk'aropke* 날카롭게 sharply; stingingly.

nallim 날림 slipshod work; careless manufacture. *nallim kongsa* 날림 공사 jerry-building.

nanip 난입 intrusion; trespass(ing). *nanip'ada* 난입하다 break into; intrude; trespass.

nallo 난로 stove; fireplace; heater.

nalmada 날마다 every day; day after day; day by day.

nalp'um 날품 day labo(u)r; daywork. *nalp'um-p'arikkun* 날품팔이꾼 day laborer.

nalssaeda 날쌔다 (be) quick; swift; nimble. *nalssaege* 날쌔게 quickly; speedily; swiftly.

nalssi 날씨 weather; weather condition.

nalssinhada 날씬하다 (be) slender; slim.

naltcha 날짜 date. *kyeyak naltcha* 계약 날짜 date of a contract.

nam 남 another person; others; unrelated person; stranger; outsider.

nam 남 south. *namŭro* 남으로 to the south. *nam-tchoge* 남쪽에 in the south.

nammae 남매 brother and sister.

nambi 남비 pot; cook-pot; pan; saucepan.

nambu 남부 southern part[district, section].

nambuk 남북 north and south. *nambuk taehwa* 남북 대화 the South-North dialogue. *nambuk t'ongil* 남북 통일 reunification of Korea.

nambukkŭrŏpta 남부끄럽다 (be) ashamed; feel

shameful.

namdaemun 남대문 the South Gate (of Seoul).

namdan 남단 the southern extremity.

namgida 남기다 ① leave (behind); bequeath ② make[get, obtain, realize] a profit (of).

Namhan 남한 South Korea.

namja 남자 man; male. *namjaŭi* 남자의 male; masculine. *namjadaun* 남자다운 manly.

namnyŏ 남녀 man and woman; male and female.

namŏji 나머지 ① the rest; the remainder; the balance ② excess.

namp'yŏn 남편 husband; one's man; one's worse half.

namsŏng 남성 male (sex); the masculine gender. *namsŏngjŏk(in)* 남성적(인) manly; virile.

namta 남다 be left over; remain.

namu 나무 ① tree; plant ② wood; timber; lumber. *namunnip* 나뭇잎 leaf; foliage.

namurada 나무라다 scold; reproach; reprimand.

namyong 남용 misuse; abuse. *namyonghada* 남용하다 misuse; abuse.

nan 난 column. *kwanggonan* 광고난 advertisement column. *tokchanan* 독자난 reader's column.

nanbang 난방 heating; heated room. *nanbang changch'i* 난방 장치 heating apparatus.

nanbong 난봉 dissipation; debauchery. *nanbong-burida* 난봉부리다 live a fast life. *nanbongkkun* 난봉꾼 libertine; prodigal son.

nanch'o 난초 orchid; orchis.

nanch'ŏ 난처. *nanch'ŏhada* 난처하다 (be) awkward; be at a loss.

nandong 난동 disturbance; commotion; riot. *nan-*

dongŭl purida 난동을 부리다 raise a disturbance; stir up a riot.

nan-gan 난간 railing; rail; parapet; balustrade.

nangbi 낭비 waste; extravagance. *nangbihada* 낭비하다 waste; squander.

nangnong 낙농 dairy; dairy farming.

nangttŏrŏji 낭떠러지 precipice; cliff.

nanmal 낱말 word; vocabulary.

nanp'a 난파 shipwreck. *nanp'ahada* 난파하다 be wrecked; wreck. *nanp'asŏn* 난파선 wrecked ship.

nanp'ok 난폭 violence; outrage. *nanp'ok'ada* 난폭하다 (be) violent; outrageous.

nant'u 난투 confused fight; scuffle.

nanuda 나누다 ① divide ② share ③ classify.

naoda 나오다 go[come, get] out; be present; leave.

nap 납 wax; beeswax.

nap'al 나팔 bugle; trumpet. *nap'alsu* 나팔수 bugler; trumpeter.

napchak'ada 납작하다 (be) flat.

napchakk'o 납작코 flat nose; snub nose.

napch'i 납치 hijacking; kidnapping. *napch'ihada* 납치하다 kidnap; hijack.

nappajida 나빠지다 grow worse; go bad.

nappu 납부 delivery; payment. *nappuhada* 납부하다 pay; deliver; supply (goods).

nappŭda 나쁘다 bad; evil; wrong; wicked; inferior (*quality*); unwell (*health*); poor, weak (*memory*); nasty, foul (*weather*).

napse 납세 tax payment. *napse kojisŏ* 납세 고지서 tax notice[papers]. *napseja* 납세자 taxpayer.

naptŭk 납득 understanding. *naptŭk'ada* 납득하다 understand; persuade oneself.

nara 나라 ① country; state; land; nation ② world; realm. *uri nara* 우리 나라 our country. *tallara* 달나라 lunar world.

naranhi 나란히 in a row[line]; side by side.

narin 날인. *narinhada* 날인하다 seal; affix one's seal. *sŏmyŏng narinhada* 서명 날인하다 sign and seal.

narŭda 나르다 carry; convey; transport.

narŭnhada 나른하다 (be) languid; weary; dull.

narutpae 나룻배 ferryboat.

nasa 나사 screw. *nasamot* 나사못 screw nail.

nassŏlda 낯설다 (be) strange; unfamiliar.

nat 낯 face; features; looks. →**ŏlgul** 얼굴.

nat 낮 daytime. *naje* 낮에 in the daytime.

nat 낫 sickle; scythe.

nat'a 낳다 ① bear; give birth to; be delivered of (a child) ② produce.

nat'anada 나타나다 come out; turn up; appear.

natcham 낮잠 nap; siesta. *natcham chada* 낮잠 자다 take a nap[siesta].

natta 낫다 (be) better (than); preferable.

natta 낫다 recover; get well; be cure (of); heal up.

natta 낮다 ① (be) low ② humble.

natton 낱돈 small[loose] money.

ne 네 four. *ne saram* 네 사람 four people.

ne 네 ① you ② your. *ne adŭl* 네 아들 your son.

ne 네 (*answer*) yes; certainly. →**ye** 예.

negŏri 네거리 crossroads; street crossing.

nemo 네모 square. *nemonan* 네모난 four-cornered; square.

netchae 네째 the fourth; No. 4; the fourth place.

no 노 oar; paddle; scull.

nŏbi 너비 width; breadth.

noch'onggak 노총각 old bachelor.

noch'ŏnyŏ 노처녀 old maid; spinster.

nodaji 노다지 ① rich mine; bonanza (*Am.*) ② run of luck; great[big, smash] success[hit].

nodong 노동 labor; work. *nodonghada* 노동하다 labor; work; toil.

nodong chohap 노동 조합 labor union(*Am.*); trade union(*Eng.*).

nodongja 노동자 laborer; worker; workingman; labor.

noe 뇌 brain; brains. *noeŭi* 뇌의 cerebral.

noeirhyŏl 뇌일혈 (cerebral) apoplexy.

noemul 뇌물 bribe; corruption.

noesŏng 뇌성 thunder; peal[rumbling] of thunder.

nogolchŏk 노골적 plain; frank; outspoken. *nogolchŏgŭro* 노골적으로 openly; broadly.

nogŭm 녹음 sound recording. *nogŭmhada* 녹음하다 record; phonograph. *nogŭmgi* 녹음기 (tape) recorder. *nogŭm t'eip'ŭ* 녹음 테이프 recording tape.

nŏguri 너구리 racoon dog.

nŏgŭrŏpta 너그럽다 (be) lenient; generous. *nŏgŭrŏi* 너그러이 generously; leniently.

nŏhŭi 너희 you all; you people[folk].

noim 노임 wages; pay. *noim insang* 노임 인상 rise [raise] in wages; wage increase (*Am.*)

noin 노인 old[aged] man. *noinpyŏng* 노인병 disease of old age.

nojŏm 노점 street-stall; booth.

nŏk 넋 soul; spirit; ghost. *nŏksŭl ilt'a* 넋을 잃다

be absent-minded.

nokchi 녹지 green track of land. *nokchidae* 녹지대 green belt[zone].

nokkŭn 노끈 string; small cord.

noksaek 녹색 green; green color.

nokta 녹다 melt; dissolve; thaw.

noktu 녹두 small green peas.

nŏkturi 넋두리 *nŏkturihada* 넋두리하다 make complaints; grumble (at, over).

nok'wa 녹화 afforestation. *nok'wahada* 녹화하다 plant trees (in).

nok'wa 녹화 video (tape) recording; videotape.

nol 놀 glow. *chŏnyŏngnŏl* 저녁놀 evening glow.

nolda 놀다 play; amuse oneself.

nŏlda 널다 spread out; stretch.

nollada 놀라다 be surprised[astonished]; be startled; be stunned. *nollal manhan* 놀랄 만한 surprising; amazing.

nolli 논리 logic. *nollijŏk(ŭro)* 논리적(으로) logical(ly). *nollihak* 논리학 logic.

nŏlli 널리 widely; far and wide; generally.

nollida 놀리다 tease; kid; laugh at; make fun of; banter; chaff; rally; ridicule.

nŏlp'ida 넓히다 widen; enlarge; broaden; extend.

nŏlppanji 널빤지 board; plank.

nŏlta 넓다 (be) broad; wide; roomy; extensive.

nŏlttwigi 널뛰기 seesaw(ing); teeter. *nŏlttwida* 널뛰다 play at seesaw.

nom 놈 fellow; chap; guy; creature.

nŏmch'ida 넘치다 ① overflow; flow[run] over; be full of ② exceed; be above[beyond].

nŏmgida 넘기다 ① hand (over); turn over; transfer; pass ② throw down; overthrow ③ pass; exceed ④ turn a page.

nŏmŏ 너머 opposite[other] side; across; beyond.

nŏmŏgada 넘어가다 ① cross; go across[over] ② sink; set; go down ③ be transferred ④ fall; be thrown down ⑤ be swallowed.

nŏmŏjida 넘어지다 fall (down) ; come down; tumble down.

nŏmŏttŭrida 넘어뜨리다 throw[tumble] down; over-throw; pull down; push down.

nŏmshilgŏrida 넘실거리다 surge; roll; swell.

nŏmta 넘다 ① cross; go over; go[get] beyond ② exceed; pass.

nŏmu 너무 too (much) ; over; excessively.

nonga 농아 deaf and dumb; deaf-mute.

nongak 농악 instrumental music of peasants. *nongaktae* 농악대 farm band.

nongbu 농부 farmer; peasant; farm hand.

nongch'on 농촌 farm village; rural community.

nongdam 농담 joke; jest; fun; prank. *nongdamhada* 농담하다 joke; jest; crack a joke.

nongdo 농도 thickness; density.

nongga 농가 farmhouse; farm household.

nonggu 농구 basketball. *nonggu sŏnsu* 농구 선수 basketball player.

nongjang 농장 farm; plantation.

nongjangmul 농작물 crops; harvest; farm produce.

nŏngk'ul 넝쿨 vine. →**tŏngul** 덩굴.

nŏngma 넝마 rags; tatters.

nongmin 농민 farmer; peasant.

nŏngnŏk'ada 넉넉하다 (be) enough; sufficient. *nŏngnŏk'i* 넉넉히 enough; sufficiently; fully.

nongŏp 농업 agriculture; farming. *nongŏbŭi* 농업의 agricultural.

nongsanmul 농산물 agricultural products; farm produce.

nongttaengi 농땡이 lazybones; do-little. *nongttaengi purida* 농땡이 부리다 shirk one's duty.

nongyak 농약 agricultural medicines[chemicals].

nonjaeng 논쟁 dispute; controversy. *nonjaenghada* 논쟁하다 dispute; argue; contend.

nonkil 논길 paddy path.

nonmun 논문 treatise; essay; dissertation; thesis.

nonsŏl 논설 discourse; leading article; editorial (*Am.*) *nonsŏl wiwon* 논설 위원 editorial writer.

nonyŏn 노년 old age; declining years.

nop'a 노파 old woman *nop'ashim* 노파심 grandmotherly solicitude.

nop'i 높이 ① (*noun*) height; altitude ② (*adverb*) high; highly.

nop'ittwigi 높이뛰기 (running) high jump.

nopta 높다 (be) high; tall; lofty; elevated.

norae 노래 song; ballad; singing. *noraehada* 노래하다 sing (a song).

norat'a 노랗다 (be) yellow.

nori 놀이 play; game; sport. *kkonnori* 꽃놀이 flower viewing. *norit'ŏ* 놀이터 playground; pleasure resort.

norida 노리다 stare at; watch (for); fix the eye on; aim at.

norigae 노리개 ① pendent trinket ② plaything; toy.

nŏrŭda 너르다 (be) wide; vast; extensive; spacious; roomy.

norŭm 노름 gambling; gaming; betting. *norŭmhada* 노름하다 gamble; play for money. *norŭmkkun* 노름꾼 gambler; gamester.

norŭnja(wi) 노른자(위) yolk of an egg.

noryŏk 노력 endeavo(u)r; effort. *noryŏk'ada* 노력하다 endeavor; strive; make efforts.

noryŏnhan 노련한 experienced; veteran; expert; skilled.

nosŏn 노선 route; line. *pŏsŭ nosŏn* 버스 노선 bus service route.

not'a 놓다 ① put; place; lay; set ② let go; set free; release.

nŏt'a 넣다 ① put in[into]; set[let] in; stuff ② send[put] (to); admit.

notkŭrŭt 놋그릇 brassware.

nŏulgŏrida 너울거리다 ① wave; roll ② flutter; undulate; waver.

noye 노예 slave; slavery. *noye kŭnsŏng* 노예 근성 servile spirit.

noyŏum 노여움 anger; offence; displeasure. *noyŏumŭl sada* 노여움을 사다 incur (a person's) displeasure.

nuda 누다 ① make[pass] water; urinate ② evacuate; relieve nature.

nŭdadŏpshi 느닷없이 abruptly; all of a sudden; unexpectedly.

nudŏgi 누더기 rags; tatters.

nue 누에 silkworm.

nugu 누구 who. *nuguŭi* 누구의 whose. *nugurŭl* 누구를 whom.

nugŭrŏjida 누그러지다 get milder; calm down; abate; subside.

nui 누이 sister; elder sister; younger sister.

nuidongsaeng 누이동생 younger[little] sister.

nujŏn 누전 electric leakage. *nujŏnhada* 누전하다 short-circuit; electricity leaks.

nŭkchangburida 늑장부리다 dawdle (over); linger; be tardy; be slow.

nŭkkida 느끼다 ① feel; be aware[conscious] (of) ② be impressed (by, with).

nŭkkol 늑골 rib; costa.　　　　　　　　　　┌placid.

nukta 눅다 ① (be) soft; limp; flabby ② (be) genial;

nŭkta 늙다 grow old; age; advance in age.

nŭktae 늑대 wolf. *nŭktae[iri]ŭi* 늑대[이리]의 lupine.

nŭl 늘 →*ŏnjena* 언제나.

nŭllida 늘리다 ① increase; add to; multiply ② extend; enlarge.

nŭlssinhada 늘씬하다 (be) slender; slim; slender and elegant.

nun 눈 snow; snowfall. *nunŭi* 눈의 snowy.

nun 눈 eye. *nunŭl ttŭda[kamta]* 눈을 뜨다[감다] open[close] one's eyes.

nŭng 능 royal mausoleum[tomb].

nŭnghada 능하다 (be) skillful; good at; proficient.

nŭnghi 능히 well; easily; ably.

nŭngmak 늑막 pleura. *nŭngmangnyŏm* 늑막염 (dry, moist) pleurisy.

nungnuk'ada 눅눅하다 (be) damp; humid.

nŭngnyŏk 능력 ability; capacity; faculty. *nŭngnyŏge ttara* 능력에 따라 according to ability. *nŭngnyŏgi itta* 능력이 있다 be able to do.

nŭngnyul 능률 efficiency. *nŭngnyulchŏgin* 능률적인 efficient.

nŭrinnŭrit 느릿느릿 slowly; sluggishly; idly.

nŭrŏnot'a 늘어놓다 ① scatter about; leave (things) lying about ② arrange; place (things) in a row.

nŭrŏsŏda 늘어서다 stand in a row; form in a line; stand abreast.

nŭrŏttŭrida 늘어뜨리다 hang down; suspend; droop.

nurŭda 누르다 ① press (down); weigh on; hold (a person) down ② stamp; seal.

nusŏrhada 누설하다 reveal; divulge; disclose; let out. *pimirŭl nusŏrhada* 비밀을 누설하다 let out [leak] a secret.

nŭsŭnhada 느슨하다 be loose; slack; relaxed.

nŭtcham 늦잠 late rising; morning sleep. *nŭtcham-jada* 늦잠자다 rise [get up] late.

nŭtch'uda 늦추다 ① loosen; unfasten; slacken ② put off; postpone; delay; defer.

nŭtta 늦다 (be) late; behind time; be slow. *nŭtke* 늦게 late. *nŭjŏdo* 늦어도 at (the) latest.

nyŏsŏk 녀석 fellow; guy; chap; boy. *I pabo nyŏsŏk* 이 바보 녀석 You fool!

O

o 오, 5 five; *cheo* 제5 the fifth.

ŏani bŏngbŏnghada 어안이 벙벙하다 be dumfounded; be struck dumb; be confused.

ŏbŏi 어버이 parents; father and mother. *ŏbŏiŭi* 어버이의 parental.

ŏbu 어부 fisherman; fisher.

ocha 오자 wrong word; erratum; misprint.

och'an 오찬 luncheon; lunch. *och'anhoe* 오찬회 luncheon party.

ŏch'ŏguniŏpta 어처구니없다 (be) amazing; dum-

founded; absurd. →**ŏiŏpta** 어이없다.
ŏch'on 어촌 fishing village.
oda 오다 come; come up[down]; come over[along].
ŏdi 어디 where; what place. 어디에나 *ŏdiena* 어디
  에나 anywhere; everywhere.
odumak 오두막 hut; shed; hovel; shanty.
ŏdupta 어둡다 (be) dark; dim; gloomy.
oebak 외박. *oebak'ada* 외박하다 stay[stop, sleep]
  out; lodging out.
oebu 외부 outside; exterior. *oebuŭi* 외부의 outside;
  outward; external.
oech'ida 외치다 shout out; cry(out); exclaim.
oech'ul 외출 going out. *oech'urhada* 외출하다 go
  out. *oech'ulbok* 외출복 street wear[clothes].
oeda 외다 recite from memory; learn by heart;
  memorize(*Am.*); commit to memory.
oedŭng 외등 outdoor lamp.
oega 외가 one's mother's family[home].
oegojip, onggojip 외고집, 옹고집. *oegojibŭi* 외고집
  의 obstinate; stubborn; obdurate.
oeguk 외국 foreign country[land]. *oegugŭi* 외국
  의 foreign; alien. *oegugin* 외국인 foreigner.
  oegugŏ 외국어 foreign language.
oegwan 외관 (external) appearance; outside view.
  oegwansang 외관상 externally; seemingly.
oegyo 외교 diplomacy. *oegyo munje* 외교 문제 diplomatic problem. *oegyo chŏngch'aek* 외교 정책 diplomatic policy. *oegyogwan* 외교관 diplomat.
oegyŏn 외견 →**oegwan** 외관.
oehwa 외화 foreign currency[money].
oein 외인 foreigner. →**oegugin** 외국인. *oein sangsa*
  외인 상사 foreign(business) firm. *oein pudae* 외인

부대 foreign legion.

oeji 외지 foreign land; oversea(s) land.

oekwa 외과 surgery; surgical department. *oekwa ŭisa* 외과 의사 surgeon.

oemo 외모 (outward) appearance; external feature.

oemu 외무 foreign affairs. *oemubu* 외무부 Ministry of Foreign Affairs.

oenson 왼손 left hand. *oensonjabi* 왼손잡이 left-handed person; southpaw (*baseball*).

oentchok 왼쪽 left (side). *oentchogŭi* 왼쪽의 left (-hand). *oentchoge* 왼쪽에 on the left side.

oerae 외래. *oeraeŭi* 외래의 foreign; imported. *oeraep'um* 외래품 imported goods.

oeropta 외롭다 (be) lonely; lonesome; solitary.

oesang 외상 credit; trust. *oesang kŏrae* 외상 거래 credit transaction.

oeshik 외식. *oeshik'ada* 외식하다 dine[eat] out; board out(*Am.*).

oeshin 외신 foreign news; foreign message[telegram].

oettal 외딸 only daughter.

oettanjip 외딴집 isolated house; solitary house.

oet'u 외투 overcoat; greatcoat; topcoat.

ogak'yŏng 오각형 pentagon.

ŏgap 억압 oppression; suppression. *ŏgap'ada* 억압하다 hold[keep] down; oppress.

ŏgida 어기다 go against; disobey; break.

ogoe 옥외. *ogoeŭi* 옥외의 outdoor; out-of-door; openair, *ogoeesŏ* 옥외에서 in the open air.

ogok 오곡 ① five grains[rice · barley · millet · bean etc.] ② grain(*Am.*); corn(*Eng.*); cereal.

ŏgu 어구 phrase; words and phrases.

ŏgul 억울. *ŏgurhada* 억울하다 suffer unfairness; feel victimized.

ŏgŭnnada 어긋나다 ① cross each other ② pass each other ③ go amiss; go wrong with.

ogŭrida 오그리다 curl up; crouch; huddle.

ŏgŭrŏjida 어그러지다 be[act] contrary to; be against; guess wrong.

ŏgwi 어귀 entrance; entry (*Am.*) *maŭl ŏgwi* 마을 어귀 entrance to a village.

ohae 오해 misunderstanding; misconception. *ohaehada* 오해하다 misunderstand.

ŏhak 어학 language study; philology; linguistics.

ohan 오한 chill; cold fit.

ohiryŏ 오히려 rather; preferably; on the contrary; instead.

ohu 오후 afternoon; p. m.; P. M.

ŏhwi 어휘 vocabulary; glossary.

oi 오이 cucumber. *oiji* 오이지 cucumbers pickled in salt.

oil 오일 five days; the fifth day (of the month).

oin 오인. *oinhada* 오인하다 misconceive; mistake [take] (A) for (B).

ŏiŏpta 어이없다 be struck dumb; be amazed (at).

ŏje 어제 yesterday. *ŏje ach'im* 어제 아침 yesterday morning.

ŏjirŏpta 어지럽다 (be) dizzy; feel giddy.

ŏjirŭda 어지르다 scatter (about); put in disorder.

ojŏn 오전 forenoon; morning; a. m.; A. M.

ŏjŏnggŏrida 어정거리다 walk leisurely along; stroll [ramble] about.

ŏjŏngtchŏnghada 어정쩡하다 (be) suspicious; doubtful; dubious; vague.

ojum 오줌 urine; piss. *ojum nuda* 오줌 누다 urinate.

ok 옥 jade. *okkarakchi* 옥가락지 jade ring.

ŏk 억 one hundred million. *shibŏk* 십억 milliard; billion (*Am.*).

ŏkche 억제 control; constraint. *ŏkchehada* 억제하다 check; control; restrain.

ŏkchiro 억지로 by force; forcibly.

ŏkkae 어깨 shoulder. *ŏkkaerŭl ŭssŭk'ada* 어깨를 으쓱하다 perk up[raise] one's shoulders.

okp'yŏn 옥편 Chinese-Korean dictionary.

oksang 옥상 roof; rooftop. *oksangesŏ* 옥상에서 on the roof.

ŏkseda 억세다 (be) strong; tough; sturdy.

ŏkta 얽다 get[be] pockmarked. *ŏlgŭn chaguk* 얽은 자국 pockmarks.

ol 올 ply; texture; strand.

ŏl 얼 spirit; mind; soul.

ŏlbŏmurida 얼버무리다 speak ambiguously; quibble.

olch'aengi 올챙이 tadpole.

olch'i 옳지 Good!; Right!; Yes!.

ŏlda 얼다 freeze; be frozen (over); be benumbed with cold.

olgamaeda 옭아매다 tie up.

olgami 올가미 trap. *olgamirŭl ssŭiuda* 올가미를 씌우다 put the rope on; trap.

olganaeda 옭아내다 cheat out of; squeeze from.

ŏlgani 얼간이 fool; half-wit; ass; dunce.

ŏlgul 얼굴 face; features; looks. *olgurŭl tollida* 얼굴을 돌리다 look away; look aside. *ŏlgurŭl pulk'ida* 얼굴을 붉히다 blush.

ŏlgulpit 얼굴빛 complexion; countenance.

ŏlgŭmbaengi 얼금뱅이 pockmarked person.

ŏlgŭnhada 얼근하다 ① (be) tipsy; slightly intoxicated ② be rather hot[peppery].

olk'e 올케 girl's sister-in-law; wife of a girl's brother.

ŏlk'ida 얽히다 be[get] entangled; get intertwined.

ŏlk'ŭnhada 얼큰하다 (be) intoxicated; be a bit spicy.

ollagada 올라가다 go up; mount; climb; rise; ascend.

ŏlle 얼레 reel; spool.

ollida 올리다 raise; lift up; put[hold] up; elevate; hoist.

ŏllon 언론 speech. *ŏllonŭi chayu* 언론의 자유 freedom of speech.

ŏlluk 얼룩 stain; spot; blot. *ŏllukchin* 얼룩진 spotted; stained; smeared.

ŏllŭn 얼른 fast; quickly; rapidly; promptly; at once.

ŏlma 얼마 ① how much; what price ② how many; what number[amount].

olmagada 옮아가다 move away; change quarters.

ŏlmana 얼마나 ① how much; what; how many ② how (far, large, old, etc.).

ŏlppaemi 올빼미 owl.

ŏlppajida 얼빠지다 (be) stunned; get absent-minded. *ŏlppajin* 얼빠진 silly; half-witted.

ŏlssaanta 얼싸안다 hug fondly; embrace.

ŏlssinmot'ada 얼씬못하다 dare not come around.

olt'a 옳다 ① (be) right; rightful ② (be) righteous; just ③ (be) correct; accurate ④ (be) proper.

ŏlttŏlttŏrhada 얼떨떨하다 (be) confused; bewildered; puzzle.

om 옴 itch; scabies.

omaksari 오막살이 living in a grass hut; hovel life.

oman 오만. *omanhan* 오만한 haughty; arrogant; overbearing.

ŏmbŏl 엄벌 severe[heavy] punishment. *ŏmbŏrhada* 엄벌하다 punish severely.

ŏmch'ŏngnada 엄청나다 (be) surprising; extraordinary; awful. *ŏmch'ŏngnage* 엄청나게 awfully; terriby.

omgida 옮기다 remove; move; transfer.

ŏmji 엄지 *ŏmjisonkarak* 엄지손가락 thumb.

ŏmkyŏk 엄격. *ŏmkyŏk'ada* 엄격하다 (be) strict; stern.

ŏmma 엄마 ma; mama; mammy; mummy.

ŏmmu 업무 business. *ŏmmuyong* 업무용 for business use.

omok'ada 오목하다 (be) hollow; dented; sunken.

ŏmŏna 어머나 Oh! Oh my! Dear me!

ŏmŏni 어머니 mother. *ŏmŏniŭi* 어머니의 mother's; motherly; maternal.

omp'ok'ada 옴폭하다 (be) hollow; sunken; dented.

ŏmsuk 엄숙 solemnity; gravity. *ŏmsuk'ada* 엄숙하다 (be) grave; solemn *ŏmsuk'age* 엄숙하게 solemnly.

omul 오물 filth; dust; dirt; garbage. *omulch'a* 오물차 garbage car.

ŏmul 어물 fishes; dried fish; stockfish. *ŏmulchŏn* 어물전 fish shop; dried-fish shop.

omulgòrida 오물거리다 mumble; chew on.

omŭrida 오므리다 pucker; purse.

omyŏng 오명 disgrace; dishonor; infamy. *omyŏngŭl ssitta* 오명을 씻다 wipe off a dishonor.

on 온 all; whole. *on sesang* 온세상 all the world. *on chiban* 온집안 whole family.

onch'ŏn 온천 hot spring; spa. *onch'ŏnjang* 온천장 hot bath[spring] resort; spa.

ondae 온대 Temperate Zone; warm latitudes.

ondo 온도 temperature. *ondogye* 온도계 thermometer; mercury.

ŏndo 언도 →**sŏn-go** 선고.

ondol 온돌 hypocaust; hot floor. *ondolpang* 온돌방 hotfloored room; ondol room.

on-gat 온갖 all; every; all sorts of; various.

ŏngdŏngi 엉덩이 buttocks; hips.

onggi 옹기 pottery; earthenware.

ŏnggida 엉기다 congeal; curdle; clot.

ongi 옹이 knot; gnarl.

ŏngk'ŭmhada 엉큼하다 (be) wily[insidious]; crafty.

ŏngmaeda 얽매다 bind[tie] up; fetter; restrict.

ŏngmang 엉망 *ŏngmangi toeda* 엉망이 되다 be spoiled; get confused; get out of shape.

ongnae 옥내. *ongnaeŭi* 옥내의 indoor. *ongnae-esŏ* 옥내에서 indoors; within doors.

ŏngnurŭda 억누르다 suppress; control; hold down.

ŏngnyu 억류 detention; detainment. *ŏngnyuhada* 억류하다 detain[keep] by force.

ŏngsŏnghada 엉성하다 (be) thin; sparse; loose.

ŏngt'ŏri 엉터리 ① fake; sham ② ground; foundation. *ŏngt'ŏri ŭisa* 엉터리 의사 quack (doctor). *ŏngt'ŏriŏmnŭn* 엉터리없는 groundless; absurd.

ŏn-gŭp 언급. *ŏn-gŭp'ada* 언급하다 refer (to); allude (to); mention.

onhwa 온화. *onhwahan* 온화한 gentle; mild; quiet; genial.

ŏnje 언제 when. *ŏnjerado* 언제라도 at any time.

ŏnjebut'ŏ 언제부터 from what time; since when.

ŏnjedŭnji 언제든지 (at) any time; whenever; always.

ŏnjekkaji 언제까지 how long; till when; by what time.

ŏnjena 언제나 always; all the time; usually.

ŏnjen-ga 언젠가 some time; some day.

onjiban 온집안 whole family; all the family.

onjongil 온종일 all day (long); whole day.

ŏnjŏri 언저리 edge; brim; bounds. *ibŏnjŏrie* 입언저리에 about one's mouth.

ŏnni 언니 elder sister.

ŏnŏ 언어 language; speech; words. *ŏnŏ changae* 언어 장애 speech defect.

onshil 온실 greenhouse; hothouse; glasshouse.

onsunhan 온순한 gentle; meek; obedient; docile.

ŏntchant'a 언짢다 (be) displeased; bad-tempered.

ont'ong 온통 all; wholly; entirely; completely.

ŏnta 얹다 put on; place[lay, set] on; load.

ŏnŭ 어느 ① a; one; certain; some ② which; what *ŏnŭ nal* 어느 날 one day. *ŏnŭ ch'aek* 어느 책 which book.

ŏnŭ chŏngdo 어느 정도 to some degree; somewhat.

onŭl 오늘 today; this day.

onŭn 오는 next; coming; to come. *onŭn t'oyoil* 오는 토요일 next Saturday.

ŏnŭsae 어느새 ① already; now; by this time ② before one knows; unnoticed.

onyuwol 오뉴월 May and June.

ŏŏp 어업 fishery; fishing (industry).
ŏpcha 업자 businessmen concerned; traders.
ŏpchŏk 업적 achievements; results.
ŏpchirŭda 엎지르다 spill; slop.
ŏp'ŏjida 엎어지다 be upset; be turned over.
ŏpshi 없이 without. *hyuildo ŏpshi* 휴일도 없이 without holidays.
ŏpta 없다 ① There is no …; cannot be found ② have no …; lack.
ŏpta 업다 carry on one's back.
ŏpta 엎다 overturn; turn over; turn upside down.
ŏptŭrida 엎드리다 prostrate oneself; lie flat.
orae 오래 long; for a long while[time].
oraettongan 오랫동안 for a long time[while].
orak 오락 amusement(s); recreation; pastime. *orak-shil* 오락실 amusement hall.
orhae 올해 this year; the current year.
orida 오리다 cut off[away]; cut out.
ŏrida 어리다 (be) young; juvenile; infant; childish.
ŏridungjŏrhada 어리둥절하다 ① (be) dazed[stunned]; bewildered ② (be) puzzled.
ŏrini 어린이 child; little one; youngster; infant.
ŏrisŏkta 어리석다 (be) foolish; silly; stupid.
ŏroe 어뢰 torpedo. *ŏroejŏng* 어뢰정 torpedo boat.
oroji 오로지 alone; only; solely; exclusively.
orŭda 오르다 go up; climb; ascend; rise; mount.
ŏrŭda 어르다 humo(u)r; fondle; amuse.
ŏrŭm 얼음 ice. *sarŏrŭm* 살얼음 thin ice. *ŏrŭm chumŏni* 얼음 주머니 ice pack[bag].
ŏrumanjida 어루만지다 stroke; caress; rub.
ŏrŭmjich'ida 얼음지치다 skate; do skating.
orŭn 오른. *orŭntchok* 오른쪽 right side. *orŭntchoge*

오른쪽에 on the right (side of). *orŭntchogŭro* 오른쪽으로 to the right (of). *orŭnson* 오른손 right hand.

ŏrŭn 어른 man; adult; grown-up (person). *ŏrŭnŭi* 어른의 adult; grown-up.

orŭnaerida 오르내리다 go up and down.

ŏrŭn-gŏrida 어른거리다 flicker; glimmer.

ŏryŏmp'ushi 어렴풋이 dimly; faintly; vaguely.

ŏryŏpta 어렵다 (be) hard; difficult.

ŏsaek 어색. *ŏsaek'ada* 어색하다 feel awkward[embarrassed]; clumsy.

oshik 오식 misprint; printer's error.

oship 오십, 50 fifty. *oshimnyŏn* 50년 fifty years.

ŏsŏ 어서 ① quickly; without delay ② (if you) please; right. *Ŏsŏ tŭrŏoshipshio* 어서 들어오십시오 Come right in, please.

osŏnji 오선지 music paper.

ossak 오싹. *ossak'ada* 오싹하다 feel[have] a chill; shiver; thrill.

ŏsŭllŏnggŏrida 어슬렁거리다 hang about[around]; wander about; loiter.

ŏsuruk'ada 어수룩하다 (be) naive; simple; unsophisticated.

ŏsusŏnhada 어수선하다 be in disorder[confusion].

ot 옷 clothes; dress; garment.

ot 옻 lacquer.

ŏtchaesŏ 어째서 why; for what reason; how.

ŏtchaettŭn 어쨌든 anyhow; anyway; at any rate.

otchang 옷장 wardrobe; clothes chest.

otcharak 옷자락 skirt; train.

otch'arim 옷차림 one's attire; personal appearance.

ŏtchi 어찌 how; in what way; by what means.

ŏtchihaesŏdŭnji 어찌해서든지 by all means; in any way.

ŏtchŏnji 어쩐지 somehow; without knowing why.

ŏtkallida 엇갈리다 pass[cross] each other.

otkam 옷감 cloth; stuff; dry goods.

otkŏri 옷걸이 coat hanger; clothes rack.

ŏtkŭje 엊그제 the day before yesterday; a few days ago.

ŏtta 얻다 get; gain; obtain; earn; achieve; win.

ŏttŏk'e 어떻게 how; in what manner[way]. *ŏttŏk'e haesŏrado* 어떻게 해서라도 at any cost; by any means.

ŏttŏn 어떤 what; what like; what sort[kind] of; any. *ŏttŏn iyuro* 어떤 이유로 why; for what reason.

ŏullida 어울리다 become; match; be becoming[suitable, fitting].

ŏŭm 어음 draft; bill; note. *yaksok ŏŭm* 약속 어음 promissory note. *pudo ŏŭm* 부도 어음 dishonored bill.

oyŏk 오역 mistranslation. *oyŏk'ada* 오역하다 mistranslate.

oyŏm 오염 pollution. *oyŏmhada* 오염하다 pollute.

P

pabo 바보 fool; ass; idiot; dunce. *pabo kat'ŭn* 바보 같은 silly; foolish.

pach'ida 바치다 give; offer; present; dedicate.

pada 바다 sea; ocean. *pada kŏnnŏ* 바다 건너 beyond[across] the sea.

padak 바닥 flat surface; bottom; bed.

pae 배 vessel; ship; boat; steamer. *paero* 배로 by ship.

pae 배 belly; abdomen; bowels; stomach.

pae 배 pear. *paenamu* 배나무 pear tree.

paeban 배반 betrayal. *paebanhada* 배반하다 betray.

paech'i 배치 arrangement; disposition. *paech'ihada* 배치하다 arrange; distribute; post.

paech'u 배추 Chinese cabbage. *paech'u kimch'i* 배추 김치 pickled cabbage.

paeda 배다 soak into[through]; spread; permeate.

paeda 배다 conceive; become pregnant. *airŭl paeda* 아이를 배다 conceive a child; be pregnant.

paedal 배달. *paedarhada* 배달하다 deliver; distribute. *paedalbu* 배달부 deliveryman; carrier; mailman.

paedang 배당 allotment; dividend. *paedanghada* 배당하다 allot; pay a dividend.

paegin 백인 white (man); Caucasian. *paeginjong* white race; the whites.

paegop'ŭda 배고프다 (be) hungry; feel hungry.

paegu 배구 volleyball.

paegŭm 배금 money worship. *paegŭmjuŭi* 배금주의 mammonism. *paegŭmjuŭija* 배금주의자 mammonist.

paegŭp 배급 distribution; rationing. *paegŭp'ada* 배급하다 distribute; ration.

paegyŏng 배경 ① background; setting ② backing; pull.

paehap 배합 combination; mixture; harmony. *paehap'ada* 배합하다 combine; match; harmonize.

paehu 배후 rear; back. *paehue* 배후에 at the back

〔rear〕; behind. *paehu inmul* 배후 인물 wirepuller.

paeje 배제 exclusion; elimination. *paejehada* 배제하다 exclude; eliminate; remove.

paekchak 백작 count; earl (*Eng.*). *paekchak puin* 백작 부인 countess.

paekchi 백지 white paper; blank sheet of paper.

paekch'i 백치 idiocy; idiot; imbecile.

paekkop 배꼽 navel; belly button.

paekku 백구 white (sea) gull.

paekkwa sajŏn 백과 사전 encyclopedia.

paekpal 백발 white〔grey〕 hair.

paeksŏ 백서 white paper; white book. *kyŏngje paeksŏ* 경제 백서 economic white book.

paektong 백동 nickel.

paekkŭm 백금 platinum; white gold.

paek'wajŏm 백화점 department store.

paem 뱀 snake; serpent.

paemjangŏ 뱀장어 eel.

paenang 배낭 knapsack; rucksack.

paengman 백만 million.

paengnyŏn 백년 one hundred years; a century.

paenmŏlmi 뱃멀미 seasickness. *paenmŏlmihada* 뱃멀미하다 get seasick.

paennori 뱃놀이 boating; boat ride.

paesang 배상 compensation; recompense; reparation. *paesanghada* 배상하다 recompense; compensate.

paesŏl 배설 excretion. *paesŏrhada* 배설하다 excrete; discharge.

paessagong 뱃사공 boatman.

paetchang 배짱 boldness; nerve; courage.

paetta 뱉다 spit out. *ch'imŭl paetta* 침을 뱉다

spit (out).

paeu 배우 actor; actress; player, *yŏnghwa*〔*yŏnguk*〕 *paeu* 영화〔연극〕 배우 film〔stage〕 actor.

paeuda 배우다 learn; take lessons (in, on); be taught; study.

paeuja 배우자 spouse; match; life partner.

paeung 배웅. *paeunghada* 배웅하다 see off; show out; give a send-off.

paguni 바구니 basket. *changpaguni* 장바구니 market〔shopping〕 basket.

paji 바지 trousers; pants(*Am.*).

pak 박 gourd; calabash.

pak 밖 ① →**pakkat** 바깥 ② outside of; exception of; except; but.

pak'a 박하 peppermint; mint.

pak'ae 박해 persecution. *pak'aehada* 박해하다 persecute; oppress.

pakcha 박자 time; rhythm; beat.

pakch'a 박차 spur. *pakch'arŭl kahada* 박차를 가하다 spur (one's horse, a person).

pakkat 바깥 outside; exterior; out-of-doors. *pakkat'ŭi* 바깥의 outside; outdoor; outer; external. *pakkat'esŏ* 바깥에서 in the open (air).

pakkuda 바꾸다 ① change; exchange; barter ② replace; alter; shift.

pakpong 박봉 small〔scanty〕 salary; poor pay.

paksa 박사 doctor〔Dr.〕; doctorate. *paksa hagwi* 박사 학위 doctor's degree.

pakshik 박식 wide knowledge; erudition. *pakshik'an* 박식한 erudite; learned; well-informed.

paksu 박수 hand clapping. *paksuch'ida* 박수치다 clap one's hands.

pakta 박다 drive in; hammer (in); set; inlay.

pakta 밝다 (be) light; bright.

pak'wi 바퀴 wheel; round[turn]. *ap*[*twit*]*pak'wi* 앞[뒷]바퀴 front[back] wheel.

pal 발 ① foot; paw; leg ② blind.

palchaguk 발자국 footprint; footmark; track (*Am.*).

palchŏn 발전 development; growth. *palchŏnhada* 발전하다 develop; grow.

palgul 발굴 excavation. *palgurhada* 발굴하다 dig up[out]; excavate; unearth.

palgyŏn 발견 discovery. *palgyŏnhada* 발견하다 find (out); discover.

paljach'wi 발자취 →**palchaguk** 발자국.

palkŏrŭm 발걸음 gait; step.

palkkŭt 발끝 tip of the toes; tiptoe.

pallan 반란 revolt; rebellion.

pallon 반론 counterargument; refutation. *pallonhada* 반론하다 argue against; refute.

palmyŏng 발명 invention. *palmyŏnghada* 발명하다 invent; devise.

palp'yo 발표 announcement; publication. *palp'yohada* 발표하다 announce; make public.

palsa 발사 firing; discharge. *palsahada* 발사하다 discharge; fire; blast-off.

palsaeng 발생 occurrence; outbreak; origination; generation. *palsaenghada* 발생하다 occur; break out; originate.

palt'op 발톱 toenail; claw.

paltal 발달 development; growth; progress; advance. *paltarhada* 발달하다 develop; grow; advance; make progress.

paltwikkumch'i, **paltwich'uk** 발뒤꿈치, 발뒤축

heel.

pam 밤 night; evening. *pame* 밤에 at night.

pamnat 밤낮 night and day. *pamnajŭro* 밤낮으로 round-the-clock.

pamsaedorok 밤새도록 all night(long); overnight; all through the night.

pamsaeuda 밤새우다 sit[stay] up all night.

pan 반 half; halfway; partial. *pan shigan* 반 시간 half an hour; half hour.

panaek 반액 half the amount[sum, price, fare]; half-price[fare].

panbak 반박 refutation; retort; confutation. *panbak'ada* 반박하다 refute; confute.

panbal 반발 repulsion. *panbarhada* 반발하다 repel; repulse; resist.

panbanhada 반반하다 (be) smooth; even; flat.

panbok 반복 repetition; reiteration. *panbok'ada* 반복하다 repeat; reiterate.

panch'an 반찬 sidedish. *kogi panch'an* 고기 반찬 meat dish. *panch'an kage* 반찬가게 grocery store.

panch'anggo 반창고 plaster. *panch'anggorŭl puch'ida* 반창고를 붙이다 apply a plaster.

pandae 반대 contrary; opposition; reverse; objection. *pandaehada* 반대하다 oppose; object to. *pandaeŭi* 반대의 opposite; contrary. *pandaero* 반대로 on the contrary.

panditpul 반딧불 glow of firefly.

pando 반도 peninsula. *Hanbando* 한반도 Peninsula of Korea.

pandong 반동 reaction; rebound. *pandongjŏk* 반동적 reactionary. *pandong punja* 반동 분자 reactionary elements.

pandŭshi 반드시 certainly; surely; without fail; necessarily; by all means. *pandŭshi ···hajinŭn ant'a* 반드시 ···하지는 않다 not always; not necessarily.

pang 방 room; chamber; apartment *setpang* 셋방 room to let.

panga 방아 mill. *mulbanga* 물방아 water mill.

pan-gam 반감 antipathy; ill feeling.

pan-gapta 반갑다 (be) happy; glad; be pleased [delighted].

pangbŏp 방법 way; method; means.

pangch'im 방침 course; line; policy; principle. *yŏngŏp pangch'im* 영업 방침 business policy.

pangch'ŏng 방청 hearing; attendance. *pangch'ŏnghada* 방청하다 hear; attend; listen to.

panggong 방공 air defense. *panggongho* 방공호 dugout; air-raid shelter. *panggong yŏnsŭp* 방공 연습 anti-air raid[air defense] drill.

panggŭm 방금 just now; a moment ago.

panggwi 방귀 wind; fart. *panggwi kkwida* 방귀 뀌다 break wind; fart.

panghae 방해 obstruction; disturbance. *panghaehada* 방해하다 obstruct; disturb; interrupt.

panghwa 방화 fire prevention. *panghwa chugan* 방화 주간 Fire Prevention Week.

panghyang 방향 direction; course.

pan-gida 반기다 rejoice (at, over); be glad (of); be delighted[pleased] (at).

pangji 방지 prevention; check. *pangjihada* 방지하다 prevent; check; stop.

pangjŏk 방적 spinning. *pangjŏk kongjang* 방적 공장 cotton (spinning) mill.

pangmangi 방망이 club; cudgel; mallet.

pangmulgwan 박물관 museum. *kungnip pangmul- gwan* 국립박물관 National Museum.

pangmun 방문 call; visit. *pangmunhada* 방문하다 (pay a) visit; make a call on; call at.

pangmyŏn 방면 direction; quarter; district. *Cheju pangmyŏn* 제주 방면 the Cheju districts.

pangmyŏng 방명 your (honored) name. *pangmyong- nok* 방명록 list of names; visitors' register[list].

pan-gong (juŭi) 반공 (주의) anti-Communism.

pangnamhoe 박람회 exhibition; exposition (EXPO) ; fair (*Am.*) *pangnamhoejang* 박람회장 fair ground.

pangsa 방사 radiation; emission. *pangsahada* 방 사하다 radiate; emit.

pangsong 방송 broadcasting; broadcast. *pangsong- hada* 방송하다 broadcast; go on the air.

pangul 방울 ① bell ② drop. *mulpangul* 물방울 water drops.

pangwi 방위 defense; protection. *pangwihada* 방 위하다 defend; protect.

pan-gyŏk 반격 counterattack. *pan-gyŏk'ada* 반격하 다 make a counterattack; strike back.

panhada 반하다 fall[be] in love (with); take a fancy (to); fall for (*Am.*).

panhang 반항 resistance; opposition; defiance. *pan- hanghada* 반항하다 resist; oppose; rebel (against).

panjep'um 반제품 half-finished goods; partly man- ufactured articles.

panji 반지 ring. *panjirŭl kkida* 반지를 끼다 put a ring on one's finger. *kyŏrhon[yak'on] panji* 결혼[약혼] 반지 wedding[engagement] ring.

panjitkori 반짇고리 work-box; housewife.

panju 반주 accompaniment. *panjuhada* 반주하다 accompany.

panmyŏn 반면 the other side; the reverse. *panmyŏne* 반면에 on the other hand.

pansa 반사 reflection. *pansahada* 반사하다 reflect; reverberate.

pansomae 반소매 half-sleeve; half-length sleeve. *pansomae syŏssŭ* 반소매 셔쓰 shirt with short (-length) sleeves.

pansŏng 반성 reflection; self-examination. *pansŏnghada* 반성하다 reflect on (oneself); reconsider.

panŭjil 바느질 needlework; sewing. *panŭjirhada* 바느질하다 sew; do needlework.

panŭl 바늘 needle; pin; hook. *ttŭgae panŭl* 뜨개 바늘 knitting needle. *nakshi panŭl* 낚시 바늘 fishhook. *panŭl pangsŏk* 바늘 방석 uncomfortable situation.

panyŏk 반역 treason; rebellion. *panyŏk'ada* 반역하다 rebel (against); rise in revolt. *panyŏkcha* 반역자 traitor.

panyŏng 반영 reflection. *panyŏnghada* 반영하다 reflect; be reflected (in).

pap 밥 boiled[cooked] rice. *pabŭl chitta* 밥을 짓다 cook[boil] rice.

papkŭrŭt 밥그릇 rice bowl.

pappŏri 밥벌이 breadwinning. *pappŏrihada* 밥벌이하다 make a living; earn one's daily bread.

pappŭda 바쁘다 (be) busy; (be) pressing; urgent. *pappŭge* 바쁘게 busily; hurriedly.

papsot 밥솥 rice pot[kettle].

papta 밟다 ① step[tread] on ② set foot on.

paraboda 바라보다 see; look (at); look out over; watch; gaze (at).

parada 바라다 ① expect; hope for; look forward to ② want; wish; desire ③ beg; request.

paraeda 바래다 fade; discolor; bleach.

param 바람 wind; breeze; gale; storm. *parami pulda* 바람이 불다 wind blows.

parammatta 바람맞다 be fooled[cheated]; be taken in; be rejected.

parhaeng 발행 publication; issue. *parhaenghada* 발행하다 publish; issue; bring out.

paro 바로 ① rightly; correctly; straight ② just; exactly ③ at once; immediately; right away.

parŏn 발언 utterance; speaking. *parŏnhada* 발언 하다 utter; speak.

parŭda 바르다 ① (be) straight; upright ② (be) right; righteous; just; correct.

parŭm 발음 pronunciation; articulation. *parŭm-hada* 발음하다 pronounce; articulate.

parŭnmal 바른말 truth; reasonable word; candid remark; plain word.

pasuda 바수다 break; smash; crush; grind.

pat'ang 바탕 ① nature; character; natural disposition ② texture; ground.

pat 밭 field; farm. *oksusubat* 옥수수밭 corn field.

patta 받다 receive; accept; be given[granted].

pawi 바위 rock; crag.

payahŭro 바야흐로 *payahŭro ...haryŏ hada* 바야흐로 …하려 하다 be going[about] to (do); be on the point of (doing).

peda 베다 cut; chop; saw; carve.

pegae 베개 pillow.

pe 베 hemp. *pet'ŭl* 베틀 loom.

pi 비 rain *piga oda[mŏtta]* 비가 오다[멎다] (It) rains

〔stops raining〕. *pie chŏtta* 비에 젖다 get wet with rain.

pi 비 broom; besom. *pitcharu* 빗자루 broom stick.

pi 비 monument. *pirŭl seuda* 비를 세우다 errect a monument.

piae 비애 sorrow; sadness; grief. *piaerŭl nŭkkida* 비애를 느끼다 feel sad.

pibida 비비다 ① rub; chafe ② make round; roll ③ mix. *sonŭl pibida* 손을 비비다 chafe〔rub〕 one's hands.

pich'am 비참. *pich'amhan* 비참한 miserable; wretched; tragic; distressful.

pich'ida 비치다 ① shine ② be reflected〔mirrored〕(in) ③ show through.

pich'uda 비추다 ① shed〔throw〕 light (on); light (up); illuminate ② reflect; mirror ③ hint; suggest.

pidan 비단 silk fabrics; silks.

pidulgi 비둘기 dove; pigeon. *pidulgip'a* 비둘기파 the doves; soft-liner.

pidŭm 비듬 dandruff; scurf.

pigida 비기다 end in a tie〔draw〕.

pigongshik 비공식 informality. *pigongshikchŏgin* 비공식적인 unofficial; informal.

pigŏp 비겁. *pigŏp'an* 비겁한 cowardly; mean.

pigŭk 비극 tragedy. *pigŭkchŏk* 비극적 tragic.

pigul 비굴. *pigurhan* 비굴한 mean; servile.

pigwan(non) 비관(론) pessimism. *pigwanhada* 비관하다 be pessimistic.

pigyo 비교 comparison. *pigyohada* 비교하다 compare (A with B). *pigyojŏk*(ŭro) 비교적 (으로) comparative(ly).

pigyŏl 비결 secret (of); key (to); tip (for).

pihaeng 비행 flying; flight; aviation. *pihaenghada* 비행하다 fly; make a flight; take the air.

pihaenggi 비행기 aeroplane(*Eng.*); airplane(*Am.*); aircraft.

pihaengjang 비행장 airfield; airport; airdrome (*Am.*); aerodrome(*Eng.*).

pihaengsŏn 비행선 airship.

pihappŏpchŏk 비합법적 (being) illegal; unlawful; illicit.

pijopta 비좁다 (be) narrow and close[confined]; cramped.

pik'ida 비키다 avoid; shun; dodge; get out of the way; evade; shirk; step aside (from).

pikkoda 비꼬다 ① twist; twine ② make cynical remarks; speak ironically.

pilda 빌다 ① pray; wish ② beg; solicit ③ ask; request; entreat.

pilda, pillida 빌다, 빌리다 borrow; have[get] the loan (of); hire; rent; lease; charter.

pimaep'um 비매품 article not for sale; not for sale.

pimangnok 비망록 memorandum; memo.

pimil 비밀 secrecy; secret. *pimirŭi* 비밀의 secret; confidential.

pimujang 비무장. *pimujangŭi* 비무장의 demilitarized. *pimujang chidae* 비무장지대 demilitarized zone(DMZ).

pimun 비문 epitaph; inscription.

pimyŏng 비명 scream; shriek. *pimyŏngŭl chirŭda* 비명을 지르다 scream; shriek.

pinan 비난 blame; censure. *pinanhada* 비난하다

blame; censure; accuse.

pinbang 빈방 empty room; vacant room.

pinbŏn 빈번. *pinbŏnhan* 빈번한 frequent; incessant. *pinbŏnhi* 빈번히 frequently.

pinbu 빈부 wealth and poverty. *pinbuŭi ch'a* 빈부의 차 the gap between the rich and the poor.

pindae 빈대 housebug; bedbug(*Am.*).

pindaek'o 빈대코 flat nose.

pindaettŏk 빈대떡 mung bean[green-bean] pancake.

pinggwa 빙과 ices; ice creams; ice cakes.

pin-gon 빈곤 poverty; want; need. *pin-gonhan* 빈곤한 poor; needy; destitute.

pinjari 빈자리 vacant seat; vacant position. → **kongsŏk** 공석.

pinnada 빛나다 ① shine; be bright; gleam ② be brilliant.

pinnaeda 빛내다 light up; make (a thing) shine; brighten.

pinnagada 빗나가다 turn away[aside]; wander[deviate] (from); miss.

pinnong 빈농 poor farmer[peasant].

pint'ŏlt'ŏri 빈털터리 penniless person.

pint'ŭm 빈틈 opening; gap; chink; crack.

pinu 비누 soap. *karu pinu* 가루 비누 soap powder.

pinŭl 비늘 scale. *pinŭri innŭn* 비늘이 있는 scaly.

pinyak'an 빈약한 poor; scant; meager. *pinyak'an chishik* 빈약한 지식 poor[scanty] knowledge.

piok 비옥. *piok'ada* 비옥하다 (be) fertile; rich; productive.

pip'an 비판 criticism. *pip'anhada* 비판하다 criticize; comment (on); pass[give] judgment (on).

pip'yŏng 비평 review; comment; critique. *pip'yŏng-*

hada 비평하다 criticize; review.
pirida 비리다 (be) fishy; (be) bloody.
pirinnae 비린내 fishy smell; bloody smell.
pirok 비록 though; if; even if.
piroso 비로소 for the first time; not … until[till].
pirye 비례 proportion; ratio. *piryehada* 비례하다 be in proportion (to).
piryo 비료 fertilizer; manure.
pisang 비상. *pisanghada* 비상하다 (be) unusual; uncommon; extraordinary.
pisŏ 비서 (private) secretary. *pisŏshil* 비서실 secretariat (office).
pisŏk 비석 tombstone; stone monument.
pissada 비싸다 (be) expensive; costly; dear; high.
pisu 비수 dagger; dirk.
pisŭt'ada 비슷하다 (be) like; similar; look like.
pit 빛 ① light; rays; beam ② color; hue.
pit 빚 debt; loan. *pijŭl chida* 빚을 지다 run[get] into debt; borrow money.
pit 빗 comb. *pitchil* 빗질 combing. *pitchirhada* 빗질하다 comb (one's hair).
pit'al 비탈 slope; incline. *pit'alkil* 비탈길 slope.
pitchang 빗장 bolt; crossbar; bar.
pitkkal 빛깔 color; shade; hue; tint.
pitmatta 빗맞다 miss the mark; guess wrong.
pitpangul 빗방울 raindrops.
pitta 빚다 ① brew (*wine*) ② shape dough for (*rice cakes*) ③ cause; give rise to; bring about.
pitturŏjida 비뚤어지다 get crooked; slant; incline; be tilted; bent; be jealous of.
pit'ŭlda 비틀다 twist; wrench; screw.
pit'ŭlgŏrida 비틀거리다 stagger; totter; reel.

piutta 비웃다 laugh at; deride; jeer (at).

piyak 비약 leap; jump. *piyak'ada* 비약하다 leap; make rapid progress.

piyŏl 비열 meanness; baseness. *piyŏrhada* 비열하다 (be) mean; base; cowardly.

piyong 비용 cost; expense(s).

piyul 비율 ratio; percentage; rate. ···*ŭi piyullo* ··· 의 비율로 at the rate[ratio] of.

pobae 보배 treasure; precious things.

pŏbin 법인 juridical[legal] person; corporation. *pŏbinse* 법인세 corporation tax.

pobok 보복 retaliation; revenge. *pobok'ada* 보복하다 retaliate; revenge oneself on.

pŏbwon 법원 court; tribunal. *pŏbwonjang* 법원장 president of a court.

pobyŏng 보병 infantry; infantryman; foot soldier.

poch'ung 보충 supplement; replacement. *poch'unghada* 보충하다 supplement; fill up.

poda 보다 see; look at; witness; stare[gaze] at; watch; read; look over; view.

podap 보답 recompense; reward; compensation. *podap'ada* 보답하다 return; repay; reward; recompense; return; compensate.

podo 보도 report; news; information.

podo 보도 sidewalk(*Am.*); pavement(*Eng.*); footpath. *hoengdan podo* 횡단 보도 marked crossing (*Am.*).

podŭmda 보듬다 embrace; hug; clasp (a person) to one's bosom.

pogi 보기 example; instance.

pogo 보고 report; information. *pogohada* 보고하다 report; inform. *pogosŏ* 보고서 report.

pogŏn 보건 (preservation of) health; sanitation;

hygienics. *segye pogŏn kigu* 세계 보건 기구 World
Health Organization (WHO).
pogŭm 복음 gospel. *pogŭm kyohoe* 복음 교회 Evan-
gelical church.
pogŭp 보급 diffusion; popularization. *pogŭp'ada*
보급하다 diffuse; pervade; popularize.
pogwan 보관 custody; (safe) keeping. *pogwan-
hada* 보관하다 take custody [charge] of; take
[have] (a thing) in charge.
pogyŏl 보결 supplement; substitute. *pogyŏrŭi* 보
결의 supplementary.
pogyong 복용. *pogyonghada* 복용하다 take (medicine); use internally.
poho 보호 protection; safeguard. *pohohada* 보호
하다 protect; shelter; safeguard.
pohŏm 보험 insurance. *pohŏmnyo* 보험료 premium.
pohŏm hoesa 보험 회사 insurance company.
poida 보이다 ① see; catch sight of; be seen [visi-
ble]; appear ② show; let (a person) see.
pojang 보장 guarantee; security. *pojanghada* 보
장하다 guarantee; secure. *sahoe pojang* 사회 보
장 social security.
pojogŭm 보조금 subsidy; bounty; grant-in-aid.
pojon 보존 preservation; conservation. *pojonhada*
preserve; conserve.
pŏjŏt'ada 버젓하다 (be) fair and square; be open.
pŏjŏshi 버젓이 fairly; overtly. ·
pojŭng 보증 guarantee; assurance; security. *pojŭng-
hada* guarantee; assure; warrant. *pojŭng sup'yo*
보증 수표 certified check. *pojŭngin* 보증인 guarantor; surety.
pok 복 felicity; bliss; blessing; good luck. *poktoen*

복된 happy; blessed.

pokchang 복장 dress; attire; clothes.

pokchap 복잡 complexity; complication. *pokcha- p'an* 복잡한 (be) complicated; complex; tangled.

pokchi 복지 (public) welfare; well-being. *pokchi shisŏl* 복지 시설 welfare facilities.

pokchik 복직 resumption of office; reappointment. *pokchik'ada* 복직하다 resume office; be reinstalled.

pokchong 복종 obedience; submission. *pokchong- hada* 복종하다 obey; submit.

pokkwon 복권 lottery ticket.

pokp'an 복판 middle; center; midst; heart. *pok- p'ane* 복판에 in the middle of.

poksa 복사 reproduction; reprint. *poksahada* 복사 하다 reproduce; copy.

poksu 복수 revenge; avenge; vengeance. *poksu- hada* 복수하다 revenge oneself (on).

poksunga 복숭아 peach. *poksungakkot* 복숭아꽃 peach blossoms.

pokta 볶다 parch; roast; fry.

pokto 복도 corridor; passage; lobby; hallway (*Am.*).

poktŏkpang 복덕방 real estate agency.

pol 볼 cheek. *polmen sori* 볼멘 소리 angry voice.

pŏl 벌 bee. *pŏltte* 벌떼 swarm of bees. *pŏlchip* 벌 집 beehive; honeycomb.

pŏl 벌 punishment; penalty. *pŏrhada[chuda]* 벌 하다[주다] punish; penalize.

pŏl 벌 set; suit. *ot han pol* 옷 한 벌 a suit of clothes.

pŏlda 벌다 earn; make (money); gain.

polgi 볼기 buttock; hip; rump.

pŏlgŭm 벌금 fine; penalty; forfeit.

pollae 본래 originally; primarily; naturally; by nature. *pollaeŭi* 본래의 original; natural.

pŏlle 벌레 insect; bug; worm; moth. *pŏlle mŏgŭn* 벌레 먹은 worm[moth]-eaten; vermicular.

pŏllida 벌리다 open; widen; leave space.

polmanhada 볼만하다 be worth seeing; be worthy of notice.

pom 봄 spring (time). *pomŭi* 봄의 spring; vernal.

pŏm 범 tiger; tigress. →**horangi** 호랑이.

pŏmhaeng 범행 crime; offense.

pŏmin 범인 criminal; offender; culprit.

pŏmjoe 범죄 crime; criminal act. *pŏmjoeŭi* 범죄의 criminal.

pŏmnyul 법률 law; statute. *pŏmnyurŭi* 법률의 legal. *pŏmnyulga* 법률가 jurist; lawyer.

pomo 보모 nurse; nursery attendant; kindergarten teacher; kindergartner.

pŏmpŏp 범법 violation of the law. *pŏmpŏp'ada* 범법하다 violate[break] the law.

pomul 보물 treasure; jewel; valuables.

pŏmwi 범위 extent; scope; sphere; range; limit; bounds. *pŏmwi nae[oe]e* 범위 내[외]에 within [beyond] the limits[scope].

ponaeda 보내다 send; forward; transmit.

ponbogi 본보기 example; model; pattern.

pŏnbŏni 번번이 every[each] time; whenever; as often as; always.

ponbu 본부 headquarters; main[head] office.

pŏnch'ang 번창 prosperity. *pŏnch'anghada* prosper; thrive; flourish.

pŏn-gae 번개 (flash of) lightning.

ponggŏn 봉건 feudalism; feudal system. *ponggŏn-*

jŏk 봉건적 feudal. *ponggŏnjuŭi* 봉건주의 feudalism. *ponggŏn chedo* 봉건 제도 feudal system.

ponggŭp 봉급 salary; pay; wages.

ponghwa 봉화 signal[beacon] fire; rocket.

pongji 봉지 paper bag.

pongmyŏn 복면 mask; disguise; veil. *pongmyŏnŭi* 복면의 masked; in disguise. *pongmyŏn kangdo* 복면 강도 masked robber.

pongori 봉오리 bud. *pongorirŭl maetta* 봉오리를 맺다 have[bear] buds. →**kkotpongori** 꽃봉오리.

pŏngŏri 벙어리 dumb person; mute.

pongsa 봉사 service; attendance. *pongsahada* 봉사하다 serve; render service; attend on.

pongsŏnhwa 봉선화 (garden) balsam; touch-me-not.

pongt'u 봉투 envelope.

ponguri 봉우리 peak; summit; top. *sanponguri* 산봉우리 mountain top[peak].

pŏnho 번호 number; mark. *pŏnhop'yo* 번호표 number ticket[plate].

ponjil 본질 essence; true[intrinsic] nature.

ponjŏk 본적 one's domicile; one's place of register.

ponjŏm 본점 ① head[main] office ② this office.

ponjŏn 본전 principal (sum); capital; prime cost.

ponin 본인 the person in question; the person himself[herself]; principal.

pŏnjida 번지다 spread; run; blot.

ponmun 본문 body (of a letter); text (of a treaty).

ponnŭng 본능 instinct. *ponnŭngjŏk[ŭro]* 본능적 [으로] instinctive[ly].

ponsa 본사 head office; main office.

ponshim 본심 one's real intention; one's heart.

pont'o 본토 mainland; the country proper.

pǒnyǒk 번역 translation. *pǒnyǒk'ada* 번역하다 translate[render] into; put (into).

pǒp 법 law; rule; custom; practice.

pǒpch'ik 법칙 law; rule.

poram 보람 worth; effect; result. *poram innǔn* 보람 있는 fruitful; effective.

poratpit 보랏빛 purple; violet. *yǒnboratpit* 연보랏빛 lilac.

pori 보리 barley. *porich'a* 보리차 barley tea.

pǒrida 버리다 ① throw[cast, fling] away ② abandon; forsake; give up.

pǒrǒjida 벌어지다 ① split; crack ② open; smile ③ occur; come about ④ become wide.

porǔm 보름 half a month.

pǒrǔt 버릇 habit; acquired tendency; propensity. *…hanǔn pǒrǔshi itta* …하는 버릇이 있다 have a habit of doing.

poryu 보류 reservation. *poryuhada* 보류하다 reserve; shelve.

posalp'ida 보살피다 take care of; look after; tend.

posang 보상 compensation; indemnity. *posanghada* 보상하다 compensate for; make up for.

posǒk 보석 jewel; gem; precious stone. *posǒksang* 보석상 jewel's (shop).

posǒk 보석 bail; bailment. *posǒk'ada* 보석하다 release (a person) on bail; bail.

pǒsǒn 버선 Korean socks.

pǒsǒt 버섯 mushroom; toadstool; fungus.

posu 보수 remuneration; reward; fee; pay.

posu 보수. *posujuǔi* 보수주의 conservatism. *posudangwǒn* 보수당원 Conservative; Tory (*Eng.*).

pǒt 벗 friend; companion; mate; company.

pot'aeda 보태다 ① supplement; make up (for); help out ② add (up); sum up.

pŏt'ida 버티다 endure; stand; bear.

pŏtkida 벗기다 ① peel; rind; pare ② take[strip] off; strip of; help off.

pot'ong 보통 ordinarily; commonly; normally. *pot'ongŭi* 보통의 usual; ordinary; common.

pŏtta 벗다 take[put] off; slip[fling] off.

poyak 보약 restorative; tonic; bracer.

poyŏjuda 보여주다 show; let (a person) see; display.

ppaeatta 빼앗다 take away from; snatch from; plunder; deprive of.

ppaeda 빼다 ① pull[take] out; draw; extract ② subtract[deduct] (from) ③ remove; wash off ④ omit; exclude.

ppaekppaek'ada 빽빽하다 (be) close[dense, thick].

ppaengsoni 뺑소니 flight; escape. *ppaengsonich'ida* 뺑소니치다 run away; take (to) flight.

ppajida 빠지다 fall[get] into; sink; go down.

ppalda 빨다 ① sip; suck; lick ② wash.

ppallae 빨래 wash; washing. *ppallaehada* 빨래하다 wash. *ppallaetchul* 빨랫줄 clothesline.

ppalli 빨리 quickly; fast; rapidly; in haste; soon; immediately.

ppaltae 빨대 straw; sipper.

ppang 빵 bread. *ppangŭl kupta* 빵을 굽다 bake [toast] bread.

ppappat'ada 빳빳하다 ① (be) stiff; straight ② (be) headstrong; unyielding.

pparŭda 빠르다 ① (be) quick; fast; swift; speedy ② (be) early; premature.

ppattŭrida 빠뜨리다 throw into (a river); trap;

tempt; lure.
ppŏkkugi, ppŏkkuksae 뻐꾸기, 뻐꾹새 cuckoo.
ppong 뽕 mulberry. *ppongnip* 뽕잎 mulberry leaves. *ppongnamu pat* 뽕나무 밭 mulberry field.
ppopta 뽑다 ① pull[take] out; draw; extract ② select; pick[single] out; elect ③ enlist; enroll.
ppŏtta 뻗다 ① lengthen; stretch; extend ② collapse; knock out ③ develop.
ppumta 뿜다 belch; emit; spout; spurt; gush out.
ppun 뿐 only; alone; merely. *ppunman anira* 뿐만 아니라 besides; moreover; in addition.
ppuri 뿌리 root. *ppuri kip'ŭn* 뿌리 깊은 deep-rooted.
ppurida 뿌리다 sprinkle; strew; scatter; diffuse.
ppyam 뺨 cheek. *ppyamŭl ch'ida* 뺨을 치다 slap (a person) on the cheek.
ppyŏ 뼈 bone. *ppyŏdae* 뼈대 frame.
pubu 부부 man[husband] and wife; married couple.
pubun 부분 part; portion; section. *pubunjŏgŭro* 부분적으로 partially.
puch'ae 부채 fan; folding fan.
puch'ida 붙이다 ① put[fix, stick] ② attach[fasten]; paste ③ apply.
puch'ida 부치다 send; mail; remit; forward. *tonŭl puch'ida* 돈을 부치다 remit money.
Puch'ŏ 부처 Buddha.
puch'ongni 부총리 Deputy Prime Minister.
puch'ugida 부추기다 incite; instigate; agitate.
pudae 부대 unit; corps; detachment. *pudaejang* 부대장 commander.
pudakch'ida 부닥치다 come upon[across]; hit upon; encounter; meet with.
pudam 부담 burden; charge; responsibility. *pudam-*

hada 부담하다 bear; shoulder; stand; share.
pudang 부당. *pudanghada* 부당하다 (be) unjust; unfair; unreasonable.
pudi 부디 without fail; by all means; in any cost.
pudich'ida 부딪히다 collide with; bump against [into].
pudo 부도 dishonor. *pudonada* 부도나다 be dishonored. *pudo sup'yo* 부도 수표 dishonored check.
pudongsan 부동산 immovable property; real estate; realty. *pudongsanŏpcha* 부동산업자 realtor (*Am.*)
pudu 부두 quay; pier; wharf; water front.
pudŭrŏpta 부드럽다 (be) soft; tender; mild; gentle. *pudŭrŏpke* 부드럽게 softly; mildly; tenderly.
pugi 부기 book-keeping.
pugo 부고 obituary; announcement of death.
pugun 부군 one's husband.
pugŭn 부근 neighborhood; vicinity. *pugŭnŭi* 부근의 neighboring; nearby; adjacent.
pugyŏl 부결 rejection. *pugyŏrhada* 부결하다 reject; turn down; decide against; vote down.
puha 부하 subordinate; follower.
puho 부호 rich man; man of wealth.
puho 부호 sign; mark; cipher; symbol.
puhŭng 부흥 revival; reconstruction; restoration; rehabilitation; renaissance. *puhŭnghada* 부흥하다 be reconstructed; be revived.
puim 부임. *puimhada* 부임하다 leave[start] for one's (new) post.
puin 부인 woman; lady. *puinpyŏng* 부인병 women's disease[ailments].
puin 부인 Mrs. ; Madam; wife; lady. *Kimssi puin* 김씨 부인 Mrs. Kim.

puin 부인 denial; disapproval. *puinhada* 부인하다 deny; disapprove; say no.

puja 부자 rich man; man of wealth.

pujang 부장 head[chief, director] of a department.

puji 부지 (building) site; plot; lot. *kŏnch'uk puji* 건축 부지 building site.

pujirŏnhada 부지런하다 (be) industrious; diligent. *pujirŏnhi* 부지런히 diligently; industriously; hard.

pujo 부조 ① help; aid; support ② congratulatory gift; condolence money.

pujok 부족 shortage; deficiency; deficit; lack. *pujok'ada* 부족하다 be short (of); lack.

pujŏktang 부적당 unfitness; unsuitableness. *pujŏktanghada* 부적당하다 (be) unfit (for).

pujŏng 부정 injustice; dishonest; unlawfulness. *pujŏnghan* 부정한 unjust; foul; unlawful.

pujŏnggi 부정기. *pujŏnggiŭi* 부정기의 irregular; nonscheduled.

pukkŭk 북극 the North Pole. *pukkŭgŭi* 북극의 arctic; polar. *pukkŭksŏng* 북극성 polestar.

pukkŭrŏpta 부끄럽다 (be) shameful; disgraceful.

pukta 붉다 (be) red; crimson; scarlet.

pul 불 fire; flame; blaze. *purŭl puch'ida* 불을 붙이다 light a fire.

pulch'injŏl 불친절 unkindness. *pulch'injŏrhan* 불친절한 unkind; unfriendly.

pulch'ungbun 불충분 insufficiency; inadequacy *pulch'ungbunhan* 불충분한 insufficient; not enough.

pulda 불다 blow; breathe. *nap'arŭl pulda* 나팔을 불다 blow a trumpet.

pulganŭng 불가능 impossibility. *pulganŭnghada* 불가능하다 (be) impossible[unattainable].

pulgil 불길. *pulgirhan* 불길한 unlucky; ominous.

pulgong 불공 Buddhist mass.

pulgongp'yŏng 불공평. *pulgongp'yŏnghada* 불공평하다 (be) partial; unfair; unjust.

pulgu 불구 deformity. *pulguŭi* 불구의 deformed; cripple; disabled. *pulguja* 불구자 disabled[deformed] person; cripple.

pulgusok 불구속. *pulgusogŭro* 불구속으로 without physical restraint.

pulgyo 불교 Buddhism. *pulgyodo* 불교도 Buddhist.

pulgyŏl 불결. *pulgyŏrhada* 불결하다 (be) dirty; unclean; filthy; unsanitary.

pulgyŏnggi 불경기 hard[bad] time; slump; dullness; depression.

pulgyuch'ik 불규칙 irregularity. *pulgyuch'ik'ada* 불규칙하다 (be) irregular; unsystematic.

puljadongch'a 불자동차 →**sobangch'a** 소방차.

pulk'wae 불쾌 unpleasantness; displeasure. *pulk'waehada* 불쾌하다 feel unpleasant[displeased].

pulli 분리 separation; segregation. *pullihada* 분리하다 separate (from); isolate; segregate.

pullyang 분량 quantity; measure; dose.

pulman 불만 dissatisfaction; discontent. *pulmanŭi* 불만의 dissatisfied.

pulmo 불모. *pulmoŭi* 불모의 barren; sterile. *pulmoji* 불모지 barren[waste] land.

pulmyŏnchŭng 불면증 insomnia. *pulmyŏnchŭng hwanja* 불면증 환자 insomniac.

pulmyŏngye 불명예 dishonor; disgrace; shame. *pulmyŏngyehan* 불명예한 dishonorable; shameful; disgraceful.

pulp'iryo 불필요 *pulp'iryohan* 불필요한 unnecessary; needless. *pulp'iryohage* 불필요하게 unnecessarily; needlessly.

pulpŏp 불법 unlawfulness; illegality. *pulpŏbŭi* 불법의 unlawful; illegal; unjust. *pulpŏp ipkuk* 불법 입국 illegal entry〔immigration〕.

pulp'yŏn 불편 inconvenience. *pulp'yŏnhada* 불편하다 (be) inconvenient.

pulp'yŏng 불평 discontent; complaint; grievance. *pulp'yŏnghada* 불평하다 grumble; complain.

pulp'yŏngdŭng 불평등 inequality. *pulp'yŏngdŭnghada* 불평등하다 (be) unequal; unfair.

pulsang 불상 image of Buddha; Buddhist image.

pulson 불손 insolence. *pulsonhan* 불손한 insolent; haughty; arrogant.

pulssanghada 불쌍하다 (be) poor; pitiful; pitiable; miserable.

pulssuk 불쑥 suddenly; unexpectedly; abruptly.

pult'ada 불타다 burn; blaze; be on fire〔in flames〕.

pultan 불단 Buddhist altar.

pumbida 붐비다 (be) crowded; congested; jammed; packed; thronged.

pumo 부모 father and mother; parents. *pumoŭi* 부모의 parental.

pumun 부문 section; department; class; group; category.

pun 분 minute (of an hour). *shibobun* 15분 quarter; fifteen minutes.

punbae 분배 distribution; sharing. *punbaehada* 분배하다 distribute; divide; allot.

punch'im 분침 minute hand.

pun-gae 분개 indignation; resentment. *pun-gaehada* 분개하다 (be) indignant; resent.

pungdae 붕대 bandage; dressing. *pungdaerŭl kamta* 붕대를 감다 apply a bandage (to); dress (a wound).

punhae 분해 analysis. *punhaehada* 분해하다 analyze; dissolve.

punhyang 분향. *punhyanghada* 분향하다 burn [offer] incense (for the dead).

punjae 분재 potted plant; pot-planting.

punjang 분장 make up; disguise. *punjanghada* 분장하다 make[dress] up as; disguise oneself as.

punji 분지 basin; hollow; valley.

punjŏm 분점 branch shop; branch office.

punju 분주. *punjuhada* 분주하다 (be) busy; busily engaged.

punmal 분말 powder; flour; dust

punmyŏng 분명 clearness. *punmyŏnghada* 분명하다 (be) clear; distinct; obvious. *punmyŏnghi* 분명히 clearly; apparently.

punno 분노 fury; rage; indignation. *punnohada* 분노하다 get[be] angry; be enraged.

punp'il 분필 chalk.

punshik 분식 powdered food; flour.

punshil 분실 loss. *punshirhada* 분실하다 lose; be lost; be missing.

punsŏk 분석 analysis. *punsŏk'ada* 분석하다 assay; analyze; make an analysis (of).

punsu 분수 fountain; jet (of water).

punswae 분쇄 *punswaehada* 분쇄하다 shatter (a thing) to pieces; crush; smash.

punwigi 분위기 atmosphere; surroundings.

punya 분야 sphere; field; province. *yŏn-gu punya* 연구 분야 field[area] of study.

punyŏ 부녀 father and daughter.

punyŏja 부녀자 woman; womenfolk; fair sex.

puŏk 부엌 kitchen.

puŏp 부업 sideline; subsidiary business.

pup'ae 부패 putrefaction; rotting. *pup'aehada* 부패하다 rot; addle.

pup'i 부피 bulk; volume; size.

purak 부락 village; village community. *purangmin* 부락민 village folk.

puran 불안 uneasiness; anxiety; unrest. *puranhan* 불안한 uneasy; anxious.

purhaeng 불행 unhappiness; misfortune; ill-luck. *purhaeng* 불행한 unhappy; unfortunate. *purhaenghi(do)* 불행히 (도) unfortunately.

purhamni 불합리 *purhamnihan* 불합리한 irrational; illogical; unreasonable.

purhapkyŏk 불합격 failure; rejection. *purhapkyŏk'ada* 불합격하다 (be) disqualified; fail to pass.

purhwa 불화 trouble; discord. *purhwahada* 불화하다 be on bad terms (with); be in discord (with); be at strife[odds] (with).

purhwang 불황 depression; slump; recession. *purhwangŭi* 불황의 inactive; dull; stagnant.

puri 부리 bill; beak.

purida 부리다 ① keep (person, horse, etc.) at work; set[put] to work; hire; employ ② manage; handle; run ③ exercise; yield.

purip 불입 payment. *purip'ada* 불입하다 pay in; pay up. *puripkŭm* 불입금 money due.

purŏ 부러 on purpose; intentionally; deliberately. *purŏ kŏjinmarhada* 부러 거짓말하다 lie deliberately. → **ilburŏ** 일부러.

purok 부록 supplement; appendix (to a book).
purŏnada 불어나다 increase; gain; grow.
purŏpta 부럽다 (be) enviable. *purŏun dŭshi* 부러운 듯이 enviously; with envy.
purŭda 부르다 ① call; hail ② name; designate ③ bid; offer ④ sing ⑤ shout ⑥ send for; invite ⑦ full; inflated.
purŭjitta 부르짖다 shout; cry; exclaim.
purun 불운 misfortune; ill-luck. *purunhan* 불운한 unfortunate; unlucky.
purut'unghada 부루퉁하다 ① (be) swollen; bloated ② (be) sulky. *purut'unghan ŏlgul* 부루퉁한 얼굴 swollen face; sulky look.
purwanjŏn 불완전 imperfection; incompleteness. *purwanjŏnhan* 불완전한 imperfect; incomplete.
puryaburya 부랴부랴 hurriedly; in a great hurry.
pusang 부상 wound; injury; cut; bruise. *pusanghada* 부상하다 be wounded; get hurt.
pusanmul 부산물 by-product; residual product.
pushida 부시다 dazzling; glaring.
pusŏjida 부서지다 break; be smashed [broken, wrecked]; go [fall] to pieces.
pusok 부속. *pusok'ada* 부속하다 belong (to); be attached to. *pusogŭi* 부속의 attached; belonging to; dependent.
pusu 부수 number of copies; circulation.
pusuip 부수입 additional [side] income.
pusŭrŏgi 부스러기 bit; fragment; scraps; adds and ends; crumbs; chips.
pusŭrŏm 부스럼 boil; ulcer; abscess; tumor.
put 붓 writing brush; brush; pen.
putta 붙다 stick (to); adhere [cling] (to); attach

oneself to; glue; paste.

putta 붓다 pour (into, out); fill with; put (water in a bowl); feed (a lamp with oil).

putta 붓다 swell; become swollen; bloat.

put'ak 부탁 request; favor; solicitation. *put'ak'a-da* 부탁하다 ask; request; beg.

putchapta 붙잡다 seize; grasp; catch; take hold of.

puttŭlda 붙들다 ① catch; seize; take hold of; grasp[grab] ② arrest; capture.

puŭi 부의 obituary gift. *puŭigŭm* 부의금 condolence money.　　　　　　　　　　　　　　⌐staff man.

puwon 부원 member of the staff; staff (member);

puyang 부양 support; maintenance. *puyanghada* 부양하다 support; maintain. *puyang kajok* 부양 가족 dependent family.

puyu 부유. *puyuhada* 부유하다 be rich; wealthy.

pyŏ 벼 rice plant; paddy.

pyŏk 벽 wall; partition. *pyŏkpo* 벽보 bill; poster.

pyŏl 별 star. *pyŏlpit* 별빛 starlight.

pyŏlchang 별장 villa; country house; cottage (*Am.*).

pyŏlgwan 별관 annex; extension; outhouse.

pyŏllo 별로 especially; particularly; in particular.

pyŏndong 변동 change; fluctuation. *pyŏndonghada* 변동하다 change; alter.

pyŏnduri 변두리 outskirts; border. *Sŏurŭi pyŏnduri* 서울의 변두리 outskirts of Seoul.

pyŏng 병 bottle; jar.

pyŏng 병 disease; sickness (*Am.*); illness (*Eng.*). *pyŏngdŭn* 병든 sick (*Am.*); ill (*Eng.*); unwell.

pyŏngguwan 병구완 nursing; tending (a sick person).

pyŏn-gi 변기 chamber pot; night stool.

pyŏngja 병자 sick person; patient.

pyŏngp'ung 병풍 folding screen.

pyŏngsa 병사 soldier; private.

pyŏngshil 병실 sickroom; (sick) ward; sick bay.

pyŏngshin 병신 deformed person; cripple; disabled person.

pyŏngwon 병원 hospital; nursing home. *pyŏng-wone ibwonhada* 병원에 입원하다 go into hospital.

pyŏngyŏk 병역 military service.

pyŏn-gyŏng 변경 change; alteration. *pyŏn-gyŏng-hada* 변경하다 change; alter.

pyŏnhada 변하다 change; undergo a change; vary. *pyŏnhagi shwiun* 변하기 쉬운 changeable.

pyŏnho 변호 defense; justification. *pyŏnhohada* 변호하다 plead; defend; speak for.

pyŏnhosa 변호사 lawyer; attorney (*Am.*); barrister. the bar;

pyŏnhwa 변화 change; variation; alteration. *pyŏnhwahada* 변화하다 change; turn.

pyŏnjang 변장 disguise. *pyŏnjanghada* 변장하다 disguise oneself (as); be disguised (as).

pyŏnjŏl 변절 betrayal; treachery. *pyŏnjŏrhada* 변절하다 apostatize; change[turn] one's coat.

pyŏnjŏnso 변전소 (transformer) substation.

pyŏnsang 변상 payment; compensation. *pyŏnsang-hada* 변상하다 pay for; reimburse.

pyŏnso 변소 lavatory; water closet; toilet room; rest room.

pyŏrak 벼락 thunder; thunderbolt. *pyŏrak kat'ŭn* 벼락 같은 thunderous.

pyŏrak puja 벼락 부자 mushroom[overnight] millionaire; upstart.

pyŏrang 벼랑 cliff; precipice; bluff.

pyŏru 벼루 inkstone; ink slab. *pyŏrutchip* 벼룻집 inkstone case.

pyŏsŭl 벼슬 government post[service].

pyŏt 볕 sunshine; sunlight.

P

p'a 파 ① branch of a family[clan] ② party; faction; sect. *churyup'a* 주류파 main stream faction.

p'a 파 Welsh onion.

p'abŏl 파벌 clique; faction.

p'abyŏng 파병 dispatch of forces[troops]. *p'abyŏng-hada* 파병하다 dispatch troops[forces].

p'ach'ul 파출 *p'ach'urhada* 파출하다 dispatch; send out. *p'ach'ulbu* 파출부 visiting housekeeper. *p'ach'ulso* 파출소 police box.

p'ada 파다 dig; excavate; drill.

p'adakkŏrida 파닥거리다 flap; flutter; flop.

p'ado 파도 waves; billows; surge.

p'ae 패 ① tag; tablet ② group; gang; company.

p'aebae 패배 defeat; reverse.

p'aeda 패다 ① strike; batter ② chop firewood ③ come to ears ④ be dug[hollowed].

p'aejŏn 패전 defeat. *p'aejŏn-guk* 패전국 defeated nation. *p'aejŏn t'usu* 패전 투수 losing pitcher.

p'aemul 패물 personal ornament; trinkets.

p'aenggaech'ida 팽개치다 throw away[aside]; fling away; cast away.

p'agoe 파괴 destruction. *p'agoehada* 파괴하다 destroy; break. *p'agoejŏgin* 파괴적인 destructive. *p'agoeja* 파괴자 destroyer.

p'ahon 파혼. *p'ahonhada* 파혼하다 break (off) engagement.

p'al 팔 arm. *p'arŭl kkigo* 팔을 끼고 with folded arms; (walk) arm in arm (with).

p'alda 팔다 sell; deal in.

p'alkkumch'i 팔꿈치 elbow.

p'alship 팔십, 80 eighty. *chep'alship* 제80 the [eightieth.

p'altchi 팔찌 bracelet; armlet(*Eng.*).

p'alttukshigye 팔뚝시계 wrist watch.

p'amutta 파묻다 bury; inter.

p'amyŏl 파멸 ruin; destruction. *p'amyŏrhada* 파멸하다 be ruined[wrecked]; go to ruin.

p'andan 판단 judgment; decision. *p'andanhada* 판단하다 judge.

p'an-gŏmsa 판검사 judges and public prosecutors.

p'an-gyŏl 판결 judgment; decision. *p'an-gyŏrhada* 판결하다 decide (on a case).

p'anja 판자 board; plank. *p'anjachip* 판자집 barrack; shack.

p'anmae 판매 sale; selling. *p'anmaehada* 판매하다 sell; deal in.

p'ansa 판사 judge; justice.

p'ansori 판소리 Korean (classical) solo opera drama.

p'aŏp 파업 strike; walkout(*Am.*). *p'aŏp'ada* 파업하다 go on strike; walk out.

p'ap'yŏn 파편 (broken) piece; fragment; splinter.

p'arae 파래 green laver; sea lettuce.

p'arang 파랑 blue(color); green. *p'arangsae* 파랑새 bluebird.

p'arat'a 파랗다 ① (be) blue; green ② (be) pale; pallid.

p'ari 파리 fly. *p'ariyak* 파리약 flypoison. *p'ari-*

ch'ae 파리채 fly flap.

p'arwol 팔월 August.

p'aryŏmch'i 파렴치. *p'aryŏmch'ihan* 파렴치한 ① shameless; infamous ② shameless fellow.

p'asan 파산 bankruptcy; insolvency. *p'asanhada* 파산하다 become bankrupt.

p'ason 파손 damage; injury; breakdown. *p'ason-doeda* 파손되다 be damaged; break down.

p'ayŏl 파열 explosion; bursting. *p'ayŏrhada* 파열하다 explode; burst (up); rupture.

p'i 피 blood. *p'iga nada* 피가 나다 bleed; blood runs[flows] out.

p'ibu 피부 skin. *p'ibusaek* 피부색 skin color.

p'igon 피곤 fatigue; tiredness. *p'igonhada* 피곤하다 (be) tired; fatigued.

p'ihada 피하다 avoid; dodge; evade; keep away from; shirk; shun.

p'ihae 피해 damage; injury; harm. *p'ihaerŭl ipta* 피해를 입다 be damaged[injured] (by).

p'iim 피임 contraception. *p'iimnyak* 피임약 contraceptive. *p'iimhada* 피임하다 prevent conception.

p'ilsup'um 필수품 necessaries; requisites. *saeng-hwal p'ilsup'um* 생활 필수품 daily necessaries.

p'ilt'ong 필통 pencil[brush] case; brush[pen] stand.

p'inan 피난 refuge. *p'inanhada* 피난하다 take refuge. *p'inanmin* 피난민 refugee.

p'inggye 핑계 excuse; pretext. *p'inggyerŭl taeda* 핑계를 대다 make[find] an excuse.

p'injan 핀잔 *p'injanŭl chuda* 핀잔을 주다 rebuke; snub; scold.

p'iri 피리 pipe; flute. *p'iri sori* 피리 소리 sound

of a flute.

p'iro 피로 fatigue; weariness; exhaustion. *p'irohan* 피로한 (be) tired; weary.

p'iryo 필요 necessity; need. *p'iryohan* 필요한 necessary; essential.

p'isŏ 피서 summering. *p'isŏ kada* 피서 가다 go to a summer resort.

p'iuda 피우다 ① make[build] a fire ② smoke; burn (incense) ③ bloom.

p'ŏbutta 퍼붓다 ① pour[shower, rain] upon ② rain in torrents.

p'odo 포도 grape. *p'odobat* 포도밭 vineyard. p'odoju 포도주 (grape)wine; port(wine).

p'ogi 포기 abandonment. *p'ogihada* 포기하다 give up; abandon.

p'ogŭnhada 포근하다 ① (be) mild; warm ② (be) soft and comfortable.

p'ogyo 포교 missionary work. *p'ogyohada* 포교하 다 preach.

p'oham 포함. *p'ohamhada* 포함하다 contain; include. *…ŭl p'ohamhayŏ* …을 포함하여 including.

p'ojang 포장 packing. *p'ojanghada* 포장하다 pack; wrap (up). *p'ojangji* 포장지 packing[wrapping] paper.

p'ojang 포장 pavement; paving. *p'ojanghada* 포 장하다 pave. *p'ojang toro* 포장 도로 pavement.

p'ŏjida 퍼지다 spread out; get broader; be propagated; get abroad.

p'ok 폭 width; breadth. *p'ogi nŏlbŭn* 폭이 넓은 wide; broad. *p'ogi chobŭn* 폭이 좁은 narrow.

p'ŏk 퍽 very (much); quite; awfully; highly.

p'ok'aeng 폭행 (act of) violence. *p'ok'aenghada*

폭행하다 do violence; commit an outrage.

p'okkun 폭군 tyrant; despot.

p'okkyŏk 폭격 bombing. *p'okkyŏk'ada* 폭격하다 bomb; make a bombing raid.

p'okpal 폭발 explosion. *p'okparhada* 폭발하다 explode; burst; blow up; erupt.

p'okp'o 폭포 waterfall; falls.

p'okp'ung 폭풍 storm; tempest; typhoon; hurricane. *p'okp'ung chuŭibo* 폭풍 주의보 storm alert.

p'okshinhada 폭신하다 (be) soft; spongy; cushiony.

p'okt'an 폭탄 bomb. *wonja[suso] p'okt'an* 원자[수소] 폭탄 atomic[hydrogen] bomb.

p'oktong 폭동 riot; uprising; disturbance.

p'ŏllŏkkŏrida, **p'ŏllŏgida** 펄럭거리다, 펄럭이다 flutter; flap; flicker; waver.

p'omok 포목 dry goods(*Am.*); drapery(*Eng.*). *p'omokchŏm* 포목점 dry goods store(*Am.*); draper's shop (*Eng.*).

p'ŏnaeda 퍼내다 bail[dip, scoop] out; pump out.

p'ongno 폭로 exposure; disclosure. *p'ongnohada* 폭로하다 expose; disclose; lay bare.

p'ongnyŏk 폭력 force; violence. *p'ongnyŏgŭro* 폭력으로 by force. *p'ongnyŏkpae* 폭력배 hooligans.

p'oro 포로 prisoner of war(POW). *p'oro suyongso* 포로 수용소 prisoner's[concentration] camp.

p'osu 포수 ① catch(er) ② gunner; shooter.

p'ot'al 포탈 evasion of tax. →**t'alse** 탈세.

p'ot'an 포탄 shell; cannonball.

p'ŏttŭrida 퍼뜨리다 spread; diffuse; circulate.

p'udaejŏp 푸대접 inhospitality; cold treatment. *p'udaejŏp'ada* 푸대접하다 treat coldly.

p'ul 풀 grass; weed. *p'ulppuri* 풀뿌리 grass root.

p'ullip 풀잎 grass leaf.

p'ul 풀 paste; starch.   *p'ullo puch'ida* 풀로 붙이다 stick with paste; paste (up).

p'ulbat 풀밭 grass field; meadow; lawn.

p'ulda 풀다 ① untie; unpack; undo ② solve.

p'umta 품다 hold in one's bosom; embrace; hug.

p'umjil 품질 quality.   *p'umjil kwalli* 품질 관리 quality control.

p'ungbu 풍부 abundance; plenty.   *p'ungbuhan* 풍부한 abundant; rich; wealthy.

p'ungch'a 풍차 windmill; penwheel.

p'unggŭm 풍금 organ.   *p'unggŭmŭl ch'ida* 풍금을 치다 play (on) the organ.

p'unggyŏng 풍경 landscape; scenery; view.

p'ungjak 풍작 good[rich] harvest.

p'ungmun 풍문 rumor; hearsay; (town) talk.

p'ungno 풍로 (portable) cooking stove; small kitchen range.

p'ungsok 풍속 manners; customs; public morals.

p'ungsŏn 풍선 balloon.   *komu p'ungsŏn* 고무 풍선 rubber[toy] balloon.

p'ungsŭp 풍습 →**p'ungsok** 풍속.

p'ungt'o 풍토 natural features; climate.

p'unnagi 풋나기 greenhorn; novice; green hand.

p'unton 푼돈 loose cash; odd money; broken money; pennies.

p'unyŏm 푸념 idle complaint.   *p'unyŏmhada* 푸념하다 complain; grumble; grievance.

p'urŏjuda 풀어주다 set (a person) free; liberate.

p'urŭda 푸르다 (be) blue; azure; pale.

p'ye 폐 lungs. *p'yeam* 폐암 cancer of lung. *p'yepyŏng[kyŏrhaek]* 폐병[결핵] tuberculosis.

p'yech'a 폐차 disused[useless] car; scrapped car [vehicle]; out-of-service car.

p'yegyŏrhaek 폐결핵 tuberculosis (T. B.).

p'yehoe 폐회 closing of meeting. *p'yehoesa* 폐회사 closing address.

p'yeji 폐지 abolition. *p'yejihada* 폐지하다 abolish; do away with; discontinue.

p'yemak 폐막. *p'yemak'ada* 폐막하다 end; close; come to a close; The curtain falls.

p'yemul 폐물 waste material; refuse; junk.

p'yeryŏm 폐렴 pneumonia. *kŭpsŏng p'yeryŏm* 급성 폐렴 acute pneumonia.

p'yo 표 table; list. *shiganp'yo* 시간표 time table. *chŏngkap'yo* 정가표 price list.

p'yobŏm 표범 leopard; panther.

p'yobon 표본 specimen; sample.

p'yŏda 펴다 spread (out); open; unfold.

p'yohyŏn 표현 expression. *p'yohyŏnhada* 표현하다 express; be representative[expressive] of.

p'yoje 표제 title; heading; caption (*Am.*).

p'yoji 표지 cover; binding. *kajuk p'yoji* 가죽 표지 leather cover.

p'yojŏng 표정 expression; look. *sŭlp'ŭn p'yojŏng* 슬픈 표정 sad expression.

p'yojun 표준 standard; level. *p'yojunŏ* 표준어 standard language.

p'yŏlli 편리 convenience; facilities. *p'yŏllihan* 편리한 convenient; expedient.

p'yŏnan 편안. *p'yŏnanhan* 편안한 peaceful; tranquil. *p'yŏnanhi* 편안히 peacefully; quietly.

p'yŏnch'ant'a 편찮다 (be) ill; unwell; indisposed.

p'yŏndo 편도 one way. *p'yŏndo sŭngch'akwon* 편

도 승차권 one-way ticket(*Am.*); single ticket (*Eng.*).

p'yŏndŭlda 편들다 side; take sides with; stand by; support; back; favor; assist.

p'yŏngbŏm 평범. *p'yŏngbŏmhan* 평범한 common; ordinary; mediocre; flat; featureless.

p'yŏngdŭng 평등 equality; parity. *p'yŏngdŭnghan* [*hage*] 평등한〔하게〕 equal〔ly〕; even〔ly〕.

p'yŏnghwa 평화 peace. *p'yŏnghwasŭrŏn* 평화스런 peaceful; tranquil. *p'yŏnghwajŏgŭro* 평화적으로 peacefully; at〔in〕 peace.

p'yŏngil 평일 weekday. *p'yŏngire* (*nŭn*) 평일에 (는) on weekdays; on business〔ordinary〕 days.

p'yŏnggyun 평균 average. *p'yŏnggyunhayŏ* 평균하여 on an〔the〕 average.

p'yŏngka 평가 valuation; appraisal. *p'yŏngkahada* 평가하다 value; estimate; appraise.

p'yŏngmyŏn 평면 plane; level. *p'yŏngmyŏndo* 평면도 plane figure.

p'yŏngnon 평론 review; criticism. *p'yŏngnonhada* 평론하다 review; criticize; comment (on).

p'yŏngp'an 평판 reputation; fame; popularity.

p'yŏngya 평야 plain; open field.

p'yŏn-gyŏn 편견 prejudice. *p'yŏn-gyŏn innŭn* 편견 있는 partial; prejudiced; biased.

p'yŏnhada 편하다 (be) comfortable; easy. *p'yŏnhage* 편하게 comfortably; at ease.

p'yŏnji 편지 letter. *p'yŏnjirŭl puch'ida* 편지를 부치다 mail〔post〕 a letter.

p'yŏnjip 편집 editing; compilation. *p'yŏnjip'ada* 편집하다 edit; compile.

p'yŏnmul 편물 knitting; knitwork; crochet. →ttŭ-

gaejil 뜨개질.
p'yŏnŭi 편의 convenience; facilities. *p'yŏnŭisang* 편의상 for convenience' sake.
p'yoŏ 표어 motto; slogan; catchphrase; catchword.

⋙ R ⋘

radio 라디오 radio〔*Am.*〕; wireless(*Eng.*).
raemp'ŭ 램프 lamp. *sŏgyu raemp'ŭ* 석유 램프 oil lamp.
raengk'ing 랭킹 ranking. *raengk'ing irwi* 랭킹 1 위 the first ranking.
rait'ŏ 라이터 (cigarette) lighter. *rait'ŏ tol* 라이터 돌 lighter flint.
rait'ŭ 라이트 light. *rait'ŭrŭl k'yŏda* 라이트를 켜 다 switch on the light.
reink'ot'ŭ 레인코트 raincoat.
rek'odŭ 레코드 record.
renjŭ 렌즈 lens; lenses.
resŭt'orang 레스토랑 restaurant.
ribŏrŏllijŭm 리버럴리즘 liberalism.
ribon 리본 ribbon.
ridŭm 리듬 rhythm.
rillei 릴레이 relay (*race*).
rinch'i 린치 lynch; lynching.
ring 링 ring(*boxing*). *ringsaidŭ* 링사이드 ringside.
risepsyŏn 리셉션 reception. *risepsyŏnŭl yŏlda* 리셉 션을 열다 hold〔give〕 a reception.
robot 로봇 robot.
rŏbŭ ret'ŏ 러브 레터 love letter.
Roma 로마 Rome. *Romacha* 로마자 Roman letters. *Roma sucha* 로마 수자 Roman numerals.

romaensŭ 로맨스 romance; love[romantic] affair.
rŏnch'i 런치 lunch; luncheon.
rŏning 러닝 running (*race*). *rŏning syassŭ* 러닝샤
쓰 gym[athletic] shirt.
rŏshi 러시 rush. *rŏshi awo* 러시 아워 rush hours.
ruksaek 룩색 rucksack.
Rŭnesangsŭ 르네상스 Renaissance.
rut'ŭ 루트 route; channel. *chŏngshik rut'ŭ* 정식
루트 legal channels.

❦ S ❧

sa 사, 4 four. *chesa* 제 4 the fourth.
sabang 사방 four sides; all directions[quarters].
sabip 삽입 insertion. *sabip'ada* 삽입하다 insert.
sabŏm 사범 teacher; master; coach. *kwont'u sabŏm*
권투 사범 boxing instructor.
sabŏp 사법 administration of justice. *sabŏbŭi* 사
법의 judicial.
sabyŏn 사변 accident; incident. *yugio sabyŏn* 6·25
사변 the June 25th Incident of Korea; Korean
sabyŏng 사병 soldier; private.   ⌊War.
sach'ae 사채 personal debt[loan]; private liabilities.
sach'ang 사창 unlicensed prostitution; streetwalker.
sach'anggul 사창굴 brothel.
sach'i 사치 luxury; extravagance. *sach'isŭrŏpta*
사치스럽다 (be) luxurious; extravagant.
sach'inhoe 사친회 Parent-Teacher Association
(P. T. A.)
sach'on 사촌 cousin. *oesach'on* 외사촌 cousin on
the mother's side.
sachŭng 사증 visa; visé. *ipkuk[ch'ulguk] sa-*

chŭng 입국〔출국〕 사증 entry〔exit〕 visa.
sach'un-gi 사춘기 adolescence; (age of) puberty.
sada 사다 buy; purchase.
sadaktari 사닥다리 ladder.
sadan 사단 (army) division. *sadanjang* 사단장 division(al) commander.
sadon 사돈 relatives by marriage.
sae 새 bird; fowl; poultry.
sae 새 new; fresh; novel; recent.
saeagi 새아기 one's new daughter-in-law; bride.
saeam 새암 jealousy; envy. *saeamhada* 새암하다 be jealous (of); be envious (of).
saebom 새봄 early spring; early springtime.
saebyŏk 새벽 dawn; daybreak. *saebyŏge* 새벽에 at dawn〔daybreak〕.
saech'igi 새치기 cutting in. *saech'igihada* 새치기하다 cut in (a line); break into the queue.
saech'imtegi 새침데기 indifferent person; ostensibly modest person.
saeda 새다 ① dawn; break ② leak(out); run.
saedal 새달 next month; the coming month.
saegida 새기다 ① sculpture; carve; engrave ② bear in mind.
saegin 색인 index.
saegŭn-gŏrida 새근거리다 ① gasp; pant ② feel a slight pain.
saehae 새해 new year; New Year.
saejang 새장 (bird) cage; birdcage. 「〔house〕.
saejip 새집 ① nest; birdhouse ② new building
saek, saekch'ae 색, 색채 colo(u)r; hue; tint; tinge.
saekki 새끼 straw rope. *saekkirŭl kkoda* 새끼를 꼬다 make〔twist〕 a (straw) rope.

saekki 새끼 ① young; litter; cub ② guy; fellow. *kaesaekki* 개새끼 You beast!

saekshi 색시 ① bride ② wife ③ maiden; girl ④ barmaid; hostess.

saemaŭl undong 새마을 운동 the new community [village] movement; Saemaul Movement.

saemmul 샘물 spring water; fountain water.

saengae 생애 life; career; lifetime.

saengch'ae 생채 vegetable salad.

saenggak 생각 ① thinking; thought; ideas ② opinion ③ mind; intention.

saenggangnada 생각나다 come to mind; occur to one; be reminded of.

saenggida 생기다 ① get; obtain; come by ② arise; occur; happen ③ come into being.

saenggye 생계 livelihood; living. *saenggyebi* 생계비 cost of living; living expenses.

saenghwal 생활 life; living; livelihood. *saenghwarhada* 생활하다 live; make a living.

saengil 생일 birthday. *saengil chanch'i* 생일 잔치 birthday party.

saengjil 생질 one's sister's son; nephew.

saengjon 생존 existence; life. *saengjonhada* 생존하다 exist; live; survive.

saengmaekchu 생맥주 draught[draft] beer.

saengmul 생물 living thing; creature; life. *saengmurhak* 생물학 biology.

saengmyŏng 생명 life; soul; vitality.

saengni 생리 physiology. *saengnijŏk yokku* 생리적 욕구 physiological desire. *saengnihak* 생리학 phy

saengsa 생사 life and death. ⌊siology.

saengsaek 생색. *saengsaengnaeda* 생색내다 ① make

a merit of ② patronizing; condescending.

saengsan 생산 production; manufacture.

saengshik 생식 reproduction; generation.

saengsŏn 생선 fish; fresh[raw] fish. *saengsŏnhoe* 생선회 sliced[slices of] raw fish.

saengnyak 생략 omission; abbreviation. *saengnyak'ada* 생략하다 omit; abbreviate.

saengnyŏnp'il 색연필 colored pencil.

saero 새로 newly; new; afresh; anew.

saeropta 새롭다 (be) new; fresh; vivid. *saeropke* 새롭게 newly; afresh.

saetkil 샛길 byway; side road; lane.

saeu 새우 lobster; prawn; shrimp. *saeujŏt* 새우젓 pickled shrimp.

saeuda 새우다 sit[stay] up all night; keep vigil.

saga 사가 historian; chronicler.

sagak 사각 square; rectangular. *sagak'yŏng* 사각형 square.

sagam 사감 dormitory dean[inspector]; house-mother.

sagi 사기 swindle; fraud; deception. *sagihada* 사기하다 swindle; impose.

sagi 사기 china; chinaware; porcelain.

sago 사고 incident; accident; trouble.

sagong 사공 boatman; oarman; ferryman.

sagŭrajida 사그라지다 ① subside; go down ② melt away; decompose.

sagwa 사과 apple. *sagwaju* 사과주 cider.

sagwa 사과 apology. *sagwahada* 사과하다 apologize; beg (a person) pardon.

sagwan 사관 (military, naval) officer. *sagwan hakkyo* 사관 학교 military[naval] academy.

sagwida 사귀다 associate with; keep company with.

sagwolse 삭월세 monthly rent[rental]. *sagwolsepang* 삭월세방 rented room.

sagyo 사교 social intercourse[life]. *sagyojŏgin* 사교적인 social.

sagyo 사교 bishop; pontiff.

sagyŏk 사격 firing; shooting. *sagyŏk'ada* 사격하다 shoot; fire at.

sahoe 사회 society; world; public. *sahoejŏk* 사회적 social.

sahŭl 사흘 ① three days ② →**sahŭnnal** 사흘날.

sahŭnnal 사흘날 the third day of the month.

sahyŏng 사형 death penalty[sentence]; capital punishment.

sai 사이 ① interval; distance; space ② time; during ③ between; among.

saim 사임 resignation. →**sajik** 사직.

sajae 사재 private funds[property].

sajang 사장 president (of company). *pusajang* 부사장 vice-president.

saje 사제 priest; pastor.

saji 사지 limbs; legs and arms; members.

sajik 사직 resignation. *sajik'ada* 사직하다 resign (from).

sajin 사진 photograph; picture; photo; snapshot. *sajinŭl tchikta* 사진을 찍다 take a photograph of. *sajin-ga* 사진가 photo artist; cameraman.

sajŏl 사절 emissary; delegate; envoy. *ch'insŏn sajŏl* 친선 사절 good-will envoy[mission].

sajŏl 사절 denial; refusal. *sajŏrhada* 사절하다 refuse; decline; turndown.

sajŏn 사전 dictionary; lexicon; wordbook. *sajŏnŭl*

ch'atta 사전을 찾다 consult[refer to] a dictionary.
sajŏng 사정 circumstances; conditions; reasons.
sajŏngŏpta 사정없다 (be) merciless; ruthless.
sak 삯 wages; pay; charge; fare. *sakchŏn* 삯전 wages; pay.
sakche 삭제 elimination; deletion. *sakchehada* 삭제하다 eliminate; strike[cross] out.
sakkam 삭감 reduction; curtailment.
sakŏn 사건 event; matter; occurrence; affair; case. *sarin sakŏn* 살인 사건 murder case.
sakpanŭjil 삯바느질 needle work for pay.
sal 살 flesh; muscles. *sari tchin* 살이 찐 fleshy; fat.
salda 살다 ① live; be alive ② make a living; get along ③ dwell; inhabit; reside.
salgu 살구 apricot.
salgŭmŏni 살그머니 furtively; stealthily; in secret.
sallida 살리다 save; spare (a person's) life.
sallim 살림 living; housekeeping. *sallimhada* 살림하다 run the house; manage a household.
sallim 산림 forest. *sallim poho* 산림 보호 forest conservation.
salp'ida 살피다 take a good look at; look about; inspect closely.
salp'o 살포 scattering; sprinkling. *salp'ohada* 살포하다 scatter; sprinkle.
sam 삼 hemp.
samagwi 사마귀 mole; wart.
samak 사막 desert.
samang 사망 death; decease. *samanghada* 사망하다 die; decease; pass away.
sambae 삼배 three times; thrice.
samch'on 삼촌 uncle (on the father's side). *oe-*

samch'on 외삼촌 uncle (on the mother's side). →
sukpu 숙부.
samch'ŭng 삼층 three stories [floors]; the third floor
(*Am.*); the second floor (*Eng.*).
samdae 삼대 three generations.
samdŭng 삼등 third class [rate]. *samdŭng yŏlch'a*
삼등 열차 third class compartment.
samgada 삼가다 ① be discreet [cautious] ② restrain
oneself.
samgak 삼각 triangle. *samgagŭi* 삼각의 triangular
samgak'yŏng 삼각형 triangle.
samgŏri 삼거리 three-way junction [intersection].
samta 삶다 boil; cook. *talgyarŭl samta* 달걀을 삶
다 boil an egg.
samilchŏl 삼일절 Anniversary of the Samil Independence Movement.
samil undong 삼일 운동 the 1919 Independence
Movement.
samin 삼인 three persons. *saminjo* 삼인조 trio.
samjung 삼중. *samjungŭi* 삼중의 threefold; triple.
samk'ida 삼키다 swallow; gulp down; gulp.
samnyŏn 삼년 three years. *samnyŏnmada* 삼년마
다 every three years.
samnyunch'a 삼륜차 tricycle.
samo 사모. *samohada* 사모하다 long for; yearn
after; burn with love.
samp'alsŏn 삼팔선 the 38th parallel.
samship 삼십, 30 thirty. *chesamship* (*ŭi*) 제30 (의)
the thirtieth.
samship'altosŏn 38도선 38 degrees north latitude
→**samp'alsŏn** 삼팔선.
samu 사무 business; affairs; office work. *samu-*

shil 사무실 office (room). *samuwon* 사무원 clerk; deskworker.

samwol 삼월 March.

samyŏng 사명 mission; commission; errand. *samyŏnggam* 사명감 sense of duty.

san 산 mountain; hill.

san 산 acid.

sana 산아 newborn baby. *sana chehan* 산아 제한 birth control.

sanaeai 사내아이 boy; lad; kid.

sanai 사나이 man; male. *sanaidaun* 사나이다운 manly; manlike; manful.

sanapta 사납다 (be) fierce; wild; violent.

sanponguri 산봉우리 mountain peak.

sanbuinkwa 산부인과 obsterics and gynecology. *sanbuinkwa ŭisa* 산부인과 의사 ladies' doctor.

sang 상 prize; reward. *sangŭl t'ada* 상을 타다 win[get] a prize.

sang 상 figure; statue; image; portrait.

sang 상 (dining, eating) table; small table.

sanga 상아 ivory. *sangat'ap* 상아탑 ivory tower.

sangbanshin 상반신 upper half of the body; bust.

sangbok 상복 mourning clothes[dress]; sables.

sangch'i 상치 lettuce. *sangch'issam* 상치쌈 lettuce wrapped rice.

sangch'ŏ 상처 wound; injury; cut; scar.

sangdae 상대 ① companion; mate ② the other party; opponent.

sangdam 상담 consultation; counsel; conference. *sangdamhada* 상담하다 consult (with); confer.

sangdang 상당. *sangdanghan* 상당한 respectable; decent. *sangdanghi* 상당히 pretty; fairly; considerably.

sangdŭng 상등 first class; best grade. *sangdŭngp'um* 상등품 top grade article.

sangga 상가 downtown; business section〔quarters, center〕.

sanggi 상기. *sanggihada* 상기하다 remember; recollect; call to mind.

sanggong 상공 commerce and industry. *sanggongbu* 상공부 Ministry of Commerce and Industry.

sanggong 상공 upper air; sky.

sanggŏrae 상거래 commercial transaction; business deal.

sanggŭm 상금 reward; prize money.

sanggwan 상관 senior〔superior〕 officer; higher officer〔official〕.

sanghae 상해 injury; harm. *sanghae ch'isa* 상해 치사 bodily injury resulting in death.

sangho 상호 firm〔trade〕 name.

sangho 상호 mutually; each other; one another. *sanghoŭi* 상호의 mutual.

sanghoe 상회 company; firm. *Chongno sanghoe* 종로 상회 the Chongno company.

sanghwang 상황 state of things〔affairs〕; conditions; situation; circumstances.

sangi 상이. *sangi kunin* 상이 군인 wounded soldier; disabled veteran.

sangin 상인 merchant; trader; dealer; tradesman; shopkeeper.

sangja 상자 box; case.

sangjing 상징 symbol; emblem. *sangjinghada* 상징하다 symbolize.

sangjŏm 상점 shop; store (*Am.*). *sangjom chuin*

상점 주인 shopkeeper (*Eng.*); storekeeper (*Am*).
sangju 상주 chief mourner.
sangk'wae 상쾌. *sangk'waehan* 상쾌한 refreshing; exhilarating; invigorating; bracing.
sangmal 상말 vulgar words; vulgarism.
sangnyanghada 상냥하다 (be) gentle; tender; amiable; sweet.
sangnyu 상류 ① upper stream ② upper[higher] classes. *sangnyu sahoe* 상류사회 high society.
sangnyuk 상륙 landing. *sangnyuk'ada* 상륙하다 land (at); go on shore.
sango 상오 forenoon; morning; a.m.; A.M.
sangŏ 상어 shark. *sangŏ kajuk* 상어 가죽 sharkskin.
sangŏp 상업 commerce; trade; business. *sangŏbŭi* 상업의 commercial; business.
sangp'ae 상패 medal; medallion.
sangp'um 상품 goods; merchandise; commodity.
sangp'yo 상표 trademark; brand.
sangsa 상사 firm; trading company. *oeguk sangsa* 외국 상사 foreign firm.
sangsa 상사 sergeant.
sangsa 상사 superior authorities; one's superior.
sangsang 상상 imagination; fancy. *sangsanghada* 상상하다 imagine; fancy.
sangse 상세 details; particulars. *sangsehada* 상세하다 (be) detailed; particular. *sangsehi* 상세히 in detail; minutely.
sangshik 상식 common sense; good sense.
sangso 상소 appeal. *sangsohada* 상소하다 appeal to (a higher court).
sangsok 상속 succession; inheritance. *sangsok'ada* 상속하다 succeed (to); inherit.

sangsŭrŏpta 상스럽다 (be) vulgar; base; indecent.

sangt'ae 상태 condition; state; situation. *kŏn-gang sangt'ae* 건강 상태 state of health.

sangchang 상장 certificate of merit; honorary certificate.

sangt'u 상투 topknot. *sangt'ujangi* 상투장이 man with a topknot.

sangyŏgŭm 상여금 bonus; reward. *yŏnmal sang-yŏgŭm* 연말 상여금 year-end bonus.

sangyong 상용. *sangyonguro* 상용으로 on busi-ness. *sangyongmun* 상용문 commercial〔business〕 correspondence〔term〕.

sanho 산호 coral. *sanhoch'o* 산호초 coral reef.

sanji 산지 place of production. *ssarŭi sanji* 쌀의 산지 rice-producing district.

sankkoktaegi 산꼭대기 mountain top; top〔summit〕 of a mountain.

sankoltchagi 산골짜기 mountain valley; ravine.

sanmaek 산맥 mountain range.

sanmaru 산마루 top of a mountain.

sanmul 산물 product; production; produce.

sanŏp 산업 industry. *sanŏbŭi* 산업의 industrial.

sansam 산삼 wild ginseng.

sanso 산소 oxygen.

sanso 산소 ancestral graveyard.

sansul 산술 arithmetic. *sansurŭi* 산술의 arithmetical.

santtŭt'ada 산뜻하다 (be) clean; fresh; bright. *santtŭt'an ot* 산뜻한 옷 neat dress.

sanyang 사냥 hunting; shooting. *sanyanghada* 사냥하다 hunt; shoot.

saŏp 사업 enterprise; undertaking; business. *saŏp-ka* 사업가 man of enterprise.

sap'wa 삽화 illustration; cut.

sarhae 살해 murder; killing. *sarhaehada* 살해하다 murder; kill; slay.

sarajida 사라지다 disappear; vanish; be gone.

saram 사람 man; person; human being.

sarang 사랑 love; affection. *saranghada* 사랑하다 love; be fond of; be attached to.

sarin 살인 murder; homicide. *sarinhada* 살인하다 commit murder.

sarip 사립 private establishment. *saribŭi* 사립의 private. *sarip hakkyo* 사립 학교 private school.

sarojapta 사로잡다 ① catch (an animal) alive; capture ② captivate.

saryŏng 사령 command. *saryŏnggwan* 사령관 commander. *saryŏngbu* 사령부 headquarters.

sasaek 사색 contemplation; meditation. *sasaek'ada* 사색하다 contemplate; speculate.

sasaenga 사생아 illegitimate child; bastard.

sasaenghwal 사생활 private[personal] life.

sasal 사살 shooting to death. *sasarhada* 사살하다 shoot (a person) dead[to death].

sasang 사상 thought; idea. *sasangga* 사상가 thinker. *sasangbŏm* 사상범 political offense[offender].

sasang 사상 death and injury; casualties. *sasangja(su)* 사상자(수) (number of) casualties.

sashil 사실 fact; actual fact; truth. *sashilsang* 사실상 in fact; actually.

sashin 사신 envoy. *oeguk sashin* 외국 사신 foreign envoys.

saship 사십, 40 forty. *chesaship* 제40 the fortieth.

sasŏl 사설 leading article; editorial; leader(*Eng.*).

sasŭl 사슬 chain.

sasŭm 사슴 deer; stag; buck. *sasŭm ppul* 사슴뿔 antler. *sasŭm kajuk* 사슴 가죽 deer skin.

sat 샅 crotch; groin. *satpa* 샅바 Korean wrestler's thigh band.

sat'ae 사태 situation; state[position] of affairs.

sat'ang 사탕 sugar. →**sŏlt'ang** 설탕.

sat'oe 사퇴 ① declination; refusal ② resignation. *sat'oehada* 사퇴하다 ① decline; refuse to accept ② resign.

sat'uri 사투리 dialect; brogue; provincial accent.

sawi 사위 son-in-law.

sawol 사월 April.

sawon 사원 member; employee; clerk. *shinip sawon* 신입 사원 incoming partner[employee].

sayang 사양. *sayanghada* 사양하다 decline (with regrets); refuse courteously.

sayong 사용 use; employment. *sayonghada* 사용하다 use; employ; apply.

sayu 사유 private ownership. *sayuhada* 사유하다 possess oneself of. *sayu chaesan* 사유 재산 private property.

se 세 tax; duty (on goods). *sodŭkse* 소득세 individual income tax.

se 세 rent; hire. *chip[pang]se* 집[방]세 house [room] rent.

se 세 three. *se saram* 세 사람 *three men*.

sebae 세배 New Year('s) greetings.

sech'a 세차 car washing. *sech'ahada* 세차하다 wash down a car.

seda 세다 count; calculate; enumerate.

seda 세다 (be) strong; powerful; mighty. *sege* 세게 hard; strongly.

sedae 세대 generation. *chŏlmŭn sedae* 젊은 세대 rising[younger] generation.

segi 세기 century. *ishipsegi* 20세기 the twenties century. *segimal* 세기말 the end of the century [fin-de-siècle.

segŭm 세금 tax. →**se** 세.

segwan 세관 customhouse; customs. *segwan chŏlch'a* 세관 절차 customs formalities.

segye 세계 world. *segyejŏk* 세계적 world-wide; international; universal.

segyun 세균 bacillus; germ; bacterium.

seje 세제 cleaning material; detergent.

semil 세밀. *semirhan* 세밀한 minute; detailed; elaborate. *semirhi* 세밀히 minutely; in detail.

sep'o 세포 cell. *sep'oŭi* 세포의 cellular.

serye 세례 baptism; christening. *seryemyŏng* 세례명 baptismal name.

seryŏk 세력 influence; power. *seryŏk innŭn* 세력 있는 powerful; influential.

sesang 세상 world; life; society. *sesange* 세상에 in the world; on earth.

sesu 세수. *sesuhada* 세수하다 wash oneself; have a wash.

set 셋 three. *setchae(ro)* 세째 (로) third(ly).

set'ak 세탁 wash(ing); laundry. *set'ak'ada* 세탁하다 wash; do washing. *set'akki* 세탁기 washing machine.

setchip 셋집 house for rent (*Am.*); house to let (*Eng.*).

setpang 셋방 room to let; room for rent.

seuda 세우다 ① raise; set[put] up; erect ② stop; hold up ③ build; construct.

sewol 세월 time; time and tide; years.

shi 시 poetry; poem; verse.

shi 시 o'clock; hour; time. *tushi* 두시 two o'clock.

shi 시 city; town. *shiŭi* 시의 municipal; city. *shich'ŏng* 시청 city hall.

shibi 십이, 12 twelve. *cheshibi* 제12 the twelfth.

shibiwol 십이월 December.

shibil 십일, 11 eleven. *cheshibil* 제11 the eleventh.

shibirwol 십일월 November.

shibo 십오, 15 fifteen. *cheshibo* 제15 the fifteenth.

shibumo 시부모 parents of one's husband.

shich'al 시찰 inspection. *shich'arhada* 시찰하다 inspect; observe.

shich'e 시체 corpse; dead body.

shida 시다 (be) sour; acid; tart.

shidae 시대. age; era; period; times; days. *uju shidae* 우주 시대 space age.

shido 시도 attempt. *shidohada* 시도하다 attempt; try out.

shidŭlda 시들다 wither; wilt; fade (away).

shiga 시가 streets of a city; city; town. *shigaji* 시가지 urban district.

shigan 시간 time; hour. *yŏngŏp shigan* 영업 시간 business hour. *shiganp'yo* 시간표 time table.

shikkŭrŏpta 시끄럽다 (be) noisy; boisterous. *shikkŭrŏpke* 시끄럽게 clamorously.

shigi 시기 season; time; period; occasion.

shigol 시골 country(side); rural district. *shigol saram* 시골 사람 country-man; rustic.

shigolttŭgi 시골뜨기 country bumpkin; hick; yokel.

shigŭmch'i 시금치 spinach; spinage.

shigungch'ang 시궁창 ditch; sink; cesspool.

shigye 시계 clock; watch. *sonmok shigye* 손목 시

계 wristwatch. *t'aksang shigye* 탁상 시계 table clock.
shigyok 식욕 appetite; desire to eat.
shigyong 식용. *shigyongŭi* 식용의 edible; eatable.
shihap 시합 →**kyŏnggi** 경기.
shihŏm 시험 examination; exam; test. *shihŏmhada* 시험하다 examine; test.
shihŏmgwan 시험관 test tube.
shiil 시일 ① time; days; hours ② date; the time. *shiilgwa changso* 시일과 장소 time and place.
shiin 시인 poet. *yŏryu shiin* 여류 시인 poetess.
shiin 시인 approval. *shiinhada* 시인하다 approve of; admit.
shijak 시작 beginning; commencement. *shijak'ada* 시작하다 begin; commence; start.
shijang 시장 market (place); fair.
shijang 시장 mayor. *Sŏul shijang* 서울 시장 Mayor of Seoul.
shijang 시장. *shijanghada* 시장하다 be hungry; feel empty.
shijip 시집 collection of poems; anthology.
shijo 시조 founder; originator; progenitor.
shijung 시중 attendance; service. *shijungdŭlda* 시중들다 attend; wait on; serve.
shikchang 식장 hall of ceremony; ceremonial hall.
shik'ida 시키다 make[let] a person do; have[get] a person do.
shik'ida 식히다 cool; let (a thing) cool.
shikki 식기 tableware; dinner set.
shikkwon 식권 meal[food]-ticket.
shikpi 식비 food expenses[cost].
shiksa 식사 meal; diet. *shiksahada* 식사하다 have

[take] a meal; dine.

shiksaenghwal 식생활 dietary[food] life.

shikta 식다 (become) cool; get cold; cool off.

shikt'ak 식탁 (dinner) table. *shikt'akpo* 식탁보 table cloth.

shiktan 식단 menu; bill of fare.

shiktang 식당 dining room[hall]; mess hall; restaurant; eating house; lunch counter.

shil 실 thread; yarn; string.

shilbi 실비 actual expense; (real) cost.

shilche 실제 truth; fact; reality. *shilcheŭi* 실제의 real; true; actual; practical. *shilchero* 실제로 really; actually.

shilchik 실직 →**shirŏp** 실업.

shilchŏk 실적 actual results[accomplishments]. *shilchŏgŭl ollida* 실적을 올리다 bring about good results.

shilch'ŏn 실천 practice. *shilch'ŏnhada* 실천하다 practice; put into practice.

shilchong 실종 disappearance; missing. *shilchonghada* 실종하다 disappear; be missing.

shilchŭng 싫증 dislike; detestation; tiredness. *shilchŭngnada* 싫증나다 get tired of; be weary[sick] of; get disgusted (with).

shilk'ŏt 실컷 to one's heart's content; as much as one wishes[likes].

shillae 실내 interior of a room. *shillaeŭi* 실내의 indoor.

shillang 신랑 bridegroom. *shillang shinbu* 신랑 신부 bride and bridegroom; new couple.

shilloe 신뢰 confidence; trust; reliance. *shilloehada* 신뢰하다 trust; believe in.

shillye 실례 example; instance; concrete case.

shillye 실례 rudeness; discourtesy.

shillyŏk 실력 real ability. *shillyŏgi innŭn* 실력이 있는 able; capable; talented.

shilmang 실망 disappointment. *shilmanghada* 실망하다 be disappointed in[at].

shilmari 실마리 clue. *shilmarirŭl ch'atta* 실마리를 찾다 find a clue to.

shilmul 실물 real thing; actual object.

shilp'ae 실패 failure; mistake; error; blunder. *shilp'aehada* 실패하다 fail; go wrong.

shilsaenghwal 실생활 real[actual] life; realities of life.

shilshi 실시 execution; enforcement. *shilshihada* 실시하다 enforce; put in operation[force].

shilsu 실수 mistake; blunder; fault. *shilsuhada* 실수하다 make a mistake; commit a blunder.

shilsŭp 실습 practice; exercise; drill. *shilsŭp'ada* 실습하다 practice; have(practical) training.

shilt'a 싫다 (be) disagreeable; disgusting; reluctant.

shimburŭm 심부름 errand; message. *shimburŭmhada* 심부름하다 go on an errand.

shimhada 심하다 (be) violent; intense; excessive; severe.

shimin 시민 citizen; townsmen; townfolks.

shimjang 심장 heart. *shimjang mabi* 심장마비 heart attack.

shimni 심리 mental state; psychology. *shimnijŏk (ŭro)* 심리적 (으로) mental(ly); psychological(ly).

shimnihak 심리학 psychology.

shimnyuk 십육, 16 sixteen.

shimsa 심사 inspection; examination. *shimsahada* 심사하다 examine; judge; investigate.

shimshimhada 심심하다 be bored; feel ennui.

shimshimp'uri 심심풀이 killing time; passtime.

shimuruk'ada 시무룩하다 (be) sulky; sullen; ill-humo(u)red.

shin 신 shoes; boots. →**kudu** 구두.

shin 신 god. *yŏshin* 여신 goddess. *shinŭi* 신의 divine; godly.

shinae 시내 brook; creek; stream.

shinae 시내 (in, within) the city. *shinae pŏsŭ* 시내 버스 urban bus. *shinae chŏnhwa* 시내 전화 local phones.

shinang 신앙 faith; belief. *shinang saenghwal* 신앙 생활 life of faith; religious life.

shinbi 신비 mystery. *shinbihan* 신비한 mystic; mysterious.

shinbu 신부 (holy) father.

shinbu 신부 bride; newly-wed wife.

shinbun 신분 social position[standing, status].

shinch'e 신체 body. *shinch'eŭi* 신체의 bodily; physical. *shinch'e kŏmsa* 신체 검사 physical check-up (*Am.*).

shinch'ŏng 신청 application. *shinch'ŏnghada* 신청하다 apply (for). *shinch'ŏngsŏ* 신청서 (written) application. *shinch'ŏngin* 신청인 applicant.

shinch'ŏnji 신천지 new world.

shinch'ullagi 신출나기 newcomer; green hand; novice; beginner.

shindo 신도 →**shinja** 신자.

shindong 신동 (infant) prodigy; wonder child.

shin-gan 신간 new publication. *shin-ganŭi* 신간의 new; newly-published.

shin-girok 신기록 new record. *segye shin-girok* 세계 신기록 new world record.

shinggŏpta 싱겁다 (be) insipid; taste flat.

shingmin 식민 colonization; settlement. *shingminji* 식민지 colony.

shingmo 식모 kitchenmaid; domestic servant.

shingmok 식목 forestation; tree planting. *shing-mogil* 식목일 Arbor Day.

shingmul 식물 plant; vegetation. *shingmurŭi* 식물의 vegetational.

shingnyang 식량 food; provisions; foodstuffs.

shin-go 신고 report; statement. *shin-gohada* 신고하다 state; report; make[file] a return.

shingshinghada 싱싱하다 (be) fresh; lively; full of life.

shin-gyŏng 신경 nerves. *shin-gyŏngsŏng(ŭi)* 신경성(의) nervous. *shin-gyŏngjil* 신경질 nervous temperament.

shinhak 신학 theology.

shinhakki 신학기 new (school) term; new semester.

shinho 신호 signal; signal(l)ing. *shinhohada* 신호하다 (make a) signal.

shinhon 신혼 new marriage. *shinhonŭi* 신혼의 newly married[wedded]. *shinhon yŏhaeng* 신혼여행 honeymoon.

shinhwa 신화 myth; mythology.

shinja 신자 believer; devotee.

shinjang 신장 kidneys. *shinjangpyŏng* 신장병 kidney trouble.

shinjang 신장 stature; height.

shinjo 신조 creed; credo; principle. *saenghwal*

shinjo 생활 신조 one's principles of life.
shinjung 신중 prudence; discretion. *shinjunghan* 신중한 prudent; careful; cautious.
shinmun 신문 newspaper; paper; press.
shinmun 신문 examination. *shinmunhada* 신문하다 question; examine.
shinnada 신나다 get in high spirits; get elated.
shinnyŏm 신념 belief; faith; conviction.
shinnyŏn 신년 new year. →**saehae** 새해.
shinsa 신사 gentleman. *shinsajŏk* 신사적 gentlemanly; gentlemanlike.
shinsaenghwal 신생활 new life. *shinsaenghwal undong* 신생활 운동 new-life movement.
shinse 신세 debt of gratitude; favor. *shinserŭl chida* 신세를 지다 be indebted to; be obliged (to).
shinsegye 신세계 new world; the New World.
shinshik 신식 new style[type, method]. *shinshigŭi* 신식의 new (style, type); modern.
shinsok 신속. *shinsok'an* 신속한 rapid; swift. *shinsok'i* 신속히 rapidly; promptly; quickly.
shinsŏng 신성 sacredness; sanctity. *shinsŏnghan* 신성한 sacred; holy; divine.
shinta 신다 wear; put[have] on. *kudurŭl[yangmarŭl] shinta* 구두를[양말을] 신다 put on one's shoes[socks].
shint'ong 신통. *shint'onghada* 신통하다 (be) wonderful; marvelous.
shinwon 신원 one's identity. *shinwon chohoe* 신원 조회 personal inquiries.
shinyong 신용 confidence; trust. *shinyonghada* 신용하다 trust (in); give credit to; rely on.
shinyung 시늉 mimicry; imitation. *shinyunghada*

시늉하다 mimic; ape; feign.

shioe 시외 outskirts of a city; suburbs. *shioeŭi* 시외의 suburban.

ship 십, 10 ten. *cheship* 제10 the tenth.

shipchaga 십자가 cross; Holy Cross.

shipchang 십장 foreman; chief workman.

shipku 십구, 19 nineteen. *shipkusegi* 19세기 the nineteenth century.　　　　　　　　　　　　　　　「teenth.

shipsa 십사, 14 fourteen. *cheshipsa* 제14 the four-

shipsam 십삼, 13 thirteen. *cheshipsam* 제13 the thirteenth.

shipta 싶다 want, wish; hope; desire; would [should] like to (do).

shiptae 십대 teens. *shiptaeŭi ai* 십대의 아이 teen-ager; teen-age boy[girl].

shirhaeng 실행 practice; execution; fulfil(l)ment. *shirhaenghada* 실행하다 practice; carry out.

shirhŏm 실험 experiment; laboratory work. *shirhŏmhada* 실험하다 experiment (on).

shirhyŏn 실현 realization. *shirhyŏnhada* 실현하다 realize; materialize; come true.

shirip 시립. *shiribŭi* 시립의 city; municipal. *shirip pyŏngwon* 시립 병원 municipal hospital.

shirŏhada 싫어하다 dislike; hate; loathe; be un-

shirŏng 시렁 wall shelf; rack.　　　　　　　　Lwilling.

shirŏp 실업 unemployment. *shirŏpcha* 실업자 man out of work; the unemployed; the jobless.

shiryŏk 시력 (eye) sight; vision. *shiryŏk kŏmsa* 시력 검사 eyesight test.

shiryŏn 시련 trial; test; ordeal.

shiryŏn 실연 disappointed love; broken heart. *shiryŏnhada* 실연하다 be disappointed in love.

shiryong 실용 practical use. *shiryongjŏgin* 실용적인 practical; useful.

shishihada 시시하다 ① (be) dull; flat; uninteresting ② (be) trifling; trivial ③ (be) worthless; poor.

shisok 시속 speed per hour; velocityper hour.

shisŏl 시설 establishment; facilities; equipment. *shisŏrhada* 시설하다 establish; equip.

shitta 싣다 load; take on; take on board; ship.

shiwi 시위 demonstration. *shiwihada* 시위하다 demonstrate; show off.

shiwonhada 시원하다 (be) feel cool[refreshing].

shiya 시야 visual field; one's view.

shwida 쉬다 rest; take a rest; lay off (*Am.*).

shwida 쉬다 get[grow] hoarse; become husky.

shwipsari 쉽사리 easily; readily; without difficulty.

shwipta 쉽다 ① (be) easy; simple; without difficulty [effort] ② be apt to; be liable to.

so 소 cow; bull; ox; cattle.

soa 소아 infant; little child. *soa mabi* 소아 마비 infantile paralysis; poliomyelitis.

soakwa 소아과 pediatrics. *soakwa ŭisa* 소아과 의사 child specialist; pediatrician.

sobang 소방 fire fighting. *sobanggwan* 소방관 fireman; fire fighter. *sobangch'a* 소방차 fire engine. *sobang yŏnsŭp* 소방 연습 fire drill.

sobi 소비 consumption. *sobihada* 소비하다 consume; spend; expend.

sobyŏn 소변 urine; piss. *sobyŏnŭl poda* 소변을 보다 urinate; pass urine[water].

soch'ong 소총 rifle; musket; small arms.

sŏda 서다 ① stand (up); rise (to one's feet) ②

stop; halt; run down ③ be built〔erected〕.

sŏdo 서도 calligraphy.

sodok 소독 disinfection. *sodok'ada* 소독하다 disinfect; sterilize.

Sŏdok 서독 West Germany.

sodong 소동 disturbance; riot. *sodongŭl irŭk'ida* 소동을 일으키다 raise a disturbance.

sodŭk 소득 income; earnings. *kungmin sodŭk* 국민 소득 national income.

sŏdurŭda 서두르다 hurry (up); hasten; make haste. *sŏdullŏ* 서둘러 hurriedly; in haste.

soebuch'i 쇠붙이 metal things; ironware.

soegogi 쇠고기 beef. *soegogijŭp* 쇠고기즙 beef tea

soegorang 쇠고랑 handcuffs; manacles. └〔bouillon〕.

soegori 쇠고리 iron ring; clasp; metal hoop.

soemangch'i 쇠망치 iron hammer.

soeyak 쇠약 weakening; emaciation. *soeyak'an* 쇠약한 weak; weakened.

sŏga 서가 book shelf; bookstand.

sogae 소개 introduction. *sogaehada* 소개하다 introduce. *sogaechang* 소개장 letter of introduction.

sŏgi 서기 clerk; secretary. *sŏgijang* 서기장 head clerk; chief secretary.

sŏgi 서기 christian era; Anno Domini (A. D.).

sogida 속이다 deceive; cheat; swindle.

sogimsu 속임수 trickery; deception. *sogimsurŭl ssŭda* 속임수를 쓰다 cheat; play a trick on.

sogŏ 속어 slang; colloquial expression.

sŏgok 서곡 prelude; overture.

sogon-gŏrida 소곤거리다 whisper; talk in whispers.

sogot 속옷 underwear; underclothes; undergarment; undershirt (*Am.*).

Sŏgu 서구 Western Europe; the West; the Occident.

soguk 소국 small country; minor[lesser] power.

sogŭk 소극. *sogŭkchŏk(ŭro)* 소극적 (으로) negative (ly); passive(ly). ⌈hotbed of crime.

sogul 소굴 den; nest; lair. *pŏmjoe sogul* 범죄 소굴

sogŭm 소금 salt. *sogŭme chŏrin* 소금에 절인 salted; pickled with salt.

sogyŏng 소경 blind man. →**changnim** 장님.

sŏgyu 석유 oil; petroleum; kerosene. *sŏgyu nallo* 석유 난로 kerosene stove; oil stove.

sohaeng 소행 conduct; behavior. ⌈careless; rash.

sohol 소홀. *sohorhada* 소홀하다 (be) negligent;

sohwa 소화 digestion. *sohwahada* 소화하다 digest.

sŏhwa 서화 paintings and calligraphic works.

sohwan 소환 summons; call. *sohwanhada* 소환하다 summon; call.

sohyŏng 소형 small size. *sohyŏngŭi* 소형의 small (-sized); tiny; pocket(-size).

soit'an 소이탄 incendiary; incendiary bomb.

sŏjae 서재 study; library.

sojak 소작 tenancy. *sojak'ada* 소작하다 tenant.

sojang 소장 major general (*army*); rear admiral (*navy*); air commodore (*air-force*).

sŏjang 서장 head; chief; marshal. *kyŏngch'alsŏjang* 경찰서장 chief of police station.

soji 소지 possession. *sojihada* 소지하다 have; possess. *sojip'um* 소지품 one's belongings.

sojil 소질 making(s); character; tendency; aptitude.

sojip 소집 call; summons; convocation; levy. *sojip'ada* 소집하다 call; convene; summon.

sŏjŏk 서적 books; publications. *sŏjŏksang* 서적상 bookshop; bookstore.

sŏjŏm 서점 bookshop; bookstore; bookseller's.
soju 소주 (distilled) spirits; 'soju'.
sok 속 interior; inner part; inside. *soge* 속에 in; within; amid (st).
sok'ada 속하다 belong (to); appertain (to).
sokch'ima 속치마 underskirt; chemise.
sokkae 속개 resumption. *sokkaehada* 속개하다 resume; continue.
sŏkkan 석간 evening paper; evening edition (of).
sokki 속기 shorthand; stenography.
sŏkko 석고 plaster; gypsum. *sŏkkosang* 석고상 plaster bust[statue].
sŏk'oe 석회 lime. *sŏk'oesŏk* 석회석 limestone.
sokkuk 속국 dependency; subject[tributary] state.
sokkye 속계 earthly world; mundane world.
sokpak 속박 restriction. *sokpak'ada* 속박하다 restrict; restrain.
sŏkp'an 석판 lithography; lithograph.
sŏkpang 석방 release; acquittal. *sŏkpanghada* 석방하다 set (a person) free; release.
sokpo 속보 prompt[quick] report; (news) flash.
sokp'yŏn 속편 sequel; follow-up; serial film.
sŏksa 석사 Master. *munhak sŏksa* 문학 석사 Master of Arts (M. A.).
soksagida 속삭이다 ① whisper; speak in a whisper. ② murmur; ripple.
sokta 속다 be cheated[deceived, fooled].
sokta 솎다 thin (out); weed out.
sŏkta 섞다 mix; blend; mingle.
soktal 속달 express[special] delivery.
soktam 속담 proverb; (common) saying; maxim.
sŏkt'an 석탄 coal. *sŏkt'anchae* 석탄재 coal cinders.

sokto 속도 speed; velocity; tempo.

sol 솔 pine (tree). *sollip* 솔잎 pine needle.

sol 솔 brush. *soljil* 솔질 brushing. *sollo t'ŏlda* 솔로 털다 brush off.

sŏl 설 New Year's Day; New Year.

sŏlbi 설비 equipment(s); arrangements; facilities. *sŏlbihada* 설비하다 equip; provide; install.

sŏlch'i 설치 establishment; institution. *sŏlch'ihada* 설치하다 establish; set up; found.

sŏlgye 설계 plan; design. *sŏlgyehada* 설계하다 plan; design; layout.

sŏlgyo 설교 sermon; preaching. *sŏlgyohada* 설교하다 preach. *sŏlgyosa* 설교사 preacher.

sŏllip 설립 foundation; establishment. *sŏllip'ada* 설립하다 found; establish.

sŏllo 선로 railroad[railway] line; railroad track.

sŏlmyŏng 설명 explanation. *sŏlmyŏnghada* 설명하다 explain; account for.

sŏlsa 설사 diarrhea; loose bowels. *sŏlsahada* 설사하다 have loose bowels.

sŏlt'ang 설탕 sugar. *kaksŏlt'ang* 각설탕 lump [cube] sugar. *hŭksŏlt'ang* 흑설탕 muscovado.

solchik 솔직 *solchik'an* 솔직한 plain; frank; candid; straight and honest.

som 솜 cotton; cotton wool.

sŏm 섬 island; isle.

somae 소매 retail (sale). *somaehada* 소매하다 retail; sell at[by] retail.

somae 소매 sleeve. *somaega kin[tchalbŭn]* 소매가 긴[짧은] long[short]-sleeved.

somaech'igi 소매치기 pickpocket. *somaech'igidanghada* 소매치기당하다 have one's pocket picked.

somo 소모 consumption. *somohada* 소모하다 consume; use up.

sonmok 손목 wrist. *sonmogŭl chapta* 손목을 잡다 take (a person) by the wrist.

sŏmŏk'ada 서먹하다 feel awkward[embarrassed]; (be) unfamiliar; be ill at ease.

somssi 솜씨 skill; make; workmanship. *somssi innŭn* 솜씨 있는 skillful; dexterous; tactful.

sŏmu 서무 general affairs. *somukwa* 서무과 general affairs section.

somun 소문 rumo(u)r; report; hearsay. *somunnan* 소문난 (very) famous.

sŏmun 서문 preface; foreword; introduction.

somyŏl 소멸. *somyŏrhada* 소멸하다 disappear; vanish; cease to exist.

sŏmyŏng 서명 signature; autograph. *sŏmyŏnghada* 서명하다 sign one's name.

sŏmyu 섬유 fiber. *injo sŏmyu* 인조 섬유 staple fiber.

son 손 hand. *orŭn[oen]son* 오른[왼]손 right[left] hand. *sone nŏt'a* 손에 넣다 get; obtain.

sŏn 선 line; route. *p'yŏnghaengsŏn* 평행선 parallel line. *kyŏngbusŏn* 경부선 kyŏngbu line.

sŏn 선 interview with a view to marriage.

sonagi 소나기 shower. *sonagirŭl mannada* 소나기를 만나다 be caught in a shower.

sonamu 소나무 pine (tree). → **sol** 솔.

sonarae 손아래. *sonaraeŭi* 손아래의 younger; junior. *sonaraet saram* 손아랫 사람 one's junior [inferiors, subordinates].

sŏnbae 선배 senior; elder; old-timer (*Am.*).

sŏnbak 선박 vessel; ship; shipping; marine. *sŏnbak hoesa* 선박 회사 shipping company.

sŏnbal 선발 selection; choice. *sŏnbarhada* 선발하다 select; choose.

sŏnban 선반 shelf; rack.

sŏnbul 선불 payment in advance. *sŏnburhada* 선불하다 pay in advance.

sonchit 손짓 gesture; signs; hand signal. *sonjit'ada* 손짓하다 (make a) gesture; beckon.

sŏnch'ul 선출 election. *sŏnch'urhada* 선출하다 elect; return (*Eng.*).

sondokki 손도끼 hand ax; hatchet.

sŏndong 선동 instigation; agitation. *sŏndonghada* 선동하다 instigate; agitate.

sŏndu 선두 head; top; lead. *sŏndu t'aja* 선두 타자 lead-off (batter); first batter.

sondŭlda 손들다 ① raise[hold up] one's hand ② yield[submit] (to).

sŏng 성 castle; fortress; citadel.

sŏng 성 family name; surname.

sŏng 성 gender; sex. *sŏngchŏk* 성적 sexual.

sŏng 성 anger; wrath; rage. *sŏngi nada* 성이 나다 grow angry.

sŏn-gaek 선객 passenger. *idŭng sŏn-gaek* 2등 선객 second-class passenger.

songaji 송아지 calf.

sŏngbun 성분 ingredient; component; constituent.

songbyŏl 송별 farewell; send-off. *songbyŏrhoe* 송별회 farewell party[meeting].

sŏngpyŏng 성병 venereal disease (V.D.); sexual disease; social disease (*Am.*).

songch'ungi 송충이 pine caterpillar.

sŏngdae 성대 vocal cords[bands].

sŏngdang 성당 church; catholic church; sanctuary.

songduritchae 송두리째 all; completely; thoroughly. *songduritchae kajyŏgada* 송두리째 가져가다 take away everything.

sŏnggashida 성가시다 (be)troublesome; annoying; bothersome.

sŏnggong 성공 success. *sŏnggonghada* 성공하다 succeed; be successful.

songgot 송곳 gimlet; drill; awl.

songgŭm 송금 remittance. *songgŭmhada* 송금하다 send money; remit money.

sŏnggyo 성교 sexual intercourse.

sŏnggyŏng 성경 (Holy) Bible; Scriptures.

songhwan 송환 sending back; repatriation. *songhwanhada* 송환하다 send back; repatriate.

songi 송이. *songibŏsŏt* 송이버섯 pine mushroom.

songi 송이 cluster; bunch; flake (of snow).

sŏngin 성인 sage; saint; holy man.

sŏngjang 성장 growth. *sŏngjanghada* 성장하다 grow (up). *sŏngjanghan* 성장한 grown-up.

sŏngjik 성직 holy orders; ministry. *sŏngjikcha* 성직자 churchman; clergyman.

sŏngjil 성질 nature; character.

sŏngjogi 성조기 Stars and Stripes; Star-spangled Banner.

sŏngjŏk 성적 result; record; merit. *sŏngjŏkp'yo* 성적표 list of students' record; grade sheet.

sŏngkwa 성과 result; fruit; outcome.

sŏngkyŏk 성격 character; personality.

songmul 속물 vulgar person; snob; worldling.

sŏngmyo 성묘. *sŏngmyohada* 성묘하다 visit one's ancestor's grave.

sŏngmyŏng 성명 declaration; statement. *sŏng-*

myŏnghada 성명하다 declare; announce.

sŏngmyŏng 성명 (full) name.

sŏngnip 성립. *sŏngnip'ada* 성립하다 be formed [organized]; be effected.

songnunssŏp 속눈썹 eyelashes. *injo songnunssŏp* 인조 속눈썹 false eyelashes.

sŏngnyang 성냥 matches. *sŏngnyangkap* 성냥갑 match box. *sŏngnyang kaebi* 성냥 개비 match ⌐stick.

songnyo 송료 carriage; postage.

songnyŏk 속력 →**sokto** 속도. *chŏnsongnyŏgŭro* 전속력으로 (at) full speed.

sŏn-go 선고 sentence; verdict. *sŏn-gohada* 선고하다 sentence; condemn.

sŏn-gŏ 선거 election. *sŏn-gŏhada* 선거하다 elect; vote for.

sonkŏul 손거울 hand mirror.

songp'ung 송풍 ventilation. *songp'unggi* 송풍기 ventilator; blower; fan.

sŏngshil 성실 sincerity; honesty. *sŏngshirhan* 성실한 sincere; faithful.

sŏngsŏ 성서 (Holy) Bible; Scripture.

songsuhwagi 송수화기 hand set.

sŏngsuk 성숙. *sŏngsuk'ada* 성숙하다 ripen; get ripe. *sŏngsuk'an* 성숙한 ripe; mature.

sŏngt'anjŏl 성탄절 Christmas (day).

sŏngŭi 성의 sincerity; faith.

sŏn-guja 선구자 pioneer; forerunner.

sŏn-gŭm 선금 advance; prepayment. *sŏn-gŭmŭl ch'irŭda* 선금을 치르다 pay in advance.

sŏn-gyo 선교 missionary work. *sŏn-gyohada* 선교하다 evangelize. *sŏn-gyosa* 선교사 missionary.

sŏngyok 성욕 sexual desire(s)[appetite].

songyu 송유 oil supply. *songyugwan* 송유관 (oil) pipeline.

sonhae 손해 damage; injury; loss. *sonhae paesang* 손해 배상 compensation for damages.

sŏninjang 선인장 cactus.

sŏnipkyŏn 선입견 preconception; preoccupation; prejudice; preconceived idea.

sonjabi 손잡이 handle; knob; gripe.

sŏnjang 선장 captain; skipper; master mariner.

sŏnjo 선조 ancestor; forefather.

sŏnjŏn 선전 propaganda; publicity; advertisement. *sŏnjŏnhada* 선전하다 propagandize; advertise.

sonkabang 손가방 briefcase (*Am*); brief bag (*Eng.*); handbag; gripsack (*Am.*).

sonkarak 손가락 finger. *ŏmjisonkarak* 엄지손가락 thumb. *chipke[kaundet, yak, saekki]sonkarak* 집게[가운뎃, 약, 새끼]손가락 index[middle, ring, little] finger.

sonkkopta 손꼽다 count on one's fingers. *sonkkomnŭn* 손꼽는 leading; prominent.

sŏnmul 선물 present; gift. *sŏnmurhada* 선물하다 give[send] a present.

sonnim 손님 ① guest; caller; visitor ② customer; client; audience ③ passenger.

sŏnmyŏng 선명. *sŏnmyŏnghada[hage]* 선명하다[하게] distinct(ly); clear(ly); vivid(ly).

sonnyŏ 손녀 granddaughter.

sŏnnyŏ 선녀 fairy; nymph.

sonppyŏkch'ida 손뼉치다 clap (one's) hands.

sŏnp'unggi 선풍기 fan; electric fan.

sonsaek 손색 inferiority. *sonsaegi ŏpta* 손색이 없다 bear[stand] comparison (with); be equal (to).

sŏnsaeng 선생 teacher; instructor; schoolmaster; schoolmistress(*Am.*).

sonshil 손실 loss; disadvantage; damage. *k'ŭn sonshil* 큰 손실 great〔heavy, serious〕 loss.

sonsu 손수 with one's own hands; personally.

sŏnsu 선수 player; athlete(*Eng.*); champion.

sonsugŏn 손수건 handkerchief.

sŏnt'aek 선택 selection; choice; option. *sŏnt'aek'ada* 선택하다 select; choose.

sont'op 손톱 fingernail. *sont'op kkakki* 손톱 깎이 nail clipper.

sontŭng 손등 back of the hand.

sŏnttŭt 선뜻 lightly; readily; willingly; offhand.

sŏnŭi 선의 favo(u)rable sense; good faith. *sŏnŭiŭi* 선의의 well-intentioned.

sŏnŭrhada 서늘하다 (be) cool; refreshing; chilly.

sŏnŏn 선언 declaration; proclamation. *sŏnŏnhada* 선언하다 declare; proclaim.

sonwi 손위. *sonwiŭi* 손위의 older; elder; senior *sonwit saram* 손윗 사람 senior; superior.

sŏnwon 선원 seaman; crew; sailor.

sŏnyak 선약 previous engagement.

sonyŏ 소녀 (young) girl; lass; maid.

sonyŏn 소년 boy; lad. *sonyŏnŭi* 소년의 juvenile.

sŏnyul 선율 melody. *sŏnyulchŏk* 선율적 melodious.

sop'o 소포 parcel; package; packet.

sŏpsŏp'ada 섭섭하다 (be) sorry; sad; disappointed; regrettable; reproachful.

sŏpssi 섭써 Celsius(C.); centigrade.

sop'ung 소풍 outing; excursion; picnic. *sop'ung kada* 소풍 가다 go on an excursion〔a picnic〕.

sora 소라 top〔wreath〕 shell.

soran 소란 disturbance; commotion. *soranhada* 소란하다 (be) noisy; disturbing.

sŏrap 서랍 drawer.

sori 소리 ① sound; noise ② voice; cry. *k'ŭn[chagŭn] soriro* 큰[작은] 소리로 in a loud[low] voice.

sŏri 서리 frost; white frost.

sorich'ida 소리치다 →**sorijirŭda** 소리지르다.

sŏrida 서리다 steam up; get steamed.

sorijirŭda 소리지르다 shout; cry[call] (out);scream; roar; yell.

sŏro 서로 mutually; each other; one another.

sŏron 서론 introduction; introductory remarks.

sŏrŭn 서른 thirty. *sŏrŭnsal* 서른살 thirty years of age.

soryang 소량 small quantity[amount]. *soryangŭi* 소량의 little; small quantity[amount] of.

soryŏng 소령 major(*army*); lieutenant commander (*navy*); wing commander(*air*).

sŏryu 서류 documents; papers. *sŏryu kabang* 서류 가방 briefcase(*Am.*); brief bag(*Eng.*).

sosaeng 소생 revival; reanimation. *sosaenghada* 소생하다 revive; come to oneself.

sosang 소상 earthen[clay] image.

soshik 소식 news; tidings; information.

sŏshik 서식 (fixed) form; formula. *sŏshige ttara* 서식에 따라 in due form.

sŏsŏhi 서서히 slowly. →**ch'ŏnch'ŏnhi** 천천히.

sosok 소속. *sosok'ada* 소속하다 belong to; be attached to. *sosogŭi* 소속의 attached[belonging] to.

sosŏl 소설 novel; story; fiction. *sosŏlga* 소설가 novelist.

sosong 소송 lawsuit; legal action. *sosonghada* 소

송하다 sue; bring a lawsuit.

sŏsŏnggŏrida 서성거리다 walk up and down rest-lessly; go back and forth uneasily.

sosu 소수 minority; few; small number. *sosu min-jok*[*p'a*] 소수민족[파] minority race[faction].

sosu 소수 decimal. *sosuchŏm* 소수점 decimal point.

sot 솥 iron pot; kettle. *sottukkŏng* 솥뚜껑 lid of a kettle.

sotta 솟다 ① rise[soar, tower] high ② gush [spring] out; well out.

sŏttal 섣달 December. *sŏttal kŭmŭm* 섣달 그믐 New Year's Eve.

sŏt'urŭda 서투르다 (be) unfamiliar; (be) awkward; clumsy; unskil(l)ful; stiff; poor.

Sŏul 서울 Seoul (capital of Korea).

soŭm 소음 noise. *soŭm pangji* 소음 방지 arrest of noise. *soŭm konghae* 소음 공해 noise pollution.

sowi 소위 second lieutenant (*army*); ensign (*navy*); second sublieutenant (*Eng.*).

sowi 소위 what is called; so-called.

sŏyak 서약 oath; pledge. *sŏyak'ada* 서약하다 swear; vow; pledge.

sŏyang 서양 the West; the Occident. *sŏyangŭi* 서양의 Western; Occidental. *sŏyang saram* 서양 사람 Westerner; European.

soyongdori 소용돌이 whirlpool; swirl.

soyu 소유 possession. *soyuhada* 소유하다 have; possess; own; hold.

ssada 싸다 wrap up[in]; do up; bundle; pack up.

ssada 싸다 (be) inexpensive; cheap; low-priced. *ssage* 싸게 cheaply; at a low cost.

ssada 싸다 excrete (urine or feces); void; discharge.

ssaida 쌓이다 be piled up; be heaped.

ssak 싹 bud; sprout; shoot. *ssagi t'ŭda* 싹이 트 다 bud; shoot; sprout.

ssal 쌀 (raw, uncooked) rice. *ssalkage* 쌀가게 rice store. *ssalt'ong* 쌀통 rice chest.

ssalssarhada 쌀쌀하다 ① (be) chilly; (rather) cold ② distant; coldhearted; indifferent.

ssangan-gyŏng 쌍안경 binoculars; field glasses.

ssangbang 쌍방 both parties[sides]; either party. *ssangbangŭi* 쌍방의 both; either; mutual.

ssangkŏp'ul 쌍거풀 double eyelid.

ssat'a 쌓다 ① pile[heap] (up); stack; lay ② ac- cumulate; store up.

ssauda 싸우다 fight; make war; struggle; quarrel.

ssi 씨 seed; stone; kernel; pit; pip. *ssi ŏmnŭn* 씨 없 는 seedless.

ssi 씨 Mr. ; Miss; Mrs. *Kimssi* 김씨 Mr. Kim.

ssiat 씨앗 seed. →**ssi** 씨.

ssikssik'ada 씩씩하다 (be) manly; manful; brave.

ssipta 씹다 chew; masticate.

ssirŭm 씨름 wrestling; wrestling match. *ssirŭm- hada* 씨름하다 wrestle.

ssitta 씻다 wash; wash away; cleanse.

ssoda 쏘다 shoot; fire; discharge.

ssŏk 썩 ① right away; at once ② very much; exceedingly.

ssŏkta 썩다 go bad; rot; decay; corrupt. *ssŏgŭn* 썩은 bad; rotten; stale.

ssollida 쏠리다 ① incline; lean ② be disposed to; tend to; get enthusiastic (about).

ssŏlmae 썰매 sled; sleigh; sledge.

ssotta 쏟다 ① pour out; spill; shed; drop ② concentrate; devote; effort.

ssŭda 쓰다 use; make use of; spend (money) on.

ssŭda 쓰다 write; scribe; describe; compose.

ssŭda 쓰다 put on; wear; cover.

ssŭdadŭmta 쓰다듬다 stroke; pat; smooth; caress.

ssŭiuda 씌우다 put on; cover.

ssuksŭrŏpta 쑥스럽다 (be) unbecoming; indecent.

ssŭlda 쓸다 sweep (up, away, off). *pangŭl ssŭlda* 방을 쓸다 sweep a room.

ssŭlssŭrhada 쓸쓸하다 (be) lonely; lonesome.

ssŭlteŏpta 쓸데없다 be of no use[value]; (be) useless; worthless.

ssŭnusŭm 쓴웃음 bitter[grim] smile.

ssŭrebatki 쓰레받기 dustpan.

ssŭregi 쓰레기 garbage; rubbish; trash (*Am.*). *ssŭregit'ong* 쓰레기통 garbage can; dustbin.

ssŭrida 쓰리다 smart; burn; ache; be tingling.

ssŭrŏjida 쓰러지다 ① collapse; fall down ② sink [break] down ③ fall dead ④ go bankrupt.

ssushida 쑤시다 ① pick; poke ② throb with pain; twinge; tingle; ache.

sswaegi 쐐기 wedge; chock.

su 수 embroidery. *sunot'a* 수놓다 embroider.

subae 수배 make[spread] (a) search (for). *subae inmul* 수배 인물 criminal wanted by the police.

subak 수박 watermelon.

subi 수비 defense. *subihada* 수비하다 defend; guard. *subidae* 수비대 garrison.

subu 수부 mariner. → **subyŏng** 수병.

subun 수분 moisture; juice; water. *subuni manŭn* 수분이 많은 watery; juicy.

subyŏng 수병 sailor; seaman; blue jacket.
such'aehwa 수채화 water colo(u)r (painting).
such'i 수치 shame; disgrace. *such'isŭrŏn* 수치스
런 shameful; disgraceful.
sŭch'ida 스치다 graze; glance (off); go past by.
such'ul 수출 export; exportation. *such'urhada* 수
출하다 export; ship abroad.
sudan 수단 means; way; measure; step.
sudang 수당 allowance; bonus. *kajok sudang* 가족
수당 family allowance.
sudasŭrŏpta 수다스럽다 (be) talkative; chatty.
sudo 수도 capital; metropolis. *sudoŭi* 수도의 metropolitan.
sudo 수도 waterworks; water service[supply].
sudo 수도 asceticism. *sudowon* 수도원 monastery;
cloister. *sudosŭng* 수도승 monk.
sudong 수동 passivity. *sudongjŏk(ŭro)* 수동적 (으로)
passive(ly).
suduruk'ada 수두룩하다 (be) abundant; plentiful.
sugap 수갑 handcuffs; manacles.
sugi 수기 note; memoirs; memorandum.
sugo 수고 trouble; pains; efforts. *sugohada* 수고
하다 take pains[trouble].
sugŏ 숙어 idiom; (idiomatic) phrase.
sugŏn 수건 towel. *sesu sugŏn* 세수 수건 face towel.
sugŏn kŏri 수건 걸이 towel horse[rack].
sugong 수공 handicraft; manual work. *sugongŏp*
수공업 manual industry.
sugŭm 수금 bill collection. *sugŭmhada* 수금하다
collect bills[money].
sugun-gŏrida 수군거리다 talk in whispers; speak
under one's breath.

sugŭrŏjida 수그러지다 ① droop; be bowed; hang (down) ② subside; abate; dwindle.

suhae 수해 damage by a flood; flood disaster.

suhak 수학 mathematics.

suhamul 수하물 luggage (*Eng.*); baggage (*Am.*).

suho 수호. *suhohada* 수호하다 protect; guard.

suhŏm 수험. *suhŏmhada* 수험하다 take[undergo, sit for] an examination.

suhwagi 수화기 (telephone) receiver; earphone.

suhwak 수확 harvest; crop. *suhwak'ada* 수확하다 harvest; reap; gather in.

suhyŏl 수혈 blood transfusion. *suhyŏrhada* 수혈하다 transfuse blood.

suil 수일 a few days; several days.

suip 수입 income; earnings. *suipkwa chich'ul* 수입과 지출 income and outgo.

suip 수입 importation; import. *suip'ada* 수입하다 import. *suipp'um* 수입품 imported articles[goods].

sujae 수재 genius; talented[brilliant] man.

suji 수지 income and outgo; revenue and expenditure. *suji mannŭn* 수지 맞는 profitable.

sujik 수직. *sujigŭi* 수직의 perpendicular; vertical. *sujiksŏn* 수직선 vertical line.

sujip 수집 collection. *sujip'ada* 수집하다 collect. *sujipka* 수집가 collector.

sujŏng 수정 crystal. *chasujŏng* 자수정 amethyst.

sujŏng 수정 amendment; modification. *sujŏng-hada* 수정하다 amend; modify.

sujŏnno 수전노 miser; niggard.

sujun 수준 ① water level ② level; standard. *mun-hwa sujun* 문화 수준 cultural level.

sujupta 수줍다 (be) shy; bashful; timid.

sukche 숙제 homework; home task. *panghak sukche* 방학 숙제 holiday task.

sukchik 숙직 night duty[watch]. *sukchik'ada* 숙직하다 be on night duty; keep night watch.

sutkarak 숟가락 spoon. *papsutkarak* 밥숟가락 tablespoon. *ch'assutkarak* 찻숟가락 teaspoon.

sukpak 숙박. *sukpak'ada* 숙박하다 lodge; stay. *sukpangnyo* 숙박료 lodging charge; hotel charges.

sukpu 숙부 uncle.

sukso 숙소 place of abode; one's address.

sul 술 wine; rice wine; liquor. *surŭl mashida* 술을 마시다 have a drink. *sure ch'wihada* 술에 취하다 get drunk.

sulchan 술잔 wine cup; liquor glass; goblet.

sulchip 술집 bar (room); saloon (*Am.*); public house (*Eng.*); tavern.

sŭlgiropta 슬기롭다 (be) wise; prudent; sensible.

sŭlgŭmŏni 슬그머니 stealthily; secretly; furtively.

sulkkun 술꾼 (heavy) drinker; tippler.

sulpyŏng 술병 liquor bottle.

sŭlp'ŭda 슬프다 (be) sad; sorrowful; pathetic.

sŭlp'ŭm 슬픔 sorrow; sadness; grief.

sullaejapki 술래잡기 tag; blindman's buff.

sŭlsŭl 슬슬 slowly; gently; lightly.

sum 숨 breath; breathing. *sumŭl shwida* 숨을 쉬다 breathe; respire.

suman 수만 tens[scores] of thousands.

sumta 숨다 hide[conceal] oneself; take cover. *sumŭn* 숨은 hidden; unknown.

sumbakkokchil 숨바꼭질 hide-and-(go)-seek; I-spy; hy-spy.

sumch'ada 숨차다 pant; be out[short] of breath.

sumgida 숨기다 hide; conceal; shelter.
sŭmida 스미다 soak; permeate through; ooze out.
sumilto 수밀도 juicy peach.
sumok 수목 trees(and shrubs); arbors.
sumyŏng 수명 life; span of life; life expectancy.
sun 순 pure; genuine. *sunhan-gukshik* 순한국식 purely Korean style.
sunan 수난 suffering; ordeals; crucifixion.
sunbak 순박. *sunbak'an* 순박한 naive; unsophisticated; homely; simple and honest.
sunbŏn 순번 order; turn. →**ch'arye** 차례.
sun-gan 순간 moment; instant; second. *sun-ganjŏk* 순간적 momentary; instantaneous.
sungbae 숭배 worship; adoration. *sungbaehada* 숭배하다 worship; admire; adore.
sŭngbu 승부 victory or defeat; match; game; bout. *musŭngbu* 무승부 drawn[tie] game; draw.
sŭngch'a 승차. *sŭngch'ahada* 승차하다 take[board] a train; get on a car.
sŭnggaek 승객 passenger; fare.
sŭngin 승인 recognition; acknowledg(e)ment; approval. *sŭnginhada* 승인하다 recognize; approve.
sŭngjin 승진 promotion; advancement. *sŭngjinhada* 승진하다 rise (in rank); be promoted[advanced].
sŭngma 승마 riding; horse riding.
sŭngmuwon 승무원 trainman; carman; crew.
sungmyŏng 숙명 fate; destiny; fatality.
sŭngnak 승낙 consent; assent; approval. *sŭngnak'ada* 승낙하다 consent[agree, assent] to.
sŭngni 승리 victory; triumph. *sŭngnihada* 승리하다 win; win[gain] a victory.

sungnyŏ 숙녀 lady; gentlewoman. *sungnyŏdaun* 숙녀다운 ladylike.

sŭngnyŏ 승려 Buddhist monk; priest.

sungnyung 숭늉 scorched-rice tea.

sungnyŏn 숙련 skill; dexterity. *sungnyŏn-gong* 숙련공 skilled worker.

sŭngsan 승산 chance[prospect] of victory; chances of winning.

sun-gŭm 순금 pure gold; solid gold.

sun-gyŏl 순결 purity; chastity; virginity. *sun-gyŏrhan* 순결한 pure; chaste; clean; unspotted.

sunhwan 순환 circulation; rotation; cycle. *hyŏraek sunhwan* 혈액 순환 circulation of blood.

suniik 순이익 net profit[gain]; clear profit.

sŭnim 스님 Buddhist priest[monk]; bonze.

sunjik 순직. *sunjik'ada* 순직하다 die[be killed] at one's post of duty; die in harness.

sunjin 순진. *sunjinhan* 순진한 naive; pure; innocent; genuine.

sunjong 순종. *sunjonghada* 순종하다 obey; submit tamely.

sunmo 순모 pure wool. *sunmoŭi* 순모의 all-wool; pure-wool(en).

sunsŏ 순서 order; sequence. *sunsŏrŭl ttara* 순서를 따라 in proper sequence.

sunwi 순위 order; ranking; grade.

sunyŏ 수녀 nun; sister. *sunyŏwon* 수녀원 nunnery; convent. *sunyŏwonjang* 수녀원장 abbess.

sunyŏn 수년 several years; some[a few] years. *sunyŏn chŏn* 수년 전 some years ago.

sŭngyongch'a 승용차 passenger car; private car; motorcar for riding.

suŏp 수업 teaching; instruction; lesson. *suŏp'ada* 수업하다 teach; instruct.

sup 숲 wood; forest; grove.

sŭpchi 습지 swampy land; boggy ground; marsh.

sup'il 수필 essay. *sup'ilga* 수필가 essayist.

sŭpki 습기 moisture; dampness; humidity.

sŭpkwan 습관 habit; custom. *sŭpkwanjŏgin* 습관적인 habitual; customary. *sŭpkwanjŏguro* 습관적으로 habitually; from habit.

sŭpkyŏk 습격 attack; assault; raid. *sŭpkyŏk'ada* 습격하다 attack; raid; charge.

sup'ok 수폭, **suso p'okt'an** 수소 폭탄 hydrogen bomb; H-bomb.

supŏp 수법 technique; style; way; trick.

sup'yo 수표 check (*Am.*); cheque (*Eng.*). *pojŭng sup'yo* 보증 수표 certified check. *pudo sup'yo* 부도 수표 dishonored check.

sup'yŏng 수평 water level; horizon. *sup'yŏngsŏn* 수평선 sea line; horizon.

surak 수락 acceptance; agreement. *surak'ada* 수락하다 accept; agree to.

sure 수레 wagon; cart. *surebak'wi* 수레바퀴 wheel.

suri 수리 repair; mending. *surihada* 수리하다 repair; mend; have (a thing) mended. *surigong* 수리공 repairman.

surip 수립 establishment. *surip'ada* 수립하다 establish; found; set up.

suro 수로 waterway; watercourse.

suryang 수량 quantity; volume.

suryo 수료 completion. *suryohada* 수료하다 complete; finish (course).

suryŏk 수력 water power; hydraulic power. *su-*

ryŏk palchŏnso 수력 발전소 hydraulic plant.

suryŏn 수련 training; practice. *suryŏnhada* 수련하 다 train; practice. *suryŏnŭi* 수련의 intern; apprentice doctor.

suryŏng 수령 leader; head; chief; boss.

suryŏp 수렵 shooting (*Eng.*); hunting (*Am.*). *suryŏp'ada* 수렵하다 hunt.

suryut'an 수류탄 hand grenade; pineapple (*mil.*).

susa 수사 criminal investigation; search. *susahada* 수사하다 investigate; search.

susaek 수색 search; investigation. *susaek'ada* 수색하다 look[hunt, search] for.

susan 수산. *susanmul* 수산물 marine products. *susan taehak* 수산 대학 fisheries college. *susanŏp* 수산업 fisheries.

susang 수상 prime minister; premier.

susang 수상. *susanghan* 수상한 suspicious(-looking); doubtful; questionable.

suse 수세. *suseshik pyŏnso* 수세식 변소 flush toilet; water closet.

sushin 수신 receipt of message. *sushinhada* 수신 하다 receive a message. *sushin-gi* 수신기 receiver. *sushinin* 수신인 addressee.

susok 수속 →**chŏlch'a** 절차.

susŏk 수석 head; chief; top[head] seat.

susŏn 수선 repair; mending. *susŏnhada* 수선하다 repair; mend; have (a shoe) mended.

susong 수송 transportation. *susonghada* 수송하다 transport; convey.

susŏnhwa 수선화 daffodil; narcissus.

susukkekki 수수께끼 riddle; puzzle; mystery. *susukkekki kat'ŭn* 수수께끼 같은 enigmatic; mysterious; riddling.

susul 수술 (surgical) operation. *susurhada* 수술하
다 operate on; perform a surgical operation. *su-
sulshil* 수술실 operating room.

sŭsŭng 스승 teacher; master; mistress.

sŭsŭro 스스로 (for) oneself; in person. *sŭsŭroŭi*
스스로의 one's own; personal.

susuryo 수수료 commission; fee; service charge.

sut 숯 charcoal. *sutpul* 숯불 charcoal fire.

sucha 수자 figure; numeral.

sut'ong 수통 water flask; canteen.

suu 수우 (water) buffalo. →**mulso** 물소.

suŭn 수은 mercury; quicksilver. *suŭnju* 수은주
mercurial thermometer.

suwan 수완 ability; talent; capacity. *suwan-ga* 수
완가 man of capacity; go-getter (*Am.*).

suwi 수위 guard; doorkeeper; gatekeeper.

Sŭwisŭ 스위스 Switzerland, Swiss Confederation.

suworhada 수월하다 (be) easy; be no trouble. *su-
worhage* 수월하게 easily; with ease.

suyo 수요 demand. *suyo konggŭp* 수요 공급 demand
and supply. *suyoja* 수요자 user.

suyoil 수요일 Wednesday.

suyong 수용 accommodation. *suyonghada* 수용하다
accommodate; receive. *suyongso* 수용소 asylum;
camp.

suyŏng 수영 swimming; swim. *suyŏnghada* 수영
하다 swim; have a swim. *suyŏngbok* 수영복
swimming suit.

syassŭ 샤쓰 shirts; undershirts; vest (*Eng.*).

syawo 샤워 shower. *syaworŭl hada* 샤워를 하다
have[take] a shower.

T

ta 다 ① all; everything; everybody ② utterly; completely. *tahaesŏ* 다해서 in all; all told. *tagach'i* 다같이 together.

tabang 다방 tearoom; teahouse; coffee house; coffee shop (of hotel).

tach'ida 다치다 be[get, become] wounded[hurt, injured, damaged]; bruised.

tadari 다달이 every month; monthly.

tadŭmta 다듬다 ① make beautiful; embellish; adorn; trim up ② prune.

tae 대 bamboo. *taebaguni* 대바구니 bamboo basket.

taebi 대비 provision; preparation. *taebihada* 대비하다 be ready for.

taebŏbwon 대법원 Supreme Court. *taebŏbwonjang* 대법원장 Chief Justice.

taebu 대부 loan(ing). *taebuhada* 대부하다 lend; loan; (make an) advance.

taebubun 대부분 most; major part (of); mostly; largely; for the most part.

taebyŏn 대변 excrement; feces. *taebyŏnŭl poda* 대변을 보다 go to stool; evacuate.

taech'aek 대책 countermeasure. *taech'aegŭl seuda* 대책을 세우다 work out a countermeasure.

taech'e 대체. *taech'ejŏgin* 대체적인 general; main; rough. *taech'ero* 대체로 generally; as a whole.

taech'ung 대충 almost; nearly; about; roughly.

taedae 대대 battalion. *taedaejang* 대대장 battalion commander.

taedae 대대. *taedaero* 대대로 from generation to

generation; for generations.

taedaejŏk 대대적. *taedaejŏgin* 대대적인 great; grand; wholesale. *taedaejŏgŭro* 대대적으로 extensively; on a large scale.

taedam 대담. *taedamhan* 대담한 bold; daring. *taedamhage* 대담하게 boldly; daringly.

taedanhada 대단하다 (be) enormous; severe; intense; grave. *taedanhi* 대단히 very; seriously; exceedingly; awfully.

taedap 대답 answer; reply. *taedap'ada* 대답하다 answer; reply; respond (to); give an answer.

taedasu 대다수 large majority; greater part.

taedongmaek 대동맥 main artery.

taegada 대가다 arrive on time; be in time (for).

taegae 대개 mostly; for the most part; in general.

taegang 대강 ① general principles; outline; general features. ② generally; roughly.

taegŏmch'alch'ŏng 대검찰청 Supreme Public Prosecutor's Office.

taegŭm 대금 price; charge; money. *taegŭm ch'ŏnggusŏ* 대금 청구서 bill; check (*Am.*).

taegyumo 대규모 large scale. *taegyumoro* 대규모로 on large scale.

taehak 대학 university; college. *taehaksaeng* 대학생 university student. *taehagwon* 대학원 graduate school; (post) graduate course; *taehak pyŏngwon* 대학 병원 university hospital.

Taehan 대한 Korea. *Taehanmin-guk* 대한민국 Republic of Korea.

taehang 대항 opposition; rivalry. *taehanghada* 대항하다 oppose; cope with.

taehapshil 대합실 waiting room.

taehoe 대회 great[grand] meeting; mass meeting; rally; convention. *taehoerŭl yŏlda* 대회를 열다 hold a mass meeting.

taehwa 대화 conversation; dialogue. *taehwahada* 대화하다 talk[converse] with. 「success.

taeinki 대인기 great popularity; big hit; great

taejang 대장 general (*army*, *air*); admiral (*navy*).

taejang 대장 ledger; register.

taejangbu 대장부 (brave) man; manly[great] man.

taejangjangi 대장장이 smith; blacksmith.

taejangkan 대장간 blacksmith's shop; smithy.

taeji 대지 site; lot; plot. *kŏnch'uk taeji* 건축 대지 building[housing] site[lot, land].

taejo 대조 contrast; collation. *taejohada* 대조하다 contrast; check; collate.

taejŏn 대전 great war; the World War. *cheich'a segye taejŏn* 제2차 세계 대전 World War Ⅱ.

taejŏp 대접 treatment; entertainment; reception. *taejŏp'ada* 대접하다 treat; entertain; receive.

taejugyo 대주교 archbishop.

taejung 대중 masses; populace; multitude. *kŭllo taejung* 근로 대중 working masses.

taek 댁 ① (your, his, her) house; residence ② you ③ the wife of (a person); Mrs ….

taemaech'ul 대매출 special bargain; great sale.

taemŏri 대머리 bald head; bald-headed person.

taemuncha 대문자 capital letter.

taenggi 댕기 pigtail ribbon.

taep'o 대포 gun; cannon; artillery. *taep'orŭl ssoda* 대포를 쏘다 fire a gun.

taep'yo 대표 representation; representative. *taep'yohada* 대표하다 represent; stand[act] for.

taeri 대리 procuration; representation; agency. *taeriin* 대리인 proxy; substitute; deputy; agent. *taerijŏm* 대리점 agency.

taerip 대립 opposition; rivalry; confrontation; antagonism. *taerip'ada* 대립하다 be opposed to.

taerisŏk 대리석 marble.

taeryang 대량 large quantity. *taeryang saengsan* 대량 생산 mass production.

taeryŏng 대령 colonel (*army*); captain (*navy*); flight colonel (*air*).

taeryuk 대륙 continent. *taeryukkan t'andot'an* 대륙간 탄도탄 intercontinental ballistic missile.

taesa 대사 ambassador. *chumi〔chuil, chuyŏng〕 taesa* 주미〔주일, 주영〕 대사 ambassador to the United States〔Japan, Great Britain〕.

taesagwan 대사관 embassy. *Miguk taesagwan* 미국 대사관 American Embassy.

taesang 대상 object; target.

taeshin 대신 (Cabinet) minister. →**changgwan** 장관.

taesŏyang 대서양 the Atlantic (Ocean).

taet'ongnyŏng 대통령 president. *taet'ongnyŏngŭi* 대통령의 presidential. *taet'ongnyŏng sŏn-gŏ* 대통령 선거 presidential election. *taet'ongnyŏng yŏngbuin* 대통령 영부인 first lady.

taettŭm 대뜸 at once; immediately; outright.

taeu 대우 treatment; reception; pay; service. *taeuhada* 대우하다 treat; receive; pay. *nomuja taeu kaesŏn* 노무자 대우 개선 improvement of labor condition.

taewi 대위 captain (*army, air*); lieutenant (*navy*).

taeyong 대용 substitution. *taeyongp'um* 대용품 substitute article.

taeyŏsŏt 대여섯 about five or six.

tagalsaek 다갈색 (yellowish) brown; liver-color.

tagaoda 다가오다 approach; draw[come] near; draw close.

tagŭp'ada 다급하다 (be) imminent; urgent; pressing.

tagwa 다과 tea and cake; light refreshments.

tahaeng 다행 good fortune[luck]. *tahaenghada* 다행하다 (be) happy; lucky; fortunate. *tahaenghi* 다행히 happily; fortunately; luckily.

tajida 다지다 ① ram; harden (the ground) ② mince; chop (up) ③ make sure of; press (a person) for a definite answer.

tajim 다짐 promise; pledge; assurance. *tajimhada* 다짐하다 assure; pledge; (make a) vow.

tak 닭 hen; cock[rooster]. *takkogi* 닭고기 chicken. *takchang* 닭장 coop; henhouse.

takch'ida 닥치다 approach; draw[come] near; be at hand.

takta 닦다 ① polish; shine; burnish; brush; wipe; scrub ② improve; cultivate; train.

tal 달 ① moon. *porŭmtal* 보름달 full moon ② month. *k'ŭn[chagŭn]dal* 큰[작은]달 odd[even] month. *chinandal* 지난달 last month.

talda 달다 weigh. *chŏullo talda* 저울로 달다 weigh (a thing) in the balance.

talda 달다 (be) sweet; sugary.

talda 달다 ① attach; affix; fasten ② fix; set up ③ put on; wear ④ register ⑤ burn.

talguji 달구지 cart; ox-cart.

talk'omhada 달콤하다 (be) sweet; sugary; honeyed.

tallaeda 달래다 appease; soothe; coax; beguile; calm; amuse; pacify; dandle.

tallajida 달라지다 change; undergo a change; alter;

tallida 달리다 run; dash; gallop.　　　　　　⌊vary.

tallyŏdŭlda 달려들다 pounce on; fly at; jump[leap, spring] at[on].

tallyŏk 달력 calendar; almanac.

tallyŏn 단련 ① temper; forging ② training; drilling; discipline.　*tallyŏnhada* 단련하다 ① temper; forge ② train; drill; discipline.

talp'aengi 달팽이 snail.

talsŏng 달성 achievement. *talsŏnghada* 달성하다 accomplish; achieve; attain.

talt'a 닳다 ① be worn out[down]; be rubbed off [down]; wear threadbare ② be boiled down ③ lose (one's) modesty.

tam 담 wall; fence. *toldam* 돌담 stone[brick] wall. *hŭktam* 흙담 mud[earthen] wall.

tam 담 phlegm; sputum.

taman 다만 ① only; merely; simply ② but; however; and yet; still.

tambae 담배 tobacco; cigaret(te). *tambaerŭl p'iuda* 담배를 피우다 smoke (tobacco). *tambae kage* 담배 가게 cigar store.

tambo 담보 security; mortgage; guarantee; warrant. *tamborŭl chapta* 담보를 잡다 take security.

tamdang 담당 charge. *tamdanghada* 담당하다 take charge (of); be in charge of.

tamgŭda 담그다 ① soak[steep, dip, immerse] (in water) ② pickle; brew.

tamhwa 담화 talk; conversation; statement. *tamhwamun* 담화문 official statement.

tamjaengi 담쟁이 ivy. *tamjaengi tŏnggul* 담쟁이 덩굴 ivy vines.

tamta 담다 put in; fill. *kwangjurie tamta* 광주리에 담다 put into a basket.

tamulda 다물다 shut; close (one's lips). *ibŭl tamulda* 입을 다물다 hold one's tongue.

tan 단 bundle; bunch; sheaf; faggot.

tanbal 단발 bob; bobbed hair. *tanbarhada* 단발하다 bob one's hair.

tanch'e 단체 group; organization. *tanch'e haengdong* united action. *tanch'e yŏhaeng* 단체 여행 group trip.

tanchŏm 단점 weak point; shortcoming; defect; fault.

tanch'u 단추 button; stud. *tanch'urŭl ch'aeuda* 단추를 채우다 button up; fasten a button. *tanch'urŭl kkŭrŭda* 단추를 끄르다 unbutton (a coat).

tanch'uk 단축 reduction; shortening. *tanch'uk'ada* 단축하다 reduct; shorten; curtail.

tandanhada 단단하다 (be) hard; solid; strong; firm. *tandanhi* 단단히 hard; solidly; firmly.

tando 단도 dagger; short sword.

tandok 단독. *tandogŭro* 단독으로 independently; separately; individually; alone; singly.

tangch'ŏm 당첨 prize winning. *tangch'ŏmhada* 당첨하다 win a prize; draw a lucky number.

tangdanghada 당당하다 (be) grand; imposing; fair. *tangdanghi* 당당히 stately; fairly.

tanggida 당기다 pull; draw; tug; haul.

tanggu 당구 billiards. *tanggurŭl ch'ida* 당구를 치다 play at billiards.

tangguk 당국 authorities (concerned). *hakkyo tangguk* 학교 당국 school authorities.

tanghwang 당황. *tanghwanghada* 당황하다 be confused[upset]; lose one's head.

tan-gi 단기 short term[time]. *tan-giŭi* 단기의 short (-term); short-dated.

tangjik 당직 being on duty[watch]. *tangjik'ada* 당직하다 be on duty[watch].

tangmil 당밀 molasses.

tan-gol 단골 custom; connection; patronage. *tan-gol sonnim* 단골 손님 customer; client; patron; regular visitor.

tangshi 당시 then; that time; those days. *tangshiŭi* 당시의 of those days; then.

tangsŏn 당선. *tangsŏnhada* 당선하다 be elected; win the election.

tangwon 당원 member of a party; party man.

tan-gyŏl 단결 union; combination; cooperation. *tan-gyŏrhada* 단결하다 unite[hold, get] (together); combine[cooperate] (with a person).

tangyŏn 당연. *tangyŏnhan* 당연한 reasonable; right; proper; natural. *tangyŏnhi* 당연히 justly; naturally; deservedly.

tanhwa 단화 shoes. →**kudu** 구두.

tanida 다니다 ① go to and from (a place); go[walk] about[around] ② ply (between) ③ commute.

tanji 단지 housing development[estate (*Eng.*)]; collective[public] housing area. *kongŏp tanji* 공업 단지 industrial complex.

tanjo 단조 monotony; dullness. *tanjoropta* 단조롭다 monotonous; flat; dull.

tanmat 단맛 sweetness; sweet taste. *tanmashi nada* 단맛이 나다 be[taste] sweet; have a sweet taste.

tanŏ 단어 word; vocabulary. *kibon tanŏjip* 기본 단

어집 collection of basic words; basic wordbook.

tanp'a 단파 short wave. *tanp'a sushin-gi* 단파 수신기 short wave receiver.

tanp'ung 단풍 maple. *tanp'ung tŭlda* 단풍 들다 turn red[crimson, yellow]. *tanp'ungnip* 단풍잎 maple leaves.

tanp'yŏn 단편 short piece; sketch. *tanp'yŏn sosŏl* 단편 소설 short story.

tanshik 단식 fast; fasting. *tanshik'ada* 단식하다 fast; abstain from food.

tansŏ 단서 ① beginning; start; first step ② clue; key. *tansŏrŭl chapta* 단서를 잡다 have[get, find] a clue (to, for).

tansok 단속 control; regulation; management; supervision. *tansok'ada* 단속하다 control; supervise; oversee; keep order.

tansume 단숨에 at a stretch[stroke]; at[in] a breath; at one effort.

tansun 단순. *tansunhada* 단순하다 (be) simple; simple-minded. *tansunhi* 단순히 simply; merely.

tanwi 단위 unit; denomination.

tanyŏn 다년 many years. *tanyŏn-gan* 다년간 for many years.

tap 답 answer; reply; solution. *tap'ada* 답하다 answer; reply; give an answer; respond.

tapchang 답장 written reply; reply letter.

tapsa 답사 survey; exploration; field investigation. *tapsahada* 답사하다 explore; survey.

taptap'ada 답답하다 be stifling; suffocating; stuffy. *kasŭmi taptap'ada* 가슴이 답답하다 feel heavy in the chest.

tarak 다락 loft; garret.

taramjwi 다람쥐 squirrel; chipmunk.

taranada 달아나다 run away; flee; escape; take to flight; break[get] loose; fly away.

tari 다리 bridge. *tarirŭl kŏnnŏda* 다리를 건너다 cross a bridge.

tari 다리 leg; limb.

tarida 달이다 boil down; decoct; infuse. *yagrŭl tarida* 약을 달이다 make a medical decoction.

tarimi 다리미 iron; flatiron. *chŏn-gi tarimi* 전기 다리미 electric iron.

taruda 다루다 handle; manage; deal with; treat.

tarŭda 다르다 differ (from, with); be different (from, with); vary; unlike.

tashi 다시 again; overagain; once more[again]; again and again.

tasŏt 다섯 five. *tasŏtchae* 다섯째 the fifth *tasŏt pae(ŭi)* 다섯 배(의) fivefold.

tasu 다수 large[great] number; many; majority. *tasuŭi* 다수의 many; large number of; numerous.

tat 닻 anchor. *tatchul* 닻줄 cable; hawser.

tat'uda 다투다 ① brawl; quarrel; have words (with) ② contend; compete; struggle.

taŭm 다음 next; following; second. *taŭmnal* 다음 날 next[following] day.

tchada 짜다 wring; squeeze. *sugŏnŭl tchada* 수건을 짜다 wring a towel.

tchada 짜다 (be) salty; briny.

tchajŭng 짜증 fret; irritation; vexation.

tchak 짝 pair; couple; partner.

tchaksarang 짝사랑 one-sided love; unrequited love. *tchaksaranghada* 짝사랑하다 love in vain [without return].

tchaksu 짝수 even number.

tchalta 짧다 (be) short; brief. *tchalke* 짧게 short; briefly.

tchaptcharhada 짭짤하다 ① (be) nice and salty; saltish ② suitable.

tchetchehada 쩨쩨하다 ① (be) miserly; stingy; niggardly ② commonplace; dull; foolish.

tchinggŭrida 찡그리다 frown; scowl; (make a) grimace[wry face].

tchikta 찍다 ① stamp; seal; impress ② stab; stick ③ (take a) photograph.

tchip'urida 찌푸리다 ① grimace; frown[scowl] ② cloud over; get cloudy.

tchirŭda 찌르다 pierce; stab; thrust; prick.

tchit'a 찧다 pound (rice); hull; ram (against).

tchitta 찢다 tear; split; cleave; rip.

tchodŭllida 쪼들리다 be troubled[annoyed]; be hard pressed; importune.

tchoeda 쬐다 ① shine on[over] ② bask in the sun.

tchogaeda 쪼개다 split; chop; crack.

tchok 쪽 direction; side; way. *orŭn*[*oen*]*tchok* 오른[왼]쪽 right[left] side.

tcholttak 쫄딱 totally; completely; utterly.

tchotta 쫓다 ① drive away ② chase; pursue.

tchugŭrŏttŭrida 쭈그러뜨리다 press[squeeze] out of shape; crush.

teda 데다 get burnt; have a burn; scald oneself.

teryŏgada 데려가다 take (a person) with.

teryŏoda 데려오다 bring (a person) along.

teuda 데우다 warm; heat (up); mull.

tŏ 더 more(*quantity*); longer(*time*); farther(*distance*). *tŏ mani* 더 많이 much more. *tŏhan-*

ch'ŭng 더한층 more and more; still more.

toan 도안 design; sketch. *toan-ga* 도안가 designer.

tobak 도박 gambling; gaming. *tobak'ada* 도박하다 gamble; play for money.

tobal 도발. *tobarhada* 도발하다 provoke; arouse; incite. *tobalchŏk* 도발적 provocative.

tobo 도보 walking. *toboro* 도보로 on foot. *tobo yŏhaeng* 도보 여행 walking tour.

tŏburŏ 더불어 together; with; together with.

tŏburuk'ada 더부룩하다 (be) tufty; bushy; shaggy.

toch'ak 도착 arrival. *toch'ak'ada* 도착하다 arrive (in, at, on); reach; get to.

toch'ŏ 도처. *toch'ŏe* 도처에 everywhere; all over; throughout.

todaech'e 도대체 on earth; in the world.

todal 도달 arrival. *todarhada* 도달하다 arrive in [at]; reach; get to.

todŏk 도덕 morality; virtue; morals. *todŏkchŏk* 도덕적 moral; ethical. *todŏksang* 도덕상 morally.

toduk 도둑 thief; burglar; robber; sneak. *toduk matta* 도둑 맞다 be stolen; be robbed (of).

tŏdŭmta 더듬다 feel[grope] for; grope about[around] for; fumble for.

tŏdŭmgŏrida, **ttŏdŭmgŏrida** 더듬거리다, 떠듬거리다 stammer; stutter; falter.

toeda 되다 ① become; get; grow ② turn[change] into; develop ③ be realized; be accomplished ④ turn out; result; prove ⑤ come to; reach.

toeda 되다 (be) thick; tough; hard. *toenchuk* 된죽 thick gruel.

toeda 되다 measure.

toenjang 된장 soybean paste.

toenŭndaero 되는대로 at random; roughly; slovenly; suitably; adequately.

toep'uri 되풀이 repetition; reiteration. *toep'urihada* 되풀이하다 repeat.

toesaegida 되새기다 chew over and over again.

togi 도기 china(ware); earthenware; pottery.

Togil 독일 Germany. *Togirŏ* 독일어 German (language). *Togirin* 독일인 German; the Germans.

togu 도구 tool; implement; utensil; instrument.

togŭm 도금 gilding; plating. *togŭmhada* 도금하다 plate (with gold); gild.

tŏgundana 더군다나 besides; moreover; furthermore; in addition.

togyak 독약 poison; poisonous drug[medicine].

tŏhada 더하다 ① add (up); sum up ② get worse; grow harder.

tohap 도합 (grand, sum) total; in all; all told; altogether; in the aggregate.

tojang 도장 seal; stamp. *tojangŭl tchikta* 도장을 찍다 seal; put one's seal to.

tojisa 도지사 provincial governor.

tojung 도중 on the way; on one's way.

tok 독 poison; venom. *togi innŭn* 독이 있는 poisonous; venomous; harmful.

tok 독 jar; jug; pot.

tok'ak 독학 self-education; self-study. *tok'ak'ada* teach oneself; study[learn] by oneself.

tokcha 독자 reader; subscriber.

tokch'ang 독창 (vocal) solo. *tokch'anghada* 독창하다 sing a solo. *tokch'anghoe* 독창회 (vocal)

tokchik 독직 corruption; bribery; graft. ⌊recital.

tokch'ok 독촉 demand. *tokch'ok'ada* 독촉하다 press

〔urge〕 (a person to do).

tokchŏm 독점 monopoly; exclusive possession. *tokchŏmhada* 독점하다 monopolize.

tokkaebi 도깨비 bogy; ghost; spectre.

tokkam 독감 influenza; bad cold; flu.

tokki 도끼 ax; hatchet.

tokpack 독백 monolog(ue); soliloquy. *tokpaek'ada* 독백하다 talk〔speak〕 to oneself.

tokpon 독본 reader. *Yŏngŏ tokpon* 영어 독본 English reader.

toksal 독살 poisoning. *toksarhada* 독살하다 poison; kill by poison.

tokshin 독신. *tokshinŭi* 독신의 single; unmarried. *tokshinja* 독신자 bachelor; spinster (*female*).

toksŏ 독서 reading. *toksŏhada* 독서하다 read (books). *toksŏ chugan* 독서 주간 book week.

tŏkt'aek 덕택. *tŏkt'aegŭro* 덕택으로 due to; thanks to; by (a person's) favor〔help, aid〕.

tol 돌 stone; pebble. *rait'ŏ tol* 라이터 돌 flint for the lighter.

tolboda 돌보다 take care of; care for; look after; attend to; back up; assist; protect.

tolda 돌다 ① turn round; rotate; revolve.

tŏlda 덜다 ① diminish; reduce; mitigate; lighten ② subtract; deduct; take off.

tolgyŏk 돌격 charge; dash; rush. *tolgyŏk'ada* 돌격하다 charge; dash; rush.

tollida 돌리다 ① turn; revolve; roll; spin ② pass (round); hand round. *sulchanŭl tollida* 술잔을 돌리다 pass a glass round.

tolp'a 돌파 *tolp'ahada* 돌파하다 break through; pass (an exam).

tolp'ari 돌팔이. *tolp'ari ŭisa* 돌팔이 의사 quack (doctor); charlatan.

toltchŏgwi 돌쩌귀 hinge.

tomae 도매 wholesale. *tomaehada* 도매하다 sell wholesale. *tomaesang* 도매상 wholesale dealer.

tomang 도망 escape; flight; desertion. *tomangch'ida[hada]* 도망치다[하다] run away; flee; fly; desert. *tomangja* 도망자 fugitive.

tŏmbul 덤불 thicket; bush. *kashi tŏmbul* 가시 덤불 thorny bush.

tŏmi 더미 heap; pile; stack. *ssŭregi tŏmi* 쓰레기 더미 rubbish[trash] heap.

ton 돈 money; cash; coin. *tonŭl pŏlda* 돈을 벌다 make[earn] money; make a fortune.

tonan 도난. *tonandanghada* 도난당하다 be robbed; have (one's money) stolen; be stolen.

tong 동 copper. *tongp'an* 동판 sheet copper.

tongan 동안 ① period; span; interval ② time; space ③ for; during; while.

tongbaek 동백 camellia.

tongbok 동복 winter clothes; winter wear[suit].

tongch'ang 동창 classmate; school fellow; fellow student. *tongch'anghoe* 동창회 old boys' association (*Eng.*); alumni[almunae] association (*Am.*).

tongch'imi 동치미 turnips pickled in salt water.

tongdŭng 동등 equality; parity. *tongdŭnghada* 동등하다 (be) equal.

tonggam 동감 same opinion; sympathy. *tonggamida* 동감이다 agree; be of the same opinion.

tonggap 동갑 same age. *tonggabida* 동갑이다 be (of) the same age.

tonggi 동기 motive; incentive; motivation.

tonggi 동기 same class. *tonggisaeng* 동기생 classmate; graduates of the same year.

tonggul 동굴 cavern; cave; grotto.

tŏnggul 덩굴 vine; tendril.

tonggŭrami 동그라미 circle; ring; loop. *tonggŭramip'yo* 동그라미표 circle symbol.

tonghoe 동회 village assembly. *tonghoe samuso* 동회 사무소 village office.

tonghwa 동화 fairy tale; nursery story[tale].

tongjak 동작 action; movement(s); manners.

tongjang 동장 town-block headman; village headman.

tongji 동지 the winter solstice.

tongji 동지 comrades; friend.

tŏnjida 던지다 throw; hurl; fling; cast.

tongjŏn 동전 copper coin.

tongjŏng 동정 sympathy; compassion. *tongjŏnghada* 동정하다 sympathize; have compassion (on).

tongmaek 동맥 artery. *taedongmaek* 대동맥 main artery.

tongmaeng 동맹 alliance; union; league. *tongmaenghada* 동맹하다 ally with; be allied[leagued] with; combine. *tongmaengguk* 동맹국 allied power. *tongmaeng p'aŏp* 동맹 파업 strike.

tongmin 동민 villager; village folk.

tongmu 동무 friend; companion; comrade. *yŏja tongmu* 여자 동무 girl friend.

tongmul 동물 animal; beast. *tongmurwon* 동물원 zoological garden; zoo.

tongmyŏn 동면 hibernation; winter sleep. *tongmyŏnhada* 동면하다 hibernate.

tongnan 동란 disturbance; upheaval; riot; war.

Han-guk tongnan 한국 동란 the Korean War.

tongnip 독립 independence; self-reliance; self-support. *tongnip'ada* 독립하다 become independent (of); stand alone. *tongnibŭi* 독립의 independent.

tongnyo 동료 associate; colleague; comrade; fellow; co-worker; companion. worker.

tongnyŏk 동력 (motive) power. *tongnyŏksŏn* 동력선 power vessel. *tongnyŏk chawonbu* 동력 자원부 Ministry of Energy and Resources.

tŏngŏri 덩어리 lump; mass; clod.

tongp'o 동포 brethren; one's fellow countryman.

tongsa 동사 death from çold. *tongsahada* 동사하다 be frozen to death.

tongsang 동상 frostbite; chilblains. *tongsange kŏllida* 동상에 걸리다 be[get] frostbitten.

tongsang 동상 bronze statue; copper image.

tongshi 동시 the same time. *tongshiŭi* 동시의 simultaneous; concurrent. *tongshie* 동시에 at the same time; simultaneously with.

tongshingmul 동식물 animal and plants; fauna and flora.

tongtchok 동쪽 east. *tongtchogŭi* 동쪽의 east; eastern; easterly. *tongtchoguro* 동쪽으로 to[in, on] the east.

tongŭi 동의 consent; assent; agreement. *tongŭihada* 동의하다 consent[assent, agree] (to).

tongwon 동원 mobilization. *tongwonhada* 동원하다 mobilize. *tongwon haeje* 동원 해제 demobilization.

tongyang 동양 the Orient; the East. *tongyangin* 동양인 Oriental; the Orientals.

tongyo 동요 shake; quake; tremble. *tongyohada* 동요하다 shake; quake; stir; tremble.

tongyo 동요 children's song; nursery rhyme.
top'i 도피 escape; flight. *top'ihada* 도피하다 escape; flee.
tŏpkae 덮개 covers; coverlet; lid. →**ttukkŏng** 뚜껑.
topta 돕다 ① help; aid; assist ② relieve; give relief to ③ promote.
top'yo 도표 chart; diagram; graph.
toraboda 돌아보다 look back; turn one's head; turn round.
toradanida 돌아다니다 wander[roam] about; walk [go] about; make a round.
toragada 돌아가다 go back; return; turn back.
toraji 도라지 (Chinese) balloon flower; Chinese bellflower.
torang 도랑 ditch; gutter; drain; dike.
toriŏ 도리어 on the contrary; instead; rather; all the more.
toro 도로 road; street; highway.
tŏrŏpta 더럽다 (be) unclean; dirty; filthy; foul; soiled.
tŭryŏbonaeda 들여보내다 send (a person) into; let (a person) in.
toryŏn 돌연 suddenly; on[all of] a sudden; all at once. *toryŏnhan* 돌연한 sudden; abrupt; unexpected; unlooked-for.
toryŏnaeda 도려내다 scrape out; cut off[out, away], cleave.
tosaek 도색 pink; rose colo(u)r. *tosaek yŏnghwa* 도색 영화 sex film; blue movies. *tosaek chapchi* 도색 잡지 yellow journal.
toshi 도시 cities; towns.
toshirak 도시락 lunch box; lunch.

tosŏ 도서 books. *tosŏgwan* 도서관 library.
tot 돛 sail; canvas.
tŏt 덫 trap; snare.
tŏnni 덧니 double[side] tooth.
totpogi 돋보기 long-distance glasses.
tŏuk 더욱 more; more and more; still more.
towajuda 도와주다 help; assist[aid]; relieve; give relief to; support.
tŏwi 더위 heat; hot weather.
ttabunhada 따분하다 ① (be) languid; dull ② (be) boring; tedious; wearisome.
ttada 따다 ① pick; pluck; nip ② open; cut out ③ get; take; obtain.
ttadollida 따돌리다 leave (a person) out (in the cold); cut (a person) out.
ttae 때 ① time; hour; moment ② case; occasion ③ chance; opportunity.
ttae 때 dirt; filth; grime.
ttaemun 때문. *ttaemune* 때문에 on account of; because of; owing to.
ttaerida 때리다 strike; beat; hit; slap.
ttaettaero 때때로 occasionally; now and then; at times; from time to time.
ttajida 따지다 ① distinguish (between right and wrong); demand an explanation of ② calculate.
ttak 딱 ① accurately; exactly; just ② firmly; stiffly ③ flatly; positively.
ttak'ada 딱하다 ① (be) annoying; embarrassing ② (be) pitiable; pitiful; sorry; regrettable.
ttakchi 딱지 ① stamp; sticker; label; tag ② picture card. *up'yo ttakchi* 우표 딱지 postage stamp.
ttakchi 딱지 ① scab ② shell; carapace ③ case.

ttakkŭmhada 따끔하다 smart; prick; bite.

ttakttak'ada 딱딱하다 ① (be) hard; solid; stiff; tough ② strict; rigid ③ (be) stiff; bookish.

ttalgi 딸기 strawberry.

ttalkkukchil 딸꾹질 hiccup; hiccough.

ttam 땀 sweat; perspiration. *ttamŭl hŭllida* 땀을 흘리다 sweat; perspire.

ttan 딴 another; other; different. *ttande[got]* 딴데〔곳〕 another place. *ttansaram* 딴사람 another person; someone else.

ttang 땅 ① earth; ground ② land; territory; soil.

ttangk'ong 땅콩 peanut; groundnut.

ttanim 따님 your[his] (esteemed) daughter.

ttaogi 따오기 sacred[crested] ibis.

ttaragada 따라가다 go with; accompany; follow (a person).

ttarasŏ 따라서 ① accordingly; therefore ② in accordance with; according to.

ttaro 따로 apart; separately; besides; in addition; additionally.

ttarŭda 따르다 ① accompany; follow; go along with ② model (after) ③ obey; yield to.

ttattŭt'ada 따뜻하다 ① (be) mild; warm; genial ② (be) kindly; cordial; heart-warming.

ttawi 따위 ① and such like; such (a thing) like [as]··· ② and so on[forth]; and[or] the like.

tte 떼 group; crowd; throng; herd; flock. *tterŭl chiŏsŏ* 떼를 지어서 in crowds[flocks].

tteda 떼다 ① take off[away]; remove ② part; pull apart; pluck[tear] off ③ break[open] the seal; cut (a letter) open.

ttemilda 떼밀다 push; thrust; elbow (a person)

out.

tti 띠 belt; sash; girdle; band.

tto 또 ① again; once more; repeatedly ② too; also; as well ③ and; moreover.

ttŏdŭlda 떠들다 make a noise; clamo(u)r; make a fuss[disturbance].

ttoeyakpyŏt 뙤약볕 scorching[broiling, burning] sunshine.

ttŏk 떡 rice cake. *ttŏkkuk* 떡국 rice-cake soup.

ttŏkkalnamu 떡갈나무 oak (tree).

ttokparo 똑바로 straight; in a straight line; erect; upright.

ttokttok'ada 똑똑하다 ① (be) clever; sharp; bright ② (be) distinctive; vivid; plain.

ttŏlda 떨다 shake; tremble; shiver; quake; shudder.

ttŏmatta 떠맡다 undertake; assume; take (a thing) upon oneself.

ttŏnada 떠나다 ① leave; start from; set out; depart ② quit; resign (from); part from[with].

ttong 똥 feces; stool; excrement; dung.

ttŏrŏjida 떨어지다 ① fall; drop; come down ② come[fall] off ③ go down; decline.

ttŏrŏttŭrida 떨어뜨리다 ① drop; throw down; let fall ② lose; miss.

ttŭda 뜨다 ① float (on the water, in the air) ② rise; come up.

ttŭda 뜨다 open (one's eyes); wake up; awake.

ttŭgŏpta 뜨겁다 (be) hot; heated; burning.

ttŭiuda 띄우다 fly; let fly; make fly. *yŏnŭl ttŭiuda* 연을 띄우다 fly a kite.

ttujangi 뚜장이 pimp; pander.

ttukkŏng 뚜껑 lid; cover; cap; shield; case. *ttu-*

kkŏngŭl yŏlda 뚜껑을 열다 lift[take off] a lid; uncover. *ttukkŏngŭl tatta* 뚜껑을 닫다 put on the lid.

ttult'a 뚫다 bore; punch; make[drill] a hole.

ttungttungbo 뚱뚱보 fatty[plump] person.

tturŏjige poda 뚫어지게 보다 stare (at); look hard (at); gaze (at, into).

tturyŏshi 뚜렷이 clearly; distinctly; evidently.

tturyŏt'ada 뚜렷하다 (be) clear; vivid; evident; obvious.

ttŭt 뜻 ① intention; intent ② meaning; sense.

ttŭtpak 뜻밖. *ttŭtpakkŭi* 뜻밖의 unexpected; surprising; accidental. *ttŭtpakke* 뜻밖에 unexpectedly; all of a sudden.

ttŭtta 뜯다 ① take down; tear apart ② pluck; pick ③ play; perform on ④ bite[gnaw] off ⑤ clamor for; importune.

ttwida 뛰다 ① run; dash ② jump; leap; skip.

ttwiŏgada 뛰어가다 run; rush; dash; dart.

ttwiŏnada 뛰어나다 (be) superior (to); excel (in).

tubu 두부 bean-curd. *tubu changsu* 두부 장수 bean-curd seller[dealer].

tuda 두다 put; place; lay; set.

tŭdiŏ 드디어 finally; at last; eventually; at length.

tudŏlgŏrida, t'udŏlgŏrida 두덜거리다, 투덜거리다 grumble; mutter; complain.

tudŭrida, ttudŭrida 두드리다, 뚜드리다 strike; beat; hit; knock.

tudŭrŏgi 두드러기 nettle rash.

tugŭn-gŏrida 두근거리다 palpitate; throb.

tuk 둑 bank; dike; embankment.

tŭkchŏm 득점 marks; point; score. *tŭkchŏmhada*

득점하다 score (a point).

tukkŏpta 두껍다 (be) thick; thick and heavy. *tukkŏpke* 두껍게 thickly; heavily. *tukkŏun ch'aek* 두꺼운 책 thick book.

tul 둘 two. *tulssik* 둘씩 by[in] twos.

tŭl 들 field; plain; green.

tŭlda 들다 take[have, carry] in one's hand; hold.

tŭlda 들다 clear (up); stop (raining).

tŭlkŏt 들것 litter; stretcher.

tŭlguk'wa 들국화 wild chrysanthemum.

tulle 둘레 circumference; girth. *tullee* 둘레에 round; around; about.

tŭllil 들일 farm work; field labor.

tŭllori 들놀이 picnic; outing. *tŭllori kada* 들놀이 가다 go on a picnic.

tŭllŭda 들르다 drop[look] in at; stop by[in] (*Am.*); visit; stop over

tultchae 둘째 the second; number two(No. 2). *tultchaero* 둘째로 second(ly); in the second place.

tŭltchuknaltchuk'ada 들쭉날쭉하다 (be) uneven; rugged; indented.

tumok 두목 chief; head; leader; boss; ringleader.

tŭmulda 드물다 (be) rare; scarce; unusual; uncommon. *tŭmulge* 드물게 rarely; seldom.

tŭmundŭmun 드문드문 occasionally; once in a while; at (rare, long) intervals.

tŭng 등 ① back ② ridge.

tŭngdae 등대 lighthouse; beacon.

tŭndŭnhada 든든하다 ① (be) strong; firm; stout; solid ② heartening; feel safe[secure].

tunggŭlda 둥글다 (be) round; circular; globular.

tŭngjang 등장. *tŭngjanghada* 등장하다 enter[appear] on the stage. *tŭngjang inmul* 등장 인물 dramatis personae; characters; cast.

tungji 둥지 nest.

tŭnggi 등기 registration; registry. *tŭnggi up'yŏn* 등기 우편 registered mail.

tŭngkol 등골 spine; line of the backbone.

tŭngnamu 등나무 wisteria.

tŭngnok 등록 registration; entry. *tŭngnok'ada* 등록하다 register; enroll.

tŭngpul 등불 lamplight; lamp. *tŭngpurŭl k'yŏda* 등불을 켜다 light a lamp.

tŭngsa 등사 copy; transcription. *tŭngsahada* 등사하다 copy; make a copy; reproduce; mimeograph. *tŭngsap'an* 등사판 mimeograph (machine).

tŭngsan 등산 mountain climbing; mountaineering. *tŭngsanhada* 등산하다 climb a mountain.

tunguri 둥우리 (square) basket; cage.

tunhada 둔하다 (be) dull; slow; slow-witted; stupid; thick-headed; dumb (*Am.*).

tunoe 두뇌 head; brains. *chŏnja tunoe* 전자 두뇌 electronic brain.

turebak 두레박 well-bucket.

tŭribatta 들이받다 run[bump] (a thing) into; butt; knock (a thing) against.

turibŏn-gŏrida 두리번거리다 look about[round].

tŭrida 드리다 give; offer up; present; dedicate.

tŭrik'ida 들이키다 drink up; drain; swallow.

tŭrŏgada 들어가다 ① enter; go[get, walk, step] in[into] ② join; enter.

turŏng 두렁 levee; bank of a rice-paddy.

tŭrŏnupta 드러눕다 lie down; lay oneself down; lie oneself down; lie on one's back.

turŭda 두르다 enclose; encircle; surround.
turumari 두루마리 roll (of paper); scroll.
turumi 두루미 (white) crane; sacred crane.
tŭryŏdaboda 들여다보다 ① peep [look, peek] into; see through [into] ② gaze [stare] (at); observe; watch.
turyŏwohada 두려워하다 fear; be afraid of; dread.
tusŏnŏ, tusŏnŏt 두서너, 두서넛 two or three; a few.
tut'ong 두통 headache. *tut'ongi nada* 두통이 나다 have a (bad, slight) headache.
tŭtta 듣다 ① hear; listen (to); lend an ear to ② obey; accede to ③ be good [effective] (for).
twaeji 돼지 pig; swine; hog. *twaejigogi* 돼지고기 pork. *twaejigirŭm* 돼지기름 lard.
twi 뒤 back; rear; next; after; future; tail; reverse. *twie* 뒤에 afterwards; later.
twiboda 뒤보다 go to stool; ease [relieve] oneself.
twich'uk 뒤축 heel. *twich'ugi nop'ŭn [najŭn]* 뒤축이 높은 [낮은] high [low]-heeled.
twidŏpta 뒤덮다 cover; overspread; veil; hang over; wrap; muffle. ⌈out; turn upside down.
twijipta 뒤집다 turn over; turn (a coat) inside
twinggulda 뒹굴다 roll (about); tumble about.
twiŏpta 뒤엎다 upset; overturn; overthrow.
twisŏkta 뒤섞다 mix up; mingle together.
twisungsunghada 뒤숭숭하다 ① (be) confused; disturbed ② be [feel] restless; uneasy.
twitchim 뒷짐. *twitchimjida* 뒷짐지다 fold one's hands behind one's back.
twitchotta 뒤쫓다 follow; go after; pursue; chase.
twitkolmok 뒷골목 back alley [lane, street].

twittari 뒷다리 hind leg.

twittŏlmi 뒷덜미 nape; back[scruff] of the neck.

twittŏrŏjida 뒤떨어지다 ① fall[drop] behind; be backward ② stay behind.

twit'ŭlda 뒤틀다 twist; wrench.

T'

t'ada 타다 burn; blaze.

t'ada 타다 ride; take; take[have] a ride in; get in[on]; go[get] aboard; embark in[on].

t'ada 타다 play (on); perform on.

t'aea 태아 embryo; unborn child.

t'aedo 태도 attitude; manner; behavior; bearing.

t'aegŭkki 태극기 national flag of Korea.

t'aek'ada 택하다 choose; make choice (of); select.

t'aeman 태만 negligence; neglect. *t'aemanhan* 태만한 neglectful; negligent.

t'aeŏnada 태어나다 be born; come into the world.

t'aep'yŏngnyang 태평양 Pacific (Ocean).

t'aesaeng 태생 ① viviparity ② birth; origin; lineage. *oeguk t'aesaengŭi* 외국 태생의 foreign-born.

t'aeuda 태우다 carry; let ride; take on board.

t'aeuda 태우다 burn; kindle. *hyangŭl t'aeuda* 향을 태우다 burn incense.

t'aeyang 태양 sun. *t'aeyangŭi* 태양의 solar. *t'aeyangnyŏl* 태양열 solar heat. *t'aeyangnyŏl chut'aek* 태양열 주택 solar house.

t'agaso 탁아소 day[public] nursery.

t'agonada 타고나다 be born[gifted] (with)

t'agyŏk 타격 blow; hit; shock. *t'agyŏgŭl chuda* 타격을 주다 strike a blow.

t'ahyang 타향 strange[foreign] land.

t'ain 타인 another person; stranger.

t'airŭda 타이르다 reason; admonish; advise.

t'aja 타자 batter; batman.

t'ajagi 타자기 typewriter. *yŏngmun t'ajagi* 영문 타 자기 English character typewriter.

t'ajasu 타자수 typist.

t'akcha 탁자 table; desk.

t'akchu 탁주 →**makkŏlli** 막걸리.

t'akku 탁구 ping-pong; table tennis.

t'al 탈 mask. *t'arŭl ssŭda* 탈을 쓰다 wear a mask.

t'alchimyŏn 탈지면 absorbent[sanitary] cotton.

t'alse 탈세 evasion of taxes. *t'alsehada* 탈세하 다 evade[dodge] a tax.

t'alsŏn 탈선 ① derailment ② digression. *t'alsŏn-hada* 탈선하다 (be) derailed; make a digression.

t'alt'oe 탈퇴 secession; withdrawal. *t'alt'oehada* 탈퇴하다 secede; withdraw; leave.

t'amgu 탐구 search; investigation. *t'amguhada* 탐 구하다 search for; seek for.

t'amhŏm 탐험 exploration; expedition. *t'amhŏmhada* 탐험하다 explore.

t'amnaeda 탐내다 want; wish; covet; be greedy [hanker] for (money).

t'anap 탄압 oppression; suppression. *t'anap'ada* 탄 압하다 suppress; oppress; bring pressure upon.

t'anhaek 탄핵 impeachment; denunciation.

t'anhwan 탄환 shot; bullet; shell.

t'ansaeng 탄생 birth; nativity. *t'ansaenghada* 탄생 하다 be born; come into the world.

t'anshik 탄식 sigh; lamentation. *t'anshik'ada* 탄 식하다 (heave[draw] a) sigh; lament; deplore.

t'anso 탄소 carbon. *t'ansoŭi* 탄소의 carbonic.

t'anyak 탄약 (a round of) ammunition. *t'anyakko* 탄약고 (powder) magazine.

t'ap 탑 tower; pagoda; steeple.

t'apsŭng 탑승. *t'apsŭnghada* 탑승하다 board[get on] (a plane). *t'apsŭnggaek* 탑승객 passenger.

t'arae 타래 bunch; skein; coil. *shil han t'arae* 실 한 타래 a skein of thread.

t'arak 타락 degradation; corruption. *t'arak'ada* 타락하다 be corrupted; degenerate. *t'arak'an* 타락한 corrupt; fallen; depraved.

t'arŭi 탈의. *t'arŭishil* 탈의실 dressing[changing] room. *t'arŭijang* 탈의장 bathing booth.

t'awon 타원 oval; elliptic. *t'awonhyŏng* 타원형 oval; ellipticity.

t'e 테 ① hoop; band; stripe ② rim; brim; frame.

t'ikkŭl 티끌 dust; mote.

t'ŏ 터 site; place; ground; lot. *chipt'ŏ* 집터 building lot[site, land].

t'ŏbŏkt'ŏbŏk 터벅터벅 ploddingly; trudgingly.

t'odae 토대 foundation; base; groundwork.

t'odam 토담 earthen wall; mud wall; dirt wall.

t'oegŭn 퇴근. *t'oegŭnhada* 퇴근하다 leave one's office; go home from work.

t'oehak 퇴학. *t'oehak'ada* 퇴학하다 leave[give up, quit] school (halfway).

t'oejik 퇴직 retirement; resignation. *t'oejik'ada* 퇴직하다 retire from office.

t'oewon 퇴원. *t'oewonhada* 퇴원하다 leave (the) hospital.

t'ogŏnŏp 토건업 civil engineering and construction.

t'ogul 토굴 cavern; cave; den; grotto.

t'ohada 토하다 vomit; spit; throw[fetch] up.

t'oji 토지 land; soil; earth.

t'ŏjida 터지다 explode; burst; erupt; blowup; break-out; rip; tear; collapse; disclosed; be struck; split.

t'ŏk 턱 jaw; chin. *t'ŏkppyŏ* 턱뼈 jawbone. *araet'ŏk* 아래턱 lower jaw.

t'okki 토끼 rabbit; hare.

t'okkip'ul 토끼풀 clover.

t'okt'ok'i 톡톡히 much; lot; great deal. *t'okt'ok'i pŏlda* 톡톡히 벌다 make quite a lot of money.

t'ŏl 털 hair. *t'ŏri manŭn* 털이 많은 hairy; haired.

t'ŏlbo 털보 hairy[shaggy] man.

t'ŏlda 털다 shake off; throw off; dust; brush up.

t'ŏljanggap 털장갑 fur[woolen] gloves.

t'ŏlshil 털실 wool(l)en yarn; knitting wool.

t'ŏlt'ŏrhada 털털하다 (be) unaffected; free and easy.

t'omak 토막 piece; bit; block. *t'omangnaeda* 토막 내다 sever; cut in pieces.

t'omnibak'wi 톱니바퀴 toothed wheel; cogwheel.

t'omok 토목 engineering works. *t'omok kongsa* 토목 공사 public (engineering) works.

t'ŏmuniŏpta 터무니없다 (be) groundless; unreasonable; absurd.

t'ong 통 tub; barrel; pail; bucket. *mult'ong* 물통 water bucket. *sult'ong* 술통 wine-barrel.

t'ongch'i 통치 rule; government. *t'ongch'ihada* 통치하다 rule; reign over.

t'ongdak 통닭. *t'ongdakkui* 통닭구이 roast chicken; chicken roasted whole.

t'onggam 통감. *t'onggamhada* 통감하다 feel keenly.

t'onggŭn 통근. *t'onggŭnhada* 통근하다 attend office; commute. *t'onggŭn pŏsŭ*[*yŏlch'a*] 통근 버스[열차] commuters' bus[train].

t'onggwa 통과 passage; passing. *t'onggwahada* 통과하다 pass; pass by[through].

t'onggwan 통관. *t'onggwanhada* 통관하다 pass the customs. *t'onggwan chŏlch'a* 통관 절차 customs formalities; clearance.

t'onggye 통계 statistics. *t'onggye*(*sang*)*ŭi* 통계 (상)의 statistic(al).

t'onghada 통하다 ① run[lead] to ② be understood ③ be familiar (with).

t'onghaeng 통행 passing; traffic. *t'onghaenghada* 통행하다 pass (by); go along.

t'onghak 통학. *t'onghak'ada* 통학하다 attend[go to] school.

t'onghwa 통화 currency; current coins[money].

t'onghwa 통화 (telephone) call. *t'onghwajung* 통화중 The line is busy.

t'ongil 통일 unity; unification. *t'ongirhada* 통일하다 unify. *nambuk t'ongil* 남북 통일 unification of North and South (Korea).

t'ongjang 통장 passbook. *yegŭm t'ongjang* 예금 통장 bankbook; deposit passbook.

t'ongji 통지 notice; report; notification; information. *t'ongjihada* 통지하다 inform; notify.

t'ongjorim 통조림 canned goods. *t'ongjorimhan* 통조림한 canned; tinned. *soegogi t'ongjorim* 쇠고기 통조림 canned[tinned] beef.

t'ongk'wae 통쾌. *t'ongk'waehan* 통쾌한 extremely delightful; thrilling; very exciting.

t'ongnamu 통나무 log. *t'ongnamu tari* 통나무 다리 log bridge. *t'ongnamujip* 통나무집 log cabin.

t'ongno 통로 passage; passageway; way; path; aisle.

tongsang 통상 commerce; trade; commercial relations. *t'ongsanghada* 통상하다 trade with. *t'ongsang choyak* 통상 조약 commercial treaty.

t'ongshin correspondence; communication. *t'ongshinhada* 통신하다 correspond (with).

t'ungso 퉁소 bamboo flute.

t'ongsol 통솔 command; leadership. *t'ongsorhada* 통솔하다 command; control; lead.

t'ongtchae(ro) 통째(로) whole; wholly; bodily. *t'ongtchaero mŏkta* 통째로 먹다 eat (something) whole.

t'ongt'onghada 통통하다 (be) plump; chubby.

t'ongyŏk 통역 interpretation. *t'ongyŏk'ada* 통역하다 interpret. *t'ongyŏkcha* 통역자 interpreter.

t'op 톱 saw; handsaw. *t'oppap* 톱밥 sawdust.

t'ŏpsuruk'ada 텁수룩하다 (be) unkempt; untrimmed; shaggy; bushy.

t'orajida 토라지다 pout; sulk; get sulky[cross].

t'oron 토론 discussion; debate. *t'oronhada* 토론하다 debate (on); discuss (with). *t'oronhoe* 토론회 forum; debate.

t'ŏrot 털옷 fur[woolen] garment.

t'osanmul 토산물 local products; native produce.

t'oshilt'oshil 토실토실. *t'oshilt'oshirhan* 토실토실한 plump; chubby; puffy.

t'ŏttŭrida 터뜨리다 explode; burst; break.

t'oŭi 토의 discussion; debate. *t'oŭihada* 토의하다 discuss; debate[deliberate] upon.

t'oyoil 토요일 Saturday.

t'ubak'ada 투박하다 ① (be) crude; vulgar ② (be)

coarse; unseemly; unshapely.
t'uch'ang 투창 javelin throw(ing). *t'uch'ang sŏnsu* 투창 선수 javelin thrower.
t'ŭda 트다 ① sprout; bud out ② be chapped.
t'udŏlgŏrida 투덜거리다 grumble (at, about, over); complain (of); murmur.
t'ŭgi 트기 hybrid; half-breed[blood]; mulatto.
t'ŭgyakchŏm 특약점 special agent; agency.
t'uja 투자 investment. *t'ujahada* 투자하다 invest; put[sink] in; lay out.
t'ujaeng 투쟁 fight;strife; struggle. *t'ujaenghada* 투쟁하다 fight; struggle.
t'ŭjip chapta 트집 잡다 find fault with; pick flaws [holes] in.
t'ŭkching 특징 characteristic; special feature. *t'ŭkching innŭn* 특징 있는 characteristic; peculiar.
t'ŭkchŏn 특전 privilege; special favo(u)r.
t'ŭkkongdae 특공대 commando; ranger corps(*Am.*).
t'ŭkkŭp 특급 limitted[special] express. *t'ŭkkŭp yŏlch'a* 특급 열차 special express (train).
t'ŭkkwon 특권 privilege. *t'ŭkkwon gyegŭp* 특권 계급 privileged class(es).
t'ŭk'ŏ 특허 patent. *t'ŭk'ŏkwon* 특허권 patent right. *t'ŭk'ŏp'um* 특허품 patented article.
t'ŭkpyŏl 특별. *t'ŭkpyŏrhan* 특별한 special; particular. *t'ŭkpyŏrhi* 특별히 particularly; specially.
t'ŭksa 특사 amnesty; special pardon. *t'ŭksahada* 특사하다 grant an amnesty.
t'ŭksaek 특색 →**t'ŭkching** 특징.
t'ŭksang 특상 special prize[reward].   「ciality.
t'ŭksanmul 특산물 special product; (local) spe-
t'ŭksu 특수. *t'uksuhan* 특수한 special; particular;

specific; peculiar.

t'ŭktŭng 특등 special class[grade]; top grade.

t'ŭl 틀 ① frame; framework ② mold.

t'ŭllida 틀리다 go wrong[amiss]; be mistaken[erroneous]. *t'ŭllin* 틀린 mistaken; wrong; false.

t'ŭm 틈 crevice; crack; gap; opening.

t'umyŏng 투명. *t'umyŏnghan* 투명한 transparent; lucid; limpid; clear.

t'ŭnt'ŭnhada 튼튼하다 ① (be) robust; sturdy; stout ② solid; firm; strong.

t'up'yo 투표 vote. *t'up'yohada* 투표하다 vote; ballot (for); give[cast] a vote[ballot].

t'ŭrim 트림 belch. *t'ŭrimhada* 트림하다 belch; burp.

t'ŭrŏmakta 틀어막다 ① stop up; stuff; plug ② muzzle; gag ③ obstruct; disturb; binder.

t'usŏ 투서 anonymous letter. *t'usŏhada* 투서하다 send (a note) anonymously.

t'usu 투수 pitcher.

t'uu 투우 bullfight. *t'uusa* 투우사 bullfighter; matador. *t'uujang* 투우장 bull ring.

t'wida 튀다 ① spring; bound; hop; bounce ② run away; flee; sneak away.

t'wigida 튀기다 ① flip; snap ② splash; spatter.

t'wigim 튀김 (batter) fried food; fried dish; fry.

◄◄ U ►►

ua 우아 elegance. *uahan* 우아한 elegant; graceful.

ubang 우방 friendly nation; ally; allied nation.

uch'e 우체. *uch'eguk* 우체국 post office; *uch'et'ong* 우체통 post; mailbox (*Am.*).

uch'ŭk 우측 right side. *uch'ŭk t'onghaeng* 우측 통행 "keep to the right."

udae 우대 special[warm] treatment. *udaehada* 우대하다 treat warmly[cordially]. *udaekwon* 우대권 complimentary ticket.

udu 우두 cowpox; vaccinia.

uduk'ŏni 우두커니 absent-mindedly; vacantly; blankly; idly.

udumŏri 우두머리 top; head; boss; chief.

udŭng 우등 top[superior] grade; excellency. *udŭngŭi* 우등의 excellent; superior. *udŭngsang* 우등상 honor prize.

ugida 우기다 demand one's own way; force; persist in; assert; stick to; be obstinate.

ugŏjida 우거지다 be[grow] thick; dense; luxuriant; be overgrown with.

ugŏjisang 우거지상 frown[wry] face; scowl.

ugŭlgŏrida 우글거리다 swarm; be crowded; be alive with.

ugŭrŏjida 우그러지다 be crushed out of shape; be dented; hollowed; depressed.

uhwa 우화 fable; allegory.

ŭibok 의복 clothes; garments; clothing.

ŭich'i 의치 false[artificial] tooth; denture.

ŭido 의도 intention; design; aim. *ŭidohada* 의도하다 intend (to do); aim at.

ŭigi yangyang 의기 양양. *ŭigi yangyanghada* 의기 양양하다 (be) triumphant; be in high spirits.

ŭigyŏn 의견 opinion; view; idea. *ŭigyŏnŭi taerip [ch'ungdol]* 의견의 대립[충돌] disagree[opposition, conflict, split, clash] of opinion.

ŭihak 의학 medical science; medicine.

ŭihoe 의회 National Assembly(*Korea*) ; Parliament (*Eng.*) ; Congress(*Am.*) ; Diet(*Jap.・Den.・Swed*).

ŭija 의자 chair; bench. *kin ŭija* 긴의자 sofa; couch.

ŭijang 의장 chairman; Speaker.

ŭiji 의지 will; volition.

ŭiji 의지 leaning; trust; reliance. *ŭijihada* 의지하다 lean on; depend[rely] on[upon].

uik 우익 right wing[flank, column]; rightists. *uiksu* 우익수 right fielder.

ŭikwa 의과 medical department. *ŭikwadaehak* 의과 대학 medical college.

ŭimi 의미 meaning; sense; significance. *ŭimihada* 의미하다 mean; imply; signify.

ŭimu 의무 duty; obligation. *ŭimujŏk* 의무적 obligatory; compulsory.

ŭimun 의문 question; doubt. *ŭimunŭi* 의문의 doubtful; questionable.

ŭinon 의논 consultation; conference. *ŭinonhada* 의논하다 consult (with); counsel (with).

ŭioe 의외. *ŭioeŭi* 의외의 unexpected; unforeseen. *ŭioero* 의외로 unexpectedly.

ŭiri 의리 duty; obligation; justice.

ŭiroe 의뢰 request; trust. *ŭiroehada* 의뢰하다 request; ask; entrust; commission.

ŭiryo 의료 medical treatment. *ŭiryo pohŏm* 의료 보험 medical (care) insurance. *ŭiryobi* 의료비 medical expenses[fee].

ŭisa 의사 doctor; physician; surgeon. *ŭisa chindansŏ* 의사 진단서 medical certificate.

ŭisa 의사 intention; mind; purpose.

ŭisang 의상 clothes; dresses; garments; costume.

ŭishik 의식 consciousness; senses. *ŭishik'ada* 의

식하다 be conscious[aware] of.
ŭishikchu 의식주 food, clothing[clothes] and shelter [housing].
ŭishim 의심 doubt; question. *ŭishimhada* 의심하다 doubt; be doubtful of; suspect.
ŭiwon 의원 member of the Assembly; assemblyman; Congressman; Senator (*Am.*); member of Parliament (M.P.).
ŭiyak 의약 medicine; physic. *ŭiyakp'um* 의약품 medical supplies.
ŭiyok 의욕 volition; will; desire. *ŭiyokchŏgin* 의욕적인 ambitious; aspiring.
ujŏng 우정 friendship; fellowship. *ujŏngi innŭn* 우정이 있는 amicable; friendly.
uju 우주 universe; cosmos; aero space. *ujuŭi* 우주의 universal; cosmic. *uju yŏhaeng* 우주 여행 space travel[flight].
ulda 울다 cry; weep.
ult'ari 울타리 fence; hedge.
ŭm 음 sound; note; tone.
ŭmak 음악 music. *ŭmakchŏk* 음악적 musical. melodious. *ŭmakka* 음악가 musician.
ŭmban 음반 phonograph record.
umch'ŭrida 움츠리다 shrink; hang back; recoil.
ŭmdok 음독. *ŭmdok chasal* 음독 자살 (commit) suicide by taking poison.
ŭmhyang 음향 sound; noise. *ŭmhyang hyokwa* 음향 효과 sound effect.
umjigida 움직이다 ① move; stir; shift ② work; operate; run ③ be moved[touched, affected].
ŭmjŏl 음절 syllable. *taŭmjŏrŏ* 다음절어 polysyllable.
ŭmju 음주 drinking. *ŭmju unjŏn* 음주 운전 drunken

driving.

umk'yŏ chapta umk'yŏ chwida 움켜 잡다 움켜 쥐다 seize; grab; clench; grasp; grip; hold.

ummak 움막 hut; dugout; hovel; shack.

ŭmmo 음모 plot; conspiracy. *ŭmmohada* 음모하다 plot; intrigue. *ŭmmoga* 음모가 conspirator; schemer.

ŭmnyo 음료 beverage; drink. *ŭmnyosu* 음료수 drinking water.

ŭmnyŏk 음력 lunar calendar.

ŭmshik 음식 food; foodstuff; diet.

ŭmsŏng 음성 voice. →**moksori** 목소리.

ŭmt'ang 음탕. *ŭmt'anghan* 음탕한 dissipated; lewd; obscene; wanton.

umul 우물 well. *umulmul* 우물물 well-water.

umulgŏrida 우물거리다 mumble; mump.

umultchumul 우물쭈물 hesitantly; hesitatingly. *umultchumurhada* 우물쭈물하다 hesitate; waver.

un 운 fortune; luck. *uni chok'e* 운이 좋게 fortunately; luckily; by good luck. *uni nappŭge* 운이 나쁘게 unluckily; unfortunately; by ill luck.

ŭn 은 silver. *un-gŭrŭt* 은그릇 silverware.

unban 운반 conveyance; transportation. *unbanhada* 운반하다 carry; convey; transport.

ŭnban 은반 ① silver plate ② skating rink.

ŭnch'ong 은총 favo(u)r; grace. *ŭnch'ongŭl ipta* 은총을 입다 be in favor with.

undong 운동 ① motion; movement ② sports; exercise. *undonghada* 운동하다 take exercise; move. *undonghoe* 운동회 athletic meet.

undonghwa 운동화 sports shoes; sneakers(*Am.*).

ungbyŏn 웅변 eloquence; fluency. *ungbyŏn-ga* 웅변가 eloquent speeker.

ŭnggŭp 응급 emergency. *ŭnggŭp ch'iryŏ* 응급 치료 first aid; first-aid treatment.

ungjang 웅장. *ungjanghan* 웅장한 grand; magnificent; sublime; majestic.

ŭngjŏp 응접 reception; interview. *ŭngjŏp'ada* 응접하다 receive (a visitor).

ŭngmo 응모 subscription; application. *ŭngmohada* 응모하다 apply for; make an application.

ungŏlgŏrida 웅얼거리다 mutter; murmur.

ŭngŏri 응어리 knot[cramp] in a muscle.

ŭngshi 응시. *ŭngshihada* 응시하다 apply for an examination.

ŭngsŏkpurida 응석부리다 play the baby; presume upon another's love.

ŭn-gŭp 은급 →**yŏn-gŭm** 연금.

ŭngwon 응원 aid; help; support. *ŭngwonhada* 응원하다 aid; assist; support.

ŭngyong 응용 (practical) application. *ŭngyonghada* 응용하다 apply. *ŭngyong munje* 응용 문제 applied question.

unha 운하 canal; waterway (*Am.*).

ŭnhaeng 은행 bank. *ŭnhaengkwon* 은행권 bank bill[note]. *ŭnhaengju* 은행주 bank stock.

ŭnhonshik 은혼식 silver wedding (anniversary).

ŭnhye 은혜 favor; benefit; grace.

unim 운임 ① fare ② freight rates (*Am.*); goods rates; freightage; shipping charge[expenses].

ŭnin 은인 benefactor; patron.

unjŏn 운전. *unjŏnhada* 운전하다 drive; operate. *unjŏn kisa* 운전 기사 driver; chauffeur.

ŭnmak 은막 (silver) screen; filmdom.

unmyŏng 운명 fate; destiny; fortune; one's lot.

ŭnŏ 은어 secret language; jargon; argot; cant.

ŭnpit 은빛 silver (color). *ŭnpich'ŭi* 은빛의 silver-colored; silvery.

ŭnsa 은사 hermit; recluse.

ŭnsa 은사 one's (respected) teacher; one's former teacher.

ŭnt'oe 은퇴 retirement. *ŭnt'oehada* 은퇴하다 retire.

unyŏng 운영 operation; management. *unyŏnghada* 운영하다 manage; run; operate.

up'yo 우표 postage-stamp; stamp.

up'yŏn 우편 post(*Eng.*); mail(*Am.*). *up'yŏn paedalbu* 우편 배달부 mailman.

uri 우리 we. *uriŭi* 우리의 our. *uriege* 우리에게 us. *urirŭl* 우리를 us.

uri 우리 cage; pen; fold; corral.

ŭriŭrihada 으리으리하다 (be) magnificent; majestic; stately; be overawed (by); gorgeously.

uroe 우뢰 thunder. *uroe kat'ŭn* 우뢰 같은 thunderous.

urŏnada 우러나다 soak out; come off; draw.

urong 우롱 mockery; derision. *uronghada* 우롱하다 mock (at); fool; make fun[a fool] of.

urŏngch'ada 우렁차다 (be) resounding; resonant.

urŏrŏboda 우러러보다 look up (at); look upward.

ŭrŭda 으르다 threaten; menace; intimidate.

urŭm 울음 crying; weeping. *urŭmŭl t'ŏttŭrida* 울음을 터뜨리다 burst out crying.

ŭrŭrŏnggŏrida 으르렁거리다 roar; growl; howl.

ŭrye 으레 habitually; usually; all the time.

uryŏ 우려 worry; anxiety; fear. *uryŏhada* 우려하다 worry over; be anxious about.

usan 우산 umbrella. *usanŭl ssŭda* 우산을 쓰다 put up[raise] an umbrella.

usang 우상 idol; image. *usanghwahada* 우상화하다 idolize. *usang sungbae* 우상 숭배 idol worship.

use 우세 superiority; predominance. *usehada* 우세하다 (be) superior; predominant.

usŏn 우선 first (of all); in the first place.

usu 우수. *usuhan* 우수한 good; excellent; superior.

usŭgae 우스개 jocularity. *usŭgaessori* 우스갯소리 joke; jest; fun; pleasantry.

usŭm 웃음 laugh; laughter; smile; ridicule.

usŭng 우승 victory; championship. *usŭnghada* 우승하다 win the championship.

usŭpta 우습다 (be) funny; amusing; laughable.

ŭsŭsŭ 으스스. *ŭsŭsŭhan* 으스스한 chilly; chill; be thrilled.

utta 웃다 ① laugh; smile; chuckle; grim ② laugh [sneer] at; ridicule; jeer at.

uttuk 우뚝 high; aloft. *uttuk'ada* 우뚝하다 (be) high; lofty; towering.

ŭttŭm 으뜸 first; top; head. *ŭttŭmganŭn* 으뜸가는 the first; the best; top; leading.

uul 우울. *uurhan* 우울한 melancholy; gloomy.

uyŏl 우열 superiority and inferiority. *uyŏrŭl tat'uda* 우열을 다투다 vie for superiority.

uyŏn 우연 chance; accident. *uyŏnhan* 우연한 casual; accidental; unexpected. *uyŏnhi* 우연히 accidentally; by chance[accident]; incidental.

uyu 우유 (cow's) milk. *punmal uyu* 분말 우유 milk *pow*der.

W

wae 왜 why; how; for what reason.

waejŏng 왜정 Japanese rule. *waejŏng shidae* 왜정 시대 Japanese administration period.

waeshik 왜식 Japanese food. *waeshikchip* 왜식집 Japanese restaurant.

wagŭlgŏrida 와글거리다 ① throng; swarm; crowd ② be clamorous; noisy.

wanch'i 완치. *wanch'idoeda* 완치되다 be completely cured[recovered].

wandu 완두 pea. *p'udwandu* 풋완두 green pea.

wang 왕 king; monarch. *wangŭi* 왕의 royal.

wangbok 왕복 going and returning; round trip. *wangbok'ada* 왕복하다 go and return. *wangbok ch'ap'yo* 왕복 차표 return ticket.

wangbi 왕비 queen; empress.

wanggung 왕궁 king's[royal] palace.

wanggwan 왕관 crown.

wangja 왕자 (Royal, Imperial) prince.

wangjin 왕진 doctor's visit (to a patient). *wangjinhada* 왕진하다 call on one's patient.

wangjo 왕조 dynasty. *wangjoŭi* 왕조의 dynastic.

wan-go 완고 obstinacy; stubbornness. *wan-gohan* 완고한 stubborn; obstinate.

wangshil 왕실 royal family[household].

wanjang 완장 armband; brassard.

wanjŏn 완전 perfection; completeness. *wanjŏnhan* [*hi*] 완전한[히] perfect[ly]; complete[ly].

wannap 완납 full payment. *wannap'ada* 완납하다 pay in full.

wansŏng 완성 completion; perfection; accomplishment. *wansŏnghada* 완성하다 complete; accomplish; finish.

wennil 웬일 what matter; what business. *wenni-*

rinya 웬일이냐? what is the matter?

wi 위 stomach.

wi 위 upside; upper part. *wiŭi* 위의 upper; upward. *wie* 위에 above; over; on; upon.

wiban 위반 violation. *wibanhada* 위반하다 violate; disobey; break; be against.

wibŏp 위법 violation of law. *wibŏbŭi* 위법의 illegal; unlawful.

wich'i 위치 situation; location; position; place; site. *wich'ihada* 위치하다 be situated[located].

wich'uk 위축 withering. *wich'uk'ada* 위축하다 ① wither (away); shrink; dwindle ② be daunted.

widae 위대 greatness; mightiness. *widaehan* 위대한 great; mighty; grand.

wido 위도 latitude. *widoŭi* 위도의 latitudinal.

widok 위독. *widok'ada* 위독하다 (be) serious; critical; be seriously ill.

wigi 위기 crisis; critical moment.

wihada 위하다 do for the sake of; respect; value. *wihayŏ* 위하여 for; for the sake of.

wihŏm 위험 danger; peril; risk. *wihŏmhan* 위험한 dangerous; perilous.

wihyŏp 위협 menace; threat; intimidation. *wihyŏp'ada* 위협하다 menace; threaten; frighten.

wiim 위임 trust; commission; charge. *wiimhada* 위임하다 entrust; delegate to.

wiin 위인 great man; hero; mastermind.

wijang 위장 stomach and intestines.

wijo 위조 forgery; fabrication. *wijohada* 위조하다 forge; counterfeit. *wijochoe* 위조죄 forgery.

wimun 위문 consolation; consolatory visit. *wimunhada* 위문하다 console.

wiro 위로 consolation; solace; comfort. *wirohada* 위로하다 console; comfort.

wiryŏk 위력 great power; mighty force.

wisaeng 위생 hygiene; sanitation. *wisaengjŏk* 위생적 sanitary; hygienic.

wishin 위신 prestige; dignity; authority.

wisŏn 위선 hypocrisy. *wisŏnja* 위선자 hypocrite.

wisŏng 위성 satellite. *wisŏngguk* 위성국 satellite state. *wisŏng chungge* 위성 중계 satellite telecast.

wiwon 위원 member of a committee. *wiwonhoe* 위원회 committee; commission.

wolbu 월부 monthly instalment[payment].

wolbuk 월북. *wolbuk'ada* 월북하다 go to North Korea.

wolgan 월간 monthly publication. *wolganŭi* 월간의 monthly. *wolgan chapchi* 월간 잡지 monthly (magazine.).

wolgŭp 월급 monthly salary[pay].

wolgyŏng 월경 menstruation; menses[flowers].

wollam 월남. *wollamhada* 월남하다 come down to South Korea.

wolli 원리 principle; theory.   [timer.

wollo 원로 elder statesman; senior (member); old-

wollyŏ 원료 raw material; materials.

wolmal 월말. *wolmare[kkaji]* 월말에[까지] at[by] the end of the month.

wolse 월세 monthly rent.

wolsegye 월세계 lunar world; moon.

won 원 desire; wish. *wonhada* 원하다 desire; wish.

wonbon 원본 original(work; copy; text; document).

wonch'ik 원칙 principle; fundamental rule[law]; general rule.

wondongnyŏk 원동력 motive power[force].

won-gi 원기 vigo(u)r; energy; vitality; spirits.

won-go 원고 manuscript (MS.); copy; draft. *wongoryo* 원고료 copy money; contribution fee.

won-go 원고 accuser; plaintiff.

won-gŭm 원금 capital; principal.

wonhan 원한 grudge; bitter feeling; spite.

wonhyŏng 원형 archetype; prototype; model.

wonin 원인 cause; origin. *wonin-gwa kyŏlgwa* 원인과 결과 cause and effect.

wonja 원자 atom. *wonjaryŏk* 원자력 atomic energy. *wonja p'okt'an* 원자 폭탄 atom(ic) bomb; A-bomb.

wonjang 원장 director[president; superintendent] (of a hospital; an institution).

wonjo 원조 help; support; assistance; aid. *wonjohada* 원조하다 assist; help; support.

wonjŏng 원정 playing tour; expedition; visit.

wonka 원가 (prime) cost; cost price.

wonman 원만. *wonmanhan* 원만한 amicable; smooth; peaceful. *wonmanhi* 원만히 amicably; harmoniously; smoothly.

wonmang 원망 grudge; resentment. *wonmanghada* 원망하다 reproach; bear a grudge against.

wonŏ 원어 original language[word].

wonsaek 원색 primary color; original color(s).

wonshi 원시. *wonshijŏgin* 원시적인 primitive. *wonshi shidae* 원시 시대 primitive times.

wonsŏ 원서 (written) application; application form.

*won*su 원수 chief of state; sovereign; ruler.

wonsu 원수 general of the army; fleet admiral (*Am.*); (field) marshal; admiral of the fleet (*Eng.*).

wonsungi 원숭이 monkey; ape.
woryoil 월요일 Monday.

Y

ya 야 Oh, dear!; O my!; Hey (you)!; Hi; Hello.
yabi 야비. yabihan 야비한 vulgar; mean; coarse.
yach'ae 야채 vegetables; greens. *yach'ae kage* 야채 가게 greengrocery.
yadam 야담 unofficial historical romance[story].
yadang 야당 opposition party.
yagan 야간 night; night time. *yaganŭi* 야간의 night; nocturnal. *yagane* 야간에 at night.
yagollida 약올리다 make (a person) angry; fret; irritate; provoke.
yagu 야구 baseball. *yagu kyŏnggi* 야구 경기 baseball game. *yakujang* 야구장 baseball ground; ball park.
yagŭn 야근 night duty; night work. *yagŭnhada* 야근하다 take night duty; be on night work.
yahoe 야회 evening party. *yahoebok* 야회복 evening dress[suit].
yak 약 medicine; remedy; drug. *yakpang* 약방 drugstore; pharmacy.
yak 약 about; some; nearly; around (*Am.*).
yak'ada 약하다 (be) weak; frail; delicate; faint. *yak'age* 약하게 weakly; feebly; faintly.
yak'ada 약하다. →**saengnyak'ada** 생략하다.
yakcha 약자 the weak; weak person.
yakcha 약자 simplified character.
yakche 약제 drugs; medicine. *yakchesa* 약제사 druggist; pharmacist (*Am.*); chemist (*Eng.*).

yakch'o 약초 medical herbs[plants].

yakchŏm 약점 weak point; disadvantage; one's blind side; weakness.

yakchu 약주 ① rice wine ② medicinal liquor.

yakkap 약값 charge for medicine; medical[drug] fee; pharmacy's bill.

yakkan 약간 some; little; bit; few; somewhat.

yakkuk 약국 pharmacy; drugstore (*Am.*); chemist's shop (*Eng.*).

yak'on 약혼 engagment; betrothal. *yak'onhada* 약혼하다 engage oneself to; getengaged. *yak'on panji* 약혼반지 engagement ring.

yakpang 약방. → **yakkuk** 약국.

yakp'um 약품 medicines; drugs; chemicals.

yakso 약소. *yaksohan* 약소한 small and weak. *yakso kukka* 약소 국가 lesser[minor] power.

yaksok 약속 promise; engagement. *yaksok'ada* 약속하다 promise. *yaksogŭl chik'ida* 약속을 지키다 keep one's promise.

yaksom 약솜 sanitary cotton. →**t'alchimyŏn** 탈지면.

yakt'al 약탈 plunder; pillage. *yakt'arhada* 약탈하다 plunder; loot; sack; strip.

yakto 약도 rough sketch; sketch map.

yalgutta 얄궂다 (be) perverse; eccentric; queer. *yalgujŭn saram* 얄궂은 사람 queer[odd] fish.

yalmipta 얄밉다 (be) offensive; hateful; detestable.

yaman 야만. *yamanjŏk* 야만적 savage; barbarous. *yamanin* 야만인 barbarian; savage.

yamang 야망 personal ambition; aspiration.

yamjŏnhada 얌전하다 (be) gentle; well-behaved; modest. *yamjŏnhi* 얌전히 gently; modestly.

yamujida 야무지다 (be) stout; sturdy; staunch.

yamujige 야무지게 firmly; steadily.
yang 양 sheep; lamb. *yanggajuk* 양가죽 sheepskin. *yanggogi* 양고기 mutton. *yangt'ŏl* 양털 wool.
yang 양 quantity; amount; volume.
yangban 양반 nobility; nobleman. *chuin yangban* 주인 양반 master (of a house).
yangbo 양보 concession; compromise. *yangbohada* 양보하다 concede (to); make a concession.
yangbok 양복 Western[European] clothes. *yangbokchŏm* 양복점 tailor; tailor's (shop); slopshop.
yangbuin 양부인 →**yanggalbo** 양갈보.
yangbun 양분 nourishment; nutriment.
yangch'in 양친 parents. *yangch'inŭi* 양친의 parental.
yangch'o 양초 candle; taper.
yangch'ŏl 양철 galvanized iron; tin plate. *yangch'ŏl chibung* 양철 지붕 tin roof.
yangdo 양도 transfer; conveyance. *yangdohada* 양도하다 transfer (to); convey.
yangdon 양돈 hog[pig]-farming. *yangdonhada* 양돈하다 raise[rear] hogs.
yanggalbo 양갈보 foreigners' whore.
yanggok 양곡 corn; grain; cereals; provisions. *yanggoksang* 양곡상 grainmerchant.
yanggung 양궁 western-style archery.
yanggwaja 양과자 Western confectionary[cakes].
yanggye 양계 poultry farming; chicken raising. *yanggyehada* 양계하다 raise poultry.
yanghae 양해 understanding; comprehension. *yanghaehada* 양해하다 understand; comprehend.
yanghwa 양화 →**kudu** 구두. *yanghwajŏm* 양화점 shoe store.
yangja 양자 foster child; adopted son.

yangjae 양재 dressmaking. *yangjaesa* 양재사 dressmaker.

yangjang 양장 foreign[Western] style of dress. *yangjanghada* 양장하다 be dressed in Western style. *yangjangjŏm* 양장점 dressmaker's (shop).

yangjo 양조 brewing; brewage; distillation. *yangjohada* 양조하다 brew; distill.

yangju 양주 foreign wine[liquors].

yangmal 양말 socks; stockings.

yangmo 양모 wool. *yangmoŭi* 양모의 woolen.

yangmul 약물 drugstuffs; medicines. *yangmul chungdok* 약물 중독 medical poisoning.

yangmyŏn 양면 both faces[sides]. *yangmyŏnŭi* 양면의 double[both]-sided.

yangnyŏ 양녀 foster daughter; adopted daughter.

yangnyŏm 양념 spices; flavo(u)r; seasoning; condiments.

yangnyŏk 양력 solar calendar.

yangnyŏk 약력 brief (personal) history[record].

yangok 양옥 Western-style house.

yangp'um 양품 foreign articles[goods]. *yangp'umjŏm* 양품점 fancy(-goods) store.

yangsan 양산 parasol. *yangsanŭl p'yŏda[chŏpta, ssŭda]* 양산을 펴다[접다, 쓰다] open[close, put-up] a parasol.

yangshik 양식 form; style; mode. *saenghwal yangshik* 생활 양식 style[mode] of living.

yangshik 양식 Western[European] style.

yangshik 양식 Western food; foreign dishes; foreign cookery. *yangshikchŏm* 양식점 foreign-style[Western] restaurant.

yangshik 양식 provisions; food. *yangshigŭl taeda*

양식을 대다 provide (a person) with food.

yangshim 양심 conscience. *yangshimŭi kach'aek* 양심의 가책 pangs[pricks] of conscience.

yangsŏ 양서 foreign[Western] book.

yangsŏ 양서 good book; valuable work.

yangt'anja 양탄자 carpet; rug. *yangt'anjarŭl kkalda* 양탄자를 깔다 spread a carpet[rug].

yangtchok 양쪽 both sides; either side. *yangtchogŭi* 양쪽의 both; either.

yaoe 야외 field; open air. *yaoeŭi* 야외의 outdoor; open air. *yaoe-esŏ* 야외에서 in the open air.

yarŭt'ada 야릇하다 (be) queer; odd; curious.

yashim 야심 ambition; designs; treason; treachery. *yashimjŏk* 야심적 ambitious.

yasu 야수 wild beast. *yasu kat'ŭn* 야수 같은 beastly; brutal.

yatchapta 얕잡다. →**yatpoda** 얕보다.

yatpoda 얕보다 look down on[upon]; make light of; despise; neglect; hold in contempt.

yatta 얕다 (be) shallow. *yat'ŭn kaeul[kŭrŭt, mot]* 얕은 개울[그릇, 못] shallow stream[dish, pond].

yawida 야위다 →**yŏwida** 여위다.

yayŏng 야영 camp; camping. *yayŏnghada* 야영하다 camp (out); encamp.

yayu 야유 picnic; outing. *yayuhoe* 야유회 picnic party.

yayu 야유 banter; jeer. *yayuhada* 야유하다 banter; make fun of; tease; chaff; rally.　　　「dent.

ye 예 instance; example; practice; custom; prece-

yebae 예배 worship; church service. *yebaedang* 예배당 chapel. *yebaeja* 예배자 worshipper.

yebang 예방 prevention; protection. *yebanghada*

예방하다 prevent; keep off; protect. *yebang chusa* 예방 주사 preventive injection.

yebi 예비 preparation; reserve. *yebihada* 예비하다 prepare[provide] for.

yebo 예보 forecast(ing). *yebohada* 예보하다 forecast; predict. *ilgi yebo* 일기 예보 weather forecast.

yebok 예복 full-dress; ceremonial dress.

yegam 예감 premonition; presentiment. *yegami tŭlda* 예감이 들다 have a presentiment (of).

yego 예고 advance[previous] notice. *yegohada* 예고하다 announce[inform] beforehand.

yegŭm 예금 deposit; bank account. *yegŭmhada* 예금하다 deposit money.

yejŏng 예정 plan; program; schedule. *yejŏngdaero* 예정대로 according to program.

yekwa 예과 preparatory course. *taehak yekwa* 대학 예과 preparatory course of a college.

yemae 예매 advance sale. *yemaehada* 예매하다 sell (ticket) in advance.

yennal 옛날 ancient times; old days. *yennare* 옛날에 once upon a time.

yennil 옛일 things of the past; bygones; past event.

yeoe 예외 exception. *yeoeŭi* 예외의 exceptional.

yeŏn 예언 prophecy; prediction.

yeppŭda 예쁘다 (be) pretty; lovely; shapely; nice.

yeri 예리. *yerihan* 예리한 sharp; acute; keen.

yesan 예산 estimate; budget.

yesang 예상 expectation; forecast; anticipation. *yesanghada* 예상하다 expect; foresee. *yesang oero* 예상 외로 beyond all expectations.

yesŏn 예선 ① previsional elect; pre-election ② preliminary (contest); tryout (*Am.*).

yesul 예술 art; fine arts. *yesulchŏk* 예술적 artistic. *yesulga* 예술가 artist.

yesŭp 예습 preparations for[of] lessons.

yeŭi 예의 courtesy; etiquette; manners; politeness. *yeŭibarŭn* 예의바른 courteous; polite.

yeyak 예약 booking; reservation; subscription. *yeyak'ada* 예약하다 reserve; subscribe.

yo 요 mattress; baddings.

yŏbaek 여백 space; blank; margin.

yŏbaeu 여배우 actress.

yŏbi 여비 travel(ing) expenses.

yŏbo 여보 hello; say(*Am.*); I say; hey (there).

yŏbun 여분 excess; extra; surplus. *yŏbunŭi* 여분의 extra; spare.

yochŏm 요점 point; essential[main] point.

yoch'ŏng 요청 demand; request. *yoch'ŏnghada* 요청하다 request; claim; demand.

yŏdan 여단 brigade. *yŏdanjang* 여단장 brigade commander.

yŏdang 여당 government[ruling] party.

yodaŭm 요다음 next. *yodaŭmŭi* 요다음의 next; coming. *yodaŭme* 요다음에 next; next time.

yŏdongsaeng 여동생 younger sister.

yŏdŭrŭm 여드름 pimple.

yŏga 여가 leisure; spare time; off hours. *yŏga-e* 여가에 at one's leisure.

yŏgan 여간. *yŏgananida* 여간아니다 (be) uncommon; unusual; remarkable.

yŏgi 여기 this place; here. *yŏgie[esŏ]* 여기에[에서] here; at[in] this place. *yŏgisŏbut'ŏ* 여기서부터 from here. *yŏgiro* 여기로 to this place.

yŏgija 여기자 lady[woman] reporter.

yŏgijŏgi 여기저기 here and there; from place to place; up and down; back and forth.

yŏgong 여공 factory girl; woman worker.

yogu 요구 demand; claim; request. *yoguhada* 요구하다 demand; request.

yogŭm 요금 charge; fee; fare. *chŏn-gi*[*sudo*] *yogŭm* 전기[수도] 요금 power[water] rates.

yŏgun 여군 woman soldier; Women's Army Corps.

yŏgŭp 여급 waitress; barmaid; maid.

yŏgwa 여과 filtration; filtering. *yŏgwahada* 여과하다 filter; filtrate.

yŏgwan 여관 hotel; inn. *yŏgwane mukta* 여관에 묵다 stay[put up] at a hotel. *yŏgwan chuin* 여관 주인 hotel keeper; host; hostess; landlady.

yŏgyosa 여교사 schoolmistress; lady teacher.

yohaeng 요행 (good) luck; chance; good fortune.

yŏhaeng 여행 travel; traveling; journey; tour. *yŏhaenghada* 여행하다 travel; make a trip to.

yŏhakkyo 여학교 girls' school.

yŏhaksaeng 여학생 girl student; schoolgirl.

yoil 요일 day of the week; weekday.

yoin 요인 factor; element; main cause.

yŏin 여인 woman. *pamkŏriŭi yŏin* 밤거리의 여인 streetwalker; woman of the streets.

yŏinsuk 여인숙 inn; lodging house.

yŏja 여자 woman; girl; female. *yŏjaŭi* 여자의 female; feminine.

yŏjangbu 여장부 heroine; brave[manly] woman.

yŏjŏmwon 여점원 saleswoman; shop girl.

yojŏng 요정 (Korean-style) restaurant; kisaeng house.

yŏjuin-gong 여주인공 heroine.

yok 욕 abuse; slander. *yogŭl hada* 욕을 하다 call names; speak ill of.

yŏk 역 (railroad; railway) station.

yŏk'al 역할 part; role.

yŏkcha 역자 translator.

yŏkchang 역장 stationmaster; station agent (*Am.*).

yokchigi 욕지기 nausea. *yokchiginada* 욕지기나다 feel nausea[sick, queasy]; retch.

yŏkchŏk 역적 rebel; traitor; insurgent.

yŏkki 역기 weight lifting.

yŏkkyŏng 역경 adversity; adverse circumstances.

yokŏn 요건 necessary [indispensable] condition; essential factor; important matter.

yokpoda 욕보다 ① have a hard time ② be put to shame ③ be raped[violated].

yŏksa 역사 history. *yŏksasangŭi* 역사상의 historical. *yŏksajogin* 역사적인 historic.

yŏkshi 역시 ① too; also; not either ② still; all [just] the same ③ after all.

yokshil 욕실 bathroom.

yokshim 욕심 greed; avarice. *yokshim manŭn* 욕심 많은 greedy; avaricious.

yŏksŏl 역설 assertion. *yŏksŏrhada* 역설하다 urge; emphasize; accentuate; lay[put] stress on[upon].

yŏksŭp 역습 counterattack. *yŏksŭp'ada* 역습하다 (make a) counterattack.

yŏkwon 여권 passport. *yŏkwŏnŭl shinch'ŏng[palbu]hada* 여권을 신청[발부]하다 apply for[issue, take out] a passport.

yŏl 열 ten. *yŏlpŏntchae* 열번째 the tenth.

yŏl 열 heat; temperature; fever.

yŏl 열 line; row; rank; column; queue. *yŏrŭl*

chitta 열을 짓다 form a line[queue]; line up.

yŏlbyŏng 열병 fever. *yŏlbyŏnge kŏllida* 열병에 걸리다 catch[suffer from] a fever.

yŏlch'a 열차 train. *yŏlch'a sago* 열차 사고 train[railroad] accident →**kich'a** 기차.

yŏlda 열다 ① open; uncover; unlock ② hold; give.

yŏlda 열다 bear (fruit); grow.

yŏlgi 열기 heat; hot air.

yŏlgwang 열광 (wild) excitement; frenzy; craze. *yŏlgwanghada* 열광하다 be[grow] wildly excited.

yŏllak 연락 connection; liaison; communication; correspondence. *yŏllak'ada* 연락하다 connect; liaise. *yŏllaksŏn* 연락선 ferryboat.

yŏllam 열람 reading; perusal. *yŏllamhada* 열람하다 read; peruse.

yŏllida 열리다 ① open; be opened; be unlocked ② be held; take place.

yŏllyo 연료 fuel. *yŏllyobi* 연료비 cost of fuel.

yŏllyŏl 열렬. *yŏllyŏrhan[hi]* 열렬한[히] ardent[ly]; fervent[ly].

yŏllyŏng 연령 age; years. *p'yŏnggyun yŏllyŏng* 평균 연령 average age.

yŏlmae 열매 fruit; nut; seed.

yŏlshim 열심 eagerness; enthusiasm. *yŏlshimin* 열심인 eager; earnest. enthusiastic.

yŏlsoe 열쇠 key. *yŏlsoerŭl ch'aeuda* 열쇠를 채우다 *lock*; turn a key on.

yŏlsŏng 열성 ardo(u)r; zeal; devotion. *yŏlsŏng-jŏgin* 열성적인 warm; earnest.

yŏlta 엷다 (be) thin. *yŏlke* 엷게 thinly.

yŏltae 열대 Torrid Zone; tropics. *yŏltae shingmul* 열대 식물 tropical plants[flora].

yŏltŭng 열등 inferiority. *yŏltŭnggam* 열등감 inferiority complex.

yŏmbul 염불 Buddhist invocation〔prayer〕.

yŏmch'i 염치 sense of honor〔shame〕. *yŏmch'iga ŏpta* 염치가 없다 be shameless.

yŏmju 염주 rosary. *yŏmjual* 염주알 bead.

yŏmmosŭp 옆모습 profile; side face.

yŏmnyŏ 염려 anxiety; worry; care. *yŏmnyŏhada* 염려하다 be〔feel〕 anxious about; worry.

yŏmsaek 염색 dyeing. *yŏmsaek'ada* 염색하다 dye.

yŏmso 염소 goat.

yŏnae 연애 love; amour. *yŏnaehada* 연애하다 be〔fall〕 in love with; lose one's heart to.

yŏnan 연안 coast; shore. *yŏnane* 연안에 on〔along〕 the coast. *yŏnanŭi* 연안의 coastal.

yŏnbang 연방 federal state; union; confederation; commonwealth.

yŏnbong 연봉 annual〔yearly〕 salary.

yŏnch'ak 연착 late arrival; delay. *yŏnch'ak'ada* 연착하다 arrive late; be delayed〔overdue〕.

yŏnch'ul 연출 production. *yŏnch'urhada* 연출하다 produce; perform; represent.

yŏndae 연대 regiment. *yŏndaejang* 연대장 regimental commander.

yŏndae 연대 age; epoch; era. *yŏndaep'yo* 연대표 chronological table.

yŏndan 연단 platform; rostrum.

yŏndara 연달아 one after another; successively.

yŏndusaek 연두색 yellow green.

yŏng 영 zero; nought. *iltae yŏngŭro* 1 대 0 으로 by score of one to zero.

yŏng 영 spirit; soul. *yŏngtchŏgin* 영적인 spiritual.

yŏn-gam 연감 yearbook; annual.

yŏngcha 영자 English letter. *yŏngcha shinmun* 영자 신문 English newspaper.

yongdo 용도 use; service. *yongdoga mant'a* 용도가 많다 have various[many] uses.

yonggam 용감 bravery. *yonggamhan[hi]* 용감한 [히] brave[ly]; heroic[ally].

yŏnggam 영감 inspiration; brain wave.

yonggi 용기 courage; bravery. *yonggi innŭn* 용기 있는 courageous; brave.

yonggi 용기 instrument; tool.

yonggu 용구 tool; instrument; appliance.

yŏnggu 영구 coffin; hearse; casket. *yŏngguch'a* 영구차 funeral car; (motor) hearse.

yŏnggu 영구. *yŏngguhi* 영구히 eternally; forever; permanently.

yŏngguk 영국 England; (Great) Britain; United Kingdom. *yŏnggugŭi* 영국의 English; British. *yŏnggugin* 영국인 Englishman; the English.

yŏnggwang 영광 hono(u)r; glory. *yŏnggwang-sŭrŏun* 영광스러운 glorious; honorable.

yŏngha 영하 below zero; sub-zero.

yŏnghan 영한 English-Korean. *yonghan sajŏn* 영한 사전 English-Korean dictionary.

yŏnghon 영혼 soul; spirit.

yŏnghwa 영화 movie; (motion) picture; film. *yŏnghwa paeu* 영화 배우 movie actor[actress]. *yŏnghwagwan* 영화관 movie theatre; cinema.

yŏnghwa 영화 glory. *yŏnghwaropta* 영화롭다 be glorious; pompous.

yŏnghyang 영향 influence; effect. *yŏnghyangŭl mich'ida* 영향을 미치다 influence; affect.

yongi 용이. *yongihan* 용이한 easy; simple. *yongi-hage* 용이하게 easily; readily; with ease.

yon-gi 연기 smoke. *yŏn-giga nanŭn* 연기가 나는 smoky; smoking.

yŏn-gi 연기 performance; acting; playing. *yŏn-gija* 연기자 performer; actor.

yŏn-gi 연기 postponement; deferment. *yŏn-gihada* 연기하다 postpone; put off; adjourn; suspend.

yongji 용지 paper (to use); (blank) form; printed form; blank (*Am.*).

yŏngjŏn 영전 promotion. *yŏngjŏnhada* 영전하다 be promoted to; be transferred[raised] to.

yŏngju 영주 permanent residence. *yŏngjuhada* 영주하다 reside permanently; settle down.

yongmang 욕망 desire; ambition; wants.

yŏngmi 영미 Britain and America. *yŏngmiŭi* 영미의 English and American; Anglo-American.

yongmo 용모 face; looks; features.

yongmu 용무 business; matter of business.

yŏngmun 영문 English (writing); English sentence.

yŏngni 영리. *yŏngnihan* 영리한 wise; clever; smart; bright.

yongnyang 용량 capacity; volume.

yongŏ 용어 term; terminology. *chŏnmun yongŏ* 전문 용어 technical terms.

yŏngŏ 영어 English; English language. *yŏngŏŭi* 영어의 English. *yŏngŏro* 영어로 in English.

yŏngŏp 영업 business; trade. *yŏngŏp'ada* 영업하다 do[carry on] business.

yŏn-gŏp'u 연거푸 continuously; successively.

yongpŏp 용법 way to use; usage; direction for use.

yongp'um 용품 supplies; article. *kajŏng yongp'um*

가정 용품 household goods.
yongsa 용사 brave man; warrior; hero.
yŏngsa 영사 consul. *yŏngsagwan* 영사관 consulate.
yŏngshi 영시 English poetry; English poem.
yongsŏ 용서 pardon; forgiveness. *yŏngsŏhada* 용서하다 pardon; forgive; excuse.
yŏngsu 영수 receipt. *yŏngsuhada* 영수하다 receive. *yŏngsujŭng* 영수증 receipt.
yŏngchang 영장 warrant; writ. *kusok yŏngchang* 구속 영장 warrant of arrest.
yŏngt'o 영토 territory; domain.
yongton 용돈 pocket money; spending money.
yŏn-gu 연구 study; research. *yŏn-guhada* 연구하다 (make a) study; investigate.
yŏn-gŭk 연극 play; drama. *yŏn-gŭgŭl hada* 연극을 하다 play; act (a play).
yŏn-gŭm 연금 annuity; pension.
yŏngung 영웅 hero. *yŏngungjŏgin* 영웅적인 heroic.
yŏngwon 영원 eternity; permanence. *yŏngwonhan* [*hi*] 영원한[히] eternal[ly].
yŏngyang 영양 nourishment; nutrition.
yŏn-gyŏl 연결 connection. *yŏn-gyŏrhada* 연결하다 connect; attach; join.
yŏnha 연하. *yŏnhachang* 연하장 New Year's card.
yŏnhada 연하다 ① (be) tender; soft ② (be) light. *yŏnhan pitkkal* 연한 빛깔 light color.
yŏnhap 연합 combination; incorporation; alliance. *yŏnhap'ada* 연합하다 combine; join; union.
yŏnhoe 연회 feast; banquet; dinner party.
yŏnin 연인 sweetheart; lover.
yŏnjang 연장 tool; inplement; utensil.
yŏnjang 연장 extension. *yŏnjanghada* 연장하다

extend; lengthen; prolong; continue.

yŏnju 연주 musical performance. *yŏnjuhada* 연주하다 perform; play. *yŏnjuhoe* 연주회 concert.

yŏnmaeng 연맹 league; federation; union.

yŏnmal 연말 end of the year; year-end.

yŏnmibok 연미복 tail coat; evening coat.

yŏnmot 연못 lotus pond; pond.

yŏnp'il 연필 (lead) pencil. *yŏnp'ilkkakki* 연필깎이 pencil sharpener.

yŏnsa 연사 speaker; orator.

yŏnsang 연상 association (of ideas). *yŏnsanghada* 연상하다 asssociate; be reminded (of).

yŏnsok 연속 continuity; continuation. *yŏnsok'ada* 연속하다 continue; last.

yŏnsŏl 연설 (public) speech; address. *yŏnsŏrhada* 연설하다 make a speech.

yŏnsŭp 연습 practice; exercise; training. *yŏnsŭp'ada* 연습하다 practice; exercise.

yŏnt'an 연탄 briquet. *yŏnt'an kasŭ chungdok* 연탄 가스 중독 briquet gas poisoning.

yŏp 옆 side; flank. *yŏp'ŭi* 옆의 side; next; adjoining. *yŏp'esŏ* 옆에서 by the side (of); by. *yŏpŭro* 옆으로 on[to] one side; aside.

yŏpchip 옆집 next door[house]; neighboring house. *yŏpchip saram* 옆집 사람 neighbor.

yŏpch'ong 엽총 hunting gun; shotgun.

yŏpkil 옆길 byroad; sideway.

yŏpkuri 옆구리 flank; side (of the chest).

yopŏp 요법 remedy; cure. *min-gan yopŏp* 민간 요법 folk remedy.

yŏpsŏ 엽서 postcard; postal card.

yoram 요람 survey; outline; handbook; manual.

yori 요리 ① cooking; cookery ② dish; food; fare. *yorisa* 요리사 cook. *yorichip* 요리집 restaurant.

yŏrŏ 여러 many; several; various.

yŏrŏbŏn 여러번 often; several[many] times; repeatedly; over and over again.

yŏrŏkaji 여러 가지 various; all kinds of; several.

yorŏn 요런 such; this; like this.

yŏron 여론 public[general] opinion. *yŏron chosa* 여론 조사 public opinion poll[survey].

yŏrŭm 여름 summer; summertime.

yoryŏng 요령 (main) point; essentials. *yoryŏng innŭn* 요령 있는 sensible; pointed. *yoryŏng ŏmnŭn* 요령 없는 pointless; vague.

yŏryu 여류 lady; woman; female. *yŏryu shiin* 여류 시인[작가] poetess[authoress]. *yŏryu pihaengsa* 여류 비행사 woman aviator.

yŏsa 여사 Lady; Madame; Mrs.; Miss. *Kim yŏsa* 김여사 Mrs.[Miss] Kim; Madame Kim.

yosae 요새 fortress; stronghold; fortification.

yosae 요새 recently; lately; these days.

yŏsaeng 여생 rest[remainder] of one's life.

yŏsamuwon 여사무원 office girl; female clerk.

yoso 요소 element; factor; essential part.

yŏsŏng 여성 womanhood; women. *yŏsŏngŭi* 여성의 female. *yŏsŏngyongŭi* 여성용의 for ladies' use.

yŏsŏt 여섯 six. *yŏsŏtchae* 여섯째 the sixth.

yosul 요술 magic; witchcraft; sorcery. *yosuljangi* 요술장이 magician; sorcerer.

yŏt'aekkaji 여태까지 till[until] now; up to the present; by this time; hitherto.

yŏtpoda 엿보다 watch[look] for; spy on; steal a glance at.

yŏttŭtta 엿듣다 overhear; eavesdrop; listen secretly.

yŏŭida 여의다 lose [be bereaved of] one's parents [husband, wife, etc.].

yŏwang 여왕 queen. *sagyogyeŭi yŏwang* 사교계의 여왕 queen of society.

yŏwida 여위다 grow thin[lean]. *yŏwin* 여윈 thin; lean; skinny; slender.

yŏu 여우 fox. *yŏu kat'ŭn* 여우 같은 foxy; sly.

yoyak 요약. summary; digest. *yoyak'ada* 요약하다 summarize; epitomize; abridge.

yoyang 요양 recuperation. *yoyanghada* 요양하다 recuperate; receive medical treatment. *yoyangso* 요양소 sanatorium; sanitarium (*Am.*).

yŏyu 여유 surplus; room. *yŏyuga itta* 여유가 있다 have in reserve; have time[money] to spare.

yua 유아 baby; infant; child[children].

yubang 유방 (woman's) breast(s).

yuch'ang 유창. *yuch'anghan* 유창한 fluent; flowing; smooth; eloquent. *yuch'anghage* 유창하게 fluently; smoothly.

yuch'i 유치. *yuch'ihan* 유치한 infantile; childish; crude; immature. *yuch'iwŏn* 유치원 kindergarten.

yudo 유도 judo.

yuga 육아 childcare; nursing; child-rearing.

yugajok 유가족 bereaved family.

yugam 유감 regret; pity. *yugamsŭrŏun* 유감스러운 regrettable; deplorable; pitiful.

yugi 유기 abandonment; desertion. *yugihada* 유기하다 abandon; desert; leave.

yugoe 유괴 kidnap(p)ing; abduction. *yugoehada* 유괴하다 abduct; kidnap; carry off.

yugyo 유교 Confucianism.

yuhae 유해 remains of the dead.

yuhaeng 유행 fashion; vogue. *yuhaenghada* 유행
하다 be in fashion[vogue]; prevail; be prevalent.

yuhak 유학 studying abroad. *yuhak'ada* 유학하다
study abroad; go abroad to study.

yuhok 유혹 temptation; lure. *yuhok'ada* 유혹하다
tempt; allure; entice; seduce.

yuhwa 유화 oil painting[color].

yuhyo 유효 validity; efficiency. *yuhyohada* 유효하
다 be effective; hold good; remain valid. *yuhyo-
hage* 유효하게 effectively; efficiently.

yuik 유익. *yuik'an* 유익한 profitable; beneficial.
yuik'age 유익하게 usefully; profitably.

yuim 유임 remaining in office. *yuimhada* 유임하
다 remain[continue] in office.

yuin 유인 temptation; allurement. *yuinhada* 유인
하다 tempt; induce; invite; attract.

yujok 유족 →**yugajok** 유가족.

yujŏk 유적 remains; relics; ruins; historic spots.

yujŏn 유전 oil field.

yujŏn 유전 heredity. *yujŏnhada* 유전하다 be inher-
ited; run in the blood.

yuk 육 six; *che yuk* 제6 the sixth.

yuk'aegonggun 육해공군 army[land], navy[sea],
and air force; armed forces.

yukch'e 육체 flesh; *body. yukch'eŭi[jŏk]* 육체의
[적] bodily; physical.

yukchi 육지 land; shore.

yukkak 육각 sexangle; hexagon.

yukkam 육감 the sixth sense.

yukkun 육군 army; miltary service. *yukkunŭi* 육

군의 military.

yuksang 육상 land; ground. *yuksang kyŏnggi* 육상 경기 athletic sports. ⌜sixtieth.

yukship 육십〔60〕 sixty. *che yukship* 제 60 the

yuk'wae 유쾌. *yuk'waehan* 유쾌한 pleasant; joyful; cheerful; jolly.

yukwonja 유권자 voter; elector.

yul 율 rate; ratio; proportion. *t'up'yo〔samang, ch'ulsan〕yul* 투표〔사망, 출산〕율 voting〔death, birth〕rate.

yulli 윤리 ethics; morals. *yullijŏk* 윤리적 ethical; moral.

yultong 율동 rhythm; rhythmic movement.

yumang 유망. *yumanghan* 유망한 promising; hopeful.

yumul 유물 relic; remains.

yumyŏng 유명. *yumyŏnghan* 유명한 famous; noted; renowned; notorious.

yundal 윤달 leap〔intercalary〕month.

yungdan 융단 carpet; rug.

yungno 육로 overland〔land〕route. *yungnoro* 육로로 by land; overland.

yungt'ongsŏng 융통성. *yungt'ongsŏng innŭn* 융통성 있는 adaptable; versatile; flexible.

yun-gwak 윤곽 outline; contour; general idea.

yunhwa 윤화 traffic〔car〕accident.

yunŭng 유능. *yunŭnghan* 유능한 able; capable; competent; talented.

yuŏn 유언 will; testament; last words. *yuŏnhada* 유언하다 make〔leave〕a will.

yup'a 유파 school; sect.

yurae 유래 origin; history; source. *yuraehada* 유

래하다 originate (in).

yuram 유람 sightseeing; excursion. *yuramhada* 유람하다 go sightseeing.

yurang 유랑 vagrancy; roaming. *yuranghada* 유랑하다 roam[wander, rove] about.

yuri 유리. *yurihan* 유리한 profitable; advantageous. *yurihage* 유리하게 profitably.

yurin 유린. *yurinhada* 유린하다 violate; infringe upon; trample; overrun; devastate.

yuryŏk 유력. *yuryŏk'an* 유력한 powerful; influential; strong; leading.

yuryŏng 유령 ghost; specter; apparition.

yusa 유사 similarity; resemblance; likeness; analogy. *yusahada* 유사하다 be similar (to).

yusan 유산 abortion. *yusanhada* 유산하다 miscarry; abort; produce abortion.

yusan 유산 inheritance; legacy; bequest.

yuse 유세 canvassing; stump-speaking (*Am.*). *yusehada* 유세하다 go canvassing; stump.

yushik 유식. *yushik'an* 유식한 learned; educated; well-informed.

yusŏ 유서 (written) will; testament; suicide note.

yut 윷 Four-Stick Game; Yut.

yut'an 유탄 stray bullet[shot].

yuŭi 유의. *yuŭihada* 유의하다 bear[keep] in mind; care about; be mindful of; take care[notice].

yuwol 유월 June.

yuwonji 유원지 amusement park; resort.

yuyong 유용. *yuyonghan* 유용한 useful; valuable; serviceable.

yuyong 유용 diversion. *yuyonghada* 유용하다 divert; misappropriate; apply to.